Native American Placenames of the United States

Consulting Editors

Native American Placenames of the United States

William Bright

University of Oklahoma Press : Norman

Also by William Bright

The Karok Language (Berkeley, 1957)
Studies in Californian Linguistics (Berkeley, 1964)
Sociolinguistics (The Hague, 1966)
A Luiseño Dictionary (Berkeley, 1968)
Variation and Change in Language (Stanford, 1976)
Coyote Stories (Chicago, 1978)
Bibliography of the Languages of Native California (Metuchen, N.J., 1982)
American Indian Linguistics and Literature (Berlin, 1984)
A Coyote Reader (Berkeley, 1993)

Library of Congress Cataloging-in-Publication Data

Bright, William, 1928–
Native American placenames of the United States / William Bright.
p. cm.
ISBN 0-8061-3576-X (alk. paper)
1. Names, Indian—United States. 2. Names, Geographical—United States. 3. United States—History, Local. I. Title.

E98.N2.B75 2004
917.3'001'4—dc22

2003061395

The paper in this book meets the guidelines for permanence and durability of the Committee on Production Guidelines for Book Longevity of the Council on Library Resources, Inc. ∞

1 2 3 4 5 6 7 8 9 10

This book is dedicated to

LIBRARIANS

past, present, and future

Contents

Acknowledgments

I AM INDEBTED to many people and institutions for making this work possible. First I must name my teachers, Murray Emeneau and Mary Haas, at the University of California, Berkeley, whose initiative, starting in the late 1940s, gave rise to the Survey of California Indian Languages (later California and Other Indian Languages). Then come my fellow Americanists who have been associated with that program down to the present day, especially those who assisted so generously with my earlier books on the placenames of Colorado (Bright 1993) and of California (Gudde 1998); they are identified by name in the list below. Then come the Consulting Editors of this work—several of whom, in fact, are also members of the preceding group. I am especially grateful to the Department of Linguistics, University of Colorado, Boulder, for providing my academic home since 1988; and special thanks go to the Interlibrary Loan Department, Norlin Library, Boulder, for much good help. I am likewise grateful to the University of Hunan, Changsha, China, for use of its facilities while I was a Visiting Scholar there in 2000. For specific information, my thanks go to the following scholars, local historians, librarians, and Native American speakers:

Leonard Adams, University of Massachusetts, Amherst
Jim Anderson, Florida State University, Tallahassee
Haruo Aoki, University of California, Berkeley
James Armagost, Mount Vernon, Washington
Virginia Beavert, Yakima Tribe, Washington
Michael Bell, University of Colorado, Boulder
Joan Brooks, University of Maine, Orono
Catherine Callaghan, Ohio State University, Columbus
Edward Callary, Northern Illinois University, DeKalb
Brian Compton, University of British Columbia, Vancouver
Rhoda Compton, Otoe Tribe, Edmond, Oklahoma
Bill Copeley, New Hampshire Historical Society, Concord
David Costa, University of California, Berkeley
William Cowan, Carleton University, Ottawa
Andrew Cowell, University of Colorado, Boulder
Don Cunningham, Nebraska State Historical Society, Lincoln
Irvine Davis, Albuquerque, New Mexico
Rose-Marie Déchaine, University of British Columbia, Vancouver
Scott DeLancey, University of Oregon, Eugene
Willem de Reuse, University of North Texas, Denton
Barry Dunbar, Coopersville, New York
John Dyson, Indiana University, Bloomington

Steven M. Egesdal, Honolulu, Hawai'i
Elaine Emerson, Colville Confederated Tribes, Washington
John Enrico, Oliver, British Columbia
Catherine Fowler, University of Nevada, Reno
Donald Frantz, Lethbridge University, Alberta
Kay French, Portland, Oregon
T. Wayne Furr, Oklahoma Board on Geographic Names, Norman
James Given, Ohio Geographic Names, Columbus
Victor Golla, Humboldt State University, Arcata, California
Lynn Gordon, Washington State University, Pullman
Randolph Graczyk, Pryor, Montana
Philip Greenfeld, San Diego State University, California
Yvonne Hajda, Portland, Oregon
Sharon Hargus, University of Washington, Seattle
Barbara Harris, University of Victoria, British Columbia
Dixie Henry, Maryland Commission on Indian Affairs, Crownsville
Thom Hess, University of Victoria, British Columbia
Vi Hilbert, Skagit Tribe, Seattle, Washington
Leanne Hinton, University of California, Berkeley
Eugene Hunn, University of Washington, Seattle
Bruce Ingham, University of London, England
William Jacobsen, University of Nevada, Reno
Karen Jania, University of Michigan, Ann Arbor
Larry Jones, Idaho State Historical Society, Boise
Robert Julyan, Albuquerque, New Mexico
Frances Karttunen, Nantucket, Massachusetts
John Koontz, National Institute of Standards & Technology, Boulder, Colorado
Donald Lance, University of Missouri, Columbia
Julian Lang, Humboldt State University, Arcata, California
Margaret Langdon, University of California, San Diego
Jeff Leer, University of Alaska, Fairbanks
Wayne Leman, Busby, Montana
Lewis L. McArthur, Portland, Oregon
Monica Macaulay, University of Wisconsin, Madison
Michael McCafferty, Indiana University, Bloomington
Pauleena MacDougall, University of Maine, Orono
Mary Marchand, Colville Indian Reservation, Washington
Jack Martin, College of William and Mary, Williamsburg, Virginia
Anthony Mattina, University of Montana, Missoula
Margaret Mauldin, Muscogee Tribe, Oklahoma
Lise Menn, University of Colorado, Boulder
Karen Michelson, University of Buffalo, New York
Jay Miller, Seattle, Washington
Kenneth Miner, University of Kansas, Lawrence
Timothy Montler, University of North Texas, Denton
Mary Morgan, South Carolina State Library, Columbia
John Nichols, University of Minnesota, Minneapolis
Tim Norton, Arizona State Place Name Board, Phoenix

Michael O'Donnell, Western Michigan University, Kalamazoo
John O'Meara, Lakehead University, Thunder Bay, Ontario
Dean Osterman, Kalispel Tribe of Indians, Usk, Washington
Robert Oswalt, Kensington, California
Douglas Parks, Indiana University, Bloomington
Lee Pederson, Emory University, Atlanta, Georgia
Jay Powell, University of British Columbia, Vancouver
Roberta Quigley, U.S. Forest Service, Salt Lake City, Utah
Carolyn Quintero, Big Spring, Texas
Jim Rementer, Bartlesville, Oklahoma
John T. Ritter, Yukon Native Language Center, Whitehorse, Yukon
David Rood, University of Colorado, Boulder
Roger Roulette, Aboriginal Languages of Manitoba, Winnipeg
Maude Rowe, Kaw Tribe, Shidler, Oklahoma
Noel Rude, Federated Tribes of the Umatilla Indian Reservation, Pendleton, Oregon
Blair Rudes, University of North Carolina, Charlotte
Johnny Rulland, Anaktuvuk Pass, Alaska
Janine Scancarelli, San Francisco, California
William R. Seaburg, University of Washington, Bothell
Emory Sekaquaptewa, Hopi Tribe, Arizona
Alice Shepherd, Oakland, California
William Shipley, University of California, Santa Cruz
Alice Snow, Seminole Tribe of Florida
Sava Stephan, Anchorage, Alaska
Wayne Suttles, Portland State University, Portland, Oregon
Jake Tansy, Cantwell, Alaska
Sarah Grey Thomason, University of Michigan, Ann Arbor
Tim Thornes, University of Oregon, Eugene
Tom Thornton, University of Alaska Southeast, Juneau
Joseph Tingley, Nevada Bureau of Mines & Geology, Reno
Michael Toomey, East Tennessee Historical Society, Knoxville
Utah State Board on Geographic Names, Salt Lake City
Ren Vasiliev, State University of New York, Geneseo
Laurel Watkins, Colorado College, Colorado Springs
Parrish Williams, Marland, Oklahoma
Catherine Willmond, Los Angeles, California
Adrian Wilson, Gallup, New Mexico
Yukihiro Yumitani, Sanyo Gakuen University, Japan
Henry Zenk, Portland, Oregon
Ofelia Zepeda, University of Arizona, Tucson

Pronunciation

Native American Languages: Key to Phonetic Symbols

In addition to the phonetic symbols used for English, a separate set—the International Phonetic Alphabet (IPA)—is commonly used to transcribe the pronunciations of Native American words as well as words from other foreign languages. In some cases, the sounds in question are nearly the same as familiar English sounds. In other cases, their pronunciation can only be approximated by English speakers. (The practical spelling systems of some Indian languages use still other symbols, which are described below.) Note the values of the following symbols:

[a] English *spa,* Spanish *padre.*
[æ] English *bad, cat.*
[c] a sound that may vary from *ts,* in English *gutsy,* to *ch* in English *church.*
[č] English *church* (the sound written *ch* in English). The symbol is called "c-wedge."
[ḍ] a sound like *d,* but with the tip of the tongue slightly turned back.
[ð] the sound of *th* in English *then, whether.* The symbol is called "edh," pronounced [ɛð].
[e] English or French *sauté,* Spanish *bebe.*
[ɛ] English *bet,* French *bête, bette.* The symbol is called "epsilon" or "open e."
[ɢ] a sound like *g,* but formed farther back in the mouth.
[ɣ] a sound like *g*, but made without closing off the air stream, as in Spanish *lago.* The symbol is called "gamma."
[ħ] like an *h,* but made with constriction of the pharynx.
[i] English *machine,* Spanish *sí.*
[ɪ] English *it, bid.*
[ɨ] a "mid central" or "high central" vowel, impressionistically between English [i], [ə], and [ʊ]. Some English speakers make a vowel like this in the initial syllable of *pretty, children, Wilshire.* The symbol is called "barred eye."
[ǰ] English *j* in *judge.*
[ɬ] a sound like *l,* but voiceless, without the vocal cords vibrating (represented in Welsh by *Ll,* as in *Lloyd).* The symbol is called "barred ell."
[ñ] as in Spanish *señor.*
[ŋ] like English *ng* in *sing* or *n* in *sinker.* The symbol is called "eng."
[o] English *solo,* Spanish *sólo.*
[ɔ] like the vowel of English *dawn, launch, brought.* The symbol is called "open oh."
[q] a sound like *k,* but formed farther back in the mouth, as in Arabic *Iraq.*
[r] in many languages indicates a "vibrant" *r,* as in Spanish *toro.*
[ʀ] a sound like [ɣ], but formed farther back in the mouth; comparable to the "uvular" *r* of French.

[š] English *ship, shore* (the sound written *sh* in English). The symbol is called "esh" or "ess-wedge."
[ṣ] a sound like *s,* but formed with the tip of the tongue slightly turned back.
[ṭ] a sound like *t,* but formed with the tip of the tongue slightly turned back.
[θ] like English *th* in *thin, theater.* The name of the symbol is "theta."
[u] as in English *dune, boot, soup.*
[ʊ] as in English *put, book, look.*
[ʌ] as in English *but, bud.*
[x] like a *k,* but made without closing off the airstream; like the *j* in Spanish *José* or the *ch* in German *Bach.*
[x̣] like [x], but made farther back in the mouth.
[x̭] like [x], but made farther forward in the mouth, like German *ch* in *ich.*
[ž] like the medial consonant in English *azure, vision, leisure.* The name of the symbol is "z-wedge."
[ʒ] like English *dz* in *adze.*
[ǯ] like English *j* in *judge.*
[ʔ] a *glottal stop*, i.e., a closure of the vocal cords, as in the middle of English *oh-oh!*
[ʕ] like a glottal stop, but made with constriction of the pharynx.

The colon [:], when written after a vowel in some languages, indicates that the vowel is long (i.e., pronounced with extra duration); the same length is written in other languages simply by doubling the vowel.

The apostrophe ['], when written next to certain consonants, indicates that the sound is *glottalized* (i.e., accompanied in pronunciation by a brief closure of the vocal cords).

The raised *w* [^{w}] is written in some languages in combinations like [k^{w}, g^{w}, x^{w}, q^{w}]; these are pronounced very similarly to [kw, gw, xw, qw], respectively.

The raised *y* [^{y}] is written in some languages in combinations like [t^{y}, d^{y}, l^{y}]; these are pronounced very similarly to [ty, dy, ly].

The *apostrophe*, in the transcription systems of many languages, is not only used to indicate glottalization of an adjacent consonant (as indicated above) but also represents the *glottal stop* [ʔ] (i.e., the interruption of breath that occurs in English expressions like *oh-oh!*).

Accent marks usually indicate accent or pitch. Usually, the *acute* accent [á] marks strong accent or high pitch; the *grave* accent [à] marks low pitch; and the *circumflex* accent [â] marks falling pitch. In some languages, a *breve* (ă) marks an extra-short vowel.

The *hook* indicates that a vowel is nasalized. Thus [ǫ] is nasalized, as in French *mouton* 'sheep'.

Capital letters indicate that a sound is voiceless (i.e., pronounced without vibration of the vocal cords).

Square brackets are used [like this] to mark *phonetic* transcriptions of words; in the case of foreign words, this means "close transcriptions," which give a relatively great amount of detail about pronunciation. By contrast, for some languages, *slashes* are used /like this/ to mark *phonemic* or "broad" transcriptions; these give phonetic details only to the extent that they serve to distinguish meaning in a particular language.

Native American Languages: Comments on Spelling Systems

Some Native American languages employ practical spelling systems that use additional symbols or use symbols shown above with other pronunciations. These are presented below.

Abenaki. Following Day 1994–95, the symbol *ô* represents [ǫ], a nasalized [o].

Ahtna. Following Kari 1990, the following special usages appear:

ae represents a low front vowel [æ], as in English *bad.*
c represents an aspirated front-velar stop, IPA [k̂].
g represents an unaspirated front-velar stop, IPA [g].
gg represents an unaspirated back-velar stop, IPA [ɢ̂].
gh represents a voiced back-velar fricative, IPA [ɣ].
k represents an aspirated back-velar stop, IPA [q].

Aleutian. Following Bergsland 1994, *ĝ* is a voiced back-velar fricative, IPA [ɣ]; *x̂* represents a voiceless back-velar fricative, IPA [χ].

Blackfoot. Following Frantz and Russell 1995, the symbol *h* represents IPA [x], the German *ch* in *Bach.*

Cherokee. The symbol *v* represents IPA [ʌ̨], the vowel [ʌ] of English *bud* with added nasalization (Alexander 1971; Feeling 1975).

Dakotan (Dakota, Lakhota). Symbols used are those of Colorado 1976 (these are similar to but partly different from those of Buechel and Manhart 2002; Ingham 2001; Riggs 1890; and Williamson 1902):

ǧ represents IPA [ɣ], a voiced velar fricative.
ȟ represents IPA [x], a voiceless velar fricative, like German *ch* in *Bach.*

Diegueño. The system of Couro and Hutcheson 1973 includes the symbol *e* in the value of schwa [ə], as in English *elope,* and *ll* for the voiceless lateral [ɬ].

Iñupiaq (Eskimo). The system used here is that of MacLean 1980; words from Fortescue et al. 1994 and fromWebster and Zibell 1970 are rewritten accordingly. Special usages are as follows:

c represents IPA [č], as in English *church.*
g represents IPA [ɣ], a voiced velar fricative
ġ is a fricative produced farther back in the mouth than *g*; it resembles the French "uvular" *r* in *rose.* Note that this sound is represented in Yupik Eskimo spelling by *r.*
ḷ represents IPA palatal [ʎ], approximately as in English *million.*
ł̣ represents IPA voiceless palatal [ʎ̥].
r resembles a range of sounds, from a retroflex glide [ɹ], as in English *red,* to a voiced palatal fricative [ž], as in English *beige.*
sr resembles a voiced retroflex fricative [ʂ].
v represents IPA [β], like an English *v* produced by using the two lips rather than the lips and teeth (i.e., like Spanish *v* in *lavar* 'to wash').

Karuk. The sequence *th* represents IPA [θ], the sound of English *think.*

Koyukon. Following Jetté and Jones 2000, the following special usages occur:

e represents a phoneme /ə/, varying phonetically between [ə], [ɨ], and [ʌ].
ee represents a phoneme /i:/, varying phonetically between [i:] and [e:].

gg represents IPA [ɢ], an unaspirated back-velar stop.
gh represents IPA [ɣ], a voiced velar fricative.
h represents IPA [χ], a voiceless velar fricative.
kk represents IPA [q], an aspirated back-velar stop.
oo represents a phoneme /u:/, varying phonetically between [u:] and [o:].

Munsee (Delaware). Following O'Meara 1996, the letter *u* is used to represent [ʌ], the vowel of English *bud.*

Muskogee (Creek). Following Martin and Mauldin 2000, words are given both in the practical spelling system and in a phonemic transcription (e.g., *yvhv* /yʌhʌ́/ 'wolf'). Special usages of the practical system are as follows:

c represents a phoneme /č/, as in English *church.*
e represents a phoneme /i/, like the vowel of English *if.*
ē represents a phoneme /i:/, like the vowel of English *feet.*
ī formerly pronounced as /ai/, as in English *pine*; now pronounced as /ei/, as in English *hey.*
r represents a phoneme /ɬ/, "voiceless ell".
ue represents a phoneme /oi/, as in English *boy.*
v represents short /a/, pronounced [ʌ], as in English *bud.*

Navajo. Following Young and Morgan 1987, the sequence *gh* is used to represent [ɣ], a voiced velar fricative.

Ojibwa. Following Nichols and Nyholm 1995, the sequence *nh* indicates nasalization of a preceding vowel (e.g., *aanh* is [ą:]).

O'odham (Pima, Papago). In the official spelling, the symbol *ĭ* represents voiceless *i.*

Osage. The vowel *ü* is pronounced like German *ü* in *früh* 'early'.

Penobscot. The vowel α (Greek alpha) is a nasalized low back vowel, IPA [ą].

Shoshoni. Following Miller 1972, as well as Crum and Dayley 1993, the letter *e* is used to represent IPA [ɨ], a vowel as in English *just.*

Tlingit. Following Davis and Leer 1976, the following system is used:

ee represents IPA [i:] as in English *seek.*
ei represents IPA [e:]; cf. English *ei* in *rein.*
g̲ represents IPA [ɢ], a sound produced farther back in the mouth than English *g.*
k̲ represents IPA [q], a sound produced farther back in the mouth than English *k.*
oo represents IPA [u:]; cf. English *boot.*
x̲ represents IPA [χ], a voiced back-velar fricative, produced farther back in the mouth than the German *ch* in *Bach.*

Yupik (Eskimo). The system used here is that of Jacobson 1984:

c represents IPA [č], as in English *church.*
g represents IPA [ɣ], a voiced velar fricative.
r is IPA [ʀ], produced farther back in the mouth than *g*; it resembles the French "uvular" *r* in *rose.* Note that this sound is represented in Iñupiaq Eskimo spelling by *ġ.*
v represents IPA [β]; see under Iñupiaq (Eskimo) above.

Key to English Pronunciation

The pronunciation of some U.S. placenames is obvious from their spelling. In most names derived from American Indian languages, however, pronunciations are indicated here phonetically within back slashes, following a simplified form of the transcription system used in the *Random House*

Dictionary (*RHD* 1987). Some of the same symbols are used in transcriptions of Indian languages; but see below for more specific information. Note the values of the following letters:

\a\ *cap*, *bad*, *act*.
\ā\ *day*, *wait*, *cape*.
\ä\ *far*, *father*, *spa*.
\âr\ *air*, *fare*, *there*.
\ch\ *child*, *church*.
\dh\ *th* as in *then*, *bathe*, *rather*.
\e\ *set*, *red*, *left*.
\ē\ *tree*, *east*, *eve*.
\ə\ *a* as in *sofa*, *agenda*. The symbol is called "schwa."
\g\ *go*, *give*, *gag*.
\i\ *it*, *bid*, *ink*.
\ī\ the vowel sound of *eye*, *sigh*, *side*, *bite*, *line*.
\j\ as in *just*, *judge*.
\N\ nasalization as in French *bon* 'good' (in La. placenames).
\ng\ *sing*, *long*.
\o\ *don*, *fond*, *cot*. Some people pronounce this the same as \ä\ in *spa*.
\ô\ *law*, *dawn*, *caught*. Many people pronounce this the same as the \ä\ in *cot*.
\ôr\ *or*, *soar*, *tore*.
\o͝o\ *book*, *put*, *foot*.
\o͞o\ *boot*, *soon*, *coop*.
\ou\ *cow*, *down*, *out*.
\oi\ *boy*, *coin*, *soil*.
\s\ *sun*, *case*, *miss*—not the \z\ sound of *rose*, *boys*.
\sh\ *shin*, *hash*, *dish*.
\th\ *thin*, *thick*, *think*—not the sound of *then*, *bathe*, which is written as \dh\.
\u\ *but*, *sun*, *rug*.
\ûr\ *fur*.
\yo͞o\ *use*, *Yuma*, *Europe*.
\zh\ *measure*, *azure*.

The syllable with principal accent has an accent mark following it; that is, the pronunciation of *Mono* is shown as \mō´ nō\.

References for English Pronunciations

Alabama: Hartsook 1976; W. Read 1984
Alaska: Duncan et al. 1975, Phillips 1973
Arizona: Granger 1983
Arkansas: Whaley 1950
California: Gudde 1998
Colorado: Bright 1993
Florida: W. Read 1934
Idaho: Ryan 1975
Illinois: Brown & Schooley 1957, Cresswell 2000, A. Read 1981

Indiana: Baker 1995, J. Beauchamp 1900
Iowa: Barnes 1959
Kansas: Kansas 1955
Kentucky: Rennick 1984
Louisiana: W. Read 1927
Maine: Eckstorm 1941
Minnesota: Lenmark 1953
Mississippi: Waite 1973
Missouri: Picinich 1951
Montana: Bue 1959
Nebraska: Christensen et al. 1953
New York: DeCamp 1944
North Dakota: Losk 1951
Oklahoma: Holland 1950
Oregon: Monaghan 1961, Webber 1995
Pennsylvania: Froke & Bodow 1962, Zawadzki 1982
South Carolina: Neuffer & Neuffer 1983
South Dakota: South Dakota 1963
Texas: Aschbacher 1978, Bradfield n.d., Hickerson 1979, Ramos 2001, Stokes 1977, Tarpley 1980
Washington: Phillips 1976, Rundell 1964
West Virginia: *A Guide* 1972, West Virginia 1995
Wisconsin: Engel 1969

Native American Placenames of the United States

Abbreviations and Symbols

BGN Board on Geographic Names (US Geological Survey)
CAC Central Atlantic Coast
cf. compare
Co. County
Eng. English
Fr. French
HNAI *Handbook of North American Indians*
Is. Island(s)
Mt. Mount
Mtn. Mountain
NEng. New England
Par. Parish (in La.)
p.c. personal communication
RHD *Random House Dictionary*
SNEng. Southern New England
Span. Spanish
USGS United States Geological Survey

The names of states in the United States are abbreviated. In Alaska, in lieu of identification of locations by county, topographic quadrangles and coordinates are given (e.g., "Juneau A-2").

\ \ back slashes, indicating dictionary pronunciation; see the chapter on Pronunciation above.
[ ] square brackets, indicating pronunciation in terms of the International Phonetic Alphabet; see the chapter on Pronunciation above.
< > angle brackets, indicating English spellings or other ambiguous transcriptions, where the true pronunciation cannot be determined.
/ / slashes, indicating phonemic transcription; see the chapter on Pronunciation above.

Introduction

Aims

This work is the first comprehensive dictionary of the origins of US placenames, used in English, which have American Indian origins or associations. (This includes origins in Latin America: for example, terms like *coyote*, borrowed through Spanish from Aztec.) My work began with data from existing publications, but I've added authoritative information on the origins of these words, based on current field research by anthropological linguists who specialize in Native American languages, as well as native speakers of those languages.

Among published reference works on American placenames, there are a few which cover the entire US, and many devoted to particular states; but in general these do not give special attention to Native American names. A handful of books deal with Native names in particular states, but they are grounded primarily in historical and literary research. What I've done in creating the present book is described below (see also Bright 1999, 2001a, 2002).

Materials

Four main kinds of published information are especially relevant to the project:

The Geographical Names Information System (GNIS)

My basic inventory of terms is drawn from the Geographical Names Information System (USGS 2002), the digital database of placenames which is available via the Internet from the US Board on Geographic Names. I have not included every possible Indian name that occurs in that database or on available maps, however. Some entries in the GNIS or on maps are erroneous; or refer to long-vanished railroad sidings where no one ever lived or have fallen out of use and memory. I do include the names that people are likely to encounter—in books, on maps, or on the land—and about which they feel curious. In addition, I've included some names relevant to regional history that are not in GNIS.

U.S. Placename Dictionaries

Another source consists of placename dictionaries of the United States as a whole, such as those by George Stewart (1970) and by Kelsie Harder (1976). These give some information about the best-known names, such as *Chicago* and *Oklahoma*; but since they try to cover placenames of every type, they cannot devote much attention to lesser-known names.

Regional Placename Dictionaries

Still another source consists of placename dictionaries of individual parts of the United States, such as well-known state placename books; good examples are Byrd Granger's work for Arizona (1983) and Lewis McArthur's for Oregon (1992). These books vary, however, in the attention they give to names of Native American origin. A problem with both these types of dictionaries is that most of the compilers had little specialist knowledge about American Indian languages and often were not able to make use of existing linguistic resources on those languages. As a result, the information that all these sources provide on placenames of Indian origin is likely to be somewhat deficient.

Regional Indian Placename Dictionaries

A final source includes a relatively limited number of volumes devoted specifically to placenames of Indian origin in particular U.S. states or other defined geographical areas, such as the excellent volumes published by Virgil Vogel for Illinois (1963), Iowa (1983), Michigan (1986), and Wisconsin (1991). These works are usually quite comprehensive for the areas they cover and in some cases have been prepared by scholars with considerable sophistication in American Indian linguistics. I can especially mention the older books by William A. Read on Louisiana (1927), Florida (1934), and Alabama (1937, revised 1984) as well as the more recent work on names of the Navajo Reservation by Alan Wilson (1995).

It should be mentioned here that Virgil Vogel also completed the manuscript of a book with the title "Their Name Is on Your Waters: A Narrative of Native American Place Names in the United States and Canada" (1982b). The manuscript is now in the Newberry Library, Chicago. Its scope is comparable to that of the present volume; but it is organized in topical chapters ("Ceremonies," "Indian Chiefs," "Commemorative Names," etc.) rather than as a dictionary. Vogel's book is a valuable compilation of historical data from works previously published by himself and others, but it does not advance much beyond them with regard to linguistic information.

Procedures

My procedure in preparing this book began with consolidating material from sources of all the above types into a single computerized database. The resulting files were "raw" in the sense of coming from many sources (which sometimes contradicted each other) and being at that stage unedited. Concurrently with this compilation, I also compiled a unified computerized bibliography of all my published sources. The references at the end of the present volume represent a subset of that larger bibliography. Both the database and the bibliography, of course, have been updated continually during the preparation of the work.

The next major part of the project was to send relevant portions of the database to the consulting editors and other qualified authorities, asking for input derived from their personal knowledge of various languages and from information they could obtain from native speakers. As my consultants have returned such input to me over the years during which this volume was being prepared, I have consolidated the entire body of data and then edited it to create entries for this dictionary.

Selection of Entries

Most entries are, of course, terms borrowed from American Indian words. These can be divided into several subtypes, which are discussed in the section on typology. Some particular varieties should be mentioned here.

Loan Translations

These formations, also called "calques," are terms that, instead of attempting to reproduce the sounds of an American Indian original, attempt to reproduce the meaning.

The commonest kind of example is that where a simple Indian placename is simply translated into English: a stream called by an Indian name meaning 'deer creek' is named *Deer Creek* in English. In such cases, to be sure, there is a good chance that the English name was applied independently, simply because there were many deer in the vicinity; but sometimes we have direct evidence that an English placename is modeled on a Native American one. For instance, the name *Black Hills* in South Dakota represents a loan translation from Lakhota (Sioux) *pahá-sapa,* literally 'hill(s)-black'. In many cases, French or Spanish acts as an intermediary language in translating a Native American name into English. For example, the placename *Des Plaines* in Illinois is an English adapatation of a French name—not with the apparent meaning 'of the plains' but rather *des pleines* 'of the maple trees' (using a word now obsolete in France)—which is in turn a translation of an Algonquian original.

Folk-Etymologies

This is the process by which an English name represents a phonetic and semantic "re-formation" of a Native American name. In the same way, English word *cockroach* represents a conversion of Spanish *cucaracha* into two English words of known meaning, *cock* and *roach* (perhaps in the sense of a hairstyle). A somewhat comparable example in toponymy is the placename *Seneca*. This was, first of all, a name applied to an Iroquoian nation of New York, and was derived from a derogatory term applied to the Senecas by their Algonquian neighbors; it meant 'wood-eaters'. Subsequently the word was applied by white settlers as a placename, but with the spelling and associations of the English name *Seneca*, referring to an ancient Roman philosopher and dramatist. This process of folk-etymology has sometimes taken place first in French or Spanish, with the result then being passed into English.

Terms Associated with Native American Culture and History

Under this heading I include English placenames that are not based directly on Indian names at all but rather refer to cultural items associated with Native American culture. A very simple example is *Fence*, occurring in Michigan and Wisconsin, which refers to traditional fish-weirs built by Indians or to brush enclosures used to trap game. An example that enters English through French is *calumet* 'Indian pipe,' found as a placename in Illinois; the term is from a dialectal French word.

Invented Words

Especially in areas close to political boundaries, placenames have often been invented by combining parts of names already in use—which may, of course, have Indian origins. A well-known example is *Texarkana*, which combines the words *Texas*, *Arkansas*, and *Louisiana*; the first two of these come from Native American sources.

Bogus Words

Some placenames have been coined from non-Native American elements to resemble Indian words. Some of these are simply jokes; thus a certain "draw" or small stream in New Mexico is called

Beechatuda Draw, the joke being apparent when the name is pronounced rapidly. Other examples represent more deliberate attempts to mystify; again in New Mexico, the placename *Zuzax*, supposedly referring to an obscure Indian tribe, was actually a complete invention.

Content of Entries

Entries in the dictionary contain material of the following types.

Headword

The first word of an entry is a placename as spelled in the GNIS. I have also entered variant or alternative names when these appear as headwords in widely used regional placename dictionaries or when they are otherwise likely to be found in historical and anthropological reference works. The headword may be followed by a generic term, as in *Mississippi River* or *Appalachian Mountains*, but only when that combination is the earliest common usage of the word.

Location

The first element here is the state or states in which the feature is located. The second element is the name of the principal county in which the feature is located, unless it is spread over several counties (e.g., the Yukon River in Alaska).

Let me note here that I have covered forty-nine states—every state except Hawai'i. To be sure, the Hawai'ian language may properly be considered "Native American"; however, an excellent dictionary of Hawai'ian placenames is already available (Pukui et al. 1974), and its contents are not repeated here. The present work does include Hawai'ian names given to places on the US mainland, including *Hawaii* as well as names like *Aloha Creek* and *Oahu Island.*

Pronunciation

Pronunciation is indicated by using a phonetic system based on that of the Random House dictionaries (e.g., *RHD* 1987). Many placename dictionaries lack this information, and some scholars may have been reluctant to provide it because many placenames are locally pronounced in more than one way; thus *Missouri* is pronounced not only as \mi zŏŏr´ē\ but also traditionally (and especially in Missouri) as \mi zŏŏr´ə\ (see Lance 1999). In such cases I list alternative pronunciations; the order in which they are given should not be taken as significant, since multidimensional historical and sociolinguistic factors are involved.

Bibliographical references to pronunciation are not given in the dictionary itself; but see the chapter on Pronunciation above. Sometimes it has been impossible to get reliable information about the pronunciation of placenames; in those cases, no phonetic transcription is attempted here.

Etymology

This is the main body of the entry. Unfortunately, for many placenames we do not have reliable information or sometimes have no information at all. This is especially true in the Atlantic coastal areas, where Native American languages tended to become extinct soonest and where reliable data are therefore scarcest; the English spellings of Indian words there tend to be the most degraded and unreliable. For many placenames in this area, we have to reconcile ourselves to the likelihood that we will never know a clear etymology. In some cases, we may never even know whether a name is Indian or not. For example, *Hoboken* looks like a Delaware (Algonquian) word for 'tobacco pipe', but it also may be transferred from a place in Belgium.

The other especially difficult area is Alaska, which perhaps has as many placenames of Native American origin as all the rest of the continental United States. Furthermore, many of the Alaskan languages are still spoken, and our libraries contain excellent grammars and dictionaries. Nevertheless, as a result of the huge number of Native American derived placenames in Alaska, along with the difficulty of fieldwork there, etymologies are available for only a minority of such names. In Alaska, however, by contrast with New England, it seems likely that many new placename etymologies will become available in future years.

The first element of an etymology is the identification of the source language. I use the spellings currently accepted by the Smithsonian Institution's *Handbook of North American Indians*; thus I use *Ojibwa*, rather than *Ojibway* or *Chippewa*. What follows is the name of the linguistic family to which the language refers: for example, "Ojibwa (Algonquian)." When the name of the linguistic family is directly based on the name of the language, it is omitted here: therefore, instead of "Muskogee (Muskogean)," I write simply "Muskogee."

Many names of Indian tribes and languages are, of course, also placenames. In such cases they are listed as headwords; thus *Seminole* is identified both as a Muskogean language and as a placename in both Florida and Oklahoma. The names of some languages or tribes that are not currently used as placenames are also listed here. Thus, when readers find that the placename *Klondike* (actually a name transferred from Canada) is borrowed from the Gwich'in language, they can look up *Gwich'in* to find its identification as an Athabaskan language of Alaska and Canada.

Most etymologies are accompanied by bibliographical references to published sources or personal communications ("p.c.") from knowledgeable individuals. In references to alphabetically ordered dictionaries and books with adequate indexes, no page numbers are given; otherwise, page references are provided. In cases where no such source is given, the origin stated is based on my own research in the languages concerned.

Following the etymological element of each entry, information is given about occurrence of the placename in other parts of the United States. Very often we can speak of *transfers* from one state to another (e.g., *Oneida*, originating in an Iroquoian language of New York, has been borrowed in many parts of the nation); if many places have been named after an original site, I only mention a few of them. Although most such transfers are from East to West, they also occur in other directions. Thus the names of some Civil War battlefields in the South were later applied to placenames in the North, such as *Iuka*, in Mississippi, which also occurs in Illinois. Also, Gold Rush names from California were applied in the East; *Yosemite*, *Yolo*, and *Yuba* all are found in the Midwest. In still other cases, we cannot specify the direction in which a transfer occurred. Thus *Manitou*, derived from the word for 'divine spirit' in Algonquian languages such as Ojibwa, has been used as a placename in Michigan, Wisconsin, Minnesota, and other states. We cannot be sure whether it was first applied in one area and then transferred to others or whether it was in part adopted independently in separate areas.

Finally, information is given about possibly related placenames with different spellings (and sometimes different pronunciations). There is a *Cheboygan* in Michigan and a *Sheboygan* in Wisconsin (pronounced alike), both derived from an Ojibwa word for 'tobacco pipe'. It is not known whether one of these represents a transfer of the other or whether the two places were named independently.

The following sample entry illustrates these components in a sample entry.

Headword	*State*	*County*	*Pronunciation(s)*
CHICAGO	(Ill.,	Cook Co.)	\shi kô´gō, shi kä´gō\

Etymology
From Miami/Illinois (Algonquian), written by early French explorers as <*chicagou*>, meaning 'wild garlic'; it may be related to <*chicagoua, chicagoueia*> 'skunk'.

Source of Information
(Vogel 1963; Swenson 1991).

Occurrence in Other States
The name has been transferred to many other states (e.g., Colo., Clear Creek Co.; Mont., Liberty Co.).

Related Names
Chicago Lake (Mich., Delta Co.), however, probably takes its name independently from the Ojibwa (Algonquian) word for 'onion'; see **Chicagon** below.

Why Has No One Done This Before?

I can think of several possible answers to this question. One answer is that such an ambitious project was unthinkable before recent advances in computers. Another answer is that most people working in the field have been writing for local audiences, frequently defined in terms of either state university presses or state and county historical societies; and their ambitions have been correspondingly restrained. Another point is that local writers who have studied regional toponymy generally have not had access to the research methods of American Indian linguistics or to the bibliographical resources available in that field; this is a major respect in which I hope this volume contributes something new. Finally, a possible reason why there has been no previous American Indian placenames volume is that—if one thinks of a totally comprehensive and perfect work—the job is indeed too daunting for anyone to undertake. But that is not what I have undertaken. This is intended to be a large reference work but not necessarily the largest or most complete that could ever be published.

Will This Book Settle All the Problems?

No, of course not; but at the same time, I do not knowingly repeat old errors. It is clear that many such errors already in print have resulted from ignoring available knowledge of American Indian languages. With the help of linguist colleagues, however, I feel confident that I have resolved many such problems. But especially in eastern states, where many Native American languages have been long extinct, some problems can never be solved with certainty. In these cases, I can only cite etymologies that have been suggested by earlier writers, adding appropriate qualifiers such as "perhaps." I will always prefer to admit a gap in knowledge rather than to offer unqualified speculations like some that have appeared in print.

What Should Be Included?

The question arises as to whether this book should include only words borrowed from Indian languages or whether it should also include names *translated* from Indian languages and words with even less definite association with Indian languages. For example, many states have an *Indian Creek*, perhaps so named because someone encountered an Indian or a group of Indians or an Indian village there—but the name carries little information of a cultural or historical sort. The general question remains: What are the criteria for inclusion? My intention here has been to include all names from the GNIS that appear to be derived from Indian words and also to include loan translations from Native American languages, like *Black Hills*, when there is evidence to identify them as such. Other types of cultural and historical associations are recognized only when they are rather specific; for example, the name *Medicine Lodge* in Kansas may not be the translation of an Indian term, but it refers to a specifically Native American cultural object: the sacred sweathouse in which Indian ceremonialists carried out their rituals.

A Possible Typology and Its Elaboration

It is useful to think of the placenames in this book as falling into a number of types (cf. Smith 1996). To be sure, typologies should not be carved in stone. They have value only to the extent that they are helpful in research, and any proposed typology needs to be tested in terms of its continuing usefulness. With this in mind, the following classification can be considered.

Traditional Native American Placenames

These can be defined as terms that we believe were used as placenames in the Native American languages, like *Chicago*, probably 'wild onion place', and *Tucson*, 'black (mountain) base'. But as this category is defined here, it includes an immense number of names—tens of thousands, at the very least—that have never entered English usage. Indeed, only a relatively small number of them have been recorded, typically by anthropologists, under the heading of *ethnogeography*. Exemplary works of this genre include T. T. Waterman's *Yurok Geography* (1920, for a tribe of California) and Eugene Hunn's *Nch'i-wana, "The Big River": Mid-Columbia Indians and Their Land* (1990).

Several American Indians have told me that their tribes need research on their native placenames and have asked whether I can help them. I agree that such work is important, and I have in fact done such research for the Karuk tribe in California. But unfortunately the present book is not able to address this need; since the scope of this work is very broad in one sense—covering the entire United States—it has to be limited in another sense—restricted to those Indian placenames that have entered English usage.

A problem that occasionally arises is that we are not sure whether an ostensible Indian placename may have a European source. For instance, *Galice* is the name of an Athabaskan Indian tribe, a settlement, and a creek in Oregon, and it is explained by McArthur (1992) as a French surname. In the 1950s, however, the last surviving speaker of the Galice language told the anthropologist Harry Hoijer that the name represented an Indian pronunciation *galiis* of the English word *Kelly's*—the settlement was named after a miner called Kelly. A search of the Paris phonebook shows that *Galice* is indeed a French surname, although a rare one. To the extent that the derivation from *Kelly's* may be valid, we have the possibility of a placename that has an Indian history, although its ultimate source is European.

Native American Derivations

This class can be defined as terms derived from the Native American languages of an area, though we may not be sure that they were used as placenames by the Indian people. This clearly includes a large number of the placenames covered in the present book. But several subtypes can be distinguished:

1. Some are names of prominent Indian individuals, such as *Seattle* and *Spokane*.

2. Some are derived from other words of local Indian languages, such as *Chittamo* (Wisconsin) from Ojibwa *ajidamoo* 'red squirrel'. It should be noted, however, that the English word *chipmunk,* found in placenames of Wisconsin and other states, is itself derived from the same Ojibwa word. In the case of a particular place called *Chipmunk Rapids*, we may not be able to tell whether the term was borrowed directly from Ojibwa or is simply the English word.

3. A special category consists of placenames in which white explorers evidently interpreted Indian generic terms as if they were specific. Thus when John C. Fremont's party first saw Lake Tahoe in 1844, they asked a Washo Indian what it was called. The Indian said *dá'aw* 'a lake', which was written down in English as *Tahoe*. In 1877 the Wheeler surveying party in the same area asked another Washo to identify a California mountain; the Indian said *dalá'ak* 'a mountain', which became *Mount Tallac*.

Pidgin Derivations

These names are derived from Amerindian-based pidgin languages (mixed languages used between Native American people and European immigrants). Many cases involve the Chinook Jargon, a trade language of the Pacific Northwest, containing elements of several Native American languages, especially Chinookan and Salishan, as well as French and English. Again some subtypes can be distinguished.

1. A name may come from the pidgin, which in turn takes it from a Native American language. Thus the word and toponym *Skookum*, occurring in many northwestern placenames, represents the Chinook Jargon for 'strong, powerful', borrowed in turn from a Salishan language.

2. A name may come from the pidgin but have its ultimate origin in a European language. For example, the word *Siwash*, again occurring in many northwestern placenames, represents the Chinook Jargon word for 'Indian', borrowed from French *sauvage*.

Transferred Derivations

These are terms that have been borrowed from a Native American language into a European language and are then applied as placenames outside the original geographic area. These are very common and constitute a large proportion of the names included in this work. Again some subtypes can be distinguished.

1. Common nouns used in English are often carried from one region to another. For example, *Tepee Flats* (Idaho) uses the Siouan term *thípi* 'house', which is native to the Great Plains. *The Pogonip*, a frequently foggy hillside overlooking Santa Cruz, California, is an application of a word that English speakers in the Great Basin had borrowed from Numic *pakɨnappɨ* 'fog'. (For a historical account of such words, apart from their use as placenames, see Cutler 1994.)

2. Transferred placenames are common. For example, *Milwaukee*, transferred from Wisconsin to Oregon, and *Chicago*, as applied to *Port Chicago* in California, were originally Algonquian placenames. Some names are borrowed from Latin American sources into North America; thus *Mexico*, *Lima*, and *Peru* are frequent on the map of the United States.

3. Some names are locally thought to be of Indian origin but actually have European origins. Thus, as noted above, *Calumet* (Illinois, Michigan), understood as a word for 'Indian pipe', is borrowed by English from a Norman French dialect word, related to Standard French *chalumeau* 'type of flute'. Such a word, then, does not actually have an Indian origin, but was applied as a placename because of its Indian cultural associations.

Dubious Native American Terms

These are imaginative, sometimes even fraudulent, attempts to imitate Indian models. I have given examples above, but again there are subtypes.

1. Complete inventions are sometimes found. An example is *Lake Itasca*, the Minnesota origin of the Mississippi River; the name was coined by Henry R. Schoolcraft, who also gave imaginary Indian names to several counties in Michigan. In the case of *Itasca*, he took letters from an intended but ungrammatical Latin phrase: *veritas caput*, supposed to mean 'true head(waters)' (cf. Vogel 1991; better Latin would be *verum caput*).

2. Some supposedly Indian names were originally given currency by literary works, especially Henry Wadsworth Longfellow's *Hiawatha* (see Cowan 1987). Some of these, however, have been considerably distorted in sound or meaning. An example is the word *Hiawatha* itself, now found as a placename in many states. In this case the name was not originally fictitious; it was borne by a famous Iroquois leader in New York, but apparently the poet liked the sound of it and applied it to the hero of his epic, who was supposed to be an Algonquian of the Great Lakes area. In other cases, names taken from Longfellow cannot be traced to any genuine Indian origin at all.

3. Some placenames are based on English words that are supposedly literal translations of Native American concepts, but they may be of varying authenticity. One type consists of terms like *Medicine Lodge Mountains* (Kansas), as noted above; this may translate a Native American term or may not. *Pipestone Creek* (Wisconsin) is supposed to translate an Algonquian word for a type of stone from which the Indians made pipe-bowls; but we cannot confirm the original Indian name of the place. White settlers could simply have coined the term *pipestone*, as a common noun, under Native American inspiration, and later applied the word as a placename.

4. Some cases have still more dubious origins. A widespread name like "Badger Creek" is sometimes assumed on very little evidence to represent a translation of an Indian name. A particular stream may or may not have had an Indian name meaning 'badger creek'; but if it was frequented by badgers, it was very likely to be given such a name in English. If a name has no clearly documented Indian association, either linguistic or cultural, I have not included it here.

Adopted European Names

These are placenames referring to Native American people who have adopted European names. In this category falls a placename like *Adams* (Massachusetts), named for an otherwise obscure Indian with that family name. Other types of adopted names, however, may be of greater linguistic or historical interest.

1. Some names reflect cases where English has borrowed an Indian personal name, which was borrowed in turn from a European language; an example is *Lolo Pass* (Montana), said to be from a Salish personal name *Lolo,* from French *Laurent*. (Salish has no *r* sound, so it replaces French *r* with *l*; but in fact *Lolo* may be a perfectly good French nickname.) A somewhat more complex case is *Stanislaus* (river and county in California); this is an English adaptation of *Estanislao,* the Spanish baptismal name of an Indian who became famous for his successful raids on Spanish missions.

2. Other names are simple loan translations; thus *Black Hawk* and *Big Foot Beach* (Wisconsin) are translations of the names of Algonquian leaders.

3. Some placenames are only ambiguously of Indian origin. For instance, is *Saint Germain* (Wisconsin) named after the French soldier Jean François St. Germain who arrived in the area in the seventeenth century or after one or more of his mixed-blood descendants who have lived in Wisconsin ever since?

English < Spanish/French < Indian

Some placenames are borrowings from Spanish or French common nouns that are in turn borrowed from Native American languages. We can recognize the following categories.

1. Some placenames are borrowed through Spanish or French but ultimately come from Indian languages of the same area; for example, *Abalone Point* (California) reflects California Spanish *aulón(es)*, from Rumsen *aulon*.

2. Some placenames are transferred, through Spanish or French, from some other colonized area; thus, *Temescal Canyon* (California) is from Mexican Spanish *temescal* 'sweathouse', from Aztec *temaxcalli.* A possible example involving French is *Muskellunge* (Michigan, Wisconsin), from the English name of a type of fish resembling a pike—from French *masquinonge*, from Ojibwa *maashkinoozhe* 'evil(-looking) pike'.

3. Some names involve transformation via folk-etymology in Spanish or French, based on an earlier Indian name; thus *Temetate Creek* (California) takes its name from the Mexican Spanish word *temetate* 'stone grinding-slab', ostensibly from Aztec *temetlatl.* But this is probably in fact a reworking of the original Chumash placename, which was /stemeqtatimi/; its original meaning is unknown. Another example is the name of the *Canadian River* (Colorado, Oklahoma), from Sp. *canadiano,* seemingly from the name of the country *Canada* (transmitted through French but originally Iroquoian); however, the name is probably in fact a folk-etymological reshaping of Caddo /káyántinu'/, the name of the nearby Red River.

4. Some names, borrowed by English through Spanish or French, are specifically derived from American Indian placenames in colonies outside the United States. This is then a special category of *transfer* placenames, of two types.

a. As noted above, names borrowed through Spanish from Latin America include placenames such as *Mexico* (Missouri) and *Lima* (Ohio, originally from *Lima* in Peru).

b. Names borrowed from French Canada include familiar ones like *Quebec* and *Ontario.* These names require some special attention, however, since most of them come from Iroquoian or Algonquian languages that are spoken in both Canada and the United States; there may sometimes be doubt as to whether a name was first borrowed in the United States, or on the Canadian side of the border.

Hybrid Indian Names

These are coined from parts of two or more other names, at least one of which is of Indian origin. The motive for such coinages is usually that the site is located at or near the places whose names are represented in the hybrid; examples are *Texarkana* (Texas, Arkansas) and *Clackamette* (Oregon, from *Clackamas* plus *Willamette*). Such names of course have no motivation in American Indian culture or history. They are included in this book, however, because of their interest as curiosities and because they may occasionally be mistaken for genuine Indian names.

Why the Linguistic Details?

Some entries in some placename publications, including the present one, read more or less like this: "The term 'Tallahassee' may be from Creek, meaning 'old town'." This amount of information may indeed satisfy the curiosity of some readers. The question then arises: Except in the rare case where the reader may be a speaker of Creek, or a specialist in the language, why should any effort be made to specify the regional variety of Creek involved—whether the Muskogee of Oklahoma, or the Seminole of Oklahoma, or the Seminole of Florida? Why should the native Muskogee name be presented both in the traditional orthography as *tvlvhasse* and in a technical notation as /talahá:ssi/? Why is it noted that the name was probably that of an original tribal town in Georgia but was first reported in Florida in 1799 in the form "Sim-e-no-le-tallau-has-see" (i.e., "Seminole Tallahassee")? Why is the etymology specified as probably involving a shortened form of *etvlwv* /(i)tálwa/ 'tribal town' plus *vhvssē* 'rancid, old'? Why is it stated that the name *Tallahassee* is probably connected to *Tullahassee* in Oklahoma (McIntosh Co.), *Talisi* in Alabama (Lowndes Co.), *Tulse* in Alabama (Shelby Co.), and *Tulsa* in Oklahoma? And why are there specific bibliographic references to Read 1934, Goff 1975, and Martin and Mauldin 2000?

The answer to the question about bibliography is of course self-evident: this information is given so that readers can check on me—they can go back to these books and see whether I have reported them right. In fact, the references to related placenames in Oklahoma and Alabama also lend themselves to bibliographical checking: one can look up books on the placenames of Oklahoma and Alabama and see to what extent they agree about this family of related names.

But beyond these matters of bibliography, the other details given in my entries have a similar purpose: to help readers validate the accuracy of what I say and evaluate the likelihood of the etymologies that I offer. If readers are speakers of Muskogee or Seminole, or if they can find speakers of those varieties, then they can see and hear for themselves whether those speakers write and pronounce the words in the ways indicated and use them with the meanings indicated.

To put the matter bluntly: in all placename books, again including this one, there is a large proportion of uncertain etymologies, doubtful ones, and sometimes even nonsensical ones. The purpose of giving such detailed information is for the sake of those readers who hold the proverbial attitude of people from Missouri (or Missoura): they want to be shown the evidence.

Must Every Name Have an Etymology?

A persistent bit of folklore about language in general is that the meaning of words on some essential level is to be found in their histories rather than in their use. This idea has been raised recently in discussion of the stigmatized word *squaw*—which some people believe to originate in an Iroquoian word meaning 'vagina'; it is actually from an Algonquian word for 'woman' (Bright 2000c). Such belief in the covert significance of etymology also turns up in discussions of Native American placenames.

One of the most prominent scholars in the field of placenames was Erwin G. Gudde (1889–1969), a professor of German literature at Berkeley who became an authority on California history; he was the founding editor of *Names* (the journal of the American Name Society) and the author of *California Place Names,* one of the most respected state placename dictionaries. Gudde's dictionary, published by the University of California Press, went through three editions between 1949 and 1969; a fourth edition (revised by me) came out in 1998. Gudde often seemed reluctant to examine possible American Indian etymologies for California placenames, however, and indeed his attitudes toward

Native American cultures were sometimes off the mark. Thus he stated in his preface (3rd ed., 1969: xiv): "The original inhabitants had very few geographical names, and practically all of these were descriptive . . . Mountains themselves were of no practical importance to the Indians and probably had no names."

This statement is remarkable, considering that Gudde was familiar with such works as T. T. Waterman's *Yurok Geography* (Berkeley, 1920), which lists over 900 placenames (including mountains) used in the rather limited territory of the Yurok tribe and language. For years I was puzzled as to how Gudde could have said that American Indians "had very few geographical names." Only more recently, while reading extensively on American toponymy, have I realized that Gudde's statement reflects a long-standing attitude among onomastic scholars. In recent years, Leonard Ashley (1996:1403) has written: "What we think of as placenames may differ considerably from names Amerindians put upon the land. The red man [*sic*] considered himself a part of nature, not the master of it. . . . The names he gave were more like descriptions: any large river might be 'big river'. . . . It is arguable that an Amerindian name that translates 'where there is a heap of stones' . . . is no more a name in our strict sense than the expression 'the corner grocery that stays open until midnight'."

The ethnocentric message of these quotations seems to be that American Indians, seen as children of nature, did not have real placenames; to the extent that such names had clear etymologies, they could be regarded as mere "descriptions." We might say the same of American English placenames like *Long Island, Great Falls,* or *Grand Canyon.* But two other points can be made. First, many Native American placenames were indeed morphologically complex and semantically "descriptive," but they are not fairly represented by such translations as 'where there is a heap of stones'. Thus the Karuk placename *asánaamkarak,* on the Klamath River in northwestern California, can be interpreted etymologically as 'where a rocky flat place extends into the water'. Thanks to the "polysynthetic" character of the Karuk language, however, the Native American name is not a cumbersome phrase like the English translation; it is a single word and a single lexical item and as much a proper name as *Rocky Flats.*

Second, Native Americans used many placenames that were not descriptive. They consisted of single morphemes, with no meaning except their toponymic reference. Karuk village names included terms such as *Píptaas, Kíinik, Útkee, Tíih, Kúuyiv, Túuyvuk,* and *Vúpam.* These are just as unanalyzable, whether by the linguist or by the native speaker, as European placenames like *London, Paris,* or *Rome.* To be sure, all these names may have once been "descriptive"—but their etymologies, whether American Indian or European, have long been irrelevant to their usage. Their meanings are, to quote one of my favorite clichés, "lost in the mists of antiquity."

The same principle applies to many names of Native American tribes and languages, such as Cherokee and Choctaw. (Some of these have also come to be used by white people as placenames.) It is clear that English borrowed the first of these terms from the Cherokee self-designation *Tsalagi,* and the second from the Choctaw self-designation *Chahta.* In their respective languages, these words mean nothing more or less than 'Cherokee' and 'Choctaw'. Some commentators on Indian ethnic names and placenames have strained their imaginations to propose fanciful etymologies. So it has been said that *Cherokee* comes from a Creek (Muskogee) word meaning 'people of a different speech'. The Creek word for 'Cherokee' is *Cvlakke* /čalá:kki/, however, probably borrowed from Cherokee *Tsalagi*; and the unrelated word meaning 'to speak a different language' is *celokketv* /čilo:kk-itá/ (Martin and Mauldin 2000). As for the Choctaw word *Chahta,* it has been said that "its meaning is unknown"; but, as Pamela Munro (p.c.) points out, one might as well just say that its meaning is 'Choctaw'. Of course such names must have had *some* remote historical origins; but those are lost to us and are irrelevant to the speakers of Cherokee or Choctaw. The same label, "meaning unknown," could be attached to European ethnic names such as *German* or *Greek.*

For such reasons, I have simply stated in this book that some English placenames are derived from Indian terms that, as such, had no etymology. The buck, so to speak, stops with the Indian placename itself.

Conclusion

The main defects of this volume, with regard to inadequate or nonexistent etymologies, have been noted above. Some of them, especially in Alaska, can certainly be remedied by further research. Others, especially on the Atlantic seaboard, may never be remedied.

Nevertheless, I think it is clear that the present book goes much further, in both inclusiveness and accuracy, than any earlier reference source on placenames of American Indian origin. The perfect etymological dictionary of such names will never exist; but better books of this type will exist in the future, and I trust that my work will help to make them possible.

Native American Placenames

A

A'AI STO (Ariz., Pima Co.). O'odham (Piman) *a'ai sto* 'white on both sides'; cf. *a'ai* 'on both sides', *s-toha* 'white' (J. Hill p.c.) A possible variant is **Asai Sto.**

AASAYII Wash (Ariz., Navajo Co.) \ä sä´ yē\. Probably Navajo (Athabaskan) *ásaayi'* 'in a bowl', from *ásaa'* 'bowl, pot, kettle', *-yi'* 'in it' (A. Wilson p.c.). A related name is **Asayi** (N.Mex., McKinley Co.).

AATS Bay (Alaska, Craig D-7) \äts\. From Tlingit *áat dàa* 'Coronation Island', containing *dàa* 'island' (T. Thornton p.c.).

ABACOOCHEE (Ala., Talladega Co.) \ab ə ko͞o´ chē\. Muskogee *apehkuce* /a:pihkočí/, a traditional Creek "tribal town"; from *apehkv* /a:píhka/ 'Arbeka, name of a tribal town' and *-uce* /očí/ 'little' (Martin and Mauldin 2000). A related name is **Arbacoochee** (Ala., Cleburne Co.).

ABACOTNETIC Stream (Maine, Somerset Co.). Said to reflect an Abenaki (Algonquian) name meaning 'stream opening out from between mountains' (Rutherford 1970); the Native American name consists of /apak-/ 'flat', /atən/ 'mountain', and /-atak/ 'stream place' (P. MacDougall p.c.).

ABAGADASSET River (Maine, Sagadahoc Co.) \ab ə gə das´ ət\. Written in early times as <Abbacadusset, Abagadassic> (etc.) (Eckstorm 1941). The native form is Abenaki (Algonquian) /apakatehset/ 'where it lies flat'; cf. /apakatehsin/ 'it lies flat' (P. MacDougall p.c.)

ABAK'IN SHILOW IM'A (N.Mex., McKinley Co.). The Zuni placename perhaps contains /šilowa/ 'be red' (Ferguson and Hart 1985, Newman 1958).

ABALONE \ab ə lō´ nē\. The name of a large mollusk found on the California coast, valued for its meat and for its shell lined with mother-of-pearl; the term is reflected in the names of several points and coves. It comes from the Rumsen language (Costanoan family), in which *awlun* means 'red abalone'. The Indian word became Spanish *aulón, avalone,* and both versions entered English (Gudde 1998). As a placename, **Abalone** occurs in Calif. (Monterey Co.), and also in Alaska (Dixon Entrance D-2).

ABANAKA (Ohio, Van Wert Co.) \ab ə nak´ ə\. Perhaps from Miami/Illinois (Algonquian) /waapanahkia/ 'Delaware Indian', lit. 'easterner' (M. McCafferty p.c.). The term is related to the tribal name **Abenaki**; see **Abenaki Brook** below.

ABANAKEE, Lake (N.Y., Hamilton Co.) \ab ə nak´ ē\. From the same origin as **Abenaki Brook**; see below.

ABARAMIUT (Alaska, Nunivak Island B-5). The Yupik (Eskimo) name was reported in 1949 (Orth 1967); the ending *-miut* means 'people'.

ABBIE Creek (Ala., Henry Co.) \ab´ ē\. A shortening of earlier <Yattayabba, Pattayaba>; apparently from a Muskogean language, but the derivation is unclear (Read 1984).

ABENAKI Brook (N.H., Coös Co.) \ä bə nä´ kē, ab ə nak´ ē\. The name is that of an Algonquian group, also spelled **Abnaki,** who are native to upper N.Y. state, the province of Ontario, and adjacent areas. The origin is in the group's own name *wǫbanakii,* perhaps adapted from <ouabanăkiouek> 'dawn-land people, easterners', as used in the Montagnais (Algonquian) language of Canada (*HNAI* 15:148). Related placenames are **Abenaquis Dam** (Maine, Somerset Co.) and **Abeniki Mountain** (N.H., Somerset Co.). Also related are the names **Abanaka** (Ohio, Van Wert Co.), **Abanakee** (N.Y., Hamilton Co.), and **Wapanacki** (Ver., Lamoille Co.).

ABERJONA River (Mass., Middlesex Co.). Said to be from SNEng. Algonquian, meaning 'junction, confluence' (Huden 1962).

ABIACA Creek (Miss., Holmes Co.). Also written <Abyatchie, Abiacha, Abyache> (etc.) (BGN 7503). Perhaps from Choctaw (Muskogean) *abayyaci* 'to go along the side'; cf. *abayyaka* 'side of a swamp or creek' (Seale 1939; P. Munro p.c.).

ABIHKA (Ala., Talladega Co.) \ə bē´ kə\. Muskogee *apehkv* /a:píhka/ (Martin & Mauldin 2002).

ABIKUDSHI (Ala., Talladega Co.) \ab i kōō´ chē\. From Choctaw (Muskogean) *aayabikoshi* 'little place of sickness' (Read 1984), with the diminutive ending *-oshi* (P. Munro p.c.).

ABINODJI Falls (Mich., Gogebic Co.) \ab i nō´ jē\. From Ojibwa (Algonquian) *abinoojiinh* 'child' (Vogel 1986, Nichols and Nyholm 1995).

ABIQUA Creek (Ore., Marion Co.) \ab´ i kwä, ə bē´ kwə\. Perhaps from Tualatin (Kalapuyan) /mámp^h^kwi, ámp^h^kwi/ 'hazelnut' (H. Zenk p.c.).

ABIQUIU (N.Mex., Rio Arriba Co.) \ä´ bi kyōō, ä bi kyōō´\. The Spanish spelling represents Tewa (Tanoan) /ávéšúʔ/ (HNAI 9:199).

ABITA Springs (La., St. Tammany Par.) \ə bē´ tə\. Perhaps from Choctaw (Muskogean) *ibiitop* 'end, tip' (P. Munro p.c.). The name also occurs in Minn. (Cook Co.).

ABITOSSE Creek (Mich., Gogebic Co.). The Ojibwa (Algonquian) name is said to mean 'it comes to or arrives to the middle' (Vogel 1986).

ABO (N.Mex., Torrance Co.) \ä bō´\. From the extinct Tompiro language, said to have meant 'water bowl' (Julyan 1998).

ABOITE River (Ind., Allen Co.). From French *rivière à boite* 'muddy river', with *boite, bouette* 'mud', corresponding to Miami/Illinois (Algonquian) /neekawasiipi/ 'sand river', with /neekaw-/ 'sand' (McCafferty 2002).

ABOL Falls (Maine, Piscataquis Co.) \ā´ bôl\. Shortened from Abenaki (Algonquian) <Aboljackarnegassic> (Rutherford 1970); the Native American name is /apaləčehkamikéhsihtək^y^/ 'where there is a small stream on a small barren knoll' (P. MacDougall p.c.).

ABOTCAPUTA Creek (Miss., Carroll Co.). Perhaps from Choctaw (Muskogean) *apokta* 'something doubled' and *patha* 'broad', referring to a broad creek consisting of two branches (Seale 1939; P. Munro p.c.). Also written as **Abotcaputta.**

ABRAQUIDASSAT Point (Maine, Washington Co.) Perhaps from Penobscot (Algonquian) /apəlahk^y^ítasset/ 'where it is barren and juts into the water' (P. MacDougall p.c.).

ABSARAKA (N.Dak., Cass Co.) \ab sə rä´ kə\. A name related to **Absaroka**; see **Absaroka Range** below. Another related name is **Absarraca Lake** (Wyo., Laramie Co.) \ab sə rak´ ə\.

ABSAROKA Range (Wyo., Park Co.) \ab sâr´ ə kə\. Named for the Crow (Siouan) people, who call themselves *apsa'alooka* 'crow, raven' (R. Graczyk p.c.) A related placename is **Absarokee** (Mont., Stillwater Co.); other related names are **Absaraka** (N.Dak., Cass Co.); and **Absarraca** (Wyo., Laramie Co.).

ABSECON (N.J., Atlantic Co.). Also recorded as **Absecom;** the derivation from a Delaware (Algonquian) origin is unclear (Becker 1964). A possibly related name is **Lake Absegami** (N.J., Burlington Co.).

ABYATCHIE Creek (Miss., Holmes Co.). A name related to **Abiaca**; see **Abiaca Creek** above.

ACABONACK Cliff (N.Y., Suffolk Co.). Said to take its name from an Algonquian word for a kind of edible root or tuber, sometimes called 'ground nut'; also written **Accaponack** (Beauchamp 1907; Tooker 1911).

ACADIA \ə kā´ dē ə\. This placename, corresponding to French *Acadie,* was originally applied to the maritime provinces of Canada plus adjacent parts of Quebec and Maine. Its origin may involve borrowing of a Micmac (Algonquian) term as well as confusion with the classical Greek placename *Arcadia.* In 1755 the British government deported several thousand French-speaking Acadians from the area; many subsequently settled in Louisiana (Read 1927). There they were known in French as *acadiens,* giving rise to the English word *Cajun.* In the United States, the placename Acadia is found in Maine (Aroostook Co.) and La. (Lafourche Par.).

ACALA (Tex., Hudspeth Co.) \ə kä´ lə\. The name is from "Acala cotton," a variety originating in Mexico (Tarpley 1980). The Mexican placename represents Nahuatl (Aztecan) *acallan* 'place of boats', from *acalli* 'boat', lit. 'water-house', composed of *a(tl)* 'water' and *calli* 'house'.

ACALANES (Calif., Contra Costa Co.) \ä kə lā´ nēz\. The name is from an Indian group within the Miwokan family, now usually referred to as Saklan. Spanish *Los Sacalanes* 'the Saklans' was reinterpreted as *Los Acalanes* in a document of 1834 (Gudde 1998).

ACAPESKET (Mass., Barnstable Co.) \ak ə pes´ kət\. From SNEng. Algonquian, containing <aucupaese-> 'small cove' and <-et> 'place' (W. Cowan p.c.).

ACAPULCO (S.C., Lexington Co.) \ak ə po͞ol´ kō\. Named for the city in Mexico; from Nahuatl (Aztecan) *acapulco* 'place of the large canes', with *aca(tl)* 'cane (plant)', *-pul* 'large', and *-co* 'place'.

ACCABEE Flats (S.C., Charleston Co.) \ak´ ə bē\. Earlier written <Ickerby>, <Ickaby> (Waddell 1980). Perhaps from an unidentified Indian language (Pickens 1963:37).

ACCACEEK (Va., Richmond Co.). A form related to **Accokeek**; see below.

ACCAPONACK (N.Y., Suffolk Co.). A variant of **Acabonack Cliff** (N.Y., Suffolk Co.).

ACCOKEEK (Md., Prince George's Co.) \ak´ ə kēk\. Earlier <Acquakick>; apparently Algonquian, perhaps meaning 'at the edge of the hill' (Kenny 1984). The placename also occurs in Va. (Stafford Co.). A related name is **Accaceek** (Va., Richmond Co.).

ACCOMAC (Va., Accomack Co.) \ak´ ə mak\. Perhaps from CAC Algonquian <acaume-> 'the other side', <-auk> 'land' (Trumbull 1879, W. Cowan p.c.). While the name of the town is spelled **Accomac**, the county is **Accomack** (Hagemann 1988). The name **Accomac** is also found in Pa. (York Co.).

ACCOMPSETT (N.Y., Suffolk Co.) \ə komp´ sət\. Abbreviated from a SNEng. Algonquian placename <Nesaquaque Accompsett>, translated as 'the place opposite Nesaquaque', otherwise known as **Nissequogue** (Tooker 1911).

ACHARON Channel (Alaska, Black C-1). The Yupik (Eskimo) name "may be derived from the word for slough" (Orth 1967).

ACHI (Ariz., Pima Co.) \ä´ chē\. From O'odham (Piman) *aji* 'thin, narrow' (J. Hill p.c.).

ACHIMIN Basin (WA, Okanogan Co.). Possibly from an Okanagan (Salishan) toponym /ʕacmín/ (D. Kinkade p.c.).

ACHONEE, Mount (Colo., Grand Co.) \ə chō´ nē\. Probably named for a Cheyenne (Algonquian) leader, Ochanee or Ochinee, meaning 'one-eye', who was killed at the Sand Creek Massacre in 1864 (Bright 1993).

ACHUNACHI (Ala., De Kalb Co.) \ach ə nach´ ē\. From Choctaw (Muskogean) *achnąchi* 'perseverance, resolution' (Read 1984; P. Munro p.c.).

ACIPCO (Ala., Jefferson Co.) \ə sip´ kō\. Perhaps from Muskogee *acvpko* /a:-čápko:/ 'place where it is long' (P. Munro p.c.).

ACKAN MANANGAHA (Del., New Castle Co.). A Delaware (Algonquian) name, possibly meaning 'the land of the large owl' (Heck et al. 1966).

ACOAXET (Mass., Bristol Co.). Perhaps from a SNEng. Algonquian word meaning 'at the fishing promontory' (Huden 1962).

ACOCK Pond (Ala., Houston Co.). Perhaps from Choctaw (Muskogean) *hohtaak* 'pond' (Read 1984; P. Munro p.c.).

ACOMA Pueblo (N.Mex., Cibola Co.). \ä´ kō mə, ak´ ō mə, ak´ ə mə\. From Spanish *Ácoma,* from Acoma (Keresan) *áak'úume* 'a person from Acoma', containing *áak'u* 'Acoma pueblo' (I. Davis p.c.). **Acoma** is found elsewhere as a transfer name (Ariz., Maricopa Co.; Minn., McLeod Co.).

ACOMILLA (N.Mex., Socorro Co.) \ä kə mē´ yə\. A Spanish diminutive of *Ácoma*, the term for the pueblo. Another diminutive is **Acomita** (N.Mex., Cibola Co.).

ACQUACKANONK, Lake (N.J., Sussex Co.) \ə kwak´ ə nongk\. Earlier <Haquequenunck>, with some eighty other spellings (Becker 1964). The derivation from Delaware (Algonquian) is obscure, but there may be a relationship to <achgonican, achquanican> 'fish dam' (Brinton and Anthony 1888); cf. Munsee Delaware *akwaaníikan* 'fishing net' (O'Meara 1996).

ACTEON Ridge (N.H., Grafton Co.). The name of a leader of the Pemigewasset (Algonquian) Indians (Julyan and Julyan 1993); perhaps modeled on Acteon, a figure in Greek mythology.

ACUSHNET (Mass., Bristol Co.) \ə ko͞osh´ nət\. From SNEng. Algonquian, 'at the wet place', containing <ogqushki-> 'it is wet', <-et > 'place' (W. Cowan p.c.).

ADADKA Spring (Ariz., Navajo Co.) \ə däd´ kə\. Navajo (Athabaskan) *adáá' dik'ą́* 'slanted ridge', from *adáá'* 'ridge, edge, ledge', *dik'ą́* 'it is slanted' (A. Wilson p.c.).

ADAGDAK, Cape (Alaska, Adak C-2). From the Aleut placename *adagdax̂* (Bergsland 1994).

ADAHCHIJIYAHI Canyon (Ariz., Navajo Co.). From Navajo (Athabaskan) *adah ch'íjíyáhí* 'where someone walked off a cliff', containing *adah* 'downward', *ch'í* 'outward horizontally', and *jíyá* 'someone walked' (A. Wilson p.c.).

ADAH HILLINI (Utah, San Juan Co.). From Navajo (Athabaskan) *adahiilí, adahiilíní* 'water dropping down' (Linford 2000).

ADAK Island (Alaska, Adak C-2) \ā´ dak\. From the Aleut placename *adaax, addaagix̂* (Bergsland 1994).

ADANAC Creek (Alaska, Ketchikan D-1). Probably **Canada** spelled backward.

ADENA (Ohio, Jefferson Co.) \ə dē´ nə\. This name is applied to a mound-building culture of prehistoric North America and to the **Adena Mound** in Ohio. It bears an accidental similarity to a widely distributed Algonquian word for 'mountain', exemplifed by Abenaki *aden,* but in fact it was coined from ancient Greek *ádēn* 'enough' (Kenny 1967).

ADIRONDACK Mountains (N.Y., St. Lawrence Co.) \ad i ron´ dak\. The term is a back-formation from *Adirondacks,* treated as if it were a plural. In origin, however, the word is from Mohawk (Iroquoian) *adirǫ́:daks* 'tree-eaters', a name applied to neighboring Algonquian groups. This is derived from *ratirǫ́:taks* 'they eat trees', containing *rati-* 'masculine plural agent', *-ati-* 'tree', *-ak-* 'to eat', and *-s* 'imperfective' (Heller 1989; M. Mithun p.c.).

ADOIS (La., Natchitoches Par.) \ad ē ōs`\. Earlier recorded as <Adayes>; originally a French or English plural form of *Adai,* a Caddo subgroup, said to be derived from <hadai> 'brushwood'. The local pronunciation apparently results from a confusion with Spanish *adiós* 'goodbye' (Read 1927).

ADRIGIGON Creek (Alaska, Wainwright A-2). The Iñupiaq (Eskimo) name was reported in 1926 (Orth 1967).

ADUGAK Island (Alaska, Samalga Island D-4). From the Aleut placename *adugax̂* (Bergsland 1994).

ADULTERY Dune (AZ, Apache Co.). Corresponds to Navajo (Athabaskan) *séí adiléhé* 'adultery sand', because the dune was a secluded place visited by illicit lovers (Linford 2000). The name contains *séí* 'sand' (Young and Morgan 1987).

AENEAS (Wash., Okanogan Co.) \ē´ nē əs\. Named for an Indian, Aeneas Somday, who died around 1880. His name is said to have been a distortion of French *Ignace* [iñás] 'Ignatius' (Hitchman 1985). The English spelling is apparently inspired by the name of Aeneas, a hero of ancient Roman legend.

AFFONEE Creek (Ala., Bibb Co.) \af´ nē\. Perhaps from Choctaw (Muskogean) *naafoni* 'bone' (Read 1984; P. Munro p.c.).

AFOGNAK (Alaska, Afognak A-3) \ə fog´ nak\. The name is probably Alutiiq (Eskimo); it was first recorded as <Afagnack> in 1780 (Orth 1967).

AGAAK Creek (Alaska, Killik River A-2). The Iñupiaq (Eskimo) name was recorded in 1956 (Orth 1967).

AGA Cove (Alaska, Attu A-1). An abbreviation of the name of **Agattu Island** (see below), on which the cove is located (Orth 1967).

AGAGRAK Creek (Alaska, Noatak C-4). The Iñupiaq (Eskimo) name is *aakagraq* 'stepmother'; cf. **Agarak,** below.

AGAI PAH Hills (Nev., Mineral Co.) \ə gī´ pä\. From Northern Paiute (Numic) /akaipa'a/ [aɣaiva'a], lit. 'trout water', the name for Walker Lake. It contains /akai/ 'trout' and /paa/ 'water' (J. McLaughlin p.c.).

AGAKLAROK (Alaska, Kwiguk C-6). The Yupik (Eskimo) name was recorded in 1899 (Orth 1967).

AGAMENTICUS, Mount (Maine, York Co.) \ag ə men´ ti kəs\. The name may reflect an Abenaki (Algonquian) word meaning 'the other side of the little river' (Rutherford 1970).

AGAMGIK Bay (Alaska, Unalaska C-2). From Aleut *agamgix̂* 'red chiton, gum boot', a mollusk (Bergsland 1994).

AGAMOK Lake (Minn., Lake Co.) \ä´ gə mok\. Perhaps from Ojibwa (Algonquian) *aagimaak* 'black ash tree' (Upham 2001; Nichols and Nyholm 1995).

AGAMSIK, Cape (Alaska, Gareloi Island C-1). The Aleut name was published in 1852 (Orth 1967).

AGARAK Creek (Alaska, Point Hope A-2). Perhaps from Iñupiaq (Eskimo) <akaroaq> 'mother-in-law' (Orth 1967); cf. *aakagraq* 'stepmother', *aakaruaq* 'mother-in-law' (L. Kaplan p.c.).

AGASHASHOK River (Alaska, Noatak B-2). The Iñupiaq (Eskimo) name is *iġġiitch isuam kuuŋa* (Burch 1998).

AGATHLA Peak (Ariz., Navajo Co.) \ə gath´ lə\. From Navajo (Athabaskan) *aghaałą́* 'much wool', from *aghaa'* 'wool', *łą́* 'much' (Wilson 1995).

AGATTU Island (Alaska, Attu A-2) \ag´ ə to͞o\. From Aleut *angatux̂* 'has big sides'; cf. *anga-* 'side' (Bergsland 1994).

AGAWAM (Mass., Hampden Co.) \ag´ ə wäm\. From SNEng. Algonquian, containing <-woonki> 'crooked' (W. Cowan p.c.). The placename also occurs in N.Y. (Suffolk Co.), with the variant spelling **Agawan. Agawam** also occurs as a transfer name: for example, in Ky. (Clark Co.), Okla. (Grady Co.), and Mont. (Teton Co.).

AGEKLAROK (Alaska, Kwiguk C-6). The Yupik (Eskimo) name was recorded in 1899 (Orth 1967).

AGEKLEKAK (Alaska, St. Michael A-6). The Yupik (Eskimo) name was reported in 1950 (Orth 1967).

AGENCY (Iowa, Wapello Co.) Named for the federal agency established here in 1838 to supervise the Sauk and Fox (Algonquian) Indians.

AGENUK Mountain (Alaska, Dillingham D-7). The Yupik (Eskimo) name was reported around 1931 (Orth 1967).

AGGIPAH Mountain (Idaho, Lemhi Co.) \ag´ i pä\. Shoshoni (Numic, Uto-Aztecan) /akai-paa/ 'salmon water' (Boone 1988).

AGHALUK Mountain (Alaska, Sleetmute C-7). The Yupik (Eskimo) name was obtained in 1945 (Orth 1967).

AGHIK Island (Alaska, Sutwik Island A-3). The name is probably Alutiiq (Eskimo); it was published in 1888 (Orth 1967).

AGHILEEN Pinnacles (Alaska, Cold Bay B-1). The Alutiiq (Eskimo) name was reported in 1880 (Orth 1967).

AGHIYUK Island (Alaska, Sutwik Island A-3). Said to be the Aleut word for 'cormorant' (Orth 1967), specifically *agayuk* 'black cormorant' (Geoghegan 1944).

AGHNAGHAK Lagoon (Alaska, ST. Lawrence C-6). From the same stem as **Aghnuk;** see **Aghnuk River** below.

AGHNUK River (Alaska, St. Lawrence C-6). Supposedly from Yupik (Eskimo) <akhankhak> 'two women', reported in 1949 (Orth 1967); cf. Yupik *arnaq* 'woman' (Jacobson 1984). A related form is the nearby **Aghnaghak Lagoon.**

AGHSIT Point (Alaska, St. Lawrence D-6). The Yupik (Eskimo) name, recorded in 1965, is said to mean 'resting place', referring specifically to seals (Orth 1967).

AGIAGIAK Creek (Alaska, Killik River A-1). The Iñupiaq (Eskimo) name, reported in 1956, has been translated as 'route to Agiak' (Orth 1967).

AGIAK Lagoon (Alaska, De Long Mountains D-5). Reported in 1956; from Iñupiaq (Eskimo) *agik, agiaq-* 'to rub, file', *agiaq* 'grindstone' (Fortescue et al. 1994).

AGIAPUK River (Alaska, Teller A-2). The Iñupiaq (Eskimo) name was recorded in 1827 as <Agee-ee-puk> (Orth 1967).

AGINAW Lake (Mich., Shiawassee Co.) \ag´ i nô\. Perhaps formed from the name **Saginaw** by dropping the initial letter (Vogel 1986).

AGIUKCHUK (Alaska, Baird Inlet B-7). The Yupik (Eskimo) name was reported in 1878 (Orth 1967).

AGLIGADAK Island (Alaska, Seguam C-3). Reported in 1852; from the Aleut placename *aĝlig adax*, from *aĝligax* 'albatross' (Bergsland 1994).

AGLUNGAK Hills (Alaska, Misheguk Mountain A-2). The Iñupiaq (Eskimo) name, reported in 1956, is said to refer to the hole in the top of a tent (Orth 1967).

AGNAYAGHIT Point (Alaska, St. Lawrence C-2). The Yupik (Eskimo) name was reported in 1949 (Orth 1967).

AGTAPUK Point (Alaska, St. Lawrence D-6). The Yupik (Eskimo) name was recorded in 1949 (Orth 1967).

AGUANGA (Calif., Riverside Co.) \ə wäng´ gə\. Spanish spelling for a Luiseño (Takic) village, called *awáanga* 'dog place', from *awáal* 'dog', *-nga* 'place' (Gudde 1998).

AGUCHIK Island (Alaska, Mt. Katmai B-1). The Aleut name was published in 1847 (Orth 1967).

AGULIAK Island (Alaska, Seward B-3). The Alutiiq (Eskimo) name was reported in 1917 (Orth 1967).

AGULIGIK Island (Alaska, Mt. Katmai B-1). Probably from Alutiiq (Eskimo) *aarulik* 'hawk' (Orth 1967; Leer 1978).

AGULIUK Point (Alaska, Umnak B-2). From the Aleut placename *aguulux̂,* perhaps from *agu-* 'to do, work' (Bergsland 1994).

AGULOWAK River (Alaska, Dillingham B-8). The Yupik (Eskimo) name is said to mean 'many rapids' (Orth 1967); cf. *qurrlur-* 'to cascade down', *qurrlugtaq* 'waterfall' (Jacobson 1984).

AGULUKPAK River (Alaska, Dillingham C-7). The Yupik (Eskimo) name was reported in 1890 (Orth 1967).

AGUMSADAK, Cape (Alaska, Atka B-6). From the Aleut placename *aagamchiidax̂* (Bergsland 1994).

AGUNTANG Brook (R.I., Washington Co.). Perhaps from SNEng. Algonquian <agwonk> 'under a tree', containing <agwu> 'earthward, under' plus <-unk> 'tree' (W. Cowan p.c.).

AGUTIROAK Creek (Alaska, Meade River A-2). The Iñupiaq (Eskimo) name was reported in 1956 (Orth 1967).

AHAGATEYEIT Lake (Alaska, Chandler Lake B-4). Koyukon (Athabaskan) *aaĥaage teyet* 'old squaw-duck place' (J. Kari p.c.).

AHA KWIN Park (Calif., Riverside Co.) \ə hä kwin\. Contains Mojave (Yuman) *'ahá* 'water' and *aakwín-* 'to bend' (Gudde 1998).

AHALAPAM Cinder Field (Ore., Lane Co.) \ä hal´ ə pam\. The name represents Central Kalapuyan /anhálpam/ 'upland people, upriver people', a name for the Santiam Kalapuyas (D. Kinkade p.c.).

AHALIKNAK Creek (Alaska, Baird Mountains C-6). The Iñupiaq (Eskimo) name was obtained in 1955 (Orth 1967).

AHALIORAK Lake (Alaska, Chandler Lake D-3). The Iñupiaq (Eskimo) name is *aaqhaaliuraq* 'little old squaw (duck)' (L. Kaplan p.c.).

AHAN OWUCH (Ariz., Pima Co.). From O'odham (Piman) *a'an owij,* lit. 'feather awl' (J. Hill p.c.).

AHAYU:T A:CHIYA' DELASHHIN'A (NM, McKinley Co.) The Zuni placename is that of a shrine to the War Gods (Ferguson and Hart 1985). Another such placename is **Ahayu:t An Yalanne** (Catron Co.), containing /yala-nne/ 'mountain' (Ferguson and Hart 1985; Newman 1958).

AHDING River (Alaska, Nunivak Island B-5). The Yupik (Eskimo) name was recorded in 1949. The placename **Ahdingmiut** in the same area means 'people of Ahding' (Orth 1967).

AHDUCK Bay (Alaska, Yakutat C-5). From Tlingit *aadáq* (J. Leer p.c.).

AHE VONAM (Ariz., Pima Co.). O'odham (Piman) *a'ai wonamĭ* 'hat on both ends', from *a'ai* 'both ends, sides', *wonamĭ* 'hat' (J. Hill p.c.).

AH-GUDE-LE-ROCK (Alaska, Teller D-6). The Iñupiaq (Eskimo) name was recorded in 1908 (Orth 1967).

AH HOL SAH (Ariz., Coconino Co.) Perhaps from Navajo (Athabaskan) *ahoodzą́* 'hole, cavity' (Brian 1992; A. Wilson p.c.).

AHJUMAWI State Park (Calif., Shasta Co.). \ä jo͞o mä´ wē\. Named for a local Indian group, also called the Pit River people, of the Shastan family; the spellings **Achumawi** and **Achomawi** also occur. The term is from the Native American name *ajumaawi* 'river people', from *ajuma* 'river', originally referring to the Fall River band (Gudde 1998).

AHKITOOK (Alaska, Nunivak Island B-4). The Yupik (Eskimo) name was reported in 1949 (Orth 1967).

AHKIULKSNUK Lake (Alaska, Nunivak Island A-4). The Yupik (Eskimo) name was reported in 1949 as <Ahkiwixnux> (Orth 1967).

AHKLUN Mountains (Alaska, Goodnews Bay B-5). The Yupik (Eskimo) name was reported in 1898 as <Oklune> (Orth 1967).

AHKOLIKOTAK Head (Alaska, Nunivak Island A-6). The Yupik (Eskimo) name was recorded in 1949 (Orth 1967).

AHLIK River (Alaska, Nunivak Island A-6). The Yupik (Eskimo) name, reported in 1949, was said to mean 'stream' (Orth 1967).

AHLOSO (Okla., Pontotoc Co.) \ə los´ ō\. From the Chickasaw (Muskogean) placename *haalooso* (Shirk 1974; P. Munro p.c.).

AHMEEK (Mich., Keweenaw Co.) \ä´ mēk\. From Ojibwa (Algonquian) *amik* 'beaver' (Vogel 1986; Nichols and Nyholm 1995). The placename is also found in Wis. (Bayfield Co.). From the same source is **Ahmik** in Mich. (Keweenaw Co.) \ä´ mik\ and Minn. (St. Louis Co.). Probably related names are **Amik** (Mich., Price Co.) and **Ahmikwam** (Mich., Lake Co.).

AHMIKDOLIGAMIUT (Alaska, Nunivak Island A-2). The Yupik (Eskimo) name was reported in 1949 (Orth 1967); the suffix *-miut* means 'people'.

AHMIKWAM Lake (Mich., Lake Co.). Probably from the same source as **Ahmeek** (Vogel 1986); see above. The name is also written as **Ahmikwan.**

AHMOO Creek (Minn., Lake Co.) \ä´ mo͞o\. Probably from Ojibwa (Algonquian) *aamoo* 'bee, wasp' (Upham 2001; Nichols and Nyholm 1995).

AHNAPEE (Wis., Kewaunee Co.) \ä´ nə pē\. Possibly from Ojibwa (Algonquian) *aanapii* 'when?' (Vogel 1991, Nichols and Nyholm 1995).

AHNEWETUT Lake (Alaska, Ambler River A-6). The Iñupiaq (Eskimo) name was reported in 1956 (Orth 1967).

AHNOWIKSAT Rocks (Alaska, Nunivak Island B-5). The Yupik (Eskimo) name was recorded in 1949 (Orth 1967).

AHOLI Park (Ariz., Maricopa Co.) \ə hō´ lē\. Hopi (Uto-Aztecan) *áhooli* is the name of a kachina (K. Hill p.c.).

AHOSKIE (N.C., Hertford Co.) \ə hos´ kē\. The name is said to be of Indian origin, but no details are available (Powell 1968).

AHPAH Creek (Calif., Humboldt Co.) \ä´ pä\. From Yurok *ohpo,* the name of a large flat near the creek (Gudde 1998).

AHPEATONE (Okla., Cotton Co.) \ə pē´ ə tōn\. Said to have been the name of a Kiowa (Kiotanoan) leader; his Native American name was /á:-pí:thǫ̂/, lit. 'lance-wood'. He was also called "Wooden Lance" in English (Shirk 1974:5; L. Watkins p.c.).

AHQUABI, Lake (Iowa, Warren Co.) \ä kwä´ bē\. Said to be an Indian word meaning 'resting place' (Vogel 1983); cf. Meskwaki (Algonquian) /a:kwapiwa/ 'he rests, sits to rest' (I. Goddard p.c.). The name is also reminiscent of Ojibwa (Algonquian) *akwaabiigad* 'to be a certain length' (Nichols and Nyholm 1995), but the Ojibwas did not live in Iowa.

AHRAYUKSOOKWIT Bluff (Alaska, Nunivak Island B-4). The Yupik (Eskimo) name was recorded as <Ahrayuxsooxwit> in 1949 (Orth 1967).

AHRNKLIN River (Alaska, Yakutat B-5). From Tlingit *aan tlein* 'land big' (J. Leer p.c.).

AHSAHKA Mountain (Idaho, Clearwater Co.) \ə sä´ kə\. From the Nez Perce (Sahaptian) placename /asáqa/ (D. Kinkade p.c.).

AH-SHE-SLE-PAH (NM, San Juan Co.) A variant writing of **Ah-Shi-Sle-Pah Wash** \ā shē shlep´ ə\. Navajo (Athabaskan) *áshı̨̨́h łibá* 'gray salt', from *áshı̨̨́h* 'salt', *łibá* 'it is gray' (A. Wilson p.c.).

AHTANUM (Wash., Yakima Co.) \ə tan´ əm, ə ten´ əm\. From a Sahaptin toponym [átanɨm] (D. Kinkade p.c.).

AHTELL Creek (Alaska, Nabesna C-6) \ä tel´, ä´ tel\. The name is perhaps Ahtena (Athabaskan); it was reported in 1903 (Orth 1967).

AHTENA (Alaska) Also written **Ahtna** \ät´ nə, at´ nə\; a name applied to an Athabaskan people of Alaska, from *atna',* their name for the Copper River. The people call themselves *atnahwt'aene* 'people of the Copper River' (HNAI 6:662). The placename **Atna** (Alaska, McCarthy C-6) has the same source.

AHTUN Point (Alaska, Craig D-4). This name, probably Tlingit, was published in 1964 (Orth 1967).

AHWAHNEE (Calif., Madera Co.) \ä wä´ nē\. From Southern Sierra Miwok /awooni, owooni/ 'Yosemite Valley', from /awwo, owwo/ 'mouth' (Gudde 1998).

AHWATUKEE (Ariz., Maricopa Co.) \ä wä to͞o´ kē\. The settlement was built around a house called in Spanish *Casa de Sueños* 'house of dreams', and the name is said to represent a translation of that phrase into Crow (Siouan), a language of Mont. The closest counterpart identifiable in Crow, however, is *awachúhka* 'flat land, prairie' (R. Graczyk p.c.).

AHWIYAH Point (Calif., Madera Co.) \ə wī´ yə\. From Southern Sierra Miwok /awaaya/ 'lake; deep'. Reference may be to Mirror Lake (Gudde 1998).

AH-YEH-LI A-LO-HEE (Ga., Hart Co.). Originally a Cherokee (Iroquoian) assembly ground; said to mean 'center of the world' (Krakow 1975).

AHYOSUPSUCK Pond (Conn., New London Co.). Said to be Mohegan (Algonquian) for 'place of wild hemp' (Trumbull 1881; Huden 1962). A variant form is **Wyassup Lake**.

AHZWIRYUK Bluff (Alaska, Nunivak Island A-6). The Yupik (Eskimo) name was recorded in 1949 (Orth 1967).

AIAK, Cape (Alaska, Unalaska A-5). The Aleut name, also written as <Ayak>, was recorded in 1852 (Orth 1967).

AIAKTALIK (Alaska, Trinity Islands C-1) \ī ak ´ tə lik\. The name, probably Alutiiq (Eskimo), was recorded in 1802 as <Anayachtalak> and in 1826 as <Anayakhtakh> (Orth 1967).

AIALIK Bay (Alaska, Blying Sound D-8). The Alutiiq (Eskimo) name has also been written as Ayalik (Orth 1967).

AICHILIK River (Alaska, Demarcation Point D-2). The Iñupiaq (Eskimo) name was recorded in 1918; it has also been spelled <Aitshillik> (Orth 1967).

AIKTAK Island (Alaska, Unimak A-3) \ī´ ək tuk\. The Aleut name was transcribed in 1852 (Orth 1967); it may be from *aix̂a-lix* 'to travel' (Bergsland 1994).

AIUGNAK Columns (Alaska, Sutwik Island D-2). This name, probably Alutiiq (Eskimo), was first recorded as <Augnak> in 1849 (Orth 1967).

AIVICHTIK River (Alaska, St. Lawrence C-3). The Yupik (Eskimo) name has also been written as Aivikhtak or Iveetok (Orth 1967).

AIVIK Creek (Alaska, Point Hope C-2). From Iñupiaq (Eskimo) *aiviq* 'walrus' (Orth 1967; MacLean 1980).

AJIBIKIKA Falls (Mich., Gogebic Co.). Apparently from an Ojibwa (Algonquian) word meaning 'rocky place' (Vogel 1986); cf. Ojibwa *aazhibik* 'rock cliff' (Nichols and Nyholm 1995).

AJO (Ariz., Pima Co.) \ä´ hō\. This may represent a Spanish spelling of an O'odham (Piman) word referring to the use of a red ore for body painting and has nothing to do with Spanish *ajo* 'garlic'. The O'odham name for the town of Ajo is in fact *mu'i wawhia*, lit. 'many wells' (Granger 1983; J. Hill p.c.).

AKABA Tank (Ariz., Coconino Co.). From the surname of a Havasupai (Yuman) family (L. Hinton p.c.).

AKAHAMUT (Alaska, Russian Mission C-8). The Yupik (Eskimo) name was recorded in 1916 as <Okhnagamiut>, said to mean 'people on the other side (of the river)' (Orth 1967); the element *-miut* means 'people'.

AKAIYAN Falls (Mont., Flathead Co.). The name is that of a Blackfoot (Algonquian) mythic hero; it has been translated as 'Old Robe' (Holterman 1985); cf. Blackfoot *áka* 'old', *aan* 'robe' (Frantz and Russell 1995).

AKA Lake (Alaska, Yakutat C-5) \ä´ kä\. From Tlingit *áa ká* '(area) on the lake' (J. Leer p.c.).

AKALOLIK Creek (Alaska, Point Hope B-3). The Iñupiaq (Eskimo) name is probably *akàlulik* 'one that has fish' (L. Kaplan p.c.).

AKALUGRAK PANGA (Alaska, Noatak D-5). The Iñupiaq (Eskimo) name is probably *aqalugruam paaŋa* 'salmon river-mouth' (L. Kaplan p.c.). A probably related name is **Akalugram Creek** (Alaska, Noatak D-5); also probably related is **Akalura Lake;** see below.

AKALUOVIK Lakes (Alaska, Misheguk Mountain A-2). The Iñupiaq (Eskimo) name was reported in 1956 (Orth 1967).

AKALURA Lake (Alaska, Karluk A-1). The Iñupiaq (Eskimo) name meaning 'salmon' may be *agalugruaq*, a dialect form of *iqaluqruaq* 'salmon' (L. Kaplan p.c.). A probably related name is **Akalugrak Panga;** see above.

AKANUKLINUK Slough (Alaska, Kwiguk D-6). The Yupik (Eskimo) name was reported in 1952 to mean 'all women' (Orth 1967); cf. *arnaq* 'woman' (Jacobson 1984).

AKARGICHEK Mountain (Alaska, Noatak A-3). The Iñupiaq (Eskimo) name is probably *aqargitchiaq* 'young ptarmigan' (L. Kaplan p.c.).

AKASKA (S.Dak., Walworth Co.) \ə kas´ kə\. Perhaps from Dakota (Siouan) *akáska* 'to be greedy, voracious' (B. Ingham p.c.).

AK CHIN (Ariz., Pinal Co.) \äk chin`\. From O'odham (Piman) *akĭ ciñ*, lit. 'arroyo-mouth' (J. Hill p.c.).

AK CHUT VAYA (Ariz., Pima Co.) \äk chut vä´ yə\. From O'odham (Piman) *akiceḍ wahia*, lit. 'arroyo-well' (J. Hill p.c.).

AKEFTAPAK (Alaska, St. Lawrence D-6). From St. Lawrence Island Yupik (Eskimoan) *aqeftaghaaq* 'bag' (Orth 1967; Jacobson 1987).

AKEKU Point (Alaska, Prince Rupert D-2). This possibly Tlingit name was reported in 1936 (Orth 1967).

AKEONIK (Alaska, Wainwright B-5). The Iñupiaq (Eskimo) name was reported in 1924 (Orth 1967).

AKFAYEGAK Creek (Alaska, St. Lawrence C-6). The Yupik (Eskimo) name was reported in 1949 (Orth 1967).

AKHIOK (Alaska, Trinity Islands D-1) \ak´ ē ok\. The Alutiiq (Eskimo) name is perhaps the same as the name reported in 1814 as <Ooha-iack> (Orth 1967).

AKIACHAK (Alaska, Bethel D-7) \ak´ ē ə chuk\. Reported in 1890; from the Yupik (Eskimo) placename *akiacuar,* from *aki-* 'other side; to reciprocate' (Jacobson 1984).

AKIAK (Alaska, Bethel D-6) \ak´ ē ak\. Reported in 1956; from the Yupik (Eskimo) placename *akiaq,* from *aki-* 'other side; to reciprocate' (Jacobson 1984). Another name, **Akiak Stream** (Alaska, Ambler River B-6), is apparently from Iñupiaq (Eskimo), recorded in 1956 (Orth 1967).

AKIKNAAK Peaks (Alaska, Ambler River D-4). The Iñupiaq (Eskimo) name has been translated as 'against (alongside)', reported in 1956 (Orth 1967).

AKIKUKCHIAK Creek (Alaska, Baird Mountains D-5). The Iñupiaq (Eskimo) name, reported in 1956, has been translated as 'going to the new (other) side' (Orth 1967).

AKILLIK River (Alaska, Ambler River A-6). The Iñupiaq (Eskimo) name, reported in 1956, is said to mean 'something on the other side' (Orth 1967).

AKILLOAQ (Alaska, Barrow A-5). The Iñupiaq (Eskimo) name was reported in 1959 (Orth 1967).

AKJEMGUIGA Cove (Alaska, Iliamna A-4). The Alutiiq (Eskimo) name was reported in 1923 (Orth 1967).

AK KOMELIK (Ariz., Pima Co.) \äk kō´ mə lik\. O'odham (Piman) *akĭ komalik* 'flat arroyo', with *akĭ* 'arroyo' and *komalĭ* 'flat' (J. Hill p.c.).

AKLEK, Cape (Alaska, Karluk C-5). Probably an Aleut name, reported in 1831 (Orth 1967).

AKLUMAYUAK Creek (Alaska, Baird Mountains D-3). The Iñupiaq (Eskimo) name is *aglaq mayuġaaq* 'grizzly bears climbing up' (Burch 1998); cf. *akłaq* 'brown bear, grizzly' (MacLean 1980).

AKLUT (Alaska, Baird Inlet A-1). The Yupik (Eskimo) name, reported in 1878, supposedly means 'ammunition' or 'provisions' (Orth 1967).

AKMAGOLIK Creek (Alaska, Chandler Lake B-3). The Iñupiaq (Eskimo) name was recorded in 1956 (Orth 1967).

AKMAKTAKSRAK Bluff (Alaska, Killik River C-1). The Iñupiaq (Eskimo) name is said to mean 'supplied with flint' (Orth 1967); cf. *agmaaq* 'flint' (MacLean 1980). Probably related is the placename **Akmalik Creek** (Alaska, Killik River B-2).

AKMIUT (Alaska, Sleetmute C-7). The Yupik (Eskimo) name was reported in 1880 (Orth 1967); the element *-miut* means 'people'.

AKOKALA Creek (Mont., Flathead Co.). This name, also transcribed *aquk'ała,* is said to represent the Kutenai name for Bowman Lake (Holterman 1985).

AKULA Lake (Alaska, Kenai C-3) \ə kōō´ lə\. From a Dena'ina (Athabaskan) source (J. Kari p.c.).

AKUN (Alaska, Unimak A-5). Perhaps from Aleut *akungan,* 'on the side over there' (*aku-* 'over there') or perhaps from *akungax̂* 'ochre' (Bergsland 1994).

AKUTAN (Alaska, Unimak A-6). The Aleut placename is *akutanax̂,* perhaps from *aku(n) tanax̂* 'the island over there'; cf. *aku-* 'over there', *tanax̂* 'island' (Bergsland 1994).

AKUYAN, Cape (Alaska, Adak D-1). From the Aleut placename *aakuyang* (Bergsland 1994).

AKWAŁINA: YALA:WE (N.Mex., Cibola Co.). The Zuni placename consists of /akwałi-na/ 'light blue-green' plus /yala-weʔ/ 'mountains' (Ferguson and Hart 1985; Newman 1958).

AKWE RIVER (Alaska, Yakutat B-3). From Tlingit ['akʷe], perhaps a borrowing from an Athabaskan language (De Laguna 1972:83).

ALABAHA River (Ga., Pierce Co.) \ə lä´ bə hä\. From the same source as the **Alapaha River** (Ga., Berrien Co.).

ALABAM (Ark., Madison Co.) \al ə bam\. An abbreviation of **Alabama**; see below. The name **Alabam** also occurs in Alaska (Livengood C-3).

ALABAMA \al ə bam´ ə\. The state of **Alabama** is named for a people affiliated with the Creeks; their language is Muskogean. The name is probably from a Choctaw term meaning 'plant cutters' (Read 1984). The present-day Choctaw form is *albaamu,* from *albah* 'plant', *amo* 'to clear'; the word *albah* may refer specifically to medicinal plants (P. Munro p.c.) There is an **Alabama River** in the state. The placename is found elsewhere: for example, La. (St. Landry Par.), N.Y. (Genesee Co.), and Wis. (Polk Co.).

A'LABATTSI'A (N.Mex., Cibola Co.). The Zuni placename designates a spring sacred to the Galaxy Society (Ferguson and Hart 1985).

ALACHUA County (Fla.) \ə lach´ o͞o ə\. The name was originally that of a Muskogee town in southern Ga., recorded in 1715 as <Allachua> (Read 1934).

ALACULSA (Ga., Murray Co.) \al ə ko͞o´ sə\. Perhaps from Cherokee (Iroquoian), but the derivation is unclear.

ALAFIA River (Fla., Hillsborough Co.) \al ə fī´ ə\. The name was that of a Seminole (Muskogean) village (Read 1934).

ALAGA (Ala., Houston Co.). The name is a combination of Ala., short for **Alabama**, and Ga., short for *Georgia* (Goff 1975).

ALAGANIK (Alaska, Cordova B-4) \ə lag´ ə nik\. Tlingit /anax̱anaq/, said to be from Eyak ['ᴀnᴀx̣ᴀnᴀ́g̹]; cf. also Aluutiq (Eskimo) *alaaRanaq* 'mistake, wrong turn' (De Laguna 1972:105).

ALAGNAK River (Alaska, Dillingham A-3). Perhaps from Yupik (Eskimo) *alagnaq* 'type of red berry' (Jacobson 1984).

ALAGOGSHAK Creek (Alaska, Mt. Katmai A-4). The Yupik (Eskimo) name was published in 1922 (Orth 1967).

ALAI, Mount (Alaska, Ugashik B-2). A Native American name, probably Alutiiq (Eskimo), recorded in 1832 (Orth 1967).

ALAKANUK (Alaska, Kwiguk C-6) \ə lak´ ə nuk\. From the Yupik (Eskimo) placename *alarneq,* from *alar-* 'to be in error' (Jacobson 1984).

ALAKTAK River (Alaska, Teshekpuk D-4) \ə lak´ tak\. The Iñupiaq (Eskimo) name was reported in the 1940s; the name is said to refer to the river's meandering (Orth 1967); cf. *alaqtaq* 'something turned away from', with *alaq-* 'to turn away from', *-taq* 'passive nominalizer' (L. Kaplan p.c.).

ALAKUCHAK River (Alaska, Nunivak Island C-1). The Yupik (Eskimo) name said to mean 'elder sister' (Orth 1967); cf. *alleqaq, alqaq* 'elder sister' (Jacobson 1984).

ALAMANCE County (N.C.) \al´ ə mans\. Named for **Alamance Creek,** of possible but unidentified Indian origin. The name was recorded as <Aramancy> in 1728 (Powell 1968).

ALAMO (N.Mex., Socorro Co.) \al´ ə mō\. Spanish for 'cottonwood tree'. The name corresponds to Navajo (Athabaskan) *t'iistsoh* 'big cottonwood tree' (Linford 2000), from *t'iis* 'cottonwood', *-tsoh* 'big' (Young and Morgan 1987).

ALAMOOSAK (Maine, Hancock Co.) A variant of **Alamoosook** (Maine, Hancock Co.) \al ə mo͞o´ sək\. The name is said to represent a Malecite (Algonquian) term meaning 'at the fish spawning place' (Rutherford 1970).

ALAMOROSA (N.Mex., Otero Co.) \al ə mə rō´ sə\. So called because it is between **Alamo**

Gordo, Spanish for 'fat cottonwood', and **Tularosa** 'full of tule patches', from Nahuatl **Tule** (R. Julyan p.c.). The resulting pseudo-Spanish name appears to mean 'pink cottonwood'.

ALAMUCHA (Miss., Lauderdale Co.) \al ə much´ə\. From the same source as **Alamuchee** (Ala., Sumter Co.) \al ə much´ē\. Said to be the name of a Choctaw (Muskogean) town in Miss. called 'little hiding place'(Read 1984); it can be derived from *aloma* 'hiding place' (*aa-* 'there', *loma* 'to be hidden') and *-oshi* 'small' (P. Munro p.c.) Related names may include **Armuchee** (Ga., Floyd Co.).

ALAPAHA River (Ga., Berrien Co.; Fla., Hamilton Co.) \ə lä´ pə hä\. After a Seminole (Muskogean) settlement in northern Florida, recorded in 1821 as <A-lapa-ha> (Goff 1975, Read 1934). A related name is **Alabaha River** (Ga., Pierce Co.). A related placename is **ALAPAHOOCHEE River** (Ga., Lowndes Co.; Fla., Hamilton Co.) meaning 'little Alapaha' (Krakow 1975), containing *-uce* /-očí/ 'little'.

ALAPAH Mountain (Alaska, Chandler Lake A-2). From Iñupiaq (Eskimo) *alappaa* 'it's cold weather!' (L. Kaplan p.c.).

ALAPOCAS (Del., New Castle Co.) \al ə pō´ kəs\. Perhaps from Delaware (Algonquian), but of unclear derivation (Heck et al. 1966).

ALAQUA Bayou (Fla., Walton Co.) \ə lä´ kwä\. Possibly from a word meaning 'gum, wax' in Seminole (Muskogean); cf. Read 1934. The Native American form is *helokwv* /hilókwa/ (Martin and Mauldin 2000). A perhaps related name is **Hilokee Creek** (Ga., Lee Co.).

ALASKA \ə las´ kə\. The name was applied by Russian explorers in the eighteenth century, first to the **Alaska Peninsula**, in the forms <Alaksu> and <Alakshak>; it was later applied to what is now the entire state of **Alaska**. The name is derived from Aleut *aláxsxaq*, lit. 'the object toward which the action of the sea is directed' (Ransom 1940; Orth 1967). The current Aleut spelling is *alaxsxix̂* (Bergsland 1994). The placename **Alaska** occurs as a transfer elsewhere: for example, Minn. (Beltrami Co.), Wash., (Kittitas Co.), and Wis. (Kewaunee Co.). A related placename is **Mount Alyeska** (Alaska, Seward D-6).

ALATKROK River (Alaska, Wainwright B-2). The Iñupiaq (Eskimo) name, also written **Alataktok,** was reported in 1924 (Orth 1967).

ALATNA River (Alaska, Bettles C-6) \ə lat´ nə\. The Koyukon (Athabaskan) name was reported in 1899 (Orth 1967). The Native American name is *aalatne*; cf. the Iñupiaq (Eskimo) name *aalaasuk* (Jetté and Jones 2000).

ALCACHUSKA Creek (Ala., Talladega Co.) \al kə cho͞os´ kə\. Also known as Blue Eye Creek. The name may be from a Muskogee term meaning 'broken pot' (Read 1984:85); the form would be *vrkvs-kvcke* /ałkas-káčk-i/, from *vrkvswv* /ałkáswa/ 'clay pot', *kackē* /káčkē/ 'broken' (Martin and Mauldin 2000). An alternative connection is to Choctaw *alhkocha* 'odd one, remainder' (P. Munro p.c.).

ALCAN Highway (Alaska) \al´ kan\. An abbreviation of **Alaska-Canada**. Each element has its own Native American origin.

ALCHESAY Canyon (Ariz., Maricopa Co.) \al chi sā\. The name is taken from a White Mountain Apache (Athabaskan) leader whose name meant 'little one' (Granger 1983). The form is *ałch'ísé* or *ałts'ísé,* from the stem *-ts'isé* 'little' (P. Greenfeld p.c.).

ALCKEE Creek (Wash., Clallam Co.) \al´ kē\. The name, probably assigned by the U.S. Forest Service, is from Chinook Jargon <al-kie, al´-ki, al´kee> [álki] 'by and by, afterward, presently', perhaps from Lower Chinook [áłki] 'later on' (D. Kinkade p.c.). A related placename is **Alki** (Wash., King Co.).

ALCONA County (Mich.) \al kō´ nə\. This is an artificial name, supposedly compounded of Native American and other elements (Vogel 1986).

ALCOVY River (Ga., Newton Co). The 1818 spelling <Ulco-fau-hatchee> suggests a derivation from Muskogee *orko* /óiko/ 'pawpaw', *-ofv* /-ó:fa/

'location', and *hvcce* /háčči/ 'stream' (Martin and Mauldin 2000).

ALECK Island (Ga., Wayne Co.) \al´ ik\. From the same source as **Alecks Creek** (Ga., Wayne Co.). The name refers to an eighteenth-century Muskogee leader who was given the English name *Alleck* or *Alex,* based on a Creek word for 'doctor' (Goff 1975). The Muskogee form is *vlēkcv* /alí:kča/ (Martin and Mauldin 2000). Related placenames include **Alex Creek** (Ga., Wayne Co.) and **Alikchi** (Okla., McCurtain Co.).

ALEKNAGIK, Lake (Alaska, Dillingham B-7) \ə lek´ nə gik\. From the Yupik (Eskimo) placename *alaqnaqiq* (Jacobson 1984).

ALEKSASHKINA (Alaska, Kodiak D-2). The name was given to an Alutiiq (Eskimo) village in 1852 by a Russian naval expedition (Orth 1967).

ALEUT \al´ ē o͞ot\. This name for the Native American people of the **Aleutian Islands** \ə lo͞o´ shən\ is not a word of Aleut origin. It was applied by the Russians around 1750, perhaps based on the name of Alut, a village on the coast of Kamchatka, in Siberia. In their own language (Atkan dialect), the Aleuts are called *unangax̂* (Bergsland 1994). The Aleut language is related to Eskimo in a family called Eskimo-Aleut. As a placename, **Aleut** occurs in **Aleut Point** (Alaska, Rat Islands B-5). Derivative placenames are **Aleutika Island** (Alaska, Seldovia B-4); **Aleutkina Bay** (Alaska, Sitka A-4), with the Russian term for 'an Aleut woman' (Orth 1967); and **Aleutski Island** (Alaska, Sitka A-5), with the Russian word for 'Aleutian'.

ALEXAUKEN (N.J., Hunterdon Co.) Perhaps from Delaware (Algonquian) *alàxhàking* 'barren land' (Kraft and Kraft 1985); cf. <haki> 'earth'> (Brinton and Anthony 1888).

ALEX Creek (Ga., Wayne Co.) \al´ iks\. From the same source as **Alecks Island**; see above.

ALGANSEE (Mich., Branch Co.) \al´ gən sē\. This is apparently an artificial name, with the element **Algan**- intended to suggest **Algonquian.**

ALGODONES (Calif., Imperial Co.) \al gə dō´ nəs\. Reflects the name of a Yuman group that once dwelt on both sides of the Colorado River; the term is not from Spanish *algodón* 'cotton'. The name was recorded as <Achedomas> in 1758 and as <Jalchedunes> in 1774. In anthropological literature, the term is found as <Halchidhoma> (Gudde 1998).

ALGOMA (Mich., Kent Co.) \al gō´ mə\. The term was invented by Henry R. Schoolcraft in the nineteenth century, with **Algo**- suggesting **Algonquian**; he unsuccesfully tried to give this name to Lake Superior (Vogel 1986). It has been widely adopted as a transfer name: for example, in Ore. (Klamath Co.), Idaho (Bonner Co.), and Wis. (Kewaunee Co.).

ALGONA (Iowa, Kossuth Co.) \al gō´ nə\. Apparently a variant of the name of **Algoma** (Mich., Kent Co.). There is another **Algona** in Wash. (King Co.), with a similar origin (Hitchman 1985).

ALGONAC (Mich., St. Clair Co.) \al´ gə nak\. The name was coined by Henry R. Schoolcraft from **Algonquian** plus an Algonquian element that can be identified with Ojibwa *aki* 'earth' (Vogel 1986, Nichols and Nyholm 1995).

ALGONKIAN Regional Park (Va., Loudoun Co.) \al gong´ kē ən\. From the same origin as **Algonquian**; see below.

ALGONKIN Lake (N.J., Salem Co.) \al gong´ kin\. The name also occurs in **Algonquin Lake** (Mich., Barry Co.), where it is is \al gong´ kwin\. From the same origin as **Algonquin**; see below.

ALGONQUIAN \al gong´ kē ən, al gong´ kwē ən\. This name is applied to a widespread North American Indian language family, also written as **Algonkian.** The term is derived from **Algonquin**; see below. The spelling **Algonquian** is not currently used in any U.S. placenames.

ALGONQUIN Peak (N.Y., Essex Co.) \al gong´ kwin, al gong´ kin\. This name, also spelled **Algonkin,** was first applied by the French to an Indian people of the Ottawa River, in Ontario and Québec, Canada. Later the word was extended to designate the large language family to which the Algonkin language belongs; the name of the family is commonly written **Algonquian. Algonquin** is from the term <Algoumequin>, perhaps representing Maliseet (Algonquian) [εlægómogwik] 'they are our relatives or allies' (Day 1972). As a placename, **Algonquin** is widespread: for example, in Ill. (Cook Co.), Mich. (Barry Co.), and Wis. (Milwaukee Co.).

ALI AK CHIN (Ariz., Pima Co.) \ä lē äk chin\. O'odham (Piman) *ali akĭ ciñ* 'little Ak Chin'; see the placename **Ak Chin** above.

ALIAKSIN, Cape (Alaska, Port Moller B-3). Perhaps of Aleut origin; recorded by a Russian naval expedition as <Aliakska> in 1836 (Orth 1967).

ALI CHUK (Ariz., Pima Co.) \ä lē chuk\. From O'odham (Piman) *ali jeg* 'small hole', from *ali* 'small' plus *jeg* 'hole, opening' (J. Hill p.c.).

ALI CHUKSON (Ariz., Pima Co.) \ä lē cho͞ok´ son\. O'odham (Piman) *ali cukṣon* 'little Tucson', from *ali* 'little', *cukṣon* 'black base, Tucson' (*cuk* 'black', *ṣon* 'base'; J. Hill p.c.).

ALIKCHI (Okla., McCurtain Co.) \ä lik´ chē, ä lik´ shē\. Choctaw (Muskogean) *alikchi* 'doctor' (Shirk 1974, P. Munro p.c.). Related placenames include **Aleck Island** (Ga., Wayne Co.).

ALIKSEMIT Island (Alaska, Sutwik Island A-3). The Native American name was recorded as **Alikhsemit** in 1888 (Orth 1967); it may be Alutiiq (Eskimo).

ALIKTONGNAK Lake (Alaska, Noatak B-2). The Iñupiaq (Eskimo) name is said to mean 'big pickerel' (Orth 1967).

ALIKULA Bay (Alaska, Craig D-7). The name is said to be Haida for 'night' (Orth 1967); cf. /ʕáalgaa/ 'dark' (Lawrence 1977).

ALI MOLINA (Ariz., Pima Co.) \ä lē mō lē´ nə\. O'odham (Piman) *ali mali:na* 'little Magdalena', with *ali* 'little' and *mali:na* 'Magdalena, a place name', from Spanish *Magdalena* (J. Hill p.c.).

ALIMUDA Bay (Alaska, Unalaska A-5). Aleut *alim udaa* 'the bay in the middle'; cf. *al-* 'middle', *udax̂* 'bay' (Bergsland 1994).

ALINCHAK Bay (Alaska, Karluk D-4). The name was recorded in 1904 (Orth 1967); it is probably Alutiiq (Eskimo).

ALI OIDAK (Ariz., Pima Co.) \ä lē oi´ däk\. From O'odham (Piman) *ali oidag,* lit. 'little field' (J. Hill p.c.).

ALIQUIPPA (Pa., Beaver Co.) \al i kwip´ ə\. This was the title of a female leader of the Delaware (Algonquian), perhaps from <alloquepi> 'hat' (Donehoo 1928); cf. Munsee Delaware *aakongwéepuy* 'hat' (O'Meara 1996). Possibly related placenames include **Allegrippus** (Pa., Blair Co.) and **Allegrippis** (Pa., Huntington Co.).

ALITAK Bay (Alaska, Trinity Islands D-1) \al´ i tak\. The Alutiiq (Eskimo) name was recorded as Alitok in 1826 (Orth 1967).

ALIULIK Peninsula (Alaska, Kaguyak D-6). The placename is in Alutiiq (Eskimo) territory but may be from Aleut *haluulux̂* 'thimble' (Orth 1967; Bergsland 1994).

ALI WUA Pass (Ariz., Pima Co.) \ä lē wo͞o´ ə\. From O'odham (Piman) *ali wua,* lit. 'little pond' (J. Hill p.c.).

ALKALUGEN Creek (Alaska, Point Hope D-2). The Iñupiaq (Eskimo) name was reported in 1950 as <Ah-kah-loo-gen> (Orth 1967).

ALKI (Wash., King Co.) \al´ kī\. From Chinook Jargon <al´ki> 'in the future, by and by'. The town was originally named New York; when it was slow in growing, it was jokingly called New York Alki 'New York by and by', and finally simply **Alki** (Hitchman 1985).

ALLAGASH River (Maine, Aroostook Co.) \al´ ə gash\. From Penobscot (Algonquian) /walakéskʸihtəkʸ/ 'bark stream' (P. MacDougall p.c.).

ALLAKAKET (Alaska, Bettles C-6) \al ə kak´ ət\. Corresponds to Koyukon (Athabaskan) *aalaa kkaakk'et* [a:la:qa:q'ət]; cf. *aalaatne* 'Alatna

River', and *aalaasuk*, the Iñupiaq (Eskimo) name for the river (Jetté and Jones 2000:17).

ALLAMAKEE County (Iowa) \al ə mə kē\. Perhaps from Meskwaki (Algonquian) <An-a-mee-kee>, a word referring to 'thunder' and to the Thunder Clan (Vogel 1983). Cf. Meskwaki *nenemehkiwa* 'thunderer, thunder being'; in the nineteenth century, *l* and *n* alternated in Meskwaki. Another possibly related form is Ojibwa (Algonquian) *animikii* 'thunderbird, thunderer' (Goddard 1994; Nichols and Nyholm 1995). A shortened form occurs as **Makee Township** (Iowa, Allamakee Co.).

ALLAMUCHY (N.J., Warren Co.). Perhaps from Delaware (Algonquian) *alemuching* 'place of cocoons' (Kraft 1985).

ALLAPATTAH (Fla., Dade Co.) From Muskogee *hvlpvtv, vlpvtv* /(h)alpatá/ 'alligator' (Martin and Mauldin 2000).

ALLATOONA Creek (Ga., Cherokee Co.) \al ə tōō´ nə\. Apparently from a Cherokee (Iroquoian) source, which cannot be identified (Krakow 1975). The name of **Altoona** (Pa., Blair Co.), founded in 1849, may be adapted from the Georgia name (Stewart 1970).

ALLAWAY Creek (Iowa, Jasper Co.) \al´ ə wā\. Perhaps from the same source as **Alloway**; see below.

ALLEGAN County (Mich.) \al´ ə gən\. An abbreviation of **Allegany** (N.Y.) or **Allegheny** (Pa.); see below.

ALLEGANY County (N.Y.) \al ə gā´ nē\. This spelling, established in N.Y. state, has the same origin as **Allegheny** in Pa. (Allegheny Co.). The name originally referred to what is now called the **Allegheny River.** The origin may be from Delaware (Algonquian) <Alligewi Hanna> 'river of the Alligewi', referring to a people said to live in the drainage of the Ohio River (Beauchamp 1907; Donehoo 1928). The spelling **Allegany** also occurs in N.Y. (Cattaraugus Co.), Md. (Allegany Co.), and Ore. (Coos Co.); the spelling **Allegheny** occurs in many states: for examples Md. (Garrett Co.), Tenn. (Greene Co.), and Nev. (Elko Co.); and the spelling **Alleghany** in Calif. (Sierra Co.).

ALLEGRIPPIS (PA, Huntingdon Co.) \al ə grip´ əs\. From the same origin as **Aliquippa** (Pa., Beaver Co.); see above. Another related placename is **Allegrippus** (Pa., Blair Co.), of which a variant form is **Alleguippas.**

ALLEQUASH Creek (Wis., Vilas Co.) \al´ ē kwash\. Perhaps from the name of the **Allagash River** (Maine, Aroostook Co.); see above.

ALLOWAY Creek (Md., Anne Arundel Co.; Pa., Cambria Co.) \al´ ō wā\. Perhaps from Delaware (Algonquian) *allŭwi* 'more' (Kraft and Kraft 1985); cf. Unami Delaware *aluwí:i* 'more' (I. Goddard p.c.); however, **Alloway** is also a placename in Scotland (Kenny 1984). The name **Alloway** also occurs in N.J. In Mich. (Keweenaw Co.) and Wis. (Douglas Co.), **Allouez** has a similar pronunciation, but is named for a French priest, Father Claude Allouez. Perhaps related are **Allaway Creek** (Iowa, Jasper Co.) and **Alluwe** (Okla., Nowata Co.).

ALMENA (Mich., Van Buren Co.) \al mē´ nə\. Probably an invented word, like **Alpena County** (Mich.), perhaps with some Ojibwa (Algonquian) component. There is a claim that the name was that of "an Indian princess"; but as Vogel (1986:84) remarks, "The red flag of caution should always be raised when an Indian princess is mentioned."

ALMONESSON (N.J., Gloucester Co.). Perhaps from Delaware (Algonquian) <allumes> 'young of any domestic animal' (Becker 1964); cf. Munsee Delaware *nd-álŭmoonz* 'my dog, my horse, my pet', *alumóonzuw* 'to keep as a pet' (O'Meara 1996).

ALMOTA (Wash., Whitman Co.) \al mō´ tə\. From a Nez Perce (Sahaptian) placename /alamóta/ (Aoki 1994:962).

ALNGEEYAK Point (Alaska, St. Lawrence C-2). The Yupik (Eskimo) name was reported in 1932 (Orth 1967).

ALOHA Creek (Alaska, Tanana B-1) \ə lō´ hä\. The Hawaiian word for 'love', used as a greeting, has also been given to places in several parts of the continental United States: for example, Mich. (Cheboygan Co.), Ore. (Washington Co.), and Wash. (Grays Harbor Co.).

ALOKUT Point (Alaska, Point Hope D-2). The Iñupiaq (Eskimo) word is said to mean 'jaw' (Orth 1967); cf. *agliġuq* 'jaw' (MacLean 1980).

ALOLUKROK (Alaska, Point Hope A-1). The Iñupiaq (Eskimo) word was reported in 1960 (Orth 1967).

ALPENA County (Mich.) \al pē´ nə\. Apparently an invented word, like **Almena** (Mich., Van Buren Co.); perhaps based in part on Ojibwa (Algonquian) *bine* 'partridge' or *binesi* 'bird' (Vogel 1986; Nichols and Nyholm 1995). **Alpena** also occurs, perhaps as a transfer name, in Ark. (Boone Co.), S.Dak. (Jerauld Co.), and W.Va. (Randolph Co.).

ALPOWA (Wash., Whitman Co.) \al´ pə wä\. From Nez Perce (Sahaptian) /alpaha/ 'Alpowa Creek' (Aoki 1994).

ALSEA (Ore., Benton Co.) \al sē´, äl´ sē\. The name of an Indian group, of the Yakonan family, that lived at the mouth of the **Alsea River**. The word is from /alsíiya/, the name applied to the **Alseas** by the neighboring Tillamook (Salishan) and Coosan peoples (McArthur 1992; D. Kinkade p.c.).

ALSEK River (Alaska, Yakutat A-2) \al´ sek\. From Tlingit ['ałsex̣yık], of unknown etymology (De Laguna 1972:87).

ALTA (Wash., Jefferson Co.) \al´ tə\. From Chinook Jargon <al´-ta> [áltə] 'now, at present', from Lower Chinook [álta] 'now' (D. Kinkade p.c.).

AL TAHOE (Calif., El Dorado Co.) \al tä´ hō\. From the Al Tahoe Hotel, built in 1907 by Almerin R. Sprague and named with his own nickname plus the word **Tahoe,** from Washo *dá'aw* 'lake' (Gudde 1998).

ALTAMAHA (Ga., Tattnall Co.) \äl´ tə mə hô\. Perhaps from Muskogee but of obscure derivation (Read 1949–50; Krakow 1975). The placename also occurs in Fla. (Polk Co.). A probably related name is **Altamahaw** (N.C., Alamance Co.).

ALTOONA (Pa., Blair Co.) \al to͞o´ nə\. Perhaps adapted from the name **Allatoona Creek** (Ga., Cherokee Co.), where it is said to be from Cherokee (Krakow 1975; Stewart 1970). Other writers, however, have suggested a derivation from the city of Altona in Germany. The name **Altoona** is found in many other locations: for example, Ala. (Etowah Co), Fla. (Lake Co.), and Wis. (Eau Claire Co.). Possibly of the same origin is **Altonah** (Pa., Northampton Co.; Utah, Duchesne Co.).

AL TSE TOH (Ariz., Apache Co.) \äl sē tō\. Apparently from Navajo (Athabaskan) *áłtsé tó* 'first water', from *áłtsé* 'first', *tó* 'water, spring' (A. Wilson p.c.).

ALUKLIK Bay (Alaska, Seward A-3) The Alutiiq (Eskimo) name was reported in 1951 (Orth 1967).

ALUMA, Lake (Okla., Oklahoma Co.) \ə lo͞o´ mə\. Said to be a shortening of Choctaw (Muskogean) <Aluma Chulosa> 'peaceful retreat' (Shirk 1974); cf. Choctaw *aaloma* 'a retreat' (*aa-* 'place', *loma* 'hidden'), *cholosa* 'calm, quiet' (P. Munro p.c.).

ALUM Lake (R.I., Providence Co.) \al´ əm\. Nipmuck (Algonquian) <allum> 'dog' (W. Cowan p.c.). There is also a **Alum Pond** in Mass. (Worcester Co.).

ALUTIIQ \ə lo͞o´ tik\. This name is applied to the Eskimo people of Alaska who live on the Upper Alaska Peninsula, the tip of the Kenai Peninsula, and Kodiak Island; they are sometimes also called Pacific Eskimos or Pacific Yupiks. It is from the word *alúutiq* of their own language, meaning 'a Pacific Eskimo person'. The term *Eskimo* is disfavored locally, however, "because of a strongly felt cultural and ethnic distinctiveness from the Eskimos to the north" (*HNAI* 5:196). **Alutiiq** should not be confused with **Aleutian,** which is used by scholars to designate the ethnically and linguistically distinct people of the Aleutian Islands.

ALYESKA, Mount (Alaska, Seward D-6) \al yes´ kə\. From the same source as **Alaska**; see above.

AMABALA (Okla., Okfuskee Co.). A reversed spelling of the name **Alabama**; see above.

AMACHE, Camp (Colo., Prowers Co.) \ä mä´ chē\. The site of **Amache Relocation Center**, where Japanese Americans were interned during World War II, is said to be named for **Amache**, the daughter of Ochinee (Lone Wolf), a Cheyenne (Algonquian) chief (Bright 1993). Also written as **Campamanche.**

AMACOY (Wis., Rusk Co.) \am´ ə koi\. Perhaps from Ojibwa (Algonquian) *amik* 'beaver' (Vogel 1991, Nichols and Nyholm 1995); cf. **Amaqua** (Iowa, Boone Co.), from Meskwaki (Algonquian) */amehkwa/* 'beaver'.

AMAGALIK, Cape (Alaska, Gareloi Island B-1). From Aleut *amagilax̂* 'has several steep hills'; cf. *aygix̂* 'hill' (Bergsland 1994).

AMAGANSETT (N.Y., Suffolk Co.). Said to be an Algonquian word meaning 'near the fishing place' (Beauchamp 1907; Tooker 1911).

AMAGAT Island (Alaska, False Pass D-3). The Aleut name was recorded in 1852 (Orth 1967).

AMAGOALIK Creek (Alaska, Wainwright C-1). The Iñupiaq (Eskimo) name, said to mean 'wolf pups', was recorded in 1956 (Orth 1967); cf. *amaġuq* 'wolf' (MacLean 1980). Possibly related placenames include **Amakomanak Creek** (Alaska, Ambler River D-4), **Amagoalik Creek** (Alaska, Wainwright C-1), **Amawk Mountain** (Alaska, Wiseman D-1), and **Amo Creek** (Alaska, Misheguk Mountain D-3).

AMAKATATEE Creek (Alaska, Goodnews Bay D-4). From Yupik (Eskimo) (Orth 1967).

AMAKDEDORI (Alaska, Iliamna B-4) \ə mak də dôr´ ē\. The Alutiiq (Eskimo) name was recorded in 1923 (Orth 1967). A probably related name is **Amakdedulia.**

AMAK Island (Alaska, Cold Bay B-4) \ə mak\. From Aleut *amax* 'high cliff' (Bergsland 1994). A possibly related name is **Amaknak Island** (Alaska, Unalaska C-2).

AMAKNAK Island (Alaska, Unalaska C-2) \ə mak´ nak\. From Aleut *amaxnax̂*; cf. *amax* 'high cliff' (Bergsland 1994).

AMAKOMANAK Creek (Alaska, Ambler River D-4). The Iñupiaq (Eskimo) name is said to mean 'wolf dung' (Orth 1967); cf. *amaġuq* 'wolf', *anaq* 'excrement' (MacLean 1980). Possibly related placenames are **Amagoalik Creek** (Alaska, Wainwright C-1), **Amawk Mountain** (Alaska, Wiseman D-1), and **Amo Creek** (Alaska, Misheguk Mountain D-3).

AMAKTUSAK Creek (Alaska, Point Hope A-2). The Iñupiaq (Eskimo) name was reported in 1962 (Orth 1967).

AMAKUK Arm (Alaska, Goodnews Bay C-1). The Yupik (Eskimo) name was reported in 1929 (Orth 1967).

AMALIK Bay (Alaska, Mt. Katmai A-2). The Alutiiq (Eskimo) name was reported in 1895 (Orth 1967).

AMANKA Lake (Alaska, Goodnews Bay A-1). The Yupik (Eskimo) name was reported in 1898 (Orth 1967).

AMAQUA (Iowa, Boone Co.). From Meskwaki (Algonquian) /amehkwa/ 'beaver' (I. Goddard p.c.). A related placename is **Amacoy** (Wis., Rusk Co.); see above.

AMATIGNAK Island (Alaska, Gareloi Island A-4) \am ə tig´ nak\. From Aleut *amatignax̂* 'chip, splinter' (Bergsland 1994).

AMATULI Cove (Alaska, Afognak D-1). The Alutiiq (Eskimo) name was recorded in 1908 (Orth 1967).

AMATUSUK Hills (Alaska, Point Lay A-3). The Iñupiaq (Eskimo) name was recorded in 1920 (Orth 1967).

AMAUNG Lake (Mich., Newaygo Co.) \ə môŋ\. Perhaps a Native American name, but of unclear derivation (Vogel 1986).

AMAWALK (N.Y., Westchester Co.). The name is apparently abbreviated from <Appamaghpogh>, from an Algonquian word meaning 'trap-fishing place' (Beauchamp 1907; Ruttenber 1906).

AMAWK Mountain (Alaska, Wiseman D-1) \ə môk⁀\. From the Iñupiaq (Eskimo) word for 'wolf' (Orth 1967); cf. *amaġuq* 'wolf' (MacLean 1980). Possibly related placenames include **Amakomanak Creek** (Alaska, Ambler River D-4) and **Amagoalik Creek** (Alaska, Wainwright C-1).

AMBAJEJUS Lake (Maine, Piscataquis Co.). From Abenaki (Algonquian) /ɑpɑ́čičohs/ 'eddy, reverse current' (P. MacDougall p.c.).

AMBEJACKMOCKAMUS Falls (Maine, Piscataquis Co.). The Abenaki (Algonquian) name has been translated 'a little pond crosswise (of the usual route)' (Huden 1962).

AMBOY \am´ boi\. This element occurs in the names of **Perth Amboy** and **South Amboy** (N.J., Middlesex Co.) The former was named in the seventeenth century for James, earl of Perth, lord high chancellor of Scotland, who founded a settlement there; to its name was added **Amboy,** representing a Delaware (Algonquian) word that has not been clearly identified (Ruttenber 1906; Becker 1964). The name **Amboy** occurs widely elsewhere (e.g., Ill., Lee Co.; N.Y., Onondaga Co.; and W.Va., Preston Co.).

AMBRESVAJUN Lake (Alaska, Table Mountain C-5). Gwich'in (Athabaskan) *Ambrose vavan* 'Ambrose's lake' (J. Kari p.c.).

AMCHITKA Island (Alaska, Rat Islands B-4) \am chit´ kə\. From the Aleut placename *amchixtax̂* (Bergsland 1994).

AMERICAN HORSE Creek (S.Dak., Shannon Co.). Probably named for an Oglala (Lakhota, Siouan) leader who died in 1876 (Sneve 1973); his Native American name was *wašį́čų-thašųka* (B. Ingham p.c.). Cf. Lakhota *wašį́čų* 'white man', *šų́ka* 'dog'.

AMICALOLA (Ga., Dawson Co.) \am i kə lō´ lə\. Said to be from Cherokee (Iroquoian) <ama kalola>, lit. 'tumbling water' (Goff 1975); cf. Cherokee *ama* 'water' (Feeling 1975).

AMICOY (Wis., Rusk Co.) \am´ i koi\. Probably derived from the Ojibwa word for 'beaver' (Vogel 1991); the form is *amik* (Nichols and Nyholm 1995). An alternative spelling is **Amacoy.** Probably related placenames are **Amaqua** (Iowa, Boone Co.) and **Amik Lake** (Mich., Gogebic Co.).

AMIDOLA:DEBOW UL'A (N.Mex., Cibola Co.). The Zuni placename contains /amitola/ 'rainbow color' (Ferguson and Hart 1985; Newman 1958).

AMIK Island (Alaska, Trinity Islands D-1) \ə mēk⁀\. From Alutiiq (Eskimo) *amiik* 'gate, door' (Orth 1967, Leer 1978).

AMIK Lake (Mich., Gogebic Co.) \ä´ mik\. From Ojibwa (Algonquian) *amik* 'beaver' (Nichols and Nyholm 1995). The name is also found in Minn. (Lake Co.) and Wis. (Douglas Co.). Probably related names include **Ahmeek** (Mich., Keweenaw Co.; Wis., Bayfield Co.), **Amaqua** (Iowa, Boone Co.); and **Amicoy** (Wis., Rusk Co.).

AMILOYAK Lake (Alaska, Chandler Lake A-5). The Iñupiaq (Eskimo) name was recorded in 1956 (Orth 1967).

AMIMENIPATJ (Del., New Castle Co.). This may be from a Delaware (Algonquian) name meaning 'where pigeons sleep' (Heck et al. 1966); cf. Delaware /ami:mi/ 'pigeon' (I. Goddard p.c.).

AMITCHIAK Lake (Alaska, Ambler River D-1). The Iñupiaq (Eskimo) name is *amitchuaq,* said to mean 'narrow' (Orth 1967; Burch 1998); cf. *amitchuq* 'narrow' (Webster and Zibell 1970).

AMITE (La., Tangipahoa Par.) \am ēt´, ā mit⁀\. The name appears in eighteenth-century records as <Amite, Mité, Amit, Amitte>. It is perhaps to be derived from Choctaw (Muskogean) *himmita* 'young', with some influence from French *amitié* 'friendship' (Read 1927). The name also occurs in Miss. (Amite Co.).

AMLIA Island (Alaska, Seguam C-5) \am lē´ ə\. From the Aleut placename *amlax, amlagix̂,* perhaps containing *am-* 'narrow' (Bergsland 1994).

AMMONOOSUC River (N.H., Grafton Co.) \am ə nōō´ sək\. Western Abenaki (Algonquian) *ômanosek* [ɔ̨manosək] 'fishing place'; cf. *ôma* 'he fishes', *-ek* 'place' (Day 1994–95).

AMNICON (Wis., Douglas Co.) \am´ ni kon\. Said to be from an Ojibwa (Algonquian) word meaning 'spawning ground (of fish)' (Vogel 1991); cf. Ojibwa *aamiwag* 'they spawn' (Nichols and Nyholm 1995).

AMO Creek (Alaska, Misheguk Mountain D-3) \ä´ mō\. Said to be abbreviated from Iñupiaq (Eskimo) *amaġuq* 'wolf' (Orth 1967, MacLean 1980). Possibly related placenames include **Amakomanak Creek** (Alaska, Ambler River D-4), **Amagoalik Creek** (Alaska, Wainwright C-1), and **Amawk Mountain** (Alaska, Wiseman D-1).

AMOLE Peak (Ariz., Pima Co.) \ə mō´ lē\. From the Spanish name of a plant, sometimes called 'soaproot', ultimately from Aztec (Nahuatl) *amolli.* The name occurs elsewhere in **Cañada de Amole** (N.Mex., Santa Fe Co.), with the Spanish plural form in **Los Amoles** (N.Mex., Doña Ana Co.), and perhaps in **Amola Ridge** (N.Mex., Mora Co.).

AMOOK Island (Alaska, Kodiak B-6) \ə mōōk\. The Alutiiq (Eskimo) name was first recorded as <Amok> in 1908 (Orth 1967).

AMOSKEAG Bridge (N.H., Hillsborough Co.) \am´ əs keg\. From Abenaki (Algonquian) *namaskik* 'at fish land'; cf. *namas* 'a fish' (Day 1995). The term also occurs as a transfer name (Ga., Dodge Co.).

AMOS Point (Alaska, Umnak A-2). Aleut *amuusix̂* 'painter (mooring rope)'; cf. *amu-lix* 'to tie up, to moor' (Bergsland 1994).

A'MOSSI'A (N.Mex., Cibola Co.). The Zuni placename designates a camping area (Ferguson and Hart 1985).

AMOTA Butte (Ore., Lake Co.) \ə mot´ ə\. From Chinook Jargon <a-mo´-ta> [amótə] 'strawberry', from a Chinookan form such as Kathlamet [amōte] (D. Kinkade p.c.).

AMOXIUMQUA (N.Mex., Sandoval Co.). The Spanish spelling reflects Jemez (Tanoan) *amun-sho-kwa* 'ant hill', containing *amun* 'ant', *sho* 'to live', and *-kwa* 'place'; or perhaps *amun-shun-kwa* 'ant hill place', containing *shuun* 'hill' (Y. Yumitani p.c.).

AMTAGIS Islands (Alaska, Atka C-2). The Aleut name was first published in 1852 (Orth 1967).

AMUGUL Bay (Alaska, Unalaska B-2). The Aleut name was recorded as <Amuglik> in 1840; it may be from *amux̂* 'lightning' (Orth 1967; Bergsland 1994).

AMUKTA Island (Alaska, Amukta B-4) \ə muk´ tə\. From the Aleut placename *amuux̂tax̂* (Bergsland 1994).

AMUSOVI Mesa (Ariz., Navajo Co.). Hopi (Uto-Aztecan) *angwus'ovi* 'high raven place', from *angwus(i)* 'raven, crow', *-'o-* 'high', and *-vi* 'place' (K. Hill p.c.).

ANACACHO Mountains (Tex., Kinney Co.) \an ə kä´ chō\. Perhaps an Indian name, but the derivation is not clear (Tarpley 1980).

ANACAPA Islands (Calif., Ventura Co.) \an ə kap´ ə\. The name was reported in 1792 as <Eneeapah> and <Enecapa>; it is derived from Chumashan /anyapax/ 'mirage, illusion' (Gudde 1998).

ANACHLIK Island (Alaska, Harrison Bay B-1). Iñupiaq (Eskimo) *aanaakłiq* 'whitefish' (Orth 1967, MacLean 1980).

ANACOSTIA River (Md., Prince George's Co.) \an ə kos´ tē ə\. From an Algonquian language, perhaps meaning 'at the trading town' (Kenny 1984).

ANADARCHE Creek (Okla., Love Co.) \an ə där´ kē\. From the same origin as **Anadarko** (Okla., Caddo Co.) \an ə där´ kō\. The source is Caddo /nadá:kuh/, originally a placename meaning 'bumblebee place', from /na-/ 'place' and /dá:kuh/ 'bumblebee' (W. Chafe p.c.). The placename also occurs in Tex. (Rusk Co.).

ANAGAKSIK Island (Alaska, Atka B-6). From the Aleut placename *anagaxsax̂* (Bergsland 1994).

ANAHUAC (Tex., Chambers Co.) \an´ ə wak\. The Spanish spelling represents Aztec (Nahuatl) *anahuac,* lit. 'near the water', from *a(tl)* 'water' and *-nahuac* 'near'; the name was applied by the Aztecs to their territory in central Mexico. The Spanish or Aztec pronunciation is [ä nä´ wäk]. By contrast, **Anahuac Spring** (Calif., San Diego Co.) \ä´ nə hwäk\ is derived from the name of **Iñaja Indian Reservation,** from Diegueño (Yuman) *'enyehaa* 'my water' (Gudde 1998); see **Iñaja** below). The term has been assimilated in pronunciation and spelling to the Aztec name.

ANAJUK Point (Alaska, Harrison Bay B-2). The Iñupiaq (Eskimo) name was reported in 1951 (Orth 1967).

ANAK Creek (Alaska, Ikpikpuk River A-2). From Iñupiaq (Eskimo) *anaq* 'excrement' (Orth 1967; MacLean 1980). A possibly related placenames include **Anakruak** (Alaska, Teshekpuk D-2), **Anaktuk** (Alaska,Wainwright A-2), and **Anuk Creek** (Alaska, Howard Pass D-3); see below.

ANAKEESTA Ridge (Tenn., Sevier Co.) \an ə kē´ stə\. Said to be Cherokee (Iroquoian) for 'place of balsams' (M. Toomey p.c.).

ANAKEKSIK Creek (Alaska, Norton Bay B-4). The Iñupiaq (Eskimo) name was reported about 1954 (Orth 1967).

ANAKRUAK (Alaska, Teshekpuk D-2). The Iñupiaq (Eskimo) name is said to mean 'old dung'. It was reported in 1955 (Orth 1967); cf. *anaq* 'excrement' (MacLean 1980). Probably related placenames include **Anak Creek** (Alaska, Ikpikpuk River A-2) and **Anuk Creek** (Alaska, Howard Pass D-3); see above and below.

ANAKSHEK Pass (Alaska, Kwiguk B-6). The Yupik (Eskimo) name was reported in 1899 (Orth 1967).

ANAKTOK Creek (Alaska, Baird Mountains C-2). The Iñupiaq (Eskimo) name was recorded in 1955 (Orth 1967). A possibly related form is **Anaktuk** (Alaska, Wainwright A-2) \ə nak´ tuk\. This Iñupiaq name, reported in 1923, is said to mean 'excrement' (Orth 1967). Probably related placenames include **Anak Creek** (Alaska, Ikpikpuk River A-2), **Anakruak** (Alaska, Teshekpuk D-2), and **Anaktok Creek** (Alaska, Baird Mountains C-2); see above. Another probably related name is **Anaktuvuk Pass** (Alaska, Chandler Lake A-3) \an ək to͞o´ vuk\, from Iñupiaq *anaqtuġvik* 'place where dung is found' (Phillips 1973). There is also a transfer name, **Anaktuvuk Saddle,** in Ore. (Curry Co.).

ANALAK Creek (Alaska, Misheguk Mountain A-3). The Iñupiaq (Eskimo) name was recorded in 1956 (Orth 1967).

ANALCO (N.Mex., Santa Fe Co.) \ə nal´ kō\. Settled around 1610 by Indians from Tlaxcala state, Mexico, who spoke Nahuatl (Aztecan); it received the name *analco* 'on the other side of the water' (Julyan 1998). The word is from *a(tl)* 'water', *-nal-* 'beyond', and *-co* 'place'.

ANALOMINK (Pa., Monroe Co.) \an ə lō´ mingk\. Probably a Delaware (Algonquian) name, of unknown origin (Donehoo 1928).

ANAMOOSE (N.Dak., McHenry Co.) \an´ ə mo͞os\. From Ojibwa (Algonquian) *animosh* 'dog' (Wick 1988, Nichols and Nyholm 1995). A probably related placename is **Anamosa** (Iowa, Jones Co.) \an ə mō´ sə\; this is apparently from a word for 'dog' in some Algonquian language (Vogel 1983), perhaps Meskwaki /anemo:ha/ (or archaic **anemosa*, I. Goddard p.c.) or Ojibwa.

ANAN Creek (Alaska, Bradfield Canal A-6). Tlingit *an.áan* 'resting village', containing *aan* 'village' (T. Thornton p.c.).

ANANGULA Island (Alaska, Samalga Island D-3). From the Aleut placename *anagulax̂* (Bergsland 1994).

ANAPAMU (Calif., Santa Barbara Co.) \an ə pə mo͞o\. From Barbareño (Chumashan) *anapamu'* 'ascending place' (Gudde 1998).

ANAQUASSACOOK (N.Y., Washington Co.) \an ə kwä´ sə ko͝ok\. An Algonquian name of uncertain derivation (Ruttenber 1906; Beauchamp 1907).

ANASAGUNTICOOK, Lake (Maine, Oxford Co.) \an ə sə gun´ ti kŏŏk\. Said to be Abenaki (Algonquian) for 'at the river with the sandy bottom' (Huden 1962).

ANASAZI Canyon (Utah, San Juan Co.) \ä nə sä´ zē\. The term refers to pueblo dwellers who flourished from around A.D. 100 to 1300. The name is borrowed from Navajo *anaasází* 'enemies' ancestors,' the term 'enemies' being used by the Navajos to designate the modern Pueblo peoples of the Southwest.

ANATONE (Wash., Asotin Co.) \an´ ə tōn\. Supposedly named after a Nez Perce woman (Hitchman 1985).

ANAYAKNAURAK Creek (Alaska, Chandler Lake C-3). The Iñupiaq (Eskimo) name was recorded in 1956 (Orth 1967).

ANCON Peak (Alaska, Petersburg B-2). The name may be Tlingit; it was reported in 1916 (Orth 1967).

ANDERSON (Ind., Madison Co.). Named for William Anderson, the son of a Delaware woman and a Swedish American trader, born in the 1750s; he came to be a Delaware leader in Ind., and died in 1821. His Native American name was <Koktowhanund>, said to mean 'making a cracking noise' (McPherson 1993).

ANDES (N.Y., Delaware Co.) \an´ dēz\. Named for the Andes Mountains in South America; the term is from the Quechua (Inca) language (Room 1997). Places called **Andes** are also found elsewhere (e.g., Mont., Richland Co.) **Andesite,** a volcanic rock, also occurs in placenames (Calif., Siskiyou Co.; Alaska, Bendeleben C-5).

ANDIATAROCTE (N.Y., Warren Co.). From a Huron (Iroquoian) adapatation of the Mohawk (Iroquoian) name for Lake George, *ganyá:daro'kde',* meaning 'the lake coming to an end' (Lounsbury 1960:41).

ANDROSCOGGIN County (Maine) \an drə skog´ in\. From Eastern Abenaki (Algonquian) /aləssíkɑntəkw, alsíkɑntəkw/ 'river of cliff rock shelters', lit. 'thus-deep-dwelling-river' (Siebert 1943); or perhaps from Penobscot (Algonquian) /aləsstkɑtək^{W}/ 'river of rock shelters' (P. MacDougall p.c.). The **Androscoggin River** flows through both Maine and N.H.

ANERTZ Lake (Alaska, Kenai C-3) The Native American name, probably Alutiiq (Eskimo), was made official around 1963 (Orth 1967).

ANESKETT Point (Alaska, Petersburg A-4). The name, perhaps from Tlingit, was reported in 1904 (Orth 1967).

ANGAYUCHAM Mountains (Alaska, Hughes D-5). The Iñupiaq (Eskimo) name is *aŋayuqaatchiam iñġii* (Burch 1998), said to mean 'old man mountains'; cf. *angayuqaksraq* 'old man' (MacLean 1980). Probably related placenames include **Angayukachak Creek** (Alaska, Hughes D-6); **Angayukak Creek** (Alaska, Point Hope A-2); **Mount Angayukaqsraq** (Alaska, Baird Mountains C-1); and **Angayutak Mountain** (Alaska, Point Hope C-2); see below.

ANGAYU Creek (Alaska, Survey Pass C-5). The Iñupiaq (Eskimo) name is reported to be the name of a dance (Orth 1967); cf. *aŋayu-* 'to dance Eskimo style' (MacLean 1980).

ANGAYUKALIK Hills (Alaska, Baird Mountains D-3). The Iñupiaq (Eskimo) name is *aŋayukalik* 'eldest brother' (Orth 1967; Burch 1998); cf. the Uummarmiut dialect forms *angayuk* 'older sibling of ego's sex' (Dorais 1990:86, 203). Probably related placenames include **Angayucham Mountains** (Alaska, Hughes D-5); see above.

ANGAYUTAK Mountain (Alaska, Point Hope C-2). The Iñupiaq (Eskimo) name is *aŋayugaatchiam iñġii* (Burch 1998), said to mean 'old man mountains'; cf. *aŋayuqaksraq* 'old man' (MacLean 1980). Possibly related placenames include **Angayucham Mountains** (Alaska, Hughes D-5).

ANGIAAK Pass (Alaska, Survey Pass B-5). From an Iñupiaq (Eskimo) word meaning 'stone scraper' (Orth 1967).

ANGMAKROK Mountain (Alaska, Point Hope B-1). The Iñupiaq (Eskimo) word is said to mean 'old flint' (Orth 1967); cf. *agmaaq* 'flint' (MacLean 1980).

ANGOLIK Creek (Alaska, Point Hope C-3). The Iñupiaq (Eskimo) name was reported in 1950 (Orth 1967).

ANGOON (Alaska, Sitka C-2) \an gōōn\. Tlingit *aangóon* 'town's portage', from *aan* 'land, town' and *góon* 'narrowest point of an isthmus, portage' (J. Leer p.c.).

ANGOYAKVIK Pass (Alaska, Ikpikpuk River A-3). From an Iñupiaq (Eskimo) name, perhaps meaning 'place where the enemy is' (Orth 1967); cf. *anguyak-* 'to wage war' (Fortescue et al. 1994).

ANGUK Island (Alaska, Kodiak C-6). From an Alutiiq (Eskimo) word meaning 'big' (Orth 1967); cf. Central Yupik *ang'uq* 'it is big' (Jacobson 1984).

ANGUNELECHAK Pass (Alaska, Survey Pass B-5). The Iñupiaq (Eskimo) name is said to mean 'for use by the man who does not hunt' (Orth 1967); cf. *aŋu-* 'to catch a game animal' (MacLean 1980).

ANGUN River (Alaska, Demarcation Point D-3). From an Iñupiaq (Eskimo) name reported in 1920 (Orth 1967).

ANGUTIKADA Peak (Alaska, Shungnak C-1). Probably a Koyukon (Athabaskan) name, reported in 1901 (Orth 1967).

ANGUVIK Island (Alaska, Chignik B-1). This name, probably Alutiiq (Eskimo), was reported in 1847 (Orth 1967).

ANGYOYARAVAK Bay (Alaska, Hooper Bay B-2). The Yupik (Eskimo) name was reported in 1951 (Orth 1967).

ANIAK (Alaska, Russian Mission C-2) \an´ ē ak\. From Yupik (Eskimo) *anyaraq* 'the way to go out', from *ane-* 'to go out' (Jacobson 1984). A perhaps related name is **Aniakchak Bay** (Alaska, Sutwik Island C-5), probably from Alutiiq (Eskimo) (Orth 1967). Other perhaps related placenames include **Aniakvik** (Alaska, Sutwik Island C-5), **Anirak Lake** (Alaska, Ambler River A-3), **Anisak River** (Alaska, Howard Pass A-5), and **Aniuk River** (Alaska, Ambler River D-4); see below.

ANIAKVIK Creek (Alaska, Killik River B-2). The Iñupiaq (Eskimo) name has been translated 'place where one goes out' (Orth 1967); cf. *aniiq-* 'be outside' (MacLean 1980). Possibly related placenames include **Aniak** (Alaska, Russian Mission C-2); see above.

ANIKOVIK River (Alaska, Teller B-6). The Iñupiaq (Eskimo) name was reported in 1900 (Orth 1967).

ANIKTUM Island (Alaska, Hooper Bay D-3). The Yupik (Eskimo) name was reported in 1951 (Orth 1967).

ANIRAK Lake (Alaska, Ambler River A-3). The Iñupiaq (Eskimo) name has been translated 'place to go out' (Orth 1967); cf. *aniiq-* 'be outside' (MacLean 1980). Possibly related placenames include **Aniak** (Alaska, Russian Mission C-2); see above.

ANIRALIK Lake (Alaska, Misheguk Mountain A-2). The Iñupiaq (Eskimo) name was recorded in 1956 (Orth 1967).

ANISAK River (Alaska, Howard Pass A-5). The *Iñupiaq* (Eskimo) name is *anisaam kuŋa,* reported to mean 'place to go out' (Orth 1967; Burch 1998); cf. *aniiq-* 'be outside' (MacLean 1980). Possibly related placenames include **Aniak** (Alaska, Russian Mission C-2), **Aniakvik Creek** (Alaska, Killik River B-2), and **Anirak Lake** (Alaska, Ambler River A-3), as well as **Aniuk River** (Alaska, Ambler River D-4); see above and below.

ANISOM Point (Alaska, Seldovia C-4). The Alutiiq (Eskimo) name is supposedly that of an Eskimo man, also written as <Anisim> (Orth 1967).

ANIUK River (Alaska, Ambler River D-4). The Iñupiaq (Eskimo) name may mean 'he goes out' (Orth 1967); cf. *aniiq-* 'be outside' (MacLean 1980). Possibly related placenames include **Aniak** (Alaska, Russian Mission C-2); see above.

ANIVIK Creek (Alaska, Chandler Lake A-3). The Iñupiaq (Eskimo) name may mean 'village place' (Orth 1967); cf. *-vik* 'place' (Webster and Zibell 1970).

ANIWA (Wis., Shawano Co.) \an´ i wä\. From an Ojibwa or Menomini (Algonquian) word referring to superiority; cf. Menomini /ani:w/ 'more, farther' (Bloomfield 1975).

ANIYUYAKTUVIK Creek (Alaska, Point Hope B-1). The Iñupiaq (Eskimo) word has been translated as 'place where wind has hardened snow, so that a snow house can be built' (Orth 1967).

ANKAU, The (Alaska, Yakutat C-5) \än kou´\. The name of this channel is from Tlingit *aan-qáawu* 'rich man, chief' (J. Leer p.c.).

ANKODOSH Creek (Mich., Chippewa Co.). Appears to be a Native American word, but the derivation is not clear (Vogel 1986).

ANMAN Creek (Alaska, Skagway B-3). Possibly from Tlingit *an.áan* 'resting village', containing *aan* 'village' (T. Thornton p.c.).

ANNABESSACOOK Dam (Maine, Kennebec Co.) \an ə bes´ ə ko͞ok\. Seems to contain Abenaki (Algonquian) /aləpéhsin/ 'it lies sideways' (P. MacDougall p.c.).

ANNAHOOTZ Mountain (Alaska, Sitka B-4) \an´ ə ho͞ots\. Said to be named for a Tlingit leader, *anaxóots,* containing *xoots* 'brown bear'.

ANNAQUATUCKET (R.I., Washington Co.) \an ə kwə tuk´ ət\. From a Massachusett (Algonquian) name meaning 'at the end of the river', from <wunnashque> 'at the end of', plus <-tuk>, a combining form of the word for 'river', plus <-et> 'place' (W. Cowan p.c.).

ANNARICKEN Brook (N.J., Burlington Co.) \an ə rik´ən\. From Delaware (Algonquian), perhaps containing *aney* 'road, path' (Becker 1964).

ANNASNAPPET Brook (Mass., Plymouth Co.) \an ə snap´ ət\. Algonquian, meaning 'at the source of the stream', containing <wanash(que)-> 'on top of', <-nip-> 'water', <-et> 'place' (W. Cowan p.c.).

ANNAWAMSCUTT (R.I., Bristol Co.) \an ə wäm´ skət\. A variant spelling of **Annawomscutt.**

ANNAWAN Rock (Mass., Bristol Co.) \an´ ə wän\. The term applied to a seventeenth-century Massachusett (Algonquian) leader, perhaps from <annoonnuwaen> 'commander' (Huden 1962; Vogel 1963). It occurs as a transfer name in Ill. (Henry Co.).

ANNAWOMSCUTT (R.I., Bristol Co.) From a Massachusett (Algonquian) word meaning 'at the end of the rocks' (i.e., 'at the top of the rocks'), from <wunnashque> 'at the end of', plus <-ompsk>, a combining form of the word for 'rock', plus <-utt> 'place' (W. Cowan p.c.). The spelling **Annawamscutt** also occurs.

ANNEEWAKEE (Ga., Douglas Co.) Probably from the surname of a Cherokee (Iroquoian) family, written as <Anne waky>, perhaps containing *wahga* 'cow' (from Spanish *vaca*) (Goff 1975; cf. Feeling 1975).

ANNEMESSEX Creek (Md., Somerset Co.) \an ə mes´ iks\. From an Algonquian language; it has been suggested that the meaning is 'it rushes beneath (the bank)' (Kenny 1984).

ANNINAN Lake (Wis., Langlade Co.) Perhaps from Ojibwa (Algonquian), but the derivation is not clear (Vogel 1991).

ANNISQUAM (Mass., Essex Co.) \an´ i skwäm\. Algonquian, meaning 'top of the rock', containing <wanashque> 'on top of', <-ompsk> 'rock' (W. Cowan p.c.).

ANNOKSEK Creek (Alaska, Mt. Fairweather B-3) The Tlingit name was reported in 1901 (Orth 1967).

ANNURSNAC Hill (Mass., Middlesex Co.). Perhaps from a Nipmuck (Algonquian) word meaning 'lookout place' (Huden 1962).

ANNUSANTONSET River (Mass., Plymouth Co.). Perhaps from Nipmuck (Algonquian), 'broken-up land' (Huden 1962).

ANNUTTELIGA Hammock (Fla., Hernando Co.) \ə nut ə lī´ gə\. Possibly from Muskogee *vnvttē* /anatt-í:/ 'obstacle' and *alikv* /a:-léyk-a/ 'sitting there' (Martin and Mauldin 2000). Also written as **Annutti Alagga** (Read 1934).

ANOGOK (Alaska, Kuskokwim Bay D-6) \ə nog´ ok\. The Yupik (Eskimo) name was reported in 1878 (Orth 1967).

ANOKA (Minn., Anoka Co.) \ə nō´ kə\. From Dakota (Sioux) *anóka* 'on both sides', applied because the city was laid out on both sides of the Rum River (Upham 2001; Riggs 1890). The name is found in many other states: for example, as the name of towns in Ind. (Cass Co.), Ore. (Columbia Co.), and Fla. (Highlands Co.).

ANORAT Creek (Alaska, Survey Pass C-5) \an´ ə rat\. The Iñupiaq (Eskimo) name is *aanġuaq* 'amulet' (L. Kaplan p.c.).

ANOTLENEEGA Mountain (Alaska, Melozitna C-4). The Koyukon (Athabaskan) name was recorded in 1956 (Orth 1967).

ANOWIK Island (Alaska, Sutwik Island A-3). The Alutiiq (Eskimo) name was published in 1888 (Orth 1967).

ANTASSAWAMOCK (Mass., Plymouth Co.). Said to be a Narragansett (Algonquian) name, but of uncertain derivation (Huden 1962).

ANTELOPE. This English word is commonly used in the western United States to refer to what is also known as the 'pronghorn antelope' or simply the 'pronghorn'. **Antelope Butte** (S.Dak., Butte Co.) is probably a loan-translation from the Lakhota (Sioux) word for 'antelope' (Sneve 1973); the form is *thathókala* (Ingham 2001). **Antelope House** (Ariz., Apache Co.) corresponds to Navajo (Athbabaskan) *jádí deíjechí kits'iilí* 'where swift ones (antelope) run along ruin' (Linford 2000); cf. *kits'iil* 'pueblo-type ruin' (Young and Morgan 1987). **Antelope Lookout Mesa** (N.Mex., McKinley Co.) corresponds to Navajo (Athabaskan) *jádí hádít'įįh* 'antelope lookout' (Linford 2000). **Antelope Pass** (Ariz., Coconino Co.) corresponds to Navajo *jádí habitiin* 'antelope ascending trail' (Linford 2000); cf. *jádí* 'antelope' (Young and Morgan 1987). **Antelope Trading Post** (Ariz., Navajo Co.) is from Navajo *jádító* 'antelope spring' (cf. *tó* 'water, spring'); This is located at the settlement of **Jeddito,** the English spelling of the Navajo name (Linford 2000).

ANTERO (Colo., Park Co.) \an târ´ ō\. The name is that of a 19th century Ute leader; its origin is not known (Bright 1993). A possibly related placename is **Antora** (Colo., Saguache Co.).

ANTIETAM (Md., Washington Co.) \an tē´ təm\. An Algonquian word, perhaps meaning something like 'swift water' (Kenny 1984). The name also occurs in Ohio (Trumbull Co.) and Pa. (Franklin Co.).

ANTIGO (Wis., Langlade Co.) \an´ ti gō\. This represents a portion of a longer name, said to be Ojibwa (Algonquian); its derivation is not clear (Vogel 1991).

ANTINGMIUT Creek (Alaska, Nunivak Island A-5) \an ting´ myo͞ot\. The Yupik (Eskimo) name was reported in 1937 (Orth 1967). The element *-miut* refers to the inhabitants of a place.

ANTITONNIE Creek (Alaska, Iliamna D-1). The Native American name may be Dena'ina (Athabaskan).

ANTLEN River (Alaska, Yakutat B-4) \an´ tlen\. From Tlingit *aan tlein,* lit. 'land big' (T. Thornton p.c.) The name has also been adapted into English as **Ahrnklin.**

ANTOKEN Creek (Ore., Wasco Co.) \än tō´ kən\. Said to have been the name of an Indian resident of the area who died in 1905 (McArthur 1992).

ANTORA Peak (Colo., Saguache Co.) \an tôr´ ə\. Perhaps from the same origin as **Antero,** name of a Ute (Numic) leader (Bright 1993).

ANUK Creek (Alaska, Howard Pass D-3) \an´ ək\. From Iñupiaq (Eskimo) *anaq* 'excrement' (Orth 1967, MacLean 1980). A probably related name is **Anuk River** (Alaska, Kwiguk B-4). Other likely related placenames are **Anak Creek** (Alaska, Ikpikpuk River A-2) and **Anakruak** (Alaska, Teshekpuk D-2).

ANUZUKANUK Pass (Alaska, Kwiguk D-6). The Yupik (Eskimo) name was recorded in 1948 (Orth 1967).

ANVIK (Alaska, Holy Cross C-3) \an´ vik\. This community of Deg Hit'an (Athabaskan) Indians has a Yupik (Eskimo) name: *anvik* means 'place to go out' (Jacobson 1984).

ANYAKA Island (Alaska, Skagway A-1) The Tlingit name was reported in 1922 (Orth 1967).

AOWA Creek (Neb., Dixon Co.) \ī´ ə wə, ou´ wə\. Earlier written as Aoway (Perkey 1995); perhaps from **Iowa, Ioway,** the name of the state and of a Siouan Indian group.

APACHE \ə pach´ ē\. A cover term for several Indian peoples speaking languages of the **Apachean** family; the family includes **Western Apache** (Ariz.), **Chiricahua** and **Mescalero** (N.Mex.), **Navajo** (Ariz., N.Mex., Utah), and **Plains Apache** (Lipan, Kiowa Apache, in Okla.). The family is part of the larger **Athabaskan** group. The Spanish form *apache* was first recorded by the Spanish explorer Juan de Oñate in 1598 at San Juan Pueblo in what is now N. Mex. **Apache**, which was originally used to include the Navajos, is not from any Apachean language but apparently from the language of some neighboring people (*HNAI* 10:385). The most plausible derivation is perhaps from Yavapai (Yuman) *'paacha* ['əpá:ča], the plural form of *'paa* ['əpa:] 'person' (P. Munro p.c.) **Apache** occurs in placenames in many states: for example, **Apache County** (Ariz.), **Apache Peak** (N.Mex., Colfax Co.), and **Apache Park** (Iowa, Linn Co.) A related placeame is **Apacheria** (Ariz., Gila Co.) \ə pach ə rē´ ə\, from Spanish *apachería* 'place of the Apaches'.

APAKSHAU Slough (Alaska, St. Michael A-4). The Yupik (Eskimo) name was reported in 1899 (Orth 1967).

APALACHE (S.C., Spartanburg Co.) \ap ə lach´ ē\. From the same origin as **Apalachee** \ap ə lach´ ē\. This is the name of a Muskogean people, allied politically with the Creeks, who formerly lived in northwestern Fla. and adjacent areas. The name may be from Apalachee *abalahci* 'other side of the river' or from Hitchiti (Muskogean) *apalwahči* 'dwelling on one side' (P. Munro p.c.; J. Martin p.c.). As a present-day placename, the term occurs in Ala. (Baldwin Co.), Ga. (Morgan Co.), and Fla. (Jefferson Co.). In the sixteenth century the Spanish applied the name, in the form *Apalachen,* to what we now call the **Appalachian Mountains.**

APALACHIA (Tenn., Polk Co.) \ap ə lach´ ē ə\. From the same source as **Apalache** or **Appalachia**; see above and below.

APALACHICOLA (Fla., Franklin Co.) \ap ə lach i kō´ lə\. The term, entering English through Spanish, means 'Apalachee people' in a Muskogean language, perhaps equivalent to 'people dwelling on the other shore'; cf. Choctaw *oklah* 'people' (P. Munro p.c.); see also **Apalache**, above. The equivalent English borrowing directly from Muskogean is **Apalatchukla** (Ala., Russell Co.).

APALACHIN (N.Y., Tioga Co.) \ap ə lā´ kin\. Probably from <Apalachen>, an earlier form for the name of the **Appalachian Mountains** (see **Appalachian** below) There is also an **Apalachin Creek** in Pa. (Susquehanna Co.).

APALATCHUKLA (Ala., Russell Co.) \ap ə lə cho͝ok´ lə\. Probably means 'Apalachee people' in a Muskogean language, perhaps equivalent to 'people dwelling on the other shore'; cf. Choctaw *oklah* 'people' (P. Munro p.c.). The same name was borrowed through Spanish as **Apalachicola** (Fla., Franklin Co.); see also **Apalache**, above.

APATIKI Camp (Alaska, St. Lawrence C-5). From the surname of a Yupik (Eskimo) family (Orth 1967).

APAVAWOOK Cape (Alaska, St. Lawrence B-0). The Yupik (Eskimo) name was reported in 1948 (Orth 1967).

APEEKWA Lake (Wis., Vilas Co.) \ə pēk´ wä\. Perhaps from a mistranscription of Apukwa, a word used in Longfellow's *Hiawatha* and translated 'bulrush'. This is apparently from an Ojibwa word, forms of which have been recorded as <apakwa> 'rush', <apakwei> 'mat, lodge mat' (Vogel 1991). Related forms in present-day Ojibwa are *apakwe* 'to put on a roof', *apakweshkway* 'cattail mat, cattail' (Nichols and Nyholm 1995). A related name is **Puckaway Lake** (Wis., Green Lake Co.).

APHREWN River (Alaska, Hooper Bay A-1). From Yupik (Eskimo) *aprun,* from *aper-* 'to say, pronounce' (Jacobson 1984).

APIATAN Mountain (Colo., Grand Co.). Supposedly named for a Kiowa leader and singer; his name is said to refer to a wooden ceremonial lance (Bright 1993),

APIKUGURUAK Creek (Alaska, Wainwright B-2). The (Eskimo) name is from *aqpik* 'cloudberry, salmonberry' (L. Kaplan p.c.).

APIKUNI Creek (Mont., Glacier Co.). Formerly spelled **Appekunny**, this was the Blackfoot (Algonquian) name of James Willard Schultz, a white man who lived for years with western Indians and wrote many books about them. Although the name has been translated 'scabby robe', it was an honorable name, given to Schultz by Running Crane, who owned it (Holterman 1985). The derivation may be from *apiikani* 'people with scabby robes (from poorly processed hides)'; cf. *aapíksssin* 'skin eruption' (D. Frantz p.c.). The name **Piegan,** referring to a subdivision of the Blackfoot people, may come from the same source.

APISHAPA River (Colo., Las Animas Co.) \ə pish´ ə pə\. Perhaps from Ute (Numic) *áapasagopaa* 'increasingly mossy water', containing *aa-* 'increasingly', *paságo(vü)* 'moss', and *paa* 'water' (J. McLaughlin p.c.) At one time folk-etymologized into "Fish-Paw River."

APOKAK (Alaska, Baird Inlet A-1) \ap´ ō kak\. The Yupik (Eskimo) name was recorded in 1878, (Orth 1967).

APOLACON Township (Pa., Susquehanna Co.) A derivation of the name has been proposed from Delaware (Algonquian) <Apelogacan> 'whence the messenger returned' (Donehoo 1982).

APONIVI (Ariz., Navajo Co.) \ə pō´ nē vē\. From Hopi (Uto-Aztecan) *apòonivi* (K. Hill p.c.).

APOOKTA Creek (Miss., Attala Co.) \ə pōōk´ tə\. Choctaw (Muskogean) *apokta* 'something doubled' (P. Munro p.c.).

APOON Pass (Alaska, St. Michael A-3). The Yupik (Eskimo) name is said to mean 'thumb' (Orth 1967).

APOPKA (Fla., Orange Co.) \ə pop´ kə\. Earlier written as **Ahapopka**, the name is Muskogee for 'potato-eating' (Read 1934), from *vhv* /ahá/ 'potato', *papkv* /pa:p-ka/ 'eating' (Martin and Mauldin 2000). The similar name **Charley Apopka Creek** (Fla., Hardee Co) means 'trout-eating', from Creek *calo* 'trout'.

APOXEE (Fla., Osceola Co.) \ə pok´ sē\. From Muskogee *vpakse* /apáksi/ 'tomorrow'. This is not an original Creek placename but was taken by whites from a Creek wordlist (Martin and Mauldin 2000).

APPALACHIA (N.H., Coös Co.) \ap ə lā´ chē ə\. From the same origin as **Appalachian Mountains;** cf. **Apalache** above. The placename also occurs in Okla. (Tulsa Co.) and Va. (Wise Co.).

APPALACHIAN \ap ə lā´ chē ən\. This term, applied to the principal mountain range of the eastern United States, was earlier written by Spanish explorers as <Apalachen> and then was rewritten to resemble an English adjective. Until the mid-nineteenth century it referred primarily to the mountains of the southern states; subsequently it was applied to what we now call the **Appalachian Mountains** (Stewart 1970). In origin it is the name of a Muskogean people, allied politically with the Creeks, who formerly lived in northwestern Fla. and adjacent areas. The name may be from Apalachee *abalahci* 'other side of the river' or from Hitchiti (Muskogean) *apalwahči* 'dwelling on one side' (P. Munro p.c.; J. Martin p.c.); see **Apalache**, above.

APPALACHIE Pond (Maine, Lincoln Co.) Perhaps a shortening of Abenaki (Algonquian)

/apaləčehkámihke/ 'barren knoll of land' (P. MacDougall p.c.).

APPALOOSA Ridge (Ariz., Coconino Co.) \ap ə lo͞o´ sə, ä pə lo͞o´ sə\. Named from a breed of horse, traditionally associated with the Nez Perce (Sahaptian) group of Idaho and the Palouse River of their region. The name is perhaps to be associated with **Opelousas**, however, a Louisiana placename (*RHD* 1987). **Palouse** is from Sahaptin *palú:s* 'what is standing up in the water'; **Opelousas** is perhaps from Choctaw *api losa* 'black body'.

APPANOOSE County (Iowa) \ap´ ə no͞os\. Named for *apeno:sa,* a leader of the Meskwaki (Algonquian) people; this is an archaic form of /apeno:ha/ 'child' (I. Goddard p.c.). The placename also occurs elsewhere (Ill., Hancock Co.; Kans., Franklin Co.).

APPISTOKI Creek (Mont., Glacier Co.) \ap i stō´ kē\. The Blackfoot (Algonquian) name has been variously interpreted. One claim is that it means 'behind the ears', from *aapát* 'behind' and *sstoki* 'ear'. Another is that it is a reduced form of *á'pistotooki* 'God, creator', lit. 'he who created us' (Holterman 1985; Frantz and Russell 1995).

APPLE River (Wis., St. Croix Co.). An abbreviated translation of French *pomme de terre,* lit. 'apple of the earth' but used to mean 'potato'. In North America early French visitors applied the term to various wild tubers or roots that were consumed by the Indians (Vogel 1991). Among the Ojibwa (Algonquian) people the 'wild potato' is now called *bagwajipin,* from *bagwaj* 'in the wilderness' plus *opin,* which was the original name of the wild plant, but now refers to the domestic potato (Nichols and Nyholm 1995).

APPLEVUN Lake (Alaska, Fort Yukon C-1). The Gwich'in (Athabaskan) name was recorded in 1956 (Orth 1967).

APPOMATTOC (Va., Chesterfield Co.) \ap ə mat´ ək\. A local subgroup of the Powhatan (Algonquian) Confederacy was called <Apamatic> by the Jamestown settlers in 1607; the plural form of this later came to be written as **Appomattox** (Va., Appomattox Co.) \ap ə mat´ əks\ (Hagemann 1988). Elsewhere there is an **Appomattox Township** (S.Dak., Potter Co.).

APPONAGANSETT (Mass., Bristol Co.) \ap ə nə gan´ sət\. The Eastern Algonquian name may mean 'where he sits, remains', containing <appu-> 'he sits', <-et> 'place' (W. Cowan p.c.).

APPONAUG Cove (R.I., Bristol Co.) \ap´ ə nôg\. Probably from Narragansett (Algonquian) <opponenauhock> 'place where he roasts oysters'; cf. <apwonau> 'he roasts' and <hogh> 'shellfish' (W. Cowan p.c.).

APPOQUINIMINK River (Del., New Castle Co.) \ap ə kwin´ ə mingk\. From Delaware (Algonquian), possibly meaning 'wounded duck' (Heck et al. 1966).

APROKA Pass (Alaska, Kwiguk D-5). The Yupik (Eskimo) name has been said to mean 'little trail' (Orth 1967); cf. Yupik *aprun* 'trail' (Jacobson 1984).

APROTHLUK River (Alaska, Hooper Bay A-1). The Yupik (Eskimo) name was recorded in 1951 (Orth 1967).

APSHAWA (N.J., Passaic Co.). The name is probably Delaware (Algonquian), of unknown derivation. There is a **Lake Apshawa** in Fla. (Lake Co.).

APTAKISIC (Ill., Lake Co.) Named for a nineteenth-century Potawatomi (Algonquian) leader whose name was reported as <Op-ta-gu-shick>, translated as **Half Day**; cf. Potawatomi <apitu> 'half', <kijik> 'day' (Vogel 1963).

APTOS (Calif., Santa Cruz Co.) \ap´ tōs\. Probably from the Rumsen (Costanoan) language; a local tradition says that the original meaning was 'the meeting of two streams' (Gudde 1998).

APTUCXET (Mass., Barnstable Co.) \ap tuk´ sət\. Eastern Algonquian, 'waiting place at the small tidal river', containing <appu-> 'he sits', <-tuck-> 'tidal river', <-s-> 'small', <-et> 'place' (W. Cowan p.c.).

APUKWA. See **Apeekwa Lake**.

AQPI (Ariz., Navajo Co.) This name of a spring may be from Hopi (Uto-Aztecan).

AQUASCO (Md., Prince George's Co.) \ə kwäs´ kō\. Perhaps from Algonquian elements meaning 'edge' and 'weed' (Kenny 1984).

AQUEBOGUE (N.Y., Suffolk Co.) \ak´ wə bōg\. The Algonquian name was written in colonial times as **Accopogue, Occopogue, Aquebauke, Ocquebauck, Ucquebaug,** and so on. It may have meant 'end-of-water place' (Ruttenber 1906; Tooker 1911).

AQUETONG (Pa., Bucks Co.) \ak´ wə tong\. The Delaware (Algonquian) name may have meant 'at an island' (Donehoo 1928). There is also a **Mount Aquetong** in N.Y. (Westchester Co.).

AQUIA (Va., Stafford Co.) \ak´ wē ə\. The Algonquian name may have meant 'muddy' (Hagemann 1988).

AQUIDNECK Island (R.I., Newport Co.) \ə kwid´ nek\. The term refers to what is otherwise called "The Island of Rhode Island." It is derived from SNEng. Algonquian /akwidnək/ 'on the island' (I. Goddard p.c.); cf. **Quidnet.**

AQUONE (NC, Macon Co.) From Cherokee *egwoni* 'sea' (Feeling 1975).

ARAMINGO Square (Pa., Philadelphia Co.) \âr ə ming´ gō\. The name is reduced from Delaware (Algonquian) <Tumanaraming>, supposedly meaning 'wolf walk'; cf. /tə́me:/ 'wolf' (Blalock et al. 1994).

ARANSAS County (Tex.) \ə ran´ zəs\. Perhaps from the Karankawa Indian language; the origin is not clear (Tarpley 1980).

ARAPAHO \ə rap´ ə hō\. The name of a Plains Indian group, of the Algonquian linguistic family; at present one branch lives in Wyo., the other in Okla. This is not the name that the Arapaho people use for themselves; it is said to be borrowed from Pawnee *tiraapuhu* 'he is bartering' or *iriiraraapuhu* 'trader'. The Pawnees do not use this term to refer to the Arapahos, however, so it may have been misunderstood by whites. Another possible source is Crow /aaraxpé-ahu/, lit. 'tattoo' (Bright 1993). The form **Arapaho** occurs as a placename in several areas: Kans. (Haskell Co.), Okla. (Custer Co.), Wyo. (Albany Co.), and even N.J. (Sussex Co.). The alternative spelling **Arapahoe** also occurs, as the name of a county in Colo. and of a town in Wyo. (Fremont Co.).

ARAPIEN Valley (Utah, Sanpete Co.) \âr ə pē´ ən\. Named for a Paiute leader, the younger half-brother of Chief Walker (Van Cott 1990).

ARATHLATULUK, Mount (Alaska, Solomon D-2). The Iñupiaq (Eskimo) name was published in 1956 (Orth 1967).

ARAVAIPA (Ariz., Graham Co.) \âr ə vī´ pə, ä rə vī´ pə\. The name is associated with a group of Apache (Athabaskan) Indians who lived in the area in the eighteenth century. The word is said to come from a Piman (Uto-Aztecan) language of Mexico, however, (Granger 1983).

ARBACOOCHEE (Ala., Cleburne Co.)) \är bə ko͞o´ chē\. From the name of a Muskogee tribal town, *apehkuce* /a:pihkocí:/, meaning 'little *apehkv*', which is itself the name of a Creek tribal town, /a:píhka/. This is itself the source of the name **Arbeca Creek** in Okla. (Hughes Co.; Shirk 1974; Martin and Mauldin 2000). A related placename is **Arbeka** (Okla., Seminole Co.).

ARCATA (Calif., Humboldt Co.) \är kā´ tə\. From Yurok *oket'oh* 'where there is a lagoon' (referring to Humboldt Bay), from *o-* 'place' plus *ket'oh* 'to be a lagoon'; the name is also applied by the Yuroks to Big Lagoon, farther up the coast (Gudde 1998).

ARCHAWAT (Wash., Clallam Co.) \arch´ ə wat\. From the Makah (Nootkan) toponym [hač'a:wa:ʔat] (W. Jacobsen p.c.). This term is itself perhaps from Quileute (Chemakuan) [hač'a:wat] 'good beach', from /hač'/ 'good' and /-awat/ 'beach' (D. Kinkade p.c.).

ARCHUELINGUK River (Alaska, Kwiguk A-4). The Yupik (Eskimo), also written <Atchuelinguk>, was reported in 1952 (Orth 1967).

ARCHUSA Creek (Miss., Clarke Co.) \är kyōō´ sə\. Perhaps from the Choctaw for 'little stream', containing *haccha* 'stream' and *-osi, -oshi* 'little' (P. Munro p.c.).

ARENAC County (Mich.) \âr´ ə nak\. The name is invented, combining Latin *arena* 'sand' with an Algonquian element meaning 'land' (Vogel 1986); cf. Ojibwa *aki* 'land' (Nichols and Nyholm 1995).

ARESKONK Creek (N.Y., Suffolk Co.). An Algonquian word, thought to be the name of an Indian resident (Tooker 1911).

ARHYMOT Lake (Alaska, Russian Mission C-4). The Yupik (Eskimo) name was reported about 1952 (Orth 1967).

ARICA Mountain (Calif., Riverside Co.) \ə rē´ kə\. Perhaps named after Arica in northern Chile, which itself may be derived from a South American Indian language (Gudde 1998).

ARICKAREE Point (S.Dak., Campbell Co.) \ə rik´ ə rē\. From the same source as **Arikara**; see below. As a placename, **Arickaree** also occurs in Colo. (Washington Co.).

ARIKARA \ə rik´ ə rä\. The name of an Indian people of the Caddoan linguistic family. A Spanish record of 1794 lists *Alicara* as the name of one band within the group. It has been claimed that the name comes from Pawnee (Caddoan) *paariiku'* 'horn' or *arikaraaru'* 'buck deer', referring to a custom of wearing two bones in the hair, standing up like horns; however, this is not in fact the Pawnee name for the Arikaras (Bright 1993); it is likely to be a folk etymology (D. Parks p.c.). Related forms include **Arickaree Point** (S.Dak., Campbell Co.) and the abbreviation **Ree.** Another related name is **Arikaree Peak** (Colo., Grand Co.).

ARIMO (Idaho, Bannock Co.) \ə rē´ mō\. Supposedly the name of an Indian leader, language not identified (Boone 1988).

ARIPEKA (Fla., Pasco Co.) \âr i pē´ kə\. Named for a nineteenth-century Mikasuki (Muskogean) leader whose name was also written <Apiaka>; he was known in English as Sam Jones (Read 1934). The Muskogee form of his name was *apvyakv* /a:payá:ka/ 'chicken snake, rat snake', but the form **Aripeka** may show some confusion with *apehkv* /a:píhka/, the name of a Muskogee tribal town, called in English **Arbeka** (Martin and Mauldin 2000).

ARIVACA (Ariz., Pima Co.) \â ri vak´ ə, â ri vä´ kə\. O'odham (Piman) *ali wag* 'little hole', from *ali* 'little', *wag(a)* 'hole' (J. Hill p.c.).

ARIZOLA (Ariz., Pinal Co.) \âr i zō´ lə\. A combination of **Arizona** with the woman's name *Ola* (Granger 1983).

ARIZONA \âr i zō´ nə\. The name of the state is from Spanish *Arizonac* (Granger 1983), probably derived from an O'odham (Piman) term meaning 'having a little spring', from *ali* 'little', *ṣona-g* 'spring-having' (J. Hill p.c.). A derivation from Basque *arizonak* 'good oaks' is also possible, however (Douglass 1979). **Arizona** occurs as a transfer name in many other states, as far away as La. (Claiborne Co.).

ARKABUTLA (Miss., Tate Co.) \är kə but´ lə\. Perhaps from Choctaw (Muskogean) *aa-kobolli* 'where they broke it', from *aa-* 'place', *kobolli* 'break, shatter' (P. Munro p.c.).

ARKANSAS \är´ kən sô\. The name of the state reflects the name of the **Arkansas River,** which flows through Colo., Kans., Okla., and Ark.; it was originally named for a Siouan tribe. The spelling of the term represents a French plural, *Arcansas,* of a name applied to the Quapaw people who lived on the **Arkansas River**; their name was also written in early times as <Akancea, Acansea, Acansa> (Dickinson 1995). This was not the name used by the Quapaws themselves, however. The term /akansa/ was applied to them by Algonquian speakers; this consists of /a-/, an Algonquian prefix found in the names of ethnic groups, plus /kką:ze/, a Siouan stem referring to members of the Dhegiha branch of the Siouan family. This stem is also the origin for the name of the Kansa tribe and of the state of **Kansas**; thus the placenames **Arkansas** and **Kansas** indirectly have the same origin (R. Rankin p.c.). In **Kansas**, by analogy with the name of the state, the **Arkansas River** is sometimes given the alternative pronunciation \är kan´ zəs\.

ARKANSAW (Wis., Pepin Co.) \är´ kən sô\. This name, assigned in 1852, represents the common pronunciation of the placename **Arkansas** (Vogel 1991).

ARKAQUA Creek (Ga., Union Co.). Said to be named after a Cherokee (Iroquoian) man who lived in the area; also written **Arcaqua** (Krakow 1975).

ARKOMA (Okla., Le Flore Co.) \är kō´ mə\. The term was coined from the names **Arkansas** and **Oklahoma**, both of Indian origin (Shirk 1974).

ARLEE (Mont., Lake Co.) \är´ lē\. Named for a Flathead (Salishan) leader; his name was also written as Alee (Cheney 1984).

ARMONCK (NY, Westchester Co.) \är´ mongk\. A variant spelling of **Armonck**, an Algonquian name variously explained as meaning 'fishing place' or as being from the Delaware word for 'beaver' (Ruttenber 1906, Beauchamp 1907); cf. Munsee Delaware *amóxkw* 'beaver' (O'Meara 1996).

ARMUCHEE (Ga., Floyd Co.) \är mo͞o´ chē\. Perhaps from a Choctaw (Muskogee) term <alumushi>, meaning 'little hiding place' (Krakow 1975); it can be derived from *aloma* 'hiding place' (*aa-* 'there', *loma* 'to hide') and *-ushi* 'small' (P. Munro p.c.). Related forms are **Alamuchee** (Ala., Sumter Co.) and **Alamucha** (Miss., Lauderdale Co.).

AROLIK River (Alaska, Goodnews Bay C-8) \ə rō´ lik\. From a Yupik (Eskimo) name recorded as <Aalalik> (Orth 1967); this may be from *araq* 'ash' (Jacobson 1984).

AROLOKOVIK (Alaska, Kwiguk B-4). The Yupik (Eskimo) name was reported in 1899 (Orth 1967).

AROOSTOOK County (Maine) \ə ro͞o´ sto͝ok\. Perhaps from Abeṇaki /wəláhstək^{y}/ 'beautiful river' (P. MacDougall p.c.) or from *walastegw* 'shallow river'; cf. *waaskad* 'it is shallow water', *-tegw* 'river' (Day 1994–95).

AROPUK Lake (Alaska, Marshall A-5). The Yupik (Eskimo) name was recorded in 1948 (Orth 1967).

AROTAK Creek (Alaska, Misheguk Mountain A-2). The Iñupiaq (Eskimo) name was recorded as <argoag> 'windy and cold' (Orth 1967); cf. *argu* 'windward side' (MacLean 1980).

AROVIRCHAGK (Alaska, Kwiguk C-6). The Yupik (Eskimo) was recorded in 1952 (Orth 1967).

ARRIGETCH Peaks (Alaska, Survey Pass B-3). The Iñupiaq (Eskimo) name was reported as meaning 'fingers extended' (Orth 1967); cf. *argaich* 'fingers', from *argak* 'hand', *-ich* 'plural' (L. Kaplan p.c.) A related name is **Artigotrat** (Alaska, Point Hope A-2).

ARROWHEAD. This term, referring to a stone projectile point as used by Native Americans, occurs in many U.S. placenames: for example, **Arrowhead Butte** (S.Dak., Perkins Co.).

ARROWMINK Creek (Pa., Montgomery Co.). The name in this form appears to be a popular etymology; it has also been written as **Arronemink** and in the seventeenth century as <Aroenemeck>. It is probably from Delaware (Algonquian) (Donehoo 1928).

ARROWSIC (Maine, Sagadahoc Co.) \ə rō´ sik\. The name was earlier written <Arousik>, <Arouscag>, <Arrowseag>, <Arrowsike>, and so forth (Eckstorm 1941); it is perhaps from Abenaki (Algonquian) /alə́sseke/ 'cliff, wall or rock' (P. MacDougall p.c.).

ARTICHOKE Butte (S.Dak., Sully Co.). Perhaps a loan-translation from Dakota (Siouan); the Dakota word for the 'wild artichoke' (Helianthus) is *phąǧí* (Ingham 2001).

ARTIGOTRAT (Alaska, Point Hope A-2). The Iñupiaq (Eskimo) name is said to mean 'resembling hands' (Orth 1967); cf. *argak* 'finger' (MacLean 1980). A related name is **Arrigetch Peaks** (Alaska, Survey Pass B-3); see above.

ARVESTA Creek (Alaska, Kateel River A-6) \är ves´ tə\. Perhaps a Koyukon (Athabaskan) name; or perhaps a typographic error for Spanish *arrastra* 'ore mill' (Orth 1967).

ARWIRNUK Rock (Alaska, Nunivak Island B-4). A Yupik (Eskimo) name reported in 1937 (Orth 1967).

ASAAYI Dam (N.Mex., McKinley Co.) \ə sä´ yē\. Navajo (Athabaskan) *ásaayi'* 'inside the bowl', from *ásaa'* 'bowl, pot, kettle' plus *yi'* 'inside' (Wilson 1995).

ASAI STO (Ariz., Pima Co.). Perhaps a variant of **A'ai Sto,** from O'odham (Piman); meaning 'white on both sides'; cf. *a'ai* 'both sides', *s-toha* 'white' (J. Hill p.c.).

ASAYVA (Ariz., Navajo Co) \ə sī´ və\. Hopi (Uto-Aztecan) *asayva* 'sparrow spring', from *asya, asay-* 'sparrow', *paahu, -va* 'water' (K. Hill p.c.).

ASCUTNEY (Vt., Windsor Co.) \ə skut´ nē\. Perhaps from Abenaki (Algonquian) *bemapskadena* 'where there is a rocky mountain', from *bemapska* 'rocky place', *-adena* 'mountain' (Day 1994–95).

ASHAWAY River (R.I., Washington Co.) \ash´ ə wā\. Algonquian <nashaue> 'in the middle' (W. Cowan p.c.). The name is also found in Connecticut (New London Co.). Variants include **Ashawog, Ashawaug,** and **Ashawagh.**

ASHEGON Lake (Wis., Sawyer Co.) \ash´ i gon\. From Ojibwa (Algonquian) *ashigan* 'large-mouth bass' (Vogel 1991; Nichols and Nyholm 1995).

ASHEPOO (S.C., Colleton Co.) \ash´ i pōō\. Earlier written <Asha-po>, <Ospo>, <Ishepoo> (Waddell 1980). Named for an Indian band of the Cusabo group, of unknown linguistic affiliation (Pearson 1978:63).

ASHEWAGH (R.I., Washington Co.). A variant writing of **Ashaway River** (R.I., Washington Co.); see above. Other written variants are **Ashawagh** and **Ashawog.**

ASHIIAK Island (Alaska, Ugashik A-2). The Alutiiq (Eskimo) name is reported from 1847 (Orth 1967).

ASHIMUET (Mass., Barnstable Co.). A variant of **Ashimuit.**

ASHIMUIT (Mass., Barnstable Co.). Eastern Algonquian, 'at the spring', from <ashim-> 'spring', <-et> 'place' (W. Cowan p.c.). A variant spelling is **Ashimuet.**

ASHIPPUN (Wis., Dodge Co.) \ash´ i pən\. From an Algonquian word for 'raccoon', such as Potawatomi <ä´shpun>, Menomini <ä´sepan> (Vogel 1991); cf. also Ojibwa <esiban>

ASHISHIK Point (Alaska, Umnak C-1). From the Aleut placename *asasix̂* (Bergsland 1994).

ASHIVAK (Alaska, Iliamna A-3) \ash´ i vak\. The Alutiiq (Eskimo) name was published in 1881 (Orth 1967).

ASHKUM (Ill., Iroquois Co.) \ash´ kəm\. Named for a nineteenth-century Potawatomi (Algonquian) leader called <ēchkúm>, meaning 'more and more' (Vogel 1963); cf. Ojibwa (Algonquian) *eshkam* (Nichols and Nyholm 1995).

ASHNOLA River (Wash., Okanogan Co.) \ash nō´ lə\. From an Okanagan (Salishan) toponym /nʔaysnúlaʔxw/ (D. Kinkade p.c.).

ASHOKAN (N.Y., Ulster Co.) \ə shō´ kən, ash´ ə kan\. From an Algonquian word, perhaps meaning 'outlet of a stream' (Ruttenber 1906, Beauchamp 1907). A related form is **Shokan** (N.Y., Ulster Co.).

ASHTABULA County (Ohio) \ash tə byōō´ lə\. Perhaps from Delaware (Algonquian) <ashtə-təpé-ələw/ 'there is always enough moving', perhaps referring to fish in the water; the parts are <ashə-> 'always', <-təpe-> 'enough', and <-ələw> 'it exists moving' (Mahr 1959: 370).

ASHUE (Wash., Yakima Co.). Said to be an Indian family name, language not known (Reese 1996).

ASHUELOT (N.H., Cheshire Co.) \ash wā´ lət, əsh wā´ lət\. Eastern Algonquian, perhaps 'place between two other places', containing <nashue-> 'between' (W. Cowan p.c.). A probably related form is **Ashwillet Brook** (Conn., New London Co.).

ASHUMET Pond (Mass., Barnstable Co.). Eastern Algonquian, 'at the spring', from <ashim-> 'spring', <-et> 'place' (W. Cowan p.c.).

ASHWAUBENON (Wis., Brown Co.) \ash wô´ bə nən\. Perhaps from Ojibwa (Algonquian) <ashiwabiwining> 'place where they keep a lookout' (Vogel 1991).

ASHWILLET Brook (Conn., New London Co.) \ash´ wil ət\. Perhaps a SNEng. Algonquian name meaning 'place between' (Huden 1962); a probably related form is **Ashuelot** (N.H., Cheshire Co.).

ASIGYUKPAK Spit (Alaska, Hagemeister Island C-4). The Yupik (Eskimo) name was recorded in 1948 (Orth 1967).

ASIK Mountain (Alaska, Noatak B-1) The Iñupiaq (Eskimo) name is *aasriġraġaġaaŋiq*, perhaps from *asiq* 'sleeve' (Burch 1998; Fortescue et al. 1994). A related placename is **Asikpak River** (Alaska, Noatak D-6), from Iñupiaq *asaqpam kuuŋa* 'big sleeve river'; cf. *-(q)pak* 'big' (MacLean 1980).

ASINIAK Point (Alaska, Wainwright D-1). The Iñupiaq (Eskimo) name was recorded in 1956 (Orth 1967).

ASKECKSY (Del., Sussex Co.) \ə skek´ sē\. The name is from Delaware (Algonquian); it was recorded earlier as <Ackequesame>, <Askquexence>, <Askeeksky>, and <Askakeson> (Heck et al. 1966).

ASKETUM Branch (Del., Sussex Co.) \ə skē´ təm\. From Delaware (Algonquian); nothing else is known of the name (Heck et al. 1966).

ASKINUK Mountains (Alaska, Hooper Bay D-2). The Yupik (Eskimo) name was published in 1882 (Orth 1967).

ASLIK, Cape (Alaska, Umnak B-2). From the Aleut placename *asliix* (Bergsland 1994).

ASNACOMET Pond (Mass., Worcester Co.) \as´ nə kom ət\. Earlier writings include <Asnaconcomick> and <Asnecomomet> (BGN 7203). From SNEng. Algonquian, 'at the stone building', containing <hassun-> 'stone', <-komu(k)-> 'enclosed space', <-et> 'place' (W. Cowan p.c.).

ASNEBUMSKIT Hill (Mass., Worcester Co.) \as nə bum´ skit\. From SNEng. Algonquian, of unclear derivation.

ASOTIN County (Wash.) \ə sō´ tin\. From Nez Perce (Sahaptian) /hasó:tin/, perhaps based on /hé:su/ 'eel' (Aoki 1994:99).

ASPALAGA Landing (Fla., Gadsden Co.) \as pə lä´ gə\. Written by the Spanish in 1680 as *Ospalaga* and said to be from Hitchiti (Muskogean); but the derivation is not clear (Read 1934).

ASPATUCK River (N.Y., Suffolk Co.) \as´ pə tuk\. Algonquian <ashpotaug> 'a height' (W. Cowan p.c.). Related to **Aspetuck** (Conn., Fairfield Co.).

ASPEN Canyon (Ariz., Apache Co.). Corresponds to Navajo (Athabaskan) *t'iisbáí bikooh* 'aspen wash', containing *t'iisbáí* 'aspen' (lit. gray cottonwood, cf. *t'iis* 'cottonwood') (Linford 2000).

ASPETUCK (Conn., Fairfield Co) \as´ pə tuk\. Algonquian <ashpotaug> 'a height' (W. Cowan p.c.). Also written **Aspetock** and **Aspectuc.** Related to **Aspetuck** (NY, Suffolk Co.).

ASPINOOK Pond (Conn., New London Co.) \as´ pi nŏŏk\. Algonquian, said to mean 'at the high place'; cf. <ashpunuk> 'when he lifts it up' (W. Cowan p.c.).

ASQUAMCHUMAUKE Ridge (N.H., Grafton Co.) Perhaps from Abenaki (Algonquian) *skaméskwamáakw,* "which names the sticks which the female beaver has gnawed for the bark in the house and let float to the top" (Day 1981:146).

ASSABET River (Mass., Middlesex Co.) \ə sab´ ət, as´ ə bet\. SNEng. Algonquian, 'at the miry place', containing <sabae-> 'soft, miry', <-et> 'place' (W. Cowan p.c.).

ASSABUMBEDOCK Falls (Maine, York Co.) \as ə bum´ bə dok\. Perhaps Abenaki (Algonquian), meaning 'sloping, sandy bottom' (Eckstorm 1941; Huden 1962).

ASSACORKIN Island (Md., Worcester Co.) \as´ ə kôr kin\. The Algonquian name was earlier written <Assaquakin>. Meanings suggested are 'where there is land beyond' or 'where there is brown or yellow earth' (Kenny 1984).

ASSAMOOSICK Swamp (Va., Sussex Co.) \as ə moo´ sik\. Perhaps from Algonquian (Hagemann 1988).

ASSAN DECHALI Spring (Ariz., Navajo Co.) \ə san də chä´ lē\. Possibly represents Navajo (Athabaskan) *asdzáán dijoolí* 'woman who is round', from *asdzáán* 'woman', *dijool* 'round' (A. Wilson p.c.).

ASSAPUMPSET Brook (R.I., Providence Co.) \as ə pump´ sət\. Perhaps Narragansett (Algonquian), of unclear derivation. Also written as <Ossopimsuck> (Huden 1962).

ASSATEAGUE Island (Md., Worcester Co.; Va., Accomack Co.) \as´ ə tēg\. The Algonquian name may mean 'river beyond' or perhaps 'brown/yellow river' (Kenny 1984; Hagemann 1988).

ASSAWOMAN Bay (Del., Sussex Co.; Md., Worcester Co.; Va., Accomack Co.) \as´ ə woŏm ən\. From CAC Algonquian, of unclear derivation (Heck et al. 1966; Kenny 1984; Hagemann 1988).

ASSAWOMPSET Pond (Mass., Plymouth Co.) \as ə womp´ sət\. Eastern Algonquian, 'at the big trading place', containing <(m)assa-> 'big', <-(kodtau-)wompasu-> 'he trades, barters', <-et> 'place' (W. Cowan p.c.).

ASSEKONK Brook (Conn., New London Co.) \as´ ə kongk\. Mohegan (Algonquian), perhaps referring to 'much green grass' (Trumbull 1881); cf. <ashkosque> 'green' (W. Cowan p.c.). Also written as <Ossekunk>.

ASSINIBOIN \ə sin´ ə boin\. A Dakotan (Siouan) group living in northeastern Mont. and adjacent Canada. The name is from Canadian French *assiniboine,* from Ojibwa (Algonquian) *assini:pwa:n* 'stone Sioux', equivalent to Proto-Algonquian **aʔsenyi* 'stone' plus **pwa:θa* 'enemy tribesman' (*HNAI* 13:590–92). The English name of the group is also spelled **Assiniboine,** as in the placename **Assiniboine Creek** (Mont., Phillips Co.). Possibly related terms include **Assinika Creek** and **Assonet** (see below), as well as **Ossining** and **Sing Sing Prison** (N.Y., Westchester Co.), **Stoney Indians Lake** (Mont., Glacier Co.), and **Rocky Mountains**.

ASSINIKA Creek (Minn., Cook Co.). Ojibwa (Algonquian) *asiniika* 'there are many stones', from *asin* 'stone' (Nichols and Nyholm 1995). Other related placenames include **Assinins** (Mich., Baraga Co.), from Ojibwa *asiniins* 'small stones', the diminutive of *asin* 'stone' (Nichols and Nyholm 1995); and **Assinippi** (Mass., Plymouth Co.), from Eastern Algonquian, 'rocks in water', containing <hassan-> 'rock', <nip> 'water' (W. Cowan p.c.). Possibly related terms include **Assiniboin;** see above.

ASSISCUNG Creek (N.J., Hunterdon Co.) \ə sis´ kung\. Probably from the same source as **Assiscunk Creek** (N.J., Burlington Co.) \ə sis´ kungk\. This is Munsee Delaware *asíiskong* 'in the mud', from *asíiskuw* 'mud' (O'Meara p.c.).

ASSONET (Mass., Bristol Co.) \as´ ə nət\. From SNEng. Algonquian <hassan-> 'rock', <-et> 'place' (W. Cowan p.c.). A possibly related placename is **Assunpink Creek** (N.J., Mercer Co.), perhaps from Delaware (Algonquian) *ahsŭnping* 'rocky place that is watery' (Kraft and Kraft 1985); cf. Unami Delaware /a:hsə́n/ 'stone' (Blalock et al. 1994). Possibly related terms include **Assiniboin** (see above), **Ossining** and **Sing Sing Prison** (N.Y., Westchester Co.), **Stoney Indians Lake** (Mont., Glacier Co.), and **Rocky Mountains.**

ASTATULA (Fla., Lake Co.) \as tə too´ lə\. It has been speculated that the name may represent a Seminole (Muskogean) word meaning 'people of different tribes' (Read 1934).

ASTIALKWA (N.Mex., Sandoval Co.). Jemez (Tanoan) *aa-tyole-kwa* 'place for bringing down a grinding-stone', containing *aa* 'grinding-stone', *tyole* 'to bring down', *-kwa* 'place' (Y. Yumitani p.c.).

ASTICO (Wis., Dodge Co.) \as´ ti kō\. Perhaps derived from the Maine placename **Asticou** (Maine, Hancock Co.). This is said to be the name of an Abenaki (Algonquian) leader around 1613 (Rutherford 1970); perhaps from Abenaki /asə́hətike/ 'he refuses' (P. MacDougall p.c.).

ASTICOU (Maine, Hancock Co.). Named after an Abenaki (Algonquian) Indian leader who was living around 1613, when the whites arrived (Huden 1962; Rutherford 1970).

ASUKSAK Island (Alaska, Adak C-1). From the Aleut placename ***hasux̂sax̂*** (Bergsland 1994).

A'SU'WA (NM, Cibola Co.). The Zuni placename refers to a rock mentioned in myths (Ferguson and Hart 1985).

ATA-AI-ACH Mountain (Alaska, Goodnews Bay D-3). The Yupik (Eskimo) name was reported in 1898 (Orth 1967).

ATAAKAS Camp (Alaska, St. Lawrence C-3). Named for a Yupik (Eskimo) individual (Orth 1967).

ATA DEEZA (Ariz., Apache Co.). Navajo (Athabaskan) *atah deez'á* 'among ridges, bluffs', from *atah* 'among', *deez'á* 'ridge, bluff, mesa' (A. Wilson p.c.).

ATAHGO Point (Alaska, Cape Mendenhall D-2). The Yupik (Eskimo) name was reported in 1937 (Orth 1967).

ATAKAPA \ə tak´ ə pä\. An Indian group of unclear linguistic affiliation, whose home was on the Louisiana coast. The term occurs as a placename in **Camp Atakapa** (La., East Feliciana Par.). A related form is **Attakapas Island** (La., St. Mary Par.).

ATAKU Island (Alaska, Port Alexander D-5). The Tlingit name was reported in 1826 (Orth 1967).

ATALISSA (Iowa, Muscatine Co.) \at ə lis´ ə\. Perhaps from Outalissa or Outalissi, the names of fictional Indians in early-nineteenth-century literary works (Vogel 1983).

ATANIK (Alaska, Wainwright D-1) \at´ ə nik\. Iñupiaq (Eskimo) *ataniq* 'isthmus', from *ata-* 'to be connected' plus *-niq* 'nominalization' (L. Kaplan p.c.).

ATAYAK Mountain (Alaska, Goodnews Bay D-3). The Yupik (Eskimo) name was reported in 1898 (Orth 1967).

ATCHAFALAYA (La., St. Martin Par.) \ach ə fə lī´ ə, ə chaf ə lī´ ə, chaf ə lī´ ə\. Early spellings of the name include Chafalia, Tchafalaya, and Atchafa-Laya (Read 1927). It is from the Choctaw (Muskogean) for 'long river', from *hachcha* 'river' and *falaya* 'long' (P. Munro p.c.). The name also occurs as **Atchafalaya Bayou** (Miss., Humphrey Co.).

ATCHEE (Colo., Garfield Co.) \ach´ ē\. Named for a Ute (Numic) leader (Bright 1993); perhaps to be identified with Ute *áatsi,* meaning both 'father's younger brother' and 'bow (for shooting)' (J. McLaughlin p.c.).

ATCHUELINGUK River (Alaska, Marshall D-3). Yupik (Eskimo) *ecuilnguq*, from *ecur-* 'to be murky (of liquids)' (Jacobson 1984).

ATHABASKAN \ath ə bas´ kən\. The name given to a Native North American linguistic family, consisting of a large number of languages in Alaska and subarctic Canada as well as a smaller number in the northwestern United States, plus the Apachean family (including Navajo) in the Southwest. **Athabaskan** is derived from the name of **Lake Athabasca** in northern Alberta, Canada; and this name is in turn derived from Woods Cree (Algonquian) *aðapaska:w* '(where) there are plants one after the other', referring to the delta region west of the lake (HNAI 6:168). The name of the linguistic family is also written as **Athapaskan, Athabascan,** and **Athapascan.** None of these forms occurs as a placename in the United States, though the spelling **Athabasca** is used in several placenames of Canada (Rayburn 1997).

ATHAO, Bayou (La., Natchitoches Par.). Perhaps from Natao, a division of the Caddo people; they are also known as **Adai**, from Caddo *adai* 'brushwood' (Read 1927).

ATHOL (Idaho, Kootenai Co.) \ath´ əl\. Named for a Coeur d'Alene (Salishan) leader; the name itself, however, is Scottish (D. Kinkade p.c.).

ATIGARU Point (Alaska, Harrison Bay C-3). The Iñupiaq (Eskimo) name may mean 'old coat' (Orth 1967); cf. *atigi* 'parka', *atikłuk* 'snowshirt' (MacLean 1980).

ATIGUN River (Alaska, Philip Smith Mountains C-4) \at´ i gun\. The Iñupiaq (Eskimo) name is probably from *atiq-* 'go down'.

ATKA Island (Alaska, Atka C-1) \at´ kə\. From the Aleut placename *atx̂ax̂* (Bergsland 1994).

ATKASUK (Alaska, Meade River B-3) \at´ kə suk\. From the Iñupiaq (Eskimo) placename *atqasuk.* The word also means 'outer flare of nostril', but speakers do not generally associate the two meanings (L. Kaplan p.c.).

ATKULIK Island (Alaska, Sutwik Island B-6). The Native American name, perhaps Alutiiq (Eskimo), was reported in 1827 (Orth 1967).

ATLA Creek (Alaska, Hughes A-3) \at´ lə\. From a Koyukon (Athabaskan) family name, reported in 1909 (Orth 1967).

ATLATL Rock (Nev., Clark Co.) \at´ lat əl\. A term imported from Mexico: Nahuatl (Aztecan) *atlatl* 'throwing stick, spear-thrower'. The placename was probably applied by anthropologists.

ATLIK Hill (Alaska, Howard Pass D-2) \at´ lik\. From Iñupiaq (Eskimo) *alliq* 'bottom one' (Orth 1967, MacLean 1980).

ATMAUTLUAK (Alaska, Baird Inlet D-1) \at mô´ lo͞o ak\. From the Yupik (Eskimo) placename *atmaulluaq* (Jacobson 1984).

ATMO Mountain (Alaska, Karluk D-4) \at´ mō\. Probably from Alutiiq (Eskimo), reported in 1919 (Orth 1967).

ATMUGIAK Creek (Alaska, Goodnews Bay D-3). A Yupik (Eskimo) name reported in 1898 (Orth 1967).

ATNA Peaks (Alaska, McCarthy C-6) \at´ nə, ät´ nə\. From *atna',* the name of the Copper River in the language of the **Ahtena** (Athabaskan) people (*HNAI* 6:662); their English name is derived from the same source. The word is also written **Ahtna.**

ATNEERICH Creek (Alaska, De Long Mountains B-1). The Iñupiaq (Eskimo) name was reported about 1955 (Orth 1967).

ATNUK (Alaska, Solomon B-2) \at´ nək\. From Iñupiaq (Eskimo) *atniq* or Yupik *atneq,* probably from *ati-* 'down', *-niq* (Yupik *-neq)* 'nominalizer' (L. Kaplan p.c.).

ATOKA (Tenn., Tipton Co.) \ə tō´ kə\. Perhaps from Choctaw (Muskogean) *hitoka* 'ball-ground' (i.e., a field on which a Native American game, similar to lacrosse, was played) (McClaren 1991). The name occurs elsewhere in **Atoka County** (Okla.), and in the names of towns (e.g., Ala., Geneva Co.; Ky., Boyle Co., N.Mex., Eddy Co.) A related placename is **Autauga County** (Ala.), perhaps from Alabama (Muskogean) *aatòoka* 'ball-ground, playing field' (Sylestine et al. 1993).

ATOKO Point (Ariz., Coconino Co.) \ə tō´ kō\. From Hopi *atoko* 'crane or other long-legged wading bird' (K. Hill p.c.).

ATOLE Pond (N.Mex., Rio Arriba Co.) \ə tō´ lē\. From Spanish *atole* 'a beverage made from cornmeal', from Nahuatl (Aztecan) *atolli.*

ATONGARAK Creek (Alaska, Ambler River D-3). The Iñupiaq (Eskimo) name was recorded in 1956 (Orth 1967).

ATOSIK Lagoon (Alaska, Point Hope A-1) \ə tō´ sik\. Iñupiaq (Eskimo) *atausiq* 'one' (Orth 1967; MacLean 1980).

ATQASUK (Alaska, Meade River B-3). The Iñupiaq (Eskimo) name is said to mean 'the place to dig the rock that burns', referring to a coal mine (Orth 1967).

ATRISCO (N.Mex., Bernalillo Co.) \ə tris´ kō\. The name was imported by settlers from Tlaxcala state, Mexico, around 1703; it is probably from the Nahuatl (Aztecan) placename *atlixco* [a:tlí:ško] 'on the surface of the water', with *atl* 'water'and *ixco* 'on the face or surface' (*ix-tli* 'face' and *-co* 'place') (Karttunen 1983).

ATRNAK Point (Alaska, Nunivak Island B-1). The Yupik (Eskimo) name was recorded in 1949 (Orth 1967).

ATSADAHSIDAHI (Ariz., Apache Co.) \ət sä dä si dä´ hē\. Navajo (Athabaskan) *atsá dah sidáhí* 'where the eagle sits on high', containing *atsá* 'eagle', *dah* 'up at an elevation', and *sidá* 'it sits' (A. Wilson p.c.).

ATSAKSOVLUK Creek (Alaska, Bethel D-1). The Yupik (Eskimo) name is said to mean 'place to get berries' (Orth 1967); cf. Yupik *atsaq* 'berry' (Jacobson 1984).

ATSEE NITSAA (N.Mex., McKinley Co.) \ət sā´ nit sä\. Apparently Navajo (Athabaskan) for 'big tail', from *atsee'* 'tail', *nitsaa* 'big' (A. Wilson p.c.).

ATSENA OTIE Key (Fla., Levy Co.) \ə tsē´ nə ō tē\. Muskogee for 'cedar island', from *vcenv* /acína/ 'cedar', *otē* /otí:/ 'island'.

ATSHICHLUT Mountain (Alaska, Goodnews Bay C-3). The Yupik (Eskimo) name was reported in 1898 (Orth 1967).

ATSINA \at sē´ nə\. The name of a people, also called **Gros Ventre** ('big belly'), who live in Mont. They are linguistically related to the Arapahos, within the Algonquian family. Note the placename **Atsina Falls** (Mont., Glacier Co.).

ATSINNA (N.Mex., Cibola Co.). Said to be Zuni for 'writing on the rocks' (Julyan 1998).

ATSION (N.J., Burlington Co.) \at´ sē ən\. Earlier written as **Atsionk**, **Atsayonck**, and **Axion**, probably from Delaware (Algonquian); cf. Unami Delaware /a:hsə́n/ 'stone' (Blalock et al. 1994).

ATTAKAPAS Island (La., St. Mary Par.) \ə tak´ ə pä\. Derived from **Atakapa,** the name of an Indian group; see above.

ATTAPULGUS Creek (Fla., Gadsden Co.; Ga., Decatur Co.) \at ə po͞ol´ gəs\. Perhaps from a Muskogee word meaning 'dogwood grove' (Read 1934; Goff 1975); cf. Creek *vtvpha* /atápha/ 'dogwood', *-vlke* /-alki/ 'group' (Martin and Mauldin 2000).

ATTAWAN Beach (Conn., New London Co.) \at´ ə wän\. Possibly Eastern Niantic (Algonquian), meaning 'hills, dunes' (Huden 1962).

ATTAWAUGAN (Conn., Windham Co.) \at ə wô´ gən\. Possibly Nipmuck (Algonquian), 'hill, knoll' (Huden 1962).

ATTEAN Mountain (Maine, Somerset Co.) \ā´ tē en\. For Étienne Orson, an eighteenth-century Abenaki (Algonquian) resident; cf. Western Abenaki *atian* (Day 1995). The French male given name *Étienne* corresponds to English *Stephen.*

ATTITASH Mountain (N.H., Carroll Co.) \at´ i tash\. Said to be an Algonquian word for 'blueberry' (Julyan and Julyan 1993).

ATTIUNIK Point (Alaska, Selawik C-5). This Yupik (Eskimo) name was recorded around 1885 (Orth 1967).

ATTOOGA Branch (N.C., Graham Co.) \ə to͞o´ gə\. Cherokee (Iroquoian) *aatuugi'a* 'he's taking a drink (of alcohol)' (B. Rudes p.c.).

ATTOYAC (Tex., Nacogdoches Co.) \at´ ə yak\. Perhaps imported from Mexico, where a placename *Atoyac* occurs; it is from Nahuatl (Aztecan) *atoyac* 'at the river', containing *atoyatl* 'river' and *-c* 'place' (Karttunen 1983).

ATTU Island (Alaska, Attu C-3) \at´ o͞o\. From the Aleut placename *atan, atta, atux̂* (Bergsland 1994).

ATUK Mountain (Alaska, St. Lawrence C-3) \at´ ək\. From Yupik (Eskimo) *ateq* [atɨq] 'name' (Orth 1967; Jacobson 1984).

ATUSHAGVIK, Cape (Alaska, Mt. Katmai A-1). The Native American name, probably Alutiiq (Eskimo), was published in 1836 (Orth 1967).

ATUTSAK River (Alaska, Tanana A-6). Koyukon (Athabaskan) *edets'ehulh yhno, ede-*

ts'ehoodlkk'otlno' 'where-we-spend-the-winter river' (Jetté & Jones 2000:277).

AUBBEENAUBBEE (Ind., Fulton Co.) \ô bē nô´ bē\. Named for a nineteenth-century Algonquian leader; his name was also spelled **Awbenabi**, **Obanaoby**, **Wabanaba**, and so forth (McPherson 1993).

AUCHEHACHEE River (Ga., Wheeler and Telfair Cos.) \ô chē hach´ ē\. Muskogee, meaning 'cedar stream', from *vcenv* /acína/ 'cedar' *hvcce* /háčči/ 'stream' (Martin and Mauldin 2000). Also written as **Auchenehatchee.**

AUCHUMPKEE Creek (Ga., Upson Co.) \ô chump´ kē\. Perhaps from Choctaw (Muskogean), meaning 'hickory nuts all over' (Read 1949–50); cf. *ocē* /očí:/ 'hickory nut', *hvmkvn* /hámkan/ 'all over' (Martin and Mauldin 2000).

AUCILLA (Fla., Jefferson Co.; Ga., Thomas Co.) \ô sil´ ə\. Also written <Ocilla, Oscillee>; the name of a Seminole town. Perhaps derived from a village name of the Timucua people, who previously occupied the area (Read 1934; Goff 1975).

AUCOOT Cove (Mass., Plymouth Co.) \ô´ k o͞o t\. SNEng. Algonquian, 'at the cove', from <aucu(p)> 'cove', <-et> 'place' (W. Cowan p.c.).

AUGHWICK (Pa., Huntingdon Co.). Said to be from <achweek> 'brushy, overgrown with brush' in an unidentified Indian language (Donehoo 1928).

AUGUSI Canyon (Utah, Uintah Co.) \ə go͞o´ sē\. Supposedly named after an Indian resident (Van Cott 1990).

AUKAMUNUK Creek (Alaska, Goodnews Bay D-3). The Yupik (Eskimo) name was reported in 1898 (Orth 1967).

AUK Bay (Alaska, Seward A-4) \ôk\. From *áak'w,* a division of the Tlingit Indians, although this is not in Tlingit territory (*HNAI* 7:227). The origin is the same as that of **Auke Bay** (Alaska, Juneau B-3).

AUKE Bay (Alaska, Juneau B-3) \ôk\. From *áak'w,* a division of the Tlingit Indians (*HNAI* 7:227). The origin is the same as that **Auk Bay** (Alaska, Seward A-4). **Auke Nu Cove** (Alaska, Juneau B-3) represents a Tlingit name meaning 'Auke fort' (Orth 1967).

AUKULAK Lagoon (Alaska, Noatak A-3) The Yupik (Eskimo) name is said to mean 'strip of land between two bodies of water' (Orth 1967).

AULATAURUK River (Alaska, Wainwright C-2). The Iñupiaq (Eskimo) name may mean 'many fishing lines' (Orth 1967).

AUPUK Creek (Alaska, Ikpikpuk River A-3). Named for an Iñupiaq (Eskimo) guide in a 1924 expedition (Orth 1967).

AURORA (Ill., Kane Co.) \ə rōr´ ə, ə rôr´ ə\. Perhaps a transfer name from N.Y. (E. Callary p.c); however, the choice of this Latin word for 'dawn' may have corresponded to the name of a nineteenth-century Potawatomi (Algonquian) leader. His name (written as <Waubonsie>, etc.) is said to be from Potawatomi <wápin> 'daybreak' (Vogel 1963). The Native American form of the name is reflected in **Waubonsie Creek** (Ill., Kendall Co.; Iowa, Fremont Co.) as well as in **Waubonsee Creek** (Ill., Kane Co.) and **Wauponsee** (Ill., Grundy Co.).

AU SABLE Point (Mich., Alger Co.) \ō sä´ bəl, ô sä´ bəl\. The French name, meaning 'at the sand', is an adaptation from Ojibwa (Algonquian) <negawadjing> 'at the sand mountain' (Vogel 1986); cf. *negaw* 'sand' (Rhodes 1985). A related placename is nearby **Grand Sable**.

AUTAUGA County (Ala.) \ô tô´ gə\. The name commemorates a town of the Alabama (Muskogean) people (Read 1984). A possible etymology is Alabama *aatòoka* 'ball-ground, playing field' (Sylestine et al. 1993), referring to a field for playing a Native American game similar to lacrosse. A related name is **Atoka** (occurring in several states), perhaps from Choctaw (Muskogean) *hitoka* 'ball-ground'.

AVAK Bay (Alaska, Barrow A-3). Probably from Iñupiaq (Eskimo) *avik-* 'to divide into halves' (Orth 1967; MacLean 1980).

AVALIK River (Alaska, Wainwright A-2). Iñupiaq (Eskimo) *avalliq* 'something to one side, in the surrounding area', from *avan* 'extremity, surrounding area' plus *-liq* 'one in the direction of' (L. Kaplan p.c.).

AVALITKOK Creek (Alaska, Wainwright A-1). The Iñupiaq (Eskimo) name, said to mean 'the farther stream', was recorded in 1956 (Orth 1967).

AVATANAK Island (Alaska, Unimak A-4). \ə vat´ nak\. From the Aleut placename *agutanax̂, awatanax̂*; cf. *awan* 'that one passing by' (Bergsland 1994).

AVAWATZ Mountains (Calif., San Bernardino Co.) \av´ ə wäts\. The Southern Paiute (Numic) name is *áviwats* or *ávawats* 'gypsum', from *ávi* 'white clay' (Gudde 1998).

AVENAK Mountain (Alaska, Noatak D-5). The Iñupiaq (Eskimo) name is *aġviġnaq*, said to mean 'black whale' (Orth 1967, Burch 1998); cf. *aġviq* 'bowhead whale' (MacLean 1980).

AVGUN River (Alaska, Noatak D-1) The Iñupiaq (Eskimo) name *avgun* means 'border, boundary' (L. Kaplan p.c.). A related name is **Uvgoon Creek** (Alaska, Noatak C-1).

AVICHI Arroyo (Calif., Marin Co.). The term may be from Coast Miwok *awwíč* 'crow' (Gudde 1998).

AVI COROTATH (Calif., San Bernardino Co.) \əvē´ kôr ə täth\. Contains Mojave *'avíi* 'rock, mountain' and *kwalatáth-* 'to be big and round' (Gudde 1998).

AVINGAK Creek (Alaska, Utukok River B-4). From Iñupiaq (Eskimo) *aviŋŋaq* 'lemming' (Orth 1967; MacLean 1980). A probably related name is **Avingyak Hills** (Alaska, Howard Pass A-5); see below.

AVINGORIAK Peak (Alaska, Noatak A-2). The Iñupiaq (Eskimo) name was recorded in 1956 (Orth 1967).

AVINGYAK Hills (Alaska, Howard Pass A-5) The Iñupiaq (Eskimo) term is said to be a family name (Orth 1967); cf. *aviŋŋaq* 'lemming' (MacLean 1980). A probably related placename is **Avingak Creek** (Alaska, Utukok River B-4); see above.

AVINTAQUIN Creek (Utah, Duchesne Co.) \ə vin´ tə kwin\. Presumably from Ute (Numic); the derivation is not clear (Van Cott 1990).

AVNULU Creek (Alaska, Kodiak A-5) The Alutiiq (Eskimo) name was published in 1943 (Orth 1967).

AVOCADO Creek (Fla., Monroe Co.) \ä və kä´ dō\. The name of the fruit is from Mexican Spanish *ahuacate,* derived from Nahuatl (Aztecan) *ahuacatl,* which also means 'testicle'.

AVOGON Pass (Alaska, Kwiguk C-6). The Yupik (Eskimo) name was published in 1901 (Orth 1967).

AVOYELLES Parish (La.) \ə voi´ əlz\. The name is that of an Indian group, perhaps a branch of the Natchez people who lived here in the eighteenth century. The derivation of the name is not clear (Read 1927).

AWAPA Plateau (Utah, Wayne Co.). Perhaps from Ute (Numic) /oa-ppa/, lit. 'yellow water' (J. McLaughlin p.c.).

AWATOBI (Ariz., Navajo Co.) \ə wä´ tə bē\. Refers to the Bow Clan of the Hopi (Uto-Aztecan) people (Granger 1983). The Hopi name is *awat'ovi* 'high place of the bow', from *awat-, awta* 'bow', *-'o-* 'high', *-vi* 'place' (K. Hill p.c.). Related forms are **Awatovi Spring** (Ariz., Navajo Co.) and **Awatubi Creek** (Ariz., Coconino Co.).

AWAYAK Creek (Alaska, Goodnews Bay B-5). From Yupik (Eskimo) *avayaq* 'branch, limb of tree' (Orth 1967; Jacobson 1984).

AWENDAW (S.C., Charleston Co.) \ô´ wən dô\. The Indian name has been thought to mean 'deer' (Neuffer and Neuffer 1983). The form <Avendaugh-bough>, attested from 1701, suggests Catawba (Siouan) *widebuuye* 'deer' (B. Rudes p.c.). Cf. **Wadboo, Wando.**

AWIXA Creek (N.Y., Suffolk Co.) \ə wik´ sə\. Also written <Aweeksa>; an Algonquian name, perhaps meaning 'as far as the brook' (Huden 1962).

AWLINYAK Creek (Alaska, Survey Pass C-3). The Iñupiaq (Eskimo) name, said to mean 'exit', was reported in 1931 (Orth 1967).

AWOSTING (N.J., Passaic Co.) \ə wos´ ting\. From Delaware (Algonquian), perhaps related to <awossi> 'beyond' (Becker 1964); cf. Munsee Delaware *awásii* 'the other side of something' (O'Meara 1996). The name **Awosting** also occurs in N.Y. (Ulster Co.).

AWUNA River (Alaska, Ikpikpuk River A-5). The Iñupiaq (Eskimo) name is said to mean 'westward' (Orth 1967).

AYAKALAK Creek (Alaska, Killik River A-3). The Iñupiaq (Eskimo) term is said to mean 'joint of the neck-bone', reported in 1956 (Orth 1967).

AYAKULIK (Alaska, Karluk A-2) \ə yak´ o͞o lik\. Probably an Alutiiq (Eskimo) name, first reported in 1852 (Orth 1967).

A:YAYA:KYA (N.Mex., Cibola Co.) The Zuni placename refers to a sacred spring (Ferguson and Hart 1985).

AYIYAK River (Alaska, Chandler Lake D-4). The Iñupiaq (Eskimo) name was published in 1944 (Orth 1967).

AYUGADAK Point (Alaska, Rat Islands C-5). The Aleut name was reported in 1935 (Orth 1967).

AYUGATAK Creek (Alaska, Point Hope D-2). The Iñupiaq (Eskimo) name is *ayagutaq* 'tent pole' (Burch 1998); cf. the Uummarmiut dialect form *ayak* 'post, pole' (L. Kaplan p.c.).

AYUTKA, Cape (Alaska, Mt. Katmai A-1). The Alutiiq (Eskimo) name was reported in 1900 (Orth 1967).

AZACHARUM Slough (Alaska, Kwiguk A-4). The Yupik (Eskimo) name, reported to mean 'slough', was recorded in 1899 (Orth 1967).

AZACHOROK Hill (Alaska, Kwiguk A-4). The Yupik (Eskimo) name was recorded in 1899 (Orth 1967).

AZAMIS Cove (Alaska, Adak C-1). The Aleut name was published in 1852 (Orth 1967).

AZANSOSI Mesa (Ariz., Navajo Co.) \ə zän sō´ sē\. Named for Mrs. Louise Wetherill, the wife of a trader in the area. Her Navajo (Athabaskan) name was *asdzą́ą́ts'ósí* 'slim woman', from *asdzą́ą́* 'woman', *ts'ósí* 'slender, slim' (Wilson 1995).

AZIAK Island (Alaska, Adak C-1). From the Aleut placename *haazax*; cf. *ha-azax* 'ten' (Bergsland 1994).

AZISCOHOS Lake (Maine, Oxford Co.; N.H., Coös Co.) \ə zis´ kō os\. From Penobscot (Algonquian) /asə́skoho/ 'covered with mud' (P. MacDougall p.c.). Also written as **Aziscoos.**

AZTALAN (Wis., Jefferson Co.) \az´ tə lən\. Derived from Nahuatl (Aztecan) *aztlan,* the legendary home of the Aztec people, usually thought to have been somewhere in the southwestern United States. The name was assigned in the 1830s by an amateur archaeologist, under the impression that the Aztecs might have originated in Wis. (Vogel 1991).

AZTEC (N.Mex., San Juan Co.) \az´ tek\. The English name of the Aztec people, who dominated much of central Mexico at the time of the Spanish conquest, comes from Spanish *azteca,* which in turn is from the Nahuatl (Aztecan) singular form *aztecatl,* plural *aztecah.* The name means 'coming from *aztlan',* the legendary home of the Aztecs.

AZUN River (Alaska, Hooper Bay A-1). The Yupik (Eskimo) name was recorded in 1878 (Orth 1967).

AZUSA (Calif., Los Angeles Co.) \ə zo͞o´ sə\. From Gabrielino (Takic) *ashúkshanga,* with the suffix *-nga* meaning 'place' (Gudde 1998).

B

BAADA Point (Wash., Clallam Co.) \bā ā´ də, bā hā´ də, bə hā´ də\. From Makah (Nootkan) /biʔidʔa/, a village name, perhaps meaning 'on the rocks' (W. Jacobsen p.c.).

BAATHBAKDIZUNI Creek (Alaska, Hughes A-4). This Koyukon (Athabaskan) Indian name is, said to mean 'spruce trees for good bows' (Orth 1967).

BABANTALTLIN Creek (Alaska, Hughes B-5). This is a Koyukon (Athabaskan) Indian name of unknown meaning (Orth 1967).

BABOCOMARI River (Ariz., Cochise Co.) \bä bō kō´ mə rē, bä bō kə mä´ rē\. The name was first given to a Spanish land grant in 1832, in the spelling **Babacomari**. It is from O'odham (Piman) *waw komali* 'flat bedrock', from *waw* 'bedrock' plus *komali* 'flat' (J. Hill p.c.).

BABOOSIC Brook (N.H., Hillsborough Co.) \bə bo͞o´ sik\. Probably from Abenaki (Algonquian) *babaskw* 'leech' (Day 1994–95).

BABOQUIVARI Peak (Ariz., Pima Co.) \bä bō kē´ və rē, bä bō kwi vâr´ ē\. From O'odham (Piman) *waw giwulǐk* 'bedrock constricted in the middle', from *waw* 'bedrock' plus *giwulǐ-k* 'belted, constricted in the middle' (J. Hill p.c.).

BABYBASKET Hill (Alaska, Medfra A-2). The name corresponds to Upper Kuskokwim (Athabaskan) *mik'itsotl'zitone* 'the one with a baby-basket sitting on it'. The term refers to a woven cradle-basket used by Indians (Kari 1999:97).

BABY PEE Trail (Ariz., Apache Co.). A translation of Navajo (Athabaskan) *awéé haazhilzhí* 'where a baby urinated on the way up' (Linford 2000).

BABY Rock (Ore., Lane Co.). Supposedly so named from an Indian legend: people who slept near the rock were said to receive fatal bites from some creature that left the footprints of a baby (McArthur 1992). By contrast, **Baby Rocks** (Ariz., Navajo Co.) is so called because the sandstone here appears to be composed of many small rocks rather than continuous layers. The name is a translation of Navajo (Athabaskan) *tsé awé'é* 'rock babies', from *tsé* 'rock(s)' plus *awé'é, awéé* 'baby' (Wilson 1995; Linford 2000).

BAC, San Xavier del (Ariz., Pima Co.) See **Mission San Xavier del Bac**, below.

BACABI (AZ, Navajo Co.) \bä´ kə bē\. A spelling variant of **Bacavi** (Ariz., Navajo Co.) \bä´ kə vē\. This is from Hopi (Uto-Aztecan) *paaqavi* 'place of reeds', with *paaqa* 'reed' (K. Hill). Other variants are **Bacobi** and **Bakabi.**

BACHATNA Creek (Alaska, Kenai C-6) \bä chät´ nə\. The Dena'ina (Athabaskan) name is *bajatnu,* perhaps meaning 'stone creek' (Kari and Kari 1982:29).

BACOBI (Ariz., Navajo Co.) \bä´ kə bē\. Alternative spelling of **Bacabi**; see above.

BAD. This English word has often been as an equivalent for Indian terms meaning 'supernaturally dangerous', as in the stereotyped "bad medicine." This is reflected in a number of placenames; for example, **Bad River** (Mich., Saginaw Co.) is a translation from Ojibwa (Algonquian) *mji-* 'evil' plus *ziibi* 'river' (Vogel 1986; Rhodes 1985). **Bad River** (S.Dak., Stanley Co.) is a translation of Dakota (Sioux) *wakpá-šiča,* lit.'lake-bad', referring to a flash flood around 1738 (Sneve 1973; A. Taylor p.c.) In Ariz., **Bad Trail** (Apache Co.) is a translation of Navajo (Athabaskan) *hóchxǫ́ ha'atiin* 'bad trail up' (Linford 2000). See also **Badlands** and **Badnation** below.

BADGER Lake (S.Dak., Kingsbury Co.). A translation from Dakota (Siouan) *mni-ȟóka* 'badger water', from *mni* 'water' plus *ȟoká* 'badger' (A. Taylor p.c.). In another case, **Badger Lake** (S.Dak., Kingsbury Co.) is a body of water called in Dakota *mde-ȟóka,* lit. 'badger lake', from *mde* 'lake' plus *ȟoká* 'badger' (Sneve 1973; A. Taylor p.c.).

BADLANDS (S.Dak., Pennington Co.). Corresponds to Dakota (Sioux) *šíča makhá* 'bad land', from *šíča* 'bad' plus *mahká* 'land'. It is not clear whether the English is a translation of the Dakota or vice versa. Some Dakotas have recalled that in their youth they had heard these places called *šíča ič'ímaniya* 'bad to travel', with *ič'îmaniya* 'travel' (Sneve 1973; A. Taylor p.c.).

BADNATION (S.Dak., Mellette Co.) This is said to be a translation of the name of a Lakhota (Sioux) leader, Oyatesica, who settled here (Sneve 1973). The name can be analyzed as *oyáte* 'nation, people' plus *šiča* 'bad' (A. Taylor p.c.).

BAGADUCE River (Maine, Hancock Co.) \bag´ ə do͞os\. The name apparently represents an earlier <Majabigwaduce> (Eckstorm 1941); it is probably from Penobscot (Algonquian) /mači-pikʸátohsək/ 'at the bad shoal' (P. MacDougall p.c.).

BAHALA Creek (Miss., Lawrence Co.). Probably reflects a Choctaw (Muskogean) name meaning 'mulberry tree standing', from *bihi* 'mulberry tree' plus *hiili* 'stand' (Seale 1939; P. Munro p.c.).

BAHAMA Beach (Fla., Bay Co.) \bə hä´ mə\. This name is probably borrowed from the islands in the Caribbean called the **Bahamas**, which in turn reflect the Native American name Guanahani. But another place named **Bahama** (N.C., Durham Co.) is said to have been coined from the names of three prominent families: Ball, Harris, and Nangum (Powell 1968).

BAHA Spring (Ariz., Navajo Co.). This perhaps represents Navajo (Athabaskan) *bą̨ąhí* 'place where there is an edge', from *bą̨ąh* 'border, edge' (A. Wilson p.c.).

BA HA ZOHNNIE BETOH (Ariz., Navajo Co.) \bä hə zhō´ nē bi tō´\. This spring has the Navajo (Athabaskan) name *bą̨ąh hózhóní bito'* 'alongside a pleasant spring', from *bą̨ąh* 'alongside it' plus *hózhóní* 'that which is pleasant' (*hózhǫ́* 'pleasant, beautiful') plus *bito'* 'its water' (*bi-* 'its', *to'* 'water, spring') (A. Wilson p.c.).

BAHOBOHOSH Point (Wash., Clallam Co.) \bə hō´ bə hōsh\. From the Makah (Nootkan) placename /buxú:buxš/ 'bubbling intermittently', from /bux-/ 'to boil, bubble' (W. Jacobsen).

BAHOKWUS Peak (Wash., Clallam Co.) \bə hō´ kwəs\. From Makah (Nootkan) /bix̣uqis/, perhaps meaning 'basket turned over' (W. Jacobsen p.c.).

BAITUK Creek (Alaska, Teller C-6) Reflects a Yupik (Eskimo) name, earlier reported as **Botuk** and **Bituk** (Orth 1967).

BAKABI (Ariz., Navajo Co.) Alternative spelling of **Bacavi,** a Hopi (Uto-Aztecan) village. The Native American name is *paaqavi* 'place of reeds', from *paaqa* 'reed' (K. Hill).

BAKATIGIKH Mountain (Alaska, Hughes A-4). Said to be a shortening, "for cartographic acceptability," from <Bakatigikhdalitan>, a Koyukon (Athabaskan) name reported to mean 'dry weed hill' (Orth 1967).

BAKBUK Creek (Alaska, Sleetmute A-5). The name is Yupik (Eskimo), said to mean 'stream with a big mouth' (Orth 1967).

BALA CHITTO Creek (Miss., Pike Co.) \bä lə chit´ ō\. May represent a Choctaw (Muskogean) name meaning 'big beans', from *bala* 'bean' plus *chito* 'big' (Seale 1939).

BALAKAI Mesa (Ariz., Apache Co.) \bä lə kī´\. Derived from Navajo (Athabaskan) *baalók'aa'í* 'reeds alongside it' from *baa* 'alongside it' plus *lók'aa'* 'reed(s)' (Wilson 1995). Also written as **Balokai.**

BALD RIDGE Creek (Ga., Forsyth Co.) It has been speculated that this name does not refer to a bare ridge but to a Cherokee (Iroquoian) family, which bore the English family name *Baldridge* (Goff 1975).

BALL GROUND (Ga., Cherokee Co.) This name refers to a place where Indians played the "ball game," a sport resembling lacrosse, especially popular among Indians of the southeastern United States. The same term is found elsewhere: for example, **Ball Ground Creek** (Miss., Noxubee Co.). A similar name is **Ball Play** (Tenn., Polk Co.). Placenames based on native Muskogean words for 'ballground' include **Atoka** (Tenn., Tipton Co.) and **Autauga County** (Ala.). Other placenames containing the word *ball* may in some cases have a similar origin or may reflect the English family name *Ball.*

BALLOW (Wash., Mason Co.). Perhaps from the name of a mythological personage called \bal'ǽ\. or \malǽ\. in some of the Salishan languages (D. Kinkade p.c.).

BALLPLAY (Ala., Etowah Co.) Probably refers to the Indian "ball game"; see **Ball Ground** above.

BALLY Mountain (Calif., Siskiyou Co.) \bal´ ē\. The name is derived from Wintu *buli* 'mountain'; the same term has been borrowed in other forms into other California placenames, such as **Bully Choop** in Shasta Co., **Winnibulli** in Shasta Co., and **Yolla Bolly** in Trinity Co. (Gudde 1998). It is likely that use of the term has been affected by regional Eng. *bald* 'bare peak', known especially from the southeastern United States.

BALUCTA (Miss., Scott Co.) \bə luk´ tə\. The name reflects Choctaw (Muskogean) *bolokta* 'round' (P. Munro p.c.).

BALUKAI Mesa (Ariz., Apache Co.) \bä lə kī´\. Alternative spelling of **Balakai,** from Navajo (Athabaskan) *baalók'aa'í* 'reeds alongside it' (Wilson 1995).

BANDDANA Creek (Alaska, Tanana C-5). The Tanana (Athabaskan) name is said to mean 'duck river' (Orth 1967).

BANGOOKBIT Dunes (Alaska, Cape Mendenhall D-4). The Yupik (Eskimo) name has also been written as <Bangooxthleet, Bangookthleet>; no etymology is known (Orth 1967).

BANIDA (Idaho, Franklin Co.) \ban ī´ də\. The name was coined in 1908 by combing the names of nearby **Bannock** and **Oneida Counties** (Boone 1988); both are Native American names.

BANNEG BEG Pond (Maine, York Co.) A variant of **Bauneg Beg,** perhaps from an Abenaki (Algonquian) term meaning 'spread-out lake' (Eckstorm 1941).

BANNOCK \ban´ ək\. This name refers to a division of the Northern Paiute Indian people living in southern Idaho; their language belongs to the Numic branch of the Uto-Aztecan family. The term has been applied to a county in Idaho and elsewhere to a town (Nev., Lander Co.). and a waterfall (Wyo., Teton Co.). In the spelling **Bannack,** it refers to a mountain pass (Idaho, Clark Co.) The name is derived from Northern Paiute /pannakwatɨ/, the term that the Bannocks used to distinguish themselves from their Shoshoni neighbors (J. McLaughlin p.c.). The English form, however, seems to have been assimilated to the English word *bannock,* meaning a type of flat bread.

BANTAM (Conn., Litchfield Co.) \ban´ təm\. Perhaps adapted from Natick (Algonquian) <peäntam>, lit. 'he prays', a term used to refer to Indians who had been converted to Christianity (Trumbull 1881).

BAPCHULE (Ariz., Pinal Co.) \bap cho͞ol´\. Perhaps from an O'odham (Piman) term meaning 'hooked nose' (Granger 1983).

BARABARA Cove (Alaska, Kodiak D-3). It is claimed that this term was applied by the Russians to Native American huts in Alaska but that the word is actually derived from a language of Kamchatka, in Siberia (Orth 1967). A related placename is **Barrabora** (Alaska, St. Michael B-1).

BARAGA County (Mich.) \bâr´ ə gə\. The name is not Indian, but commemorates Father Frederic Baraga, a nineteenth-century Slovene missionary to the Ojibwa (Algonquian) people and author of a major dictionary of their language (Baraga 1880).

BARBENCITA Butte (Ariz., Coconio Co.) \bär bən sē´ tə\. Derived from Spanish *Barboncito* 'little beard' (from *barba* 'beard'), a name applied to a nineteenth-century Navajo leader (McNamee 1997).

BARRABORA (Alaska, St. Michael B-1). A name related to **Barabara Cove**; see above.

BASHBISH Falls (Mass., Berkshire Co.) \bash´ bish\. From SNEng. Algonquian, of unclear derivation.

BATON ROUGE (La., East Baton Rouge Par.) \bat ən ro͞ozh´\. The French name, meaning 'red stick', is a translation of the Choctaw (Muskogean) phrase *itti homma* 'red pole', from *itti* 'stick, tree, wood', *homma* 'red' (P. Munro p.c.). The Indians are said to have erected a pole near here, painted red, perhaps as a boundary marker (Read 1927). The same Choctaw phrase gives rise to **Istrouma**, another placename in the area.

BATTLE. This word forms part of many placenames, referring to places where battles occurred between Indian groups, or between Indians and whites. One of the best known is **Battle Creek** (Mich., Calhoun Co.) (Vogel 1986).

BATZALNETAS (Alaska, Nabesna C-6) \bat səl nē´ təs, ban zə nē´ tə\. From an Ahtna (Athabaskan) personal name (J. Kari p.c.).

BATZA River (Alaska, Melozitna D-3) \bat´ sə\. From an Ahtna (Athabaskan) source (J. Kari p.c.).

BAUNEG BEG (Maine, York Co.). A variant of **Banneg Beg;** see above.

BAYOU \bä´ yo͞o, bä´ yō, bä´ yə\. This English term for a sluggish stream is borrowed from French, which took it from an early Choctaw (Muskogean) form *bayuk* 'creek, river' (Read 1927:xii). In specific placenames, it generally occurs before a modifying noun, on the French pattern; thus **Bayou Chêne** (La., St. Martin Parish), meaning 'oak bayou'. **Bayou Talla** (Miss., Hancock Co.) may mean 'palmetto bayou', from Choctaw *tala* 'palmetto' (Seale 1939). The word *bayou* is also used as a generic term, especially in La. and adjacent states. There are a few examples of the term in more distant areas once visited by French explorers: for example, **The Bayou** (Mich., Osceola Co.) as well as other places in Mich. (Chippewa Co.) and Colo. (Douglas Co.). The placename **Bayou Salado** (Colo., Park Co.) is bilingual, containing Spanish *salado* 'salty'. The Choctaw term *bayuk* has the historically later variant *book,* which entered French and English as **Bogue** and is used in many placenames; see entries below.

BAYOU GOULA (La., Iberville Par.) \go͞o´ lə\. Not the name of a bayou, but from an ethnic name <Bayogoula>, folk-etymologized as from Choctaw *bayuk oklah* 'river people' (Read 1927; I. Goddard p.c.).

BEANBLOSSOM (Ind., Brown Co.). Corresponds to Unami Delaware (Algonquian) <Hakiachhanne>, perhaps 'bean stream'; cf. /hakiyaaláxkwsiit/ 'a type of bean' (McCafferty 2002).

BEAR. This term, referring either to the grizzly bear or to the black bear, occurs in placenames throughout North America. For example, **Bear Butte** (S.Dak., Meade Co.) corresponds to Lakhota (Siouan) *mathó pahá,* lit. 'bear hill'; it is said to look like a sleeping bear (Sneve 1973; A. Taylor p.c.).

BEARPAWS Peaks (Colo., Jackson Co.) is a translation of Arapaho (Algonquian) *woxéihtoo* 'bear paw' (A. Cowell, p.c.).

BEAVER Creek (Ind., Lawrence Co.). Corresponds to Unami Delaware (Algonquian) <Tamaquehanne> 'it is a beaver stream', with /təmaakwe/ 'beaver' (McCafferty 2002).

BEAVER Lake (Alaska, Nabesna A-2) Corresponds to Upper Tanana *tsa' männ',* lit. 'beaver lake' (J. Kari p.c.).

BEGAY Well (Ariz., Apache Co.) \bi gā´\. A common Navajo (Athabaskan) surname, literally from Navajo *bighe', biye'* 'his son', from *bi-* 'his' plus *ye'* 'son' (A. Wilson p.c.) Originally, the Navajos did not use surnames; but when Anglo administrators asked their names, they got answers such as *Pedro biye'* 'son of Pedro'. The administrators interpreted *biye'* as a surname, writing it as **Begay**.

BEMIDJI, Lake (Minn., Beltrami Co.) \bə mij´ ē\. From Ojibwa (Algonquian) *bimijigamaa* 'be a crosswise lake', from *bimid-* 'crosswise' and *-gam-aa* 'be a lake' (J. Nichols p.c.).

BENA (Minn., Cass Co.) \bē´ nə\. From Ojibwa (Algonquian) *bine* 'ruffed grouse', locally called 'partridge'. The term may have been popularized by its occurrence as Bena in Longfellow's *Hiawatha,* translated 'pheasant' (Upham 2001; Nichols and Nyholm 1995). The same name is applied to **Bena Lake** (Wis., Vilas Co.) \ben´ ə\. Alternative spellings are **Bine** (Minn.) and perhaps **Bina** (N.C.).

BENALLY (Ariz., Coconino Co.) \bi nal´ ē, bi nä´ lē\. This common Navajo (Athabaskan) surname is from *binálí* 'his son's son, his paternal grandparent', from *bi-* 'his' plus *nálí* 'son's son, paternal grandparent' (A. Wilson p.c.; Young and Morgan 1987). Originally, the Navajos did not use surnames; but when Anglo administrators asked their names, they got answers such as *Pedro binálí* 'grandson of Pedro'. The administrators interpreted *binálí* as a surname, writing it as **Benally**. See also **Begay Well** above.

BENCO (Alaska, Talkeetna A-1) \ben´ kō\. From Dena'ina (Athabaskan) *ben ka'a* 'big lake' (Orth 1967, Kari and Kari 1982:39). Also written as **Benka.**

BEN DAVIS Creek (Ind., Rush Co.). This was the name of a Delaware (Algonquian) leader, known in his own language as <Petchekekepon>, who died around 1820. The Delaware name for the stream was *mahoning* 'salt lick' (McPherson 1993), which became an English placename elsewhere; see **Mahoning** below. In Marion Co., Ind., the village of **Ben Davis** is said to be named after a railroad superintendent, Benjamin Davis (Baker 1995).

BENEWAH (Idaho, Benewah Co.) \ben´ ə wä\. The name is derived from that of a historic Coeur d'Alene (Salishan) leader, Benoit, pronounced \binwá\. and derived from French *Benoît* 'Benedict'. His Coeur d'Alene name has been given as /cilčpú/ 'five buttes' (D. Kinkade p.c.).

BENKA (Alaska, Talkeetna A-1) \ben´ kə, bung´ kə\. From Dena'ina (Athabaskan) *ben ka'a* 'big lake' (Orth 1967, Kari and Kari 1982:39). Also written as **Benco**.

BENONA Township (Mich., Oceana Co.) \bə nō´ nə\. Probably named for a fictitious Indian heroine; the term is likely to be artificial (Vogel 1986).

BEOWAWE (Nev., Eureka Co.) \bē´ ə wä wē, bā´ ə wä wē\. The name is probably from Northern Paiute or Shoshoni (both Numic languages of the Uto-Aztecan family), but several etymologies have been proposed. One is from Shoshoni /pia-waa-wia/ 'big pinyon pass' (/pia-/ 'big', /waa/ 'pinyon pine', /wia/ 'pass'). Another is from Northern Paiute /piawavi/ 'elderly married woman'. Still another is from Shoshoni /piawopin/ 'big wagon', from /pia/ 'big' plus /wopin/ 'wagon' (Carlson 1974; J. McLaughlin p.c.).

BERINO (N.Mex., Dona Ana Co.) \bə rē´ nō\. The name has been said to come from a word meaning 'ford' in an unspecified Indian language or to be a contraction of the placename **Chamberino,** itself of unclear origin (Julyan 1998).

BERTRAND (Mich., Berrien Co.). This is the family name of a prominent mixed-blood family, founded by a French-Canadian named Joseph Bertrand (Vogel 1986).

BESA CHITTO Creek (Miss., Choctaw Co.). \bē sə chit´ ə\. From Choctaw (Muskogean) *bissa chito,* lit. 'blackberries-big' (P. Munro p.c.).

BESECK Lake (Conn., Middlesex Co.) Said to be from Mohegan (Algonquian), meaning 'at the water-place' (Huden 1962).

BESH-BA-GOWAH Ruins (Ariz., Gila Co.) \besh bä gō´ wə\. Although these are the ruins of a Pueblo settlement, the name is from Western Apache (Athabaskan) *bésh baaghowąh* 'house for metal', from *bésh* 'metal' and *baaghowąh* 'house for it' (containing *goghąh* 'wickiup', related to Navajo *hooghan* 'hogan'. It probably refers to the ore smelter at Globe, Ariz. (P. Greenfeld p.c.).

BESHBITO Wash (Ariz., Navajo Co.) \besh´ bi tō\. Navajo (Athabaskan) *béésh bito'* 'spring of flint or metal' from *béésh* 'flint, metal' plus *bito'* 'its spring' (*bi-* 'its', *to'* 'water, spring'; A. Wilson p.c.).

BESHTA Bay (Alaska, Tyonek A-4) \besh´ tə, bäsh´ tə\. Adapted from Dena'ina (Athabaskan) *bashda q'atl'u* 'coal bay' (Kari & Fall 1987:47).

BESZIVIT (Alaska, Melozitna C-5). Said to be a Koyukon (Athabaskan) Indian name (Orth 1967).

BETATAKIN Ruin (Ariz., Navajo Co.) \bə tä´ tə kin, bə tat´ ə kin\. This is the ruin of a Pueblo settlement but has been given the Navajo (Athabaskan) name *bitát'ahkin* 'house(s) on a rock ledge, or on rock ledges' from *bitát'ah* 'rock ledge(s)' plus *kin* 'house(s)' (Wilson 1995). Hopis say that the Navajo term is borrowed from Hopi *pitataki* 'houses clinging', from *pita-* 'adhere flatly' (reduplicated to *pita-ta-*) plus *kii* 'house' (K. Hill p.c.).

BETAW Plantation (S.C., Berkeley Co.) \bē´ tô\. The name is said to mean 'honeybee' or 'alligator' in an unidentified Indian language (Neuffer and Neuffer 1983).

BETAY (Ariz., Coconino Co.) \bi tī´, bə tā´\. The name of this summit is possibly from Navajo (Athabaskan) *bidáá'í* 'its edge', containing *bi-* 'its' and *adáá'* 'edge' (A. Wilson p.c.).

BETONNIE TSOSIE Wash (N.Mex., San Juan Co.) \bə tō´ nē tsō´ sē\. Named after a Navajo man, Slim Bitani, referred to in Navajo (Athabaskan) as *baadaaní ts'ósí* 'his/her slim son-in-law', from *badaaní* 'her daughter's husband' (*adaaní* 'daughter's husband') plus *ts'ósí* 'slim'. The place is referred to in Navajo as *k'ai' naaschii' bikooh* 'meandering red willow wash', from *k'ai'* 'willow', *naashchii'* 'serpentine or meandering red line' and *bikooh* 'canyon, arroyo, wash' (Wilson 1995). Also written as **Bitani Tsosie.** A related name is **Betony Butte** (Ariz., Navajo Co.), probably from the same Navajo surname. This family name is written in English as **Betonnie**, **Bitani**, **Betony**, and so forth.

BEWABIC Park (Mich., Iron Co.) \bi wä´bik\. From Ojibwa (Algonquian) *biiwaabik* 'iron' (Vogel 1986; Nichols and Nyholm 1995). Related placenames include **Biwabik** (Minn., St. Louis Co.), **Pewabic Falls** (Mich., Houghton Co.) and **Pewabeck** (Mich., Ontonagan Co.).

BIACHOUA Bayou (Miss., Harrison Co.) \bī ə choo͞´ ə\. Perhaps from Choctaw (Muskogean) *bayyi* 'white oak' plus *showa* 'rotten' (P. Munro p.c.).

BIBA WILA Creek (Miss., Oktibbeha Co.) \bib ə wī´ lə, bī bə wī´ lə\. Perhaps Choctaw (Muskogean) *bihi* 'mulberries' plus *bayalli* 'to go along in rows' (P. Munro p.c.).

BIBON Lake (Wis., Bayfield Co.) \bib´ ən\. From Ojibwa (Algonquian) *biboon* 'be winter' (Vogel 1991, Nichols and Nyholm 1995).

BIBYAK (Ariz., Pima Co.) \bib´ ē äk\. O'odham (Piman), perhaps from *bibbi* 'served-out food, plates of food' plus *akĭ* 'arroyo' (J. Hill p.c.).

BIDAAII TO HAALI (Ariz., Coconino Co.) \bi dä´ ē tō hä´ lē\. This spring has the Navajo (Athabaskan) name *bidáá'í tó háálį́* 'ledge(s) where water flows up and out', containing *bidáá'* 'its ledge(s)' (*adáá'* 'ledge'), *tó* 'water', and *háálį́* 'it flows up and out' (A. Wilson p.c.).

BIDAHOCHI (Ariz., Navajo Co.) \bid´ ə hō chē, bid ə hō´ chē\. Navajo (Athabaskan) *bidahóóchii'* 'a red area coming down, extending downward', from *bidah* 'down, downward', *hó(ó)* 'space, area', *chii'* 'the color of red ochre' (Wilson 1995). Also written **Bidahochee.**

BIDARKA Point (Alaska, Cordova D-8) \bi där´ kə\. This name refers to a sealskin boat used by indigenous peoples in southeastern Alaska (Orth 1967) The word is not Native American, however, it is from Russian *baidarka.* Another form of the word occurs in the placename **Bidark Creek** (Alaska, Seldovia C-5); see also **Boidarkin** (Alaska, Sitka A-4).

BIGBEE (Miss., Monroe Co.) \big´ bē\. An abbreviation of **Tombigbee** (Seale 1939), from a Choctaw (Muskogean) term meaning 'coffin makers'. There is another Bigbee in Ala. (Washington Co.) (Read 1984).

BIG CAVE (Ariz., Apache Co.). Corresponds to Navajo (Athabaskan) *tsé'áántsoh* 'big space under rock (cave)' (Linford 2000).

BIG COTTONWOOD Canyon (AZ, Apache Co.) corresponds to Navajo (Athabaskan) *t'iis nitsxaaz sikaad nástłah,* lit. 'huge-cottonwood-spreads cove' (Linford 2000).

BIG FLOW Canyon (Ariz., Apache Co.) corresponds to Navajo (Athabaskan) *nááli hatsoh nástł'ah* 'big it-flows-downward-area cove', referring to a waterfall (Linford 2000).

BIG FOOT Hill (S.Dak., Jackson Co.). Named for a nineteenth-century Minniconjou (Siouan) leader; Big Foot is a translation of his Lakhota name, *sí-thąka,* lit. 'foot-big' (A. Taylor p.c.). **Big Foot Wall** (S.Dak., Pennington Co.) is also named after him.

BIG FOOT Prairie (Ill., McHenry Co.). Named for a Potawatomi (Algonquian) leader in the early nineteenth century (Vogel 1963). **Big Foot Beach** (Wis., Walworth Co.) is also named for him (Vogel 1991).

BIGHEART Creek (Okla., Osage Co.). Named for Chief James Bigheart, an Osage (Siouan) leader (BGN 1998). The Native American name is /nące łąðe/, lit. 'heart big', but is used to mean 'brave' (R. Rankin p.c.).

BIG HILL Lake (Kans., Labette Co.). Named for the Big Hill band of the Osage (Siouan) people; their Native American name was /hpasó:łį/, from /hpasü´ olį/ 'they dwell on the top' (R. Rankin p.c.). They were supposedly so called because they once took refuge from a flood on high ground (Rydjord 1968).

BIG Lake (Alaska, Pribilof Islands D-4). Corresponds to Aleut *anilgux̂*; cf. *hanix̂* 'lake', *-lgu-, -lĝu-* 'big' (Bergsland 1994). **Big Mountain** (Ariz., Navajo Co.) corresponds to Navajo (Athabaskan) *dził ntsaa,* from *dził* 'mountain' plus *ntsaa* 'big' (Wilson 1995).

BIG Meadows (Colo., Grand Co.) is a translation of Arapaho (Algonquian) *toonóóxuuté'* 'meadow' (A. Cowell p.c.).

BIG SPRING Creek (Kans., Kingman Co.). Corresponds to Osage (Siouan) /nį́ hnį htąk(a)/, lit. 'water cold big' (R. Rankin p.c.).

BIG STONE Lake (Minn., Big Stone Co.). The term may correspond to Dakota (Siouan) *mde íyą-thąka* 'lake of the big stone'; from *mde* 'lake', *įyą* 'stone', *thąka* 'big'; this refers to stone outcrops in the lake valley, which lies on the boundary with S.Dak. (Upham 2001, Sneve 1973; A. Taylor p.c.).

BIHILINIE Canyon (Ariz., Apache Co.) \bi hə lē´ nē\. Possibly from Navajo (Athabaskan) *bįįh háálíní* 'deer spring', containing *bįįh* 'deer' and *háálį́* 'it flows up and out' (A. Wilson p.c.).

BIJAADIBAE (Ariz., Apache Co.) \bi jä di bī\. Possibly from Navajo (Athabaskan) *bijáádíbáí* 'gray legs', containing *bijáád* 'its leg(s)' (*jáád* 'leg') and *(ł)bá* 'gray' (A. Wilson p.c.).

BI KEESH Wash (Ariz., Apache Co.) \bi kēsh\. Possibly Navajo (Athabaskan) *bik'iish* 'his, her, its alder tree', from *bi-* 'his, her, its' and *k'iish (k'ish)* 'alder' (A. Wilson p.c.).

BIKO HODO KLIZH (Ariz., Coconino Co.) \bi kō hō dō´ klizh\. This valley takes its name from Navajo (Athabaskan) *bikooh hodootł'izh* 'blue canyon' from *bikooh* 'canyon' plus *ho-* 'space, area' plus *dootł'izh* 'blue, it is blue' (A. Wilson p.c.).

BILAN AKKWE'A (N.Mex., Cibola Co.). The Zuni placename probably contains /ʔakkweʔ/ 'groove, ditch' (Ferguson and Hart 1985; Newman 1958).

BILLENA:WA (N.Mex., Cibola Co.). The Zuni placename refers to a place where timber was gathered (Ferguson and Hart 1985).

BILL MOOSE Run (Ohio, Franklin Co.). Named for Bill Moose, a Wyandot (Iroquoian) resident who died in 1937 (BGN 1999).

BILLY BOY Dam (Wis., Sawyer Co.). Named for William Billy Boy, a Chippewa (Ojibwa, Algonquian) resident (Vogel 1991).

BILLY CHINOOK Lake (Ore., Jefferson Co.). Named for Billy Chinook, a Wasco (Chinookan) resident of the area (McArthur 1992).

BILOXI \bi luk´ sē, bi lok´ sē\, the name of a Siouan people of the lower Mississippi valley. It ccurs as a placename in Miss. (Harrison Co.) and La. (St. Bernard Par.). The ethnic name occurs first in 1699 as <Annocchy> and <Bilocchy> (Seale 1939). It may have come from Muskogean sources: Chickasaw *bilokshi'*, Koasati *biloksi* (P. Munro p.c.).

BIMAHYOOK Creek (Alaska, Nunivak Island A-5). A Yupik (Eskimo) name recorded in 1959 (Orth 1967).

BIMIUT (Alaska, Black A-2) \bī´ myōōt\. Probably from Yupik (Eskimo) *paimiut* 'river-mouth people', with *pai-* 'mouth, outlet' and *-miut* 'people' (Orth 1967; Jacobson 1984). A related placename is **Paimiut** (Alaska, Hooper Bay C-3).

BINA (N.C., Ashe Co.) \bē´ nə\. Perhaps a transfer, with altered spelling, of the name **Bena,** found in Wis. and Minn., from Ojibwa (Algonquian) *bine* 'partridge'; or perhaps from Choctaw (Muskogean) *bina* 'camp' (Seale 1939).

BINAGAMI (MN, Cook Co.) \bi nä´ gə mē\. Formerly known as Clearwater Lake (Upham 2001:747); the name is from Ojibwa (Algonquian) *biinaagami* 'to be clean, as a liquid' (Nichols and Nyholm 1995).

BINAJOAKSMIUT (Alaska, Cape Mendenhall D-5). A Yupik (Eskimo) name reported in 1937 (Orth 1967).

BINAKSBAK Bluff (Alaska, Nunivak Island A-7). A Yupik (Eskimo) name said to mean 'big bluff' (Orth 1967); cf. *peńak* 'bluff' (Jacobson 1984).

BINAKSLIT Bluff (Alaska, Nunivak Island A-6). A Yupik (Eskimo) name said to mean 'steep bluff' (Orth 1967); cf. *peńak* 'bluff' (Jacobson 1984).

BINALIK Crater (Alaska, Nunivak Island A-4). A Yupik (Eskimo) name reported in 1973 (Orth 1967).

BINAT-INGRAT Hill (Alaska, Cape Mendenhall D-5). A Yupik (Eskimo) name said to mean 'bluff mountain' (Orth 1967); cf. Yupik *peńak* 'bluff', *ingriq* 'mountain' (Jacobson 1984).

BINE Lake (Minn., Lake Co.) \bē´ nə\. Formerly called Partridge Lake (Upham 2001:747). The name is from Ojibwa (Algonquian) *bine* 'partridge' (Nichols and Nyholm 1995), also written as **Bena** (Minn., Wis.), and perhaps as **Bina** (N.C.).

BINNE ETTENI Canyon (Ariz., Coconino Co.) \bi nē´ et´ ə nē\. Probably from a Navajo (Athabaskan) personal name. There are three possibilities: *binii'ádinii* 'no face', containing *bi-* 'his, her, its', *anii'* 'face', and *ádin* 'it does not exixt'; or *biníí'ádinii* 'no waist', containing *biníí'* 'his, her, its waist'; or *bíni'ádinii* 'no mind', contaiining *bíni'* 'his, her, its mind' (A. Wilson p.c.).

BIRCH COOLEY (Minn., Renville Co.). This township was named for a stream earlier called **Birch Coulee**. The reference to the birch tree is a loan translation from Dakota (Siouan) *tą̨pá* 'white birch' (Upham 2001).

BIRCH Hill (Alaska, Fairbanks D-2). Probably a literal translation of Lower Tanana (Athabaskan) *k'iyh ddheł* (J. Kari p.c.).

BIRD HEAD Rock (Ariz., Apache Co.). Corresponds to Navajo (Athabaskan) *tsídii binii'í* 'bird's face' (Linford 2000).

BIRD SPRING (AZ, Navajo Co.). Corresponds to Navajo (Athabaskan) *tsídiito'i,* containing *tsídii* 'bird' and *to'* 'water, spring' (Wilson 1995).

BISANABI Lake (Wis., Racine Co.) \bi sä´ nə bē\. Ojibwa (Algonquian) *bizaanabi* 'sits quietly' (J. Nichols p.c.).

BI:SHU'K'YAY'A (N.Mex., Cibola Co.). A Zuni placename referring to a sacred spring (Ferguson and Hart 1985).

BIS II AH Wash (Ariz., Apache Co.) \bis ē´ ä\. Navajo (Athabaskan) *bis íí'á* 'standing adobe formation, adobe pinnacle' from *bis* 'adobe' plus *íí'á* 'it juts upward, stands up' (A. Wilson p.c.).

BISTINEAU Lake (La., Webster Par.) \bis´ ti nō\. This name, first recorded in 1807 as **Bistiono**, perhaps reflects a Caddo term for 'big broth', referring to froth on the water (Read 1927).

BISUKA (Idaho, Ada Co.) \bi sōō´ kə\. Shoshoni (Numic) /pia-sukkuh/ 'big-there', used ironically (McLaughlin p.c.).

BITHLO (Fla., Orange Co.) \bith´ lō\. Not a Native American placename but a term chosen from a Creek (Muskogean) wordlist; the source is *perro* /píɬɬo/ 'boat' (J. Martin p.c.).

BITLABITO (Ariz., Apache Co.) \bi klä´ bi tō\. Navajo (Athabaskan) *bitł'ááh bito'* 'a spring underneath' from *bitł'ááh* 'beneath it' (*tł'ááh* 'underside, bottom') plus *bito'* 'its water' (*to'* 'water, spring') (Wilson 1995). Also written as **Beclabito**.

BITSIHUITOS Butte (Ariz., Apache Co.) \bit sē wē´ tōs\. Navajo (Athabaskan) *bitsį́į́h hwii-ts'os* 'an area or hill that tapers at its base' from *bitsį́į́h* 'its base' (*tsį́į́h* 'base') and *hwii-* 'area, space' plus *ts'os* 'it tapers' (Wilson 1995).

BITTERROOT River (Mont., Ravalli Co.). The name refers to a plant with a bitter but edible root. The name of the river in Flathead (Salishan) is <spet-lm-seulko> 'bitterroot water', derived from <spet-lm> 'bitterroot plant' (D. Kinkade p.c.).

BITZLA River (Alaska, Kateel River) \bits´ lə\. A shortening of a Koyukon (Athabaskan) name written in 1887 as **Bitzlatoiloeta** and **Bitzlatoilocta** (Orth 1967).

BITZSHTINI Mountains (Alaska, Kantishna River B-5) \bi chi stē´ nē\. From Koyukon (Athabaskan) *bedzesh tene,* lit. 'caribou trail' (Kari 1999:109).

BIWABIK (Minn., St. Louis Co.) \bi wä´ bik\. From Ojibwa (Algonquian) *biiwaabik* 'iron' (Upham 2001; Nichols and Nyholm 1995).

BLACK Creek (Ga., Bulloch Co.). Many streams in the United States bear this name because of their dark waters, but this Ga. stream was previously given the name <Weelustie>, apparently from a Muskogee name meaning 'black water' (Goff 1975:290). The Native American elements are *uewv* [óiwa, wí:wa] 'water' and *lvstē* /lásti:/ 'black' (Martin and Mauldin 2000).

BLACK DOG Lake (Minn., Dakota Co.). Named for a Dakota (Siouan) Indian residing in the area (Upham 2001:168).

BLACKFEET. A name given to an Indian people who speak an Algonquian language, living in Mont. and in Alberta, Canada. The term is a literal translation of the Native American name *sik-siká,* lit. 'black-foot'. The official name of the group is **Blackfeet** in the United States and **Blackfoot** in Canada, but the two forms are used in both countries as singulars and as plurals, and the language is usually called **Blackfoot** (D. Frantz p.c.). The form **Blackfoot** is also used as a placename (Mont., Glacier Co.).

BLACKFISH Lake (Alaska, Mt. McKinley C-6). Corresponds to Upper Kuskokwim (Athabaskan) *hozrighe mina',* lit. 'blackfish lake' (Gudgel-Holmes 1991:119).

BLACKFOOT Creek (S.Dak., Corson Co.). This name, also occurring as **Blackfeet** (see above), refers not to the Algonquian-speaking people of Mont., but to a division of the Teton Sioux in S.Dak. (Sneve 1973). Their Native American name is *sihá-sapa,* lit. 'sole-black', from *sihá* 'sole of the foot' (*si* 'foot', *ha* 'skin') plus *sápa* 'black' (A. Taylor p.c.).

BLACK HAWK. A leader of the Sac or Sauk people (Algonquian), born in 1767, who in 1832 led some of his people from Iowa into Ill., from which they had been previously expelled by white settlers; the resulting conflict became known as the Black Hawk War. He died in 1838 (Vogel 1991). His Sauk name was *mahkate:wi-meši-ke:hke:hkwa,* from *mahkate:wi* 'black' plus *meši-ke:hke:hkwa*; this in turn consists of *meši-* 'big' plus *ke:hke:hkwa,* a species of hawk. The name **Black Hawk** has been given to several locations in Ill.; to one in Scott Co., Iowa; and to one in Sauk Co., Wis. The township of **Black Hawk** in Haakon Co., S.Dak., may commemorate the Sauk leader or may have been named for a Santee (Siouan) leader known as Black Hawk.

BLACK Hills (S.Dak., Lawrence Co.). Probably a loan-translation from Lakhota (Siouan) *pahá-sapa,* lit. 'hill(s) black', supposedly applied because the dense forest on their slopes makes the hills appear dark from a distance (Sneve 1973; A. Taylor p.c.).

BLACK Lake (Ariz., Apache Co.). Corresponds to Spanish *laguna negra* and Navajo (Athabaskan) *be'ek'id halzhiní,* lit. 'lake that is black' (Linford 2000).

BLACK LASSIC Peak (Calif., Trinity Co.). Named after nearby **Mount Lassic,** which was named in turn for Lassik, leader of an Athabaskan Indian group (Gudde 1998).

BLACK LICK (Pa., Indiana Co.). Corresponds to Delaware (Algonquian) <Naeskahoni>, said to mean 'black lick', referring to a deer-lick or salt-lick, a natural salt deposit frequented by deer (Donehoo 1928). Cf. Munsee Delaware *nzúkeew* 'black' (O'Meara 1996), Unami Delaware /ma:ho:nink/ 'deer-lick place' (M. McCafferty p.c.). A related placename is **Mahoning** (Pa., Fayette Co.).

BLACK Mesa (Ariz., Navajo Co.). Corresponds to Navajo (Athabaskan) *dziłijiin* 'the mountain is black; black mountain', from *dził* 'mountain', *(y)ijiin* 'it is black' (Wilson 1995).

BLACK OAK Lake (Minn., Stearns Co.). The name is said to translate the term used by the Dakota (Siouan; Upham 2001:106); cf. Dakota *utuhu* 'oak', *sapa* 'black' (Riggs 1890).

BLACK PARTRIDGE Woods (Ill., Cook Co.). Named for a Potawatomi (Algonquian) leader of the early nineteenth century. His Native American name has been given as <mucketeypokee> 'black partridge' (Vogel 1963).

BLACK River (Wis., Jackson Co.). Corresponds to Ho-Chunk (Winnebago, Siouan) *niišéep,* from *níi* 'water, river' and *séep* 'black, dark-colored' (Vogel 1991, K. Miner p.c.).

BLACK Rock (Ariz., Apache Co.). Corresponds to Navajo (Athabaskan) *chézhiní,* lit. 'rock that is black', containing *tsé, ché* 'rock' (A. Wilson p.c.). **Black Rock Trail** (Ariz., Apache Co.) corresponds to Navajo (Athabaskan) *tsézhin ha'atiin* 'black rock trail up out', containing *tsé-zhin,* lit. 'rock-black' (Linford 2000).

BLACK SALT Valley Ariz., Apache Co.). Corresponds to a Navajo (Athabaskan) name given as *áshį́į́shzhiin* 'black salt' (Linford 2000); cf. *áshįįh* 'salt' (Young and Morgan 1987).

BLACKWARRIOR River (Ala., Hale Co.). This is a translation of the Choctaw (Muskogean) placename written in English as **Tuscaloosa,** from *tvshka* 'warrior' and *lusa* 'black'. The river is also called simply "The Warrior" (Read 1984).

BLACK WOLF (Wis., Winnebago Co.). Named for a Winnebago (Siouan) leader of the early nineteenth century; probably a translation of *šuukǰą́ksepga,* containing *šuukǰą́k* 'wolf,' *séep* 'black' (Vogel 1991; K. Miner p.c.).

BLOOD Creek (Kans., Barton Co.). The name is supposed to commemorate a bloody battle between the Cheyenne and Pawnee peoples in 1849 (Rydjord 1968).

BLOODY Run (Iowa, Humboldt Co.). The name refers to a stream where a Dakota (Siouan) family was murdered by a white man, "a whiskey seller and frontier ruffian," in 1854 (Vogel 1983).

BLUEBERRY (Minn., Wadena Co.). The name of this township corresponds to an Ojibwa (Algonquian) word (Upham 2001), also reflected in the local placename **Menahga** (Upham 2001). Ojibwa has *miinan* 'blueberries', *miinagwaawanzh* 'blueberry plant', and *miinikaa* 'there are lots of blueberries' (J. Nichols p.c.).

BLUE BLANKET Creek (S.Dak., Walworth Co.). Said to be a translation from Dakota (Siouan) *šiná-tho,* lit. 'blanket-blue'. Various stories are told as to the reason for the name (Sneve 1973; A. Taylor p.c.).

BLUE Canyon (Ariz., Coconino Co.). Corresponds to Navajo (Athabaskan) *bikooh hodootł'izh* 'a canyon area that is of a greenish or bluish cast', from *bikooh* 'canyon, wash, arroyo', *hodootł'izh* 'it is a blue area' (*ho-* 'space, area' plus *dootł'izh* 'it is green, blue)' (Wilson 1995).

BLUE CLOUD Abbey (S.Dak., Grant Co.). This Benedictine monastery is named for a Yankton Sioux leader who died in 1918 (Sneve

1973). The name would apparently be better translated as 'Blue Sky' (Sneve 1973); cf. Dakota *mahpíya thó*, lit. 'sky blue' (A. Taylor p.c.).

BLUE DOG Lake (S.Dak., Day Co.). The name was that of a Dakota (Siouan) resident called *šųk-thó wįyųpi* 'the dog that was painted blue'; cf. *šų́ka* 'dog', *tho* 'blue', *wįyųpi* 'paint' (Sneve 1973; A. Taylor p.c.).

BLUE EARTH. A translation from the Dakota (Siouan) placename **Mankato**, referring to bluish-green earth used as a pigment (Upham 2001, Vogel 1983). The term is from *mąkhá* 'earth' plus *tho* 'blue, green' (R. Rankin p.c.). The name is applied to a river in Iowa and Minn., and to a county in Minn.

BLUE JACKET Crossing (Kans., Douglas Co.). Named for the Reverend Charles Bluejacket, of Shawnee (Algonquian) descent. The family name was originally borne by a white man who joined the Shawnee people in Ohio in 1794; a Shawnee name meaning 'blue jacket' was given to him because of a garment that he wore (Rydjord 1968).

BLY (Ore., Klamath Co.) \blī\. Klamath *blay* 'above, up high' (Barker 1963).

BOBIDOSH Lake (Wis., Vilas Co.) \bō´ bi dosh\. The lake was given the surname of a local Ojibwa (Algonquian) family. It is possibly related to the placename **Obadash Lake** (Wis., Iron Co.), which seems to be abbreviated from the Ojibwa word for 'dragonfly' (Vogel 1991). The Ojibwa form is *oboodashkwaanishinh* 'dragonfly' (Nichols and Nyholm 1995).

BODCAU (Ark., Nevada and Lafayette Cos.; La., Bossier Par.) \bod´ kô\. Probably from Choctaw (Muskogean) *patkah* 'wide' (P. Munro p.c.), referring to **Bodcau Creek** in Ark. The spelling **Bodcaw Creek** in Ala. is also used. The placename **Bodka** seems to have the same source.

BODELTEH Islands (Wash., Clallam Co.). From Makah (Nootkan) /ba:diƚta/ 'fishing (for black bass, cod, halibut)' (W. Jacobsen p.c.).

BODKA Creek (Ala., Sumter Co.) \bod´ kə\. Probably from the Choctaw (Muskogean) word for 'wide' (Read 1984); the form is *patka* (P. Munro p.c.). The placename **Bodcau** or **Bodcaw** (Ark., La.) probably has the same origin.

BODOWAY Mesa (Ariz., Coconino Co.) \bod´ ə wā\. Named for a nineteenth-century leader of the Southern Paiute (Numic) people (Granger 1983). His Native American name was *potokwai* [poroɣwai] 'they travel away', from *poto* 'to travel' (plural subject), *-kwai* 'away' (J. McLaughlin p.c.).

BOGACHIEL River (Wash., Jefferson Co.) \bō´ gə chēl, bō´ gə shēl\. Quileute (Chimakuan) /boq'ʷač'íƛ/, lit. 'muddy water', from /bó:q'ʷa/ 'muddy' and /číƛowa/ 'water' (D. Kinkade p.c.).

BOGAHOMA (Ala., Lowndes Co.) \bō gə hō´ mə\. Choctaw (Muskogean) for 'red stream', from *book* 'creek, river', *homma* 'red'. The same name occurs in several counties of Mississippi as **Bogue Homa**, or **Boga Homo**.

BOGALUSA (La., Washington Par.) \bō gə lo͞o´ sə\. Choctaw (Muskogean) for 'black stream' (Read 1927), from *book* 'creek' and *losa* 'black' (P. Munro p.c.). Variant spellings include **Bogaloosa** and **Bogue Lusa**. Related placenames are **Bogue Loosa** (Ala., Choctaw Co.) and **Bulgosa** (Ala., Butler Co.).

BOGATA (Tex., Red River Co.) \bə gō´ tə\. It was intended to name the town after Bogotá, Colombia. The current pronunciation reflects the vowel qualities of the intended spelling (Tarpley 1980).

BOGOTA (Ill., Jasper Co.) \bō gə tä´\. Named for Bogotá, the capital of Colombia in South America. That city was originally named Santa Fe de Bogotá in honor of a Chibcha Indian leader, Bogotá or Bacatá (Room 1997).

BOGUE \bōg\. This generic term for 'creek' is widespread in the southeastern United States; it is from Choctaw (Muskogean) *book* (Read 1984; P. Munro p.c.). Examples include **Bogue Creek** (Ala., Lamar Co.); however, **Bogue** in

N.C. (Carteret Co.) may have a European origin (Payne 1985). An earlier form of the Choctaw word was *bayuk*, whence French and English *bayou*; this also occurs in many placenames (as listed above).

BOGUE CHITTO (Ala., Dallas Co.) \bōg chit´ ə, bōg´ chit ə\. Choctaw (Muskogean) for 'big stream' (Read 1927), containing *chito* 'big' (P. Munro p.c.). The name also occurs in Miss. (Lincoln Co.) and in Ala. as **Boguechitta** (Bullock Co.).

BOGUE FALAYA (La., St. Tammany Par.) \bōg fə lä´ yə\. Choctaw (Muskogean) for 'long stream' (Read 1927), containing *book* 'stream', *falaya* 'long' (P. Munro p.c.). Several placenames in Mississippi (Seale 1939) probably represent the same form: **Bogue Fallah** (Oktibbeha and Choctaw Cos.), **Bogue Fala** (Lee Co.), **Bogue Faliah** (Scott Co.), and **Bogue Phalia** (Washington Co.).

BOGUEGABA Creek (Miss., Itawamba Co.) \bōg gä´ bə\. Perhaps short for Choctaw (Muskogean) *book kabak aachi* 'creek that says *kabak*', where *kabak* is an onomatopoetic element, referring to the sound of hitting or knocking (P. Munro p.c.).

BOGUE HOMA (Miss., Hancock Co.) \bō gə hō´ mə\. Choctaw (Muskogean) for 'red stream' (Seale 1939), containing *homma* 'red'. The name is also written as **Bogahoma** (Ala., Lowndes Co.) and **Boga Homo** (Miss., Wayne and Clarke Cos.).

BOGUE LOOSA (La., Washington Par.) \bōg lo͞o´ sə\. Choctaw (Muskogean) for 'black stream', containing *losa* 'black' (P. Munro p.c.). The name also occurs in Ala. (Choctaw Co.). Other spellings used in La. are **Bogalusa** and **Bogue Lusa.**

BOGUE PHALIA (Miss., Washington Co.) \bō gə fə lī´ ə\. Choctaw (Muskogean) for 'long stream' (Seale 1939), containing *falaya* 'long'; also written in other ways: for example, **Bogue Falaya** (La., St. Tammany Par.).

BOHEET (Neb., Platte Co.) \bō hēt\. From Pawnee (Caddoan) word *pahiitu'* 'quiet, slow' (D. Parks p.c.).

BOHEMOTASH Mountain (Calif., Shasta Co.) \bō hē´ mə tash\. From (Northern) Wintu *bohema thoos* 'big camp' (Gudde 1998).

BOHICKET Creek (S.C., Charleston Co.) \bō´ hik ət\. Earlier written <Bohekit>, <Bohickock> (Waddell 1980). Perhaps from CAC Algonquian <picohicora>, a milky drink made from hickory nuts; **Hickory** is from this source (Pickens 1964:33; *RHD* 1987). Another possible source is a Cusabo word meaning 'curer' (B. Rudes p.c.).

BOIDARKIN Island (Alaska, Sitka A-4) \boi där´ kin\. Derived from Russian *baidarka,* a word applied to Alaskan sealskin boats (Orth 1967). The placename **Bidarka Point** (Alaska, Cordova D-8) has a similar origin.

BOIS BLANC Island (Mich., Mackinac Co.) \boi´ blängk, boiz blängk\. The French name, meaning 'white wood', corresponds to an Ojibwa (Algonquian) word meaning 'basswood tree' (Vogel 1986); the form is *wiigob* (Nichols and Nyholm 1995). An old-fashioned pronunciation is \bä´ blō\.

BOIS DE SIOUX River (Minn., Wilkin Co.) \boi də so͞o\. The French name, meaning 'woods of the Sioux', refers to nearby settlements of the Dakota people (Upham 2001:554).

BOKCHITO (Okla., Bryan Co.) \bok´ chē tō, bok chē´ tō\. From Choctaw (Muskogean), meaning 'big stream' (Shirk 1974); composed of *book* 'stream', *chito* 'big' (P. Munro p.c.). The name occurs elsewhere as **Bogue Chitto** (Ala., Miss.) and as **Boguechitta** (Ala., Bullock Co.).

BOKENGEHALAS Creek (Ohio, Logan Co.). This represents the name of an eighteenth-century Delaware (Algonquian) leader, also written **Buckongehelas** (L. Miller 1972); the Native American name is Unami Delaware /pahkancíhəla:s/ 'one who goes directly' (M. McCafferty p.c.). The name **Buckhannon** (W.Va., Upshur Co.) may be related to this (Kenny 1945).

BOKHOMA (Okla., McCurtain Co.) \bōk´ hō mə, bōk hō´ mə\. From Choctaw (Muskogean) *book* 'stream', *homma* 'red' (P. Munro p.c.). The same form is reflected by the names **Bogahoma** (Ala., Lowndes Co.), **Bogue Homa** (Miss., Hancock Co.), and **Bogahoma** or **Boga Homo** (Ala., Lowndes).

BOKOSHE (Okla., Le Flore Co.) \bō kō´ shē\. Choctaw (Muskogean) for 'little stream' (Shirk 1974), containing *ushi* 'diminutive' (Byington 1915).

BOKTUKLO Creek (Okla., McCurtain Co.) \bok to͞ok´ lō\. Choctaw (Muskogean) for 'two creeks' (Shirk 1974); cf. *tuklo* 'two' (P. Munro p.c.).

BOLAPUSHA Creek (Miss., Scott Co.) \bol ə push´ ə\. From Choctaw (Muskogean) *balup asha* 'slippery elms are there', containing *balup* 'slippery elm' (Seale 1939). Also written as **Bollybusha.**

BOLATUSHA (Miss., Leake Co.) \bol ə tush´ ə, bō lə to͞o´ shə\. Said to be from a "war name" borne by a Choctaw (Muskogean) man, meaning 'one who strikes and cuts to pieces', from *booli* 'to strike', *tusha* 'to cut to pieces' (Seale 1939).

BOLIGEE (Ala., Greene Co.) \bō li jē´, bō´ li jē\. Possibly from Choctaw (Muskogean) *baluhchi* 'hickory bark' (Read 1984).

BOLINAS (Calif., Marin Co.) \bō lē´ nəs\. First recorded in 1834 as **Baulenes**, the name of a Coast Miwok Indian band that lived in the area. **Bolinas Creek** (Calif., Alameda Co.), however, is named for Antonio Bolena, of Portugal (Gudde 1998).

BOLINGCHESSA (Miss., Clarke Co.) \bol ing ches´ ə\. From Choctaw (Muskogean) *balohchi asha* 'place where there are strips of hickory bark', containing *balohchi* 'hickory bark' (Seale 1939; P. Munro p.c.).

BOLLIBOKKA Mountain (Calif., Shasta Co.) \bol ē bok´ ə\. From (Northern) Wintu *buli* 'mountain', *phaqa* 'manzanita' (Gudde 1998).

BOLLYBUSHA Creek (Miss., Scott Co.) \bol i bush´ ə\. From Choctaw (Muskogean) *balup asha* 'slippery elms are there', containing *balup* 'slippery elm' (Seale 1939). Also written as **Bolapusha.**

BOMBAZINE Island (Maine, Cumberland Co.) \bom´ bə zēn\. Derived from the name of an Abenaki (Algonquian) leader who lived in the eighteenth century; his name has also written as *Obam-Saween, Obum-Saween, Abomazine, Abomazeen, Bombazeen,* and *Bomazeen*; it has been said to mean 'keeper of the ceremonial fire'. The related form **Bomoseen** is also found (Vt., Rutland Co.; Eckstorm 1941; Huden 1962). The form Bombazeen is evidently influenced by the English word *bombazine,* the name of a fabric, of Greco-Latin origin.

BONE Creek (Alaska, Nabesna D-6). An adaptation of Athna (Athabaskan) *c'eggaan' ts'enn' na',* lit. 'arm bone creek' (J. Kari p.c.).

BONEY Creek (Alaska, Tanana A-5). Probably adapted from Upper Koyukon (Athabaskan) *taatl'enhledlo no',* lit. 'bones-are-in-water creek' (J. Kari p.c.).

BONFOUCA (La., St. Tammany Par.) \boN fo͞o kä\. Said to be the name of a Choctaw chief in the eighteenth century. This is perhaps a mistranscription of a Choctaw (Muskogean) placename, written <Boukfouca> in 1932 (Read 1927). It probably means 'near the river'; the elements would be *book* 'stream', *fokka* 'around, near' (P. Munro p.c.).

BONHOMME Creek (Mo., St. Louis Co.) \bon´ əm, bō´ nəm\. The French term, meaning 'good man', may here be a translation of Osage (Siouan) /níkka dą̧he/, the title given to a prominent man of the group (Ramsay 1952; R. Rankin p.c.).

BONNE FEMME Creek (Mo., Howard Co.) \bun fäm\. The French term, meaning 'good woman', here may be a translation of the Omaha (Siouan) word for a prominent woman (Ramsay 1952).

BOOSHU Camp (Alaska, St. Lawrence C-6). This is the surname of a Yupik (Eskimo) family living in the area (Orth 1967).

BORREGO Pass (N.Mex., McKinley Co.) \bôr ā´ gō\. The Spanish word for 'yearling lamb' corresponds to Navajo (Athabaskan) *dibé yázhí habitiin* 'ascending lamb trail' (Linford 2000); it contains *dibé yázhí* 'lamb', lit. 'sheep small', from *dibé* 'sheep', *yázhí* 'small' (Young and Morgan 1987).

BOSEBUCK Mountain (Maine, Oxford Co.). Perhaps from Penobscot (Algonquian) /pósəpek/ 'where it is wet' (P. MacDougall p.c.).

BO'SHO'WA (NM, Cibola Co.). The Zuni placename designates an area used in religious pilgrimages (Ferguson and Hart 1985).

BOSS Creek (Alaska, Sleetmute A-7). Said to be a translation of the Yupik (Eskimo) name <Adanarayak> (Orth 1967).

BOSTON Creek (Wash., Skagit Co.). Chinook Jargon <boston, pos-ton> /bástən, pástən/, 'American, white man', from English *Boston*, as distinguished from <king george man, kin-chautsch> 'British, Canadian' (D. Kinkade p.c.).

BOTNA (Iowa, Shelby Co.) \bot´ nə\. A shortening of the name of the **Nishnabotna River** (Vogel 1983); another place is named **Nishna.** For the name of this stream, cf. Osage (Siouan) /nį-hnį-pošta/, probably meaning 'spouting spring', from /nį-hni/ 'spring' (lit. 'water-cold'), /pošta/ 'spouting' (J. Koontz p.c.).

BOTTENINTNIN Lake (Alaska, Kenai C-2). From Dena'ina (Athabaskan) *begh tinitin* 'trail goes by it' (Kari and Kari 1982:31).

BOULDER Lake (Alaska, Gulkana B-4). An adaptation of Ahtna (Alaska) *ts'es cogh z'aan bene'*, lit. 'big boulder is-there lake' (J. Kari p.c.).

BOURBONNAIS (Ill., Kankakee Co.) \bər bō´ nəs, bər´ bə nā, bər bə nā´\. Named for the Bourbonnais family of the early nineteenth century, of mixed French and Potawatomi (Algonquian) ancestry. Elsewhere the name is also written **Bourbonais** (Kans., Shawnee Co.).

BOWL CANYON Creek (N.Mex., McKinley Co.). Corresponds to Navajo (Athabaskan) *ásaayi'* 'in the bowl' (Linford 2000), *ásaa'* 'bowl' (Young and Morgan 1987).

BOWLEGS (Okla., Seminole Co.). Named for Billy Bowlegs, a Seminole (Muskogean) leader (Martin and Mauldin 2000).

BOYGAN Lake (Wis., Vilas Co.) \boi´ gən\. The name reflects an Algonquian word meaning 'pipe (for smoking)', perhaps Menomini *ohpuakan* (Vogel 1991); cf. also Ojibwa *opwaagan* (Nichols and Nyholm 1995). The name is elsewhere written as **Poygan Lake** (Wis., Winnebago Co.).

BOY Lake (Minn., Cass Co.). Said to be a translation of the Ojibwa (Algonquian) name, given because some small boys were once killed there by a group of Sioux (Upham 2001). The Native American name contains the term for 'boy', Ojibwa *gwiiwizens* (Nichols and Nyholm 1995). The nearby **Woman Lake** was supposedly named for a similar incident.

BOYSAG Point (Ariz., Mohave Co.) \boi´ sag\. From Southern Paiute /paɨsaka/ [páɨsaɣa, páɨsaxA] 'bridge' (J. McLaughlin p.c.).

BRANDT (Pa., Susquehanna Co.). Probably named for the famous Mohawk (Iroquoian) chief, Thayendanegea, known in English as Joseph Brandt (Donehoo 1928).

BRASSTOWN (N.C., Clay Co.). Supposedly so named in an attempt to translate the Cherokee (Iroquoian) word for 'green', but it was confused with a word for 'brass' (Powell 1968). The former is Cherokee *ije'i* 'green' (Feeling 1975); the latter has been written <untsai'yi>.

BRASSUA (Maine, Somerset Co.) \bras´ o͞o ā\. Perhaps from an Abenaki (Algonquian) pronunciation of the French male given name *François* (Huden 1962); cf. Western Abenaki *blaswa* (Day 1994–95).

BREAD Springs (N.Mex., McKinley Co.). Corresponds to Navajo (Athabaskan) *bááh háálį́* 'bread flows up and out', from *bááh* 'bread', *háálį́* 'it flows up and out' (Wilson 1995).

BRIDGE Lake (Alaska, Fairbanks D-4). Probably a literal translation of Lower Tanana (Athabaskan) *dwxteni mena'* (J. Kari p.c.).

BROCKATONORTON Bay (Md., Worcester Co.) \bog ə när´ tən\. From a placename in the Va. Algonquian language, written <Bauchitinaughton> in 1670. Since a Va. Algonquian word <boketawh> has been recorded as meaning 'fire', it has been speculated that the name means 'fire people' (Kenny 1984).

BROKEN ARROW Creek (Ala., Russell Co.). This translates the name of a Lower Creek (Muskogean) town, recorded as <Likachka> (Read 1984). This can be analyzed as *rē* /łi:/ 'arrow', *kvckē* /káčki:/ 'broken' (Martin and Mauldin 2000). Other locations with the same name, in Ala. and elsewhere, may also be loan-translations from Native American names.

BROUILLETTS Creek (Ind., Vermillion Co.) \broo lets\. This name is intended as possessive, *Brouillett's*. It may have been named for Michael Brouillette, an Indian interpreter (Baker and Carmony 1975).

BRULE \brool\. From French *brulé* 'burnt', representing a loan-translation from Dakota (Siouan). The **Brule River** (Minn., Cook Co.) is said to be based on Ojibwa (Algonquian) <Wissakode> 'half burnt' (Upham 2001). The placename **Brule Lake** also occurs in Mich. (Iron Co.) **Brule County** in S.Dak., however, is named after the Brulé division of the Teton Sioux (Sneve 1973), known in Dakota as *sičhą́ ǧú,* lit. 'thigh(s) burnt' (A. Taylor p.c.).

BRUSHKANA Creek (Alaska, Healy B-3) \brush kan´ ə\. From Ahtna (Athabaskan) *bes ce'e na* [bəškə'əna], lit. 'bank-big creek' (Kari 1983:77). Probably from the same origin is **Bruskasna Creek** (Alaska, Healy B-3) \brush kaz´nə\.

BUCATUNNA (Miss., Clarke Co.) \buk ə tun´ ə\. Perhaps Choctaw (Muskogean) *book* 'river', *ittanaha* 'to meet, gather' (P. Munro p.c.). The name is also written **Buckatunna** (Miss., Wayne Co.; Ala., Choctaw Co.).

BUCKALOONS (Pa., Warren Co.) \buk ə loonz\. From *Buckaloon*, once the site of an Iroquoian village. It is said that the original Seneca name was <Kachuidagon> 'broken reed', which was partially translated by speakers of Delaware (Algonquian) as <Poquihhilleu> 'broken' (Donehoo 1928; Brinton and Anthony 1888); cf. Munsee Delaware *kaxkihleew* 'broken' (O'Meara 1996), which was then transformed further by English speakers into *Buckaloon.*

BUCKATAHPON Dam (Wis., Vilas Co.) \buk ə tä´ bən\. Said to be from an Ojibwa (Algonquian) word for 'hunger'; the placename is also written as **Buckatabon** (Vogel 1991); cf. Ojibwa *bakade* 'to be hungry' (Nichols and Nyholm 1995). Perhaps from the same origin is **Buckaton Creek** (Wis., Vilas Co.).

BUCKATUNNA (Miss., Wayne Co.; Ala., Choctaw Co.) \buk ə tun´ ə\. The name was written in 1764 as <Bacatune> and in 1772 as <Bogue-aithee-Tanne>. It perhaps represents a Choctaw (Muskogean) phrase, 'stream where baskets are woven' (Read 1984); a modern transcription is *book aatana,* containing *book* 'stream' and *tana* 'to weave' (P. Munro p.c.). The name is also written **Bucatunna** (Miss., Clarke Co.).

BUCKHANNON (W.Va., Upshur Co.) \buk han´ ən\. The origin of this placename is unclear, and some believe it is from the English surname *Buchanan*. Others, however, believe that it represents the name of an eighteenth-century Delaware (Algonquian) leader whose name is recorded as <Buck-on-go-ha-non>. It is possible that this individual can be identified with a better-known Delaware leader whose name has been written as <Buckongahelas>, said to mean 'breaker in pieces' (Kenny 1945). The latter name may also be reflected in **Bokengahalas Creek** and **Buckongehelas** (Ohio, Logan Co.).

BUCKONGEHELAS (Ohio, Logan Co.). A variant spelling of **Bokengehelas Creek**; see above. The name **Buckhannon** (W.Va., Upshur Co.) may be related to this (Kenny 1945).

BUCKSHUTEM (N.J., Cumberland Co.) \buk´ shoo təm\. Perhaps from Delaware (Algonquian); however, a definite source has not been identified (Becker 1964).

BUCKSTOCK River (Alaska, Russian Mission B-1) \buk´ stäk\. Supposedly from Yupik (Eskimo} <buksta(k)> 'swampy river' (Orth 1967).

BUFFALO. Although the buffalo or bison is closely associated with Native American culture, the English term is derived from Latin *bufalus, bubalus,* originally a type of African antelope. Many U.S. placenames are loan translations from American Indian names that refer to the buffalo: for example, **Buffalo Creek** (Pa., Armstrong Co.), corresponding to Delaware (Algonquian) <Sisiliehanna> 'buffalo stream' (Donehoo 1928); cf. Unami Delaware /si:si:li:e/ 'buffalo' (Blalock et al. 1994), <-hanne, -hanneck> 'creek' (Brinton and Anthony 1888). In S.Dak. (Custer Co.), **Buffalo Gap** translates Dakota (Siouan) *okó thathą́ka,* lit. 'hole [of the] buffalo' (Sneve 1973; A. Taylor p.c.).

BUGOMOWIK Pass (Alaska, Kwiguk D-6). The Yupik (Eskimo) name was written <Pagomawik> in 1899 (Orth 1967).

BULCHITNA Lake (Alaska, Tyonek D-3) \bo͞ol chit´ nə\. The name was assigned by the USGS in 1954 (Orth 1967); it was originally coined by whites, on the basis of English *bullshit,* with Athabaskan *-na'* 'stream' (J. Kari p.c.).

BULGOSA (Ala., Butler Co.) \bul gō´ sə\. Probably derived from **Bogueloosa**, found as a placename in both La. and Ala. It is from Choctaw (Muskogean) *book losa,* lit. 'stream black' (P. Munro p.c.). See **Bogue Loosa** above.

BULL Creek (S.Dak., Gregory Co.). The term *bull* is used in several midwestern placenames that translate Native American names and specifically refer to the male buffalo. The name cited from S.Dak. corresponds to Dakota (Siouan) *thathą́ka-bdoka,* lit. 'buffalo-male' (A. Taylor p.c.).

BULLY CHOOP Mountain (Calif., Shasta and Trinity Cos.) \bo͞ol ē cho͞op\. Represents Wintu *buli č'uup* 'mountain peak' (Gudde 1998).

BUMYOK Ridge (Alaska, Dillingham B-8) \bum´ yok\. The Yupik (Eskimo) name was first reported in 1932 (Orth 1967); cf. Yupik *pamyuq* 'tail (of animal or kayak)' (Jacobson 1984).

BUNCHED FEATHERS (Ariz., Apache Co.). Corresponds to Navajo (Athabaskan) *t'á' náásééł* 'a crowd of people is moving back with feathers', from *t'a'* 'feather(s)' plus *náásééł* 'a crowd is moving back' (Wilson 1995).

BUNCO Lake (Alaska, Talkeetna C-2) \bung´ kō\. From Dena'ina (Athabaskan) *ben ka'a,* lit. 'lake big' (Kari 1999:73). Another writing is found in **Bunka Lake** (Alaska, Tyonek A-4).

BUNGAMUG Brook (Maine, Cumberland Co.) \bung´ gə mug\. The name was recorded in 1735 as <Bungomungomug>. It is said to be from an Abenaki (Algonquian) name meaning 'fishing place at the boundary' (Ekstorm 1941). It has also been written as **Bungamic.**

BUNGANUT Pond (Maine, York Co.) \bung´ gə nut\. Perhaps containing Abenaki (Algonquian) /pɑk/ 'bump' or /pɑkahk/ 'indented' (P. MacDougall p.c.). The name **Bunganock** (Maine, Oxford Co.) is likely to have a similar origin (Huden 1962).

BUNGY Rock (Maine, Washington Co.). Perhaps from Abenaki (Algonquian), referring to the idea of 'boundary' (Huden 1962).

BUNITLANA Lake (Alaska, Kenai D-5) \bun ē tlä´ nə\. From Dena'ina (Athabaskan) *ben'idlen* 'lake current flows' (Kari and Kari 1982).

BUNKA Lake (Alaska, Tyonek A-4) \bung´ kə\. Dena'ina (Athabaskan) *ben ka'a,* lit. 'lake big' (Kari & Fall 1987:50); another writing is found in **Bunco Lake** (Alaska, Talkeetna C-2).

BURIBURI Ridge (Calif., San Mateo Co.) \bûr ē bûr´ ē, byo͞o rē byo͞o´ rē\. The term is from a Costanoan language; it is perhaps related to *purris* 'needle' (Gudde 1998).

BURNETT Mound (Kans., Shawnee Co). Named for Abram Burnett, of mixed French and Potawatomi (Algonquian) ancestry; he left Ind. in 1838 and settled in Kans. (Rydjord 1968). **Burnetts Creek** (Ind., Cass Co.) is also named after him (McPherson 1993).

BURNT CABINS (Pa., Fulton Co.). Named for the log cabins that white squatters built without authorization on Indian lands at this location, which were burned by the local Indians (Donehoo 1928).

BURNT CORN Wash (Ariz., Navajo Co.). Corresponds to Navajo (Athabaskan) *naadą́ą́ diilid* 'corn is burnt', from *naadą́ą́* 'corn' (*naa* 'enemy', *dą́ą́* 'food') and *diilid* 'it is burnt' (Wilson 1995).

BURNT WATER (Ariz., Apache Co.). Corresponds to Navajo (Athabaskan) *tó díílidí* 'water that is burnt'. A burnt ramada fell into a well here (Linford 2000).

BURRO, Mount (Ariz., Coconino Co.). Probably named for a Havasupai (Yuman) family with the surname *Burro* (L. Hinton p.c.).

BURRO Springs (Ariz., Coconino Co.). Corresponds to Navajo (Athabaskan) *télii bito'* 'burro's spring' (Linford 2000); from *télii* 'burro', *bito'* 'its spring, its water' (*to'* 'water'; Young and Morgan 1987).

BUSHLEY, Bayou (La., Catahoula Par.) \bush´ lē\. From Choctaw (Muskogean) *bashli* 'to cut; (as a noun) a cut' (P. Munro p.c.).

BUSHY HEAD Mountain (Ga., Gilmer and Fannin Cos.). The name is that of a Cherokee (Iroquoian) resident (BGN 8701). In Okla., the placename **Bushyhead** (Rogers Co.) commemorates Dennis Bushyhead, a Cherokee leader in the late nineteenth century (Shirk 1974).

BUTTAHATCHEE (Ala., Lamar and Marion Cos.) \but ə hach´ ē\. From the Choctaw (Muskogean) for 'sumac river' (Read 1984); cf. *bati* 'sumac', *hahcha* 'river' (P. Munro p.c.). The name occurs elsewhere in **Buttahatchee Creek** (Miss., Lamar Co.), also written as **Buttahatchie.**

BUTTE DES MORTS (Wis., Winnebago Co.) \byōōt´ i môr\. The French name, meaning 'hill of the dead', commemorates a battle between the French and the Meskwaki or Fox (Algonquian) in the early eighteenth century (Vogel 1991).

BUXAHATCHEE Creek (Ala., Chilton Co.) \buk sə hach´ ē\. Probably means 'chickensnake creek' in a Muskogean language: either in Choctaw, where the elements would be *abaksha* 'chicken snake', *hahcha* 'river'; or in Alabama-Koasati, where they would be *abaksa* 'chicken snake', *hahcí* 'river' (P. Munro p.c.).

BUZODOC Slough (Alaska, Bettles C-6). The Koyukon (Athabaskan) Indian name was recorded in 1956 (Orth 1967).

BUZZARD FLAPPER Creek (Ga., Cherokee Co.). This was reported as a Cherokee (Iroquoian) man's given name in the early nineteenth century; the reason for the name is not known (Goff 1975). It is also written as **Buzzard Flopper.**

BUZZARD ROOST (Ala., St. Clair Co.). Corresponds to Choctaw (Muskogean) *sheki a nusi* 'where buzzards sleep' (Read 1984); cf. *sheki* 'buzzard', *nusi* 'to sleep' (P. Munro p.c.).

BYHALIA (Miss., Marshall Co.) \bī hā´ lē ə\. From Choctaw (Muskogean), meaning 'white oaks stand'; cf. *bayyi* 'white oak', *hiili* 'to stand' (P. Munro p.c.). There is also a **Byhalia** in Ohio (Union Co.) [bə hā´ lyə], perhaps transferred from Miss.

BYLAS (Ariz., Graham Co) \bī´ ləs\. This is the name of a nineteenth-century Apache (Athabaskan) leader (Granger 1983); the Native American origin of the name has not been traced.

BYWY (Miss., Choctaw Co.) \bī´ wī\. From Choctaw (Muskogean) *bayyi wayya* 'white-oak leaning', from *bayyi* 'white oak', *wayya* 'to lean' (P. Munro p.c.). The name is also written **Bywiah,** pronounced \bī wī´ ə\ (Seale 1939).

C

CABABI Mine (Ariz., Pima Co.) \kä bä´ bē, kə bä´ bē\. From O'odham (Piman), meaning 'badger well', containing *ka:w* 'badger' and *wahia* 'well' (J. Hill p.c.).

CABANOCEY (La., St. James Par.) \kab ə nō´ sē\. Previously written <Cabahannosé>; perhaps meaning 'where the blacksmith sleeps' (Read 1927), from Choctaw (Muskogean) *kabaha* 'beater, hammerer', *aa-nosi* 'where he sleeps' (P. Munro p.c.).

CABAZON (Calif., Riverside Co.) \kab´ ə zon\. Spanish *cabezón* 'big head', from *cabeza* 'head'. Named for a leader of the Cahuilla (Takic) Indians of southern California (Gudde 1998).

CACAPON River (W.Va., Morgan Co.) \kə kā´ pən, kā´ pən\. Said to be a contraction of Shawnee (Algonquian) <Cape-cape-pe-hon> 'medicine water' (Kenny 1945). A related form is **Cacapehon** (W.Va., Hampshire Co.).

CACAWAY Island (Md., Kent Co.). From CAC Algonquian, possibly meaning 'porcupine quills' (Kenny 1984).

CACHAGUA Creek (Calif., Monterey Co.) \kə chä´ gwə\. Perhaps an Esselen name, variously spelled as <Tasshaguan, Jachaguan, Xasauan>; a local tradition is that it means something like 'hidden waters' (Gudde 1998).

CACHUMA (Calif., Santa Barbara Co.). \kə cho͞o´ mə\. From the Barbareño (Chumashan) village name that the Spanish spelled <Aquitsumu>, Barbareño /aqitsu'm/ 'sign' (Gudde 1998).

CADAUGHRITY (N.Y., Montgomery Co.). Perhaps Iroquoian, meaning 'steep banks' (Beauchamp 1907).

CADDO \kad´ ō\. An Indian group who formerly occupied eastern Tex., southern Ark., and the Red River Valley of La.; they now live in Okla. The family to which their language belongs is named, after them, **Caddoan.** The language name is from the first two syllables of /kaduhdá:ču'/, the name of a tribal division; the last two syllables mean 'sharp' (W. Chafe p.c.). As an English placename, **Caddo** is widespread: for example, Ala. (Lawrence Co.), Ariz. (Navajo Co.), and Mo. (Webster Co.). A related placename is **Caddoa** (Colo., Bent Co.) \kə dō´ ə\.

CADOSIA (N.Y., Delaware Co.) \kə dō´ shə, kə dō´ zē ə\. Perhaps Iroquoian, 'covered with a blanket' (Beauchamp 1907).

CADOTT (Wis., Chippewa Co.) \kä dot´\. Named for a family of mixed French and Ojibwa (Algonquian) descent, prominent in the area from the early eighteenth century. The French name was originally *Cadeau* (Vogel 1991).

CAHABA (Ala., Dallas Co.) \kə hä´ bə\. Perhaps from Choctaw (Muskogean), of unclear derivation (Read 1984); cf. Choctaw *kaha* '(pl.) to lie down, sleep' (P. Munro p.c.). There is another **Cahaba** in N.C. (Bertie Co.).

CAHINNIO Camp (Ark., Logan Co.) \kə hin´ ē ō\. The name refers to a band of Indians living in the area in 1687; the name has also been written as <Cahaynohoua> and <Cahinoa>. The language of the group is not known (Dickinson 1995).

CAHOKIA (Ill., St. Clair Co.) \kə hō´ kē ə\. The name refers to a division of the Miami/Illinois (Algonquian) Indians, referred to in early records as <Caoukiaki> (*HNAI* 15:680); a modern reconstruction of the name is /kawakiwa/ or /kawakia/ (Costa 2000:45). A possibly related name is **Kahoka** (Mo., Clark Co.).

CAHOLA (Kans., Chase Co.) \kə hō´ lə\. The name refers to a group of Kansa (Siouan) Indians; the Native American term is /gaxo:ļi/, from /gaxá olį̨/, lit. 'by-the-creek they-dwell' (R. Rankin p.c.).

CAHOULA Creek (La., Ouachita Par.) \ko͞o´ lē\. The pronunciation may have been influenced by English *coulee,* from French *coulée,* used in Louisiana to refer to a seasonal stream (Read 1927). The probable origin is Choctaw (Muskogean) 'sacred stream', from *oka* 'water', *hollo* 'sacred, taboo' (P. Munro p.c.).

CAHTO (Calif., Mendocino Co.) \kä´ tō\. From Northern Pomo /khaṭo/ 'lake', containing /khá/ 'water' (Gudde 1998). There is also a **Cahto Creek** (Calif., Humboldt Co.). As the name of a local Indian group, of the Athabaskan family, the name is usually written **Kato**.

CAHUENGA (Calif., Los Angeles Co.). \kə hung´ gə, kə weng´ gə\. From Gabrielino (Takic) *kawé'nga*; this is possibly cognate with Luiseño *qawíinga* 'at the mountain', from *qawíicha* 'mountain', and Cahuilla *qáwinga'* 'at the rock', from *qáwish* 'rock' (Gudde 1998).

CAHUILLA \kə wē´ ə\. An Indian group of southern Calif., belonging to the Takic linguistic family, a part of the Uto-Aztecan stock. The term is sometimes thought to be from Cahuilla *qáwiy'a* 'leader, chief'; but in fact it is borrowed from Spanish *cahuilla* 'unbaptized Indian', a local term used in mission days; this term itself was apparently derived from an extinct Indian language of Baja Calif. (Gudde 1998). As a geographical term, the name was first published, in the form **Cohuilla,** in 1859, applied to what is now called the **Coachella Valley**; see **Coachella** below. In 1873 it was published as **Coahuila,** showing confusion with the state so named in northeastern Mexico. The current spelling, **Cahuilla,** has been used since 1888 for several locations (Calif., Riverside Co.). The name **Cahuilla** has no relationship to **Kaweah** (Calif., Tulare Co.), the name of a Yokuts subgroup, although they are similarly pronounced.

CAHULGA Creek (Ala., Cleburne Co.) \kə hul´ gə\. The name may be Muskogee for 'canebrake', from *koh-vlke* /koh-âlki/ 'canebrake', from *kohv* /kohá/ 'cane', *-vlke* /-âlki/ 'group' (Read 1984, Martin and Mauldin 2000).

CAJALCO Canyon (Calif., Riverside Co.) \kə hal´ ko\. This appears to be a Spanish spelling of a name also written as <Keihal, Keihalker> (etc.). One could consider a relationship to forms for 'quail' in Takic (Uto-Aztecan) languages of the area: Luiseño *qaxáal,* Cahuilla *qáxal* (Gudde 1998).

CAKESOSTA Rock (Wash., Clallam Co.) \kāk sōs´ tə\. From Quileute (Chemakuan) /kikc'ó:stal/ 'canoe landing place', containing /kì:kíʔ/ 'to land a canoe', /-c'oʔ/ 'land', and /-tal/ 'place' (D. Kinkade p.c.).

CALAMUT Lake (Ore., Douglas Co.) \kal´ ə mut\. Perhaps from the same source as **Klamath River** (McArthur 1992); see below.

CALAPOOYA \kal ə pōō´ yə\. The name refers to a group of Indian peoples native to the Willamette Valley of Ore.; the term is usually written **Kalapuya** by anthropologists. The name probably entered English from Clackamas Chinook /itk'alapúyawaykš/, from the stem /-galapúywi-/ or /-k'alapúywa-/, of unknown origin; cf. Santiam (Kalapuyan) /k'alaphúya/ (D. Kinkade p.c.; Henry Zenk p.c.). In placenames, the spellings **Calapooya** (Ore., Douglas Co.) and **Calapooia** (Ore., Linn Co.) both occur.

CALAWAH River (Wash., Clallam Co.) \kə lä´ wä\. From Quileute (Chimakuan) /qàlóʔwa:/ 'in between' (D. Kinkade p.c.).

CALCASIEU (La., Rapides Par.) \kal´ kə shōō\. Said to be the name of an Atakapa leader, meaning 'crying eagle', from [katkōsh] 'eagle', [yōk] 'to cry' (Read 1927).

CALDWELL (Ill., Cook Co.). Named for Billy Caldwell, a nineteenth-century Potawatomi (Algonquian) leader (Vogel 1963).

CALEBEE (Ala., Macon Co.) \kə lē´ bē\. Earlier written as <Calobe>, <Caloebee> (Read 1984). Possibly from Creek (Muskogean) *kvlvpe* /kalápi/ 'a type of oak' (Martin and Mauldin 2000).

CALEDONIA (N.Y., Livingston Co.) \kal ə dō´ nē ə\. This Latin name for Scotland is a popular etymology based on **Canawaugus,** which also occurs as a placename in the area. The origin is Seneca (Iroquoian) *ga:nǫwǫgę́s* 'smelly rapids' (W. Chafe p.c.)

CALIBOGUE (S.C., Beaufort Co.) \kal´ i bōg\. Perhaps from an unidentified Indian language (Neuffer and Neuffer 1983).

CALIMUS Butte (Ore., Klamath Co.) \kal´ i məs\. From the Klamath placename /kelmas/ (Barker 1963).

CALIPEEN (Idaho, Shoshone Co.) \kal´ i pēn\. Chinook Jargon <cal´-li-peen> [kælapín] 'rifle', from French *carabine* 'rifle' (D. Kinkade p.c.).

CALISPELL (Wash., Pend Oreille Co.) \kal´ i spel\. Named for a division of the Pend Oreille

(Salishan) people; the Native American name is /qlispél/ (D. Kinkade p.c.). Related forms include **Kalispel** (Wash., Pend Oreille Co.) and **Kalispell** (Idaho, Bonner Co.; Mont., Flathead Co.).

CALISTOGA (Calif., Napa Co.) \kal i stō´ gə\. Said to be a combination of the names *California* (derived from Spanish) and **Saratoga**, a name from N.Y. state of Iroquoian origin (Gudde 1998).

CALLAO (Utah, Juab Co.). Named for **Callao** in Peru, the seaport of the city of Lima; the word may be from a local Indian language. There is also a **Callao** in Va. (Northumberland Co.).

CALLEGUAS Creek (Calif., Ventura Co.) \kä yā´ gəs\. The origin is Ventureño (Chumashan) /kayɨwiš/ 'the head' (Gudde 1998).

CALOOSA (Fla., Sarasota Co.) \kə lo͞o´ sə\. The name of an Indian group that once lived in the southeastern United States. Related names are **Calusa Keys** (Fla., Monroe Co.), **Colusa** (Ill., Hancock Co.), and perhaps **Colusa County** in Calif. The **Caloosahatchee River** (Fla., Monroe Co.) \kə lo͞o sə hach´ ē\ seems to contain the same name (Read 1934), plus Muskogee *hvcce* /háčči/ 'river' (J. Martin p.c.).

CALOWAHCAN, Mount (Mont., Lake Co.). Flathead (Salishan) 'beaver head', from /sqaléw'/ 'beaver' and /-q(i)n/ 'head' (D. Kinkade p.c.).

CALPELLA (Calif., Mendocino Co.) \kal pel´ ə\. Named for the leader of a Northern Pomo village. The word is from Northern Pomo /khál phíila/ 'carrying mussels down', containing /khál/ 'mussels' (Gudde 1998).

CALUMET \kal´ yo͞o met, kal´ yə met, kal yə met´\. The word refers to the ceremonial pipe for smoking tobacco used by Indians of the central states. Although sometimes thought to be an Indian word, it is from a dialectal French word *calumet* 'pipe', derived from Latin *calamus* 'reed'. The word occurs as a placename in several states: for example, Iowa (O'Brien Co.), Mich. (Houghton Co.), and S.Dak. (Pennington Co.).

CALUSA Keys (Fla., Monroe Co.) \kə lo͞o´ sə\. The name of an Indian group that once lived in the southeastern United States. Related names occur in **Caloosa** (Fla., Sarasota Co.) and in **Colusa** (Ill., Hancock Co.); cf. also **Colusa County** (Calif.).

CALVA (Ariz., Graham Co.) \kal´ və\. Named for a San Carlos Apache (Athabaskan) leader. The name may be short for Spanish *Calvario* 'Calvary' (Granger 1983).

CAMAJAL (Calif., San Diego Co.) \kä mä häl´\. A Spanish landgrant established in 1846; the name is from an unidentified Indian language (Gudde 1998).

CAMANCHE (Iowa, Clinton Co.) \kə man´ chē\. From the same source as **Comanche**, a people of the Numic (Uto-Aztecan) family. The name is from Ute (Numic) /kɨmánci, kɨmáci/ 'enemy, foreigner' (J. McLaughlin p.c.). As a transfer name, **Camanche** also occurs in Calif. (Calaveras and Kern Cos.).

CAMAS \kam´ əs\. A plant with an edible bulb, of genus *Camassia*, growing in the Pacific Northwest and in the adjacent Plateau; it was much used as food by the Indian peoples. The ultimate source of the name is probably Nez Perce (Sahaptian) /qém'es/ 'camas', from which it entered both English and Chinook Jargon; the latter has the form <kam´-ass> [kámas] (Hartley 2001). It is widespread as a placename, (e.g., Idaho, Jefferson Co.; Mont., Sanders Co.; and Wash., Clark Co.). A related form is **Lacamas** (Wash., Lewis Co.). **Camassia** (Ore., Clackamas Co.) takes its name from the botanical Latin name of the genus to which the camas belongs.

CAMATTA Creek (Calif., San Luis Obispo Co.) \kə mat´ ə\. From <Camate, Comate>, the name of an Indian village in the the border area between the Migueleño (Salinan) and Obispeño (Chumashan) peoples (Gudde 1998).

CAMBOLASSE Pond (Maine, Penobscot Co.). From Penobscot (Algonquian) /ékapəlálahsik/ 'that which is a small rough uneven course of water', from a root /akapəl-/ (P. MacDougall p.c.).

CAMEAHWAIT, Lake (Wyo., Fremont Co.). Named for a Shoshoni (Numic) man, the brother of Sacajawea. Possibly /kammuahwaittɨ/ 'he who misses jackrabbits when shooting at them', from /kammu/ 'jackrabbit', /ahwai/ 'to miss a target', /-(t)tɨ/ 'nominalizer' (J. McLaughlin p.c.).

CAMIACA Peak (Calif., Tuolumne Co.) \kä mē ä´ kə\. Possibly from Southern Sierra Miwok /kamya-ka/ 'from the yarrow', from /kamya/ 'yarrow' (Gudde 1998).

CAMOTE (Ariz., Pima Co.) \kə mō´ tē\. From Mexican Spanish *camote* 'sweet potato', from Nahuatl (Aztecan) *camohtli.*

CAMPAMANCHE (Colo., Prowers Co.) \kam pə man´ chē\. The site of **Amache Relocation Center**, where Japanese Americans were interned during World War II, is said to be named for **Amache**, the daughter of Ochinee or Lone Wolf, a Cheyenne (Algonquian) leader (Bright 1993). Also written as **Camp Amache.**

CAMPGAW (N.J., Bergen Co.) \kamp´ gô\. From a Delaware (Algonquian) word of unclear derivation (Becker 1964).

CAMPTI (La., Natchitoches Par.) \kamp´ tī\. This name, also written <Compti>, may to a leader of the Natchitoches band of the Caddo people (Read 1927).

CAMULOS (Calif., Ventura Co.) \kə myōō´ ləs\. From Ventureño (Chumashan) /kamulus/ 'the juniper' (Gudde 1998).

CANACADEA Creek (N.Y., Allegany Co.) \kan ə kə dē´ ə\. Perhaps Iroquoian, of unknown derivation (Beauchamp 1907).

CANACHAGALA Brook (N.Y., Herkimer Co.) \kan ə chə gā´ lə\. Said to be Iroquoian, meaning 'one-sided kettle' (Beauchamp 1907).

CANADA \kan´ ə də\. This name was taken from French, which took it in turn from a word meaning 'settlement, town' in Laurentian, the Iroquoian language first encountered by Jacques Cartier on the St. Lawrence River in 1534. That language is no longer spoken, but most present-day Iroquoian languages have a similar word: for example, Mohawk *kaná:ta'* 'town' (M. Mithun p.c.). The word has been applied as a placename in several parts of the United States, including N.Y. (Fulton Co.), Maine (Cumberland Co.), and Wis. (Buffalo Co.).

CANADARAGO Lake (N.Y., Otsego Co.). Mohawk (Iroquoian) *kanyatarâ:ke,* from *kanyá:tare'* 'lake', from the root *-nyatar-* 'lake' (Lounsbury 1960:51).

CANADAWAY Creek (N.Y., Chautauqua Co.) \kan ə dou´ ē\. The Iroquoian name has been written <Kanandaweron> and <Ka-na-da-wa-o> (Beauchamp 1907). A modern recording is *kanę̨́tawęǫ'*, perhaps containing *-nę̨'t(a)-* 'hemlock' (Morrison 1983).

CANADIAN \kə nā´ dē ən\. This term is widespread as a U.S. placename and in many cases may commemorate Canadian explorers and trappers; an example is the more northern of the two streams called the **Canadian River** in Colo. (Jackson Co.). The name of the **Canadian River** of southern Colo., northern Tex., and Okla., however, is probably from Spanish *Río Canadiano*, a popular etymology from Caddo /káyántinu'/, used by the Indians to refer not the Canadian River but to the nearby Red River (D. Rood p.c.).

CANADICE (N.Y., Ontario Co.) \kan´ ə dīs\. The Iroquoian name has been written <Ska-ne-a-di-ce>, <Conyeadice>, and <Aionyedice>; it is said to mean 'long narrow lake' (Beauchamp 1907). Cf. **Skaneateles** (N.Y., Cayuga Co.), from Oneida *skanyátales* 'long lake' (M. Mithun p.c.).

CANADOHTA, Lake (Pa., Crawford Co.) \kan ə dō´ tə\. Perhaps an Iroquoian name, of unclear derivation (Beauchamp 1907).

CANAGERE (N.Y., Montgomery Co.). The Iroquoian name has been written <Gandagiro, Gandagora, Canagora>; it is perhaps derived from <Ganniagwari> 'grand bear' (Ruttenber 1906) or from <Gannagare> 'great pole' (Beauchamp 1907). Cf. Mohawk *ohkwa:ri* 'a bear', *kaná:kare* 'a stick' (Michelson 1973).

CANAJOHARIE (N.Y., Montgomery Co.) \kan ə jō hâr´ ē\. The name has been written <Ga-na-jo-hi´-e>, perhaps from Mohawk (Iroquoian) <gannatsiohare> 'to wash the kettle' (Beauchamp 1907). The present-day Mohawk form would be *kana'tsióhare'* 'washed kettle' (M. Mithun p.c.).

CANALASKA Mountain (Alaska, Coleen B-1) \kan ə las´ kə\. From the combination of **Canada** and **Alaska**, both words of Indian origin (Orth 1967).

CANANDAIGUA (N.Y., Ontario Co.) \kan ən dā´ gwə\. The Seneca (Iroquoian) name has been written as <Ga´-nun-da-gwa> 'place selected for a settlement' (Beauchamp 1907). A modern transcription is *tganǫdæ:gwęh* 'at the chosen town' (W. Chafe p.c.). There is also a **Canandaigua** in Mich. (Lenawee Co.).

CANAPITSIT Channel (Mass., Dukes Co.) \kan ə pit´ sit\. From SNEng. Algonquian, 'at the long trap', containing <qunni> 'long', <appeh> 'trap', <-et> 'place' (W. Cowan p.c.).

CANARSIE (N.Y., Kings Co.) \kə när´ sē\. The Munsee Delaware (Algonquian) name has been variously translated as 'long small grasses' (Ruttenber 1906) and 'fenced place' (Tooker 1911; cf. Grumet 1981).

CANASAWACTA Creek (N.Y., Chenango Co.) \kan ə sə wäk´ tə\. The Iroquoian name is also written <Canasaweta>; it is of unknown derivation (Beauchamp 1907).

CANASERAGA (N.Y., Allegany Co.) \kan ə sə rô´ gə\. The Iroquoian name has also been written as <Ga-nus´-ga-go>, perhaps meaning 'among the milkweeds' (Beauchamp 1907); cf. Seneca *onǫ:skę'* 'milkweed' (Chafe 1967). Another place in N.Y. state called **Canaseraga Creek** (Madison Co.), also written <Ka-na´-so-wa´-ga, Canassaderaga>, may have a different derivation, with the translation 'several strings of beads with a string lying across' (Beauchamp 1907).

CANASTOTA (N.Y., Madison Co.) \kan ə stō´ tə\. Onondaga (Iroquoian) *ganasdooda'* 'standing or protruding post or stake', from *ga-* 'it', *-nasd-* 'stake, post, rafter', *-od-* 'stand upright, protrude', *-a'* 'stative aspect' (H. Woodbury p.c.).

CANAWAUGUS (N.Y., Livingston Co.) \kan ə wô´ gəs\. From Seneca (Iroquoian) *ga:nǫwǫgęs* 'smelly rapids' (W. Chafe p.c.).

CANCHARDEE (Ala., Talladega Co.) \kan chär´ dē\. A traditional Creek (Muskogean) tribal town (Read 1984), from *kvnchate* /kancá:ti/ 'red earth', from *ēkvnv* /i:kaná/ 'earth', *catē* /čá:ti:/ 'red' (Martin and Mauldin 2000). The related form **Concharty** occurs in Okla. (Wagoner Co.).

CANDUTCHKEE Creek (Ala., Tallapoosa Co.) \kan duch´ kē\. Creek (Muskogean) *ēkvntvchkv* /(i:)kantácka/ 'division of land'; cf. *ēkvnv* /i:kaná/ 'land, earth', *tvckē* /táčki:/ 'to cut' (Martin and Mauldin 2000). A related form is **Econtuchka** (Okla., Pottawatomie Co.).

CANEMAH (Ore., Clackamas Co.) \kä nē´ mə\. Said to have been the name of an Indian leader, language unidentified (McArthur 1992).

CANESTO Brook (Mass., Worcester Co.) \kə nes´ tō\. From SNEng. Algonquian, probably 'place where there are pickerel', from <qunosu> 'pickerel', lit. 'he is long' (W. Cowan).

CANIADERIGUARUNTE (N.Y., Essex Co.) Mohawk (Iroquoian) *kaniatarakwá:ronte'* 'Lake Champlain', lit. 'the lake/river has a bulge in it' or 'bulge in the lake/river'. The root *-niatar-* refers to a lake, river, or any large body of water, but not a creek (Lounsbury 1960; M. Mithun p.c.).

CANISTEO (N.Y., Steuben Co.) \kə nis´ tē ō, kan is tē´ ō\. Possibly from Seneca (Iroquoian) *gane:sdyo'* 'board in the water' (W. Chafe p.c.); cf. *gane:sdę'* 'board' (Chafe 1967). There is also a **Canisteo Township** in Minn. (Dodge Co.).

CANIVUS Banks (Alaska, Tyonek D-3). The Dena'ina (Athabaskan) name is perhaps *tsani bes* 'cliff bank' (J. Kari p.c.).

CANNISNIA Lake (La., Caddo Par.). Recorded in 1806 as <Canasenihan>, the name may refer to the Lipan Apaches (Athabaskan), who lived northwest of the present state of La. (Read 1927).

CANNON Falls (Minn., Goodhue Co.) \kan´ ən\. A garbling of the name that was published in 1832 as <Cano>, and in 1855 as <Chemaun> or <Ocano>. In fact the form <Canot> represents French *canot* 'canoe'; <Ocanot> represents French *aux canots* 'of the canoes'. These correspond to the Ojibwa (Algonquian) word for 'canoe' (Upham 2001), which is *jiimaan* 'canoe' (Nichols and Nyholm 1995). Both English *canoe* and French *canot* are from Spanish *canoa,* a borrowing from the Taino (Arawakan) language of the Caribbean area.

CANOA Ranch (Ariz., Pima Co.) \kə nō´ ə\. From Spanish *canoa,* which can mean either 'canoe' or 'trough' (Granger 1983). The Spanish word is borrowed from an Arawakan language of the Caribbean area. **Canoas Creek** (Calif., Fresno Co.) \kə nō´ əs\. represents the Spanish plural form.

CANOBIE Lake (N.H., Rockingham Co.). Said to be Abenaki (Algonquian) for 'abundant water' (Huden 1962).

CANOE \kə no͞o´\. The word for a portable boat, like those made by Native Americans, was borrowed from French *canot,* from Spanish *canoa,* from the Taino (Arawakan) language of the Caribbean. It is widespread in placenames (e.g., Ill., Rock Island Co.; Mich., Chippewa Co.; and N.Y., Ulster Co.).

CANOGA (N.Y., Seneca Co.) \kə nō´ gə\. Perhaps from Seneca (Iroquoian) *ga:nó'geh* 'place of oil in the water' (W. Chafe p.c.). The name also occurs in **Canoga Park** (Calif., Los Angeles Co.). Another spelling is found in **Ganoga Lake** (Pa., Luzerne Co.).

CANONCHET (R.I., Washington Co.) Named for a seventeenth-century SNEng. Algonquian leader (Huden 1962).

CANOOCHEE (Ga., Emanuel Co.) \kə no͞o´ chē\. Perhaps from Creek (Muskogean) meaning 'little ground' (Goff 1975; Krakow 1975); cf. Creek *ēkvnv* /i:kaná/ 'earth, ground', *-ocē* /-učí/ 'little' (Martin and Mauldin 2000).

CANOPUS Hill (N.Y., Putnam Co.) \kə nō´ pəs\. Said to be named after an Indian leader, language not identified (Beauchamp 1907). Perhaps a popular etymology on the basis of *Canopus* (from Greek), the name of a star.

CANOSIA Township (Minn., St. Louis Co.) \kə nō´ shə\. From an Ojibwa (Algonquian) word for 'pike (a fish)'; the form is *ginoozhe* (Nichols and Nyholm 1995). Related placenames include **Kenosha** (Wis., Kenosha Co.) and **Kenoza Lake** (Mass., Essex Co.).

CANTIAGUE (N.Y., Nassau Co.). An earlier spelling is <Cantiaque>. The SNEng. Algonquian name perhaps means 'where trees are being blazed' (Tooker 1911).

CANYON DE CHELLY. See **DeChelly, Canyon.**

CAPAC (Mich., St. Clair Co.) \kā´ pak\. Supposedly named for Manco Capac, the legendary founder of the Inca dynasty in Peru; the name is from the Quechua language (Vogel 1986).

CAPAHA Village (Mo., New Madrid Co.) \kap´ ə hä\. From the same source as **Quapaw**, the name of a Siouan people (Ramsay 1952).

CAPAHOSIC (Va., Gloucester Co.) \kap ə hō´ sik\. The name of a tribal group of the CAC Algonquian people (Hagemann 1988); also written as **Cappahosic** and as **Capahowasic.**

CAPALOA Creek (Alaska, Point Hope C-3) \kap ə lō´ ə\. The Iñupiaq (Eskimo) name was reported in 1906 (Orth 1967); the variants **Kapaloak** and **Kapalowa** also occur.

CAPAUM Pond (Mass., Nantucket Co.). Earlier written <Cuppammet>, <Cuppame> (Little 1984). SNEng. Algonquian <koppomuk> 'harbor' (W. Cowan p.c.).

CAPAY (Calif., Yolo Co.) \kə pā´\ From a Patwin (Wintuan) word for 'stream' (Gudde 1998).

CAPELL Creek (Calif., Humboldt Co.) \kə pel´\. The name, also spelled **Cappell,** is derived from that of the Yurok village *kep'el* (Gudde 1998).

CAPE NEWAGEN (Maine, Lincoln Co.). The name does not originally refer to a cape but is modified from <Capanewagen>, an Abenaki (Algonquian) term, perhaps meaning 'interrupted route' (Eckstorm 1941:123–24); cf. *gebem* 'it is closed', *gebinigen* 'it is shut; a dam' (Day 1994–95). The shortened form **Newagen** also occurs.

CAPE POGE Bay (Mass., Dukes Co.) \kāp pōg\. The name does not originally refer to a cape but is modified from **Capoag;** cf. SNEng. Algonquian <koppomuk> 'harbor' (W. Cowan p.c.).

CAPISIC Pond (Maine, Cumberland Co.). Perhaps from Abenaki (Algonquian), meaning 'dammed-up stream' (Huden 1962); cf. /kəp-/ 'to close up, to shut' (P. MacDougall p.c.).

CAPOUSE Reservoir (Pa., Lackawanna Co.). Said to be named for a Munsee Delaware (Algonquian) leader (Donehoo 1928).

CAPSHAW (Ala., Limestone Co.) \kap´ shô\. Perhaps Chickasaw (Muskogean) *oka' kapassa'* 'cold water', from *oka'* 'water', *kapassa* 'cold' (P. Munro p.c.).

CAPULIN (Colo., Conejos Co) \kap yōō lēn\. Mexican Spanish *capulín* 'wild cherry', from Nahuatl (Aztecan) *capolin* (Gudde 1998). The name also occurs in N.Mex. (Rio Arriba Co.).

CARATUNK Lake (Maine, Somerset Co.) \kâr´ ə tungk\. From Abenaki (Algonquian) /kálətak^y/ 'hidden stream' (P. MacDougall p.c.).

CARAWAY Creek (N.C., Randolph Co.) \kâr´ ə wā\. Said to be adapted from <Keyauwee>, the name of an Indian group (Powell 1968).

CARCAJOU (Wis., Jefferson Co.) \kär kə zhōō´, kär kə jōō\. From Canadian French *carcajou* 'wolverine', from Montagnais (Algonquian) /kwi:hkwaha:če:w/ (*RHD* 1987). As a placename, the term also occurs in Mont. (Glacier Co.).

CARIBOO (Kans., Butler Co.) \kâr´ i bōō\. From the same source as **Caribou,** an animal similar to the reindeer. The writing with <-boo> reflects the spelling used for the **Cariboo** Mountains in British Columbia, Canada, the scene of a gold rush in the 1860s (Rayburn 1997).

CARIBOU \kâr´ i bōō\. Canadian French *caribou,* an animal similar to the reindeer, from the Micmac (Algonquian) language of the Canadian maritime provinces. The Micmac form of the name is *ĝalipu,* lit. 'snow-shoveler', because the animal paws the snow to find food (*RHD* 1987; DeBlois 1996). The term is widespread as a placename (e.g., Maine, Aroostook Co.; Idaho, Caribou Co.; and Mich., Chippewa Co.); there is even a **Caribou Creek** in the Mojave Desert (Calif., San Bernardino Co.). Related placenames are **Magalloway River** (Maine, Oxford Co.) and **Magurrewock Lakes** (Maine, Washington Co.).

CARIMONA Township (Minn., Fillmore Co.) \kâr i mō´ nə\. Named for a nineteenth-century leader of the Ho-Chunk (Winnebago, Siouan) people, whose name is also recorded as <Car-a-mau-nee>; the Native American name was *kéeramąnį́* 'walking turtle', from *kéé* 'turtle', *ra* 'definitizer', *mąąnį́* 'walk' (Upham 2001, K. Miner p.c.).

CARNE HUMANA (Calif., Napa Co.) \kär´ nā ōō mä´ nä\. Spanish for 'human flesh', the name of an 1841 land grant, is a popular etymology from an Indian name (language not identified) that was written as <Huilic Noma, Caligolman, Colijolmanoc> (Gudde 1998).

CARNUEL (N.Mex., Bernalillo Co.) \kärn wel\. A Spanish spelling for a Tiwa (Tanoan) village name, <Carna-aye>, said to mean 'badger place' (Julyan 1998).

CARONDOWANNA, Camp (Pa., Beaver Co.). The name refers to the Iroquoian group more often called the **Susquehannock;** the name also appears in French spelling as <Carantouan>, adjectival <Carontouannais> (Donehoo 1928). The Iroquoian name appears to mean 'big, grassy flat', as in Mohawk *skahętó:wanę* 'great field' (HNAI 15:362); cf. Mohawk *kahéhta* 'field' (Michelson 1973).

CARQUINEZ (Calif., Solano and Contra Costa Cos.) \kär kē´ nəs\. This is originally a Spanish plural, *Carquines,* of a tribal name, *Carquín* (Karquin, Karkin), based on a Costanoan word meaning 'barter'. The current spelling **Carquinez** imitates Spanish family names like *Martínez* (Gudde 1998).

CARRABASSETT (Maine, Franklin Co.) \kâr ə bas´ ət\. From Abenaki (Algonquian), of unclear derivation (Huden 1962).

CARTECAY Mountain (Ga., Gilmer Co.) \kär´ tə kā\. Said to be from Cherokee (Iroquoian), meaning 'bread valley' (Krakow 1975); cf. Cherokee *gadu* 'bread' (Feeling 1975).

CARTOOGECHAYE Creek (N.C., Macon Co.). Said to be Cherokee (Iroquoian) for 'corn fields' (Powell 1968).

CASADEPAGA (Alaska, Solomon D-5) \kas ə dē pä´ gə\. The name resembles Spanish *casa de paga* 'house of payment', but it represents Iñupiaq (Eskimo) *qaqsuqtam paaga* 'mouth of the Qaqsuqtaq River'; the etymology of the river name is not known (L. Kaplan p.c.).

CASCO (Maine, Cumberland Co) \kas´ kō\. Perhaps from Abenaki (Algonquian) *gasko* 'heron' (Day 1994–95). The word is found elsewhere as a transfer name (e.g., Mich., St. Clair Co.; Wis., Kewaunee Co.).

CASHIE River (N.C., Bertie Co.) \kash´ ē\. Said to be from Tuscarora (Iroquoian) *kę̨yhę̨heh* 'river' (B. Rudes p.c.).

CASHKA Lake (Alaska, Kenai C-3). From Dena'ina (Athabaskan) *geshga bena* 'rich-man lake' (J. Kari p.c.).

CASLAMAYOMI (Calif., Sonoma Co.) \käs lä mä yō´ mē\. A land grant of this name was recorded in 1844. The element *yomi* means 'place' in Lake Miwok and Bodega Miwok (Gudde 1998).

CASMALIA (Calif., Santa Barbara Co.) \kaz māl´ yə\. The name, from Purisimeño (Chumashan) /kasma'li/ 'it is the last', appeared in 1837 (Gudde 1998).

CASSADAGA (N.Y., Chautauqua Co.) \kas ə dä´ gə, kas ə dā´ gə\. Possibly from Seneca (Iroquoian) *gasháda'geh* 'in the mist' (W. Chafe p.c.); cf. *osha:ta'* 'steam, mist, cloud' (Chafe 1967). There is also a **Cassadaga** in Fla. (Volusia Co.).

CASSADORE Mountain (Ariz., Gila Co.) \kas´ ə dôr\. Named after a nineteenth-century Apache (Athabaskan) leader (Granger 1983). The term may be from Spanish *cazador* 'hunter', from *cazar* 'to hunt'.

CASTAFFA Creek (Miss., Jasper Co.) \kas taf´ ə\. Perhaps related to Choctaw (Muskogean) *kashofa* 'to be clean', *kashoffi* 'to clean' (P. Munro p.c.).

CASTAIC (Calif., Los Angeles Co.) \kas tāk´\. From Ventureño (Chumashan) /kaštɨq/ 'the eye, the face' (Gudde 1998). A related form is **Castac Lake** (Calif., Kern Co.).

CASTINE Bayou (La., St. Tammany Par.) \kas´ tēn\. Choctaw (Muskogean) *kashti įbayok* 'river of fleas', from *kashti* 'flea', *bayuk, book* 'river' (Read 1927; P. Munro p.c.).

CASTLE Hill (N.Y., Bronx Co.). The term *castle* was applied to Indian fortifications by Europeans who arrived in the Hudson River valley in early days (Grumet 1981).

CASWAY (Wash., Kittitas Co.) \kas´ wā\. The term is said to be a combination of *Cascade* and **Teanaway**, Sahaptin for 'drying place' (Hitchman 1985, D. Kinkade p.c.).

CATACOONAMUG Brook (Mass., Middlesex Co.). SNEng. Algonquian <(nquitte-)connauog> 'eels' (W. Cowan p.c.).

CATACULA (Calif., Napa Co.) \kä tä ko͞o´ lä\. This land grant, dated 1844, has a name said to be from Patwin (Wintuan) (Gudde 1998).

CATAHOULA Bay (La., St. Martin Par.) \kat ə ho͞o´ lə\. Probably represents a Choctaw (Muskogean) term meaning 'sacred lake', from *okhata* 'lake, ocean' and *hollo* 'sacred' (Read 1927; P. Munro p.c.). The name also occurs in Mississippi (Hancock Co.).

CATALE (Okla., Rogers Co.). Said to be Cherokee (Iroquian) for 'in the valley' (Shirk 1974).

CATALOOCHEE (N.C., Haywood Co.) \kat ə lo͞o´ chē\. From Cherokee *gaadaluugi'a* 'he is plowing it' (B. Rudes p.c.). The name also occurs in Ga. (Haywood Co.).

CATALPA \kə tal´ pə\. This name for a flowering tree is probably from Creek (Muskogean) *kvtvrpv* /katáɬpa/, lit. 'head-wing'; cf. *eka* /iká/ 'head', *tvrpv* /(i)táɬpa/ 'wing'. It has sometimes been confused with **Catawba**, the term for a Siouan group and language in the southeastern United States; see below. **Catalpa** is widely used as a placename, especially in the southeastern states (Ala., Pike Co.; Ark., Johnson Co.; Neb., Holt Co.).

CATAOUATCHE, Lake (La., St. Charles Par.) \kat ə wô´ chē\. Also written as <Cataouache>, this may be a combination of two names: **Catahoula Bay,** from Choctaw (Muskogean) 'sacred lake', and **Lake Ouache.** The latter term, no longer in use, may have been the name of a local Indian group (Read 1927; P. Munro p.c.).

CATASAUQUA (Pa., Lehigh Co.) \kat ə sä´ kwə\. Said to be from Delaware (Algonquian) <Gattoshacki> 'thirsty earth' (Donehoo 1928); cf. Delaware <gattosomuin> 'to be thirsty', <haki> 'earth, ground'. Compare also Munsee Delaware *katóosŭmuw* 'to be thirsty', *áhkuy* 'land, earth' (O'Meara 1996); Unami Delaware /ka:tu:səmwi:-/ 'to be thirsty' (Blalock et al. 1994).

CATATOGA Estates (Ala., St. Clair Co.) \kat ə tō´ gə\. Said to be Cherokee (Iroquoian) for 'new settlement place' (Krakow 1975).

CATAULA (Ga., Harris Co.) \kə tô´ lə\. Said to be from Creek (Muskogean) *kētali* /ki:táli:/ 'withered mulberry', from *kē* /ki:/ 'mulberry', *tvlē* /talí:/ 'withered' (Goff 1975; Martin and Mauldin 2000). A related placename is **Mulberry Creek** (Ga., Harris Co.).

CATAUMET (Mass., Barnstable Co.) \kə tô´ mət\. From SNEng. Algonquian 'by the sea', from <kettahhann-> 'sea', <-it> 'place' (W. Cowan p.c.).

CATAWBA \kə tô´ bə\. This name of an Indian group and language of the southeastern United States, of the Siouan linguistic family, is derived from their word *katapu* 'fork of a stream', which is itself a borrowing from a Muskogean language, where the word means 'separate' (B. Rudes p.c.). The term has sometimes been confused with **Catalpa,** the name of a tree, also used as a placename; see above. As a placename, **Catawba** occurs in **Catawba County** (N.C.) and in several other states (e.g. Fla., Citrus Co.; N.J., Atlantic Co.; and Ohio, Clark Co.).

CATAWISSA (Pa., Columbia Co.) \kat ə wis´ ə\. Probably an Algonquian name, perhaps from <gatawisi> 'growing fat'; or perhaps, in the form <Ganawese>, a term referring to the Conoy, a little-known Algonquian group of the area (Donehoo 1928; *HNAI* 15:249). Cf. Unami Delaware (Algonquian) /wi:si:-/ 'to be fat' (Blalock et al. 1994), Munsee Delaware *wíisuw* 'to be fat' (O'Meara 1996).

CATEECHEE (S.C., Pickens Co.) \kə tē´ chē\. The name was originally given to a fictitious Cherokee (Iroquoian) woman in a story written by James Henry Rice in the 1890s; the name was further popularized in 1898, in a poetic treatment by James Walter Daniel (Pearson 1978; Neuffer and Neuffer 1983).

CATHANCE (Maine, Sagadahoc Co.) \kat´ hans\. Said to from Abenaki (Algonquian) <keght-nik> 'the principal fork (of a river)' (Eckstorm 1941:140, 225).

CATHERINE Creek (N.C., Hertford Co.). A popular etymology from a term previously written <Cautaking, Catokinge, Cataking>; from Tuscarora (Iroquoian) *kataakrę'* 'tribe' (B. Rudes p.c.).

CATHLAMET Bay (Ore., Clatsop Co.) \kath lam´ ət\. From Kathlamet Chinook *gaɬámat,* the people of the village at Cathlamet Head (D. Kinkade p.c.). There is also a Cathlamet in Wash. state (Wahkiakum Co.).

CATOCTIN Creek (Md., Frederick Co.) \kə tok´ tin\. The CAC Algonquian name perhaps means 'speckled mountain' (Kenny 1984). The name is also found in Va. (Loudoun Co.).

CATOMA (Ala., Montgomery Co.) \kə tō´ mə\. Perhaps from Alabama (Muskogean) *oki* 'water' and <Tohome>, the name of a Muskogean subgroup (Read 1984).

CATOOSA County (Ga.) \kə to͞o´ sə\. From Cherokee (Iroquoian) *gadusi* 'hill' (Krakow 1975; Alexander 1971). There is also a **Catoosa** in Okla. (Rogers Co.).

CATTARAUGUS County (N.Y.) \kat ə rô´ gəs\. Clearly from a Northern Iroquoian word meaning 'smelly clay', referring to the banks of **Cattaraugus Creek**. The word looks intriguingly like an earlier form of Seneca, reconstructable as **ka'daragęs,* before the loss of *r* from that language. The corresponding word in current Seneca is *ga'dæ:gęs* 'smelly clay'. The **Cattaraugus Seneca Reservation** is called in Seneca *ga'dæ:gę́sgę:ǫ?,* with a suffix meaning 'formerly'. There may have been a village on **Cattaraugus Creek** called *ga'dæ:gęs* that the Senecas who were moved to that area from the Buffalo Creek Reservation later referred to as *ga'dæ:gę́sgę:ǫ'* 'where *ga'dæ:gęs* used to be' (W. Chafe p.c.).

CATUMB Rocks (R.I., Washington Co.). Probably from SNEng. Algonquian <keht-> 'big' plus <-ompsk> 'rock' (W. Cowan p.c.).

CAUCOMGOMOC Lake (Maine, Piscataquis Co.) \kok´ mə gom ik\. From Penobscot (Algonquian) /káhk^{y}ɑkamok/ 'at gull lake' (P. MacDougall p.c.).

CAUGHDENOY (N.Y., Oswego Co.) \kô´ də noi\. Probably an Iroquoian name; it has been written <Quaquendena> and <T'kah-koon-goon-da-nah´-yea> and translated as 'where the eel is lying down' (Beauchamp 1907).

CAUGHNAWAGA (N.Y., Montgomery Co.) \kô nə wä´ gə\. Mohawk (Iroquoian) *kahnawà:ke* 'place of the rapids', originally referring to the rapids of the Mohawk River in N.Y. state. When the Mohawks moved to Canada, they took the village name with them, and it now applies to a community across the St. Lawrence River from Montreal—where, however, there are no rapids (M. Mithun p.c.). Cf. also Mohawk *ohna:wa* 'rapids' (G. Michelson 1973).

CAUMSETT State Park (N.Y., Suffolk Co.) \kum´ sət\. Perhaps from SNEng. Algonquian <ketumpset> 'near the sharp rock' (Tooker 1911).

CAYADUTTA Creek (N.Y., Fulton Co.) \kā ə dut´ ə\. The Iroquoian name, which has also been written as <Caniadutta>, may mean 'standing stone' (Ruttenber 1906; Beauchamp 1907); cf. Mohawk *oně:ya* 'stone' (Michelson 1973).

CAYENNE (Mass., Hampden Co.) \kā yen´\. The name perhaps refers to *cayenne* pepper, the name of which comes from *kyinha* in the Tupí Indian language of South America. There is also a long association with *Cayenne*, the capital of French Guiana (*RHD* 1987), however. This word has the same origin as the name *Guiana* or *Guyana,* also derived from a South American Indian language (Room 1997).

CAYMUS (Calif., Napa Co.) \kī´ mo͞os\. The landgrant of 1836 was named after an Indian village, language not identified (Gudde 1998).

CAYOTE (Tex., Bosque Co.) \kā´ ōt\. From the same source as *coyote (*the animal), from Mexican Spanish *coyote,* from Nahuatl (Aztecan) *coyotl.* The word is written **Coyote** in a large number of other placenames.

CAYUCOS (Calif., San Luis Obispo Co.) \kī yo͞o´ kəs\. Spanish *cayucos,* plural of *cayuco* 'small boat, kayak', borrowed from Inuit (Eskimo) *kayaq* (Gudde 1998).

CAYUGA County (N.Y.) \kā yo͞o´ gə, kī yo͞o´ gə\. From the Cayuga (Iroquoian) name for their own group, *kayohkhó:nǫ'* or less commonly *kayokhwęhó:nǫ',* of unclear derivation (*HNAI* 15:503). The term occurs as a transfer name elsewhere (Ill., Livingston Co.; Okla., Delaware Co.; Wis., Ashland Co.) In Tex. (Anderson Co.), the pronunciation \kā yo͝og´ ə\. is reported. A possibly related name is **Keuka** (N.Y., Steuben Co.; Fla., Putnam Co.).

CAYUSE \kä´ yo͞os, kä yo͞os´\. This name for an Indian group and language is of unclear origin

(*RHD* 1987). It has also been applied to a type of Indian pony. When the term is used as a placename, it is often unclear whether it refers to the people or the horse (Idaho, Clearwater Co.; Ore., Umatilla Co., Wash., Okanogan Co.).

CEBALOP (Wash., Pierce Co.) \sə bä´ ləp\. From Lushootseed (Salishan) \šəbáləp\ 'dry tree trunk', containing /šáb(a)-/ 'dry' and /-ap/ 'bottom, base' (D. Kinkade p.c.).

CEBOLLETA (N.Mex., Cibola Co.) \seb ō yet´ ə\. Spanish for 'wild onion', a diminutive of *cebolla* 'onion'. The name corresponds to Navajo (Athabaskan) *tł'ohchin* 'onion', from *tł'oh* 'grass' (Wilson 1995); cf. *halchin* 'to have an odor' (Young and Morgan 1987). The spelling **Seboyeta** is also used. **Cebolletita** (N.Mex., Cibola Co.) means 'little wild-onion', so named because it was settled by people from Cebolleta (Julyan 1998).

CEDAR County (Iowa). Meskwaki (Algonquian) /meškwa:wa:hkwi-si:po:wi/ 'Cedar River', from /meškwa:wa:hkwa/ 'red cedar tree', containing /meškwa:wi/ 'red' (/meškwi/ 'blood'; I. Goddard p.c.). A related term is /meškwahki:ha/, the name of the Meskwaki people. **Cedar Creek** (Ind., Allen Co.) has a similar origin, from Potawatomi (Algonquian) /mskwawazibə/, lit. 'cedar creek' (McCafferty 2002). Elsewhere in Ind. (Lake Co.) **Cedar Lake** corresponds to Potawatomi /mskwawak nbəs/, lit. 'cedar lake' (McCafferty 2000). See also the related term **Meskwaki.**

CEE CEE AH Creek (Wash., Pend Oreille Co.) \sē sē ä´\. From Kalispel (Salishan) /ciciá/, a man's name (D. Kinkade p.c.). The placename is also written as **C.C.A. Creek.**

CELILO, Lake (Ore., Wasco Co.; Wash., Klickitat Co.) \sə lī´ lō\. From Wishram (Chinookan) \sílailo:\, the name of a Wayam Sahaptin village (D. Kinkade p.c.).

CELO (N.C., Yancey Co.) \sē´ lō\. From Cherokee (Iroquoian) *seelu* 'corn' (B. Rudes p.c.).

CEMETERY Hill (Ore., Polk Co.). Said to have been named because of an Indian burial ground in the area (McArthur 1992).

CEMOCHECHOBEE Creek (Ga., Clay Co.) \sə mō chō´ bē\. From Hitchiti (Muskogean) *samo:či-čo:bi*, lit. 'sand-big' (Read 1949–50, J. Martin p.c.).

CENCHAT (Ga., Walker Co.) \sen´ chat\. A combination of the names of two railroads, the Central of Georgia and the Chattanooga Southern (Goff 1975). See **Chattanooga**.

CENTEOTL, Point (Ariz., Coconino Co.) \sen tā´ ō təl\. **Centeotl** is the name of the goddess of corn in Aztec mythology.

CENTIMUDI Bay (Calif., Shasta Co.) \sen tē mo͞o´ dē\. Perhaps from Wintu *kenti* 'down, inside' plus *mute* 'hear, listen' (Gudde 1998).

CENTRAHOMA (Okla., Coal Co.) \sen trə hō´ mə\. Coined from the phrase "central Oklahoma" (Shirk 1974). The name **Oklahoma** itself was coined from Choctaw (Muskogean), meaning 'red people'.

CENTRALHATCHEE (Ga., Heard Co.) \sen trəl hach´ ē\. A folk etymology from earlier **Sundalhatchee,** from the Muskogee, for 'perch stream', from *svntalakwv* /santa:lákwa/ 'perch (fish)', *hvcce* /hácci/ 'stream' (Read 1949–50; Martin and Mauldin 2000).

CERBAT (Ariz., Mohave Co.) \sûr´ bat\. Perhaps from the Maricopa (Yuman) word for 'bighorn sheep, mountain sheep' (Granger 1983); the form is *svaat* [səva:t] (L. Gordon p.c.). This and a number of other words for 'mountain sheep' in southwestern Indian languages are borrowed from Spanish *chivato* 'he-goat', from *chivo* 'kid, young goat' (Bright 2000a).

CETAHOMA Landing (Ala., Marengo Co.) \sē tə hō´ mə\. Possibly Choctaw (Muskogean) for 'red snake', from *sįti* 'snake', *homma* 'red' (P. Munro p.c.).

CETEAHLUSTEE Creek (Ala., Chambers Co.) \sē tə lus´ tē\. Perhaps Muskogee for 'black persimmon' (Read 1984); the form would be *svtv-lvste* /sata-lásti/, from *svtv* /satá/ persimmon, *lvste* /lásti/ 'black' (Martin and Mauldin 2000).

CHACALOOCHEE Bay (Ala., Baldwin Co.) \chä kə lo͞o´ chē\. Choctaw (Muskogean) for 'little cypress' (Read 1984), from *shąkolo* 'cypress', *-oshi* 'little' (P. Munro p.c.).

CHA-CHOO-SEN (Wash., Whatcom Co.). This island has a Lummi (Salishan) name, said to mean 'low swampy island' (Hitchman 1985).

CHACO Canyon (N.Mex., San Juan Co.) \chä´ kō\. Navajo (Athabaskan) *tsékooh* 'rock canyon', from *tsé* 'rock', *kooh* 'canyon' (Julyan 1998; A. Wilson p.c.).

CHA Creek (Utah, San Juan Co.) \chä\. From Navajo (Athabaskan) *chaa'* 'beaver' (Linford 2000).

CHACUACO Creek (Colo., Las Animas Co.) \chə kwä´ kō\. From New Mexican Spanish, meaning 'elderberry'; perhaps from a Native American source.

CHAFFIE Creek (Ark., Ouachita Co.) \chaf´ ē\. Named for a nineteenth-century Choctaw (Muskogean) leader called *cheffo* 'runner' (Dickinson 1995). A spelling variant is **Cheffie Creek.**

CHAGAK Cape (Alaska, Umnak C-1). From the Aleut placename *chaxax, chagax*; cf. *chagax̂* 'obsidian' (Bergsland 1994).

CHAGEE (S.C., Oconee Co.). Also written <Chagu>; cf. Cherokee (Iroquoian) *dlayhga* (Pickens 1961–62:4–5, Feeling 1975). A probably related placename is the nearby **Chauga River**; see below.

CHAGOOPA (Calif., Tulare Co.) \chə go͞o´ pə\. Said to be the name of a Mono (Numic) leader (Gudde 1998).

CHAGULAK Island (Alaska, Amukta C-4). From the Aleut placename *chugaaĝinax̂*, perhaps meaning 'lying north'; cf. *chug-* 'north' (Bergsland 1994).

CHAGVAN Bay (Alaska, Hagemeister Island D-6). The Yupik (Eskimo) name was published in 1826 (Orth 1967).

CHAHALIE Lake (Alaska, Black River C-6). From Gwich'in (Athabaskan), of unclear derivation (Orth 1967).

CHAHINKAPA Park (N.Dak., Richland Co.) \chə hingk´ pä pä\. Said to be Dakota (Siouan) for 'end of the woods' (Wick 1988). The Native American term is probably *čhą-įkpa*, from *čhą* 'wood' plus *įkpa* 'end' (Riggs 1890).

CHAHOVUN Lakes (Alaska, Fort Yukon D-5). The Gwich'in (Athabaskan) name is *ch'aghoo van* 'egg lake(s)' (J. Kari p.c.).

CHAIK Bay (Alaska, Sitka B-2). The Tlingit name was published as <Cha-ik> in 1896 (Orth 1967).

CHAKACHAMNA Lake (Alaska, Tyonek A-7) \chak ə cham´ nə, chä kə chäm´ nə\. Dena'ina (Athabaskan) *ch'akaja bena* 'tail-extends-out lake' (Kari and Kari 1982:17, Kari and Fall 1987). A related placename is **Chakachatna River** (Alaska, Kenai D-5) \chak ə chat´ nə, chä kə chät´ nə\, from Dena'ina *ch'akajatnu* 'tail-comes-out river' (Kari and Kari 1982:29).

CHAKAKTOLIK (Alaska, Marshall D-5). The Yupik (Eskimo) name is said to mean 'many animal bones' (Orth 1967).

CHAKCHAK (Alaska, Baird Inlet C-7). The Yupik (Eskimo) name is said to mean 'mouth' (Orth 1967).

CHAKIK Cape (Alaska, Adak C-1). From the Aleut placename *chaaqix̂* (Bergsland 1994).

CHAKINA River (Alaska, McCarthy B-6) \chə kī´ nə\. From the Ahtna (Athabaskan) placename *hwts'a'i na'* 'brushy creek' (J. Kari p.c.).

CHAKOK River (Alaska, Seldovia D-5) \chā´ kok\. From the Dena'ina (Athabaskan) placename *chakaq', ch'akaq'* (Kari and Kari 1982:30).

CHAKWAKAMIUT (Alaska, Cape Mendenhall D-5). The Yupik (Eskimo) name was reported in 1949 (Orth 1967).

CHALANEY Creek (Calif., Tulare Co.) \chə lā´ nē\. Previously known as Chilean Creek, possibly from Spanish *chileno* 'Chilean' (Gudde 1998), derived from the name of the country *Chile,* taken from a South American Indian language (Room 1997).

CHALCHIHUITL, Mount (N.Mex., Santa Fe Co.) \chäl´ chi wē təl\. From Nahuatl (Aztecan) *chalchihuitl* [čalčíwitɬ] 'precious green stone' (Julyan 1998).

CHALIT (Alaska, Kuskokwim Bay D-5). The Yupik (Eskimo) name was reported in 1878 (Orth 1967).

CHALKYITSIK (Alaska, Black River C-6) \chal kēt´ sik\. From Gwich'in (Athabaskan) *jaɬk'iitsik* 'mouth of fish-hooking place' (Caulfield et al. 1983); cf. *jaɬ* 'fish hook' (Peter 1979).

CHALONE (Calif., San Benito Co.) \shə lōn´, chə lōn´\. The name of an Indian group, speaking a language of the Costanoan family (Gudde 1998).

CHALUGAS Bay (Alaska, Seguam C-5) \chə lo͞o´ gəs\. From the Aleut placename *chaluugis*; cf. *chalu-* 'corner of bay, narrow bight' (Bergsland 1994).

CHAMA (N.Mex., Rio Arriba Co.) \chä´ mə\. A shortening of Tewa (Tanoan) [tsą̨mą̨' ǫŋwį̨keyi] 'wrestling pueblo-ruin', from [tsą̨ma] 'to wrestle' and [ǫŋwį̨keyi] 'pueblo ruin' ([ǫŋwį̨] 'pueblo', [keyi] 'old'; Harrington 1916:147). Nearby is **Chamita** (N.Mex., Rio Arriba Co.), the Spanish diminutive, meaning 'little Chama' (Julyan 1998).

CHAMNA Natural Preserve (Wash., Benton Co.). From Sahaptin [čamná], the name of a village (D. Kinkade p.c.).

CHAMOKANE Creek (Wash., Stevens Co.) \shim´ ə kən\. Perhaps from Okanogan (Salishan) /ac'mqin/ 'brains' (A. Mattina p.c.). A related form is **Tshimakain.**

CHAMPEPADAN Creek (Minn., Rock Co.) \cham pə pan´ də\. From Dakota (Siouan), meaning 'thorny wood' (Upham 1969); cf. *čhą* 'wood, tree' and *phephé* 'prickly' from *phe* 'sharp' (Riggs 1890, Ingham 2001).

CHAMPOEG (Ore., Marion Co.) \sham po͞o´ ig, sham po͞o´ ē\. Kalapuyan [čʰámpuik], perhaps an abbreviation of [čʰa-čʰíma-púičuk], referring to an edible root called [púičuk], known in English as *yampa* (H. Zenk p.c.).

CHANARAMBIE Township (Minn., Murray Co.) \chan ə ram´ bē\. From Dakota (Siouan), meaning 'concealed trees' (Upham 2001); cf. *čhą* 'wood, tree', *anáȟbe* 'to conceal' (Williamson 1902; Ingham 2001).

CHANCHELULLA Mountain (Calif., Trinity Co.) \chän chə lo͞o´ lə\. Wintu /son čuluula/, lit. 'rock black' (Gudde 1998).

CHANDALAR (Alaska, Chandalar C-3) \chan´ də lär, shan´ də lär\. The name refers to the Gwich'in (Athabaskan) Indians of the area, but it is from French *gens de large* 'people of the wide-open', that is, 'nomadic people' (Orth 1967).

CHANEANDEPECO Inlet (N.C., Dare Co.). Perhaps derived from a CAC Algonquian word referring to a shallow area (Payne 1985).

CHANHASSEN (MN, Carver Co.) \chan has´ ən\. Abbreviated from Dakota (Siouan) *čąhásą* 'sugar maple tree' (Upham 2001; Riggs 1890). The abbreviated form **Hassan** is also a township in Minn. (Hennepin Co.); and a related name is **Tenhassen Township** (Minn., Martin Co.); see below.

CHANILIUT (Alaska, St. Michael A-3) \chə nil´ yo͞ot\. Yupik (Eskimo) *caniliaq*, from *cani-* 'area beside' (Jacobson 1984).

CHANKLIUT Island (Alaska, Chignik A-1). Probably from Yupik (Eskimo), recorded in 1847 (Orth 1967).

CHANNAHATCHEE Creek (Ala., Elmore Co.) \chin i hach´ i\. From Muskogee *vcenv-hvcce* /acina-hácci/ 'cedar creek', from *vcenv* /ačína/ 'cedar', *hvcce* /háčči/ 'stream' (Martin and Mauldin 2000).

CHANNAHON (Ill., Will Co.) \shan´ ə hon\. Perhaps from a Delaware (Algonquian) placename meaning 'confluence' (Vogel 1963).

CHAN OWAPI (N.Dak., McLean Co.) \chän ō wä´ pē\. Dakota (Siouan) *čhą́ owápi* 'marked tree, painted tree', lit 'tree marked' (D. Parks p.c.; Riggs 1890).

CHANTA PETA Creek (N.Dak., Adams Co.) From the Lakhota (Siouan) personal name of a

Roman Catholic man, *čhąté pheta* 'fire heart', from *čhąté* 'heart' and *phéta* 'fire', a metaphor for a the Sacred Heart of Jesus (D. Parks p.c.).

CHANUK Creek (Alaska, Lake Clark C-8). Perhaps a Dena'ina (Athabaskan) name, reported in 1950 (Orth 1967).

CHAONIA (Mo., Wayne Co.) \kā´ ō nə\. Said to be named for an Indian leader, language unspecified (Ramsay 1952).

CHAPANOKE (N.C., Perquimans Co.) \chap´ ə nōk\. Said to be an Indian word, in an unspecified language, for 'land of the dead' (Powell 1968).

CHAPELUK Slough (Alaska, Kwiguk D-4). The Yupik (Eskimo) name was published in 1901 (Orth 1967).

CHAPPAQUA (N.Y., Westchester Co.) \chap´ ə kwä\. Perhaps from Delaware (Algonquian), meaning 'well-watered land' (Beauchamp 1907); cf. Delaware <schaphackamigueu> 'wet ground' (Brinton and Anthony 1888). Cf. also Munsee Delaware *skápeew* 'to be wet', *áhkuy* 'land' (O'Meara 1996).

CHAPPAQUIDDICK (Mass., Dukes Co.) \chap´ ə kwid ik\. From SNEng. Algonquian, 'island adjacent to the mainland'; cf. <chippi-> 'separate', <-aquid(ne)-> 'island', <-auke> 'land' (W. Cowan p.c.).

CHAPPAQUOIT (Mass., Barnstable Co.) \chap´ ə kwoit\. From SNEng. Algonquian, 'at the separate land'; cf. <chippi-> 'separate', <-auke> 'land', <-it> 'place' (W. Cowan p.c.).

CHAPPO (Calif., San Diego Co.) \chap´ ō\. Perhaps from Mexican Spanish *chapo* 'a short person', from Nahuatl (Aztecan) *tzapa* 'dwarf' (Gudde 1998).

CHAPTICO (Md., St. Mary's Co.) \chap´ tē kō\. From CAC Algonquian, perhaps meaning 'big stream' (Kenny 1984).

CHAPULTEPEC (Wis., Trempealeau Co.) \chə po͞ol´ tə pek\. From the placename **Chapultepec** in Mexico City, a fortress captured during the U.S. invasion of Mexico in 1847. The Nahuatl (Aztecan) name means 'grasshopper-hill-place', from *chapol(in)* 'grasshopper', *tepe(tl)* 'hill', and *-c* 'place'.

CHARGOGGAGOGGMANCHAUGGAGOGGCHAUBUNAGUNGAMAUG, Lake (Mass., Worcester Co.). This name is displayed locally as the name of a lake, otherwise known as Lake Webster, near the town of Webster, Mass., but the long name is not recognized as official by U.S. government mapmakers. It is said to be Nipmuck (Algonquian), meaning 'the fishing place at the boundaries and neutral meeting grounds'. There is evidence, however, that the name as given here was invented in the 1920s by a local newspaper reporter, who claimed that the name came from *Chargoggagogg* 'you fish on your side', *Manchauggagogg* 'I fish on my side', *Chaubunagungamaugg* 'nobody fish in the middle' (Randall 1993; Tynan 2000). The official name of the lake is **Chaubunagungamaug Lake**.

CHARLEY APOPKA Creek (Fla., Hardee Co.) \chär´ lē ə pop´ kə\. Muskogee *calo apapkv* 'where trout are eaten', from *calo* /čá:lo/ 'trout', *apapkv* /a:-pá:pka/ 'eating there'; cf. *pvpeta* /papitá/ 'to eat (something)' (Read 1934; Martin and Mauldin 2000). A related form is **Tsala Apopka Lake** (Fla., Citrus Co.).

CHARLEY Creek (Ind., Wabash Co.). Named for a (Algonquian) leader, also known as <Ke-tun-ga> or <Ke-tun-ga>, who died around 1826 (McPherson 1993).

CHARLIESKIN (Alaska, Nabesna D-2). From Upper Tanana (Athabaskan) *chaałį niign* 'current-flows creek' (J. Kari p.c.).

CHARLO (Mont., Lake Co.). Named for a leader of the Flathead (Salishan) people. The term may be for French *Charlot*, a nickname for *Charles* (Cheney 1984).

CHARTEE Creek (Ala., Talladega Co.) \chär´ tē\. Perhaps shortened from Creek (Muskogean) *kvncate* /kancá:ti/ 'Concharty, a Creek tribal town', lit. 'red land', from *ēkvnv* /i:kaná/ 'land' plus *catē* /cá:ti:/ 'red' (Martin and Mauldin 2000). Related placenames are **Canchardee**

(Ala., Talladega Co.) and **Concharty Creek** (Okla., Wagoner Co.).

CHARTIERS Creek (Pa., Allegheny Co.). This placename represents the possessive *Chartier's*; it refers to Peter Chartier, an eighteenth-century trader of mixed Shawnee (Algonquian) and French descent (Donehoo 1928).

CHASINA, Point (Alaska, Craig B-1). Probably a Tlingit name, published in 1852 (Orth 1967).

CHASKA (Minn., Carver Co.) \chas´ kə\. From Dakota (Siouan) *časké* 'firstborn child if a son' (Upham 2001; Riggs 1890).

CHASKI Bay (Ore., Klamath Co.) \chas´ kē\. From Klamath /č'asgaay/ 'weasel' (McArthur 1992; Barker 1963).

CHATAHOSPEE Creek (Ala., Tallapoosa Co.) \chat ə hos´ pē\. Muskogee *cvtohospv* /čato-hó:spa/ 'rock wall', from *cvto* /čató/ 'rock' and *hospv* /hó:spa/ 'wall' (Read 1984, Martin and Mauldin 2000). The name has been confused with **Chattasofka Creek** (Ala., Tallapoosa Co.).

CHATANIKA (Alaska, Livengood A-1) \chat ə nē´ kə\. The Lower Tanana (Athabaskan) name was recorded in 1903 (Orth 1967); perhaps *dradlaya nik'a* 'round whitefish river' (J. Kari p.c.).

CHATAWA (Miss., Pike Co.) \chat´ ə wô\. Possibly from Choctaw (Muskogean) *chahta* 'Choctaw', *aay-* 'place', *owwatta* 'to hunt', meaning 'where the Choctaws hunt' (P. Munro p.c.).

CHATEAUGAY (N.Y., Franklin Co.) \shä´ tə gā\. The name looks like French *chateau gai* 'gay castle' but is possibly a popular etymology from an Iroquoian name, written at one time as <Chateuaga> (Beauchamp 1907).

CHATHENDA Creek (Alaska, Nabesna A-3) \chə thān´ də\. From Upper Tanana (Athabaskan) *chiithii nda'*, lit. 'low-point stream' (J. Kari p.c.).

CHATIEMAC Brook (N.Y., Warren Co.) \shat´ i mak\. The name was coined by Henry R. Schoolcraft, who claimed it to be an Algonquian name for the lower Hudson River. He defined it as 'stately swan'; but elsewhere he identified it with the name **Shatemuc** (N.Y., Westchester Co.) which he said meant 'pelican river' (Beauchamp 1907). Schoolcraft may have been thinking of Ojibwa *zhede* 'pelican' (Nichols and Nyholm 1995).

CHATRITT, Lake (Alaska, Black River C-6). From Gwich'in (Athabaskan), recorded in 1956 (Orth 1967).

CHATTAHOOCHEE River (Ga., Muscogee Co.; Ala.; Houston Co.) \chat ə hōō´ chē\. Muskogee *cato-hocce hvcce* /čato-ho:čči-háčči/ 'marked-rock river', from *cato-hocce* /čato-hó:čči/ 'marked rock' (*cvto* /čató/ 'rock', *hocce* /hó:čči/ 'marked') plus *hvcce* /háčči/ 'stream' (Read 1984; Martin and Mauldin 2000). The name is also given to a place in Fla. (Gadsden Co.).

CHATTANOOGA (Tenn., Hamilton Co.) \chat ə nōō´ gə\. The name has been said to be from Cherokee (Iroquoian) and from Muskogee and to mean 'rock rising to a point'; but its derivation remains unclear (McClaren 1991). Cf. Muskogee *cato* /čató/ 'rock' (Martin and Mauldin 2000). There is also a **Chattanooga** in Okla. (Comanche Co.).

CHATTAROY (W.Va., Mingo Co.) \chat´ ə roi\. The name has been recorded since 1775 (as <Tattaroy, Tatterio, Chatterio, Chattarawha> etc.). The term referred to the Big Sandy River as well as to the Indian group called the **Tutelo,** of the Siouan linguistic family (Kenny 1945). There is also a **Chattaroy** in Wash. (Spokane Co.), established in the early 1880s (Hitchman 1985).

CHATTASOFKA Creek (Ala., Tallapoosa Co.) \chat ə sôf´ kə\. Muskogee *cvto aksofkē*, a tribal town, lit. 'rock hole', from *cvto* /čató/ 'rock', *aksofkē* /aksófki/ 'deep place, hole' (from *sofkē* /sófki:/ 'deep') (Read 1984, Martin and Mauldin 2000). This term has sometimes been confused with **Chatahospee Creek** (Ala., Tallapoosa Co.).

CHATTERDOWEN Creek (Calif., Shasta Co.) \chat´ ər dou ən\. Wintu *čati tawin,* lit.

'pine-nut flat' (Gudde 1998). Also written **Chatterdown.**

CHATTOKA (N.C., Craven Co.) \chə tō´ kə\. Tuscarora (Iroquoian) *ujatuukę'* 'shoreless', from *ujaateh* 'shore' (B. Rudes p.c.).

CHATTOLANEE (Md., Baltimore Co.) \chat ə lä´ nē\. The name is imported from the Muskogean languages of the southeastern states, intended to translate the Md. placename *Green Spring* (Kenny 1984). Muskogee *cvto lanē* actually means 'green rock', from *cvto* /čató/ 'rock', *lanē* /lá:ni:/ 'green' (Martin and Mauldin 2000).

CHATTOOGA County (Ga.) \chə to͞o´ gə\. The name may be Cherokee (Iroquoian) or Muskogee (Read 1984); cf. Muskogee *cato* /čató/ 'rock' (Martin and Mauldin 2000). The name is also given to the **Chattooga River** (Ala., Cherokee Co.). The **Chattooga River** in S.C. (Oconee Co.), however, and Ga. (Rabun Co.) is said to get its name from Cherokee *jitaaga* 'chicken' (B. Rudes p.c.). The name also occurs in **Chatooga Ridge** and **Chatuge Lake** (N.C., Jackson Co.).

CHAUBUNAGUNGAMAUG Lake (Mass., Worcester Co.) \chô bə nə gung´ ə môg\. Nipmuck (SNEng. Algonquian) for 'divided-island lake', i.e. a lake divided by islands. The name is also written **Chaubanakongkomun** or **Chabanakongkomuk**; and it is labeled locally as **Lake Chargoggagoggmanchauggagoggchaubunagungamaugg**; see above.

CHAUEKUKTULI, Lake (Alaska, Taylor Mountains A-8). Probably a Yupik (Eskimo) name, written <Chauiskuktuli> in 1915 (Orth 1967).

CHAUFCHIVAK, Mount (Alaska, Taylor Mountains A-7). The Yupik (Eskimo) name was reported in 1931 (Orth 1967).

CHAUGA River (S.C., Oconee Co.) \chô´ gə\. Also written <Chawgee>; perhaps from Cherokee (Iroquoian) *dlayhga* (Pickens 1961–62:4–5; Feeling 1975). A probably related placename is the nearby **Chagee**; see above.

CHAUGHTANOONDA Creek (N.Y., Schenectady Co.) \chôk tə no͞on´ də\. Also written **Chuctanunda,** perhaps an Iroquoian name meaning 'stony places' (Beauchamp 1907).

CHAUIK Mountain (Alaska, Bendeleben A-4). Perhaps an Iñupiaq (Eskimo) name, reported in 1900 (Orth 1967).

CHAUTAUQUA County (N.Y.) \shə tô´ kwə\. Seneca (Iroquoian) *ja'dáhgwęh,* possibly derived from a word meaning 'raised body' (W. Chafe p.c.). The name has been transferred to places all over the United States, including Colo. (Boulder Co.), Fla. (Pinellas Co.), and Ohio (Montgomery Co.).

CHAVOLDA Creek (Alaska, Nabesna A-3) \chə vōl´ də\. The name is Upper Tanana (Athabaskan), recorded in 1902 (Orth 1967).

CHAWANAKEE (Calif., Fresno Co.) \chə wä´ nə kē, shə wä´ nə kē. Said to be an Indian word, but of unknown origin (Gudde 1998).

CHAWEKAT Mountain (Alaska, Goodnews Bay A-7). The Yupik (Eskimo) name was published in 1951 (Orth 1967).

CHEAHA Creek (Ala., Talladega Co.) \chē´ hô\. A Muskogee tribal town, *cēyahv* /či:yá:ha/ (Martin and Mauldin 2000). Possibly related forms are **Chehaw** (Ala., Macon Co.) and **Chiaha** (Ala., Russell Co.).

CHEBACCO Lake (Mass., Essex Co.) \chə bä´ kō\. SNEng. Algonquian, 'separate land', from <chippi-> 'separate', <-auke> 'land' (W. Cowan p.c.).

CHEBANIKA Creek (Alaska, Hughes D-1). Probably a Koyukon (Athabaskan) name, obtained in 1956 (Orth 1967).

CHEBANSE (Ill., Kankakee Co.) \shə bäns´\. Named for a nineteenth-century Potawatomi (Algonquian) leader whose name was written <Chee-banse>, perhaps meaning 'little duck' (Vogel 1963); cf. Ojibwa (Algonquian) *zhiishiib, zhiishiibenh* 'duck', *-s* 'little' (Rhodes 1985).

CHEBOYGAN County (Mich.) \shə boi´ gən\. Probably Ojibwa (Algonquian) for 'big pipe' (Vogel 1986); cf. *gichi-, chi-* 'big', *opwaagan* 'pipe' (Nichols and Nyholm 1995). The same form appears in Wisconsin as **Sheboygan County.**

CHEBOYGANING Creek (Mich., Bay Co.) \shə boi´ gə ning\. Perhaps Ojibwa, 'big pipe place' (Vogel 1986).

CHECATS Creek (Alaska, Ketchikan B-3). The Tlingit name was reported in 1897 (Orth 1967).

CHECHING (Alaska, Baird Inlet A-6). The Yupik (Eskimo) name was reported in 1949 (Orth 1967).

CHE-CHU-PIN-QUA Woods (Ill., Cook Co.). Named for a nineteenth-century Potawatomi (Algonquian) resident, known in English as Alexander Robinson (Vogel 1963).

CHECOTAH (Okla., McIntosh Co.) \shi kō´ tə\. Named for Samuel Checote, a Muskogee leader (Shirk 1974). The Muskogee form of the placename is *cokotv* /čokó:ta/ (Martin and Mauldin 2000). Possibly related is **Chicota** (Tex., Lamar Co.).

CHEDATNA Lakes (Alaska, Tyonek B-3) \chə dat´ nə\. From Dena'ina (Athabaskan) *ts'idatnu* 'Lewis River', containing *-tnu* 'river' (Kari & Fall 1987:57).

CHEDISKI Peak (Ariz., Navajo Co.) \ched´ i skī\. Probably from Western Apache (Athabaskan) /tsee deesgai/ 'white stones extend horizontally', with /tsee/ 'stone', /dee-/ 'extends in a line', and /s-gai/ 'white' (Granger 1983; P. Greenfeld p.c.).

CHEDOTLOTHNA Glacier (Alaska, Talkeetna D-4) \chə dot loth´ nə\. Perhaps from Upper Kuskokwim (Athabaskan) *ch'idotl'uł no'* 'braided-string river' (J. Kari p.c.).

CHEECHAKO Gulch (Alaska, Talkeetna B-3) \chē chä´ kō\. Chinook Jargon for 'newcomer', from <chee> [či] 'new' (Lower Chinook *čxi* 'straightaway') plus <chako> [čako] 'come' (Nootka *čokwaa* 'come!') (*RHD* 1987).

CHEECHILGEETHO (N.Mex., McKinley Co) \chē chil gē´ thō\. Probably from Navajo (Athabaskan) *chéch'ilgitó* 'spring at the oak trees', with *chéch'il* 'oak tree' (*tsé, ché* 'rock', *ch'il* 'plant'), *-gi* 'at', and *tó* 'water, spring' (A. Wilson p.c.). Another current name for this place is **Chi Chil Tah**; see below.

CHEEKA Peak (Wash., Clallam Co.). From Makah (Nootkan) /č'ik'a/, the name of a Makah man (W. Jacobsen p.c.).

CHEEKTOWAGA (N.Y., Erie Co.) \chēk tō wä´ gə\. Seneca (Iroquoian) *jóíkdowá'geh* "crabapple place"; cf. *jóíkdowa'* 'crabapple' (W. Chafe p.c.).

CHEENEETNUK River (Alaska, Sleetmute D-1) \chē nēt´ nuk\. From Deg Hit'an (Athabaskan) *jonetno'* 'murky river' (J. Kari p.c.).

CHEENIK Creek (Alaska, Solomon C-3) \chē´ nik\. The Iñupiaq (Eskimo) name was published in 1908 (Orth 1967).

CHEESECOTE Mountain (N.Y., Rockland Co.) \chēz´ kōt\. Also written as <Cheesecocks>, perhaps from Delaware (Algonquian), of unclear derivation (Ruttenber 1906; Beauchamp 1907). Possibly related is **Cheesequake** (N.J., Middlesex Co.) \chēz´ kwāk\, perhaps from Delaware (Algonquian) *chiskhake* 'land that has been cleared' (Kraft and Kraft 1985).

CHEETDEEKAHYU, Mount (Alaska, Skagway B-4). The Tlingit name was published in 1952 (Orth 1967).

CHEE Well (N.Mex., McKinley Co.) \chē\. Probably represents a Navajo (Athabaskan) given name *chii,* short for *łichíí'* 'red' (A. Wilson p.c.) **Chee Dodge School** (N.Mex., McKinley Co.) was named for a Navajo leader; his Native American name was *hastiin adiits'a'ii'* 'the man who hears or understands' (A. Wilson p.c.).

CHEFFIE Creek (Ark., Ouachita Co.) \chef´ ē\. Named for a nineteenth-century Choctaw (Muskogean) leader called *cheffo* 'runner' (Dickinson 1995). A spelling variant is **Chaffie Creek;** see above.

CHEFORNAK (Alaska, Baird Inlet A-7) \chə fôr´ nək\. Yupik (Eskimo) *cevv'arneq,* from *cevv'arte-* 'to emerge into an open area' (Jacobson 1984).

CHEHALEM (Ore., Washington Co.) \chə hā´ ləm, shə hā´ ləm\. Tualatin (Kalapuyan) \čʰahé:lim\ 'place out, outside', a village name (D. Kinkade p.c.).

CHEHALIS (Wash., Lewis Co.) \chə hā´ lis, shə hā´ lis\. From Lower Chehalis (Salishan) /c'x̣íl's/ [c'(ə)x̣íl'(ə)s] 'sand', the name of a village near present-day Westport. The name was extended to the **Chehalis River** and then to the city of **Chehalis** in the territory of the Upper Chehalis language, in which the cognate word for 'sand' is /c'ax̣éʔs/ (D. Kinkade p.c.). A related placename is **Mox Chehalis Creek** (Wash., Grays Harbor Co.), meaning 'two sands', with Chinook Jargon *mox* 'two'.

CHEHAW (Ala., Macon Co.) \chē´ hô\. Muskogee *cēyahv* /či:yá:ha/, a tribal town (Martin and Mauldin 2000). There is also a **Chehaw** in Ga. (Lee Co.) and a **Chehaw River** in S.C. (Colleton Co.). Other related placenames are **Cheaha Creek** (Ala., Talladega Co.) and **Chiaha** (Ala., Russell Co.).

CHEHULPUM Creek (Ore., Marion Co.) \chə hul´ pəm\. Northern Kalapuyan \čʰahálpam\, referring to a place 'upstream' or 'upland' (H. Zenk p.c.).

CHEKEPA Creek (S.Dak., Day Co.). Named for a family belonging to the Santee-Sisseton branch of the Dakota (Siouan); from *čhekpá* 'a twin' (D. Parks p.c.).

CHEKHECHUNNJIK Creek (Alaska, Christian B-6). The Gwich'in (Athabaskan) name was recorded in 1956 (Orth 1967).

CHEKOK (Alaska, Iliamna D-4) \chē´ kok\. Dena'ina (Athabaskan) *chix kaq'* 'ochre mouth' (Kari and Kari 1982:24).

CHELAN County (Wash.) \shə lan´\. From Moses-Columbian (Salishan) /cl'án/ [čəl'án], originally meaning 'lake' (D. Kinkade p.c.). **Chelan Bank** (Alaska, Unalaska D-2) was named after a USGS cutter (Orth 1967), which in turn was named for the place in Wash.

CHELATCHIE (Wash., Clark Co.) From Sahaptin [č'álača] 'fern' (D. Kinkade p.c.).

CHELATNA Lake (Alaska, Talkeetna B-3) \chə lat´ nə\. Dena'ina (Athabaskan) *ch'alintnu,* the name for Coffee Creek (J. Kari p.c.).

CHELLY, CANYON DE. See **De Chelly, Canyon.**

CHELUNGINIK River (Alaska, Hooper Bay C-2). The Yupik (Eskimo) name was reported in 1951 (Orth 1967).

CHEMAWA (Ore., Marion Co.) \chə mä´ wə\. Kalapuyan [čʰaméewi] 'place of low-lying, frequently overflowed ground', related to /méewi/' 'camas-digging site' (H. Zenk p.c.). **Chemawa** also occurs, apparently as a transfer name, in Calif. (Riverside Co.).

CHEMEHUEVI \chem ə wā´ vē\. The name of a Numic (Uto-Aztecan) group closely related to the Southern Paiutes, repeatedly mentioned by this name in Spanish and early American times under a great variety of spellings. The source is Mojave *'achiimuuév,* said to mean 'those who work with fish', containing *'achíi-m* 'with fish' and *uu-év-* 'plural-work' (Gudde 1998). The term occurs in several placenames, such as **Chemehuevi Valley** (Calif., San Bernardino Co.).

CHEMEKETA (Ore., Yamhill Co.) \chə mek´ ə tə\. This represents [čʰamíkiti], the name of the Santiam (Kalapuyan) village at what is now the city of Salem (H. Zenk p.c.).

CHEMQUASABAMTICOOK Lake (Maine, Piscataquis Co.) From Penobscot /kčiməkʸásəpemtəkok/ 'stream belonging to a large lake' (P. MacDougall p.c.).

CHEMULT (Ore., Klamath Co.) \chə mult´, shə mult´\. Named for a leader of the Klamath people (McArthur 1992).

CHEMUNG County (N.Y.) \shə mung´\. Supposedly from the Delaware (Algonquian) for 'horn' (Beauchamp 1907); cf. Delaware <oschummo, wschummo> (Brinton and Anthony 1888). The term occurs elsewhere (e.g., Pa., Bradford Co.; Mass., Norfolk Co.; and Mich., Livingston Co.).

CHENANGO County (N.Y.) \shə nang´ gō\. Said to be from Onondaga (Iroquoian) <ot-seningo>, from <o-che-nang> 'bull thistles' (Beauchamp 1907). The term occurs as a transfer name in several states, including Alaska (Ketchikan A-5) and Mich. (Livingston Co.). Probably related is **Cheningo** (N.Y., Cortland Co.).

CHENA River (Alaska, Fairbanks D-2) \chē´ nə\. From Lower Tanana (Athabaskan) *ch'eno'*, lit. 'something river' (J. Kari p.c.).

CHENEATHDA Hill (Alaska, Tanacross A-2). From Upper Tanana (Athabaskan) *sheh nia*, perhaps meaning 'long hill' (J. Kari p.c.).

CHENEGA (Alaska, Seward B-3) \chə nē´ gə\. Perhaps an Alutiiq (Eskimo) name.

CHENEQUA (Wis., Waukesha Co.) \chə nē´ kwä\. From Ojibwa (Algonquian) *zhingwaak* 'white pine' (Nichols and Nyholm 1995).

CHENGWATANA Township (Minn., Pine Co.). From Ojibwa (Algonquian), meaning 'pine town' (Upham 2001); cf. *zhingwaak* 'white pine', *oodena* 'town' (Nichols and Nyholm 1995).

CHENIK (Alaska, Iliamna A-4). The Yupik (Eskimo) name was reported in 1925 (Orth 1967).

CHENINGO (N.Y., Cortland Co.) \shə ning´ gō\. Said to be from Onondaga (Iroquoian) <Otsiningo>, from <o-che-nang> 'bull thistles' (Beauchamp 1907). Probably related is **Chenango County** (N.Y.).

CHENNEBY, Chief (Ala., Talladega Co.) \chen´ ə bē\. A spelling variant of the name **Chinnabee**; see below.

CHENOA (Ky., Bell Co.) \chə nō´ ə\. Supposedly an Indian name, but otherwise unidentified. Another town called **Chenoa** (Ill., McLean Co.) is likely to be a transfer from the Ky. location (Vogel 1963:176).

CHENOIS Creek (Wash., Grays Harbor Co.) \shə nōōs´\. From Lower Chehalis (Salishan) \čənús\, the name of a local leader (D. Kinkade p.c.).

CHENOKABY Creek (Miss., Newton Co.) \chi nuk´ ə bi\. Choctaw (Muskogean) *chinakbi* 'crooked' (P. Munro p.c.).

CHENTANSITZTAN (Alaska, Nulato B-2). From Koyukon (Athabaskan), of unclear derivation.

CHENUNDA Creek (N.Y., Allegany Co.) \chə nun´ də\. Perhaps an Iroquoian name (Beauchamp 1907).

CHEOAH (N.C., Graham Co.) Perhaps from Cherokee (Iroquoian) *tsiya* 'otter' (Powell 1968; Alexander 1971). A possibly related placename is **Cheohee** (SC, Oconee Co.; Pickens 1961:4).

CHEPACHET (R.I., Providence Co.) \chi pach´ it, shi pash´ ē\. Probably related to Narragansett (Algonquian) <chippachausin> 'it divides (as a path)', <-et> 'place' (W. Cowan p.c.) There is also a **Chepachet** in N.Y. (Herkimer Co.).

CHEPANUU (N.C., Perquimans Co.) Said to refer to a settlement of the Weapemeoc (Algonquain) Indian group (Powell 1968).

CHEPETA Lake (Utah, Duchesne Co.) \chə pē´ tə\. From the same source as **Chipeta,** the wife of **Ouray**, a nineteenth-century Ute (Numic) leader (Van Cott 1990). Derived from Ute /tsip-píttɨ/ 'a spring', from /tsíppi/ 'to come out' (J. McLaughlin p.c.) The related form **Chipeta** also occurs as a placename (Utah, Uintah Co.; Colo., Delta Co.).

CHEPIWANOXET (R.I., Bristol Co.). From SNEng. Algonquian, meaning 'small separate place', containing <chippi> 'separate', <ohke> 'land', <-s-> 'small', <-et> 'place' (W. Cowan p.c.).

CHEQUIT Point (N.Y., Suffolk Co.) \chā´ kwit\. The term refers to a type of fish and is perhaps of SNEng. Algonquian origin (Tooker 1911).

CHERAW (S.C., Chesterfield Co.) \shə rô´\. Earlier written as <Xuala, Saraw> (etc.); from Catawban (Siouan) /sá:ra:'/ 'peninsula' (Pearson 1978; B. Rudes p.c.) The name also occurs in N.C. (Caldwell Co.) and in Miss. (Marion Co.).

CHERICOKE (Va., King William Co.) \châr´ i kōk\. The Indian name is of unknown origin (Hagemann 1988).

CHEROKEE \châr´ ə kē\. An Indian group of the southeastern United States, of the Iroquoian linguistic family. At the time of first contact with white settlers, the Cherokees lived in the southern Appalachians. In the early nineteenth century, many of them were forced to resettle in what is now the Cherokee Nation of Okla.; however, some remain on a reservation in N.C. The Cherokee term is *tsalagi.* As a placename, **Cherokee** is widespread in the United States; there are counties called **Cherokee County** in many states (e.g., Ala., Iowa, and Tex.).

CHESACO Park (Md., Baltimore Co.) \ches´ ə kō\. The term is coined from **Chesapeake Bay** (Kenny 1984); see below.

CHESANING (Mich., Saginaw Co.) \ches´ ə ning\. From the Ojibwa (Algonquian) for 'big rock' (Vogel 1986); cf. *gichi-* 'big', *asin* 'rock' (Nichols and Nyholm 1995).

CHESAPEAKE Bay (Md., Va.) \ches´ ə pēk\. From CAC Algonquian, earlier written <Chesepiooc, Chesupioc>; perhaps meaning 'great shellfish bay' (Kenny 1984; Hagemann 1988).

CHESHNINA River (Alaska, Valdez C-2) \chesh´ ni nä, chesh nē´ nə\. From Ahtna (Athabaskan) *tsesnen' na',* containing *na'* 'stream' (Kari 1983:20).

CHESLINA River (Alaska, Nabesna D-3) \ches´ li nä, ches lī´ nə\. From Ahtna (Athabaskan) *ttheeth̲äł niign*, lit. 'steambath creek' (J. Kari p.c.).

CHESNIMNUS Creek (Ore., Wallowa Co.) \ches nim´ nəs\. Nez Perce /sisnímex̣s/ 'thornberry mountain, area at the head of Thorn Creek', from /sísnim, císnim/ 'black hawthorn, black thornberry' plus a shortened form of /mée̓x̣sem/ 'mountain' (Aoki 1994).

CHESTER Creek (Alaska, Anchorage A-8) Dena'ina (Athabaskan) *chanshtnu* 'grass creek' (J. Kari p.c.).

CHE Spring (Ore., Grant Co.) \chē\. Possibly from Chinook Jargon <chee> [či] 'lately, just now, new, fresh, original' in its 'fresh' sense; from Lower Chinook <tchi> 'lately, just now' (D. Kinkade p.c.).

CHESTOA (Tenn., Unicoi Co.). From Cherokee *jisdu* 'rabbit' (M. Toomey p.c.; Feeling 1975). A variant spelling occurs in the placename **Chestuee Creek** (Tenn., Monroe and McMinn Cos.).

CHESUNCOOK (Maine, Piscataquis Co.) \chi sun´ ko͝ok\. From Penobscot /kčí-sɑkok/ 'at the big outlet' (P. MacDougall p.c.).

CHETAC Lake (Wis., Sawyer Co.) \chə tak´\. From Ojibwa (Algonquian) *zhede* 'pelican' (Vogel 1991; Nichols and Nyholm 1995). A related form is **Chetek** (Wis., Barron Co.).

CHETASLINA River (Alaska, Valdez C-2) \chi tas´ li nä\. From Ahtna (Athabaskan) *ts'itaẕdlen na'* 'straight-current river' (J. Kari p.c.).

CHETCO River (Ore., Curry Co.) \chet´ kō\. Chetco (Athabaskan) [čidxu], a self-designation, from [čedi-xwad] 'čedi-river'. The first part consists of [če] 'tail' used metaphorically for 'the mouth of a river'; [-d(i)] is a locative enclitic, thus [če-d(i)] means 'at the river-mouth' (D. Kinkade p.c.; V. Golla p.c.).

CHETEK (Wis., Barron Co.) \shə tek´\. From the Ojibwa (Algonquian) word for 'pelican' (Vogel 1991); the form is *zhede* 'pelican' (Nichols and Nyholm 1995). A related name is **Chetac Lake** (Wis., Sawyer Co.).

CHETIMACHES (La., St. Mary Par.). From the name of the **Chitimacha** Indian tribe; see below.

CHETLECHAK Island (Alaska, Livengood D-5). Koyukon (Athabaskan) *tootl'eets'ege,* lit. 'water straight shortcut' (Matthew et al. 1999).

CHETLO, Lake (Ore., Lane Co.) \chet´ lō\. Chinook Jargon <chet´lo> [čǽtlo] 'oyster', from Lower Chehalis (Salishan) /č'ə́ƛ'əxʷ/ 'oyster' (D. Kinkade p.c.). There is also a **Chetlo Harbor** in Wash. (Pacific Co.).

CHETOLAH Creek (Kans., Ellis Co.). Perhaps contains Kansa (Siouan) /čči/ 'house' (Rydjord 1968; R. Rankin p.c.).

CHETOPA (Kans., Labette Co.) \shə tō´ pə\. From the name of an Osage (Siouan) leader, /hcí tó:pa/ 'four houses', from /hci/ 'house' plus /tó:pa/ 'four' (R. Rankin p.c.).

CHETTRO KETTLE (N.Mex., San Juan Co.) \chet´ rō ket´ əl\. The Navajo (Athabaskan) name is *tsé bidádi'ní'ání* 'rock that is plugged or sealed up', containing *tsé* 'rock', *bidádi'* 'blocking it', *ní'á* 'solid objects lie in a row or line' (Julyan 1998; Wilson 1995).

CHETWOOT Lake (Wash., King Co.). Chinook Jargon <chetwoot> [čɛ´twʊt] 'black bear', from Lower Chehalis (Salishan) [čə́tx^{w}ən'] 'black bear' (D. Kinkade p.c.). The same name occurs in **Chetwot Creek** (Wash., Snohomish Co.).

CHEVAK (Alaska, Hooper Bay C-2) \chē´ vak\. Yupik (Eskimo) *cev'aq* 'cut-through place where the river has carved a new channel' (Jacobson 1984).

CHEWACK Falls (Wash., Okanogan Co.) \chē´ wak\. From Moses-Columbian (Salishan) [čwáx] 'creek' (D. Kinkade p.c.). Related forms occur in **Chewuch River** (Wash., Okanogan Co.) and **Cheweka Creek** (Wash., Stevens Co.).

CHEWACLA Creek (Ala., Lee Co.) \chə wäk´ lə\. The name was recorded in 1844 as <Sawacklahatchee> (Read 1984). Perhaps from Muskogee *svwokle* /sawókli/, a tribal town (Martin and Mauldin 2000); or perhaps from Choctaw (Muskogean) *chowahla* 'cedar' (P. Munro p.c.).

CHEWALLA Creek (Ala., Tuscaloosa Co.) \chi wô´ lə\. Recorded in 1719 as <Ho-ith-le-wau-le>, in 1814 as <Clewwalle>, from the name of a Muskogee town <Holiwahali>, perhaps from elements meaning 'war' and 'divide' (Read 1984). Modern Muskogee has *horre* /hóɬɬi/ 'war', *waretv* /wa:ɬ-itá/ 'to cut', and a tribal town name *rewahle* /ɬiwáhli/ (Martin and Mauldin 2000). The placename **Chewalla** also occurs in Miss. (Marshall Co.), where it has been associated with Choctaw *chowahla* 'cedar' (Seale 1939), and in Tenn. (McNairy Co.).

CHEWAUCAN (Ore., Lake Co.) \shə wô´ kən\. From Klamath /čwaknii/, perhaps meaning 'wild potato people', from /čwa/ 'wapato, wild potato' and /-knii/ 'people or person from' (Barker 1963).

CHEWAWAH Creek (Miss., Chickasaw Co.) \chə wä´ wä\. Perhaps from the same source as **Chihuahua,** a state of northern Mexico, which is also used as a placename in the United States (e.g., Calif., San Diego Co.).

CHEWEKA Creek (Wash., Stevens Co.) \chə wē´ kə\. Okanagan (Salishan) /(c)cwíxaʔ/ 'little creek', from /cwíx-/ 'creek' (D. Kinkade p.c.). Related forms are **Chewack Falls** and **Chewuch River** (Wash., Okanogan Co.).

CHEWELAH (Wash., Stevens Co.) \chə wē´ lə\. From Spokane (Salishan) [sč'ew'íl'eʔ] 'watersnake, gartersnake' (D. Kinkade p.c.). The term also occurs, apparently as a transfer name, in Wis. (Vilas Co.; Vogel 1991).

CHEWILIKEN Creek (Wash., Okanogan Co.). Named for a Colville (Salishan) leader (Hitchman 1985).

CHEWUCH River (Wash., Okanogan Co.). From Moses-Columbian (Salishan) /cwáx/ [čwáx] 'creek' (D. Kinkade p.c.). A related form occurs in **Chewack Falls** (Wash., Okanogan Co.).

CHEYAVA Falls (Ariz., Coconino Co.) \chā yä´ və\. Hopi *tsiyakva*, from *tsiyak-* 'to crack' (K. Hill p.c.).

CHEYENNE \shī en´, shī an`\. An Indian people of the Algonquian linguistic family, living in the Great Plains. At present there are Cheyenne communities in Wyo. and in Okla. The English name comes from French *cheyenne*, originally recorded in 1679 as <Chaiena>, from Dakota (Siouan) *šahíyena.* This is the diminutive of *šahíya*, a Dakotan name for the Cree people (W. Leman p.c.; J. Koontz p.c.). The term is widespread as a placename; there are counties called

Cheyenne County in Colo., Kans., and Neb. The city of **Cheyenne** (Wyo., Laramie Co.) is the state capital.

CHIAHA (Ala., Russell Co.) \chē´ hô\. A Muskogee tribal town, *cēyahv* /či:yá:ha/ (Martin and Mauldin 2000). Related forms are **Cheaha Creek** and **Chehaw** (both in Ala., Talladega Co.). According to Booker et al. (1992: 426–27), **Chiaha** was in the chiefdom of Coosa, a part of the Creek Federation, but the people may have spoken another Muskogean language, such as Hitchiti or Koasati.

CHIAKTUAK Creek (Alaska, Chignik B-3). The Alutiiq (Eskimo) name was recorded in 1928 (Orth 1967).

CHIAVRIA Point (Ariz., Coconino Co.). Named for Juan Chiavria, a nineteenth-century leader of the Maricopa (Yuman) people (McNamee 1997).

CHIAWANA Park (Wash., Franklin Co.) \chi wä´ nə\. From Sahaptin /nč'iwána/ 'Columbia River', lit. 'big river', from /nč'i/ 'big', /wána/ 'river, water' (D. Kinkade p.c.).

CHIBAHDEHL Rocks (Wash., Clallam Co.). From Makah (Nootkan) /sa:dapadiƚ/ 'kelp fishline wrapped around neck', from /sadʔaƚ/ 'kelp fishline' (W. Jacobsen p.c.).

CHIBUKAK Point (Alaska, St. Lawrence D-6). The Yupik (Eskimo) name is probably from *sivu* 'front, bow of boat' (L. Kaplan p.c.).

CHICACOAN (Va., Northumberland Co.). This name, earlier written <Sekacawone>, referred to a local Indian group, speaking a CAC Algonquian language (Hagemann 1988).

CHICAGO (Ill., Cook Co.) \shi kô´ gō, shi kä´ gō\. Fox (Algonquian) /šeka:ko:heki/ 'at the wild onion place' or Ojibwa /šika:konk/ 'at the skunk place' (Afable & Beeler 1996:191; cf. Swenson 1991). The name has been transferred to many other states (e.g. Colo., Clear Creek Co.; Mont., Liberty Co.); **Port Chicago** occurs in Calif. (Contra Costa Co.). **Chicago Lake** (Mich., Delta Co.), however, probably takes its name independently from the Ojibwa (Algonquian) word for 'onion'; see **Chicagon** below.

CHICAGON (Mich., Iron Co.). Perhaps from Ojibwa (Algonquian) *zhgaagwanzh, zhgaagwinzh* 'onion' or from *zhgaag, zhgaagoo* 'skunk' (Vogel 1986; Rhodes 1985). The word for 'skunk' is related, through Proto-Algonquian */šeka:kwa/, to the Massachusett (SNEng. Algonquian) word from which English *skunk* was borrowed (*RHD* 1987); see **Skunk** as a placename below.

CHICAMACOMICO River (Md., Dorchester Co.). A CAC Algonquian name, speculated to mean 'dwelling place by the big water' (Kenny 1984). There is also a **Chicamacomico Channel** in N.C. (Dare Co.) Perhaps related is the name of **Chickinacommock Inlet** (N.C., Dare Co.).

CHICAMUXEN (Md., Charles Co.). A CAC Algonquian name, recorded in 1650 as <Chingomuxon>; the derivation is not known (Kenny 1984).

CHICHANTNA River (Alaska, Tyonek B-5) \chi chant´ nə\. Dena'ina (Athabaskan) *ƚich'antnu* 'from-glacier stream', with *-tnu* 'stream' (Kari and Fall 1987:55).

CHI CHIL TAH (N.Mex., McKinley Co.) \chē´ chil tä\. From Navajo *chéch'il-tah,* lit. 'oaks-among'; the word *chéch'il* 'oak' is from *ché, tsé* 'rock' plus *ch'il* 'plant' (Julyan 1998; Young and Morgan 1987). This name refers to the same place as the related **Cheechilgeetho**.

CHICHITNOK River (Alaska, Taylor Mountains B-4) The Yupik (Eskimo) name was published in 1826 (Orth 1967).

CHICHOKNA River (Alaska, Valdez D-2) \chi chok´ nə\. From Ahtna (Athabaskan) *tsitsox na',* lit. 'yellow-head stream' (J. Kari p.c.).

CHICKABALLY Mountain (Calif., Shasta Co.) \chik´ ə bä lē\. Probably contains Wintu *ƚikup'uri* 'a fight', *buli* 'mountain' (Gudde 1998).

CHICKAHOMINY (Va., Henrico Co.) \chik ə hom´ ə nē\. The name of a CAC Algonquian subgroup; the derivation is not known (Hagemann 1988:49). There is also a **Chickahominy Creek** in Ore. (Harney Co.).

CHICKAK River (Alaska, Tyonek D-7). Perhaps Dena'ina (Athabaskan) *chik'a qilantnu* 'firewood-is-there river' (J. Kari p.c.).

CHICKALAH (Ark., Yell Co.) \shi kē´ lə\. Named for a Cherokee (Iroquoian) leader; also written as <Chikileh> (Dickinson 1995).

CHICKALOON River (Alaska, Anchorage D-4) \chik´ ə lo͞on\. Named for a Dena'ina (Athabaskan) leader known as *chiklu*; the name may have been derived from Russian (Kari and Fall 1987:262).

CHICKAMAUGA River (Ga., Tenn.) \chik ə mô´ gə\. Perhaps from Chickasaw (Muskogean) *chokma* 'good' (Munro and Willmond 1994). The name also occurs in Ohio (Gallia Co.) Probably related names are **Chickamaw Bend** (La., Madison Par.) and **Chickima** (La., Rapides Par.); see below.

CHICKAMAW Bend (La., Madison Par.) \chik´ i mô\. Probably from Choctaw (Muskogean) *achukma* 'good' (Read 1927; P. Munro p.c.) The name occurs as a transfer in Minn. (Cass Co.). Probably related names are **Chickamauga River** (Ga., Tenn.) and **Chickima** (La., Rapides Par.).

CHICKAMIN River (Alaska, Ketchikan D-3) \chik´ ə min, chik´ ə mən\. Chinook Jargon <chik´-a-min> [číkəmən, číkəmɪn] 'iron, metal, money', from Nootka *cikimin* 'iron' (D. Kinkade p.c.). A related placename is **Chikamin Creek** (Wash., Chelan Co.).

CHICKASAW \chik´ ə sô\. A people of the Muskogean language family, originally living in northern Miss. and western Tenn.; the Chickasaw Nation is now in Oklahoma. The term comes from the Chickasaws' name for themselves, which is *chikashsha* (P. Munro p.c.). There are counties called **Chickasaw** in Miss. and Iowa. Other occurrences of the placename are widespread (e.g., Ohio, Mercer Co.; Okla., Carter Co.; and Tenn., Monroe Co.). **Chickasaw Bogue** (Ala., Marengo Co.) means 'Chickasaw stream', containing Choctaw (Muskogean) *book* 'stream'. As the name of a town in Okla. (Grady Co.), the term has the form **Chickasha** \chik´ ə shā\.

CHICKASAWBA (Ark., Mississippi Co.) \chik ə sô´ bə\. Named for a Chickasaw (Muskogean) leader (Dickinson 1995). The final syllable remains unexplained.

CHICKASAWHAY River (Miss., George Co.) \chik´ ə sə hā\. Choctaw (Muskogean) *chikashsha-ahi,* lit. 'Chickasaw potato' (P. Munro p.c.).

CHICKASHEEN Brook (R.I., Washington Co.) \chik´ ə shēn\. Probably contains Narragansett (Algonquian) <chekasu> 'northeast' (W. Cowan p.c.).

CHICKATAWBUT Hill (Mass., Norfolk Co.) \chik ə tô´ bət\. From SNEng. Algonquian, contains <chikohteau-> 'it (fire) rages violently', <-ut> 'place' (W. Cowan p.c.).

CHICKIMA (LA, Rapides Par.) \chik´ i mô\. Probably from Choctaw (Muskogean) *achukma* 'good' (Read 1927; P. Munro p.c.). Likely related names are **Chickamaw Bend** (La., Madison Par.) and **Chickamauga River** (Ga., Tenn.).

CHICKINACOMMOCK Inlet (N.C., Dare Co.) \chik i nə kom´ ək\. Probably of CAC Algonquian origin; the name has been written <Chickinockcominock, Chickinoke, Chicomok> (Payne 1985). Perhaps related are the names of **Chicamacomico Channel** (N.C., Dare Co.) and **Chicamacomico River** (Md., Dorchester Co.).

CHICKNEY Creek (Wis., Menominee Co.) \chik´ nē\. A shortening of **Machickanee,** the name of a Menominee (Algonquian) leader, perhaps meaning 'bad eagle' (Vogel 1991); cf. /mace:q-/ 'bad', /kene:w/ 'eagle' (Bloomfield 1975). The written form **Chickeney** also occurs.

CHICKWAN Bight (Alaska, Dixon Entrance C-3). The Tlingit name was published in 1911 (Orth 1967).

CHICKWOLNEPY Stream (N.H., Coös Co.) \chik wol´ nə pē\. The Abenaki (Algonquian) name is said to mean 'frog pond' (Huden 1962); cf. Western Abenaki *cegwal* 'frog', *nebi* 'water' (Day 1994–95).

CHICO \chē´ kō\. This Spanish word means 'small' and can also be a nickname for someone called *Francisco.* In the Southwest it is used as the name of a native bush, in English called black greasewood; this is probably the source of the placename **Chico** in N.Mex. (Colfax Co.; Julyan 1998). An Indian origin for the name of the bush is possible. A Spanish adjective derived from the name of the plant occurs in **Chicosa Lake** (N.Mex., Harding Co.). Elsewhere, **Chico** (Wash., Kitsap Co.) was named for an Indian leader who died in 1909; the derivation of his name is not known. In Calif. **Chico** (Butte Co.) gets its name from Spanish *arroyo chico* 'small creek'.

CHICOG (Wis., Washburn Co.) \shi kog´\. Perhaps named for an Ojibwa (Algonquian) Indian), whose name may have been the word for 'skunk' (Vogel 1991); cf. Ojibwa *zhigaag* (Nichols and Nyholm 1995). This word is of course related to the word **Skunk,** of Algonquian origin, which occurs in placenames elsewhere.

CHICOMA Mountain (N.Mex., Rio Arriba Co.) \chi kō´ mə\. Perhaps from a Tewa (Tanoan) word meaning 'flint, obsidian' (Julyan 1998).

CHICONE Creek (Md., Dorchester Co.) \chi kōn´\. A CAC Algonquian name, perhaps meaning 'big snow' (Kenny 1984).

CHICOPA Creek (Miss., Holmes Co.) \chi kō´ pə\. Perhaps from Choctaw (Muskogean) <shikopa> 'feather' (Seale 1939).

CHICOPEE (Mass., Hampden Co.) \chik´ ə pē\. From SNEng. Algonquian, perhaps meaning 'violent water'; cf. <chikka-> 'violently', <pa-> 'water'. The name has been transferred to many areas (e.g., Ga., Hall Co.; Kans., Crawford Co.; and Idaho, Bonner Co.).

CHICORA (S.C., Berkeley Co.) \shi kō´ rə\. The name given by the Spanish to an Indian group that they encountered on the coast of present-day S.C. in the early sixteenth century (Neuffer and Neuffer 1983). The name also is found in Miss. (Wayne Co.) and Pa. (Butler Co.) The town of **Chicora** in Mich. (Allegan Co.) [chi kō´ rə] was named for a passenger steamer that sank in Lake Michigan in 1895.

CHICORICA Creek (N.Mex., Colfax Co.) \chik ə rē´ kə\. Perhaps from a Plains Apache (Athabaskan) term for 'turkey', equivalent to Navajo *tsídii łíkizh* 'bird-spotted' (Young and Morgan 1987). This may have become Spanish **chiti-riqui,* changed by assimilation to **chiquiriqui,* and then folk-etymologized to *chico rico* 'rich child'. English pronunciation resulted in **Chicorica** (Bright and de Reuse 2002). The same term has been adapted into English as **Sugarite** \sho͞og´ ə rē͞et\.

CHICOSA Lake (N.Mex., Harding Co.) \chi kō´ zə\. The Spanish adjective is derived from *chico* 'black greasewood', perhaps an Indian name in origin. The masculine form of the adjective, **Chicoso,** also occurs as a placename in N.Mex. (Colfax Co.).

CHICOTA (Tex., Lamar Co.) \chi kō´ tə\. Possibly a variant of **Checotah** (Okla., McIntosh Co.). This is perhaps from a Muskogee placename *cokotv* /čokó:ta/ (Martin and Mauldin 2000). Another possible origin is from American Spanish *chicote* 'whip'.

CHICOT County (Ark.) \shē´ kō\. Perhaps from an unidentified Indian language; or perhaps from French *chicot* 'stub, stump' (Deane 1986:20).

CHICWILLASAW Creek (Miss., Clarke Co.) \chik wil´ ə sô\. May be from Chickasaw *chokkilissa, chokkillissa* 'to be quiet, lonely' or from Choctaw *chokkilissa, chokkillissa* 'vacant house, solitude', perhaps containing *chokka* 'house' (P. Munro p.c.).

CHIDAGLEKNE Creek (Alaska, Nabesna D-2). From Upper Tanana (Athabaskan), of unclear derivation.

CHIDEK Lake (Alaska, Nabesna D-2). From Upper Tanana (Athabaskan) *tidettsoh männ',* lit. 'yellow-water lake' (J. Kari p.c.).

CHIEF. A term often applied by whites to Indian leaders or jocosely to male Indians in general; in the latter usage, it is now generally considered patronizing and unacceptable. The word has been widely used in placenames: for example, **Chief Creek** (Mich., Manistee Co.) and **Chiefs Lake** (i.e., Chief's Lake; Ohio, Warren Co.) It also occurs when the full name of an Indian leader is used as a placename, such as **Chief Joseph Mountain** (Ore., Wallowa Co.); to find such names, refer to the element following **Chief**.

CHIEFS HEAD Peak (Colo., Boulder Co.) is based on Arapaho (Algonquian) *nííthe'ééno* 'heads' (A. Cowell, p.c.).

CHIGINAGAK Bay (Alaska, Sutwik Island D-3). The Yupik (Eskimo) name was recorded as <Tchighinagac> in 1827 (Orth 1967).

CHIGLEY (Okla., Murray Co.) \chig´ lē\. Named for Nelson Chigley, a prominent Chickasaw (Shirk 1974).

CHIGMIT Mountains (Alaska, Lake Clark A-2) \chig´ mit\. The name is probably Yupik (Eskimo); it was first recorded in 1850 (Orth 1967).

CHIGNAKI Pond (Alaska, Anchorage C-7). The name is probably Ahtena (Athabaskan), of unknown derivation (BGN 8002).

CHIGNIK (Alaska, Chignik B-2) \chig´nik\. The Alutiiq (Eskimo) name was reported in 1847 (Orth 1967).

CHIGOORHALIGAMIUT (Alaska, Cape Mendenhall D-3). The Yupik (Eskimo) name was reported in 1949 (Orth 1967).

CHIHUAHUA Valley (Calif., San Diego Co.) \chi wä´ wä\. Named after a state in northern Mexico, perhaps meaning 'dry place', derived from an unidentified Indian language (Room 1997). There is also a **Chihuahua** in Tex. (Hidalgo Co.).

CHIJUK Creek (Alaska, Tyonek D-2). Named for a Dena'ina (Athabaskan) leader who died in the 1930s (BGN 8502). The term is said to mean 'curly hair' (Kari 1999:69).

CHIKAMIN Creek (Wash., Chelan Co.) \chik´ ə min\. Chinook Jargon <chik´-a-min> [číkəmən, číkəmɪn] 'iron, metal, money', from Nootka *cikimin* 'iron' (D. Kinkade p.c.). A related placename is **Chickamin River** (Alaska, Ketchikan D-3).

CHIKAMING Township (Mich., Berrien Co.) \chik´ ə ming\. Said to be Potawatomi (Algonquian) for 'big lake' (Vogel 1986); cf. Ojibwa *gichi-, chi-* 'big', *agamiing* 'at the lake' (Nichols and Nyholm 1995).

CHIKAPANAGI Mesa (Ariz., Coconino Co.). From Havasupai (Yuman) /jgbañg/ 'bat' (McNamee 1997; Hinton et al. 1984).

CHIKASANOXEE Creek (Ala., Chambers Co.) \chik ə sô nok´ si\. Earlier written <Cohoasanocsa, Konuckse>, perhaps Muskogee for 'cane-ridge', and later confused with the tribal name Chickasaw (Read 1984). Cf. Muskogee *kohv* /kohá/ 'cane', *cvnakse* /čanák-si/ 'ridged' (Martin and Mauldin 2000).

CHIKASKIA River (Okla., Kay Co.) \chi kas´ kē ə, shi kas´ kē ə\. This name has been said to be Osage (Siouan) for 'white spotted deer' (Shirk 1974), but that origin cannot be confirmed. Possibly it is an invented name, incorporating elements of two Ill. names, **Chicago** and **Kaskaskia**.

CHIKOOTNA Creek (Alaska, Anchorage D-4) \chi ko͞ot´ nə\. The Dena'ina (Athabaskan) name was reported in 1932 (Orth 1967).

CHIKULULNUK Creek (Alaska, Taylor Mountains D-7). The Yupik (Eskimo) name was reported in 1844 (Orth 1967).

CHIKUMINUK Lake (Alaska, Taylor Mountains A-8). The Yupik (Eskimo) name was reported in 1915 (Orth 1967).

CHIKUNGAMIUT (Alaska, Cape Mendenhall D-4). The Yupik (Eskimo) name was reported in 1949 (Orth 1967); the suffix *-miut* means 'people'.

CHILAO (Calif., Los Angeles Co.) \chi lā´ ō\. Previously written <Chileo, Chilleo>, the name of a local bandit, perhaps from Spanish *chileno* 'Chilean', from the nation of *Chile,* originally a South American Indian word (Gudde 1998).

CHILATCHEE Creek (Ala., Dallas Co.) \chi lach´ i\. Probably from Choctaw *cholah-hahcha,* lit. 'fox river' (P. Munro p.c.).

CHILCHITNA River (Alaska, Lake Clark B-8) \chil chit´ nə\. From the Dena'ina (Athabaskan) placename *chaɬchitnu* (Kari and Kari 1982).

CHILCHUKABENA Lake (Alaska, Mt. McKinley D-4) \chil cho͞o kə bin´ ə\. From Koyukon (Athabaskan) *ch'elkoghee bene',* perhaps referring to a 'fat animal'; with *bene'* 'lake' (Kari 1999:119).

CHILCOOT \chil´ ko͞ot\. From the same source as **Chilkoot,** an Alaskan placename made famous at the time of the Yukon Gold Rush around 1900. The term originally referred to a subdivision of the Tlingit Indians. Placenames using the spelling **Chilcoot** occur in Calif., Trinity Co.; Idaho, Valley Co.; and Ore., Douglas Co.

CHILE \chil´ ē\. The name of this South American nation is probably derived from a local Indian language. The term has sometimes been confused with Mexican Spanish *chile* 'chili pepper', derived from Nahuatl (Aztecan) *chilli,* and the spellings **Chili** and **Chilli** have been used in English for both the country and the vegetable. The large number of Chilean miners who came to Calif. during the Gold Rush inspired names like **Chili Bar** (Calif., El Dorado Co.) There is also a **Chilean Mill** in Ariz. (Yavapai Co.).

CHILENO Valley (Calif., Marin Co.) \chi lē´ nō\. From the Spanish designation for a native of Chile (Gudde 1998).

CHILHOWEE Mountain (Tenn., Polk Co.) \chil hô´ wē, chil hou´ wē, chil ə wē`\. The name is probably derived from Muskogean or from Cherokee (Iroquoian); it was first reported as **Chalahume** by a Spanish explorer, but the Muskogean form has also been written in English spelling as <Chilhoe> (Booker et al. 1992: 432). There is also a town called **Chilhowee** in Mo. (Johnson Co.) Probably also related is **Chilhowie,** a town in Va. (Smyth Co.).

CHILI \chil´ ē\. This spelling has been used in English both for the South American nation of Chile, derived from an Indian language of the area, and as the counterpart of Mexican Spanish *chile* 'chili pepper', derived from Nahuatl (Aztecan) *chilli.* **Chile, Chili,** and **Chilli** have been used in English for both the country and the vegetable. U.S. placenames that use **Chili** include towns in N.Mex. (Rio Arriba Co.), Ind. (Miami Co.), and Wis. (Clark Co.).

CHILICOTAL Mountain (Tex., Brewster Co.) \chil i kō täl`\. Mexican Spanish, 'where the *chilicote* grows', referring to a squash-like plant. The term also occurs in **Chilicote Canyon** (Tex., Presidio Co.) \chil i kō´ tē\. This is a variant of *chilicayote,* from Nahuatl (Uto-Aztecan) *chilicayotl* 'a type of squash' (Karttunen 1983).

CHILIKADROTNA River (Alaska, Lake Clark C-7) \chil i kə drot´ nə\. From Dena'ina (Athabaskan) *tsilak'idghutnu,* perhaps with *-tsila* 'tongue' (Kari and Kari 1982; Wassillie 1979).

CHILILI (N.Mex., Bernalillo Co.) \chi li lē`\. Perhaps from a Tiwa (Tanoan) word meaning 'sound of water barely trickling' (Julyan 1998).

CHILIWIST (Wash., Okanogan Co.) \chil´ ə wist\. From the same source as **Chillowist:** Okanagan (Salishan) [sləx^{w}íʔst] 'bluff with holes' (D. Kinkade p.c.).

CHILKAT (Alaska, Skagway A-2) \chil´kat\. Eyak /jiɬqaat/ 'the Bering River'. The name is not to be confused with **Chilkoot** (Skagway B-2) [chil´ ko͞ot]; this term refers to a clan of the Tlingit Indians, called /ǯiɬqut/ in their own language (*HNAI* 7:227). There is also a **Chilkoot Pass** (Ore., Grant Co.).

CHILLICOTHE (Ohio, Ross Co.) \chil i kôth´ ē, chil i koth´ ē\. From Miami/Illinois (Algonquian) /čalaka:θe/ 'member of the /čalaka/ subgroup', referring to a division of the Shawnee people (also Algonquian; M. McCafferty p.c.). The placename **Chillicothe** has been transferred to several states (e.g., Ill., Peoria Co.; Mo., Livingston Co.; and Tex., Hardeman Co.).

CHILLI Creek (Miss., Benton Co.) \chil´ ē\. Perhaps from **Chile,** the South American country, or from Mexican Spanish *chile* 'chili pepper', from Nahuatl (Aztecan) *chilli.* Other placenames written **Chile** and **Chili** are widespread in the United States.

CHILLIGAN River (Alaska, Tyonek A-8). Named for an Indian resident, probably Dena'ina (Athabaskan); reported in 1919 (Orth 1967).

CHILLISQUAQUE (Pa., Northumberland Co.). Formerly written <Chelisquaqua, Shallyschohking, Zilly-squachne> (etc.); said to represent <Chililisuagi> 'place of snow-birds' in some Algonquian language (Donehoo 1928).

CHILLIWACK River (Wash., Whatcom Co.) \chil´i wak\. Formerly written <Chillukweyuk>; the name is probably Indian, but the derivation is not clear (Hitchman 1985).

CHILLOWIST (Wash., Okanogan Co.) \chil´ ə wist\. From Okanagan (Salishan) [sləx^{w}í?st] 'bluff with holes', containing /ləx^{w}-/ 'hole', /-i?st/ 'rock' (D. Kinkade p.c.). The variant **Chiliwist** also occurs.

CHILNUALNA (Calif., Mariposa Co.) \chil nōō äl´ nə\. Perhaps containing Southern Sierra Miwok /čɨli/ 'mosquito' (Gudde 1998).

CHILOCCO (Okla., Kay Co.) \chi luk´ ō, chi lok´ ō\. Muskogee *cerakko* /čiłákko/ 'horse', lit. 'big deer', from *eco* /ičó/ 'deer', *-rakko* /-łákko/ 'big' (Martin and Mauldin 2000).

CHILOQUIN (Ore., Klamath Co.) \chil´ ə kwin\. From the name of a Klamath man, *čiiloqin* (Barker 1963).

CHILOWAY (N.Y., Delaware Co.) \chil´ ə wā\. Said to be the name of an Indian converted by the Moravian Mission, linguistic affiliation unknown (Beauchamp 1907).

CHILTIPIN Creek (Tex., Jim Wells Co.) \chil ti pēn´\. From Mexican Spanish *chiltepín,* a variant of *chiltipiquín* 'a type of chili pepper', from Nahuatl (Aztecan) *chiltecpin,* from *chilli* 'chili pepper' plus *tecpin(tli)* 'flea' (Santamaría 1959).

CHIMACUM (Wash., Jefferson Co.) \chim´ ə kəm\. Named for a people of the area; their name is generally written **Chemakum** by anthropologists and linguists, and their language has been assigned to the Chemakuan linguistic family. The English word, however, comes from the term used by their Salishan neighbors to designate them; cf. Twana [cə́bqəb], Lushootseed [cə́bəqəb] (D. Kinkade p.c.). These forms reflect the alternation between *m* and *b* that characterizes languages of the area.

CHIMAL, Valle (N.Mex., San Miguel Co.) \chē mäl´\. New Mexican Spanish *chimal* 'a homemade shield made of rawhide' (Cobos 1983), from Nahuatl (Aztecan) *chimalli* 'shield' (Julyan 1998).

CHIMAYO (N.Mex., Rio Arriba Co.) \chim ə yō´\. From Spanish *Chimayó,* name of a former Tewa (Tanoan) pueblo, said to mean 'good flaking stone' (Julyan 1998). The name of **Chimayosos Peak** (N.Mex., Rio Arriba Co.) \chim ə yō´ sōs\ contains a Spanish word meaning 'people from Chimayó' (Julyan 1998).

CHIMENCHUN Creek (Alaska, Naknek C-3). The Yupik (Eskimo) name was reported in 1952 (Orth 1967).

CHIMILES (Calif., Napa Co.) \chi mē´ lās\. The name, of unknown Indian origin, was given to a land grant dated 1846 (Gudde 1998).

CHIMMEKANEE Creek (Calif., Humboldt Co.) \chim ə kə nē´\. From the Karuk village *chamiknîinach* (Gudde 1998).

CHINATI (Tex., Presidio Co.) \chi nä´ tē\. Perhaps from Mexican Spanish *chanate, zanate* 'blackbird', from Nahuatl (Aztecan) *tzanatl* 'grackle' (Santamaría 1959; Karttunen 1983).

CHINCHAHOMA Creek (Miss., Oktibbeha Co.) \ching kə hō´ mə\. Said to be a Choctaw (Muskogean) personal name, literally meaning 'red post-oak' (Seale 1939). The derivation is apparently from Choctaw *chisha* 'post-oak', *homma* 'red' (P. Munro p.c.).

CHINCHALO (Ore., Klamath Co.) \chin chä´ lō\. Named for a nineteenth-century Klamath leader (McArthur 1992).

CHINCHONTE, Arroyo (N.Mex., Torrance Co.) \chin chon´ tā\. New Mexican Spanish *chinchonte* 'mocking bird' (Cobos 1983), from Mexican Spanish *sinsonte, zenzontle* (Santamaría 1959), abbreviated from Nahuatl (Aztecan) *centzon-tlahtoleh,* lit. 'having four hundred languages', containing *centzontli* 'four hundred' plus *tlahtolli* 'word, language' (Julyan 1998).

CHINCOPIN Branch (N.J., Cumberland Co.) Probably from the same source as **Chinquapin** \ching´ kə pin\, a type of chestnut; in that spelling, the term is widespread as a placename. It is from CAC Algonquian <chechinquamins> (*RHD* 1987).

CHINCOTEAGUE Bay (Va., Accomack Co.) \shing kō tēg´\. From CAC Algonquian, perhaps meaning 'large inlet' (Hagemann 1988). The term is associated with "Chincoteague ponies" and "Chincoteague oysters." Perhaps related is **Cinquoteck** (Va., King William Co.).

CHINDAGLEKNE Creek (Alaska, Nabesna D-2). The name is Upper Tanana (Athabaskan) (Orth 1967).

CHINDAGMUND Lake (Alaska, Tanacross A-3). From Upper Tanana (Athabaskan) *ch'inaagn männ'* 'mineral-lick lake' (J. Kari p.c.).

CHINDE (N.Mex., San Juan Co.) \chin dē´, chēn´ dē\. From Navajo (Athabaskan) *ch'į́įdii* 'evil spirit, devil, ghost', also used as an expletive, 'Damn! Hell!' (A. Wilson p.c.).

CHINEEKLUK Mountain (Alaska, Sleetmute B-6). The Yupik (Eskimo) name is said to mean 'pointed' (Orth 1967); cf. Yupik *cingik* 'point' (Jacobson 1984). Related placenames include **Chingeeruk Point** (Alaska, Nunivak Is. B-5) and **Chingekigtlik** (Alaska, Goodnews Bay B-6).

CHINGARORA Creek (N.J., Monmouth Co.) \ching gə rôr´ ə\. The derivation from Delaware (Algonquian) is not clear (Becker 1964).

CHINGEERUK Point (Alaska, Nunivak Island B-5). The Yupik (Eskimo) name is said to mean 'point of land' (Orth 1967); cf. Yupik *cingig-* 'to be sharp', *cingik* 'point' (Jacobson 1984). A probably related placename is **Chingekigtlik Mountain** (Alaska, Goodnews Bay B-6). Other probably related names include **Chineekluk Mountain** (Alaska, Sleetmute B-6).

CHINIAK Bay (Alaska, Kodiak C-2). Although this site is in Alutiiq (Eskimo) territory, the name has been interpreted as coming from Aleut *chihngax̂* 'crag, impassable spot' (Orth 1967; Bergsland 1994). A possibly related form is **Cape Tuniak** (Alaska, Kodiak C-1).

CHINIDERE Mountain (Ore., Hood River Co.) \chin´ i dēr\. Named for a nineteenth-century leader of the Wasco (Chinookan) people (McArthur 1992).

CHINIGYAK, Cape (Alaska, Nunivak Island B-1). The Yupik (Eskimo) name was recorded in 1949 (Orth 1967).

CHINIKLIK, Mount (Alaska, Russian Mission D-6). The Koyukon (Athabaskan) name was reported in the nineteenth century (Orth 1967).

CHINIKLUK Slough (Alaska, Kwiguk D-5). The Yupik (Eskimo) name was recorded in 1952 (Orth 1967).

CHINITNA Bay (Alaska, Iliamna D-1) \chi nit´ nə\. From Dena'ina (Athabaskan) *tsanitnu* 'cliffs-are-there stream', with *-tnu* 'stream' (Kari and Kari 1982:26).

CHINIT Point (Alaska, Nunivak Island C-1). The Yupik (Eskimo) name is said to mean 'points of land' (Orth 1967); cf. Yupik *chingik* 'point' (Jacobson 1984).

CHINKAPIN Creek (N.C., Hertford Co.) \ching´ kə pin\. From the same source as **Chinquapin**; see below.

CHINKELYES Creek (Alaska, Iliamna C-3) \ching´ kəl gash\. From Dena'ina (Athabaskan) *ch'ank'elyashtnu* 'things-are-carried-out stream', with *-tnu* 'stream' (Kari and Kari 1982:25).

CHINLE Creek (Ariz., Apache Co.; Utah, San Juan Co.) \chin lē´, chin´ lē, shin´ lē\. Navajo

(Athabaskan) *ch'ínílį́* 'it flows outward', from *chi* 'outward', *nílį́* 'it flows' (Wilson 1995).

CHINNABEE (Ala., Talladega Co.) \chin´ ə bē\. Named for a Muskogee leader and meaning 'cedar tree' (Read 1984); cf. *vcenv* /acína/ 'cedar', *vpe* /apí/ 'tree' (Martin and Mauldin 2000). Also written **Chinneby, Chief Chenneby**.

CHINOM Point (Wash., Kitsap Co.) Earlier written <Tchinom>; possibly a Twana (Salishan) name, of unknown derivation (Hitchman 1985).

CHINOOK \chi nōōk´, shi nōōk´\. This name for a group of related Indian peoples, living in Wash. and Ore. on the lower Columbia River, is from Lower Chehalis (Salishan) /činúk/, a village site on Baker Bay (D. Kinkade p.c.). The term has given rise to many placenames (e.g., Wash., Pacific Co.; Ore., Lincoln Co.; and Alaska, Talkeetna Mountains D-5). The word **Chinook** also refers to a kind of salmon and to warm winds that blow in spring in the Pacific Northwest and Rocky Mountain states. The term **Chinook Jargon** designates a trade language containing elements from Chinook and other Indian languages as well as from French and English that was once used in the Pacific Northwest; locally it was often called simply "Chinook" or "Jargon."

CHINQUAPIN \ching´ kə pin, shing´ kə pin\. The name of a kind of wild chestnut, recorded in CAC Algonquian as <chechinquamins> in colonial times (*RHD* 1987). As a placename, the term occurs in Md. (Baltimore Co.), N.C. (Duplin Co.), and Calif. (Mariposa Co.). The related forms **Chincopin Branch** and **Chinkapin Creek** occur in several states.

CHINTIMINI Creek (Ore., Benton Co.) \chin tim´ i nē\. Central Kalapuyan *čhantímanwi,* the name of a mountain where spiritual power was sought (H. Zenk p.c.).

CHINUBEE (Tenn., Lawrence Co.). The term has been said to mean 'land of the mighty wind' in an unidentified Indian language (Siler 1985).

CHIPETA (Colo., Delta Co.) \chi pē´ tə\. The name is probably from the same source as **Chepeta Lake,** which also occurs as a placename; it refers to the wife of Ouray, the nineteenth-century Ute (Numic) leader. From Ute /cipittɨ/ 'a spring', derived from /cippi/ 'to come out' (J. McLaughlin p.c.). The name also occurs in Utah (e.g., Uintah Co.).

CHIPMUNK \chip´ mungk\. A type of small squirrel; the name was earlier written <chitmunk>. It is apparently from Ojibwa (Algonquian) *ajidamoo* 'red squirrrel', containing *ajid-* 'upside down', because the animal's manner of descending trees (*RHD* 1987; Nichols and Nyholm 1995). As a placename, the word is widespread (e.g., Wis., Vernon Co.; Utah, Garfield Co.; and Wash., Yakima Co.).

CHI Point (Alaska, Lake Clark A-5) \chē\. Perhaps from a Dena'ina (Athabaskan) pronunciation of Russian *chai* 'tea' (J. Kari p.c.).

CHIPOLA Creek (Ala., Barbour Co.) \chi pō´ lə\. Perhaps from Choctaw (Muskogean) *chipolli* 'feast' (Read 1984, P. Munro p.c.) The name also occurs in Fla. (Calhoun Co.).

CHIPPEKOKEE Park (Ind., Knox Co.) \chip ə kō´ kē\. From Miami/Illinois (Algonquian) /čiipihkaahki/ 'root land', with /čiipihka/ 'root' and /-ahki-/ 'land' (McCafferty 2002).

CHIPPEWA \chip´ ə wô\. The name of a people of the Great Lakes area, speaking a language of the Algonquian family. The word is synonymous with and cognate with the terms **Ojibwa** and **Ojibwe,** all going back to the self-designation *ojibwe.* A Native American explanation connects this term with a root meaning 'puckered up', referring to the form of Ojibwa moccasins (*HNAI* 15:768, Nichols and Nyholm 1995). Some Chippewas today prefer to describe themselves as *anishinaabe* 'original people'. The form **Chippewa** is widespread in placenames (e.g., Ill., Cook Co.; Mich., Cheboygan Co.; and Wis., Dunn Co.) A related form occurs in **Chippeway Park** (N.Mex., Otero Co.).

CHIPPEWANUCK Creek (Ind., Kosciusko Co.) \chip ə wä´ nək\. From Potawatomi

(Algonquian) *jibəywanəg* 'at the corpse hole', that is, 'at the grave' (McCafferty 2002).

CHIPPOKES (Va., Surry Co.). Said to be named after a CAC Algonquian resident named <Choupouke> in the seventeenth century (Hagemann 1988).

CHIPUXET River (R.I., Washington Co.) \chi puk´ sət\. From SNEng. Algonquian for 'little separate place'; cf. <chippe> 'separate', <uhke> 'land', <-s-> 'small', <-et> 'place' (W. Cowan p.c.).

CHIRICAHUA (Ariz., Cochise Co.) \chir ə kä´ wə\. The name of an Apache (Athabaskan) group; from Spanish *Chiricagui,* a name applied to mountains in Sonora, Mexico, derived from the Ópata (Uto-Aztecan) language of that region (*HNAI* 10:417).

CHIRPCHATTER (Calif., Shasta Co.) \chûrp´ chat ər\. From Wintu /t'arap č'araw/, lit. 'cottonwood field', from /t'arap/ 'cottonwood tree' and /č'araw/ 'green place' (Gudde 1998).

CHISAGO County (Minn.) \ši sä´ gō\. Supposedly from Ojibwa (Algonquian) <Ki-chi-sago>, lit. 'big lovely' (Upham 2001); cf. *gichi-* 'big', *zaagi'-* 'to love' (Nichols and Nyholm 1995).

CHISAK Bay (Alaska, Adak C-1) The Aleut name was reported as <Kchisakh> in 1868 (Orth 1967).

CHISANA (Alaska, Nabesna A-3) \chi san´ ə, sho͞o shan´ ə\. Ahtna (Athabaskan) *tsetsaan' na'* 'copper river', from *tsetsaan'* 'copper' (*tse* 'rock', *tsaan* 'excrement') plus *na'* 'stream' (Kari 1990).

CHISCA (Ala., Colbert Co.) \chis´ kə\. Muskogee *ceskv* /číska/ 'edge, base, end' (Martin and Mauldin 2000).

CHISE (N.Mex., Sierra Co.) \chēz\. Perhaps from Navajo (Athabaskan) *chíshí,* referring to the Chiricahua Apaches (Athabaskan) (*HNAI* 10:417); or perhaps from Chiricahua Apache (Athabaskan) *chizh* 'firewood' (W. de Reuse p.c.). A possibly related placename is **Cochise County** (Ariz.).

CHISHE:NA:/ A'L'AKKWE'A (N.Mex., Catron Co.). The Zuni placename may contain /ʔakkweʔ/ 'groove, ditch' (Ferguson and Hart 1985; Newman 1958).

CHISIK Island (Alaska, Kenai A-7) \chē´ sik\. From Dena'ina (Athabaskan), of unclear derivation (Orth 1967).

CHISKIAC (Va., York Co.) \kis´ kē ak\. The name of a CAC Algonquian village, recorded in 1622 (Hagemann 1988). The variant spellings **Chischiak** and **Kiskiack** also occur.

CHISMAHOO Creek (Calif., Ventura Co.) \chis´ mə ho͞o\. Probably from Ventureño (Chumashan) /ts'ismuhu/ 'it streams out' (Gudde 1998).

CHISNA (Alaska, Mt. Hayes A-2) \chis´ nə, chēz´ nə\. From Ahtna (Athabaskan) *tsiis na',* lit. 'ochre creek' (Kari 1983:87).

CHISSOVUN Lake (Alaska, Fort Yukon B-4). The Gwich'in (Athabaskan) name was recorded in 1956 (Orth 1967).

CHISTOCHINA (Alaska, Gulkana C-2) \chis tō chē´ nə\. Ahtna (Athabaskan) *tsiis tl'edze' na',* from *tsiis tl'edze',* lit. 'pigment-blue', plus *na'* 'stream' (J. Kari p.c.).

CHITA (Miss., Attala Co.) \chit´ ə\. Perhaps from Choctaw (Muskogean) *chito* 'big' (P. Munro p.c.).

CHITANANA River (Alaska, Kantishna River D-4) \chit ə nan´ ə\. From Koyukon (Athabaskan) *ch'edenaano',* with *no'* stream' (Kari 1999: 108).

CHITANATALA Mountains (Alaska, Kantishna River C-5). From Koyukon (Athabaskan) *ch'edenaa dlele',* with *-dlele'* 'mountain' (Kari 1999:108).

CHITIMACHA (La.) \shi ti mə shä´, chi ti mä´ chə\. The name of an Indian tribe. As a placename, the word occurs in the form **Chetimaches** (La., St. Mary Par.).

CHITINA (Alaska, Valdez C-2) \chit´ nə, chi tē´ nə\. Ahtna (Athabaskan) *tsedi na'* 'copper river', from *tsedi* 'copper' plus *na'* 'stream' (Kari 1990).

CHITIOK, Mount (Alaska, Survey Pass B-5). The Iñupiaq (Eskimo) name is said to mean 'long ears' (Orth 1967); cf. *siun* 'ear', *taki-* 'be long' (MacLean 1980).

CHITISTONE River (Alaska, McCarthy B-5) \chit´ i stōn\. Ahtna (Athabaskan) *tsedi ts'ese' na'* 'copper stone creek'; cf. *tsedi* 'copper', *ts'ese'* 'stone', *na'* 'stream' (Kari 1990).

CHITITU Creek (Alaska, McCarthy B-5). Ahtna (Athabaskan) *tsedi tu',* lit.'copper water' (Kari 1990).

CHITKA Point (Alaska, Rat Islands B-4). Abbreviated from the Aleut name of **Amchitka Island** (Orth 1967).

CHITNA Creek (Alaska, Anchorage D-3) \chit´ nə\. From Ahtna (Athabaskan) *tsit-na'* 'head creek' (J. Kari p.c.).

CHITSIA Mountain (Alaska, Mt. McKinley D-1) \chit sē´ ə\. From Koyukon (Athabaskan) *ch'edzaaye'* 'heart' (Kari 1999:115).

CHITTAMO (Wis., Washburn Co.) \chit´ ə mō\. From Ojibwa (Algonquian) *ajidamoo* 'red squirrel' (Vogel 1991; Nichols and Nyholm 1995).

CHITTO, Bogue (Ala., Choctaw Co.) \chit´ ō\. Choctaw (Muskogean) *book chito,* lit. 'stream big' (P. Munro p.c.). There is also a **Bogue Chitto** in Miss. (Lincoln Co.).

CHITUTAH (N.Dak., McLean Co.) \chi too͞´ tə\. From Arikara (Caddoan) *čitúta'* 'otter' (D. Parks p.c.).

CHIUKI River (Alaska, Bering Glacier A-5). The name is probably Tlingit, reported in 1904 (Orth 1967).

CHIWAPA (Miss., Pontotoc Co.) \chi wô´ pə\. Also written as <Chowappa>; perhaps from Choctaw (Muskogean) *shawi aay-apa* 'where they eat raccoons', containing *shawi* 'raccoon', *apa* 'to eat' (Seale 1939; P. Munro p.c.).

CHIWAUKEE Prairie (Wis., Kenosha Co.) \shi wô´ kē\. A combination of elements from **Chicago** and **Milwaukee,** both names of Algonquian origin (Vogel 1991).

CHIWAUKUM (Wash., Chelan Co.) \chi wä´ kəm, shi wä´ kəm\. From a Moses-Columbian (Salishan) placename, containing /cwáx/ [čwáx] 'creek' (D. Kinkade p.c.). Related names are **Chewack Falls** and **Chewuch River** (Wash., Okanogan Co.) and **Cheweka Creek** (Wash., Stevens Co.).

CHIWAWA River (Wash., Chelan Co.) \chi wä´ wä, shi wä´ wä\. From Moses-Columbian (Salishan) [čwáx t wáwaʔ], containing /cwáx-/ 'creek' (D. Kinkade p.c.).

CHLANAK, Cape (Alaska, Adak B-4). From the Aleut placename *chlanax̂* (Bergsland 1994).

CHLECA Lakes (Alaska, Medfra C-1). Perhaps from Upper Kuskokwim (Athabaskan).

CHLOYA Lake (Alaska, Fort Yukon A-4). The Gwich'in (Athabaskan) name is *tl'oo ghyaa van* 'hollow grass lake' (Caulfield et al. 1983).

CHOCCOLOCCO (Ala., Calhoun Co.) \chok ō lok´ ō\. Perhaps from a Muskogee term meaning 'big shoal' (Read 1984); *cahkē-rakko* /čahki:-ɬákko/, lit. 'shoal-big', is a Muskogee tribal town (Martin and Mauldin 2000).

CHOCKAHOMA (Miss., Tallahatchie Co.) \chok ə hō´ mə\. Perhaps from a Choctaw (Muskogean) clan name <Chakchiuma>; cf. *shaakchi* 'crawfish', *homma* 'red' (Seale 1939).

CHOCKALOG (R.I., Providence Co.) \chôk´ ə lôg\. Perhaps from the SNEng. Algonquian for 'fox place' (Huden 1962). There is also a **Chockalog Pond** in Mass. (Worcester Co.).

CHOCKEYOTTE (N.C., Halifax Co.). The name is believed to be from Tuscarora (Iroquoian) (Powell 1968). An alternative spelling is **Chockoyotte**.

CHOCKTOOT Creek (Ore., Lake Co.) \chok´ too͞t\. Named for a Paiute (Numic) leader (McArthur 1992).

CHOCOLATE \chok´ lət\. From Spanish *chocolate,* of unclear derivation from Nahuatl (Aztecan). In placenames, the word is used to refer to dark brown coloring of earth or water, as in **Chocolate Mountains** (Calif., Imperial Co.) and **Chocolate**

Creek (Wash., Snohomish Co.) In Tex. (Calhoun Co.) **Chocolate Bay** is said to have been so named through a confusion with Mexican Spanish *chiltepín, chiltipiquín* 'a type of chili pepper', from Nahuatl (Aztecan) *chiltecpin* (Tarpley 1980).

CHOCOLAY Creek (Mich., Marquette Co.) \chō´ kō lā\. Perhaps a reflection of English *chocolate* and/or French *chocolat,* both derived from Spanish *chocolate* (Vogel 1986), from Nahuatl.

CHOCONUT Creek (Pa., Susquehanna Co.; N.Y., Broome Co.) \chō´ kə nut\. The name may be from SNEng. Algonquian; it has also been written <Choconotte, Chokenote, Chugnut, Cokonnuck> (etc.) (Beauchamp 1907; Donehoo 1928).

CHOCORUA (N.H., Carroll Co.) \chə kôr´ o͞o ə\. Named for an eighteenth-century Abenaki (Algonquian) leader, of whom many legends are told (Julyan 1993).

CHOCOWINITY (N.C., Beaufort Co.). Of undetermined Indian origin, said to mean 'fish from many waters' (Powell 1968).

CHOCTAFAULA Creek (Ala., Macon Co.) \chok tə fô´ lə\. Perhaps meaning 'tall Choctaw', from Choctaw (Muskogean) *chahta* 'Choctaw', *falaya* 'long, tall' (P. Munro p.c.).

CHOCTAHATCHEE Creek (Ala., Macon Co.) \chok tə hach´ ē\. Meaning 'Choctaw stream', from Choctaw (Muskogean) *chahta* 'Choctaw', *hahcha* 'stream' (P. Munro p.c.). A related placename is **Lake Choctawhatchee** (Ala., Henry Co.); see below.

CHOCTAW \chok´ tô\. A people of the southeastern United States, now living in Miss. and Okla.; their language is of the Muskogean family; the Native American name is *chahta,* an unanalyzable word (P. Munro p.c.). The word is widespread in placenames; there are counties so named in Ala., Miss., and Fla. A related placename is **Lake Choctawhatchee** (Ala., Henry Co.) \chok tô hach´ ē\; this is literally 'Choctaw stream', from Choctaw *chahta* 'Choctaw' and *hahcha* 'stream' (P. Munro p.c.). In Fla. (Walton Co.) **Choctawhatchee Bay** is said to be pronounced \chok tə wä´ chē\.

CHOCWICH Campground (Wash., Snohomish Co.). Perhaps from Lushootseed (Salishan) (Hitchman 1985).

CHOKIO (Minn., Stevens Co.) \shə kī´ ō\. Earlier <Chokago>, probably from Dakota (Siouan) *čhokáka,* a form of *čhoká* 'middle' (Upham 2000; Riggs 1890).

CHOKOSNA River (Alaska, McCarthy B-8) \chō kos´ nə\. From Ahtna (Athabakan) *tsetggaasi na'* 'rough-rock river', with *na'* 'stream' (Kari 1983:8).

CHOKOTONK River (Alaska, Lake Clark B-2) \chō kə tongk\. From Dena'ina (Athabaskan) *chuqutenghehtnu* 'trail-cache stream', with *-tnu* 'stream' (Kari and Kari 1982).

CHOKOYIK Island (Alaska, Melozitna A-2). The Koyukon (Athabaskan) name was reported in 1869 (Orth 1967).

CHOKUP Pass (Nev., Eureka Co.) \chō´ kup\. Named for a nineteenth-century Shoshoni (Numic) leader whose name was also written <Sho-kup> (Carlson 1974). The term is possibly from Shoshoni /tsokɨpa/, from /tso-/ 'with the head' plus /kɨppaa/ 'to break (intr.)' (J. McLaughlin p.c.).

CHOLAME (Calif., Monterey Co.) \chō lä´ mē\. A Salinan Indian village; the name is from Migueleño (Salinan) *č'olám,* said to refer to evil people (Gudde 1998).

CHOLOCCO LITABIXEE (Ala., Tallapoosa Co.) \chə lok´ kō lit ə bik´ sē\. Muskogee *corakko le-tvpeksē* /čoɬákko litapíksi:/ 'horse's flat foot', from *corakko* 'horse', *ili* 'foot', *tvpekse* 'flat' (Martin and Mauldin 2000).

CHOPAKA (Wash., Okanogan Co.) \chō pak´ ə\. Probably from Okanagan (Salishan), perhaps meaning 'high mountain' (Hitchman 1985).

CHOPMIST (R.I., Providence Co.) \chop´ mist\. A Narragansett (Algonquian) name of unclear derivation (Huden 1962).

CHOPPEE (S.C., Georgetown Co.) \chop ē \. Perhaps from an unidentified Indian language (Neuffer and Neuffer 1983).

CHOPTANK River (Md., Caroline Co.; Del., Kent Co.) \chop´ tangk\. From a CAC Algonquian name for a tidal stream, perhaps meaning 'it flows back strongly' (Kenny 1984).

CHOPTIE Prairie (Ore., Klamath Co.) \chop´ tē\. Klamath /čapdi/ 'the place of a certain plant', from /čap/, the name of the plant, plus /-di/ 'place of' (Barker 1963).

CHOSKA (Okla., Wagoner Co.) \cho͞os´ kə, chōs´ kə\. The Muskogee name, meaning 'post oak' (a species of oak tree), is said to commemorate Polly Postoak, the townsite owner (Shirk 1974); the Native American name is *coskv* /čó:ska/ 'post oak' (Martin and Mauldin 2000).

CHOTA (Tenn., Blount Co.) \chō´ tə\. Originally the name of a Cherokee village (M. Toomey p.c.). Possibly related is **Echota** (Ga., Gordon Co.), also said to be Cherokee.

CHOTTSIK Lake (Alaska, Arctic A-3). The Gwich'in (Athabaskan) name is *ch'ootsik van* 'soft-mushy-whitefish lake' (Caulfield et al. 1983).

CHOTZATDHAH (Alaska, Christian D-3). The Gwich'in (Athabaskan) name *ch'adzah ddhaa* 'dance mountain' (Caulfield et al. 1983).

CHOWAN County (N.C.). Named for the Chowanoc Indians of the area; the term may be derived from the Algonquian word for 'south', which elsewhere has the form **Shawnee** (Powell 1968).

CHOWCHILLA (Calif., Madera Co.) \chou chil´ ə\. The term refers to a Yokuts subgroup and/or village, whose name was recorded by the Spanish as <Chausila, Chauciles>, perhaps meaning 'killers' (Gudde 1998).

CHOWIET Island (Alaska, Sutwik Island A-3). The Alutiiq (Eskimo) name was reported in 1874 (Orth 1967).

CHUAL, Mount (Calif., Santa Clara Co.) \cho͞o´ əl\. From Mexican Spanish *chual* 'pigweed', from Nahuatl (Aztecan) *tzohualli* (Santamaría 1959). The name **Chualar** (Calif., Monterey Co.) is Mexican Spanish for 'place where pigweed grows' (Gudde 1998).

CHUAR Butte (Ariz., Coconino Co.). Said to be the name of a Southern Paiute (Numic) leader (McNamee 1997).

CHUATHBALUK (Alaska, Russian Mission C-1). Yupik (Eskimo) *curarpalek,* from *curaq* 'blueberry' (Jacobson 1984).

CHUBBEHATCHEE Creek (Ala., Elmore Co.) \chub ē hach´ ē\. Seems to be a scrambled version of Muskogee *hvcce cvpv* /hačči-čápa/, perhaps meaning 'river-edge', from *hvcce* /hačči/ 'stream', *cvpa* /čápa/ 'edge' (Martin and Mauldin 2000).

CHUBBY Creek (Miss., Itawamba Co.) \chub´ ē\. Perhaps an abbreviation of the name of a Choctaw (Muskogean) leader, <Lucha Chuhubi> 'turtle killer' (Seale 1939); cf. *loksi* 'turtle', *abi* 'to kill' (P. Munro p.c.).

CHUCHUPATE (Calif., Kern Co.) \cho͞o cho͞o pat´ ē\. From Spanish *chuchupate,* the name of a local plant; the term is probably from Nahuatl (Aztecan) *xoxouhca-pahtli,* lit. 'blue-medicine' (Gudde 1998).

CHUCHUWANTEEN Cabin (Wash., Okanogan Co.). Perhaps from Okanagan (Salishan) (Hitchman 1985).

CHUCKAHO Creek (Okla., Lincoln Co.). Said to be named for a local Sauk (Algonquian) Indian called <Che-ka-ko> (Shirk 1974).

CHUCKANUT (Wash., Whatcom Co.) \chuk´ ə nut\. From a Lummi (Salishan) placename [xwcə́k^{W}ənəč], perhaps containing /-nəč/ 'bottom, base, butt, bay'; the word may have been borrowed from Nooksack, another Salishan language (D. Kinkade p.c.).

CHUCKATUCK (Va., Suffolk Co.) \chuk´ ə tuk\. Said to be a CAC Algonquian word meaning 'crooked creek' (Hagemann 1988).

CHUCKCHANSI Indian Reservation (Calif., Fresno Co.) \chuk chan´ sē\. From *čhukčhansi,* the name of a Yokuts subgroup (Gudde 1998).

CHUCKEY Creek, Little (N.C., Greene Co.) \chuk´ ē\. An abbreviation for the name of the **Nolichucky River,** of which it is a tributary; cf. the Cherokee (Iroquoian) town <Na-na-tsu-gun>, lit. 'spruce tree place' (M. Toomey p.c.).

CHUCKFEE Bay (Ala., Baldwin Co.) \chuk´ fē\. Choctaw (Muskogean) *chokfi* 'rabbit' (Read 1984, P. Munro p.c.).

CHUCK River (Alaska, Sumdum C-5) \chuk\. Chinook Jargon <chuck> [čʌk] 'water', derived from Nootka (Thomas 1935). The term occurs in other placenames of Alaska and the Pacific Northwest, such as **Salt Chuck** 'salt water' (Alaska, Craig C-2).

CHUCKSEY Branch (Ala., Choctaw Co.) \chuk´ sē\. Perhaps from Choctaw (Muskogean) *chokka* 'house', *-usi* 'small' (P. Munro p.c.).

CHUCKSNEY Creek (Ore., Lane Co.) \chuk´ snē\. Perhaps from Klamath *čakġeenknii* 'serviceberry-area people', used to refer to the Molala people (H. Zenk p.c.).

CHUCKWALLA Mountains (Calif., Riverside Co.) \chuk´ wä lə\. The term refers to a species of lizard native to the California desert. It may come from local Spanish *chacahuala* or directly from Cahuilla (Takic) *cháxwal* (Gudde 1998). The word is also found in places called **Chuckwalla Canyon** (Calif., Inyo Co.; Ariz., Maricopa Co.; Nev., Nye Co.).

CHUCTANUNDA (N.Y., Montgomery Co.) \chuk tə nun´ də\. Also written **Chaughtanoonda**; perhaps Iroquoian, meaning 'stone house' (Beauchamp 1907).

CHUGACH Mountains (Alaska, Valdez A-4) \cho͞o´ gach\. The Alutiiq (Eskimo) name is of uncertain derivation (Orth 1967); it may be from *cuungaaciq* 'Cook Inlet' (*HNAI* 5:195). The name **Chugachik Island** (Alaska, Seldovia C-3) may have the same origin.

CHUGIAK (Alaska, Anchorage B-7) \cho͞og´ yak\. Perhaps from Alutiiq (Eskimo), of unknown derivation (Orth 1967).

CHUGINADAK Island (Alaska, Samalga Island D-6) \cho͞o gin´ ə dak\. Aleut *chuginadax* 'simmering', referring to the constantly smoking Mt. Cleveland; cf. *chugi-* 'to simmer' (Bergsland 1994).

CHUG Spring (Wyo., Sweetwater Co.) \chug\. The word *chug* is used locally to refer to a "buffalo drop," a cliff over which Indian hunters chased buffalo so that they could be slaughtered. The term is said to represent the sound made by the buffalos when they hit the bottom. Related placenames include **Chugwater** (Wyo., Platte Co.) and **Wahkpa Chug'n** (Mont., Hill Co.).

CHUGUL Island (Alaska, Atka B-6). From the Aleut placename *chiĝulax̂,* perhaps meaning 'chasing in a baidarka' (i.e., a boat made of skin), from *chiĝulix* 'to chase in a baidarka' (Bergsland 1994).

CHUGWATER (Wyo., Platte Co.). From the same source as **Chug Spring** (Wyo., Sweetwater Co.); see above.

CHUILNUK River (Alaska, Sleetmute A-4). From Yupik (Eskimo) *cuignilnguq* 'otter' (Orth 1967; Jacobson 1984).

CHUIMUND Lake (Alaska, Tanacross A-4) \cho͞o ē mund\. From Upper Tanana (Athabaskan) *chuyh mänh,* lit 'down-feathers lake' (J. Kari p.c.).

CHUIT Creek (Alaska, Tyonek A-5) \cho͞o´ it\. An abbreviation of Dena'ina (Athabaskan) *ch'u'itnu* 'Chuitna River', containing *-tnu* 'river' (Kari and Fall 1987:52). Related names in the same area are **Chuitna River** (Tyonek A-3) and **Chuitbuna Lake** \cho͞o it bun´ ə\, containing *-bena* 'its lake' (Alaska, Tyonek A-4).

CHUITKILNACHNA Creek (Alaska, Kenai D-5) \cho͞o it kil näch´ nə\. Compare the Dena'ina (Athabaskan) *ch'k'e'uła betnu* 'we-chew-something stream' (Kari and Fall 1987:44).

CHUITNA River (Alaska, Tyonek A-3). From Dena'ina (Athabaskan) *ch'u'itnu,* containing *-tnu* 'stream' (Kari and Kari 1982:52).

CHUKAJAK Creek (Alaska, Solomon D-1). The Iñupiaq (Eskimo) name was published in 1901 (Orth 1967).

CHUKOWAN River (Alaska, Taylor Mountains D-5). The Yupik (Eskimo) name was recorded in 1903 (Orth 1967).

CHUKWUGWAHLIK River (Alaska, Baird Inlet B-4). Yupik (Eskimo) *cuukvagtalek* 'place with many pike', from *cuukvak* 'pike' (a type of fish) (Jacobson 1984).

CHULA (Ark., Yell Co.) \cho͞o´ lə\. From Choctaw (Muskogean) *cholah* 'fox' (P. Munro p.c.). The name occurs elsewhere (e.g., Okla., McCurtain Co.; and Va., Amelia Co.). In some places it may have been confused with Spanish *chula* 'pretty'.

CHULAFINNEE (Ala., Cleburne Co.) \cho͞o lə fin´ ē\. Muskogee for 'pine bridge', from *cule* /čolí/ 'pine', *fenv* /finá/ 'footbridge' (Martin and Mauldin 2000).

CHULAHOMA (Miss., Marshall Co.) \cho͞o lə hō´mə\. Said to be named for a Choctaw (Muskogean) called 'red fox' (Seale 1939); cf. Choctaw *cholah* 'fox', *homma* 'red' (P. Munro p.c.).

CHULITNA River (Alaska, Lake Clark A-5) \cho͞o lit´ nə\. Dena'ina (Athabaskan) *ch'alitnu* 'flows-out stream', with *-tnu* 'stream' (Kari and Kari 1982:24). Another stream in Alaska is also called the **Chulitna River** (Talkeetna Mountains D-6); the derivation is from Dena'ina (Athabaskan) *ts'ilutnu* (Kari and Fall 1987:173).

CHULTIKANA Creek (Alaska, Valdez C-5) From Ahtna (Athabaskan) *tsihwcik'aan na'*, lit. 'where-it-burned-to-the shore creek' (Kari 1983:30).

CHULUOTA (Fla., Seminole Co.) \cho͞o lot´ ə\. Perhaps from an unidentified Indian language (Read 1934).

CHUMASH Peak (Calif., San Luis Obispo Co.) \cho͞o´ mash\. Named for a group of Indian peoples and languages of the southern Calif. coast (Gudde 1998); it includes the Barbareño, Ventureño, and others. The term **Chumashan** is also used with reference to the language family but is not currently used as a placename.

CHUM Lake (Alaska, Kenai D-2) \chum\. Perhaps referring to a type of salmon called the *chum salmon*; the name is from Chinook Jargon <chum> [čʌm] 'variegated in color', from Lower Chinook *c'əm* (*RHD* 1987). A related placename is **Chumstick** (Wash., Chelan Co.).

CHUMSTICK (Wash., Chelan Co.) \chum´ stik\. A Chinook Jargon placename meant to mean 'marked tree'. The components are <chum, tsum> 'mark(ed), write, paint, spot, color', from Lower Chinook *c'əm* 'striped, figured'; and Chinook Jargon <stick> [stɪk] 'tree, wood', from English *stick*. A related placename is **Chum Lake** (Alaska, Kenai D-2).

CHUMUCKLA (Fla., Santa Rosa Co.) \cho͞o muk´ lə\. Perhaps from an unidentified Indian language (Read 1934).

CHUNAK Point (Alaska, Cold Bay A-5). From the Aleut placename *chunax̂* (Bergsland 1994).

CHUNCHULA (Ala., Mobile Co.) \chun cho͞o´ lə\. Perhaps from Choctaw (Muskogean) *hachǫchobah* 'alligator' (Read 1984; P. Munro p.c.).

CHUNEKUKLEIK Mountain (Alaska, Skagway B-3). Said to be from Tlingit <Tschuh-nek-kutsch-kleh-eek> 'notch-in-the-arrow mountain' (Orth 1967).

CHUNIKSAK Point (Alaska, Attu C-4). The Aleut name was published in 1852 (Orth 1967).

CHUNILNA Creek (Alaska, Talkeetna B-1) \chə nil´ nə\. From Dena'ina (Athabaskan) *ch'aniltnu*, with *-tnu* 'stream', or Ahtna *ts'anilna'*, with *-na'*, meaning 'stream that flows out' (Kari and Fall 1987:201).

CHUNKA Creek (S.Dak., Todd Co.) \chung´ kə\. Probably from Lakhota (Siouan) *šų́ka* 'dog' (Ingham 2001).

CHUNKY (Miss., Newton Co.) \chung´ kē\. From Choctaw (Muskogean) *cǫki* 'martin, a type of bird' (Seale 1939; P. Munro p.c.).

CHUNNENUGGEE (Ala., Bullock Co.) \chun ē nug´ ē\. Muskogee *cvnvnvkē* /čananakí:/ 'a ridge' (Martin and Mauldin 2000).

CHUNU Bay (Alaska, Adak B-5). The Aleut name was published in 1956 (Orth 1967).

CHUQUATONCHEE Creek (Miss., Clay Co.) \cho͞o kə ton´ chē\. From Choctaw (Muskogean) *shokha* 'hog', *tǫchi* 'corn', referring to beech mast, prized as food for hogs (Seale 1939; P. Munro p.c.). There are many alternative writings of the name, including **Sookatonchie.**

CHURUBUSCO (Ind., Whitley Co.) \châr ə bus´ ko, châr yo͞o bus´ kō\. The name refers to a place near Mexico City, now the center of the Mexican film industry. The Spanish name is derived from Nahuatl (Aztecan) *huitzilopochco* 'place of Huitzilopochtli', referring to a major deity of the Aztecs. The name of the god is derived from *huitzil(in)* 'hummingbird' and *opochtli* 'left-hand side' (Karttunen 1983). There is also a place called **Churubusco** in N.Y. (Clinton Co.).

CHUSCA, Rio (N.Mex., San Juan Co.) \cho͞o´ skə\. A Spanish spelling for the name of the **Chuska Mountains,** derived from Navajo (Athabaskan) *ch'óshgai* 'white spruce' (Wilson 1995).

CHUSICK (Mass., Hampshire Co.). Said to be SNEng. Algonquian for 'mountain place' (Huden 1962).

CHUSINI Cove (Alaska, Craig D-4). The Tlingit name was published in 1964 (Orth 1967).

CHUSKA Mountains (N.Mex., San Juan Co.) \cho͞o´ skə, chus´ kə\. Navajo (Athabaskan) *ch'óshgai* 'white spruce', from *ch'ó* 'spruce tree', *(sh)gai* '(it is) white' (Wilson 1995).

CHUTLA Peak (Wash., Lewis Co.) \chut´ lə\. From Southern Lushootseed (Salishan) /č'ə́ƛ'əʔ/ 'rock, boulder' (D. Kinkade p.c.).

CHUTTOH Bluffs (Alaska, Chandalar A-1). Gwich'in (Athabaskan) *ch'at'oh* 'nest' (Caulfield et al. 1983).

CIBECUE (Ariz., Navajo Co.) \sib i kyo͞o´, sib´ i kyo͞o, sē´ bē kyo͞o\. From Western Apache (Athabaskan) *deshchíí' bikǫ* 'canyon of horizontally red-things', from *deshchíí'* 'horizontally red things' (*de-* 'things in a line', *s-* 'perfective', *chíí'* 'red') plus *bikǫ* (*bi-* '3rd person possessor', *kǫ* 'canyon, valley') (P. Greenfeld p.c.).

CIBOLA County (N.Mex.) \sē´ bə lə\. From New Mexican Spanish *cíbola* '(female) buffalo, from earlier *vaca de Cíbola* 'cow of Cíbola', referring to the legendary cities of Cíbola that were sought by the conquistadores (Julyan 1998). It has been suggested that *Cíbola* may be derived from the Zuni name for Zuni pueblo, which is *šiwin'a* (*HNAI* 9:480–81). The related form *cíbolo* 'male buffalo' occurs in the names of the **Cibolo Mountains** (N.Mex., DeBaca Co.) \sē´ bə lō\ and **Cibolo Creek** (Tex., Guadalupe Co.) \sē´ bō lō\.

CIGAR Creek (Mont., Dawson Co.) **Cigar** occurs in several American placenames and also in the diminutive **Cigarette**, as in **Cigarette Hills** (Calif., San Diego Co.). The word is borrowed from **cigarro**, Spanish from Yucatec (Mayan) *sik'ar* 'to smoke', from *sik'* 'tobacco' (Gómez 1988).

CINNAMINSON (N.J., Burlington Co.). The name was earlier written <Sinamensinck, Synamensick> (Becker 1964). The source is perhaps Delaware (Algonquian) *ahsënamènsing* 'rocky place of fish' (Kraft and Kraft 1985); cf. Unami Delaware /a:hsə́n/ 'stone', /namés/ 'fish' (Blalock et al. 1994).

CINQUOTECK (Va., King William Co.) \sing´ kə tek\. The name was that of a CAC Algonquian town (Hagemann 1988). Perhaps related is **Chincoteague Bay** (Va., Accomack Co.).

CISCA Lake (Alaska, Kenai C-3) \sis´ kə\. Perhaps from Dena'ina (Athabaskan) *ses ka'a* 'big ridge' (J. Kari p.c.).

CISCO \sis´ kō\. The term refers to a kind of whitefish and is from Canadian French *cisco,* a back-formation from the pseudo-diminutives *ciscoette, ciscaouette,* shortened from Ojibwa (Algonquian) *beemideewiskaweet,* lit. 'fish with oily flesh' (*RHD* 1987); cf. Minnesota Ojibwa *bimide* 'oil' (Nichols and Nyholm 1995). As a placename, **Cisco** occurs in Mich. (Gogebic Co.), Ill. (Piatt Co.), and Utah (Grand Co.) The Ojibwa name of the fish is also borrowed into English as *siscowet* 'a type of lake trout', which also occurs as a placename: for example, as **Siskiwit Bay** (Wis., Bayfield Co.).

CISPUS River (Wash., Lewis Co.) \sis´ pəs\. From Sahaptin [šíšpas], the name of the river (D. Kinkade p.c.).

CITICO (Tenn., Monroe Co.) \sit´ i kō\. Perhaps the name of a Cherokee (Iroquoian) settlement, earlier transcribed as <sitiku, sutagu> (Read 1984). According to Booker et al. (1992:432), the name was also used by Muskogean speakers. It was first recorded by a Spanish explorer as *Satapo,* and later written in English as both **Citico** and **Settico**. The origin probably involves loan-translation; cf. Muskogean *sat(t)a* 'mayhaw, a fruit' and Cherokee /se:ti/ 'a type of fruit'. The placename **Citico** also occurs in Ala. (Etowah Co.).

CLACKAMAS County (Ore.) \klak´ ə məs\. Clackamas Chinook /gitɬáq'imaš, giɬaq'imaš/ 'those of the Clackamas River', based on /niq'ímašix/ 'Clackamas River' (D. Kinkade p.c.).

CLACKAMETTE Cove (Ore., Clackamas Co.). This site lies where the Clackamas River joins the Willamette River, and the name merges the two words (McArthur 1992).

CLALLAM County (Wash.) \klal´ əm\. The term refers to an Indian group that speaks a Salishan language. The name is probably not their own term but the term applied to them by neighboring Salishan peoples; it may be from Songish /x^{w}sƛ̓'éləm/. It is said to mean 'strong people' (D. Kinkade p.c.).

CLAQUATO (Wash., Lewis Co.) \klə kwā´ tō, klak´ wə tō\. From an Upper Chehalis (Salishan) placename /ɬak^{w}ítu/ [ɬak^{w}íto] (D. Kinkade p.c.).

CLASSET Creek (Wash., Clallam Co.). This site is in Makah (Nootkan) territory, but the name is from the Nootka language of Vancouver Island; it is /tl'a:ʔasatx̣/ 'southerly people', the term which the Nootkas applied to the Makahs (W. Jacobson p.c.).

CLATSKANIE River (Ore., Columbia Co.) \klats´ kə nī\. From a Lower Chinook ethnic name, /iɬáck'ani/ 'those of the region of small oaks' (D. Kinkade p.c.). A related form is **Klatskanine River** (Ore., Clatsop Co.).

CLATSOP County (Ore.) \klat´ sop\. From a Lower Chinook ethnic name, /tɬác'əp/, /ɬác'p/ 'those who have pounded salmon' (D. Kinkade p.c.).

CLAWANMENKA Lake (Alaska, Bettles C-3). The Koyukon (Athabaskan) name was recorded in 1956 (Orth 1967).

CLAXTAR (Ore., Marion Co.) \klak´ stər\. From a Lower Chinook ethnic name, /iɬá'aqštaq/ 'roundheads' (D. Kinkade p.c.).

CLAYHATCHEE (Ala., Dale Co.) \klā hach´ ē\. The site is located where Claybank Creek meets the Choctawhatchee River, and the name merges those terms (Read 1984).

CLAYMORE Creek (Kans., Montgomery Co.). Derived from the name of an Osage (Siouan) leader known in English as <Clermont> or <Claremont>. This may have been derived in turn from an Osage name <Gra Mo'n>, of unclear meaning (Rydjord 1968). In Okla. the same name is written **Claremore** (Rogers Co.).

CLEAR Lake (S.Dak., Deuel Co.). Corresponds to the Dakota (Siouan) name, containing *mdéza* 'clear' (Sneve 1973; A. Taylor p.c.). In Alaska (Tanacross A-4).

CLEAWOX Lake (Ore., Lane Co.) \klē´ ə woks\. The name of the lake in the Siuslaw language has been recorded as [tɬ'ú'wɑwɑx̣] and [tɬ́w'a:x] (D. Kinkade p.c.).

CLE ELUM (Wash., Kittitas Co.) \klē el´ əm\. From the Sahaptin placename /ƛ̓iílam/ (D. Kinkade p.c.).

CLEVA Bay (Alaska, Dixon Entrance D-3). The Tlingit name, published in 1923, has been written <Clevak, Tlevak> (Orth 1967). A related name is **Tlevak Narrows** (Alaska, Craig B-4).

CLIFFORD Creek (S.Dak., Shannon Co.). Named for Sybil Clifford, a Sioux woman (Sneve 1973).

CLIFTY Creek (Ind., Rush Co.). The English name seems to refer to cliffs, corresponding to Unami Delaware (Algonquian) /ahsə́n(a) ahaanhúkwi/ 'rocks over and over again' (McCafferty 2002).

CLISTOWACKIN (Pa., Northampton Co.) \klis´ tə wak in\. The Delaware (Algonquian) name perhaps means 'fine land' (Donehoo 1928).

CLOCHACOHUA Lake (Alaska, Beaver B-4). Koyukon (Athabaskan) *tlojə kayəx* 'old village' (Kari 2000).

CLO-CHEW-TAH Ranch (N.Mex., McKinley Co.) \klō cho͞o´ tä\. Navajo (Athabaskan) *tł'ohchintah* 'among the wild onions', from *tł'ohchin* 'wild onion' (*tł'oh* 'grass', *-chin* 'smell') plus *-tah* 'among' (A. Wilson p.c.).

CLOQUALLUM (Wash., Mason Co.). From Upper Chehalis (Salishan) /łaq'ʷə́lm/ [łaq'ʷə́ləm] 'break up, divide', containing /łə́q'ʷ-/ 'to break, pull apart' (D. Kinkade p.c.).

CLY Butte (Ariz., Navajo Co.) \klī\. Perhaps from a Navajo (Athabaskan) personal name *tł'aa'í*, originally meaning 'left-handed', now used in the spelling *Cly* as a family name (A. Wilson p.c.).

COACHELLA (Calif., Riverside Co.) \kō chel´ ə, kō ə chel´ ə\. Derived from **Cahuilla,** the name of the local Indian group, speakers of a Takic language; the term is also used as a placename in the area. The term has sometimes been confused with Spanish *conchilla* 'little shell' (Gudde 1998).

COAGIE Branch (Ala., Coosa Co.) \kō´ gi\. Possibly from Muskogee *kohv* /kohá/ 'cane' plus *hake* /há:ki/ 'noise' (Read 1984); or from *kowike* /ko:wéyki/ 'quail, guinea fowl' (Martin and Mauldin 2000); or from Alabama (Muskogean) *kowi* 'panther' plus *oki* 'water' (P. Munro p.c.).

COAHOMA County (Miss., Coahoma Co.) \kō ə hō´ mə\. Choctaw (Muskogean) for 'red panther', from *kowi* 'panther', *homma* 'red' (Seale 1939; P. Munro p.c.) There is also a **Coahoma** in Tex. (Howard Co.), where it is pronounced \kō hō´ mə, kə hō´ mə\.

COALCA (Ore., Clackamas Co.) \kō al´ kə\. Named for an Indian man, language unknown (McArthur 1992).

COAN (Va., Northumberland Co.). Abbreviated from **Chicacoan**, the name of a CAC Algonquian Indian group (Hagemann 1988).

COASSUK (Vt., Orange Co.) \kō´ ə suk\. A historical name for the place now called *Newbury*. Derived from Western Abenaki (Algonquian) *goasek* [goasək] 'place of small white pines'; cf. *goa* 'white pine', *goas* 'small white pine'; also written **Coösuck** (Day 1994–95). The placename is perhaps cognate with **Cohas Brook** (N.H., Hillsborough Co.), **Cohasset** (Mass., Norfolk Co.), **Cohoes** (N.Y., Albany Co.), and **Coös County** (N.H.).

COATICOOK River (Vt., Essex Co.). Western Abenaki (Algonquian) *goategok* 'at white-pine river'; cf. *goa* 'white pine', *-tegw-* 'river' (Day 1994–95).

COATOPA (Ala., Sumter Co.) \kō ə tō´ pə\. Probably from Choctaw (Muskogean) *kowi aa(ho)ttopa* 'where the panther was wounded', from *kowi* 'panther', *aa-* 'place', *hottopa* 'to be wounded' (Read 1984; P. Munro p.c.).

COATUE (Mass., Nantucket Co.). From SNEng. Algonquian; earlier written <Coatuit, Cotuit, Coituate> (cf. Little 1984); cf. <koowa-> 'pine tree' (Huden 1962; W. Cowan p.c.).

COBBOSSEECONTEE Lake (Maine, Kennebec Co.) \kō bos ē kon´ tē\. Also written <Cobeskonte, Cobasseeconteag, Cobosseconte> (Eckstorm 1941); from Penobscot /kapahséhkαhti/ 'sturgeon gathering place' (P. MacDougall p.c.).

COBMOOSA Lake (Mich., Oceana Co.) \kob mo͞o´ sə\. Named for an Ottawa (Algonquian) leader who died in 1872. His name was also written <Cawpemossay, Caw-ba-mo-say>, translated 'the walker' (Vogel 1986).

COBSCOOK (Maine, Washington Co.) \kobz´ ko͝ok\. Said to be from Malecite (Algonquian) <kapscook> 'rock under water' (Eckstorm 1941).

COCALICO (Pa., Lancaster Co.) \kō kal´ i kō\. Said to be an abbreviation of Delaware (Algonquian) <Achgookwalico> 'snake hole' (Donehoo 1928); cf. Munsee Delaware /axkook-waalakuw/ 'there is a snake-hole', containing /áxkook/ 'snake' (J. O'Meara p.c.).

COCASSET Lake (Mass., Norfolk Co.) \kō kas´ ət\. Perhaps SNEng. Algonquian for 'at the small kettle' (Huden 1962).

COCHECO (N.H., Strafford Co.) \kō chē´ kō\. Said to be Abenaki (Algonquian), 'place of the rapid current' (Huden 1962).

COCHECTON (N.Y., Sullivan Co) \kō kek´ tən\. Earlier written <Cashieghtunk, Cashington> (etc.); a Delaware (Algonquian) name, perhaps meaning 'washing' (Ruttenber 1906; Beauchamp 1907); cf. Munsee Delaware *kshíix-toow* 'to wash' (O'Meara 1996). Related forms include **Coshecton** (Pa., Wayne Co.) and **Cushetunk** (N.J., Hunterdon Co.).

COCHESETT (Mass., Plymouth Co.) \kō ches´ ət\. SNEng. Algonquian, probably from <kutchissitau> 'he washes' (W. Cowan p.c.).

COCHETOPA Pass (Colo., Saguache Co.) \kō chi tō´ pə, koch i tō´ pə\. Probably from Ute (Numic) *kuchútupa* 'buffalo emerging', from *kúchu* 'buffalo', *túpa* 'to emerge' (J. McLaughlin p.c.).

COCHGALECHEE Creek (Ala., Russell Co.) \koch gə lē´ chē\. A Muskogee name, possibly 'lower Broken Arrow' (referring to a tribal town), from *rē kackv* /ɬi:-ka:čka/ (*rē* 'arrow', *kackv* 'broken') plus *lecv* /líča/ 'lower' (Read 1984; Martin and Mauldin 2000).

COCHICHEWICK Lake (Mass., Essex Co.). From SNEng. Algonquian, perhaps 'place where people wash'; cf. <kutchiss(itau)> 'he washes', <-wog> 'plural' (W. Cowan p.c.).

COCHIKUACK Brook (Conn., New London Co.). Also written <Cockichiwake, Caukitchewonk> (etc.); perhaps Mohegan (Algonquian) for 'violent current' (Trumbull 1881).

COCHISE County (Ariz.) \kō chēs´\. Named for a leader of the Chiricahua Apache (Athabaskan) people. The term may be derived from *chizh* 'firewood', *ko-chizh* 'his firewood'; or from *ch'izhí* 'the rough one' (from *dich'izh* 'rough'; P. Greenfeld p.c.). A possibly related placename is **Chise** (N.Mex., Sierra Co.).

COCHITI (N.Mex., Sandoval Co.) \kō´ chi tē\. A pueblo of the Keresan language family; the Native American name is /k'údyîiti/, perhaps meaning 'stone kiva' (I. Davis p.c.).

COCHITUATE (Mass., Middlesex Co.) \kə chit´ yo͞o ət\. From SNEng. Algonquian, perhaps 'where he washes'; cf. <kutchi(ss)itau> 'he washes', <-t> 'place' (W. Cowan p.c.).

COCHNEWAGON Lake (Maine, Kennebec Co.) Said to be Abenaki (Algonquian), meaning 'closed-up route' (Huden 1962).

COCHPINNECOTE (Mass., Barnstable Co.). Wampanoag (Algonquian), perhaps meaning 'at the green bank' (Huden 1962).

COCKAPONSET (Conn., Middlesex Co.). \kok´ ə pon sət\. The name is from SNEng. Algonquian, of unclear derivation (Trumbull 1881).

COCKENOE Harbor (Conn., Fairfield Co.) \kok´ ə nō\. Named for a SNEng. Algonquian man who helped to arrange land transfers in 1652. Also written <Cockeno, Cokenoe>, the name means 'interpeter'; cf. <kuhkinneam> 'he observes' (Trumbull 1881; W. Cowan p.c.).

COCOA Beach (Fla., Brevard Co.) \kō´ kō\. The name appears to contain the word *cocoa,* the name of a beverage; but in fact it reflects the former spelling *cocoanut* for a type of palm and its fruit, now usually spelled *coconut* (Read 1934). Elsewhere in Fla. we find both **Cocoanut**

Key (Monroe Co.) and **Coconut Creek** (Brevard Co.). The name of the coconut is from Portuguese, but the name of the cocoa bean is from Spanish *cacao,* based on Nahuatl (Uto-Aztecan) *cacahuatl* 'cocoa bean'.

COCOLALLA (Idaho, Bonner Co.) \kō kō lä´ lə\. Said to be from Coeur d'Alene (Salishan), meaning 'very cold' (Boone 1988).

COCOLAMUS (Pa., Juniata Co.) \kō kə lā´ məs\. Also written <Cockalamus, Kakonlamus>; an Indian term from an unidentified language (Donehoo 1928).

COCOMUNGA Canyon (Ariz., Gila Co.) \kō kə mung´ gə\. Perhaps a transfer name from **Cucamonga** (Calif., San Bernardino Co.).

COCONINO County (Ariz.) \kō kō nē´ nō\. The term <Coninas, Cogninas, Cosninos> applies to the Havasupai people (Yuman) in early Spanish documents (*HNAI* 10:24); cf. Hopi (Uto-Aztecan) *kòonina* 'Havasupai person' (K. Hill p.c.). A related placename is **Cosnino** (Ariz., Coconino Co.).

COCOPAH Mountains (Calif., Imperial Co.) \kō kō pä´, kō kə pä´, kō´ kō pä, kō´ kə pä\. Named for a Yuman Indian group; their Native American name is *kokwapá* (*HNAI* 10:111). The English spelling generally used by anthropologists and linguists is **Cocopa;** this also occurs in **Cocopa Point** (Ariz., Coconino Co.).

COCUMCUSSOC (R.I., Washington Co.) \kō kə mus´ək\. From SNEng. Algonquian, perhaps 'place of high rock' (Huden 1962).

C.O.D. Lake (Alaska, Livengood A-5). A folk-etymology from Lower Tanana (Athabaskan) *tho'odi mena',* lit. 'all-the-time lake' (J. Kari p.c.).

CODORUS Creek (Pa., York Co.) \kə dôr´ əs\. Said to be an Indian word, from an unidentified source, meaning 'rapid water' (Donehoo 1928).

COE (Wash., King Co.) \kō\. From Lushootseed (Salishan) /q^{W}úʔ/ '(fresh) water' (D. Kinkade p.c.).

COES Reservoir (Mass., Worcester Co.) \kōz\. From SNEng. Algonquian, 'small pine tree', from <koowa-> 'pine tree', <-s> 'small' (W. Cowan p.c.). Related placenames include **Coös County** (N.H.).

COESSE (Ind., Whitley Co.) \kō es´ ē\. Named for a (Algonquian) leader, <Ko-wa-zi, Ku-wa-zi>, supposed to mean 'old man' (Baker 1995).

COEUR D'ALENE (Idaho, Kootenai Co.) \ko͞or də len´, ko͞or´ də len\. The name refers to a Salishan group of the area. It is French for 'heart of (like) an awl', applied for reasons that are now unclear (Boone 1988).

COFACHIQUI (Ga., Richmond Co.). The site of a village ruled by a woman Muskogee leader, encountered by the Spanish explorer Hernando de Soto in the seventeenth century; also written <Cofitachequi>, perhaps meaning 'dogwood town' (Krakow 1975). Cofachiqui also occurs as a transfer name in Kans. (Allen Co.).

COFFADELIAH (Miss., Neshoba Co.) \kof ə də lī´ ə\. Choctaw (Muskogean), meaning 'sassafras thicket', from *kafi* 'sassafras', *talaaya* 'to stand' (Seale 1939; P. Munro p.c.).

COFFEE BOGUE (Miss., Scott Co.) \kof´ ē bōg\. Choctaw *kafi book* 'sassafras stream', from *kafi* 'sassafras', *book* 'stream' (Seale 1939; P. Munro p.c.).

COFFIN Rock (Ore., Columbia Co.). Said to have been so named because it was an Indian burial site (McArthur 1992).

COGINCHAUG River (Conn., Middlesex Co.). The name is from Wangunk (Algonquian), perhaps meaning 'at the place where they cure fish' (Huden 1962).

COHABIE Creek (Ala., Talladega Co.) \kō hab´ ē\. Muskogee, meaning 'cane stalk', from *kohv* /koha/ 'cane', *vpe* /api/ 'stalk' (Read 1984; Martin and Mauldin 2000).

COHANNET (Mass., Bristol Co.) \kō han´ət\. Narragansett (Algonquian), perhaps 'at the long place' (Huden 1962).

COHANSEY (N.J., Salem Co.) \kō han´ sē\. Said to be named for a Delaware (Algonquian) leader whose name was written <Cohanzick, Conochockink> (etc.) (Becker 1964).

COHAS Brook (N.H., Hillsborough Co.) \kō´ häs\. Abenaki (Algonquian) *goas* 'small white-pine', diminutive of *goa* 'white pine' (Day 1994–95). Related names include **Cohoes Brook** (N.Y., Albany Co.) and **Coös County** (N.H.).

COHASSET (Mass., Norfolk Co.) \kō has´ ət\. From NEng. Algonquian, perhaps meaning 'small pine place'; cf. Massachusett <koo, koowa> 'pine' (Trumbull 1903), Abenaki *goa* 'white pine', diminutive *goas* (Day 1994–95). Possibly related names are **Cohas Brook** (N.H., Hillsborough Co.), **Cohoes** (N.Y., Albany Co.), and **Coös County** (N.H.). The name has been transferred to several states: Calif. (Butte Co.), Minn. (Itasca Co.), and N.Y. (Orange Co.) A probably related placename is **Cohassett** (Wash., Grays Harbor Co.).

COHATTA (Miss., Itawamba Co.) \kō hat´ ə\. Choctaw (Muskogean) for 'white panther', from *koi* 'panther', *hata* 'white' (Seale 1939).

COHELEE (Ga., Early Co.). Perhaps from Muskogee *kohv* /kohá/ 'cane, reed', *herē* /hiɬí:/ 'good' (Goff 1975; Martin and Mauldin 2000).

COHOBADIAH Creek (Ala., Randolph Co.) \kō hob ə dī´ ə\. Probably from Muskogee; cf. *kohv-vpvtake* /koha-apatá:k-i/ 'cane up against (a hill etc.)' (Martin and Mauldin 2000). A possibly related placename is **Upatoi** (Ga., Muscogee Co.).

COHOCKSINK Creek (Pa., Philadelphia Co.) \kō hock´ singk\. Perhaps from Delaware (Algonquian) <Cuwenhasink> 'where there are pine trees' (Donehoo 1928); cf. Unami Delaware *kú:we:* 'pine' (Blalock et al. 1994).

COHO Cove (Alaska, Ketchikan B-5) \kō´ hō\. Refers to the species of fish called the *coho salmon*. The fish was earlier called <cohoes>, from the Halkomelem (Salish) language of Wash. state, in which the term is /k^{w}'ə́x^{w}aθ/ (*RHD* 1987). There is a **Cohoe** in Alaska (Kenai B-4).

COHOCTAH (Mich., Livingston Co.) \kō hok´ tə\. Possibly from the same source as **Cohocton** (N.Y., Steuben Co.) \kō hok´ tən\. This name, previously written <Conhocton>, perhaps of Iroquoian origin (Beauchamp 1907).

COHOES (N.Y., Albany Co.) \kō´ hōz\. Possibly from an Algonquian word referring to pine trees (Ruttenber 1906); cf. Unami Delaware /kú:we:/ 'pine', Western Abenaki *goa* 'white pine'. The writings <Kahoos, Kahoes> also occur. Probably related is **Cohoos Pond** (N.H., Cheshire Co.) \kō hōz´\, from Abenaki (Algonquian) *goas* 'small white-pine', diminutive of *goa* 'white pine' (Day 1994–95). Other possibly related placenames include are **Cohas Brook** (N.H., Hillsborough Co.) and **Coös County** (N.H.).

COHUTTA (Ga., Whitfield Co.) \kə hut´ ə\. Perhaps from Cherokee (Iroquoian) <cohutta> 'frog' (Krakow 1975).

COILA (Miss., Carroll Co.) \kō ī´lə\. Perhaps Choctaw (Muskogean) 'where the panther arrives', from *kowi* 'panther', *aa(y)-* 'place', *ala* 'to arrive' (Seale 1939; P. Munro p.c.). There is also a **Coila** in N.Y. (Washington Co.).

COKATO (Minn., Wright Co.) \kō kā´ tō\. From Dakota (Siouan) *čhokáta* 'at the middle', from *čhoká* 'middle' (Upham 2001, Riggs 1890).

COKER (Tenn., Monroe Co.) \kō´ kər\. Perhaps from Cherokee (Iroquoian) *kuku* 'squash' (vegetable). Another **Coker** (Ala., Tuscaloosa Co.) is said to reflect an English family name (Read 1984).

COKEY Swamp (N.C., Edgecombe Co.) \kō´ kē\. Perhaps abbreviated from the name of an Indian village, written <Tiancok, Tyancoka, Tiancoco, Tincoco>; the Native American language has not been identified (Powell 1968).

COLAPARCHEE Creek (Ga., Monroe Co.) \kol ə pär´ chē\. Muskogee *kvlvpi* /kalápi/ 'white oak', *hacce* /háčči/ 'stream' (Read 1949–50; Martin and Mauldin 2000).

COLCHUCK Lake (Wash., Chelan Co.) \kōl´ chuk\. The Chinook Jargon placename was coined with the meaning 'cold water', from <cold, cole> [kol] 'cold' plus <chuck> [čʌk] 'water' (D. Kinkade p.c.).

COLD Spring (Ariz., Apache Co.). Corresponds to Navajo (Athabaskan) *tó sik'az háálį́* cold water flows up and out', containing *tó* 'water', *sik'az* 'it is cold', *háálį́* 'it flows up and out' (Granger 1983).

COLEOATCHEE Creek (Ga., Talbot Co.). From Muskogee *kvlv* /kalá/ 'white oak', *hacce* /háčči/ 'stream' (Read 1949–50; Martin and Mauldin 2000). The spelling **Coleothcee** also occurs.

COLEWA Bayou (La., West Carroll Par.) \kōl´ wä\. Possibly from Choctaw (Muskogean) *oka lawa* 'lots of water', from *oka* 'water', *lawa* 'much' (P. Munro p.c.). There may be a connection with an Indian group called <Koroa> (Dickinson 1995:153).

COLIMA (Ga., Gordon Co.) \kō lē´ mə\. Probably a transfer name from *Colima,* a state in Mexico; the term is from an Indian language of the area (Krakow 1975).

COLLAWASH River (Ore., Clackamas Co.) \kol´ ə wôsh\. Perhaps named after a Sahaptin leader, whose name has been written as <Colwash> (McArthur 1992); the Native American form of the name is [q'álwaš] (N. Rude p.c.).

COLLAYOMI Valley (Calif., Lake Co.) \kol ə yō´ mē\. Probably from Lake Miwok /koyáayomi/ 'song place' (Gudde 1998).

COLLE Canyon (N.Mex., Sandoval Co.) \kō´ yā\. New Mexican Spanish *coye* 'roof-door', from Tewa (Tanoan) *k'oyi* (Harrington 1916:436). Also written **Coye Canyon.**

COLLICUT Brook (Maine, Aroostook Co.) \kol´i kut\. Abenaki (Algonquian), 'at the place of flames' (Huden 1962).

COLMA (Calif., San Mateo Co.) \kōl´ mə\. Perhaps from the San Francisco dialect of Costanoan, meaning 'moon' (Gudde 1998).

COLOHATCHEE Park (Fla., Broward Co.) \kō lə hach´ ē\. Perhaps from Seminole (Muskogean) *kvlv* /kalá/ 'white oak' and *hvcce* /háčče/ 'stream' (Read 1934; Martin and Mauldin 2000).

COLOMA (Calif., El Dorado Co.) \kə lō´ mə\. The name was that of a Nisenan (Maiduan) village and became famous after the discovery of gold there in 1848 (Gudde 1998). **Coloma** is found as a transfer name (e.g., Ala., Cherokee Co.; Kans., Woodson Co.; and Wis., Waushara Co.).

COLOMOKEE (Ga., Early Co.). Perhaps from <Kolomi>, a Muskogee tribal town (Krakow 1975); a probably related placename is **Kolomoki Creek** (Ga., Clay Co.).

COLOROW Mountain (Colo., Rio Blanco Co.) \kə lə rō`\. Named for a nineteenth-century Ute (Numic) leader of Comanche origins, who was suspected of murdering a U.S. Indian agent at White River. In spite of these associations, the name **Colorow** is given to six features in various parts of Colo. (Bright 1993). The name may be from Spanish *colorado* 'red'.

COLOTOCHES (Ark., Prairie Co.). Named for a nineteenth-century Muskogee leader; his name has also been written as <Callaches, Callachee, Kealedji> (Dickinson 1995).

COLUCKUM Creek (Wash., Chelan Co.). Moses-Columbian (Salishan) /nq'ʷul'áqaʔm/ [nq'ʷol'áqaʔəm] 'raven place', from /na-/ 'place', /q'ʷul'áqaʔ/ 'raven' (D. Kinkade p.c.).

COLUSA (Ill., Hancock Co.) \kə lo͞o´ sə\. Perhaps derived from **Caloosa** (Fla., Sarasota Co.), originally the name of an Indian group in the southeastern United States (Vogel 1963). The placename **Colusa**, of whatever origin, also occurs in Kans. (Haskell Co.), Mont. (Granite Co.), and N.Mex. (Santa Fe Co.).

COLUSA County (Calif.) \kə lo͞o´ sə\. Perhaps from a Patwin (Wintuan) village named <Koru>; the names <Kolus, Coluses, Kolussas> were applied to Mexican landgrants in 1844–45 (Gudde 1998). A connection with the name **Caloosa** from the southeastern United States is also possible.

COLVILLE (Wash., Okanogan Co.) \kol´vil\. This term is used both as a placename and as the name for an Indian subgroup of the Salishan language family in eastern Wash. (Hitchman

1985). The name of **Fort Colville** was given to honor Andrew Colvile (note the difference in spelling), a governor of the Hudson's Bay Company.

COMA-A Spring (Ariz., Navajo Co.). Said to be from a Navajo (Athabaskan) pronunciation of a Numic word for 'jackrabbit' (Linford 2000); cf. Southern Paiute (Numic) /kamɨ/ (Sapir 1930).

COMAL (Tex., Comal Co.) \kō´ mal\. From Mexican Spanish *comal,* referring to the griddle on which tortillas are cooked (Tarpley 1980). The word is from Nahuatl (Aztecan) *comalli.*

COMANCHE \kə man´ chē\. The name of a Native American people in the southern Plains states, now living in Okla.; their language belongs to the Numic branch of the Uto-Aztecan family. The name is from Ute (Numic) /kɨmánci, kɨmáci/ 'enemy, foreigner' (J. McLaughlin p.c.). The word occurs in the placenames of many states (e.g. Ariz., Coconino Co.; Colo., Larimer Co.; and Mont., Yellowstone Co.). A related spelling is **Camanche** (Iowa, Clinton Co.; Calif., Calaveras Co.) A name given to the Comanche people by some of their Indian neighbors was <Padouca>, and this gave rise to the placename **Paducah** found in several states. The Spanish term **Comancheros** (N.Mex., San Miguel Co.) \kō mən chär´ ōs\ refers to Hispanic and Anglo entrepreneurs who carried on trade with the Comanches in the nineteenth century (Julyan 1998).

COMBAHEE River (S.C., Colleton Co.) \kum´ bē\. Earlier written <Cumbohee>, <Combohe> (Waddell 1980). Named for a division of the Cusabo Indian people (Pearson 1978; B. Rude p.c.).

COMMACK (N.Y., Suffolk Co.) \kō´ mak\. Perhaps a shortened form of **Winnecomac,** a SNEng. Algonquian village name, possibly meaning 'good field' (Tooker 1911); cf. also **Accomac**.

COMMANCHE Village (Ill., Sangamon Co.). From the same source as **Comanche**; see above.

COMOBABI (Ariz., Pima Co.) \kōm ə bä´ bē\. O'odham (Piman) *ko:m wahia* 'hackberry well', from *ko:m* 'hackberry', *wahia* 'well' (J. Hill p.c.).

COMPETINE (Iowa, Wapello Co.). Said to be named for a Meskwaki (Algonquian) Indian (Vogel 1983).

COMPO (Conn., Fairfield Co.) \kom´ pō\. Perhaps from SNEng. Algonquian, meaning 'long pond' (Huden 1962).

COMPOUNCE Lake (Conn., Hartford Co.) \kom´ pouns\. Earlier <Compound's>, referring to a SNEng. Algonquian man whose name was written <Compound, Acompound>; he lived in the area in the seventeenth century (Trumbull 1881).

COMPTCHE (Calif., Mendocino Co.) \komp´ chē\. Probably an Indian name, possibly from the Pomo village <Komacho> (Gudde 1998).

CONANICUT Island (R.I., Newport Co.) \kə nan´ i kət\. From SNEng. Algonquian, containing <qunni>, <-ut> 'place' (W. Cowan p.c.).

CONASAUGA (Ga., Gilmer Co.) \kon ə sô´ gə\. Probably from a Cherokee (Iroquoian) village name, variously written as <Conasagua, Gansagi, Gansagigi>, perhaps from *kanesga* 'grass' (Read 1934; Alexander 1971). The name also occurs in Tenn. (Polk Co.) and Fla. (Manatee Co.). Perhaps related is **Kennesaw Mountain** (Ga., Cobb Co.).

CONASKONK Point (N.J., Middlesex Co.). Perhaps from Delaware (Algonquian) *kwënàskung* 'place of tall grass' (Kraft and Kraft 1985); cf. Munsee Delaware *kwŭnáskwat* 'be long grass' (O'Meara 1996).

CONBOY Lake (Wash., Klickitat Co.) \kon´ boi\. The term is the surname of a Klickitat (Salishan) family (Reese 1996).

CONCHARTY Creek (Okla., Wagoner Co.) \kən chär´ tē\. From the name of a Muskogee tribal town, *kvncate* /kančá:ti/, perhaps from /i:kaná/ 'land, earth' and /čá:ti/ 'blood' (Martin and Mauldin 2000). Related placenames are

Chartee Creek and **Canchardee** (both Ala., Talladega Co.).

CONCHAS (N.Mex., San Miguel Co.) \kōn´ chəs\. The Spanish word *conchas* means 'shells', and it is possible that the placename refers to shells used by Indians for ornament. There may also be confusion with *Conchos*, however, a term used by the Spanish as a name for an Indian group that they encountered in southern N.Mex. in the seventeenth century (Julyan 1998).

CONCOBONA Creek (Miss., Newton Co.) \kông kə bō´ nə, kō kə bō´ nə\. Perhaps a Choctaw (Muskogean) name meaning 'where the chicken-hawk comes', from *akąkabi* 'chicken-hawk' (*akąka* 'chicken', *abi* 'to kill') plus *aay-* 'place' and *ona* 'to come' (Seale 1939; P. Munro p.c.).

CONCOMLY (Ore., Marion Co.) \kon kom´ lē\. Named for a Chinook leader; his Native American name was /qánqm̍li/ (D. Kinkade p.c.). There is also a **Concomly Lake** in Wash. (Skamania Co.).

CONCONULLY (Wash., Okanogan Co.) \kon kə nul´ ē, kon kə nel´ ē\. From Okanagan (Salishan) /q^{w}únq^{w}unɬp/ [q^{w}ónq^{w}onɬp], the Native American name for Salmon Creek and for the town of Okanogan (D. Kinkade p.c.).

CONCOW (Calif., Butte Co.) \kon´ kow, kong´ kow\. An Indian group of the Maiduan language family. The name in their language is *koyoom k'awi* 'valley earth', from *koyoo* 'valley, flat place', *k'aw* 'earth, ground' (Gudde 1998).

CONECUH County (Ala.) \kə nā´ kə\. Perhaps from a Muskogee name meaning 'skunk's head', from *kono* /konó/ 'skunk', *ekv* /iká/ 'its head' (Read 1984; Martin and Mauldin 2000). The **Conecuh River** is partly in Fla. (Santa Rosa Co.).

CONEHATTA (Miss., Newton Co.) \kō ni hat´ ə\. Probably a Choctaw (Muskogean) name meaning 'white skunk', from *konih* 'skunk', *hata* 'white' (Seale 1939; P. Munro p.c.).

CONEJOHELA Valley (Pa., York Co.). Said to be the name of an Indian village in an unidentified language, recorded as <Conejoholo> 'kettle on a long upright object' (Donehoo 1928).

CONEMAUGH (Pa., Cambria Co.) \kon´ ə mô\. From the name of a Delaware (Algonquian) village, also written <Conemach, Conemough> (etc.), perhaps derived from the word for 'otter'; cf. Unami Delaware *kwənámuxkw* (Blalock et al. 1994).

CONESTEE (S.C., Greenville Co.) \kon´ ə stē\. Perhaps from Cherokee (Iroquoian) <kanosita> 'dogwood' (Pickens 1961–62:4).

CONESTOGA (Pa., Lancaster Co.) \kon i stō´ gə\. The name of an Iroquoian group, also written <Kanastoge, Andastoegue, Gandastoques> (etc.), sometimes said to mean 'people of the cabin pole'. The place called **Conestoga** gave its name to the "Conestoga wagon," a type of covered vehicle commonly used in the nineteenth century by westward migrants in the United States. The Conestoga people have been identified with the **Susquehanna,** a term also used as a placename (Donehoo 1928; *HNAI* 15:367).

CONESUS (N.Y., Livingston Co.) \kə nē´ səs\. Perhaps from Seneca (Iroquoian) *ga'nyéhse:s* 'long (string of?) nannyberries' (*Viburnum lentago*); cf. *ga'nyéhsa'* 'nannyberry' (W. Chafe p.c.).

CONETOE (N.C., Edgecombe Co.) \kon´ ə tō\. Tuscarora (Iroquoian) *kahnehtuu'* 'loblolly pine in water', a variant in the northern Tuscarora dialect of *kahtehnuu'*, a principal town of the Tuscarora during the wars of 1711–13 (B. Rudes p.c.).

CONEWAGO (Pa., Lancaster Co.) \kon ə wä´ gō\. From Seneca (Iroquoian) *ga:nǫwǫgǫ:h* 'in the rapids' (W. Chafe p.c.). The form **Conewango** \kon i wäng´ gō\. occurs elsewhere in Pa. (Warren Co.) and in N.Y. (Cattaraugus Co.). The form **Conowingo** (Pa., Lancaster Co.; Md., Cecil Co.) may be related; cf. also **Konawaugus Valley** (N.Y., Wyoming Co.).

CONGAHBUNA Lake (Alaska, Tyonek A-4). Dena'ina (Athabaskan) *k'enq'a bena,* lit. 'fishing-hole lake', containing *bena* 'lake' (Kari and Fall 1987:47).

CONGAMUCK Lakes (Conn., Hartford Co.) \kon´ gə muk\. SNEng. Algonquian, perhaps meaning 'long fishing place' (Trumbull 1881). The related form **Congamond** \kong´ gə mond\ occurs in Mass. (Hampden Co.).

CONGAREE (S.C., Richland Co.) \kong´ gə rē\. Catawba (Siouan) *kų̄karii* 'it's over there, far distant' (B. Rudes p.c.).

CONICASHNI Creek (S.Dak., Bennett Co.). Lakhota (Siouan) *čho-níčhešni* 'flesh does not exist', supposedly referring to thin horses (Sneve 1973; A. Taylor p.c.).

CONIMICUT (R.I., Bristol Co.) \kə nim´ i kət\. Said to be named for <Quenimiquet>, a SNEng. Algonquian woman, the granddaughter of the famous leader Canonicus (Huden 1962).

CONIOTT Creek (N.C., Bertie Co.). From Tuscarora (Iroquoian) *kanuhuu'* 'floating white-flowering dogwood', from *nuhi'* 'white-flowering dogwood' (B. Rudes p.c.).

CONNARITSA (N.C., Bertie Co.). Earlier <Conneritsat>, apparently an Indian name for an unidentified group (Powell 1968).

CONNEAUT (Ohio, Ashtabula Co.) \kon´ ē ôt, kon´ ē ət\. Perhaps from Onondaga (Iroquoian) <(wa)-koano-hote> 'there is increase' or <kanawoate> 'mud' (Mahr 1957:155); cf. /-gowanę-/ 'to be large', /ganawa:de'/ 'swamp, pond' (H. Woodbury p.c.). The name also occurs in Pa. (Crawford Co.).

CONNECTICUT \kə net´ i kət\. The name originally referred to the **Connecticut River**, which rises in N.H., separates it from Vt., and finally flows through the states of Mass. and Conn. The term is SNEng. Algonquian, 'on the long tidal river', reflecting **kwən-* 'long', **-əhtəkw* 'tidal river', **-ənk* 'place' (Afable & Beeler 1996:193). A related form is **Connetquot River** (N.Y., Suffolk Co.).

CONNEROSS (SC, Oconee Co.). Said to be from Cherokee (Iroquoian) <kawan-uri-sun-yi> 'where the duck fell' (Pickens 1961–62:5); cf. *kawonu* 'duck' (Feeling 1975).

CONNESENA Creek (Ga., Bartow Co.). The term was the surname of a Cherokee (Iroquoian) family, named after an ancestor; it is said to mean 'dragging canoe' (Goff 1975).

CONNESTEE Falls (N.C., Transylvania Co.). Said to have been named for an "Indian princess," language unidentified (Powell 1968).

CONNETQUOT River (N.Y., Suffolk Co.) \kə net´ kwot\. The SNEng. Algonquian name means 'long tidal-river place' (Tooker 1911); it is from the same source as **Connecticut**.

CONNOISARAULEY Creek (N.Y., Cattaraugus Co.) \kan i sə rô´ lē\. The name, also written <Connoirtoirauley>, is probably Iroquoian, of unclear derivation (Beauchamp 1907).

CONOCOCHEAGUE Creek (Pa., Franklin Co.; Md., Washington Co.) \kon´ ə kə chēg\. Earlier forms were <Conigochego, Conegocheek>. The Algonquian term has been speculatively translated as 'a dull sound is heard far off' (Donehoo 1928; Kenny 1984).

CONODOGUINET Creek (Pa., Cumberland Co.). The name is perhaps Delaware (Algonquian), meaning 'winding stream' (Donehoo 1928).

CONOHO (N.C., Martin Co.) \kō´ nə hō\. Earlier written as <Coneyhoe>, probably of Indian origin, from an unidentified language (Powell 1968).

CONOMO Point (Mass., Essex Co.). From SNEng. Algonquian, perhaps containing <qunni-> 'long' (W. Cowan p.c.).

CONOQUENESSING (Pa., Butler Co.) \kon ə kwə nes´ ing\. A Delaware (Algonquian) name, earlier written <Canaghqunesa, Conaquanosshan> (etc.), of unclear derivation (Donehoo 1928).

CONOTTON (Ohio, Harrison Co.). Said to be from an Indian name, also written <Kannoten>, of unknown origin (Miller 1996).

CONOWINGO Creek (Pa., Lancaster Co.) \kon ə wing´ gō\. The term is probably related to **Conewago** (Pa., Lancaster Co.); see above. Possibly related placenames include **Conowingo** (Md., Cecil Co.) and **Konawaugus Valley** (N.Y., Wyoming Co.).

CONOY Creek (Pa., Lancaster Co.) \kə noi´\. From the name of an Algonquian people; they have been identified with the **Piscataway,** a term that is also used as a placename (Donehoo 1928). In Md. there is a **Conoy Lake** (St. Marys Co.).

CONRAD Creek (Wash., Snohomish Co.). Named for Jimmy Conrad, an Indian resident (Hitchman 1985).

CONSHOHOCKEN (Pa., Montgomery Co) \kon shə hok´ ən\. Perhaps from Delaware (Algonquian) *kanshihàking* 'elegant land' (Kraft & Kraft 1985).

CONTENTNEA (N.C., Greene Co.) \kən tent´ nē\. From Tuscarora (Iroquoian) *kęjęę'nye'* 'fish going by' (B. Rudes).

COOCHIE (La., Concordia Par.) \ko͞o´ chē\. An abbreviation of **Withlacoochee River,** a term transferred from Fa. The name represents Muskogee *ue-rakkuce* /oy-ɬakk-ocí, wi:-/ 'small river', from *ue-rakko* /oy-ɬákko/ 'river' (*ue* 'water', *rakko* 'big') plus *-uce* /-oci/ 'small' (Read 1927; Martin and Mauldin 2000).

COOCHIE Brake (La., Winn Par.) \ko͞o´ chē\. The name of this swamp is from Choctaw (Muskogean) *kǫshak* 'reed' (Read 1927; P. Munro p.c.).

COOLEEMEE (N.C., Davie Co.). Perhaps derived from Muskogee *kvlv* /kalá/ 'white oak' (Powell 1968; Martin and Mauldin 2000).

COOLEEWAHEE (Ga., Baker Co.) \ko͞o lē wä´ hē\. Said to be Muskogee, meaning 'where white-oak acorns are scattered'; cf. *kvlv* /kalá/ 'white oak (acorn)', *vwahē* /awá:hi:/ 'scattered' (Read 1949–50; Martin and Mauldin 2000).

COON \ko͞on\. The term is an abbreviation of *raccoon,* the name of a nocturnal mammal found throughout the United States. The term was originally recorded by Captain John Smith in Va. as <Aroughcun>, from a CAC Algonquian language (*RHD* 1987). As a placename, it is widespread (e.g., Iowa, Wapello Co.; Kans., Douglas Co.; and Mich., Ingham Co.). In some placenames, the term may reflect a secondary meaning, in which *coon* is used as a derogatory term for an African American.

COONAMESSETT Pond (Mass., Barnstable Co.) \ko͞o nə mes´ ət\. SNEng. Algonquian, perhaps containing <qunni-> 'long', <-ss-> 'small', <-et> 'place' (W. Cowan p.c.).

COONEWAH Creek (Miss., Lee Co.) \ko͞o´ ni wô\. Perhaps a Choctaw (Muskogean) personal name *akkanowa* 'walker', from the verb *akkanowa* 'to walk' (Seale 1939; P. Munro p.c.).

COONSA Creek (Mont., Glacier Co.) \ko͞on´ sä\. Said to be named for a Flathead (Salishan) man (Holterman 1985).

COONSHUCK Creek (Miss., Neshoba Co.) \ko͞on´ shäk\. An abbreviation of a Choctaw (Muskogean) name meaning 'cane bulge', from *kǫshak* 'cane' (the plant) plus *tikpi* 'bulge, swelling, bend in a stream' (P. Munro p.c.).

COOSADA (Ala., Elmore Co.) \ko͞o sô´ də\. From the name of a Muskogean people better known as the **Koasati;** that term also occurs as a placename. The placename **Coosada** also occurs in Fla. (Washington Co.).

COOSA River (Ala., Elmore Co.) \ko͞o´ sə\. The probable origin is Choctaw *kǫshak* 'cane' (the plant; Read 1984; P. Munro p.c.). The placename **Coosa** also occurs in La. (Concordia Par.) and Okla. (Latimer Co.), and the form **Coosha** occurs in Miss. (Lauderdale Co.). Related placenames are **Coosawhatchie** (S.C., Jasper Co.) and **Kusa** (Okla., Okmulgee Co.).

COÖSAUK Fall (N.H., Coös Co.) \kō´ ə sôk\. It is said that an early explorer thought the Abenaki (Algonquian) word <coos> meant 'jolt' or 'rough' and joined it with the word <auke> 'place' to give the meaning 'rough place'. In fact *goas* means 'small white-pine' (from *goa* 'white pine'), as in the name of **Coös County** (Julyan and Julyan 1993).

COOSAW (SC, Beaufort Co.) \ko͞o´ sô\. Earlier written <Cozao>, <Cooso>, <Kussah> (Waddell 1980). Perhaps from a Muskogean word for 'cane'; see **Coosawhatchie** (S.C., Jasper Co.) below.

COOSAWATTEE (Ga., Gordon Co.) \ko͞o sə wä´ tē\. Perhaps from a Cherokee (Iroquoian) name <Kusawetiyi> 'old creek place' (Krakow 1975).

COOSAWHATCHIE (S.C., Jasper Co.) \ko͞o sä hach´ ē\. Perhaps from a Muskogean name meaning 'cane stream' (Pearson 1978); cf. Choctaw *kǫshak* 'cane', *hahcha* 'stream' (P. Munro p.c.). Probably related placenames include **Coosa River** (Ala., Elmore Co.) and **Coosaw** (S.C., Beaufort Co.) as well as **Coosha** (Miss., Lauderdale Co.) \ko͞o´ shə\.

COÖS County (N.H.) \kō´ os\. Western Abenaki (Algoquian) *goas* 'small white-pine', diminutive of *goa* 'white pine' (Day 1994–95). Probably related placenames include **Cohas Brook** (N.H., Hillsborough Co.), **Cohasset** (Mass., Norfolk Co.), and **Cohoes** (N.Y., Albany Co.).

COOS County (Ore.) \ko͞os\. The name of an Indian people, earlier written <Cook-koo-oose, Koo'as, Kowes, Koos> (etc.). In 1844 the French explorer Duflot de Mofras misunderstood **Coos River**, translating it into French as *Rivière des Vaches* 'river of cows' (McArthur 1992). The term Coos may be from Oregon Athabaskan [kŭs] 'bay', or from Hanis (Coosan) [kuᵘs] 'south' (D. Kinkade p.c.).

COOSKIE Mountain (Calif., Humboldt Co.). Supposedly from Mattole (Athabaskan), of unclear derivation (Gudde 1998).

COOSTON (Ore., Coos Co.) \ko͞os´ tən\. From **Coos County** (see above) plus English *-ton*, short for *town* (McArthur 1992).

COÖSUCK (Vt., Orange Co.) \kō´ ə suk\. A historical name for the place now called *Newbury*. Derived from Western Abenaki (Algonquian) *goasek* [goasək] 'place of small white pines'; cf. *goa* 'white pine', *goas* 'small white pine' (Day 1994–95). Also written **Coassuk**; a probably related placename is **Cohasset** (Mass., Norfolk Co.).

COOWEESCOOWEE (Okla., Rogers Co.). The term is said to have been the personal name of a prominent Cherokee (Iroquoian) man, known in English as John Ross (Shirk 1974).

COO-Y-YAH (Okla., Mayes Co.) \kyo͞o´ ē yä\. Said to be from Cherokee (Iroquoian) <kuwahiyi> 'mulberry grove' (Shirk 1974); cf. *kuwa* 'mulberry' (Alexander 1971).

COPAHEE Sound (S.C., Charleston Co.). Perhaps from a word <kopa> 'creek' in an unidentified Indian language (Pickens 1961–62:5).

COPAKE (N.Y., Columbia Co.) \kō´ pāk\. Earlier written <Achkookpeek, Ukhkokpeck, Kookpake> (etc.); from a Mohegan (Algonquian) name, probably meaning 'snake pond' (Ruttenber 1906).

COPALIS River (Wash., Grays Harbor Co.) \kō pā´ lis, kə pā´ lis\. From Quinault (Salishan) [k'ʷpíls], containing /-ils/ 'rock' (D. Kinkade p.c.).

COPAN (Okla., Washington Co.) \kō´ pan\. From Spanish *Copán*, the name of a town in Honduras, famous for its Mayan ruins (Hitchman 1985).

COPASSAW (Ala., Choctaw Co.) \kop´ ə sô\. Abbreviated from Choctaw (Muskogean) *oka kapassa* 'cold water', from *oka* 'water', *kapassah* 'to be cold' (Read 1984; P. Munro p.c.). The form **Bayou Copassaw** occurs in La. (Terrebonne Par.).

COPEECHAN Pond (Pa., Lehigh Co.) \kō pē´ chən\. Said to be derived from an Indian personal name, from an unidentified language (Donehoo 1928).

COPEMISH (Mich., Manistee Co.) \kō´ pə mish\. Perhaps abbreviated from Ojibwa (Algonquian) *wiigobimish* 'basswood' (Vogel 1986; Nichols and Nyholm 1995).

COPIAG (N.Y., Suffolk Co.). A variant of **Copiague** \kō´ peg\. This is perhaps from a SNEng. Algonquian name meaning 'a place shut in' (Tooker 1911). The variant **Coppiag** also occurs.

COPICUT River (Mass., Bristol Co.). SNEng. Algonquian, probably from <kuppohquodt> 'cloudy weather' (W. Cowan p.c.).

COPPEI (Wash., Walla Walla Co.). From a Sahaptin placename /kapyú, kapyə́y/ (D. Kinkade p.c.).

COPPIAG (N.Y., Suffolk Co.). A variant of **Copiag**; see above.

COQUILLE (Ore., Coos Co.) \kō kwēl´, kō kēl\. The spelling suggests French *coquille* 'shell'. The name is probably derived from that of a local Indian group, however, which has been written <Coquel, Coquel, Kiguel> (McArthur 1992).

CORAM (N.Y., Suffolk Co.) \kôr´ əm\. Perhaps a shortened form of <Moncorum>, from a SNEng. Algonquian name meaning 'low country' (Tooker 1911). There is also a **Coram** in Conn. (Fairfield Co.).

CORN Creek (S.Dak., Bennett Co.). Said to be a translation of Lakhota (Siouan) *wagmíza* 'corn' (Sneve 1973; Ingham 2001).

CORNHOUSE (Ala., Randolph Co.) Corresponds to Muskogee *tohto-kake* /tohto-ká:ki/ 'sitting corncribs', from tohto /tóhto/ 'corncrib', *kake* /ká:ki/ 'sitting (of two)' (Read 1984; Martin and Mauldin 2000).

CORNPLANTER Run (Pa., Warren Co). Named for the eighteenth-century Seneca (Iroquoian) leader called Cornplanter; his Native American name was *gayę̨́thwahgeh,* which means something like 'it's used for planting' (W. Chafe p.c.).

CORONACA (S.C., Greenwood Co.). Perhaps from Cherokee (Iroquoian) <karun-egwa> 'great raven' (Pickens 1961:5); cf. *golanv* 'raven', *equa* 'great' (Alexander 1971).

CORROTOMAN River (Va., Lancaster Co.). Named for a CAC Algonquian subgroup (Hagemann 1988). Also written as **Corotoman.**

CORRUMPA (N.Mex., Union Co.) \kə rum´ pə\. Said to represent an Indian word, language unidentified, meaning 'wild, isolated' (Julyan 1998).

CORTINA (Calif., Colusa Co.) \kôr te´ nə\. Named for <Kotina>, a Patwin (Wintuan) leader (Gudde 1998).

COS COB (Conn., Fairfield Co.) \kos´ kob\. From SNEng. Algonquian <kussohkiompsk>, containing <kous-> 'pointed', <-ompsk 'rock'> (W. Cowan p.c.).

COSHECTON (Pa., Wayne Co.) \kə shek´ tən\. Perhaps from the same source as **Cochecton** (N.Y., Sullivan Co.), of Algonquian origin, meaning 'washing place' (Donehoo 1928); cf. Munsee Delaware *kshíixtoow* 'to wash' (O'Meara 1996).

COSHOCTON County (Ohio) \kō shok´ tən\. Perhaps from Delaware <kosh´-ochk-t-oon> 'river-crossing device, i.e. a ferry' (Mahr 1957:145). It is possible that the name is related to **Cochecton** (N.Y., Sullivan Co.) or **Coshecton** (Pa., Wayne Co.).

COSKAKAT (Alaska, Kantishna River D-3) \kō skä´ kət\. Koyukon (Athabaskan) *kk'os kaakk'et* [q'oscka:q'ət], lit. 'schist streammouth', from *kk'os* 'schist rock' plus *-kaakk'et, -chaakk'et* 'stream mouth' (Jetté and Jones 2000:289, 366); cf. the nearby **Cosna** 'schist river'; see below. Also written as **Cos Jacket, Crossjacket**.

COSKATA (Mass., Nantucket Co.). Earlier written <Coscaty>, <Causkata> (Little 1984). Perhaps from Wampanoag (Algonquian), of unclear derivation (Huden 1962).

COSMIT (Calif., San Diego Co.) \kōz mēt\. From a Diegueño (Yuman) name, of unclear derivation (Gudde 1998).

COSMOPOLIS (Wash., Grays Harbor Co.) \koz mop´ ə lis\. From Lower Chehalis (Salishan) [qaysúl'məš, qay'sál'məš] 'fine pebbles, gravel bar', containing /qáys/ 'stone, rock' and /-mš/ 'earth, land' (D. Kinkade p.c.).

COSNA (Alaska, Kantishna River D-3) \kos´ nə, koz´ nə\. Koyukon (Athabaskan) *kk'os no'* [q'osno'], lit. 'schist river', from *kk'os* 'schist rock', *no'* 'river' (Jetté and Jones 2000). Cf. **Coskakat**; see above.

COSNINO (Ariz., Coconino Co.) \kōz nē´ nō, koz nē´ nō\. From Hopi *kòonina* 'Havasupai person' (K. Hill p.c.). A related placename is **Coconino County** (Ariz.).

COSO (Calif., Inyo Co.) \kō´ sō\. From Panamint (Numic) *kosoowa* 'to be steamy', referring to hot springs in the area (Gudde 1998).

COSSADUCK Hill (Conn., New London Co.) \kos´ ə duk\. From SNEng. Algonquian <kowas-'htugk> 'pine trees', from <kowas-> 'pine', <-htuck> 'tree' (W. Cowan p.c.). The placename has also been written <Cosattuck, Cosaduck, Coassatuck> (Huden 1962).

COSSAYUNA (N.Y., Washington Co.) \kos ə yōō´ nə\. An Abenaki (Algonquian) name, said to mean 'lake at our pines' (Beauchamp 1907); cf. Abenaki *goas* 'little pine', diminutive of *goa* 'pine' (Day 1994–95).

COSTAPIA, Bayou (Miss., Harrison Co.) \kə stä´ pē ə\. Perhaps from a Choctaw (Muskogean) name meaning 'being among fleas' (Seale 1939); cf. *kashti* 'flea', *abiha* '(plural) to be in' (P. Munro p.c.).

COSUMNES (Calif., El Dorado Co.) \kə sum´ nəs\. Referring to a local Indian group (with Spanish plural *-s*); probably from Plains Miwok or Northern Sierra Miwok *kooso* 'holly berries, toyon berries' (Gudde 1998).

COTACO Creek (Ala., Morgan Co.) \kō tä´ kō\. Perhaps abbreviated from a combination of Cherokee (Iroquoian) *ikati* 'swamp', *kunahita* 'long' (Read 1984).

COTAHAGA Landing (Ala., Sumter Co.) \kō tə hā´ gə\. Perhaps from Choctaw (Muskogean) *kati aahikkiiya* 'where the locust tree stands', from *kati* 'locust tree', *aa-* 'place', *hikkiiya* '(singular) to stand' (Read 1984; P. Munro p.c.).

COTAHOMA Creek (Ala., Choctaw Co.) \kō tə hō´ mə\. Perhaps Choctaw (Muskogean) for 'red locust tree', from *kati* 'locust tree', *homma* 'red' (P. Munro p.c.).

COTATI (Calif., Sonoma Co.) \kō tä´ tē\. Named for a Coast Miwok village, <Kotati> (Gudde 1998).

COTE BAS (S.C., Berkeley Co.) \kōt bä\. The name is written as if it were French *côte bas* 'lower slope'; however, earlier spellings <Coatbaw, Cutbaw, Cortbaw> suggest an Indian origin, from an unidentified language (Neuffer and Neuffer 1983).

COTE SANS DESSEIN (Mo., Callaway Co.) \kōt san´ də san, kōt san də sen\. The name looks as if it were French, 'slope without design', but may be a popular etymology from Osage (Siouan) /zą́:ce/ 'upland forest'. The same Osage name was later adapted into French, by another popular etymology, as *Rivière Cent Deux,* subsequently translated into English as *The Hundred and Two* (Ramsay 1952).

COTOPAXI (Colo., Fremont Co.) \kō tō pak´ sē\. Named for **Mt. Cotopaxi in Ecuador**. The name is from Quechua, a South American Indian language, and is said to mean 'shining mountain' (Room 1997).

COTOXEN, Lake (N.J., Burlington Co.). The name has also been written as <Crossweeksung, Criswicks, Crosswicks>; it may be from a Delaware (Algonquian) word meaning 'separation' (Becker 1964).

COTTANEVA (Calif., Mendocino Co.) \kot ə nē´ və\. The name may be from Kato (Athabaskan) *kaatəneebi* 'place where the trail goes over the hill', from *təni* 'trail' (Gudde 1998).

COTTAQUILLA (Ala., Calhoun Co.) \kot ə kwil´ ə\. Perhaps from a Muskogee name meaning 'dead honey-locusts', from *kvtohwa* /katóhwa/ 'honey locust', *elē* /ilí:/ 'dead' (Read 1984).

COTTONWOOD County (Minn.) Corresponds to Dakota (Siouan) *wáǧachą* 'cottonwood' (Upham 2001, Riggs 1890). The placename **Cottonwood Tank** (Ariz., Coconino Co.) corresponds to Navajo (Athabaskan) *t'iis* *sitání* 'the place where the cottonwood is lying', containing *t'iis* 'cottonwood tree(s)', *sitą́* 'it is lying' (Wilson 1995). Again, **Cottonwood Wash** (Utah, San Juan Co.) is from Navajo (Athabaskan) *t'iis bikooh* 'cottonwood's wash', with *t'iis* 'cottonwood' and *bi-kooh* 'its-canyon' (Linford 2000).

COTUIT (Mass., Barnstable Co.) \kə to͞o´ it, kot´ yo͞o it\. Wampanoag (SNEng. Algonquian), perhaps meaning 'at the long planting fields' (Huden 1962).

COUCHSACHRAGA Peak (N.Y., Essex Co.). Also written <Coughsarage, Coughsagrage>; an Iroquoian name of unclear derivation (Beauchamp 1907).

COUDERAY (Wis., Sawyer Co.) \ko͞o´ də rā\. An English adaptation of French *courte-oreilles* 'cut-ears', a name given by explorers in 1659 to a group of Ottawa (Algonquian) Indians, supposedly because they had cut the rims off their ears. Their territory was later occupied by an Ojibwa (Algonquian) group (Vogel 1991). The placename now occurs in the forms **Couderay** and **Courte Oreilles.**

COUGAR \ko͞o´ gər\. This large member of the cat family is known in various parts of North America as the *cougar, puma, panther,* or *mountain lion.* **Cougar** is from French *cougouar,* adapted from a neo-Latin (zoological) name *Cuguacu ara,* apparently a misinterpretation of the term *guaçu ara,* used in the Guaraní language of South American Indians (*RHD* 1987). **Cougar** is widespread in North American placenames (e.g., Ill., Cook Co.; and Utah, Beaver Co.).

COUNCIL \koun´ sil\. As used in North American placenames, this term usually refers to a site where meetings were held between Indian groups or between Indians and white settlers; an example is **Council Bluffs** (Iowa, Pottawattamie Co.).

COURTE OREILLES (Wis., Sawyer Co.) \ko͞o´ tə rā\. From French *courte-oreilles* 'cut-ears', a name given by explorers in 1659 to a group of Ottawa (Algonquian) Indians, supposedly because they had cut the rims off their ears. Their territory was later occupied by an Ojibwa (Algonquian) group (Vogel 1991). The placename now occurs in the forms **Couderay** and **Courte Oreilles.**

COUSE \kous\. This term is applied to a plant with an edible root, sometimes called 'biscuit root', used by Indians of the Pacific Northwest to make a type of bread (Hitchman 1985). It originates in Nez Perce (Sahaptian) *qaaws* 'a native root used for food' (Aoki 1994). As a placename, **Couse** occurs in Ore. (Umatilla Co.) and in Wash. (Asotin Co.).

COUSHATTA (La., Red River Par.) \ko͞o shat´ ə\. The name of a Muskogean people, formerly living in Ala.; most of the Coushattas now live on the Alabama-Coushatta Reservation in southeast Tex. The name is from a Choctaw (Muskogean) word meaning 'white cane', from *kǫshak* 'cane', *hata* 'white' (Read 1927; P. Munro p.c.). A related form is **Koasati** (Ala., Elmore Co.); this form of the name is the one now most commonly used by anthropologists and linguists.

COWANESQUE Creek (N.Y., Steuben Co.; Pa., Tioga Co.) \kō ə nesk´\. Also written <Gowanisque>; from Seneca (Iroquoian) *ga:wé:nesgeh* 'at the long island' (W. Chafe p.c.).

COWANSHANNOCK (Pa., Armstrong Co.). Perhaps from Delaware (Algonquian), meaning 'brier stream' (Donehoo 1928).

COWASSIT (Conn., New London Co.) \kō wä´ sit\. From Mohegan (Algonquian), probably meaning 'pine place' (Trumbull 1881). Related placenames include **Cowesett** (R.I., Bristol Co.) and **Coös County** (N.H.).

COWEE (N.C., Macon Co.) \kou´ ē\. Probably from Cherokee (Iroquoian) *ahawi'i* 'deer place', from *ahawi* 'deer' (B. Rudes p.c.).

COWEE Creek (Alaska, Juneau C-3). Said to be named for a leader of the Auk group of the Tlingit Indians (Orth 1967).

COWEEMAN River (Wash., Cowlitz Co.). Said to be named for a Cowlitz (Salishan)

Indian man called <Co-wee-na> 'short one' (Hitchman 1985).

COWEETA Creek (N.C., Macon Co.) \kō wē´ tə\. Probably from the same source as **Coweta County** (Ga.); see below.

COWESETT (R.I., Bristol Co.) \kō´ wə set\. From Narragansett (Algonquian) <cowawesuck>, probably meaning 'at the place of a young pine tree' (W. Cowan p.c.). Related placenames include **Cowassit** (Conn., New London Co.) and **Coös County** (N.H.).

COWETA County (Ga.) \kō wē´ tə, kou ē´ tə\. From Muskogee *kvwetv* /kawíta/, the name of a tribal town (Martin and Mauldin 2000). There is also a **Coweta** in Okla. (Wagoner Co.). The related form **Koweta Lake** also occurs in Ga. (Fulton Co.).

COWICHE (Wash., Yakima Co.) \kou ich´ ē\. Sahaptin [tkʷáywayčaš] 'lying-across place', from /-tkʷáy-/ 'lying, spread out on ground', /-way-č/ 'across', and /-aš/ 'place' (D. Kinkade p.c.).

COWIKEE (Ala., Barbour Co.) \kau ī´ kē\. Perhaps from Muskogee *kowike* /ko:wéyki/ 'quail', now also 'guinea fowl' (Read 1984; Martin and Mauldin 2000).

COWLIC (Ariz., Pima Co.) \kou´ lik\. From O'odham (Piman) *kawlĭk* 'hilly' (J. Hill p.c.).

COWLITZ County (Wash.) \kou´ lits\. The name of a Salishan subgroup; the Native American name is /káwlic/ [káwlɪts] (D. Kinkade p.c.).

COWSEAGAN Narrows (Maine, Lincoln Co.) \kou sē´ gən\. Derived from Abenaki /kaw-/ 'to lie prostrate' or homophonous /kaw-/ 'rough, uneven' (P. MacDougall p.c.). Also written **Cowsigan, Cowsegan.**

COW Springs (Ariz., Coconino Co.). Corresponds to Navajo (Athabaskan) *béégashii bito'* 'cow's spring', from *béegashii* 'cow', *bi-to'* 'its-water'. Navajo *béégashii* 'cow' is a borrowing from the Spanish plural *vacas* 'cows'.

COXIT Creek (Wash., Okanogan Co.) \kok´ sit\. Chinook Jargon <kok´-shut, cock´-sheet> [kákšət] 'broken, beat, hit, hurt', from Nootka [kiƛ̓šiƛ̓] 'to crack something' (D. Kinkade p.c.).

COXSACKIE (N.Y., Greene Co.) \ko͝ok sak´ ē, kok sak´ ē\. A Delaware (Algonquian) name of unclear derivation (Ruttenber 1906; Beauchamp 1907).

COYE Canyon (N.Mex., Sandoval Co.) \kō´ yā\. New Mexican Spanish *coye* 'roof-door', from Tewa *k'oyi* (Harrington 1916:436). Also written **Colle Canyon**.

COYOTE \kī ō´ tē, kī´ ōt\. An animal of the dog family, found over much of North America. The word is from Spanish *coyote,* from Nahuatl (Aztecan) *coyotl.* It is widespread as a placename, especially in the western United States (e.g., Calif., Santa Clara Co.; and Kans., Osage Co.) In N.Mex. **Coyote Canyon** (McKinley Co.) corresponds to Navajo (Athabaskan) *mą'ii téeh yítłizhí* 'where the coyote fell into deep water', containing *mą'ii* 'coyote', *téeh* 'deep water', *yítłizh* 'he fell in' (Wilson 1995).

CRACKATUXET Cove (Mass., Dukes Co.) \krak ə tuk´ sət\. From SNEng. Algonquian; contains <-tuk-> 'tidal river', <-s-> 'small', <-it> 'place' (W. Cowan p.c.).

CRANBERRY Lake (N.Y., St. Lawrence Co.). Corresponds to Western Abenaki (Algonquian) *popokwanebes,* from *popokwa* 'cranberry plant', *nebes* 'lake' (Day 1994–95).

CRAZY HORSE Canyon (S.Dak., Todd Co.). Named for a famous war leader of the Teton Lakhota (Siouan) people who died in 1877. He is usually called *thašų̨ka witko,* lit. 'his-horse is-crazy' (B. Ingham p.c.); cf. *šų́ka* 'horse', *witkó* 'to be crazy, foolish' (cf. Buechel and Manhart 2002).

CREDIT Island (Iowa, Scott Co.). Said to be so named because an early French trading post here extended credit to Indian customers (Vogel 1983).

CREEK. The name of a major Indian group of the southeastern United States belonging to the

Muskogean language family. They formerly lived mostly in Ga. and Ala.; now they are in the Creek and Seminole Nations of Okla., and in the Seminole community of Florida. The name **Creek** was abbreviated from "Ochese Creek Indians," referring to a stream in Ga. where the group was first contacted by English traders; that stream is now called the **Ocmulgee River.** As a placename, **Creek Indian** occurs in Ga. (Douglas Co.). The Creek people are also called **Muskogee,** a word of unclear derivation (Wright 1951), and that name is used elsewhere in this volume for the people and the language. As a placename, it occurs widely (e.g., in **Muskogee County,** Okla.).

CREE Spring (Ore., Baker Co). Named for the Cree Indians, an Algonquian-speaking group of Canada. The term is from French *Cris,* an abbreviation of an Ojibwa (Algonquian) term /kiristino:/, originally referring to a Cree-speaking group in the Hudson Bay region (*HNAI* 6:227).

CROATAN (N.C., Craven Co.) \krō´ ə tan\. The name first appears on an English map in 1585; it is derived from that of a CAC Algonquian village, said to be from <Krō-ōtän> 'talk town', indicating the chief's residence (Powell 1968; Payne 1985).

CROMESET Point (Mass., Plymouth Co.). From Wampanoag (SNEng. Algonquian), of uncertain derivation (Huden 1962).

CRONOMER Valley (N.Y., Orange Co.) \kron´ ə mər\. Said to have been named after an Indian resident, language unknown; his name may have been a version of Dutch *Hieronymus* 'Jerome' (Beauchamp 1907).

CROOKED Creek (Pa., Armstrong Co.). Said to be a translation of Delaware (Algonquian) <Woak-hanne> 'crooked-stream', from <woaku> 'crooked', <hanne> 'stream' (Donehoo 1928).

CROOKED FINGER Prairie (Ore., Marion Co.). Said to be named for a leader of the Molala people in the nineteenth century (H. Zenk p.c.).

CROSS CANYON Trail (N.Mex., Apache Co.). Navajo (Athabaskan) *ałnaashii ha'atiin* 'a trail that goes up on opposite sides', from *ałnaashii* 'on opposite sides', *ha-* 'up' plus *atiin* 'trail, road' (Wilson 1995).

CROSSJACKET (Alaska, Kantishna River D-3) \kros´ jak ət\. A popular etymology from Koyukon (Athabaskan) *kk'os chaakk'et* [q'osča:q'ət], lit. 'schist stream-mouth', from *kk'os* 'schist rock', *-kaakk'et, -chaakk'et* 'stream mouth' (Jetté and Jones 2000:289, 366). Also written as **Coskakat, Cos Jacket.** A related term is **Cosna** 'schist river'.

CROTON River (N.Y., Westchester Co.) \krō´ tən\. Perhaps from Munsee Delaware (Algonquian) <kenotin, knoton> 'wind' (Beauchamp 1907). The term also occurs in N.J. (Hunterdon Co.) and as a transfer name elsewhere (e.g., Iowa, Lee Co.; and Mich., Newaygo Co.).

CROW. This term, as it appears in placenames, may sometimes refer directly to the bird; at other times, it may translate Indian names that refer to the bird or to human beings called **Crow**, after the bird; at still other times, it may be taken from an English family name. In the northern Plains, it may refer to the Crow Indian people, who speak a language of the Siouan family. Their name in Indian languages of the area is usually derived from the word for the bird: for example, Lakhota (Siouan) *khąǧí* 'crow' (bird), *khąǧí wičhaša* 'Crow people' (Ingham 2001).

CROW Canyon (Colo., Montezuma Co.). Corresponds to Navajo (Athabaskan) *gáagii bikooh,* lit. 'crow's canyon', from *gáagi* 'crow', *bi-kooh* 'its canyon' (Linford 2000).

CROW Creek (Iowa, Scott Co.). Translated from French *Rivière du Corbeau,* itself a translation of Meskwaki (Algonquian) /ka:ka:kiwisi:po:wi/ 'crow river', containing /ka:ka:kiwa/ 'crow' (I. Goddard p.c.).

CROWHEART Butte (Wyo., Fremont Co.). So named because of a legend concerning the Shoshoni (Numic) leader Washakie, who is supposed to have challenged a Crow (Siouan) warrior to a combat here. Upon killing the Crow, Washakie is supposed to have eaten his heart (Urbanek 1974).

CROW Island (Mich., Chippewa Co.). Named after an Ojibwa (Algonquian) leader called <Kakawiskou>, or in English 'Crow' (Vogel 1986); the Native American stem is actually *gaagaagiw* 'raven' (Nichols and Nyholm 1995).

CROW Peak (S.Dak., Lawrence Co.). Corresponds to Lakhota (Siouan) *pahá khąǧí okakteyapi* 'hill where they killed the crows, or the Crows, or the enemies' (A. Taylor p.c.).

CROWS NEST Peak (S.Dak., Pennington Co.). Possibly based on Lakhota (Siouan) *khąǧí toka* 'bluish crow' or 'first crow' or 'enemy crow' (Sneve 1973; B. Ingham p.c.).

CROW Trail (Ariz., Apache Co.). Navajo (Athabaskan) *gáagii haayáhí* '(where) the crow ascended' (Linford 2000).

CROW WING River (Minn.). A translation from French *Rivière à l'Aile de Corbeau,* itself based on Ojibwa (Algonquian) <Gagagiwigwuni> 'raven's wing' (Upham 2001). The elements are *gaagaagiw* 'raven', *-igwan* 'feather' (Nichols and Nyholm 1995).

CRUMBLED HOUSE (N.Mex., San Juan Co.). Corresponds to Navajo (Athabaskan) *kin náázhoozhí* 'sliding house' (Linford 2000); cf. *kin* 'house'.

CRYSTAL (N.Mex., San Juan Co.). Corresponds to Navajo (Athabaskan) *tóniłts'ílí* 'sparkling water', from *tó* 'water', *niłts'ílí* 'it sparkling' (Wilson 1995). Other occurrences of **Crystal** in U.S. placenames are probably also based on Indian terms referring to clear or sparkling water (e.g., **Crystal River** in Fla., Citrus Co.), given the Muskogee name <Wewakiahakee>, from /oywa-haya:yakí:/ 'clear water', from *uewv* /óywa/ 'water', *hvyayvkē* /haya:yakí:/ 'bright, clear' (J. Martin p.c.).

CUASLUI (Calif., Santa Barbara Co.) \kwäs lī \. Earlier written <Guaslay>; from Purisimeño Chumashan /awašla'y, wašlayɨk/ 'net sack with wooden mouth-ring' (Gudde 1998).

CUATE \kwä´ tē\. This Mexican Spanish word means 'twin', from Nahuatl (Aztecan) *coatl,* which also means 'snake'. The Spanish term has been applied to a variety of native plants (Gudde 1998). In Calif. it occurs in the names of three Mexican land grants: for example, **Corral del Cuate** (Santa Barbara Co.), 'corral of the twin'; cf. also **Cuate Canyon** (N.Mex., Socorro Co.). A variant spelling is **Quate.** From this is derived Spanish *cuatal, quatal* 'place where *cuate* grows', found as the placename **Quatal Canyon** (Calif., Santa Barbara Co.). The plural **Cuates** also occurs (N.Mex., Union Co.).

CUBA \kyōō´ bə\. The name of this island nation in the Caribbean Sea became a popular placename in the United States at the time of the Spanish-American War, at the end of the nineteenth century. The term is said to be from the Taino (Arawakan) name *Cubanacan,* referring to the people who occupied the island. Examples are in Calif. (Merced Co.), Ill. (Lake Co.), and N.Dak. (Barnes Co.). Spanish *cuba* can also mean 'trough, tank', however, and this may be the source of the placename **Cuba** in N.Mex. (Sandoval Co.), which was named prior to the Spanish-American War (Julyan 1998). A related placename is **Cuban Gulch** (Alaska, Eagle C-1); see below.

CUBAHATCHEE Creek (Ala., Macon Co.) \kyōō bā hach´ ē\. Possibly from Muskogee *kvpe* /kapí/ 'lye', *hvcce* /háčči/ 'stream' (Martin and Mauldin 2000).

CUBAN Gulch (Alaska, Eagle C-1). The name was reported in 1898, perhaps referring to the Caribbean island (Orth 1967); see **Cuba** above.

CUBERANT Lake (Utah, Summit Co.) \kōō´ bə rənt\. Said to be from a Ute (Numic) word meaning 'long' (Van Cott 1990); but this may be a confusion with /kúwaagati/ 'sharp-edged' (Givón 1979).

CUCA (Calif., San Diego Co.) \kōō´ kə\. Earlier recorded as <Cucam>; perhaps a Diegueño

(Yuman) name for an edible plant (Gudde 1998).

CUCAMONGA (Calif., San Bernardino Co.) \ko͞o kə mung´ gə, ko͞o kə mong´ gə\. From Gabrielino (Takic) *kúkamonga*, containing *-nga* 'place' (Gudde 1998). Possibly related forms also occur in some neighboring states: for example, **Cocamonga** (Ore., Harney Co.), **Cucamonga** (Ariz., Coconino Co.), and **Cucomungo** (Nev., Esmeralda Co.) \ko͞o kə mung´ gō\.

CUDEI (N.Mex., San Juan Co.) \kə dī´\. From Navajo (Athabaskan) *gad íí'áí* 'juniper sticking-up', containing *gad* 'juniper, cedar', *íí'á* 'it sticks up' (Wilson 1995). Also written **Cudai.**

CUERNA VERDE Park (Colo., Pueblo Co.) \kwâr´ nə vâr´ dē\. A garbling of Spanish *Cuerno Verde* 'green horn', the name of a Comanche (Numic) leader killed nearby in the eighteenth century. His name is also reflected in nearby **Greenhorn Mountain.** His Native American name may have been /taivo narɨkatɨ/ 'white men are afraid of him' (J. McLaughlin p.c.).

CUFFAWA Creek (Miss., Marshall Co.) \kə fä´ wä\. Choctaw (Muskogean) *kafi aawaaya* 'where sassafras grows', from *kafi* 'sassafras', *aa-* 'place', *waaya* 'to grow' (Seale 1939; P. Munro p.c.).

CUITIN Creek (Wash., Yakima Co.) \kwē´ tin\. From Chinook Jargon <ku-i-tan> 'horse' (Hitchman 1985); also written **Cuitan**, as in **Cuitan Creek** (Ore., Crook Co.).

CULLABY Creek (Ore., Clatsop Co.) \kul´ ə bē\. Named for an Indian resident of the area; the language involved is not known (McArthur 1992).

CULLASAJA (N.C., Macon Co.) \kul ə sä´ jə\. From Cherokee (Iroquoian) *kalseeji* 'sugar' (Powell 1968, B. Rudes p.c.).

CULLEOKA (Tenn., Maury Co.) \kul ē ō´ kə\. Perhaps from Choctaw (Muskogean) *kali-oka* 'spring water' (P. Munro p.c.). The term occurs as a transfer name in Tex. (Collin Co.).

CULLEY, Bogue (Miss., Chickasaw Co.) \kul´ ē\. From Choctaw (Muskogean) *kali* 'spring' (of water), *book* 'stream' (Seale 1939).

CULLOWHEE (N.C., Jackson Co.). The name was earlier written <Kullaughee>, said to be from an unidentified Indian language, meaning 'place of the lilies' (Powell 1968).

CULSTIGH Creek (Ala., Cherokee Co.). Perhaps from Cherokee (Iroquoian) *kulsetsi* 'honey locust', a flowering tree (Read 1984).

CULTAS Creek (Alaska, Charlet River A-4) \kul´ təs\. From the same origin as **Cultus Creek** (Ore., Jefferson Co.). This is Chinook Jargon <cul´-tus, kul´tus> [kə́ltəs] 'bad, worthless', from Lower Chinook *káltas* 'in vain; worthless; only' (D. Kinkade p.c.). The term occurs in other placenames of the northwestern states (e.g., Idaho, Valley Co.; and Wash., Jefferson Co.).

CUMA, Arroyo (N.Mex., Santa Fe Co.) \ko͞o´ mə\. Perhaps a Spanish spelling of Tewa (Tanoan) *t'oma,* a name for the promontory called Red Hill (Harrington 1916:459).

CUMERO Canyon (Ariz., Santa Cruz Co.) \ko͞o mâr´ ō\. From local Spanish *cumero* 'hackberry tree', from O'odham (Piman) *ko:m* 'hackberry tree' (Saxton et al. 1983). A related form is **Cumaro Canyon** (Ariz., Pima Co.).

CUMMAQUID (Mass., Barnstable Co.) \ko͝om´ ə kwid\. From SNEng. Algonquian, 'at an enclosed space'; cf. <koomuk-> 'enclosed space', <-it> 'place' (W. Cowan p.c.).

CUMMOCK Island (R.I., Washington Co.) \ko͝om´ ək\. From SNEng. Algonquian <koomuk> 'enclosed space' (W. Cowan p.c.).

CUMTUX (Ore., Curry Co.) \kum´ tuks\. From Chinook Jargon <kum´-tux, kum´-tuks> [kə́mtəks] 'to know, understand', based on Nootka /kamat/ 'known' (D. Kinkade p.c.). A related name is **Kumtux** (Wash., Clark Co.).

CUNDAYÓ (NM, Santa Fe Co.). A variant of **Cundiyo** (N.Mex., Santa Fe Co.) \ko͞on dē´ yō\. This is from the Tewa (Tanoan) placename *kų̱diyo* (Harrington 1916:378).

CUNNEO TUBBY Creek (Okla., Latimer Co.) \kun ə tub´ ē\. Perhaps from the "war name" of a Choctaw (Muskogean) man, of the form *kaniya-t-abi* '(one who) went away and killed', containing *kaniya* 'to go away', *abi* 'to kill' (P. Munro p.c.).

CUPIT MARY Mountain (Ore., Lane Co.) \kyo͞o pit mâr´ ē\. Named for an Indian woman who resided in the area; her ethnic group is not known. The name is from Chinook Jargon <ko-pet´> [kopít] 'stop, the end, enough', from Chinookan *kupat* 'enough, as much', supposedly because she was the youngest child in her family (McArthur 1992; D. Kinkade p.c.).

CUPSAW Brook (N.J., Passaic Co.) \kup´ sô\. Probably from Delaware (Algonquian); the derivation is not clear (Becker 1964).

CUPSOQUE Beach (N.Y., Suffolk Co.) \kup´ sok\. From SNEng. Algonquian, also written <Cupsawege, Cupsaoge, Cupsage> (etc.), perhaps meaning 'a closed-up inlet' (Tooker 1911).

CUPSUPTIC (Maine, Oxford Co.) \kup sup´ tik\. Perhaps from Abenaki (Algonquian), meaning 'a closed-up stream' (Huden 1962).

CURECANTI Pass (Colo., Gunnison Co.). \ko͞or i kan´ tē\. Said to be named for a Ute (Numic) leader called <Curicata>; the Native American form is /kudáganti/ or /kudágati/, lit. 'has a neck', from /kuda/ 'neck' (J. McLaughlin p.c.).

CURRAHEE Mountain (Ga., Stephens Co.) \kûr´ ə hē\. Said to be from Cherokee (Iroquoian) <gurahiyi>, perhaps meaning 'watercress place', or perhaps 'standing alone' (Krakow 1975). A related form is **Curry Hee Mountain** (Tenn., Blount Co.).

CURRATUCK Creek (Va., Accomack Co.) \kûr´ ə tuk\. From the same source as **Currituck County** (N.C.). This is said to be from a CAC Algonquian word meaning 'wild geese'. Older spellings of the term are <Coratock, Carotank, Coratank> (Powell 1968; Payne 1985). A related placename is **Curratuck** (Va., Accomack Co.).

CURRY HE Mountain (Tenn., Blount Co.) \kûr´ ē hē\. A form related to **Currahee Mountain** (Ga., Stephens Co.); see above.

CUSABO \ko͞o sä´ bō\. The name given by the Spanish to a tribe formerly living around Charleston Bay in S.C.; it has been speculated that they were related to the Taino (Arawakan) Indians of the Caribbean area (B. Rudes p.c.). The term **Cusabo** is not currently used as a placename.

CUSHETUNK (N.J., Hunterdon Co.). Perhaps from a Delaware (Algonquian) word meaning 'washing'; cf. Munsee Delaware *kshíixtoow* 'to wash' (O'Meara 1996). Possibly related names are **Cochecton** (N.Y., Sullivan Co.), **Coshecton** (Pa., Wayne Co.), and **Coshocton County** (Ohio).

CUSHTUSHA (Miss., Neshoba Co.) \kush tush´ ə\. Probably Choctaw (Muskogean), meaning 'fleas are there', from *kashti* 'flea', *asha* 'they are there' (Seale 1939; P. Munro p.c.). Also written as **Cushtusia.**

CUSSETA (Ala., Chambers Co.) \kə sē´ tə\. From Muskogee *kvsehtv* /kasíhta/, the name of a tribal town (Read 1984; Martin and Mauldin 2000). There is also a **Cusseta** in Ga. (Chattahoochee Co.). The alternative writing **Cussetaw** occurs.

CUSSEWAGO Creek (Pa., Crawford Co.). From the name of a Munsee Delaware (Algonquian) village of the eighteenth century (Donehoo 1928).

CUSTALOGA (Ohio, Wayne Co.) \kus tə lō´ gə\. This was the Iroquoian name of the Unami Delaware (Algonquian) leader <Pakanke>. It may be from Mohawk *kahstaró'kwa'* 'necklace of big beads' or from Oneida *kastóla'ke* 'single-feathered headdress of chiefs' (M. McCafferty p.c.).

CUTCA Valley (Calif., San Diego Co.) \kut´ kə\. An earlier form of the name is <Whitka>; it is probably of Indian origin, but the language is not identified (Gudde 1998).

CUTCHOGUE (N.Y., Suffolk Co.) \kə chōg´\. Earlier written <Corchaki, Corchoge, Cor-

choagg, Curchaulk> (etc.); perhaps from a SNEng. Algonquian name meaning 'principal place' (Tooker 1911).

CUT FOOT SIOUX Lake (Minn., Itasca Co.). Translated from the Ojibwa (Algonquian) name for a Sioux with a wounded foot, who was killed at this lake in a battle of 1748 (Upham 2001).

CUTMAPTICO Creek (Md., Wicomico Co.) \kut map´ tē kō\. Earlier written <Cutty Mock-tico>; perhaps from CAC Algonquian elements meaning 'big tree' (Kenny 1984).

CUT MEAT Creek (S.Dak., Todd Co.). A translation of the Dakotan (Siouan) name, perhaps Lakhota *thaló-waksa,* from *thaló* 'fresh meat' and *waksá* 'to cut off' (Ingham 2001).

CUTTATAWOMEN (Va., Lancaster Co.) \kə tat´ ə wo͝om ən\. The name of a CAC Algonquian subgroup, also written **Cuttawoman,** of unclear derivation (Hagemann 1988).

CUTTYHUNK (Mass., Dukes Co.) \kut´ ē hungk\. From SNEng. Algonquian, perhaps 'place where someone speaks'; cf. <kut-toowonk> 'speech, utterance' (W. Cowan p.c.).

CUXABESIS Lake (Maine, Piscataquis Co.). From Malecite (Algonquian), meaning 'little swift water' (Huden 1962).

CUYAHOGA County (Ohio) \kī ə hō´ gə\. Perhaps from Wyandot (Iroquoian) /kažáʔke/ 'at the wing' (M. McCafferty p.c.). The term occurs elsewhere as a transfer name (e.g. Mich., Ontonagon Co.).

CUYAMA (Calif., Santa Barbara Co.) \kwē yä´ mə, ko͞o yä´ mə, kwē yam´ ə\. From Chumashan /kuyam/ 'clam', referring to freshwater shellfish (Gudde 1998).

CUYAMACA (Calif., San Diego Co) \kwē ə mak´ ə, ko͞o yə mä´ kə\. From Diegueño (Yuman) *wiiyemak* 'behind the clouds', from *'ekwii* 'cloud, rain' plus *'emak* 'behind' (Gudde 1998).

CUYAMUNGUE (N.Mex., Santa Fe Co.) \ko͞o yə mo͝ong´ gā\. Tewa (Tanoan) [k'uyemuɣe] 'where they threw down the stones', from [k'u] 'stone', [yemu] 'to throw things down', [-ɣe] 'down at' (Harrington 1916:332).

CUYAPAIPA (Calif., San Diego Co.). A spelling variant of **Cuyapipe** (Calif., San Diego Co.) \ko͞o´ yə pīp, kwē ə pī´ pə\. This is from Diegueño (Yuman) *'ewiiy-aapaayp* 'leaning rock', containing *'ewiiy* 'rock' and *aapaayp* 'to lean' (Gudde 1998). Also written as **Guyapipe.**

CUZCO (Ind., Dubois Co.) \kuz´ kō\. Named for a city in Peru, the ancient capital of the Inca empire. The name also occurs elsewhere (Va., Louisa Co.).

D

DAAQUAM (Maine, Aroostook Co.) \dak´ wäm\. Said to be Abenaki (Algonquian) for 'your beaver' (Huden 1962); cf. W. Abenaki *demakwa* 'beaver' (Day 1994–95).

DABOB (Wash., Jefferson Co.) \dä´ bob\. From the Twana (Salishan) placename /táʔbax^{W}/ (D. Kinkade p.c.). Perhaps related names are **Tabook Point** and **Tarboo Creek** (Wash., Jefferson Co.).

DACHIKJOWARUK Cove (Alaska, Nunivak Island A-5). The Yupik (Eskimo) name was recorded in 1949 (Orth 1967). A probably related name is **Dachirowruk Cove** (Alaska, Nunivak Island A-5).

DACOMA (Okla., Woods Co.) \də kō´ mə\. From a combination of **Dakota,** of Siouan origin, and **Oklahoma,** of Choctaw (Muskogean) origin (Shirk 1974).

DADASOA Spring (N.Mex., McKinley Co.). Perhaps from Navajo (Athabaskan) *dah ast'os* 'cone shaped', containing *dah* 'up' (A. Wilson p.c.).

DADINA River (Alaska, Valdez D-3) \dä dē´ nə\. From Ahtna (Athabaskan) *hwdaadi' na',* lit. 'downriver stream' (Kari 1983:22).

DAGISLAKHNA Creek (Alaska, Tanana C-5). The Koyukon (Athabaskan) name was recorded in 1956 (Orth 1967).

DAGITLI River (Alaska, Kateel River C-2). The Koyukon (Athabaskan) name was reported as <Doggetlooscat> in 1887 (Orth 1967).

DAHDAYLA Island (Wash., Clallam Co.). From the Quileute (Chimakuan) placename /da:dila/, referring to Jagged Island (D. Kinkade p.c.).

DAHINDA (Ill., Knox Co.) \dä hin´ də, də hin´ də\. The term is probably taken from Longfellow's *Hiawatha,* where this word is given the meaning 'bullfrog' (Vogel 1963); cf. Ojibwa (Algonquian) *dende* 'bullfrog' (Rhodes 1985).

DAHLONEGA (Ga., Lumpkin Co.) \dä lon´ ə gə, də lon´ ə gə\. The name of this Gold Rush town of the 1830s is from Cherokee (Iroquoian); cf. *adel dalonige* 'gold', lit. 'money-yellow' (Krakow 1975; J. Scancarelli p.c.). The term has been transferred to other states (e.g., Iowa, Wapello Co.; and Idaho, Lemhi Co.), and the pronunciation \də long´ gə\ is reported from Idaho. The spelling **Delonegha** occurs in Calif. (Kern Co.).

DAHLOONGAMIUT (Alaska, Cape Mendenhall D-6). The Yupik (Eskimo) name was reported about 1949 (Orth 1967).

DAHOGA (Pa., Elk Co.) \dä hō´ gə\. Perhaps a alternate form of **Tioga** (see below), from an Iroquoian name meaning 'where it forks' (Donehoo 1928).

DAHTEH (Alaska, Black River C-5). The Gwich'in (Athabaskan) name was recorded in 1956 (Orth 1967).

DAHTKIT Cove (Alaska, Nunivak Island B-5). The Yupik (Eskimo) name is said to mean 'small bay' (Orth 1967).

DAKAI Well (N.Mex., McKinley Co.) \dä´ kī\. Perhaps from Navajo (Athabaskan) *ndaakai* 'they wander around' (A. Wilson p.c.). A related placename is **Nokai Canyon** (Ariz., Navajo Co.), meaning 'Mexican', lit. 'those who wander around' (Granger 1983).

DAKANEEK Bay (Alaska, Petersburg D-6). The Tlingit name was published in 1943 (Orth 1967).

DAKAVAK Lake (Alaska, Mount Katmai A-3). The Alutiiq (Eskimo) name was reported in 1904 (Orth 1967).

DAKEEKALIK Creek (Alaska, Nunivak Island B-3) \də kēk´ ə lik\. The Yupik (Eskimo) name was recorded in 1949 (Orth 1967).

DAKEEKATHLRIMJINGIA Point (Alaska, Nunivak Island B-3). The Yupik (Eskimo) name was recorded in 1949 (Orth 1967).

DAKLI River (Alaska, Kateel River D-l) \däk´ lē\. Probably abbreviated from Koyukon (Athabaskan) <Dakliakakat>, as recorded in 1885 (Orth 1967).

DAKOTA \də kō´ tə\. This term refers to a group of peoples, forming a major branch of the Siouan language family, living in the northern Plains states. The term **Lakota** or **Lakhota** represents the pronunciation of the word **Dakota** in western dialects such as that of the Teton subgroup, and *Nakota* or *Nakhota* the pronunciation in other dialects such as **Assiniboine.** The term *Dakotan* is sometimes used by linguists to include all dialects of the language. The source of the English term is a word often translated as 'allies'; cf. Dakota *dakhóta* 'friendly' (Riggs 1890), Santee Dakota *kodá* 'friend' (Riggs 1890), Lakhota *kholá* (Ingham 2001). As a placename, **Dakota** occurs not only in the names of the states **North Dakota** and **South Dakota,** but in many other areas (e.g., Neb., Dakota Co.; Iowa, Humboldt Co.; and Mich., Baraga Co.). The term has also given its name to a type of geological formation, which in tum has been used as a placename, as in **Dakota Ridge** (Colo., Boulder Co.) and **Dakota Hill** (Utah, Kane Co.).

DA KO TAH, Lake (S.Dak., Hand Co.) \dä kō´ tä\. From the same source as **Dakota**; see above.

DALASUGA Island (Alaska, Skagway A-l) \dä lə so͞o´ gə\. The Tlingit Indian name is said to mean 'barnacle-infested' (Orth 1967); cf. /s'uuk/ 'barnacle' (Davis and Leer 1976).

DALCO, Point (Wash., King Co.) \däl´ kō\. The name may be Indian, recorded in 1841, but the language of origin is not clear (Reese 1996). A possibly related name is **Tahlequah** (Wash., King Co.), with assimilation in pronounciation and spelling to the town in Okla. (Cherokee Co.).

DALIMALOAK Creek (Alaska, Survey Pass D-2). Perhaps from the Iñupiaq (Eskimo) word for 'five' or 'seven' (Orth 1967); cf. *tallimat* 'five', *tallimat malġuk* 'seven' (MacLean 1980).

DAMARISCOTTA (Maine, Lincoln Co.) \dam ər i skot´ ə\. Perhaps from Penobscot (Algonquian) <Nahmayskontik> 'plenty of fishes' or <D'amaswakkontee> 'plenty of alewives' (a type of fish); cf. <madames> 'alewife', <n'mays> 'fish in general'. This name has been confused with **Damariscove** \dam ə ris kōv´\. (also in Lincoln Co.), which may actually be from English *Damarill's Cove,* named after Humphrey Damarill, a seaman who lived in the area around 1614 (Eckstorm 1941).

DAMUNDTALI Lake (Alaska, Tanacross A-2). The Upper Tanana (Athabaskan) name is *daamänhdeedlay* 'lakes that are up above' (J. Kari p.c.).

DANCING RABBIT Creek (Miss., Madison Co.). A partial translation of Choctaw (Muskogean) <chukfi-luma-hilhlah-book>, containing *chukfi* 'rabbit', *luma* 'hidden', *hilha* 'dance', and *book* 'creek' (Seale 1939; P. Munro p.c.).

DANEKA Lake (Alaska, Talkeetna Mountains C-4) \dan´ ə kə\. The name is Ahtna (Athabaskan) *deniigi* 'moose' (J. Kari p.c.).

DAOKOAH Point (Wash., Clallam Co.). Makah (Nootkan) /t'uku:ʔa/, translated as 'hard to get in', with the root /t'uk-/ 'small' (W. Jacobsen p.c.).

DAPRAKMIUT (Alaska, Nunivak Island B-3). The Yupik (Eskimo) name was reported in 1949 (Orth 1967).

DARGUN Point (Alaska, Craig D-4). The Tlingit name was published in 1964 (Orth 1967).

DARIEN (N.Y., Genesee Co.) \dâr´ ē ən\. From Spanish *Darién,* a name referring to the Isthmus of Panama; derived from an Indian language of the area. The placename occurs in several other states (e.g., Conn., Fairfield Co.; and Ill., DuPage Co.).

DASANI Island (Alaska, Craig D-4). The Tlingit name was published in 1956 (Orth 1967).

DASHA Island (Alaska, Ruby D-4). The name, perhaps from Koyukon (Athabaskan), was published in 1940 (Orth 1967).

DASHOGA Ridge (N.C., Swain Co.). Perhaps an Indian name, from an unidentified language (Powell 1968).

DATHA Island (S.C., Beaufort Co.). Earlier written <Dataw, Dawtaw>; said to have been named for an Indian leader of a Muskogean group; the term reportedly means 'green wood' (BGN 8604).

DATHEEKOOK Point (Alaska, Nunivak Island A-7). The Yupik (Eskimo) name was reported in 1949 (Orth 1967).

DATHLALMUND Lake (Alaska, Tanacross A4). From Upper Tanana (Athabaskan) *daałäl männ'*, lit. 'floating-moss lake' (J. Kari p.c.).

DATKOKAN Lake (Alaska, Beaver A-5). Koyukon (Athabaskan) *dotsoka dənh*, borrowed from Gwich'in (Athabaskan), meaning 'place with no cache' (Kari 2000); cf. Koyukon *denh* [dəN] 'place where' (Jetté and Jones 2000), Gwich'in *dehtsii* 'raised cache with house' (Peter 1979).

DATZKOO Islands (Alaska, Dixon Entrance C-3). The Tlingit name was published in 1911 (Orth 1967).

DAUFUSKEE Island (S.C., Beaufort Co.) \dô fus´ kē\. Perhaps a word meaning 'fork' (of a river), in an unidentified Indian language (Neuffer and Neuffer 1983).

DAWHO River (S.C., Charleston Co.). Also written <Dawhaw>; perhaps from Muskogee *tahwv* /tá:hwa/ 'lamb's-quarters', an edible green plant (Pickens 1963:37; Martin and Mauldin 2000).

DAYEHAS Creek (Alaska, Skagway B-l). The Tlingit name was published in 1923 (Orth 1967).

DAYKOO Islands (Alaska, Dixon Entrance C-3 \dā´ ko͞o\. The name, perhaps from Tlingit, was published in 1911 (Orth 1967).

DEAD INDIAN Creek (Ore., Jackson Co.). Named in memory of two Rogue River Indians found dead here by settlers around 1854 (McArthur 1992).

DEAD River (Mich., Marquette Co.). From Fench *Rivière de Mort* 'river of death', said to be from Ojibwa <gi-nibo-manitou-sibi> 'river of the spirits of the dead' (Vogel 1986); cf. *manidoo* 'spirit' (Nichols and Nyholm 1995).

DEBEBEKID (Ariz., Navajo Co.) \di bā´ bə kid\. Navajo (Athabaskan) *dibé be'ek'id* 'sheep lake' (Linford 2000), containing *dibé* 'sheep' and *be'ek'id* 'small lake' (Young and Morgan 1987).

DEBSCONEAG Falls (Maine, Piscataquis Co.) \deb´ skə neg\. Abenaki (Algonquian), perhaps meaning 'ponds at the high place' (Rutherford 1970).

DE CHELLY, Canyon (Ariz., Apache Co.) \də shā´, dē shā\. The Hispanic spelling represents Navajo (Athabaskan) *tséyi'* 'canyon', with *tsé* 'rock' and *-yi'* 'inside' (Wilson 1995). Details on the placenames of this area are given in Jett 2001.

DECORAH (Iowa, Winneshiek Co.) \də kôr´ ə\. From the surname of a Winnebago (Siouan) family, originally living in Wis. The name is said to derive from that of a Frenchman, Sabrevoir de Carrie, who took a Winnebago wife in 1729 (Vogel 1983). The placename also occurs in Idaho (Adams Co.) Altemative spellings are found in the village of **Decorra** (Ill., Henderson Co.) and in **Decoria Township** (Minn., Blue Earth Co.).

DEER. This term, widespread in American placenames, is likely to represent a translation from American Indian placenames in many cases. A settlement in Ariz. called simply **Deer** (Navajo Co.) corresponds to Navajo (Athabaskan) *bįįh bito'* 'deer's spring', from *bįįh* 'deer' and *bi-to'* 'its water' (*to'* 'water, spring') (Wilson 1995). **Deer Lake** (Minn., Itasca Co.) is said to be a translation of the Ojibwa (Algonquian) name <Wawashkeshiwi> (Upham 2001); cf. *waawaashkeshi* 'deer' (J. Nichols p.c.). In Ind. (Carroll Co.) **Deer Creek** probably corresponds to Miami/Illinois /apeehskionki/ 'at the fawn' (McCafferty 2002).

DEG HIT'AN \deg hi tän\The term refers to an Athabaskan group of the lower Kuskokwim River drainage in western Alaska, otherwise known as **Ingalik**; see below. The expression represents /deg hət'an/ 'people from here' (*HNAI* 6:614).

DEGUYNOS Canyon (Calif., San Diego Co.) \də gē´ nōs\. From Spanish *diegueños* 'those of San Diego (Mission)', applied to the local Indian people, of the Yuman language family (Gudde 1998).

DEKKAS Creek (Calif., Shasta Co.) \dek´ əs\. From Wintu /dekes/ '(the act of) climbing', from /dek-/ 'to climb' (Gudde 1998).

DELATE (Idaho, Shoshone Co.) \də lāt\. From Chinook Jargon <de-late> [dilét] 'straight, direct, true, sure', from Canadian French *dret* 'straight, right', equivalent to Standard French *droit.* The name was applied by a Forest Service officer in 1927 (Boone 1988; D. Kinkade p.c.).

DELAWARE \del´ ə wâr\. This word, orginally the surname of the British nobleman Thomas West, Lord De la Warr, was first applied as a placename to the **Delaware River** and to what later came to be the state. The British, however, also applied it to an Indian people who spoke an Algonquian language, who occupied much of the **Delaware River** valley of Pa. in colonial times as well as all of N.J. and the area around New York city. Some Delaware people moved to Canada in subsequent migrations, and others to Okla. During the white exploration of the West, the U.S. Army employed a number of Delaware scouts who were involved in placenaming. As a toponym, the term frequently refers to the Indian people rather than to the river or the state; examples occur in Ohio (Delaware Co.), Mich. (Keweenaw Co.), and Ark. (Logan Co.).

DELNAZINI Spring (N.Mex., San Juan Co.) \del nä zē´ nē\. Navajo (Athabaskan) *dééł naazíní* 'standing cranes', containing *dééł* 'crane' and *naazį́* 'they stand erect' (A. Wilson p.c.). A related form occurs in **De-na-zin Wash** (also in San Juan Co.).

DELONEGHA Hot Springs (Calif., Kern Co.) \də lon´ ə gə\. Named after **Dahlonega** (Ga., Lumpkin Co.); see above.

DEL SHAY Basin (Ariz., Gila Co.) \del shā´\. Named for a Western Apache leader who died in 1874. His name was *de'iłché'é* 'red ant', probably with the literal meaning 'red ones in a line' (P. Greenfeld p.c.).

DELYNDIA Lake (Alaska, Tyonek C-2) \də lin´ dē ə\. Named for Shem Pete, a Dena'ina (Athabaskan) man whose Native American name was *delindin,* from Russian "Derenty" (Kari and Fall 1987:229), probably *Terentij* 'Terence'.

DENAGIEMINA Lake (Alaska, Medfra A-2). From Upper Kuskokwim (Athabaskan) *dineje mina',* lit. 'moose lake'. This Indian name actually refers to a small lake south of what is called **Denagiemina Lake** in English, however; the latter is called *ch'idrohtane mina* 'heart-hill lake' by the Indians (Kari 1999:97).

DENALI (Alaska, Healy A-l) \də nä´ lē\. Koyukon (Athabaskan) *deenaalee* 'the tall one', from *-naał-* 'to be long, tall' (Jetté and Jones 2000:432). Regarding the controvery over this name, see Kari 1986.

DE-NA-ZIN Wash (N.Mex., San Juan Co.) \den ə zēn´\. From the same source as **Delnazini Spring**; see above.

DENEKI Lake (Alaska, Healy C-4) \də nē´ kē\. From Ahtna (Athabaskan) *deniigi bene'* 'moose lake' (Kari 1999:45).

DENIKTOW Ridge (Alaska, Melozitna D-5). The Koyukon (Athabaskan) name was recorded in 1956 (Orth 1967).

DENLUMUNGUT (Alaska, Kateel River B-2). From Koyukon (Athabaskan), of unclear derivation (Orth 1967).

DENNEHOTSO (Ariz., Apache Co.) \dā ni hōt´ sō, den ā hōt´ sō\. Navajo (Athabaskan) *deinihootso* 'yellow area extending upward', from *dei* 'upward', *niho(o)* 'space, area', and *tso* 'yellow' (Wilson 1995). The spelling variant **Dennihotso** also occurs.

DEPOE Bay (Ore., Lincoln Co.) \dē´ pō\. Named for Charley DePoe, an Indian of the Siletz Reservation, said to be from the Tututni (Athabaskan) people (McArthur 1992; D. Kinkade p.c.).

DES ARC (Mo., Iron Co.) \des´ ärk, dez´ ärk, dez ärk´\. From French *des Arcs* 'of the Arks', with the abbreviated name that the French used to refer to the **Arkansas** (Siouan) Indians (Ramsay 1952). The term is parallel to **Ozark Mountain**, from French *aux Arcs* 'at the Arks', referring to the same group. As a placename, **Des Arc** occurs in Ark. (Prairie Co.).

DESATOYA Peak (Nev., Lander Co.) \des ə toi´ ə\. Possibly Shoshoni /tɨasɨ-toya/ 'frozen mountain', from /tɨasɨ/"to be frozen', /toya(-pi)/ 'mountain' (J. McLaughlin p.c.).

DESCHUTES River (Wash., Thurston Co.) \dā sho͞ot´\. This apparently represents French *Rivière des Chutes* 'river of the (water)falls'. It is possibly a folk-etymology, however, from Southern Lushootseed (Salishan) [dəx^{w}scə́tx^{w}ad], the name of the river, lit. 'black-bear place'; it contains /cə́tx^{w}əd/ 'black bear' (D. Kinkade p.c.). There is also a **Deschutes River** (and County) in Ore., and the French etymology may be the correct one there.

DESHA Creek (Utah, San Juan Co.) \dā shā´\. From Navajo (Athabaskan) *deez'á* 'ridge' (Linford 2000). A related name is **Deza Bluffs** (N.Mex., McKinley Co.).

DESHGISH (Ariz., Navajo Co) \desh´ gish\. From Navajo (Athabaskan) *deeshgizh* 'gapped butte' (Linford 2000).

DESHKA River (Alaska, Tyonek C-l) \desh´ kə\. From Dena'ina (Athabaskan) *dashq'e* 'on the shoal' (Kari 1999:68).

DESHU Isthmus (Alaska, Skagway A-2). The Tlingit Indian name supposedly means 'trail end' (Orth 1967).

DES MOINES (Iowa, Polk Co.) \di moin´, di moinz´\. From French *Rivière des Moines,* which could be interpreted as 'river of the monks' or 'river of the mills'. In fact, however, *Moines* is here an abbreviation used by the French for *Moingouena* (Eng. <Moingwena>), an Algonquian subgroup (Vogel 1983). The Native American term is /mooyiinkweena/, and it was a derogatory name applied to the Moingouenas by the Peorias, another subgroup. Its meaning, as an early French writer said is, 'visage plein d'ordure'—or in plain English 'shitface' (Costa 2000:45); see also **Moingona** below. The placename Des Moines also occurs in Mo. (Clark Co.).

DES PLAINES (Ill., Cook Co.) \dez plānz´, des plānz´\. The name appears to be from French *des plaines* 'of the plains'. A more accurate derivation, however, is probably from French Canadian *plaines,* referring to a variety of maple, the sap of which flows freely in the spring. The French placename may represent a translation of Potawatomi <Sheshikmaoshike Sepe>, translated as 'river of the tree that exudes liquid' (Vogel 1963). The name is thus parallel to **Eau Pleine River** (Wis., Marathon Co.), which can be interpreted as *aux plaines* 'at the maple trees'.

DE TOUR Passage (Mich., Chippewa Co.) \də to͞or´\. Said to be a translation of Ojibwa (Algonquian) <Giwideonaning> 'point where we go around in a canoe' (Vogel 1986).

DEUNQUAT (Ohio, Wyandot Co.). Said to have been named for a Wyandot (Iroquoian) leader; his name was also written <Doanquod> (Miller 1996).

DEVIL. This term referring to evil beings was often applied by Christian English speakers to supernatural beings of Indian belief, though they may have been benign from the Native American viewpoint; some examples are given in the following entries. Note that in some placenames the English term *devil* has been used to translate Algonquian *manito,* which might more properly be translated as 'spirit' or 'god'. Thus **Devil Canyon** (Utah, San Juan Co.) is a translation of Navajo (Athabaskan) *ch'į́į́dii bikooh* 'evil spirit's canyon', containing *ch'į́į́dii* 'evil spirit, ghost' (Linford 2000). **Devil Track River** (Minn., Cook Co.) corresponds to Ojibwa <Manido bimadagakowini zibi> 'spirit walking-on-the-ice river' (Upham 2001). **Devils Lake** (Wis., Sauk Co.) is a white interpretation of a Ho-Chunk (Winnebago, Siouan) name, probably *teewákąčągrá* 'the sacred lake', with *tée* 'lake', *wakąčą́k* 'sacred, holy,' and *-ra* 'the' (Vogel 1991; K. Miner p.c.). **Devils Lake Fork** (Ore., Lincoln Co.) probably refers to a peak with the Kalapuyan name [č^{h}awá'lakč^{h}i méfu] 'forked mountain', said to be the home of a monstrous supernatural being called [amúulukw] (H. Zenk p.c.).

DEWATTO (Wash., Mason Co.) \dē wā´ tō\. From a Twana (Salishan) placename /du?wátax^{w}/ (D. Kinkade p.c.).

DEZA Bluffs (N.Mex., McKinley Co.) \də zā´\. From Navajo (Athabaskan) *deez'á* 'point, promontory, elongated ridge' (Linford 2000). A related name is **Desha Creek** (Utah, San Juan Co.).

DHAHEDSE Ridge (Alaska, Arctic A-3). The Gwich'in (Athabaskan) name is *ddhah edzii* (J. Kari p.c.).

DIBE CHAA Valley (Ariz., Apache Co.) \di bā´ chä\. Perhaps from Navajo (Athabaskan) *dibé ntsaa,* lit. 'sheep-big', a name also given by the Navajo to La Plata Mountain in Colorado (Linford 2000).

DICKEY Creek (Wash., Kittitas Co.). An abbreviation of an earlier <Dickodochteder> (Reese 1996), from a Quileute (Chemakuan) placename /dix^{w}odáčtada/ (D. Kinkade p.c.).

DICK Point (Ore., Tillamook Co.). Named for an Indian man, affiliation not known, called "Indian Dick" (McArthur 1992).

DIFJAKAMIUT (Alaska, Cape Mendenhall D-4). The Yupik (Eskimo) name was reported in 1932 (Orth 1967).

DILCON (Ariz., Navajo Co.) \dil´ kon, dil kon\. A spelling variant of **Dilkon** (Ariz., Navajo Co.). This is a shortening of Navajo (Athabaskan) *tsézhin dilkǫǫh* 'smooth black rock', from *tsé* 'rock', *zhin* 'black', *dilkǫǫh* 'it is smooth' (Granger 1983; Wilson 1995).

DINETAH (N.Mex.) \di nā´ tä\. The term refers to the Navajo (Athabaskan) homeland in northwestern N.Mex. (Julyan 1998); it represents Navajo *dinétah* 'among the Navajos', from *diné* 'human being, Navajo', *-tah* 'among' (Young and Morgan 1987). Related placenames include **Dinne Mesa** (Ariz., Apache Co.); see below.

DINGLISHNA Hill (Alaska, Tyonek B-2) \ding lish´ nə, ding lēsh´ nə\. Dena'ina (Athabaskan) *dinlishla* 'little ridge' (Kari and Fall 1987:96).

DINNE Mesa (Ariz., Apache Co.) \di nā\. From Navajo (Athabaskan) *diné* 'human being, Navajo' (Granger 1983). Related placenames include **Dinnebito Wash** (Ariz., Coconino Co.) \din ā bē´ tō\, from *diné bito'* 'Navajo's spring', containing *to'* 'water, spring' (Wilson 1995); and **Dinnehotso** (Ariz., Navajo Co.) \di nā´ hot sō, di nā hot´ sō\. Navajo (Athabaskan) *diné hotso* 'upper end of meadow' (Granger 1983; Young and Morgan 1987). Related placenames include **Dinetah** (N.Mex.); see above.

DIOBSUD Creek (Wash., Skagit Co.). Perhaps a Lushootseed (Salishan) placename (Hitchman 1985).

DIRT LODGE Creek (S.Dak., Corson Co.). The name refers to a semisubterranean dwelling also known as an 'earth lodge' or 'dugout house' (Sneve 1973). The English word *lodge* is used to refer to an Indian house. The corresponding Lakhota (Siouan) name is *makhá-thipi*, lit. 'earth-house' (A. Taylor p.c.).

DISHKAKAT (Alaska, Ophir C-3) \dish´ kak ət\. From Holikachuk (Athabaskan) *diyh kagg* 'spruce-hen stream-mouth' (J. Kari p.c.). A related placename is **Dishna River** (Alaska, Ophir C-3) \dish´ nə\, from *diyhno'* 'spruce-hen river' (J. Kari p.c.).

DISHNO Pond (Alaska, Anchorage A-8) \dish´ nə\. Perhaps from Dena'ina (Athabaskan), of unclear derivation (Orth 1967).

DISIGUOY Creek (Nev., Elko Co.) \dis i goi\. Shoshoni (Numic) /tɨsi-ko'i/ 'saltgrass hill', from /tɨsi(-ppɨ)/ 'salt grass', /ko'i/ 'hill' (J. McLaughlin p.c.).

DISTIK, Mount (Alaska, Sitka B-1) \dis´ tik\. The Tlingit name was reported in 1926 (Orth 1967).

DIX Hills (N.Y., Suffolk Co.) \diks\. This apparently stands for "Dick's Hills." The name appears in 1689 as <dickepechegans>, for "Dick Pechegan's," referring to the home of an SNEng. Algonquian resident (Tooker 1911).

DOCK (Ariz., Pinal Co.) \dok\. From O'odham (Piman) *dak* 'sitting' (J. Hill p.c.).

DOG Butte (S.Dak., Dewey Co.). A translation of Lakhota (Siouan) *pahá šų́ka,* lit. 'butte [of the] dog' (A. Taylor p.c.) A related placename is **Dog Ear Creek** (S.Dak., Tripp Co.), named for a Lakhota leader; the term corresponds to *nakpá šų́ka,* lit. 'ear [of the] dog' (A. Taylor p.c.). Elsewhere **Dog Creek** (Alaska, Gulkana C-4) corresponds to Ahtna (Athabaskan) *łi'ke na',* lit. 'dogs creek' (J. Kari p.c.).

DOGUE (Va., King George Co.). From the name of a local Indian group; the word is of unknown derivation (Hagemann 1988).

DO HA HI BITOH (Ariz., Navajo Co.) \dō hä´ bi tō\. From Navajo (Athabaskan), probably 'slow man's water' (Linford 2000); cf. *doo hahí* 'slowly' (*doo* 'not', *hahí* quickly') plus *bitó'* 'his water' (Young and Morgan 1987).

DOK Point (Alaska, Skagway B-2). An abbreviation of Tlingit <doq xaku, dok-haku>, said to mean 'cottonwood point' (Orth 1967); cf. /dúq/ 'cotttonwood', /x'aa/ 'point of land' (Davis and Leer 1976).

DONCHELOK Creek (Alaska, Mount McKinley D-5) \don´ chə lok\. The Upper Kuskokwim (Athabaskan) name is *donch'elah no'*, perhaps 'suckers-run creek' (J. Kari p.c.).

DONNAHA (N.C., Forsyth Co.). Supposedly named for an Indian leader, language not identified (Powell 1968). The name has also been written as **Donnoha** and **Donnahee**.

DOOKSOOK River (Alaska, Nunivak Island A-7). The Yupik (Eskimo) name was recorded in 1949 (Orth 1967).

DOOLTH Mountain (Alaska, Sitka C-7) \do͞olth\. The Tlingit name is said to refer to abundance of natural resources (Orth 1967).

DOONERAK, Mount (Alaska, Wiseman D-2) \do͞o´ nə rak\. The Iñupiaq (Eskimo) word is said to refer to a supernatural being (Orth 1967); cf. *tuunġaq* 'helping spirit of a shaman; devil' (Webster and Zibell 1970:43).

DOOR Village (Ind., La Porte Co.). The name is a translation of French *la porte* 'the door', which is also reflected in the name of the county. This in turn may be a translation of a Potawatomi (Algonquian) village name <Ish-Kwan-dom> 'the door', said to refer to an opening in the woods (McPherson 1993). In Wis., **Door County** represents French *La Porte des Morts* 'the door of the dead', referring to a legend about how Indian warriors met their deaths in this area (Vogel 1991).

DORCHEAT, Bayou (Ark., Columbia Co.; La., Webster Par.) \dôr´ chēt\. Earlier written <Dacheet, Dauchite> (etc.); perhaps from the Caddo language, but the derivation is not clear (Read 1927, Dickinson 1995).

DOSENNAUGHTEN Lake (Alaska, Bettles C-6). The Koyukon (Athabaskan) name was recorded in 1956 (Orth 1967).

DOSEWALLIPS River (Wash., Jefferson Co.) \dōs ē wä´ lips\. From Southern Coast Salishan, for a Twana (Salishan) placename /čduswáylupš/ (HNAI 7:487).

DOU-PAH-GADE, Lake (Nev., Eureka Co.) \do͞o pä´ gə dē\. Shoshoni (Numic) /tuupaa-katɨ/ 'black lake', lit. 'black-water sitting', from /tuu-paa/ 'black water' (/tuu-/ 'black', /paa/ 'water'), /katɨ/ 'to sit' (J. McLaughlin p.c.).

DOVELAWIK Bay (Alaska, Saint Lawrence D6). The Yupik (Eskimo) name was reported in 1944; perhaps from <tivlarak> 'portage' (Orth 1967). A variant form of the name is **Tiflighak Bay.**

DOWAGIAC (Mich., Cass Co.) \də wä´ zhē ak\. Possibly from Potawatomi (Algonquian) <dwagek, tetwakuk> 'autumn' (Vogel 1986); cf. Ojibwa (Algonquian) *dagwaagin* 'autumn' (Nichols and Nyholm 1995). There is also a **Dowagiac** in Ky. (Hart Co.).

DOWA YALANNE (N.Mex., Cibola Co.) \dō wə yä´ lə nā\. Said to be Zuni for 'corn mountain' (Julyan 1998); cf. /a:-towa/ 'corn' (/towa/ 'ancient', /yala-nne/ 'mountains') (Newman 1958).

DOWOZHIEBITO Canyon (Ariz., Navajo Co.). Navajo (Athabaskan) *diwózhii bii' tó* 'spring in the greasewood' (Linford 2000), from *diwózhii* 'greasewood', *bii'* 'in it', and *tó* 'water, spring' (Granger 1983).

DRIFTWOOD River (Ind., Johnson Co.). Corresponds to a Miami/Illinois (Algonquian) form reconstructed as */aankwaahsakwa/ 'driftwood' (McCafferty 2002).

DUBAKELLA (Calif., Trinity Co.) \do͞o bə kel´ ə\. From Wintu /duubit kiili/, the name of a type of 'wild potato'; /duubit/ refers to such edible roots (Gudde 1998).

DUCHESNE County (Utah) \də shān´\. Derivation from Ute (Numic) has been suggested but not confirmed (Van Cott 1990); the word may be a French surname, as the spelling suggests.

DUCHIKMIUT (Alaska, Cape Mendenhall D-4). The Yupik (Eskimo) name was reported in 1932 (Orth 1967); the element *-miut* means 'people'.

DUCHIKTHLUK Bay (Alaska, Cape Mendenhall D-4). The Yupik (Eskimo) name was reported in 1937 (Orth 1967).

DUCKABUSH (Wash., Jefferson Co.) \duk´ ə bo͝osh\. From Southern Coast Salishan, for the Twana (Salishan) placename /dəx^{w}yabús/ 'place of the crooked-jaw salmon', from /dax^w-/ 'place' and /yabús/ 'crooked-jaw salmon' (*HNAI* 7:487, D. Kinkade p.c.).

DUCK Creek (Ind., Madison Co.). Perhaps an error for *Buck Creek*, referring to the eighteenth-century Delaware (Algonquian) leader known in English as **Killbuck** (see **Killbuck Run** below) (McCafferty 2002).

DUCKTOWN (Tenn., Polk Co.). Said to be named for a Cherokee (Iroquoian) leader known to white settlers as Chief Duck (McClaren 1991).

DUITATUK Lake (Alaska, Arctic A-3). The Gwich'in (Athabaskan) name was recorded in 1956 (Orth 1967).

DUKTOTH River (Alaska, Bering Glacier A-5). From Eyak /da<u>x</u>ta'ł/.

DULBATNA Mountain (Alaska, Melozitna B-5) \dul bät´ nə\. The Koyukon (Athabaskan) name is *dolbaat no'* 'gosling river' (Jetté & Jones 2000).

DULBI River (Alaska, Kateel River B-2) \dol´ bē\. The Koyukon (Athabaskan) name is related to **Dulbatna,** above.

DULL KNIFE (Wyo., Johnson Co.). Named for a nineteenth-century Cheyenne (Algonquian) leader who was so called by white settlers. His Cheyenne name was *vooheheve* 'morning star' (W. Leman p.c.).

DUMARCE Lake (S.Dak., Marshall Co.). Said to be from the surname, of French origin, of a Dakota man (Sneve 1973).

DUNANDA (Wyo., Teton Co.) \də nan´ də\. From Shoshoni (Numic) /tunnantɨ/ [tunnándɨ] 'straight' (J. McLaughlin p.c.).

DUNLIN Lake (Alaska, Kenai D-3) \dun´ lin\. Perhaps from Dena'ina (Athabaskan); the derivation is not clear (Orth 1967).

DUNUKCHAVUK Slough (Alaska, Saint Michael A-5). The Yupik (Eskimo) name was recorded in 1952 (Orth 1967).

DUNULETAK Creek (Alaska, Iliamna A-4). The Dena'ina (Athabaskan) name was recorded in 1923 (Orth 1967).

DUNULIMJINGIA Point (Alaska, Nunivak Island B-3). The Yupik (Eskimo) name was recorded in 1949 (Orth 1967).

DU QUOIN (Ill., Perry Co.) \do͞o koin´\. Named for Jean Baptiste Ducoigne, an early-nineteenth-century leader of the Kaskaskia subgroup of the Algonquian people (Vogel 1963).

DUSHKOT Island (Alaska, Unalaska C-2). Perhaps from Aleut *duxsxan* 'hipbone' (Bergsland 1994).

DUTCH Creek (Ark., Yell Co.). Named for William Dutch, a nineteenth-century Cherokee (Iroquoian) leader. **Dutch** was from his Cherokee name, written <Tahchee> (Dickinson 1995).

DUWAMISH River (Wash., King Co.) \də wä´ mish\. This name of a Salishan subgroup is from Lushootseed /dx^{w}dawʔábš, dx^{w}duʔábš/, lit. 'people inside the bay' (D. Kinkade p.c.). The alternation between *b* and *m* is characteristic of languages in the area.

DUWEE Falls (Ore., Klamath Co.) \do͞o´ ē\. From Klamath /diwii/ 'flows and spreads out', with from /di-/ 'drip, flow' and /-(o)wi/ 'spreading out' (Barker 1963).

DYEA (Alaska, Skagway C-l) \dī ē´\. From a Tlingit term, earlier written <Dyaytahk>, said to mean 'carrying place' (Phillips 1973).

DZIL DASHZHINII (Ariz., Navajo Co.) \dzil däsh´ ji nē\. Navajo (Athabaskan) *dziłdashzhinii* 'black mountain' (Linford 2000); cf. *dził* 'mountain' and *dashzhin* 'to be black', of an area or surface (Young and Morgan 1987). Related terms include **Dzil Nda Kai Mountain** (N.Mex., McKinley Co.) \dzil dā´ kī\, perhaps from Navajo *dził ndaakai* 'mountains walk around' (cf. *ndaakai* 'they walk around'; A. Wilson p.c.); **Dzilth-Na-O-Dith-Hle** (N.Mex., San Juan Co.) \dzil nä ō´ dith lē\ from *dził ná'oodiłii* 'Huerfano Mountain', lit. 'the mountain around which people move' (cf. *ná'oodiłł* 'people circle around') (Wilson 1995); and **Dzilntsahah**

Summit (N.Mex., San Juan Co.) \dzil nə tsä´ hä\ from *dziɬ ntsaa* 'big mountain' (cf. *ntsaa* 'it is big') (A. Wilson p.c.).

E

EAGLE. Since the eagle had symbolic importance both for Native Americans and for white Americans, it is understandable that it frequently figures in placenames, including many in which the English term is a loan-translation from Indian languages. Examples are **Eagle Butte** (S.Dak., Ziebach Co.), based on Lakhota (Siouan) *wąblí* 'eagle', *pahá* 'butte, hill' (Ingham 2001); and **Eagle River** (Wis., Vilas Co.), based on Ojibwa (Algonquian) *migizi* 'eagle', *ziibi* 'river' (Nichols and Nyholm 1995). In other cases, *eagle* was part of the given name of an Indian individual, as in **Eagle Township** (Iowa, Sioux Co.), probably named for War Eagle, a Dakota (Siouan) leader who died in 1851 (Vogel 1983; Koontz p.c.).

EAGLE CHASING Draw (S.Dak., Ziebach Co.). Named for a Lakhota (Siouan) man, Joseph Eagle Chasing, who worked as a scout for the U.S. Army (Sneve 1973).

EAGLES NEST Butte (S.Dak., Harding Co.). Corresponds to Lakhota (Siouan) *wąblí-hoȟpila,* lit. 'eagle nesting-place' (Sneve 1973; A. Taylor p.c.); cf. *hoȟpí* 'nest' (Ingham 2001).

EARL, Lake (Calif., Del Norte Co.) \ûr´ əl\. Although this is in Tolowa (Athabaskan) territory, the term is derived from a Yurok placename /r:ɬ/ (Gudde 1998).

EASTABOGA (Ala., Calhoun Co.) \ē stə bō´ gə\. From Muskogee, perhaps meaning 'lake where people died in the water', from *este* /ísti/ 'person', *ak-* /ak-/ 'in water or a low place', *pokv* /po:ka/ 'being gone, dying' (Read 1934; Martin and Mauldin 2000). A spelling variant is **Estaboga.** A related placename is **Istokpoga** (Fla., Highlands Co.).

EASTABUCHIE (Miss., Forrest Co.) \ē stə buch´ ē\. Probably from Choctaw (Muskogean) *hashtap, hishtap* 'fallen leaves' plus *hachcha* 'river' (Seale 1939, P. Munro p.c.).

EASTANOLA (Ga., Stephens Co.) \ē stə nō´ lə\. Perhaps from a Cherokee (Iroquoian) word referring to shoals (Goff 1975). Alternative spellings are **Eastanolee** and **Eastanollee.** A related placename is **Oostanaula** (Ga., Gordon Co.).

EASTATOE (S.C., Pickens Co.) \ē´ stə toi\. Probably from the same source as **Eastertoy** (Ga., Rabun Co.). This is a folk etymology for the name of a Cherokee (Iroquoian) village site, earlier written as <Estatowih, Estatohe> (etc.) (Krakow 1975); a written variant is **Estatoah Falls**; related forms include **Estatoe** (N.C., Mitchell Co.).

EAU CLAIRE County (Wis.) \ō klâr´\. The French name, meaning 'clear water', is said to be a translation of an Ojibwa (Algonquian) name <Wayokomig> (Vogel 1991).

EAU PLEINE River (Wis., Marathon Co.) \ō plīn´\. The name seems to represent French *eau pleine* 'full water' (whatever that might mean); however, an earlier spelling is *aux plaines.* This could be translated as 'at the plains', but a more likely translation is 'at the maple trees', from Canadian French *plaine* 'a type of maple'. The French placename may represent a translation of Potawatomi <Sheshikmaoshike Sepe> 'river of the tree that exudes liquid' (Vogel 1963). The name is thus parallel to **Des Plaines** (Ill., Cook Co.), which can be interpreted as '(river) of the maples'.

EAVOK Channel (Alaska, Selawik C-6). Perhaps from Iñupiaq (Eskimo) *iyavraq* (Burch 1998).

EAYAGIT Point (Alaska, Saint Lawrence B-0). The Yupik (Eskimo) name was reported in 1932 (Orth 1967).

EBEEMEE Lake (Maine, Piscataquis Co.) \ə bē´ mē\. Earlier given as <Ebeemin>, the name may be Abenaki (Algonquian) for 'berries' (Huden 1962); cf. Abenaki *-men, -min* 'berry', *ômwaimen* 'service berry' (Day 1994–95).

EBENECOOK Harbor (Maine, Lincoln Co.). Perhaps Abenaki (Algonquian), meaning 'opens out behind the entrance-place', from <apanna> 'spreads out wide' (Eckstorm 1941).

ECHASHOTEE (Fla., Pasco Co.) \ē chäs hō´ tē\. From Seminole (Muskogean) *eccaswv* /iččá:swa/ 'beaver, manatee' plus *(i)hute* /hóti/ 'home' (Read 1934; Martin and Mauldin 2000).

ECHAW Creek (S.C., Beaufort Co.) \ē´ chô\. Earlier written <Ectchew>, <Itshaw> (Waddell 1980). Perhaps from an unidentified Indian language (Pickens 1963:37).

ECHECONNEE (Ga., Peach Co.) \ē chē kon´ ē\. Probably from a Muskogee word meaning 'deer trap', from *eco* /ičó/ 'deer', *kvnhv* /kánha/ 'trap' (Read 1949–50; Martin and Mauldin 2000).

ECHETA (Wyo., Campbell Co.) \ə chē´ tə\. Said to mean 'horse' in an unidentified Indian language (Urbanek 1974).

ECHO Cave (Ariz., Navajo Co.). Corresponds to Navajo (Athabaskan) *tséyaa hodiits'a'í* 'rock under which there is an echo' (Linford 2000); cf. *tsé* 'rock', *-yaa* 'under', *hodiits'a'* 'to echo' (Young and Morgan 1987). The placename **Echoing Lake** (Alaska, Beaver B-5) translates Koyukon (Athabaskan) *məts'ənh dəlitłish mən'* 'echo-comes-from-it lake' (Kari 2000); cf. *hʉdellaał* 'the place echoes', *mən'* 'lake'.

ECHOOKA River (Alaska, Sagavanirktok B-3). The Iñupiaq (Eskimo) name is from *isaġuq* 'wing' (Orth 1967; MacLean 1980).

ECHOTA (Ga., Gordon Co.) \ē chō´ tə\. Said to be a Cherokee name, of unclear derivation (Krakow 1975). There is also an **Echota** in Okla. (Adair Co.), and **Chota** in Tenn. (Blount Co.) may be related.

ECOLA Creek (Ore., Clatsop Co.) \ē kō´ lə\. The name suggests the Chinook Jargon word <eh´-ko-lie> 'whale', from Chinookan [ék'uale]. The placename, however, was probably borrowed into English directly from Clatsop Chinook [ékole, ékoli] 'whale' (McArthur 1992; D. Kinkade p.c.).

ECONFENA (Fla., Taylor Co.). Probably from the same source as **Econfina** (Fla., Bay Co.) \ē kon fē´ nə\. This is a Muskogee word meaning 'earth bridge', from *ēkvnv* /i:kaná/ 'land, earth', *fenv* /finá/ 'foot log, bridge' (Read 1934; Martin and Mauldin 2000).

ECONLOCKHATCHEE River (Fla., Seminole Co.) \ē kon lok hach´ ē\. The spelling <Econ-like Hatchee> is recorded from 1839, and this may represent a Muskogee name meaning 'earth-mound stream'. On this hypothesis, <Econ-like> 'earth-mound' contains *ēkvnv* /i:kaná/ 'earth, land' plus *like* /léyki/ 'sitting'; the remainder is *hvcce* /háčči/ 'stream' (Read 1934; Martin and Mauldin 2000).

ECORSE (Mich., Wayne Co.) \ē´ kôrs\. From French *Rivière des Écorces* 'river of bark', referring to the material for canoes. This may correspond to Ojibwa (Algonquian) <wigwass-sibi>, lit. 'bark-river' (Vogel 1986); cf. *wiigwaas* 'birch bark', *ziibi* 'river' (Nichols and Nyholm 1995).

EDAHO Mountain (Idaho, Boise Co.) \ē´ də hō\. From the same origin as the word **Idaho** (Boone 1988). The term is a transfer name from Colo., where it is derived from a Plains Apache (Athabaskan) word for 'enemy' (Bright 1993).

EDA HUGKAM SWADAG (Ariz., Pima Co.). O'odham (Piman) *eḍa hugkam swadagĭ* 'half wet', containing *eḍa hugkam* 'half' and *wadagĭ* 'wet' (J. Hill p.c.).

EDISTO River (S.C., Charleston Co.) \ed´ i stō\. Earlier written <Adusta>, <Audusta>, <Orista> (Waddell 1980). Perhaps named for a subgroup of the Cusabo people (Pearson 1978; B. Rudes p.c.).

EDIZ Hook (Wash., Clallam Co.) \ē´ diz\. From the Klallam (Salishan) placename /ʔiʔínas/, translated as 'a spit' or 'good beach' (D. Kinkade). A related placename is **Ennis Creek** (Wash., Clallam Co.); note that *n* and *d* often alternate in languages of this area.

EDUCKET Creek (Wash., Clallam Co.) \ē duk´ ət\. From the Makah (Nootkan) placename /ʔidakat/ (W. Jacobsen p.c.).

EEK (Alaska, Baird Inlet A-l) \ēk\. Yupik (Eskimo) *iik* 'two eyes', from *ii* 'eye' (Jacobson 1984).

EEKAYRUK Mountain (Alaska, Wiseman D1). The Iñupiaq (Eskimo) name was reported in 1930 (Orth 1967).

EEL River (Ind., Allen Co.). The name of this stream is a translation of Miami/Illinois (Algonquian) /kineepikwameekwa siipiiwi/, lit. 'snake-fish river' (McCafferty 2002). Another **Eel River,** in southern Ind. (Clay Co.), takes its name from Unami Delaware (Algonquian) /šɔ́ɔxxameekw/ 'eel', lit. 'slippery fish' (McCafferty 2002).

EENA Creek (Idaho, Benewah Co.) \ē´ nə\. The stream was named by the Forest Service with the Chinook Jargon word <ee´na> [ína] 'beaver', from Lower Chinook <i-i-na> (Boone 1988; D. Kinkade p.c.).

EENAYARAK River (Alaska, Baird Inlet A-l). The Yupik (Eskimo) name was reported in 1910 (Orth 1967).

EEVWAK Point (Alaska, Saint Lawrence D-4). The Yupik (Eskimo) name is said to mean 'to go around' (Orth 1967).

EFAW (Fla., Okeechobee Co.) \ē´ fô\. From Muskogee *efv* /ifá/ 'dog'; not an original Indian placename but a word chosen from a published vocabulary (Martin and Mauldin 2000).

EFFIGY Mounds (Iowa, Clayton Co.). Named for the forms of birds and animals that prehistoric Native Americans gave to many of the mounds on this site (Vogel 1983).

EGA Draw (Wyo., Fremont Co.) \ē´ gə\. Shoshoni (Numic) /ɨkɨ/ [ɨ́ɣɨ] 'new' (Urbanek 1974; J. McLaughlin p.c.).

EGAKSRAK River (Alaska, Demarcation Point D-2). The Iñupiaq (Eskimo) name was reported in 1948 (Orth 1967).

EGAUPAK Lake (Alaska, Shungnak D-5). The Iñupiaq (Eskimo) name was reported in 1927 (Orth 1967).

EGAVIK (Alaska, Norton Bay A-4) \ē gä´ vik\. Iñupiaq (Eskimo) *igaavik*, probably meaning 'cooking place, kitchen', from *iga-* 'to cook' and *-vik* 'place', with influence from the corresponding Yupik (Eskimo) term *egavik* [ga:vik] (L. Kaplan p.c.).

EGEGIK (Alaska, Naknek A-5) \ē´ gə gik\. The Yupik (Eskimo) name has also been written as <Igagik> and <Ugaguk> (Orth 1967).

EGGEMOGGIN (Maine, Hancock Co.) \eg ə mog´ in\. Earlier written <Archimagau, Agemogen, Algomongan, Edgamoggan, Edgemaroggan> (etc.); perhaps from Malecite (Algonquian), meaning 'fish-weir place' (Eckstorm 1941).

EGIN (Idaho, Fremont Co.) \ē´ jin\. From Shoshoni (Numic) /ɨitsɨi/ [ɨ́ižɨi] 'cold' (Boone 1988; Miller 1972).

EGOMA SABA (Kans., Pottawattomie Co.). This variant name for Vermillion Creek represents Kansa (Siouan) /égomą sábe/ 'black paint', lit. 'paint-black' (R. Rankin p.c.).

EGONIAGA Creek (Ala., Calhoun Co.) \eg ō nē ā´ gə\. Perhaps from a Muskogee word for 'cave', with *ēkana* /i:kaná/ 'earth' and *hvokē* /háwki:] 'opening' (Read 1984; Martin and Mauldin 2000).

EGOZUK Creek (Alaska, Sleetmute B-7). The Yupik (Eskimo) word is said to mean 'elbow' (Orth 1967).

EGUMEN Lake (Alaska, Kenai C-2). Perhaps from Dena'ina (Athabaskan), of unclear derivation (Orth 1967).

EGUNK Hill (Conn., New London Co.). From SNEng. Algonquian, perhaps meaning 'at the turn or bend' in a river or trail (Huden 1962). Perhaps related is the name **Ekonk** (Conn., Windham Co.).

EIGALORUK (Alaska, Noatak A-4). From Iñupiaq (Eskimo) *igalauraq* 'window' (Orth 1967; MacLean 1980).

EKAKEVIK Mountain (Alaska, Howard Pass C-2) \ē kä´ kə vik\. From Iñupiaq (Eskimo) *iqaqqivik* 'wash basin' (Orth 1967; MacLean 1980); cf. *iqaġi-* 'to wash the hands or face', *-vik* 'place'.

EKALAKA (Mont., Carter Co.). Named for a Lakhota (Siouan) woman; her name is said to mean 'swift one' (Cheney 1984).

EKALGRUAK Lake (Alaska, Meade River D-1). The Iñupiaq (Eskimo) name was recorded in 1956 (Orth 1967).

EKALUAKAT River (Alaska, Demarcation Point D-2). The Iñupiaq (Eskimo) name is said to mean 'small fish place' (Orth 1967); cf. *iqaluk* 'fish' (MacLean 1980).

EKANEETLEE Creek (N.C., Swain Co.). The name is of possibly Cherokee but unidentified origin (Powell 1968).

EKASHLUAK Creek (Alaska, Hooper Bay D3). The Yupik (Eskimo) name was reported in 1949 (Orth 1967).

EKASLUKTULI River (Alaska, Hooper Bay C3). The Yupik (Eskimo) name is said to mean 'trout' (Orth 1967).

EKICHUK Lake (Alaska, Selawik D-6). From Iñupiaq (Eskimo) *ikkitchiaq* (Burch 1998).

EKIEK Creek (Alaska, Shungnak B-6). From Iñupiaq (Eskimo) *ikkik* (Burch 1998).

EKILUKRUAK Entrance (Alaska, Barrow A-3). The Iñupiaq (Eskimo) name is said to mean 'wide, rough inlet' (Orth 1967).

EKLUTNA (Alaska, Anchorage B-7) \ē klo͞ot′ nə\. Fom Dena'ina (Athabaskan) *idluytnu* 'plural-objects river', with *-tnu* 'river' (Kari and Fall 1987:282).

EKOKPUK Creek (Alaska, Chandler Lake A-4). The Iñupiaq (Eskimo) name is said to mean 'split in two' (Orth 1967).

EKOLINA Creek (Alaska, Medfra A-2) \ē kō′ li nə\. The Upper Kuskokwim (Athabaskan) name *ek'aleno'* refers to nearby Jones Creek (J. Kari p.c.).

EKONK (Conn., Windham Co.). Perhaps SNEng. Algonquian, meaning 'a bend or turn' (Huden 1962). A probably related form is **Egunk Hill** (Conn., New London Co.).

EKUK (Alaska, Nushagak Bay D-2) \ē′ kuk\. From Yupik (Eskimo) *iquk* 'end' (Jacobson 1984).

EKWOK (Alaska, Dillingham B-4) \ek′ wok\. From Yupik (Eskimo) *iquaq,* based on *iquk* 'end' (Jacobson 1984).

ELA (N.C., Swain Co.). Perhaps from Cherokee (Iroquoian) *elohi* 'earth' (B. Rudes p.c.).

ELAKTOVEACH Channel (Alaska, Harrison Bay B-2). The Iñupiaq (Eskimo) name is said to mean 'the wide stream in the middle' (Orth 1967); cf. the Uummarmiut dialect form *hiliktuq* 'wide' (Dorais 1990:5), Barrow dialect *siḷik-* 'to be wide' (MacLean 1980).

ELARONILUK Creek (Alaska, Baird Mountains A-2). The Iiiupiaq (Eskimo) name was reported in 1955 (Orth 1967).

ELEUTAK (Alaska, Kwiguk B-6). The Yupik (Eskimo) name was reported in 1899 (Orth 1967).

ELGHI Island (Alaska, Craig D-4). The Tlingit name was published in 1964 (Orth 1967).

ELILAKOK (Alaska, Dillingham C-3) \el il′ ə kok\. The Yupik (Eskimo) name was reported in 1910 (Orth 1967).

ELIM (Alaska, Solomon C-l) Celim\. The Iñupiaq (Eskimo) name was reported around 1915 (Orth 1967).

ELIP Creek (Idaho, Benewah Co.) \ē′ lip\. From Chinook Jargon <e′-lip> [ílɪp] 'first, before, ahead', from Lower Chehalis or Cowlitz (Salishan) /ʔílp/ 'first, in front'. So named by the Forest Service because this was the first of three tributaries to Eena Creek (Boone 1988; D. Kinkade p.c.). Another stream called **Elip Creek** (Wash., Jefferson Co.) was similarly named in contrast with nearby **Kimta Creek**, from the Chinook Jargon word for 'behind, later' (Hitchman 1985).

ELI River (Alaska, Noatak B-3). The Iñupiaq (Eskimo) name is *uaim kuuŋa* (Burch 1998).

ELKAHATCHEE (Ala., Tallapoosa Co.) \el kə hach´ ē\. Also written <Alkehatchee>; perhaps from a Muskogee name meaning 'sweet-potato stream'; cf. *vhvlvk* 'sweet potato', *hvcce* /háčči/ 'stream' (Read 1984; Martin and Mauldin 2000).

ELKATAWA (Ky., Breathitt Co.) \el´ kə tä wə\. Supposedly derived from <Ellskwatawa>, itself a corruption of <Tenskwautawa>, a Shawnee (Algonquian) Indian leader known as "The Prophet" (Rennick 1984).

ELK Creek (S.Dak., Lawrence Co.). Perhaps a translation of Lakhota (Siouan) *wakpálatha,* supposedly meaning 'creek [of the] elk' (Sneve 1973; A. Taylor p.c.); cf. *wakpála* 'creek' (Ingham 2001).

ELKHART County (Ind.) \el´ kärt\. Corresponds to Potawatomi (Algonquian) /mžəweodəʔik/ 'at the elk heart', with /mžəwe/ 'elk' (McCafferty 2002).

ELKUGU Bay (Alaska, Sitka C-7). The Tlingit name was published in 1928 (Orth 1967).

ELLEMEHAM Mountain (Wash., Okanogan Co.). From Okanagan (Salishan) [ilmíx^{w}əm] 'chief', from the stem /ylmíx^{w}-/ 'chief' (D. Kinkade p.c.).

ELLIGO, Lake (Vt., Orleans Co.) \el´ i gō\. Perhaps from Abenaki (Algonquian), meaning 'a birch-bark dish' (Huden 1962); cf. *walagaoo* 'there is bark on', from *wala* 'bark, shell' (Day 1994–95).

ELLIJAY (N.C., Macon Co.) \el´ i jā\. From a Cherokee (Iroquoian) name meaning 'green earth', from *elohi* 'earth' and *ijee'i* 'green (of plants), new' (B. Rudes p.c.).

ELLOREE (S.C., Orangeburg Co.) \el´ ə rē\. Perhaps from an unidentified Indian language (Neuffer and Neuffer 1983).

ELOCHOMAN River (Wash., Wahkiakum Co.) \ē lō´ kə mən\. From a Cathlamet (Chinookan) village named /ilóx̣umin/ (Hitchman 1985). Another currently used spelling is **Elokomin.**

ELOIKA Lake (Wash., Spokane Co.) \i loi´ kə\. This supposedly reflects the name given to the lake by the Pend Oreille (Salishan) Indians (Hitchman 1985).

ELONGOZHIK Slough (Alaska, Saint Michael A-5). The Yupik (Eskimo) name was reported in 1899 (Orth 1967).

ELOWAH Falls (Ore., Multnomah Co.) \ē lō´ wə\. Perhaps an Indian name, but of unknown derivation (McArthur 1992).

ELTERPOM Creek (Calif., Trinity Co.) \el´ tə pom\. From Wintu /eltipom/ 'place on the other side', from /elti/ 'inside, on the other side' plus /-pom/ 'place' (Gudde 1998).

ELTOPIA (Wash., Franklin Co.) \el tō´ pē ə\. Perhaps a placename from an unidentified Indian language, <El-To-Pai> (Hitchman 1985), probably with assimilation to English *utopia.*

ELUITKAK Pass (Alaska, Barrow B-4). The Iñupiaq (Eskimo) name is said to mean 'it's bad, difficult' (Orth 1967); cf. *(g)iiḻi* 'bad' (MacLean 1980).

ELUKOZUK Slough (Alaska, Kwiguk C-6). The Yupik (Eskimo) name is said to mean 'having many branches' (Orth 1967).

ELUKSINGIAK Point (Alaska, Wainwright D-1). The Iñupiaq (Eskimo) name is said to mean 'Eluk's entrance' (Orth 1967).

ELUPAK (Alaska, Barter Island A-5). The Iñupiaq (Eskimo) name was reported in 1952 (Orth 1967).

ELUTULI Creek (Alaska, Sleetmute C-3). The Yupik (Eskimo) name was reported in 1948 (Orth 1967).

ELUWAKTAK Mountain (Alaska, Bethel B-5). The Yupik (Eskimo) name was reported in 1955 (Orth 1967).

ELWA (Ala., Mobile Co.) \el´ wə\. Perhaps from Choctaw (Muskogean) *halwa* 'soft-shelled turtle' (Read 1984; P. Munro p.c.).

ELWHA River (Wash., Jefferson Co.) \el´ wä\. From Klallam (Salishan) /ʔéʔɬx̣^{w}ə, /ʔíɬx̣^{w}a/ (D. Kinkade p.c.).

EMAIKSOUN Lake (Alaska, Barrow A-4). The Iñupiaq (Eskimo) name may be derived from *imiq* 'fresh water, drinking water' (Orth 1967; MacLean 1980).

EMANVICROK Channel (Alaska, Selawik C6). From Iñupiaq (Eskimo) *imaaġvigruaq* (Burch 1998).

EMATHLA (Fla., Marion Co.) \ē math´ lə\. Named for Charley Emathla, a Seminole (Muskogean) leader who died in 1835. The Native American name is *emarv* /imá:ɬa/, a title of leadership (Read 1934; Martin and Mauldin 2000).

EMAUHEE (Ala., Talladega Co.) \ē mô´ hē\. Possibly from Muskogee *em mahe* /im má:hi/ 'his/her father-in-law' (Read 1984; Martin and Mauldin 2000).

EMEGHEE Point (Alaska, Saint Lawrence A-2). The Yupik (Eskimo) name was reported in 1949 (Orth 1967).

EMEKYALOK Point (Alaska, Saint Lawrence B-3). The Yupik (Eskimo) name was reported in 1949 (Orth 1967).

EMGETEN Island (Alaska, Sitka A-4). The name, probably from Tlingit, was published in 1826 (Orth 1967).

EMGHEM Mountain (Alaska, Saint Lawrence A-2). The Yupik (Eskimo) name was reported in 1949 (Orth 1967).

EMIKA (Ariz., Pima Co.) \ē´ mi kə\. From O'odham (Piman) *i:miga* 'kinship terms' (J. Hill p.c.).

EMILY, Mount (Ore., Union Co.) \em´ i lē\. Tolowa (Athabaskan) /nanəmai/, possibly meaning 'undulating earth' (D. Kinkade p.c.), with assimilation to the English given name *Emily.*

EMMONAK (Alaska, Kwiguk D-6) \ē mon´ ək\. From Yupik (Eskimo) *imangaq* 'blackfish' (Jacobson 1984).

EMNAVAK Ridge (Alaska, Howard Pass D-3). The Iiiupiaq (Eskimo) name was reported in 1956 (Orth 1967).

EMUCKFAW (Ala., Tallapoosa Co.) \ē muk´ fô\. Possibly from a Hitchiti (Muskogean) word referring to an ornament made of shell (Read 1984).

EM'URLUQ Bay (Alaska, Seward B-4). The Alutiiq (Eskimo) placename was made official by the BGN in 1995.

EMUSSA (Ala., Houston Co.) \ē mus´ ə\. Perhaps from Muskogee *im-osa* /imosá:/ 'his pokeweed' or from Choctaw (Muskogean) *im-ǫssi* 'his eagle' (P. Munro p.c.).

ENATALIK Creek (Alaska, Taylor Mountains D-7). The Yupik (Eskimo) name was reported in 1945 (Orth 1967).

ENDION (Minn., St. Louis Co.) \en´ dē ən\. From Ojibwa (Algonquian) *endaayaan* 'my home' (lit. 'where I dwell') or *endaayan* 'your home'; cf. *daa* 'to live in a certain place' (J. Nichols p.c.).

ENEKALIKRUAK Creek (Alaska, Killik River A-2). The Iñupiaq (Eskimo) name was reported in 1956 (Orth 1967).

ENEMY Creek (S.Dak., Hanson Co.). A translation of Dakota (Siouan) *thóka wakpála,* lit. 'enemy creek' (Sneve 1973; A. Taylor p.c.). The placename **Enemy Swim Lake** (S.Dak., Day Co.) corresponds to Dakota (Siouan) *thóka khiníwa bde* 'enemy swim-home lake' (Sneve 1973; A. Taylor p.c.).

ENENTAH, Mount (Colo., Grand Co.) \ə nen´ tä\. Based on Arapaho (Algonquian) *hinenítee* 'man, person' (A. Cowell p.c.).

ENETAI (Wash., Kitsap Co.) \en´ ə tī\. Chinook Jargon <in-a-ti, inataï> [ínatay, ɛ́natay] 'across, outside, other side'; cf. Lower Chinook [-nata] 'on the other side', Kathlamet Chinook [ínata] 'one side' (D. Kinkade p.c.). A related name is **Inati Bay** (Wash., Whatcom Co.).

ENGA Creek (Wyo., Fremont Co.) \eng´ gə\. Shoshoni (Numic) /ainka/ 'red' (Urbanek 1974; Miller 1972).

ENGLISH River (Iowa, Washington Co.). Recorded in 1835 as <Sacanashisippo>, reflecting Meskwaki (Algonquian) /sa:kana:ši-si:po:wi/ 'English river', containing /sa:kana:ša/ 'Englishman', a loan from early Ojibwa (Algonquian)—a pejorative formed from French *les anglois* 'the English', an archaic counterpart to modern French *les anglais* (I. Goddard p.c.). Cf. Ojibwa *zhaaganaash* 'Englishman' (Nichols and Nyholm 1995).

ENITACHOPCO (Ala., Clay Co.) \ē nit a chop´ kō\. Possibly from Muskogee *vnvttē-cvpko* /anatti:-čápko/ 'long thicket', from *vnvttē* /anátti:/ 'thicket, hindrance' plus *cvpko* /-čápko/ 'long' (Read 1984, Martin and Mauldin 2000).

ENNIS Creek (Wash., Clallam Co.) \en´ is\. From the Klallam (Salishan) placename /ʔiʔínəs/, translated as 'a spit' or 'good beach' (D. Kinkade p.c.). A related placename is **Ediz Hook** (Wash., Clallam Co.); note that *n* and *d* often alternate in languages of this area.

ENO (N.C., Orange Co.) \en´ ō\. Probably from Catawba (Siouan) /énu/ 'little crow' (B. Rudes p.c.). The name is apparently related to **Enoree** (S.C., Spartanburg Co.); see below.

ENOLA, Lake (Fla., Lake Co.) \ə nō´ lə\. Perhaps a variant of **Inola** (Okla., Rogers Co.), said to be Cherokee (Iroquoian) for 'black fox' (Shirk 1974); **Enola** also occurs as a woman's name, however, and has sometimes been explained as the word *alone* written backward. The placename **Enola** also occurs in Ark. (Faulkner Co.).

ENOREE (S.C., Spartanburg Co.) \en´ ə rē\. From Catawba (Siouan) /enuree/, which has been translated as 'it is little crow' (B. Rudes p.c.). A related name is **Eno** (N.C., Orange Co.).

ENSAWKWATCH Creek (Wash., Whatcom Co.) \en sôk´ wäch\. Probably from an unidentified Indian language (Hitchman 1985).

ENTIAT (Wash., Chelan Co.) \en´ tē at\. From Moses-Columbian (Salishan) /nt'yátk^{W}/ [nt'iátk^{W}] 'place of grassy water', from /na-/ 'place', /st'íyaʔ/ 'tall grass, hay', and /-atk^{W}/ 'water' (D. Kinkade p.c.).

ENUMCLAW (Wash., King Co.) \ē´ nəm klô\. Sahaptin /inɨmɬá/ 'he who makes noise', containing /ínɨmn/ 'to neigh, bray, sing', /-ɬa/ 'he who' (N. Rude p.c.).

EPIZETKA River (Alaska, Point Lay C-2) \ep i zet´ kə\. The Iñupiaq (Eskimo) name has been given as <qipigsatqaq> 'crooked' (Orth 1967).

EQUINUNK (Pa., Wayne Co.) \ek´ i nungk\. Said to be from a Delaware (Algonquian) name meaning 'where articles of clothing were distributed' (Donehoo 1928); cf. *akwúneew* 'to dress someone' (O'Meara 1996).

ERCHAKRTUK Mountain (Alaska, Baird Inlet C-8). The Yupik (Eskimo) name was reported in 1949 (Orth 1967).

ERIE \ē´ rē\. The name is that of an Iroquoian people who were largely dispersed during the seventeenth century. The English name is from French *Erie* or *Erié,* abbreviations of the Native American term <Rhiienhonons>, often translated as *la nation de Chat* 'the Cat nation'. Early descriptions of *chats sauvages* 'wild cats', however, makes it clear that the term referred to raccoons, and Canadian French *chat sauvage* is still used to mean 'raccoon' (*HNAI* 15:416). **Erie** appears in many placenames, including **Lake Erie** and other far-flung examples (Fla., Manatee Co.; Ill., Whiteside Co.; and Mich., Monroe Co.).

ESALEN Institute (Calif., Monterey Co.) \es´ ə lən\. From the name of a local Indian group, otherwise spelled **Essalen** (Gudde 1998). In the twentieth century, the name was applied to an institution dedicated to "personal growth."

ESCAMBIA River (Ala., Fla.) \es kam´ bē ə\. The Native American origin of the name is obscure (Read 1934, 1984). A possible derivation is from Chickasaw (Muskogean) *ishkobohomma,* lit. 'head red', the name of a medicinal plant (P. Munro p.c.). The stream gives its name to units called **Escambia County** in both Ala. and Fla.

ESCANABA (Mich., Delta Co.) \es kə nä´ bə\. Presumably from Ojibwa (Algonquian), but the derivation is unclear. A possible origin is in <Oshqua na be konk> 'slippery rock' (Peters 1996; Vogel 1986); cf. *ozhaashaa* 'be slippery' (Nichols and Nyholm 1995). The name occurs as a transfer in Wis. (Vilas Co.).

ESCATAWPA River (Ala., Washington Co.; Miss., Jackson Co.) \es kə tô´ pə\. Probably from Choctaw (Muskogean) *oski aatapa* 'where the cane was cut', from *oski* 'cane' plus *aa-tapa* 'cutting place' (*aa-* 'place', *tapa* 'to cut') (Read 1984; P. Munro p.c.).

ESCHITA (Okla., Tillman Co.) \esh´ i tä\. Named for a nineteenth-century Comanche (Numic) leader whose name is also rendered as <Ishatai>; the Native American term is /isa-tai/, lit. 'wolf-vulva' (J. McLaughlin p.c.).

ESCOHEAG (R.I., Bristol Co.) \es´ ko hēg\. The SNEng. Algonquian term has been translated 'this is as far as the fish-spearing goes' (Huden 1962).

ESCUMBUIT Island (N.H., Rockingham Co.). Perhaps from Micmac (Algonquian), meaning 'at the watching place' (Huden 1962).

ESETUK Creek (Alaska, Mount Michelson B-1). Named for an Iñupiaq (Eskimo) man; the name was reported in 1960 (Orth 1967).

ESHAMY Bay (Alaska, Seward B-3). The Alutiiq (Eskimo) name is said to mean 'good fishing grounds' (Orth 1967).

ESKA Lake (Wis., Taylor Co.) \es´ kə\. Said to be from Ojibwa (Algonquian) <ishkwa> 'end, last in a row' (Vogel 1991); cf. *ishkwaaj* 'last' (Nichols and Nyholm 1995). Related names include **Eskwagama Lake** (Minn., Lake Co.). There is also an **Eska Creek** in Alaska (Anchorage C-6), derived from Dena'ina (Athabaskan) *ts'es tuk'ilaght* 'where fish run among rocks' (J. Kari p.c.).

ESKALAPIA (Ky., Lewis Co.) \es kə lä´ pē ə\. Perhaps from Shawnee (Algonquian) /škaa-laap-piye/ 'soggy terrain over a long stretch', from /škaa-/ 'raw', soft, wet', /-laap-/ 'the same repeated', and /-piye/ 'long extended area' (Mahr 1960:162).

ESKILIDA Creek (Alaska, Valdez B-2) \es ki lē´ də\. From Ahtna (Athabaskan), from a personal name (J. Kari p.c.).

ESKIMINZIN Wash (Ariz., Pinal Co.) \es kə min´ zin\. Named for a Western Apache (Athabaskan) leader; his name has also been spelled <Hackibanzin> (Granger 1983). This can be interpreted as a "war name" of the form /hašké baanzįn/ 'they stand in line for him who is angry', containing *hašké* 'angry, fierce' (P. Greenfeld p.c.).

ESKIMO \es´ ki mō\. This term refers to an ethnic and linguistic grouping of peoples who live in Arctic areas and speak a distinctive set of language varieties. They fall into two linguistic groups, one living in areas bordering the Arctic Ocean from Greenland westward, across Canada and into Alaska, as far as the Bering Straits; the other group lives in southwestern Alaska, in areas bordering the Chukchi Sea and the Gulf of Alaska. **Eskimo** has its first English attestation in 1584, in the form <Esquimawes>; this was later written <Esquimaux> and was used as a singular and a plural in both French and English. **Eskimo** became commoner after the mid-nineteenth century. It is likely that the word entered both French and English from Montagnais (Algonquian), in which the early use of <aiachkimeou> and <aiachtchimeou> was recorded for the Micmac. Some Algonquian languages refer to the Eskimos by a term that means 'eaters of raw meat' (e.g., Eastern Ojibwa *ashkipook*); and in this connection some Eskimo people prefer to be referred to by other terms (*HNAI* 5:5–6). In Canada official usage has adopted the term *Innuit* for the people and *Inuktitut* for the language. In Alaska **Iñupiaq** (see below) refers to the people on the Arctic coast north of the Bering Straits, and *Yupik* to those in southeastern Alaska. Eskimo speakers on the Gulf of Alaska are more specifically referred to as **Alutiiq** (see below), a term that derives historically from the fact that the Russians identified them with the Aleuts (who in fact speak a separate language). As a placename, **Eskimo** is attached to many places in Alaska and to a few elsewhere:

for example, **Eskimo Hill** (Calif., Shasta Co.) and **Eskimo Tank** (N.Mex., Otero Co.).

ESKIPPAKITHIKI (Ky., Clark Co.) \es kip´ ə kə thē´ kə\. Perhaps from Shawnee (Algonquian) /škipak-eθi-ʔki/ 'where it is green all over', from /škipaky-/ 'blue, green', /-eθi-/ 'all over', and /-ʔki/ 'place' (Mahr 1960:161).

ESKOTA (N.C., Yancey Co.) \es kō´ tə\. Perhaps an Indian name, but without identification (Powell 1968). There is also an Eskota in Tex. (Fischer Co.).

ESKUTASSIS Pond (Maine, Penobscot Co.) \es kə tas´ is\. Said to be Abenaki (Algonquian) for 'small trout' (Huden 1962); cf. Abenaki *skotam* 'speckled trout' (Day 1995).

ESKWAGAMA Lake (Minn., Lake Co.) \es kwä´ gə mə, es kwə gä´ mə\. Said to be Ojibwa (Algonquian), meaning 'the last' of a series of lakes (Upham 2001); cf. *ishkwaaj* 'last' (Nichols and Nyholm 1995). Probably related names include **Esquagama Lake** (Minn., St. Louis Co.), **Esquagamah** (Minn., Aitkin Co.), and **Eska Lake** (Wis., Taylor Co.).

ESOPUS (N.Y., Ulster Co.) \ē sō´ pəs\. Earlier written <Sopus, Soopus>, from the Munsee Delaware (Algonquian) placename /só:pəs/ (*HNAI* 15:237). The modern form **Esopus** is influenced by Latin *Aesopus,* the author of Aesop's fables.

ESQUAGAMA Lake (Minn., St. Louis Co.). From the same source as **Eskwagama Lake**; see above.

ESSOWAH Harbor (Alaska, Dixon Entrance D-3). The Tlingit name was reported in 1897 (Orth 1967).

ESTABOGA (Ala., Calhoun Co.) \ē stə bō´ gə\. A spelling variant of **Eastaboga**; see above.

ESTABUTCHIE (Miss., Jones Co.). Possibly from a Choctaw (Muskogean) word meaning 'what they mourn with', from *isht-* 'instrument', *tabashi* 'to mourn' (P. Munro p.c.).

EASTANAULA (Tenn., Hayward Co.). Said to be Cherokee (Iroquoian) for 'here we cross' (Miller 2001).

ESTATOAH Falls (Ga., Rabun Co.). A written variant of **Eastatoe;** see above.

ESTATOE (N.C., Mitchell Co.). A placename related to **Eastertoy** (Ga., Rabun Co.); see **Eastatoe** above.

ESTIFFANULGA (Fla., Liberty Co.) \es tə fə nul´ gə\. Perhaps from Muskogee <Isfanvlgi>, referring to one of the Muskogee clans (Read 1934); but the derivation is not clear.

ETACH Creek (Wash., Skagit Co.). Perhaps derived from a Lushootseed (Salishan) placename (Hitchman 1985).

ETCHEPUK River (Alaska, Solomon D-3). The Iñupiaq (Eskimo) name was reported in 1910 (Orth 1967).

ETICUERA Creek (Calif., Napa Co.) \et i kwâr´ ə\. The name is shown on a Mexican land grant as *Etécuero*; it may be transferred from Michoacán state in Mexico, where *etúcuero* is Tarascan for 'salt place', from *etúcua* 'salt' (Gudde 1998).

ETIGONIK Mountain (Alaska, Howard Pass D4). The Iñupiaq (Eskimo) name is from *itivliq* 'ortage' (L. Kaplan p.c.). A related placename is the nerby **Etivluk River.**

ETIKAMIUT (Alaska, Cape Mendenhall D-3). The Yupik (Eskimo) name, reported in 1932, contains *-miut* 'people' (Orth 1967).

ETIVLIK Lake (Alaska, Howard Pass A-l). The Iñupiaq (Eskimo) name is from *itivliq* 'portage' (L. Kaplan p.c.). A related placename is the nearby **Etivluk River**.

ETIWANDA (Calif., San Bernardino Co.) \et i wän´ də\. Said to be named for a leader of an unidentified Indian group near Lake Michigan (Gudde 1998). No comparable placename has been identified in the Great Lakes area.

ETOI KI (Ariz., Pima Co.) \ē toi kē\. From O'odham (Piman) *i'itoi ki* 'house of I'itoi', referring to the culture hero so named; cf. *ki* 'house' (J. Hill p.c.).

ETOKEK Slough (Alaska, Kwiguk D-4). The Yupik (Eskimo) name was recorded in 1952 (Orth 1967).

ETONIAH Creek (Fla., Putnam Co.) \et ə nī´ ə\. An earlier form of the name is <It-tun-wah>. It seems likely to be from a Muskogean language (Read 1934); cf. Muskogee *etvlwv* /itálwa/ 'tribal town' (Martin and Mauldin 2000).

ETOTULGA (Fla., Madison Co.) \ē tə tul´ gə\. Possibly Muskogee *eto-tolkē* /ito-tólki/ 'felled tree', from *eto* /itó/ 'tree' and *tolkē* /tólki:/ 'knocked over' (J. Martin p.c.).

ETOWAH River (Ga., Floyd Co.) \et´ ō wä, et´ ə wä\. Said to be named for a Cherokee (Iroquoian) settlement <Itawa> (Krakow 1975); however, the word may be a borrowing from Catawban (Siouan) /itá:wą/ 'longleaf pine tree' (B. Rudes p.c.). The name was also used by Muskogean speakers, recorded by Spanish explorers as *Itaba* (Booker et al. 1992:432). There is an **Etowah County** in Ala., and the term occurs as a transfer name in several states (e.g., Ark., Mississippi Co.; Fla., Lake Co.; and N.C., Henderson Co.) It has been folk-etymologized as **Hightower** (Ga., Forsyth Co.); it is perhaps also related to **Ettawa** (Calif., Lake Co.) and **Eutaw** (S.C., Orangeburg Co.).

ETTAHOMA Creek (Miss., Marion Co.) \et ə hō´ mə\. Probably from Choctaw (Muskogean) *itihomi* 'sourwood tree', from *itti* 'tree', *homi* 'sour' (Seale 1939).

ETTAWA (Calif., Lake Co.) \et´ ə wə\. Perhaps from Lake Miwok *éetaw* 'hot' (Gudde 1998), or perhaps a transfer name from **Etowah River**; see above.

ETTRAIN Creek (Alaska, Charley River B-1). Said to be an Indian (Athabaskan) word for 'mosquito' (Orth 1967).

EUARYE (Wyo., Fremont Co.). Said to be Shoshoni (Numic) for 'warm valley' (Urbanek 1974); cf. /yuai/ 'warm' (Miller 1972).

EUCHA (Okla., Delaware Co.) \yo͞o´ chə\. From the same source as **Euchee** \yo͞o´ chē\. This is the name of a people, once politically affiliated with the Muskogees in Ga. but speaking a distinct language. The Euchee/Yuchi community now lives in Okla. The term is usually spelled **Yuchi** by anthropologists and linguists. In Fla. (Walton Co.) there is a **Euchee Valley** and a **Eucheeanna** \yo͞o chē ä´ nə\. The Muskogee form of the name is *yocce* /yóčči/ (Martin and Mauldin 2000).

EUCHRE Creek (Ore., Cuny Co.) \yo͞o´ kər\. From the Tututni (Athabaskan) placename [yúgwi], folk-etymologized under the influence of English *euchre,* a once-popular card game (D. Kinkade p.c.).

EUCLAUTUBBA Creek (Miss., Lee Co.) \yo͞o klô tub´ ə, ō klə tub´ ə\. Perhaps fom a Choctaw (Muskogean) "war name" *hoklitabi* 'he captures and kills', containing *hokli* 'to capture' and *abi* 'to kill' (Seale 1939; P. Munro p.c.).

EUCUTTA (Miss., Wayne Co.) \yo͞o kut´ ə\. Perhaps from a Choctaw (Muskogean) word meaning 'slave-born' (Seale 1939); cf. *yoka* 'slave', *atta* 'to be there' (P. Munro p.c.).

EUFALA (Fla., Calhoun Co.). From the same source as **Eufaula** (Ala., Barbour Co.) \yo͞o fô´ lə\. This is from Muskogee *yofalv* /yofá:la/, the name of a tribal town (Read 1984; J. Martin p.c.). The name also occurs in Ga. (Stewart Co.), Okla. (McIntosh Co.), and Wash. (Cowlitz Co.). The spelling **Eufola** occurs in N.C. (Iredell Co.).

EUHARLEE (Ga., Bartow Co.). The name has been said to be Cherokee (Iroquoian) for 'she laughs as she runs' (Krakow 1975). The term was first recorded by Spanish explorers, however, as a Muskogean placename, *Ulibahali* (Booker et al. 1992:432).

EULACHON Slough (Alaska, Petersburg C-l) \yo͞o´ lə kon\. Refers to a kind of fish, also called candlefish because of its high oil content. The term is borrowed from Chinook Jargon, which takes it from Clatsop (Chinookan) /u-tlalxwa(n)/ 'brook trout' (*RHD* 1987). A related placename is **Hulakon River** (Alaska, Bradfield Canal A-4).

EUPHAUBEE (Ala., Macon Co.) \yōō fô´ bē\. Also written <Euphaube, Uphapee>; perhaps related to Hitchiti (Muskogean) <nofàpi> 'beech tree' (Read 1984).

EUTACUTACHEE Creek (Miss., Rankin Co.). Perhaps from a Choctaw (Muskogean) word meaning 'chestnut pond', from *oti* 'chestnut' plus *hohtak oshi* 'small pond' (*hohtak* 'lake', diminutive *-oshi*) (Seale 1939; P. Munro p.c.).

EUTAH Bend (Miss., Tallahatchie Co.). Probably from the same source as **Eutaw Creek** (S.C., Orangeburg Co.) \yōō´ tä\. This is apparently from an earlier writing <Etiwaw> (Pearson 1978), perhaps from Cherokee (Iroquoian) *iitaawaa* 'longleafed pine tree' (B. Rudes p.c.); if so, it is related to the name **Etowah,** widespread in the southeastern United States. The placename **Eutaw** also occurs in Ala. (Greene Co.) and Miss. (Bolivar Co.). Probably related is **Eutah Bend** (Miss., Tallahatchie Co.). The name **Eutaw** is pronounced very much like **Utah**, but there is no connection.

EVELUKPALIK River (Alaska, Noatak A-4). The Iñupiaq (Eskimo) name is said to mean 'place of big clams' (Orth 1967); cf. *iviḷuq* 'clamshell' (Webster and Zibell 1970).

EVGHINAK Point (Alaska, Saint Lawrence B-6). The Yupik (Eskimo) name was recorded in 1949 (Orth 1967).

EVRULIVIK Lake (Alaska, Barrow A-4). The Iñupiaq (Eskimo) name was also recorded as <Ivirulivik>, said to mean 'place where there is moss' (Orth 1967); cf. *ivruq* 'sod for house building', *-vik* 'place' (Webster and Zibell 1970:98).

EWAKLALIK, Mount (Alaska, Russian Mission D-6). The Yupik (Eskimo) name was reported in 1918 (Orth 1967).

EWAUNA, Lake (Ore., Klamath Co.) \ē wô´ nə\. From Klamath /ihwawna/ 'is propped up against' (Barker 1963).

EXSHO (Ala., Washington Co.) \ek´ shô\. Perhaps a joke; Choctaw (Muskogean) *ikshoh* means 'there's nothing' (P. Munro p.c.).

EYAK (Alaska, Cordova C-5) \ē´ yak\. This village bears the name of an Indian people, who last lived here as a group. The Eyak name of the village was /iiyaaɢ/, a borrowing from Alutiiq (Eskimo) *igya'aq* 'throat; outlet of a lake' (*HNAI* 7:196, Leer 1978).

EYESE (Calif., Siskiyou Co.) \ī´ ēz\. From the Karuk village name *áyiith* (Gudde 1998).

EYOTA (Minn., Olmsted Co.) \ē yō´ tə\. From Dakota (Siouan) *iyótą* 'great, most'; the name was apparently applied by white settlers (Upham 2001; Riggs 1890).

F

FACE Rock (Ariz., Apache Co.). Corresponds to Navajo (Athabaskan) *tsé binii'í* 'rock's face' (Linford 2000); cf. *tsé* 'rock', *bi-nii'* 'its face' (Young and Morgan 1987).

FAHKAHHATCHEE (Fla., Collier Co.). A variant of **Fakahatchee** (Fla., Collier Co.). This is from Seminole (Muskogean) *fvkv* /fáka/ 'vine', or perhaps from *fakke* /fákki/ 'soil', plus *hvcce* /háčči/ "tream' (Read 1934; Martin and Mauldin 2000). An alternative spelling is **Fahkahhatchee.** A related name is **Faka Union Bay** (Fla., Collier Co.).

FAKIT CHIPUNTA (Ala., Clarke Co.) \fä kit chi pun´ tə\. Choctaw (Muskogean) *fakit chipǫta* 'young/little turkeys', from *fakit* [fʌkit] 'turkey' and *chipǫta* 'little'. This word for 'turkey' has now become stigmatized because of its resemblance to an English taboo expression (Read 1984; P. Munro p.c.). A related placename is **Turkey Creek** (Ala., Choctaw Co.).

FALAKTO (Ala., Chilton Co.) \fə lak´ tō\. From Choctaw (Muskogean) *falakto(h)* 'to be forked' (Read 1984, P. Munro p.c.).

FALIAH (La., Washington Par.) \fə lī´ ə\. From Choctaw (Muskogean) *falaya* 'long' (P. Munro p.c.). This is probably an abbreviation of a placename that occurs as **Bogue Falaya** (La., St. Tammany Par.), lit. 'stream-long', as well as in the related forms **Bogue Fallah** (Miss., Oktibbeha and Choctaw Cos.), **Bogue Fala** (Miss., Lee Co.), **Bogue Faliah** (Miss., Scott Co.), and **Bogue Phalia** (Miss., Washington Co.).

FALL Creek (Ind., Henry Co). A translation of a Munsee Delaware (Algonquian) term reconstructed as */susuukpéhəlaak/ '(water) spilling down' (McCafferty 2002). Similarly, **Fall River** (S.Dak., Fall River Co.) corresponds to Lakhota (Siouan) *mní ȟiȟé*, lit. 'water-fall' (Sneve 1973; A. Taylor p.c.).

FALLING IRON Cliffs (Ariz., Apache Co.). Corresponds to Navajo (Athabaskan) *béésh nahałdaas* 'falling iron', with *béésh* 'flint, iron' (Young & Morgan 1987).

FALL LEAF (Kans., Leavenworth Co.). Named for a Delaware (Algonquian) scout employed in Kans. by the U.S. Army; his Native American name has been given as <Po-na-kah-ko-wah> (Rydjord 1968).

FANNEGUSHA Creek (Miss., Holmes Co.) \fan i gush´ ə\. A Choctaw (Muskogean) name, perhaps meaning 'good-tasting squirrel', from *fani* 'squirrel' plus *kashaha* 'delicious' (P. Munro p.c.). A related placename is **Phenatchie Creek** (Ala., Pickens Co.).

FAQUETAÏQUE, Prairie (La., Acadia Par.) \fä ki tā ēk\. From Choctaw (Muskogean) *fakit tiik* 'turkey hen', from *fakit* 'turkey' plus *tiik* 'female' (Read 1927; P. Munro p.c.).

FAR SPIRAL Canyon (Ariz., Apache Co.). Corresponds to Navajo (Athabaskan) *nízaa'ali-wozh nástł'ah* 'far spiral cove' (Linford 2000); cf. *nízaad* 'to be far', *nástł'ah* 'cove' (Young and Morgan 1987).

FATHER Rock (Ariz., Apache Co.). Corresponds to Navajo (Athabaskan) *tsé bazhei* 'rock's father' (Linford 2000); cf. *tsé* 'rock', *azhé'é* 'father' (Young and Morgan 1987).

FEMME OSAGE Creek (Mo., St. Charles Co.) \fem ē ō sāj\. French for 'Osage woman'; the French pronunciation would be approximately [famozáž] (Ramsay 1952).

FENACHE Creek (Ala., Sumter Co.) \fē nach´ ē\. Perhaps from Choctaw (Muskogean), meaning 'squirrels are there'; cf. *fani* 'squirrel', *asha* 'are there' (Read 1984). The spelling **Phenatchie Creek** is also used (Ala., Pickens Co.). A related placename is **Fannegusha Creek** (Miss., Holmes Co.).

FENCE. This English word refers to Native American hunting and fishing practices; it designates a barrier made of stakes and brush used to herd game or to trap fish. Among placenames, the settlement called **Fence** (Wis., Florence Co.) is said to be named after such a barrier used in hunting (Vogel 1991). **Fence River** (Mich., Iron Co.) refers to a fish-dam or weir, translating Ojibwa (Algonquian) <mitchikan> (Vogel 1986); cf. Ottawa (Algonquian) *mjigkan* 'fence' (Rhodes 1985).

FENCED UP HORSE Valley (N.Mex., McKinley Co.). Corresponds to Navajo (Athabaskan) *łį́į́ biná'asht'ih* 'horse enclosed in fence' (Linford 2000); cf. *łį́į́* 'horse', *biná'ázt'i'* 'to be fenced in' (Young and Morgan 1987).

FENHOLLOWAY (Fla., Taylor Co.) \fen hol´ ə wā\. A Muskogee word meaning 'high bridge', from *fenv* /finá/ 'foot-log, bridge', *hvlwe* /hálwi/ 'high' (Read 1934; Martin and Mauldin 2000).

FINIKOCHIKA Creek (Ala., Coosa Co.) \fin i kos´ kə\. Muskogee *fenv-kvcēke* /fina-kačí:ki/ 'broken footbridges', from *fenv* /finá/ 'foot-bridge', *kvcēke* /kačí:ki/ 'broken', of two or more (Read 1984; Martin and Mauldin 2000).

FIRESTEEL (S.Dak., Dewey Co.). Corresponds to Lakhota (Siouan) *čhąká* 'flint', which could be struck with steel to make fire (Sneve 1973; Ingham 2001).

FISHEATING Bay (Fla., Glades Co.). Corresponds to Muskogee *rvro-papkv hvcce* /łało-pa:pka háčči/ 'fish-eating stream', from *rvro* /łałó/ 'fish', *papkv* /pá:pka/ 'eating', and *hvcce* /háčči/ 'stream' (Martin and Mauldin 2000).

FISHING Creek (Pa., York Co.). Perhaps translated from the Delaware (Algonquian) name <Namescesepong> (Donehoo 1928); cf. Unami Delaware *namés* 'fish' (Blalock et al. 1994), Munsee Delaware *namées* (O'Meara

1996). In Ind. (Orange Co,.) **Fishing Creek** reflects Delaware (Algonquian) /namèeshánee/ 'it is a fish river' (McCafferty 2002).

FISH Lake (Alaska, Tancross A-4). From Tanacross (Athabaskan) *łuug menn'*, literally 'fish lake' (J. Kari p.c.).

FISHNET Lake (Alaska, Beaver A-4). Corresponds to Koyukon (Athabaskan) *tabil k'at* 'fishnet place' (Kari 2000).

FITEE (Ala., Washington Co.) \fit´ ē\. Perhaps from Hitchiti (Muskogean) /fiiti/ 'turkey' (P. Munro p.c.).

FIXICO Creek (Ala., Randolph Co.) \fik´ si kō\. This represents a common surname used by Muskogee families. It is from *fekseko* /fiksikó/, sometimes translated 'heartless', used in men's "war names"; cf. *fēke* 'heart', *seko* /sikó/ 'nonexistent' (Martin and Mauldin 2000).

FLAMBEAU River (Wis., Iron Co.) \flam´ bō\. The French term for 'torch' refers to the Indian practice of using pine torches while spear-fishing in lakes at night (Vogel 1991). Related terms are **Lac du Flambeau** (Wis., Vilas Co.) as well as **Torch Lake** (Wis., Vilas Co.) and **Torch River** (Mich., Kalkaska Co.).

FLATHEAD County (Mont.). Named for an Indian people, called *Têtes Plattes* in French, belonging to the Salishan linguistic family. The term seems to refer to the practice of flattening children's heads in cradleboards, which was practiced by some American Indian groups; the Flathead people did not have such a custom, however, and the name seems to have been given to them through a misunderstanding (Cheney 1984).

FLAT Lake (Alaska, Beaver B-4). Corresponds to Koyukon (Athabaskan) *mənh t'ʌsjə* 'flat lake' (Kari 2000).

FLESHLANANA Creek (Alaska, Tanana C-3). Perhaps from Koyukon (Athabaskan); the name was recorded in 1956 (Orth 1967).

FLINT. The term refers to a type of hard rock used by Indians to make arrowheads and spearheads. In some parts of North America, it is also used to refer to other types of hard rock used for similar purposes, especially obsidian. **Flint** occurs in many placenames, translating Native American terms for such rocks. **Flint Creek** (Iowa, Des Moines Co.) corresponds to Meskwaki (Algonquian) <Shoquokon, Shokokan> 'flint hill' (Vogel 1983). **Flint River** (Mich., Genesee Co.) is equivalent to Ojibwa (Algonquian) <Peonigoing sebe, Biwânag sibi> 'river of the place of flint' (Vogel 1986); cf. *biiwaanag* 'flint', *ziibi* 'river' (Nichols and Nyholm 1995). **Flint Hill** (S.Dak., Fall River Co.) is a translation of Lakhota (Siouan) *wąhí pahá*, from *wąhí* 'flint, arrowhead' (*wą* 'arrow', *hi* 'tooth') plus *pahá* 'hill' (A. Taylor p.c.).

FLORALA (Ala., Covington Co.). Represents a merger of *Florida* and **Alabama**, the second of which is of American Indian (Muskogean) origin.

FLOWERS (Ind., Miami Co.). Named for a leader of the Wea people, a subgroup of the Miami/Illinois (Algonquian) Indians. His English name was Billy Flowers, and his Native American name <Na-go-to-cup-wah, No-ka-me-nah> also referred to 'flowers' (McPherson 1993).

FODDER Creek (Ga., Towns Co.). Said to be named for a Cherokee (Iroquoian) individual who used the English word *fodder* as a surname; his Native American name is supposed to have been <Saluwaugah> (Goff 1975).

FOND DU LAC County (Wis.) \fon´ də lak\. French for 'end of the lake', translating Menominee (Algonquian) <wanika miu>, referring to Lake Winnebago (Vogel 1991).

FONTANELLE (Iowa, Adair Co.) \fon tə nel´\. Named for a nineteenth-century Omaha (Siouan) leader whose English name was Logan Fontanelle. His Native American name was /šąge ska/, lit. 'horse-white' (Vogel 1983; R. Rankin p.c.).

FORDOCHE (La., Pointe Coupee Par.) \fô dôsh´\. Possibly from a Caddo source, of unclear derivation (Read 1927); or possibly from

Choctaw (Muskogean) *folosh* 'clamshell, spoon' (P. Munro p.c.).

FOREST Lake (Ariz., Navajo Co.). Corresponds to Navajo (Athabaskan) *tsinyi' be'ek'id* 'lake within the trees or woods', from *tsin* 'trees, woods', *yi'* 'within', and *be'eki'd* 'lake' (Wilson 1995).

FOSHEE (Ala., Escambia Co.) \fô´ shē, fō´ shē\. From Chickasaw (Muskogean) *foshi'* 'bird' (Read 1984, P. Munro p.c.). The name also occurs in La. (Natchitoches Par.).

FOUR KILLER Creek (Ga., Fulton Co.). From the name of a Cherokee (Iroquoian) leader. The term is a "war name" derived from Cherokee <Nunggihtehe, Nankeeteehee>, indicating that the person so named had killed four enemy warriors. The English name has sometimes had the variant "Foe Killer" (Goff 1975). Cf. Cherokee *nvhgi* [nʌ̰hgi] 'four' (Feeling 1975).

FOUR-LEGGED Lake (Minn., Clearwater Co.). Said to be named for an Ojibwa (Algonquian) man called <Nio-gade> (Upham 2001); cf. *niiyo-* 'four', *-gaad-* 'leg' (Nichols and Nyholm 1995).

FOX. The name of this Algonquian people, closely linked to the Sac (or Sauk), is a translation of French *renards,* which in turn may be a translation of an Iroquoian term meaning 'red-fox people'. The name of the Fox people for themselves is /meškwahki:-haki/ 'red-earths', which has entered English as **Mesquakie** or **Meskwaki** (*HNAI* 15:646); the latter spelling is used in this book. Several U.S. placenames containing *fox* may refer to this group rather than to the animal; examples are **Fox River** (Iowa, Van Buren Co.), **Fox Lake** (Ill., Lake Co.), and **Fox River** (Wis., Kenosha Co.). **Fox** also occurs in some placenames translated directly from Indian terms referring to the animal: for example, **Fox Lake** in Wis. (Dodge Co.) is named after a Winnebago (Siouan) leader called Big Fox; his Native American name was *wašerekéga,* lit. 'the fox', from *wašereké* 'fox' (Vogel 1991; K. Miner p.c.); cf. **Waushara County** (Wis.).

FROG Creek (S.Dak., Butte Co.). Corresponds to Lakhota (Siouan) *gnašká* 'frog' (Sneve 1973; Ingham 2001). **Frog Rock** (Ariz., Apache Co.) corresponds to Navajo (Athabaskan) *chał sitą́* 'frog sits' (Linford 2000); cf. *chał* 'frog', *sitą́* 'it sits' (Young and Morgan 1987).

FU GYO Spring (Ariz., Coconino Co.) \fo͞o´ gyō\. From Havasupai (Yuman) /'fú gyo/, lit. 'willow place' (L. Hinton p.c.).

FUMECHELIGA (Fla., Orange Co. \fum i chə lī´ kə\. From Muskogee *fvmēcv-like* /fami:ča-léyki/ 'sitting muskmelon', from /famí:ča/ 'muskmelon' and /léyki/ 'sitting' (Read 1984, Martin and Mauldin 2000).

FUNMAKER Flowage (Wis., Jackson Co.). Named for George Funmaker Sr., a Winnebago (Siouan) who died in 1947. The name is said to be badly translated: "Actually, it refers to the antics of a bear cub; [it] probably means 'Laughing-at-his-antics', [perhaps] Old Funmaker's vision-quest name" (Vogel 1991:62).

FUNNY Creek (Miss., Pontotoc Co.) \fun´ i\. From Choctaw (Muskogean) *fani* 'squirrel' (Seale 1939; P. Munro p.c.). This Choctaw word occurs in other place names, such as **Bayou Funny Louis** (La., La Salle Par.) \fun ē lo͞o´ ē\, perhaps meaning 'burnt squirrel', with *lowa* 'burnt' (Read 1927). **Funny Yockana Creek** (Miss., Neshoba Co.) [fun i yok´ nə] means 'squirrel country', containing Choctaw *yaakni* 'country' (Seale 1939; P. Munro p.c.). Related placenames are **Fenache Creek** (Ala., Sumter Co.), **Phenatchie Creek** (Ala., Pickens Co.), and **Fannegusha Creek** (Miss., Holmes Co.).

FUSHACHEE Creek (Ga., Stewart Co.) \fus hach´ ē\. From a Muskogee band name *fus'hvcce* /fos-háčči/ 'bird creek'; cf. *fuswv* /fóswa/ 'bird', *hacce* /háčči/ 'stream' (Martin and Mauldin 2000). The related form **Fusihatchi** \fus i hach´ ē\ occurs in Ala. (Elmore Co.).

FUZZY Mountain (N.Mex., McKinley Co.). Corresponds to Navajo (Athabaskan) *dził ditłł'oii* 'fuzzy mountain', containing *dził* 'mountain', *ditł'o* 'it is fuzzy, hairy' (Wilson 1995). Also called **Zilditloi Mountain.**

G

GABIMICHIGAMI Lake (Minn., Cook Co.) \gab´ ē mish´ ē gam´ ē\. Probably from Ojibwa (Algonquian) *gaa-bimijigam(aag),* a name for Lake Bemidji, lit. 'cross lake' (i.e., a lake with a river crossing it); cf. *bimid-* 'across', *-gami* 'body of water' (J. Nichols p.c.).

GAGARA Lake (Alaska, Kenai C-3). Perhaps from Dena'ina (Athabaskan); the derivation is unclear (Orth 1967).

GAGARYAH River (Alaska, Lime Hills C-8) \gär´ gə rī\. From Dena'ina (Athabaskan) *k'ezghaxtnu* 'fish-harvest river', with *-tnu* 'river' (Kari and Kari 1982:14).

GAHANNA (Ohio, Franklin Co.) \gə han´ ə\. Possibly shortened from a Delaware (Algonquian) name, containing <hanna> 'stream' (M. McCafferty p.c.).

GAKONA (Alaska, Gulkana B-3) \gə kō´ nə\. From Ahtna (Athabaskan) *ggax* [ɢax] *kuna',* lit. 'rabbit river' (Kari 1990).

GALAS Point (Alaska, Adak C-2). A shortened form of the name of Kagalaska Island; the full form is from the Aleut placename *qigalaxsxix̂, qigalaxsxan* (Bergsland 1994).

GALICE (Ore., Josephine Co.) \gə lēs´\. The name is perhaps from a French surname, *Galice.* The last speaker of the Galice (Athabaskan) language, however, claimed that it represented an Indian pronunciation of *Kelly's.*

GAMBLER'S Spring (N.Mex., San Juan Co.). A translation of Navajo (Athabaskan) *nááhwiłbį̨į̨hí bitooh* 'the gambler's spring', from *nááhwiłbį̨į̨hí* 'the gambler' (lit. 'he who won them again and again') plus *bi-tooh* 'his spring' (*bi-* 'his', *tooh* 'spring, water'). The name refers to a figure in Navajo legend called the Gambler (Wilson 1995). The trail that leads to the spring is called Gambler's Trail, from Navajo *nááhwiłbį̨į̨hí bitiin* 'the gambler's trail', with *(a)tiin* 'trail, path' (Wilson 1995).

GANEER Township (Ill., Kankakee Co.) \jə nēr´\. Named for a Potawatomi (Algonquian) woman whose name was written <Je-neir> (Vogel 1963).

GANOGA Lake (Pa., Luzerne Co.) \gə nō´ gə\. Perhaps from Seneca (Iroquoian) *ga:noó'geh* 'place of oil in the water' (W. Chafe p.c.); cf. *ó:nǫ* 'oil' (Chafe 1967). The name has the same origin as **Canoga** (N.Y., Seneca Co.).

GANSETT Point (Mass., Barnstable Co.) \gan´ sət\. From Wampanoag (Algonquian), perhaps meaning 'at the drinking place' (Huden 1962).

GAOHI Islands (Alaska, Craig D-4). The Tlingit name was published in 1956 (Orth 1967).

GAP Rock (Ariz., Apache Co.). Corresponds to Navajo (Athabaskan) *tsé' ńdeshgizh* 'rock gap' (Linford 2000), with *tsé'* 'rock'.

GARDEAU Overlook (N.Y., Wyoming Co.) \gär´ dō\. Said to be named for an Indian resident, affiliation not known; the name may be a borrowing from French (Beauchamp 1907).

GARDEN (Mich., Delta Co.). So named by early white visitors because of the vegetable gardens that they found being cultivated by the Algonquian peoples of the Great Lakes area (Vogel 1986); cf. Ojibwa *gitigaan* (Nichols and Nyholm 1995). Another example of the placename is in **Garden Lake** (Wis., Bayfield Co.).

GAROGA (N.Y., Fulton Co.) \gə rō´ gə\. Perhaps from an Iroquoian name meaning 'on this side' (Beauchamp 1907).

GASSABIAS Lake (Maine, Hancock Co.). Abenaki (Algonquian), said to mean 'small clearwater lake' (Rutherford 1970).

GATAGAMA Point (Ariz., Coconino Co.). From the surname of a Havasupai (Yuman) family (Brian 1992).

GATLENA Gap (Alaska, Livengood D-4) \gəd lē´ nə\. Koyukon (Athabaskan) *gaadlee no',* with *no'* 'stream' (Matthew et al. 1999).

GEANQUAKIN Creek (Md., Somerset Co.) \jin kō´ kin\. The Algonquian name is of unclear derivation (Kenny 1984).

GEAUGA County (Ohio) \jē ô´ gə\. Possibly from Seneca (Iroquoian) *jo'ę:ga* 'raccoon' (W. Chafe p.c.).

GECHIAK Creek (Alaska, Goodnews Bay A-4). The Yupik (Eskimo) name was reported in 1898 (Orth 1967).

GEESE Lake (Alaska, Beaver A-5). Corresponds to Koyukon (Athabaskan) *dach'əx mənə'* 'white-fronted-goose lake', with *mənə'* 'lake' (Kari 2000).

GEMODEDON Island (Alaska, Nulato D-4). The Koyukon (Athabaskan) name was reported in 1954 (Orth 1967).

GEMUK Mountain (Alaska, Bethel C-l). The Yupik (Eskimo) name was reported in 1945 as meaning 'lone' (Orth 1967).

GENEROSTEE Creek (S.C., Anderson Co.) \jen ə ros´ tē\. Also folk-etymologized as **Generosity Creek**; perhaps from an unidentified Indian language (Pickens 1961–62:5).

GENESEE County (N.Y.) \jen ə sē´, jen´ ə sē\. Apparently from Seneca (Iroquoian) *jonéshi:yo:h* 'good valley' (W. Chafe p.c.); cf. *-awiyo-, -iyo-* 'to be good, beautiful' (Chafe 1967). The name has spread widely as a transfer name (e.g., Calif., Plumas Co.; R.I., Washington Co.; and Wis., Waukeksha Co.). Related forms are **Genessee** (La., Tangipahoa Par.) and **Gennessee** (Minn., Kandiyohi Co.). A related name is **Geneseo** (N.Y., Livingston Co.) \jen ə sē´ ō\; this form of the word also occurs in Iowa (Tama Co.), Ill. (Henry Co.), and Kans. (Rice Co.).

GEODUCK Creek (Wash., Jefferson Co.) \g o͞o´ ē duk, gwē´ duk\. The term is used in local English as the name of a clam, from Puget Salish /gwidəq/ (*RHD* 1987).The eccentric spelling of the name is said to be by analogy with words such as *geology* (Parratt 1984).

GEOHENDA Creek (Alaska, Nabesna A-3) \jē ō hen´ də\. The Upper Tanana (Athabaskan) name, which has been written <Gehoenda, Genaenda>, was reported in 1902 (Orth 1967).

GEORGETOWN (Ind., Cass Co.). Named for George Cicott, a trader of mixed Indian and French ancestry, who lived among the Potawatomis (Algonquian) in the early nineteenth century (McPherson 1993).

GEORGICA (N.Y., Suffolk Co.) \jôr´ ji kə\. The name has been written as <Jorgke, George cake, Jeorgeke> (etc.); it is said to have been named for an Indian, probably Algonquian, named <Jeorgkee> (Tooker 1911).

GERMAINE, Saint (Wis., Vilas Co.) \jər mān´\. For French *Saint Germain,* the surname of a family of mixed Ojibwa (Algonquian) and French descent (Vogel 1991).

GERONIMO (Ariz., Graham Co.) \jə ron´ i mō\. From the name of the famous nineteenth-century Western Apache leader. **Geronimo** is from Spanish *Gerónimo, Jerónimo,* corresponding to English *Jerome.* His Native American name was *goyą̨ąłé,* perhaps meaning 'the wise one', from *-yą̨ął* 'to be wise' (P. Greenfeld p.c.). As a placename, **Geronimo** also occurs in N.Mex. (San Miguel Co.) and in Tex. (Guadalupe Co.).

GETMUNA (Alaska, Sleetmute D-6). The name is said to be an abbreviation of Deg Hit'an (Athabaskan) <Get-munna-yam-al'ia> 'stream which flows in the opposite direction' (Orth 1967).

GETUKTI Cliff (Alaska, Prince Rupert D-2). The name, probably Tlingit, was reported in 1955 (Orth 1967).

GEUDA Springs (Kans., Sumner Co.) \gyo͞o´ də\. From Ponca or Omaha (Siouan); the Native American name is /giúdą/ 'it is good for one' (R. Rankin p.c.).

GHEENA Point (Alaska, Saint Lawrence B-3) \gē´ nə\. The Yupik (Eskimo) name was reported in 1949 (Orth 1967).

GHOST DANCE Ridge (Nev., Mineral Co.). The name refers to a ceremony that became popular in the nineteenth century among Indians of the western United States, in the belief that it would bring the spirits of the dead back to life (cf. **Wovoka**).

GIANTTRACK Mountain (Colo., Larimer Co.) is based on Arapaho (Algonquian) *hinenítee tohnooxéiht* 'man where-he-made-tracks' (A. Cowell p.c.).

GIJIK Creek (Mich., Gogebic Co.) \gij´ ik\. From Ojibwa (Algonquian) *giizhik* 'white cedar' (Vogel 1986; Nichols and Nyholm 1995). There is also a **Gijik Lake** in Minn. (Cass Co.).

GILAHINA River (Alaska, McCarthy B-8) \gil ə hē´ nə\. From Ahtna (Athabaskan) *keghiil na'*, perhaps 'steps river' (J. Kari p.c.).

GILANTA Rocks (Alaska, Prince Rupert D-3). The name, perhaps from Tlingit, was published in 1943 (Orth 1967).

GILA River (Ariz.) \hē´ lə\. The name occurs in early Spanish records as <Xila, Gila, Hyla> etc.; it was probably borrowed from an Indian language, but the source cannot now be identified (Granger 1983). The name also occurs in N.Mex. (Grant Co.) and Ill. (Jasper Co.).

GINGOTEAGUE Creek (Va., King George Co.) \ging´ gə tēg\. From the same source as **Chincoteague Bay** (Va., Accomack Co.), perhaps meaning 'large inlet' (Hagemann 1988).

GISASA River (Alaska, Kateel River B-4) .The Koyukon (Athabaskan) name was published in 1887 (Orth 1967).

GISH (Alaska, Craig D-7) \gish\. From Tlingit [gi:š] 'kelp' (Orth 1967; Davis and Leer 1976).

GISHNA Creek (Alaska, Tanana C-3) \gish´ nə\. The Koyukon (Athabaskan) word was recorded in 1956 (Orth 1967).

GITCHEGUMEE, Lake (Mich., Wexford Co.) \gich ē goo͞´ mē\. The name is probably taken from Longfellow's *Hiawatha,* which popularized the Ojibwa (Algonquian) term said to mean 'big sea water'; cf. *gichigamii* 'large lake, one of the Great Lakes', containing *gichi-* 'big', *gamii* 'lake' (Nichols & Nyholm 1995). A related name is **Gitchie Manitou** (Iowa, Lyon Co.): although this state preserve is in Siouan territory, it was given an Algonquian name by white settlers (Vogel 1991). It represents an Ojibwa term meaning 'great spirit'; cf. *gichi* 'great', *manidoo* 'spirit' (Nichols and Nyholm 1995). Other probably related names include **Kitchi Gammi Park** (Minn., St. Louis Co.), **Tichigan** (Wis., Racine Co.) and **Michigan**.

GITHGIDUNKA Creek (Alaska, Hughes A-l) From a Koyukon (Athabaskan) name that has been translated as 'fished with a hook' (Orth 1967).

GIUSEWA (N.Mex., Sandoval Co.) \joo͞´ sə wä\. From Jemez (Tanoan) [gįųsewa] 'hot place', referring to hot springs (Harrington 1916:394).

GIZOQUIT Brook (Maine, Aroostook Co.). Perhaps Abenaki (Algonquian), meaning 'eel weir place' (Rutherford 1970).

GLAMAN Lake (Alaska, Tanacross B-5) \glä´ mən\. From Tanacross (Athabaskan) *dlaa menn'*, lit. 'algae lake' (J. Kari p.c.).

GNADENHUTTEN (Ohio, Tuscarawas Co.) \gə nä´ dən hut ən, jə nä´ dən hut ən\. From German *Gnadenhütten* 'tabernacles of grace', the name applied by Moravian missionaries to Indian missions here in 1772 (Donehoo 1928; Miller 1996).

GOGEBIC County (Mich.) \gō gib´ ik, jō jē´ bik\. A possible earlier spelling was <Agogebic>. The word is probably from Ojibwa (Algonquian), but the derivation is not clear. Possibly related terms are *agidaabik* 'on something mineral (rock, metal)', *aazhibik* 'rock cliff' (Vogel 1986; Nichols and Nyholm 1995). The placename also occurs in Minn. (Cook Co.) and Wis. (Ashland Co.).

GOGOMAIN River (Mich., Chippewa Co.). Perhaps from Ojibwa (Algonquian) <kâgwaiân> 'porcupine skin', with <kâg> 'porcupine' (Baraga 1880; Vogel 1986); cf. *gaag* 'porcupine' (Nichols and Nyholm 1995).

GOGUAC Lake (Mich., Calhoun Co.) \gō´ gō ak\. Earlier spellings were <Coquaiack, Goguagick>. The name may be from Ojibwa (Algonquian), but the derivation is not clear (Vogel 1986).

GOING SNAKE (Okla., Adair Co.). Named for a Cherokee (Iroquoian) leader (Shirk 1974).

GOKACHIN Creek (Alaska, Ketchikan B-4). The Tlingit name was published in 1902 (Orth 1967).

GOKEE Creek (Mich., Cheboygan Co.). The name may be from Ojibwa (Algonquian), but the derivation is not clear (Vogel 1986).

GOMANCHE Creek (Mich., Baraga Co.) \gə man´ chē\. From the same origin as **Comanche**, an Indian people of the Numic (Uto-Aztecan) family; it is originally derived from Ute /kɨmánci, kɨmáci/ 'enemy, foreigner' (J. McLaughlin p.c.).

GONAKADETSEAT Bay (Alaska, Yakutat C-5). The Tlingit name was published in 1959 (Orth 1967).

GONIC (N.H., Strafford Co.) \gon´ ik\. Abbreviation from **Squamanagonic**, a nearby placename; from Abenaki (Algonquian), perhaps meaning 'salmon spearing place' (Huden 1962).

GOOD HART (Mich., Emmet Co.). Named for an Ottawa (Algonquian) individual, otherwise known as Good Heart (Vogel 1986).

GOODLATA Peak (Alaska, McCarthy A-6) \gŏŏd´ lə tä\. From Ahtna (Athabaskan), from a personal name (J. Kari p.c.).

GOOD THUNDER (Minn., Blue Earth Co.). Named for a nineteenth-century Winnebago (Siouan) leader. The name also referred to a Dakota (Siouan) leader in the same area and period, called in his own language <Wa-kin-yan-was-te>, and the two have sometimes been confused (Upham 2001). Cf. Dakota *wakį́yą* 'thunder', *wašté* 'good' (Riggs 1890).

GOOSE Creek (S.Dak., Dewey Co.). Corresponds to Lakhota (Siouan) *máğa wakpála,* lit. 'goose stream' (Sneve 1973; Ingham 2001). **Goose Creek** (Alaska, Talkeetna Mountains C-2) is a folk-etymology based on Ahtna (Athabaskan) *gguus kulaen na* 'creek where there is celery' (Kari and Fall 1987:190); cf. *gguus* \ɢu:s\ 'wild celery', *na* 'stream' (Kari 1990).

GOOSMUS Creek (Wash., Ferry Co.). Named for an Indian leader, language not identified (Hitchman 1985).

GOPHER Canyon (Ariz., Apache Co.) Corresponds to Navajo (Athabaskan) *na'azísí nástłah* 'gopher cove' (Linford 2000); cf. *na'azísí* 'gopher', *nástłah* 'cove' (Young and Morgan 1987). The placename **GOPHER Valley** (Ore., Yamhill Co.) translates Tualatin (Kalapuyan) [óofpi túnu], lit. 'gopher's place' (H. Zenk p.c.).

GOSHOOT Canyon (Utah, Juab Co.). From the same origin as **Goshute** (Nev., White Pine Co.; Utah, Juab Co.) \gō´ shōōt\. The term refers to a subgroup of the Shoshoni (Numic) people; the name is from Shoshoni /kusiutta/ (J. McLaughlin p.c.) another variant is **Gosiute** (Nev., Elko Co.).

GOSSIP Hills (N.Mex., McKinley Co.). Translates Navajo (Athabaskan) *aseezí* 'gossip, rumor, news' (Wilson 1995).

GOTEBO (Okla., Kiowa Co.) \gō´ tə bō\. Named for a leader of the Kiowa people (Shirk 1974).

GOWANDA (N.Y., Cattaraugus Co.) \gō wän´ də\. Apparently from Seneca (Iroquoian) *ogǫwǫde'* 'ridge, knoll' (W. Chafe p.c.). There is also a **Gowanda** in Colo. (Weld Co.).

GOWANUS Bay (N.Y., Kings Co.) \gō wä´ nəs\. From an Algonquian name of unclear derivation (Grumet 1981).

GRAND FORKS County (N.Dak.). Said to correspond to the Ojibwa (Algonquian) name for the junction of two rivers, <Kitchi-madawang> 'big forks' (Upham 2001).

GRAND MARAIS (Mich., Alger Co.) \grand mə rā´\. French for 'big swamp'; however, the placename may have entered English usage as a mistranscription of *grand mare* 'big pond', corresponding to Ojibwa <kitchi-bitobig> (Vogel 1986). Similarly, **Grand Sable** (Mich., Alger Co.) \grand sä´ bəl\ is French for 'great sand', an adaptation from Ojibwa (Algonquian) <negawadjing> 'at the sand mountain' (Vogel

1986); cf. *negaw* 'sand' (Rhodes 1985). A related placename is nearby **Au Sable Point.** Again, **Grand Traverse County** (MI) \grand trav´ ərs\. is from French *grand travers* 'big crossing'; *travers* 'crossing' is common in placenames of the Great Lakes area and in some cases may represent a translation of Ojibwa (Algonquian) *niminâgan* 'place of crossing over a bay, lake, etc.' (Baraga 1880).

GRAN QUIVIRA (N.Mex., Torrance Co.) \gran kē vē´ rə\. The Spanish phrase meaning 'great Quivira' refers to a legendary city sought by the Spanish explorer Francisco de Coronado, now thought to have been in Kans. The origin of the name, possibly Native American, is obscure (Julyan 1998); cf. **Quivira Lake** (Kans., Johnson Co.).

GRASS Creek (S.Dak., Shannon Co.). Corresponds to Lakhota (Siouan) *wakpá wathó-thąka* 'big-grass creek', from *wakpá* 'stream' plus *wathó-thąka,* lit.'grass-big' (Sneve 1973; A. Taylor p.c.).

GRAY CLOUD Island (Minn., Washington Co.). Named for a Dakota (Siouan) woman whose name was <Mahkpia-hoto-win> (Upham 2001); cf. *mah̆píya* 'cloud', *h̆óta* 'gray' (Riggs 1890).

GRAY HORSE (Okla., Osage Co.). Named for an Osage (Siouan) man; his Native American name was /hkáwa xó:ce/, lit. 'horse gray' (Shirk 1974; R. Rankin p.c.). The Osage word /hkáwa/ 'horse' is a borrowing from Spanish *caballo.*

GRAYLING Lake (Alaska, Medfra A-l). The name corresponds to Upper Kuskokwim (Athabaskan) *ts'idat'ana mina',* lit.'grayling lake' (Kari 1999:98). The grayling is a fish.

GRAY WHISKERS Butte (Ariz., Navajo Co.). Corresponds to Navajo (Athabaskan) *dághaa' łibáí* or *bidághaa łibáí* 'gray whiskers' (Linford 2000); cf. *dághaa'* 'his whiskers'; *bidághaa* 'his whiskers', *łibáí* 'gray' (Young and Morgan 1987).

GREASEWOOD (Ariz., Navajo Co.). This name for a native shrub corresponds to Navajo (Athabaskan) *diwózhii bii' tó* 'a spring in the greasewood', from *diwózhii* 'greasewood', *bii'* 'in it', *tó* 'water, spring' (Wilson 1995).

GREAT LAKES. The term corresponds to Ojibwa (Algonquian) *gichigamii* 'large lake', referring in particular to Lake Superior, but also to any of the Great Lakes (Nichols and Nyholm 1995).

GREEN COTTONWOOD Canyon (Ariz., Apache Co.). Corresponds to Navajo (Athabaskan) *t'iis ndiitsoi ntista'ah* 'yellow-green cottonwoods extending downward (in a line) cove' (Linford 2000), from *t'iis* 'cottonwood' and *ndiitsoi* 'yellow-green'.

GREEN GRASS (S.Dak., Dewey Co.). A translation of Lakhota (Siouan) *wakpála pheží,* lit. 'creek [of the] grass' (Sneve 1973; Ingham 2001). A related name is **Greenwood** (S.Dak., Charles Mix Co.), perhaps a translation of Dakota (Siouan) *čhą-phéži,* lit. 'wood [of] grass' (B. Ingham p.c.).

GREYLOCK Mountain (Mass., Berkshire Co.). Named for a SNEng. Algonquian leader of the eighteenth century; his Native American name may have been <Wabantep>, lit. 'white head' (Huden 1962).

GRIGNON Lake (Wis., Oconto Co.). Named for a family of mixed Menominee (Algonquian) and French descent, established in the area since the eighteenth century (Vogel 1991).

GRIKHDALITNA Creek (Alaska, Melozitna D4). The Koyukon (Athabaskan) name was recorded in 1956 (Orth 1967).

GRINDSTONE Butte (S.Dak., Haakon Co.). The term translates Lakhota (Siouan) *izúza* 'grindstone', referring to rocks used as whetstones (Sneve 1973; Ingham 2001).

GRIZZLY Creek (S.Dak., Custer Co.). Corresponds to Lakhota (Siouan) *mathó-h̆ota,* lit. 'bear-gray' (Sneve 1973; Ingham 2001).

GROMKOPA (Alaska, Nulato D-3). The Koyukon (Athabaskan) name is of unclear derivation.

GROS VENTRES Island (N.Dak., McLean Co.) \grō´ vänt\. The French term, meaning 'big bellies', has been used to refer to two different peoples of the northern Plains: the Hidatsas (Siouan) and the Atsinas (Algonquian) (*HNAI* 13:692–94). The latter are closely related to the Arapahos. A related placename in Wyo. (Teton Co.) is **Grovont,** an English spelling of the tribal name.

GROUNDHOUSE River (Minn., Kanabec Co.). The term refers to houses covered with earth, at one time used by members of the Siouan language family (Upham 2001).

GUACAMALLA Canyon (N.Mex., Sandoval Co.) \gwä kə mä´ yə\. A variant spelling of Spanish *guacamaya* 'macaw, a type of parrot', originally borrowed from Taino (Arawakan), a language of the West Indies (Julyan 1998). The Spanish masculine form occurs in **Guacamayo Historic Site,** also in Sandoval County.

GUACHAMA (Calif., San Bernardino Co.) \gwä chä´ mə\. The name was that of a subgroup of the Serrano (Takic) Indians (Gudde 1998).

GUACHE, El (N.Mex., Rio Arriba Co.) \wä´ chā\. Also written as **El Guacho;** perhaps an abbreviation of **Guachupangue** (Julyan 1998); see below.

GUACHUPANGUE (N.Mex., Rio Arriba Co.) \gwä cho͞o päng´ gā\. Earlier written **Guachepanque**; a Spanish adaptation of Tewa (Tanoan) [p'otsip'ą'nge] 'down at the mud-string place', from [p'otsi] 'mud', [p'ą'] 'thread, string', and [-ɣe] 'down at' (Harrington 1916:233).

GUADALASCA (Calif., Ventura Co.) \gwä də läs´ kə\. Perhaps from Ventureño (Chumashan) /šuwalaxšo/, a village in Big Sycamore Canyon; the etymology is unknown, but cf. /xšo/ 'sycamore' (Gudde 1998). The Spanish form of the name seems to contain *guad-,* from Arabic *wâdî* 'river', found in numerous placenames, such as *Guadalupe.*

GUAGUS Stream (Maine, Hancock Co.) \gwag´ əs\. From Micmac (Algonquian), perhaps meaning 'little stream' (Rutherford 1970).

GUAJALOTE, Arroyo (N.Mex., San Miguel Co.) \gwä hə lō´ tē\. From Mexican Spanish *guajolote* 'turkey', from Nahuatl (Aztecan) *huehxolotl* 'male turkey' (Karttunen 1983).

GUAJATOYAH Creek (Colo., Las Animas Co.) \gwä hə toi´ ə\. Comanche (Numic) /wahatoya/, the name of Spanish Peaks, lit. 'two mountains', from /waha-/ 'two' and /toya/ 'mountain' (J. McLaughlin p.c). A related name is **Wahatoya Creek** (Colo., Huerfano Co.).

GUAJE Canyon (N.Mex., Santa Fe Co.) \gwä´ hā\. Apparently from Spanish *guaje* 'gourd' (Julyan 1998), from Nahuatl (Aztecan) *huaxin* [wášin].

GUAJOME (Calif., San Diego Co.) \wä hō´ mē\. Apparently from Luiseño (Takic) *waxáawumay* 'little frog', from *waxáawut* 'frog' (Gudde 1998).

GUALALA (Calif., Sonoma Co.) \wä lä´ lə\. From Kashaya (Pomo) /walaali/, a shortening of /qhawalaali/, an Indian village; it is derived from /ahqha walaali/ 'water go-down-place'. English speakers folk-etymologized the name to *Walhalla,* and this in turn was re-spelled as **Gualala** under the mistaken impression that it was Spanish (Gudde 1998).

GUANO Creek (Ore., Lake Co.) \gwä´ nō\. From American Spanish *guano, huano* 'dung, fertilizer', from the word *wanu* in Quechua, a language of the Andean region (*RHD* 1987).

GUAPA (Calif., Riverside Co.) \wä´ pə\. The name of a Gabrielino (Takic) village, first written as *Guapia* and *Haupa* (Gudde 1998). The present spelling and pronunciation are like that of Spanish *guapa* 'pretty' (fem.).

GUATAY (Calif., San Diego Co.) \gwä tī´\. Probably from Diegueño (Yuman) *wataay* 'big house' (i.e., 'ceremonial house'), from *ewaa* 'house' plus *'etaay* 'big' (Gudde 1998).

GUAYULE Creek (Tex., Brewster Co.) \gwä yo͞o´ lē\. From the name of a desert plant that is a source of rubber; a Mexican Spanish word, from Nahuatl (Aztecan) *cuauh-olli* 'wood-rubber', from *cuauh-tli* 'tree, wood' and *olli* 'rubber', or *huauh-olli* 'amaranth-rubber', with *huauh-tli* 'amaranth, an edible plant' (*RHD* 1987).

GUEJITO (Calif., San Diego Co.) \wā hē´ tō\. Perhaps for Spanish *güejita,* a diminutive of *güeja,* which in northwest Mexico refers to a gourd vessel (Gudde 1998); it is a borrowing from Yaqui (Uto-Aztecan) *bweha'i* 'half gourd, for dipper or resonator' (Molina et al. 1999).

GUENOC (Calif., Lake Co.) \gwen´ok\. The name was applied in Mexican land grants to a lake that the Lake Miwoks called /wénok pólpol/ 'Guenoc lake' (Gudde 1998). This name may contain Lake Miwok /wéne/ 'medicine'; or it may be a borrowing from Wappo (Yukian) /wénnokh/, referring to the neighboring Southern Pomos.

GUERO Peak (Colo., Gunnison Co.) \wâr´ ō\. From *Güero,* the Spanish name of a Ute (Numic) leader. The Spanish term (also spelled *huero*) means 'fair in complexion' (Bright 1993).

GUEVAVI Canyon (Ariz., Santa Cruz Co.). This name was given to the first Spanish mission founded in Ariz., in 1701. Its Indian source has not been established (BGN 8201).

GUFMUT (Alaska, Baird Inlet B-2). The Yupik (Eskimo) name was reported in 1949 (Orth 1967).

GUGUAK Bay (Alaska, Seward A-3). The Alutiiq (Eskimo) name was reported in 1951 (Orth 1967).

GUHAO Inlet (Alaska, Craig D-4). The Tlingit name was published in 1964 (Orth 1967).

GUILICOS (Calif., Sonoma Co.) \wil´ i kōs\. From Lake Miwok /wiilok/ 'dusty' plus the Spanish masculine plural suffix /-os/ (Gudde 1998).

GUIQUE, El (N.Mex., Rio Arriba Co.) \gē´ kā\. Probably from a Tewa (Tanoan) placename, not otherwise identified; also written as **Quiqui**, **Guyqui** (Julyan 1998).

GUISHIEMANA Lake (Alaska, Beaver A-6). Koyukon (Athabaskan) *k'ish yi bənə,* lit. 'birch-in lake' (Kari 2000).

GUKTU Point (Alaska, Craig D-4). The Tlingit name was published in 1956 (Orth 1967).

GUKYUK (Alaska, Kwiguk D-5). The Yupik (Eskimo) name was published in 1899 (Orth 1967).

GULKANA (Alaska, Gulkana B-3) \gul kan´ ə\. From Ahtna (Athabaskan) *c'uul c'ena'* [k'uul k'əna'], lit. 'tearing river' (J. Kari p.c.).

GULL Island (Alaska, Beaver A-4). Corresponds to Koyukon (Athabaskan) *bats nu'u* 'gull's island' (Kari 2000).

GUNGYWAMP Hill (Conn., New London Co.) \gun´ jē wämp\. From SNEng. Algonquian <qunnuckqompsk> 'high rock', containing <qunni-> 'long', <ompsk> 'rock' (W. Cowan p.c.).

GUN Lake (Mich., Mason Co.). Perhaps a translation of Ojibwa (Algonquian) <Pashkisigan Sagaigan> (Vogel 1986); cf. *baashkizigan* 'gun' (from *baashkide* 'to explode'), *zaaga'igan* 'lake' (Nichols and Nyholm 1995).

GUNNUK Creek (Alaska, Petersburg D-6). The name, probably Tlingit, was recorded in 1951 (Orth 1967).

GUSDAGANE Point (Alaska, Dixon Entrance D-2). The Haida name was recorded in 1901 (Orth 1967).

GUSHDOIMAN Lake (Alaska, Beaver A-5). Koyukon (Athabaskan) *k'ałdoy bənə'* 'lake-outlet lake' (Kari 2000).

GUSHIATE Lake (Alaska, Beaver A-4). Koyukon (Athabaskan) *k'ush yeet bene'* 'in-the-willows lake' (Kari 2000).

GUTCHI Creek (Alaska, Craig D-4). The Tlingit name was recorded in 1949 (Orth 1967).

GUYANDOT River (W.Va., Wyoming Co.) \gī´ ən dot\. From the same origin as **Wyandot,** the name of an Iroquoian people. The placename **Guyandot** also occurs in Ohio (Lawrence Co.). Another related form **Guyandotte**, is found in W.Va. (Cabell Co.).

GWEEK River (Alaska, Bethel D-7) \gwēk\. The Yupik (Eskimo) name is *kuik* 'river' (L. Kaplan p.c.).

GWICH'IN (Alaska) \gwich´ in\. This name refers to an Indian people of central Alaska, speaking a language of the Athabaskan family; the term is also written **Kutchin.** It is derived from the Native American word *gwich'in,* meaning 'people of, dwellers at [a specified place]' (*HNAI* 6:530). Although the language has furnished many placenames to the topographic vocabulary of Alaska, the name of the people itself has not yet been used as a placename.

H

HA AMAR Creek (Calif., Humboldt Co.) \hä ə mär´\. From the Yurok placename *ho'omer* (Gudde 1998).

HACHASOFKEE Creek (Ga., Talbot Co.) \hach ə sof´ kē\. A Muskogee name meaning 'deep stream', from *hvcce* /háčči/ 'stream' and *sofkē* /sófki:/ 'deep' (Goff 1975; Martin and Mauldin 2000). A related form is **Hatchsophka** (Ala., Elmore Co.).

HACHEMEDEGA Creek (Ala., Coosa Co.) \hach i mə dē´ gə\. Muskogee *hvcce imvtēkē* /háčči (i)m-ati:kí:/ 'stream's edge', from *hvcce* 'stream', *im-* 'its', *vtēkē* 'edge' (Read 1984; Martin and Mauldin 2000).

HACKENSACK (N.J., Bergen Co.) \hak´ ən sak\. Perhaps from Unami Delaware (Algonquian) *ahkinkèshaki* 'place of sharp ground' (Kraft and Kraft 1985); cf. Munsee Delaware *kíineew* 'be sharp', *áhkuy* 'earth' (O'Meara 1996). The name also occurs in N.Y. (Rockland Co.) and in Minn. (Cass Co.).

HACKMATACK Pond (Maine, Waldo Co.) \hak´ mə tak\. The term refers to a dense undergrowth of native shrubs, such as tamarack and juniper; it may be from Western Abenaki (Algonquian; *RHD* 1987).

HADOKHTEN Lake (Alaska, Melozitna C-6). The Koyukon (Athabaskan) name was recorded in 1956 (Orth 1967). Perhaps related is **Hadotohedan Lake** (Alaska, Melozitna C-6), from the same source.

HADWEENZIC River (Alaska, Fort Yukon B-6) \həd wēn´ zik\. Gwich'in (Athabaskan) *oozrii njək* 'name stream' (Kari 2000); cf. *voozhri'* 'his name' (Peter 1979).

HAHANUDAN Lake (Alaska, Melozitna C-6). The Koyukon (Athabaskan) name was reported in 1956 (Orth 1967).

HAHATONKA (Mo., Camden Co.) \hä hä tong´ kə\. The name was probably coined by whites from Dakota (Siouan) elements (Ramsay 1952); cf. *ȟaȟá* 'waterfall', *tháka* 'large' (Riggs 1890).

HA HO NO GEH Canyon (Ariz., Coconino Co.). The Navajo (Athabaskan) name, recorded since about 1858, is said to mean 'too many washes', but the derivation is not clear (Granger 1983). The current Navajo name is said to be *nahonsheeshjéél* 'rough rocky canyon' (Linford 2000).

HAIDA \hī´ də\. The name of an Indian group living mainly on the northern coastline of British Columbia (Canada), with a small extension into southeastern Alaska. Their language may be remotely related to the Athabaskan family. The name **Haida** is from Northern Haida /háat'e:, háade:/ 'the people' (*HNAI* 7:258). As a placename, the term occurs in **Haida Point** (Wash., San Juan Co.), also written as **Haidah.**

HAITI Island (N.Y., Cayuga Co.) \hā´ tē\. Probably borrowed from the name of the Caribbean nation, from a Taino (Arawakan) term. Possibly from the same source is **Hayti** (S.Dak., Hamlin Co.) \hā´ tī\, folk-etymologized as "hay-tie" (i.e., 'to tie hay').

HAIVANA NAKYA (Ariz., Pima Co.) \hī vä nä näk´ yä\. O'odham (Piman) *hawañ naggia* 'crow hang' from *hawañ* 'crow' plus *naggia* 'hanging' (J. Hill p.c.).

HAIVAN VAYA (Ariz., Pima Co.) \hī vän vä´ yä\. O'odham (Piman) *haiwañ wahia* 'cow well', from *haiwañ* 'cow, cattle' and *wahia* 'well' (J. Hill p.c.).

HAIWEE (Calif., Inyo Co.) \hā´ wā\. Panamint (Numic) *heewi* 'dove' (Gudde 1998).

HAIYAHA Lake (Colo., Larimer Co.) \hä yä´ hä\. From an Arapaho (Algonquian) *hóó'óooy* 'it is rocky' (A. Cowell p.c.).

HAKATAI Canyon (Ariz., Coconino Co.) \hä´ kə tī\. Perhaps the Havasupai (Yuman) name for the Colorado River, meaning 'big water', containing *ha* 'water', *tay* 'big' (P. Munro p.c.).

HAKIHOKAKE Creek (N.J., Hunterdon Co.). Perhaps from a Delaware (Algonquian) word meaning 'plantation, field' (Becker 1964).

HALAGOW (Calif., Humboldt Co.) \hal´ ə gou\. From Yurok *helega'a,* the 'boat dance' that formed part an annual world renewal ceremony (Gudde 1998).

HALAWAKEE Creek (Ala., Lee Co.) \hal ə wak´ ē\. From Muskogee *holwvkē* /holwakí:/ 'bad' (Read 1984; Martin and Mauldin 2000). The writing **Halawaka** also occurs.

HALCHITA (Utah, San Juan Co.) \hal chē´ tə\. Navajo (Athabaskan) *halchíítah* 'among the red areas' (Linford 2000); cf. *łichíí'* 'red' (Young and Morgan 1987).

HALELANI (Utah, Salt Lake Co.) \hä lā lä´ nē\. Hawaiian, meaning 'house of the sky', from *hale* 'house', *lani* 'sky' (Pukui et al. 1974).

HALELEA (Utah, Salt Lake Co.) \hä lā lā´ ä\. Hawaiian, meaning 'house of joy', from *hale* 'house', *le'a* 'joy' (Pukui et al. 1974).

HALFBREED Rapids (Wis., Oneida Co.). The term has traditionally been used for a person of mixed Native American and European ancestry but is now considered offensive; terms like *mixed-blood* are sometimes used instead.

HALF DAY (Ill., Lake Co.). Named for a Potawatomi (Algonquian) leader; the term is said to be a translation of his Native American name, <Aptakisic>; cf. Potawatomi *apte'* 'half', *gizhguk* 'day' (Vogel 1963; Kansas 1997). **Half Day** also occurs in Kans. (Shawnee Co.). In addition, **Aptakisic** occurs as a placename (Ill., Lake Co.).

HALF PONE Point (Md., St. Mary's Co.). Perhaps a popular etymology from Va. Algonquian <apones, appoans> 'bread', from Proto-Algonquian **apwa:n-* 'thing roasted or baked', from **apwe-* 'to roast' (*RHD* 1987). The term *pone* itself entered English in the meaning 'bread', as in *corn pone* 'corn bread'.

HALGAITOH SPRING (Utah, San Juan Co.) \häl gī´ tō\. Navajo (Athabaskan) *halgai tó,* lit. 'plains water' (Linford 2000).

HALI MURK (Ariz., Pima Co.) \hä lē mûrk\. O'odham (Piman) *ha:lĭ mek* 'burnt squash', from *ha:lĭ* 'squash', *mek* [mɨk] 'burnt' (J. Hill p.c.).

HALLOCA Creek (Ga., Chattahoochee Co.) \hā´ lō kə\. Although in Muskogee territory, the name may be from Choctaw (Muskogean) *haloka* 'sacred, dear' (Goff 1975).

HALO Creek (Ore., Lane Co.) \hā´ lō\. From Chinook Jargon <ha´-lo> [hélo] 'no, not, none, without'. Perhaps from a Shoalwater Bay dialect of the Chinook language (D. Kinkade p.c.).

HALPATA (Fla., Columbia Co.) \hal pat´ ə\. From Hitchiti (Muskogean) *halpati* 'alligator' (J. Martin p.c.).

HALPATIOKEE River (Fla., Martin Co.) \hal pat ē ō´ kē\. Recorded in 1839 as <Al-pa-ti-okee>, from Hitchiti (Muskogean) *halpati-oki,* lit. 'alligator water' (Read 1934; J. Martin p.c.).

HALTHALDA Hill (Alaska, Nabesna D-3). From Upper Tanana (Athabaskan) *x̲aal ddhäl',* lit. 'cisco mountain'. The nearby **Halthmund Lake** is from *x̲aal männ',* meaning 'cisco (a fish) lake' (J. Kari p.c.).

HALU Creek (Alaska, Tanana D-2). From Koyukon (Athabaskan), of unclear derivation (Orth 1967).

HALUTU Ridge (Alaska, Skagway B-2). The Tlingit name, said to mean 'promontory', was reported in 1923 (Orth 1967).

HAMIDRIK (Ariz., Coconino Co.). This is the surname of a Havasupai (Yuman) family, said to mean 'nighthawk' (Brian 1992). Also written as **Hamidreek.**

HAMMA HAMMA River (Wash., Mason Co.) \ham ə ham´ ə\. An abbreviation of Twana (Salishan) /dəxʷχəbχábay/ 'place of the giant horsetail plant', from /dəxʷ-/ 'place', /χəbχáb/ 'horsetail tuber', and /-ay/ 'plant' (D. Kinkade p.c.). The alternation of *b* and *m* is characteristic of languages in the area.

HAMMONASSET Beach (Conn., New Haven Co.) \ham ə nas´ ət\. An Algonquian name, perhaps meaning 'at the place of small islands' (Huden 1962).

HANAGITA Lake (Alaska, McCarthy A-8) \hä nē git´ ə\. Named for an Ahtna (Athabaskan) leader; reported in 1911 (Orth 1967).

HANAUPAH (Calif., Inyo Co.) \hə nōō´ pä, han´ ə pä\. From Panamint (Numic); cf. *hunuppin* 'canyon', *paa* 'water' (Gudde 1998). Perhaps related is **Hannapah** (Nev., Nye Co.).

HANDSOME LAKE Campground (Pa., Warren Co.). Named for a Seneca (Iroquoian) leader; his Native American name was *ganyodaiyo'*, derived from *ganyodaiyo:h* 'good, nice, or beautiful lake' (W. Chafe p.c.). There is also a **Handsome Lake** in Mich. (Oakland Co.).

HANEY (Okla., Seminole Co.) \hā´ nē\. Named to have been named for a Seminole (Muskogean), the Reverend Willie Haney (Shirk 1974).

HANNAHATCHEE Creek (Ga., Stewart Co.) \han ə hach´ ē\. Perhaps from Muskogee *vcenv* /ačína/ 'cedar', *hvcce* /háčči/ 'stream' (Read 1949–50).

HANNAPAH (Nev., Nye Co.) \han´ ə pä\. Possibly from Shoshoni (Numic) /honoppaa/ 'bat springs', from /hono-ppittsih/ 'bat' (/-pittsih/ 'scary thing'), /paa/ 'water' (J. McLaughlin p.c.). Perhaps related is **Hanaupah** (Calif., Inyo Co.).

HANO (Ariz., Navajo Co.) \hä´ nō\. This community on First Mesa in the Hopis Reservation, also called **Tewa Village,** is occupied by descendants of Tewa (Tanoan) Indians from the Rio Grande valley of New Mexico, who took refuge with the Hopi during the days of Spanish colonial rule. The people of Hano, also called "Hopi-Tewa" or "Arizona Tewa," speak both Hopi (Uto-Aztecan) and Tewa. **Hano** is from Hopi *haano,* borrowed from Tewa *tháanu,* referring to an abandoned pueblo in N.Mex.; this is the source of the word *Tanoan* as a name for the language family to which Tewa belongs (*HNAI* 9:601).

HANSKA, Lake (Minn., Brown Co.) \han´ skə\. From Dakota (Siouan) *hą́ska* 'long' (Upham 2001; Riggs 1890).

HAPAHA (Calif., San Diego Co.) \hä´ pə hä\. Perhaps a Diegueño (Yuman) placename, but its derivation has not been traced (Gudde 1998).

HAPPOGUE (N.Y., Suffolk Co.) \hä´ pog, hap´ og\. The Algonquian name may refer to 'overflowed land' (Beauchamp 1907; Tooker 1911). The variant writing **Hauppaugue** also occurs.

HARCUVAR (Ariz., La Paz Co.) \här kə vär´, här´ kə vär\. Mojave (Yuman) *ha-kavaar,* shortened from *'ahá kaváar* 'there's no water', containing *'ahá* 'water', *kaváar* 'be not' (P. Munro p.c.).

HARD GROUND Canyon (N.Mex., McKinley Co.). Corresponds to Navajo (Athabaskan) *ni' hóttizí* 'hard ground' (Linford 2000); cf. *ni'* 'earth', *hóttiz* '(area) to be hard' (Young and Morgan 1987).

HARJO (Okla., Pottawatomie Co.) \här´ jō, här´ ō\. A Muskogean surname, originally a title, *haco* /há:čo/, sometimes translated as 'berserk, crazy' (Shirk 1974; Martin and Mauldin 2000).

HARQUA (Ariz., Maricopa Co.) \här´ kwä\. This seems to contain Mojave (Yuman) *'ahá, ha-* 'water', but otherwise its derivation is unclear (P. Munro p.c.). Possibly it is an abbreviated form of the same Mojave name that appears in English as **Harquahala Mountain** (Ariz., La Paz Co.).

HARQUAHALA Mountain (Ariz., La Paz Co.) \här´ kwə hā lə, här kwə hā´ lə\. Probably from Mojave (Yuman) *'avií hakwahél,* the name of a mountain range. This seems to mean 'rock where water flows', containing *'avií* 'rock', *ha-* 'water', and a verb root *-hel* that apparently means 'to flow' (P. Munro p.c.).

HARRASEEKET River (Maine, Cumberland Co.) \hâr ə sē´ kət\. Perhaps Abenaki (Algonquian), meaning 'full of obstacles' (Huden 1962).

HASBIDITO Creek (Ariz., Apache Co.) \häs bi dē´ tō\. Navajo (Athabaskan) *hasbídí tó,* lit. 'turtle-dove spring' (Linford 2000).

HASGOX Point (Alaska, Gareloi Island A-3). Aleut *haasxux̂* 'spear-thrower' (Bergsland 1994).

HASHAMOMUCK Beach (N.Y., Suffolk Co.). The Algonquian name is of disputed derivation (Ruttenber 1906; Beauchamp 1907; Tooker 1911).

HASHAN CHUCHG (Ariz., Pima Co.) \hä´ sän chōōchk\. O'odham (Piman), meaning 'standing saguaro cactus', from *ha:ṣañ* 'saguaro', *cu:ck* 'standing' (J. Hill p.c.).

HASHAWHA (Md., Carroll Co.). The Algonquian name may mean 'the place over across' (Kenny 1984).

HASHUQUA (Miss., Noxubee Co.) \hä shōō´ kwə\. Perhaps from Choctaw (Muskogean) *hashshok* 'grass', *waaya* 'to grow' (P. Munro p.c.).

HASKA Creek (Alaska, Skagway A-2) \has´ kə\. The Tlingit name, said to mean 'little falls', was reported in 1912 (Orth 1967).

HASSAN Township (Minn., Hennepin Co.) \hə sän\. Abbreviated from Dakota (Siouan) *cąhasą* 'sugar maple tree' (Upham 2001; Riggs 1890). The fuller form **Chanhassen** is also a placename in Minn. (Carver Co.); cf. also **Tenhassen Township** (Martin Co.).

HASSAYAMPA (Ariz., Maricopa Co.) \has ə yam´ pə, häs ə yäm´ pə\. Perhaps from Yavapai (Yuman) *'ha syáamvoo,* containing *'ha* 'water'; it may mean something like 'smooth running water' (Granger 1983; P. Munro p.c.). The variant **Hassiamp** also occurs.

HASSIAH Inlet (Alaska, Craig A-2). The Tlingit name was reported in 1905 (Orth 1967).

HASSIAMP (Ariz., Maricopa Co.) \has´ ə yamp\. A variant of **Hassayampa**; see above.

HATCHAPALOO Creek (Miss., Smith Co.) \hach ə pə lōō\. Perhaps from Choctaw (Muskogean), meaning 'river where (fish) are netted', from *hahcha* 'river', *aa-* 'place', *pihli* 'to sweep up, scoop up' (e.g., fish) (Seale 1939; P. Munro p.c.).

HATCHECHUBBEE (Ala., Russell Co.) \hach ə chub´ ē\. The name of a Muskogee village, *hvcce cvpv* /hačči-čapa/, said to mean 'stream-edge', containing *hacce* /háčči/ 'stream' (Martin and Mauldin 2000).

HATCHEE Branch (Ala., Butler Co.) \hach´ē\. Probably from Muskogee *hvcce* /háčči/ 'stream'.

HATCHEETIGBEE Landing (Ala., Washington Co.) \hach i tig´ bē\. A variant of **Hatchetigbee**; see below.

HATCHET Creek (Ala., Coosa Co.) \hach´ ət\. Said to be a translation of Muskogee *pocoshvcce* /počos-háčči/, a tribal town; lit. 'ax creek', from *pocoswv* /počóswa/ 'ax', *hacce* /háčči/ 'creek' (Read 1984; Martin and Mauldin 2000).

HATCHETIGBEE (Ala., Washington Co.) \hach i tig´ bē\. From Choctaw *hahcha-tikpi*, translated as 'river knob', from *hachcha* 'river', *tikpi* 'bend in water course' (Read 1984; P. Munro p.c.) A variant spelling is **Hatcheetigbee**.

HATCHETT Creek (Ala., Coosa Co.) \hach´ ət\. A variant spelling of **Hatchet Creek**; see above.

HATCHIE (Miss., Tippah Co.) \hach´ ē\. Probably from Choctaw (Muskogean) *hachcha* 'river' (Seale 1939; P. Munro p.c.). The name also occurs in Tenn. (Madison Co.).

HATCHIE COON (Ark., Poinsett Co.) \hach´ ē kōōn\. Perhaps derived from Choctaw *hachcha* 'river' plus *koni* 'young cane' or *konih* 'skunk' (Dickinson 1995; P. Munro p.c.).

HATCHINEHA, Lake (Fla., Osceola Co.) \hə chin´ ə hô\. Possibly from Muskogee *vcenvho* /ačinahó:/ 'cypress tree' (Read 1934; Martin and Mauldin 2000).

HATCHITIGBEE Bar (Ala., Washington Co.) \hach i tig´ bē\. A variant of **Hatchetigbee Landing**, from Choctaw (Read 1984).

HATCHSOPHKA (Ala., Elmore Co.) \hach sof´ kə\. The name is related to **Hachasofkee Creek** (Ga., Talbot Co.); see above.

HAT Creek (Calif., Shasta Co.). Perhaps from the Achumawi (Shastan) placename /hatiwîwi/ (Gudde 1998). Another **Hat Creek** (S.Dak., Fall River Co.) is said to be a translation of Lakhota (Siouan) *waphóštą* 'hat, bonnet' (Sneve 1973; B. Ingham p.c.).

HATDOLITNA Canyon (Alaska, Hughes A-3). The Koyukon (Athabaskan) name was reported in 1956 (Orth 1967).

HAT LIE Lake (Alaska, Fort Yukon B-4). From Gwich'in (Athabaskan), of unclear derivation (Orth 1967).

HATOBI (Okla., McCurtain Co.) \hä´ tō bē\. Perhaps from a Choctaw (Muskogean) "war name" *hattak-abi* 'person killer', containing *hattak* 'person', *abi* 'to kill' (Shirk 1974; P. Munro p.c.).

HATSEEGATLOTH Lake (Alaska, Kateel River B-2). The Koyukon (Athabaskan) name was reported in 1955 (Orth 1967).

HATTERAS, Cape (N.C., Dare Co.) \hat´ ə rəs\. The name may be Algonquian, referring to sparse vegetation (Payne 1985).

HATWAI Creek (Idaho, Nez Perce Co.) \hat´ wā\. The name is from Nez Perce (Sahaptian) *héetwey*, perhaps containing *-wey* 'creek' (Aoki 1994).

HAUANI Creek (Okla., Marshall Co.) \hə wä´ nē\. From Chickasaw (Muskogean) *hayowani'* 'worm' (P. Munro p.c.). Also written as **Hauwani Creek**.

HAULAPAI Island (Ariz., Mohave Co.) \wä´ lə pī\. From the same source as **Hualapai**; see below.

HAUNTED Butte (S.Dak., Corson Co.). Corresponds to Lakhota (Siouan) *wanáǧi-s'e*, lit. 'ghost-like', referring to images inscribed on a rock (Sneve 1973; A. Taylor p.c.).

HAUPPAUGUE (N.Y., Suffolk Co.). The Algonquian name may refer to 'overflowed land' (Beauchamp 1907; Tooker 1911). The variant writing **Happogue** also occurs.

HAUTI Island (Alaska, Craig D-4). The Tlingit name was published in 1964 (Orth 1967).

HAUWANI Creek (Okla., Marshall Co.) \hə wä´ nē\. A variant of **Hauani;** see above.

HAVANA \hə van´ ə\. From Spanish *La Habana,* the capital of Cuba; originally from the Taino (Arawakan) language of the West Indies. The name occurs in several parts of the United States (e.g., Fla., Gadsden Co.; Ill., Mason Co.; and Kans., Montgomery Co.).

HAVASU Creek (Ariz., Coconino Co.) \hav´ ə sōō\. From Havasupai (Yuman) *havasu* 'blue water', from *ha-* 'water' and *vasu* 'blue' (P. Munro p.c.). The name of the **Havasupai** \hav ə sōō´ pī\ people and language means 'Havasu people', containing *-pai* 'person, people'. Note, however, that the name of **Lake Havasu** on the Colorado River (Ariz., Mohave Co.; Calif., San Bernardino Co.) is from Mojave (Yuman) *havasúu* 'blue'; cf. *'ahá havasúu* 'blue water', referring to the Colorado River south of Parker Dam (Gudde 1998).

HAWAII \hə wī´ ē\. Apart from its occurrence in the name of the state of **Hawai'i** and the island of **Hawai'i**, plus many other placenames in that state, **Hawaii** occurs as a placename in a few locations of the mainland United States; thus there is a **Hawaii Park** in Ill. (Cook Co.) **Hawaiian** occurs in **Hawaiian Gardens** (Calif., Los Angeles Co.) and **Hawaiian Island** (Mo., Miller Co.). Terms related to the placename **Hawai'i** occur in many parts of Polynesia (e.g., in New Zealand Maori *Havaiki* and Samoan *Savai'i*; the original Polynesian form was probably *Savaiki*). In some areas, but not in **Hawai'i**, this name refers to the homeland of the Polynesian people, or to the underworld home of the dead (Pukui et al. 1974).

HA WHI YALIN Wash (Ariz., Navajo Co.). The Navajo (Athabaskan) name is said to be *hahoyílíní,* translated as 'up well flow' (Linford 2000).

HAWIKUH (N.Mex., Cibola Co.) \hä´ wi ko͞o\. This archaeological site was once a Zuni village encountered by Spanish explorers in 1539. The name was later written <Aguico> (Julyan 1998).

HAWK Creek (Minn., Renville Co.). Corresponds to the Dakota (Siouan) name <Chetamba> (Upham 2001); cf. *cetą* 'chicken-hawk' (Riggs 1890).

HAWKEYE (N.Y., Clinton Co.). This perhaps goes back to James Fenimore Cooper's novel *Last of the Mohicans*; in which the name was given by Delaware (Algonquian) Indians to a fictitious white scout and trapper. There is also a **Hawkeye** in Iowa (Fayette Co.), and the term is used to refer to natives of that state. This usage may refer to Cooper's creation or may echo the name of **Black Hawk**, a Sauk (Algonquian) leader whose name is attached to many other locations in Iowa (Vogel 1983).

HAW River (N.C., Chatham Co.). Shortened from Saxapahaw, a tribal name (I. Goddard, p.c.).

HAWZERAH Lake (Alaska, Bettles C-4). The Koyukon (Athabaskan) name was reported in 1931 (Orth 1967).

HAYMOCK Lake (Maine, Piscataquis Co.) \hā´ mok\. Abbreviated from the Abenaki (Algonquian) placename <Pongokwahemook>, meaning 'woodpecker place' (Rutherford 1970).

HAYNACH (Colo., Grand Co.) \hā´ nak\. From Arapaho (Algonquian) *hííínech* 'snow water' (Bright 1993).

HAYO-WENT-HA Point (Mich., Antrim Co.) \hā yō wen´ tə\. Probably from an unidentified Indian language (Vogel 1986).

HAYSOP Creek (Ala., Bibb Co.) \hā´ sop\. Probably from Choctaw (Muskogean) *hoshapa* 'black gum tree' (Read 1984; P. Munro p.c.).

HAYTI (S.Dak., Hamlin Co.) \hā´ tī\. Possibly borrowed from the name of the Caribbean nation of Haiti, of Taino (Arawakan) Indian origin, and folk-etymologized as "hay-tie" (i.e., 'to tie hay'). Perhaps from the same source is **Haiti Island** (N.Y., Cayuga Co.).

HAYWITCH Creek (Wash., King Co.) \hā´ wich\. Said to have been named for a Native American man noted as a shaman, language not identified (BGN 1999).

HEAD Island (N.Y., Clinton Co.). Corresponds to Western Abenaki (Algonquian) *odébsék,* lit. 'where their heads are', from *o-* '3rd singular posssessor', *-deb-* 'head', *-sek* 'place'. The historic name **Head Island** has been replaced by **Ash Island** (Day 1981:151). The placename **Head Rock** (Ariz., Apache Co.) corresponds to Navajo (Athabaskan) *tsé bitsii'í* 'rock's head', with *tsé* 'rock' plus *bitsii'* 'its head' (Linford 2000).

HEAGAN Mountain (Maine, Waldo Co.). Possibly named for Sampson Heagan, a seventeenth-century Algonquian leader (Huden 1962).

HEBADIN'A (N.Mex., Cibola Co.). The Zuni name of a shrine used by a religious society (Ferguson and Hart 1985).

HECKATOO Landing (Ark., Lincoln Co.) \hek´ ə to͞o\. Named for a leader of the Quapaw (Siouan) people in the early nineteenth century; from /heka ttǫ/ 'big buzzard' (Dickinson 1995; R. Rankin p.c.).

HEEBEECHEECHE, Lake (Wyo., Fremont Co.) \hē bə chē´ chē\. Said to be named for a Shoshoni (Numic) leader (Urbanek 1974). His name may have been *hipi-ttsi-ttsi* [hivittšittši] 'little drinker', from *hipi* 'to drink' plus a doubled diminutive suffix *-tsi.* Another possibility, even as a man's name, is /hɨpittsittsi/ [hɨvittšittši] 'little old woman', from /hɨpittsi/ 'old woman' plus /-ttsi/ 'little' (J. McLaughlin p.c.).

HE HE Mountain (Wash., Okanogan Co.) \hē´ hē\. From Chinook Jargon <he´-he> [híhi] 'to laugh', from Chinookan /héhe/ (D. Kinkade p.c.). Related spellings occur in **Hehe Creek**

(Ore., Lane Co.) and **Hee Hee Creek** (Wash., Jefferson Co.).

HEINTOGA (N.C., Swain Co.) \hīn tō´ gə\. Supposedly from Cherokee (Iroquoian) <i-yen-to-ga> 'hiding place' (M. Toomey p.c.).

HEK'O YAL'A (N.Mex., Cibola Co.). A Zuni placename; cf. /yala/ 'mountain' (Ferguson and Hart 1985; Newman 1958).

HELISWA (Okla., Seminole Co.) \hə lis´ wə\. From Muskogee *heleswv* /hilíswa/ 'medicine' (Martin and Mauldin 2000).

HELOTES (Tex., Bexar Co.) \hel ō´ tis\. From Mexican Spanish *elotes* 'ears of sweet corn' (Tarpley 1980), the plural of *elote,* from Nahuatl (Aztecan) *elotl.*

HENCOOP Creek (S.C., Anderson Co.). Probably a folk-etymology from earlier <Hencub>; perhaps from Cherokee <hungu, hinku> 'how much?' (Pickens 1961–62:6).

HERON Lake (Minn., Crow Wing Co.). Corresponds to Dakota (Siouan) <Okabena> 'herons' nests', from *hok'á* 'heron' and *be* 'to hatch' (Upham 2001; Riggs 1890).

HESHODA BITSULLIYA (N.Mex., San Juan Co.). The Zuni name means 'round house', from /hešota/ 'house' and /pitsulliya/ 'be round' (Ferguson and Hart 1985; Newman 1958).

HESHODA YALT'A (N.Mex., Cibola Co.). The Zuni name contains /hešota/ 'house' (Ferguson and Hart 1985; Newman 1958).

HESHOTAUTHLA Historic Site (N.Mex., McKinley Co.). Perhaps Zuni for 'nearby house', from /hešota/ 'house' and /uɬɬa/ 'to be near, close' (Ferguson and Hart 1985; Newman 1958).

HETCH HETCHY (Calif., Tuolumne Co.) \hech hech´ ē\. The original form was <Hatchatchie>, perhaps from Southern Sierra Miwok *aččačča* 'magpie' (Gudde 1998).

HETTA (Alaska, Craig A-2) \het´ ə\. The name is perhaps Tlingit, reported in 1905 (Orth 1967).

HETTEN (Calif., Trinity Co.) \het´ ən\. From Wintu *xetin* 'camas', referring an edible root. Derived from this is **Hettenshaw** (CA, Trinity Co.) \het´ ən shô\, from Wintu /xetin č'aaw/ 'camas sing'; the plants were said to sing in that location (Gudde 1998).

HIACK Creek (Ore., Tillamook Co.) \hī´ ak\. Chinook Jargon <hy-ak> [háiæk] 'quick, fast, hurry', from Chinookan *áyaq* 'quickly' (D. Kinkade p.c.). Another spelling is used in **Hyaak Creek** (Idaho, Latah Co.).

HIAGI (Ala., Russell Co.) \hī´ ə gē\. Said to be the name of a former Muskogee town, also written <Hiaggee, Haihagi, Ihagi>, perhaps meaning 'groaners', from *hihketv* /heyhkitá/ 'to groan' (Read 1984; Martin and Mauldin 2000).

HIALEAH (Fla., Dade Co.) \hī ə lē´ ə\. Perhaps from Muskogee *hvyakpo* /hayakpó:/ 'prairie' plus *here* /-hiɬí/ 'good' (Read 1934; Martin and Mauldin 2000); but little seems to be left of the first part of the compound.

HIAMOVI Mountain (Colo., Grand Co.) \hē ə mō´ vē\. Supposedly the name of a Cheyenne (Algonquian) leader (Bright 1993).

HIAWASSEE (Ga., Towns Co.) \hī ə wä´ sē, hī wä´ sē\. From Cherokee (Iroquoian) <ayuh-wasi> 'meadow' (Read 1934; Krakow 1975). The name is written differently in the name of the **Hiwassee River** (Ga., Towns Co.; N.C., Cherokee Co.; Tenn., Meigs Co.) and is also written as **Hiawassie** (Ill., Randolph Co.).

HIAWATHA \hī ə wä´ thə\. This term became popular as a placename because of Longfellow's popular narrative poem *Hiawatha.* Although Longfellow took most of the features of his story from the Ojibwa (Algonquian) people of the Great Lakes area, he borrowed the name of his protagonist from a legendary hero of the Iroquois, called in Onondaga *hayę́hwàtha* (*HNAI* 15:422). Some of the places that have been named after Hiawatha are in Iowa (Linn Co.), Pa. (Wayne Co.), and Wis. (Vilas Co.).

HICHITEE Creek (Ga., Chattahoochee Co.) \hich´ ə tē\. Also written **Hitchiti** and **Hitchita**

Creek; the term refers to a Muskogean people and language of Ga., and to their tribal town in the Creek Confederacy (Krakow 1975). The language is still spoken among the Seminole community of Fla. Derivation of the term is from Muskogee *hecete* /hičíti/ or *hecetv* /hičíta/, the name of the tribal town (Martin and Mauldin 2000).

HICKIWAN (Ariz., Pima Co.) \hik´ i wän\. From O'odham (Piman) *hikiwañ* 'jagged cut' (J. Hill p.c.).

HICKORY. The name of the tree and of its edible nuts, native to the eastern United States, is shortened from CAC Algonquian <pocohicora>, a milky drink made from hickory nuts (*RHD* 1987). Among placenames based on **Hickory** are those found in Iowa (Allamakee Co.), La. (Avoyelles Par.), and Wis. (Oconto Co.). A possibly related name is **Bohicket Creek** (S.C., Charleston Co.).

HICO (Tex., Hamilton Co.) \hī´ kō\. The origin of the name is unclear, but it may be related to the name of a Caddoan Indian group, written as <Hico> or <Hueco> (Tarpley 1980) or now as in the placename **Waco** (Tex., McLennan Co.). There is also a **Hico** in W.Va. (Fayette Co.), which may or may not be related (Kenny 1945).

HICORUM (Calif., San Bernardino Co.) \hī´ kôr əm\. Named for <Hi-corum>, a Chemehuevi (Numic) Indian; the term is apparently /haiku-rɨmpa/ 'white-man mouth', from /haiku/ 'white man' plus /tɨmpa/ 'mouth' (Gudde 1998). A perhaps related placename is **Hiko** (Nev., Lincoln Co.).

HICPOCHEE, Lake (Fla., Glades Co.) \hīk pō´ chē\. The Muskogee name means 'little prairie', from *hvyakpo* /hayakpó:/ 'prairie' plus *-uce* /-oči/ 'small' (Martin and Mauldin 2000).

HIDDEN TIMBER (S.Dak., Todd Co.). Probably a translation of Lakhota (Siouan) *čhą náȟmapi,* containing *čhą* 'tree' and *naȟma* 'to hide' (B. Ingham p.c.).

HIGGANUM (Conn., Middlesex Co.) \hig´ ə nəm\. A shortening from SNEng. Algonquian <Tomheganompsket, Tomheganomset> 'at the axe rock', from <tomhegun-> 'axe, tomahawk', <-ompsk> 'rock', <-et> 'place' (Trumbull 1881; W. Cowan p.c.).

HIGHTOWER (Ga., Forsyth Co.) \hī´ tou ər\. A folk-etymological transformation of the name of a Cherokee (Iroquoian) settlement <Itawa> (Krakow 1975); the word may be a borrowing from Catawba (Siouan) *iitaawaa* 'longleaf pine tree' (B. Rudes p.c.). There is also a **Hightower Creek** in Ga. (Towns Co.), but the settlement of **Hightower** in Alabama (Cleburne Co.) is said to derive from an English family name. The Cherokee term <Itawa> was also adopted as an English placename in **Etowah County** (Ala.), **Etowah River** (Ga.), and at other locations (Ark., Mississippi Co.; Fla., Lake Co.; N.C., Henderson Co.; and Tenn. (McMinn Co.).

HIKO (Nev., Lincoln Co.) \hī´ kō\. From a word meaning 'white man' in several Indian languages of the area; cf. Chemehuevi (Numic) *háiku(u).* Perhaps from Spanish *mexicano* 'Mexican'. A possibly related name is **Hicorum** (Calif., San Bernardino Co.).

HILINE Lake (Alaska, Tyonek C-4). Perhaps shortened from Ahtna (Athabaskan) *bak'elghiłi bena,* lit. 'lake in which something is clubbed', with *bena* 'lake' (Kari 1999:80).

HILLABAHATCHEE Creek (Ala., Randolph Co.; Ga., Heard Co.) \hil ə bə hach´ ē\. The Muskogee name means 'Hillabee creek', derived from *helvpe* /hilapi/, the tribal town called **Hillabee** in English, plus /háčči/ 'stream' (Krakow 1975; Martin and Mauldin 2000).

HILLABEE Creek (Ala., Tallapoosa Co.) \hil´ ə bē\. A Muskogee tribal town, adapted from *helvpe* /hílapi/ (Read 1984; Martin and Mauldin 2000). There is also a **Hillabee** in Okla. (McIntosh Co.), and a **Hillabi** in Ala. (Tallapoosa Co.). **Hillabeehago Branch** (Ala., Randolph Co.) appears also to be based on the tribal town *helvpe,* but the derivation is not clear.

HILOKEE Creek (Ga., Lee Co.) \hi lō´ kə\. Possibly from Muskogee *helokwv* /hilókwa/ 'gum, wax' (Read 1949–50; Martin and Mauldin 2000) An alternative spelling is **Hiloka**

Creek (Ga., Terrell Co.). The placename **Alaqua Bayou** (Fla., Walton Co.) may be related.

HILOLO (Fla., Okeechobee Co.) \hi lō´ lō\. From Muskogee *hvlolo* /halólo/ 'curlew', a word chosen out of a published vocabulary as a name for a railroad station (Read 1934; Martin and Mauldin 2000).

HIMMONAH (Okla., Garvin Co.) \him´ ə nä\. Perhaps abbreviated from an expression meaning 'new place'; cf. Chickasaw (Muskogean) *himona(')* 'new' (Shirk 1974; P. Munro p.c.).

HIOUCHI (Calif., Del Norte Co.) \hī o͞o´ chē\. Named with an Indian word, language unidentified, supposedly meaning 'blue waters' (Gudde 1989).

HITCHITA (Okla., McIntosh Co.) \hich´ i tə, hi chē´ tə\. The term refers to a Muskogean people and language of Ga., also written **Hitchiti**, and to their tribal town in the Creek Confederacy (Krakow 1975). The language is still spoken among the Seminole community of Fla. Derivation of the term is from Muskogee *hecete* /hičíti/ or *hecetv* /hičíta/, the name of the tribal town. The placename is also written **Hichitee Creek**. There is a **Hitchiti Creek** in Ga. (Jones Co.).

HITESHITAK Mountain (Alaska, Skagway C-4). The Tlingit name was published in 1952 (Orth 1967).

HIWASSEE River (Ga., Towns Co; N.C., Cherokee Co.; Tenn., Meigs Co.) \hī wä´ sē\. From Cherokee (Iroquoian) <ayuhwasi> 'meadow' (Read 1934; Goff 1975). The name is spelled differently in the community of **Hiawassee** (Ga., Towns Co.) as well as in **Hiawassie** (Ill., Randolph Co.) and **Hiwasse** (Ark., Benton Co.). In Mo. (Oregon Co.) there is a **Hi Wassie**—and logically enough, a nearby **Low Wassie** (Ramsay 1952).

HIYU Mountain (Ore., Clackamas Co.) \hī´ yo͞o\. Chinook Jargon <hy-iu´, hi-yu> [haiú] 'much, many', from Nootka /ḥayo/ 'ten', perhaps confused with Nootka *aya* 'much, many' (D. Kinkade p.c.). The name also occurs in Idaho (Boise Co.) Another spelling is used in **Hi Yu Spring** (Ore., Grant Co.).

HOA MURK (Ariz., Pima Co.) \hō ə mûrk\. O'odham (Piman) *hoa mek* 'burnt basket', from *hoa* 'basket', *mek* [mɨk] 'burnt' (Granger 1983; J. Hill p.c.).

HOBCAW Creek (S.C., Charleston Co.) \hob´ kô\. Earlier written <Habcaw> (Waddell 1980). Perhaps from an unidentified Indian language (Pickens 1961–62:6).

HOBOKEN (N.J., Hudson Co.) \hō´ bō kən\. Perhaps from Delaware (Algonquian) <hupokën> 'tobacco pipe'; or perhaps from a place called *Hoboken* in the Netherlands (Ruttenber 1906; Becker 1964). Cf. also **Pipe Creek** (Ind., Madison Co.).

HOBOLOCHITTO Creek (Miss., Pearl River Co.) \hə bō lə chit´ ə\. Perhaps Choctaw (Muskogean) for 'big thicket', from *aabohli* 'thicket', *chito* 'big' (Seale 1939; P. Munro p.c.).

HOBOMOCK Pond (Mass., Plymouth Co.) \hob´ ə mok\. From SNEng. Algonquian, perhaps 'the place where Hobomock dwells', referring to an evil spirit, also written as <Hobbomock> (W. Cowan p.c.).

HOBUCK Creek (Miss., Yalobusha Co.) \hō´ buk\. From Choctaw (Muskogean) *hobak* 'castrated animal or person' (Seale 1939, P. Munro p.c.).

HOBUCKEN (N.C., Pamlico Co.) \hō´ buk ən\. Named for **Hoboken**, N.J. (Hudson Co.; Powell 1968), which may have either an Algonquian or a Dutch origin.

HOCHANDOCHTLA Mountain (Alaska, Melozitna C-4). The Koyukon (Athabaskan) name was recorded in 1956 (Orth 1967).

HOCHATOWN (Okla., McCurtain Co.) \hō´ chə toun\. The first element may be from Choctaw (Muskogean) *hachcha* 'river' (Shirk 1974; P. Munro p.c.).

HOCHILAGOK Hill (Alaska, Marshall C-7). The Yupik (Eskimo) name is said to refer to the lesser sandhill crane; it has been translated as 'color body red' (Orth 1967).

HOCHUBBEE (Okla., Le Flore Co.) \hō chub´ bē, hoch´ ə bē\. From Choctaw (Muskogean) *hochokbi* 'cave, cavern' (Shirk 1974; P. Munro p.c.).

HO-CHUNK \hō´ chungk\. This is the preferred self-designation of the people and language otherwise called **Winnebago,** of the Siouan linguistic family, living primarily in Wis. (The term **Winnebago** is of Algonquian origin.) **Ho-Chunk** is an English spelling of the native term *hoočąk*; the people as a whole are usually called *hoočą́gra* (K. Miner p.c.).

HOCKANUM (Conn., Hartford Co.) \hok´ ə nəm\. Probably derived from an Algonquian word meaning 'a hook' (Trumbull 1881).

HOCKESSIN (Del., New Castle Co.) \hō kes´ in\. The name has been written <Okesian, Hocesion, Okesan> (etc.); it is probably from Delaware (Algonquian), but the derivation is not clear (Heck et al. 1966).

HOCKHOCKSON Brook (N.J., Monmouth Co.) \hok hok´ sən\. Perhaps from Delaware (Algonquian), meaning 'a plantation', written as <hakihakan> (Becker 1964).

HOCKING County (Ohio) \hok´ ing\. Perhaps abbreviated from a Delaware (Algonquian) term <hockhocking> (Miller 1996); cf. Unami Delaware /hákhakənk/ 'bottle-gourd place', from /hákhakw/ 'bottle gourd'; or perhaps from Unami /há:kiŋ/ 'on the land' (M. McCafferty p.c.). The placename **Hocking** also occurs in Pa. (Somerset Co.) and Iowa (Monroe Co.).

HOCKOMOCK River (Mass., Plymouth Co.) \hok´ ə mok\. From SNEng. Algonquian, meaning 'fish-hook land'; cf. <hoquaun-> 'fish-hook', <-auke> 'land' (W. Cowan p.c.). Also written as **Hockmock, Hockamock. A Hockomock** in Maine (Sagadahoc Co.) was earlier written as <Hobbomocca>, said to be an Abenaki (Algonquian) word meaning 'hell'. A place called **Hell Gate** is nearby (Eckstorm 1941). A probably related name is **Hockomonco Pond** (Mass., Worcester Co.) \hok ə mong´ kō\.

HODATIC River (Alaska, Kateel River C-3). The Koyukon (Athabaskan) name was reported in 1900 (Orth 1967).

HODCHODKEE Creek (Ga., Quitman Co.). Perhaps from Muskogee *hvcce* /háčči/ 'stream', *cutke* /-čótk-i/ 'small' (Martin and Mauldin 2000).

HODEGADEN Creek (Alaska, Nulato D-4). The Koyukon (Athabaskan) name was reported in 1954 (Orth 1967).

HODZANA River (Alaska, Beaver B-2) \hōd zan´ ə\. Koyukon (Athabaskan) *oodzaa' no'*, containing *no'* 'stream' (Kari 2000).

HOGAN \hō´ gän, hō´ gən\. A term for a traditional Navajo (Athabaskan) house; the Navajo word is *hooghan* 'home' (Young and Morgan 1987). This is probably the origin of placenames such as **Hogan Ridge** (Ariz., Coconino Co.), **Hogan Well** (N.Mex., McKinley Co.), and **Hogan Mesa** (N.Mex., San Juan Co.); elsewhere, **Hogan** is more likely to represent an English surname of Irish origin.

HOGANSAANI Spring (Ariz., Apache Co.) \hō gən sä´ nē\. The name is supposedly Navajo (Athabaskan) for 'lone hogan', but more correct Navajo would be *sahdii hooghani* (Linford 2000). The English word *hogan*, referring to a traditional house, is from Navajo *hooghan* 'someone's house'.

HOGATZA (Alaska, Hughes A-6) \hō gät´ sə\. The Koyukon (Athabaskan) name is *hʉgaadzaat no'*, meaning uncertain (Jetté & Jones 2000). The presumably related name **Hogatzakhotak** (Alaska, Hughes A-5) was said in 1900 to mean 'little hog river' (Orth 1967).

HOG Creek (Mich., Branch Co.). Corresponds to Ojibwa (Algonquian) <Kokoshi minissing> 'hog island place' (Vogel 1986); cf. *gookoosh* 'pig', *minis* 'island' (Nichols and Nyholm 1995).

HOH (Wash., Jefferson Co.) \hō\. From the Quinault (Salishan) placename /húx^{W}/ (D. Kinkade p.c.).

HO HO KAM Village (Ariz., Maricopa Co.) \hō hō käm´, hō hō´ kəm, hō´ hō kəm\. The term is applied by archaeologists to the ancient cultures of the Southwest that preceded the Pueblo peoples; it is derived from O'odham (Piman) *huhugkam* 'those who have perished', from *huhug* 'to perish' (J. Hill p.c.).

HOHOKUS Brook (N.J., Bergen Co.) \hō hō´ kəs\. Perhaps from a Delaware (Algonquian) word <mehokhokus> 'red cedar' (Becker 1964); also written **Ho-Ho-Kus.**

HOHOLITNA River (Alaska, Sleetmute C-3) \hō hō lit´ nə\. From Dena'ina (Athabaskan) *tleghtitnu* 'oil-water stream', containing *tlegh* 'oil', *-tnu* 'stream' (Wassillie 1979; Kari and Kari 1982); a related name is **Holitna River** (Alaska, Sleetmute C-4).

HOI OIDAK (Ariz., Pima Co.) \hoi oi´ däk\. O'odham (Piman) *ho'i oidak* 'thorn field', from *ho'i* 'thorn', *oidak* 'field' (J. Hill p.c.).

HOKAH (Minn., Houston Co.) \hō´ kə\. Perhaps from Dakota (Siouan) *hutką* 'root' (Upham 2001; Riggs 1890).

HOKDOLONI Hills (Alaska, Hughes A-4). The Koyukon (Athabaskan) name was reported in 1956 as meaning 'hills above' (Orth 1967).

HOKENDAUQUA (Pa., Northampton Co.) \hok´ ən dô kwə\. Perhaps a Delaware (Algonquian) name, meaning 'searching for land' (Donehoo 1928).

HOKNEDE Mountain (Alaska, Lake Clark A-6) \hōk nē´ dē\. From Dena'ina (Athabaskan) *unhnidi* 'the one farthest upriver' (Kari and Kari 1982).

HOKO River (Wash., Clallam Co.) \hō´ kō\. From Makah (Nootkan) /hu:qu:/, perhaps a borrowing from a nearby Salishan language (W. Jacobsen p.c.).

HOKTAHEEN Creek (Alaska, Mt. Fairweather A-2). The Tlingit name was reported in 1901 (Orth 1967).

HOLAKI Knob (Idaho, Benewah Co.) \hol´ ə kē\. The name was given by the Forest Service, supposedly from a Chinook Jargon meaning 'open' (Boone 1988). This may have been a misreading of the Jargon word <háh-lakl> [hálakl], from Chinookan /-xálaqtł/ 'to open' (D. Kinkade p.c.).

HOLANNA Creek (Ga., Quitman Co.) \hə lä ´ nə\. Muskogee *vhv-lane* /aha-lá:ni/ 'yellow potato', from *vhv* /ahá/ 'potato', *lane* /lá:ni/ 'green, yellow, brown' (Read 1949–50; J. Martin p.c.).

HOLDEYEIT Lake (Alaska, Bettles C-6). The Koyukon (Athabaskan) name is *hʉlde yeet* 'in burned timber' (J. Kari p.c.).

HOLETAH Creek (Ala., Sumter Co.) \hō lē´ tə\. From Choctaw (Muskogean) *holihta* 'fence, barricade' (Read 1984; P. Munro p.c.).

HOLIKACHUK (Alaska, Holy Cross D-2) \hol´ i kə chuk, hō´ li kə chuk\. The term refers to a people and language of the Athabaskan language family. It is derived from the name of an earlier village in the area, written as <Khuligichagat, Holiaktzag, Holiktsak, Hologochaket> (*HNAI* 6:616); cf. Upper Kuskokwim (Athabaskan) *holjichak'* (Kari 1999:84).

HOLITNA River (Alaska, Sleetmute C-4) \hō lit´ nə\. From Deg Hit'an (Athabaskan) *haghaletno, xagheletno, xoletno* 'grease-flows river' (J. Kari p.c.); a related name is **Hoholitna River** (Sleetmute C-3).

HOLLOLLA, Lake (Ala., Sumter Co.) \hä lä´ lə\. Perhaps from Choctaw (Muskogean) *halǫlabi* 'bullfrog' (Read 1984; P. Munro p.c.).

HOLLY Creek (Ga., Murray Co.). Probably a translation of the Cherokee (Iroquoian) name, recorded in 1798 as <Oose tus te> (Goff 1975).

HOLOKUK Mountain (Alaska, Sleetmute B-7). The Yupik (Eskimo) name was reported in 1945 (Orth 1967).

HOLONADA Creek (Alaska, Bettles A-5). The Koyukon (Athabaskan) name was reported in 1956 (Orth 1967).

HOLOPAW (Fla., Osceola Co.) \hol´ ə pô\. The name was taken from a published Muskogee vocabulary in which it was given the translation 'walk (pavement)'. It may be related to *hvlvtetv*

/halatitá/ 'to hold' (Read 1934; Martin and Mauldin 2000).

HOLTILYET Slough (Alaska, Nulato D-4). The Koyukon (Athabaskan) name was reported in 1954 (Orth 1967).

HOLTNAKATNA Creek (Alaska, Kateel River B-2). The Koyukon (Athabaskan) name was reported in 1955 (Orth 1967).

HOMBOGUE Creek (Ala., Sumter Co.) \hom´ bōg\. Possibly a coinage based on Choctaw (Muskogean) *homma* 'red', *book* 'stream', but the adjective should follow the noun in Choctaw (P. Munro p.c.).

HOMINY \hom´ i nē\. The term refers to hulled corn from which the bran and germ have been removed by soaking in lye or by grinding and sifting. The word is from Va. Algonquian <uskatahomen, usketchamun> 'that which is treated' (in a way specified by a preceding element), probably 'that which is ground or beaten' (*RHD* 1987). The term occurs as a placename in several states (e.g., N.J., Monmouth Co.; and Fla., Flager Co.). But in Okla. (Osage Co.), the term is from an Osage (Siouan) personal name /hą mąni/, lit. 'night walker' (R. Rankin p.c.).

HOMLY (Ore., Umatilla Co.) \hōm´ lē\. Named for a nineteenth-century Walla Walla (Sahaptian) leader; his Native American name was [xúmlay] (N. Rude p.c.).

HOMOCHITTO (Miss., Amite Co.) \hō mə chit´ ə\. Abbreviated from Choctaw (Muskogean) *book homma chito* 'big red river', containing *book* 'river', *homma* 'red', and *chito* 'big' (Seale 1939; P. Munro p.c.).

HOMOLOBI (Ariz., Navajo Co.) \hə mol´ ə vē, hə mō´ lə vē\. Hopi (Uto-Aztecan) *homol'ovi* 'high mounded place', from *homol-* 'to be mounded', *-'o-* 'high', and *-vi* 'place' (K. Hill p.c.). The spelling **Homolovi** also occurs.

HOMOSASSA (Fla., Citrus Co.) \hō mə sä´ sə\. From a Muskogee name meaning 'some pepper', from *homv* /homá/ 'pepper', *sasv* /sá:sa/ 'some' (Martin and Mauldin 2000).

HOMOWACK Kill (N.Y., Sullivan Co.) \hom´ ō wak\. Perhaps from an Algonquian word <aumauog> 'they fish' (Beauchamp 1907).

HONAN (Ariz., Coconino Co.). From Hopi (Uto-Aztecan) *honani* 'badger' (K. Hill p.c.).

HONCUT (Calif., Yuba Co.) \hon´kut\. From the name of a Maidu village, also written <Hoan´kut> (Gudde 1998).

HONEA PATH (S.C., Anderson Co.). Perhaps from an Indian word meaning 'path' (Pickens 1961–62:6); cf. Cherokee (Iroquoian) *ganvnvi* 'path' (Alexander 1971), *nunohi* 'road' (Feeling 1975).

HONEOYE (N.Y., Ontario Co.) \hun´ ē oi\. The Iroquoian name has been written <Ha´-ne-a-yah, Hah´-nyah-yah, Hanyaye> (etc.), supposedly meaning 'finger lying' (Beauchamp 1907). A related placename is **Honeyoey** (Mich., Gratiot Co.).

HONEY Lake (Calif., Lassen Co.). Perhaps from Maidu /hanɨlekim/, mentioned in the Native American creation myth as the name for the lake and its valley; it is from /hanɨlek/ 'to carry (an object) swiftly away' (Gudde 1998).

HONEYOEY (Mich., Gratiot Co.) \hun´ ē oi\. The placename is related to **Honeoye** (N.Y., Ontario Co.); see above.

HONGA (Md., Dorchester Co.) \hong´ gə\. Perhaps an abbreviation of Powhatan (Algonquian) <kahunge, kahangoc> 'goose' (Kenny 1984).

HONHOSA River (Alaska, Kateel River B-4). The Koyukon (Athabaskan) name was published in 1959 (Orth 1967).

HONK Hill (N.Y., Ulster Co.) \hongk\. Perhaps from earlier <Honeck>, derived from Delaware (Algonquian) <hannek> 'stream' (Ruttenber 1906).

HONNEDAGA (N.Y., Oneida Co.) \hon ə dä´ gə\. Perhaps an Iroquoian term meaning 'hilly place' (Beauchamp 1907).

HONOBIA (Okla., Le Flore Co.) \hō´ nə bə, hə nō´ bə\. Said to be named for a Choctaw

(Muskogean) individual named <O-no-bi-a> (Shirk 1974).

HONOLULU \hon ə lo͞o´ lo͞o\. The name of the capital of Hawai'i turns up occasionally as a placename on the mainland (e.g., Alaska, Healy A-6; and Ohio, Highland Co.) The name means 'protected bay' (Pukui et al. 1974).

HONTOKALO Creek (Miss., Scott Co.) \hon tok´ ə lō\. From Choctaw (Muskogean) *ǫtoklo* 'seven' (Seale 1939; P. Munro p.c.).

HONTUBBY (Okla., Le Flore Co.) \hon´ tub ē, hon tub´ ē\. Probably the "war name" of a Choctaw (Muskogean) man, perhaps *ǫtabi* 'arrived and killed', containing *ona* 'to arrive', *abi* 'to kill' (P. Munro p.c.).

HOOKSETT (N.H., Merrimack Co.) \ho͝ok´ sət\. Perhaps abbreviated from <Annahooksett, Onnahooksett>, Abenaki (Algonquian) for 'at the place of beautiful trees' (Huden 1962).

HOOKS Pond (S.C., Horry Co.). Perhaps from a word meaning 'lower river people' in an unidentified Indian language (Pickens 1961–62:6).

HOOLIGAN Creek (Alaska, Bendeleben A-6) \ho͞o´ li gən\. A supposed Tlingit name <euchalon> was recorded in 1948 (Orth 1967), perhaps involving some confusion with English *eulachon* 'candlefish', which also occurs as a placename (Alaska, Petersburg C-1). The term *eulachon* is Chinook Jargon, probably from Clatsop (Chinookan) /u-tłalxwə́(n)/, said to mean 'brook trout' (*RHD* 1987). A related placename is **Hulakon River** (Alaska, Bradfield Canal A-4).

HOONAH (Alaska, Juneau A-5) \ho͞o´ nə\. The name of a village and subdivision of the Tlingits; the Native American name is *xunaa,* said to mean 'cold lake' (*HNAI* 7:227).

HOONAWPA (Ariz., Navajo Co.). Hopi (Uto-Aztecan *hoonàwpa* 'bear spring', from *hoonaw* 'bear' (K. Hill p.c.).

HOOPA (Calif., Humboldt Co.) \ho͞o´pä\. The placename is not from the language of the resident **Hupa** (Athabaskan) people; rather, it represents the name of the valley in the language of the neighboring Yurok people, *hup'oo* (Gudde 1998).

HOOP AND POLE GAME Rock (Ariz., Apache Co.). Navajo (Athabaskan*) tséyaa nda'azhǫǫshí* 'rock under which the hoop and pole game is played', containing *na'azhǫǫsh* 'hoop and pole game' (Linford 2000).

HOOSAC Range (Vt., Bennington Co.) \ho͞o´ sak\. Perhaps Mahican (Algonquian), meaning 'stone place' (Huden 1962); cf. SNEng. Algonquian <hassu(nn)ek> 'cave', from <hassun-> 'stone' (W. Cowan p.c.). The term also occurs in Mass. (Berkshire Co.). and N.H. (Rockingham Co.) Perhaps related is **Hosac Mountain** (Maine, York Co.).

HOOSIC River (N.Y., Rensselaer Co.; Mass., Berkshire Co.) \ho͞o´ sik, ho͞o´ zik\. Perhaps from Mahican (Algonquian), meaning 'rim of the kettle'; confusion with the name **Hoosac Range** is possible (Beauchamp 1907; Huden 1962). The spelling **Hoosick** also occurs.

HOOSIMBIM Mountain (Calif., Trinity Co.) \ho͞o´ sim bim\. From Wintu /huusun meem/, lit. 'buzzard's water' (Gudde 1998).

HOOSKANADEN Creek (Ore., Curry Co.) \ho͞os´ kə nä dən\. From Tututni (Athabaskan) /xusteneten/ 'gravel place' (D. Kinkade p.c.).

HOPATCONG (N.J., Sussex Co.). From Delaware (Algonquian), of unclear derivation (Becker 1964).

HOPI \hō´ pē\. The name of this Pueblo people, of the Uto-Aztecan language family, is also the name of their reservation in northern Ariz. The term represents their own word *hopi,* meaning 'well-mannered, civilized' (K. Hill p.c.). There is evidence that, at an earlier period the Hopis called themselves *mookwi,* and this term entered Spanish in the sixteenth century, in the form *moqui,* pronounced [mókwi] By the nineteenth century this had been reinterpreted in Spanish as [moki], however, and had entered English as **Moqui**, pronounced \mō´ kē\; see below. It also occurs in placenames, as in **Moqui Spring**

(Ariz., Coconino Co.). The Hopi people found this pronunciation offensive because of its similarity to their word *mooki* 'dies, is dead'; and at the instance of J. Walter Fewkes, the name was officially changed to **Hopi** (*HNAI* 9:550).

HOPOCA (Miss., Leake Co.) \hō pok´ ə\. From Choctaw (Muskogean) *hopaaki* 'far, distant' (P. Munro p.c.).

HOPOKOEKAU Beach (Wis., Fond du Lac Co.). Named for an eighteenth-century female leader of the Ho-Chunk or Winnebago (Siouan) people. Her name is said to be more correctly ***h*ą́ą*p hoguwį́ga,*** meaning 'day-where-comes woman' (referring to the false dawn that precedes sunrise), from *hą́ąp* 'day,' *ho-* nominalizer, *gúu* 'leave returning,' *-wį* 'feminine', *-ga* personal name ending (Vogel 1991; K. Miner p.c.).

HOPPAW Creek (Calif., Del Norte Co.) \hop´ou\. Named for the Yurok village *ho'pew* (Gudde 1998).

HOPSEWEE Plantation (S.C., Georgetown Co.) \hop´ sə wē\. Perhaps from an unidentified Indian language (Pickens 1961–62:6).

HOQUARTEN Slough (Ore., Tillamook Co.) \hō kwôr´ tən\. From the Tillamook (Salishan) placename /t'əhúuqaatən/ (D. Kinkade p.c.).

HOQUIAM (Wash., Grays Harbor Co.) \hō´ kwē əm, hō´ kē əm\. From Lower Chehalis (Salishan) [x̣ʷə́qʷyamc] 'driftwood', lit. 'hungry for wood', from /x̣ʷə́qʷ-/ 'hungry' and /yámc/ 'Douglas fir, wood' (D. Kinkade p.c.).

HORICON (N.Y., Warren Co.) \hôr´ i kən\. This name was made popular by the nineteenth-century novelist James Fenimore Cooper, who took it to be an Iroquoian name for Lake George. Subsequently it has been applied as a placename in several states (e.g., Mich., Otsego Co.; N.J., Ocean Co.; and Wis., Dodge Co.).

HORNOLUCKA Creek (Miss., Prentiss Co.) \hôr nə luk´ ə\. Possibly a Choctaw (Muskogean) expression meaning 'sacred food', from *honni* 'food', *haloka* 'sacred' (Seale 1939; P. Munro p.c.).

HORSE. This animal was not known to the American Indians in pre-Columbian times but was introduced by the Spanish at an early date. By the time that Anglo-Americans began to explore the Great Plains, the horse had already become part of the Native American cultures in that area. American Indian languages created words for 'horse' from their native resources; in some areas, the native word for 'dog' was adapted to mean 'horse', and a modified form of the word was used to mean 'dog'. An example occurs in the placename **Horse Rock** (Ariz., Apache Co.), which corresponds to Navajo (Athabaskan) *tsé łįįłí* 'horse rock' (Linford 2000). Here the original Navajo word *łįį* 'dog, pet' has come to mean 'horse'; a new word *łééchąą'í* (lit. 'shit pet') has been coined to mean 'dog'.

HORSE LINTO Creek (Calif., Humboldt Co.) \hos lin´ tən\. A popular etymology from Hupa *xahslin-ding* (Athabaskan) 'riffles-place'. The mapmakers' spelling **Horse Linto** has given rise to a current spelling-pronounciation, \hôrs´ lin tō\.

HOSA, Chief (Colo., Jefferson Co.) \hō ´ sə\. The site honors an Arapaho (Algonquian) leader named *hóuu-sóó* 'crow-child' (A. Cowell p.c.).

HOSAC Mountain (Maine, York Co.) \hō´ sak\. Perhaps from Mahican (Algonquian), meaning 'stone place'; similar terms are **Hoosac Range** and **Hoosic River** in other New England states (Rutherford 1970).

HOSKININNI Mesa (Ariz., Navajo Co.) \hos´ ki nē nē\. Named for a Navajo (Athabaskan) leader who died in 1909 (Granger 1983). His Native American name was *hashké neiniihí* 'he distributed them with angry insistence', referring to Hoskinini's giving sheep to returning Navajos after they were confined at Bosque Redondo (Linford 2000). An alternative spelling occurs in **Hoskinnini Mesa** (Utah, Garfield Co.).

HOSPAH (N.Mex., McKinley Co.) \hōs´ pä, hos´ pä\. Navajo (Athabaskan) *haasbá* 'gray area slopes upward', from *ha-* 'upward', *-a-* 'space', *-ł(s)bá* 'it is gray' (A. Wilson p.c.).

HOSPILIKA Creek (Ala., Lee Co.) \hos pi lī´ kə\. From Muskogee *hospv-like* /ho:spa-léyki/ 'sitting wall' (Martin and Mauldin 2000). A variant writing is **Hospelaga.**

HOSTA Butte (N.Mex., McKinley Co.) \hōs´ tə\. Named for a nineteenth-century leader of Jemez Pueblo (Tanoan), also known as Francisco; his Jemez name was /hót^{y}i/ 'lightning' (HNAI 9:425).

HOSTEEN BEGAY Well (Ariz., Apache Co.) \hos tēn´ bə gā´\. Named for a Navajo (Athabaskan) man called *hastiin bighe',* lit. 'man's son', from *hastiin* 'man' and *bighe'* 'his son' (*bi-* 'his', *-ghe', -ye'* 'son of male'; Young and Morgan 1987). The word *hastiin* is, as in this case, used as an equivalent of English 'mister', and *bighe'* **Begay** is used as a family name. Similarly, **Hosteen Tso Canyon** (Ariz., Apache Co.) \hos tēn´ sō\ is named for a Navajo (Athabaskan) man called *hastiin-tsoh* 'big man', lit. *hastiin* 'man; Mr.' and *-tsoh* 'big' (Young and Morgan 1987).

HOTASON VO (Ariz., Pima Co.) \hō tə son vō´\. O'odham (Piman) *hodai ṣon wo'o* 'rock-spring pond', from *hodai* 'rock', *ṣon* 'spring', *wo'o* 'pond' (J. Hill p.c.).

HOTAUTA Canyon (Ariz., Coconino Co.) \hō tou´ tə\. Named for a leader of the Havasupai (Yuman) people (Brian 1992). The placename is also spelled **Hotouta.**

HOTEVILA (Ariz., Navajo Co.) \hō´ tə vil ə, hot ə vil´ ə, hōt´ vil ə\. Hopi (Uto-Aztecan) *hotvela,* from *hó'atvela* 'juniper slope', the name of this location before it was established as a village; cf. *ho(-hu)* 'juniper', *(a)tvela* 'slope' (K. Hill p.c.). The spelling **Hotevilla** is also used.

HOT NA NA Wash (Ariz., Coconino Co.) \hot nä´ nä\. Navajo (Athabaskan) *ha'naa na'ní'á* 'bridge across' (Linford 2000); cf. *ha'naa* 'across', *na'ní'á* 'bridge' (Young and Morgan 1987).

HOTULKEE (Okla., Pottawatomie Co.) \hə tō´ kē\. Named for a Muskogee leader, called Hotulkee Martha or Edward Bullette. The term **Hotulkee** refers to his membership in the Wind Clan, *hotvlkvlke* /hotalkâlke/; cf. *hotvlē* /hotalí:/ 'wind' (Martin and Mauldin 2000).

HOULKA (Miss., Chickasaw Co.) \hōl´ kə\. Perhaps from Choctaw (Muskogean) *holhki* 'calf of the leg' (Seale 1939; P. Munro p.c.).

HOUMA (La., Terrebonne Par.) \hōō´ mə, hō´ mə\. The term refers to a Muskogean group that once lived in La.; from Choctaw *homma* 'red' (Read 1927; P. Munro p.c.). The word also occurs in the placenames **Bogue Homa, Bogahoma, Boga Homo,** all intended for *book homma* 'red stream'.

HOUSATONIC River (Conn., Litchfield Co.; Mass., Berkshire Co.) \hōō sə ton´ ik\. Perhaps from SNEng. Algonquian <hasseuneutunk> 'stone wall', containing <hassun-> (W. Cowan p.c.); but cf. Abenaki (Algonquian) *awasadenek* 'beyond the hill', from *awasi* 'beyond', *-aden* 'hill, mountain', *-ek* 'place' (Day 1994–95).

HOVENWEEP Canyon (Colo., Montezuma Co.) \hō´ vən wēp\. Probably from Ute or Southern Paiute (Numic), meaning 'bone canyon'; both languages have /ooviɨ/ 'bone', /uippi/ 'canyon' (J. McLaughlin p.c.).

HÖWIIPA (Ariz., Navajo Co.). Hopi (Uto-Aztecan) *höwìipa* 'dove spring', from *höwi* 'dove' and *-pa, paa-hu* 'water, spring' (K. Hill p.c.).

HOWKAN (Alaska, Dixon Entrance D-3). From Haida /ʔ^{h}áwk'ya:n/ (*HNAI* 7:258). Also written as **Howkwan.**

HOWLOCK Creek (Ore., Klamath Co.) \hou´luk\. Named for a Northern Paiute (Numic) leader (McArthur 1992). Another spelling appears in **Howluk Butte** (Ore., Harney Co.).

HOYA Creek (Alaska, Bradfield Canal A-6). The name, possibly Tlingit, was reported in 1955 (Orth 1967).

HOYADAZZITHETHNO Creek (Alaska, Hughes A-1). The Koyukon (Athabaskan) name was reported in 1956 (Orth 1967).

HOYPUS Point (Wash., Island Co.) \hoi´ pəs\. The name was recorded in 1841 as <Hoipus>; its possible Indian origin has not been traced (Hitchman 1985).

HOYUBY (Okla., Hughes Co.) \hoi ub´ ē, hoi´ ə bē\. Named for a Choctaw (Muskogean) resident whose name was written <Ho-yw-bbee> (Shirk 1974); it may be a war name, 'looked for and killed', containing *hoyo* 'to look for' and *abi* 'kill' (P. Munro p.c.).

HOZATKA Lake (Alaska, Kateel River A-2). The Koyukon (Athabaskan) name was reported in 1955 (Orth 1967).

HOZOMEEN Creek (Wash., Whatcom Co.) \hoz´ ə mēn\. From a Thompson River Salishan word meaning 'sharp (like a knife)', derived from /x̣ʷəz-/ 'sharp' (D. Kinkade p.c.).

HUACHUCA Peak (Ariz., Cochise Co.) \wä cho͞o´ kə\. The Spanish spelling is said to represent an O'odham (Piman) name meaning 'it rains here' (Granger 1983); cf. O'odham *ju:k* 'to rain' (Saxton et al. 1983).

HUAJI Cliff (Alaska, Dixon Entrance C-1). The name is said to be Tlingit for 'grizzly bear sitting down' (Orth 1967); cf. Tlingit *xóots* 'grizzly bear' (Davis & Leer 1976).

HUALAPAI \wä lə pī´, wä´ lə pī\. The term refers to a Yuman people living in northern Ariz. The name is from Mojave (Yuman) *huuwaalya-pay* 'pine tree people', from *huwaaly* 'pine tree', *-apay* 'people'. It occurs as a placename in Ariz. (Coconino Co.) and in Nev. (Pershing Co.). Related forms are **Haulapai Island** (Ariz., Mohave Co.); **Hualpai** (Ariz., Yavapai Co.; Nev., Clark Co.); and **Walapai** (Ariz., Mojave Co.).

HUASNA (Calif., San Luis Obispo Co.) \wäz´ nə\. The Spanish spelling represents a Purisimeño (Chumashan) village name, /wasna/ (Gudde 1998).

HUDEUC Lake (Alaska, Nabesna D-2). From Upper Tanana (Athabaskan), of unclear derivation (Orth 1967).

HUENEME, Port (Calif., Ventura Co.) \wī nē´ mə, wī nē´ mē\. From Ventureño (Chumashan) /wene'mu/ 'sleeping place' (Gudde 1998). An older spelling and pronunciation was **Wynema,** probably by confusion with **Winema,** an Indian woman who played an important role in the Modoc War of the late nineteenth century.

HUERHUERO Creek (Calif., San Luis Obispo Co.) \wâr wâr´ ō\. Possibly from an Obispeño (Chumashan) village name, /elewexe/ (Gudde 1998).

HUITZIL, Point (Ariz., Coconino Co.) \wēt sēl´\. From Nahuatl (Aztecan) *huitzilin* 'hummingbird'.

HUK OVI (Ariz., Navajo Co.) \huk ō´ vē\. Hopi (Uto-Aztecan) *huk'ovi* 'high windy place', from *huk-* 'wind', *-'o-* 'high', *-vi* 'place' (K. Hill p.c.).

HULAH (Okla., Osage Co.) \hyo͞o´ lə, ho͞o´ lə\. Perhaps from Osage (Siouan) /xüðá/ 'eagle' (R. Rankin p.c.).

HULAHULA River (Alaska, Flaxman Island A-1) \ho͞o lə ho͞o´ lə\. From Hawaiian *hulahula,* a type of dance, also called simply *hula* (Orth 1967, *RHD* 1987).

HULAKON River (Alaska, Bradfield Canal A-4) \yo͞o´ lə kən\. Refers to a kind of marine fish, also called *candlefish* because of its high oil content. The term is borrowed from Chinook Jargon, which takes it from Clatsop (Chinookan) /u-tlalxwə(n)/ 'brook trout' (*RHD* 1987). An alternative spelling is found in **Eulachon Slough** (Alaska, Petersburg C-1). A related placename is **Hooligan Creek** (Alaska, Bendeleben A-6).

HULGOTHEN Bluffs (Alaska, Bettles C-3). The Koyukon (Athabaskan) name was recorded in 1956 (Orth 1967).

HUMP Butte (S.Dak., Corson Co.). Corresponds to Dakota (Siouan) *pažó* 'hump of a buffalo' (Sneve 1973; Williamson 1902).

HUMPTULIPS (Wash., Grays Harbor Co.) \hump to͞o´ lips\. From a Lower Chehalis (Salishan) placename [xʷəmtúlapš], containing /-apš/ 'stream' (D. Kinkade p.c.).

HUNK-PA-PA Creek (S.Dak., Corson Co.) \ho͝ongk´ pä pä\. From /hų́kpapha/, the name of a Teton Lakhota (Siouan) subgroup, Sitting Bull's band, on the Standing Rock Reservation (D. Parks p.c.). A related placename is **Unkpapa Peak** (S.Dak., Custer Co.).

HUNODIM Peak (Calif., Plumas Co.). From Maidu /hɨ́nodi/ 'that which is gathered' (of plants), from /hɨ́-/ 'to gather' (W. Shipley p.c.); the name was made official by the BGN in 1999.

HU-PWI Wash (Nev., Mineral Co.) \ho͞o´ pwē\. From Northern Paiute (Numic) *huuppin* 'wood, brush' or *huuppi* 'boxthorn' (J. McLaughlin p.c.).

HUSLIA (Alaska, Kateel River C-1) \ho͞os´ lē ə\. The Koyukon (Athabaskan) name is *hʉlyekk'etne,* meaning uncertain (Jetté & Jones 2000).

HUSPA Creek (S.C., Beaufort Co.). Earlier written <Hospa>; perhaps the name of an Indian leader, language not identified (Pickens 1961–62:6).

HUTLINANA Creek (Alaska, Tanana A-1) \ho͞ot li nan´ ə\. From Lower Tanana (Athabaskan) *hwlde nilanh no',* lit. 'burned-timber-exists creek', with *no'* 'stream' (Kari 1999:112).

HYAMPOM (Calif., Trinity Co.) \hī´ əm pom\. Perhaps from Wintu *xayiin-pom* 'slippery place', from *xay-* 'to slip' (Gudde 1998).

HYANNIS (Mass., Barnstable Co.) \hī an´ is\. The term commemorates a seventeenth-century SNEng. Algonquian leader whose name was written <Anayanough> or <Iyanogh>, perhaps meaning 'he who wages war'. The placename was originally possesssive, **Iyanogh's Place** (Huden 1962). There is a **Hyannis Peak** in Colo. (Pitkin Co.).

HYAS Creek (Wash., Clallam Co.) \hī´ əs\. From Chinook Jargon <hias, haías> [háyəs] 'big, large, great, very', from Nootka /aya/, /ayaʔaš/ 'lots' (D. Kinkade).

HYDABURG (Alaska, Craig A-3) \hī´ də bûrg\. Named for the Haida people, who live principally on the Queen Charlotte Islands in British Columbia, Canada. Reference to them also occurs in the name of **Haida Point** (Wash., San Juan Co.).

I

IAQUA (Calif., Humboldt Co.) \ī´ ə kwā\. From a Wiyot exclamation [ayakwi:], used when one suddenly notices or remembers something (J. Lang p.c.). The word was adapted as a greeting in other Indian languages of northwestern Calif.; thus Yurok *oyekwi',* Karuk *ayukîi* 'hello!' (Gudde 1998).

IASLAKTOLI River (Alaska, Marshall D-8). The Yupik (Eskimo) name was reported in 1949 (Orth 1967).

IATAN (Mo., Platte Co.) \ī´ ə tan\. Named for an Oto (Siouan) leader (Ramsay 1952), supposedly so named because of his battles with the Comanche people (Numic), who were sometimes called <Ietan> or <Hietan> (Rydjord 1968). This word is probably related to **Iatt** (La., Grant Par.). **Iatan** has also been used to name a place in Tex. (Mitchell Co.), where it is said to be pronounced \ī tan´\. A related placename may be **Yutan** (Neb., Saunders Co.).

IATT (La., Grant Par.) \ī´ ət\. The name was recorded in 1816 as <Hietan>. It therefore probably has the same origin as **Iatan**; see above.

IBANTIK Reservoir (Utah, Summit Co.) \ī ban´ tik\. Said to be of Ute (Numic) origin (Van Cott 1990).

IBAPAH (Utah, Tooele Co.) \ī´bə pä, ī´bə pə\. From Shoshoni (Numic) /aipimpa/ 'white-clay water', with /aipin/ 'white clay' and /-pa/ 'water' (J. McLaughlin p.c.). A related name is **Ivanpah** (Calif., San Bernardino Co.); see below.

IBKIKWIT Lava Bed (Alaska, Cape Mendenhall D-4). The Yupik (Eskimo) name was recorded in 1949 (Orth 1967).

IBRULIKORAK Creek (Alaska, Point Hope A-2). The Iñupiaq (Eskimo) name is said to mean 'little sod house' (Orth 1967); cf. *ivruq* 'sod for house-building' (Webster and Zibell 1970:98).

ICHABUCKLER Creek (Ga., Stewart Co.) \ich ə buk´ lər\. From Muskogee *hecepakwv* /hičipákwa/ 'tobacco pipe'; cf. *hece* /hiči/ 'tobacco' (Goff 1975; Martin and Mauldin 2000).

ICHAWAYNOCHAWAY Creek (Ga., Baker Co.) \ich ə wā noch´ ə wā\. Perhaps a Muskogee name meaning 'deer sleeping' (Read 1949–50:130); cf. *eco* /ičó/ 'deer', *nucē* /nočí:/ 'asleep' (Martin and Mauldin 2000).

ICHETUCKNEE River (Fla., Suwannee Co.) \ich ə tuk´ nē\. Possibly from Muskogee *hacce-toccēne* /hačči-toččí:ni/ 'three streams'; cf. /háčči/ 'stream', /toččí:ni/ 'three' (J. Martin p.c.).

ICICLE Creek (Wash., Chelan Co.) \ī´ sik əl\. A folk-etymology from Moses-Columbian (Salishan) /nsíq'l't/ [nsíq'əl't] 'split canyon', containing /na-/ 'place', /síq'-/ 'split' (D. Kinkade p.c.).

IDAHO \ī´ də hō\. The name of the state is not native to that area but was first applied to part of eastern Colo.; it is from the Kiowa-Apache (Athabaskan) word *ídaahę́* 'enemy', a name that they applied to the Comanches (Numic) (Bright 1993, 1999c). It survives in the placename **Idaho Springs** (Clear Creek Co.) and as a transfer name elsewhere (e.g., N.Y, Livingston Co.; Ohio, Pike Co.; and Alaska, Talkeetna Mountains A-1). The name **Idahome** (Idaho, Cassia Co.) \ī´ də hōm\. is a fusion of **Idaho** and *home* (Boone 1988).

IDAK Creek (Alaska, Unalaska A-6). From the Aleut placename *iidax, idax* (Bergsland 1994).

IDALIUK Point (Alaska, Samalga Island D-4). From the Aleut placename *idalukax̂*, from *idalux̂* 'long flat cape' (Bergsland 1994).

IDALUG, Cape (Alaska, Seguam C-5). From Aleut *idalux̂* 'long flat cape' (Bergsland 1994).

IDANHA (Ore., Marion Co.) \ī dan´ ə\. Named for a brand of mineral water bottled in Soda Springs, Idaho, called "Idan-Ha water"; the name was supposedly derived from an Indian legend (McArthur 1992).

IDAVADA (Idaho, Twin Falls Co.) \ī də vā´ də\. A fusion of **Idaho** and Nevada, from being on the state boundary; the former name is of Indian origin (Boone 1988).

IDDO (Ala., Pike Co.) \id´ ō\. Possibly from Muskogee *eto* /itó/ 'tree' (P. Munro p.c.).

IDELAKUKYA DEY'A (N.Mex., Cibola Co.). The name of a place referred to in Zuni prayer (Ferguson and Hart 1985).

IDITAROD (Alaska, Iditarod C-5) \ī dit´ ə rod\. From Holikachuk (Athabaskan) *xidedhod* 'distant place' (J. Kari p.c.).

IDIWA DAHN'A (N.Mex., Cibola Co.). The Zuni name perhaps contains /itiwa/ 'center' (Ferguson and Hart 1985; Newman 1958). A perhaps related placename is **Idiwananne** (also Cibola Co.); see also **Idwa K'yan'a** below.

IDMON (Idaho, Clark Co.) \id´ mən\. A combination of **Idaho** and *Montana* (Boone 1988).

IDWA K'YAN'A (N.Mex., Cibola Co.). The Zuni name perhaps contains /itiwa/ center (Ferguson and Hart 1985; Newman 1958); see **Idiwananne** above.

IFCONJO Creek (Ga., Monroe Co.) \if kon´ jō\. Recorded in 1818 as <If-con-jo-hatchee>, for Muskogee *ēfkvnco* /i:fkánčo/ 'tick', *hvcce* /háčči/ 'stream' (Read 1949–50:130, Martin and Mauldin 2000).

IGALIK Island (Alaska, Barrow A-2). The Iñupiaq (Eskimo) name is said to mean 'window' (Orth 1967); cf. *igaliq* 'skylight window' (Fortescue et al. 1994:99).

IGGIRUK Mountains (Alaska, Misheguk Mountain B-1). The Iñupiaq (Eskimo) name is *iġġigrut* (Burch 1998).

IGIAK (Alaska, Hooper Bay C-3) \ig´ ē ak\. The Yupik (Eskimo) name was reported in 1878 (Orth 1967).

IGIAYAROK Pass (Alaska, Hooper Bay D-2). From Yupik (Eskimo) *igyaraq* 'throat', from *ige-* 'to swallow' (Orth 1967; Jacobson 1984). A related form is **Igiugig** (Alaska, Iliamna B-8).

IGICHUK Hills (Alaska, Noatak A-2). The Iñupiaq (Eskimo) name was reported in 1913 (Orth 1967).

IGIGLOGRUK Mountain (Alaska, Noatak C-4). The Iñupiaq (Eskimo) name is said to mean 'old mountain' (Orth 1967); cf. *iġġi* 'mountain' (MacLean 1980). A probably related placename is **Mt. Igikpak** (Alaska, Survey Pass B-4), said to refer to 'two big peaks' (Orth 1967). Possibly related placenames include **Igisukruk Mountain** (Alaska, Noatak A-2) and **Iikhkluk Mountain** (Alaska, Nunivak Island A-6).

IGILATVIK Creek (Alaska, Demarcation Point D-5). The Iñupiaq (Eskimo) name is said to mean 'place where parts of a house are found' (Orth 1967); cf. *iglu* 'house' (MacLean 1980). A related placename is **Igloo** (Alaska, Teller A-1).

IGILERAK Hill (Alaska, Point Hope B-2). The Iñupiaq (Eskimo) name was recorded in 1960 (Orth 1967).

IGISUKRUK Mountain (Alaska, Noatak A-2). The Iñupiaq (Eskimo) name is said to mean 'big mountain' (Orth 1967); cf. *iġġi* 'mountain' (MacLean 1980). Possibly related names include **Igiglogruk Mountain** (Alaska, Noatak C-4) and **Iikhkluk Mountain** (Alaska, Nunivak Island A-6).

IGITKIN Island (Alaska, Atka B-6). From the Aleut placename *igitxix̂* (Bergsland 1994).

IGITNA River (Alaska, Tyonek A-8) \ē gĕt′ nə\. The Dena'ina (Athabaskan) name is *igitnu*, containing *-tnu* 'river' (Kari and Kari 1982:22).

IGIUGIG (Alaska, Iliamna B-8) \ig ē ug′ ig\. From Alutiiq (Eskimo) *igya'aq* 'throat' (Leer 1978). A related form is **Igiayarok Pass** (Alaska, Hooper Bay D-2).

IGKLO River (Alaska, Wainwright D-1). The Iñupiaq (Eskimo) name is said to mean 'large intestine' (Orth 1967); cf. *iqłu* 'colon' (Webster and Zibell 1970:11).

IGLOO \ig′ lo͞o\. The word for an Eskimo house probably entered English from an Inuit dialect of northeastern Canada (*RHD* 1987). Related forms used in Alaska include Alutiiq *engluq* [ɨŋluq] 'house', Iñupiaq *iglu* (MacLean 1980). As a placename, **Igloo** occurs in Alaska (Teller A-1) and in S.Dak. (Fall River Co.).

IGLUPAK Creek (Alaska, Point Hope B-2). From Iñupiaq (Eskimo) *iglupiaq* 'sod house' (Burch 1998, Fortescue et al. 1994).

IGMIUMANIK River (Alaska, Goodnews Bay C-4). The Yupik (Eskimo) name was reported in 1954 (Orth 1967).

IGNEK Creek (Alaska, Mt. Michelson C-4). From Iñupiaq (Eskimo) *igniq* 'fire' (MacLean 1980). Probably related is **Igning River** (Alaska, Survey Pass C-6) \ig′ ning\; the Iñupiaq name was reported in 1956 as meaning 'fire' or 'match' (Orth 1967). Also probably related is **Ignisirok Creek** (Alaska, Misheguk Mountain B-2); the Iñupiaq (Eskimo) name is said to mean 'material for fire' (Orth 1967).

IGOKLUK Slough (Alaska, Kwiguk B-6). The Yupik (Eskimo) name was recorded in 1899 (Orth 1967).

IGRAROK Creek (Alaska, Point Hope D-2). The Iñupiaq (Eskimo) name was reported to mean 'low hills' (Orth 1967); cf. *iġġi* 'mountain' (MacLean 1980).

IGRIKCHUM Slough (Alaska, Kwiguk A-5). The Yupik (Eskimo) name was reported in 1949 (Orth 1967).

IGRUGAIVIK Creek (Alaska, Noatak C-5). The Iñupiaq (Eskimo) name was reported in 1966 (Orth 1967).

IGRUIVOTALIK Creek (Alaska, Point Hope B-2). The Iñupiaq (Eskimo) name was reported in 1960; it has also been written as **Igruwotalik** (Orth 1967).

IGUSHIK (Alaska, Nushagak Bay C-3) \i go͞o′ shik\. From Yupik (Eskimo) *iyussiiq* (Jacobson 1984). There is another **Igushik** in northern Alaska

IHAGEE Creek (Ala., Russell Co.) \ī haj´ ē\. An alternative form of **Hiagi,** the name of a former Muskogee town (Read 1984).

IIKHKLUK Mountain (Alaska, Nunivak Island A-6). The Yupik (Eskimo) name, also written <i-ikh-qluq>, was reported as meaning 'rough mountain' (Orth 1967); cf. *irriq* 'mountain' (Fortescue et al. 1994). Possibly related placenames include **Igiglogruk Mountain** (Alaska, Noatak C-4) and **Igisukruk Mountain** (Alaska, Noatak A-2).

IISIKTOK Creek (Alaska, Baird Inlet C-7). The Yupik (Eskimo) name, said to mean 'he enters', was reported in 1965 (Orth 1967).

IKAGIAK Creek (Alaska, Chandler Lake B-5). From Iñupiaq (Eskimo) *ikaaġiaq* 'ford' (Burch 1998), from *ikaaq-* 'to cross over' (MacLean 1980).

IKAGLUIK Creek (Alaska, Mt. Katmai C-4). The Alutiiq (Eskimo) name was reported in 1919 (Orth 1967).

IKAKNAK Pond (Alaska, Point Hope A-2). The Iñupiaq (Eskimo) name was reported to mean 'north wind' (Orth 1967); cf. *ikaŋnaq* 'northeast wind' (MacLean 1980).

IKALOOKSIK River (Alaska, St. Lawrence C-5). The Yupik (Eskimo) name was reported in 1932 (Orth 1967).

IKALUGTULIK River (Alaska, Nunivak Island C-1). The Yupik (Eskimo) name, said to mean 'having humpbacked salmon', was recorded in 1949 (Orth 1967).

IKATAN (Alaska, False Pass C-4) \ik´ ə tan\. From an Aleut placename *ikatan, ikatux̂* (Bergsland 1994). A related name is **Ikatok Peak,** located nearby.

IKATHLEEWIK Bay (Alaska, Nunivak Island B-2). The Yupik (Eskimo) name was recorded in 1949 (Orth 1967). The neighboring **Ikathleewimjingia** was recorded in the same period.

IKATOK Peak (Alaska, False Pass C-4). From an Aleut placename *ikatan, ikatux̂* (Bergsland 1994). A related name is **Ikatan,** located nearby.

IKES Creek (Calif., Humboldt Co.) \īks\. The name represents "Ike's Creek," after a Karuk resident known as Little Ike, from his Karuk name, *éehkan* (Gudde 1998).

IKIAK (Alaska, Barrow A-1). The Iñupiak (Eskimo) name, also recorded as <Ikikak>, is said to refer to a strait (Orth 1967); cf. *ikiq* 'bay, sound' (Fortescue et al. 1994).

IKIAKPAURAK Valley (Alaska, Mt. Michelson B-4). The Iñupiaq (Eskimo) name was reported in 1919 as meaning 'small valley' (Orth 1967).

IKIGINAK Island (Alaska, Atka B-5). From the Aleut placename *ikiiĝinax̂,* perhaps meaning 'lying across over there' (Bergsland 1994).

IKIJAKTUSAK Creek (Alaska, Point Hope A-2). The Iñupiaq (Eskimo) name was reported in 1962 as meaning 'young gull' (Orth 1967).

IKIKILERUK Creek (Alaska, De Long Mountains D-4). The Iñupiaq (Eskimo) name was reported in 1956 to mean 'narrow' (Orth 1967).

IKLAUYAK Creek (Alaska, Killik River A-1). The Iñupiaq (Eskimo) name was reported in 1956 (Orth 1967).

IKLAUYAURAK Creek (Alaska, Chandler Lake A-5). The Iñupiaq (Eskimo) name was reported in 1956 (Orth 1967).

IKMAKRAK Lake (Alaska, Meade River B-3). The Iñupiaq (Eskimo) name was recorded in 1956 (Orth 1967).

IKNIVIK Creek (Alaska, Chandler Lake B-3). The Iñupiaq (Eskimo) name, said to mean 'pointed place', was published in 1951 (Orth 1967); cf. *-vik* 'place'.

IKNUTAK Mountain (Alaska, Solomon B-3). The Iñupiaq (Eskimo) name was reported about 1940 (Orth 1967).

IKO Bay (Alaska, Barrow A-3). The Iñupiaq (Eskimo) name is *iqu* 'end' (L. Kaplan p.c.).

IKOOK Point (Alaska, Nunivak Island A-7). The Yupik (Eskimo) name was reported about 1908 (Orth 1967).

IKOOKSMIUT (Alaska, Nunivak Island A-7). The Yupik (Eskimo) name was reported in 1949 (Orth 1967). It appears to be related to **Ikook Point;** the suffix *-miut* means 'people'.

IKOOKSTAKSUAK Cove (Alaska, Nunivak Island A-7). The Yupik (Eskimo} name was recorded in 1949; the spelling **Ikookstakswak** is also recorded (Orth 1967).

IKOYGAK Creek (Alaska, St. Lawrence D-6). The Yupik (Eskimo) name was reported in 1949 (Orth 1967).

IKPEK (Alaska, Teller D-5) \ik´ pek\. The Iñupiaq (Eskimo) name was published in 1956 (Orth 1967); cf. *ikpik* 'river bank' (L. Kaplan p.c.) Probably related placenames in Alaska include **Ikpik Hill** (Karluk A-2), **Ikpikpuk River** (Teshekpuk D-3), and **Ikpitcheak Creek** (Wainwright B-2).

IKPIK Hill (Alaska, Karluk A-2) \ik´ pik\. The Alutiiq (Eskimo) name is said to mean 'cliff, bluff' (Orth 1967); cf. Central Yupik (Eskimo) *ekvik* 'cliff' (Jacobson 1984). Probably related placenames in Alaska include **Ikpek** (Teller D-5), **Ikpikpuk River** (Teshekpuk D-3), and **Ikpitcheak Creek** (Wainwright B-2).

IKPIKPUK River (Alaska, Teshekpuk D-3) \ik pik´ puk\. From Iñupiaq (Eskimo) *ikpikpak* 'big bluff, bank', from *ikpik* 'river bank', *-(q)pak* 'big' (Orth 1967; L. Kaplan p.c.). Probably related placenames include **Ikpitcheak Creek** (Alaska, Wainwright B-2).

IKPILGOK (Alaska, Wainwright C-2). The Iñupiaq (Eskimo) name was published in 1958 (Orth 1967).

IKPITCHEAK Creek (Alaska, Wainwright B-2). The Iñupiaq (Eskimo) name, said to mean 'new bank', was recorded in 1956 (Orth 1967); cf. *ikpik* 'river bank' (L. Kaplan p.c.). Probably related placenames in Alaska include **Ikpek** (Teller D-5), **Ikpik Hill** (Karluk A-2), and **Ikpikpuk River** (Teshekpuk D-3).

IKROAVIK Lake (Alaska, Barrow A-4). The Iñupiaq (Eskimo) name was reported around 1950 as meaning 'a place where one gets in a boat to travel' (Orth 1967).

IKSIAK Point (Alaska, Unalaska B-3). Probably from Aleut *hixsix* 'to burn' (Bergsland 1994).

IKT Butte (Ore., Deschutes Co.) \ikt\. This is Chinook Jargon for 'one'; the site was named by the Forest Service, along with several other points named with Chinook Jargon numbers (McArthur 1992). The term comes from Chinookan *-ixt* (D. Kinkade p.c.).

IKTI Cape (Alaska, Stepovak Bay D-2). The Aleut name was published as <Ikhti> in 1847, and as <Itkhi> in 1852 (Orth 1967).

IKTLIYAGAK Mountain (Alaska, Goodnews Bay A-7). The Yupik (Eskimo) name was reported in 1954 (Orth 1967).

IKTUA Bay (Alaska, Seward A-3). The Native American name, perhaps Alutiiq (Eskimo), was reported in 1951 (Orth 1967).

IKUKTLITLIG Mountain (Alaska, Goodnews Bay B-7). The Yupik (Eskimo) name, perhaps meaning 'old end mountain', was recorded about 1951 (Orth 1967); cf. *ikuq* 'end' (Jacobson 1984).

ILAK Island (Alaska, Gareloi Island A-1). From the Aleut placename *iilax̂* (Bergsland 1994).

ILANIK Lakes (Alaska, Goodnews Bay A-7). The Yupik (Eskimo) name was reported in 1954 (Orth 1967).

ILERUM Lake (Alaska, Kenai D-2). The Native American name, perhaps Dena'ina (Athabaskan), was made official around 1963; the writing **Ilerun** is also found (Orth 1967).

ILIAMNA (Alaska, Iliamna D-6) \il ē am´ nə, ē lē am´ nə\. Perhaps from Dena'ina (Athabaskan) *nila vena* 'islands lake' (Kari and Kari 1982:23); cf. *ni* 'island' (Wassillie 1979).

ILIASIK Passage (Alaska, Port Moller A-6). The Aleut name was reported in 1897 (Orth 1967).

ILIGLURUK Creek (Alaska, De Long Mountains D-1). The Iñupiaq (Eskimo) name, said to refer to a 'burnt-looking' area, was reported in 1925 (Orth 1967); cf. *ilik-* 'to become scorched' (MacLean 1980).

ILIKRAK Creek (Alaska, Point Hope B-2). The Iñupiaq (Eskimo) name is said to refer to 'the death struggle of an animal' (Orth 1967).

ILINGNORAK Ridge (Alaska, Misheguk Mountain C-5). The Iñupiaq (Eskimo) name is said to refer to a 'burned' area (Orth 1967); cf. *ilik-* 'to get burnt' (Fortescue et al. 1994).

ILIUK Arm (Alaska, Mt. Katmai C-5). The Alutiiq (Eskimo) name was published in 1922 (Orth 1967).

ILIULIUK Bay (Alaska, Unalaska C-2). From Aleut *iluulux̂, iluulax̂* '(bay) going in a half circle' (Bergsland 1994).

ILIVIT Mountains (Alaska, Holy Cross A-4). The Native American name, perhaps Koyukon (Athabaskan), was reported in 1842–44 (Orth 1967).

ILKOGNAK Rock (Alaska, Kodiak D-3). The Alutiiq (Eskimo) name was reported around 1840 (Orth 1967).

ILLABOT Creek (Wash., Skagit Co.). From Northern Lushootseed (Salishan) /x̣əlábac/ 'hollow cedar tree' (D. Kinkade p.c.).

ILLAHAW (Fla., Osceola Co.) \i lä´ hô\. From Muskogee *yvlahv* /yalá:ha/ 'orange', from Spanish *naranja* (Read 1934; Martin and Mauldin 2000). The form **Yalaha** also occurs as a placename (Fla., Lake Co.).

ILLAHE (Ore., Curry Co.) \il´ ə hē\. Chinook Jargon <il´-la-hee>, <illihie>, <ilahe> 'land, earth, country', probably from Lower Chinook [i-lé'e] 'country' (D. Kinkade p.c.). The spelling **Illahee** also occurs (Wash., Kitsap Co.).

ILLILOUETTE Fall (Calif., Mariposa Co.) \i lil o͞o et´\. The name was earlier written <Tululowehäck> and <Tooluluwack>, from Southern Miwok /ṭiṭilwiyak/, lit. 'something shiny'; cf. /ṭululli/ 'shiny' (Gudde 1998).

ILLINOIS \il i noi´\. The name refers to an Indian people, a division of what are often called the Miami/Illinois peoples, belonging to the Algonquian linguistic family. Their name for themselves was recorded in 1725 as <Inoca>. They were early referred to as <Ilinoüek>, Old Ottawa (Algonquian) for 'ordinary speaker'. The modern form "Illinois" represents a seventeenth-century French spelling, pronounced [ilinwe] at that time (HNAI 15:679; cf. also Costa 2000: 46–47). Placenames derived from these forms include the name of the state and of the **Illinois River** (Ill., Calhoun Co.); **Illiopolis** (Ill., Sangamon Co.), a combination with Greek *polis* 'city'; **Illiniwek Forest Preserve** \i lī´ ni wek\. (Ill., Rock Island Co.); and **Illini Township** (Ill., Macon Co.) \i lī´ nī\. Outside the state, there is an **Illinois Bayou** (Ark., Pope Co.).

ILLIPAH (Nev., White Pine Co.) \il´ i pä\. The name is said to be from Shoshoni (Numic), containing /paa/ 'water', but the derivation is not clear (Carlson 1974).

ILMALIANUK, Cape (Alaska, Umnak B-2). From the Aleut placename *idmalanax̂,* perhaps meaning 'contents along', from *idmax̂* 'contents, what is in it' (Bergsland 1994).

ILNIK (Alaska, Chignik C-5) \il´ nik\. The Yupik (Eskimo) name was reported in 1951 (Orth 1967).

ILPUT Island (Alaska, Port Alexander D-5). The Tlingit name was reported in 1809 (Orth 1967).

ILWACO (Wash., Pacific Co.) \il wä´ kō\. Named for a Lower Chinook leader, also called "El-wah-ko Jim"; his Native American name was [ʔɪlwək^{W}o] (D. Kinkade p.c.). The placename also occurs in Ore. (Clatsop Co.).

ILYIRAK Creek (Alaska, Point Hope B-2). The Iñupiaq (Eskimo) name was recorded as <Eelyeerat> in 1960 (Orth 1967).

IMAGE Creek (Ore., Clackamas Co.). Formerly the site of a rock carved in the shape of an Indian woman with a cougar (or bear) on her back; it is said that the carving was vandalized and is no longer to be found (H. Zenk p.c.).

IMAIKNIK Lake (Alaska, Umiat C-2). The Iñupiaq (Eskimo) name was reported in 1956 and said to mean 'dried up place' (Orth 1967).

IMAKRUAK Lake (Alaska, Teshekpuk D-2). The Iñupiaq (Eskimo) name is probably *imaǵruaq* 'big old body of water' (L. Kaplan p.c.). A perhaps related name is **Imelyak River** (Ambler River C-5), from Iñupiaq *imiaq,* said to mean 'little water' (Orth 1967; Burch 1998). Other probably related names include **Imik Lagoon** (Alaska, Noatak B-4); see below.

IMIAKNIKPAK Lake (Alaska, Killik River B-2). The Iñupiaq (Eskimo) name, said to mean 'big dry lake', was recorded in 1956 (Orth 1967); cf. *-(q)pak* 'big'.

IMIK Lagoon (Alaska, Noatak B-4) \im´ ik\. From Iñupiaq (Eskimo) *imiq* 'drinking water' (Orth 1967; MacLean 1980). Probably related names in Alaska include **Imikneyak Creek** (Misheguk Mountain A-3), said to mean 'has no water'; **Imikpuk Lake** (Barrow B-4) \im ik´ puk\, said to mean 'big freshwater lake', with *-(q)pak* 'big'; **Imikrak Creek** (Point Hope A-2), said to mean 'warm water'; and **Imikruk Creek** (Noatak C-5), said to mean 'freshwater place'. Other probably related placenames include **Imakruak Lake** (Alaska, Teshekpuk D-2); see above.

IMMOKALEE (Fla., Collier Co.) \i mō´ kə lē\. The site was settled by William Allen in 1872 and became known as Allen's Place; this was translated into Hitchiti (Muskogean) as *Allen im-okli* 'Allen's home', from *im-* 'his, her' plus *okli* 'home' (Goff 1975; J. Martin p.c.).

IMNAHA (Ore., Wallowa Co.) \im nä´ hə, im nä´ hä\. From Nez Perce (Sahaptian) /imnáha/, the name of a village (Aoki 1994).

IMNAITCHIAK Creek (Alaska, Killik River C-3). The Iñupiaq (Eskimo) name, said to mean 'young mountain sheep', was reported in 1956 (Orth 1967); cf. *imnaiq, ipnaiq* 'mountain sheep' (Fortescue et al. 1994). Related forms in Alaska include **Imnatchiak Bluff** (Killik River D-1) and **Ipnavik River** (Howard Pass D-1).

IMNAK Bluff (Alaska, Noatak D-4) \im´ nak\. From Iñupiaq (Eskimo) *imnaq* 'cliff', reported in 1966 (Orth 1967; Webster and Zibell 1970). A related name is **Imnakpak Cliff** (Alaska, Point Hope A-2), reported in 1962 as meaning 'big cliff' (Orth 1967); cf. *-(q)pak* 'big' (Webster and Zibell 1970). Also probably related is **Imnakuk Bluff** (Alaska, Noatak D-6), reported in 1966 (Orth 1967).

IMNATCHIAK Bluff (Alaska, Killik River D-1). The Iñupiaq (Eskimo) name, said to mean 'young mountain sheep', was reported in 1956 (Orth 1967); cf. *imnaiq, ipnaiq* 'mountain sheep' (Fortescue et al. 1994). Related forms in Alaska include **Imnaitchiak Creek** (Killik River C-3) and **Ipnavik River** (Howard Pass D-1).

IMNAVAIT Mountain (Alaska, Philip Smith Mountains D-5). The Iñupiaq (Eskimo) name was reported in 1956 (Orth 1967).

IMPACH (Wash., Ferry Co.). From Okanagan (Salish) /npáq/ 'alkaline area', lit. 'white place', from /n-/ 'place' and /páq-/ 'white' (D. Kinkade p.c.).

IMPAGHUK Point (Alaska, St. Lawrence C-4) The Yupik (Eskimo) language was reported in 1949 (Orth 1967).

IMURUK Basin (Alaska, Teller A-2). Iñupiaq *imaǵruk* 'something which is not quite a sea', from *imaq* 'sea, large body of water' plus *-ruk* 'almost, not quite' (L. Kaplan p.c.).

IMUYA Bay (Alaska, Ugashik A-2). The Yupik (Eskimo) name was published in 1835 (Orth 1967).

INADU Knob (N.C., Haywood Co.) \in´ ə do͞o\. From Cherokee (Iroquoian) *inada* 'snake' (B. Rudes p.c.).

IÑAJA (Calif., San Diego Co.) \in´yə ħä\. From Diegueño (Yuman) *'enyehaa* 'my water' (or perhaps 'my tears'), from *'iñ-* 'my' plus *'ehaa* 'water' (Gudde 1998). A related placename is **Anahuac Spring** in Calif.; see above.

INAKPUK (Alaska, Dillingham C-4). The Yupik (Eskimo) name was recorded in 1930 (Orth 1967).

INALIK (Alaska, Teller D-8). The Yupik (Eskimo) name was reported in 1880 (Orth 1967).

INAM (Calif., Siskiyou Co.) \i näm´\. From Karuk *inaam* 'site of the annual world renewal ceremony' (Gudde 1998).

INANUDAK Bay (Alaska, Umnak B-2). From the Aleut placename *inganudax̂*, perhaps from *ingan udax̂* 'the bay there in front'; cf. *inga* 'right there in front', *udax̂* 'bay' (Bergsland 1994).

INARU River (Alaska, Meade River D-1). The name may be a miscopying of <Kuaru>, reported in 1885, from Iñupiaq (Eskimo) <Kugaarug> (Orth 1967).

INATI Bay (Wash., Whatcom Co.) \in´ ə tī\. From Chinook Jargon <in-a-ti, inataï> [ínətay, ɛ́nətay] 'across, over, outside, other side', from Chinookan; cf. Lower Chinook root [-nata] 'on the other side', Kathlamet [ínata] 'one side' (D. Kinkade). The same name occurs as **Enetai** (Wash., Kitsap Co.).

INCHELIUM (Wash., Ferry Co.) \in chə lē´ əm\. From an Okanagan (Salishan) placename [ncaʔlíwm], perhaps related to [ncaʔlíʔm] 'water hitting against something' (D. Kinkade p.c.).

INDIAN \in´ dē ən, in´ din\. This word was originally an adaptation of Spanish *indio,* used by early explorers to refer to the inhabitants of *las Indias* 'the Indies'. The term occurs in many combinations in placenames, said to occur in every state except Hawai'i; one of the commonest is **Indian Creek.** The term **Indian Fields** occurs in several states, designating lands originally cultivated by Indians (e.g., Md., St. Marys Co.); (Kenny 1984). In the same state and county, **Indian Queen** refers to the wife of an Algonquian chieftain in colonial times (Kenny 1984). Some places in various states are named after Indian residents who were called "Indian so-and-so" by local white people: for example, a meadow in Wash. (Pierce Co.) is called **Indian Henrys Hunting Ground** (Hitchman 1985). In addition, a number of placenames combine **Indian** with other elements, including **Indiahoma** (Okla., Comanche Co.), a fusion with **Oklahoma**; the city of **Indianapolis** (Ind., Marion Co.), with Greek *polis* 'city'; and **Indianola,** with the "euphonic" suffix *-ola,* in several states (e.g., Okla., Pittsburg Co.; Wash., Kitsap Co.).

INDIO (Calif., Riverside Co.) \in´ dē ō\. From Spanish *indio* 'Indian' (Gudde 1998). There is also an **Indio Canyon** (N.Mex., Catron Co.) and an **Inditos Draw** (N.Mex., McKinley Co.), from the Spanish diminutive plural, meaning 'little Indians'.

INDOOLI Mountain (Alaska, Nunivak Island A-5). The Yupik (Eskimo) name was recorded in 1959 (Orth 1967).

INEREVUK Mountain (Alaska, Shungnak D-2). The Iñupiaq (Eskimo) name was reported after 1940 (Orth 1967).

INGAKSLUGWAT Hills (Alaska, Marshall B-6). The Yupik (Eskimo) name, reported in 1948, is said to mean 'little old mountains' (Orth 1967); cf. *ingriq* [iŋʀiq] 'mountain' (Jacobson 1984).

INGALIK \ing gä´ lik\. This term, referring to an Athabaskan people of the lower Kuskokwim River drainage, in western Alaska, is from Yupik (Eskimo) *iŋqilig* 'Indian' (*HNAI* 6:613). It is now often replaced by **Deg Hit'an**, lit. 'people from here'.

INGALUAT Creek (Alaska, Umiat C-3). The Iñupiaq (Eskimo) name was reported in 1956 (Orth 1967).

INGLOOTHLOOGRAMIUT (Alaska, Cape Mendenhall D-3). The Yupik (Eskimo) name was reported in 1932 (Orth 1967). The suffix *-miut* means 'people'.

INGLUTALIK River (Alaska, Norton Bay D-4). Iñupiaq (Eskimo) *iglutalik* 'place with sod houses', from *iglu* '(sod) house', *-talik* 'having many'; or from Yupik (Eskimo) *englutalek,* with the same meaning (*englu, ngellu* 'sod house') (L. Kaplan p.c.).

INGRAKAKLAK (Alaska, Kiguk C-6). The Yupik (Eskimo) name was reported in 1898 as <Ingrakaghamiut> (Orth 1967).

INGRICHERK Mountain (Alaska, Ambler River A-4). Iñupiaq (Eskimo) *iñġitchiaq* 'new mountain' (L. Kaplan p.c.).

INGRICHUAK Hill (Alaska, Kwiguk A-5). The Yupik (Eskimo) name, meaning 'little mountain', was recorded in 1842–44 (Orth 1967); cf. *ingriq* [iŋʀiq] 'mountain' (Jacobson 1984). Several other Alaska placenames seem related, including **Ingrihak** (Marshall D-1) \ing´ grə häk\, published in 1880 (Orth 1967); **Ingrijoak Hill** (Cape Mendenhall D-4), recorded in 1949 (Orth 1967); **Ingrilukat Hills** (Nunivak Island A-5), recorded in 1949, said to mean 'small hills close together' (Orth 1967); **Ingrimiut** (Nunivak Island A-2) \ing´ gri myo͞ot\, said to mean 'mountain people' (Orth 1967), with *-miut* 'people' (Jacobson 1984); **Ingriruk Hill** (Cape Mendenhall D-3), meaning 'little mountain' (Orth 1967); and **Ingrisarak Mountain** (Hooper Bay C-1), reported in 1951 (Orth 1967).

INGRUKSUKRUK Creek (Alaska, Shungnak B-5). The Yupik (Eskimo) name was recorded in 1927 (Orth 1967).

INGUADONA (Minn., Cass Co.) \ing gwə dō´ nə\. This name may be of Indian origin, but its derivation has not been traced (Upham 2001).

INIAKUK River (Alaska, Survey Pass A-1). The Iñupiaq (Eskimo) name is probably *inyukuq*, from *inyuk* 'person' (L. Kaplan p.c.).

INIAM Point (Alaska, Naknek C-3). The Yupik (Eskimo) name is probably *inyukuq,* from *iñuk* 'person' (L. Kaplan p.c.).

INICOK Creek (Alaska, Harrison Bay A-5). The Iñupiaq (Eskimo) name, said to mean 'it goes somewhere', was reported in 1956 (Orth 1967). The variant **Inigok** also occurs.

INIKAKLIK Creek (Alaska, Killik River B-1). The Iñupiaq (Eskimo) name, said to mean 'camping place', was reported in 1950 (Orth 1967).

INIKLA Island (Alaska, False Pass B-2). The Aleut name was reported in 1901 (Orth 1967).

INKOM (Idaho, Bannock Co.) \ing´ kəm, in´ kum\. From Shoshoni (Numic) /ɨn kimma/ 'you (singular) come' (J. McLaughlin p.c.).

IN-KO-PAH (Calif., Imperial Co.) \ing´ kō pä\. Named by the Division of Highways on the basis of Diegueño (Yuman) *'enyaak 'iipay,* lit. 'east people' (Gudde 1998).

INMACHUK (Alaska, Kotzebue A-2) \in´ mə chuk\. Iñupiaq (Eskimo) *ipnatchiaq* 'new cliff', from *ipnaq* 'cliff', *-tchiaq* 'new' (L. Kaplan p.c.).

INNOKO River (Alaska, Holy Cross A-2) \in ō´ kō, ē nō´ kō\. From Deg Hit'an (Athabaskan) *eniq, enigg, yooniq* 'upland' (J. Kari p.c.).

INOLA (Okla., Rogers Co.) \ī nō´ lə\. Said to be from a Cherokee (Iroquoian) word meaning 'black fox' (Shirk 1974). Perhaps related is the placename **Lake Enola** (Fla., Lake Co.).

INOWAK Creek (Alaska, Sleetmute C-3). From Yupik (Eskimo) *iinruq* 'medicine' (J. Kari p.c.).

INSELNOSTLINDE (Alaska, Holy Cross C-2). From Deg Hit'an (Athabaskan), of unclear derivation (Orth 1967).

INTENLEIDEN (Alaska, Holy Cross C-2). From Deg Hit'an (Athabaskan), of unclear derivation (Orth 1967).

INTUN Cone (Alaska, Dixon Entrance C-1). Possibly an abbreviation of nearby **Intungidi Hill,** a name of Haida origin (Orth 1967).

INUKPAK Rock (Alaska, Point Hope A-2). The Iñupiaq (Eskimo) name, said to mean 'big man', was reported about 1962 (Orth 1967); cf. *iñuk* 'person', *-(q)pak* 'big' (MacLean 1980).

INUKPASUGRUK Creek (Alaska, Chandler Lake A-3). From Iñupiaq (Eskimo) *iñukpasr̄ugr̄uk* 'giant' (Orth 1967; Webster and Zibell 1970).

INUKTAK Creek (Alaska, Point Hope A-10). The Iñupiaq (Eskimo) name is *iñuktaq* 'murder victim' (L. Kaplan p.c.).

IÑUPIAQ \i no͞o´ pē ak, i no͞o´ pē äk\. The term refers to a speaker of the Eskimo language of northern Alaska or to the language itself; it is derived from Iñupiaq *iñuk* 'person' (MacLean 1980). The related peoples of northern Canada are called **Inuit**, and their language is called **Inuit** or **Inuktitut**. The plural of **Iñupiaq** is **Iñupiat**, which occurs in the placename **Inupiat Mountain** (Alaska, Chandler Lake A-5) \i no͞o´ pē at, i no͞o´ pē ät\

INVUT Mountain (Alaska, St. Lawrence B-2). The Yupik (Eskimo) name was reported in 1932 (Orth 1967).

INYAN KARA Mountain (Wyo., Crook Co.) \in´ yən kâr ə\. From Lakhota (Siouan) *íyą́-kağa* 'stone made', from *íyą* 'stone', *káğa* 'to make' (Urbanek 1974; Ingham 2001).

INYO County (Calif.) \in´ yō\. Probably from Panamint (Numic) /ɨnɨ-yun/ 'it's dangerous' (Bright and McLaughlin 2000). The name also occurs in Idaho (Lemhi Co.).

INYORURAK Lakes (Alaska, Howard Pass A-1). The Iñupiaq (Eskimo) term, said to be a personal name, was recorded in 1956 (Orth 1967).

INYUGAKULIGIT Creek (Alaska, Killik River B-1). The Iñupiaq (Eskimo) term is *iñugaqutligich,* plural of *inyugaqutligik* 'mythical dwarf' (L. Kaplan p.c.).

INYUILAK Creek (Alaska, Survey Pass A-4). The Iñupiaq (Eskimo) name is *iñuiḷaq* 'deserted place' (L. Kaplan p.c.).

INYURAKTOAK Creek (Alaska, Killik River A-5). The Iñupiaq (Eskimo) name was reported in 1954 (Orth 1967).

IOKA (Utah, Duchesne Co.) \ī ō´ kə\. The name was supposedly "named for a Ute headman and means 'bravado'" (Van Cott 1990:200).

IOLA (Fla., Gulf Co.) \ī ō´ lə\. From Muskogee *yvholv* /yahó:la/ 'shouter', a title appearing in war names, such as that of the famous Seminole leader **Osceola** (*Vsse Yvholv* /assi-yahó:la/ 'black-drink shouter'; Read 1934:13; Martin and Mauldin 2000). A related form is **Iolee** (Fla., Calhoun Co.).

IOLAND (Okla., Ellis Co.) \ī´ ō land\. Coined from the placename **Iowa** (of Siouan origin) plus *land* (Shirk 1974).

IOLEE (Fla., Calhoun Co.) \ī ō´ lē\. An alternative form of **Iola**; see above.

IONA (S.Dak., Lyman Co.) \ī ō´ nə\. Perhaps an adaptation of Lakhota (Siouan) *oná* 'prairie fire' (Sneve 1973; A. Taylor p.c.). The Scottish island *Iona* and the English female name *Iona* or *Ione* are also possible sources, however.

IOSCO County (Mich.) \ī os´ kō\. The term refers to an Ottawa (Algonquian) hero in a legend published by Henry R. Schoolcraft; however, the name seems to have been invented by Schoolcraft himself (Vogel 1986). There is also an **Iosco Township** (Minn., Waseca Co.) and a **Lake Iosco** (N.J., Passaic Co.).

IOSEPA (Utah, Tooele Co.) \ē ō sā´ pā\. This name for what was once a community of Hawai'ian converts to Mormonism is from Hawai'ian *Iosepa* 'Joseph' (Van Cott 1990).

IOWA \ī´ ō wə, ī´ ō wā\. This name refers first of all to the **Iowa** Indian people, of the Chiwere branch of the Siouan linguistic family; it was then applied to the **Iowa River**, to the state, and to many local features. The origin of the term may be Santee Dakota (Siouan) *ayúxba* 'sleepy ones'; however, the name may also come from Algonquian forms such as Miami/Illinois /aayohoowia/ (*HNAI* 13:445; Costa 2000:31).

IOWITHLA River (Alaska, Dillingham A-5). The Yupik (Eskimo) name was recorded as <Ai-u-wath-lok> in 1910 (Orth 1967).

IPASHA Falls (Mont., Glacier Co.). The name refers to a woman leader of the Mandan (Siouan) people, written as <Ipashá> and translated as 'good eagle tail' (Holterman 1985).

IPEWIK River (Alaska, Point Hope B-2). Iñupiaq (Eskimo) *ipivik* 'drowning place', from *ipi-* 'to drown', *-vik* 'place' (L. Kaplan p.c.).

IPIUTAK (Alaska, Point Hope B-3). The Iñupiaq (Eskimo) name is *ipiutaaq* (L. Kaplan p.c.).

IPNAVIK River (Alaska, Howard Pass D-1) \ip´ nə vik\. The Iñupiaq (Eskimo) name, recorded in 1925, is said to mean 'a place where young mountain sheep are raised' (Orth 1967); cf. *imnaiq, ipnaiq* 'mountain sheep' (Fortescue et al. 1994), *-vik* 'place' (Webster and Zibell 1970). Related Alaska placenames include **Ipnek Creek** (Wiseman B-2) and **Ipnelivik** (Ambler River C-1), said to mean 'mountain sheep raising place' (Orth 1967).

IPSOOT Creek (Idaho, Latah Co.) \ip´ so͞ot\. Chinook Jargon *ip´-sut, ip-sut* [ípsut] 'to hide; hidden', from Chinookan *-pšut* 'to hide' (D. Kinkade p.c.). There is also an **Ipsoot Butte** (Ore., Klamath Co.) and an **Ipsoot Lake** (Wash., Whatcom Co.). Related forms include **Ipsut Creek** (Wash., Pierce Co.).

IRAK Creek (Alaska, Wainwright B-1). The Iñupiaq (Eskimo) word is *irrak* 'two eyes' (L. Kaplan p.c.).

IRETEBA Peaks (Nev., Clark Co.) \ēr ə tē´ bə\. Named for a Mojave (Yuman) leader named *'aratev,* a short form of *'ichiyer aatev,* lit. 'freed bird' (P. Munro p.c.). His name is also written <Iretaba, Iritaba>.

IRGKIVIK Creek (Alaska, Chandler Lake B-3). The Iñupiaq (Eskimo) name was recorded in 1956 (Orth 1967).

IRGNYIVIK Lake (Alaska, Chandler Lake B-3). The Iñupiaq (Eskimo) name was reported in 1956 (Orth 1967).

IRIVIK Creek (Alaska, Killik River A-2). The Iñupiaq name, reported in 1956, is said to mean 'place where there is a cave' (Orth 1967).

IROGAMI Lake (Wis., Waushara Co.) \ēr ə gä´ mē\. The name is a combination of **Iroquois**, referring to a group of Native American peoples, and <Outagami>, a name that the Ojibwa (Algonquian) used to refer to the Fox or Meskawaki people (Vogel 1991). The latter term, written **Outagamie**, is the name of a county in Wis.; cf. Ojibwa /otaka:mi:k/ 'people of the other shore' (*HNAI* 15:646).

IRONDEQUOIT (N.Y., Monroe Co.) \ə ron´ də kwät, ə ron´ də kwoit\. The Iroquoian name has been written <Neo-da-on-da-quot>, <Nidenindequeat>, <Irondequot> (etc.), perhaps referring to a bay or cove (Beauchamp 1907).

IRON NATION (S.Dak., Lyman Co.). Named for a leader of the Brulé Lakhota (Siouan) people; his Native American name was *máza oyáte,* lit. 'iron nation' (Sneve 1973; Ingham 2001).

IROQUOIS \ēr´ ə kwoi\. The term refers to a number of Indian groups, living mainly in upper N.Y. state and adjacent areas of Canada, speaking closely related languages of a family known as **Iroquoian.** In colonial times, the nucleus of these formed a confederacy known as the Five Nations; this consisted of the Cayuga, Mohawk, Onondaga, Oneida, and Seneca peoples. Around 1713, this was expanded to the Six Nations by the addition of the Tuscaroras, who speak a more distantly related Iroquoian language. The prototype of **Iroquois** was apparently neither an Iroquoian word nor an Algonquian one; it was learned by the French explorer Samuel Champlain as early as 1603. He wrote it <Irocois> and <Yrocois>, probably pronounced [irokwe] in seventeenth-century French (*HNAI* 15:319; Day 1968). As a U.S. placename, **Iroquois** is widespread: for example, N.Y. (Erie Co.), Pa. (Perry Co.), W.Va. (Wyoming Co.), and farther afield in **Iroquois County** (Ill.) and **Point Iroquois** (Minn., Chippewa Co.).

IRWAKYARUK Point (Alaska, Cape Mendenhall D-3). The Yupik (Eskimo) name was reported in 1949 (Orth 1967).

ISACHELUICH Mountains (Alaska, Misheguk Mountain A-3). The Iñupiaq (Eskimo) name is from *isa* 'moulting duck' (L. Kaplan p.c.).

ISAHULTILA Mountains (Alaska, Melozitna D-4). The Koyukon (Athabaskan) name was recorded in 1956 (Orth 1967).

ISANOTSKI Strait (Alaska, False Pass D-5). Probably a Russian adaptation of Aleut *isanax̂* 'hole, gap' (Orth 1967; Bergsland 1994).

ISANTI County (Minn.) \i san´ tē\. Probably from Dakota (Siouan) *isą́-ati,* referring to a division of the Dakotas usually called the Santees; it has been derived from *isą́* 'knife', *atí* 'to pitch camp' (Riggs 1890; Upham 2001). Related placenames include **Izatys** (Minn., Mille Lacs Co.), **Kathio Township** (Minn., Mille Lacs Co.), and **Santee** (Neb., Knox Co.).

ISAOKTUVIK Creek (Alaska, Baird Mountains D-3). The Iñupiaq (Eskimo) name is *isaġuqtuġvik* 'place to eat wings' (Burch 1998); cf. *isaġuq* 'wing' (MacLean 1980).

ISAQUEENA Falls (S.C., Oconee Co.) \is ə kwē´ nə\. A fictional Choctaw (Muskogean) name for the fictional Cherokee (Iroquoian) heroine of a long narrative poem by James Walter Daniel, published in 1898 (Neuffer and Neuffer 1983).

ISCHUA (N.Y., Cattaraugus Co.) \ish´ o͞o ə, ish´ o͞o ā\. Supposedly an Iroquoian name, translated as 'coating nettles', written earlier as <Asueshan> and <He´-shoh> (Beauchamp 1907).

I-SEE-O Tank (Okla., Comanche Co.) \ī sē ō\. Named for Sergeant I-See-O (perhaps the initials I. C. O.), a Kiowa scout with the U.S. Army (BGN 1992).

ISHAN'AN DEK'YAPBOW'A (N.Mex., Cibola Co.). The Zuni name probably contains /tek'appowa/ 'hill' (Ferguson and Hart 1985; Newman 1958).

ISHAWOOA Cone (Wyo., Park Co.) \ish ə wo͞o´ ə\. Probably from Shoshoni (Numic) /isawɨa/ 'coyote's penis', from /isa/ 'coyote' and /wɨa/ 'penis' (J. McLaughlin p.c.).

ISHI Caves (Calif., Tehama Co.) \ish´ ē\. Named for Ishi, a member of the **Yahi** tribe, the last "wild Indian" in Calif., who came to the attention of whites in 1911.

ISHKOTE Lake (Mich., Iron Co.) \ish kō´ tə\. From Ojibwa (Algonquian) *ishkode* 'fire' (Vogel 1986; Nichols and Nyholm 1995).

ISHKOWIK River (Alaska, Kuskokwim Bay D-2). The Yupik (Eskimo) name was reported in 1951 (Orth 1967).

ISHPEMING (Mich., Marquette Co.) \ish´ pə ming\. From Ojibwa (Algonquian) *ishpiming* 'above' (Vogel 1986; Nichols and Nyholm 1995).

ISHTALITNA Creek (Alaska, Tanana D-4) \ish tə lit´ nə\. The Koyukon (Athabaskan) name was recorded in 1956 (Orth 1967).

ISHUKPAK Bluff (Alaska, Umiat D-3). The Iñupiaq (Eskimo) name was reported in 1956, said to mean 'big end one' (Orth 1967); cf. *isu* 'end', *-(q)paq* 'big' (MacLean 1980). A probably related placename is **Isuk Creek** (Alaska, Point Hope A-2).

ISHUKTAK Creek (Alaska, Teshekpuk A-5). From Iñupiaq (Eskimo) *isuqtuq* 'it is muddy' (Orth 1967; Webster and Zibell 1970).

ISHUT Creek (Alaska, Teller C-6). The Iñupiaq (Eskimo) name was reported in 1899 (Orth 1967).

ISIAK Lake (Alaska, Ambler River C-1). From Iñupiaq (Eskimo) *isigak* 'foot' (Orth 1967; MacLean 1980). Related placenames include **Isikut Mountain** (Howard Pass A-1).

ISLAY Creek (Calif., San Luis Obispo Co.) \iz´ lā\. Borrowed through Spanish from Salinan *slay'* 'wild cherry bush'. The Spanish plural is reflected in **Islais Creek** (Calif., San Francisco Co.) \is´ lis\. (Gudde 1998).

ISLETA (N.Mex., Bernalillo Co.) \iz let´ ə\. The name applied by white people to this Tiwa (Tanoan) pueblo represents the Spanish for 'little island' (cf. *isla* 'island'). The Tiwa name for the place is [šiehwíb-àg]'flint kick-stick place', referring to pieces of flint kicked along in a race (Julyan 1998; *HNAI* 9:364).

ISOM Lake (Okla., Bryan Co.) \ī´ səm\. The reservoir was named for Isom Springs, named in turn for Isom O'ky-um-ba, a Chickasaw resident (Shirk 1974).

ISRATHORAK Creek (Alaska, Russian Mission B-5). The Yupik (Eskimo) name was reported in 1949 (Orth 1967).

ISSAQUAH Creek (Wash., King Co.) \is´ ə kwä\. From the Southern Lushootseed (Salishan) placename /sq^{W}áx^{W}/ (D. Kinkade p.c.).

ISSAQUENA County (Miss.) \is ə kwē´ nə\. Probably from Choctaw *isi-okhina* 'deer creek', from *isi* 'deer' and *okhina* 'creek' (Seale 1939); there is also a place called **Issaquena** in Sharkey Co. An alternative spelling occurs in **Issaqueena Lake** (S.C., Oconee Co.).

ISSICK Creek (Idaho, Benewah Co.) \is´ ik\. Short for Chinook Jargon *is'ick stick* 'alder tree' (also 'ash, maple, elm'), from *is'sik* [ísɪk] 'paddle, oar' (Lower Chinook *í-sik*) plus English *stick* (D. Kinkade p.c.).

ISSORTULIK Slough (Alaska, Hooper Bay B-3). The Yupik (Eskimo) name was reported in 1951 (Orth 1967).

ISTACHATTA (Fla., Hernando Co.) \is ti chat´ ə\. From Muskogee *este-cate* [isti-čá:ti] 'Indian', lit. 'man-red', from *este* 'man' and *cate* 'red' (Read 1934; Martin and Mauldin 2000); probably a loan-translation from English *redman.*

ISTKU Point (Alaska, Craig D-4). The Tlingit name was published in 1964 (Orth 1967).

ISTOKPOGA (Fla., Highlands Co.) \is tok pō´ gə\. From Muskogee, perhaps meaning 'lake where people died in the water', from *este* /ísti/ 'person', *ak-* /ak-/ 'in water or a low place', *pokv* /po:ka/ 'being gone, dying' (Read 1934; Martin and Mauldin 2000). A related placename is **Eastaboga** (Ala., Calhoun Co.).

ISTROUMA (La., East Baton Rouge Par.) \i stro͞o´ mə\. This represents the Choctaw (Muskogean) for 'red stick', from *itti* 'stick, tree, wood' and *homma* 'red' (P. Munro p.c.). Its French equivalent is the placename **Baton Rouge** (La.).

ISUK Creek (Alaska, Point Hope A-2). The Iñupiaq (Eskimo) name, reported in 1950, is said to mean 'end, last one' (Orth 1967); cf. *isu* 'end' (MacLean 1980). A probably related placename is **Ishukpak Bluff** (Alaska, Umiat D-3).

ISURIK Creek (Alaska, Goodnews Bay B-6). From Yupik (Eskimo) *issuriq* 'spotted seal' (Orth 1967; Jacobson 1984).

ITA (Miss., Itawamba Co.) \it´ ə\. An abbreviation of the placename **Itawamba,** representing Choctaw (Muskogean) *itombi* 'box, chest' (Seale 1939).

ITAK (Ariz., Pima Co.) Probably from O'odham (Piman), but of unclear derivation (Granger 1983).

ITALIO River (Alaska, Yakutat B-4). **Italio** was a surname used in English by a Tlingit family (De Laguna 1972:81).

ITASCA, Lake (Minn., Clearwater Co.) \ī tas´ kə, i tas´ kə\. The name of this body of water, considered the headwaters of the Mississippi River, was invented by Henry R. Schoolcraft in 1832, combining the *-itas* of Latin *veritas* 'truth' and the *ca-* of *caput* 'head'. The original Ojibwa (Algonquian) name is said to have been <Omushkos> 'elk' (Upham 2001); this can be more accurately written as *omashkooz* 'elk' (Nichols and Nyholm 1995). The name **Itasca** was subsequently applied to **Itasca County** in Minn., and to several other places (e.g., Ill., Du Page Co.; Wis., Douglas Co.; and Tex., Hill Co.) The alternative spelling **Itaska** occurs in N.Y. (Broome Co.).

ITAWAMBA County (Miss.) \it ə wôm´ bə\. Named after a Choctaw (Muskogean) leader called <Itawamba Minco> or in English Levi Colbert. The term **Itawamba** is perhaps from *itombi* 'box, chest, bench'; cf. *iti* 'wood' (Seale 1939). An apparently abbreviated form occurs as **Ita** (Miss., Itawamba Co.).

ITCHEPACKESASSA Creek (Fla., Hillsborough Co.) \ich ə pak ə sä´ sə\. From Muskogee *hecepakwv* /hičipákwa/ 'pipe' (or *hece-pakpvkē* /hiči-pakpakí:/ 'a medicinal plant') plus *sasv* /sá:sa/ 'some' (Martin and Mauldin 2000).

ITERIAK Creek (Alaska, Killik River C-5). From Iñupiaq (Eskimo) *itiġiaq* 'weasel, ermine' (Orth 1967; MacLean 1980).

ITHAGSUTLEK Lake (Alaska, Goodnews Bay D-8). The Yupik (Eskimo) name was published in 1951 (Orth 1967).

ITIGAKNIT Mountain (Alaska, Philip Smith Mountains C-5). The Iñupiaq (Eskimo) name was reported in 1956 (Orth 1967).

ITIKMALAIYAK Creek (Alaska, Chandler Lake B-3). The Iñupiaq (Eskimo) name, reported in 1951, is said to mean 'little rectum' (Orth 1967); cf. *itiq* 'anus' (Fortescue et al. 1994). Probably related Alaska names are **Itikmalak River** (Philip Smith Mountains B-5), reported in 1956 (Orth 1967), and **Itikmalakpak Creek** (Chandler Lake B-3), published in

1951 and said to mean 'big rectum' (Orth 1967); cf. *-(q)paq* 'big' (Fortescue et al. 1994).

ITILYIARGIOK Creek (Alaska, Killik River A-5). The Iñupiaq (Eskimo) name has also been written <Itkilyiargiak> and is said to mean 'go to visit Indians' (Orth 1967); cf. *itqiḷiq* 'Indian' (MacLean 1980). Probably related placenames include **Itkilikruich** (Alaska, Killik River C-3).

ITIMTIKRAK Creek (Alaska, Howard Pass A-5). The Iñupiaq (Eskimo) name was recorded in 1956 (Orth 1967).

ITINIK Lake (Alaska, Meade River C-5). The Iñupiaq (Eskimo) name is said to mean 'rim of water around a still frozen lake' (Orth 1967).

ITKILIKRUICH (Alaska, Killik River C-3). The Iñupiaq (Eskimo) name is said to mean 'old Indian mountain' (Orth 1967); cf. *itqiḷiq* 'Indian' (MacLean 1980). Probably related Alaska placenames are **Itkillik River** (Harrison Bay A-2) and **Itkilyariak Creek** (Mt. Michelson D-1), said to mean 'Indian route' (Orth 1967). Possibly related Alaska names include **Itilyiargiok Creek** (Killik River A-5) and **Killik River** (Ikpikpuk River A-2).

ITSALIK, Mount (Alaska, Point Hope C-2). The Iñupiaq (Eskimo) name was published in 1964 (Orth 1967).

ITSAMI Ledge (Wash., Thurston Co.). The name was given in 1841, based on an unidentified Indian language (Hitchman 1985).

ITSWOOT Creek (Wash., Jefferson Co.) \its´ wo͞ot\. From Chinook Jargon <its´-hoot, atchhoat> [íts-hut, ítswut] 'black bear', from Lower Chinook [-ítsxut] 'black bear' (D. Kinkade p.c.).

ITTA BENA (Miss., Leflore Co.) \it ə bē´ nə\. Perhaps from Choctaw (Muskogean) *iti* 'forest, wood' and *bina* 'a camp' (Seale 1939). A possibly related placename is **Bina** (N.C., Ashe Co.); see above.

ITTAR Rock (Alaska, Sitka C-7). The name, perhaps from Tlingit, was published in 1928 (Orth 1967).

ITTITALAH (Okla., Johnston Co.) \it i tä´ lə\. Perhaps from Choctaw (Muskogean) *ittitakla* 'between' (P. Munro p.c.).

ITUBLARAK (Alaska, Point Hope B-2). The Iñupiaq (Eskimo) name was reported about 1962 (Orth 1967).

ITULILIK (Alaska, Sleetmute B-3). The Yupik (Eskimo) name was reported in 1903; it refers to a species of small fish (Orth 1967).

ITUMA (Miss., Holmes Co.) \ĭ to͞o´ mə\. Probably from Choctaw (Muskogean), perhaps 'red stick', from *iti* 'stick, tree' and *humma* 'red', and thus related to **Istrouma** (La., East Baton Rouge Par.), which enters French and English as **Baton Rouge.**

IUKA (Miss., Tishomingo Co.) \ī o͞o´ kə, ī o͝ok´ ə\. Perhaps a shortening of the name of a Choctaw or Chickasaw (Muskogean) leader, such as one named <Ishtoki Yukatubi> (Dyson 1994); this may be a Choctaw "war name" meaning 'great-one, prisoner-killer', from <ishtokaka> 'the great one' (said to be from Chickasaw *ishto* 'great') plus *yoka'* 'prisoner, slave' and *abi* 'kill' (Seale 1939; Munro and Willmond 1994). A battle here during the Civil War seems to have led to the name's being transferred to several other places (e.g., Ill., Marion Co.; Ohio, Franklin Co.; and Ky,. Livingston Co.).

IUMKRARAK Slough (Alaska, Kwiguk C-5). The Yupik (Eskimo) name was reported in 1899 (Orth 1967).

IVANPAH (Calif., San Bernardino Co.) \ī´ vən pä\. Chemehuevi (Numic) /avimpa, aavimpa/ 'white clay water', from /avi/ 'white clay' and /pa/ 'water' (Gudde 1998). The name also occurs in Nev. (Clark Co.) and in Kans. (Greenwood Co.) Probably related is **Ibapah** (Utah, Tooele Co.); see above.

IVEKAN Mountain (Alaska, St. Lawrence C-6). The Yupik (Eskimo) name, also written <Aivikan>, was recorded in 1944 (Orth 1967).

IVIANGIK Mountain (Alaska, Point Hope C-3). From Iñupiaq (Eskimo) *iviaŋŋiq* 'breast' (Orth 1967; Fortescue et al. 1994).

IVIK Creek (Alaska, Survey Pass B-6). From Iñupiaq (Eskimo) *ivik* 'blade of grass' (Orth 1967; Fortescue et al. 1994).

IVISAK Creek (Alaska, Killik River B-2). From Iñupiaq (Eskimo) *ivisaaq* 'red mineral, iron oxide paint' (Orth 1967; L. Kaplan p.c.). Probable variants of the same word are found in **Ivisaruk River** (Alaska, Wainwright B-2), early written as <Ivisaurk>; and in **Ivishak River** (Alaska, Sagavanirktok B-3).

IVOTUK Creek (Alaska, Killik River C-5). The Iñupiaq (Eskimo) name is *ivutuq* 'lamb' (L. Kaplan p.c.).

IWAKTOK Hill (Alaska, Marshall B-7). The Iñupiaq (Eskimo) name, reported in 1965, is said to mean 'game searching place' (Orth 1967); cf. *ivaq-* 'to hunt, search for' (MacLean 1980).

IWARAWIRAMIUT (Alaska, Cape Mendenhall D-4). The Yupik (Eskimo) name was reported in 1932 (Orth 1967).

IWOONUT Point (Alaska, St. Lawrence B-6). The Yupik (Eskimo) name, reported in 1944, has also been written <Aikhwunat> (Orth 1967).

IWOORIGAN Camp (Alaska, St. Lawrence D-7). The Yupik (Eskimo) name was reported in 1932 (Orth 1967).

IYAHUNA Creek (Alaska, Survey Pass C-5). The Iñupiaq (Eskimo) personal name was recorded in 1956 (Orth 1967).

IYANBITO (N.Mex., McKinley Co.) \i yän´ bi tō\. Navajo (Athabaskan) *ayání bito'* 'buffalo's spring', from *ayáni* 'buffalo, bison' plus *bito'* 'its spring' (*bi-* 'his, her, its', *to'* 'water' (Wilson 1995).

IYESKA (S.Dak., Shannon Co.) \i yes´ kə\. Named for a Dakota (Siouan) man called *iyeska* 'interpreter', lit. 'speech-clear', from *iye* 'speech', *ska* 'white, clear' (B. Ingham p.c.).

IYOUKEEN Cove (Alaska, Sitka D-3). The Tlingit name was also reported as <I-you-keen> and <Iyukin> (Orth 1967).

IYOUKTUG Creek (Alaska, Sitka D-3). The Tlingit name was reported in 1958 as meaning 'stream this side of point' (Orth 1967).

IZATYS (Minn., Mille Lacs Co.) \i zä´ tis\. The name is related to that found in **Isanti County** (Minn.), derived from Dakota (Siouan) *isą́-ati*, referring to a subgroup of the Sioux usually called the Santees. Related names are **Santee** (e.g., Neb., Knox Co.) and **Kathio Township** (Minn., Mille Lacs Co.).

IZAVIEKNIK River (Alaska, Goodnews Bay C-2). The Yupik (Eskimo) name was published in 1951 (Orth 1967).

IZAVIKNEK River (Alaska, Marshall A-5). The Yupik (Eskimo) name was reported in 1949 (Orth 1967).

IZHIGA Cove (Alaska, Umnak B-2). The Aleut name was reported in 1840 (Orth 1967).

IZHUT Bay (Alaska, Afognak A-1). The Alutiiq (Eskimo) name was reported around 1840 (Orth 1976).

J

JABISH Brook (Mass., Bristol Co.) \jā´ bish\. Perhaps from Mahican (Algonquian), of unclear derivation (Huden 1962).

JACAL DE PALO Spring (N.Mex., Rio Arriba Co.) \hə käl´ də pä´ lō\. The Spanish phrase means 'wooden hut', containing Mexican Spanish *jacal* 'hut', from Nahuatl (Aztecan) *xacalli* and *palo* 'wood, tree, stick' (Julyan 1998).

JACALITOS Creek (Calif., Fresno Co.) \jak ə lē´ təs\. A plural diminutive, meaning 'little huts', from Spanish *jacal* 'hut', from Nahuatl (Aztecan) *xacalli* (Gudde 1998).

JACKSINA Creek (Alaska, Nabesna B-4) \jak´ si nä, jak sī´ nə\. Perhaps derived from English *Jack's* plus Ahtna (Athabaskan) *-na* 'stream' (Orth 1967).

JACOBS Creek (Pa., Westmoreland Co.). Named for a Delaware (Algonquian) leader known in English as "Captain Jacobs" (Donehoo 1928).

JACONA (N.Mex., Santa Fe Co.) \hä kō´ nə\. The Spanish spelling corresponds to Tewa (Tanoan) \sekǫnæ\ 'at the tobacco barranca', from [sa] 'tobacco', [ko] 'barranca', [-næ] 'place' (Harrington 1916:330). The adjacent community of **Jaconita** is named with the Spanish diminutive.

JACQUEZ Canyon (N.Mex., San Juan Co.) \hä´ kəz\. Named for a Navajo, Candalero Jacquez (or Jaques), who owned grazing allotments here (Julyan 1998).

JACUMBA (Calif., San Diego Co.) \hə kum´ bə, hə ko͞om´ bə\. From the name of a Diegueño (Yuman) village, perhaps containing *ha-* 'water' (Gudde 1998).

JADITO (Ariz., Navajo Co.) \jed´ i tō, jə dit´ ō\. From Navajo (Athabaskan) *jádító* 'antelope spring', from *jádí* 'antelope', *tó* 'water' (Linford 2000; Young and Morgan 1987). Alternative writings are **Jedito** and **Jeddito.**

JALAMA (Calif., Santa Barbara Co.) \hə lä´ mə\. From Purisimeño (Chumashan) /xalam/, a village name meaning 'bundle' (Gudde 1998).

JALAMUND Lake (Alaska, Nabesna C-2) \jä lə mund´\. From Upper Tanana (Athabaskan) *ch'ilah männ'*, containing *männ'* 'lake' (J. Kari p.c.).

JALAPA (Ind., Grant Co.) \jə lap´ ə\. Named for the Mexican city of *Jalapa* [xalápa] in Veracruz state, which was invaded by U.S. forces during the Mexican War of the 1840s. The origin is in Nahuatl (Aztecan) *xalapan,* lit. 'sand-spring place', from *xal(li)* 'sand', *a(tl)* 'water', *-pan* 'place'. There is also a **Jalapa** in S.C. (Newberry Co.), and the spelling **Jalappa** occurs in Pa. (Berks Co.).

JAMACHA (Calif., San Diego Co.) \ham´ ə shô\. From Diegueño (Yuman) *hemechaa* 'a type of gourd used for soap' (Gudde 1998).

JAMAICA (N.Y., Queens Co.) \jə mā´ kə\. Perhaps an abbreviation of a Delaware (Algonquian) word meaning 'beaver pond'; cf. Unami Delaware /təmá:kwe/ 'beaver', Munsee Delaware /amóxkw/ (I. Goddard p.c.). In any case the placename was probably modified in English to resemble **Jamaica**, the West Indian island, a name derived from the Taino (Arawakan) language. The placename **Jamaica** is found in several other states; these may be transfers from N.Y. or from the West Indies (e.g., Iowa, Guthrie Co.; Mass., Suffolk Co.; and Maine, Kennebec Co.).

JAMUL (Calif., San Diego Co.) \hə mo͞ol´\. From Diegueño (Yuman) *hemull,* a village name meaning 'foam, lather' (Gudde 1998).

JAPACHA (Calif., San Diego Co.) \hä´ pə chä\. From Diegueño (Yuman) *hapechaa* 'handstone for grinding', equivalent to Spanish *mano de metate* (Gudde 1998).

JAPATUL Valley (Calif., San Diego Co.) \hä pə to͞ol´\. Perhaps from Diegueño (Yuman) *hatepull* 'woodpecker' (Gudde 1998).

JARBIDGE Mountains (Idaho, Owyhee Co.) \jär´ bij\. From Shoshoni (Numic) /tso'apittsɨh/ 'ghost monster', a supernatural being associated with these mountains; cf. /tso'a/ 'ghost' (J. McLaughlin p.c.).

JA SHE Creek (Calif., Shasta Co.) \jä´ shē\. The Wintu name replaced earlier "Squaw Creek" (BGN 8802).

JATAHMUND Lake (Alaska, Nabesna C-3). From Upper Tanana (Athabaskan) *ch'atx̱ą̈ą' männ',* perhaps meaning 'moldy lake' (J. Kari p.c.).

JAYALIK Hill (Alaska, Cape Mendenhall D-5). The Yupik (Eskimo) name was reported in 1949, said to mean 'silver salmon' (Orth 1967); cf. *caayuryaq* 'silver or coho salmon' (Jacobson 1984).

JEDDITO (Ariz., Navajo Co.) \jed´ i tō\. An alternative writing for **Jadito**, reflecting Navajo (Athabaskan) *jádító* 'antelope spring', from *jádí* 'antelope', *tó* 'water' (Linford 2000; Young and Morgan 1987). Another alternative spelling is **Jedito.**

JEHOSSEE Island (S.C., Charleston Co.). Earlier written <Chebasah>, <Johoowa>, <Johasse> (Waddell 1980). Perhaps from an unidentified Indian language (Pickens 1963:37).

JELLOWAY (Ohio, Knox Co.) \jel´ ə wā\. Named for Tom Jelloway, an Indian resident, affiliation unknown (Miller 1996).

JEMEZ Pueblo (N.Mex., Sandoval Co.) \hā´ məs, hā´ məz\. From Towa (Tanoan) /hiimiš/ 'Jemez people', containing /hiim/ 'Jemez person' and /-iš/ 'plural' (Y. Yumitani p.c.).

JEREMY Island (S.Car., Charleston Co.) Named for an Indian leader of around 1700 (Waddell 1980).

JEWN River (Alaska, Baird Inlet B-2). The Yupik (Eskimo) name was reported in 1949 (Orth 1967).

JHUS Canyon (Ariz., Cochise Co.). Named for a nineteenth-century Apache (Athabaskan) leader; the term reflects Western Apache *hosh* [x^{W}ʊš] (P. Greenfeld p.c.).

JICARILLA (N.Mex., Lincoln Co.) \hik ə rē´ yə\. The term refers to an Apache (Athabaskan) group as well as being a placename. The Mexican Spanish word means 'little cup', the diminutive of *jícara* 'drinking cup, originally made of gourd'; this in term is from Nahuatl (Aztecan) *xicalli.* Another diminutive, **Jicarita Creek** \hik ə rē´ tə\. is also a placename (N.Mex., Taos Co.).

JIGWALLICK Marsh (Vt., Addison Co.). From Abenaki (Algonquian) *cegwal* 'frog', pl. *cegwalak,* loc. *cegwalek* (Day 1994–95).

JIM THORPE (Pa., Carbon Co.). Named for the famous American Indian athlete of the early twentieth century, of Sauk-Fox (Algonquian) descent. Before 1954 the community was called **Mauch Chunk**, perhaps from Delaware (Algonquian), meaning 'at the hill of the bears'.

JINGEERUK Point (Alaska, Nunivak Island B-3). The Yupik (Eskimo) name was recorded in 1949 (Orth 1967).

JINGWAK Lake (Mich., Gogebic Co.) \jing´ gwäk\. From Ojibwa (Algonquian) *zhingwaak* 'white pine' (Vogel 1986; Nichols and Nyholm 1995). There is also a **Jingwak Lake** in Wis. (Vilas Co.).

JINHI Bay (Alaska, Craig D-4). The Tlingit name was published in 1964 (Orth 1967).

JISKOOKSNUK Hill (Alaska, Nunivak Island A-6). The Yupik (Eskimo) name was recorded in 1949 (Orth 1967).

JOCASSEE (S.C., Oconee Co.) \jō kas´ ē\. The name may come from a Cherokee (Iroquoian) legend, but the derivation is not clear (Neuffer and Neuffer 1983).

JOCINAH Creek (Ind., Grant Co.) \jō sē´ nä\. From Miami/Illinois (Algonquian) /tohseenia/ 'an Indian' (McCafferty 2002). It has also been written as **Josina.** A related placename is **Metocinah** (Ind., Grant Co.).

JOE GEE Hill (N.Y., Orange Co.). Named for an eighteenth-century Delaware (Algonquian) leader, known as <Kegh-ge-ka-po-well> in his own language, as *Joghem* 'Joachim' in Dutch, and as **Jogee** or **Joe Gee** in English (Beauchamp 1907).

JOE MOSES Creek (Wash., Okanogan Co.). Named for an Indian resident of Salishan affiliation; his Native American name was [paʔtskstíya] (D. Kinkade p.c.).

JOE POKUM Pond (Maine, Somerset Co.). Named for a local Indian resident of unknown affiliation (Rutherford 1970).

JOHNSON (Ore., Lincoln Co.). Named for Jakie Johnson, a local Indian from the Siletz Reservation (McArthur 1992).

JOJOBA Boating Site (Ariz., Maricopa Co.) \hō hō´ bə\. The name of a desert plant, from O'odham (Piman) *hohowai* (Saxton et al. 1983).

JOKAKI (Ariz., Maricopa Co.) \jō kä´ kē\. Hopi (Uto-Aztecan) *tsöqaki* 'mud house', from *tsöqa* 'mud' plus *-kihu* 'house' (K. Hill p.c.).

JOKINAUGH Island (Alaska, Beaver A-4) \jō´ ki nô\. Koyukon (Athabaskan) *joxka nu'*, borrowed from Gwich'in (Athabaskan), probably containing a word for 'island' (Kari 2000); cf. *njuu, juu* 'island' (Peter 1979).

JOKOEI Lake (Alaska, Black River C-6). From Gwich'in (Athabaskan), of unclear derivation (Orth 1967).

JOLON (Calif., Monterey Co.) \hə lōn\. From Antoniano Salinan /xolon/ 'it leaks; a leak; a channel where water cuts through' (Gudde 1998).

JONATA (Calif., Santa Barbara Co.) \hō nä´ tə, hon´ ə tə\. Spanish *jonjonata,* from Barbareño (Chumashan) /xonxon'ata/ 'tall oak' (Gudde 1998).

JONIVE Hill (Calif., Sonoma Co.). Probably a Spanish spelling of the name of an Indian village, language unknown (Gudde 1998).

JOSEPH Creek (Wash., Asotin Co.). Named for Chief Joseph, also known as Young Joseph (1840–1904), the famous Nez Perce (Sahaptian) leader. His Nez Perce name was /hinmatóowyalahtq/ 'thunder traveling to higher areas' (Aoki 1994:155 and p.c.), from /hinmét-/ 'thunder', /wiyée-/ 'as one travels', /láhtaq'i/ 'move up out of water or lower areas', /-t/ 'nominalizer' (Aoki 1994:155). There is another place called **Joseph** in Ore. (Wallowa Co.). There are also places called **Chief Joseph** in Idaho (Lemhi Co.), Wash. (Okanogan Co.), and Ore. (Wallowa Co.).

JUAB County (Utah) \jo͞o´ ab\. From Ute /yuapi/ [yuavI] 'level place, valley' (J. McLaughlin p.c.).

JUANITA BEGAY Spring (Ariz., Coconino Co.) \wä nē´ tə bə gā\. Apparently named after a Navajo (Athabaskan) woman. **Begay** is a common Navajo family name; see **Begay,** above.

JUAN TABO Canyon (N.Mex., Bernalillo Co.) \wän tə bō\. Possibly abbreviated from the name of an eighteenth-century resident named Juan Taboso. The term *Taboso* referred to an Indian group, akin to the Apaches, in southeastern New Mexico (Julyan 1998).

JUAQUAPIN Creek (Calif., San Diego Co.) \wä kwə pēn\. Perhaps from Diegueño (Yuman) *hakupin* 'warm water' (Gudde 1998).

JUCQA-VA (Ariz., Navajo Co.) \jə kwä´ vä\. Hopi (Uto-Aztecan) *tsöqava,* perhaps from *tsöqa* 'mud' plus *-va, paa-hu* 'water, spring'; cf. *tsöqavö* 'earthen dam or reservoir' (K. Hill p.c.).

JUDACULLA Mountain (N.C., Jackson Co.). The name is thought to be of Indian origin, but the language is not known (Powell 1968).

JUMANOS, Mesa de los (N.Mex., Torrance Co.) \ho͞o mä´ nōs\. Refers to a Pueblo group encountered by early Spanish explorers, of unknown linguistic affiliation. Their name is also written <Humanos>, <Juamanes>, <Jumanes> (Julyan 1998).

JUMPER (Okla., Pottawatomie Co.). Named for John Jumper, a Seminole (Muskogean) leader (Shirk 1974).

JUNALUSKA Creek (N.C., Cherokee Co.). Named for a Cherokee (Iroquoian) leader of the early nineteenth century (Powell 1968).

JUNCTION, The (Ariz., Apache Co.). Corresponds to Navajo (Athabaskan) *ahidiidlíní* 'the confluence' (Linford 2000:55); cf. *ahidiilį́* 'they flow together', with *ahidii-* 'together' (Young and Morgan 1987).

JUNEKAKAT Creek (Alaska, Ruby D-4). The Koyukon (Athabaskan) name is *ts'oon kkaakk'et,* meaning uncertain (J. Kari p.c.).

JUNGJUK Creek (Alaska, Sleetmute D-6). The Yupik (Eskimo) name was given in 1898 as <Yukwonilnuk> 'stream where no man is'; the present-day name was reported in 1944 (Orth 1967).

JUNIATA County (Pa.) \jo͞o nē yat´ ə\. From Seneca (Iroquoian) <Tyunayate> 'projecting rock' (Donehoo 1928). The name has been transferred to several other states (e.g., Ala., Talladega Co.; Iowa, Buena Vista Co.; and Miss., Tuscola Co.). In some places the name seems to have been confused with the Spanish female name *Juanita.*

JUNINGGULRA Mountain (Alaska, Sleetmute D-7). The Dena'ina (Athabaskan) name, reported in 1944, is said to mean 'crosswise' (Orth 1967).

JUNJIK River (Alaska, Arctic A-3) \jōōn´ jik\. The Gwich'in (Athabaskan) name is *njuu njik* 'island river' (Caulfield et al. 1983).

JURISTAC (Calif., Santa Clara Co.) \hōō ri stäk\. The Spanish spelling is perhaps from Chocheño (Costanoan), with /huri/ 'to take off, let go' and /-tak/ 'place' (Gudde 1998).

JURUPA (Calif., Riverside Co.) \hə rōōp´ ə\. The Spanish spelling is probably from Gabrielino (Takic) or a related language, meaning 'sagebrush place'; cf. Gabrielino *horúvar* 'sagebrush' (Gudde 1998).

JWA QWAW GWA Spring (Ariz., Coconino Co.). From Havasupai (Yuman), of unclear derivation (L. Hinton p.c.).

K

KABEKONA Lake (Minn., Hubbard Co.) \kab ə kō´ nə\. From Ojibwa (Algonquian) *gabekana* 'at the end of the road' (Upham 2001; Nichols and Nyholm 1995).

KABETOGAMA (Minn., St. Louis Co.) \kab ə tō´ gə mə\. From Ojibwa (Algonquian), perhaps meaning 'abreast, alongside' (Upham 2001).

KABUCH Point (Alaska, False Pass D-5). The Aleut name was published as <Khaboutcha> in 1852 (Orth 1967).

KABUSIE Creek (Wash., Clallam Co.). Probably a Native American name, from an unidentified language (BGN 8502).

KABUSTASA Lake (Minn., St. Louis Co.). Probably a Native American name, from an unidentified language (Upham 2001).

KABYAI Creek (Calif., Shasta Co.) \kä bē ī\. From a Wintu placename /xebeyay'/ (Gudde 1998).

KACHAUIK River (Alaska, Solomon C-3). The Iñupiaq (Eskimo) name was published in 1908 (Orth 1967).

KACHEMACH River (Alaska, Harrison Bay B-2) \kach´ ə mak\. The Iñupiaq (Eskimo) name was reported in 1950 (Orth 1967).

KACHEMAK (Alaska, Seldovia C-4) \kach´ ə mak\. Perhaps an Alutiiq (Eskimo) name, published in 1847 as <Kochekmak> (Orth 1967).

KACHESS River (Wash., Kittitas Co.) \kə chiz\. From a Sahaptin placename [k'ácis] (D. Kinkade p.c.).

KACHIKSUK Bluffs (Alaska, Barrow A-2). The Iñupiaq (Eskimo) name, recorded in 1951, is said to mean 'high bluffs' (Orth 1967); cf. *qutchiksuq* 'is high' (Webster and Zibell 1970).

KACHINA Point (Ariz., Apache Co.) \kə chē´ nə\. From Hopi (Uto-Aztecan) *katsina* 'spirit being' (K. Hill p.c.) There is a natural arch called **Kachina Bridge** (Utah, San Juan Co.).

KACHWONA Creek (Alaska, Wiseman D-2). The Iñupiaq (Eskimo) term is perhaps a girl's name (Orth 1967).

KACROWTUK Lake (Alaska, Selawik C-3). The Iñupiaq (Eskimo) name was recorded in 1955 (Orth 1967).

KADACHAN Glacier (Alaska, Mount Fairweather D-4). Perhaps a variant writing of the name found in **Kadashan Bay**; see below.

KADAKE Creek (Alaska, Petersburg D-6). The name, probably of Tlingit origin, was published in 1943 (Orth 1967).

KADAKINA Creek (Alaska, Bettles B-5). The Koyukon (Athabaskan) name was reported in 1956 (Orth 1967).

KADASHAN Bay (Alaska, Sitka C-4) \kä´ də shän\. Named in 1919 for Paul Kadashan, a Tlingit resident (Orth 1967). A probably related name is **Kadachan Glacier** (Alaska, Mount Fairweather D-4).

KADI Creek (Alaska, Unalaska B-6). Perhaps an abbreviation of Aleut <kadigukuq> 'it stands against, it is in front of' (Orth 1967).

KADLEROSHILIK River (Alaska, Beechey Point A-2). The Iñupiaq (Eskimo) has been said to mean 'possesses something on top' (Orth 1967).

KADOKA (S.Dak., Jackson Co.) \kə dō´ kə\. Perhaps from Dakota (Siouan) *kaȟdóka* 'to make a hole by striking' (Sneve 1973; Riggs 1890).

KADRUAKVIK Creek (Alaska, Killik River A-3). The Iñupiaq (Eskimo) name was reported in 1956 (Orth 1967).

KAGALUK Lake (Alaska, Baird Inlet D-4). The Yupik (Eskimo) name was reported in 1949 (Orth 1967).

KAGALURPAK Lake (Alaska, Baird Inlet D-6). The Yupik (Eskimo) name, reported in 1949, is said to mean 'river's end' (Orth 1967).

KAGALUS, Cape (Alaska, Atka B-6). Abbreviated from Aleut *chiĝulam-kagalungis,* lit. 'the heels of *chiĝulax̂,* Chugul Island '; cf. *kagalux̂* 'heel' (Bergsland 1994).

KAGAMIL Island (Alaska, Samalga Is. D-6). From the Aleut placename *qagaamila* (Bergsland 1994).

KAGANKAGUTI Lake (Alaska, Hooper Bay C-1). The Yupik (Eskimo) name, reported in 1951, is said to mean 'the source' (Orth 1967); cf. *kangiq* 'source (of river)' (Jacobson 1984).

KAGA Point (Alaska, Adak B-2). An abbreviated form of the name of **Kagalaska Island** (Alaska, Adak B-2). The term is from the Aleut placename *qigalaxsix̂, qigalaxsxan* (Bergsland 1994).

KAGATI Lake (Alaska, Goodnews Bay D-3). The Yupik (Eskimo) name, reported in 1898, is said to mean 'source' (Orth 1967).

KAGAYAN Flats (Alaska, Port Moller C-3). The Yupik (Eskimo) or Aleut name was reported in 1916 (Orth 1967).

KAGEET Point (Alaska, Bering Glacier A-1). The name is likely to be of Tlingit origin (Orth 1967).

KAGEVAH Peak (Wyo., Fremont Co.) \kə jē´ və\. From Shoshoni (Numic) /ko'ittsipaa/ [ko'ittšivaa] 'little-summit water', with /ko'i/ 'summit', /-ttsi/ 'little', and /paa/ 'water' (J. McLaughlin p.c.).

KAGHASUK Lake (Alaska, Baird Inlet D-5). The Yupik (Eskimo) name was reported in 1949 (Orth 1967).

KAGHKUSALIK Point (Alaska, St. Lawrence C-4). The Yupik (Eskimo) name was recorded in 1965 and said to mean 'crown of the head'; cf. Central Yupik *kakangcaq, kakgaq* (Jacobson 1984).

KAGHOOPALIK Point (Alaska, St. Lawrence D-6). From St. Lawrence Is. Yupik (Eskimo) *qaguq* 'brow' (Jacobson 1987).

KAGIGIKAK, Cape (Alaska, Adak B-3). From Aleut *qagaaĝix̂* 'eastern', containing *qaga* 'outside, east' (Bergsland 1994).

KAGILUAK Creek (Alaska, Demarcation Point C-1). The Iñupiaq (Eskimo) name was recorded in 1952 (Orth 1967).

KAGLUGRAK Deep (Alaska, Noatak C-5). The Iñupiaq (Eskimo) name, reported in 1966, is said to mean 'old deep place' (Orth 1967).

KAGUK Cove (Alaska, Craig C-4). The Tlingit name was recorded in 1949 (Orth 1967).

KAGUYAK (Alaska, Kaguyak D-6) \kə gī´ ək\. The Alutiiq (Eskimo) name was reported in 1880 (Orth 1967).

KAGVIK Creek (Alaska, Misheguk Mt. B-5). The Iñupiaq (Eskimo) name was reported in 1956 (Orth 1967).

KAHACHI MILIUK (Ariz., Pima Co.). From O'odham (Piman) *ge* 'big', *aji* 'skinny', and *meliwkuḍ* 'place where runners end a race, finish line' (J. Hill p.c.).

KAHATCHEE (Ala., Talladega Co.) \kä hach ´ ē\. Perhaps from Muskogee *kohv-hvcce* /kohaháčči/, lit. 'cane stream' (Read 1984; Martin and Mauldin 2000).

KAHGEATAK Creek (Alaska, Point Lay A-3). The Iñupiaq (Eskimo) name, also written <Kahkatak>, was reported in 1949 (Orth 1967).

KAHILTNA Creek (Alaska, Point Lay A-4) \kə hilt´ nə\. From Dena'ina (Athabaskan) *kagheltnu* 'flows-directly river', with *-tnu* 'river' (Kari and Fall 1987:145).

KAHKWA Creek (Wash., Jefferson Co.) \kä´ kwä\. From Chinook Jargon <cakua, kāh-kwa> [kákwa] 'thus, the same, alike'; perhaps from Nootka (D. Kinkade p.c.).

KAHLOTUS (Wash., Franklin Co.) \kal ō´ təs, kə lō´ təs\. From the Sahaptin placename /kalú:t'as/ (D. Kinkade p.c.).

KAHNEETA Hot Springs (Ore., Wasco Co.) \kä nē´ tə\. From Sahaptin [x̣níta] 'go digging (roots)', from /x̣ní/ 'to dig roots', /-ta/ 'go for a purpose'—the personal name of a woman who was called Mollie David in English (N. Rude p.c.).

KAHNIRUK River (Alaska, Nunivak Is. B-5). The Yupik (Eskimo) name, reported in 1949, is said to mean 'corner (of the cove)'; cf. *kangiraq* 'corner' (Jacobson 1984). The nearby placename **Kahnirukmiut** means 'people (or village) of the corner'.

KAHOKA (Mo., Clark Co.) \kə hō´ kə\. The name may be related to **Cahokia**, a subdivision of the Miami-Illinois (Algonquian) people.

KAH SHAKES Cove (Alaska, Ketchikan A-3). The name was borne by a former Tlingit village and by its leader (Orth 1967). The nearby **Shakes Village** takes its name from the same source.

KAH SHEETS Creek (Alaska, Petersburg C-4). The Tlingit name was reported in 1897 (Orth 1967).

KAHUNTLA Lake (Alaska, Cordova A-2). The Tlingit name was reported in 1903 (Orth 1967).

KAIBAB Plateau (Ariz., Mohave Co.; Utah, Kane Co.) \kī´ bab\. An abbreviated form of Southern Paiute (Numic) /kaipapittsi/ [kaivavittsI] 'plateau', from /kaipa/ [kaivA] 'mountain' (J. McLaughlin p.c.). The name also occurs in Colo. (Eagle Co.).

KAIBITO (Ariz., Coconino Co.) \kī bē´ tō\. Navajo (Athabaskan) *k'ai' bii' tó* 'a spring within the willows', from *k'ai'* 'willow', *bii'* 'inside', and *tó* 'water, spring' (Wilson 1995).

KAINA Creek (Alaska, Valdez D-7) \kī´ nə\. From Ahtna (Athabaskan) *k'aay na'* 'ridge creek' (Kari 1990).

KAIPAROWITZ Peak (Utah, Garfield Co.) \kə pâr´ ə wits\. From Southern Paiute (Numic) /kaippatuwattsi/, lit. 'mountain son', from /kaipa/ 'mountain', /tua/ 'son', and /-tsi/ 'diminutive' (Sapir 1930; J. McLaughlin p.c.).

KAKNA Lake (Alaska, Kenai B-2) \käk´ nə\. From Dena'ina (Athabaskan) *kahtnu* 'the Kenai River' (J. Kari p.c.).

KAKOON Lake (Alaska, Kenai D-2). Perhaps from Dena'ina (Athabaskan); the derivation is not clear (Orth 1967).

KALA Creek (Alaska, Nulato C-2). Perhaps from Koyukon (Athabaskan), of unclear derivation (orth 1967).

KALALOCH (Wash., Jefferson Co.) \kə lā´ lok\ Quinault (Salishan), of unclear derivation.

KALAMAZOO County (Mich.) \kal ə mə zo͞o´\. There is a local tradition that this represents the Ojibwa (Algonquian) name of the **Kalamazoo River**, given as <Ke-kanamazoo> and translated 'boiling pot'; but this derivation has not been confirmed (Vogel 1986). The name **Kalamazoo** also occurs in Fla. (Volusia Co.), Kans. (Sedgwick Co.), and Nev. (White Pine Co.).

KALAMINK Creek (Mich., Ingham Co.). The name is of obscure Algonquian origin; there may be some relationship to **Kalamazoo** (Vogel 1986).

KALAMUT Island (Wash., Island Co.). Said to be derived from <Cal-a-met>, meaning 'stone' or 'rocky ground' in an unidentified Indian language (Hitchman 1985).

KALAPUYA \kal ə pōō´ yə\. The name refers to a group of Indian peoples native to the Willamette Valley of Ore.; the term **Kalapuyan** is also used with reference to the language family to which the groups belonged. The Native American name was [k'alap^h^úya] (McArthur 1992). Spellings used in placenames are **Calapooya** (Ore., Douglas Co.) and **Calapooia** (Ore., Linn Co.).

KALARVIK Point (Alaska, Baird Inlet C-6). The Yupik (Eskimo) name was reported in 1949 (Orth 1967).

KALASIK Lake (Alaska, Marshall A-1). From Yupik (Eskimo) *qallaciq* 'navel' (Orth 1967, Jacobson 1984).

KALDACHABUNA Lake (Alaska, Tyonek A-4) The Dena'ina (Athabaskan) name is *k'qalt'ats'a bena* 'water-lily lake' (J. Kari p.c.).

KALDOLYEIT Lake (Alaska, Bettles B-4). The Koyukon (Athabaskan) name was recorded in 1956 (Orth 1967).

KALEETAN Butte (Ore., Deschutes Co.) \kal´ ē tan\. This form is apparently based on a mistaken spelling-pronunciation of Chinook Jargon <kalitan> [kəláitən] 'arrow', from Lower Chinook [-kalaitan] (D. Kinkade p.c.). **Kaleetan** also occurs in Wash. (King Co.). The related form **Kalitan Creek** is found in Ore. (Lane Co.).

KALEKTA Bay (Alaska, Unalaska C-1). From Aleut *kalix̂tax̂*, perhaps 'had as bottom'; cf. *qalixtix̂* 'bottom' (Bergsland 1994).

KALGIN Island (Alaska, Kenai B-6) \kal´gin\. From Dena'ina (Athabaskan) *qelghin,* perhaps meaning 'greasy' (Kari and Kari 1982:28).

KALHABUK Creek (Alaska, Chandalar C-6). The term represents the Native American name of an Iñupiaq (Eskimo) woman, Florence Jonas (Orth 1967).

KALHAGU Cove (Alaska, Skagway A-1). The Tlingit name, translated 'skunk-cabbage beach', was published in 1923 (Orth 1967).

KALHOMA (Okla., Pontotoc Co.) \kal hō´ mə\. Chickasaw (Muskogean) *kali homma* 'red spring', from *kali* 'spring, well' and *homma* 'red'; also written **Kalihoma** (P. Munro p.c.).

KALIAKH River (Alaska, Bering Glacier A-5). From Tlingit /ɢaɬyax̣/, a village name first published in 1849 (*HNAI* 7:227). This may be from the same source as **Kulthieth River**; see below.

KALIFORNSKY (Alaska, Kenai B-4) \kal i fôrn´ skē\. This is a Dena'ina (Athabaskan) family name, derived from Russian *kalifornskij* 'Californian'; the name was given because of a Dena'ina man who in the early nineteenth century participated in the Russian colony at Fort Ross in northern Calif. (Schorr 1986). The spelling **Kalifonsky** also occurs.

KALIGAGAN Island (Alaska, Unimak A-3). Perhaps from Aleut *qigalĝan, qagalĝa,* referring to the nearby **Tigalga Island;** cf. *qigaaĝix̂* 'eastern' (Bergsland 1994).

KALIGURICHEARK River (Alaska, Baird Mountains A-1). The Iñupiaq (Eskimo) name is *qalugraitchauram kuuŋa,* said to refer to a kind of fish (Orth 1967; Burch 1998).

KALIHOMA (Okla., Pontotoc Co.) \kal ē hō´ mə\. Chickasaw (Muskogean) *kali homma* 'red spring', from *kali* 'spring, well' and *homma* 'red'; also written **Kalhoma** (P. Munro p.c.).

KALIKPIK River (Alaska, Harrison Bay B-4). The Iñupiaq (Eskimo) name, reported in 1951, is said to refer to the stream's 'being without banks' (Orth 1967).

KALIK River (Alaska, Kotzebue C-6). The Iñupiaq (Eskimo) name, said to mean 'nasal mucus', was reported in 1901 (Orth 1967).

KALIKSNEETHNOOK River (Alaska, Nunivak Is. A-2). The Yupik (Eskimo) name was reported in 1949 (Orth 1967).

KALIOKA Springs (Ala., Mobile Co.) \kal ē ō´ kə\. From Choctaw (Muskogean) *kalih* 'well', *oka* 'water' (P. Munro p.c.).

KALISPEL (Wash., Pend Oreille Co.) \kal´i spel\. The term refers to a division of the Pend

Oreilles (Salishan) people; the Native American name is /qlispél/ (D. Kinkade p.c.). An alternative spelling is **Calispell** and **Kalispell**; the latter also occurs in Idaho (Bonner Co.) and in Mont. (Flathead Co.).

KALITAN Creek (Ore., Lane Co.) \kə lī´ tən\. From Chinook Jargon <ka-li´-tan> 'arrow, shot, bullet', from Lower Chinook [-kalaitan] 'arrow' (D. Kinkade p.c.). A related name is **Kaleetan** \kal´ ē tan\, found in Ore. (Deschutes Co.) and Wash. (King Co.).

KALKA Island (Alaska, Tanana D-1) \käl´ kə\. Perhaps from Koyukon (Athabaskan); the name was reported in 1956 (Orth 1967).

KALKASKA County (Mich.) \kal kas´ kə\. Possibly from an Ojibwa (Algonquian) form meaning 'burned over', or perhaps a "made-up" word based on the English surnames *Calcraft* and *Cass* (Vogel 1986).

KALLA (Alaska, Shungnak D-2) \kal´ ə\. The Iñupiaq (Eskimo) name is *qala* 'churning water' (L. Kaplan p.c.).

KALLARICHUK River (Alaska, Baird Mountains A-2). The Iñupiaq (Eskimo) name is *qalugraitchiam kuuŋa,* said to refer to 'reeds' (Orth 1967; Burch 1998).

KALOKUT Creek (Alaska, Demarcation Point D-2). The Iñupiaq (Eskimo) name was recorded in 1919 (Orth 1967).

KALSKAG (Alaska, Russian Mission C-4) \kal´ skag\. From the Yupik (Eskimo) placename *qalqaq* (Orth 1967; Jacobson 1984).

KALTAG (Alaska, Nulato B-6) \kal´ tag\. From Koyukon (Athabaskan) *ggaał doh* 'camp for king salmon fishing', from *ggaał* 'king salmon' (Orth 1967; Jetté and Jones 2000:199–200).

KALUBIK Creek (Alaska, Harrison Bay B-1). The Iñupiaq (Eskimo) name was reported in the late 1940s (Orth 1967).

KALUCHAGUN (Alaska, Kwiguk C-6). The Yupik (Eskimo) name was recorded in 1948 (Orth 1967).

KALUICH Creek (Alaska, Ambler River D-5). The Iñupiaq (Eskimo) name is *qaluich,* plural of *qaluk* 'fish' (L. Kaplan p.c.).

KALUKNA River (Alaska, Tanacross A-4) \kə lo͞ok´ nə\. From Upper Tanana (Athabaskan) *x̱aal niign,* lit. 'cisco (fish) stream' (J. Kari p.c.).

KALUKRUATCHIAK Point (Alaska, Killik River D-1). The Iñupiaq (Eskimo) name is *qalugruatchiaq* 'new salmon' (L. Kaplan p.c.).

KALUKTAVIK River (Alaska, Baird Mountains D-4). Iñupiaq (Eskimo) *qiruktaġvik,* perhaps from *qaluk* 'fish' (L. Kaplan p.c.).

KALU Lake (Alaska, Kenai D-2). From Dena'ina (Athabaskan), of unclear derivation (Orth 1967).

KALURIVIK Creek (Alaska, Ambler River A-3). The Iñupiaq (Eskimo) name was reported in 1955 (Orth 1967).

KALUSUK Creek (Alaska, Candle C-2). The Iñupiaq (Eskimo) name was reported in 1949 (Orth 1967).

KALUTNA River (Alaska, Tanacross A-3) \kə lo͞ot´ nə\. The Athabaskan name was reported in 1955 (Orth 1967).

KALUVARAWLUK Mountain (Alaska, Sleetmute B-7). The Yupik (Eskimo) name was recorded in 1948 (Orth 1967).

KALUYUT Mountains (Alaska, Baird Inlet C-8). The Yupik (Eskimo) name was reported in 1949 (Orth 1967).

KAMANKEAG Brook (Maine, Oxford Co.). Perhaps from Abenaki (Algonquian), meaning 'near the weir' (Huden 1962).

KAMAS (Utah, Summit Co.) \kam´ əs\. The term represents an alternative spelling of *camas,* referring to an edible root best known from the Pacific Northwest states. The ultimate source of the name is probably Nez Perce (Sahaptian) *qém'es* 'camas', from which it entered both English and Chinook Jargon. In the spelling **Camas,** it is widespread as a placename (e.g., Idaho, Jefferson Co.; Mont., Sanders Co.; and Wash., Clark Co.).

KAMELA (Ore., Union Co.) \kam´ ə lä\. From Nez Perce /kimíle/ 'tamarack, Western larch' (Aoki 1994).

KAMERCHILUK Slough (Alaska, Kwiguk D-4). The Yupik (Eskimo) name was recorded in 1899 (Orth 1967).

KAMIACHE Creek (Wash., Whitman Co.). The name is related to **Kamiakan**; see **Kamiak Butte** below.

KAMIAH (Idaho, Lewis Co.) \kam´ ē ī\. From a Nez Perce (Sahaptian) placename /qémyex̣p/, perhaps derived from /qé:mu/ 'Indian hemp; rope or string made of hemp' (Aoki 1994).

KAMIAK Butte (Wash., Whitman Co.) \kə mī´ ək\. The name is a variant form of **Kamiakan Butte** (Wash., Yakima Co.) \kə mī´ ə kən\, named for a nineteenth-century Yakima (Sahaptian) leader; his Native American name was [k'amáyaaqɨn]. The word is Spokane (Salishan) in origin, however (N. Rude p.c.). Related forms include **Kamiache Creek** (Wash., Whitman Co.).

KAMIKTUNGITAK Creek (Alaska, Misheguk Mt. D-2). The Iñupiaq (Eskimo) name was reported in 1956 (Orth 1967).

KAMILCHE (Wash., Mason Co.) \kə mil´ chē\. From Upper Chehalis (Salishan) /k'amíɬči/ 'Skookum Bay', lit. 'narrow water', from /k'ém-/ 'narrow' (D. Kinkade p.c.).

KAMISHAK (Alaska, Iliamna A-4) \kam´ i shak\. The name, perhaps Alutiiq (Eskimo), was recorded in 1826 (Orth 1967).

KAMLOOPS Island (Wash., Stevens Co.) \kam´ lo͞ops\. Perhaps from Okanagan (Salishan), or perhaps transferred from the town of Kamloops, British Columbia, where the name is said to be from Shuswap (Salishan) <Kahmoloops> 'meeting of the waters' (Rayburn 1997). In Mich. **Kamloops Island** (Keweenaw Co.) is named for a Canadian ship that sank near there in 1927 (Vogel 1986).

KAMMA Mountains (Nev., Pershing Co.) \kam´ ə\. From Northern Paiute (Numic) /kammɨ/ 'jackrabbit' (J. McLaughlin p.c.).

KAMPESKA (S.Dak., Codington Co.) \kam pes´ kə\. From Dakota (Siouan) *khąpéska* 'shell, abalone shell'; cf. Lakhota (Siouan) *phąkéska* 'shell, chinaware' (D. Parks p.c.).

KANAA Valley (Ariz., Coconino Co.) \kə nä´ ä\. From Hopi (Uto-Aztecan) *ka'naskatsina* 'name of a kachina', possibly of Keresan origin (K. Hill p.c.). Also written **Kana-a.**

KANAB Creek (Utah, Kane Co.; Ariz., Mohave Co.) \kə nab´\. From Southern Paiute (Numic) /kannapɨ/ [kannávɨ] 'willow' (J. McLaughlin p.c.).

KANABEC County (Minn.) \kə nā´ bek, kan´ ə bek\. From Ojibwa (Algonquian) *ginebig* 'snake' (Nichols and Nyholm 1995).

KANAGA, Lake (Ill., Effingham Co.) \kə nä´ gə\. Possibly a transfer name, with altered spelling, from **Kanauga** (Ohio, Gallia Co.) or from **Canoga** (N.Y., Seneca Co.), both names of Native American origin.

KANAGA Island (Alaska, Adak B-5) \kan´ ə gə\. From an Aleut placename *kanaga* (Bergsland 1994).

KANAGTATLEK Creek (Alaska, Goodnews Bay D-8). The Yupik (Eskimo) name was published in 1951 (Orth 1967).

KANAGUNUT Islnd (Alaska, Prince Rupert C-3). The Tlingit name was reported in 1869 (Orth 1967).

KANAKA Creek (Wash., Skamania Co.) \kə nak´ ə\. From the English word *Kanaka*, referring to Hawai'ians who worked as miners in the Pacific Northwest during the nineteenth century; borrowed from Hawai'ian *kanaka* 'human being, person'. As a placename, the term also occurs in Ore. (Jackson Co.) and Utah (Tooele Co.).

KANAKANAK (Alaska, Dillingham A-7). From the Yupik (Eskimo) placename *kanaqnaq,* perhaps from *kanar-* 'to emerege from the woods, coming down to a body of water' (Jacobson 1984).

KANAK Island (Alaska, Cordova A-1). From Tlingit [g̣ɪnʌ̀q´], said to mean 'egg island' (cf. Eyak /ginaq/; or from Alutiiq (Eskimo) *keneq* 'fire' (De Laguna 1972:103; Leer 1978).

KANAKNOLL Point (Alaska, Naknek C-3). The Yupik (Eskimo) name was reported in 1952 (Orth 1967).

KANAKTOK Creek (Alaska, Baird Mountains D-2). The Iñupiaq (Eskimo) name is *qaniqtuq* (Burch 1998).

KANALKU Bay (Alaska, Sitka C-2). The Tlingit name was published in 1891 (Orth 1967).

KANAPAHA (Fla., Alachua Co.) \kə nä´ pə hä\. Probably from Seminole (Muskogean), but of unclear derivation (Read 1934).

KANAPAK (Alaska, Marshall D-4). The Yupik (Eskimo) name was reported in 1949 (Orth 1967).

KANARANZI Creek (Minn., Rock Co.; Iowa, Lyon Co.). Of unclear derivation; perhaps from Dakota (Siouan) *khą́ze,* referring to the Kaw or Kansa people, after whom the state of **Kansas** is named (Vogel 1983; J. Koontz p.c.).

KANARRA Creek (Utah, Washington Co.) \kə nâr´ ə\. From Ute (Numic) /kannatɨ/ [kannárɨ̵] 'willow canyon-mouth' (J. McLaughlin). From the same origin is the name of **Kanarraville** (Utah, Iron Co.).

KANASKAT (Wash., King Co.) \kə nas´ kət\. Named for a Yakima (Sahaptian) leader from central Wash., who is said to have had a wife living in western Wash. His name may have been Interior Salishan in origin, containing /-asq't/ 'sky, day' (Hitchman 1985; D. Kinkade p.c.). The name is also written **Kanasket.**

KANATAK (Alaska, Ugashik C-1) \kan´ ə tak\. The Yupik (Eskimo) name was reported in 1890 (Orth 1967).

KANATON Ridge (Alaska, Adak C-4). The Aleut name was published in 1951 (Orth 1967).

KANAUGA (Ohio, Gallia Co.) \kə nô´ gə\. Perhaps adapted from the name of the **Kanawha River**. The term is said to refer to an Algonquian Indian group, appearing also as the placename **Conoy Lake** (Md., St. Marys Co.) and **Conoy Creek** (Pa., Lancaster Co.).

KANAUGUK River (Alaska, Teller B-6). The Iñupiaq (Eskimo) name was reported in 1900 (Orth 1967).

KANAWAUKE, Lake (N.Y., Rockland Co.) \kä nə wô´ kə\. Probably from Mohawk (Iroquoian) *kahnawà:ke* 'place of the rapids', a name that also enters English as **Caughnawaga** (N.Y., Montgomery Co.).

KANAWHA River (W.Va.) \kə nô´ wə\. The term refers to an Algonquian group also known as the **Conoy.** The placename **Kanawha** occurs as a transfer in Iowa (Hancock Co.) and Tex. (Red River Co.); the term **Conoy Lake** similarly occurs in Md. (St. Marys Co.) and **Conoy Creek** in Pa. (Lancaster Co.).

KANAYAT Creek (Alaska, Baird Mountains D-3). The Iñupiaq (Eskimo) name was recorded in 1955 (Orth 1967).

KANAYUT River (Alaska, Chandler Lake C-2). Iñupiaq (Eskimo) *kanayut,* plural of *kanayuq* 'sculpin' (L. Kaplan p.c.).

KANCAMAGUS (N.H., Grafton Co.) \kang kə mä´ gəs, kang kə mang´ gəs\. Named for a seventeenth-century leader of the Pennacook band of the Abenaki (Algonquian) Indians (Julyan and Julyan 1993).

KANCHEE Point (Alaska, Anchorage A-8) \kan´ chē\. From Dena'ina (Athabaskan) *qanchi* 'porcupine'; the name was given by the Mountaineering Club of Alaska in 1967 (Kari and Fall 1987:293).

KANDIK River (Alaska, Charley River B-4) \kan´dik\. The Han (Athabaskan) name was recorded in 1885 (Orth 1967).

KANDIOTA (N.Dak., Sargent Co.) \kan dē ō´ tə\. From Santee Dakota (Siouan) *khą̣dí* 'buffalo fish', *óta* 'many' (Wick 1988; B. Ingham p.c.). The spelling **Kandiotta** also occurs.

KANDIYOHI County (Minn.) \kan di yō´ hī, kan di yō hī´\. Contains Dakota (Siouan) *khądí* 'buffalo fish', *hi* 'to arrive' (Upham 2001; Riggs 1890). There is also a **Kandiyohi Township** in N.Dak. (Burke Co.).

KANDOTA Township (Minn., Todd Co.) \kan dō´ tə\. The name, bestowed in 1856, is said to mean 'here we rest' in an unspecified Indian language (Upham 2001).

KANEAROK Creek (Alaska, Ambler River A-4). The Iñupiaq (Eskimo) name was reported in 1956 (Orth 1967).

KANEETAKSMIUT (Alaska, Nunivak Is. B-3). The Yupik (Eskimo) name was reported in 1949; the suffix *-miut* means 'people' (Orth 1967).

KANEKTOK River (Alaska, Goodnews Bay C-8). The Yupik (Eskimo) name, reported in 1898, was said to mean 'snowy' (Orth 1967); cf. Yupik *qanikcaq* 'snow on the ground' (Jacobson 1984).

KANELIK (Alaska, Kwiguk C-6). The Yupik (Eskimo) name was reported as <Kaneglik> in 1899 (Orth 1967).

KANEM Point (Wash., Jefferson Co.) \kä´ nəm\. From Chinook Jargon *kanim, ca-nim* [kánəm] 'canoe, boat', from Chinookan *i-kánim* (D. Kinkade p.c.).

KANETUCHE Creek (Ala., Clarke Co.). Both this placename and **Kanetuck** (Ala., Jefferson Co.) may be from Choctaw (Muskogean) *kantak* 'smilax', a kind of brier from which bread is made (Read 1984). Also possible is a relationship to **Kentuck**; see below.

KANGEE Camp (Alaska, St. Lawrence C-4). From Yupik (Eskimo) *kangiraq* 'corner' (Jacobson 1987). Probably related Alaska placenames include **Kangeeghuk Bay** (St. Lawrence A-2) and **Kangighsak Point** (St. Lawrence B-1).

KANGEEKIKSATHARUK Cove (Alaska, Nunivak Is. B-3). The Yupik (Eskimo) name, reported in 1949, is said to mean 'small boat shelter' (Orth 1967). A possibly related name is **Kangeekiktharuk Cove** (Alaska, Nunivak Is. B-4).

KANGIGHSAK Point (Alaska, St. Lawrence B-1). The Yupik (Eskimo) name was reported in 1932 (Orth 1967). This placename may be related to **Kangik River** (Alaska, St. Lawrence C-4) and to **Kangee Creek** (Alaska, St. Lawrence C-4); see above.

KANGIK (Alaska, Wainwright A-2) \kan´gik\. The Iñupiaq (Eskimo) name is *kaŋiq,* reported as meaning 'river head' (Orth 1967; Burch 1998).

KANGIKTOOLIKMIUT (Alaska, Cape Mendenhall D-4). The Yupik (Eskimo) name was reported about 1949 (Orth 1967); the suffix *-miut* means 'people'.

KANGILIPAK Lake (Alaska, Baird Mountains D-1). The Iñupiaq (Eskimo) name is *kaŋiliqpak,* said to mean 'big lake end' (Orth 1967; Burch 1998).

KANGIRLVAR Bay (Alaska, Nunivak Is. C-1). The Yupiq (Eskimo) name was reported in 1949 (Orth 1967).

KANGNAKSNAK Point (Alaska, Nunivak Is. B-3). The Yupik (Eskimo) name was recorded in 1949 (Orth 1967).

KANGOKAKLI Pass (Alaska, Kwiguk D-6). The Yupik (Eskimo) name was reported in 1899 (Orth 1967).

KANGUKHSAM Mountain (Alaska, St. Lawrence B-0). The Yupik (Eskimo) name was reported in 1949 (Orth 1967).

KANICK (Calif., Humboldt Co.) \kā´ nik\. From the Yurok village name *kenek* (Gudde 1998). Also written as **Kenick.**

KANIK Creek (Alaska, Selawik A-5) \kan´ ik\. Iñupiaq (Eskimo) *qannik* 'snowflake' (MacLean 1980). A related term is **Kaniksrak Lake** (Alaska, Killik River A-2), from *qanniksraq* 'something that will become (falling) snow' (L. Kaplan p.c.). More distantly related is **Kanik River** (Alaska, Nushagak Bay D-5), from Yupik (Eskimo) *qanuk* 'snowflake' (Jacobson 1984).

KANIKSU (Wash., Stevens Co.) \kə nik´ sōō\. From the name given by local Indians, possibly

Kutenai, to a Jesuit missionary, Father John Roothan (Hitchman 1985). The name also occurs in Idaho (Boundary Co.).

KANIKULA Glacier (Alaska, Talkeetna C-3) \kə ni ko͞o´ lə\. From Dena'ina (Athabaskan) *k'enik'ela* 'that which breaks off' (Kari 1999:73).

KANIKYAKSTALIKMIUT (Alaska, Nunivak Is. A-2). The Yupik (Eskimo) name was reported about 1949 (Orth 1967). The suffix *-miut* means 'people'.

KANIMA (Okla., Haskell Co.) \kə nē´ mə\. From Choctaw (Muskogean) *kanihma* 'somewhere' (Shirk 1974; P. Munro p.c.).

KANIM Creek (Wash., King Co.) \kan´ im\. Named for Bill Kanim, a Snoqualmie (Salishan) healer of the early twentieth century; his surname was probably from Chinook Jargon *kanim, ca-nim* [kánəm] 'canoe, boat', from Chinookan /i-kánim/ (BGN 1994; D. Kinkade p.c.). The same word is found in **Kanem Point** (Wash., Jefferson Co.).

KANISAKROK Lake (Alaska, Selawik C-2). The Iñupiaq (Eskimo) name was reported in 1955 (Orth 1967).

KANKAKEE River (Ill., Kankakee Co.; Ind., La Porte Co.) \kang kə kē´, kang´ kə kē\. Earlier written <Teatíki>, <Theatiki>; the modern spelling is a distortion.

KANKAPOT Creek (Wis., Outagamie Co.). This term was a family name among the "Stockbridge" Indians, originally Mahicans (Algonquian) from Stockbridge, Mass., who settled in Wisconsin in the early nineteenth century (Vogel 1991); see **Konkapot.**

KANKONE Peak (Alaska, Mount McKinley C-2) \kan kō´ nē\. The Koyukon (Athabaskan) name is *hedenee'one* 'that which is attached', i.e. a black birch fungus (J. Kari p.c.).

KANLOYAK (Alaska, Baird Inlet B-8). The Yupik (Eskimo) name was reported in 1949 (Orth 1967).

KANNAH (Colo., Mesa Co.) \kan´ ə\. Perhaps from Ute *kanávɨ* 'willow', or *kanáwiya* 'valley with willows' (Bright 1993).

KANOKOLUS Bog (Maine, Waldo Co.). Named for an Abenaki (Algonquian) Indian; the term perhaps meant 'long flame' (Huden 1962).

KANONA (N.Y., Steuben Co.) \kə nō´ nə\. Perhaps from Mohawk (Iroquoian) *ka'nuhkwá:ke* 'at the bottom' (Michelson 1973).

KANONGIKSUK Creek (Alaska, Killik River A-2). The Iñupiaq (Eskimo) name was reported in 1956 (Orth 1967).

KANOSH (Utah, Millard Co.) \kə nōsh´, kə nosh´\. Named after a Southern Paiute (Numic) leader; the Native American term is /kana-'oša/ 'willow basket', from /kana(-pɨ)/ 'willow' and /oša/ 'carrying basket' (Sapir 1930).

KANOUSE MOUNTAIN (N.J., Passaic Co.). Perhaps from Delaware (Algonquian), of unclear derivation (Becker 1964).

KANSAS \kan´ zəs\. The name of the state is derived from the name of an Indian group, also called the **Kaw**, belonging to the Dhegiha branch of the Siouan linguistic family. The term is a French or English plural of /kką:ze/, an ancient ethnonym (cf. **Arkansas**). The alternative term **Kaw** originated as a French abbreviation of the tribal name (*HNAI* 13:474). The placename has been transferred to many other states: for example, **Kansas Creek** (Okla., Bryan Co.) as well as Ill. (Vermillion Co.) and Mo. (Jackson Co.) In Minn. the name of **Kansas Lake** (Watonwan Co.) is said to be derived from "Kensie's lake," after a resident named John Kensie (Upham 2001).

KANTANGNAK Creek (Alaska, Misheguk Mtn. D-5). The Iñupiaq (Eskimo) name is probably *qattaġnaq* 'like a bucket' (L. Kaplan p.c.).

KANTISHNA (Alaska, Mount McKinley C-2) \kan tish´ nə\. From Koyukon (Athabaskan) *hentooɫ no'* 'uncertain stream', with *no'* 'stream' (Jetté & Jones 2000).

KANUGA Lake (N.C., Henderson Co.). Said to be named for a Cherokee (Iroquoian) town, supposedly meaning 'meeting place of many peoples' (Powell 1968).

KANU Island (Alaska, Adak C-1). The name was derived by the U.S. Navy in 1936 by the backward spelling of the Aleut name <Unak>, to distinguish it from nearby placenames <Ulak> and <Umak> (Orth 1967). The original Aleut form is *hunax̂* 'wound' (Bergsland 1994).

KANUKTIK Creek (Alaska, Goodnews Bay D-4). The Yupik (Eskimo) name was reported in 1898 (Orth 1967).

KANUNUK (Alaska, St. Michael A-4). The Yupik (Eskimo) name was reported in 1899 as <Kanuhnukaili> (Orth 1967).

KANUTI River (Alaska, Bettles B-6) \kə no͞o´ tē\. From Koyukon (Athabaskan) *kk'oonootne* [q'u:nu:tnə] (Orth 1967; Jetté and Jones 2000). Names in the area derived from this include **Kanuti Chalatna Creek** and **Kanuti Kilolitna River.**

KANUWALEM KUIYA Creek (Alaska, Cordova B-7). The Native American name is said to mean 'copper creek', perhaps from Alutiiq (Eskimo); it was made official by the BGN in 1990.

KANYAK River (Alaska, Kwiguk C-6). The Yupik (Eskimo) name was recorded in 1952 (Orth 1967).

KAOLAK River (Alaska, Wainwright A-2). The Iñupiaq (Eskimo) name was reported in 1924 (Orth 1967).

KAOLEDOLY Slough (Alaska, Kwiguk D-5). The Yupik (Eskimo) name was reported in 1899 (Orth 1967).

KAPALOAK Creek (Alaska, Point Hope C-3). The Iñupiaq (Eskimo) name was reported in 1906 as **Capaloa** (Orth 1967); the writing **Kapalowa** also occurs.

KAPHO Mountains (Alaska, Bradfield Canal A-5). The Tlingit name, said to mean 'brothers', was reported in 1886 (Orth 1967).

KAPIOMA Township (Kans., Atchison Co.). Named for a leader of the Kickapoo (Algonquian) people (Rydjord 1968).

KAPKA Butte (Ore., Deschutes Co.) \käp´ kə\. From Klamath /ɢapɢa/ 'jack pine' (Barker 1963).

KAPOON Creek (Alaska, Wiseman D-1). From Iñupiaq (Eskimo), a man's name (Orth 1967).

KAPOSIA Park (Minn., Dakota Co.) \kə pō´ zhə\. From Dakota (Siouan) *kap'oja* 'light (in weight)', used to refer to a tribal group, understood to mean 'those who traveled light' (Upham 2001; Riggs 1890).

KAPOWSIN (Wash., Pierce Co.) \kə pou´ sin, kə pou´ zin\. Perhaps from a Puyallup (Salishan) word meaning 'shallow' (Hitchman 1985).

KAPSUKALIK Lake (Alaska, St. Lawrence C-3). The Yupik (Eskimo) name, said to mean 'constricted in the middle', was recorded in 1949 (Orth 1967).

KARAMIN (Wash., Ferry Co.). Perhaps an Okanagan (Salishan) word meaning 'cutting instrument', from /k'ər-/ 'to cut' (D. Kinkade p.c.).

KARHEEN (Alaska, Craig D-4) \kär hēn´\. Possibly from Tlingit <ta-hin> 'salmon stream'; cf. *t'a* 'king salmon', *héen* [hí:n] 'water, stream' (Davis and Leer 1976:7, 32).

KARILLYUKPUK Creek (Alaska, Wiseman D-1). The Iñupiaq (Eskimo) name, reported in 1956, is said to mean 'very rugged' (Orth 1967).

KARLUK (Alaska, Karluk C-2) \kär´ luk\. The Alutiiq (Eskimo) name was reported in 1805 (Orth 1967).

KARMUK Point (Alaska, Wainwright C-2). The Iñupiaq (Eskimo) name was reported in 1924 (Orth 1967).

KARON Lake (Alaska, Cape Mendenhall D-4). The Yupik (Eskimo) name, said to mean 'river head', was reported in 1949 (Orth 1967).

KARTA Bay (Alaska, Craig C-2). The Tlingit name was published as <Kasa-an> in 1883 (modern **Kasaan),** but later became **Karta** by a copying error (Orth 1967).

KARTAR Creek (Wash., Okanogan Co.). From an Okanagan (Salishan) placename [katár], of unclear derivation (D. Kinkade p.c.).

KARUK Indian Reservation (Calif., Siskiyou Co.) \kä´ ro͞ok\. The name of this people on the upper Klamath River is from the word *káruk* 'upriver', contrasting with *yúruk* 'downriver'—which was applied by white settlers to the linguistically unrelated Yurok people on the lower Klamath (Gudde 1998). The writing <Karok> was formerly used by anthropologists and linguists.

KARUMNULIMA Creek (Alaska, Survey Pass C-6). The Iñupiaq (Eskimo) name, said to refer to a broken arrow, was reported in 1956 (Orth 1967); cf. *qaġruq* 'arrow' (MacLean 1980).

KASAAN (Alaska, Craig C-2) \kə san´\. From Tlingit *kasa'aan* 'pretty town' (*HNAI* 7:259). The nearby placename **Karta Bay** is from the same source.

KASEGALUK Lagoon (Alaska, Wainwright A-6). The Iñupiaq (Eskimo) name, said to mean 'spotted seal place', was recorded as <Kasegarlik> in 1923; cf. *qasigiaq* 'spotted seal' (MacLean 1980).

KASHAGNAK, Mount (Alaska, Skagway B-2). The Tlingit name was published in 1952 (Orth 1967).

KASHAIAK Mountains (Alaska, Goodnews Bay B-4) The Yupik (Eskimo) name was reported in 1954 (Orth 1967).

KASHEGA (Alaska, Unalaska A-4) \kə shē´ gə\. From the Aleut placename *qusiix* (Bergsland 1994).

KASHEGELOK (Alaska, Taylor Mountains D-5) \kə shē´ gə lo͝ok\. From a Yupik (Eskimo) name, reported in 1903 (Orth 1967).

KASHIAGAMIUT (Alaska, Goodnews Bay B-3) \kə shē´ əg myo͞ot\. The Yupik (Eskimo) name was reported as <Kissiak> in 1880; the ending *-miut* means 'people' (Orth 1967).

KASHIA Indian Reserve (Calif., Sonoma Co.) \kə shī´ ə\. The name refers to the Southwestern Pomo Indians; it is from their self-designation /k'ahšáaya/ 'agile people', from /k'ahša/ 'agile, nimble' (Gudde 1998).

KASHONG Creek (N.Y., Ontario Co.) \kə shong´\. Probably an Iroquoian name, earlier written as <Gaghcoughwa, Gahgsonghwa> (etc.); perhaps meaning 'the limb has fallen' (Beauchamp 1907).

KASHOTO Glacier (Alaska, Mount Fairweather D-4). Named for a leader of the Tlingit (Orth 1967).

KASHUNUK River (Alaska, Hooper Bay B-2). From the Yupik (Eskimo) placename *qissunaq* (Orth 1967; Jacobson 1984).

KASHVIK Bay (Alaska, Karluk D-4). The Alutiiq (Eskimo) name was published as <Katvik> in 1852 (Orth 1967).

KASHWITNA (Alaska, Tyonek D-1) \kash wit´ nə\. From Dena'ina (Athabaskan) *kiłbitnu*, containing *kił* 'boy' and *-tnu* 'river' (Kari and Fall 1987:163).

KASIANA Island (Alaska, Sitka A-5). The Tlingit name was recorded in 1809 (Orth 1967).

KASIDAYA Creek (Alaska, Skagway B-1). The Tlingit name <Kasidayiya>, translated as 'slide-front', was published in 1923 (Orth 1967).

KASIGLUK (Alaska, Baird Inlet D-2) \kə sig´ lo͝ok\. From Yupik (Eskimo) *kassigluq* 'confluence of rivers' (Jacobson 1984).

KASIK Lagoon (Alaska, Noatak A-4). From Iñupiaq (Eskimo) *kiasik* 'shoulder blade' (Orth 1967; MacLean 1980).

KASILOF River (Alaska, Kenai B-4) \kə sil´ of\. From Dena'ina (Athabaskan) *ggasilatnu*, with *-tnu* 'river' (Kari and Kari 1982:14), apparently adapted to resemble a Russian surname.

KASINUK Mountain (Alaska, Baird Inlet C-8). The Yupik (Eskimo) name was reported in 1949 (Orth 1967).

KASITSNA Bay (Alaska, Seldovia B-5) \kə sit´ nə\. From Dena'ina (Athabaskan) *k'tsits'ena* 'skull' (Kari and Kari 1982:30).

KASKANAK Creek (Alaska, Dillingham B-1) \kas´ kə nak\. The Yupik (Eskimo) name was reported as <Kaskinakh> in 1880 (Orth 1967).

KASKASKIA (Ill., Randolph Co.) \kas kas´ kē ə\. The name is that of a branch of the Miami-Illinois (Algonquian) people, first recorded in 1672 as <Kakachkiouek> (*HNAI* 15:680). The Native American name is /kaaskaaskiiwa, kaahkaahkia/ 'katydid' (Costa 2000:48).

KASKELA (Ore., Wasco Co.) \kas kel´ ə\. Named for a nineteenth-century leader of the Wasco (Chinookan) people at Warm Springs Reservation; his name is also written <Cush Kella> (McArthur 1992).

KASKUTU Point (Alaska, Skagway A-2). The Tlingit name was reported in 1922 as <Kashkulu Khaku>, supposedly meaning 'man's-scalp-off point' (Orth 1967).

KASLOKAN Point (Alaska, Cold Bay A-2). Perhaps from an Alutiiq (Eskimo) word meaning 'low' (Orth 1967); cf. Yupik (Eskimo) *qas-* 'low in volume' (Jacobson 1984).

KASNA Creek (Alaska, Lake Clark A-3). The Dena'ina (Athabaskan) name is *kazhnatnu* 'lynx stream' (J. Kari p.c.).

KASNYKU Bay (Alaska, Sitka A-3). The Tlingit name was reported in 1895 (Orth 1967).

KASOAG (N.Y., Oswego Co.) \kə sōg´\. Possibly from a word meaning 'sky' in an Algonquian language, although the location is outside the Algonquian area (Beauchamp 1907); cf. Abenaki (Algonquian) *asokw* 'sky', *kakasokw* 'clear sky' (Day 1994–95).

KASOOK Lake (Alaska, Craig A-3). The Tlingit name was recorded in 1897 (Orth 1967).

KASOTA City (Minn., LeSueur Co.) \kə sō´ tə\. Said to be from a Dakota (Siouan) placename meaning 'cleared off' (Upham 2001); cf. *kasóta* 'to cut off trees from an area' (Riggs 1890).

KASSA Inlet (Alaska, Dixon Entrance D-2). The Tlingit name was recorded in 1905 (Orth 1967).

KASSAN Island (Alaska, Craig D-4). The Tlingit name was published in 1962 (Orth 1967).

KASSIANMUTE (Alaska, Goodnews Bay B-4). The Yupik (Eskimo) name was reported in 1880 (Orth 1967); the ending *-miut* means 'people'.

KASSON Creek (Alaska, Solomon C-5). The Iñupiaq (Eskimo) name was reported in 1900 (Orth 1967).

KATAGUNI Island (Alaska, Skagway A-1). The Tlingit name was reported in 1883 (Orth 1967).

KATAHDIN, Mount (Maine, Piscataquis Co.) \kə tä´ din\. Eastern Abenaki (Algonquian) *ktàtən* 'large mountain', from *kt-* 'large' and *-atən* 'mountain' (I. Goddard p.c.). The name also occurs in Mass. (Middlesex Co.). A possibly related name is **Kitattiny** (Pa., Carbon Co.).

KATAK Creek (Alaska, Mount Michelson B-1). From Iñupiaq (Eskimo) *katak-* 'to fall, to drop' (Orth 1967; Fortescue et al. 1994).

KATAKITEKON (Mich., Gogebic Co.). From Ojibwa (Algonquian) <Ketekitiganing> 'old field place', because Indians once planted crops here on a lakeshore; the lake still bears the French name **Lac Vieux Désert** 'lake (of the) old deserted-place' (Vogel 1991). The Native American name is from Ojibwa *gete-* 'old', *gitigaan* 'field' (Nichols and Nyholm 1995).

KATAKTURUK River (Alaska, Mount Michelson D-2). The Iñupiaq (Eskimo) name perhaps contains *katak-* 'to fall, to drop' (Orth 1967; MacLean 1980).

KATAKWA Point (Alaska, Prince Rupert D-3). The Tlingit name was published in 1869 (Orth 1967).

KATALA Hills (Ala., Talladega Co.) \kə tal´ ə\. Perhaps Muskogee for 'dead mulberry', from *kē* /ki:/ 'mulberry', *tale* /tá:li/ 'dead (of wood)' (Martin and Mauldin 2000).

KATALAHOSA Lake (Alaska, Bettles B-5). The Koyukon (Athabaskan) name was recorded in 1956 (Orth 1967).

KATALLA (Alaska, Cordova A-2) \kə tal´ ə\. From Tlingit [qatána']; no etymology is known (De Laguna 1972:104).

KATALSTA Ridge (N.C., Swain Co.). Said to be the name of an Indian woman, language not identified (Powell 1968).

KATAMA (Mass., Dukes Co.). From a SNEng. Algonquian placename, probably containing <keht-> 'great' (W. Cowan p.c.).

KATCHIN Creek (Alaska, Kenai B-7). The name, perhaps from Dena'ina (Athabaskan), was reported in 1958 (Orth 1967).

KATEEKUK Island (Alaska, Sutwik Is. A-3). The Yupik (Eskimo) name was reported as <Kateekhuk> in 1874 (Orth 1967).

KATEEL River (Alaska, Kateel River B-4) \kə tēl´\. From Koyukon (Athabaskan) *kodeel no'*, perhaps literally 'river that provides for the stomach'; cf. *-konh, ko-* 'abdomen', *no'* 'river' (Jetté and Jones 2000).

KATEMCY (Tex., Mason Co.) \kə tem´ sē\. Said to be named for an Indian leader, <Katumse>, language not identified (Stokes 1977).

KATENAI Hill (Alaska, Afognak A-3). The Alutiiq (Eskimo) name was reported in 1952 (Orth 1967).

KATETE River (Alaska, Bradfield Canal C-6). The Tlingit name was first published in 1883 as <Kwahteetah> (Orth 1967).

KATHAKNE (Alaska, Nabesna D-2). The Upper Tanana (Athabaskan) name was reported in 1955 (Orth 1967).

KATHIO Township (Minn., Mille Lacs Co.) \kath´ ē ō\. The name is based on a mistranscription of the nearby placename **Izatys** (Upham 2001), which in turn is from Dakota (Siouan) *isą́-ati,* referring to a division of the Sioux usually called the **Santee** (see the placename in Neb., Knox Co., below). Another related placename is **Isanti County** in Minn.

KATHUL Mountain (Alaska, Charley River B-3). The Han (Athabaskan) name was recorded in 1883 (Orth 1967).

KATIKTAK (Alaska, Chandler Lake A-2). From Iñupiaq (Eskimo) *qatiqtuq* 'is white' (Orth 1967; Webster and Zibell 1970).

KATIMIN (Calif., Siskiyou Co.) \kä´ ti mēn\. From Karuk *ka'tim'îin,* lit. 'upriver-edge falls', from *ka'* 'upriver', *tiim* 'edge', and *îin* 'falls', referring to a major rapids in the Klamath River (Gudde 1998).

KATLIAN, Mount (Alaska, Sitka A-4) \kat´ lē ən\. Named for an eighteenth-century Tlingit leader (Orth 1967).

KATLITNA River (Alaska, McGrath D-6). From Upper Kuskokwim (Athabaskan) *k'esh-dzotno',* perhaps meaning 'birch river', with *-no'* 'river' (Kari 1999:86).

KATMAI, Mount (Alaska, Mount Katmai B-3) \kat´ mī\. The Alutiiq (Eskimo) name refers to a village site south of the volcano, abandoned after the 1912 eruption. The term was recorded by Russian explorers in 1827 (Orth 1967).

KATO \kä´ tō\. An Indian group of northern Calif., belonging to the Athabaskan language family; from Northern Pomo /khaṭo/ 'lake', containing /khá/ 'water' (Gudde 1998). As a placename it is written **Cahto** (Calif., Mendocino Co.). There is also a **Cahto Creek** (Calif., Humboldt Co.).

KATOLINAT, Mount (Alaska, Mount Katmai B-5). The name, perhaps Alutiiq (Eskimo), was reported as <Kakhtolinat> in 1880 (Orth 1967).

KATONAH (N.Y., Westchester Co.) \kə tō´ nə\. Named for a seventeenth-century Indian leader, perhaps of the Munsee Delaware (Algonquian) people. The name has been translated 'great mountain' (Grumet 1981); cf. Munsee *kihchi-, kihchu-* 'very big' (O'Meara 1996).

KATOYA Lake (Mont., Glacier Co.). From Blackfoot (Algonquian) *katoyi(s), kátoyiss* 'balsam fir, sweet pine' (Holterman 1985; D. Franz p.c.).

KATRIKIORAK Creek (Alaska, Wainwright A-2). The Iñupiaq (Eskimo) name was published in 1958 (Orth 1967).

KATSUCK Creek (Idaho, Benewah Co.) \kat´ suk\. Named by the U.S. Forest Service, from Chinook Jargon <katsuk> [kátsak] 'middle', from Lower Chinook [ká:tsak] 'middle' (D. Kinkade p.c.). The same name occurs as **Katsuk Butte** (Ore., Deschutes Co.) as **Katsuk Peak** (Wash., Skagit Co.). A related placename is **Kotsuck Creek** (Wash., Pierce Co.).

KATZEHIN River (Alaska, Skagway A-1). The Tlingit name was reported as <Chkazehin> in 1883 (Orth 1967); cf. *héen* [hí:n] 'river' (Davis and Leer 1976:6).

KAUBASHINE Creek (Wis., Oneida Co.) \kô´ bə shēn\. Possibly from Ojibwa (Algonquian) *gabeshiwin* 'campsite', from *gabeshi* 'to set up camp' (Nichols and Nyholm 1995).

KAUDA Point (Alaska, Craig D-4). The name, perhaps Tlingit, was published in 1956 (Orth 1967).

KAUKAUNA (Wis., Outagamie Co.) \kô kô´ nə\. This represents the Menominee (Algonquian) placename /oka:hkoneh/ 'place of pike (fish)', from /oka:w/ 'pike' (Vogel 1991; Bloomfield 1975).

KAUK River (Alaska, Selawik B-5). The Iñupiaq (Eskimo) name was recorded in 1901 (Orth 1967).

KAULTUI Mountain (Alaska, Table Mt. B-4). The Gwich'in (Athabaskan) name is *ga'al tąįį ddhaa* 'mountain where game passes by trail' (J. Kari p.c.). Probably related is nearby **Kaultuinjek Creek.**

KAUNEONGA (N.Y., Sullivan Co.). Perhaps from a Munsee Delaware (Algonquian) form meaning 'two wings', earlier written as <Kau-na-ong-ga> (Ruttenber 1906); cf. Munsee *lóngwan* 'my wing' (O'Meara 1996).

KAVACHURAK Creek (Alaska, Ambler River D-2). The Iñupiaq (Eskimo) name, said to mean 'red hill', was reported in 1956 (Orth 1967); cf. *qaviqsuq* 'is red' (Webster and Zibell 1970).

KAVAKSURAK Mountain (Alaska, Howard Pass B-2). The Iñupiaq (Eskimo) name is from *kaviksuq* 'is red' (L. Kaplan p.c.).

KAVALGA Island (Alaska, Gareloi Is. B-3). From Aleut *qawalĝa* 'the one to the east'; cf. *qawa-* 'east' (Bergsland 1994).

KAVALGHAK Bay (Alaska, St. Lawrence D-6). The Yupik (Eskimo) name, said to mean 'sleeping place', was reported in 1965 (Orth 1967); cf. *qavagh-* [qavaʀ-] 'to sleep' (Jacobson 1987). The placename is also written as **Kavalrok.**

KAVEARAK Point (Alaska, Beechey Point C-4). Said to be from Iñupiaq (Eskimo) <qaviaraq> 'sand', reported in 1951 (Orth 1967); cf. *qavia* 'fine sand' (MacLean 1980).

KAVET Creek (Alaska, Baird Mountains A-1). The Iñupiaq (Eskimo) name was recorded as <Kau-vet> in 1901 (Orth 1967).

KAVIAK Creek (Alaska, Mount Michelson C-2). From Iñupiaq (Eskimo) *kavviaq* 'red fox' (Orth 1967; Fortescue et al. 1994).

KAVIK River (Alaska, Beechey Point A-1) From Iñupiaq (Eskimo) *qavvik* 'wolverine' (Orth 1967; MacLean 1980).

KAVIKTIT Mountain (Alaska, Survey Pass D-2). From Iñupiaq (Eskimo), perhaps meaning 'like a quoit' (Orth 1967).

KAVIRUK River (Alaska, Teller A-1). The Iñupiaq (Eskimo) name is probably *qaviaraq* 'sand hill' (L. Kaplan p.c.).

KAVOLIK (Ariz., Pima Co.). From O'odham (Piman) *kawelǐk* 'hilly, hill' (J. Hill p.c.).

KAVRORAK Hill (Alaska, Noatak D-6). The Iñupiak (Eskimo) name, said to mean 'the pointed part of a woman's parka', was reported in 1950 (Orth 1967).

KAW \kô\. The term is an alternative name of the **Kansas** (Siouan) people, originating as a French abbreviation of the native term <Kansa>

(*HNAI* 13:474). **Kaw River** is an alternative name of the Kansas River. The placename **Kaw** occurs in other states: for example, in **Kaw City** (Okla., Kay Co.), as well as in Mo. (Jackson Co.) and Neb. (Dundy Co.).

KAWA (Kans., Montgomery Co.). Perhaps Osage (Siouan) /hkáwa/ 'horse', reduced from Spanish *caballo* (Rydjord 1968; R. Rankin p.c.).

KAWAGUESAGA Lake (Wis., Oneida Co.) \kə wô gə sä´ gə\. Perhaps from an Ojibwa (Algonquian) name meaning 'clearwater lake' (Vogel 1991); cf. Eastern Ojibwa *waaseyaagmig* 'to be clear water', *zaaghigan* 'lake' (Rhodes 1985).

KAWAIKA-A (Ariz., Navajo Co.) \kə wī´ kə ə\. From Hopi (Uto-Aztecan) *kawàyka'a,* the same as the name for Laguna, a Keresan pueblo in New Mexico. Cf. names for that pueblo in Keresan languages: Acoma /k'áwa'yka/, Santa Ana /k'áwàyka/ (K. Hill p.c.).

KAWAK Butte (Ore., Deschutes Co.) \kā´ wôk\. The Chinook Jargon name <ka-wa´k>, probably [kawák] 'to fly', was assigned by the U.S. Forest Service (McArthur 1992); it is derived from Lower Chehalis (Salishan) /sqáw'əq/ 'to fly' (D. Kinkade p.c.).

KAWAMEEH Park (N.J., Union Co.). Said to be named for a Delaware (Algonquian) leader (Becker 1964).

KAWANAK Channel (Alaska, St. Michael A-6). The Yupik (Eskimo) name was reported in 1899 (Orth 1967).

KAWANERA (Alaska, Pribilof Is. A-2) The Aleut name was reported in 1903 as meaning 'sea lions' boat' (Orth 1967); cf. Aleut *qawax̂* 'sea lion' (Bergsland 1994).

KAWBAWGAM, Lake (Mich., Marquette Co.). Named for a nineteenth-century Ojibwa leader, Charles Kawbawgam (Vogel 1986).

KAWEAH (Calif., Tulare Co.) \kə wē´ ə\. The name, earlier written <Kawia> and <Ga´wia>, originally referred to a Yokuts subgroup. It is now pronounced the same as **Cahuilla,** an Indian people and placename in southern Calif., but it is unrelated to that term.

KAWEEHNALI Slough (Alaska, St. Michael A-4). The Yupik (Eskimo) name was first reported as "Kaweenah Slough" in 1952 (Orth 1967).

KAWIAKPAK Creek (Alaska, Hooper Bay D-3). The Yupik (Eskimo) name was reeported in 1949 (Orth 1967).

KAWIALIK Lake (Alaska, Hooper Bay C-1). The Yupik (Eskimo), said to mean 'sandy', was reported in 1949 (Orth 1967); cf. *qaugyaq* 'sand' (Jacobson 1984).

KAWICHIARK River (Alaska, Selawik C-1). The Iñupiaq (Eskimo) name is *kuutchiaq* 'new river' (Burch 1998); cf. *kuuk* 'river', *-tchiaq* 'new' (MacLean 1980). Probably related Alaska names include **Kucheak Creek** (Meade River C-3) and **Kuchiak Creek** (Point Lay B-3).

KAWICH Range (Nev., Nye Co.) \kä´ wich\. Said to be called after a Shoshoni (Numic) leader whose name meant 'mountain' (Carlson 1974). The Native American term may have been Southern Paiute /kaipa-cci/ [káivattši] 'little mountain', diminutive of /kaipa/ 'mountain' (J. McLaughlin p.c.).

KAWISHIWI River (Minn., Lake Co.) \kə wish´ i wē\. The Ojibwa (Algonquian) name has been defined as 'river full of beavers' houses' (Upham 2001).

KAWKAWAK, Lake (Wash., Skagit Co.). From Chinook Jargon <káw-ka-wak> [káwkawak] 'yellow, green, pale', from Lower Chinook <kau-kau-ak> 'yellow' (Reese 1996; D. Kinkade p.c.).

KAWKAWLIN (Mich., Bay Co.) \kə kô´ lin\. Perhaps from Ojibwa (Algonquian) *gaagaagiw* 'raven' (Vogel 1986; Nichols and Nyholm 1995).

KAWOKHAWIK Island (Alaska, Kwiguk D-6). The Yupik (Eskimo) name is said to mean 'overnight camp' (Orth 1967); cf. *qavartar-* 'to stay overnight' (Jacobson 1984).

KAWUNEECHEE Valley (Colo., Grand Co.) \kä wo͞o nē´ chē\. From an Arapaho (Algonquian) term meaning 'coyote river', *koo'óhwuu-niicii* (A. Cowell p.c.).

KAYADEROSSERAS Creek (N.Y., Saratoga Co.) \kā yə də rôs´ ə rəs\. From Mohawk (Iroquoian) *kanyataróseras,* perhaps meaning something like 'lake mouth'; from the root *-nyatar-,* noun form *kanyá:tare'* 'lake' (Ruttenber 1906, Lounsbury 1960:51). A related name is **Kaydeross Park** (N.Y., Saratoga Co.).

KAYAK \kī´ ak\. This term for a type of Eskimo canoe was probably first borrowed by English from Greenlandic or Eastern Canadian Inuktitut (Eskimo) *qayaq*, although the equivalent words in the Eskimo languages of Alaska are similar—Yupik *qayaq,* Iñupiaq *qayaq* (Fortescue et al. 1994). The term is used as a placename at several sites in Alaska, such as **Kayak Island** (Middleton Is. D-2), and at **Kayak Point** in Wash. (Snohomish Co.). **Kayak Cape** (Alaska, Unalaska B-2), however, may be from Aleut *qayax̂* 'hill, mountain', not from *iqyax̂* 'kayak' (Orth 1967; Bergsland 1994).

KAYAKSAK Mountain (Alaska, Point Hope B-2). The Iñupiaq (Eskimo) name is probably *qayaksraq* 'material for a kayak' (L. Kaplan p.c.).

KAY CHEE Draw (N.Mex., McKinley Co.). Perhaps a Navajo personal name, containing the surname *Chee*. This is a shortened form of *łichíí'* 'red' (A. Wilson p.c.).

KAY Creek (Alaska, Point Hope D-2) \kā\. Apparently an abbreviation of an Iñupiaq (Eskimo) placename, <Keak> or <Kayniktouk> (Orth 1967).

KAYDEROSS Park (N.Y., Saratoga Co.) \kā´ də rôs\. The name is related to that of the nearby **Kayaderosseras Creek**, from the Mohawk (Iroquoian) placename *kanyataróseras*; cf. *kanyá:tare'* 'lake'.

KAYENTA (Ariz., Navajo Co.) \kā yen´ tə, kä yen´ tə\. From Navajo (Athabaskan) *téé'ndééh* '(animals) fall into the water' (Wilson 1995). A related placename is **Tyende Creek** (Ariz., Apache Co.).

KAYIGYALIK Lake (Alaska, Baird Inlet D-2). The Yupik (Eskimo) name was reported in 1951 (Orth 1967).

KAYOSKH Lake (Minn., Lake Co.). From Ojibwa (Algonquian) *gayaashk* 'gull' (Nichols and Nyholm 1995).

KAYUTA Lake (N.Y., Oneida Co.) \kā yo͞o´ tə\. Probably from an Iroquoian language; cf. Mohawk *kanyá:tare'* 'lake' or Seneca *kęhǫ:te'* 'creek' (Beauchamp 1907; Chafe 1967).

KAZHUTAK (Alaska, Kwiguk A-4). The Yupik (Eskimo) name was reported in 1899 (Orth 1967).

KAZIK Hill (Alaska, Taylor Mountains D-6). The Yupik (Eskimo) name, said to mean 'little house', was reported in 1945 (Orth 1967); cf. *qasgiq* 'men's community house, steambath house' (Jacobson 1984).

KEALAVIK River (Alaska, Marshall A-8). The Yupik (Eskimo) name was reported in 1949 (Orth 1967); it contains *-vik* 'place'.

KEARSARGE, Mount (N.H., Merrimack Co.) \kēr´ särj\. From Abenaki (Algonquian) *gôwizawajo* 'rough mountain'; cf. *gôwigen* 'it is rough', *wajo* 'hill, mountain' (Day 1994–95). The name was given to a U.S. naval vessel that won a sea battle against the Confederate warship *Alabama* in 1864; perhaps for this reason the term appears in several areas as a transfer name: Calif. (Inyo Co.), Mich. (Houghton Co.), and Pa. (Erie Co.).

KEATCHIE (La., De Soto Par.) \kē´ chē\. The term refers to an Indian group of the Caddoan language family (Read 1927); it is sometimes written **Kichai** in the anthropological literature. Probably related placenames include **Kechi** (Kans., Sedgwick Co.), **Keechi Creek** (Okla., Caddo Co.), **Keechie** (Tex., Anderson Co.), and **Quihi** (Tex., Medina Co.).

KEBO Brook (Maine, Hancock Co.). Perhaps from an Abenaki (Algonquian) form related to *gibosa* 'it falls over' (Huden 1962; Day 1994–95).

KECHE Mountain (Alaska, Christian D-6). The Gwich'in (Athabaskan) name was recorded in 1956 (Orth 1967).

KECHI (Kans., Sedgwick Co.) \kē´ chī\. The term refers to an Indian group of the Caddoan language family (Rydjord 1968); it is sometimes written **Kichai** in the anthropological literature. There is also a **Kechi** in Okla. (Grady Co.). Related names include **Keatchie** (La., De Soto Par.), **Keechi Creek** (Okla., Caddo Co.), and **Keechie** (Tex., Anderson Co.).

KECHIBA:WA Ruin (N.Mex., Cibola Co.) \kech´ i bä wə\. The Zuni name probably contains /kečipa/ 'chalky stone' (Kari and Fall 1987; Newman 1958).

KECHUMSTUK (Alaska, Eagle A-4) \kech´ əm stuk\. A Tanacross (Athabaskan) version of English *catching stock,* i.e. capturing caribou (J. Kari p.c.).

KECOUGHTAN (Va., Hampton Co.). Earlier spelled <Kiccowtqan>, the name of a Va. Algonquian village visited by the English in 1607 (Hagemann 1988).

KEDINKET ISLAND (R.I., Washington Co). Probably from SNEng. Algonquian <kitonuck> 'ship' (W. Cowan p.c.).

KEECHELUS (Wash., Kittitas Co.) \kech´ ə ləs\. Said to be from a Sahaptin name meaning 'few fish', supposedly contrasting with the placename **Kachess River,** meaning 'many fish' (Hitchman 1985).

KEECHI (Tex., Leon Co.) \kē´ chī\. The term refers to an Indian people of the Caddoan language family (Tarpley 1980); it is sometimes written **Kichai** in the anthropological literature. There is also a **Keechi Creek** in Okla. (Caddo Co.) As a placename, it is also written as **Keatchie** (La., De Soto Par.), **Kechi** (Kans., Sedgwick Co.), and **Keechie** (Tex., Anderson Co.).

KEEGO Lake (Wis., Vilas Co.) \kē´ gō\. From Ojibwa (Algonquian) *giigoonh* [gi:gǫ:] 'a fish' (Nichols and Nyholm 1995). The term was written <Keego> in Longfellow's *Hiawatha* and in that form was applied as a placename in several areas, including Mich. (Oakland Co.) and Ala. (Escambia Co.) There is also a **Kego Township** in Minn. (Cass Co.).

KEEKWULEE Falls (Wash., King Co.) \kēk´ wə lē\. The name, given by a mountaineering club in 1916, represents Chinook Jargon <kekulle, keekwully, kīkwīlī> [kíkwɪli, kíkwɪli, kíkwəli, kíkwəli] 'below, under, down, low', from Lower Chinook <kík-hwil-li, kik-hwi-li> 'below, under' (Hitchman 1985; D. Kinkade p.c.).

KEESIN Peak (Alaska, St. Lawrence B-3). The Yupik (Eskimo) name was reported in 1930 (Orth 1967),

KEESUS, Lake (Wis., Waukesha Co.) \kē´ səs\. From Potawatomi (Algonquian) <kises> 'the sun' (Kansas 1997); cf. Ojibwa *giizis* (Nichols and Nyholm 1995).

KEETE Island (Alaska, Craig A-2). The name, possibly from Tlingit, was reported in 1951 (Orth 1967).

KEET SEEL (Ariz., Navajo Co.) \kēt sēl\. Navajo (Athabaskan) *kits'iilí* 'the place of the shattered houses', containing *ki* (*kin*) 'house' and *ts'iil* 'fragment, sherd' (Wilson 1995). The placename is also written as **Kit Sili** and **Kitsillie**.

KEEWAHDIN (Mich., St. Clair Co.) \kə wä´ din\. From Ojibwa (Algonquian) *giiwedin* 'north; the north wind' (Nichols and Nyholm 1995). In the form <Keewaydin>, translated as 'northwest wind', the term was popularized in Longellow's *Hiawatha.* It has been used as a placename in a variety of pronunciations and spellings: for example, in **Keewatin** (Minn., Itasca Co.) \kē wä´ tin\. and **Keewayden** (Mich., Baraga Co.). In Maine (Oxford Co.) **Keewaydin Lake** was supposedly named for a Mrs. Virginia Keewaydin Jones (Rutherford 1970); and the same spelling occurs in other states (e.g., Fla., Collier Co.; Mich., Baraga Co.; and Pa., Clearfield Co.).

KEEYUK Creek (Alaska, Candle D-5). The Iñupiaq (Eskimo) name was reported in 1949 (Orth 1967).

KEGAN Creek (Alaska, Craig A-1). Named in 1897 for an Indian resident, probably Tlingit (Orth 1967).

KEGONSA (Wis., Dane Co). From Ojibwa (Algonquian) *giigoons* 'little fish', diminutive of *giigoonh* 'fish' (Vogel 1991; Nichols and Nyholm 1995).

KEGO Township (Minn., Cass Co.) \kē´ gō\. From Ojibwa (Algonquian) *giigoonh* [gi:gǫ:] 'a fish' (Upham 2001; Nichols and Nyholm 1995). In the spelling **Keego,** the name also occurs as **Keego Lake** in Wis. (Vilas Co.) as well as in Mich. (Oakland Co.) and Ala. (Escambia Co.).

KEGUK River (Alaska, Baird Inlet A-6). The Yupik (Eskimo) name was reported in 1949 (Orth 1967).

KEGUM KAGATI Lake (Alaska, Baird Inlet B-7). The Yupik (Eskimo) name, meaning 'head of the Keguk (River)', was reported in 1949 (Orth 1967).

KEHUKEE Swamp (N.C., Halifax Co.). From Tuscarora (Iroquoian) *kęyhuu'ke* 'at the river' (B. Rudes p.c.).

KEJULIK River (Alaska, Karluk D-6). The Alutiiq (Eskimo) name was reported in 1904 (Orth 1967).

KEKAWAKA Creek (Calif., Trinity Co.) \kik´ ə wä kə\. From Wintu /kiki waqat/ 'frozen creek', containing /kik-/ 'to freeze' and /waqat/ (Gudde 1998).

KEKEGAMA Lake (Wis., Washburn Co.). Appears to be a coinage based on Ojibwa (Algonquian) *giigoonh* 'fish' and *-gami* 'lake' (Vogel 1991; Nichols and Nyholm 1995).

KEKEKABIC Lake (Minn., Lake Co.) \kek ə kä´ bik\. Probably from Ojibwa (Algonquian) *gakaabikaa* 'there is a rock ledge, e.g. at a waterfall' (J. Nichols p.c.).

KEKIKTUK River (Alaska, Mount Michelson C-2). From Iñupiaq (Eskimo) *qikiqtaq* 'island' (Orth 1967, MacLean 1980).

KEKIONGA Lake (Ind., Allen Co.). Probably from Miami/Illinois (Algonquian) /(ah)kihkionki/ 'on the earth', with /(ah)kihkiwi/ 'earth' (McCafferty 2002).

KEKOSKEE (Wis., Dodge Co.) \kē kos´ kē\. The name of a Winnebago (Siouan) village, of unclear derivation (Vogel 1991).

KEKU Creek (Alaska, Petersburg C-6). The Tlingit name was published in 1869 (Orth 1967).

KEKUR Island (Alaska, Kodiak C-1). The term was used by Russian explorers of Alaska to designate a high isolated rock or rocky islet; it may be taken from a native language of Kamchatka, in Siberia (Orth 1967).

KELEDZHICHAGAT (Alaska, Sleetmute D-5). The Deg Hit'an (Athabaskan) name is of unknown derivation (Orth 1967).

KELEZ, Mount (Alaska, Mount Katmai B-6). The Alutiiq (Eskimo) name was published in 1951 (Orth 1967).

KELGAYA Point (Alaska, Skagway A-1). The Tlingit name was reported in 1883 as <Ketlgakhya> 'dog-howl place' (Orth 1967); cf. *keitl* [ke:tl] 'dog' (Davis and Leer 1976).

KELL Bay (Alaska, Port Alexander A-1). The Tlingit name was reported in 1886 (Orth 1967).

KELUCHE Creek (Calif., Shasta Co.) \kə lōō´ chē\. Named for Charlie Klutchie or Keluche, a Wintu shaman; his Wintu name was /tl'učuheres/. It is derived from Wintu /tl'uči/ 'sticking, stabbing', from /tl'u-/ 'to stick, stab' (Gudde 1998).

KEMA (Okla., Ottawa Co.) \kē´ mə\. Said to be from Miami/Illinois (Algonquian) /(a)kima/ (Shirk 1974; M. McCafferty p.c.).

KEMAH (Tex., Galveston Co.) \kē´ mə\. Said to mean 'facing the winds' in an unidentified Indian language (Tarpley 1980).

KEMAH, Lake (N.J., Sussex Co.). Possibly from Unami Delaware (Algonquian) *kimí* 'secretly' (Becker 1964; Blalock et al. 1994).

KEMEGRAK Hills (Alaska, Point Hope B-2). The Iñupiaq (Eskimo) is probably *qimiġaq* 'hill' (L. Kaplan p.c.).

KEMIK Creek (Alaska, Sagavanirktok B-1). From Iñupiaq (Eskimo) *qimiq* 'hill' (Orth 1967; Lowe 1984a).

KEMUK Mountain (Alaska, Dillingham C-6). The Yupik (Eskimo) name was reported in 1965 (Orth 1967).

KENABEE, Lake (Wis., Polk Co.) \ken′ ə bē\. Perhaps from Ojibwa (Algonquian) *ginebig* 'snake' (Vogel 1991; Nichols and Nyholm 1995). The Indian term appears as <Kenabeek> in Longfellow's *Hiawatha* and occurs as a placename in **Kenabeek Creek** (Mich., Gogebic Co.), pronounced \ken′ ə bek\.

KENAI (Alaska, Kenai C-4) \kē′ nī\. The English name was adapted from Russian *kenaiets* (sg.), *kenaitsy* (pl.) 'Kenai Indian' or from the corresponding adjective *kenaiskii*; this in turn was borrowed from Dena'ina (Athabaskan) *kahtnu* 'river-mouth river' (J. Kari p.c.).

KENAKUCHUK Creek (Alaska, Dillingham B-6). The Yupik (Eskimo) name was recorded in 1910 as <Ki-nuk-tu-cha-rok> (Orth 1967).

KENASNOW Rocks (Alaska, Sitka B-2). The name is related to the nearby **Killisnoo**; see below.

KENDUSKEAG (Maine, Penobscot Co.) \ken′ dəs kēg\. From Penobscot (Algonquian) /kα′teskik/ 'at the place or land of the eel weirs', probably borrowed from Passamaquoddy (Algonquian), which has /kat/ 'eel' (Siebert 1943:506).

KENEBEC Creek (Calif., Butte Co.) \ken′ ə bek\. Probably related to the name **Kennebec** in Maine (Washington Co.); see below.

KENESAW (Ga., Cobb Co.) \ken′ ə sô\. Probably related to the name of nearby **Kennesaw Mountain**, perhaps named for the Cherokee (Iroquoian) village of **Conasauga** (Ga., Gilmer Co.), from *kanesga* 'grass' (Read 1934; Alexander 1971).

KENIBUNA Lake (Alaska, Tyonek A-8) \kə nē′ bə nä\. Dena'ina (Athabaskan) *hni bena,* lit. 'island lake' (Kari and Kari 1982:22).

KENICK (Calif., Humboldt Co.) \kā′ nik\. From the Yurok village name *kenek* (Gudde 1998). Also written as **Kanick.**

KENNAKEET Township (N.C., Dare Co.) \ken′ ə kēt\. Probably from a placename in the CAC Algonquian language (Payne 1985).

KENNEBAGO (Maine, Franklin Co.) \ken ə bā′ gō\. From Western Abenaki (Algonquian) *ginebagw* 'large lake' (Huden 1962; Day 1994–95); cf. *gini* 'much, strong'. A related form is **Kennebec** (Maine, Washington Co.).

KENNEBEC (Maine, Washington Co.) \ken′ ə bek\. From Eastern Abenaki /kínipek^{W}/ 'large body of still water, large bay' (Eckstorm 1941:142–43; *HNAI* 15:146). The term occurs as a transfer name in Iowa (Monona Co.) and S.Dak. (Lyman Co.). Related forms are **Kenebec Creek** (Calif., Butte Co.) and **Kennebago** (Maine, Franklin Co.).

KENNEBUNK (Maine, York Co.) \ken′ ə bungk\. The name may be from Abenaki or Micmac (both Algonquian), but the derivation is not clear (Eckstorm 1941).

KENNEKUK (Kans., Atchison Co.). Named for a Kickapoo (Algonquian) leader called /keenehkaka/ (Ives Goddard p.c.).

KENNESAW Mountain (Ga., Cobb Co.) \ken′ ə sô\. Perhaps named for the Cherokee (Iroquoian) village of **Conasauga** (Ga., Gilmer Co.), from *kanesga* 'grass' (Read 1934; Alexander 1971). A related placename is the nearby **Kenesaw**.

KENNEWICK (Wash., Benton Co.) \ken′ ə wik\. The name is probably from Sahaptin; it has been translated as 'grassy place' (Hitchman 1985); cf. also Sahaptin /čanúwi/ 'to weave' (N. Rude p.c.).

KENNYETTO Creek (N.Y., Fulton Co.) \ken ē et′ ō, ken ē at′ ō\. The name may be of Iroquoian origin, meaning 'stone lying flat in the water'; it has also been written <Kenneattoo> and <Kininyitto> (Beauchamp 1907).

KENOCKEE (Mich., St. Clair Co.). Possibly from Ojibwa (Algonquian) for 'long land' (Vogel 1986); cf. *ginoozi* 'be long', *aki* 'land' (Nichols and Nyholm 1995).

KENO Creek (Alaska, Goodnews Bay C-7). The Yupik (Eskimo) name was reported in 1919 (Orth 1967).

KENOGAMA Lake (Minn., Itasca Co.). Perhaps Ojibwa (Algonquian) for 'long lake'; cf. Eastern Ojibwa *gnoo-zid* 'be long', *gamii* 'lake' (Rhodes 1985). A probably related form is **Kinogami Lake** (Minn., Cook Co.).

KENONG GO MONG Lake (Wis., Racine Co.) \kə nong´ gō mong\. Perhaps from a Potawatomi (Algonquian) word meaning 'long lake' (Vogel 1991); cf. Ojibwa **Kinogami Lake,** with that meaning.

KENOSHA County (Mich.) \kə nō´ shə\. Adopted from the term for 'pike' (fish) in Longfellow's *Hiawatha,* derived in turn from Ojibwa (Algonquian) *ginoozhe* (Vogel 1986; Nichols and Nyholm 1995). The term occurs in Mich. (Newaygo Co.) and as a transfer name, with the alternative spelling **Kanosha,** in Neb. (Cass Co.). The alternative **Kenosia** occurs in Conn. (Fairfield Co.). **Canosia Township** (Minn., St. Louis Co.) represents still another spelling. More distantly related is **Kenoza Lake** (Mass., Essex Co.), from the Abenaki (Algonquian) word for 'pike'.

KENOVA (W.Va., Wayne Co.) \kə nō´ və\. The name was coined to designate the meeting place of three states: Ky., Ohio, and W.Va. The first two of these have Indian origins. The term also occurs as a transfer name in Ark. (Union Co.) and Wash. (Whitman Co.).

KENOZA Lake (Mass., Essex Co.) \kə nō´ zə\. Probably from Abenaki *kwenoza* 'great northern pike (fish)' (Day 1994–95); the term also occurs as a placename in N.Y. (Sullivan Co.). Related placenames include **Kenosha County** (Wis.), from the Ojibwa (Algonquian) word for 'pike'; see above.

KENTUCK (Ala., Talladega Co.) \ken´tuk\. Perhaps an abbreviation of **Kentucky**; see below. The name occurs in several other states (e.g., Md., Dorchester Co.; Ore., Coos Co.; and W.Va., Jackson Co.) Also possibly related names include **Kanetuche Creek** (Ala., Clarke Co.); see above.

KENTUCKY \ken tuk´ ē, kən tuk´ ē\. The name was perhaps originally Iroquoian, referring to the Shawnee (Algonquian) village in Clark County, Ky., known to the Shawnees as **<Eskippakithiki>** (Read 1984:91). It may have been a Wyandot (Iroquoian) word meaning 'plain, meadowland'; cf. Seneca *gę̨dá'geh* 'at the field' (Vogel 1991; W. Chafe p.c.). The term occurs as a transfer name in several areas (e.g., Kans., Jefferson Co.; Ore., Douglas Co.; and Wis., Lafayette Co.). The abbreviation **Kentuck** is also widespread.

KENTUCTAH Creek (Miss., Madison Co.) \kin tuk´ tə\. Perhaps from Choctaw (Muskogean), meaning 'beaver dam'; cf. *kįta* 'beaver', *oktapah* 'dam' (Seale 1939:109, 223; P. Munro p.c.).

KENU Lake (Wis., Vilas Co.). Probably from Ojibwa (Algonquian) *giniw* 'golden eagle' (Vogel 1991; Nichols and Nyholm 1995).

KENUNGA Creek (Alaska, Chandler Lake A-2). The Iñupiaq (Eskimo) name, said to mean 'knife edge', was reported in 1956 (Orth 1967).

KEOKA Lake (Maine, Oxford Co.). Perhaps from Abenaki (Algonquian), meaning 'where they get red earth for pots' (Huden 1962).

KEOKEE (Va., Lee Co.). Said to have been named for Mrs. Keokee Perrin, who was of Indian descent, language unknown (Hagemann 1988).

KEOKLEVIK River (Alaska, Hooper Bay B-3). The Yupik (Eskimo) name was reported in 1951 (Orth 1967); contains *-vik* 'place'.

KEOKUK County (Iowa) \kē´ ō kuk\. The name is that of a Sauk (Algonquian) leader of the early nineteenth century, said to mean 'one who moves about alertly' (Vogel 1983). His Native American name was /ki:yohkaka/; cf. /ki:w-/ 'about, in places', and /-ehk/ 'to step on (it)' (I. Goddard p.c.). There is also a **Keokuk Falls** (Okla., Pottawatomie Co.). A related name is **Keota**; see below.

KEOMAH Village (Iowa, Mahaska Co.). The name was created by combining the first part of the name **Keokuk**, a Sauk (Algonquian) leader, and the last part of the name **Mahaska**, an Iowa (Siouan) leader (Vogel 1983).

KEO Point (Alaska, Wainwright B-2). The Iñupiaq (Eskimo) term was reported in 1956 (Orth 1967).

KEOSAUQUA (Iowa, Van Buren Co.) \kē ō sä´ kwə\. This was apparently an old Meskwaki (Algonquian) name for the Des Moines River (Vogel 1983); it has been more accurately written as [kiwashokue] (I. Goddard p.c.).

KEOTA (Iowa, Keokuk Co.) \kē ō´ tə\. The site was earlier named **Keoton**, derived from a combination of **Keokuk** (see above) and *Washington* (Vogel 1983). As a transfer name, **Keota** occurs in Colo. (Weld Co.), Mo. (Macon Co.), N.Mex. (Colfax Co.), and Okla. (Haskell Co.).

KEOWEE (S.C., Oconee Co.) \kē´ ō wē\. Said to be the name of a Cherokee village, perhaps meaning 'mulberry-grove place' (Neuffer and Neuffer 1983; Pearson 1978); cf. *kuwa* 'mulberry' (Feeling 1975).

KERCHURAK Creek (Alaska, Shungnak D-5). The Iñupiaq (Eskimo) name was reported in 1927 (Orth 1967).

KERES (N.Mex.) \kâr´ əs\. This name, which also occurs in the form **Keresan** [kâr´ ə sən], refers to a family of closely related language varieties, spoken in the pueblos of Laguna, Acoma, Zia, Santa Ana, San Felipe, Santo Domingo, and Cochiti. The term was first recorded by the Spanish in the sixteenth century as <Quirix, Quires, Quereses>; it is probably from the Pecos (Tanoan) equivalent of Jemez /kél'iš/ 'Keresans' (HNAI 9:234). **Keres** does not occur in any present-day English placename.

KERHONKSON (N.Y., Ulster Co.) \kər hongk´ sən\. The name has also been written as <Kerhonkton, Kahanksen, Kahanckasink> (etc.), perhaps meaning 'shallow place' (Ruttenber 1906); cf. Unami Delaware (Algonquian) /ka:han/ 'it is shallow' (Blalock et al. 1994).

KERULUK Creek (Alaska, Shungnak B-6). The Iñupiaq (Eskimo) name is probably *qiruiḷaq* 'having no wood' (L. Kaplan p.c.).

KESCAYOGANSETT Pond (Mass., Barnstable Co.). From SNEng. Algonquian, perhaps meaning 'return to fishing place' (Huden 1962).

KESHENA (Wis., Menominee Co.) \kə shē´ nə\. Named after a nineteenth-century Menominee (Algonquian) leader (Vogel 1991). The Native American name is /kesi:ʔnɛh/, from the personal name /kesi:ʔnɛw/, lit. 'flies fast'. The nearby **Keshena Falls** has the Menominee name /kahka:pɛhkatoh/, lit. 'at the waterfall', from /kahka:pɛhkat/ 'it is a sharply cut-off rock' (Bloomfield 1975).

KESHEQUA Creek (N.Y., Livingston Co.) \kesh´ ə kwä\. Said to be from an Iroquoian word written as <gah-she-gweh> 'a spear' (Beauchamp 1907). The spelling **Keshaqua** also occurs.

KESHOTEE Island (Ark., Mississippi Co.) \kə shō´ tē\. Probably refers to a Muskogean people, whose name is more commonly written **Coushatta** or **Koasati**, originally living in Alabama (Dickinson 1995); see above and below.

KESKI Island (Alaska, Craig D-5). Probably from Tlingit *k̲eix̲'é* [qe:x̣'é] 'dawn' (Orth 1967; Davis and Leer 1976).

KESSISO (Wash., Clallam Co.). From the Makah (Nootkan) placename /kisisʔu/ (W. Jacobsen p.c.).

KETA River (Alaska, Ketchikan B-2) The name, perhaps from Tlingit, was reported in 1961 (Orth 1967).

KETCHEPEDRAKEE Creek (Ala., Randolph Co.) \kech ē pə drā´ kē\. The name refers to a Muskogee tribal town, *keco pvtake* /kičo-patá:ki/ 'mortar (for grinding) lying flat', from *keco* /kičó/ 'mortar', *pvtaketv* /pata:kitá/ 'to be lying flat, to be spread out' (Read 1984; Martin and Mauldin 2000).

KETCHIKAN (Alaska, Ketchikan B-5) \kech´i kan\. The Tlingit name, said to mean 'eagle-wing river', was reported as <Kitschk-hin> in 1881 (Orth 1967).

KETCHKETCH Butte (Ore., Deschutes Co.) \kech´ kech\. Said to be from Klamath <ketch-kitchli> 'rough' or <ketchkatch> 'gray fox' (McArthur 1992).

KETIK River (Alaska, Wainwright A-2). The Iñupiaq (Eskimo) name was reported in 1924 (Orth 1967).

KETILI River (Alaska, Bradfield Canal C-6). The Tlingit name, said to mean 'hot spring', was published in 1927 (Orth 1967).

KETLKEDE Mountain (Alaska, Nulato B-2). The Koyukon (Athabaskan) name was reported as <R(kh)etlela> in 1903 (Orth 1967).

KETOK Mountain (Alaska, Dillingham D-4). Abbreviated from Yupik (Eskimo) <Ketokecheegilinguk> 'the mountain we cannot go around' (Orth 1967).

KETTENPOM Valley (Calif., Trinity Co.) \ket´ ən pom\. From Wintu /xetin-pom/ 'camas place', containing /xetin/ 'camas', an edible bulb (Gudde 1998).

KETTLE River (Minn., Pine Co.) \ket´ əl\. Corresponds to the Ojibwa (Algonquian) <Akiko zibi> (Upham 2001); cf. *akik* 'kettle', *ziibi* 'river' (Nichols and Nyholm 1995).

KEUKA (N.Y., Steuben Co.) \ki yo͞o´ kə\. Perhaps an alternative form of **Cayuga,** from the Cayuga (Iroquoian) language, in which the name is *kayohkhó:nǫ* (W. Chafe p.c.) There is also a **Keuka**, apparently as a transfer name, in Fla. (Putnam Co.).

KEVINJIK Creek (Alaska, Black River C-3). The Gwich'in (Athabaskan) name is *kii vee njik* 'gray rock stream' (Caulfield et al. 1983).

KEVUK Creek (Alaska, Wiseman D-6). The Iñupiaq (Eskimo) name, said to mean 'large intestine', was reported in 1956 (Orth 1967).

KEWA (Wash., Ferry Co.) \kē´ wə\. From the Okanagan (Salishan) placename [kíwaʔ] (D. Kinkade p.c.).

KEWADIN (Mich., Antrim Co.) \kə wä´ din\. Named for a nineteenth-century Ottawa (Algonquian) leader (Vogel 1986); the term is probably derived, or abbreviated, from *giiwedin* 'north wind' (Rhodes 1985). Related placenames are **Keewatin** (Minn., Itasca Co.), **Keewayden** (Mich., Baraga Co.), and **Keewaydin** (Maine, Carroll Co.), all probably from Ojibwa (Algonquian) *giiwedin* 'north; the north wind' (Nichols and Nyholm 1995).

KEWAGEK Creek (Alaska, St. Lawrence C-5). The Yupik (Eskimo) name, said to mean 'growing river', was recorded in 1965 (Orth 1967).

KEWAHATCHIE (Ala., Shelby Co.) \kē wô hach´ ē\. Probably from Muskogee; the second part is *hvcce* /hačči/ 'stream' (Read 1984; Martin and Mauldin 2000).

KEWANEE (Ill., Henry Co) \kē wä´ nē\. Perhaps from Ottawa (Algonquian) <ke-won-nee> 'prairie chicken' (Vogel 1963). The term occurs elsewhere, apparently as a transfer name (Ga., Laurens Co.; Miss., Lauderdale Co.). Perhaps related terms are **Kewanna** (Ind., Fulton Co.) and **Kewaunee County** (Wis.).

KEWANNA (Ind., Fulton Co.) \kē wä´ nə, kə wä´ nə\. Named for a Potawatomi (Algonquian) leader called <Ki-wa-na>; the name is said to mean 'prarie chicken' (McPherson 1993). Perhaps related terms are **Kewanee** (Ill., Henry Co.) and **Kewaunee County** (Wis.).

KEWASKUM (Wis., Washington Co.). Named for a nineteenth-century Potawatomi (Algonquian) leader; the term is said to mean 'turning back on his tracks' (Vogel 1991).

KEWAUNEE County (Wis.) \kē wô´ nē\. Probably from a term meaning 'prairie chicken' in some Algonquian language (Vogel 1991). Likely related terms are **Kewanee** (Ill., Henry Co.) and **Kewanna** (Ind., Fulton Co.).

KEWEENAW County (Mich.) \kē´ wə nô\. The Objibwa (Algonquian) name has been translated as 'a bend' or 'a detour' (Vogel 1986).

KEYA PAHA River (S.Dak., Tripp Co.; Neb., Keya Paha Co.) \kē yə pä´ hä, kip´ ə hä\. From Lakhota (Siouan) *khéya pahá,* lit. 'turtle hill' (Sneve 1973; B. Ingham p.c.).

KGUN Lake (Alaska, Marshall C-5) \kə gun´\. From Yupik (Eskimo) *qagan* 'source of river' (Orth 1967; Jacobson 1994).

KHAALI Lake (Alaska, Arctic A-3). The Gwich'in (Athabaskan) name is *khaalii van,* perhaps 'it-is-pulled-out-by-hook lake' (Caulfield 1983).

KHADILOTDEN (Alaska, Iditarod C-5). The Koyukon (Athabaskan) name is of unclear derivation (Orth 1967).

KHANTAAK Island (Alaska, Yakutat C-5). From Tlingit, probably [xAntA'Ax'] 'strawberry point', originally from Eyak (De Laguna 1972: 63).

KHOTOL River (Alaska, Nulato A-4) \hō tōl´\. The Koyukon (Athabaskan) name was recorded in 1903 (Orth 1967). A related placename is **Rodo River** (Alaska, Nulato B-6).

KHOTYLKAKAT (Alaska, Kateel River B-4). From Koyukon (Athabaskan) *kodeel kaakk'et,* with *-kaakk'et* 'mouth of stream' (Jetté and Jones 2000).

KHUCHAYNIK Creek (Alaska, McGrath C-4) \hə chī´ nik\. From Upper Kuskokwim (Athabaskan) *hwtsah nek'* or *hwtsash hnek',* possibly meaning 'first creek' (J. Kari p.c.).

KHULIKAKAT (Alaska, Kateel River B-4). The Koyukon (Athabaskan) placename contains *-kaakk'et* 'mouth of stream' (Jetté and Jones 2000).

KI-A-CUT Falls (Ore., Washington Co.) \kē´ ə kət\. A variant writing of **Ki-a-kuts Falls**; see below.

KIAGNA River (Alaska, McCarthy A-5) \kī ag´ nə\. From Ahtna (Athabaskan) *kayaxi na',* lit. 'village creek' (Kari 1983:10).

KIAHANIE Campground (Ore., Lane Co.). Probably a mistranscription of **Klahanie**, a placename derived from Chinook Jargon (D. Kinkade p.c.).

KI-A-KUTS Falls (Ore., Washington Co.) \kē´ ə kəts\. Named after a nineteenth-century Tualatin (Kalapuyan) leader called [k'áyak'ač] (McArthur 1992, D. Kinkade p.c.). The placename also has the form **Ki-a-cut.**

KIALEGAK Mountains (Alaska, St. Lawrence A-2). The Yupik (Eskimo) name was reported in 1849 (Orth 1967).

KIAMENSI (Del., New Castle Co.) \kī ə men´ sē\. Perhaps from Delaware (Algonquian) <kwiskakimensi> 'young tree' (Heck 1966); cf. Unami Delaware /wə́ski:/ 'new, young' (Blalock et al. 1994).

KIAMICHI River (Okla., Pushmataha Co.; Ark., Polk Co.) \kī ə mē´ chē, kī ə mē´ shē, kī ə mish´ ē\. The name of a Caddo village (I. Goddard, p.c.). Perhaps also related is **Kiomatia** (Tex., Red River Co.); **Kiamesha Lake** (N.Y., Sullivan Co.) \kī ə mē´ shə\ is probably a transfer name.

KIANA (Alaska, Selawik D-3) \kē an´ ə\. The name, perhaps from Iñupiaq (Eskimo), was reported in 1910 (Orth 1967). The current Iñupiaq name for the place, however, is *katyaak* (Webster and Zibell 1970:iv).

KIANGOLEVIK Pass (Alaska, Black B-1). The Yupik (Eskimo) name was recorded in 1899 (Orth 1967).

KIANTONE Creek (N.Y., Chautauqua Co.; Pa., Warren Co.) \kin´ tōn, kī´ ən tōn\. Perhaps Iroquoian, written earlier as <Ke-on-to-na, Ca-yon-to-na> (Beauchamp 1907).

KIAPOT Point (Wash., Clallam Co.). Chinook Jargon <kīapōt, keep´wot, akaepooit> [káyəpot, kípwot] 'needle, pin, thorn', from Lower Chinook <o-kwe´-po-wa> 'needle' (D. Kinkade p.c.). A related form is **Klapot Point**, from a Chinook Jargon form <kla´-pote, kla´-pite> 'thread'; see below.

KIASHITA (N.Mex., Sandoval Co.) \kē äsh´ ə tä\. From Towa (Tanoan) *k'yaashota* 'place where sheep live', containing *k'yaa* 'sheep', *sho* 'to live', and *-ta* 'place'; but *k'yaa* also means 'rock' (Y. Yumitani p.c.).

KIAVAH MOUNTAIN (Calif., Kern Co.) \kī´ ə vä\. Said to have been named in 1906 for an Indian leader; the term may contain Panamint (Numic) /kiya-/ 'to play' plus /pa/ 'water, spring' (Gudde 1998).

KIAVAK Bay (Alaska, Kodiak A-5). The Alutiiq (Eskimo) placename was recorded in 1805 (Orth 1967).

KIAWAH Island (S.C., Charleston Co.) \kē´ ə wä\. Earlier written <Cayagua>, <Cayaque>, <Cayegua> (Waddell 1980). Perhaps from Cusabo, meaning 'palmetto bay' (Pearson 1978; B. Rudes p.c.).

KIAWA Mountain (N.Mex., Rio Arriba Co.) \kī´ ə wə\. Perhaps a variant writing of **Kiowa,** the name of an Indian people; see below.

KIBESILLAH (Calif., Mendocino Co.) \kib ə sil´ ə\. Northern Pomo for 'flat rock', from /khabé/ 'rock' plus /silá/ 'flat' (Gudde 1998).

KICHAI \kē´ chī\. The term refers to an Indian people of the Caddoan language family. Alternative forms in placenames include **Keatchie** (La., De Soto Par.), **Kechi** (Kans., Sedgwick Co.), **Keechi Creek** (Okla., Caddo Co.), and **Keechie** (Tex., Anderson Co.).

KICHATNA River (Alaska, Talkeetna A-4) \kē chät´ nə\. Dena'ina (Athabaskan) *k'its'atnu,* containing *-tnu* 'river' (Kari and Fall 1987:140).

KICHLULIK (Alaska, Russian Mission D-6\. \kich lo͞o´ lik\. The Yupik (Eskimo) word was reported in 1919 (Orth 1967).

KICKAMUIT River (Mass., Bristol Co.; R.I., Bristol Co.). Perhaps from SNEng. Algonquian <kehkomau-> 'he slanders him', <-it> 'place' (W. Cowan p.c.).

KICKAPOO \kik´ ə po͞o\. The name of an Algonquian people that once lived in central Ill.; the Native American name is /kiikaapoa/, sometimes interpreted as 'wanderers' (Vogel 1963; *HNAI* 15:667). Groups of Kickapoo later moved to Kans., Okla., Tex., and northern Mexico. The placename **Kickapoo** occurs in several states (e.g., Ill., Peoria Co.; Kans., Leavenworth Co.; and Okla., Caddo Co.).

KIDAZQENI Glacier (Alaska, Tyonek B-6). The name is said to be from the Dena'ina (Athabaskan) word for the volcanic Mount Spurr, meaning 'the one that is burning inside' (Schorr 1996).

KIDZIIBAHI (Ariz., Apache Co.). Perhaps Navajo (Athabaskan) for 'gray streak mountain' (Linford 2000); cf. *dzíbá* 'to be a gray strip across' (Young and Morgan 1987).

KIGALIK River (Alaska, Ikpikpuk River B-3). The Iñupiaq (Eskimo) name was recorded in 1886 (Orth 1967).

KIGEZRUK Creek (Alaska, Teller C-6). The Iñupiaq (Eskimo) term was recorded in 1900 as <Kivyearzruk, Kivyearuk>, said to be a man's name (Orth 1967).

KIGIGAK Island (Alaska, Baird Inlet D-8). The Yupik (Eskimo) name was recorded in 1949 (Orth 1967).

KIGIKTOWK Creek (Alaska, De Long Mountains D-5). The Iñupiaq (Eskimo) name is probably *kiŋiktuaq* 'high one' (L. Kaplan p.c.).

KIGLAPAK Mountains (Alaska, Goodnews Bay A-8). The Yupik (Eskimo) name, said to mean 'big sawtooth mountains", was recorded around 1951 (Orth 1967); cf. *kegglaq* 'a saw' (Jacobson 1984).

KIGLUAIK Mountains (Alaska, Nome D-1). The Iñupiaq (Eskimo) name was reported in 1927 (Orth 1967).

KIGOUMIUT (Alaska, Nunivak Is. A-6) \kig´ ō myo͞ot\. The Yupik (Eskimo) name was reported in 1932 (Orth 1967); the ending *-miut* means 'people'.

KIGRAGRAK (Alaska, De Long Mountains A-4). The Iñupiaq (Eskimo) name is probably *kigragraq* 'old path through willows' (L. Kaplan p.c.).

KIGTSUGTAG Mountain (Alaska, Goodnews Bay A-8). The Yupik (Eskimo) name was reported in 1956 (Orth 1967).

KIGUGA, Cape (Alaska, Adak C-3). The Aleut placename was reported in 1852 (Orth 1967).

KIGUL Island (Alaska, Umnak A-2). From the Aleut placename *kiigalux̂* (Bergsland 1994).

KIGUN, Cape (Alaska, Atka C-4). From the Aleut placename *kiiĝun,* related to *kiiĝusix̂* 'mountain' (Bergsland 1994).

KIGUNAK, Cape (Alaska, Umnak B-2). From the Aleut placename *qigunax̂* (Bergsland 1994).

KIGUSHIMKADA, Cape (Alaska, Umnak A-3). From Aleut *kiiĝusim-kadaa* 'point of the mountain', with *kiiĝuusix̂* 'mountain' and *kadax̂* 'point' (Bergsland 1994).

KIINGYAK Lake (Alaska, Howard Pass A-2). From Iñupiaq (Eskimo) *kiiñaq* 'face' (Orth 1967; MacLean 1980).

KIIQO (Ariz., Navajo Co.). Hopi *kiiqö* 'a ruin', from *kii(-hu)* 'house' and *qö(hi)* 'to break' (K. Hill p.c.).

KIJIK (Alaska, Lake Clark B-4) \kē´ jik\. The Dena'ina (Athabaskan) name is *qizhjeh,* perhaps 'they came on the run' (J. Kari p.c.).

KIKAHE River (Alaska, Bradfield Canal C-6). The Tlingit name was reported in 1955 (Orth 1967).

KIKAK Creek (Alaska, Umiat C-3). The Iñupiaq (Eskimo) name was reported in 1956 (Orth 1967).

KIKAKPAK Bluff (Alaska, Killik River D-1). The Iñupiaq (Eskimo) name was recorded in 1949 (Orth 1967).

KIKALRODIK Hill (Alaska, Nunivak Island A-5). The Yupik (Eskimo) name was reported in 1949 (Orth 1967).

KIKARTAMJINGIA Point (Alaska, Nunivak Island B-3). The Yupik (Eskimo) name is probably *qikertam cingia* 'point of island' (L. Kaplan p.c.).

KIKARTIK Rock (Alaska, Nunivak Island A-5). From Yupik (Eskimo) *qikertaq* 'island ' (Orth 1967; Jacobson 1984); cf. **Kikegtek Island** below.

KIKDOOLI Butte (Alaska, Nunivak Is.). The Yupik (Eskimo) name was recorded in 1949 (Orth 1967).

KIKEGTEK Island (Alaska, Kuskokwim Bay D-7). Perhaps from Yupik (Eskimo) *qikertaq* [qikəʀtaq] 'island ' (Orth 1967; Jacobson 1984). A possibly related placename is **Kikertalik Lake** (Alaska, Nushagak Bay C-4), from *qikertalek* 'one that has an island' (L. Kaplan p.c.).

KIKET Island (Wash., Skagit Co.). From an Indian placename, language not identified (Hitchman 1985).

KIKIAKRORAK River (Alaska, Umiat D-3). The Iñupiaq (Eskimo) name was reported in 1947 (Orth 1967).

KIKIKTAK Island (Alaska, Teshekpuk D-5). From Iñupiaq (Eskimo) *qikiqtaq* 'island' (Orth 1967; MacLean 1980). A related form is **Kekiktuk River** (Alaska, Mount Michelson C-2). Possibly related Alaska forms include: **Kikiktalik Rock** (Nunivak Is. B-5); **Kikiktat Mountain** (Mount Michelson B-2), from Iñupiaq *qikiqtat* 'islands'; **Kikikyak Hill** (Nunivak Is. A-5), from Yupik (Eskimo), meaning 'island-like' (Orth 1967), with *qikertaq* 'island' and *-yak* 'similar' (Jacobson 1984); **Kikitaliorak Lake** (Howard Pass A-1), from Iñupiaq, meaning 'has an island' (Orth 1967); and **Kodiak Island** (Kodiak D-2, see below).

KIKKU Creek (Alaska, Goodnews Bay C-8). The Yupik (Eskimo) name may be *qiku* 'clay' (L. Kaplan p.c.).

KIKLUKH River (Alaska, Bering Glacier A-8). The Tlingit or Eyak name was reported in 1904 (Orth 1967).

KIKLUPIKLAK Hills (Alaska, Point Lay B-1). The Iñupiaq (Eskimo) name was published in 1955 (Orth 1967).

KIKMIKSOT Mountain (Alaska, Noatak D-3). From Iñupiaq (Eskimo) *kimmiksut,* said to mean 'resembling heels' (Orth 1967; Burch 1998); cf. *kikmik, kimmik* 'heel' (Webster and Zibell 1970). Related placenames include **Kiknik Creek**, from Yupik (Alaska, Taylor Mtns. D-5).

KIKMIKTALIKAMIUT (Alaska, Nunivak Is. B-3). The Yupik (Eskimo) name was reported in 1949 (Orth 1967); the ending *-miut* means 'people'.

KIKNEAK River (Alaska, Hooper Bay D-1). The Yupik (Eskimo) name was reported in 1952 (Orth 1967).

KIKNIK Creek (Alaska, Taylor Mtns. D-5) \kik´ nik\. From Yupik (Eskimo) *kitngik* 'heel' (Orth 1967; Jacobson 1984). Related placenames include **Kikmiksot Mountain**, from Iñupiaq (Alaska, Noatak D-3).

KIKOLIK Creek (Alaska, Meade River D-3). From Iñupiaq (Eskimo) *kikkuliq* 'seal hole in ice' (Orth 1967; Fortescue et al. 1994). The nearby placename **Kikoligarak** is derived from the same base.

KIKOOJIT Rocks (Alaska, Nunivak Is. B-5). The Yupik (Eskimo) name was reported in 1949 (Orth 1967).

KIKPYAT Creek (Alaska, Killik River B-1). The Iñupiaq (Eskimo) name was reported in 1956 (Orth 1967).

KIKTAK Island (Alaska, Bethel D-7) \kik´ tak\. The Yupik (Eskimo) name was reported in 1879 as <Kikkhtagamute> 'island people' (Orth 1967); cf. *qikertaq* 'island', *-miut* 'people' (Jacobson 1984). Related Alaska placenames include **Kikiktak Island** (Teshekpuk D-5; see above), as well as **Kikuktok Mountain** (Hooper Bay C-3), and **Kodiak Island** (Kodiak D-2; see below).

KIKTOYA Creek (Alaska, Point Hope A-1). The Iñupiaq (Eskimo) name was reported in 1952 (Orth 1967).

KIKUKTOK Mountain (Alaska, Hooper Bay C-3) \ki kuk´ tok\. The Yupik (Eskimo) name, reported in 1951, is from *qikertaq* [qikəʀtaq] 'island' (Orth 1967; Jacobson 1984). Related placenames include **Kikiktak Island** (Teshekpuk D-5) and **Kiktak Island** (Bethel D-7), as well as **Kodiak Island** (Kodiak D-2); see above and below.

KI Lake (Wash., Snohomish Co.) \kī\. The original Indian name, in an unidentified language, is said to have been <Kah> (Hitchman 1985).

KILANGNAK Bluff (Alaska, Noatak A-3). The Iñupiaq (Eskimo) name was reported in 1966 (Orth 1967).

KILBUCK Run (Pa., Allegheny Co.) \kil´ buk\. The name is related to **Killbuck** (Pa., Cambria Co.) the nickname of an eighteenth-century Delaware (Algonquian) leader. There is also a **Kilbuck Creek** in Ill. (Winnebago Co.). The **Kilbuck Mountains** (Alaska, Bethel C-3) were named in 1898 for the Reverend John Kilbuck, a Moravian missionary in the area (Orth 1967).

KILCHIS River (Ore., Tillamook Co.) \kil´chis\. Named for a Tillamook (Salishan) Indian leader (McArthur 1992); his Native American name was [gə́lšəs, gə́lčəs] (D. Kinkade p.c.).

KILICH Point (Alaska, Wainwright B-2). The Iñupiaq (Eskimo) name was published in 1958 (Orth 1967).

KILIGMAK Creek (Alaska, Noatak B-4) \kil´i mak\. The Iñupiaq (Eskimo) name is *qiliġmiam kuuŋa* (Burch 1998).

KILIGUAK Creek (Alaska, Point Hope A-2). From Iñupiaq (Eskimo) *qiḷḷuq* 'carcass' (Orth 1967; Fortescue et al. 1994); cf. **Kili Hill** (Noatak D-5).

KILI Hill (Alaska, Noatak D-5). Perhaps from Iñupiaq (Eskimo) *qiḷḷi-* 'to find a carcass', reported in 1950 (Orth 1967; Fortescue et al. 1994).

KILIKMAK Creek (Alaska, Noatak B-4). From Iñupiaq (Eskimo) *qiliġmiaq,* named after a person (Burch 1998).

KILIKRALIK Point (Alaska, Point Hope C-3). Probably from Iñupiaq (Eskimo) *iqirġaq* 'corner' (Orth 1967; MacLean 1980).

KILIKTAGIK Island (Alaska, Sutwik Is. A-3). The Alutiiq (Eskimo) name was recorded in 1874 as <Keelikhtagikh> (Orth 1967).

KILIKTAKGOT Creek (Alaska, Point Hope C-2). The Iñupiaq (Eskimo) name, said to mean 'jointed', was reported in 1950 (Orth 1967).

KILIOVILIK Creek (Alaska, Shungnak B-4). The Iñupiaq (Eskimo) name was recorded in 1927 (Orth 1967).

KILISUT Harbor (Wash., Jefferson Co.). From Chinook Jargon <kīlitsūt, kil-it ´-sut> [kɪlítsət] 'bottle, glass, flint'; cf. Kathlamet Chinook [ik'ilẋcutk] (D. Kinkade p.c.).

KILIUDA Bay (Alaska, Kodiak B-3). The name was recorded as <Kiluden> in 1805. Although in Alutiiq (Eskimo) territory, it may be from Aleut *qilax̂* 'morning' plus *udax̂* 'bay' (Bergsland 1994).

KILLAK River (Alaska, Shungnak D-1). The Iñupiaq (Eskimo) name was reported in 1956 (Orth 1967).

KILLAMACUE Creek (Ore., Baker Co.) \kil´ ə mə kyōō\. Perhaps an Indian name, but from an unidentified language (McArthur 1992).

KILLBUCK Run (Pa., Cambria Co.) \kil´ buk\. Named for an eighteenth-century Delaware (Algonquian) leader, nicknamed Killbuck by white people; his Native American name was <Gelelemend> (Donehoo 1928). Places in a number of states are named for him or members of his family (e.g., Ill., Ogle Co.; Ind., Delaware Co.; and N.Y., Cattaraugus Co.) An alternative spelling is **Kilbuck Run** (Pa., Allegheny Co.).

KILLEAK Lakes (Alaska, Kotzebue B-5). From Iñupiaq (Eskimo) *kialiik* (Burch 1998).

KILLESTOK Creek (Alaska, Teller B-4). The Iñupiaq (Eskimo) word is said to mean 'fossil-shell creek' (Orth 1967).

KILLI Creek (Alaska, Meade River D-4). The Iñupiaq (Eskimo) name is *killi* (Burch 1998).

KILLIK River (Alaska, Ikpikpuk River A-2) \kil´ ik\. The Iñupiaq (Eskimo) name is *killium kuuŋa* (Burch 1998).

KILLINUPAK Mountain (Alaska, Nunivak Is. C-1). The Yupik (Eskimo) name was reported in 1951 (Orth 1967).

KILLISNOO (Alaska, Sitka B-2). The Tlingit name was earlier written as <Khutz-n'hu>, said to mean 'bear fort' (Orth 1967); cf. Tlingit *xoots* [xu:ts] 'grizzly bear' (Davis and Leer 1976). The term also appears in the nearby placename **Kenasnow Rocks**.

KILLOQUAH (N.Y., Hamilton Co.). Perhaps from the Mohawk (Iroquoian) word for 'the sun' (Beauchamp 1907); cf. *karáhkwa* 'sun' (Michelson 1973).

KILLSNAKE River (Wis., Calumet Co.). Named for John Killsnake, a Munsee Delaware (Algonquian) leader (Vogel 1991).

KILMANTAVI (Alaska, Wainwright B-3). The Iñupiaq (Eskimo) name was first recorded in 1844 as <Kylyamigtagvik>, apparently with the ending *-vik* 'place'. In 1890 it was said to refer to 'a throwing weapon like a sling or bola' (Orth 1967); cf. *qiḷamitautit* 'bola' (Webster and Zibell 1970). Another modern writing for the placename is **Kilimantavi.**

KILOKAK Rocks (Alaska, Ugashik A-2). The Alutiiq (Eskimo) name was reported in 1827 (Orth 1967).

KILOKNAK Lagoon (Alaska, St. Lawrence B-0). The Yupik (Eskimo) name, said to mean 'mainland lake', was reported in 1965 (Orth 1967).

KILOKUYAK Creek (Alaska, Goodnews Bay C-6). The Yupik (Eskimo) name was published in 1951 (Orth 1967).

KIL-SO-QUAH (Ind., Huntington Co.). Named for an Indian woman, language not identified, born in Indiana in 1810 (Dunn 1919).

KILULIKPUK Creek (Alaska, Candle D-4). The Iñupiaq (Eskimo) name was reported in 1949 (Orth 1967).

KILUSIKTOK Lake (Alaska, Meade River D-2). The Iñupiaq (Eskimo) name was reported in 1956 (Orth 1967).

KILYAKTALIK Peaks (Alaska, Baird Mountains D-6). The Iñupiaq (Eskimo) name was recorded in 1955 (Orth 1967).

KIMAMA (Idaho, Lincoln Co.) \ki mam´ ə\. The name was given in the late nineteenth century by railroad officials; it was thought to mean 'butterfly' in an unidentified Indian language (Boone 1988).

KIMBETO (N.Mex., San Juan Co.) \kim bē´ tō\. From Navajo (Athabaskan) *giní bit'ohí* 'hawk's nest', containing *giní* 'hawk', *bit'oh* 'its nest' (*bi-* 'its', *t'oh* 'nest') (Wilson 1995). Also written as **Kinbito.**

KIMIJOOKSUK Butte (Alaska, Nunivak Is. A-4). The Yupik (Eskimo) name, reported in 1949, was said to mean 'two hills with the same base' (Orth 1967); cf. *qemiq* 'hill' (Jacobson 1984).

KIMIKPAURAUK River (Alaska, Demarcation Point D-3). The Iñupiaq (Eskimo) name is perhaps *qimiqpauraq* 'big hill' (L. Kaplan p.c.).

KIMIKSTHEK Hill (Alaska, Nunivak Is. A-6). The Yupik (Eskimo) name was recorded in 1949 (Orth 1967). Probably related is **Kimikthak Hills** (Nunivak Is. B-4). Cf. Yupik *qemiq* 'hill' (Jacobson 1984).

KIMIROK Hill (Alaska, Noatak A-3). From Iñupiaq (Eskimo) *qimiġaq* 'hill' (Orth 1967; MacLean 1980).

KIMIT Hills (Alaska, Nunivak Is. A-4). The Yupik (Eskimo) name is *qemit* 'hills' (L. Kaplan p.c.).

KIMIXTHORUK Hill (Alaska, Nunivak Is. A-6). The Yupik (Eskimo) name was reported in 1949 (Orth 1967).

KIM-ME-NI-OLI Ruins (N.Mex., McKinley Co.) \kim ə nī ō´ lē\. Navajo (Athabaskan) *kin bii' naayolí* 'house in which the wind blows around', from *kin* 'house, building', *bii'* 'in it', *naayolí* 'the wind blows about' (Wilson 1995). Also written as **Kin Bineola**.

KIMOUKSIK (Alaska, Barrow A-4). Said to be named for an Iñupiaq (Eskimo) resident; recorded in 1956 (Orth 1967).

KIMSHEW Creek (Calif., Butte Co.) \kim´ shōō\. Konkow (Northwestern Maidu) /kiwim sewi/ 'the stream on the other side', from /kiw/ 'behind, on the other side' and /sew/ 'stream'. A related placename is the nearby **Nimshew**.

KIMTA Creek (Wash., Jefferson Co.) \kim´ tä\. The name was given by the U.S. Forest Service, based on Chinook Jargon <kim´-tah> 'behind, after, last', in contrast to **Elip Creek,** meaning 'before, first' (Parratt 1984). The name of **Kimta Creek** in Idaho (Benewah Co.) was given under similar circumstances (Boone 1988).

KINA Creek (Alaska, Craig B-2). The name, perhaps from Tlingit, was reported in 1897 (Orth 1967).

KINAK Bay (Alaska, Mount Katmai A-2) \kē´ nak\. From Alutiiq (Eskimo) *giinaq* 'face' (Orth 1967; Leer 1978). There is also a place called **Kinak** in Central Yupik territory (Baird Inlet B-2).

KINAKHULANTAN Lake (Alaska, Ruby D-4). The Koyukon (Athabaskan) name is of unclear origin (Orth 1967).

KINANI Point (Alaska, Craig D-4). The name, probably Tlingit, was published in 1964 (Orth 1967).

KINARUK Lake (Alaska, Baird Inlet C-7). The Yupik (Eskimo) name was reported in 1949 as meaning 'something to look through' (Orth 1967).

KINCHAFOONEE Creek (Ga., Dougherty Co.) \kin chə fōō´ nē\. Perhaps from a Muskogee word meaning 'pestle' (Goff 1975:121); cf. *keco* /kičó/ 'mortar, grinding bowl', *fone* /fóni/ 'bone' (Martin and Mauldin 2000).

KINDANINA Lake (Alaska, Kantishna River D-1). From Koyukon (Athabaskan) *kendo' no'*, lit. 'canoe-seat stream', with *no'* 'stream'; the lake is called *kendo' bene'* 'canoe-seat lake' (Kari 1999:112).

KINEEGHIT Point (Alaska, St. Lawrence D-4). The name was recorded in 1932 as <Kinnit> and in 1965 as <Kannit>, said to mean 'near' (Orth 1967); cf. *ukani* 'near' (Jacobson 1984).

KINEGNAK (Alaska, Hagemeister Is. D-5) \kin´ig nak\. The Yupik (Eskimo) name was reported in 1890 (Orth 1967).

KINEO, Mount (Maine, Piscataquis Co.) \kin´ ē ō\. From an Abenaki (Algonquian) term, said to mean 'sharp peak' (Rutherford 1970); cf. *ginô-* 'steep' (Day 1994–95). The pacename occurs elsewhere: N.H. (Grafton Co.), Colo. (El Paso Co.).

KINGAGLIA Lake (Alaska, Marshall C-5). The Yupik (Eskimo) name was reported in 1965 as meaning 'the last one' (Orth 1967).

KINGAK Mountain (Alaska, Howard Pass C-1). From Iñupiaq (Eskimo) *qiŋaq* 'nose' (Orth 1967, MacLean 1980).

KINGAKTAKAMIUT (Alaska, Cape Mendenhall D-4). The Yupik (Eskimo) name was reported in 1942 (Orth 1967).

KINGASIVIK Mountains (Alaska, Misheguk Mt. A-2). The Iñupiaq (Eskimo) name, recorded in 1956, is said to mean 'the high place' (Orth 1967); cf. *kiŋik-* 'to be high' (Fortescue et al. 1994). A probably related name is the nearby **Kingaviksak Mountain** (Alaska, Misheguk Mt. B-4).

KINGMETOLIK Creek (Alaska, Norton Bay C-3). The Iñupiaq (Eskimo) name was reported about 1954 (Orth 1967).

KINGOKAKTHLUK Lake (Alaska, Hooper Bay C-1). The Yupik (Eskimo) name was reported in 1951 (Orth 1967).

KING PHILLIP Mountain (Conn., Hartford Co.). Named for a seventeenth-century SNEng. Algonquian leader; his Native American name was rendered as <Metacom>, <Metacomet>, or <Pometacom> (Huden 1962).

KINGSESSING (Pa., Philadelphia Co.). This name of a Delaware (Algonquian) village was first recorded as <Kingeesingh> in 1656 (Donehoo 1928).

KIN HOCHO'I (N.Mex., McKinley Co.) \kin hōch´ kē\. Navajo (Athabaskan) *kin hoóchxǫ́ǫ́'í* 'ugly house' (Linford 2000).

KINIA River (Alaska, Baird Inlet A-7). This is said to be a misapplication of a Yupik (Eskimo) placename <Kinak>, properly applied to another stream in the area (Orth 1967).

KINIKINIK (Colo., Larimer Co.) \kin´i ki nik\. A variant spelling of **Kinnickinick**; see below.

KINIKLIK (Alaska, Seward D-2) \ki nik´ lik\. From an Alutiiq (Eskimo) village name (Orth 1967).

KIN Indian Ruin (N.Mex., San Juan Co.). Coined from Navajo (Athabaskan) *kin* 'house', generally used to refer to Pueblo houses as opposed to Navajo hogans (Linford 2000). The same word *kin* forms part of many Navajo placenames, as listed below.

KINIPAGHULGHAT Mountains (Alaska, St. Lawrence B-0). The Yupik (Eskimo) name was reported in 1932 (Orth 1967).

KIN KLETSO (N.Mex., San Juan Co.) \kin klet´ sō\. Navajo (Athabaskan) *kin łitsooí* 'yellow house(s)', with *łitso(o)* 'yellow' (Wilson 1995).

KIN KLIZHIN (N.Mex., San Juan Co.) \kin kli zhin´, kin klich´ in\. Navajo (Athabaskan) *kin łizhiní* 'black house(s)', with *łizhin* 'black' (Wilson 1995).

KINLICHEE (Ariz., Apache Co.) \kin´ li chē, kin lē´ chē\. Navajo (Athabaskan) *kin dah łichí'í* 'red house(s) up at an elevation', with *dah* 'up (at an elevation)' and *łichí'í* 'red' (Wilson 1995).

KIN NAA DAA (N.Mex., Rio Arriba Co.) \kin nä dä\. Possibly Navajo (Athabaskan) *kin naadą́ą́'* 'corn house', with *naadą́ą́'* 'corn', lit. 'enemy food' (A. Wilson p.c.).

KIN NAHASBASD (N.Mex., San Juan Co.). Navajo (Athabaskan) *kin názbąs* 'circular house', with *názbąs* 'circle, it is circular' (A. Wilson p.c.).

KIN NAHZIN (N.Mex., McKinley Co.) \kin nä´ zin\. Navajo (Athbaskan) *kin náázíní* 'house standing erect', with *náázį́* 'it stands erect' (A. Wilson p.c.).

KINNICKINNICK \kin i ki nik´, kin´ i ki nik\. The term refers to a mixture of plant substances, sometimes including tobacco, which was formerly used as a smoking mixture by Indians and frontiersmen. It is derived from Unami Delaware (Algonquian) /kələk:əní:k:an/ 'admixture' (*RHD* 1987). The terms occurs in various adapatations, used as placenames in several states: **Kinnickinnic** (Mich., Gogebic Co.; Wis., Pierce Co.); **Kinnickinnick** (Ill., Boone Co.; Mont., Lewis and Clark Co.); **Kinniconick** (Ky., Lewis Co.); **Kinnikinic** (Idaho, Custer Co.); **Kinnikinnic** (Ore., Deschutes Co.); **Kinnikinnick** (Idaho, Idaho Co.; Ohio, Ross Co.); **Kinikinik** (Colo., Larimer Co.), and **Pinnickinnick Mountain** (W.Va., Harrison Co.).

KINNICUM Pond (N.H., Rockingham Co.) \kin´ i kəm\. Perhaps from Abenaki (Algonquian) *ginigômo-* 'to be very fat' (Day 1994–95).

KIN NIZHONI Ruin (N.Mex., McKinley Co.) \kin ni zhō´ nē\. Navajo (Athabaskan) *kin nizhóní* 'beautiful house' (Linford 2000), with *nizhóní* 'it is beautiful' (Young and Morgan 1987).

KINNORUTIN Pass (Alaska, Wiseman D-1). Said to be derived from an Iñupiaq (Eskimo) expression meaning 'you are crazy' (Orth 1967); cf. *qinnak-* 'to be angry' (MacLean 1980).

KINOGAMI Lake (Minn., Cook Co.). Ojibwa (Algonquian) *ginoo-gami,* lit. 'long lake' (J. Nichols p.c.). A probably related form is **Kenogama Lake** (Minn., Itasca Co.).

KINSACKS Creek (Ala., Pickens Co.) \kin´ saks\. From Choctaw (Muskogean) *kǫshak* 'cane, reed' (Read 1984; P. Munro p.c.).

KINSHUDA Hill (Alaska, Nabesna D-3) \kēn shōō´ də\. The Upper Tanana (Athabaskan) name is *k'i̯i̯shüh ddhäl'* perhaps 'birch ridge mountain' (J. Kari p.c.).

KINTA (Okla., Haskell Co.) \kin´ tə\. From Choctaw (Muskogean) *ki̯tah* 'beaver' (Shirk 1974; P. Munro p.c.).

KINTANGA Bay (Alaska, St. Lawrence C-2). The Yupik (Eskimo) name was reported in 1949 (Orth 1967).

KINTAYAKNI (Ala., Shelby Co.) \kin tə yäk´ nē\. From Choctaw (Muskogean), meaning 'beaver country'; cf. *ki̯tah* 'beaver', *yaakni* 'land' (P. Munro p.c.).

KIN TEEL (N.Mex., McKinley Co.) \kin tēl\. Navajo (Athabaskan) *kinteel* 'wide house' (Linford 2000), with *-teel* 'wide' (Young and Morgan 1987). A related name is **Wide Ruins** (Ariz., Apache Co.).

KINTERBISH (Ala., Sumter Co.) \kin´ tə bish\. From Choctaw (Muskogean), meaning 'beaver mound'; cf. *ki̯tah* 'beaver', *ibish* 'mound' (Read 1984; P. Munro p.c.).

KINTLA Creek (Mont., Flathead Co.) \kin´ tlə\. From a Kutenai word meaning 'sack' (Holterman 1985).

KINUK Island (Alaska, Noatak A-1). From Iñupiaq (Eskimo) *qinnak-* 'to be angry' (Orth 1967; MacLean 1980).

KINWAMAKWAD Lake (Mich., Gogebic Co.). Perhaps from Ojibwa (Algonquian) *ginwaakwad* 'to be long (speaking of wood)' (Vogel 1986; Nichols and Nyholm 1995).

KIN YA-AH (N.Mex., McKinley Co.) \kin yä´ ä\. Navajo (Athabaskan) *kin yaa'á* 'house that sticks up', with *yaa'á* 'it sticks up' (Wilson 1995).

KINZUA (Pa., Warren Co.) \kin´ zōō ə, kin zōō\. From Seneca (Iroquoian) *tgę̨dzó:a'* 'fish on the end of a pole' (W. Chafe p.c.). The term also occurs as a transfer placename in Ore. (Wheeler Co.).

KIOKEE (Ga., Columbia Co.). Earlier written as <Okiokee> (Krakow 1975); perhaps from Hitchiti (Muskogean), containing <oki> 'water' (Read 1949–50:130).

KIOKLUK Mountains (Alaska, Sleetmute A-6). The Yupik (Eskimo) term is said to mean 'rocky mountains' (Orth 1967).

KIOLIK Hill (Alaska, Nunivak Is. B-4). The Yupik (Eskimo) name is said to mean 'rocky top' (Orth 1967); cf. *qai-* 'top' (Jacobson 1984).

KIOMATIA (Tex., Red River Co.) \kī ə mē´ shē, kē ō mä´ shē ə\. Perhaps related to **Kiamichi** (Okla., Pushmataha Co.); see above.

KIONA (Wash., Benton Co.) \kē´ ō nə\. From Sahaptin /káyuna/, a personal name (D. Kinkade p.c.). There is another **Kiona** in Lewis Co., said to have been named for an Indian called "Columbia Kionee" (Hitchman 1985); it is not clear whether these names have a single source.

KIOWA \kī´ ō wä, kī´ ō wə\. The term refers to an Indian people of the southern Plains, of the Kiowa-Tanoan language family. Their name appears in early records as Spanish *Caigua,* English <Kae-gua> (etc.). As a placename, it occurs in several states (Kans., Barber Co.; Okla., Pittsburg Co.; Alaska, Anchorage B-8).

KIPMIK Lake (Alaska, Ambler River D-1) \kip´ mik\. From Iñupiaq (Eskimo) *kimmik, kipmik* 'heel' (Orth 1967; Fortescue et al. 1994).

KIPNIARAK River (Alaska, Marshall D-7). The Yupik (Eskimo) name was reported in 1951 (Orth 1967).

KIPNUK (Alaska, Kuskokwim Bay D-6) \kip´ nuk\. From an Yupik (Eskimo) placename *qipneq,* from *qipe-* 'to twist' (Jacobson 1984).

KIPNUKTULI Creek (Alaska, Goodnews Bay C-2). The Yupik (Eskimo) name was published in 1951 (Orth 1967).

KIPTOPEKE (Va., Northampton Co.). Named for a seventheenth-century leader of the Va. Algonquian leaders (Hagemann 1988).

KIPUNGOLAK River (Alaska, Marshall D-7). The Yupik (Eskimo) name was reported in 1951 (Orth 1967).

KIRK (Ore., Klamath Co.). Named for the family of Jesse Kirk, a Klamath Indian and Methodist minister (McArthur 1992).

KIRUKTAGIAK River (Alaska, Chandler Lake C-4). The Iñupiaq (Eskimo) name was reported in 1944 (Orth 1967).

KISARALIK River (Alaska, Bethel D-6). The Yupik (Eskimo) name was reported in 1914 as <Kiselalik> (Orth 1967).

KISATCHIE (La., Natchitoches Par.) \ki sach´ē\. Perhaps from Choctaw (Muskogean), meaning 'little reed', from *kǫshak* 'reed, cane' plus *oshi* 'child, little' (Read 1927; P. Munro p.c.).

KISAYMARUKTUK Mountain (Alaska, Noatak D-6). The Iñupiaq (Eskimo) name was reported in 1960 (Orth 1967).

KISCO (N.Y., Westchester Co.) \kis´ kō\. Perhaps from a Munsee Delaware (Algonquian) placename <Kishkituck-ock> 'land on the edge of a creek', containing <kishke> 'by the side' (Beauchamp 1907).

KISHACOQUILLAS (Pa., Mifflin Co.) \kish ə kə kwil´ əs\. Named for an eighteenth-century Shawnee (Algonquian) leader. The term, also written as <Kissikahquelas>, has been said to be derived from <Gisch-achgook-walieu, Gischichgakwalis> 'the snakes are already in their dens' (Donehoo 1928).

KISHENEHN Creek (Mont., Flathead Co.). The stream rises in Canada, where it is written **Kishinena.** The word is from Kutenai, but is of unclear derivation.

KISHWALKS (Ore., Wasco Co.) \kish´ wôks\. Probably the surname of a Wasco (Chinookan) family on the Warm Springs Reservation (D. Kinkade p.c.).

KISHWAUKEE (Ill., Winnebago Co.) \kish wô´ kē\. Probably from a Meskwaki (Algonquian) word for 'sycamore tree' (Vogel 1963); cf. /ki:šowa:hkowiwa/ 'he is a sycamore' (Goddard 1994). A related placename is **Sycamore** (Ill., DeKalb Co.).

KISIMIGIUKTUK Hill (Alaska, Noatak D-5). The Iñupiaq (Eskimo) name is *kisimġiuqtuq* 'stands alone' (L. Kaplan p.c.).

KISIMILAT Creek (Alaska, Noatak D-5). The Iñupiaq (Eskimo) name was reported in 1966 (Orth 1967); it may be related to **Kisimilok Creek.**

KISIMILOK Creek (Alaska, Point Hope A-1). This Iñupiaq (Eskimo) name, reported in 1950, has been said to be derived from <kisimulowk>

'poke (bag)', but also from a term meaning 'stands alone' (Orth 1967); cf. *kisi-* 'only' (Fortescue et al. 1994).

KISKADINNA Lake (Minn., Cook Co.) \kis kə dē´ nə\. From Ojibwa (Algonquian) *giishkadinaa* 'to be a steep bank' (Upham 2001; Nichols and Nyholm 1995).

KISKA Island (Alaska, Kiska C-2) \kis´ kə\. This represents an Aleut placename *qisxa, qixsa,* perhaps from *qit-, qisix* 'to contract, be cramped' (Bergsland 1994).

KISKATOM (N.Y., Greene Co.) \kis´ kə tom\. Abbreviated from earlier <Kiskatammeeche, Kiskatamenakoak>, perhaps Munsee Delaware (Algonquian) forms, meaning 'place of shagbark hickory nuts' (Ruttenber 1906); cf. Munsee *kéhtaam* 'hazelnut' (O'Meara 1996).

KISKIACK (Va., York Co.) \kis´ kē ak\. A variant spelling of **Chiskiak,** a term designating a group of Va. Algonquian Indians. It has also been written <Chischiack, Kiskyacke> (Hagemann 1988).

KISKIMERE (Pa., Armstrong Co.) \kis´ ki mēr\. The form is related to **Kiskiminetas River** (Pa., Westmoreland Co.); see below.

KISKIMINETAS River (Pa., Westmoreland Co.) \kis ki mi nē´ təs\. The Delaware (Algonquian) name was recorded in 1756 as <Kee-ah-kshee-man-nit-toos>. A suggested meaning is 'plenty of walnuts' (Beauchamp 1907); cf. Munsee Delaware *kéhtaam* 'hazelnut' (O'Meara 1996). Related placenames include **Kiskimere** and **Kiskiminitas River** (both Pa., Armstrong Co.).

KISLOWRUT Hills (Alaska, Noatak A-3). The Iñupiaq (Eskimo) name, recorded in 1950, is said to mean 'without cover, bare of trees' (Orth 1967).

KISMALIUK Bay (Alaska, Unalaska A-4). The Aleut name was reported by Russian explorers in 1826 (Orth 1967).

KISSACOOK Hill (Mass., Middlesex Co.) \kis´ ə ko͞ok\. From SNEng. Algonquian <kussohkoi> 'summit, point of rock' (W. Cowan p.c.).

KISSAWAUG Swamp (Conn., New Haven Co.) \kis´ ə wôg\. Perhaps SNEng. Algonquian, 'place of big stones', containing <qussuk> 'stone' (W. Cowan p.c.).

KISSELEN Bay (Alaska, Unalaska B-2). From the Aleut placename *kisalax̂* (Bergsland 1994).

KISSENA Lake (N.Y., Queens Co.) \kis´ ə nä\. The term was apparently borrowed from Ojibwa (Algonquian) of the Great Lakes region, with the meaning 'it is cold' (Grumet 1981); cf. *gisinaa* 'it is cold (weather)' (Nichols and Nyholm 1995).

KISSIMMEE (Fla., Osceola Co.) \ki sim´ ē\. Perhaps from Seminole (Muskogean), containing *kē* /kí:/ 'mulberry' (Read 1934; Martin and Mauldin 2000). The word occurs as a transfer name in Pa. (Snyder Co.).

KITALITNA Creek (Alaska, Melozitna D-4). The Koyukon (Athabaskan) ws reported in 1956 (Orth 1967).

KITCHAWAN (N.Y., Westchester Co.) \kich´ ə wän\. The name has also been written as <Kith-a-wan, Kicktawank, Kitchawanc, Kitchiwan> (etc.); it may be from Munsee Delaware (Algonquian) and has been defined as meaning 'rapid stream' (Ruttenber 1906; Beauchamp 1907).

KITCHI Creek (Minn., Beltrami Co.) \kich´ ē\. Perhaps contracted from a name beginning with Ojibwa (Algonquian) *gichi-* 'big' (Upham 2001; Nichols and Nyholm 1995). **Kitchi Gammi Park** (Minn., St. Louis Co.) is from Ojibwa (Algonquian) *gichigamii* 'big lake', referring to Lake Superior or the other Great Lakes (Nichols and Nyholm 1995). This corresponds to the <Gitche Gumee> 'big sea-water' of Longfellow's *Hiawatha.* Related names include **Lake Gitchegumee** (Mich., Wexford Co.) and **Gitchie Manitou** (Iowa, Lyon Co.).

KITEMAUG (Conn., New London Co.) \kit´ ə môg\. Represents SNEng. Algonquian <kehteamaug> 'great fishing place', from <kehte-> 'great' plus <-amaug>, a combining form for the word for 'fish' (W. Cowan p.c.).

KITINGIRAK Gap (Alaska, Noatak D-5). The Iñupiaq (Eskimo) name *kitiŋuruaq* is said to mean 'old skin scraper', from a stem *kitik* (Orth 1967; Burch 1998).

KITIRAM IPITANGA Hills (Alaska, Noatak D-5). The Iñupiaq (Eskimo) name was reported in 1966 (Orth 1967).

KITKONAK Hill (Alaska, Point Hope D-1). The Iñupiaq (Eskimo) name was reported in 1956 as meaning 'between (sea and land)' (Orth 1967); cf. *qitiq* 'middle' (MacLean 1980).

KITKUN Bay (Alaska, Craig A-1). The Tlingit name was reported in 1901 (Orth 1967).

KITLIK River (Alaska, Baird Mountains A-2) \kit´ lik\. The Iñupiaq (Eskimo) name was reported in 1955 (Orth 1967).

KITLUK River (Alaska, Kotzebue C-5). The Iñupiaq (Eskimo) name was recorded in 1950 (Orth 1967).

KITNAGAK Bay (Alaska, St. Lawrence B-0). The Yupik (Eskimo) name was reported in 1919 (Orth 1967).

KITNEPALUK (Alaska, St. Lawrence C-6). The Yupik (Eskimo) name was reported in 1965 (Orth 1967).

KITNIK Mountain (Alaska, Nunivak Is. C-1) \kit´ nik\. From Yupik (Eskimo) *kitngik* 'heel' (Orth 1967; Jacobson 1984). There is also a **Kitnik River** (Alaska, St. Lawrence D-3).

KITSAP County (Wash.) \kit´sap\. Named after a Lushootseed (Salishan) leader; his Native American name was [k'c'áp] (Hitchman 1985; D. Kinkade p.c.).

KIT SILI Wash (Ariz., Apache Co.). A variant writing of **Keet Seel**; see above. Another variant is **Kitsillie** (Navajo Co.).

KITTAHUTTY Creek (Miss., Calhoun Co.) \kit ə hut´ ē\. Choctaw (Muskogean), meaning 'white mortar (grinding bowl)', from *kitti* 'mortar', *hata* 'white' (Seale 1939; P. Munro p.c.).

KITTANNING (Pa., Armstrong Co.) \ki tan´ing\. From Delaware (Algonquian), meaning 'great river place' (Donehoo 1928); cf. <kittan> 'great river', <kit-> 'great' (Brinton and Anthony 1888).

KITTANSET (Mass., Plymouth Co.) \ki tan´ sət\. SNEng. Algonquian, 'at the sea', from <kehtahannash-> 'sea', <-et> 'place'(W. Cowan p.c.).

KITTATINNY (Pa., Carbon Co.) \kit´ ə tin ē\. Perhaps from Delaware (Algonquian) *kitahtëne* 'big mountain' (Kraft and Kraft 1985). A possibly related placename is **Mount Katahdin** (Maine, Piscataquis Co.), from Abenaki (Algonquian) *gitaaden, gitaden, gtaden* 'great mountain'; cf. *git(a)-* 'great', *-aden* 'mountain' (Day 1994–95). There is also a **Kittatinny** in N.J. (Sussex Co.).

KITTILNGOOK Bay (Alaska, St. Lawrence D-6). The Yupik (Eskimo) name was reported in 1932 (Orth 1967).

KITTINELBE (Calif., Humboldt Co.) \kit ə nel´ bē\. From the name of an Indian village. The site is in Athabaskan territory, but the name is apparently from the neighboring Wintu language, in which /xetin-elba/ means 'camas-eating', referring to an edible root (Gudde 1998). A related name is **Hetten** (Calif., Trinity Co.), also referring to the camas root.

KITTITAS County (Wash.) \kit´i tas\. From the Sahaptin placename [k'ɨtɨtáš], with [-aš] 'place', referring to a gravel bank in a shoal of the Yakima River (Hitchman 1985; D. Kinkade p.c.).

KITTY HAWK (N.C., Dare Co.) \kit´ ē hôk\. The name has also been written as <Chicahauk, Chickahawk, Kettyhauk> (etc.); it was probably the name of a CAC Algonquian village (Payne 1985).

KIUGILAK, Cape (Alaska, Adak D-1). From an Aleut placenamne *kyugalux̂* (Bergsland 1994).

KIUGTLUGTULIT Mountain (Alaska, Goodnews Bay B-7). The Yupik (Eskimo) name was reported in 1954 (Orth 1967).

KIUKPALIK Island (Alaska, Afognak C-5). The Alutiiq (Eskimo) name was recorded by a Russian navigator in 1847 as <Ukayukhpalyk> (Orth 1967).

KIUP Spring (Nev., Clark Co.) \kē´ əp\. Possibly from Southern Paiute (Numic) /kia/ 'to laugh' plus /-ppɨh/ 'perfective' (J. McLaughlin p.c.).

KIVALIK Inlet (Alaska, Noatak D-6). The Iñupiaq (Eskimo) name was reported in 1966 (Orth 1967).

KIVALINA (Alaska, Noatak C-5) \kē və lē´ nə\. The Iñupiaq (Eskimo) placename is *kivaliñiq*, probably from *kivalliq* 'one up the coast, to the east' plus *-niq* 'nominal ending' (L. Kaplan p.c.).

KIVA School (Ariz., Maricopa Co.) \kē´ və\. From Hopi *kiva* 'ceremonial chamber (K. Hill p.c.).

KIVEEPUK Bay (Alaska, St. Lawrence D-4). The Yupik (Eskimo) name, reported in 1944, is said to mean 'jammed, packed in' (Orth 1967).

KIVIDLO (Alaska, Kotzebue C-6). The Iñupiaq (Eskimo) name was reported in 1950 (Orth 1967).

KIVIVIK Creek (Alaska, Baird Mountains D-6). The Iñupiaq (Eskimo) name is *kivikik* 'place where something sank' (L. Kaplan p.c.).

KIVLIKTORT Mountain (Alaska, Howard Pass B-1). The Iñupiaq (Eskimo) name is *qivliqtuat* 'things that glitter' (L. Kaplan p.c.).

KIWA Creek (Idaho, Latah Co.) \kī´ wə\. The name was given by the U.S. Forest Service; it is from Chinook Jargon <ki´wa> 'crooked', perhaps derived from Wasco (Chinookan) (Boone 1988; D. Kinkade p.c.). The name also occurs in Ore. (Deschutes Co., Lane Co.) In the spelling **Kiwah**, it is found in Valley Co., Idaho.

KIWAIKULUK/A (N.Mex., Cibola Co.). The Zuni site is used for Medicine Society prayers (Ferguson and Hart 1985).

KIWALIK Lagoon (Alaska, Selawik A-6) \kē wä´ lik\. The Iñupiaq (Eskimo) name is *kivallium imaġruŋa* (Burch 1998).

KIWANDA Creek (Ore., Tillamook Co.) \kī wän´ də\. From Tillamook (Salishan) [k'awə́ndiʔ], a man's name (D. Kinkade p.c.).

KIWANIS Park (Ill., Cook Co.) \ki wä´ nis\. Named for the Kiwanis Club, a civic organization. The term is alleged to be from Ojibwa (Algonquian), meaning 'to make oneself known' (*RHD* 1987); but in fact it resembles an entry in the dictionary of Baraga (1880:198): "*Kiwanis (nin).* I make noise; I am foolish and wanton" (Vogel 1963); cf. modern Ojibwa *gii-wanaadizi* 'to be crazy' (Nichols and Nyholm 1995). The placename occurs in several states (e.g., Mich., Genesee Co.; Wis., Waupaca Co.; and Pa., York Co.).

KIWASSA Lake (N.Y., Franklin Co.) \ki wä´ sə\. Perhaps from Abenaki (Algonquian), of unclear derivation (Beauchamp 1907).

KIWOOK Pass (Alaska, St. Lawrence C-5). The Yupik (Eskimo) name is said to mean 'growing river' (Orth 1967); cf. St. Lawrence Is. Yupik *kiikw* 'river' (Jacobson 1987).

KIYAKYALIKSAMIUT (Alaska, Cape Mendenhall D-6). The Yupik (Eskimo) name, with the ending *-miut* 'people', was reported about 1949 (Orth 1967).

KIZHUCHIA Creek (Alaska, Port Alexander D-5). The name, perhaps from Tlingit, was reported in 1809 by a Russian navigator (Orth 1967).

KIZHUYAK Bay (Alaska, Kodiak D-3). The Alutiiq (Eskimo) name was reported in 1852 (Orth 1967).

KLACHOPIS Point (Wash., Clallam Co.). From Makah (Nootkan) /tl'a:čapi:s/, from the root /tl'a:č-/ 'to fold; (waves) to break' (W. Jacobsen).

KLADEIN Flats (Alaska, Craig D-4). The name, probably Tlingit, was published in 1964 (Orth 1967).

KLAG Bay (Alaska, Sitka C-7). The Tlingit name was reported in 1908 (Orth 1967).

KLAGETOH (Ariz., Apache Co.) \klag ə tō´, klag´ tō\. Navajo (Athabaskan) *łeeyi'tó* 'water in the ground', from *łee(zh)* 'ground, soil', *yi'* 'inside', and *tó* 'water' (Wilson 1995).

KLAHANIE (Wash., King Co.) \klä´ hə nē\. Chinook Jargon <kla-ha-nee, kla´-ha-nie, klaghanie> 'outdoors, outside' (Hitchman 1985); from Lower Chinook [k^{W}ɬáxane] 'outside' or from Kathlamet Chinook [ɬáx̢ane] (D. Kinkade p.c.).

KLAHINI River (Alaska, Bradfield Canal A-4). The name, probably Tlingit, was reported in 1900 (Orth 1967).

KLAHOWYA Creek (Wash., Pend Oreille Co.) \klə hou´ yə\. Chinook Jargon <klahāwēm, tlahawiam, kla-how-yah> [klaháwya, kləháwyə, tláhawyəm] 'poor; to sympathize with'; also used as a greeting, 'hello, good-bye'. The term is from Lower Chinook [-xauyam] 'what excites sympathy' (D. Kinkade p.c.).

KLAKAS Lake (Alaska, Craig A-2). The Tlingit name was recorded in 1897 (Orth 1967).

KLAK Butte (Ore., Deschutes Co.) \kläk\. Named by the U.S. Forest Service, from Chinook Jargon <klak> [klak] 'off, out, away; to take off' (McArthur 1992); from Lower Chinook [tɬəx] 'to cut'; cf. Kathlamet Chinook [tɬx̢^{W}áp] 'cut' (D. Kinkade p.c.).

KLAK Creek (Alaska, Goodnews Bay D-5). The Yupik (Eskimo) name was recorded in 1898 as <Chlach> (Orth 1967).

KLALBAIMUNKET Lake (Alaska, Hughes A-3). The Koyukon (Athabaskan) name, recorded in 1956, is said to mean 'grayling lake', referring to a type of fish (Orth 1967); cf. *tleghelbaaye* 'grayling', *benh* 'lake', *-k'et* 'place' (Jetté and Jones 2000).

KLALUTHYIIT Bluff (Alaska, Hughes B-1). The Koyukon (Athabaskan) name is said to refer to the narrowing of the Koyukuk River (Orth 1967).

KLAMATH River \klam´ əth\. This name for an Indian people in southern Ore. is from the Upper Chinookan /ɬámaɬ/, the name applied to the Klamath people, lit. 'they of the river', from /-maɬ/ 'river' (*HNAI* 12:464). The term occurs in placenames including the **Klamath Lakes** and **Klamath County** in Ore., as well as the **Klamath River** in Ore. and Calif.

KLANELNEECHENA Creek (Alaska, Valdez C-7) \klä nel nēch´ nə\. From Ahtna (Athabaskan) *tl'ahwdinaesi na'*, lit. 'rear-one-that-is-tall creek' (J. Kari p.c.).

KLAN Hill (Alaska, Prince Rupert D-3). An abbreviation of a Tlingit placename <Sitklan>, reported in 1883 (Orth 1967).

KLAPATCHE Ridge (Wash., Pierce Co.). Named for a Puyallup (Salishan) leader (Hitchman 1985).

KLAPOT Point (Wash., Clallam Co.). From Chinook Jargon <kla-pote, kla´-pite> 'thread', from Lower Chinook [-pait] 'rope' (D. Kinkade p.c.). A related form is **Kiapot Point**, from Chinook Jargon <kīapōt, keep´wot] 'needle', from Lower Chinook <o-kwe´-po-wa> 'needle'; see above.

KLASKANINE River (Ore., Clatsop Co.) \klas´ kə nīn\. From a Lower Chinook ethnic name, /iɬáck'ani/ 'those of the region of small oaks' (D. Kinkade p.c.). A related form is **Clatskanie River** (Ore., Columbia Co.).

KLAS Rock (Wash., Jefferson Co.). Probably from Chinook Jargon <klās, glass> [klas, glas] 'mirror, looking glass, window', from English *glass* (D. Kinkade p.c.).

KLATAKHNA Creek (Alaska, Tanana C-6). The Koyukon (Athabaskan) name was reported in 1956 (Orth 1967).

KLATSUTA River (Alaska, Melozitna A-2). The Koyukon (Athabaskan) name was reported in 1869 (Orth 1967.

KLAWA Creek (Idaho, Latah Co.) \klä´ wə\. The name was given by the U.S. Forest Service, based on Chinook Jargon <klah-wa> 'slow' (Boone 1988; Thomas 1935).

KLAWASI River (Alaska, Valdez D-4) \klä wä´ sē \. From Ahtna (Athabaskan) *kolghosi na'*, lit. 'boiling creek' (Kari 1983:31).

KLAWHOP Butte (Ore., Deschutes Co.) \klô´ hop\. Named by the U.S. Forest Service on the basis of Chinook Jargon <kla-whop> [klahwɔ́p, kláwap] 'hole', from Lower Chinook [tɬoáp] 'to dig', or from Kathlamet Chinook [tɬx̣ʷáp] 'hole' (D. Kinkade p.c.).

KLAWOCK (Alaska, Craig C-4) \klə wok'\. The Tlingit village name was referred to by a Russian navigator in 1853 as <Klyakkhan>, in 1855 as <Thlewakh> (Orth 1967). The Native American form of the name is /ɬawa:k/, a subgroup of the Tlingit nation) (*HNAI* 7:227).

KLAXTA (Wash., Lincoln Co.) \klak´ stə\. Chinook Jargon <klaksta, klaxta> [kláksta] 'who, somebody', from Lower Chinook <tluk-sta> 'who' (Hitchman 1985; D. Kinkade p.c.).

KLEHINI River (Alaska, Skagway B-3) \klə hē´ nē\. The Tlingit placename was reported in 1883 as <Kluhini, T'lehini> (Orth 1967).

KLETHLA Valley (Ariz., Coconino Co.) \kleth´ lə\. Navajo (Athabaskan) *ɬį́į́'ɬání* 'many horses' (Linford 2000), from *ɬį́į́'* 'horse', *ɬání* 'many' (Young and Morgan 1987).

KLETSAN Creek (Alaska, McCarthy C-1) \klāt´ sän\. The Upper Tanana (Athabaskan) name is *ttheetsą̨ą̨' ndiig* 'copper creek' (J. Kari p.c.).

KLICKITAT County (Wash.) \klik´i tat\. Probably from Sahaptin /ɬátaxat/, the name of the **Klickitat River** (D. Kinkade p.c.). There is also a **Klickitat Creek** in Ore. (Clatsop Co.).

KLICKTON Divide (Wash., Yakima Co.) \klik´ tən\. A combination of the names of the **Klickitat River** and the **Tieton River** (D. Kinkade p.c.).

KLIKHTENTOTZNA Creek (Alaska, Hughes B-4). The Koyukon (Athabaskan) name was reported in 1956 as meaning 'bow-and-arrow river' (Orth 1967); cf. *tl'eeɬten'* 'bow for archery' (Jetté and Jones 2000).

KLIKITARIK (Alaska, Unalakleet B-5). The Yupik (Eskimo) name is *qikiqtaaruk* 'peninsula' (L. Kaplan p.c.).

KLINKWAN (Alaska, Dixon Entrance D-2) \kling kwän'\. From Tlingit /ɬenquaʔa:n/ 'tide-flats-place-town' (HNAI 7:259); cf. *léin* [ɬe:n] 'tide flats' (Davis and Leer 1976).

KLIPCHUCK (Wash., Okanogan Co.) \klip´ chuk\. The name is a combination of Chinook Jargon elements meaning 'deep water': <klip> 'deep', from Lower Chehalis (Salishan) [tɬ'ə́p, tɬ'ə́pəɬ] 'deep' or Lower Chinook [tɬ'ep] 'under water'; and Chinook Jargon <chuck> 'water' (D. Kinkade p.c.).

KLIPSAN Beach (Wash., Pacific Co.) \klip´ sən\. The name was assigned by the U.S. Coast Guard; it is from Chinook Jargon <klip sun> 'sunset', from <klip> 'deep, going down' plus English *sun* (Hitchman 1985; D. Kinkade p.c.).

KLISKON, Mount (Alaska, Talkeetna B-4) \klis´ kon\. From Dena'ina (Athabaskan) *tseles qan* 'ground-squirrel lodge' (Kari and Fall 1987: 142).

KLOAN (Ore., Wasco Co.) \klōn\. This railway station was named with the Chinook word <klone> 'three', as being the third station from the north end of the line (McArthur 1992). Another form of the name is found in **Klone Butte** (Ore., Deschutes Co.); see below.

KLOH KUTZ, Mount (Alaska, Mount Fairweather D-1). The name was reported in 1941 as the name of a Chilkat (Tlingit) leader, said to mean 'hole in the cheek' (Orth 1967).

KLONAQUA (Wash., Chelan Co.) \klə nä´ kwə\. The name, applied by the U.S. Forest Service, is apparently intended to mean 'three lakes', from Chinook Jargon <klone> [klon] 'three' plus Moses-Columbian (Salish) /-atkʷ/ 'water' (D. Kinkade p.c.).

KLONDIKE \klon´ dīk\. The name of the **Klondike River** in Yukon Territory, Canada, was recorded in 1913 as <Throndiuck>, said to mean 'hammer-water', referring to the practice of driving stakes in the river to support fish-traps. The name is from Gwich'in (Athabaskan), and the original form was probably [tr'ondiëk]; in present-day dialects it occurs as *tr'ondëk, tr'odëk, tr'oju.* The first element, [tr'o-] 'hammer stone', no longer occurs in isolation; the second element is *-ndëk, -dëk, -ju* 'stream' (J. Ritter p.c.). Because of the famous Klondike

Gold Rush of the 1890s, the placename was borrowed widely in the United States (e.g., Iowa, Lyon Co.; Mass., Essex Co.; and Ore., Sherman Co.). The spelling **Klondyke** also occurs (Ind., Parke Co.; Wis., Grant Co.).

KLONE Butte (Ore., Deschutes Co.) \klōn\. The name was assigned by the U.S. Forest Service, based on Chinook Jargon <klone> [klon] 'three', from Chinookan /tlun/ 'three', as one of a series of prominences named at the same time (McArthur 1992; D. Kinkade p.c.). The name of **Klone Creek** (Wash., Chelan Co.) has a similar origin (Hitchman 1985). Another spelling is found in **Kloan** (Ore., Wasco Co.).

KLOOCHMAN Creek (Wash., Chelan Co.) \klo͞och´ mən\. Chinook Jargon <klootch-man> [klúčman] 'woman, female', from Nootka /ɬu:cma/, with <-man> perhaps by analogy to English *woman.* The name was given by the U.S. Forest Service (Hitchman 1985; D. Kinkade p.c.). Related placenames include **Klootch Creek** (Idaho, Boundary Co.) and **Klootchman Creek** (Ore., Crook Co.); see below. As slang terms for 'woman' in the Northwest, both *kloochman* and *klootch* are now considered offensive.

KLOOQUEH Rocks (Ore., Curry Co.). Probably from Tututni (Athabaskan), meaning 'grass on-top' (D. Kinkade p.c.).

KLOOTCH Creek (Idaho, Boundary Co.) \klo͞och\. A shortening of Chinook Jargon <klootchman> 'woman'; see **Kloochman Creek** (Wash., Chelan Co.) above. Probably related placenames include **Klootchie Creek** (Ore., Clatsop Co.) and **Klootchman Creek** (Ore., Crook Co.).

KLOSHE Creek (Wash., Clallam Co.) \klōsh\. Chinook Jargon <kloshe, klosh> [kloš] 'good, beautiful', from Nootka /tɬuɬ/ 'pretty, good' (D. Kinkade p.c.). **Kloshe Chuck Reservoir** (Ore., Clackamas Co.) is from the Chinook Jargon for 'good water', with <chuck> 'water'. **Kloshe Nanich** (Wash., Clallam Co.) is intended as Chinook Jargon for 'good view', with <nanitch, noneneech> [nánıč, nǽnıč] 'look, see', from Nootka [n'an'a:nic] 'looking at something' (D. Kinkade).

KLUANIL (Alaska, Craig B-1). The name, perhaps from Tlingit, was published in 1927 (Orth 1967).

KLUCHMAN Mountain (Alaska, Taku River C-6) \klo͞och´ mən\. The term is related to **Kloochman Creek** (Wash., Chelan Co.); see above.

KLUKTAK Creek (Alaska, Bethel A-8). The Yupik (Eskimo) name was reported in 1951 (Orth 1967).

KLUKWAH Mountain (Alaska, Skagway C-3). The Tlingit name was published in 1954; it may be a variant writing of **Klukwan** (Orth 1967); see below.

KLUKWAN (Alaska, Skagway B-3) \kluk´ wän\. The Tlingit name, reported in 1880, is said to mean 'old town' (Orth 1967).

KLUNATHKADĄ Hill (Alaska, Nabesna D-2). The Upper Tanana (Athabaskan) name is of unclear derivation (Orth 1967).

KLUNISTANA Creek (Alaska, Healy B-3). From Ahtna (Athabaskan), based on a name for the upper Nenana River, *łuyinanest'aani na* 'one-that-extends-into-glacier creek' (J. Kari p.c.).

KLU River (Alaska, McCarthy A-6) \klo͞o\. From Ahtna (Athabaskan) *łuu* 'glacier' (Orth 1967; Kari 1990). A possibly related name is **Klutlan Glacier** (Alaska, McCarthy B-1).

KLUTINA River (Alaska, Valdez D-4) \klo͞o tē´ nə\. Ahtna (Athabaskan) *tl'ati-na',* lit. 'headwaters river' (J. Kari p.c.).

KLUTLAN Glacier (Alaska, McCarthy B-1). The name is from Ahtna (Athabaskan) *łuułaan* 'glacier is there' (J. Kari p.c.). Possibly related names are **Klu River** (Alaska, McCarthy A-6) and **Kluvesna Glacier** (Alaska, McCarthy D-8).

KLUTSHAH Mountain (Alaska, Skagway C-3). The Tlingit name was published in 1952 (Orth 1967).

KLUTUK Creek (Alaska, Dillingham B-4). The Yupik (Eskimo) name was reported in 1930 (Orth 1967).

KLUTUSPAK Creek (Alaska, Taylor Mountains A-4). The Yupik (Eskimo) name was reported in 1952 (Orth 1967).

KLUVESNA Glacier (Alaska, McCarthy D-8) \klo͞o vas´ nə\. Ahtna (Athabaskan) *łubaedzi na'* 'glacier-brown stream'; cf. *łuu* 'glacier', *na'* 'stream' (Kari 1983:13).

KLYMUNGET Lake (Alaska, Melozitna C-5). The Koyukon (Athabaskan) name was recorded in 1956 (Orth 1967).

KNIFE River (Minn., St. Louis Co.). The name corresponds to Ojibwa (Algonquian) <Mokomani zibi> (Upham 2001); cf. *mookomaan* 'knife', *ziibi* 'river' (Nichols and Nyholm 1995).

KNIK (Alaska, Anchorage B-8) \kə nik´\. Dena'ina (Athabaskan) *k'enaka nen* 'Knik area', with *nen* 'land' (Kari and Fall 1987:238).

KNOCKHOCK (Alaska, Kwiguk D-6). An Eskimo village, now abandoned and replaced by one called "New Knockhock" (Orth 1967). Cf. Yupik (Eskimo) *nunaqerraq,* from *nuna* 'land' (Jacobson 1984).

KNOPKI Creek (Calif., Del Norte Co.) \kə nop´ kē\. Perhaps of Indian origin, but this has not been confirmed (Gudde1998).

KNOYA Peak (Alaska, Anchorage A-8). From Dena'ina (Athabaskan) *k'nuy'a* 'beaver'; the name was suggested by the Mountaineering Club of Alaska in 1967 (Kari and Fall 1987: 293).

KNULTHKARN Creek (Calif., Humboldt Co.) \kə nulth´ kärn\. From the Yurok placename <knułkenok> (Gudde 1998).

KNUTRUIN Rock (Alaska, Kenai C-5). The name is perhaps from Dena'ina (Athabaskan); it was reported in 1958 (Orth 1967).

KOASATI (Ala., Elmore Co.) \kō ə sä´ tē\. The name designates a people of the Muskogean language family, formerly living in Alabama; see **Coushatta** above.

KOBEH Valley (Nev., Eureka Co.) \kō´ bē\. From Shoshoni (Numic) /kopai/, pronounced [kóvai] or [kóve] 'face' (Carlson 1974; J. McLaughlin p.c.).

KOBOLUNUK (Alaska, Kwiguk A-3). The Yupik (Eskimo) name was reported in 1899 (Orth 1967).

KOBUK (Alaska, Shungnak D-2) \kō´ buk\. Iñupiaq (Eskimo) *kuuvak* 'big river', containing *kuuk* 'river' and *-vak* 'big' (L. Kaplan p.c.). Possibly related Alaska placenames include **Koyuk** (Norton Bay D-5), **Kogru River** (Harrison Bay C-4), and **Kuzitrin River** (Teller A-1).

KOCHILAGOK Hill (Alaska, Marshall C-7). Perhaps from Iñupiaq (Eskimo) *tatirgaq* 'crane (bird)' (Orth 1967; MacLean 1980).

KOCHLUK Pass (Alaska, St. Michael A-6). The Yupik (Eskimo) name was reported in 1952 (Orth 1967).

KOCHU Island (Alaska, Skagway A-2). The name, perhaps from Tlingit, was reported in 1848 (Orth 1967).

KODIAK Island (Alaska, Kodiak D-2) \kō´ dē ak\. From Russian <Kadiak>, from Alutiiq (Eskimo) *qikertaq* 'island' (Orth 1967; Leer 1978). The term occurs as a transfer name (e.g., Idaho, Clearwater Co.; and Ore., Klamath Co.). Related Alaska placenames include **Kikiktak Island** (Teshekpuk D-5), **Kiktak Island** (Bethel D-7), and **Kikuktok Mountain** (Hooper Bay C-3); see above.

KODOSIN MINNKOHWIN Lake (Alaska, Bettles B-5). The Koyukon (Athabaskan) name was reported in 1956 (Orth 1967). Probably related is nearby **Kodosin Nolitna Creek.**

KODUIT Lake (Alaska, Fort Yukon C-2). The Gwich'in (Athabaskan) name is *goondit* (Caulfield et al. 1983).

KOGISH Mountain (Alaska, Craig C-4). Named for an Indian leader, perhaps Tlingit (Orth 1967).

KOGOK River (Alaska, St. Michael B-2). The Yupik (Eskimo) name was reported in 1898 (Orth 1967).

KOGOLUKTUK River (Alaska, Shungnak D-2). From Iñupiaq (Eskimo) *quġluqtuq* 'waterfall' (Webster and Zibell 1970; Burch 1998).

KOGOSUKRUK (Alaska, Umiat D-3). The Iñupiaq (Eskimo) name was reported in 1946 (Orth 1967).

KOGOTPAK River (Alaska, Demarcation Point D-3). The Iñupiaq (Eskimo) name was reported in 1956 (Orth 1967).

KOGOYUK Creek (Alaska, Sleetmute B-7). From Yupik (Eskimo) *qugyuk* 'swan' (Orth 1967; Fortescue et al. 1994).

KOGRU River (Alaska, Harrison Bay C-4) \kō´ grōō\. The Iñupiaq (Eskimo) name was recorded as <kogru> in 1854, and as <kogruak> in 1855; it was said to mean 'creek' or 'old river' (Orth 1967). Cf. *kuuk* 'river', *kuuġuq* 'tributary river', *kuuġuuraq* 'creek' (Webster and Zibell 1970). Related placenames probably include **Kogruk Creek** (Alaska, Misheguk Mt. C-4), probably from Iñupiaq *kuuġuq* 'tributary river' (Webster and Zibell 1970); and **Kogruk-luk River** (Alaska, Taylor Mountains D-5), probably from *kuuġuq* 'tributary river', *-luk* 'bad' (Webster and Zibell 1970). Other related Alaska names may include **Kobuk** (Shungnak D-2), **Koyuk** (Norton Bay D-5), and **Kuzitrin River** (Teller A-1).

KOHATK (Ariz., Pinal Co.) \kō´ hatk\. From O'odham (Piman) *kohadk* 'hollow' (Granger 1983; J. Hill p.c.).

KOHI KUG (Ariz., Pima Co.) \kō hē kuk`\. O'odham (Piman) *gohi ke:k,* lit. 'mulberry standing' (Granger 1983; J. Hill p.c.).

KOHOKACHALLA Mountain (Alaska, Hughes B-1). The Koyukon (Athabaskan) name, said to mean 'heart', was recorded in 1956 (Orth 1967).

KOIANGLAS (Alaska, Dixon Entrance D-3). The Haida name was also written as <Koranhunglus> (Orth 1967). The Native American form is /q'wí: ʕántla:s/; cf. /q'wí:/ 'water', /ʕántl/ 'water' (*HNAI* 7:258, Lawrence 1977).

KOIP Peak (Calif., Mono Co.) \koip\. From Northern Paiute (Numic) /kóipa/ 'mt. sheep'; or from Mono (Numic) /koippɨ/ 'mt. sheep', lit. 'that which is killed', from /koi-/ 'kill plural' (Gudde 1998).

KOITLAH (Wash., Clallam Co.). From a Makah (Nootkan) placename /q'ʷitl'a/ 'rock-slide' (W. Jacobsen p.c.).

KOIYAKTOT Mountain (Alaska, Howard Pass A-1). The Iñupiaq (Eskimo) name was reported in 1856 (Orth 1967).

KOKACHO Creek (Alaska, Fort Yukon D-4). The Gwich'in (Athabaskan) name was recorded in 1956 (Orth 1967).

KOKADJO (Maine, Piscataquis Co.) \kō kaj´ ō\. Said to be Abenaki (Algonquian) for 'kettle mountain' (Huden 1962); cf. *kokw* 'kettle' (Day 1994–95).

KOKANEE, Lake (Wash., Mason Co.). Perhaps a placename from the Twana (Salishan) language (D. Kinkade p.c.).

KOKECHIK Bay (Alaska, Hooper Bay C-3). The Yupik (Eskimo) name, reported in 1949, is said to mean 'has wood' (Orth 1967); cf. *equk* [əqok] 'wood' (Jacobson 1984).

KOKHANOK Bay (Alaska, Iliamna B-5). From the Yupik (Eskimo) placename *qarr'unaq* (Jacobson 1984).

KOKINHENIK (Alaska, Cordova A-4). The name, perhaps from Tlingit, was reported in 1897 as <Coquenhena> (Orth 1967).

KOKIRAT Creek (Alaska, Point Hope B-2). The Iñupiaq (Eskimo) name was recorded in 1960 (Orth 1967).

KOKNUK Flats (Alaska, Petersburg C-2). The name, perhaps from Tlingit, was recorded in 1952 (Orth 1967).

KOKO Lake (Ore., Jefferson Co.) \kō´ kō\. Probably from Chinook Jargon <ko´-ko> [kóko] 'to knock', from Lower Chinook <ko-ko> 'to knock' (D. Kinkade p.c.).

KOKOLIK River (Alaska, Point Lay D-2). From Iñupiaq (Eskimo) *qaqalium kuuŋa* (Burch 1998).

KOKOMO (Ind., Howard Co.) \kō´ kə mō\. Said to be the name of a Miami/Illinois (Algonquian) leader, appearing in early documents as <Co-ka-maw, Ko-ko-maw, Ko-ke-maw>; the Native American form was probably /mahkokima/, lit. 'bear-chief' (M. McCafferty p.c.). The placename occurs as a transfer in Alaska (Livengood A-1), Ark. (Lee Co.), and Tex. (Eastland Co.) In Colo. (Lake Co.) there is a place called **Kokomo**, but it is pronounced \kō kō´ mō\, and is said to have been the name of a local Indian (Bright 1993). There is a place called **Kokomo** \kō kō´ mō\ in Hawai'i (Maui Co.), but it is from Hawai'ian *koa-komo* 'koa-tree entering' (Pukui et al. 1974).

KOKOPNYAMA (Ariz., Navajo Co.) \kō kōp nyä´ mə\. From Hopi *kookopngyamu* 'the Fire Clan', containing *ngyam* 'clan members' (K. Hill p.c.).

KOKOPUK Creek (Alaska, Selawik C-4). The Iñupiaq (Eskimo) name is *kuuqquqpaat* (Burch 1998).

KOKOSING River (Ohio, Knox Co.) \kō kō´ sing\. Delaware (Algonquian) /ko:khó:s:ink/ 'owl place' (I. Goddard p.c.).

KOKOSTICK Butte (Ore., Deschutes Co.) \kō´ kō stik\. Chinook Jargon <kokostick> [kókostɪk] 'woodpecker', from <ko´-ko> 'to knock' (from Lower Chinook <ko-ko> 'to knock') plus <stick> [stɪk] 'tree, wood, stick, etc.' from English (D. Kinkade p.c.).

KOKOWEEP Peak (Calif., San Bernardino Co.) \kō´ kō wēp\. Perhaps from Southern Paiute (Numic) /koko/ 'gopher snake' plus /uippi/ 'canyon' (Gudde 1998).

KOKRUAGAROK (Alaska, Teshekpuk D-1). The Iñupiaq (Eskimo) placename is probably *kuugruaġruk* 'big river' (L. Kaplan p.c.).

KOKSETNA River (Alaska, Lake Clark A-6) \kōk set´ nə\. From Dena'ina (Athabaskan) *q'uk'tsatnu*, with *-tnu* 'river' (Kari and Kari 1982: 24).

KOKTAYA (Alaska, Anchorage A-7). From Dena'ina (Athabaskan) *k'uhda'i* 'moose'; suggested by the Mountaineering Club in Alaska in 1967 (Kari and Fall 1987:296).

KOKUMPAT Creek (Alaska, Hughes D-6). The Iñupiaq (Eskimo) name was recorded in 1956 as meaning 'the south one' (Orth 1967).

KOKWOK River (Alaska, Dillingham B-5). The Yupik (Eskimo) name was reported as <Kukuak> in 1880 (Orth 1967).

KOLANA (Calif., Tuolumne Co.) \kō lä´ nə\. Perhaps from Southern Sierra Miwok /kuluunaw/, the name of the location now called Coarsegold (Gudde 1998).

KOLAVINARAK River (Alaska, Baird Inlet B-8). The Yupik (Eskimo) name was reported in 1949 as meaning 'silting' (Orth 1967).

KOLCHAN \kol chan\. The name of an Athabaskan people of the **Upper Kuskokwim River** in western Alaska; from Dena'ina /ɣ̌əlcana/ 'interior Athabaskans' (*HNAI* 6:622). The people and language are now often called **Upper Kuskokwim.**

KOLCHICHET Mountain (Alaska, Goodnews Bay D-3). The Yupik (Eskimo) name was reported in 1898 (Orth 1967).

KOLELEMOOK Lake (N.H., Sullivan Co.). Said to be from Abenaki (Algonquian), meaning 'shining pond' (Huden 1962).

KOLIGANEK (Alaska, Dillingham C-4) \kō lig´ ə nek\. Yupik (Eskimo) *qalirneq* 'one on top; roof', from *qaliq* 'top layer' (Jacobson 1984).

KOLIPSUN Creek (Alaska, Wainwright C-1). The Iñupiaq (Eskimo) name is *qulipsiun* 'old style clay pot' (L. Kaplan p.c.).

KOLLIOKSAK River (Alaska, Shungnak D-2). The Iñupiaq (Eskimo) name was reported in 1925 (Orth 1967).

KOLLUTUK Mountain (Alaska, Chandler Lake A-4). The Iñupiaq (Eskimo) word was reported in 1930 as meaning 'sheep horn dipper' (Orth 1967); cf. *qallun* 'cup, dipper', *qallutaun, qayuutaq* 'ladle' (Webster and Zibell 1970).

KOLOKEE (Fla., Seminole Co.) \kol´ ə kē\. From Muskogee *kulkē* /kolkí:/ 'light, lamp'; not a Native American placename, but a word chosen by white people from a Muskogee wordlist (Martin and Mauldin 2000).

KOLOLA Springs (Miss., Lowndes Co.). Perhaps from Choctaw (Muskogean) *kolohli* 'to be cut off, cut up' (Seale 1939; P. Munro p.c.).

KOLOMAK River (Alaska, Hooper Bay C-3). The Yupik (Eskimo) name was reported in 1951 (Orth 1967).

KOLOMOKI Creek (Ga., Clay Co.). Possibly derived from <Kolomi>, a Muskogee tribal town (Krakow 1975). A probably related placename is **Colomokee** (Ga., Early Co.).

KOLOSH (Alaska, Port Alexander D-5) \kō´ losh\. From Russian *kolosh,* a word used to designate the Tlingit Indians. The term was derived from Russian *kalusha,* referring to the wooden disks worn in their lips by Tlingit women. This in turn was a Russian diminutive of Aleut *kalukax̂* 'dish, plate' (*HNAI* 7:226; Bergsland 1994).

KOLOTUK Creek (Alaska, Mount Michelson B-1). The Iñupiaq (Eskimo) name was reported in 1960 (Orth 1967).

KOLOVIK (Alaska, Teshekpuk D-1). The Iñupiaq (Eskimo) name was reported in 1951; it is said to mean 'tipping place (where boats are emptied of water)' (Orth 1967).

KOLUKTAK Lakes (Alaska, Ikpikpuk River C-2). The Iñupiaq (Eskimo) name was reported in 1956 (Orth 1967).

KOMAKAK Creek (Alaska, Ambler River C-1). The Iñupiaq (Eskimo) name, said to mean 'outgoing trail', was reported in 1956 (Orth 1967).

KOMA KULSHAN´ (Wash., Whatcom Co.). The name appears to be made up of Salishan words referring to Mount Ranier and Mount Baker, who were wife and husband in a Native American myth. The element **Koma** may represent Lummi [qʷúʔmə], Lushootseed [təqʷúbəʔ], which also appears in the placename **Tacoma**; see below. The element **Kulshan,** which also occurs alone as a placename (see below), is from a Salishan form such as Lummi [kʷəlšé:n] (D. Kinkade p.c.).

KOMAK WUACHO (Ariz., Pima Co.). From O'odham (Piman) *komaḍk weco,* lit. 'flats beneath' (J. Hill p.c.).

KOMALTY (Okla., Kiowa Co.) \kō mäl´ tē\. Named for <Ko-mal-te>, a Kiowa leader (Shirk 1974).

KOMATKE (Ariz., Maricopa Co.) \kō mät´ kē\. From O'odham (Piman) *komaḍk* 'flats' (J. Hill p.c.).

KOMELIK Mountain (Ariz., Pima Co.) From O'odham (Piman) *komal̆k* 'low flat place' (J. Hill p.c.) There is a place called **North Komelik** in Pinal Co. (BGN 7801).

KOM KUG (Ariz., Pima Co.) \kōm kug\. From O'odham (Piman) *ko:m ke:k,* lit. 'hackberry standing' (J. Hill p.c.).

KOMOIARAK Slough (Alaska, Hooper Bay C-2). The Yupik (Eskimo) name was reported in 1951 (Orth 1967).

KOMO Point (Ariz., Coconino Co.) \kō´ mō\. Perhaps the surname of a Havasupai (Yuman) family (Granger 1983).

KOM VO (Ariz., Pima Co.) \kōm vō\. From O'odham (Piman) *ko:m wo'o,* lit. 'hackberry pond' (J. Hill p.c.).

KONARUT Mountain (Alaska, Bethel A-1). The Yupik (Eskimo) name, said to mean 'the source', was reported in 1932 (Orth 1967).

KONAWA (Okla., Seminole Co.) \kon´ ə wä, kə nä´ wä\. From Muskogee *konawv* /koná:wa/ 'bead(s)' (Shirk 1974; Martin and Mauldin 2000).

KONAWAUGUS Valley (N.Y., Wyoming Co.) \kon ə wô´ gəs\. Perhaps related to **Conewago**

(Pa., Lancaster Co.), from Seneca (Iroquoian) *ga:nǫwǫgǫ:h* 'in the rapids' (W. Chafe p.c.); possibly related placenames include **Conowingo Creek** (Pa., Lancaster Co.), as well as **Conewango** (Pa., Warren Co.).

KONCHANEE Lake (Alaska, Kenai C-2) \kōn chä´ nē\. Perhaps from Dena'ina (Athabaskan) *qunsha ni* 'ground-squirrel island' (J. Kari p.c.).

KONEDSIN MINNKOHWIN Lake (Alaska, Bettles B-4). The Koyukon (Athabaskan) name was reported in 1956 (Orth 1967).

KONGAKUT River (Alaska, Demarcation Point D-2). The Iñupiaq (Eskimo) name was reported in 1919 as meaning 'deer pond' (Orth 1967). A possibly related placename is **Konganevik Point** (Alaska, Flaxman Is. A-3), reported in 1912 as meaning 'place where there is a deer pond' (Orth 1967).

KONGERUK River (Alaska, Baird Inlet C-1). From Iñupiaq (Eskimo) *kaŋiʀaq* 'corner, corral' (Orth 1967; Fortescue et al. 1994).

KONGIGANAK (Alaska, Kuskokwim Bay D-3). This is the Yupik (Eskimo) placename *kangirnaq,* from *kangiq* 'source, headwaters' (Jacobson 1984).

KONGISHLUK Bay (Alaska, Hooper Bay D-3). The Yupik (Eskimo) name was reported in 1949 (Orth 1967).

KONGKOK Bay (Alaska, St. Lawrence C-6). The Yupik (Eskimo) name was reported in 1944 (Orth 1967).

KONGSCUT Mountain (Conn., Hartford Co.). Perhaps from SNEng. Algonquian <kogsŭhkoag> high place' (Trumbull 1881).

KONGUMAVIK Creek (Alaska, Chandler Lake A-3). The Iñupiaq (Eskimo) name is *kanŋuumavik* 'gathering place' (L. Kaplan p.c.).

KONIAG Glacier (Alaska, Kodiak B-4). From Aleut *kanaax̂* 'Eskimo people of Kodiak and Alaska Peninsula' (Bergsland 1994).

KONIUJI Island (Alaska, Kodiak D-3) \kon yo͞o´ jē\. Although the island is in Alutiiq (Eskimo) territory, the name, assigned by the Russians, is from Aleut *kunugyux̂* 'crested auklet', the name of a sea bird (Bergsland 1994).

KONKAPOT River (Conn., Litchfield Co.) \kong´ kə pot\. Named for an eighteenth-century Mahican (Algonquian) leader; the term may have meant 'long spout' (Huden 1962). The name also occurs in Mass. (Berkshire Co.). See **Kankapot.**

KONOCTI, Mount (Calif., Lake Co.) \kə nok´ tī\. The Pomo name has also been written <knok´tai>, from /kno/ 'mountain' plus /xatai/ 'woman' (Gudde 1998).

KONOMOC Hill (Conn., New London Co.). Perhaps from a SNEng. Algonquian word referring to lamprey eels (Huden 1962).

KONOOTENA Village (Alaska, Hughes B-1). The Koyukon (Athabaskan) name is *kk'oonootne*; cf. **Kanuti.**

KONSIN Beach (Wis., Calumet Co.) \kon´ sin\. An abbreviation of **Wisconsin**; see below.

KONTEKA Creek (Mich., Ontonagan Co.). Named for an Ojibwa (Algonquian) leader of the early nineteenth century (Vogel 1986).

KONTRASHIBUNA Lake (Alaska, Lake Clark A-3) \kon trash i bo͞o´ nə\. From Dena'ina (Athabaskan) *qenłghishi vena,* lit. 'water-sloshes lake' (Kari and Kari 1982:17).

KOOBUK Creek (Alaska, Candle D-5). The Iñupiaq (Eskimo) name was reported in 1949 as meaning 'big river' (Orth 1967). This is probably an alternative form of **Kobuk**; see above.

KOOCHICHING County (Minn.) \ko͞o´ chi ching\. The name was applied by the Ojibwa (Algonquian) Indians to Rainy Lake and Rainy River. The term was earlier written <Ouchichiq>, perhaps meaning 'neighbor lake', and is said to have been originally from the Cree (Algonquian) language (Upham 2001).

KOOISK Point (Alaska, Yakutat C-5). The name may be from Tlingit (BGN 7702).

KOOKJILIK Point (Alaska, Nunivak Is. B-3). The Yupik (Eskimo) name was reported in 1949 (Orth 1967).

KOOKOOLIGIT Mountains (Alaska, St. Lawrence C-3). The Yupik (Eskimo) name was reported in 1921 (Orth 1967). The name may be related to **Kookoolik**; see below.

KOOKOOLIK (Alaska, St. Lawrence D-3). From the St. Lawrence Is. Yupik (Eskimo) *kukulget* (Jacobson 1987). A possibly related placename is **Kookooliktook River** (Alaska, St. Lawrence C-5).

KOOKU Beach (Alaska, St. Lawrence A-2). The Yupik (Eskimo) name was reported in 1949 (Orth 1967).

KOOKUKLUK Creek (Alaska, Hagemeister Is. D-5). The Yupik (Eskimo) name, said to refer to 'a small stream', was reported in 1938 (Orth 1967); cf. *kuik* 'river' (Jacobson 1984). Probably related Alaska placenames, derived from Iñupiaq (Eskimo) *kuuk* 'river', include **Kobuk** (Shungnak D-2), **Kogru River** (Harrison Bay C-4), **Koyuk** (Norton Bay D-5), and **Kuzitrin River** (Teller A-1).

KOOMLANGEELKUK Bay (Alaska, St. Lawrence D-4). The Yupik (Eskimo) name was reported in 1944 (Orth 1967).

KOONKAZACHEY (Okla., Kiowa Co.). Named for a Kiowa-Apache (Athabaskan) leader known in English as "Apache John"; his Native American name was probably [koka yik'a hásče] 'mean over his camp' (W. De Reuse p.c.).

KOOSAH Mountain (Ore., Lane Co.) \ko͞o´ sä\. Chinook Jargon <koo´sah> [kúsa, kúsə] 'sky', from Chinook [ikúsax] 'sky' (D. Kinkade p.c.). There is also a **Koosah Falls** in Linn Co. Probably related is **Kosa Point** (Wash., Pierce Co.).

KOOSHAREM (Utah, Sevier Co.) \kə shâr´ əm\. From the name of a Ute (Numic) band, /kusatumpɨ/ [kusárumpɨ̥], lit. 'bindweed, rope' (Sapir 1930; J. McLaughlin p.c.).

KOOSKIA (Idaho, Idaho Co.) \ko͞o´ skē\. The name is shortened from \ko͞os ko͞os´ kē ə, ko͞os ko͞os´ kē\, which also occurs in the area as a placename. It is said to be from Nez Perce (Sahaptian), referring to 'clear water' (Boone 1988). From the same source is **Kooskooskie** (Wash., Walla Walla Co.).

KOOTENAI \ko͞o´ tə nē, ko͞ot´ nē, ko͞o´ tə nā\. The term refers to a people living in the area where Idaho, Mont., and Canada come together; their language has no close relationships. **Kootenai**, from Blackfoot (Algonquian) *kotonaa'* (Frantz and Russell 1995), is usually written as **Kutenai** by linguists and anthropologists (Boone 1988). **Kootenai** is found as the name of a county in Idaho, and is also applied to several features in Mont.

KOOTZNAHOO Head (Alaska, Sitka C-2). From Tlingit /xucnu:wú/, lit. 'brown bear's fort', from /xú:c/ 'brown bear, grizzly bear' and /nu:w/ 'fortified place' (Orth 1967; *RHD* 1987). An English adaptation of the name is <Hoochinoo>, which is the origin of the term *hooch* 'illicit liquor'.

KOOVUKSELUK Point (Alaska, St. Lawrence D-4). The Yupik (Eskimo) name was reported as <Kooviksilik> in 1932 (Orth 1967).

KOOZATA Lagoon (Alaska, St. Lawrence C-4). Named for Warren Koozata, a Yupik (Eskimo) leader (Orth 1967).

KOPACHUCK State Park (Wash., Pierce Co.) \kō pə chuk´\. The term is a combination of Chinook Jargon terms, intended to mean 'at the water'. The first element is <ko-pa, kwapa> [ko´ pə] 'place, at', from Lower Chinook <kó-pa> 'at'; the second element is <chuck> [čək] 'water'; cf. **Chuck River** above.

KOPSHESUT Creek (Alaska, Ambler River A-5). The Iñupiaq (Eskimo) name was reported in 1955 (Orth 1967).

KORNUI Lake (Alaska, Arctic A-3). The Gwich'in (Athabaskan) name is *goonąįį vavan* 'the lake of (a person named) *goonąįį*' (J. Kari p.c.).

KOSAKUTS River (Alaska, Bering Glacier A-6). The name, probably from Tlingit, was reported lin 1903 (Orth 1967).

KOSA Point (Wash., Pierce Co.) \kō´ sə\. Probably from the same source as **Koosah Mountain** (Ore., Lane Co.); see above.

KOSHKONONG (Wis., Jefferson Co.) \kosh´ kə nong\. Probably from Ojibwa (Algonquian) <kackäwanung> 'where there is a heavy fog' (Cassidy 1948; Vogel 1991); cf. *gashkawan* 'heavy fog' (Nichols and Nyholm 1995).

KOSHOPAH (Neb., Brown Co.) \kosh´ ō pô\. Said to be an Indian word, from an unidentified language (Perkey 1995). This is possibly from the Ojibwa (Algonquian) family name *Kashpaw,* from Cree (Algonquian) *kâspâw* 'it is brittle, crisp' (J. Nichols p.c.).

KOSINA Creek (Alaska, Talkeetna Mountains D-2). Ahtna (Athabaskan) *cets'i na'* [kets'ina'] 'spearing creek' (Kari and Fall 1987:189).

KOSKATANTNA Creek (Alaska, Hughes B-4). The Koyukon (Athabaskan) name was recorded in 1956 (Orth 1967).

KOSOMA (Okla., Pushmataha Co.) \kō sō´ mə\. From Choctaw (Muskogean) *kosoma* 'stink' (Shirk 1974; P. Munro p.c.).

KOSON VAYA (Ariz., Pima Co.) From O'odham (Piman) *koson wahia,* lit. 'packrat well' (J. Hill p.c.).

KOSTA Lake (Fla., Polk Co.) From Muskogee *kaccv* /ká:čča/ 'panther, cougar', locally called 'tiger' (Read 1934; Martin and Mauldin 2000).

KOTAN (Ore., Klamath Co.) \kō´ tän\. Probably represents Chinook Jargon <kiu´-a-tan, kuitan, cuitin>, from Chinook [ikiuatan] 'horse' (McArthur 1992; D. Kinkade p.c.). A related placename is **Kuitan Lake** (Ore., Linn Co.).

KOTIL (Alaska, Iditarod B-4). The Koyukon (Athabaskan) name is of unclear derivation (Orth 1967).

KOTLIK (Alaska, St. Michael A-4) \kot´lik\. From Yupik (Eskimo) *qerrullik,* from *qerrulliik* 'pants', said to have been so named because the river there is shaped like a pair of trousers (Orth 1967; Jacobson 1984). Also written as **Kothlik.**

KOTSINA River (Alaska, Valdez C-2) \kət sē´ nə\. Ahtna (Athabaskan) *k'a'si na',* lit. 'cold river' (J. Kari p.c.).

KOTS KUG (Ariz., Pima Co.) \kots kug´\. O'odham (Piman) *kots ke:k* 'standing cross', from *kots* 'cross' (Sp. *cruz*) plus *ke:k* [kɨ:k] 'standing' (J. Hill p.c.).

KOTSUCK (Wash., Pierce Co.). The name is related to **Katsuck Creek** (Idaho, Benewah Co.); see above.

KOTYITI (N.Mex., Sandoval Co.). The name represents the Native American pronunciation of **Cochiti** (see above), one of the Keresan-speaking pueblos.

KOUGACHUK Creek (Alaska, Kotzebue B-4). The Iñupiaq (Eskimo) name is *kuugaatchiaq* (Burch 1998).

KOUGAROK River (Alaska, Bendeleben B-6). The Iñupiaq (Eskimo) name is *kuugruaq* 'big river' (L. Kaplan p.c.). See also **Kugruk River** below.

KOUSK Island (Alaska, Petersburg D-6). The name, probably Tlingit, was reported in 1947 (Orth 1967).

KOUWEGOK Slough (Alaska, Unalakleet D-4). The Yupik (Eskimo) name was reported in 1952 (Orth 1967).

KO VAYA (Ariz., Pima Co.) \kō vä´ yə\. O'odham (Piman) *ka:w wahia,* lit. 'badger well' (Granger 1983; J. Hill p.c.).

KOWALIGA (Ala., Elmore Co.) \kō ə lī´ jə\. This name, also written <Kowaligi>, may be from Muskogee, but the derivation is unclear (Read 1984).

KOWEE Creek (Alaska, Juneau B-2). Named for a nineteenth-century Tlingit leader (Orth 1967).

KOWEEJOONGAK River (Alaska, Nunivak Is. B-3). The Yupik (Eskimo) name was recorded in 1949 (Orth 1967).

KOWEELIK Bluff (Alaska, Nunivak Is. A-6). The Yupik (Eskimo) name, reported in 1949, refers to the fact that "the bluff is cut by streams" (Orth 1967).

KOWETA Lake (Ga., Fulton Co.) \kə wē´ tə\. Has the same source as **Coweta County** (Ga.), from Muskogee *kvwetv,* a tribal town (Martin and Mauldin 2000).

KOWIGILIKALIK (Alaska, Baird Inlet B-4). The Yupik (Eskimo) name was reported in 1949 (Orth 1967).

KOWIKARURMIUT (Alaska, Cape Mendenhall D-4). The Yupik (Eskimo) name was recorded in 1949 (Orth 1967); the ending *-miut* means 'people'.

KOWKOW Creek (Alaska, Goodnews Bay B-7). The Yupik (Eskimo) name was reported in 1921 (Orth 1967).

KOWTUK Point (Alaska, Point Hope B-3). The Iñupiaq (Eskimo) name was reported in 1950 to mean 'little point' (Orth 1967).

KOYANA Creek (Alaska, Solomon C-4). The name may be Iñupiaq (Eskimo) *quyaana* 'thanks!' (L. Kaplan p.c.).

KOYUK (Alaska, Norton Bay D-5) \koi´yuk\. The Iñupiaq (Eskimo) name was recorded as <Kvyguk> in 1852 (Orth 1967). Probably from Central Alaskan Yupik *kuiyuk* or Iñupiaq *kuuyuk,* derived from *kuik, kuuk* 'river' plus Central Alaskan Yupik *-yuk* 'thing like that'. Possibly related Alaska placenames include **Kobuk** (Shungnak D-2), **Kookukluk Creek** (Hagemeister Is. D-5), and **Kuzitrin River** (Teller A-1).

KOYUKON \koi yo͞o kon´\. The name of an Indian people and language of the Athabaskan family, living in central Alaska. The term is from Russian *kuyukantsy,* derived from *kuyukuk,* the name given by the Russians the **Koyukuk River**; see below. The spelling **Koyukon** was introduced in 1936, suggesting a reference to the **Yukon River** as well (*HNAI* 6:599); see below.

KOYUKTOLIK Bay (Alaska, Seldovia A-6). The Alutiiq (Eskimo) name was reported in 1908 (Orth 1967).

KOYUKUK River (Alaska, Nulato D-4) \koi´ yə kuk\. From Russian *kuyukak,* applied in 1838, on the basis of an Iñupiaq (Eskimo) word *kuvyukuq*, of unclear meaning (Jetté & Jones 2000:1). Probably related placenames include **Kobuk** (Shungnak D-2); see above.

KOZAKAKAT Slough (Alaska, Kateel River B-2). The Koyukon (Athabaskan) name was reported in 1955 (Orth 1967); cf. *-kaakk'et* 'stream mouth' (Jetté and Jones 2000).

KRAVAKSARAK (Alaska, Kwiguk D-5). The Yupik (Eskimo) name was reported in 1899 (Orth 1967).

KREKATOK Island (Alaska, Black A-2). The Yupik (Eskimo) name was reported in 1923 (Orth 1967).

KROTO Creek (Alaska, Tyonek C-1). Named after a Dena'ina (Athabaskan) leader; his Native American name was *k'ghudu* (Kari and Fall 1987:156).

KSHALIUK Point (Alaska, Umnak A-3). The Aleut name was published in 1852 (Orth 1967).

KUAKAN Point (Alaska, Petersburg A-1). From Tlingit /quwakaan/ 'deer' (Orth 1967, Davis and Leer 1976).

KUAKATCH (Ariz., Pima Co.). From O'odham (Piman) *ku:kaj* 'its end' (i.e., end of the mountain) (Granger 1983; J. Hill p.c.).

KUAKAT Ridge (Alaska, Howard Pass D-3). The Iñupiaq (Eskimo) name was reported in 1956 (Orth 1967).

KUAMAKSI Butte (Ore., Deschutes Co.) \kwä mä´ skē\. Klamath /ɢome:ksi/ 'cave place', from /ɢome/ 'cave' and /-ksi/ 'place' (Barker 1963).

KUAPA Ruin (N.Mex., Sandoval Co.). From a Cochiti (Keresan) placename (Harrington 1916: 435).

KUAUA (N.Mex., Sandoval Co.) \ko͞o ä´ wä\. From the Tiwa (Tanoan) placename <gho-wye> 'evergreen' (Julyan 1998).

KUBUGAKLI Cape (Alaska, Karluk D-4). The name, perhaps from Alutiiq (Eskimo), was published in 1835 (Orth 1967).

KUCHAURAK Creek (Alaska, Point Lay B-2). The Iñupiaq (Eskimo) name, said to mean 'new small stream', was reported in 1949 (Orth 1967). Related placenames may include **Kobuk** (Alaska, Shungnak D-2); see above.

KUCHEAK Creek (Alaska, Meade River C-3). The Iñupiaq (Eskimo) name was reported in 1956 (Orth 1967). This may be related to **Kucher Creek** (Alaska, Killik River D-5); the Iñupiaq (Eskimo) name, also written as <koo-che-ak, kugchiak>, is *kuutchiaq* 'new river' (L. Kaplan p.c.). A likely related name is **Kuchiak Creek** (Alaska, Point Lay B-3). There is another **Kuchiak Creek** (Alaska, Selawik C-3), perhaps with the same etymology. Related Alaska placenames may include **Kawichiark River** (Selawik C-1) and **Kobuk** (Shungnak D-2); see above.

KUCHUK Creek (Alaska, Shungnak C-6). The Iñupiaq (Eskimo) name is *arguqłiq kuutchauraq* (Burch 1998); see **Kuchaurak Creek** above.

KUCKUP Spring (Ore., Wasco Co.) \kuk´ əp\. Named for a nineteenth-century leader on the Warm Springs Reservation (McArthur 1992).

KUDUGNAK, Cape (Alaska, Atka C-1). From the Aleut placename *kudugnax̂,* perhaps meaning 'shaped like a shank'; cf. *kudux̂* 'shank, lower leg' (Bergsland 1994).

KUGACHIAK Creek (Alaska, Point Lay D-1). The Iñupiaq (Eskimo) name was reported in 1956, perhaps meaning 'new stream' (Orth 1967); see **Kucheak Creek,** above.

KUGARAK River (Alaska, Selawik C-1). The Iñupiaq (Eskimo) name is *kuugruaq* 'big old river' (L. Kaplan p.c.).

KUGIRAROK Creek (Alaska, Point Hope B-2). The Iñupiaq (Eskimo) name was reported in 1956, said to mean 'flint arrowheads' (Orth 1967); cf. *qaġruq* 'arrow' (Webster and Zibell 1970).

KUGRAK River (Alaska, Survey Pass C-6). The Iñupiaq (Eskimo) name is *kuugruk* 'big river' (Burch 1998); cf. *kuuk* 'river' (MacLean 1980). A probably related placename is **Kugukpak Creek** (Alaska, Killik River A-1); see below.

KUGRUA River (Alaska, Wainight D-1). The Iñupiaq (Eskimo) name, reported in 1855, may be from *qugruk* 'swan' (Orth 1967; MacLean 1980).

KUGRUK River (Alaska, Kotzebue A-2). From Iñupiaq (Eskimo) *kuugruaq* 'big old river', from *kuuk* 'river' and *-ruaq* 'big, old' (L. Kaplan p.c.).

KUGRUPAGA Inlet (Alaska, Teller D-4). The Iñupiaq (Eskimo) name is *kuugruam paaŋa* 'mouth of big-old-river' (L. Kaplan p.c.).

KUGUKLIK River (Alaska, Kuskokwim Bay D-6). The Yupik (Eskimo) name was reported in 1878 (Orth 1967).

KUGUKPAK Creek (Alaska, Killik River A-1). The Iñupiaq (Eskimo) name, reported in 1956, is *kuuġuqpak* 'big tributary' (L. Kaplan p.c.). Related placenames include **Kobuk** (Alaska, Shungnak D-2).

KUGUN Point (Alaska, Craig D-4). The Indian name, probably Tlingit, was reported in 1949 (Orth 1967).

KUGURUROK River (Alaska, Baird Mountains D-6). The Iñupiaq (Eskimo) name is *kuugruaq* (Burch 1998); cf. *kuuk* 'river' (MacLean 1980). A probably related placename is **Kugukpak Creek** (Alaska, Killik River A-1); see above.

KUGUYUK Lake (Alaska, Kenai D-2). The name, perhaps Dena'ina (Athabaskan), was assigned in 1963 (Orth 1967).

KUHSUMAN Creek (Alaska, Chandler Lake B-1). The name, perhaps Koyukon (Athabaskan), was reported in 1944 (Orth 1967).

KUIAK River (Alaska, St. Michael B-1). The Yupik (Eskimo) name was recorded in 1952 (Orth 1967).

KUIKCHERK River (Alaska, Shungnak D-3). The Iñupiaq (Eskimo) name was recorded as <Kue-che-ark> in 1900 (Orth 1967).

KUIRZINJIK Lake (Alaska, Table Mtn. B-5). The Gwich'in (Athabaskan) name is *gwizhrii njik* 'clear(-view) river' (J. Kari p.c.).

KUITAN Lake (Ore., Linn Co.) \kyo͞o´ ə tən\. From Chinook Jargon <kiu´-a-tan, kuitan> [kyúətən] 'horse'. The Chinook Jargon word is written and pronounced in many different ways (D. Kinkade p.c.). Probably related is **Kotan** (Ore., Klamath Co.).

KUI TATK (Ariz., Pima Co.) \ko͞o ē tätk´\. From O'odham (Piman) *kui tatk*, lit. 'mesquite root' (J. Hill p.c.).

KUIT VAYA (Ariz., Pima Co.). O'odham (Piman) *kui wahia* 'mesquite well', from *kui* 'mesquite' and *wahia* 'well' (J. Hill p.c.).

KUIU Island (Alaska, Port Alexander C-1) \kyo͞o´ yo͞o\. From Tlingit /kuyú/, the name of a tribal division (*HNAI* 7:227).

KUIUKTA Bay (Alaska, Chignik A-2). The name, probably Alutiiq (Eskimo), was published in 1852 (Orth 1967).

KUIUKTULIK River (Alaska, Norton Bay D-5). The Iñupiaq (Eskimo) name was reported in 1900 (Orth 1967).

KUJULIK Bay (Alaska, Sutwik Is. C-6). The name, probably Alutiiq (Eskimo), was reported as <Kizhulik> in 1847 (Orth 1967).

KUKA Creek (Alaska, Marshall B-4) \ko͞o´ kə\. The Yupik (Eskimo) name, said to mean 'its middle', was reported in 1965 (Orth 1967); cf. *qukaq* 'middle' (Jacobson 1984).

KUKAK (Alaska, Mount Katmai B-1) \ko͞o´ kak\. The Alutiiq (Eskimo) name was reported in 1831 (Orth 1967); cf. *qukaa* 'the middle of it' (Leer 1978).

KUKAKLIK Lake (Alaska, Russian Mission C-5). The Yupik (Eskimo) name was reported in 1844 (Orth 1967).

KUKAKTLIK River (Alaska, Goodnews Bay B-5). The Yupik (Eskimo) name, reported in 1951, is said to mean 'middle one' (Orth 1967); cf. *qukaq* 'middle' (Jacobson 1987).

KUKAKTLIM Lake (Alaska, Goodnews Bay B-4). The Yupik (Eskimo) name was reported in 1951 (Orth 1967).

KUKE CHEHEDAGI Tank (Ariz., Pima Co.). O'odham (Piman) *ku:g cehedagĭ* 'green edges', from *ku:g* 'end, edge' plus *cehedagĭ* 'green (pl.)' (J. Hill p.c.).

KUKKAN Bay (Alaska, Sitka C-7). Named for a nineteenth-century Tlingit leader (Orth 1967).

KUKPOWRUK River (Alaska, Point Lay C-2). Probably represents Iñupiaq (Eskimo) *kuukpauraq* 'fairly large stream', from *kuuk* 'river', *-(q)pak* 'big', *-uraq* 'diminutive' (Orth 1967; L. Kaplan p.c.). Other related names probably include **Kukpuk** (Alaska, Point Hope B-2), from Iñupiaq (Eskimo) *kuukpak* 'big river' (Orth 1967; L. Kaplan p.c.); **Kukruk Creek** (Alaska, Point Hope D-1), reported to mean 'creek' (Orth 1967), containing *kuuġuq* 'tributary river' or *kuuġuuraq* 'creek' (Webster and Zibell 1970); and **Kupigruak Channel** (Alaska, Harrison Bay B-1; see below).

KUK River (Alaska, Wainwright C-2) \ko͞ok\. From Iñupiaq (Eskimo) *kuuk* 'river' (Orth 1967; MacLean 1980).

KUKTHLUK River (Alaska, Baird Inlet D-1). The Yupik (Eskimo) name was reported in 1949 (Orth 1967).

KUKUKPILAK Creek (Alaska, Misheguk Mt. B-2). The Iñupiaq (Eskimo) name was recorded in 1956 (Orth 1967).

KULAKALA Point (Wash., Clallam Co.) \kul ə kä´ lə\. Chinook Jargon <kallakalla, kalákalá> [kəlákəla] 'bird', from Lower Chinook <kal-lák-a-la> 'bird, goose' (D. Kinkade p.c.). See also **Kulla Kulla Lake** below.

KULAK Point (Alaska, Gareloi Is. B-1). The Aleut name was reported in 1852 (Orth 1967).

KULAVOK Ridge (Alaska, Mount Michelson A-2). The Eskimo name was officially adopted by the BGN in 1992.

KULIAK Bay (Alaska, Mount Katmai A-1). From an Alutiiq (Eskimo) placename, recorded in 1852 (Orth 1967).

KULI CHUK CHU (Okla., McCurtain Co.) \kul ē cho͞ok´ cho͞o\. From Choctaw (Muskogean) *kalih* 'well, spring' plus *chokcho* 'maple tree' (Shirk 1974; P. Munro p.c.).

KULI INLA (Okla., McCurtain Co.) \kul ē in´ lə\. From Choctaw (Muskogean) *kalih* 'well, spring' plus *į̨la* 'different' (P. Munro p.c.).

KULIK Lake (Alaska, Mount Katmai D-3). The name, perhaps Alutiiq (Eskimo), was reported in 1923 (Orth 1967).

KULILIAK Bay (Alaska, Unalaska A-4). Perhaps from Aleut *quliilax̂* 'sadness, grief' (Jacobson 1984).

KULLA KULLA Lake (Wash., King Co.) \kə lä kə lä\. This site and the nearby **Little Kulla Lake** probably take their names from Chinook Jargon <kullagh, kolo> [kəlá, kəláx] 'fence, enclosure', from Lower Chehalis (Salishan) [q'aláx̣] 'fence, enclosure' (Hitchman 1985; D. Kinkade p.c.) There may be some confusion with Chinook Jargon <kallakalla, kalákalá> [kəlákəla] 'bird', however; see **Kulakala Point** above.

KULLICHITO (Okla., McCurtain Co.) \kul ē chit´ ō\. From Choctaw *kalih chito,* lit. 'spring big' (P. Munro p.c.). The spelling **Kulichito** also occurs.

KULLITUKLO (Okla., McCurtain Co.) \kul ē to͞o´ klō\. From Choctaw *kalih toklo* 'two springs', from *kalih* 'spring, well' and *toklo* 'two' (Shirk 1974; P. Munro p.c.).

KULLY CHAHA Township (Okla., Le Flore Co.) \kul ē chä´ hä\. From Choctaw *kalih chaaha* 'high spring', from *kalih* 'spring, well' and *chaaha* 'tall, high' (Shirk 1974; P. Munro p.c.).

KULMOGON Slough (Alaska, St. Michael A-3). The Yupik (Eskimo) name, reported in 1952, is said to mean 'counting to ten' (Orth 1967).

KULSHAN (Wash., Whatcom Co.) \kul´ shən\. From a Salishan term for Mount Baker—for example, Nooksack [k^{W}əlšé:n] or Lummi [k^{W}əlšé:n, k^{W}əl'še'n], perhaps meaning 'shooting place' (cf. /k^{W}ə'lə'š/ 'to shoot') (D. Kinkade p.c.). See also **Koma Kulshan** (Wash., Whatcom Co.).

KULTHIETH River (Alaska, Bering Glacier A-6). From Tlingit [g̣ᴀłiyᴀ, g̣ałyᴀx̣], perhaps from Eyak [g̣ałyᴀx̣] 'the lowest' (De Laguna 1972:101). This may be from the same source as **Kaliakh River**; see above.

KULUGRA Ridge (Alaska, Lookout Ridge C-4). The Iñupiaq (Eskimo) name was reported in 1890 (Orth 1967).

KULUKAK (Alaska, Nushagak Bay D-6) \ko͞o´ lo͞o kak\. The Yupik (Eskimo) name was reported in 1880 as <Kulluk> (Orth 1967).

KULUK Bay (Alaska, Adak C-2). From the Aleut placename *qulux̂,* referring to what is now called 'Sweeper Cove' (Bergsland 1994).

KULUKBUK Hills (Alaska, Sleetmute B-4). The Yupik (Eskimo) name was reported in 1944 (Orth 1967).

KULUMI (Ala., Elmore Co.). Probably from Muskogee *kvlv* /kalá/ 'white oak' (Read 1984; Martin and Mauldin 2000).

KULURUAK (Alaska, Demarcation Point C-1). The Iñupiaq (Eskimo) name was recorded in 1952 and is said to mean 'like a thumb' (Orth 1967); cf. *kuvlu* 'thumb' (Fortescue et al. 1994).

KULVAGAVIK (Alaska, Kuskokwim Bay D-2). The Yupik (Eskimo) name was reported in 1879 (Orth 1967).

KUMLIK (Alaska, Sutwik Is. C-5). The name, probably Alutiiq (Eskimo), was recorded in 1827 (Orth 1967). Probably related is **Kumliun Creek** (Alaska, Sutwik Is. C-6), recorded in 1827 as <Komliouck>.

KUMLUNAK Peninsula (Alaska, Baird Inlet D-8). The Yupik (Eskimo) name is *kumlunaq* 'one like a thumb' (L. Kaplan p.c.).

KUMTUX (Wash., Clark Co.) \kum´ tuks\. Said to be named for a nineteenth-century Indian leader, language unknown. His name was Chinook Jargon <kum´-tux, kum´-tuks> [kə́mtəks] 'to know, understand', based on Nootka /kamat/ 'known' (D. Kinkade p.c.). A related name is **Cumtux** (Ore., Curry Co.).

KUNAGHAK Creek (Alaska, St. Lawrence C-6). The Yupik (Eskimo) name was reported in 1944 (Orth 1967).

KUNAMAKST Creek (Wash., Jefferson Co.) \kun´ ə mäkst\. Chinook Jargon <kun´-a-moxt> [kə́nəmaks] 'both, together, with', from Lower Chinook [skanasmɔ́kst] 'both' or Kathlamet Chinook /kana-mákst/ 'both' (D. Kinkade p.c.). Cf. the placenames **Mokst Butte** (Ore., Deschutes Co.), **Mox Chuck** (Wash., Grays Harbor Co.), containing Chinook Jargon <mokst, moxt> 'two'.

KUNA Peak (Calif., Tuolumne Co.) \kōō´ nə\. The name means 'fire' in several Numic languges of eastern Calif. (Gudde 1998); cf. Shoshoni *kunna* (Dayley 1989), Kawaiisu *kuna* (Zygmond et al. 1991), and Chemehuevi /kuna/ (Press 1979). The Idaho placename **Kuna** (Ada Co.) \kyōō´ nə\. may be from Shoshoni *kuna* 'fire, firewood' (Miller 1972; Crum and Dayley 1993).

KUNARAK Creek (Alaska, Meade River D-4). The Iñupiaq (Eskimo) name was reported in 1950 (Orth 1967).

KUNA River (Alaska, Howard Pass D-3) \kōō´ nə\. From Iñupiaq (Eskimo) *kaŋuq* 'snow goose' (Orth 1967; Webster and Zibell 1970); see **Kungok River,** below.

KUNAYOSH Creek (Alaska, Yakutat B-5). The Tlingit name was reported in 1901 (Orth 1967).

KUNCANOWET Hills (N.H., Hillsborough Co.) \kung kə nō´ wət\. Probably contains Abenaki (Algonquian) *gweni-gano,* lit. 'long portage' (Day 1994–95).

KUNGEALORUK Creek (Alaska, Kotzebue B-4). The Iñupiaq (Eskimo) name was reported in 1950 (Orth 1967).

KUNGIAKROK Creek (Alaska, Baird Mountains D-6). The Iñupiaq (Eskimo) name is *kaŋiġaksraq* 'something for a corral' (L. Kaplan p.c.).

KUNGKAKA Lakes (Alaska, Hughes B-1). The Koyukon (Athabaskan) name is of unclear derivation (Orth 1967).

KUNGOK River (Alaska, Wainwright B-2). From Iñupiaq (Eskimo) *kaŋuq* 'snow goose' (Orth 1967; Webster and Zibell 1970); see **Kuna River,** above.

KUNGSUGRUG River (Alaska, Selawik C-3). The Iñupiaq (Eskimo) name was reported in 1955 (Orth 1967).

KUNK Creek (Alaska, Petersburg B-2). The Tlingit placename was reported in 1901 (Orth 1967).

KUN River (Alaska, Hooper Bay D-2). The Yupik (Eskimo) name was reported in 1870 (Orth 1967).

KUNSINIALI Point (Alaska, Naknek C-3). The Yupik (Eskimo) name was reported in 1952 (Orth 1967).

KUNUK Creek (Alaska, Point Hope A-2). The Iñupiaq (Eskimo) name is perhaps *quŋuq* 'grave' (L. Kaplan p.c.).

KUNYANAK Creek (Alaska, Ambler River D-5). The Iñupiaq (Eskimo) name was reported in 1956 (Orth 1967).

KUPARUK River (Alaska, Beechey Point B-4). The Iñupiaq (Eskimo) name is perhaps *kuukpaġruk* 'big river' (L. Kaplan p.c.).

KUPIGRUAK Channel (Alaska, Harrison Bay B-1). The Iñupiak (Eskimo) name, reported in 1951, has also been written as <Kugpakruaq> 'big old river' (Orth 1967); cf. *kuuk* 'river', *-(q)pak* 'big' (MacLean 1980). Probably related Alaska placenemes include **Kobuk** (Shungnak D-2), **Kogru River** (Harrison Bay C-4), **Koyuk** (Norton Bay D-5), **Kurgorak Bay** (Barrow A-2), **Kuruk Creek** (Misheguk Mt. B-5), and **Kuzitrin River** (Teller A-1).

KUPK (Ariz., Pima Co.) \kōōpk\. From O'odham (Piman) *ku:pĭk* 'dam, dike' (Granger 1983; J. Hill p.c.).

KUPLURUAK Point (Alaska, Wainwright B-2). The Iñupiaq (Eskimo) name is *kuvluġruaq* 'big old thumb' (L. Kaplan p.c.).

KUPUK Creek (Alaska, Wiseman D-1). Named for an Iñupiaq (Eskimo) resident (Orth 1967).

KUPUNKAMINT Mountain (Mont., Glacier Co.). Said to be from Kootenai <k'upum'qamik> 'shakes himself', originally the name of Double Mt. (Holterman 1985).

KURGORAK Bay (Alaska, Barrow A-2). Probably from Iñupiaq (Eskimo) *kuuġuuraq* 'creek' (Orth 1967; Webster and Zibell 1970); see **Kuruk Creek** (Alaska, Misheguk Mt. B-5) below.

KUROPAK Creek (Alaska, Point Hope A-1). The Iñupiaq (Eskimo) name was reported in 1962, as "alluding to a big valley hidden by a narrow mouth" (Orth 1967).

KURUK Creek (Alaska, Misheguk Mt. B-5). The Iñupiaq (Eskimo) name was reported in 1955 (Orth 1967); cf. *kuuġuq* 'tributary river', from *kuuk* 'river' (Webster and Zibell 1970). Probably related Alaska placenames include **Kobuk** (Shungnak D-2), **Kogru River** (Harrison Bay C-4), **Koyuk** (Norton Bay D-5), **Kupigruak Channel** (Harrison Bay B-1), and **Kurgorak Bay** (Barrow A-2).

KURUPA River (Alaska, Ikpikpuk River A-4). The Iñupiaq (Eskimo) name may be *kuruqaq* 'pintail duck' (L. Kaplan p.c.).

KUSA (Okla., Okmulgee Co.) \ko͞o´ sə, kyo͞o´ sə\. Probably from Choctaw *kǫshak* 'cane (the plant)' (Read 1984, P. Munro p.c.). Related placenames include **Coosa** (La., Concordia Par.), **Coosha** (Miss., Lauderdale Co.), and **Coosawhatchie** (S.C., Jasper Co.).

KUSHAQUA Lake (N.Y., Franklin Co.) \ko͝osh´ ə kwä, kush´ ə kwä\. Perhaps from an Iroquoian word <gaw-she-gweh> 'spear' (Beauchamp 1907). Probably related is **Kushequa** (Pa., McKean Co.).

KUSHLA (Ala., Mobile Co.) \ko͞osh´ lə\. Perhaps from Choctaw (Muskogean) *kųshak* 'reed, cane', but of unclear derivation (Read 1984).

KUSHNEAHIN Creek (Alaska, Petersburg B-5). The Tlingit name was reported in 1901 (Orth 1967); cf. *héen* [hí:n] 'river' (Davis and Leer 1976).

KUSHTAKA Lake (Alaska, Cordova B-1). Perhaps from Eyak *kushdaqaa*.

KUSILVAK Mountains (Alaska, Kwiguk A-6). The Yupik (Eskimo) name was reported in 1870 (Orth 1967).

KUSIM Hill (Calif., Plumas Co.) \kə sim´\. From Maidu /k'ɨsím/ 'ridge' (nominative case), with the stem /k'ɨs/ 'ridge' (W. Shipley p.c.). The name was made official by the BGN in 1999.

KUSKOKUAK Slough (Alaska, Bethel D-7) The Iñupiaq (Eskimo) name was reported in 1949 (Orth 1967).

KUSKOKWAK Creek (Alaska, Baird Inlet A-1). From Yupik (Eskimo) *kusquqvak*, the name of the **Kuskokwim River**, perhaps meaning 'a small thing with a big flow' (Orth 1967; Jacobson 1984). A related placename is **Kuskovak** (Alaska, Baird Inlet A-2).

KUSKOKWIM River (Alaska, Baird Inlet A-1) \kus´ kō kwim\. Recorded by a Russian navigator in 1826 as <Kuskokvim>; from Yupik (Eskimo) *kusquqviim* 'Kuskokwim river' (relative case form; Jacobson 1984). The term **Upper Kuskokwim** is now often used for the Athabaskan people and language native to the upper course of the river; they are otherwise called **Kolchan;** see above. The lower course of the river is occupied by Eskimo peoples.

KUSKOVAK (Alaska, Baird Inlet A-2) \kus´ kō vak\. The name is related to **Kuskokwak Creek** (Baird Inlet A-1); see above.

KUSKULANA River (Alaska, Valdez B-1) \kus kə lī´ nə\. From Ahtna (Athabaskan) *gguus kulaen na'* 'celery-exists stream' (Kari 1983:7).

KUSLINA Creek (Alaska, Valdez C-2) \kus lē´ nə\. From the Ahtna (Athabaskan) placename *skostle na'*, with *na'* 'stream' (J. Kari p.c.).

KUSSAN Point (Alaska, Craig D-4) The name, probably Tlingit, was recorded in 1949 (Orth 1967).

KUSSHI Creek (Wash., Klickitat Co.). Sahaptin /k'usiyáy/ 'horse', from /k'úsi/ 'horse' and /-yáy/ 'personifier, honorific' (D. Kinkade p.c.).

KUSSU Island (Alaska, Craig D-4) The name, probably from Tlingit, was published in 1964 (Orth 1967).

KUSTATAN (Alaska, Kenai C-5) \kus´ tə tan, kus´ kə tan\. From Dena'ina (Athabaskan) *qezdegnen* 'point of land' (Kari and Kari 1982:28).

KUSUMPE Pond (N.H., Carroll Co.) \kə sum´ pē\. Perhaps from Abenaki (Algonquian), 'choked-up pond' (Huden 1962).

KUTARLAK Creek (Alaska, Ambler River B-1). The Iñupiaq (Eskimo) name, said to mean 'big drop', was recorded in 1956 (Orth 1967).

KUTCHAURAK Creek (Alaska, Howard Pass C-1). The Iñupiaq (Eskimo) name was reported in 1949 (Orth 1967).

KUTCHIK River (Alaska, Umiat B-3). From Iñupiaq (Eskimo) *kutchik* 'hip bone' (Orth 1967; Webster and Zibell 1970).

KUTCHIN \ko͞o chin\. This name for a people and language of central Alaska, of the Athabaskan linguistic family, is derived from /g^{W}ič'in/ 'people of . . .', used along with Native American placenames (*HNAI* 6:530). The practical orthography **Gwich'in** is now preferred for writing the name of the language.

KUTCHUMA Island (Alaska, Sitka A-4). The name, probably from Tlingit, was reported in 1852 (Orth 1967).

KUTEGI Point (Alaska, Craig D-4) The Native American name, probably Tlingit, was published in 1964 (Orth 1967).

KUTENAI \ko͞o´ tə nē, ko͞o´ tə nā\. The name of an Indian people of Idaho, Mont., and adjacent Canada. In placenames the term is usually written as **Kootenay**; see above.

KUTKAN Island (Alaska, Sitka A-4). The Indian term, probably Tlingit, was reported in 1883 (Orth 1967).

KUTLAKU Creek (Alaska, Port Alexander C-1). The Tlingit name was reported in 1900 (Orth 1967).

KUTMUKNUK Channel (Alaska, Black C-1) The Yupik (Eskimo) name was reported in 1898 (Orth 1967).

KUTNA Creek (Alaska, Tyonek D-3) \kut´ nə\. From Dena'ina (Athabaskan) *k'etnu* 'creek' (Kari and Fall 1987:110).

KUTOKBUNA Lake (Alaska, Lime Hills B-7). The Dena'ina (Athabaskan) name is *qedeq vena* 'upper lake' (J. Kari p.c.).

KUTTAK River (Alaska, Hooper Bay C-2). The Yupik (Eskimo) name was reported in 1952 (Orth 1967).

KUTTAWA (Ky., Lyon Co.) \kə tä´ wə\. Probably from Chickasaw (Muskogean) *kat(i) aa-waa'* 'where honey-locusts grow', containing *kati* 'honey-locust tree', *aa-* 'place', and *waa* 'grow' (P. Munro p.c.); or perhaps from a Cherokee (Iroquoian) placename <kitu'hwa, kettoowah, kittowa> (etc.) (J. Dyson).

KUTUKHUN River (Alaska, Baird Inlet C-2). The Yupik (Eskimo) name was reported in 1949 (Orth 1967).

KUTUK River (Alaska, Survey Pass C-2). The Iñupiaq (Eskimo) name was reported in 1886 as <Koo-too-ark> (Orth 1967).

KUTZKATNA Creek (Alaska, Anchorage D-3). The Dena'ina (Athabaskan) name, said to mean 'canyon river', was reported in 1932 (Orth 1967).

KUVIAK Lake (Alaska, Kenai D-2). The name, perhaps from Alutiiq (Eskimo), was officially assigned in 1963 (Orth 1967).

KUVIROK Lake (Alaska, Point Lay C-1). The Iñupiaq (Eskimo) name was published in 1955 (Orth 1967).

KUVLOMIUT (Alaska, Nunivak Is. B-3). The Yupik (Eskimo) name was reported in 1932 (Orth 1967); the ending *-miut* means 'people'.

KUVRITOVIK Entrance (Alaska, Barter Is. A-5). The Iñupiaq (Eskimo) name was reported in 1952 (Orth 1967).

KUYANAK Bay (Alaska, Meade River D-1). The Iñupiaq (Eskimo) name may be *quyanaq* 'thanks!' (L. Kaplan p.c.).

KUYUKTUVUK Creek (Alaska, Chandalar D-6). The Iñupiaq (Eskimo) name was reported in 1939 (Orth 1967).

KUYUKUTUK (Alaska, Kwiguk A-1). The Yupik (Eskimo) name was reported in 1948 (Orth 1967).

KUYUNGSIK River (Alaska, Hooper Bay B-1). The Yupik (Eskimo) name was reported in 1949 (Orth 1967).

KUYUYUKAK Cape (Alaska, Sutwik Is. D-3). The Alutiiq (Eskimo) name was reported in 1827 (Orth 1967).

KUZITRIN River (Alaska, Teller A-1). From Iñupiaq (Eskimo) *kurritqiun* 'something that was made into a river again', from *kuuk* 'river', *-li-* 'make', *-tqin-* 'again', *-un* 'nominal, instrumental' (L. Kaplan p.c.). Probably related Alaska placenames include **Kobuk** (Shungnak D-2), **Kogru River** (Harrison Bay C-4), and **Koyuk** (Norton Bay D-5), as well as derivatives from Yupik (Eskimo) *kuik* 'river', such as **Kookukluk Creek** (Hagemeister Is. D-5).

KVICHAK (Alaska, Naknek D-3) \kwē´ jak, kvē´ chak\. The Yupik (Eskimo) name was published in 1898 (Orth 1967).

KVICHAVAK River (Alaska, Marshall A-1). The Yupik (Eskimo) name was reported in 1879 as <Kivvichavak> (Orth 1967).

KVIGATLUK (Alaska, Baird Inlet D-2). The Yupik (Eskimo) name was reported in 1879 as <Kvigathlok> (Orth 1967).

KWAATZ Point (Wash., Pierce Co.) \kwäts\. From Lushootseed (Salishan) \sq^{W}ácqs\, said to mean 'crooked promontory', probably containing /-qs/ 'nose, point' (D. Kinkade p.c.).

KWADDIS, Lake (Wash., Skamania Co.) \kwä´ dis\. From Chinook Jargon <kwad´dis, kwa´h-nice> [kwádis, kwánis] 'whale', taken from a Salishan language; cf. Southern Lushootseed [q^{W}ə́dis], Straits Salish [q^{W}ə́nəs] (D. Kinkade p.c.).

KWAGUNT Creek (Ariz., Coconino Co.). Named for a Southern Paiute (Numic) resident in the nineteenth century (Brian 1992).

KWAIN Bay (Alaska, Ketchikan A-5). The name, probably Tlingit, was reported as <Khwain> in 1904 (Orth 1967).

KWA'KIN'A Historic Site (N.Mex., McKinley Co.). The site of a Zuni village occupied at the time of European contact in 1540 (Ferguson and Hart 1985).

KWASTIYUKWA Ruin (N.Mex., Sandoval Co.) \kwä sē yo͞o´ kwä\. From Jemez (Tanoan) /kwaantiyukwa/ 'pine cicada place', containing /kwaan/ 'ponderosa pine', /tiyu/ 'cicada', and /-kwa/ 'place' (Y. Yumitani p.c.).

KWATAHEIN Creek (Alaska, Port Alexander C-1). The Tlingit name was reported in 1900 as meaning 'trout river' (Orth 1967); cf. *x̱'wáat'* 'trout', *héen* 'river' (Davis and Leer 1976).

KWATI Point (Alaska, Craig D-4). The name, probably Tlingit, was published in 1964 (Orth 1967).

KWECHARAK River (Alaska, Hooper Bay C-2). The Yupik (Eskimo) name was reported in 1951 (Orth 1967).

KWEI KWEI Canyon (Wash., Ferry Co.). From the Okanagan (Salishan) placename [k^{W}ík^{W}] (D. Kinkade p.c.).

KWEMELUK Pass (Alaska, Kwiguk B-6). The Yupik (Eskimo) name was recorded as <Kuimla> in 1863 (Orth 1967).

KWEO Butte (Ore., Deschutes Co.) \kwā´ ō\. From Chinook Jargon <kweo-kweo> [kwíok-wio] 'ring, circle', taken from Lower Chinook <t'kwéo-kweo> 'ring' (D. Kinkade p.c.).

KWETHLUK (Alaska, Bethel D-7) \kweth´luk\. From the Yupik (Eskimo) placename *kuiggluk*, derived from *kuik* 'river' (Orth 1967; Jacobson 1984).

KWICHLOWAK Pass (Alaska, St. Michael A-4). The Yupik (Eskimo) name is said to mean 'good stream' (Orth 1967); cf. *kuik* 'river'.

KWIGILLINGOK (Alaska, Kuskokwim Bay D-4) \kwi gil´ing gok, kwi gil´ing guk\. From the Yupik (Eskimo) placename *kuigilnguq,* lit. 'one without a river', from *kuik* 'river' (Jacobson 1984).

KWIGORLAK (Alaska, Marshall D-4). The Yupik (Eskimo) name was reported in 1937 (Orth 1967).

KWIGUK (Alaska, Kwiguk D-6) \kwēē guk\. From Yupik (Eskimo) *kuiguk,* lit. 'big river', from *kuik* 'river' (Orth 1967; Jacobson 1984).

KWIKAK (Alaska, Black B-1). The Yupik (Eskimo) name was reported in 1898 (Orth 1967).

KWIKLOAKLOK (Alaska, Kwiguk A-3). The Yupik (Eskimo) name was reported in 1899 (Orth 1967).

KWIKLOKCHUN Channel (Alaska, Kwiguk C-6). The Yupik (Eskimo) name was reported in 1952 as meaning 'fish saltry' (Orth 1967).

KWIKLUAK (Alaska, Kwiguk C-6). The Yupik (Eskimo) name was reported as <Kvikhlyuak> in 1844, said to mean 'crooked, meandering' (Orth 1967).

KWIKOKTUK Pass (Alaska, Kwiguk C-6). The Yupik (Eskimo) name, said to mean 'blind', was reported in 1949 (Orth 1967).

KWIKPAK (Alaska, St. Michael A-5) \kwik´pak\. The Yupik (Eskimo) name is *kuigpak* 'big river' (L. Kaplan p.c.).

KWIKPAKAK Slough (Alaska, Kwiguk D-5). The Yupik (Eskimo) name was reported in 1899 (Orth 1967).

KWIKTALIK Mountain (Alaska, Solomon B-2). The Iñupiaq (Eskimo) name was reported in 1900 (Orth 1967).

KWILI YALA: A:CHI (N.Mex., Cibola Co.). The site of a Zuni War God shrine, perhaps containing /yala-/ 'mountain' (Ferguson and Hart 1985).

KWIMLILTHLA Slough (Alaska, Kwiguk C-5). The Yupik (Eskimo) name was reported in 1899 as <kwimlithkok> 'river without place or camp' (Orth 1967).

KWINIUK River (Alaska, Solomon C-1). The Iñupiaq (Eskimo) name was reported as <Quinnehuk> in 1900 (Orth 1967).

KWINNUM Butte (Ore., Deschutes Co.) \kwin´ əm\. Chinook Jargon <kw'in´num> [kwĭnəm] 'five', from Lower Chinook [qwínəm] 'five'; so named by the U.S. Forest Service because this was the fifth butte in a series (McArthur 1992; D. Kinkade p.c.).

KWITTEVUNKUD Lake (Alaska, Christian B-2). The Gwich'in (Athabaskan) name is *gwit'ee venk'at* 'lake upon underneath area' (J. Kari p.c.).

KWOLH Butte (Ore., Deschutes Co.) \kwōl\. Chinook Jargon <kwal'h> 'aunt', from Lower Chehalis (Salishan) /k^{W}áɬ/ 'aunt' (D. Kinkade p.c.).

KWONEESUM (Wash., Skamania Co.). Chinook Jargon *kwah´-ne-sum* [kwánəsəm, kwánsəm] 'always, forever, often', from Lower Chinook [gwánsəm] 'always' (D. Kinkade p.c.).

K'YA:DECHIA'A (N.Mex., Cibola Co.). The Zuni name may refer to 'smelly water', from /k'a/ 'water' and /teči/ 'to have a smell, be rotten' (Ferguson and Hart 1985; Newman 1958).

KYAGAMIUT (Alaska, Cape Mendenhall D-4). The Yupik (Eskimo) name was reported in 1942 (Orth 1967).

KYAKI:MA Historic Site (N.Mex., Cibola Co.). An ancestral site in the Zuni migration narrative (Ferguson and Hart 1985).

KYAMA:KYA (N.Mex., Cibola Co.). The Zuni site is the home of the Kamakwe kachina (Ferguson and Hart 1985).

KYANA (Ind., Dubois Co.) \kī an´ ə\. From the endings of **Kentucky** and **Indiana**.

K'YANA:WA (N.Mex., Cibola Co.). The Zuni placename may contain /k'a/ 'water' (Ferguson and Hart 1985; Newman 1958).

KYANE:LU YALA:WE (N.Mex., San Juan Co.). The Zuni name probably means 'sheep mountains', with /kane:lu/ 'sheep' (from Spanish *carnero*) and /yala-we/ 'mountains' (Ferguson and Hart1985; Newman 1958).

K'YA:TS'I'K'YAN'A (N.Mex., Cibola Co.). The Zuni placename may contain /k'a/ 'water' (Ferguson and Hart 1985; Newman 1958).

KYDAKA Point (Wash., Clallam Co.). Perhaps from Clallam (Salishan); the derivation is unclear (Hitchman 1985).

KYDIKABBIT (Wash., Clallam Co.). From the Makah (Nootkan) placename /q'idiq'abit/ (W. Jacobsen p.c.).

KYIKHGYIT, Lake (Alaska, Hughes B-4). The Koyukon (Athabaskan) name was recorded in 1956 as <k'yikh-g'yi-it> 'among the birch trees' (Orth 1967); cf. *kk'eeyh* [q'i:x̣] 'birch' (Jetté and Jones 2000).

KYKOTSMOVI (Ariz., Navajo Co.) \ki kots´ mō vē, kyə kots´ mō vē, kī kots mō´ vē\. Hopi (Uto-Aztecan) *kiqötsmovi* 'place of hills made of ruins', from *kiqö-, kiiqö* 'ruin', *-tsmo, tsomo* 'hill', *-vi* 'place' (K. Hill p.c.). Also written as **Kyakotsmovi.** The place is also known locally as **K-Town**.

KYMULGA (Ala., Talladega Co.) \kī mul´ gə\. From Muskogee, meaning 'all the mulberries'; cf. *kē* /kí:/ 'mulberry', *omvlkv* /omálka/ 'all' (Read 1984; Martin and Mauldin 2000).

KYOTE (Tex., Atascosa Co.) \kī´ ōt\. Probably from the same source as **Coyote** (see above), used in many other placenames and referring to the animal.

L

LABISH (Ore., Marion Co.) \lə bish\. From Michif *la bish* 'elk', from French *la biche* 'the doe' (D. Kinkade p.c.). Michif is a language composed of Algonquian and French elements, spoken by the *métis,* an ethnically and culturally mixed Indian-French community of Canada and adjacent areas of the United States.

LACAMAS (Wash., Lewis Co.) \lə kam´ əs\. From Chinook Jargon and/or local French *la camas,* name of a plant with an edible bulb. The term also occurs in Chinook Jargon as <kam´-ass> [kámas] and has entered English as **Camas,** also found as a placename. The ultimate source of the name is probably Nez Perce (Sahaptian) /qém'es/ 'camas' (D. Kinkade p.c.). A related form is **Lackamas Creek** (Wash., Clark).

LAC COURTE OREILLES (Wis., Sawyer Co.) \lak ko͞o´ tə rā\. French for 'cut-ears lake', a name given in the seventeenth century to a group of Ottawa (Algonquian) Indians who had supposedly cut the rims off their ears (Vogel 1991). See **Courte Oreilles** above.

LAC DU FLAMBEAU (Wis., Vilas Co.) \lak də flam´ bō\. The French term for 'lake of the torch' refers to the Indian practice of using pine torches for spear-fishing in lakes at night. The term translates Ojibwa <Wauswagaming> 'at the lake of torches' (Vogel 1991); cf. *waaswaagan* 'torch' (Nichols and Nyholm 1995). Related terms are **Flambeau River** (Wis., Iron Co.) as well as **Torch Lake** (Wis., Vilas Co.) and **Torch River** (Mich., Kalkaska Co.).

LACHBUNA Lake (Alaska, Lake Clark B-3) \läch bo͞o´ nə\. The Dena'ina (Athabaskan) name is *nl'ałi vena* '(ducks) are-swimming lake' (J. Kari p.c.).

LACKAMAS Creek (Wash., Clark Co.) \lak´ ə məs\. The name is related to **Lacamas** (Wash., Lewis Co.); see above.

LACKAWACK (N.Y., Ulster Co.) \lak´ ə wak\. From the Delaware (Algonquian) term <lechauwak> 'division, separation' (Ruttenber 1906; Brinton and Anthony 1888); cf. Munsee Delaware *lxáweew* 'to be forked' (O'Meara 1996). Related placenames are **Lackawanna County** (Pa.) and **Lehigh** (Pa., Lackawanna Co.).

LACKAWANNA County (Pa.) \lak ə wä´ nə\. Perhaps from Delaware (Algonquian) *lèkaohane* 'sandy stream' (Kraft and Kraft 1985); cf. Munsee Delaware *léekuw* 'sand'. Or perhaps from

<lechauhanne> 'fork of a river' (Donehoo 1928; Brinton and Anthony 1888); cf. [lɛxaohánɛk] 'forks of the river' (Masthay 1991:56). The placename **Lackawanna** is found in several other states (e.g., N.Y., Erie Co.; N.J., Sussex Co.; and Fla., Duval Co.) A related placename is **Lackawannock Creek** (Pa., Mercer Co.). Other probably related placenames include **Lackawack** (N.Y., Ulster Co.), **Lackawaxen** (Pa., Pike Co.), and **Lehigh** (Pa., Lackawanna Co.).

LACKAWAXEN (Pa., Pike Co.) \lak ə wak´ sən\. From Delaware (Algonquian) <lechauwak> 'division, separation' (Ruttenber 1906; Brinton and Anthony 1888); probably related to **Lackawack** (N.Y., Ulster Co.), **Lackawanna County** (Pa.) and **Lehigh** (Pa., Lackawanna Co.).

LACKEMUTE (Ore., Polk Co.) \lak´ə myōōt\. A variant writing of **Luckiamute River**; see below.

LACOOCHEE (Fla., Pasco Co.) \lə kōō´ chē\. Probably a shortened form of **Withlacoochee River** (Read 1934), which represents Muskogee *ue-rakkuce* /oy-ɬakk-očí, wi:-/ 'small river', from *ue-rakko* /oy-ɬákko/ 'river' plus *-uce* /-oči/ 'small' (Martin and Mauldin 2000).

LACOTA (Mich., Van Buren Co.) \lə kō´ tə\. From the same source as **Lakota,** referring to a branch of the Dakotan (Siouan) peoples (Vogel 1986).

LAC QUI PARLE County (Minn.) \lak kwi pär´ əl\. The French phrase, meaning 'lake that speaks', was translated from Dakota (Siouan) <mde iyedan> (Upham 2001); cf. *mde* 'lake', *eyá* 'to say' (Williamson 1902).

LACROSSE \lə krôs\. The name of the game is from French *la crosse* 'the hooked stick' (as used in games), but the game itself was borrowed from Indians of Canada and the upper Midwest (Vogel 1991); cf. Ojibwa (Algonquian) *baaga'adowe* 'to play lacrosse' (Nichols and Nyholm 1995). As a placename, spelled both **Lacrosse** and **La Crosse,** the term occurs in several states: for example, in **La Crosse County** (Wis.), as well as in Mich. (Iron Co.) and Ill. (Hancock Co.).

LAC VIEUX DESERT (Mich., Gogebic Co.). The French phrase means 'lake [of the] old deserted-place', a translation of Ojibwa (Algonquian) <Ketekitiganing> 'old field place', because Indians had earlier planted crops here (Vogel 1991); cf. *gete-* 'old', *gitigaan* 'field' (Nichols and Nyholm 1995).

LADIGA (Ala., Calhoun Co.) \lə dī´ gə\. Possibly from the name of a Muskogee leader, also written as <Ledagie>, perhaps the word for 'runner' (Read 1984); cf. *lētkv* /lí:tka/ 'runner' (Martin and Mauldin 2000).

LADY WHITE Trail (Ariz., Apache Co.). A translation of Navajo (Athabaskan) *asdzą́ą́ łigaaí habitiin* 'Lady White's trail-up-out', named for a Navajo woman called *asdzą́ą́ łigaaí* 'woman who is white' (Linford 2000).

LA FONTAINE (Ind., Wabash Co.) \lä foun´ tən\. Named for Francis La Fontaine, a Miami/Illinois (Algonquian) leader of the early nineteenth century (McPherson 1993). The French surname means 'the fountain'.

LA FRAMBOISE Woods (Ill., Cook Co.) Named for a nineteenth-century Potawatomi (Algonquian) resident, Claude La Framboise (Vogel 1963). The French surname means 'the raspberry'.

LAGRO (Ind., Wabash Co.) \lā´ grō\. The name represents French *le gros* 'the big one, the fat one', a nickname given to a Miami/Illinois (Algonquian) leader of the early nineteenth century (McPherson 1993); the Native American form is /meehcikilita/ 'one who is big' (M. McCafferty p.c.).

LAHAWAY Creek (N.J., Monmouth Co.). Probably from Delaware (Algonquian), perhaps related to the placenames **Lackawack** or **Rockaway Beach,** which in turn may be linked to <lekau> 'sand, gravel' or to <lechauwak> 'division, separation' (Becker 1964; Brinton and Anthony 1888); cf. Munsee Delaware *léekuw* 'sand' (O'Meara 1996).

LAHOMA (Okla., Garfield Co.) \lə hō´ mə\. A shortening of **Oklahoma,** from Choctaw (Muskogean), meaning 'red people' (Shirk 1974).

LA JOLLA (Calif., San Diego Co.) \lə hoi´ ə\. Ostensibly from Spanish *la hoya,* 'the hollow place, the hole', spelled to reflect a nonstandard Spanish pronunciation resembling [lä hō´ yä]. An alternative etymology, however, is from Diegueño (Yuman) *mat-ku-laahuuy* 'place that has holes or caves', related to *llehup* 'hole' (Gudde 1998).

LAKA (Ore., Umatilla Co.) \lä´ kə\. From Nez Perce (Sahaptian) /lá:qa/ 'ponderosa pine' (Aoki 1994).

LAKHOTA \lə khō´ tə\. This spelling is often used for the name of a Dakotan language (of the Siouan family), otherwise called **Lakota** (see below) or Teton Sioux.

LAKI, Mount (Ore., Klamath Co.) \lä´ kē\. From Klamath /laGi/ 'rich, powerful, chief' (Barker 1963).

LAKINA River (Alaska, McCarthy B-7) \lə kī´ nə\. From Ahtna (Athabaskan) *c'elaxi na'*, lit. 'spawning stream', containing *na'* 'stream' (Kari 1983:9).

LAKONTA (Iowa, Mahaska Co.) \lə kon´ tə\. Probably a mistranscription of **Lakota** (see below), the name of a Siouan group (Vogel 1983).

LAKOTA \lə kō´ tə\. The name refers to western groups of the Dakotan (Siouan) language family, in particular to the Teton people of the northern Plains. The Native American name is *lakhóta,* corresponding to *dakhóta* of related groups to the east; the term has been said to mean 'united, allied' (*HNAI* 13:750). As a placename, **Lakota** occurs in several states (e.g., S.Dak., Custer Co.; and Iowa, Kossuth Co.). The related placename **Lacota** is found in Mich. (Van Buren Co.).

LAKSO Slough (Alaska, Nulato B-5). The Koyukon (Athabaskan) name was reported in 1935 (Orth 1967).

LAMINGTON (N.J., Somerset Co.). Earlier written <Allametunk>, the name is probably from Delaware (Algonquian), perhaps related to <allami> 'in there', <allamawunke> 'under the hill' (Becker 1964, Brinton and Anthony 1888); cf. Munsee Delaware *aláami* 'inside' (O'Meara 1996).

LAMOILLE County (Vt.) \lə moil´\. Probably a respelling of French *la moelle* 'the marrow'; corresponds to the Western Abenaki (Algonquian) placename *wíntegók,* lit. 'at marrow river', from *win* 'marrow', *-tegw* 'river', *-ok* 'place' (Day 1981:158).

LANAHASSEE Creek (Ga., Marion Co.) \lan ə has´ ē\. Perhaps from Muskogee /oy-la:n-ahá:ssi/ 'water-yellow-old' (Read 1949–50:130); cf. *uewv* /óy(wa)/ 'water', *lanē* /lá:ni:/ 'green, yellow, brown', and *vhassē* /ahá:ssi:/ 'rancid, stale' (Martin and Mauldin 2000).

LANCE Creek (S.Dak., Stanley Co.). Said to have been named by white settlers who discovered an Indian lance or spear along the stream (Sneve 1973).

LANGLADE (Wis., Langlade Co.) \lang´ lād\. Named for Charles Michel de Langlade, a prominent figure in early Wis. history, born in 1729 of a French father and an Ottawa (Algonquian) mother (Vogel 1991).

LANKA OKA (Ala., Shelby Co.) \lang kə ō´ kə\. Perhaps a coinage intended to mean 'yellow water', based on Choctaw *laknah* 'yellow, brown' and *oka* 'water' (P. Munro p.c.).

L'ANSE (Mich., Baraga Co.) \läns, lans\. French for 'the handle; (in geography) the cove', perhaps corresponding to an Ojibwa (Algonquian) name (Vogel 1986).

LAPEER County (Mich.) \lä pēr´\. From French *rivière la pierre* 'stone river', referring to the **Flint River**. Both the French and the English names are based on Ojibwa (Algonquian) <Biwânag sibi> 'flint river' (Vogel 1986); cf. *biiwaanag* (Nichols and Nyholm 1995).

LAPOEL Point (Wash., Clallam Co.) \lä pō el´\. Chinook Jargon <la-po-el´, la poo´-el> [lapuɛ́l, lapoɛ́l] 'frying pan', from French *la poêle* 'frying pan' (D. Kinkade p.c.).

LAPOMKEAG Lake (Maine, Penobscot Co.). Said to be from Abenaki (Algonquian), meaning 'place of rocks', with the French article *la* (Rutherford 1970).

LAPPATUBBY Creek (Miss., Union Co.) \lap ə tub´ ē\. A Choctaw (Muskogean) personal name, meaning 'buck killer', from *lapitta* 'buck, male deer' and *abi* 'to kill' (Seale 1939; P. Munro p.c.).

LA PUSH (Wash., Clallam Co.) \lə po͞osh´\. Chinook Jargon <la-bush, la push> [lapúš, labúš] 'mouth, mouth of a river', from French *la bouche* 'mouth' (Hitchman 1985; D. Kinkade p.c.).

LAPWAI Creek (Idaho, Nez Perce Co.) \lap´ wā\. From Nez Perce (Sahaptian) /lé:pwey/, perhaps meaning 'butterfly creek'; cf. /lé:pɬep/ 'butterfly', /wey/ 'creek' (Aoki 1994).

LASSIC, Mount (Calif., Trinity Co.) \las´ ik\. The name refers to an Athabaskan group, said to be named after <Lassik>, their last leader; however, the name is probably not Athabaskan; in the neighboring Wintu language /lasik/ means 'bag' (Gudde 1998).

LATAH County (Idaho) \lā´ tä\. From a Nez Perce (Sahaptian) placename /lá:taw/ (Aoki 1994). The name **Latah** also occurs in Wash. (Spokane Co.).

LATAX Rocks (Alaska, Afognak C-2). Perhaps a garbling of Aleut *chngatux̂* 'sea otter' (Orth 1967; Bergsland 1994).

LATENACHE Bayou (La., Pointe Coupee Par.) \lat´ i nash\. The name was recorded earlier as <Atenache> and <Latania>. The origin may be Choctaw (Muskogean), but the derivation is not clear (Read 1927).

LA TOUTENA MARY Creek (Ore., Yamhill Co.). Named for an Indian woman, also known as "Toutney Mary" (McArthur 1992); cf. **Tututni,** the name of an Athabaskan group of southwestern Ore. (D. Kinkade).

LATUM Creek (Wash., Yakima Co.). From Sahaptin; cf. /ltat-/ 'down into' (Eugene Hunn p.c.).

LAUGHING WATER Creek (S.Dak., Custer Co.). Probably a translation from Lakhota (Siouan) *mniȟápi,* from *mni* 'water' and *iȟápi* 'to laugh' (Sneve 1973; Ingham 2001).

LAUGHING WHITEFISH River (Mich., Alger Co.). Said to be a translation from Ojibwa (Algonquian) <atikameg bapit> (Vogel 1986); cf. *adikameg* 'whitefish', *baapi* 'to laugh' (Nichols and Nyholm 1995).

LAUMECHEN Creek (Wash., Whatcom Co.). A written variant of **Liumchen Creek**; see below.

LEAF Mountain (Minn., Otter Tail Co.). Said to be adapted from Ojibwa (Algonquian) <Gaskibudgudjiwe> 'rustling leaf mountain' (Upham 2001).

LECHE-E Wash (Ariz., Coconino Co.) \lə chē´, lə chā´\. From Navajo (Athabaskan) *ɬíchíí* 'red' (Linford 2000).

LE CLAIRE (Iowa, Scott Co.) \lə klâr´\. For Antoine Le Claire, of French and Potawatomi (Algonquian) descent, born in the late eighteenth century; he was a founder of the city of Davenport (Vogel 1983).

LEELANAU County (Mich.) \lē´lə nô\. From *Leelinau,* the name of the Indian heroine in a story by the nineteenth-century writer Henry R. Schoolcraft; the word was probably Schoolcraft's invention (Vogel 1986).

LEFLORE County (Okla.) \lə flôr´\. Named for a family of mixed French and Choctaw (Muskogean) descent (Shirk 1974).

LEFT HAND Spring (Okla., Blaine Co.). Named for an Arapaho (Algonquian) leader who was called "Left Hand" in English (Shirk 1974); cf. Arapaho *nowó:θ* 'left side', *nihno:wô:θít* 'he was left-handed' (Salzmann 1983). The name is also rendered in English as **Niwot** and exists as a placename in Colo. (Boulder Co.).

LEHAMITE Creek (Calif., Mariposa Co.) \lə hä´ mi tē\. The Southern Sierra Miwok origin is *leeha'-mite* 'there are several syringa bushes', from *leeha* 'syringa, mock orange' (Gudde 1998).

LEHIGH (Pa., Lackawanna Co.) \lē´ hī\. The name comes from <Lecha> as written by German settlers, from Delaware (Algonquian) <Lechauweeki, Lechauwiechink, Lechauweing> 'forks of the river'; cf. [lɛxaohánɛk] 'forks of the river' (Masthay 1991:56), Munsee Delaware *lxáweew* 'to be forked' (O'Meara 1996). The name occurs as a transfer in several states (e.g., Iowa, Webster Co.; Ill., Kankakee Co.; and Mich., Gogegic Co.). The apparently related **Lehighton** (Pa., Carbon Co.) is probably from Delaware (Algonquian) <Lechauweting, Lechauwetank> 'at the forks' (Donehoo 1928). Other related placenames are **Lackawack** (N.Y., Ulster Co.), **Lackawanna County** (Pa.), and **Lackawaxen** (Pa., Pike Co.).

LEHUNUA Island (Alaska, Skagway A-2). The Tlingit name, also written as <Lehu-nuwu> and <Tlekuknuwu>, is said to mean 'red-ocher ford' (Orth 1967).

LELOO Lake (Ore., Douglas Co.) \lē´ lo͞o\. From Chinook Jargon <le-loo´> [ləlú] 'wolf', from French *le loup* 'the wolf' (D. Kinkade p.c.).

LEMAH (Wash., Kittitas Co.) \lē´ mä\. Chinook Jargon <limáh, la-mah> [limá, ləmá, líma] 'hand, finger, arm', from French *la main* 'the hand' (D. Kinkade p.c.).

LEMEVA (Ariz., Navajo Co.). Also written **Lemova** (BGN 1995); probably from Hopi (Uto-Aztecan) *lemova* 'hail water', from *lemo(wa)* 'hailstone' and *-va* 'water, spring' (K. Hill p.c.).

LEMISH Lake (Ore., Deschutes Co.) \lem´ ish\. From Klamath /lmeys/ 'thunder' (McArthur 1992; Barker 1963).

LEMITI Creek (Ore., Marion Co.) \lem´ i tī\. Chinook Jargon <la-món-ti, la-mó-ti> [ləmɪtí, lemɔntái] 'mountain', from French *la montagne* 'the mountain' or *les montagnes* 'the mountains' (McArthur 1992; D. Kinkade p.c.).

LEMOLO Lake (Ore., Douglas Co.) \lem´ ō lō, lē mō´ lō\. Chinook Jargon <le-mo´-lo> [lɛmólo] 'wild, untamed', from French *le marron* 'the untamed animal' or plural *les marrons* (McArthur 1992; D. Kinkade p.c.). The name **Lemolo** also occurs in Wash. (King Co.).

LEMOOSH Creek (Idaho, Benewah Co.) \lə mo͞osh\. Chinook Jargon for 'fly' or 'flies' (the insect), from French *la mouche,* plural *les mouches* (Boone 1988).

LENAPAH (Okla., Nowata Co.) \len´ ə pä\. From the same source as **Lenape,** the name of the Delaware (Algonquian) people (Shirk 1974).

LENAPE (Pa., Chester Co.) \len´ ə pē\. From the Unami Delaware (Algonquian) self-designation /ləná:p:e/ (etymologically /lən-/ 'ordinary, real, original' plus /-a:p:e/ 'person'). The term /lə̀ni-ləná:p:e/ 'real Lenape' also exists, but is rejected as redundant by modern speakers (*HNAI* 15:236). The placename **Lenape** also occurs in Kans. (Leavenworth Co.) and N.J. (Atlantic Co.). A related placename is **Lenni;** see below.

LENAWEE County (Mich.) \len´ ə wē, len´ ə wā\. From a Delaware or Shawnee (Algonquian) word for 'human being', perhaps from Shawnee *lenawe* (Vogel 1991; Pearson 1995). The name also occurs in other states (Wis., Bayfield Co.; Colo., Summit Co.

LENEXA (Kans., Johnson Co.) \lə nek´ sə\. Said to be the name of a Shawnee (Algonquian) woman, also written <Len-ag-see> (Rydjord 1968).

LENNA (Okla., McIntosh Co.) \len´ ə\. Named for Lenna Moore, a Muskogee resident (Shirk 1974).

LENNI (Pa., Delaware Co.) \len´ ē\. An abbreviation of Delaware (Algonquian) /lə̀ni-ləná:p:e/ 'real Lenape' (i.e., 'real Delaware people'); see **Lenape** above. A related placename is **Lenni-Lenape Island** (N.Y., Warren Co.).

LEOTA (Minn., Nobles Co.) \lē ō´ tə\. Said to be the name of the Indian heroine in a fictional work (Upham 2001).

LE SAUK Township (Minn., Stearns Co.) \lə sôk\. French for 'the Sauk', referring to an Algonquian people (Upham 2001); see **Sauk** below.

LESCHI Glacier (Wash., Skamania Co.) \lesh´ ī\. Said to have been named for a Nisqually (Salishan) leader (Hitchman 1985).

LESHARA (Neb., Saunders Co.) \lə shä´ rə\. Said to have been named for a Pawnee (Caddoan) leader, whose name was written more fully as <Petalesharo> (Perkey 1995).

LETOHATCHEE (Ala., Lowndes Co.) \lē tō hach´ ē\. Perhaps a Muskogee name meaning 'arrow wood stream' (Read 1984); cf. *rē* /ɬi:/ 'arrow', *eto* /itó/ 'wood', *hvcce* /háčči/ 'stream' (Martin and Mauldin 2000).

LIAKIK, Cape (Alaska, Kodiak A-5). Recorded in 1852 as <Lyakhik> (Orth 1967). From Aleut *lax* 'goose'; or from Yupik (Eskimo) *lagiq,* borrowed from Aleut (Bergsland 1994).

LIBBY (Ore., Coos Co.) \lib´ ē\. Named for Libby Tinilon, an Indian resident of the nineteenth century (McArthur 1992).

LICK. This term refers to a "salt lick" (i.e., a spring from which deer and other animals are able to drink salt water). It occurs in many placenames, often as the translation of a Native American term. Placenames containing **Lick** are especially common in the Ohio Valley (e.g., **Black Lick Creek** in Ky., Taylor Co.); in that area, names with *lick* are often loan translations from Algonquian languages of the area, especially Delaware (in which the word for 'lick' is <mahoning>) and Shawnee.

LIDA Township (Minn., Otter Tail Co.) \lī´ də\. Perhaps adapted from an Ojibwa (Algonquian) word for 'pelican', written as <Shada> in Longfellow's *Hiawatha* (Upham 2001); cf. Ojibwa *zhede* (Nichols and Nyholm 1995).

LIK Ridge (Alaska, De Long Mountains A-1). The Iñupiaq (Eskimo) name was made official by the BGN in 1990.

LILLIWAUP (Wash., Mason Co.) \lil´ ə wôp\. Twana (Salishan) /slələ́wap/ 'cove, inlet', from /s-/ 'nominalizer', diminutive reduplication, /lə́w-/ 'enter', and /-ap/ 'end' (D. Kinkade p.c.).

LIMA (Ohio, Allen Co.) \lī´ mə, lē´ mə\. From the city in Peru, derived through Spanish from Quechua *rimac.* The name occurs in several states (e.g. Ill., Adams Co.; N.Y., Livingston Co.; and Okla., Seminole Co.). The same Peruvian placename of course occurs in *lima* \lī´ mə\ *beans.*

LIMPY Creek (Ore., Douglas Co.). From the nickname of an Indian resident who walked with a halting gait (McArthur 1992).

LIPAN (Tex., Hood Co.) \li pan´, lī pan´\. Named for the Lipan (Apachean) people, an Indian group of Tex.; the name was earlier written as <Ipandes> (*HNAI* 13:951). The placename **Lipan** also occurs elsewhere (Ariz., Coconino Co.; Colo., Mesa Co.).

LIPLIP (Wash., Jefferson Co.). Chinook Jargon <liplip> [lĭplɪp] 'boil', from Chinookan [ləp] 'to boil' (Hitchman 1985; D. Kinkade p.c.).

LISES, Cape (Alaska, Adak C-1). Perhaps from Aleut *liisis* 'ways of coming in sight', from *lilix* 'to come into sight' (Bergsland 1994).

LISQUE Creek (Calif., Santa Barbara Co.) \lē´ skā\. Probably for a Spanish spelling <Lisgüey>, from the Ineseño (Chumashan) village name /aliswey/ 'in the tarweed' (Gudde 1998).

LITHKEALIK River (Alaska, Hooper Bay C-3). The Yupik (Eskimo) name was reported in 1951 (Orth 1967).

LITTLE (Okla., Seminole Co.). Named for Thomas Little, a Seminole (Muskogean) leader (Shirk 1974).

LITTLE BEAVER Creek (Pa., Beaver Co.). Perhaps a translation of Delaware (Algonquian) <tank-amochk-hanne> (Donehoo 1928); cf. Munsee Delaware *amóxkw* 'beaver' (O'Meara 1996). In many other placenames, *little* similarly refers to Native American names; thus **Little Crow Peak** (S.Dak., Lawrence Co.) was named for one of several Santee Dakota (Siouan) leaders who were called **Little Crow** in English (Sneve 1973). **Little Deer Creek** (Ind., Cass Co.) may correspond to Miami/Illinois (Algonquian) /apeehsia/ 'fawn' (McCafferty 2002). **Little Eagle** (S.Dak., Corson Co.) was named for a Lakhota (Siouan) leader (Sneve 1973).

Little Girls Point (Mich., Gogebic Co.) represents a possessive (**Girl's**) from a tradition that an Ojibwa (Algonquian) girl drowned at this place (Vogel 1986). **Little Robe Creek** (Okla., Dewey Co.) was named for a Cheyenne (Algonquian) leader (Shirk 1974); his Native American name was probably /tšeške'oomahe/, literally 'little-robed-one' (W. Leman p.c.). **Little Soldier Creek** (S.Dak., Corson Co.) is said to have been named for a Lakhota (Siouan) resident (Sneve 1973). **Little Thunder Flowage** (Wis., Jackson Co.) is derived from the name of a Winnebago (Siouan) leader of the nineteenth century (Vogel 1991); his Native American name was /wakąǰánįká/, containing /wakąǰą́/ 'thunder' and /-nįk/ 'little' (K. Miner p.c.). **Little Water** (N.Mex., San Juan Co.) is a translation of Navajo (Athabaskan) *tó'áłts'íísí* 'little water', from *tó* 'water' and *áłts'íísí* 'little, small' (A. Wilson p.c.).

LITUYA Bay (Alaska, Mount Fairweather C-5) \lə to͞o´ ə\. From Tlingit [łtu's], perhaps from [łıtu's] 'to-be-inside lake' (De Laguna 1972:93).

LIUMCHEN Creek (Wash., Whatcom Co.). Perhaps from Nooksack (Salishan) [layúmcən], related to Upriver Halkomelem [layúmθəl] 'water gushing out' (D. Kinkade p.c.). A variant is **Laumechen Creek.**

LIZARD Mound (Wis., Washington Co.). The name refers to a mound made in the shape of a lizard by prehistoric Indians (Vogel 1991).

LIZARD Spring (Ariz., Apache Co.). Navajo (Athabaskan) *na'ashǫ́'iito'í* 'lizard spring', containing *na'shǫ́'i* 'lizard'' and *tó* 'water, spring' (Wilson 1995).

LLAO Bay (Ore., Klamath Co.) \lou\. From Klamath /le:w/, a monster said to live in Crater Lake (Barker 1963).

LMUMA (Wash., Kittitas Co.) \lə mo͞o´ mə\. The name was adopted by the BGN in 1999 to replace a former "Squaw Creek"; it is from Yakima (Sahaptian) *łmuma* 'old woman' (E. Hunn p.c.).

LOA (Utah, Wayne Co.) \lō´ ə\. Named for Mauna Loa volcano in Hawai'i (Van Cott 1990). The Hawaiian name is literally translated as 'mountain long'.

LOACHAPOKA (Ala., Lee Co.) \lō chə pō´ kə\. A Muskogee tribal town, *lucv-pokv* /loča-pó:ka/, lit. 'turtles sitting', from *lucv* /ločá/ 'turtle' and *vpoka* 'to sit (of three or more)' (Martin and Mauldin 2000).

LOAKFOMA (Miss., Winston Co.) \lō kə fō´ mə\. A Choctaw (Muskogean) name meaning 'red dirt', from *lokfi* 'dirt' plus *homma* 'red' (Seale 1939; P. Munro p.c.).

LOANTAKA Brook (N.J., Morris Co.). Probably from Delaware (Algonquian), perhaps containing <lowan> 'winter' (Becker 1964; Brinton and Anthony 1888); cf. Unami Delaware /lú:wan/ 'winter' (Blalock et al. 1994).

LOBLOCKEE Creek (Ala., Lee Co.) \läb lok´ ē\. A Muskogee tribal town, *raprakko* /ła:płákko/ (Martin and Mauldin 2000); perhaps meaning 'big cane (plant)', from *rawa,* a type of cane from which blowguns were made, plus *rakko* 'big' (Read 1984).

LOBUTCHA (Miss., Winston Co.) \lə buch´ ə\. Probably a shortening of **Yalobusha,** perhaps from Choctaw (Muskogean) *yalooboshi* 'little tadpole' (Seale 1939; P. Munro p.c.).

LOCHAPOPKA Lake (Fla., Polk Co.) \lō chə pop´ kə\. From a Muskogee term meaning 'eating turtles', from *lucv* /ločá/ 'turtle' and *papkv* /pá:pka/ 'eating' (Read 1934, Martin and Mauldin 2000). A related placename is **Locktsapopka** (Fla., Hillsborough Co.).

LOCHLOOSA (Fla., Alachua Co.) \lok lo͞o´ sə\. Choctaw (Muskogean) for 'black turtle', from *loksi* 'turtle' and *losa* 'black' (Read 1934; P. Munro p.c.).

LOCHOCHEE Creek (Ga., Terrell Co.) \lō chō´ chē\. The Muskogee name may mean 'little turtle', from *lucv* /ločá/ 'turtle' and *-uce* /-oči/ 'little' (Read 1949–50:130, Martin and Mauldin 2000).

LOCHSA Creek (Idaho, Idaho Co.) \lok´ sə, lok´ sô\. Perhaps from a Flathead (Salishan) word meaning 'rough water' (Boone 1988).

LOCKATONG Creek (N.J., Hunterdon Co.) \lok´ ə tong\. Probably from Delaware (Algonquian), perhaps containing <lekau> 'sand, gravel' (Becker 1964; Brinton and Anthony 1888); cf. Munsee *léekuw* (O'Meara 1996). A probably related placename is the nearby **Locktown.**

LOCKCHELOOGE Creek (Ala., Cleburne Co.) \lok chi lo͞o´ jē\. The Muskogee name may contain *lákca* /lákča/ 'acorn' (Read 1984; Martin and Mauldin 2000).

LOCKIT (Ore., Wasco Co.) \lok´ it\. Chinook Jargon <lak´ it, lok´-it, lockit> 'four' [lɔ́kɪt], from Lower Chinook [lákit] 'four' (D. Kinkade p.c.).

LOCKTOWN (N.J., Hunterdon Co.) \lok´ toun\. This name is probably related to the nearby **Lockatong Creek** (Becker 1964).

LOCKTSAPOPKA River (Fla., Hillsborough Co.) \lok tsə pop´ kə\. Related to **Lochapopka Lake** (Fla., Polk Co.); see above.

LOCOALLOMI (Calif., Napa Co.) \lə kä´ yə mē\. Probably from a Lake Miwok placename /lakáh-yomi/ 'cottonwood place' or /lakáa-yomi/ 'goose place' (Gudde 1998).

LOCONOMA Valley (Calif., Lake Co.) \lō kō nō´ mə\. Probably from Wappo (Yukian) *lóknoma* 'goose place' (Gudde 1998).

LODGEPOLE \loj´ pōl\. The word *lodge* can refer to a typical Indian dwelling, such as a tepee; and a lodgepole is a pole used to build a tepee. The term also gives its name to the lodgepole pine, a tree that provided long poles suitable for tepees. **Lodgepole Creek** (S.Dak., Harding Co.) probably represents a translation of Lakhota (Siouan) *thuší* 'lodgepole' (Sneve 1973; B. Ingham p.c.). The placename **Lodgepole** occurs in many western states, often referring to the lodgepole pine (e.g. Calif., Lassen Co.).

LOGAN County (W.Va.) Named for a prominent Cayuga (Iroquoian) man of the eighteenth century, called Chief Logan in English (Kenny 1945).

LOGAN Valley (Pa., Blair Co.). Said to have been named for a Delaware (Algonquian) leader who was called Captain Logan in English (Donehoo 1928).

LOGSDEN (Ore., Lincoln Co.). Said to be named for a very old resident of the Siletz Indian Reservation (McArthur 1992).

LOHALI Mesa (Ariz., Apache Co.). From Navajo (Athabaskan) *ɬóó' háálį́* 'fish flow out' (Linford 2000).

LOKASAKAL Wash (Ariz., Navajo Co.) \lō kä´ sə käl\. From Navajo (Athabaskan) *lók'aa' sikaad* 'reeds spread-out' (Wilson 1995). The English spelling **Lokasakad** also occurs.

LOKOSEE (Fla., Osceola Co.) \lō kō´ sē\. Based on Muskogee *nokose* /nokósi/ 'black bear' (Read 1934; Martin and Mauldin 2000).

LOKOYA (Calif., Napa Co.) \lō koi´ ə\. Probably abbreviated from **Locoallomi** (Gudde 1998).

LOLAH Butte (Ore., Deschutes Co.) \lō´ lə\. Perhaps from Chinook Jargon <lowullo, lolo, lohlo> [lówəlo] 'round, whole, entire', from Chinookan \lólo\ 'round' (McArthur 1992; D. Kinkade p.c.). A possibly related placename is **Lowullo Butte.**

LOLAMAI Point (Ariz., Navajo Co.) \lō´ lə mī\. Said to be named for an Oraibi Hopi (Uto-Aztecan) leader (Granger 1983); cf. *lolma* 'beautiful one', reduplication of *loma-* 'beautiful' (K. Hill p.c.).

LOLETA (Calif., Humboldt Co.) \lō lē´ tə\. In 1893 a resident, Mrs. Rufus F. Herrick, chose the present name, supposed to be from the local Wiyot Indian language. The Indian name was in fact *katawóɬo't,* but an elderly Indian played a joke on Mrs. Herrick by telling her that the name was *hóš wiwítak* 'let's have intercourse!'—the latter part of which she interpreted in baby-talk fashion as **Loleta** (Teeter 1958).

LOLO Butte (Ore., Deschutes Co.) \lō´ lō\. Probably from Chinook Jargon <lo´-lo> [lólo] 'to carry, to pack', from Lower Chinook [lólo] 'to carry on the back' (D. Kinkade p.c.). The same placename occurs in Wash. (Clallam Co.).

LOLO Pass (Idaho, Clearwater Co.; Mont., Missoula Co.). The name has been said to represent an Indian pronunciation of the French male name *Laurent* or *Laurence* (Cheney 1984); however, **Lolo** may also be a perfectly good French nickname. The name **Lolo Pass** was also transferred to Ore. (Hood River Co.).

LOMAKI Ruin (Ariz., Coconino Co.) \lō mä´ kē\. Hopi (Uto-Aztecan) *lomaki* 'beautiful house', from *loma-* 'beautiful' and *-ki, kii-hu* 'house' (K. Hill p.c.).

LOMAVIK (Alaska, Baird Inlet C-1) \lō mə vik\. The Yupik (Eskimo) name was reported in 1880 (Orth 1967).

LOMPOC (Calif., Santa Barbara Co.) \lôm´ pōk, lōm´pok\. From Purisimeño (Chumashan) /lompo', olompo'/, perhaps meaning 'stagnant water' (Gudde 1998).

LONACONING (Md., Allegany Co.). Possibly from an Algonquian name meaning 'where it disappears from view' (Kenny 1984).

LONE Butte (S.Dak., Fall River Co.). Corresponds to Dakota (Siouan) *pahá išnána ų́* 'butte is alone' (Sneve 1973; A. Taylor p.c.).

LONG ALEC Creek (Wash., Ferry Co.). Named for a Colville (Salishan) man who was exceptionally tall (Hitchman 1985).

LONG Butte (S.Dak., Dewey Co.). Corresponds to Lakhota (Siouan) *pahá hą́ska,* lit. 'butte long' (Sneve 1973, A. Taylor p.c.). Elsewhere, **Long Lake** (N.Mex., San Juan Co.) corresponds to Navajo (Athabaskan) *be'ek'id hóneezi* 'long lake', containing *be'ek'id* 'lake', *ho-* 'space, area', and *neez* 'long' (Wilson 1995). In N.Y., **Long Lake** (Hamilton Co.) is a translation of Western Abenaki (Algonquian) *gwenogamak* 'it is a long lake'; cf. *gweni* 'long' (Day 1994–95). In S.Dak. (Codrington Co.), **Long Lake** corresponds to Dakota (Siouan) *mdé hą́ska,* lit. 'lake long' (Sneve 1973; A. Taylor p.c.). In Alaska **Long Point** (Beaver A-4) corresponds to Koyukon (Athabaskan) *tledonenaale* 'point that is long' (Kari 2000).

LONG HOUSE Creek (N.Y., Orange Co.). The name refers to one of the large communal dwellings built by the Iroquois (Ruttenber 1906).

LONG JIM Reservoir (Wash., Chelan Co.). Named for a Chelan (Salishan) leader; his Native American name was /səl'pímtkən/ (D. Kinkade p.c.).

LONG TOM (Ore., Lane Co.). A folk-etymology from the name of a Kalapuyan tribal group; the Native American name is [lámp^{h}tumpif], translated literally as 'spank-his-ass' (H. Zenk p.c.). In Tex. (Polk Co.,), **Long Tom Creek** was named for a Muskogee Indian leader (Tarpley 1980).

LOOKING GLASS Butte (Idaho, Idaho Co.). Named for a nineteenth-century Nez Perce (Sahaptian) leader, called **Looking Glass** in English (McArthur 1992); his Native American name was /ʔelelímyeteʔqenin'/ 'wrapped-in-wind' (Aoki 1994). The placename occurs elsewhere (Ore., Union Co.; Wash., Asotin Co.).

LOOKOUT Mountain (Tenn., Hamilton Co.). Said to have been adapted from Cherokee (Iroquoian) <Atalidandakanika> 'mountains looking at each other' (McClaren 1991).

LOOKSOOKALOO (Ala., Sumter Co.) \lo͞ok so͞o´ kə lo͞o\. Perhaps from a Choctaw (Muskogean) placename meaning 'sacred turtle-water' (Read 1984); cf. *loksi* 'turtle', *oka* 'water', *hollo* 'sacred' (P. Munro p.c.).

LOOP LOOP (Wash., Okanogan Co.) \lo͞op´ lo͞op\. Perhaps from Okanagan (Salishan) /lup lup/ 'pools of fish' (A. Mattina p.c.). The spelling **Loup Loup** also occurs.

LOOSAHATCHIE River (Tenn., Shelby Co.) \lo͞o sə hach´ ē\. Perhaps Choctaw (Muskogean) *losa* 'black' and *hachcha* 'river', but Choctaw normally puts adjectives after nouns (P. Munro p.c.).

LOOWIT Creek (Ore., Clatsop Co.). From Sahaptin /lawilayt-ɬa/ 'smoker' (D. Kinkade p.c.) The placename also occurs in Wash. (Skamania Co.).

LOOXAHOMA (Miss., Tate Co.) \lo͞ok sə hō´ mə\. Perhaps from Choctaw (Muskogean), meaning 'red turtle'; cf. *loksi* 'turtle', *homma* 'red' (Seale 1939).

LOOXAPALIA (Ala., Lamar Co.) \lo͞ok sə pä´ lē ə\. From Choctaw (Muskogean), meaning 'floating turtle'; cf. *loksi* 'turtle', *okpalalih* 'to float' (P. Munro p.c.). A related placename is **Luxapallila Creek.**

LOPATCONG Creek (N.J., Warren Co.). The name is probably Delaware (Algonquian), but is of unclear derivation (Becker 1964). A possibly related name is **Luppatatong Creek.**

LOS AMOLES Creek (Calif., Santa Barbara Co.) \ä mō´lās\. Mexican Spanish for 'the soap-root plants', from Aztec *amulli* (Gudde 1998).

LOSPE Mountain (Calif., Santa Barbara Co.) \lōs´ pē\. Purisimeño (Chumashan) /lospe/ 'flower' (Gudde 1998).

LOST Creek (S.Dak., Deuel Co.). Corresponds to Dakota (Siouan) *mní thą'į̨ šni* 'disappearing water', lit. 'water appear not' (Sneve 1973; A. Taylor p.c.).

LOST DOG Creek (S.Dak., Jackson Co.). Corresponds to Lakhota (Siouan) *šų́ka thokháȟ'ą* 'place where the dog was lost' (Sneve 1973; A. Taylor p.c.).

LOTLOH Creek (Wash., Clallam Co.) Chinook Jargon <la-tlah´> [latlá] 'noise', from French *le train* 'train'; note the Canadian French expression *faire du train* 'to make noise' (D. Kinkade p.c.).

LOTT (Wash., Lincoln Co.). Named for an Indian resident known as Chief Lott or Lot (Hitchman 1985).

LOUIS, Bayou (La., Catahoula Par.) \lo͞o´ ē\. Perhaps from Choctaw (Muskogean) *lowa* 'burnt' (P. Munro p.c.), with assimilation in spelling to the French personal name *Louis.*

LOUP LOUP Creek (Wash., Okanogan Co.) \lo͞op´ lo͞op\. Perhaps from Okanagan (Salishan) /lup lup/ 'pools of fish' (A. Mattina p.c.). The spelling **Loop Loop** also occurs.

LOUSE Rocks (Wash., Pacific Co.). An Indian legend tells that these rocks represent a man and woman who introduced lice among their people (Hitchman 1985).

LOWULLO Butte (Ore., Deschutes Co.) \lou wul´ ō\. Chinook Jargon <lowullo, lolo, lohlo> [lówəlo] 'round, whole, entire', from Lower Chinook [lólo] 'round' (McArthur 1992; D. Kinkade p.c.). A possibly related placename is **Lolah Butte.**

LOXAHATCHEE (Fla., Palm Beach Co.) \lok sə hach´ ē\. Earlier written as <Locha Hatchee>, perhaps from Muskogee *lucv* /ločá/ 'turtle' plus *hvcce* /háčči/ 'stream' (Read 1934; Martin and Mauldin 2000).

LOYALHANNA (Pa., Westmoreland Co.) \loi əl han´ ə\. The Delaware (Algonquian) name, earlier written as <Loyalhanning>, may be from <lawel> 'middle', <hanna> 'stream', and <-ing> 'place' (Donehoo 1928); cf. Munsee Delaware *leeláawii* 'in the middle' (O'Meara 1996).

LOYALSOCK (Pa., Lycoming Co.) \loi´ əl sok\. The Delaware (Algonquian) name was earlier written as <Lywasock>, perhaps meaning 'middle creek' (Donehoo 1928); see **Loyalhanna** above.

LUBBUB (Ala., Pickens Co.) \lub´ ub\. Probably from Choctaw (Muskogean) *lahbah* 'to be warm' (Read 1984; P. Munro p.c.).

LUCHEK Mountain (Alaska, Karluk A-1). The Alutiiq (Eskimo) word is said to mean 'signal' (Orth 1967).

LUCKIAMUTE River (Ore., Polk Co.) \luk´ ē myo͞ot\. The Santiam (Kalapuyan) placename /aláak'mayut/ refers to a tribal subgroup, perhaps related to /láqowa/ 'edge of timber' or /láqmi/ 'creek mouth, fish dam' (McArthur 1992; H. Zenk p.c.). The variant writing **Lackemute** also occurs.

LUDASESKA Creek (Alaska, Skagway A-2). The Tlingit placename was published in 1923 (Orth 1967).

LUKACHUKAI (Ariz., Apache Co.) \lo͞o kə cho͞o´ kī, lo͞o kə chuk´ ī\. Navajo (Athabaskan) *lók'a'ch'égai* 'reeds extending white', from *lók'aa'* 'reeds', *ch'é* (*ch'í*) 'extending', and *gai* 'white' (Wilson 1995).

LUKFATA (Okla., McCurtain Co.) \luk fä´ tə\. The Choctaw (Muskogean) placename, also written **Luk-fah-tah,** may mean 'white dirt', from *lokfi* 'dirt' and *hata* 'white' (Shirk 1974; P. Munro p.c.).

LUKLUKSUKWIK Lake (Alaska, Nunivak Island A-6). The Yupik (Eskimo) placename was reported in 1942 (Orth 1967).

LUKTHLUKRIT Marsh (Alaska, Nunivak Island A-6). The Yupik (Eskimo) name, reported in 1949, is said to mean 'moulting place of geese' (Orth 1967); cf. *lagiq* 'goose' (Jacobson 1984).

LU:K'YAN'A (N.Mex., Cibola Co.) \lo͞ok´ yän-ä\. The Zuni name refers to a sacred spring (Ferguson and Hart 1985).

LULAH Falls (Ga., Dade Co.) \lo͞o´ lə\. Shortened from **Talulah,** perhaps from Choctaw (Muskogean) *talula* 'bell' (Krakow 1975; Byington 1915).

LULULONGTURKWI (Ariz., Navajo Co.). Hopi (Uto-Aztecan) *lölöqangwtuyqa* 'bullsnake point', from *lölöqangw* 'bullsnake', *tuyqa* 'outside corner' (K. Hill p.c.).

LUMBEE \lum´ bē\. A Native American group of the Carolinas, of mixed descent. Perhaps identified with the river name early written by the Spanish as <Arambe, Ilapi, Herape>, now called the **Lumber River** (S.C., Marion Co.).

LUMKEE (Okla., Hughes Co.) \lum´ kē\. Perhaps from Muskogee *lvmhe* /lámhi/ 'eagle' (Shirk 1974; Martin and Mauldin 2000).

LUMMI (Wash., Whatcom Co.) \lum´ ē\. Named for a Salishan tribal group (Howell 1948); the Native American name is [nəx^{W}lə́miʔ] or [x^{W}lə́miʔ] (D. Kinkade p.c.).

LUMPY Ridge (Colo., Larimer Co.) is based on Arapaho (Algonquian) *theethi'ótoyóó'* 'lumpy mountain' (A. Cowell p.c.).

LUMRUM Butte (Ore., Deschutes Co.) \lum´ rum\. Said to be from a Chinook Jargon word meaning 'rum, whisky', derived from English *rum* (McArthur 1992); however, the usual Jargon word for hard liquor is simply <lum> (D. Kinkade p.c.).

LUPPATATONG Creek (N.J., Monmouth Co.). The Delaware (Algonquian) name is also written as <Luppacong, Luppatcong>, of unclear derivation (Becker 1964); a perhaps related name is **Lopatcong Creek.**

LUTAK Inlet (Alaska, Skagway B-2) \lo͞o´ tak\. The Tlingit placename was published in 1923 (Orth 1967).

LUXAPALLILA Creek (Ala., Lamar Co.; Miss., Lowndes Co.) \luk shə pə lī´ lə\. Probably from Choctaw (Muskogean), meaning 'floating turtle'; cf. *loksi* 'turtle', *okpalalih* 'to float' (P. Munro p.c.). A related placename is **Looxapalia.**

LYCOMING County (Pa.) \lī kō´ ming\. The Delaware (Algonquian) name was earlier written as <Lecamick>, possibly from <lekau> 'sand, gravel' (Donehoo 1928; Brinton and Anthony 1888); cf. Munsee Delaware *léekuw* 'sand' (O'Meara 1996). The placename also occurs in N.Y. (Oswego Co.). A perhaps related placename is **Lehigh.**

LYEEL-GHIT Cliff (Alaska, Saint Lawrence D-4). The Yupik (Eskimo) name was reported in 1932 (Orth 1967).

M

MAACAMA Creek (Calif., Sonoma Co.) \mā yak´ mə\. From the same source as **Mayacamas Mountains** (Calif., Lake Co.); see below.

MACACHEE, Lake (Ohio, Mahoning Co.) \mak´ ə chē\. From [mekoče], a Shawnee (Algonquian) subgroup (*HNAI* 15:634). Related placenames include **Macochee Creek** (Ohio, Logan Co.) and **Macacheek Castle** (Ohio, Logan Co.) \mak´ ə chēk\.

MACANIPPUCK Run (N.J., Cumberland Co.) \mak ə nip′ək\. Perhaps from Delaware (Algonquian) *mèkënipèk* 'last creek' (Kraft and Kraft 1985).

MACATAWA (Mich., Ottawa Co.) \mak ə tä′ wə\. Probably from Ojibwa *makadewaa* 'to be black' (J. Nichols p.c.).

MACE Mountain (Ore., Douglas Co.). Named for an Indian resident, Mace Tipton (McArthur 1992).

MACHEWIK Mountain (Alaska, Goodnews Bay A-8). The Yupik (Eskimo) name was reported in 1954 (Orth 1967).

MACHIAS (Maine, Washington Co.) \mə chī′ əs\. Perhaps Abenaki (Algonquian) for 'bad little falls' (Eckstorm 1941:217–19); cf. *maji-* 'bad' (Day 1994–95). The placename also occurs elsewhere (N.Y., Cattaraugus Co.; Wash., Snohomish Co.).

MACHICKANEE Flowage (Wis., Oconto Co.). Named for a Menominee (Algonquian) leader called <Match-a-ken-naew> 'bad eagle', also shortened to **Chickney Creek** (Vogel 1991); cf. /mace:q-/ 'bad', /kene:w/ 'eagle' (Bloomfield 1975).

MACHODOC (Va., Westmoreland Co.) \mə shō′ dok\. From the name of a CAC Algonquian village (Hagemann 1988).

MACKINAC County (Mich.) \mak′ i nô, mak′ i nak\. Abbreviated from <Michilimackinac>, probably Ojibwa (Algonquian) for 'many turtles'; cf. *mishiin-* 'be many', *mikinaak* 'snapping turtle' (Nichols and Nyholm 1995; I. Goddard p.c.). Possibly related placenames include **Mackinaw City** (Mich.; see below), **Meckinock** (N.Dak.), **Mekanac Point** (Wis.), and **Mokena** (Ill., Will Co.).

MACKINAW City (Mich., Cheboygan Co.) \mak′ i nô\. From the same origin as **Mackinac County**; see above. The word *mackinaw* 'a type of double-breasted coat' is derived from the placename. The name **Mackinaw** in Ill. (Tazewell Co.) is probably not a transfer from the Mich. term but a direct borrowing from Ojibwa (Algonquian) *mikinaak* 'snapping turtle' (Vogel 1963; Nichols and Nyholm 1995); see **Mackinac County**, above. **Mackinaw Bay** (Mont., Glacier Co.) probably refers to the "mackinaw trout," a fish named after the place in Mich. (Holterman 1985). Related placenames include **Mackinac County** (Mich.), **Meckinock** (N.Dak., Grand Forks Co.), **Mekanac Point** (Wis., Oneida Co.), **Mickinock Township** (Minn., Roseau Co.), **Fort Michilimackinac** (Mich., Fort Emmet Co.), and **Mokena** (Ill., Will Co.).

MACOCHEE Creek (Ohio, Logan Co.). The name is related to **Lake Macachee** (Ohio, Mahoning Co.); see above.

MACONAQUAH Park (Ind., Miami Co.) \mə kon′ ə kwä\. Miscopied from <Maconsquah>, a Miami/Illinois (Algonquian) woman; her Native American name was /mahkoonshkwa/ 'bear-cub woman' (M. McCafferty p.c.).

MACOPIN (N.J., Passaic Co.). From an Algonquian word of unclear origin, referring to a type of edible root or tuber (Becker 1964). A probably related placename is found in **Macoupin County** (Ill.) \mə ko͞o′ pin\.

MACUNGIE (Pa., Lehigh Co.). Perhaps from Delaware (Algonquian) <machk-kawunshi-i> 'bear thorn-bush', from <machk-> 'bear', <-kawunshi> 'thorn-bush', and <-i> 'emphatic'; cf. Unami Delaware /maxkw/ (Blalock et al. 1994), Munsee Delaware *máxkw* (O'Meara 1996). A related placename is **Maxatawney.**

MACWAHOC (Maine, Aroostook Co.) \mak wā′ hok\. From Abenaki (Algonquian) *megoakw* 'swamp' (Eckstorm 1941:58; Day 1994–95).

MADAGASCAL Pond (Maine, Penobscot Co.) \mad ə gas′ kəl\. Said to be Abenaki (Algonquian) for 'meadows at the mouth' (Eckstorm 1941:50).

MADAKET (Mass., Nantucket Co.). Earlier written <Mawtukkit>, <Mattakett> (Little 1984). From SNEng. Algonquian <matahquadt> 'cloudy, overcast' (W. Cowan p.c.).

MADAWASKA (Maine, Aroostook Co.) \mad ə wä´ skə\. Perhaps from Abenaki (Algonquian), 'where there is much hay' (Huden 1962). The placename occurs as a transfer in N.Y. (St. Lawrence Co.).

MAD BEAR Creek (S.Dak., Corson Co.). Named for a Lakhota (Siouan) resident (Sneve 1973).

MADELINE Island (Wis., Ashland Co.). Named for an Ojibwa (Algonquian) woman, Madeleine Cadotte (Vogel 1991).

MADEQUECHAM Pond (Mass., Nantucket Co.). Perhaps from a SNEng. Algonquian name meaning 'foothill place' (Huden 1962).

MADUSKEAG Stream (Maine, Aroostook Co.). Perhaps from Maliseet (Algonquian), 'falls at the mouth' (Rutherford 1970).

MAGAKTLEK Creek (Alaska, Goodnews Bay C-7). The Yupik (Eskimo) name was published in 1951 (Orth 1967).

MAGALLOWAY River (Maine, Oxford Co.; N.H., Coös Co.) \mə gal´ ə wā\. Abenaki (Algonquian) *magôlibo* 'caribou' (Julyan and Julyan 1993; Day 1994–95). The term is derived from an earlier Algonquian form meaning 'snow-shoveler', because the animal shovels away snow in order to graze; from the same Algonquian source come **Magurrewock Lakes** (Maine, Washington Co.) and **Caribou.**

MAGEIK, Mount (Alaska, Mt. Katmai A-4). The name, whether Yupik (Eskimo) or Aleut, was reported in 1917 (Orth 1967).

MAGITCHLIE Range (Alaska, Nulato A-5). The Koyukon (Athabaskan) name was reported in 1939 (Orth 1967).

MAGOMISCOCK Hill (Mass., Worcester Co). Probably contains SNEng. Algonquian <magi-> 'great', <-ompsk> 'rock' (W. Cowan p.c.).

MAGONK Point (Conn., New London Co.). From SNEng. Algonquian, meaning 'great tree', from <mogki-> 'large' and <-unk> 'tree' (Trumbull 1881; W. Cowan p.c.).

MAGOTSU Creek (Utah, Washington Co.) \mə got´ so͞o\. Said to be from Southern Paiute (Numic) <ma-haut-su> 'long slope' (Van Cott 1990).

MAGOWAH Creek (Miss., Lowndes Co.). Perhaps from Choctaw (Muskogean) *imaakohcha* 'his pass, ford, or ferry', from *kohcha* 'to come out' (P. Munro p.c.).

MAGUNCO Hill (Mass., Middlesex Co.). From SNEng. Algonquian <magoonk> 'gift' (W. Cowan p.c.).

MAGURIAK Creek (Alaska, Wainwright C-1). From Iñupiaq (Eskimo) *maguruq* 'it howls' (Orth 1967; Webster and Zibell 1970).

MAGURREWOCK Lakes (Maine, Washington Co.). From the same source as **Magalloway** ('caribou') **River** (Huden 1962); see above.

MAHAGONY Spring (Ore., Crook Co.). From the same source as **Mahogany Creek**; see below.

MAHALA (Calif., Humboldt Co.) \mə hä´ lə\. The term was once used in Calif. English to mean 'Indian woman'; it may be from an Indian pronunciation of Spanish *mujer* or from a Yokuts term such as Chowchila *mokheelo* 'woman' (Gudde 1998). The placename **Mahala** also exists elsewhere (Ariz., Coconino Co.; Neb., Butler Co.; Nev., Churchill Co.); some of these may be from a personal name *Mahalah,* found in the Bible.

MAHANA Peak (Colo., Boulder Co.) \mə hä´ nə\. Said to be a name for the Comanches (Numic) used by the Taos (Tanoan) Indians of N.Mex. (Bright 1993).

MAHANOY (Pa., Perry Co.) \mä´ hə noi\. A name related to **Mahoning,** from the Delaware (Algonquian) word for a salt-lick (Donehoo 1928).

MAHANTANGO (Pa., Snyder Co.). Perhaps from a Delaware (Algonquian) placename meaning 'where we had plenty of meat to eat' (Donehoo 1928).

MAHASKA County (Iowa) \mə has´ kə\. Named for an Ioway (Siouan) leader of the early nineteenth century, also known as White Cloud (Vogel 1983). The Native American name is derived from /mą́ɣu/ 'cloud' plus /ska, θka/ 'white' (R. Rankin p.c.). In Kans., the placename **Mahaska** (Washington Co.) is named for the son of the elder White Cloud (Rydjord 1968).

MAHICAN \mə hē´ kən\. The term refers to an Algonquian language and people of the upper Hudson Valley in N.Y. state, extending into western New England. The Native American term is /ma:hi:kan/ 'people of the tidal estuary', referring to tides on the Hudson River (*HNAI* 15:211). The word is also written **Mohican,** as in James Fenimore Cooper's novel *The Last of the Mohicans.* The placename **Mahican Brook** is in Mass. (Berkshire Co.). **Mahican** is not to be confused with **Mohegan,** the name of an SNEng. Algonquian group of coastal Conn.

MAHKEENAC Heights (Mass., Berkshire Co.). Said to be a Mahican (Algonquian) placename, meaning 'the abode of the Mahicans' (Huden 1962).

MAHNOMEN County (Minn.) \mə nō´ min\. From Ojibwa (Algonquian) *manoomin* 'wild rice' (Upham 2001; Nichols and Nyholm 1995). Probably related placenames are **Manomin Creek, Menominee Lake, Munnomin.**

MAHO, Lake (Ariz., Navajo Co.) \mä´ hō\. From Hopi (Uto-Aztecan) *máho,* a First Mesa personal name (K. Hill p.c.).

MAHOGANY Creek (Nev., Humboldt Co.). The term is applied to a number of native plants with hard wood resembling that of mahogany, a South American tree. The word entered English in the seventeenth century, from an Indian language of the West Indies (*RHD* 1987). In the western United States, it generally refers to a bush called *mountain mahogany.* The placename also occurs in Calif. (Inyo Co.), N.Mex. (Catron Co.), and W.Va. (Monongalia Co.).

MAHOMET (Ill., Champaign Co.) \mə hom´ ət\. **Mahomet** occurs in English as a variant form of *Mohammed,* the prophet of Islam. In U.S. history **Mahomet** occurs as an alternative spelling for the name of a Mohegan (SNEng. Algonquian) leader who lived in Conn. during the early eighteenth century. The Ill. placename may have been named for the Conn. Indian (Vogel 1963).

MAHONE Peak (Ariz., Yavapai Co.). Named for Jim Mahone, a nineteenth-century Hualapai (Yuman) scout (Granger 1983).

MAHONING (Pa., Fayette Co.) \mə hō´ ning\. From Unami Delaware (Algonquian) /ma:ho:nink/ 'salt-lick place', with /-ink/ 'place' (Donehoo 1928; M. McCafferty p.c.). The term is also found in Ohio (Portage Co.). Related placenames are **Mahanoy** (Pa., Perry Co.), **Sinnemahoning** (Pa., Cameron Co.), and names containing **Lick**, e.g. **Black Lick** (Pa., Indiana Co.).

MAHOOSUC Range (N.H., Coös Co.) \mə hōō´ sək\. The name was perhaps given by SNEng. Algonquian refugees from Conn., meaning 'pinnacle'; or it may be from Abenaki (Algonquian), meaning 'abode of hungry animals' (Huden 1962).

MAHOPAC (N.Y., Putnam Co.) \mā´ ō pak\. Perhaps from Munsee Delaware (Algonquian), earlier recorded as <Makoohpeck, Macookpack>, perhaps meaning 'snake lake' (Ruttenber 1906:36).

MAHORAS Brook (N.J., Monmouth Co.). Probably from Delaware (Algonquian), but of unclear derivation (Becker 1964).

MAHSKEEKEE Lake (Mich., Delta Co.) From Ojibwa (Algonquian) *mashkiki* 'medicine', in the American Indian sense of objects or procedures that have magical effect (Vogel 1986; Nichols and Nyholm 1995).

MAHTKWINGAK Slough (Alaska, St. Michael A-5). The Yupik (Eskimo) name was reported in 1899 (Orth 1967).

MAHTO (S.Dak., Corson Co.) \mä´ tō\. From Lakhota (Siouan) *mathó* 'bear' (Sneve 1973; Ingham 2001). Related names include **Mah-**

tomedi (Minn., Washington Co.) \män tō´ mē dī\, from Dakota (Siouan) *mathó mdi,* lit. 'bear lake' (Upham 2001; Riggs 1890); **Mahtotopa Mountain** (Mont., Glacier Co.), named for a Mandan (Siouan) leader of the early nineteenth century, also known in English as Four Bears, the translation of his Native American name (Holterman 1985); and **Mahtowa** (Minn., Carlton Co.) \mä´ tō wə\. The name is said to have been made up by taking pieces from Dakota *mathó* 'bear' and from Ojibwa (Algonquian) *makwa* 'bear' (Upham 2001; Nichols and Nyholm 1995).

MAHTSON-PI (Ariz., Navajo Co.) \mät sōn´ pē\. Hopi (Uto-Aztecan) *matsònpi,* the name of a prehistoric ruin at the foot of Hotevilla mesa (K. Hill p.c.).

MAHWAH River (N.J., Bergen Co.; N.Y., Rockland Co.). Probably from Munsee Delaware (Algonquian), earlier written <Maywayway>, perhaps to be identified with <mawewi> 'meeting place' (Ruttenber 1906); cf. Munsee *maawehléewak* 'to meet, gather together' (O'Meara 1996).

MAIDEN Rock (Wis., Pierce Co.). Supposedly named for the heroine of a Dakota (Siouan) legend; her name, widely adopted as a placename, is said to have been **Winona,** which is in fact the Dakota word for 'firstborn daughter' (Vogel 1991).

MAIDU \mī´ do͞o\. The name of a Calif. Indian people, of the Maiduan language family; the term is from the Native American word /máydɨ/ 'human being' (Shipley 1963). The term was apparently transferred to the placename **Maidu Lake** in Ore. (Douglas Co.).

MAIITOH (Ariz., Coconino Co.). From the same source as **Maito** (Ariz., Apache Co.); see below.

MA-IN-GAN Lake (Mich., Gogebic Co.). From Ojibwa (Algonquian) *ma'iingan* 'wolf' (Vogel 1986; Nichols and Nyholm 1995).

MAISH VAYA (Ariz., Pima Co.). O'odham (Piman) *ma'iṣ wahia,* lit. 'covered well' (J. Hill p.c.).

MAITO (Ariz., Apache Co.) \mī´ tō\. Navajo (Athabaskan) for 'coyote spring', from *mą'ii* 'coyote', *to'* 'water, spring' (Young and Morgan 1987). A related placename is **Maiitoh** (Ariz., Coconino Co.).

MAIYUMERAK Mountains (Alaska, Baird Mountains D-6). The Ingalik (Eskimo) name may be from *mayuq-* 'to ascend' (L. Kaplan p.c.).

MAJENICA (Ind., Huntington Co.) \mə jen´ i kə\. Named for a Miami/Illinois (Algonquian) leader of the early nineteenth century. His name has been written <Monji-ni-kia, Met-chin-e-qua> (etc.), and has been translated 'big frame' (McPherson 1993; Baker 1995).

MAKAH \mə kô´\. The name refers to a people of the Nootkan linguistic stock, living in far northwestern Wash.; the term is from Clallam (Salishan) /màq'áʔa/ 'those who eat their fill', which the Clallam people applied to the Makahs (W. Jacobsen p.c.). The placename **Makah Bay** is in Clallam Co. in Wash.

MAKAKA Point (Alaska, Cordova C-7) \mə kär´ kə\. A variant writing of **Makarka Creek** (Orth 1967); see below.

MAKAKTUK Lake (Alaska, Chandler Lake B-3). The Iñupiaq (Eskimo) lake was reported in 1956 (Orth 1967).

MAKANDA (Ill., Jackson Co.) \mə kan´ də\. Supposedly named for an Indian leader, but the language has not been identified (Vogel 1963).

MAKARKA Creek (Alaska, Cordova C-7) \mə kär´ kə\. Named for an Ahtna (Athabaskan) leader, Makarka Feodorovich Chimovitski (BGN 1991). The variant **Makaka Point** also occurs.

MAKEE Township (Iowa, Allamakee Co.) \mə kē´\. A shortened form of **Allamakee,** probably from a Meskwaki (Algonquian) word for 'thunder' (Vogel 1983).

MAKGUM HAVOKA (Ariz., Pima Co.). O'odham (Piman) *makkumĭ hawo'oga* 'pond of the caterpillars', from *makkumĭ* 'caterpillar(s)', *ha-wo'o-ga* 'their pond' (J. Hill p.c.).

MAKLAKS Creek (Ore., Klamath Co.) \mak´ laks\. From Klamath /maqlaqs/ 'human being, Indian, Klamath Indian' (Barker 1963).

MAKNEK River (Alaska, St. Lawrence B-1). The Yupik (Eskimo) name was reported in 1949 (Orth 1967). A probable variant writing is **Maknik.**

MAKOSHIKA State Park (Mont., Dawson Co.). Probably from Lakota (Siouan) *makhó-šiča* 'badlands', lit. 'land-bad' (Cheney 1984; Buechel and Manhart 2002).

MAKOTI (N.Dak., Ward Co.) \mə kō´ tē\. Said to be Mandan (Siouan), meaning 'largest of the earth lodges' (Wick 1988); cf. Dakota (Siouan) *makhá othí* 'lives in an earth lodge', lit. 'earth dwells' (D. Ingham p.c.).

MAKPIK Creek (Alaska, Howard Pass A-5). From Iñupiaq (Eskimo) *makpik* 'outlet of a lake' (Burch 1998).

MAKTAK Mountain (Alaska, Point Hope B-1). From Iñupiaq (Eskimo) *maktak* 'whale skin with blubber' (Orth 1967; MacLean 1980).

MAKUSHIN (Alaska, Unalaska C-3). Russian, probably from *makushka* 'crown of the head, top' (Orth 1967); or from the Aleut placename *magusix̂* (Bergsland 1994).

MAKWA Lake (Minn., Lake Co.) \mä´ kwə\. From Ojibwa (Algonquian) *makwa* 'bear' (Nichols and Nyholm 1995).

MALAMUTE \mal´ ə myōōt\. The term refers to Eskimo people of the Kotzebue region in northwestern Alaska; the Iñupiaq term is *mali-miut* (*HNAI* 5:318). It has also been extended to a type of dog raised by the Eskimos. The term occurs in several placenames: for example, **Malamute Fork** (Alaska, Wiseman A-4) and also outside Alaska (Idaho, Shoshone Co.). An alternative spelling is **Malemute** (Alaska, Bettles C-6; Colo., Pitkin Co.).

MALECITE \mal´ i sēt\. From the same source as **Maliseet**, an Algonquian people of Maine.

MALGA Bay (Alaska, Unalaska C-1). Probably an error for **Unalga Island,** from Aleut *unalĝa* 'the seaward one'; cf. *una* 'out there on the sea' (Orth 1967; Bergsland 1994).

MALIBU (Calif., Los Angeles Co.) \mal´ i bōō\. From a Ventureño (Chumashan) village name <Umalibo>; the Native American name may have been /(hu-)mal-iwu/ 'it makes a loud noise all the time over there', referring to the surf (Gudde 1998). The placename **Malibu** occurs as a transfer in other states (e.g., Ga., Fulton Co.; Va., Virginia Beach Co.).

MALIKFIK Bay (Alaska, Norton Bay B-5). The Iñupiaq (Eskimo) name was reported about 1954 (Orth 1967).

MALISEET \mal´ i sēt\. A language and people of the Algonquian linguistic family, living in northern Maine and adjacent areas of Canada; also written as **Malecite.** The term is from a neighboring Algonquian language, Micmac, in which it means 'lazy speakers' (*HNAI* 15:135); it is not currently used as a placename in the United States. The **Passamaquoddy** are a closely related group.

MALLEGO Brook (N.H., Strafford Co.). Probably from Abenaki (Algonquian) *molôka* 'deep place' (Day 1994–50).

MAMACOKE Cove (Conn., New London Co.). From SNEng. Algonquian <maumacock> 'a great hook' (Trumbull 1881; W. Cowan p.c.).

MAM-A-GAH (Ariz., Pima Co.). O'odham (Piman) *mamakai* 'medicine men', plural of *ma:kai* (J. Hill p.c.).

MAMAGNAK Mountains (Alaska, St. Lawrence C-6). From St. Lawrence Is. Yupik (Eskimo), meaning 'like breasts'; cf. *mamaq* 'breast', *-naq* 'like' (Orth 1967; Jacobson 1987).

MAMAKATING (N.Y., Sullivan Co.) \mam´ ə kā ting\. From a Munsee Delaware (Algonquian) placename earlier written as <Mame-catink, Mamacotton> (etc.); the derivation is unclear (Ruttenber 1906).

MAMANASCO Lake (Conn., Fairfield Co.). Perhaps from SNEng. Algonquian <mohmoeog> 'they go together' (Trumbull 1881; W. Cowan p.c.).

MAMARONECK (N.Y., Westchester Co.) \mə mâr´ ə nek\. Probably from a Munsee Delaware (Algonquian) placename, perhaps referring to 'stripes' or 'strips' (Ruttenber 1906); cf. Munsee *maamáaleew* 'to be striped' (O'Meara 1996).

MAMATOTK Mountain (Ariz., Pima Co.). Perhaps from O'odham (Piman) *mamhaḍag* 'branch' or *mamaḍhoḍ* 'algae' (J. Hill p.c.).

MAMELAK Mountain (Alaska, Noatak A-2). The Iñupiaq (Eskimo) name was reported in 1950 (Orth 1967).

MANABOZHO Falls (Mich., Gogebic Co.) \man ə bō´ zhō\. The name refers to a character of Ojibwa (Algonquian) myth, viewed as a trickster and culture hero. The Native American name in western dialects is *wenabozho* (Nichols and Nyholm 1995); in eastern dialects, it is *nenbozh, nenbozhoo* (Rhodes 1985).

MANADA Creek (Pa., Dauphin Co.). Perhaps from Delaware (Algonquian) <menatey, menach´hen> 'island' (Donehoo 1928; Brinton and Anthony 1888); cf. Munsee Delaware *mŭnáhan* (O'Meara 1996). The name has also been written as **Monody Creek.** Possibly related placenames are **Manahawkin** (N.J., Ocean Co.) and **Monocanock Island** (Pa., Luzerne Co.).

MANAHASSETT Creek (N.J., Monmouth Co.) \man ə has´ ət\. Probably related to **Manhasset** (N.Y., Nassau Co.); see below.

MANAHAWKIN (N.J., Ocean Co.) \man ə hô´ kin\. Perhaps from Delaware (Algonquian) *mënahòkin* 'where the land slopes' (Kraft and Kraft 1985). Or perhaps from <menatey, menach´hen> 'island' (Becker 1964; Brinton and Anthony 1888); cf. Munsee Delaware *mŭnáhan* 'island' (O'Meara 1996). Possibly related placenames are **Manada Creek** (Pa., Dauphin Co.) and **Monocanock Island** (Pa., Luzerne Co.).

MANAHOWIC Creek (Md., St. Mary's Co.). Probably from the name of a CAC Algonquian group, written by Captain John Smith in 1608 as <Mannahoke> (Kenny 1984).

MANAKACHA Point (Ariz., Coconino Co.). Named for a leader of the Havasupai (Yuman) people in the early twentieth century (Brian 1992); the Native American name was /manakaja/. (L. Hinton p.c.).

MANAKE Lake (Mich., Mecosta Co.). Perhaps from Ojibwa (Algonquian) *maankik* 'maple forest' (Vogel 1986; Rhodes 1985). Possibly related placenames are **Manakiki Falls, Manoka Lake,** and **Lake Manuka.**

MANAKIKI Falls (Mich., Gogebic Co.). From Ojibwa (Algonquian) *maankik* 'maple forest' (Vogel 1986; Rhodes 1985). The placename also occurs in Wis. (Wood Co.). Possibly related placenames are **Manake Lake, Manoka Lake,** and **Lake Manuka.**

MANAKIN (Va., Goochland Co.). From the name of a CAC Algonquian group (Hagemann 1988). Perhaps related placenames are **Monacan** (Va., Albemarle Co.); see also **Manokin** (Md., Somerset Co.).

MANALAPAN (N.J., Monmouth Co.). The Delaware (Algonquian) placename perhaps means 'good bread' (Becker 1964); cf. Unami Delaware /a:hpón/ 'bread' (Blalock et al. 1994). The placename also occurs in Fla. (Palm Beach Co.).

MANANA Island (Maine, Lincoln Co.). From Abenaki (Algonquian), also written as **Mananis;** the Native American form is *menahaniz* 'small island', from *menahan* 'island' (Huden 1962; Day 1994–95). The Abenaki word for 'island' is related to that in other Algonquian languages, as reflected in placenames such as **Manhasset.**

MANANTICO (NJ, Cumberland Co.). A variant spelling of **Menantico**; see **Menantic Creek** below.

MANASOTA (Fla., Sarasota Co.) \man ə sō´ tə\. A word made up from **Manatee Creek** and **Sarasota County**, the names of adjacent counties.

MANASQUAN (N.J., Monmouth Co.) \man´ ə skwän\. Perhaps from Delaware (Algonquian) *mënàskung* 'place to gather grass' (Kraft and Kraft 1985). Or perhaps the word contains

<men´achk> 'fence, fort' (Becker 1964; Brinton and Anthony 1888); cf. Munsee Delaware *meenaxk* 'fence' (O'Meara 1996).

MANASTASH Creek (Wash., Kittitas Co.) \mə nas´ tash\. Sahaptin /má:naštaš /, perhaps meaning 'we are going root digging' (E. Hunn p.c.).

MANATAWNA (Pa., Philadelphia Co.) \man ə tô´ nə\. Perhaps from the same source as **Manatawny** (Pa., Berks Co.).

MANATAWNY (Pa., Berks Co.) \man ə tô´ nē\. The Delaware (Algonquian) name has been explained as <Menhaltanink> 'where we drank liquor' (Donehoo 1928); cf. <meney> 'to drink' (Brinton and Anthony 1888), Unami Delaware /məne:-/ 'to drink' (Blalock et al. 1994). Possibly related placenames include **Manatawna** and **Manayunk** (both Pa., Philadelphia Co.).

MANATEE County (Fla.) \man´ ə tē\. The placename refers to an aquatic mammal native to Fa.; it is from Spanish *manatí,* borrowed from a Cariban language of South America (*RHD* 1987).

MANATUCK Hill (Conn., New London Co.) \man´ i tuk\. From SNEng. Algonquian, perhaps meaning 'a place of observation, a lookout' (Trumbull 1881). The variant **Manitock** also occurs.

MANAWA Lake (Iowa, Pottawattamie Co.) \man´ ə wä, man´ ə wə\. The name was given by white settlers, supposedly borrowed from an Indian language; but the source has not been identified (Vogel 1983). The placename occurs elsewhere: for example, Iowa, Pottawattamie Co.; and Neb., Sarpy Co.).

MANAYAGAVIK Slough (Alaska, Hooper Bay C-4). The Yupik (Eskimo) name was reported in 1951 as meaning 'hook fish' (Orth 1967); cf. *manar-* 'to fish with a hook' (Jacobson 1984).

MANAYUNK (Pa., Philadelphia Co.) \man´ ə yungk\. Perhaps from Delaware (Algonquian) *mëneyung* 'place to drink' (Kraft and Kraft 1985); cf. Unami Delaware /məne:-/ 'to drink' (Blalock et al. 1994). A possibly related placename is **Manatawny.**

MANCHAC (La., Tangipahoa Par.) \man´ shak\. The name may be a French adaptation of Choctaw (Muskogean) *imąshaka* 'behind it', from *im-* 'its', *ąšaka* 'rear' (Read 1927; P. Munro p.c.).

MANCHAUG (Mass., Worcester Co.) \man´ chôg\. Perhaps from SNEng. Algonquian <munnoh-> 'island', <-(mi)shaskq> 'reeds' (W. Cowan p.c.).

MANCOS Mesa (Utah, San Juan Co.) \mang´ kōs, mang´ kəs\. Named for Mancos Jim, a Southern Paiute (Numic) leader (Van Cott 1990). The nearby **Mancos Jim Butte** is named for the same person.

MANDAN \man´ dan\. The term refers to an Indian people and language of the Siouan linguistic family, living in the northern Plains. The word comes from a common Siouan designation of the group: for example, Lakhota *miwátąni,* Omaha/Ponca *mąwádani* (*HNAI* 13:362–63). The placename **Mandan** occurs in several states: for example, Mich. (Keweenaw Co.) \man´ dən\, N.Dak. (Norton Co.), and S.Dak. (Mandan Co.),

MANDAREE (N.Dak., McKenzie Co.) \man´ də rē\. The name was made up from elements in the names of three Indian groups: the **Mandan, Hidatsa,** and **Ree** or **Arikara** peoples (Wick 1988).

MANET Beach (Mass., Norfolk Co.) \man´ ət\. From SNEng. Algonquian <munnoh-> 'island', <-et> 'place' (W. Cowan p.c.).

MANETUCK (N.Y., Suffolk Co.). Perhaps from Delaware (Algonquian) <menantak> 'pine swamp' (Tooker 1911; Brinton and Anthony 1888).

MANGANIKA Lake (Minn., St. Louis Co.) \mang gə nē´ kə\. Ojibwa (Algonquian) *mangaanagaa* 'there is a big island' (J. Nichols p.c.).

MANGAS Mountain (Ariz., Gila Co.) \mang´ gəs\. Probably for Mangas Colorado ("Red Sleeves"), a prominent nineteenth-century Apache leader (Granger 1983); more correct Spanish would be *mangas coloradas.* The placename **Mangas** also occurs in N.Mex. (Catron Co.).

MANGOAK River (Alaska, Selawik B-3). The name, perhaps from Iñupiaq (Eskimo), was reported in 1886 (Orth 1967).

MANGROVE Bayou (La., Cameron Par.) \mang´ grōv\. This name for a tree that grows in swamps is borrowed from Spanish *mangle* or Portuguese *mangue,* taken in turn from the Taino Indian language of the West Indies (*RHD* 1987).

MANHANNOCK (Conn., Hartford Co.). From SNEng. Algonquian <munnoh> 'island' (Trumbull 1881; W. Cowan p.c.).

MANHANOCK Pond (Maine, Piscataquis Co.). Probably from Abenaki (Algonquian) *menahan* 'island' (Huden 1962; Day 1994–95).

MANHAN River (Mass., Bristol Co.) \man´ han\. From SNEng. Algonquian <munnoh> 'island' (Trumbull 1881, W. Cowan p.c.) The variant **Munhan River** also occurs.

MANHASSET (N.Y., Nassau Co.) \man has´ ət\. The name has also been written as <Manhansett, Manhansuck>; it may be from Munsee Delaware (Algonquian) *mŭnáhan* 'island' (O'Meara 1996). A related placename is **Manahassett Creek** (N.J., Monmouth Co.).

MANHATTAN (N.Y., New York Co.) \man hat´ ən\. It has been suggested that this name, Walt Whitman's <Mannahatta>, is from the Delaware (Algonquian) word for 'island' (Grumet 1981:23); cf. Munsee Delaware *mŭnáhan* 'island' (O'Meara 1996). It is more likely to be from <Man-ă-hă-tonh>, however, perhaps representing Munsee Delaware /é:nta mənaháhte:nk/ 'where one gathers bows', with /-aht-/ 'bow' (I. Goddard p.c.). The placename has been transferred to many other areas (e.g., Calif., Los Angeles Co.; Kans, Riley Co.).

MANIDO Falls (Mich., Gogebic Co.) \man´ i dō\. A variant of **Manito**; see below.

MANINGLIK River (Alaska, Marshall D-5). The Yupik (Eskimo) name was reported in 1937 (Orth 1967).

MANISTEE County (Mich.) \man´ i stē, man i stē´\. The term is probably from the same source as **Manistique** (Mich., Schoolcraft Co.) \man´ i stēk, man i stēk´\, a French borrowing from Ojibwa (Algonquian), perhaps referring to 'red clay', but of unclear derivation (Vogel 1986).

MANITO \man´ i tō\. This represents a word (occurring in many of the Algonquian languages) that means 'spirit, deity, supernatural being'; it first entered English as a borrowing from Unami Delaware /manə́t:u/ and was then reinforced by borrowings from other Algonquian languages (*RHD* 1987); cf. Munsee Delaware *manútoow* (O'Meara 1996), Ojibwa *manidoo* (Nichols and Nyholm 1995), Meskwaki /maneto:wa/ (Goddard 1994). The placename **Manito** occurs in several areas (e.g., Ill., Mason Co.; Mich., Oakland Co.; and Pa., Westmoreland Co.). Other placenames with this origin are written **Manido Falls** (Mich., Gogebic Co.); **Manitou** (Mich., Keweenaw Co.; Colo., Teller Co.), **Manitto** (Pa., Westmoreland Co.), **Mannetto Hills** (N.Y., Nassau Co.), and **Minito Lake** (Wis., Langlade co.). The name of **Moniteau County** (Mo.) reflects the same term.

MANITOCK Hill (Conn., New London Co.) \man´ i tok\. From SNEng. Algonquian, perhaps meaning 'a place of observation, a lookout' (Trumbull 1881); cf. <moneau> 'he looks, observes' (W. Cowan p.c.). Another form of the name is **Manitook** (Conn., Hartford Co.) The variant **Manatuck Hill** also occurs.

MANITOU \man´ i to͞o\. From the same source as **Manito**; see above. The term is widespread as a placename (e.g., Colo., Teller Co.; and Mich., Keweenaw Co.).

MANITOULIN Basin (Mich., Alcona Co.) \man i to͞o´ lin\. From **Manitoulin Island,** part of the territory of Canada, in Lake Huron. From Old Ottawa (Algonquian) /manito:wa:link/ 'at the spirit's cave' (I. Goddard p.c.).

MANITOWOC County (Wis.) \man i tō´ wok\. From the Menomini (Algonquian) placename /maneto:wak/; cf. /manɛ:to:wew/ 'he is animal-like, he has supernatural power', /manɛ:to:w/ 'game animal' (Bloomfield 1975). A related placename is **Manito.**

MANITTO (Pa., Westmoreland Co.) \man´ i tō\. Probably related to **Manito,** see above. A variant spelling is **Mannitto.**

MANIWAKI Creek (Minn., Lake Co.). Probably from Ojibwa (Algonquian) *mino-* 'good' plus *aki* 'land' (Vogel 1991; Nichols and Nyholm 1985) A related placename is **Milwaukee County.**

MANKAKVIK Creek (Alaska, Marshall D-4). The Yupik (Eskimo) name was reported in 1951 (Orth 1967).

MANKATO (Minn., Blue Earth Co.) \man kā´ tō\. The name is derived from a Dakota (Siouan) term meaning 'blue earth', which is also translated in the name **Blue Earth** (Upham 2001). The Native American name is from /mąkhá/ 'earth' and /tho/ 'blue, green' (R. Rankin p.c.). The placename was transferred to Neb. (Boyd Co.) and Kans. (Jewell Co.).

MANKO (Okla., Pottawatomie Co.) \mang´ kō\. Said to be named for <Me-an-ko>, a Potawatomi (Algonquian) resident (Shirk 1974).

MANKOMEN Lake (Alaska, Gulkana D-2) \man kō´ mən\. From Ahtena (Athabaskan) *bentgga bene'* 'lake-upper lake' (J. Kari p.c.).

MANNETTO Hills (N.Y., Nassau Co.) \mə net´ ō\. Probably from the Delaware (Algonquian) word for 'spirit, deity' (Beauchamp 1907); cf. Unami Delaware /monə́t:u/ (*RHD* 1987), Munsee Delaware *manútoow* (O'Meara 1996). Related placenames are **Manito** and **Manitou**.

MANNINGTON Creek (N.J., Salem Co.) \man´ ing tən\. Earlier written <Manneton, Mannaton>. Perhaps from the Delaware (Algonquian) word for 'spirit, deity' (Becker 1964); see **Manito** above.

MANNITTO Lake (Pa., Westmoreland Co.). A variant spelling of **Manitto**; see above.

MANOA Springs (Colo., Chaffee Co.) \mə nō´ ə\. Perhaps from the Hawai'ian placename, now part of the city of Honolulu (Bright 1993).

MANOKA Lake (Mich., Montcalm Co.). Perhaps from Ojibwa (Algonquian) *maankik* 'maple forest' (Vogel 1986; Rhodes 1985). Possibly related placenames are **Manake Lake, Manakiki Falls,** and **Lake Manuka.**

MANOKIN (Md., Somerset Co.) \mə nō´ kin\. Perhaps from the same source as **Manakin** (Va., Goochland Co.) or **Monacan** (Va., Albemarle Co.), the name of a CAC Algonquian group; the translation 'earth is dug out' has been suggested (Kenny 1984).

MANOKINAK River (Alaska, Hooper Bay A-1). The Yupik (Eskimo) name was reported in 1882 (Orth 1967).

MANOKOTAK (Alaska, Nushagak Bay D-4) \man ō kō´ tak\. From the Yupik (Eskimo) placename *manuquutaq,* containing *manu-* 'front side of something' (Jacobson 1984).

MANOMET (Mass., Plymouth Co.). From SNEng. Algonquian <munnote> 'basket' (Huden 1962; W. Cowan p.c.).

MANOMIN Creek (Minn., Beltrami Co.) \mə nō´ min\. From Ojibwa (Algonquian) *manoomin* 'wild rice' (Upham 2001; Nichols and Nyholm 1995). Probably related placenames are **Mahnomen County** (Minn.), **Menominee** (Wis.), and **Munnomin Lake** (Wis., Iron Co.).

MANSET (Maine, Hancock Co.) \man´ sət\. Perhaps Abenaki (Algonquian), meaning 'at the island' (Huden 1962); cf. *menahan* 'island' (Day 1994–95).

MANTACHIE (Miss., Itawamba Co.). From a Choctaw (Muskogean) personal name, 'he who goes and speaks' (Seale 1939); cf. *mąya* 'go', *-t-* 'participle', *achi* 'to call, speak' (P. Munro p.c.).

MANTENO (Ill., Kankakee Co.). Probably named for a Potawatomi (Algonquian) woman whose name was written <Maw-se-no> or <Maw-te-no> (Vogel 1963). The placename has also been transferred to Iowa (Shelby Co.).

MANTEO (N.C., Dare Co.). Named for a CAC Algonquian leader who was taken to England in 1584 (Payne 1985).

MANTOLOKING (N.J., Ocean Co.). The Delaware (Algonquian) name is of unclear derivation but may be related to **Mantua** (Becker 1964).

MANTUA (N.J., Gloucester Co.) \man´ tyōō ə\. Perhaps named not for the city in Italy but for a Delaware (Algonquian) group, the name of which was also written as <Manta, Mantes, Mantese> (Becker 1964).

MANUELITO (N.Mex., McKinley Co.) \man wə lē´ tō\. Named for a Navajo (Athabaskan) leader of the nineteenth-century (Julyan 1998); the Spanish name means 'little Manuel'. His Native American name was *ch'il haajiní* 'a black patch of weeds extends out and up', from *ch'il* 'plant, weeds', *haa-* 'up and out', *-jin (-zhin)* 'black' (A. Wilson p.c.).

MANUKA, Lake (Mich., Otsego Co.). Perhaps from Ojibwa (Algonquian) *maankik* 'maple forest' (Vogel 1986; Rhodes 1985). Possibly related forms are **Manake Lake, Manakiki Falls** and **Manoka Lake.**

MANUMUSKIN (N.J., Cumberland Co.). The Delaware (Algonquian) name has also been written as <Monomuskiss>; it may contain <menen> 'to drink' (Becker 1964; Brinton and Anthony 1888).

MANUNKA CHUNK (N.J., Warren Co.). Perhaps from Delaware (Algonquian) *mënàngahchung* 'where the hills are clustered' (Kraft and Kraft 1985).

MANURSING Island (N.Y., Westchester Co.). Also written <Manussing, Menassink>, perhaps Munsee Delaware (Algonquian) for 'little island place' (Ruttenber 1906; Beauchamp 1907); cf. Munsee *mŭnáhan* 'island' (O'Meara 1996). See also **Minisink.**

MANWHAGUE Swamp (Mass., Bristol Co.). Perhaps SNEng. Algonquian for 'at the refuge' (Huden 1962).

MANY ARROWS (N.Mex., McKinley Co.). Corresponds to Navajo (Athabaskan) *k'aa łaní,* lit. 'arrow(s) many' (Linford 2000).

MANYASKA Township (Minn., Martin Co.) \mən yas´ kə\. Perhaps Dakota (Siouan) for 'white bluff', from *mayá* 'steep place, bank, bluff' and *ska* 'white' (Upham 2001; Riggs 1890).

MANY CHERRY Canyon (Ariz., Apache Co.). Corresponds to Navajo (Athabaskan) *didzé łání nástłah* 'many berries cove' (Linford 2000).

MANY FARMS (Ariz., Apache Co.). Corresponds to Navajo (Athabaskan) *dá'ák'eh haláni* 'many fields or farms', from *dá'ák'eh* 'field, farm', *haláni* 'many (over an area)' (Wilson 1995).

MANY SKULLS Trail (Ariz., Apache Co.). Corresponds to Navajo (Athabaskan) *tsiits'iin łání,* lit. 'skull many' (Jett 2001:155).

MANY WATERS (Ariz., Apache Co.). Corresponds to Navajo (Athabaskan) *tó łání* 'many springs', from *tó* 'water', *łání* 'much, many' (Linford 2000).

MAPSA Lake (Alaska, Baird Mountains D-6). From Iñupiaq (Eskimo) *mapsa* 'spleen; snow cornice' (Orth 1967; Fortescue et al. 1994). Perhaps related is **Mapsorak Hill** (Alaska, Point Hope A-1); the Iñupiaq (Eskimo) name is said to mean 'overhanging' (Orth 1967).

MAPTIGAK Mountain (Alaska, Chandler Lake A-2). Named for Morry Maptigak, an Iñupiaq (Eskimo) leader (Orth 1967).

MAQUAN Pond (Mass., Plymouth Co.). From SNEng. Algonquian <mequn> 'feather' (W. Cowan p.c.).

MAQUOIT Bay (Maine, Cumberland Co.). Perhaps from an Abenaki (Algonquian) word meaning 'wet' (Eckstorm 1941:153).

MAQUOKETA (Iowa, Jackson Co.) \mə kō´ kə tə\. Perhaps from a Meskwaki (Algonquian) word meaning 'a bear' (Vogel 1983); cf. *mahkwa* 'bear' (Goddard 1994).

MAQUON (Ill., Knox Co.) \mə kwon´\. Probably from a Miami/Illinois (Algonquian) word meaning ‘spoon’ (Vogel 1963); cf. Ojibwa (Algonquian) *emikwaan* ‘ladle’ (Nichols and Nyholm 1995). The placename **Spoon River** (Ill., Champaign Co.) is based on the Indian name.

MARAIS TEMPS CLAIR (Mo., St. Charles Co.) \mə rē tän klâr´, mə rā täm klâr`\. The French name, meaning ‘clearweather swamp’, is taken from *temps clair* ‘clear weather’, the name of a Kickapoo (Algonquian) leader (Ramsay 1952).

MARAMEC (Mo., Jefferson Co.) \mär´ ə mak\. Perhaps from the same source as **Maramech Hill** (Ill., Kendall Co.); see below. There is also a **Maramec** in Okla. (Pawnee Co.).

MARAMECH Hill (Ill., Kendall Co.) \mâr´ ə mek\. From the Miami/Illinois (Algonquian) word for ‘catfish’ (Vogel 1963); cf. related words such as Meskwaki /mya:name:kwa/ (Goddard 1994), Ojibwa *maanameg* (Nichols and Nyholm 1995). Probably related names are **Maramec** (Mo., Jefferson Co.) and **Minnemac Lake** (Wis., Sawyer Co.) There may also be influence of **Merrimac,** the name of a famous Confederate warship, originally a river in New England.

MARANACOOK (Maine, Kennebec Co.). Perhaps from Abenaki (Algonquian) *môlazigan* ‘black bass (fish)’ (Huden 1962; Day 1994–95).

MARANDUS Brook (Conn., Litchfield Co.). Possibly from a SNEng. Algonquian word meaning ‘cedar swamp’ (Huden 1962).

MARASPIN Creek (Mass., Barnstable Co.). Perhaps related to **Massapeag** (Conn., New London Co.) or **Massapequa** (N.Y., Nassau Co.); see below.

MARA Wash (Nev., Nye Co.) \mä´ rə\. From Southern Paiute (Numic) /mata/ [márA] ‘grinding stone’ (Carlson 1974; J. McLaughlin p.c.). A related placename is **Metate**, Mexican Spanish for ‘grinding slab’, from Nahuatl (Aztecan) *metlatl.*

MAREEP (Calif., Humboldt Co.) \mə rēp`\. From the Yurok village name *meriip* (Gudde 1998).

MARIANO Lake (N.Mex., McKinley Co.) \mä rē ā´ nō\. Named for a Navajo (Athabaskan) leader of the late nineteenth century. The Native American placename was *be'ek'id hóteelí* ‘broad lake’, containing *be'ek'id* ‘lake’ and *teel* ‘broad’ (Wilson 1995).

MARICOPA County (Ariz.) \mâr i kō´ pə\. This name refers to a people of the Yuman linguistic family; it is short for **Cocomaricopa**, a term of unknown origin, applied by the Spanish around 1690 (*HNAI* 10:83). The Maricopas call themselves /piipáa/ ‘people’ (P. Munro p.c.). The placename **Maricopa** occurs as a transfer in Calif. (Kern Co.).

MARINETTE County (Wis.) \mâr i net`\. Named for Marinette Farnsworth (née Chevalier), a woman of mixed Menominee (Algonquian) and French ancestry who lived in the early nineteenth century (Vogel 1991).

MARINGOUIN (La., Iberville Par.) \mä räɴ gwäɴ`\. The French word means ‘mosquito’, borrowed from the Tupinambá language of Brazil, where the term is *mariwį* (D. Kinkade p.c.). A related placename is **Melakwa Lake.**

MARINUKA Lake (Wis., Trempealeau Co.) \mâr i nōō´ kə\. Named for a nineteenth-century Winnebago (Siouan) woman (Vogel 1991).

MARISSA (Ill., St. Clair Co.). Perhaps from a Miami/Illinois (Algonquian) word meaning ‘knife’ (Vogel 1963); cf. Meskwaki (Algonquian) /matesi/ ‘knife’ (Goddard 1994).

MARKAGUNT Plateau (Utah, Iron Co.) \mär´ kə gunt\. Said to be from a Southern Paiute (Numic) word meaning ‘highland of trees’ (Van Cott 1990); cf. /maa-yuakantɨ/ ‘level country covered with timber’, containing /maa-/ ‘plant’ (Sapir 1930).

MARMATON River (Mo., Vernon Co.) \mär´ mə tən, mär mat´ ən\. Said to be of Indian origin, but the details are unknown (Ramsay 1952).

MARMOT Island (Alaska, Afognak A-0). The name may be an erroneous translation of an Alutiiq (Eskimo) word for ground squirrel (Orth 1967).

MAROA (Ill., Macon Co.) \mə rō´ ə\. The name refers to a division of the Miami/Illinois (Algonquian) people; it may be simply a shortening of **Tamaroa** (*HNAI* 15:680).

MAROMAS (Conn., Middlesex Co.). Perhaps from a SNEng. Algonquian word meaning 'bare' (Huden 1962).

MARRATOOKA Pond (N.Y., Suffolk Co.) \mâr ə to͞ok´ ə\. Probably from the same source as **Mattatuck** (Conn., Litchfield Co.) or **Mattatuxet** (R.I., Washington Co.) (Tooker 1911).

MARUMSCO (Md., Somerset Co.). Earlier written <Meramscott>; probably from CAC Algonquian, but of unclear derivation (Kenny 1984). The placename also occurs in Va. (Prince William Co.).

MARYS Igloo (Alaska, Teller A-1). Named for an Iñupiaq (Eskimo) woman who held open house for travelers (Orth 1967). Here the word *igloo* does not mean 'a snow house' but simply has its basic Eskimo meaning of 'house'.

MASARDIS (Maine, Aroostook Co.) \mə sär´ dis\. Said to be from an Abenaki (Algonquian) name meaning 'place of white clay' (Huden 1962).

MASCOMA (N.H., Grafton Co.) \mas kō´ mə\. Probably from Abenaki (Algonquian) *mskwamagw* 'salmon' (Huden 1962; Day 1994–95).

MASCOUTAH (Ill., St. Clair Co.) \mas ko͞o´ tə\. From the same source as **Mascouten Forest** (Ill., Cook Co.); see below.

MASCOUTEN Forest (Ill., Cook Co.) \mas ko͞o ´ tən\. The name refers to a group related to the Kickapoo (Algonquian) people, from /maskootia, meehkootia/ 'prairie people', related to /maskooteewi, mahkoteewi/ 'prairie' (Costa 2000:47). Probably related placenames include **Muscotah** (Kans., Atchison Co.), **Mascoutah** (Ill., St. Clair Co.), and **Muscatine County** (Iowa).

MASCUPPIC Lake (Mass., Middlesex Co.). Perhaps a SNEng. Algonquian word meaning 'place of the large rocks' (Huden 1962).

MASHACKET Cove (Mass., Dukes Co.). Perhaps from SNEng. Algonquian <mashq> 'a bear', <-et> 'place' (W. Cowan p.c.).

MASHAMOQUET Brook (Conn., Windham Co.). Probably from SNEng. Algonquian, meaning 'big fishing place', from <masha> 'big', <-amaug-> 'fish', <-et> 'place' (W. Cowan p.c.).

MASHAPAUG Brook (R.I., Providence Co.). The name represents SNEng. Algonquian <mishippag> 'much water', from <meshe-> 'great' and <-pog> 'water' (W. Cowan p.c.). The name also occurs in Conn. (Tolland Co.). A probably related placename is **Massapeag.**

MASHASHIMUET Park (N.Y., Suffolk Co.). Perhaps from SNEng. Algonquian, meaning 'at the great spring' (Tooker 1911).

MASHEL River (Wash., Pierce Co.) \mə shel´\. From Sahaptin /mišáł/, the name of a subgroup (D. Kinkade p.c.).

MASHENTUCK Brook (Conn., Windham Co.) \mash´ en tuk\. From SNEng. Algonquian, meaning 'well-wooded country', containing <missi-> 'large' and <-tuck> 'tree' (Trumbull 1881; W. Cowan p.c.).

MASHIPACONG Island (N.J., Sussex Co.). The Delaware (Algonquian) placename is of unclear derivation (Becker 1964).

MASHKENODE Lake (Minn., St. Louis Co.) \mash kə nō´ də\. Perhaps from Ojibwa (Algonquian) *maashkinoozhe* 'muskellunge' (Nichols and Nyholm 1995). A related term is **Muskellunge;** see below.

MASHNEE Island (Mass., Barnstable Co.) \mash´ nē\. Perhaps SNEng. Algonquian for 'big house' (Huden 1962).

MASHOMACK Point (N.Y., Suffolk Co.). From a SNEng. Algonquian placename, perhaps containing <mushoun, mishoun> 'boat, canoe' (Tooker 1911).

MASHOOSHALLUK Creek (Alaska, Wiseman C-5). The Iñupiaq (Eskimo) name refers to the 'wild potato' plant (Orth 1967); cf. *masu, maru* 'Eskimo potato' (Webster and Zibell 1970).

MASHPEE (Mass., Barnstable Co.) \mash´ pē\. Perhaps from a SNEng. Algonquian placename meaning 'big water' (Huden 1962); cf. <missi-> 'big', <-pe> 'water' (W. Cowan p.c.).

MASHULAVILLE (Miss., Noxubee Co.) \mə shōō´ lə vil\. The name refers to *Mashula*, abbreviated from <Moshulitubbee>, a Choctaw (Muskogean) leader in the early nineteenth century. The Native American term was probably the war name *amosholi-t-abi* 'he who tries hard and kills', from *amosholi* 'to try hard' and *abi* 'to kill' (Seale 1939; P. Munro p.c.). The variant **Moshulaville** is also found. A related placename is **Moshulitubbees Prairie** (Miss., Noxubee Co.).

MASIPA Spring (Ariz., Navajo Co.) \mə sē´ pə\. Hopi (Uto-Aztecan) *masìipa* 'gray spring', from *masìi-* 'gray' and *-pa, paa-hu* 'water, spring' (K. Hill p.c.).

MASKERCHUGG River (R.I., Bristol Co.) \mas´ kər chug\. Also written as <Maskachaug, Masquachug> (etc.); probably from SNEng. Algonquian <musqueechagg> 'rushes (plant)' (W. Cowan p.c.).

MASPETH (N.Y., Queens Co.) \mas´ pəth\. Probably from Munsee Delaware, but the derivation is unclear (Grumet 1981:28).

MASSABESIC (N.H., Hillsborough Co.). Perhaps from Abenaki (Algonquian), 'near the great brook' (Huden 1962); cf. *msi* 'big' (Day 1994–95).

MASSACHUSETTS \mas ə chōō´ sits\. The name of the bay and the state was originally the plural of *Massachusett* or *Massachuset*, the name applied to a SNEng. Algonquian group. The term probably means 'at the big hill', from <mass-> 'large', <-adchu-> 'mountain', <-s-> 'little', and <-et> 'place' (Trumbull 1881; W. Cowan p.c.). The name also occurs in Maine (Franklin Co.).

MASSACO (Conn., Hartford Co.). Also written <Mussawco, Massaqua> (etc.); probably from SNEng. Algonquian, meaning 'big outlet', from <massa-> 'large', <-sauk> 'outlet' (Trumbull 1881; W. Cowan p.c.).

MASSACRE \mas´ ə kər\. The term is found in many states, applied to places where fighting between Indians and white settlers or between Indian groups produced many dead; examples are in N.Mex. (Sierra Co., Julyan 1998) and in Wash. (San Juan Co.) (Hitchman 1985).

MASSAI Point (Ariz., Cochise Co.) \mə sī´, mas´ ē\. Named for an Apache (Athabaskan) warrior known in English as Big-Foot Massai; his Native American name is not known (Granger 1983).

MASSANUTTEN Mountain (Va., Page Co.). Probably a CAC Algonquian placename; it has been interpreted as 'potato ground' and as 'basket' (Hagemann 1988).

MASSAPEAG (Conn., New London Co.) \mas´ ə peg\. Probably from SNEng. Algonquian <massa> 'big', <-pe> 'water', <-auke> 'land' (Trumbull 1881, W. Cowan p.c.). A variant is **Massapeague.** Possibly related placenames include **Maraspin Creek** (Mass., Barnstable Co.) and **Massapequa** (N.Y., Nassau Co.) \mas ə pē´ kwə\ (cf. Grumet 1981).

MASSAPOAG Lake (Mass., Norfolk Co.) \mas ə pō´ əg\. Probably SNEng. Algonquian for 'large pond', from <massa-> 'big', <paug> 'pond' (Huden 1962; W. Cowan p.c.).

MASSAPONAX (Va., Spotsylvania Co.). Named for a CAC Algonquian group; also written as **Massaponnox** (Hagemann 1988).

MASSASECUM Lake (N.H., Merrimack Co.) \mas ə sē´ kəm\. Perhaps from Abenaki (Algonquian) *msa-* 'big', *asakwam* 'moss' (W. Cowan p.c.).

MASSASOIT (Mass., Worcester Co.) \mas ə soi´ it\. Named for a SNEng. Algonquian leader of the seventeenth century; his Native American name perhaps meant 'great chief'. The placename also occurs as a transfer in Kans. (Wabaunsee Co.) (Rydjord 1968).

MASSAWEPIE Creek (N.Y., Herkimer Co.) \mas ə wē´ pē\. Perhaps from Munsee Delaware, possibly containing /(m)xw-/ 'much', /-ə́pəy/ 'water' (I. Goddard p.c.). A similar placename is **Massawippa Lake** (N.Y., Orange Co.).

MASSINACAK (Va., Powhatan Co.) \mas´ nə kak\. The name of a CAC Algonquian village, reported in 1608 (Hagemann 1988).

MASTIC (N.Y., Suffolk Co.) \mas´ tik\. Perhaps SNEng. Algonquian for 'great tidal stream', from <massa-, missi> 'big', <tuk> 'tidal stream' (Tooker 1911; W. Cowan p.c.). A related placename is **Mystic**. Perhaps related is **Mastuxet** (R.I., Washington Co.), from <massa-> 'big', <tuk> 'tidal stream', <-s> 'small', <-et> 'place'.

MASU Creek (Alaska, Chandler Lake A-4). The Iñupiaq (Eskimo) name was published in 1951 (Orth 1967); it may be from *masu, maru* 'Eskimo potato' (Webster and Zibell 1970). Probably related placenames are **Masukatalik** (Alaska, Candle C-4) and **Mashooshalluk Creek** (Alaska, Wiseman C-5). Other probably related placenames include **Matsutnak River** (Alaska, Demarcation Point C-2).

MATAGUAL Valley (Calif., San Diego Co.) \mä´ tə wäl\. Perhaps from Diegueño (Yuman) *mat-iihway* 'earth-red' (Gudde 1998).

MATANUSKA (Alaska, Anchorage C-6) \mat ə nōōs´ kə\. The term was formerly used to refer to the Ahtna (Athabaskan) Indians of the Copper River region. It seems to have been derived from Russian (Orth 1967); cf. *mednovskaja, mednaja* 'pertaining to the Copper River', from *med'* 'copper'.

MATAPONI Creek (Md., Prince George's Co.) \mat ə pō nī´\. Perhaps from a CAC Algonquian word meaning 'joined waters' (Kenny 1984). A related form is **Mattaponi** (Va., King and Queen Co.). It is possible that the placename is related to **Mattapan** (Mass., Suffolk Co.) and/or **Mattapany** (Del., Sussex Co.).

MATASSEE Branch (S.C., Berkeley Co.). Perhaps derived from an unidentified Indian language (Pickens 1963:37).

MATAWAN (N.J., Monmouth Co.) \mat´ ə wän\. The Delaware (Algonquian) name is of unclear derivation; earlier writings are <Matteawan> and <Mattawong> (Becker 1964). The placename occurs as a transfer in Minn. (Waseca Co.). Probably related placenames include **Matewan** (W.Va., Mingo Co.), **Mattawan** (Mich., Van Buren Co.), **Mattawana** (Pa., Mifflin Co.), and **Matteawan** (N.Y., Dutchess Co.).

MATCHAPONIX (N.J., Middlesex Co.). The Delaware (Algonquian) name is of unclear derivation (Becker 1964).

MATCHARAK Lake (Alaska, Ambler River C-1). The Iñupiaq (Eskimo) name was reported in 1956 (Orth 1967).

MATECUMBE (Fla., Monroe Co.) \mat ə kōōm´ bə, mat ə kum´ bē\. Perhaps from an unknown Indian language (Read 1934).

MATEWAN (W.Va., Mingo Co.) \māt´ wän\. Perhaps related to **Matawan** (N.J., Monmouth Co.); see above.

MATHLES Creek (Calif., Shasta Co.) \math´ ləs\. Probably from Wintu /maaɬas/ 'baked salmon' (Gudde 1998).

MATILIJA (Calif., Ventura Co.) \mə til´ i hä\. From a Ventureño (Chumashan) placename (Gudde 1998). The matilija poppy takes its name from this place.

MATILTON (Calif., Humboldt Co.) \mə til´ tən\. From the Hupa (Athabaskan) placename *me'dil-ding,* lit. 'canoe-place' (Gudde 1998).

MATINECOCK (N.Y., Nassau Co.). Perhaps from Munsee Delaware (Algonquian) *mahtënekung* 'place of rough ground' (Kraft and Kraft 1985). The name is also written as **Matinnekonck.**

MATINICUS (Maine, Knox Co.) \mə tin´ i kəs\. Probably from Abenaki (Algonquian) *matenaga, matnaga* 'the end of the island' (Eckstorm 1941:97–99; Day 1994–95).

MATINNEKONCK (N.Y., Nassau Co.). A variant form of **Matinecock**; see above.

MATKATAMIBA Canyon (Ariz., Coconino Co.). Named for a Hualapai (Yuman) family (Granger 1983).

MATLACHA (Fla., Lee Co.). Perhaps from Muskogee *emarv* /imá:ɬa/ 'a title appearing in war names' plus *-uce* /-oči/ 'small' (Read 1934; Martin and Mauldin 2000).

MATOACA (Va., Chesterfield Co.) \mə tō´ ə kə\. This was supposedly the private name of Pocahontas, said to be derived from CAC Algonquian <metawake> 'she amuses herself playing with something'; cf. also **Pocahantas/Pocahontas** below. An alternative spelling is in the placename **Matoaka** (Va., James City Co.), which also occurs in W.Va. (Mercer Co.), Fla. (Manatee Co.), and Okla. (Washington Co.).

MATOGAK River (Alaska, Hagemeister Is. D-3). The Yupik (Eskimo) name was reported around 1947 (Orth 1967).

MATOLES (Ore., Jefferson Co.) \mat´ ōlz\. From Sahaptin [mɨt'úla] 'spawned-out salmon' (N. Rude p.c.) Possible variant writings are **MATOLIUS** and **Metolius.**

MATS MATS (Wash., Jefferson Co.) \mats´ mats\. From Chemakum [mácmac] 'chipmunk' (D. Kinkade p.c.).

MATSUTNAK River (Alaska, Demarcation Point C-2). The Iñupiaq (Eskimo) name refers to an edible tuber (Orth 1967); cf. *masu* 'Eskimo potato' (Webster and Zibell 1970). Possibly related Alaska placenames include **Masu** (Chandler Lake A-4) and **Mashooshalluk Creek** (Wiseman C-5).

MATTABESSET River (Conn., Middlesex Co.) \mat ə bes´ ət\. Also written as <Massabesit>; from SNEng. Algonquian, perhaps meaning 'at a big brook', containing <massa-> 'big', <sepu> 'river', <-s> 'diminutive', <-et> 'place' (Trumbull 1881; W. Cowan p.c.).

MATTACHEESE (Mass., Barnstable Co.) \mat´ ə chēz\. Perhaps from SNEng. Algonquian <matta-> 'not' plus <-chise> 'old man' (W. Cowan p.c.).

MATTAGODUS Stream (Maine, Penobscot Co.) \mat ə gō´ dəs\. Probably from Abenaki (Algonquian), perhaps meaning 'bad landing place for canoes' (Eckstorm 1941:62–63).

MATTAKESET Bay (Mass., Dukes Co.). From SNEng. Algonquian, perhaps meaning 'place of black mud' (Huden 1962).

MATTAKEUNK Pond (Maine, Penobscot Co.). From Abenaki (Algonquian), translated as 'runs right straight' (Eckstorm 1941).

MATTAMISCONTIS Lake (Maine, Penobscot Co.) \mat ə mis kon´ tis\. Perhaps Abenaki (Algonquian), meaning 'plenty of alewives (a type of fish)', from <madamas> 'alewife' (Eckstorm 1941:51–52).

MATTAMUSKEET Lake (N.C., Hyde Co.) \mat ə mus´ kēt\. Said to be from an Indian word <Mata-mackya-t-wi> 'it is a moving swamp'; the language has not been identified (Powell 1968).

MATTANAWCOOK Island (Maine, Penobscot Co.) \mat ə nô´ ko͝ok\. From Abenaki (Algonquian), perhaps meaning 'long island'. Eckstorm (1941:53–55) discussed the derivations of **Mattanawcook Island, Pond,** and **Stream,** which she believed had separate derivations.

MATTANO Park (N.J., Union Co.). Supposedly named for a Delaware (Algonquian) leader; the derivation is not clear (Becker 1964).

MATTAPAN (Mass., Suffolk Co.) \mat´ ə pan\. From SNEng. Algonquian <(m)wutappin> 'he sits here' (Trumbull 1879; W. Cowan p.c.). The placename also occurs in N.Y.

MATTAPANY (Del., Sussex Co.). Probably from Delaware (Algonquian), perhaps meaning 'landing place' (Heck et al. 1966).

MATTAPEX (Md., Queen Anne's Co.) \mat´ ə peks\. From CAC Algonquian, perhaps meaning 'junction of waters' (Kenny 1984).

MATTAPOISETT (Mass., Plymouth Co.) \mat ə poi´ sit\. The SNEng. Algonquian placename perhaps means 'resting place' (Huden 1962).

MATTAPONI (Va., King and Queen Co.) \mat ə pō nī`\. From the name of a CAC Algonquian group (*HNAI* 15:268); a related name is **Mattaponi Creek** (Md., Prince George's Co.); see above. Also perhaps related placenames are **Mattapan** and **Mattapany.**

MATTASEUNK Stream (Maine, Penobscot Co.). Perhaps from an Abenaki (Algonquian) placename meaning 'rapids-at-the-mouth stream' (Eckstorm 1941).

MATTASSEE Lake (S.Car., Berkeley Co.) From an unidentified Indian language (Waddell 1980).

MATTATUCK (Conn., Litchfield Co.) \mat´ ə tuk\. From SNEng. Algonquian, perhaps meaning 'place without wood', containing <ma-> 'not' and <-tuck> 'tree' (Trumbull 1881; W. Cowan p.c.). Possibly related placenames include **Marratooka Pond** (N.Y., Suffolk Co.) and **Mattatuxet** (R.I., Washington Co.) \mat ə tuk´ sət\, perhaps with the addition of <-s> 'diminutive' and <-et> 'place' (Huden 1962).

MATTAWA Lake (Mass., Franklin Co.) \mat´ ə wä\. Perhaps from SNEng. Algonquian <matwau> 'he is an enemy' (W. Cowan p.c.). The name also occurs in Wash. (Grant Co.).

MATTAWAMKEAG (Maine, Penobscot Co.) \mat ə wäm´ keg\. Perhaps from Abenaki (Algonquian), meaning 'at the mouth, a gravel bar' (Eckstorm 1941:58–60).

MATTAWAN (Mich., Van Buren Co.) \mat´ ə wän\. Perhaps a transfer of **Matawan** (N.J., Monmouth Co.); see above.

MATTAWANA (Pa., Mifflin Co.) \mat ə wä´ nə\. Perhaps related to **Matawan** (N.J., Monmouth Co.); see above. The name **Mattawana** is found as a transfer in Ala. (Blount Co.).

MATTAWOMAN Creek (Va., Northampton Co.) \mat´ ə wo͝om ən\. From the name of a CAC Algonquian subgroup (Hagemann 1988). The placename also occurs in Md. (Charles Co.; Kenny 1984).

MATTEAWAN (N.Y., Dutchess Co.) \mat´ ə wän\. Perhaps from the same source as **Matawan** (N.J., Monmouth Co.); see above.

MATTITUCK (N.Y., Suffolk Co.) \mat´ i tuk\. Perhaps from a SNEng. Algonquian placename meaning 'no trees', containing <matta> 'no' and <-tuck> 'tree' (Tooker 1911).

MATTOLE River (Calif., Humboldt Co.) \mə tōl`\. The name refers to an Athabaskan Indian people, called *bedool* by themselves and *me'tuul* by the neighboring Wiyots (Gudde 1998).

MATTUBBY Creek (Miss., Monroe Co.) \mə tub´ ē\. Probably from a Choctaw (Muskogean) personal name *mąya-t-abi* 'he who goes and kills', from *mąya* 'to go', *-t-* 'participial', *abi* 'to kill' (Seale 1939; P. Munro p.c.).

MATUNUCK (R.I., Washington Co.). Perhaps from a SNEng. Algonquian term meaning 'high place' (Huden 1962).

MATURANGO Peak (Calif., Inyo Co.) \mat ə rang´ gō\. Perhaps from Spanish *maturrango* 'bad horseman; clumsy, rough person'; or from a Panamint (Numic) form such as /mattootoongwɨnɨ/ 'stand braced, as against the wind'; or from Panamint /muatangga/, the name for Koso Hot Springs (Gudde 1998).

MAUCH CHUNK Creek (Pa., Carbon Co.) \mäk chungk´, mô chungk´, mə chungk`\. Perhaps from Delaware (Algonquian) *màxkwchung* 'at the hill of the bears' (Kraft and Kraft 1985); cf. Unami Delaware /maxkw/ 'bear' (Blalock et al. 1994). In 1954 the communities of **Lower, Upper,** and **East Mauch Chunk** were consolidated under the name **Jim Thorpe,** in honor of the famous American Indian athlete.

MAUMEE River (Ohio, Lucas Co.) \mô mē´, mô´ mē\. From Ottawa (Algonquian) /maamii ziibi/ 'Miami River', referring to the Miami/Illinois (Algonquian) people (McCafferty 2002). The placename also occurs in Ind. (Jackson

Co.). A related placename is **Miami,** in those cases where it is derived from the name of the Algonquian people; see below.

MAUNA LOA Lake (Mich., Oakland Co.) \mô nə lō´ ə\. From the name of a volcanic mountain on the island of Hawai'i, from the Hawai'ian meaning 'long mountain' (Pukui et al. 1974).

MAUNELUK River (Alaska, Shungnak D-1). From Iñupiaq (Eskimo) *maniiḷaq* 'rough mountain' (Burch 1998).

MAUNESHA River (Wis., Jefferson Co.) Perhaps from the same source as **Menasha** (Wis., Winnebago Co.) (Vogel 1991). The source may be an Algonquian word for 'island', such as Ojibwa *minis* (Nichols and Nyholm 1995), Fox /menesi/ (Goddard 1994), or Menomini /menɛ:s/ (Bloomfield 1975).

MAUVILLA (Ala., Mobile Co.) \mô vil´ ə\. The name may be derived from the same Indian source as **Mobile County;** see below.

MAUWEE Brook (Conn., Litchfield Co.) \mô´ wē\. A family name, also written *Mahwee*. Perhaps from Mahican (Algonquian), of unclear derivation (Huden 1962).

MAWAH Creek (Calif., Humboldt Co.) \mä´ wä\. From the Yurok placename *mawa* (Gudde 1998).

MAXATAWNEY (Ohio, Gallia Co.) \mak sə tô´ nē\. From Delaware (Algonquian) <machk-siit-hane> 'bear foot stream', containing <machk-> 'a bear', <-siit-> 'foot', and <-hane> 'stream' (Mahr 1959:368); cf. Unami Delaware /maxkw/ 'bear' (Blalock et al. 1994). A related placename is **MAXATAWNY** (Pa., Berks Co.); also related is **Macungie** (Pa., Lehigh Co.).

MAXINKUCKEE (Ind., Marshall Co.) \mak´ sin kuk ē\. From Miami/Illinois (Algonquian) /meenkahsenahkiki/ 'it is big stone country' (McCafferty 2002).

MAYACA, Port (Fla., Martin Co.) \mä yak´ ə\. From the same source as **Myakka** (Fla., Manatee Co.); see below.

MAYACAMAS Mountains (Calif., Lake Co.) \mə yak´ ə məs, mā yak´ məs\. From the Wappo (Yukian) village name <Maiya'kma>, probably with an added Spanish plural (Gudde 1998). A variant spelling is **Mayacmas**; a related placename is **Maacama Creek** (Calif., Sonoma Co.).

MAYES County (Okla.). Named for Samuel H. Mayes, a Cherokee (Iroquoian) leader (Shirk 1974).

MAYOEAK River (Alaska, Barrow B-4). The Iñupiaq (Eskimo) name may be from *mayuġiaq-* 'go to ascend' (L. Kaplan p.c.). Possibly related names are **Mayoriak** and **Miguakiak** (Alaska, Teshekpuk D-2) (Orth 1967).

MAYUASANIK Creek (Alaska, Killik River D-2). The Iñupiaq (Eskimo) name is from *mayuq-* 'to ascend' (L. Kaplan p.c.).

MAYUKUIT Mountain (Alaska, Killik River A-2). The Iñupiaq (Eskimo) name is perhaps from *mayuq-* 'to ascend' (L. Kaplan p.c.).

MAZA (N.Dak., Towner Co.) \mā´ zə\. Named for a Dakota (Siouan) leader called <Maza Chante> (Wick 1988); the name probably means 'iron heart', from *máza* 'iron, metal' and *čą̨nté* 'heart' (Riggs 1890).

MAZAMA, Mount (Ore., Klamath Co.) \mə zam´ ə, mə zä´ mə\. The name refers to a prehistoric volcanic mountain; the caldera is now occupied by Crater Lake. It was named for the Mazamas, a mountaineering club based in Portland, in 1896 (McArthur 1992). The word *mazama* was used at one time to refer to the mountain sheep; but it is the species name for the brocket deer, an animal native to Latin America. It is derived from Nahuatl (Aztecan) *mazame'* 'deer (pl.)', from *mazatl* 'a deer' (Bright 1999b). The placename Mazama also occurs in Wash. (Okanogan Co.) and Alaska (Talkeetna D-1). A possibly related placename is **Mazuma Creek** (Alaska, Talkeetna mountains, A-2).

MAZASKA Lake (Minn., Rice Co.) \mə zas´ kə\. From Dakota (Sioun) *mázaska* 'silver', composed of *máza* 'metal' plus *ska* 'white' (Upham 2001; Riggs 1890).

MAZATZAL Peak (Ariz., Gila Co.) \mä zə tsäl´, mad ə zel\. The name is said to be Apache (Athabaskan) for 'bleak, barren', but the derivation is not clear (Granger 1983).

MAZOMANIE (Wis., Dane Co.) \mā zō mā´ nē\. Named for a Winnebago (Indian) resident of the early nineteenth century; his name was <Mau-ze-mon-e-ka> 'iron walker' (Vogel 1991). The Native American form was probably *máazamaníga,* from *máas* 'iron,' *hamaní* 'walk on', *-ga* 'masculine' (K. Minor p.c.).

MAZON (Ill., Grundy Co.) \mə zon\. Perhaps from a Miami/Illinois word for a plant, variously identified as 'nettle' or 'wild hemp' (Vogel 1963).

MAZUMA Creek (Alaska, Talkeetna Mountains A-2) \mə zo͞o´ mə\. Perhaps related to **Mount Mazama** (Ore., Klamath Co.) (see above), with influence from the English slang term *mazuma* 'money', of Yiddish origin.

MEAT Rock (Ariz., Apache Co.). Corresponds to Navajo (Athabaskan) *tsé-'atsį'* 'meat rock' (Linford 2000).

MEAUWATAKA (Mich., Wexford Co.). Said to be from an Ojibwa (Algonquian) word meaning 'halfway', but the derivation is unclear (Vogel 1986); cf. *megwe-* 'among, in the midst of' (Nichols and Nyholm 1995).

MECAHA (Mont., Garfield Co.) \muk´ ā hô\. Dhegiha (Siouan) /mikka ha/ 'raccoon skin' (Cheney 1984, R. Rankin p.c.).

MECAN (Wis., Marquette Co.) \mi kan\. From Ojibwa (Algonquian) *miikana* 'road' (Vogel 1991, Nichols and Nyholm 1995). A related placename is **Mikana.**

MECHAKAMIUT (Alaska, Cape Mendenhall D-4). The Yupik (Eskimo) name was reported in 1949 (Orth 1967); the ending *-miut* means 'people'.

MECKINOCK (N.Dak., Grand Forks Co.) \mek´ i nok\. From Ojibwa (Algonquian) *mikinaak* 'snapping turtle' (Wick 1988; Nichols and Nyholm 1995). Related placenames are **Mackinac County, Mackinaw City, Fort Michilimackinac** (all in Mich.), as well as **Mickinock Township** (Minn., Roseau Co.) and **Mekanac Point** (Wis., Oneida Co.).

MECOSTA County (Mich.) \mə kos´ tə\. Named for a Potawatomi (Algonquian) leader of the early nineteenth century; the name perhaps meant 'little bear' (Vogel 1986). Cf. Potawatomi *mko* 'bear' (Kansas 1997).

MECOSUKEY (Okla., Seminole Co.) \mek ə so͞o´ kē\. From the same origin as **Miccosukee** (Fla., Leon Co.); see below.

MEDDYBEMPS (Maine, Washington Co.) \med´ i bemps\. Perhaps from a Passamaquoddy (Algonquian) word meaning 'alewife (a type of fish)' (Eckstorm 1941:229–30).

MEDFRA (Alaska, Medfra A-4) \med´ frə\. Perhaps from a Upper Kuskokwim (Athabaskan) placename, but the derivation is unclear (Orth 1967).

MEDICINE. This word has been widely used in Indian English and in discussion of Indian cultures to refer not only to plant products used for curing disease but also to anything associated with ceremonial practice or with supernatural power; it could thus be translated in many contexts as 'sacred'. The term frequently occurs in placenames: for example, **Medicine River** (Iowa, Wayne Co.; Vogel 1983). In a number of cases it represents a translation of Dakotan (Siouan) *phežúta,* as in **Medicine Knoll** (S.Dak., Hughes Co.), corresponding to Dakota *pahá phežúta,* lit. 'hill [of] medicine' (Sneve 1973; A. Taylor p.c.). **Medicine Bow** (Wyo., Carbon Co.) refers to bows and arrows used for ceremonial purposes. **Medicine Lodge** (Kans., Barber Co.) designates a structure, such as a sweathouse, in which worship and healing were performed. **Medicine Man Creek** (Alaska, Nabesna A-3) is a translation of Upper Tanana (Athabaskan) *di<u>sh</u>in niign* (J. Kari p.c.); the term refers to an individual with sacred powers; the term is sometimes used for a shaman or healer, sometimes for a ceremonial practitioner.

MEDOC (Mo., Jasper Co.) \mē´ dok\. Not from the French region of Médoc but probably derived from **Modoc,** a people of Ore. and northern Calif. (Ramsay 1952); see below.

MEDOMAK (Maine, Lincoln Co.) \med om´ ak\. Perhaps Penobscot (Algonquian) for 'place of many alewives (a type of fish)' (Eckstorm 1941).

MEDO Township (Minn., Blue Earth Co.) \mē´ dō\. From Dakota (Siouan) *mdo* 'a type of edible root or tuber', sometimes called 'wild potato' (Upham 2001; Riggs 1890).

MEDUMCOOK (Maine, Knox Co.). Probably a variant writing of **Meduncook River**; see below.

MEDUNCOOK River (Maine, Knox Co.). Perhaps from Malecite (Algonquian), meaning 'blocked by sandbars' (Huden 1962); probable variant writings are **Medumcook** and **Medunkeunk.**

MEDUXNEKEAG Lake (Maine, Aroostook Co.) \mə duks´ nə keg\. Perhaps from Malecite (Algonquian), meaning 'rapids at the mouth' (Huden 1962).

MEEME (Wis., Manitowoc Co.) \mē´ mē\. From Ojibwa (Algonquian) *omiimii* 'dove, pigeon' (Vogel 1991; Nichols and Nyholm 1995). A related placename is **Mimi Lake** (Wis., Bayfield Co.).

MEENAHGA Mountain (N.Y., Franklin Co.). Perhaps from Delaware (Algonquian) <mih´ nacki> 'huckleberry land' (Ruttenber 1906); cf. <minall> 'huckleberry, <haki> 'earth, ground' (Brinton and Anthony 1874).

MEETEETSE (Wyo., Park Co.) \mə tēt´ sē\. Shoshoni (Numic) /miittii-ttsi/ 'meeting place', from English *meeting* (J. McLaughlin p.c.).

MEGANSETT (Mass., Barnstable Co.) \mə gan´ sət\. From SNEng. Algonquian, perhaps meaning 'at the fish weir' (Huden 1962).

MEGOTSOL Island (Alaska, Nulato D-4). The Koyukon (Athabaskan) name was reported in 1940 (Orth 1967).

MEGUNTICOOK Lake (Maine, Knox Co.) \meg un´ ti ko͞o k\. Perhaps from Malecite (Algonquian), meaning 'big mountain harbor' (Eckstorm 1941:71–72).

MEGUZEE Point (Mich., Antrim Co.). Perhaps from Ojibwa (Algonquian) *migizi* 'bald eagle' (Vogel 1986; Nichols and Nyholm 1995).

MEHERRIN (Va., Lunenburg Co.) \mə hâr´ in\. Named for an Indian group, perhaps of the Iroquoian family, that formerly lived in the region (Hagemann 1988).

MEHOOPANY (Pa., Wyoming Co.) \mə ho͞o´ pə nē\. Perhaps from Delaware (Algonquian) <meech> 'big' and <hoopany> 'wild potatoes' (Donehoo 1928); cf. <mechek, mechen> 'big', <hob´bin> 'potato' (Brinton and Anthony 1888) and Unami Delaware /hó:pəni:s/ 'potato' (Blalock et al. 1994).

MEKANAC Point (Wis., Oneida Co.) \mek´ ə nak\. From Ojibwa (Algonquian) *mikinaak* 'snapping turtle' (Vogel 1991; Nichols and Nyholm 1995). Related placenames are **Mackinac County, Mackinaw City, Fort Michilimackinac** (all in Mich.), as well as **Mickinock Township** (Minn., Roseau Co.) and **Meckinock** (N.Dak., Grand Forks Co.).

MEKETCHUM Creek (Alaska, Ruby A-5) The name, perhaps from Koyukon (Athabaskan), was reported in 1933 (Orth 1967).

MEKORYUK (Alaska, Nunivak Is. B-4) \mē kôr´ ē yuk\. From the Yupik (Eskimo) placename *mikuryaq,* from *mikur-* '(fish, insects) to swarm' (Orth 1967; Jacobson 1984).

MEKUSUKEY (Okla., Seminole Co.) \mek ə so͝ok´ ē\. From the same source as **Miccosukee** (Fla., Leon Co.).

MELAKWA Lake (Ore., Lane Co.) \mel´ ə kwä\. From Chinook Jargon <mel-a-kwa> [mɛ́ləkwa] 'mosquito(s)', from French *maringouin,* borrowed from the Tupinambá language of Brazil, where the term is *mariwį* (McArthur 1992; D. Kinkade p.c.). The placename also occurs in Idaho (Benewah Co.) and

Wash. (King Co.). A related placename is **Maringouin** (La., Iberville Par.).

MELATOLIK Creek (Alaska, Black A-2). The Yupik (Eskimo) name was published as <Muganolowik> in 1970 (Orth 1967).

MELOKOSHAR Point (Alaska, Naknek C-3). The Yupik (Eskimo) name was reported in 1952 (Orth 1967).

MELOZIMORAN Creek (Alaska, Melozitna C-1). A name made up from parts of two names: the **Melozitna River** and the nearby Moran Dome (Orth 1967).

MELOZI Springs (Alaska, Melozitna A-4) \mə lō´ zē\. From Koyukon (Athabaskan) *meleghozeet no'*, with *no'* 'river' (Jetté and Jones 2000); the name of the river is also borrowed into English as **Melozitna River.** The related name **Melozikakat** (Alaska, Ruby C-5) \mə lō zē kak´ ət\ contains *-kaakk'et* 'stream mouth'.

MELOZITNA River (Alaska, Ruby D-5) \mel ō zit´ nə\. From Koyukon (Athabaskan) *meleghozeet no'*, with *no'* 'river' (Jetté and Jones 2000).

MEMALOOSE (Ore., Clackamas Co.) \mem´ ə lo͞os\. Chinook Jargon <mem´-a-loost, mim´-a-loos> \mĭmalus\. 'die, dead', probably from Lower Chinook [tɬmə́məlost, tɬmə́məlust] 'dead one, corpse' (McArthur 1992; D. Kinkade p.c.). The placename also occurs in Wash. (Klickitat Co.) and in Idaho (Bonner Co.).

MEMPHREMAGOG, Lake (Vt., Orleans Co.). From Abenaki (Algonquian) *mamhlawbagok* 'at the expansive lake'; cf. *mamhlawi* 'much' (Huden 1962; Day 1995).

MENAHGA (Minn., Wadena Co.) \mə nä´ gə\. From Ojibwa (Algonquian) *miinikaa* 'there are lots of blueberries' (Upham 2001; J. Nichols p.c.) A related placename is **Blueberry.**

MENAMSHA Creek (Mass., Dukes Co.) \mə nam´ shə\. From SNEng. Algonquian, but of unclear derivation (Huden 1962).

MENAN (Idaho, Jefferson Co.) \mə nan`\. Said to be a Shoshoni (Numic) word for 'many waters' (Boone 1988).

MENANHANT (MA, Barnstable Co.). A variant of **Menauhant**; see below.

MENANTIC Creek (N.Y., Suffolk Co.) \mə nan´ tik\. Probably from SNEng. Algonquian. The term may be related to **Menantico** (N.J., Cumberland Co.) \mə nan´ ti kō\, which is perhaps from Delaware (Algonquian) <menantachk> 'a swamp with trees meeting above' (Becker 1964; Brinton and Anthony 1888). An alternative spelling is **Manantico.**

MENASHA (Wis., Winnebago Co.) \mə nash´ ə\. Perhaps from Menominee (Algonquian) /menɛ:s/ 'island' (Vogel 1991; Bloomfield 1975); or perhaps from Winnebago (Siouan) *maanásge* 'sweet grass, Glyceria' (K. Miner p.c.). A possibly related name is **Maunesha River** (Wis., Jefferson Co.); see above.

MENATCHEE Creek (Wash., Asotin Co.) \mə nach´ ē\. Perhaps related to **Wenatchee,** from Sahaptin [wi:náča] 'river issuing from a canyon' (D. Kinkade p.c.).

MENAUHANT (Mass., Barnstable Co.). From SNEng. Algonquian, perhaps containing <moonaeu-> 'it is deep' (Huden 1962; W. Cowan p.c.). A variant is **Menanhant.**

MENDELTNA Creek (Alaska, Valdez D-7) \men delt´ nə\. From Ahtna (Athabaskan) *bendilna'*, with *na'* 'stream' (Kari 1983:37).

MENDOTA (Minn., Dakota Co.) \men dō´ tə\. From Dakota (Siouan) *mdóte* 'mouth of a river, junction of one river with another' (Upham 2001; Riggs 1890). The placename was transferred to several other states (e.g., Wis, Dane Co.; and Calif., Fresno Co.).

MENEKAUNEE Shoal (Wis., Marinette Co.). From Menominee (Algonquian) /meni:ka:n/ 'settlement, village' (Vogel 1991; Bloomfield 1975). The placename is also found in Minn. (Chippewa Co.).

MENEMSHA (Mass., Dukes Co.). From SNEng. Algonquian, perhaps meaning 'middle island' (Huden 1962).

MENHADEN (N.J., Cumberland Co.) \men hā′ dən\. The name refers to a type of marine fish, commonly used for fertilizing land; it is from Narragansett (SNEng. Algonquian) <munnawhatteaûg> (Becker 1964; *RHD* 1987). Cf. <munnoquohteau> 'he fertilizes' (W. Cowan p.c.).

MENNEIKA Creek (Iowa, Wapello Co.). Perhaps from the same source as **Minneika,** below.

MENO (Ore., Hood River Co.) \men′ ō\. An abbreviation of **Menominee** in Mich. (McArthur 1992).

MENOKEN (Kans., Shawnee Co.) \mə nō′ kən\. Perhaps from Osage (Siouan) /mą̨ðį́hka/ 'earth, soil, mud' (Rydjord 1968, R. Rankin p.c.); however, it may be a transfer name from **Menokin** (Va., Richmond Co.), of obscure Algonquian origin. In N.Dak. **Menoken** (Burleigh Co.) may be a transfer name from either of the above.

MENOMINEE \mə nom′ ə ne, mə nō′ mə nē\. The name refers to an Algonquian people of Wis.; the term is from Ojibwa (Algonquian) *manoominii,* lit. 'wild rice people', from *manoomin* 'wild rice'. The Menominees' name for themselves is /omɛ:ʔnomene:w/, which is clearly not derived from their word /mano:mɛh/ 'wild rice'. The tribal name has sometimes been written **Menomini** in linguistic and anthropological literature. As a placename, **Menominee** refers to counties, cities, and other places in both Wis. and Mich.; it also occurs in Ill. (Joe Daviess Co.) and Ore. (Hood River Co.). Other related terms include **Menomonee River** (Wis., Waukesha Co.) and **Menomonie** (Wis., Dunn Co.).

MENOMIN Lake (Minn., Crow Wing Co.) \mə nō′ min\. From Ojibwa (Algonquian) 'wild rice' (Nichols and Nyholm 1995); cf. **Menominee** below. The name also occurs in Wis. (Dunn Co.).

MENONAQUA Beach (Mich., Emmet Co.) \mə non′ ə kwä\. Perhaps from an unidentified Algonquian language (Vogel 1986).

MENOTL Creek (Alaska, Ophir C-6). The Koyukon (Athabaskan) name was reported in 1954 (Orth 1967).

MENOTOMY Rocks (Mass., Middlesex Co.). Shortened from the name of a SNEng. Algonquian leader, <Wannamenotonomy> (Huden 1962).

MENTANONTLI River (Alaska, Bettles B-6). The Koyukon (Athabaskan) name was reported in 1901 (Orth 1967).

MENTASTA Lake (Alaska, Nabesna D-6) \men tas′ tə\. From Ahtna (Athabaskan) *mendaesde* 'shallows lake place'; cf. *ben, men* 'lake', *daes* 'shallows' (Kari 1990).

MENTOKAKAT (Alaska, Ruby D-5). The Koyukon (Athabaskan) name contains *-kaakk'et* 'stream mouth' (Jetté and Jones 2000).

MENUCKATUCK Reservoir (Conn., Middlesex Co.) \mə nuk′ ə tuk\. From SNEng. Algonquian, perhaps related to <munnoquohteau> 'he fertilizes', referring to the use of fish for fertilizer (Trumbull 1881; W. Cowan p.c.). A possibly related placename is **Menhaden** (N.J., Cumberland Co.).

MENUNKETESUCK Island (Conn., Middlesex Co.). From SNEng. Algonquian, perhaps meaning 'strong-flowing stream' (Huden 1962).

MEQUON (Wis., Ozaukee Co.) \mek′ won\. Perhaps from Ojibwa (Algonquian) *miigwan* 'feather' (Vogel 1991; Nichols and Nyholm 1995); or perhaps a transfer name from **Miquon** (Pa., Montgomery Co.), from Delaware (Algonquian) <miquin> 'a quill' (Brinton and Anthony 1888; cf. Unami Delaware /mí:kwən/ 'feather' (Blalock et al. 1994) and Munsee Delaware *míikwan* (O'Meara 1996).

MERAMEC River (Mo., Jefferson Co.) \mâr′ ə mak\. Probably from an Algonquian word meaning 'catfish'; cf. Ojibwa *maanameg* 'catfish' (Nichols and Nyholm 1995), Meskwaki *myanamekwa* (Goddard 1994). A possibly related placename is **Maramech Hill** (Ill., Kendall Co.).

MERIWHITICA Canyon (Ariz., Mohave Co.). From a Havasupai (Yuman) placename /mat widita/, lit. 'earth hard' (L. Hinton p.c.).

MERMENTAU (La., Acadia Par.) \mûr´ mən tô\. Perhaps from <Nementou>, the name of an Atakapa leader in the eighteenth century (Read 1927).

MERRICK (N.Y., Nassau Co.) \mer´ ik\. Earlier written <Merikoke, Merricock> (etc.); a SNEng. Algonquian name, perhaps meaning 'barren land' (Beauchamp 1907; Tooker 1911).

MERRICONEAG Sound (Maine, Cumberland Co.). Perhaps from Malecite (Algonquian), meaning 'a lazy portage' (i.e., a place where canoes could be moved without unloading) (Huden 1962).

MERRIMAC (Ill., Monroe Co.) \mer´ i mak\. Probably from a Central Algonquian word for 'catfish' (Vogel 1963); cf. Ojibwa *maanameg* (Nichols and Nyholm 1995), Meskwaki /mya:name:kwa/ (Goddard 1994). Perhaps related placenames are **Meramec River** (Mo., Jefferson Co.) and **Meramech Hill** (Ill., Kendall Co.); see above. Of a separate origin is **Merrimack River** (N.H., Hillsborough Co.; Mass., Essex Co.) \mer´ i mak\, from Abenaki (Algonquian), meaning 'place of deep water', from *molô-* 'deep' plus *-demak* 'water' (W. Cowan p.c.). The name *Merrimac(k)* was given to an ironclad ship that fought a famous naval battle during the Civil War, which caused it to be adopted as a placename in many states: for example, **Merrimac** in Iowa (Jefferson Co.) and Wis. (Sauk Co.). In some names such as **Merrimac** in Ill. (Monroe Co.), it may not be possible to separate the catfish and the ironclad as possible models.

MERUWTU Point (Alaska, St. Lawrence D-6). The Yupik (Eskimo) name was recorded in 1949 (Orth 1967).

MESABA Township (Minn., St. Louis Co.) \mə sä´ bə\. A variant of **Mesabi Ranges.**

MESABI Range (Minn., St. Louis Co.) \mə sä´ bē\. From Ojibwa (Algonquian) *misaabe* 'giant' (Upham 2001; Nichols and Nyholm 1995). The name occurs as a transfer in Ore. (Tillamook Co.).

MESAHCHIE Peak (Wash., Skagit Co.) \mə sä´ chē\. From the same source as **Mesatchee Creek** (Wash., Lewis Co.); this represents Chinook Jargon <masátsi, me-sáh-chie> [mɛsáči] 'bad, wicked, evil', from Lower Chinook <ma-sá-tchi> 'bad' (Hitchman 1985; D. Kinkade p.c.).

MESCAL \mes kal´\. The Mexican Spanish term is from Nahuatl (Aztecan) *mexcalli* and designates the fleshy edible parts of several desert plants, including species of agave and yucca. Indians used it chiefly for food but also to make rope, baskets, and so forth. As a placename, **Mescal** is widespread in the Southwest (e.g., in Ariz., Cochise Co.; Calif., San Bernardino Co.; N.Mex., Sierra Co.; and Tex., Bandera Co.).

MESCALERO \mes kə lâr´ ō\. The term refers to an Apachean (Athabaskan) people of the Southwest and is Spanish for 'maker of mescal'. As a placename it occurs in Ariz. (Coconino Co.) and N.Mex. (Otero Co.).

MESCALITAN Island (Calif., Santa Barbara Co.) \mes kal´ i tən\. From Mexican Spanish *Mexcaltitlán*, probably transferred from a place in Mexico. The term is from Nahuatl (Aztecan) *mexcal-titlan*, lit. 'mescal-among' (Gudde 1998).

MESHANTICUT (R.I., Providence Co.) \mə shan´ ti kut\. A SNEng. Algonquian placename, perhaps related to *mishauntowash* 'speak out' (W. Cowan p.c.).

MESHIK (Alaska, Chignik D-3) \mesh´ik\. The Yupik (Eskimo) name was reported as <Mishik> in 1905 (Orth 1967).

MESHINGOMESIA (Ind., Grant Co.). From Miami/Illinois (Algonquian) <Mē-shing´-gwă-min-ji>, referring to the 'bur-oak tree' (Dunn 1919). Also written as **Meshingomeshia.**

MESHOMASIC Mountain (Conn., Middlesex Co.) \mesh om´ ə sik\. From SNEng. Algonquian, perhaps meaning 'at the place of great springs' (Huden 1962).

MESHOPPEN (Pa., Wyoming Co.) \mə shop´ ən\. Perhaps from Delaware (Algonquian) <maschapi> 'bead(s)' (Donehoo 1928; Brinton and Anthony 1888); cf. Munsee Delaware *maanzháapuy* (O'Meara 1996).

MESKWAKI (Iowa, Tama Co.) \mə skwä´ kē\. This name is currently used for the Algonquian people and language otherwise called **Fox**. It is a variant spelling of **Mesquakie** (Iowa, Tama Co.), from the tribe's term for themselves, /meškwahki:ha/, lit. 'red-earth one' (Vogel 1983; *HNAI* 15:646). Probably related placenames include **Misquah Hills** (MN, Cook Co.).

MESQUITAL Tank (N.Mex., Quay Co.) \mes kē täl´\. The Mexican Spanish term means 'mesquite grove' (Julyan 1998). The term **Mesquite** \mes kēt´\. refers to a desert tree bearing edible beans; it is borrowed from Nahuatl (Aztecan) *mizquitl.* As a placename, the term is common in the Southwest (e.g., Ariz., Pima Co.; Okla., Jackson Co.; and Tex., Dallas Co.).

MESSALONSKEE Lake (Maine, Kennebec Co.) \mes ə lon´ skē\. Probably from Abenaki (Algonquian), said to mean 'white clay' ((Huden 1962); cf. *mazalôpskw* 'clay' (Day 1994–95).

METACOMET Lake (Mass., Bristol Co.) \met´ ə kom ət\. The name refers to a SNEng. Algonquian leader of colonial times, more often known in English as King Philip. The term also appears as **Metacom**; it may mean 'at a far-away place' (Huden 1962). The placename **Metacomet** is also found in Conn. (Hartford Co.) and R.I. (Providence Co.).

METALLAK Mountain (Maine, Oxford Co.) \mə tal´ ik\. Said to be named after an Abenaki Indian who died around 1850 (Huden 1962); the term may be from *madahlak* 'beaver skins' (Day 1994–95).

METAMORA \met ə môr´ ə\. The term refers to the Indian hero of a popular play, *Metamora, or, the Last of the Wampanoags,* by Augustus Stone, first performed in 1829. It was based on the name and character of **Metacomet** or King Philip, a leader of the Wampanoag (SNEng. Algonquian) group (Vogel 1986). As a placename, **Metamora** occurs, for example, in Ill. (Woodford Co.), Ohio (Fulton Co.), and Pa. (Lehigh Co.).

METATE \mə tä´ tē\. Mexican Spanish for 'grinding slab', from Nahuatl (Aztecan) *metlatl.* As a placename it occurs in several states (e.g., Calif., San Diego Co.; Ariz., Graham Co.; and Tex., Atascosa Co.). A related placename is **Mara Wash,** see above.

METAUQUE Lake (N.Y., Sullivan Co.). Perhaps Delaware (Algonquian), meaning 'small trees' (Beauchamp 1907). Cf. <mehittuk> 'tree' (Brinton and Anthony 1888), Munsee Delaware *míhtukw* 'tree' (O'Meara 1996).

METEA (Ind., Cass Co.) \mē´ tē ə\. Named for a Potawatomi (Algonquian) leader of the early nineteenth century; also written <Metawa>. The term is from Old Potawatomi /midewi/ 'he participates in the Midewiwin ceremony' (M. McCafferty p.c.). Perhaps related is **Mettawa** (Ill., Lake Co.).

METEDECONK (N.J., Ocean Co.). The Delaware (Algonquian) placename is of unclear derivation (Becker 1964).

METERVIK Bay (Alaska, Nushagak Bay D-6). The Yupik (Eskimo) name was reported in 1952 (Orth 1967).

METHOW (Wash., Okanogan Co.) \met´hou\. From the Okanagan (Salishan) placename /mítx̣aw/ (D. Kinkade p.c.); cf. /mətx^{W}ú/ 'sunflower (seeds)' (A. Mattina p.c.).

METIGOSHE Lake (N.Dak., Bottineau Co.). Probably from Ojibwa (Algonquian) *mitigomizh* 'oak tree' (Wick 1988; Nichols and Nyholm 1995).

METLAKATLA (Alaska, Ketchikan A-5) \met lə kat´ lə\. The Tsimshian placename, transferred here from British Columbia, is said to mean 'a passage joining two bodies of water' (Phillips 1973).

METLAKO Falls (Ore., Hood River Co.) \met lak´ ō\. Supposedly named for "an Indian legendary goddess of the salmon" (McArthur 1992), language not identified.

METOCINAH (Ind., Grant Co.) \met ō sē´ nə\. From Miami/Illinois (Algonquian) /tohsee-nia/ 'an Indian' (McCafferty 2002). A variant form is **Jocinah Creek** (Ind., Grant Co.).

METOLIUS (Ore., Jefferson Co.) \mə tō´ lē əs\. From Sahaptin [mɨt'úla] 'spawned-out salmon' (N. Rude p.c.). A variant form of the name is **Matoles.**

METOMEN (Wisc., Fond du Lac Co.) \mə tō´ mən\. Perhaps from Menominee (Algonquian) /atɛ:hemen/ 'strawberry', lit. 'heart berry'; cf. /-tɛ:h/ 'heart', /ese:men/ 'berry' (Vogel 1991; Bloomfield 1975).

METOMKIN Point (Va., King George Co.) \mə tom´ kin\. The name is from CAC Algonquian, said to mean 'to enter into a house' (Hagemann 1988). A variant is **Metompkin.**

METONGA Lake (Wis., Forest Co.) \mə tong´ gə\. Perhaps from Dakota (Siouan) *mathą́ka* 'I am great', from *thą́ka* 'great' (Vogel 1991; Riggs 1890).

METTACAHONTS (N.Y., Ulster Co.) \met´ ə kə honts\. Perhaps from Mahican (Algonquian), of unclear derivation (Beauchamp 1907). A variant writing is **Mettekehonks.**

METTAH Creek (Calif., Humboldt Co.) \mā´ tə\. From the Yurok village name *metaa* (Gudde 1998).

METTAWA (Ill., Lake Co.) \met´ ə wä\. Named for a Potawatomi (Algonquian) leader of the early nineteenth century; the term may be related to **Metea** (Ind., Cass Co.).

METTAWEE River (N.Y., Washington Co.; Vt., Rutland Co.) \met´ ə wē\. Perhaps from Mahican (Algonquian), possibly meaning 'black earth' (Beauchamp 1907).

METTEKEHONKS (N.Y., Ulster Co.) \met´ ə kə hongks\. Perhaps from Mahican (Algonquian), of unclear derivation (Beauchamp 1907). A variant form is **Mettacahonts.**

METUCHEN (N.J., Middlesex Co.) The Delaware (Algonquian) name, which has also been written <Matouchin, Mathuching> (etc.), is of unclear derivation (Becker 1964).

MEXHOMA (Okla., Cimarron Co.) \meks hō´ mə\. The name was made up from elements of **New Mexico** and **Oklahoma,** since it is near the state boundary.

MEXICAN \mek´ si kən\. This term, corresponding to Spanish *mexicano,* is derived from Spanish *México,* the name of both the country and its capital city. In placenames of the Southwest, **Mexican** often translates Navajo (Athabaskan) *naakai* 'Mexican', lit. 'they who walk around'. Thus **Mexican Hat** (Utah, Wilson 1995) corresponds to Navajo *naakai ch'ah* (Wilson 1995); **Mexican Springs** corresponds to Navajo *naakai bi-to',* lit. 'Mexicans their-spring', with *to'* 'spring, water' (Julyan 1998; A. Wilson p.c).

MEXICO \mek´ si kō\. The name of the nation and of its capital city is from Nahuatl (Aztecan) *mexihco* [meší?ko], the name of the ancient capital. Besides occurring in the name of the state of **New Mexico,** it has been transferred to many parts of the United States (e.g., Maine, Oxford Co.; N.Y, Oswego Co.; and Wis., Forest Co.). A related placename is **Mexico City** (N.Mex., Lea Co.).

MEYERS CHUCK (Alaska, Craig C-1). The meaning is 'Meyers' water', containing Chinook Jargon <chuck> [čʌk] 'water', derived from Nootka (Phillips 1973).

MIACCA (Fla., Manatee Co.). A variant of **Myakka City**; see below.

MIACOMET Pond (Mass., Nantucket Co.). Also written <Myacomet>, <Moyacomet>. From SNEng. Algonquian, perhaps meaning 'where we meet to fish' (Huden 1962); but cf. <Moyaucoumet> 'a meeting place' (Little 1984).

MIAKKA (Fla., Sarasota Co.). A variant form of the name of **Myakka City** (Fla., Manatee Co.); this was probably the name of a Timucua village (Read 1934:19, 31). Related placename include **Port Mayaca** (Fla., Martin Co.) and **Miacca.**

MIAMI \mī am′ ē\. This word probably first entered English as a placename in the area of Ohio (see **Miami County** below). Placenames in several other states were later adapted to resemble the original **Miami;** in addition, the placename **Miami** spread even farther as a transfer. An older pronunciation \mī am′ ə\ occurs in several areas. Separate entries are given below for the different sources of the name: for example, **Miami** (Ariz., Gila Co.) may represent a blend of *Mima,* a woman's given name, with the Ohio placename (Granger 1983).

MIAMI (Fla., Dade Co.). The placename in its present form is dated from 1838; it may be from an Indian name for **Lake Okeechobee,** written by Spanish explorers as <Maymi> in 1566, as <Mayaimi> in 1575. The language of origin is not known (Read 1934).

MIAMI County (Ohio). Named for the Miami/Illinois (Algonquian) people; the term was recorded in the eighteenth century as <miamioua> (McPherson 1993; *HNAI* 15:688). The Native American name was /myaamiwa, myaamia/ 'downstream person' (Costa 2000:50). The placename **Miami** also occurs in Ill. (Cook Co.) (Vogel 1963) and in Ind. (Miami Co.) and as a transfer name in several other states (e.g., Iowa, Monroe Co.; Okla., Ottawa Co.; and W.Va, Kanawha Co.). A related placename is **Maumee River** (Ohio, Lucas Co.).

MIAMI Mountain (Calif., Mariposa Co.). From Yokuts <Me-ah-nee>, no doubt under the influence of the placenames in Fla. and in Ohio (Gudde 1998).

MIAMI River (Ore., Tillamook Co.). The stream was earlier called <Mime Chuck>, Chinook Jargon for 'downstream water' (McArthur 1992); cf. the Jargon word <mi′-mie>, probably [máimi] 'downstream', from Lower Chinook [máeme] 'downriver, downstream' (D. Kinkade p.c.). In fact, the similarity in sound and meaning to the Ohio name is remarkable, but it may be a coincidence. The spelling of the placename has probably been assimilated to the names from Fla. and Ohio. Possibly related is **Mima** (Wash., Thurston Co.).

MIAMOGUE Point (N.Y., Suffolk Co.). From SNEng. Algonquian, perhaps meaning 'a meeting place' (Tooker 1911). Possibly related placenames are **Miantonomi Hill** and **Mianus.**

MIANTONOMI Hill (R.I., Newport Co.). From SNEng. Algonquian; cf. <mianau> 'gather together' (W. Cowan p.c.). Possibly related placenames are **Miamogue Point** and **Mianus.**

MIANUS (Conn., Fairfield Co.). Named for a SNEng. Algonquian leader in the seventeenth century; from <mayonnes> 'he who gathers people together' (Trumbull 1881; W. Cowan p.c.). Possibly related names are **Miamogue Point** and **Miantonomi Hill.**

MICANOPY (Fla., Alachua Co.) \mik ə nop′ ē\. Named for a Seminole (Muskogean) leader of the early nineteenth century; the Native American name was probably *mēkk-onvpv* /mi:kk-onápa/ 'upper chief', from *mēkko* /mí:kko/ 'chief' and *onvpv* /onápa/ 'above, upper' (Read 1934; Martin and Mauldin 2000). A probably related placename is **Micco** (Fla., Brevard Co.); see below.

MICCO (Fla., Brevard Co.) \mik′ ō\. From Muskogee *mēkko* /mí:kko/ 'chief' (Read 1934; Martin and Mauldin 2000). The name also occurs in Okla. (McIntosh Co.) and W.Va. (Logan Co.).

MICCOSUKEE (Fla., Leon Co.) \mik ə so͞o′ kē, mik ə so͝ok′ ē\. The term refers to a Muskogean people and language, now spoken among the Seminoles of southern Fla.; the language is the same as that called Hitchiti. The term refers to an old tribal town in southern Ga., perhaps derived from <miki> 'chief' (Read 1934). The alternative spelling **Mikasuki** is used by anthropologists and linguists, and the related form **Mecosukey** also occurs (Okla., Seminole Co.). A probably related placename is **Micco** (Fla., Brevard Co.); see above.

MICE Creek (Alaska, Nabesna D-4). Corresponds to Upper Tanana (Athabaskan) *cheh-*

tsädn t'oh niign, lit. 'mouse nest creek' (J. Kari p.c.).

MICH-E-KE-WIS Park (Mich., Alpena Co.). Probably from Ojibwa (Algonquian) *mjiikwis* 'eldest son' (Rhodes 1985); cf. **Mudjekeewis Mountain.**

MICHE WABUN Falls (Mont., Glacier Co.). Perhaps from Cree (Algonquian), said to mean 'great dawn' (Holterman 1985); cf. *misa-* 'be big', *mihcêt* 'many, much', *wâpani-* 'be dawn' (Wolfart and Ahenakew 1998).

MICHIANA Shores (Ind., La Porte Co.) \mish ē an´ ə\. A placename made up from elements of **Michigan** and **Indiana** (Baker 1995).

MICHICOT (Wis., Manitowoc Co.) \mish´ i kot\. Named for a Potawatomi (Algonquian) resident in the eighteenth century (Vogel 1991); an alternative spelling is **Mishikot.**

MICHIGAMME (Mich., Marquette Co.) \mish i gä´ mē\. Perhaps from the same origin as **Lake Michigan** (Vogel 1986); see below. Other probably related placenames include **Mitchie Precinct** (Ill., Monroe Co.).

MICHIGAN, Lake (Mich., Wis., Ill.) \mish´ i gən\. Perhaps from an Old Ojibwa (Algonquian) word **meshi-gami* 'big lake'; cf. modern *michaa* 'be big', *-gami* 'lake' (Nichols and Nyholm 1995). But cf. also modern Ojibwa *gichigami* 'sea; one of the Great Lakes', which was historically also 'big lake' (Nichols and Nyholm 1995, I. Goddard p.c.). The state of **Michigan** is named after the lake. The placename has been transferred to other areas (e.g., Ariz., Apache Co.; N.Y., Steuben Co.; and Vt., Rutland Co.).

MICHILIMACKINAC, Fort (Mich., Emmet Co.) \mish i li mak´ i nô, -nak\. From Ojibwa (Algonquian) <Michilimackinac> 'many turtles'; cf. *michiin-* 'be many', *mikinaak* 'snapping turtle' (Nichols and Nyholm 1995; I. Goddard p.c.). Related placenames include **Mackinac County** (Mich.), **Mackinaw City** (Mich., Cheboygan Co.), **Meckinock** (N.Dak., Grand Forks Co.), **Mekanac Point** (Wis., Oneida Co.), and **Mickinock Township** (Minn., Roseau Co.), all from the word for 'turtle'.

MICHILLINDA (Mich., Muskegon Co.) \mish i lin´ də\. Formed by combining elements of the placenames **Michigan, Illinois,** and *Indiana* (Vogel 1986).

MICHIWAUKEE Shores (Mich., Schoolcraft Co.) \mish ə wô´ kē\. Probably a word made up from Algonquian elements, *mich-* 'great', as in **Michigan,** and *-waukee* 'land' as in **Milwaukee.**

MICKINOCK Township (Minn., Roseau Co.) \mik´ i nok\. Named for an Ojibwa (Algonquian) leader (Upham 2001); his Native American name was probably *mikinaak* 'snapping turtle' (J. Nichols p.c.). Related placenames are **Mackinac County, Mackinaw City, Fort Michilimackinac** (all in Mich.), **Meckinock** (N.Dak.), and **Mekanac Point** (Wis.).

MICMAC Lake (Minn., Lake Co.) \mik´ mak\. The name refers to an Algonquian people and language, native to the Maritime Provinces of Canada. The Native American term is /mi:kəmaw/ (*HNAI* 15:121).

MIDUN Island (Alaska, False Pass D-1). From the Aleut placename *miduun,* perhaps a loanword from some other language (Bergsland 1994).

MIGUAKIAK River (Alaska, Teshekpuk C-2). The Iñupiaq (Eskimo) name was reported in 1854 (Orth 1967). Related placenames are **Mayoriak** and **Mayoeak River**; cf. *mayuq-* 'to ascend, to climb' (MacLean 1980).

MIKANA (Wis., Barron Co.) \mī´ kə nə\. From Ojibwa (Algonquian) *miikana* 'road' (Vogel 1991; Nichols and Nyholm 1995). A related placename is **Mecan.**

MIKASUKI (Fla., Jefferson Co.) \mik ə so͞o´ kē\. From the same origin as **Miccosukee** (Fla., Leon Co.); see above.

MIKCHALK Lake (Alaska, Dillingham C-8). The Yupik (Eskimo) is said to mean 'small lake' (Orth 1967); cf. *mike-* 'to be small' (Jacobson 1984).

MIKFIK Creek (Alaska, Iliamna A-4). The Yupik (Eskimo) name was reported in 1923 (Orth 1967).

MIKIGEALIAK River (Alaska, Wainwright B-1). The Iñupiak (Eskimo) name was reported in 1924 (Orth 1967).

MIKISAGIMIUT (Alaska, Nunivak Is. A-7). The Yupik (Eskimo) name was reported in 1932 (Orth 1967). The ending *-miut* means 'people'.

MILAKOKIA Lake (Mich., Mackinac Co). A variant of **Millecoquins.**

MILLECOQUINS (Mich., Mackinac Co.). The name suggests French *mille coquins* 'thousand rascals', but it may be a folk-etymology from Ojibwa <mananakoking> 'place where ironwood is plentiful' (Vogel 1986); cf. *maananoons* 'ironwood' (Nichols and Nyholm 1995). The variant **Millecoquin** also occurs.

MILLICHETAH Creek (Alaska, Survey Pass B-2). The Koyukon (Athabaskan) name was reported in 1931 (Orth 1967).

MILLICOMA River (Ore., Coos Co.) \mil i kō´ mə\. Perhaps from a Miluk (Coosan) placename approximating [mɪ́l'ʊk^{w}ʊmɛ], containing the name of the Miluk people (D. Kinkade p.c.).

MILLIMAGASSETT Lake (Maine, Penobscot Co.) \mil i mə gas´ ət\. Perhaps from Abenaki (Algonquian), said to mean 'where duckhawks abound' (Huden 1962).

MILLINOCKET (Maine, Penobscot Co.) \mil´ i nok ət\. Perhaps from Abenaki (Algonquian), translated as 'this place is admirable' (Huden 1962).

MILOKRAWLOK (Alaska, Noatak A-3). The Iñupiaq (Eskimo) name was obtained in 1950 (Orth 1967).

MILOMA (Minn., Jackson Co.) \mil ō´ mə\. The name is made up by combining elements of the words **Milwaukee County** and **Omaha** (Upham 2001).

MILPAS, Cañada de las (N.Mex., Sandoval Co.) \mil´ pəs\. The Mexican Spanish name, meaning 'creek of the cornfields', contains *milpa* 'cornfield', from Nahuatl (Aztecan) *milpan* 'in the field', from *mil(li)* 'field', *-pan* 'in, on' (Julyan 1998).

MILPITAS (Calif., Santa Clara Co.) \mil pē´ təs\. The Mexican Spanish name means 'little cornfields', from *milpa* 'cornfield', from Nahuatl (Aztecan) *milpan* 'in the field' (Gudde 1998). There is a **Milpitas Draw** in N.Mex. (McKinley Co.).

MILUET Creek (Alaska, Ambler River A-4). The Iñupiaq (Eskimo) name was reported in 1955 (Orth 1967).

MILUVEACH River (Alaska, Harrison Bay B-1). The Iñupiaq (Eskimo) name was reported in 1951 (Orth 1967).

MILWAUKEE County (Wis.) \mil wô´ kē\. The placename, also written in 1831 as <Manawauky>, is perhaps from an Algonquian language, meaning 'good land' (Vogel 1991); cf. Ojibwa *mino-* 'good, well', *aki* 'land' (Nichols and Nyholm 1995). The name also occurs in Kans. (Stafford Co.), Mich. (St. Clair Co.), and Pa. (Lackawanna Co.). A related placename is **Milwaukie** (Ore., Clackamas Co.).

MIMA (Wash., Thurston Co.) \mī´ mə, mē´ mə\. Possibly from Chinook Jargon <mi´-mie>, probably [máimi] 'downstream', from Lower Chinook [máeme] 'downriver, downstream' (Hitchman 1985; D. Kinkade p.c.). A perhaps related placename is **Miami River** (Ore., Tillamook Co.).

MIMBREÑO Point (Ariz., Coconino Co.) \mim brān´ yō\. Named for an Apache (Athabaskan) group; the Spanish name means 'having to do with willow twigs', from *mimbre* 'willow twigs, withes' (Granger 1983).

MIMI Lake (Wis., Bayfield Co.) \mē´ mē\. From Ojibwa (Algonquian) *omiimii* 'dove, pigeon' (Vogel 1991, Nichols and Nyholm 1995). A related placename is **Meeme** (Wis., Manitowoc Co.).

MIMSH WAHIA Spring (Ariz., Pima Co.) \mimsh wä´ hē ä\. Perhaps O'odham (Piman) *mimş wahia* 'Protestants' well', from *mimş* 'Protestants' (reduplicated plural) plus *wahia* 'a well' (J. Hill p.c.). The word for 'a Protestant' is *mi:ş,* rather surprisingly derived from Spanish *misa* 'Catholic mass' (Saxton et al. 1983).

MINA (S.Dak., Edmunds Co.) \mī´ nə\. From Yankton Dakota (Siouan) *mína* 'knife' (D. Parks p.c.).

MINACOMUC (R.I., Washington Co.). From SNEng. Algonquian, perhaps meaning 'field in low lands' (Huden 1962).

MINALOOSA Valley (Idaho, Benewah Co.) \min ə lōō´ sə\. Perhaps from the same source as **Minnedosa,** a placename in Manitoba province, Canada; the term refers to what is now called the Little Saskatchewan River and is derived from Dakota (Siouan) *mni* 'water' plus *dus* 'swift' (Rayburn 1997; Riggs 1890).

MINAM (Ore., Wallowa Co.) \min´ əm\. Said to be from an Indian word <e-mi-ne-mah>, language not identified, referring to a type of flower (McArthur 1992).

MINATARE (Neb., Scotts Bluff Co.) \min´ ə târ\. This is the Mandan (Siouan) name for the Hidatsa (also Siouan) people; the Native American term is /wr̨ítari/ [m¹n̨ítari]. This word is itself a borrowing into Mandan of the Hidatsa word /miríta:ri/ 'crosses the water' (*HNAI* 13:345).

MINCHUMINA Lake (Alaska, Mt. McKinley D-5) \min chōō´ mi nə\. From Upper Kuskokwim (Athabaskan) *menhche mene',* lit. 'lake-large lake', containing *menh, -mene'* 'lake' (Kari 1999:121).

MINCO (Okla., Grady Co.) \ming´ kō\. From Choctaw (Muskogean) *mįko* 'chief' (P. Munro p.c.). A related placename is **Mingo** (Okla., Tulsa Co.).

MINDOWASKIN Park (N.J., Union Co.). The Delaware (Algonquian) name is of unclear derivation (Becker 1964).

MINECHOAG Brook (Mass., Hampden Co.). A variant spelling of **Minnechoag**.

MINEOLA (N.Y., Nassau Co.) \min ē ō´ lə\. The term is of unclear origin, perhaps containing an Algonquian root *min-* 'good' (Vogel 1963). The same placename occurs in Ill. (Lake Co.), in Mo. (Montgomery Co.), and with the spelling **Minneola** (see **Minneola Township** below) in several other states.

MINGAMAHONE Brook (N.J., Monmouth Co.). The Delaware (Algonquian) name is of unclear derivation (Becker 1964).

MINGKOKET Lake (Alaska, Bettles B-5). The Koyukon (Athabaskan) name was recorded in 1956 (Orth 1967); it apparently contains *benh, m̦enh* 'lake, swamp', plus *kkokk'et* 'surface' (J. Kari p.c.).

MINGO (Okla., Tulsa Co.) \ming´ gō\. From Choctaw (Muskogean) *mįko* 'chief'. The placename **Mingo** in Miss. (Tishomingo Co.) is said to be an abbreviation for **Tishomingo,** the name of a Chickasaw (Muskogean) leader. The term is unrelated to the placename **Mingo** in Pa. (Washington Co.) \ming´ gō\, from a Delaware (Algonquian) word referring to some neighboring Iroquois groups; the Munsee Delaware form is /mé:nkwe:w/, the Unami form is /mə́nkwe/ (*HNAI* 15:320). The word has also been translated as 'treacherous' (Vogel 1983). The name was made well known in the fiction of James Fenimore Cooper and was widely used as a placename (e.g., N.Y., Ulster Co.; Ohio, Champaign Co.; and Wis., Burnett Co.) A related placename is **Minquadale**; see below.

MINGOGUT Lake (Alaska, Kateel River C-2). The Koyukon (Athabaskan) name is probably equivalent to **Mingkoket**, above.

MINIATULIK River (Alaska, Norton Bay D-5). The Iñupiaq (Eskimo) name was reported in 1900 (Orth 1967).

MINIDOKA County (Idaho) \min i dō´ kə\. Perhaps from Mandan (Siouan) *mini-* 'water' plus *-iroke* 'inside' (R. Rankin p.c.).

MINIKAHDA Creek (Ore., Clackamas Co.). Perhaps from the same source as **Minnekahta** (S.Dak., Fall River Co.).

MINISINK (N.Y., Orange Co.) \min´ i singk\. From Munsee Delaware (Algonquian) /mə̆nə́sənk/, probably an archaic word for 'on the island' (*HNAI* 15:237); cf. Munsee *mŭnáhan* 'island' (O'Meara 1996). The placename also occurs in other states (e.g., N.J., Sussex Co.; and Pa., Pike Co.). Related placenames are **Munsee, Muncie, Muncy, Munising,** and **Munnisunk Brook.**

MINI SKA (S.Dak., Tripp Co.). Lakhota (Siouan) *mni-ská* 'white water', lit. 'water-white' (D. Parks p.c.).

MINITO Lake (Wis., Langlade Co.). Probably form the same source as **Manito**; see above.

MINIWAKAN (Iowa, Dickinson Co.) \min i wä´ kən\. From Dakota (Siouan) *mni* 'water' plus *wakhą́* 'sacred' (Vogel 1983; J. Koontz p.c.). The name also occurs in Wis. (Langlade Co.) Probably related placenames include **Minnewakan** (N.Dak., Ramsey Co.), **Minnewankon Falls** (Minn., Nicollet Co.), and **Minnewaukan** (N.Dak., Benson Co.).

MINKOSHCHALITON Lake (Alaska, Beaver A-4). From Koyukon (Athabaskan) *mənh kok'ə ch'ədaghilot dənh* 'where the surface of the lake is lengthy' (Kari 2000), with *dənh* 'lake'.

MINNAWANNA Lake (Mich., Lapeer Co.) \min ə wä´ nə\. Perhaps from Ojibwa (Algonquian), but of unclear derivation (Vogel 1986).

MINNEAPOLIS (Minn., Hennepin Co.) \min ē ap´ ə lis\. The town was named in 1852; the name is a compound of Dakota (Siouan) *mni* 'water' (cf. **Minnesota** below) plus Greek *polis* 'city' (Upham 2001; R. Rankin p.c.). The placename also occurs as a transfer in Kans. (Ottawa Co.) and Mich. (Delta Co.). The element meaning 'water' also occurs in **Minnechaduza Creek** (S.Dak., Todd Co.) \min i kə do͞o´ zə\, from Dakota (Siouan) *mní čadúza,* lit. 'water rapid' (A. Taylor p.c.); the placename also occurs in Neb. (Cherry Co.).

MINNECHAUG Mountain (Conn., Hartford Co.) \min´ ə chôg\. From SNEng. Algonquian, perhaps meaning 'berry hill', from <minne> 'berry', <adchu-> 'mountain', <-auke> '-land' (Trumbull 1881; W. Cowan p.c.). A possibly related placename is **Minnechoag Mountain** (Mass., Hampden Co.).

MINNECONJOU Creek (S.Dak., Stanley Co.) \min ə kon´ jo͞o\. The name refers to a division of the Teton (Lakhota, Siouan) people; the Native American name is *mnikhówožu, mnikhó'ožu.* A proposed etymology is 'planters by the water' (Sneve 1973; *HNAI* 13:757).

MINNEHA (Kans., Sedgwick Co.). A shortening of **Minnehaha Falls**; see below.

MINNEHAHA Falls (Minn., Hennepin Co.) \min ə hä´ hä\. The name for the waterfall near Fort Snelling was reported in 1849 as <Mine-hah-hah>, said to be Dakota (Siouan) for 'laughing waters' (Upham 2001). This may have involved a misunderstanding; cf. *mni, miní* 'water', *miníh̨ihe* 'waterfall', *ȟaȟá* 'to fall', but *iȟá* 'to laugh' (Riggs 1890; Williamson 1902; cf. also *mniwóȟaȟa* 'waterfall', Buechel and Manhart 2002). In 1855 Longfellow adopted the term as the name for the heroine of his *Hiawatha;* and thereafter it was adopted as a placename in many states (e.g., Iowa, Grundy Co.; Mich., Emmet Co.; and even Ariz., Yavapai Co.).

MINNEHONK Lake (Maine, Kennebec Co.) \min´ ə hongk\. Perhaps from an Abenaki (Algonquian) placename meaning 'berries stream' (Huden 1962); cf. *mins* 'little berry' (Day 1994–95).

MINNEIKA (Iowa, Wapello Co.). Perhaps from the same source as **Minneiska** (Minn., Winona Co.) \min ē es´ kə\. This is from Dakota (Siouan) *mni* 'water' plus *ska* 'white' (Upham 2001; Riggs 1890); the term is also reflected in the name of the adjacent **Whitewater River**; see **Whitewater** below. The Dakotan word for 'water' occurs in many other placenames: for example, **Minnekahta** (S.Dak., Fall River Co.), from Lakhota (Siouan) *mni-kháta* 'water-hot' (Sneve 1973; A. Taylor p.c.); probably from the same source is **Minikahda Creek** (Ore., Clackamas Co.).

MINNEMAC Lake (Wis., Sawyer Co.) \min´ ə mak\. From Ojibwa (Algonquian) *maanameg* 'catfish' (Vogel 1991; Nichols and Nyholm 1995). Probably related placenames are **Maramech Hill** (Ill., Kendall Co.) and **Maramec** (Mo., Jefferson Co.); see above.

MINNEOLA Township (Minn., Goodhue Co.) \min ē ō´ lə\. Perhaps a garbling of **Minneota** (see below), which represents the Dakota (Siouan) for 'much water' (*mni* 'water', *óta* 'much); or this may be a respelling of **Mineola** (N.Y., Nassau Co.). The placename **Minneola** occurs in several other states (e.g., Fla., Lake Co.); the use of the term for a type of citrus fruit may come from the Fla. placename. In Calif., **Minneola** (San Bernardino Co.) is said to have been called after a woman named Minnie (Gudde 1998).

MINNEOPA Creek (Minn., Blue Earth Co.) \min ē ō´ pə\. Said to be a Dakota (Siouan) name, contracted from <minne-hinhe-nonpa> 'water falling twice', i.e. 'two waterfalls' (Upham 2001); cf. *miníhįhe* 'waterfall', *nų́pa* 'two' (A. Taylor p.c.). Another placename containing the Dakota word for 'water' is **Minneota** (Minn., Lyon Co.) \min ē ō´ tə\, perhaps from *mni* 'water' plus *óta* 'much' (Upham 2001; Williamson 1902).

MINNEQUA (Pa., Bradford Co.) \min´ i kwä\. The name may be made up from "Indian-sounding" elements (Donehoo 1928); cf. Dakotan (Siouan) *mni* 'water'. The placename also occurs in Colo. (Pueblo Co.).

MINNESAKA Valley (Idaho, Clearwater Co.). Perhaps from a Lakhota (Siouan) name meaning 'dry spring, dry well', from *mni* 'water', *sáka* 'dry' (R. Rankin p.c.). Other placenames containing the Dakotan word for 'water' are **Minnesechi Creek** (S.Dak., Shannon Co.), from Dakota *mni-šíča,* lit. 'water-bad' (A. Taylor p.c.); and **Minnesela** (S.Dak., Butte Co.), from the Lakhota for 'red water' (Sneve 1973); cf. *mni* 'water', *šayéla* 'redly' (B. Ingham p.c.).

MINNESOTA \min ə sō ´ tə\. The name was first applied to the **Minnesota River,** which gave its name to the state. The Dakota (Siouan) name of the stream was *mní sóta,* from *mní* 'river, stream' plus *sóta* 'slightly clouded' (Upham 2001; Riggs 1890). The placename has been transferred to many other states (e.g., Colo., Gunnison Co.; Ga., Colquitt Co.; and Wis., Douglas Co.).

MINNETONKA (Minn., Hennepin Co.) \min ē tong´ kə\. The name was perhaps coined by white people, intended to mean 'big water', based on Dakota (Siouan) *mni* 'water', *thą́ka* 'big' (Upham 2001; Riggs 1890). The placename occurs as a transfer in Idaho (Bear Lake Co.). A related name is **Minnetrista** (Hennepin Co.) \min ē tris´ tə\, also coined by white people, intended to mean 'crooked lake'; the element *-trista* may be an adaptation of English *twisted* (Upham 2001). Among other placenames containing the Dakotan word for 'water', **Minnewakan** (N.Dak., Ramsey Co.) \min ē wô´ kən\. is from the same source as **Miniwakan** (Iowa, Dickinson Co.); see above. A related placename is **Minnewaukan** (N.Dak., Benson Co.).

MINNEWANKON Falls (Minn., Nicollet Co.). Perhaps intended to be Dakota (Siouan) for 'sacred water'; cf. *mni* 'water', *wakį́* 'sacred' (Riggs 1890); cf. **Miniwakan** above.

MINNEWASCA Lake (Mich., Delta Co.). Probably from the same source as **Minnewashta Lake** (Iowa, Dickinson Co.) and **Minnewaska** (Minn., Pope Co.); see below. Another possibly related name is **Tonka Bay** (Minn., Hennepin Co.), said to be an abbreviation.

MINNEWASHTA Lake (Iowa, Dickinson Co.) \min ē wäsh´ tə\. From Dakota (Siouan) *mniwášte,* lit. 'water-good' (Vogel 1983; A. Taylor p.c.). The placename also occurs in Minn. (Carver Co.). Related forms are **Minnewasca** (Mich., Delta Co.), **Minnewaska** (Minn., Pope Co.), and **Minnewasta** (S.Dak., Day Co.).

MINNEWASKA (Minn., Pope Co.) \min ē wäs´ kə\. From the same source as **Minnewashta Lake** (Iowa, Dickinson Co.); see above. The placename also occurs in N.Y. (Ulster Co.). Similarly, **Minnewasta Lake** (S.Dak., Day Co.) is from the same source as **Minnewashta** (Iowa, Dickinson Co.).

MINNEWAUKAN (N.Dak., Benson Co.) \min ē wô´ kən\ is from the same source as **Miniwakan** (Iowa, Dickinson Co.); cf. Dakota (Siouan) *mni* 'water', *wakq̨* 'sacred'.

MINNEWAWA Falls (Mich., Ontonagan Co.) \min ē wä´ wä, min ə wä´ wä, min ə wä´ wə\. The name is adapted from Longfellow's *Hiawatha,* in which it is said to be an Indian word for 'a pleasant sound, as of wind in the trees' (Vogel 1986); cf. Ojibwa *minwewe* 'to sound good' (J. Nichols p.c.). The placename also occurs in N.H. (Cheshire Co.) \min ə wä´ wä\ and in Minn. (Aitkin Co.).

MINNIE Island (Conn., New London Co.) \min´ ē\. Perhaps from SNEng. Algonquian <munnoh> 'island' (Huden 1962; W. Cowan p.c.).

MINNIOLA, Lake (Fla., Pasco Co.) \min ē ō´ lə\. Perhaps from the same source as **Mineola** (N.Y., Nassau Co.).

MINNISUING (Wisc., Douglas Co.) \min´ i sung\. From Ojibwa (Algonquian), meaning 'at the island' (Vogel 1991); cf. *minis* 'island' (Nichols and Nyholm 1995). Related placenames include **Minisink** (N.Y., Orange Co.) and **Munising** (Mich., Alger Co.).

MINNISUNK Brook (Conn., Hartford Co.) \min´ i sungk\. Perhaps from SNEng. Algonquian <munnoh> 'island'; a related placename is **Minisink** (N.Y., Orange Co.).

MINNITAKI Island (Minn., St. Louis Co.). Perhaps intended to mean 'big water', from Dakota (Siouan) *mni* 'water', *thą̧ka* 'big' (Riggs 1890).

MINNKOHWIN Lake (Alaska, Bettles B-5). The Koyukon (Athabaskan) name was recorded in 1956 (Orth 1967); cf. *menh, benh* 'lake, swamp' (Jetté and Jones 2000).

MINOCQUA (Wis., Oneida Co.) \mi nok´ wä\. From Ojibwa (Algonquian) *minaakwaa* 'there is a clump of trees' (J. Nichols p.c.).

MINONG Island (Mich., Keweenaw Co.) \mī´ nong\. Perhaps Ojibwa (Algonquian) for 'good place' (Vogel 1986); cf. *mino-* 'good' (Nichols and Nyholm 1995). The placename also occurs in Wis. (Washburn Co.). A probably related placename is **Minonk** (Ill., Woodford Co.).

MINONK (Ill., Woodford Co.) \mi nungk´\. Probably from the same source as **Minong Island** (Mich., Wis.); see above. The placename **Minonk** also occurs in Wis. (Vilas Co.).

MINOOK (Alaska, Tanana C-1). Named for John Minook, a prospector of Russian and Indian descent (Orth 1967).

MINOOKA (Ill., Grundy Co.) \mi nōō´ kə\. Perhaps from Ottawa (Algonquian) <me-no auky> 'good land' (Vogel 1963); cf. *mno-* 'good', *ki* 'land' (Rhodes 1985). The placename is also found elsewhere (e.g., Ala., Chilton Co.; Kans., Russell Co.; and Wis., Waukesha Co.).

MINOTOCLOGA Lake (Alaska, Bettles C-6) The Koyukon (Athabaskan) name was reported in 1956 (Orth 1967); it may contain *benh, menh* 'lake, swamp' (Jetté and Jones 2000).

MINOTOLA (N.J., Atlantic Co.). Perhaps from Delaware (Algonquian), but the derivation is not clear (Becker 1964).

MINQUADALE (Del., New Castle Co.) \ming´ kwə dāl\. The name is derived from Minqua, a word from the Delaware (Algonquian) language, said to be applied to the Susquehanna (Iroquoian) Indians (Donehoo 1928; Heck et al. 1966). It perhaps represents Munsee Delaware /mé:nkwe:w/, Unami Delaware /ménkwe/, a term applied to various Iroquoian peoples (*HNAI* 15:320). A related placename is **Minquas Run** (Pa., Delaware Co.); another related name is **Mingo**; see above.

MINSI Lake (Pa., Northampton Co.) \min´ sē\. Perhaps from the same source as **Munsee**; see below.

MINTO Lakes (Alaska, Fairbanks D-4) \min´ tō, mēn´ tō\. From Lower Tanana (Athabaskan) *menhtwx* 'Minto Flats', lit. 'lakes-among', from *menh* 'lake' (Kari 1999:104). However, the placename **Minto** in the Yukon Territory, Canada, is said to be named for the earl of Minto, a British govenor-general of Canada in the late nineteenth century (Phillips 1973).

MIOXES Pond (Mass., Nantucket Co.). The name is said to have originally been a possessive, "Mioxe's Pond," named for a SNEng. Algonquian leader of the seventeenth century, also called <Mioxeo> (Huden 1962).

MIQUON (Pa., Montgomery Co.). Perhaps from Delaware (Algonquian) <miquin> 'a quill' (Brinton and Anthony 1888); cf. Unami Delaware /mí:kwən/ 'feather' (Blalock et al. 1994), Munsee Delaware *míikwan* (O'Meara 1996). A possibly related name is **Mequon** (Wis., Ozaukee Co.).

MIRAMICHI Lake (Mich., Osceola Co.). Probably a transfer from Quebec. Perhaps from Cree (Algonquian), meaning 'ugly beaver' (Vogel 1986); cf. *mâyi* 'bad, evil', *amiskw-* 'beaver' (Wolfart and Ahenakew 1998). The placename also occurs in Mass. (Norfolk Co.).

MISCAUNA Creek (Mich., Menominee Co.). Probably from an Ojibwa (Algonquian) word for 'red' (Vogel 1986); cf. *miskwi* 'blood', *misko-* 'red', *miskwaande* 'be colored red' (Nichols and Nyholm 1995). A probably related placename is **Miscauno** (Wis., Marinette Co.).

MISCAUNO Creek (Wis., Marinette Co.) \mis kwä´ nō\. Also written **Miscuano**; probably from the same source as **Miscauna Creek** (Mich., Menominee Co.).

MIS CHIN (Wash., Pacific Co.) \mis´ chin\. From Lower Chehalis (Salishan) \mə́šč̓ən'\. 'head louse' (Howell 1948; D. Kinkade p.c.).

MISCOE Brook (Mass., Worcester Co.) \mis´ kō\. Perhaps from SNEng. Algonquian <miskam> 'he finds it' (W. Cowan p.c.).

MISCOWAWBIC Peak (Mich., Ontonagan Co.) \mis kə wä´ bik\. Ojibwa (Algonquian) *miskwaabik* 'copper', lit. 'red metal'; cf. *misko-* 'red', *biiwaabik* 'metal, iron' (Vogel 1986; Nichols and Nyholm 1995).

MISCUANO (Wis., Marinette Co.) An alternative spelling of **Miscauno Creek**; see above.

MISHA MOKWA (Wis., Buffalo Co.) \mish ə mō´ kwə\. From "Mishe Mokwa," a monster that figures in Longfellow's *Hiawatha,* translated as 'great bear' (Vogel 1991); cf. Ojibwa *mishi-* 'big', *makwa* 'a bear' (Nichols and Nyholm 1995).

MISHAUM Ledge (Mass., Bristol Co.). Perhaps SNEng. Algonquian for 'great neck' (Huden 1962).

MISHAWAKA (Ind., St. Joseph Co.) \mish ə wô´ kə\. Perhaps from Potawatomi (Algonquian) /mžwekək/ 'at the elk land' (M. McCafferty p.c.); cf. the related Meskwaki (Algonquian) /meše:we:wa/ 'elk', /ahki/ 'land' (Goddard 1994). The placename occurs as a transfer in N.Mex. (San Miguel Co.) and Ore. (Clatsop Co.).

MISHAWUM (Mass., Middlesex Co.). From SNEng. Algonquian, perhaps meaning 'great landing place' (Huden 1962). A related form is **Mishawamut Neck.**

MISHEGUK Mountain (Alaska, Misheguk Mountain A-4). Said to be an Iñupiaq (Eskimo) personal name (Orth 1967).

MISHEVIK Slough (Alaska, Russian Mission A-6). The Yupik (Eskimo) name was reported in 1948 (Orth 1967); the ending *-vik* means 'place'.

MISHICOT (Wisc., Manitowoc Co.) \mish´ i kot\. A variant of **Mishikot**; see below.

MISHIKE Lake (Mich., Gogebic Co.). Probably from Eastern Ojibwa (Algonquian) *mshii-kenh* 'snapping turtle' (Rhodes 1985).

MISHIKOT (Wis., Manitowoc Co.) \mish´ i kot\. Named for a Potawatomi (Algonquian) resident in the eighteenth century (Vogel 1991); alternative spellings include **Michicot** and **Mishicot.**

MISHNOCK River (R.I., Bristol Co.) \mish´ nok\. From SNEng. Algonquian, perhaps representing <mishoon homwock> 'by-water they-come-and-go' (Huden 1962; W. Cowan p.c.).

MISHONAGON Creek (Wis., Vilas Co.) \mish ə nä´ gən\. Perhaps from Ojibwa (Algonquian), meaning 'big dish' (Vogel 1991); cf. *micha* 'be big', *onaagan* 'dish' (Nichols and Nyholm 1995). The spelling **Mishonagan** also occurs.

MISHONGNOVI (Ariz., Navajo Co.) \mi shong´ gō vē, mish hong´ gō vē\. From the Hopi (Uto-Aztecan) placename *musangnuvi* [mɨsáŋnɨvi], with the suffix *-vi* 'place' (K. Hill p.c.).

MISHUK Creek (Alaska, Ambler River A-4). The Iñupiaq (Eskimo) name was reported in 1955 (Orth 1967).

MISKATONIC River (Mass., Arkham Co.) \mis kə ton´ ik\. From SNEng. Algonquian, perhaps meaning 'red river', from <musqui, mishque> 'red' plus <tunkw> 'tidal stream' (Huden 1962). Miskatonic University, in the town of Arkham, is noted as a center of occult science (Manguel & Guadalupi 1987).

MISLATNAH Creek (Ore., Curry Co.). Perhaps an Athabaskan placename, containing *mish* 'its nose', referring to a promontory (D. Kinkade p.c.).

MISPILLION River (Del., Sussex Co.) \mi spil´ yən\. The name was first recorded as <Mispening> in 1664; it is probably from Delaware (Algonquian), perhaps meaning 'at the great tuber' (Heck et al. 1966).

MISQUAH Hills (Minn., Cook Co.) \mis´ kwə\. From Ojibwa (Algonquian) *miskwaa* 'be red' (Upham 2001, Nichols and Nyholm 1995). Probably related names include **Meskwaki**; see above.

MISQUAMICUT (R.I., Washington Co.). From SNEng. Algonquian <mishquammauquock> 'salmon', containing <musqui> 'red' (Huden 1962; W. Cowan p.c.).

MISSABE Mountain (Minn., St. Louis Co.) \mi sä´ bē\. A variant spelling of **Mesabi Range**; see above.

MISSAK Bay (Alaska, Mt. Katmai A-1). The Aleut name was published as <Mieshak> in 1847 (Orth 1967).

MISSAUKEE County (Mich.) \mi sô´ kē\. Named for an Ottawa (Algonquian) leader in the early nineteenth century, named <Me-sau-kee>, translatable as 'great land' (Vogel 1986); cf. *mshi-* 'big', *ki* 'land' (Rhodes 1985).

MISSISQUOI River (Vt., Franklin Co.). Western Abenaki (Algonquian) *masípskooik* 'where there is flint or chert', from *masípskw* 'flint, chert', *-oo-* 'be', and *-ik* 'where' (Day 1981: 154).

MISSISSINAWA (Ohio, Darke Co.) \mis is nä´ wä\. From the same source as **Mississinewa** (Ind., Miami Co.) \mi si sin´ ə wä, mi sin´ ə wä\. This name is from Miami/Illinois (Algonquian) /nimacihsinwi/ 'it downward-lies', a term that refers to the great fall of the river (McCafferty 2002).

MISSISSIPPI \mis i sip´ ē\. The term was first applied to the river by French missionaries when they met Algonquian peoples in the upper Mississippi drainage in the seventeenth century; it is derived from forms comparable to Ojibwa *mshi-* 'big' and *ziibi* 'river' (Vogel 1983; Rhodes 1985). Later the placename was also applied to the state of **Mississippi**.

MISSOULA County (Mont.) \mi zo͞o´ lə\. Perhaps from a Flathead (Salishan) name, possibly meaning 'awesome river' (Cheney 1984). The name also occurs in Alaska (Eagle B-4).

MISSOURI \mi zo͞o´ rē, mi zo͞o´ rə\. The name of the Missouria, a Chiwere (Siouan) Indian group, as well as the names of the **Missouri River** and of the state are from a Miami/Illinois (Algonquian) word, recorded in 1700 as <missouri> 'canoe' (*HNAI* 13:461; see also Lance 1999). A modern analysis is /mihsoori/ 'big boat', from /mihs-/ 'big', /-oor-/ 'boat, and /-i/ 'inanimate' (McCafferty 2003). The placename **Missouri** occurs in many states (e.g., Iowa, Harrison Co.; and Ill., Schuyler Co.). A derived placename is **Missouriton** (Mo., St. Charles Co.) \mə zo͞o´ rē tən\.

MISTEGUAY Creek (Mich., Saginaw Co.). Perhaps corrupted from Ojibwa (Algonquian) *mizise* 'wild turkey' (Vogel 1986; Nichols and Nyholm 1995).

MISTIC Pond (Mass., Middlesex Co.) \mis´ tik\. A variant spelling of **Mystic**; see below.

MITCHIE Precinct (Ill., Monroe Co.) \mich´ ē\. A shortening of <Mitchegamie>, the Algonquian people who once lived in the area. Related terms are **Michigamme** and **Lake Michigan** (see above), from the Ojibwa (Algonquian) for 'big lake'.

MITCHIGAN River (Mich., Iron Co.) \mich´ i gən\. From Eastern Ojibwa (Algonquian) *mjigkan* 'fence', perhaps originally referring to a fish-weir (Vogel 1986; Rhodes 1985). This placename is also reflected in the names of **Fence River** and **Fence.**

MITIGWAKI Creek (Mich., Iron Co.). Eastern Ojibwa (Algonquian) *mtigwaaki* 'forest', from *mtig* 'tree' (Vogel 1986; Rhodes 1985).

MITIK Creek (Alaska, Point Hope A-2) \mit´ ik\. From Iñupiaq (Eskimo) *mitiq* 'duck' (Orth 1967; Webster and Zibell 1970).

MITIWANGA (Ohio, Erie Co.) \mit i wäng´ gə\. Probably from an Indian source, of unclear derivation.

MITLAK Mountain (Alaska, Goodnews Bay B-7). The Yupik (Eskimo) name was published in 1951 (Orth 1967).

MITLETUKERUK (Alaska, Teller D-6). The Iñupiaq (Eskimo) name was recorded in 1901 (Orth 1967).

MITLIKTAVIK (Alaska, Wainwright B-3) \mit lik´ tə vik\. The Iñupiaq (Eskimo) name, said to mean 'place where the adze is used', was reported in 1920 (Orth 1967); cf. *mitlik* 'carving tool' (Webster and Zibell 1970).

MITTINEAGUE (Mass., Hampden Co.). From SNEng. Algonquian, perhaps meaning 'abandoned fields' (Huden 1962).

MIUKA Creek (Ala., Sumter Co.) \mī yōō´ kə\. Perhaps from Choctaw (Muskogean), but of unclear derivation (Read 1984).

MIWOK Lake (Calif., Tuolumne Co.) \mē´ wok, mē´ wuk\. Named for the Miwok Indian peoples, from Central Sierra Miwok /miwwɨk/ 'people; Indians' (Gudde 1998). Another spelling of the word occurs in **Mi-Wuk Village** (Calif., Tuolumne Co.).

MIXES FOOD Creek (S.Dak., Pennington Co.). Named for a Lakhota (Siouan) resident who was known in English as Mixes Food (Sneve 1973).

MIXSAWBAH (Ind., LaPorte Co.) \mik sô´ bä\. Named for a Potawatomi (Algonquian) leader of the early nineteenth century; his name has also been written as <Macsawbee> (McPherson 1993).

MOAB (Utah, Grand Co.) \mō´ ab\. Perhaps a biblical name (Deuteronomy 29:1), or perhaps from Southern Paiute (Numic) /moo/ 'fly' or /mooa/ 'to buzz' plus /paa/ 'water' (Van Cott 1990; J. McLaughlin p.c.). Possibly related terms are **Moap** (Utah, Uintah Co.) \mō´ ap\. and **Moapa** (Nev., Clark Co.) \mō ap´ ə\.

MOAVI Park (Calif., San Bernardino Co.) \mō ä´ vē\. Possibly from Mojave (Yuman) *muu'wáav* 'kinsperson' (P. Munro p.c.).

MOBILE County (Ala.) \mō bēl´\. The name was first reported by the Spanish in 1540, in the form *Mauvila,* as referring to an Indian group; later the term was applied to the bay, the river, the city, and the county of **Mobile**. It is perhaps derived from Choctaw (Muskogean) *moeli* 'to row, to paddle' (Read 1984).

MOCANAQUA (Pa., Luzerne Co.) \mok ə nä´ kwə\. Said to be the Delaware (Algonquian) name of Frances Sloane, who was kidnapped by Indians in 1778 (O'Hara 2000). A variant is **Moncanaqua.**

MOCCASIN \mok´ ə sin\. The term for a type of Indian footwear was originally borrowed by English in Va., from CAC Algonquian <mockasin>. Similar words for 'shoe' occur in other Algonquian languages: for example, SNEng. Algonquian <makkussin>, Munsee Delaware <mahksun> (O'Meara 1996), Ojibwa *makizin*

(Nichols and Nyholm 1995). The term was also adapted in English to refer to a type of snake (the water moccasin), as well as a fish and a flower. The use of **Moccasin** in placenames may refer to any of these meanings; examples occur in Mass. (Worcester Co.), Ill. (Effingham Co.), Calif. (Tuolumne Co.), and elsewhere.

MOCKONEMA (Wash., Whitman Co.). Possibly from Nez Perce (Sahaptian), meaning 'snow place'; cf. /mé:qeʔ/ 'snow', /-nɨme/ 'place' (N. Rude p.c.).

MOCLIPS (Wash., Grays Harbor Co.) \mō´ klips\. Shortened from Quinault [nəw'múɬapš], said to mean 'large stream', containing /nəw'-/ 'place' and /-apš/ 'stream'(Hitchman 1985; D. Kinkade p.c.).

MOC-TEL-ME, Chief (Idaho, Benewah Co.). Named for a Coeur d'Alene (Salishan) leader, known as /maχ̣təlmí/, perhaps from French *Barthélemy* 'Bartholomew'. His Native American name was /t'n't'n'mílščn/ (D. Kinkade p.c.).

MODALE (Iowa, Harrison Co.) \mō´ dāl\. Formed from **Mo**, an abbreviation of **Missouri** (Vogel 1983).

MODOC \mō´ dok\. The term refers to an Indian group, closely associated with the Klamath people, living on the Ore./Calif. border. The name is from Klamath /mo:wat'a:kkni:/ 'southerners' (Barker 1963). As a placename, **Modoc** is applied to a county in Calif. and to a creek in Ore. (Klamath Co.). The name of the group became well known because of the Modoc War in 1872–74 and was applied as a transfer name to places in many states (e.g., Ariz., Greenlee Co.; Ill., Randolph Co.; and S.C., McCormick Co.). A related name is **Medoc** (Mo., Jasper Co.).

MOENAVE (Ariz., Coconino Co.) \mō nä´ vē\. Hopi (Uto-Aztecan) *mawyavi* 'where they pick things', from *maw-* , *maawi* 'pick some', *-ya* 'plural', and *-vi* 'place' (K. Hill).

MOENKOPI (Ariz., Coconino Co.) \mō en´ kō pē, mō´ (ə)n kō pē, mō´ ən kop ē\. Hopi *mùnqapi* 'place of flowing water', from *mùn-*, *muuna* 'flow', *-qa* 'that which', and *-pi* 'place' (K. Hill).

MOGAK Creek (Alaska, Marshall B-1). From Yupik (Eskimo) *murak* 'wood' (Orth 1967; Jacobson 1984).

MOGHOWEYIK River (Alaska, St. Lawrence C-6). The Yupik (Eskimo) name was reported in 1944 (Orth 1967).

MOHANSIC Lake (N.Y., Westchester Co.). The name, also written <Mo-har-sic>, is perhaps from Munsee Delaware (Algonquian), perhaps meaning 'where two ponds meet' (Ruttenber 1906; Beauchamp 1907).

MOHAVE County (Ariz.) \mō hä´ vē, mə hä´ vē, mə hav´ ē\. Named for the **Mojave** (Yuman) Indians; the term is now officially spelled with a *j* for both the people and placenames in Calif. The word is derived from the Mojaves' name for themselves, /hamakhа́av/, perhaps containing /('a)ha-/ 'water' (P. Munro p.c.).

MOHAWK \mō´ hôk\. The term refers to a people and language of the Iroquoian linguistic stock, living in upper N.Y. and adjacent areas of Canada. The word was first used in English as <Mohowawogs> (plural) in 1638, derived from a SNEng. Algonquian word for the Mohawk people, cognate with Unami Delaware /mhuwé:yɔk/ 'cannibal monsters'. The Mohawks' own name for themselves is *kanyę'kehá:ka'* or *kanyę'kehró:no'*, meaning 'people of *kanyę̂ke'* (*HNAI* 15:478). **Mohawk** has come to be used for a haircut and for a type of military aircraft. As a placename, it is used in N.Y. (Herkimer Co.) and has been transferred to many areas (e.g., Fla., Lake Co.; Ill., Du Page Co.; and Mich., Keweenaw Co.).

MOHAWKSIN (Wisc., Lincoln Co.) \mō hôk´ sin\. Named for three rivers that meet here—the Somo, the Tomahawk, and the Wisconsin (Vogel 1991). Sometimes spelled and pronounced **Mohawkskin.**

MOHEGAN \mō hē´ gən\. The name of a SNEng. Algonquian group, formerly based in Conn. The term is a contraction of earlier <Moyanhegunnewog>, from a village name that can be reconstructed as */mōLahīkan/, of unknown etymology (*HNAI*, 15:175). As a placename, the word occurs in Conn. (New London Co.) and elsewhere as a transfer (R.I., Providence Co.; N.Y., Hamilton Co.).

MOHEPINOKE, Mount (N.J., Passaic Co.). Probably from Delaware (Algonquian), but of unclear derivation (Becker 1964).

MOHICAN \mō hē´ kən\. Refers to an Algonquian group of the upper Hudson Valley in N.Y. state and adjacent parts of New England, otherwise called **Mahican.** The form **Mohican** for the tribal name was popularized by James Fenimore Cooper's novel *The Last of the Mohicans*; it is not to be confused with **Mohegan**, the name of a different Algonquian group in Conn. **Mohican** is derived from a placename <Muhheakunnuk>, referring to the tidal flow on the Hudson River (*HNAI* 15:211). As a placename, **Mohican** is found in N.Y. (Warren Co.), and as a transfer in Md. (Montgomery Co.), Mich. (Livingston Co.), and Ohio (Coshocton Co.).

MOHONK Lake (N.Y., Ulster Co.) \mō´ hongk\. The name was earlier written <Maggonck, Moggonick> (etc.), perhaps from a Mahican (Algonquian) word meaning 'high hill' (Ruttenber 1906).

MOIESE (Mont., Lake Co.) \mō ēz´\. Named for a Flathead (Salishan) leader; perhaps from French *Moïse* 'Moses' (Cheney 1984; D. Kinkade p.c.).

MOINGONA (Iowa, Boone Co.). The term refers to a branch of the Miami/Illinois (Algonquian) people, also written <Moingoane, Moingwena> (etc.) (Vogel 1983); it may be from /mooyiinkweena/ 'shit-face', containing /mooy-/ 'face', /-iinkwee-/ 'shit', and /-na/ 'indefinite actor' (Costa 2000:46). A possibly related placename is **Des Moines.**

MOIVAVI (Ariz., Maricopa Co.). From O'odham (Piman), of unclear derivation, probably containing *wahia* 'well' (J. Hill p.c.).

MOJAVE \mō hä´ vē\. The name is that of a language and people, of the Yuman linguistic family, living on the lower Colorado River. The term is now officially spelled with a *j* both in the name of the people and in Calif. placenames; but an *h* is used in the name of **Mohave County** (Ariz.). The word is derived from the Mojave name for themselves, /hamakháav/, perhaps containing /(')a)ha-/ 'water' (P. Munro p.c.).

MOKAAC Wash (Ariz., Mohave Co.; Utah, Washington Co.). The name may be from Southern Paiute (Numic), but the derivation is unclear (BGN 7901).

MOKELUMNE River (Calif., San Joaquin Co.) \mō kel´ ə mi, mō kol´ ə mē\. The name is derived from that of a Plains Miwok village, perhaps containing /moke/ 'fish net' (Gudde 1998).

MOKENA (Ill., Will Co.) \mō kē´ nə\. Perhaps from an Algonquian word for 'turtle' (Vogel 1963); cf. Ojibwa *mikinaak* 'snapping turtle' (Nichols and Nyholm 1995). Possibly related placenames include **Mackinac County** (Mich.), **Mackinaw City** (Mich., Cheboygan Co.), and **Fort Michilimackinac** (Mich., Fort Emmet Co.).

MOKI Tank (Utah, Garfield Co.) \mō´ kī\. Perhaps related to **Moqui,** from the Southern Paiute (Numic) word /mo:kkwi/, referring to the Hopi people of Ariz. (Sapir 1930).

MOKOMA (Wyo., Natrona Co.). Perhaps from Ojibwa (Algonquian) *mookomaan* 'knife' (Stennett 1908; Nichols and Nyholm 1995). The placename **Mokoma** also occurs in Pa. (Sullivan Co.), perhaps imported from the western states.

MOKOWANIS Cascade (Mont., Glacier Co.). Probably from Blackfoot (Algonquian) *móókoan* 'stomach' (Holterman 1985; D. Franz p.c.).

MOKST Butte (Ore., Deschutes Co.) \môkst\. From the same source as **Mox Peaks** (Wash., Whatcom Co.); see below.

MOLALLA (Ore., Clackamas Co.) \mō´ lal ə, mō lä´ lə\. The name refers to an Indian people of uncertain affiliation. The term apparently comes from Clackamas Chinook /muláliš/ 'Molalla tribe' (D. Kinkade p.c.).

MOLASSES Pond (Maine, Hancock Co.). Perhaps named for an Abenaki (Algonquian) woman who was called "Molasses" in English; her Native American name may have meant 'deep' (Rutherford 1970). Cf. Abenaki *molôgek* 'deep one' (Day 1994–95).

MOLAZIGAN Island (Maine, Kennebec Co.). From Abenaki (Algonquian) *môlazigan* (Day 1994–95).

MOLLIDGEWOCK Pond (Maine, Oxford Co.) \mol´ ij wok\. Perhaps from Abenaki (Algonquian) *molôgek* 'deep' (Day 1994–95). The placename also occurs in N.H. (Coös Co.) Possibly related placenames are **Molunkus, Mona Lake.**

MOLLYOCKETT Mountain (Maine, Oxford Co.) \mol´ ē ok ət\. Perhaps from the name of an Abenaki (Algonquian) woman who lived in the area in the early nineteenth century (Huden 1962); perhaps from French *Marie Agathe* [maríagát] 'Mary Agatha'. A probably related placename is **Mollywocket** (N.H., Coös Co.).

MOLUNKUS (Maine, Aroostook Co.) \mō lung´ kəs\. Perhaps from Abenaki (Algonquian) *molôka* [molǫka] 'deep place' (Eckstorm 1941; Day 1994–95). Possibly related placenames are **Mollidgewock Pond, Mona Lake.**

MOMAUGUIN (Conn., New Haven Co.) \mō mô´ gin\. Named for a seventeenth century SNEng. Algonquian leader (Huden 1962).

MOMBACCUS (N.Y., Ulster Co.) \məm bak´ əs\. Perhaps from Mahican (Algonquian), but of unclear derivation (Ruttenber 1906).

MOMBASHA Lake (N.Y., Orange Co.). Perhaps from Munsee Delaware (Algonquian), but the derivation is unclear (Ruttenber 1906).

MOMENCE (Ill., Kankakee Co.) \mō mens´\. Named for Isadore Momence, a resident of mixed Potawatomi (Algonquian) and French descent, in the early nineteenth century (Vogel 1963).

MONACAN (Va., Albemarle Co.) \mon´ ə kən\. Perhaps related to **Manakin** (Va., Goochland Co.), the name of an Indian group (Hagemann 1988). Another possibly related placename is **Manokin** (Md., Somerset Co.); see above.

MONACHE Creek (Calif., Tulare Co.) \mō nach´ ē, mō´ nə chē\. From the name of a Numic (Uto-Aztecan) people, also called **Mono**; see below. The term is from Yokuts <monachi> 'fly people', supposedly because they ate a type of fly larvae. The spelling **Monachee** also occurs (Inyo Co.).

MONADNOCK \mə nad´ nok\. This regional term for an isolated mountain reflects Western Abenaki (Algonquian) *menadena* 'a separate mountain' cf. *men-* 'apart' *-adena* 'mountain' (*RHD* 1987; Day 1994–95). As a placename, **Monadnock** occurs in N.H. (Cheshire Co.) and Vt. (Essex Co.).

MONA Lake (Mass., Hampden Co.) \mō´ nə\. Perhaps from SNEng. Algonquian <moonaeu> 'it is deep' (Huden 1962; W. Cowan p.c.). Possibly related placenames are **Mollidgewock Pond, Molunkus.**

MONANGO (N.Dak., Dickey Co.) \mon´ əng gō\. Perhaps a shortening of **Monongahela;** see below..

MONATIQUOT River (Mass., Norfolk Co.). Perhaps from SNEng. Algonquian, meaning 'at the deep tidal river' (Huden 1962); cf. <moonaeu-> 'it is deep', <-tik-> 'tidal river', <-ot> 'place' (W. Cowan p.c.).

MONCANAQUA (Pa., Luzerne Co.) \mok ə nä´ kwə\. A variant writing of **Mocanaqua**; see above.

MONDAMIN (Iowa, Harrison Co.). From the Ojibwa (Algonquian) word for 'corn', as popularized in Longfellow's *Hiawatha* (Vogel 1983); cf. *mandaamin* 'corn' (Nichols and Nyholm 1995). The placename also occurs in Okla. (Kiowa Co.); the related form **Mondawmin** is found in Md. (Baltimore Co.).

MONEE (Ill., Will Co.) \mō nē´\. Probably an Indian pronunciation of French *Marie,* representing the name of Marie Lefevre, a Potawatomi or Ottawa (Algonquian) resident (Vogel 1963).

MONEKA (Kans., Linn Co.). Osage (Siouan) /mą̄ðį́hka/ 'earth' (R. Rankin p.c.).

MONGAUP (N.Y., Sullivan Co.) \mon´ gôp\. Also recorded as <Mongawping> and <Mingwing>; perhaps from Munsee Delaware (Algonquian), but of unclear derivation (Ruttenber 1906).

MONGO (Ind., Lagrange Co.) \mong´ gō\. An abbreviation of <Mongoquinong> (Baker 1995); from Miami/Illinois (Algonquian) /maankwahkionki/ 'at the loon land', from /maankwa/ 'loon', /-ahki/ 'land', /-onki/ 'place' (M. McCafferty p.c.).

MONGOULOIS, Lake (La., St. Martin Par.) \môngʹ gōōl ä\. From a Choctaw (Muskogean) phrase meaning 'their people are there', containing *im-* 'their', *oklah* 'people', *asha* 'they are there' (Read 1927; P. Munro p.c.). A perhaps related placename is **Moklassa** (Ala., Montgomery Co.).

MONHAGEN Brook (N.Y., Orange Co.) \mon hā´ gən\. Perhaps from the same source as **Mohegan** (Ruttenber 1906:137).

MONHEGAN (Maine, Lincoln Co.) \mon hē´ gən\. Perhaps from the Maliseet (Algonquian) word for 'island' (Eckstorm 1941:96–97).

MONIE (Md., Somerset Co.) \mə nī´\. Perhaps a shortening of the CAC Algonquian placename <Nominy> (Kenny 1984).

MONITEAU County (Mo.) \mon´ ə tō\. A variant spelling of **Manito** or **Manitou,** a widespread Algonquian word for 'spirit, deity' (Ramsay 1952); see above.

MONO (Calif.) \mō´ nō\. Refers to an Indian people speaking a language of the Numic (Uto-Aztecan) family; a related form is **Monache Creek.** The term is from Yokuts <monachi> 'fly people', supposedly because they ate a type of fly larvae. The term is applied to the placename **Mono County** and to several other features. **Mono Jim Peak** was named for a Mono Indian guide who died in 1871 (Gudde 1998).

MONOCACY (Pa., Berks Co.) \mō nok´ ə se, mə nok´ ə sē\. Perhaps from Delaware (Algonquian) <men'achk> 'fence, fort', <menachkhasu> 'fortified place' (Kenny 1984; Brinton and Anthony 1888). Cf. Munsee Delaware *méenaxk* 'fence' (O'Meara 1996). The name also occurs in Md. (Frederick Co.).

MONOCANOCK Island (Pa., Luzerne Co.). Perhaps from Delaware (Algonquian) <Menachhenonk> 'island place', from <mehach'hen> 'island' (Donehoo 1928; Brinton and Anthony 1888); cf. Munsee Delaware *mŭnáhan* 'island' (O'Meara 1996). Possibly related names are **Manada Creek** (Pa., Dauphin Co.) and **Manahawkin** (N.J., Ocean Co.).

MONODY Creek (Pa., Dauphin Co.). A variant of **Manada Creek**; see above. Possibly related names are **Manahawkin** (N.J., Ocean Co.) and **Monocanock Island** (Pa., Luzerne Co.).

MONOHANSETT Island (Mass., Dukes Co.). From SNEng. Algonquian, perhaps meaning 'at the small island' (Huden 1962).

MONOMONAC Lake (Mass., Worcester Co.) \mə nō´ mə nak\. From SNEng. Algonquian, perhaps meaning 'at the deep place' (Huden 1962). The placename also occurs in N.H. (Cheshire Co.).

MONOMOY (Mass., Nantucket Co.) \mon´ ə moi\. Earlier written <Monnument>, <Mannamoy> (Little 1984). From SNEng. Algonquian, perhaps from <moonaeu-> 'it is deep' (Huden 1962; W. Cowan p.c.).

MONON (Ind., White Co.) \mō´ non\. A shortening of <Metamonon>, probably from Potawatomi (Algonquian) /mdaamənək/ 'in the corn' (McCafferty 2002). The term occurs as a transfer name in Ore. (Jefferson Co.).

MONONA County (Iowa) \mə nō´ nə\. Perhaps derived from the name of an Indian character in a play called *Oolaita, or the Indian Heroine,* by Lewis Deffebach, published in 1821 (Vogel 1983). The name also occurs in Wis. (Dane Co.), possibly with the same source (Vogel 1991).

MONONCUE (Ohio, Wyandot Co.) \mon´ ō kyōō\. May have been named for a Wyandot (Iroquoian) leader (Miller 1996).

MONONGAH (W.Va., Marion Co.) Abbreviated from the name of the **Monongahela River** below.

MONONGAHELA River (W.Va., Monongalia Co.; Pa., Washington Co.) \mə nong gə hē´ lə\. Unami Delaware /mehəmənaːɔnkéhəlaːk/ 'the one that flows with banks that continually cave off' (Afable & Beeler 1996:191).

MONONGALIA County (W.Va.) Probably a Latinized form of **Monongahela** (Kenny 1945).

MONOOSNOC Hills (Mass., Worcester Co.). The SNEng. Algonquian name may contain <moonaeu-> 'it is deep' (Huden 1962; W. Cowan p.c.).

MONOQUET (Ind., Kosciusko Co.) \mə nok´ wət\. Named for a Potawatomi (Algonquian) leader of the early nineteenth century (McPherson 1993).

MONOWI (Neb., Boyd Co.) \mō´ nō wē, mon´ ə wē\. Said to be an Indian word for 'flower', but the language has not been identified (Perkey 1995).

MONPONSETT (Mass., Plymouth Co.). The SNEng. Algonquian name may contain <moonaeu-> 'it is deep' (Huden 1962; W. Cowan p.c.).

MONRAK (Alaska, Baird Inlet B-7). The Yupik (Eskimo) name was reported in 1949 (Orth 1967).

MONSAPEC (Maine, Washington Co.). Perhaps from Maliseet (Algonquian), meaning 'island far at sea' (Huden 1962).

MONSEY (N.Y., Rockland Co.) \mon´ sē\. From the same source as **Munsee**, the name of a Delaware (Algonquian) people.

MONTANA (Alaska, Talkeetna A-1) \mon tan´ ə\. Probably a folk-etymologized form of the Dena'ina (Athabaskan) placename *nultani* (J. Kari p.c.). The name of the state **Montana** is an adapatation of Spanish *montaña* 'mountain'.

MONTAUK (N.Y., Suffolk Co.) \mon´ tôk\. From a SNEng. Algonquian placename, earlier written <Meantacut, Meantacquit> (etc.); perhaps containing <mana-> 'island' and <-auke> 'land' (Trumbull 1879; W. Cowan p.c.). The placename occurs as a transfer in Mo. (Dent Co.).

MONTAZONA Pass (Ariz., Pima Co.) \mon tə zō´ nə\. A blend of **Arizona** and **Montana** (Granger 1983).

MONTE NE (Ark., Benton Co.) \mon tə nā\. From Italian *monte* 'mountain' plus a Siouan word for 'water' (Deane 1986).

MONTEZUMA \mon tə zōō´ mə\. The name of the Aztec ruler when the Spanish arrived in Mexico. The usual Spanish form is *Moctezuma*; the original Nahuatl (Aztecan) form was *moteuczoma,* meaning something like 'angry lord'. The term has been assigned as a placename in many areas, (e.g., Ariz., Yavapai Co.; Calif., Solano Co.; and Iowa, Poweshiek Co.). A possibly related name is **Zuma Creek** (Ill., Rock Island Co.).

MONTOUR County (Pa.) \mon tŏŏr\. Named for a family of mixed Iroquoian and French descent, who were prominent in the area during the eighteenth century. The placename also occurs in N.Y. (Schuyler Co.), and as a transfer in Iowa (Tama Co.). A variant spelling is **Monture** (Mont., Powell Co.).

MONTOWESE (Conn., New Haven Co.). Named for a SNEng. Algonquian leader of the seventeenth century; his name is from <montowese> 'little god', a diminutive of **Monito** (Huden 1962; W. Cowan p.c.).

MONTOWIBO Creek (Mich., Gogebic Co.). Said to be from Ojibwa (Algonquian) <manitowabo> 'spirit-liquid' (Vogel 1986); cf. *manidoo* 'spirit' (Nichols and Nyholm 1995).

MONTSWEAG (Maine, Sagadahoc Co.). Perhaps from Abenaki (Algonquian), but of unclear derivation (Eckstorm 1941:116).

MONTURE (Mont., Powell Co.) \mon tŏŏr\. From the same source as **Montour County** (Pa.); see above.

MOODUS (Conn., Middlesex Co.) \mo͞o´ dəs\. From SNEng. Algonquian <Machemoodus>, said to mean 'bad noise' (Huden 1962).

MOOLACK Creek (Ore., Lane Co.) \mo͞o´ lək\. Chinook Jargon <moo´-lack> [múlək] 'elk', from Lower Chinook [i-mó:lak] 'elk' (McArthur 1992; D. Kinkade p.c.). The placename also exists in Wash. (Columbia Co.). In the spelling **Moolock**, it occurs in Wash. (King Co.) and Idaho (Benewah Co.).

MOOL MOOL Spring (Wash., Yakima Co.) \mo͞ol´ mo͞ol\. From Sahaptin /múlmul/ 'bubbling spring' (D. Kinkade p.c.).

MOONACHIE (N.J., Bergen Co.). Perhaps from Delaware (Algonquian) <munhácke> 'badger' or <monacque> 'ground hog' (Becker 1964; Brinton and Anthony 1888); cf. Munsee Delaware *moonáhkeew* 'ground hog' (O'Meara 1996).

MOONAX (Wash., Klickitat Co.). Said to have been named by the Lewis and Clark expedition in 1805, from an Indian word for 'woodchuck' or 'ground hog' (Hitchman 1985); it may have the same Delaware (Algonquian) origin as **Moonachie.**

MOOREK (Calif., Humboldt Co.) \mo͞o´ rek\. From the Yurok village name *muurekw* (Gudde 1998).

MOOSA (Calif., San Diego Co.) \mo͞o´ sə\. Said to be shortened from <Pamoosa> or <Pamusi>, an Indian village, perhaps from the Diegueño (Yuman) language (Gudde 1998).

MOOSABEC Reach (Maine, Washington Co.) \mo͞o´ sə bek\. The Abenaki (Algonquian) name may mean 'moose head' (Eckstorm 1941:15–16); cf. *moz* 'moose' (Day 1994–95). Possibly related placenames include **Mt. Moosalamoo** (Vt., Addison Co.), from Abenaki (Algonquian) *mozalômo* 'he makes a sound like a moose', containing *moz* 'moose' (Day 1994–95). See also **Moose** below.

MOOSE \mo͞os\. This large type of elk gets its name from an Algonquian language, perhaps from Abenaki *moz* (Day 1994–95), reinforced by similar words in other Algonquian languages, such as Ojibwa *mooz* (*RHD* 1987, Nichols and Nyholm 1995). The English word *moose* occurs in placenames in many states (e.g., Maine, Androscoggin Co.; Mich., Keweenaw Co.; and Minn., Cook Co.). In Maine (Piscataquis Co.), **Moosehead Lake** corresponds to Abenaki *mozôdebinebes*; cf. *moz* 'moose', *-deb* 'head', *nebes* 'lake' (Day 1994–95). Possibly related placenames include: **Mooseleuk Lake** (Maine, Piscataquis Co.), from Abenaki (Algonquian), perhaps meaning 'moose place' (Huden 1962); cf. *moz* 'moose' (Day 1994–95); **Mooselookmeguntic** (Maine, Franklin Co.) \mo͞os lo͝ok mə gun´ tik\, from Abenaki, perhaps meaning 'portage to the moose's feeding place' (Huden 1962); **Moosic** (Pa., Lackawanna Co.) \mo͞o´ sik\, probably from Delaware, meaning 'elk place' (cf. Unami Delaware /mo:s/ 'elk', Blalock et al. 1994); and **Moosilauke Brook** (N.H., Grafton Co.) \mo͞o si lô´ kē, mo͞o´ si lôk\, from Abenaki *mozalhlaki* 'cow moose land' (cf. *alhla* 'female ungulate', *ki* 'land', Day 1994–95). Other possibly related placenames include **Moosabec Reach** (Maine, Washington Co.).

MOOSMOOS Creek (Ore., Clatsop Co.) \mo͞os´ mo͞os\. From Chinook Jargon <moos´-moos> [músmus] 'buffalo, cattle', presumably from an Algonquian language, but the precise history of the word is unknown (D. Kinkade p.c.); cf. Cree (Algonquian) *mostosw-* 'cattle, buffalo' (Wolfart and Ahenakew 1998).

MOOSUP (Conn., Windham Co.) \mo͞o´ səp\. Named for a SNEng. Algonquian leader, also known as Mausup (Huden 1962).

MOOVALYA (Calif., San Bernardino Co.) \mo͞o väl´ yə\. From the Mojave (Yuman) placename *muvály* (P. Munro p.c.). The placename also occurs in Ariz. (La Paz Co.).

MOPANG Stream (Maine, Washington Co.) \mō´ pang\. Perhaps from Maliseet (Algonquian), meaning 'solitary place' (Huden 1962).

MOQUAH (Wis., Bayfield Co.) \mō´ kwä\. From the same source as **Mukwa** (Wis., Waupaca Co.); see below.

MOQUAWKIE Indian Reservation (Alaska, Tyonek A-4). Apparently a non-Alaskan name imposed when the reserve was established (Kari and Fall 1987:48). The term appears to consist of Algonquian elements meaning 'bear land'; cf. Ojibwa *makwa* 'bear', *aki* 'land' (Nichols and Nyholm 1995). See also **Mukwa** (Wis., Waupaca Co.) below.

MOQUI \mō´ kē\. This term was formerly used in both Spanish and English to refer to the Hopi (Uto-Aztecan) people; it was dropped because of a confusion of words. At one time, the Hopis are said to have called themselves *mookwi,* which the Spanish transcribed as *moqui.* This transcription was also used for the Hopi word *mooki* 'to die', however, and the pronunciation \mō´ kē\ was regarded as offensive when applied to the people. It was replaced by the Native American term *hopi* 'peaceful, polite, civilized' (*HNAI* 9:551). The placename **Moqui** remains in several states (e.g., Ariz., Coconino Co.; Utah, Wayne Co.; and Colo., Montezuma Co.).

MOQUITCH Canyon (Ariz., Coconino Co.) \mō´ kwich\. From Southern Paiute (Numic) /mo:kwici/ 'Hopi' (Sapir 1930), from Hopi *mookwi.* The placename also occurs in Utah (Washington Co.).

MORA (Idaho, Ada Co.) \mô´ rə\. Perhaps from Shoshoni (Numic) /muuta/ [mu:ra] 'mule' (Crum and Dayley 1993), borrowed from Spanish *mula.*

MORAPOS Creek (Colo., Moffatt Co.) \môr ap´ əs\. Perhaps from Ute (Numic) *murápuch* 'something big' (Bright 1993).

MORATOC Park (N.C., Martin Co.). The name refers to an unknown Indian group of the region (Powell 1968). Also written as **Moratock, Morattock, Moratuc,** and **Moratuck.** A possibly related placename is **Morattico** (Va., Lancaster Co.) (Hagemann 1988).

MORICHES (N.Y., Suffolk Co.) \môr ich´ əz, mərish´ əs\. Originally a possessive, "Moriche's," referring to a SNEng. Algonquian woman resident in the seventeenth century (Tooker 1911).

MORI Mesa (Ariz., Coconino Co.). Said to be named for a Navajo (Athabaskan) resident, "Hosteen Mori" (BGN 7701). The name does not sound Navajo; it may be from Hopi (Uto-Aztecan) *mori* 'bean' (K. Hill p.c.).

MORISTUL (Calif., Sonoma Co.) \môr i sto͞ol\. The name of a Spanish land grant, reflecting the Wappo (Yukian) village name *Mutistul,* from [muti] 'north', [tul] 'large valley' (Gudde 1998).

MORONGO Valley (Calif., San Bernardino Co.) \mə rong´ gō\. Serrano (Takic) /ma:rɨŋaʔ/, a lineage name (K. Hill p.c.).

MOROYAK (Alaska, Baird Inlet B-3). The Yupik (Eskimo) name was reported in 1949 (Orth 1967).

MOSELEM (Pa., Berks Co.) \mos´ ləm\. Perhaps from Delaware (Algonquian), of unclear derivation (Donehoo 1928).

MOSES, Chief (Wash., Grant Co.) \mō´ zəz\. Named for a Columbian (Salishan) leader of the nineteenth century. His Native American name was /sə̀q'taɬk'ʷúsm/ 'split-sun', containing /sə́q'-/ 'split' and /k'ʷúsm/ 'sun' (D. Kinkade p.c.).

MOSHANNON (Pa., Centre Co.) \mə shan´ ən\. From Delaware (Algonquian) <moos-hánək> 'elk stream', from <moos> 'elk' (cf. **Moose** above) plus <-hanək> 'stream' (Mahr 1959:368).

MOSHASSUCK River (R.I., Providence Co.). The SNEng. Algonquian name has been translated 'great brook in the marshy meadow' (Huden 1962).

MOSHAWQUIT (Wis., Menominee Co.) \mō shô´ kwit\. Probably from a Menominee (Algonquian) personal name, also written <Mishakwut, Moshoquit>, from /muʔsa:hkwat/ 'bright sky' (Vogel 1991; Bloomfield 1973).

MOSHOLU Park (N.Y., Bronx Co.). Probably from Munsee Delaware (Algonquian), perhaps referring to 'smooth stones or gravel' (Grumet 1981).

MOSHULAVILLE (Miss., Noxubee Co.) \mə shōō´ lə vil\. A variant spelling of **Mashulaville;** see above.

MOSHULITUBBEES Prairie (Miss., Noxubee Co.). The name refers to *Mashula*, a Choctaw (Muskogean) leader; see **Mashulaville** above.

MOSINEE (Wis., Marathon Co.) \mō´ si nē\. Named for an Ojibwa (Algonquian) leader; the name is also written as <Mon-so-ne>. Perhaps meaning 'moose tail', from *mooz* 'moose' (Vogel 1991; Nichols and Nyholm 1995). The name also occurs in Mich. (Gogebic Co.).

MOSQUITOHAWK (R.I., Providence Co.). The name is a folk-etymology, modeled on an English dialect word for 'dragonfly', from SNEng. Algonquian <Moskituauke, Moskitauke> (etc.), meaning 'grassy land', from <meskht> 'grass' and <auke> 'land' (Huden 1962; W. Cowan p.c.).

MOSWANSICUT Pond (R.I., Providence Co.). The SNEng. Algonquian name perhaps means 'red hill' (Huden 1962).

MOTANIC (Ore., Union Co.) \mō tan´ ik\. Named for Parsons Motanic, a prominent resident of the Umatilla (Sahaptian) reservation (McArthur 1992); the Native American name was [múta:nik] (N. Rude p.c.).

MOTS'OVI (Ariz., Navajo Co.). Hopi (Uto-Aztecan) *mots'ovi* 'high yucca place' , from *mots-* 'yucca', *-'o-* 'high', and *-vi* 'place' (K. Hill p.c.).

MOUND. A number of places in the Midwest are named after the mounds built by prehistoric Indian peoples: for example, **Mound City** (Ill., Pulaski Co.) and **Moundville** (Wis., Marquette Co.).

MOUNT HOPE Bay (R.I., Bristol Co.). The name is a folk-etymology from SNEng. Algonquian <montop, montaup> 'lookout place' (Huden 1962). The name occurs also in Maine (York Co.).

MOUSAM River (Maine, York Co.). Perhaps from Abenaki (Algonquian) *-mosom* 'grandfather' (Huden 1962; Day 1994–95). The spelling **Moussam** also occurs.

MOWA'API (Ariz., Navajo Co.). Hopi (Uto-Aztecan) *mowàapi* 'moist place', from *mowàa-* 'moist', *-pi* 'place' (K. Hill p.c.).

MOWEAQUA (Ill., Shelby Co.) \mō wē´ kwə\. The name has also been written <Moawequa> and <Mowawequa>, perhaps meaning 'wolf woman' in Potawatomi (Algonquian) (Vogel 1963); cf. *mwi* 'wolf', *kwe'* 'woman' (Kansas 1997).

MOWICH (Ore., Klamath Co.) \mō´ wich\. Chinook Jargon <mow-itsh, mow-itch, mah´-witsh> [máwič] 'deer, venison', from Nootka /muwač/ 'deer' (McArthur 1992; D. Kinkade p.c.). The name also occurs in Wash. (Pierce Co.). **Mowich Illahee** (Wash., Okanogan Co.) is Chinook Jargon for 'deer country'.

MOXAHALA (Ohio, Perry Co.) \mok sə hā´ lə\. Perhaps from Delaware (Algonquian), of unclear derivation (Miller 1996).

MOXEE (Wash., Yakima Co.) \mok sē´\. From Sahaptin /maxšní/, the name of an edible root (D. Kinkade p.c.).

MOXIE Falls (Maine, Somerset Co.) \mok´ sē\. Perhaps from Abenaki (Algonquian), meaning 'dark water' (Rutherford 1970).

MOX Peaks (Wash., Whatcom Co.) \môks\. The site was named by the Forest Service with a term from Chinook Jargon, <mokst, mox> [mɔkst] 'two', probably from Lower Chinook [mɔkšt] 'two' (D. Kinkade p.c.). A related placename is **Mokst Butte** (Ore., Deschutes Co.). Related placenames include **Mox Chehalis Creek** (Wash., Grays Harbor Co.), containing **Chehalis,** a placename derived from a Salishan word for 'sand'; **Mox Chuck** (Wash., Grays Harbor Co.), with <chuck> 'water' (D. Kinkade p.c.); and **Mox La Push** (Wash., King Co.), intended to mean 'two (river) mouths' (i.e., two forks of a river); with <lapush> 'mouth', from French *la bouche* 'the mouth' (Hitchman 1985).

MOYAMENSING (Pa., Philadelphia Co.). Probably from Delaware (Algonquian), of unclear derivation (Donehoo 1928).

MOYAWANCE (Md., Prince George's Co.). From the name of a CAC Algonquian subgroup and village (written by Captain John Smith as <Mayaons, Mayaoones> etc.) (Kenny 1984).

MOYINA (Ore., Klamath Co.) \moi ī´ nə\. Klamath /mo:y'ayn'a/ 'big mountain', from /mo:/ 'very, much, big' and /y'ayn'a/ 'mountain' (Barker 1963).

MUAH Mountain (Calif., Inyo Co.) \mo͞o´ ə\. Probably from Panamint (Numic) /mɨa/ 'moon' (J. McLaughlin p.c.).

MUAV Canyon (Ariz., Coconino Co.). From Southern Paiute (Numic) /mɨa-/ 'a pass, a divide' (Granger 1983; Sapir 1930).

MUCHAKINOCK (Iowa, Mahaska Co.). Formerly written as <Muchekianoe, Muchakianock> (etc.). The name may be from an Algonquian or a Siouan language; its derivation is unknown (Vogel 1983).

MUCHATTOES Lake (N.Y., Orange Co.). Perhaps from a Delaware (Algonquian) placename meaning 'bad hill' (Ruttenber 1906).

MUCHINIPPI Creek (Ohio, Logan Co.) \much i nip´ ē\. The name may mean 'bad water' in some Central Algonquian language; cf. Ojibwa *maji-* 'bad', *nibi* 'water' (Nichols and Nyholm 1995).

MUCK (Wash., Pierce Co.). Probably an abbreviation of Chinook Jargon <muckamuck> 'food'; see **Muckamuck** (Wash., Okanogan Co.) below.

MUCKAFOONEE Creek (Ga., Dougherty Co.) \muk ə fo͞o´ nē\. The name was coined by combining elements of **Muckalee Creek** and **Kinchafoonee Creek** (both in Ga., Dougherty Co.).

MUCKALEE Creek (Ga., Dougherty Co.) \muk´ ə lē\. Perhaps from a Hitchiti (Muskogean) word meaning 'my people, my town', containing /okli/ 'people, town' (Goff 1975).

MUCKALOOCHEE Creek (Ga., Lee Co.) \muk ə lo͞o´ chē\. Probably from Hitchiti (Muskogean), meaning 'little Muckalee' (Goff 1975).

MUCKAMUCK (Wash., Okanogan Co.) \muk´ ə muk\. From Chinook Jargon <muck´ -a-muck> [mʌ́kəmʌk] 'eat, food, drink'; of unknown origin (Hitchman 1985; D. Kinkade p.c.). A perhaps related placename is **Muck** (Wash., Pierce Co.).

MUCKAWANAGO Creek (Colo., Pitkin Co.) \muk ə wä´ nə gō\. Probably from the same source as **Mukwonago** (Wis., Waukesha Co.); see **Mukwa** below.

MUCKINIPATES Creek (Pa., Delaware Co.). The name has also been written <Mokornipalas, Mackinipa, Muckinapattus>; it may be from Delaware (Algonquian), but the derivation is not clear (Donehoo 1928).

MUCKLESHOOT (Wash., King Co.) \muk ´ əl sho͞ot\. The name refers to a Salishan group, from the Lushootseed (Salishan) name /bə́qəlšuɬ/, showing an alternation of *b* and *m* that is common in languages of the area. The name may contain /bə́qsəd/ 'nose' and /šuɬ/ 'see, look, appearance' (D. Kinkade p.c.).

MUCKSHAW Ponds (N.J., Sussex Co.) \muk´ shô\. Perhaps from Delaware (Algonquian), but of unclear derivation (Becker 1964). The placename also occurs in Ohio (Knox Co.).

MUCKWA Creek (Mich., Mason Co.). From Ojibwa (Algonquian) *makwa* 'a bear' (Vogel 1986; Nichols and Nyholm 1995). The placename also occurs in Minn. (Cook Co.).

MUD Butte (S.Dak., Harding Co.). Corresponds to Lakhota (Siouan) *makhótkapa* 'sticky earth', from *makhá* 'earth' and *tkápa* 'adhesive, clammy' (Sneve 1973; Buechel and Manhart 2002). By contrast, **Mud Spring** (S.Dak., Custer Co.) corresponds to Lakhota (Siouan) *mni makhá,* lit. 'water earth' (Sneve 1973; A. Taylor p.c.). The term **Muddy Water Ruin** (N.Mex., McKinley Co.) corresponds to Navajo (Athabaskan) *hashtł'ish bii' kits'iil* 'ruin in the mud' (Linford 2000).

MUDJEKEEWIS Mountain (Ore., Klamath Co.) \muj ə kē´ wis\. The name is probably taken from Longfellow's *Hiawatha,* in which **Mudjekeewis** is the the mythical West Wind spirit. The term may represent the Ojibwa (Algonquian) term for 'first-born son' (Vogel 1986), however; cf. *mjiikwis* 'eldest son' (Rhodes 1985). A related placename is **Mich-e-ke-wis Park** (Mich., Alpena Co.).

MUDYUTOK River (Alaska, Solomon C-3). The Iñupiaq (Eskimo) name was reported about 1940 (Orth 1967).

MUGGET Hill (Mass., Worcester Co.) \mug´ ət\. Perhaps from a SNEng. Algonquian word for 'beaver' (Huden 1962).

MUGISITOKIWIK (Alaska, Teller C-6). The Iñupiaq (Eskimo) name was reported around 1940 (Orth 1967).

MUGU, Point (Calif., Ventura Co.) \mə gōō´\. From Ventureño (Chumashan) /muwu/ 'beach' (Gudde 1998).

MUGUM Peak (Alaska, St. Lawrence C-5). The Yupik (Eskimo) name was reported in 1944 (Orth 1967).

MUGWUMP Lake (Minn., Lake Co.) \mug´wump\. The term refers to a person who is neutral on political issues. It represents an artificial nineteenth-century revival of SNEng. Algonquian <mugquomp>, derived from <mug-gumquomp> 'war leader' (*RHD* 1987).

MUIK VAYA (Ariz., Pima Co.). O'odham (Piman) *moik wahiam,* lit. 'soft well' (J. Hill p.c.).

MUKACHARNI Mountain (Alaska, Teller B-3). The Iñupiaq (Eskimo) name was reported in 1896 (Orth 1967).

MUKACHIAK Creek (Alaska, Baird Mountains D-4). The Iñupiaq (Eskimo) name is said to mean 'baby diaper' (Orth 1967); cf. *maqqaq* 'diaper' (Webster and Zibell 1970).

MUKEWATER Creek (Tex., Coleman Co.). Adapted from the name of a Comanche (Numic) man, written <Mukewarrah, Mukewaka, Muguara> (Tarpley 1980).

MUKIALIK (Alaska, Kwiguk A-4). The Yupik (Eskimo) name was reported in 1899 (Orth 1967).

MUKILTEO (Wash., Snohomish Co.) \muk il tē´ ō\. From a Northern Lushootseed (Salishan) placename /bə́qɬtiyuʔ, bə́qɬtiuʔ/, showing the alternation between *m* and *b* that is characteristic of languages in the region (D. Kinkade p.c.).

MUKLASSA (Ala., Montgomery Co.). Perhaps from a Choctaw (Muskogean) phrase meaning 'their people are there', containing *oklah* 'people', *asha* 'they are there' (Read 1984; P. Munro p.c.). A possibly related placename is **Lake Mongoulois** (La., St. Martin Par.).

MUKLUK (Alaska, Nulato C-5). The term *mukluk* is now used for a kind of soft boot, but it is from Yupik (Eskimo) *maklak* 'bearded seal', incorrectly taken to refer to the sealskin from which the boots were made (RHD 1987).

MUKLUKTULIK River (Alaska, Norton Bay D-5). The Iñupiaq (Eskimo) name was reported in 1900 (Orth 1967).

MUKLUNG River (Alaska, Dillingham A-7). The Yupik (Eskimo) name was reported in 1910 (Orth 1967).

MUKNUK River (Alaska, St. Lawrence C-4). The Yupik (Eskimo) name, said to mean 'a drainage' was recorded in 1965, (Orth 1967); cf. St. Lawrence Is. Yupik *maaqe-* 'to drain out' (Jacobson 1987).

MUKSLULIK Creek (Alaska, Taylor Mountains D-5). The Yupik (Eskimo) name, said to mean 'dirty water', was reported in 1945 (Orth 1967).

MUKUKSOK Point (Alaska, Selawik C-5). The Iñupiaq (Eskimo) name was reported in 1955 (Orth 1967).

MUKUNTUWEAP Canyon (Utah, Washington Co.) \mə kōōn´ tə wēp\. From Southern Paiute (Numic), probably meaning 'straight canyon' (Van Cott 1990); cf. /mukkunta/ 'straight', /uippɨ/ 'canyon' (Sapir 1930).

MUKWA (Wis., Waupaca Co.) \muk´ wä\. From Ojibwa (Algonquian) *makwa* 'a bear' (Vogel 1991; Nichols and Nyholm 1995). A related form is **Moquah** (Wis., Bayfield Co.);

see above. Another related term is **Mukwonago** (Wis., Waukesha Co.) \muk won´ ə gō\; this name is probably Potawatomi (Algonquian), said to mean 'bear's lair' (Vogel 1991); cf. *mko* 'bear' (Kansas 1997). Related forms include **Moquawkie Indian Reservation** (Alaska, Tyonek A-4) and **Muckawanago Creek** (Colo., Pitkin Co.).

MULBERRY Creek (Ga., Harris Co.). Corresponds to the Muskogee placename, said to mean 'withered mulberry' (Goff 1975); cf. *kē* /ki:/ 'mulberry', *tvlē* /talí:/ 'withered' (Martin and Mauldin 2000). A related placename is **Cataula** (Ga., Harris Co.).

MULCHATNA River (Alaska, Dillingham C-3) \mul chat´ nə\. From the Dena'ina (Athabaskan) placename *vaŧts'atnaq'* (Kari 1986:16).

MULEHEAD Butte (S.Dak., Charles Mix Co.). Corresponds to Dakota (Siouan) *pha-šų́šuna* 'head [of a] mule' (Sneve 1973; A. Taylor p.c.).

MULE Trail (Ariz., Apache Co.). Corresponds to Navajo (Athabaskan) *dzaanééz habitin* 'mule's trail up out', containing *dzaa-nééz* 'mule', lit. 'ear-long' (Linford 2000).

MULGA (Ala., Jefferson Co.) \mul´ gə\. Said to have been named for an Indian leader; the term may have something to do with Muskogee *omvlkv* /omálka/ 'all' (Read 1984). The placename also occurs in Ohio (Jackson Co.). A possibly related name is **Mulgee Creek** (Ohio, Ross Co.).

MULGULLO Point (Ariz., Coconino Co.). Named for a Havasupai (Yuman) family (Granger 1983).

MULHOCKAWAY Creek (N.J., Hunterdon Co.) \mul hok´ ə wā\. Probably from Delaware (Algonquian), of unclear derivation (Becker 1964).

MULIK Hills (Alaska, Noatak A-1). The Iñupiaq (Eskimo) name was recorded in 1954 (Orth 1967).

MULPUS Brook (Mass., Middlesex Co.). Perhaps from SNEng. Algonquian, meaning 'little heaps' (Huden 1962).

MULTNOMAH County (Ore.) \mult nō´ mə\. From Chinook /máɬnumax̣/ 'those towards the water' (D. Kinkade p.c.). The placename also occurs in Wash. (Okanogan Co.).

MUMIK Lake (Alaska, Point Lay C-1) \mo͞o´ mik\. From Iñupiaq (Eskimo) *mumiq* 'drumstick' (Orth 1967; Fortescue et al. 1994).

MUMTRAK (Alaska, Goodnews Bay A-7) \mum´ trak\. The Yupik (Eskimo) name was reported in 1880 (Orth 1967).

MUNCIE \mun´ sē\. The name is an alternative spelling of **Munsee,** the name of a language and people, who respresent a branch of the Delaware (Algonquian) Indians. The Native American term is /mə́n'si:w/, referring to a person from **Minisink** (N.Y., Orange Co.); this is in turn from /mə̆nə́sənk/, probably an archaic word for 'on the island' (*HNAI* 15:237); cf. Munsee *mŭnáhan* 'island' (O'Meara 1996). The placename **Muncie** is found in several states (e.g., Ill., Vermilion Co.; Ind., Delaware Co.; and Kans., Wyandotte Co.). The related form **Muncy** also occurs (Pa., Lycoming Co.).

MUNDCHO Lake (Alaska, Tanacross A-3) \mun chō\. From Upper Tanana (Athabaskan) *mänh choh,* lit. 'lake big'. A related term is **Mundthag Lake** (Alaska, Nabesna D-2), from *mänh ts'eegn* 'lake narrow' (J. Kari p.c.).

MUNHAN River (Mass., Bristol Co.). From SNEng. Algonquian <munnoh> 'island' (Trumbull 1881; W. Cowan p.c.). The writing **Manhan** also occurs.

MUNISING (Mich., Alger Co.) \myo͞o´ ni sing\. From Ojibwa (Algonquian), meaning 'at the island' (Vogel 1986); cf. *minis* 'island' (Nichols and Nyholm 1995). Related placenames include **Minisink** (N.Y., Orange Co.) and **Minnisuing** (Wis., Douglas Co.).

MUNNOMIN Lake (Wis., Iron Co.) \mə nom´ in\. The name is related to **Manomin Creek** (Minn., Beltrami Co.); see above.

MUNSATLI Ridge (Alaska, Medfra C-1) \mun sat´ lē\. From Upper Kuskokwim (Athabaskan) *mintsatl'e,* perhaps meaning 'chopped' or 'stone ax' (J. Kari p.c.).

MUNSEE \mun´ sē\. The name refers to a language and people, a branch of the Delaware (Algonquian) Indians. The Native American term is Munsee /mə́n'si:w/, Unami /mwə́ns:i, mɔns:i/, referring to a person from **Minisink** (N.Y., Orange Co.); this is in turn from /mə̆nə́sənk/, probably an archaic word for 'on the island' (*HNAI* 15:236–37); cf. Munsee *mŭnáhan* 'island' (O'Meara 1996). The spelling **Muncie** is used for placenames in several states (e.g., Ill., Vermilion Co.; Ind., Delaware Co.; and Kans., Wyandotte Co.). A related placename is **Muncy** (Pa., Lycoming Co.).

MUNSUNGAN Lake (Maine, Piscataquis Co.) \mun sung´ gən\. Perhaps from Abenaki (Algonquian), meaning 'humped-up island' (Huden 1962); cf. *menahan* 'island', *menahaniz* 'little island' (Day 1994–95).

MUNT Hill (N.H., Rockingham Co.). Said to be named for a local Indian, perhaps Abenaki (Algonquian) (Huden 1962).

MUNUSCONG (Mich., Chippewa Co.). Perhaps from an Ojibwa (Algonquian) word for 'rushes (plant)' (Vogel 1986); cf. *anaakanashk* 'reed, rush' (Nichols and Nyholm 1995).

MUPU (Calif., Ventura Co.) \mo͞o´ po͞o\. From a Ventureño (Chumashan) placename, recorded in 1828 (Gudde 1998).

MUSCALLONGE Bay (Mich., Mackinac Co.) \mus´ kə lunj\. From the same source as **Muskellunge**; see below.

MUSCAMOOT Ridge (Mich., St. Clair Co.) \mus´ kə mo͞ot\. Perhaps named for Muckamoot, a Potawatomi (Algonquian) leader in the early nineteenth century (Vogel 1986).

MUSCATATUCK River (Ind., Washington Co.) \mus kat´ ə tuk\. Perhaps from Munsee Delaware (Algonquian), reconstructed as */máskeekwihtəkw/ 'swamp river' (McCafferty 2002); cf. also **Muskeg** below.

MUSCATINE County (Iowa) \mus kə tēn´\. Perhaps from **Mascouten,** a subgroup of the Miami/Illinois (Algonquian) people, from /maskootia, meehkootia/ 'prairie people', related to /maskooteewi, mahkoteewi/ 'prairie' (Costa 2000:47). Probably related placenames include **Muscotah** (Kans., Atchison Co.), **Mascoutah** (Ill., St. Clair Co.), and **Mascouten Forest** (Ill., Cook Co.).

MUSCHOPAUGE (Mass., Worcester Co.) \mus´ kō pôg\. From SNEng. Algonquian, probably meaning 'muskrat pond' (Huden 1962); cf. <mus(qu)ash-> 'muskrat', <-paug> 'pond' (W. Cowan p.c.).

MUSCLE SHOALS (Ala., Lauderdale Co.). From **Mussel Shoals,** corresponding to Cherokee (Iroquoian) *dagvnahi* 'mussel place', from *dagvna* 'mussel' (Foscue 1989; Alexander 1971).

MUSCODA (Wis., Grant Co.) \mus´ kō dā\. From an Algonquian word for 'prairie' (Vogel 1991); cf. Ojibwa *mashkode* (Nichols and Nyholm 1995). Related placenames include **Muscotah** (Kans., Atchison Co.); see below.

MUSCOGEE \mus kō´ gē\. This term refers to an Indian people and language, also spelled **Muskogee** and also called **Creek,** of the **Muskogean** language family, native to the southeastern United States. The Native American form of the name is *maskoke* [ma:skó:ki] or *mvskoke* [maskó:ki] (Martin and Mauldin 2000). The placename **Muscogee** occurs in Ga. (Muscogee Co.) and Fla. (Escambia Co.); the spelling **Muskogee** is found in Okla. (Muskogee Co.).

MUSCONETCONG Mountain (N.J., Hunterdon Co.) \mus kə net´ kong\. Probably from Delaware (Algonquian), but of unclear derivation (Becker 1964).

MUSCONGUS (Maine, Lincoln Co.) \mus kong´ gəs\. The name may be from an Abenaki (Algonquian) word meaning 'many rock ledges' (Eckstorm 1941:88–92).

MUSCOTAH (Kans., Atchison Co.) \mus kō´ tə\. From an Algonquian word for 'prairie' (Vogel 1991); cf. Ojibwa *mashkode* (Nichols and Nyholm 1995). Possibly related placenames include **Muscoda** (Wis., Grant Co.), **Muskoda**

(Minn., Clay Co.), and **Mascoutah** (Ill., St. Clair Co.) Probably from the same source is **Mascouten,** a subgroup of the Miami/Illinois (Algonquian) people (Costa 2000); this also occurs as a placename, as in **Mascouten Forest** (Ill., Cook Co.) and **Muscatine County** (Iowa).

MUSCUPIABE (Calif., San Bernardino Co.) \məs kə pi yä´ bē\. From a Serrano (Takic) placename recorded in 1843 (Gudde 1998).

MUSEMBEAH Peak (Wyo., Fremont Co.). Shoshoni (Numic) /mɨtsampia/ [mɨzámbia] 'ewe (of bighorn sheep)', from /mɨtsa/ 'lamb', /-m/ 'possessive', and /pia/ 'mother' (J. McLaughlin p.c.).

MUSHAWAY Peak (Tex., Borden Co.) \mush´ ə wā\. The name has been written <Mochaquo, Muchakooago, Mucha Koo Ave> (etc.); it may be from Comanche (Numic), but the derivation is not clear (BGN 7301; Tarpley 1980).

MUSH Creek (S.Dak., Hughes Co.). The name is shortened from Dakota (Siouan) *maštį́čala* 'cottontail rabbit' (Sneve 1973; A. Taylor p.c.). A related placename is **Mustinka River** (Minn., Traverse Co.).

MUSKALLONGE Lake (Mich., Luce Co.) \mus´ kə lunj\. From the same source as **Muskellunge**; see below.

MUSKEE Creek (N.J., Cumberland Co.) \mus´ kē\. Perhaps from Delaware (Algonquian) <maskek> 'swamp' (Becker 1964; Brinton and Anthony 1888). Possibly related placenames include **Muskeg** (Mich., Gogebic Co.), **Muskego** (Wis., Waukesha Co.), and **Muskegon County** (Mich.).

MUSKEG \mus´keg\. The term refers to a type of bog, derived from Cree (Algonquian) /maske:k/ 'swamp' (*RHD* 1987). Similar terms occur in other Algonquian languages: for example, Abenaki *mskag* (Day 1994–95), Munsee Delaware *máskeekw* (O'Meara 1996), Ojibwa *mshkiig* (Rhodes 1985), Menominee /maski:k/ (Bloomfield 1975). As a placename, it occurs in Mich. (Gogebic Co.), Minn. (Lake of the Woods Co.), Wis. (Bayfield Co.), and Alaska (Sleetmute C-2). Possibly related placenames include **Muscatatuck River** (Ind., Washington Co.), **Muskee Creek** (N.J., Cumberland Co.), **Muskego** (Wis., Waukesha Co.), and **Muskegon County** (Mich.).

MUSKEGET Channel (Mass., Dukes Co.). Earlier written <Mooskeiakit>, <Muskegit>, <Miskegitt> (Little 1984). Probably from SNE Algonquian <moskeht-> 'grass', <-auke-> 'land', <-et> 'place' (Huden 1962; W. Cowan p.c.).

MUSKEGO (Wis., Waukesha Co.) \mus kē´ gō\. Perhaps from the same source as **Muskegon County;** see below. The placename **Muskego** also occurs in Minn. (St. Louis Co.) and N.Dak. (Renville Co.).

MUSKEGON County (Mich.) \mus kē´ gən\. Probably from Ojibwa (Algonquian), meaning 'marsh-place' (Vogel 1986); cf. *mshkiig* 'marsh' (Rhodes 1985). Possibly related placenames include **Muskee Creek** (N.J., Cumberland Co.), **Muskeg** (Mich., Gogebic Co.), and **Muskego** (Wis., Waukesha Co.).

MUSKELLUNGE \mus´ kə lunj\. The term refers to a large fish of the pike family; an earlier form is <muskenonge>. It is derived from Canadian French *masquinonge,* which in turn is from Ojibwa (Algonkian) *maashkinoozhe* (*RHD* 1987; Nichols and Nyholm 1995). As a placename, the word is widespread (e.g., Mich., Montcalm Co.; Wis., Grant Co.; and Alaska, Bendeleben C-4). It also occurs in other spellings such as **Muskallonge Lake** (Mich., Luce Co.) and **Muscallonge Bay** (Mich., Mackinac Co.). The name of the fish is sometimes shortened to **Muskie**, which may also be reflected in placenames e.g., Wis., Green Lake Co.; and N.Dak., Burke Co.).

MUSKESIN Lake (Wis., Vilas Co.) \mus kē´ sin\. May be from an unidentified Indian language (Vogel 1991).

MUSKINGUM Brook (N.J., Burlington Co.) \musk ing´ əm\. Perhaps originally from Shawnee (Algonquian) <məshkeekwaaməchki> 'where the land is swampy', with <mshkeekwi-> 'lake, swamp', <-aam-> 'land, soil', and <-əchki> 'place'; but then folk-etymologized as Delaware

<mooskinkum> 'elk's eye', containing <moos-> 'elk' plus <-wəshkiink> 'an eye' (Mahr 1959: 371). Cf. also Munsee Delaware *moos* 'elk, moose', *nu-skíinjukw* 'my eye' (O'Meara 1996). The name also occurs in Ohio (Muskingum Co.) and in Tex. (Ector Co.). Related words include **Moose** and **Muskeg.**

MUSKODA (Minn., Clay Co.) \mus kō´ də\. Probably from Ojibwa (Algonquian) *mashkode* 'prairie' (Upham 2001; Nichols and Nyholm 1995). In **Lake Muskoday** (Mich., Wayne Co.), the spelling is taken from Longfellow's *Hiawatha,* where the word is translated as 'meadow'. The name is also found in N.Y. (Sullivan Co.). Probably related placenames include **Mascouten Forest** (Ill., Cook Co.), **Muscatine County** (Iowa), **Muscotah** (Kans., Atchison Co.), **Mascoutah** (Ill., St. Clair Co.), and **Oscoda** (Mich., Iosco Co.).

MUSKOGEE \mus kō´ gē\. This term, also spelled **Muscogee,** refers to a language and people of the **Muskogean** language stock, also called **Creek,** living in the southeastern United States. The Native American name is *maskokē* /ma:skó:ki/ or *mvskokē* /maskó:ki/ (Martin and Mauldin 2000). The term occurs as a placename in **Muskogee County** (Okla.); in the spelling **Muscogee**, it also is found in Ga. (Muscogee Co.) and Fla. (Escambia Co.).

MUSKOMEE Bay (Alaska, Afognak A-4). The Alutiiq (Eskimo) name was reported in 1952 (Orth 1967).

MUSKRAT. The term refers to an aquatic rodent; it represents a folk-etymology derived from **Musquash,** of Algonquian origin. **Muskrat** often occurs in placenames (e.g., Maine, Oxford Co.; N.Y., Oswego Co.; and Ore., Deschutes Co.). The animal is also sometimes called simply a **Rat,** which also occurs in placenames.

MUSKWA Village (Alaska, Seward B-7). Perhaps from Alutiiq (Eskimo) (Orth 1967).

MUSLATT Mountain (Calif., Del Norte Co.) \mus´ lat\. Perhaps from Tolowa (Athabaskan), but the derivation is not clear (Gudde 1998).

MUSQUABUCK Park (Ind., Kosciusko Co.) \mus´ kwə buk\. Named for a Potawatomi (Algonquian) leader whose name is recorded as <Mesquabuck> 'copper', perhaps derived from *me'skwak* 'red' (Dunn 1919; Kansas 1997); cf. the related Ojibwa *miskwaabik* 'copper', *misko-* 'red' (Nichols and Nyholm 1995).

MUSQUACOOK (Maine, Aroostook Co.) \mus´ kwə ko͞ok\. Perhaps from Abenaki (Algonquian) *moskwas* 'muskrat' or from *maskwa* 'birch bark' (Day 1994–95).

MUSQUAPSINK Brook (N.J., Bergen Co.) \mə skäp´ singk\. Probably from Delaware (Algonquian), but of unclear derivation (Becker 1964).

MUSQUASH \mus´kwäsh\. The term refers to an aquatic rodent, derived from Abenaki (Algonquian) *moskwas* (*RHD* 1987; Day 1994–95). As a placename, it occurs in several states (Maine, Lincoln Co.; N.H., Hillsborough Co.; and N.J., Monmouth Co.). Through folk-etymology, the word also occurs in English as **Muskrat.**

MUSQUASHCUT Brook (Mass., Plymouth Co.). The SNEng. Algonquian name is probably derived from <musquash-> 'muskrat' (W. Cowan p.c.).

MUSQUETI Point (Wash., Mason Co.). From the Twana (Salishan) placename /bəsq'^{W}íli/, lit. 'having cedar trees', from /bəs-/ 'possessive' and /sq'^{W}íli/ 'cedar tree'. The original *l* was misread and miscopied as *t* (D. Kinkade p.c.).

MUSSACHUCK Creek (R.I., Bristol Co.) \mus´ ə chuk\. The SNEng. Algonquian name may have meant 'place of rushes (plants)' (Huden 1962).

MUSSELSHELL Creek (Idaho, Clearwater Co.). A translation of Nez Perce /se:wiʔsníme/ 'mussel-place', from /se:wíʔs/ 'mussel' and /níme/, a placename formant (Aoki 1994:488, 636).

MUSTINKA River (Minn., Traverse Co.) \mus ting´ kə\. From Dakota (Siouan) *maštį́ča* 'rabbit' (Upham 2001; Riggs 1890). A related placename is **Mush Creek** (S.Dak., Hughes Co.).

MUSULACON (Calif., Sonoma Co.). From Southern Pomo /mussaalahkon/ 'Long Snake', a supernatural creature; also said to have been the name of a chief (Gudde 1998).

MUTAKTUK Creel (Alaska, De Long Mountains D-5). The Iñupiaq (Eskimo) was reported in 1960 as meaning 'no parka' (Orth 1967); cf. *mattaq-* 'to remove one's parka' (MacLean 1980).

MUZACAGA Draw (S.Dak., Ziebach Co.) \muz´ ə kä gä\. Lakhota (Siouan) *máza-kağa* 'blacksmith', lit. 'metal maker' (Sneve 1973; Buechel and Manhart 2002).

MYAKKA City (Fla., Manatee Co.) \mī ak´ kə\. Probably the name of a Timucua village (Read 1934:19, 31). A variant spelling is **Miacca.** Related placenames are **Port Mayaca** (Fla., Martin Co.) and **Miakka** (Fla., Sarasota Co.).

MYAUGHEE, Cape (Alaska, St. Lawrence D-3). The Yupik (Eskimo) name was recorded in 1965 as <Maiyure> (Orth 1967); cf. St. Lawrence Is. Yupik *mayugh-* \mayuʀ-\. 'to climb' (Jacobson 1987).

MYGHAPOWIT Mountain (Alaska, St. Lawrence B-2). The Yupik (Eskimo) name was reported in 1931 (Orth 1967).

MYSTIC (Conn., New London Co.) \mis´ tik\. SNEng. Algonquian <missituk> 'great tidal river', from <missi> 'large', <-tuk> 'tidal river' (Trumbull 1881; W. Cowan p.c.). The placename occurs in several other states (e.g., Mass., Middlesex Co.; N.H., Coös Co.; and Iowa, Appanoose Co.). A variant spelling is **Mistic Pond** (Mass., Middlesex Co.).

MYTOGE Lake (Utah, Uintah Co.) \mə tō´ gē\. Perhaps from Ute (Numic) /mɨátagoci/ 'the moon', derived from /mɨa-/ 'moon' and /toko/ 'grandfather' (Van Cott 1990; Givón 1979).

N

NAABA ANI (N.Mex., San Juan Co.) \nä bə ä´ nē\. Navajo (Athabaskan) *naabi'áání* 'the place of the enemy's cave', containing *naa'* 'enemy' and *bi'áan* 'his cave' (A. Wilson p.c.).

NAACHPUNKT Brook (N.J., Passaic Co.). Supposedly named for a Delaware (Algonquian) Indian leader, perhaps involving <nachk> 'my hand' and <ponk> 'ashes' (Becker 1964; Brinton and Anthony 1888); but it could also be derived from Dutch *naakt* 'naked, bare' plus *punt* 'point'.

NA AH TEE (Ariz., Navajo Co.) \nä ā´ tē\. Navajo (Athabaskan) *náá'á dįįh* 'toadstool, loco-weed', lit. 'eyes become none' (Linford 2000).

NAAKAI Canyon (Utah, San Juan Co.) \nä kī´, nə kī´\. From Navajo (Athabaskan) *naakai* 'Mexican(s)', lit. 'wanderers' (Young and Morgan 1987); the term is also used by Navajos as a family name. Related placenames are **Nakai Peak** (Colo., Grand Co.) and **Nokai Canyon** (Ariz., Navajo Co.).

NAAMAN Creek (Del., New Castle Co.; Pa., Delaware Co.) \nā´ mən\. Probably named for a Delaware (Algonquian) Indian leader in the seventeenth century (Donehoo 1928). The name may have been applied to him by Europeans, since *Naaman* is a Biblical name.

NAASHOIBITO (N.Mex., San Juan Co.) \nä shoi´ bi tō\. Navajo (Athabaskan) *náshdóí bito'* 'wildcat's spring', from *náshdóí* 'wildcat' and *bito'* 'its spring' (*bi-* 'his, her, its', *-to'* 'water') (A. Wilson p.c.).

NAAT'A'ANIL BIKIN (N.Mex., McKinley Co.) \nä tä´ nē bi kin\. This may be Navajo (Athabaskan) *naat'áanii bikin* 'chieftain's or leader's house', from *naat'áanii* 'chief, leader' plus *bikin* 'his house' (*bi-* 'his', *kin* 'house') (A. Wilson p.c.).

NAAUSAY Township (Ill., Kendall Co). Perhaps the name of a Potawatomi (Algonquian) leader or from Ojibwa (Algonquian) *neyaashi* 'point of land' (Vogel 1963; Nichols and Nyholm 1995).

NABAKSYALIK Point (Alaska, Nunivak Is. B-4). The Yupik (Eskimo) placename was recorded in 1949 (Orth 1967).

NABANGOYAK Rock (Alaska, Nunivak Is. A-7). The Yupik (Eskimo) name was recorded in 1949 (Orth 1967).

NABESNA (Alaska, Nabesna B-5) \nə bez´ nə\. From Ahtna (Athabaskan) *nabaes na'*, with *na'* 'stream' (Kari 1990).

NABNASSET (Mass., Middlesex Co.) \nab nas´ ət\. The SNEng. Algonquian placename may mean 'near the dry land' (Huden 1962).

NACHE (Nev., Pershing Co.) \nash\. From <Naches>, the name of a Northern Paiute (Numic) leader in the nineteenth century (Carlson 1974); possibly from /naatsi'i/ [náatši'i] 'boy' (J. McLaughlin p.c.). Possibly related is **Natchez** (Nev., Elko Co.), with the spelling of the latter influenced by **Natchez,** a tribal name and placename of the southeastern United States. Not to be confused with **Natches** (Ariz., Graham Co.), the name of a Chiricahua Apache leader.

NACHES (Wash., Yakima Co.) \nach ēz´\. Perhaps Sahaptin /naxčí:š/ 'first water' (E. Hunn, p.c.).

NACHOTTA (Wash., Pacific Co.). Equivalent to **Nahcotta**; see below.

NACHRALIK Pass (Alaska, Misheguk Mountain C-4). The Iñupiaq (Eskimo) name was published in 1962 (Orth 1967).

NACHUSA (Ill., Lee Co.) \nə cho͞o´ sə, nə cho͞o´ zə\. Said to be the Winnebago (Siouan) name of a white man, John Dixon, lit. 'white-haired' (Vogel 1963; E. Callary p.c.); cf. *nąąǰú* 'hair of the head', *saa* 'white' (K. Miner p.c.).

NACKO Creek (Calif., Humboldt Co.) \nä´ kō\. This spelling was established by BGN 8402, instead of **Natchko** or **Natchka**; but the earlier spellings seem better reflections of the Yurok original /nohčka/ (Gudde 1998).

NACLINA (Tex., Nacogdoches Co.) \nak lē´ nə\. A blending of elements from the names of **Nacogdoches County** and *Angelina County* (Tarpley 1980).

NACO (Ariz., Cochise Co.) \nä´ kō, nā´ kō\. A shortening of the placename *Nacosari* in nearby Sonora, Mexico; perhaps derived from an Ópata (Sonoran) word for 'prickly pear' (Granger 1983).

NACOGDOCHES County (Tex.) \nak ə dō´ chis\. The name is the plural of <Nacogdoche>, a division of the Caddo people (Tarpley 1980).

NACOOCHEE (Ga., White Co.) \nə ko͞o´ chē\. Perhaps from Choctaw (Muskogean) *nak-oshi* 'little arrow', from *naki* 'arrow' plus *oshi* 'child' (Krakow 1975; P. Munro p.c.). The placename also occurs in Ala. (Jackson Co.).

NACORA (Neb., Dakota Co.) \nə kôr´ ə\. Probably from *nakhóda,* occurring in the Yankton or Yanktonnais dialects of Dakotan (Siouan) as the equivalent of **Dakota** and **Lakhota** (R. Rankin p.c.).

NACOTE Creek (N.J., Atlantic Co.). Perhaps from the same source as **Nanticoke,** an Algonquian people (Becker 1964); see below.

NADATDEKWI:WA (N.Mex., Cibola Co.). The Zuni name refers to a ritual hunting area (Ferguson and Hart 1985).

NADAWAH (Ala., Monroe Co.) \nä´ də wä\. Probably a transfer of an Ojibwa (Algonquian) word applied to neighboring peoples of the Siouan and Iroquoian families; see **Nodaway** below.

NADEAU (Kans., Jackson Co.) \nə dō´\. Named for a prominent Potawatomi (Algonquian) family (Rydjord 1968); the surname may be of French origin.

NADINA River (Alaska, Valdez D-4) \nä dē´ nə\. From Ahtna (Athabaskan) *hwniidi na',* lit. 'downriver stream' (Kari 1983:23).

NADOWAY Point (Mich., Chippewa Co.) \nä´ də wā\. Probably a transfer of an Ojibwa (Algonquian) word applied to neighboring peoples of the Siouan and Iroquoian families; see **Nodaway** below.

NADVIKTAK Creek (Alaska, Noatak D-5). The Iñupiaq (Eskimo) name was reported in 1966 (Orth 1967).

NADZAHEEN Cove (Alaska, Ketchikan A-5). The Tlingit placename was published as <Nadzahin> 'Nadza river' in 1911 (Orth 1967).

NA-GAH Flat (Utah, Sevier Co.). Southern Paiute (Numic) /naka/ [naɣa] 'bighorn sheep' (J. McLaughlin p.c.).

NAGAHUT Rocks (Alaska, Seldovia A-5). Probably from Dena'ina (Athabaskan), reported in 1908 (Orth 1967).

NAGAI Rocks (Alaska, Chirikof Is. D-5) \nə gī\. The Native American name was reported in 1802; it may be Yupik (Eskimo) or Aleut (Orth 1967).

NAGA Point (Alaska, Adak C-4). Shortened from the name of **Kanaga Island** and reported in 1934 (Orth 1967).

NAGASAY Cove (Alaska, Craig C-5) \nä gə sā\. From Tlingit /naaɢas'éi/ fox' (Orth 1967, Davis and Leer 1976); a perhaps related placename is **Nagat**.

NAGAWICKA Lake (Wis., Waukesha Co.). From Ojibwa (Algonquian) *negawikaa* 'there is much sand', from *negaw* 'sand' (Vogel 1991; J. Nichols p.c.).

NAGEETHLUK River (Alaska, Kwiguk B-1). The Yupik (Eskimo) name is said to mean 'place of snares' (Orth 1967); cf. *negaq* 'a snare' (Jacobson 1984).

NAGEEZI (N.Mex., San Juan Co.) \nā gē´ zē\. Navajo (Athabaskan) *naayízí* 'a squash (vegetable), lit. 'the one that rolls around', containing *naa-* 'here and there', *-yíz* 'turn, revolve' (A. Wilson p.c.).

NAGINAK Cove (Alaska, Unalaska B-3). Aleut *naĝinax̂* 'going west', from *naagix̂* 'western' (Bergsland 1994).

NAGISHLAMINA River (Alaska, Tyonek A-7) \nä gēsh lä´ mi nə\. From Dena'ina (Athabaskan) *nahq'ashla bena* 'small-lookout lake' (J. Kari p.c.).

NAGLATUK Hill (Alaska, Noatak B-4). The Iñupiaq (Eskimo) name, said to mean 'restless', was reported in 1950 (Orth 1967).

NAGOG Brook (Mass., Middlesex Co.). The SNEng. Algonquian name perhaps means 'at the sandy place' (Huden 1962).

NAGOOLTEE Peak (N.Mex., Eddy Co.) \nä gōōl´ tē\. Probably from Western Apache (Athabaskan) /naagołtį/ 'rain' (P. Greenfeld p.c.).

NAGOSAKCHOWIK (Alaska, Kwiguk C-6). The Yupik (Eskimo) name was reported in 1952 (Orth 1967).

NAGOTLIGAGEIVIK Mountain (Alaska, Goodnews Bay B-7). The Yupik (Eskimo) name was reported in 1954 (Orth 1967).

NAGUCHIK (Alaska, Kwiguk D-4). The Yupik (Eskimo) name was reported in 1952 (Orth 1967).

NAGUGUN Creek (Alaska, Goodnews Bay C-4). The Yupik (Eskimo) name was reported in 1951 as meaning 'river that others meet' (Orth 1967).

NAGYAGAT Mountain (Alaska, Goodnews Bay B-5). The Yupik (Eskimo) name was reported around 1951 as meaning 'place to smell bear' (Orth 1967).

NAHA Bay (Alaska, Ketchikan C-5). The Tlingit name was reported in 1883 (Orth 1967).

NAHA Lake (Wash., Skamania Co.) \nä´ hä\. Lower Chinook [-naa] 'mother' (D. Kinkade p.c.).

NAHAHUM Canyon (Wash., Chelan Co.) Moses-Columbian (Salishan) /naχáʕχaʕm/ 'place of crows', with /χáʕχaʕ/ 'crow' (D. Kinkade p.c.).

NAHANT (Mass., Essex Co.). The SNEng. Algonquian name is said to mean 'almost an island' (Huden 1962); cf. <nahan-> 'almost' (W. Cowan p.c.). The placename occurs as a transfer in Iowa (Scott Co.).

NAHCOTTA (Wash., Pacific Co.)) \nä kä´ tə\. A Chinook man's name, /nákəti/ (D. Kinkade, p.c.).

NAHEOLA (Ala., Choctaw Co.) \nā hē ō´lə, nā hē´ ō lə\. From Choctaw (Muskogean) *naahollo* 'something supernatural; a white person' (P. Munro p.c.).

NAHKU Bay (Alaska, Skagway B-1). The Tlingit name was published in 1923 (Orth 1967).

NAHMA (Mich., Delta Co.) \nä´ mə\. From Ojibwa (Algonquian) *name* 'sturgeon' (Vogel 1986; Nichols and Nyholm 1995). A related name is **Nahmakanta Lake** (Maine, Piscataquis Co.). Said to be from Abenaki (Algonquian), meaning 'plenty of fish' (Huden 1962); cf. *namas* 'fish', *namagw* 'lake trout' (Day 1994–95). Other possibly related names are those beginning in *nam-*, the Algonquian stem meaning 'fish'; see below.

NAHNEKE River (Idaho, Elmore Co.) \nä nē´ kē\. Perhaps from a Shoshoni (Numic) word for 'swaybacked' (Boone 1988).

NAHSUKIN Lake (Mont., Glacier Co.). Perhaps from Kutenai <nasu´kin> 'chief' (Holterman 1985).

NAHTUK River (Alaska, Survey Pass B-2) \nä´ tək\. From Iñupiaq (Eskimo) *naataq* 'great gray owl', reported in 1902 (Orth 1967, MacLean 1980).

NAHUNTA (N.C., Wayne Co.). From Tuscarora (Iroquoian) *neyurhęhtha'* 'way-station', lit. 'one spends the night' (B. Rudes p.c.). The placename occurs as a transfer in Ga. (Brantley Co.) and Wash. (Pierce Co.).

NAHWATZEL Lake (Wash., Mason Co.). From Upper Chehalis (Salishan) /nawacál'ɬ/ 'big lake', made up of /náwa-/ 'big' and /cál'ɬ/ 'lake' (D. Kinkade p.c.).

NAJI Point (Ariz., Coconino Co.) \nä´ jē\. Equivalent to **Natchi,** the name of a Chiricahua Apache leader (McNamee 1997).

NAJALAYEGUA (Calif., Santa Barbara Co.) \nä hä lä yā´ gwä\. The name of a Barbareño (Chumashan) village was first reported in 1785 (Gudde 1998).

NAKAILINGAK Creek (Alaska, Goodnews Bay D-5). The Yupik (Eskimo) name was published in 1951 (Orth 1967).

NAKAI Peak (Colo., Grand Co.) \nä´ kī, nə kī´\. From the same source as **Naakai Canyon** (Utah, San Juan Co.); see above. Related placenames are **Nokai Canyon** (Ariz., Navajo Co.) and **Nakai Yazzie Spring (Ariz., Navajo Co.)** \nə kī yä´ zē, nä ki yä´ zē\, from Navajo (Athabaskan) *nakaai yázhí,* lit. 'Mexican small' (Young and Morgan 1987); probably a personal name.

NAKAKTUK Lakes (Alaska, Umiat A-4). The Iñupiaq (Eskimo) name was reported in 1956, said to refer to 'stones or turf "lined up" to point to something as a barrier against caribou' (Orth 1967).

NAKALILOK BAY (Alaska, Sutwik Is. D-3). The Yupik (Eskimo) name was reported by Russians as <Nakkhalilok> in 1847 (Orth 1967).

NAKARNA Mountain (Idaho, Benewah Co.) \nə kä´ nə\. This name, assigned arbitrarily by U.S. government authorities, has the same origin as the western Oregon placename **Neahkahnie Creek** (Ore., Tillamook Co.); it is said to be the name of a deity in Tillamook (Salishan) or Lower Chinook (Boone 1988; D. Kinkade p.c.).

NAKAT Inlet (Alaska, Prince Rupert D-3) \nā´ kat\. The Tlingit name, reported in 1891, may be related to **Nagasay Cove** (Orth 1967); see above.

NAKCHAMIK Island (Alaska, Sutwik Is. B-6). The Yupik (Eskimo) name was reported in 1847 (Orth 1967).

NAKEE Creek (Alaska, Goodnews Bay C-8). The Yupik (Eskimo) name was published in 1951 (Orth 1967).

NAKEEN (Alaska, Naknek D-4) \nə kēn´\. The local name, perhaps Yupik (Eskimo), was reported in 1954 (Orth 1967).

NAKMAKTUAK Pass (Alaska, Ambler River C-1). The Iñupiaq (Eskimo) name is probably *natmaktuaq* 'someone backpacking' (L. Kaplan p.c.).

NAKNEK (Alaska, Naknek C-4) \nak´ nek\. Yupik (Eskimo) *nakneq,* perhaps from *naker-* 'to be straight' (Jacobson 1984).

NAKOCHELIK Creek (Alaska, Ambler River A-5). The Iñupiaq (Eskimo) name was reported in 1955 (Orth 1967).

NAKOCHNA River (Alaska, Talkeetna A-4) \nä koch´ nə, nə kōch´ nə\. From Dena'ina (Athabaskan) *nanquq'tnu, nunquhtnu* 'moss-bar creek' or possibly 'across-surface stream', containing *-tnu* 'stream' (Kari and Fall 1987:140).

NAKOLIK Mountain (Alaska, Baird Mountains D-4). The Iñupiaq (Eskimo) name is *niaqulik* 'one with a head' (L. Kaplan p.c.). The name of nearby **Nakolikurok Creek** is said to mean 'little Nakolik' (Orth 1967). Perhaps related Alaska placenames are **Naokok** (Point Lay B-2), **Neakok Island** (Wainwright B-2), **Niak Creek** (Point Hope D-2), and **Niakuk Islands** (Beechey Point B-3).

NAKOMIS (Ga., Crawford Co.) \nə kō´ mis\. Probably from the same source as **Nokomis**; see below.

NAKOOYTOOLEKMIUT (Alaska, Cape Mendenhall D-2). The Yupik (Eskimo) name was reported in 1949 (Orth 1967); the ending *-miut* means 'people'.

NALAKACHAK Creek (Alaska, Point Hope B-2). The Iñupiaq (Eskimo) name was recorded in 1960 (Orth 1967).

NALAKIHU Ruin (Ariz., Coconino Co.) \nal´ ə kyo͞o\. From Hopi (Uto-Aztecan) *nalakihu* 'lone house', containing *nala-, naala* 'alone' and *-kihu, kiihu* 'house' (K. Hill p.c.).

NALIMIUT Point (Alaska, Meade River D-5). The Iñupiaq (Eskimo) name is from *nail* 'indirect line' and *-miut* 'people' (L. Kaplan p.c.).

NALUAKRUK Lake (Alaska, Teshekpuk D-1). The Iñupiaq (Eskimo) name, reported in 1956, is said to refer to 'a place where swimming caribou are hunted' (Orth 1967).

NALUK Creek (Alaska, Selawik D-3). The Iñupiaq (Eskimo) name was obtained in 1955 (Orth 1967).

NAŁUWALA:WA (N.Mex., Cibola Co.). The Zuni name may contain /na-/ 'deer' and /łuwala/ 'to be together on the ground' (Ferguson and Hart 1985, Newman 1958).

NAMAGOSH Lake (Wis., Bayfield Co.) \nam´ ə gush\. From Ojibwa (Algonquian) *namegos* 'lake trout' (J. Nichols p.c.); a variant writing is **Namegosh.** The related form *namaycosh* has been adopted as the species name for a variety of siscowet, a fish of the trout family (Vogel 1991). Another related placename is **Namakan Lake** (Minn., St. Louis Co.) \nam´ ə kən\, perhaps from Ojibwa (Algonquian) *namekaan* 'place of abundant sturgeon'; cf. *name* 'sturgeon' (Upham 2001; J. Nichols p.c.). A variant spelling is **Namekan Lake,** and a probably related placename is **Nimikon Falls** (Mich., Ontonagan Co.). Many placenames beginning in *nam-* are derived from the Algonquian stem meaning 'fish'; see also **Nahma** (Mich., Delta Co.) and **Naomikong Creek** (Mich., Chippewa Co.).

NAMANOCK Island (N.J., Sussex Co.). A variant of **Normanock**; see below.

NAMANU, Camp (Ore., Clackamas Co.) \nä mä´ no͞o\. Probably Chinook Jargon <ne-námooks, ninamox> [ninámuks] 'otter', from Lower Chinook [enanámuks, nemámuks] 'otter' (D. Kinkade p.c.).

NAMASKET (Mass., Plymouth Co.) \nə mas´ kət\. From SNEng. Algonquian <namohs-> 'fish', with <-et> 'place' (Huden 1962; W. Cowan p.c.) From the Algonquian stem *nam-* 'fish'; cf. **Namagosh Lake** (Wis., Bayfield Co.) above.

NAMBÉ (N.Mex., Santa Fe Co.) \näm bā´\. From Tewa (Tanoan) \nąmbe'e\ 'roundish earth' (Harrington 1916:358).

NAMEAUG (Conn., New London Co.). From SNEng. Algonquian <nameauke> 'fishing place', containing <name-> 'fish' and <auke> 'land' (Huden 1962; W. Cowan p.c.). Probably related is **Namebinag Creek** (Mich., Gogebic Co.), said to be from Ojibwa (Algonquian) for 'carp' (plural), from <namebini> 'carp' (singular) (Vogel 1986); cf. Ojibwa *namebin* 'sucker', pl. *namebinag* (Nichols and Nyholm 1995). From the Algonquian stem *nam-* 'fish'; cf. **Namagosh Lake** (Wis., Bayfield Co.), above.

NAMEGOSH Lake (Wis., Bayfield Co.). A variant writing of **Namagosh Lake**; see above.

NAMEKAGON (Wis., Bayfield Co.) \nam´ ə kä gən\. From Ojibwa (Algonquian), meaning 'place of sturgeons', containing *name* 'sturgeon' (Vogel 1991; Nichols and Nyholm 1995). From the Algonquian stem *nam-* 'fish'; cf. **Namagosh Lake** (Wis., Bayfield Co.) above.

NAMEKAN Lake (Minn., St. Louis Co.). A variant of **Namakan Lake**; see **Namagosh Lake** above.

NAMEOKE (N.Y., Nassau Co.). From SNEng. Algonquian <nameauke> 'fishing place', containing <name-> 'fish' and <auke> 'land' (Huden 1962; W. Cowan p.c.). From the Algonquian stem *nam-* 'fish'; cf. **Namagosh Lake** (Wis., Bayfield Co.) above.

NAMEOKI (Ill., Madison Co.) \nam ē ō´ kē\. Perhaps from *Nahmeokee*, the name of the wife of the leading character in the play *Metamora,* written by J. A. Stone in the early nineteenth century (Vogel 1963). The term may be from the SNEng. Algonquian placename <nameauke> 'fishing place'; cf. **Nameoke** (N.Y., Nassau Co.).

NAMEQUA Creek (Ill., Rock Island Co.). Named for a daughter of Black Hawk, the nineteenth-century Sauk (Algonquian) leader. Her name has been said to mean 'fish woman' (Vogel 1963); cf. /name:sa/ 'fish' (Goddard 1994). Probably related placenames include **Namequoit Point** (Mass., Barnstable Co.), probably from SNEng. Algonquian <nameauke> 'fishing place' (Huden 1962); and **Namkee Creek** (N.Y., Suffolk Co.), probably from the same source (Tooker 1911). From the Algonquian stem *nam-* 'fish'; cf. **Namagosh Lake** (Wis., Bayfield Co.) above.

NAMPA (Idaho, Canyon Co.) \nam´ pə\. From Shoshoni (Numic) /nampai/ [námbai, námpAI] 'foot' (Boone 1988, J. McLaughlin p.c.).

NAMSKAKET (Mass., Barnstable Co.). The SNEng. Algonquian word perhaps means 'a fishing place' (Huden 1962); cf. **Namagosh Lake** (Wis., Bayfield Co.) above.

NANACHEHAW (Miss., Warren Co.). From Choctaw (Muskogean) *nanih chaaha,* lit. 'hill high' (Seale 1939; P. Munro p.c.). Probably related placenames are **Nanafalia** (Ala., Marengo Co.) \nan ə fə lī´ ə\, from Choctaw *nanih falaya,* lit. 'hill long' (Read 1984), and **Nanahubba Bluff** (Ala., Mobile Co.) \nan ə hub´ ə\, perhaps from Choctaw *nanih aba,* lit. 'hill above' (Read 1984).

NANAHUMAS Neck (Mass., Nantucket Co.). The SNEng. Algonquian name may mean 'dry land' (Huden 1962).

NANAMKIN Creek (Wash., Ferry Co.) \nə nam´ kin\. Perhaps from Okanagan (Salishan) [nánəmtqən], a man's name (D. Kinkade p.c.).

NANEPASHEMET (Mass., Essex Co.). Named for a SNEng. Algonquian leader of the seventeenth century; the name may mean 'moon', lit. 'he who walks at night' (Huden 1962).

NANEUM Creek (Wash., Kittitas Co.) \nan´ əm\. From a Sahaptin placename /ná:nɨm/ (E. Hunn p.c.).

NANIH WAIYA (Miss., Winston Co.) \nan ə wī´ ə\. From Choctaw (Muskogean) *nanih wayya,* lit. 'hill-leaning' (Seale 1939; P. Munro p.c.).

NANIKSRAK Mountain (Alaska, Chandler Lake C-2). The Iñupiaq (Eskimo) name is *naniksraq* 'material for a lamp' (L. Kaplan p.c.).

NANIRATKOHORT Creek (Alaska, Ambler River A-3). The Iñupiaq (Eskimo) name is *naniksraq* 'material for a lamp' (L. Kaplan p.c.).

NANITA Lake (Colo., Grand Co.) \nə nē´ tə\. Perhaps from a Navajo (Athabaskan) word referring to the Plains Indians; or it may be a name used for the Comanches by a group of Tex. Indians (Bright 1993).

NANJEMOY (Md., Charles Co.) \nan´ jə moi\. From CAC Algonquian, perhaps meaning 'they go down to the river' (Kenny 1984).

NANKOWEAP Mesa (Ariz., Coconino Co.) \nang kō´ wēp, nang´ kə wēp\. Perhaps from Southern Paiute (Numic) /nakukkwippa/ [naɣukkwippA] 'a battle', or from /nakukkwi-uippi/ [naɣúkkwi-uippI] 'battle canyon' (Granger 1983; J. McLaughlin p.c.).

NANNAQUAKET Hill (R.I., Newport Co.). Perhaps from SNEng. Algonquian, 'it dries up' (Huden 1962).

NANNIE CHUFA (Ala., Washington Co). Perhaps from Choctaw (Muskogean) *nanih* 'hill' plus *achoffa* 'one' (P. Munro p.c.).

NANOOK Creek (Alaska, Mt. Michelson C-4) \nan´ ŏŏk\. From Iñupiaq (Eskimo) *nanuq* 'polar bear' (Orth 1967; MacLean 1980). Possibly related Alaska placenames are **Nanuk Lake** (Harrison Bay B-2) and **Nanuktuk Creek** (Iliamna A-7).

NANSEMOND (Va., Suffolk Co.) \nan´ sə mond\. The name of a CAC Algonquian group (Hagemann 1988). The placename also occurs in N.C. (Hertford Co.).

NANSENE (Ore., Wasco Co.) \nan sēn´\. Perhaps from an Indian name <Tinanens>, language not identified, for what is now called Fifteenmile Creek (McArthur 1992).

NANTAHALA (N.C., Swain Co.) \nan tə hā´ lə\. From Cherokee (Iroquoian) *nvvda ayeehli* [nə̨:da aye:łi], lit. 'sun middle' (i.e., 'noon') (Powell 1968; B. Rudes p.c.). The name also occurs in Ga. (Towns Co.).

NANTASKET Beach (Mass., Plymouth Co.) \nan tas´ kət\. The SNEng. Algonquian placename perhaps means 'like the ebb tide', containing <nan-> 'similar to' and <-skat> 'ebb tide' (Huden 1962; W. Cowan p.c.). The placename also occurs in Conn. (Windham Co.).

NANTICOKE \nan´ti kōk\. The name refers to an Algonquian people, related to the Delawares; the Munsee form is /wənéhtko:w/, the Unami is /wəné:tku/ (*HNAI* 15:250). As a placename, **Nanticoke** is found in several states (e.g., Pa., Luzerne Co.; Md., Wicomico Co.; and N.Y., Broome Co.). A possibly related placename is **Nacote Creek** (N.J., Atlantic Co.).

NANTOK River (Alaska, Marshall D-5). The Yupik (Eskimo) name was reported in 1951 (Orth 1967).

NANTUCKET County (Mass.) \nan tuk´ ət\. Earlier written <Natocke>, <Nantican>, <Nautican> (Little 1984). From SNEng. Algonquian, of obscure origin, perhaps meaning 'in the midst of waters' (Huden 1962).

NANTUXENT Cove (N.J., Cumberland Co.) \nan tuk´ sənt\. Earlier writings are <Nantuxit, Antuxet>; the name is from Delaware (Algonquian), but the derivation is not clear (Becker 1964).

NANUK Lake (Alaska, Harrison Bay B-2) \nan´ ŏŏk\. From Iñupiaq (Eskimo) *nanuq* 'polar bear' (Orth 1967; MacLean 1980). Possibly related Alaska placenames are **Nanook Creek** (Mt. Michelson C-4) and **Nanuktuk Creek** (Iliamna A-7).

NANUKTUK Creek (Alaska, Iliamna A-7). The Yupik (Eskimo) name, reported in 1951 (Orth 1967), perhaps contains *nanuaq* 'polar bear' (Jacobson 1984). Possibly related Alaska placenames are **Nanook Creek** (Mt. Michelson C-4) and **Nanuk Lake** (Harrison Bay B-2).

NANUSHUK River (Alaska, Umiat B-2). The Iñupiaq (Eskimo) name was reported in 1901 (Orth 1967).

NANVAK Bay (Alaska, Hagemeister Is. C-6) \nan´ vak\. From Yupik (Eskimo) *nanvaq* 'lake' (Orth 1967; Jacobson 1984). A related placename is **Nenevok Lake** (Alaska, Goodnews Bay D-3). **Nanvakfak Lake** (Alaska, Goodnews Bay A-8) is from Yupik (Eskimo) *nanvarpak* 'big lake' (Orth 1967; Jacobson 1984). **Nanvaranak Slough** (Alaska, Kwiguk C-4) may mean 'little lake' (Orth 1967). **Nanvaranak Choa** (Alaska, Marshall C-8) is said to mean 'little lake in course of river' (Orth 1967). **Nanvarnarluk** (Alaska, Baird Inlet D-3) is probably also derived from the Yupik (Eskimo) for 'lake' (Orth 1967).

NANWAKSJIAK Crater (Alaska, Nunivak Is. A-3). The Yupik (Eskimo) name, reported in 1949, is said to mean 'deep hole' (Orth 1967).

NAOKOK (Alaska, Point Lay B-2). Iñupiaq (Eskimo) *niaquq* 'head' (Orth 1967; MacLean 1980). Perhaps related placenames are **Nakolik** (Baird Mountains D-4), **Niak Creek** (Point

Hope D-2), and **Niakuk Islands** (Beechey Point B-3).

NAOMIKONG Creek (Mich., Chippewa Co.). From Ojibwa (Algonquian), perhaps meaning 'sturgeon place'; cf. *name* 'sturgeon' (Vogel 1986; Nichols and Nyholm 1995). Possibly from Algonquian */nam-/ 'fish'; cf. **Namagosh Lake** (Wis., Bayfield Co.) above.

NAPA County (Calif.) \nap´ ə\. Perhaps from a Southern Patwin (Wintuan) name meaning 'homeland' (Gudde 1998).

NAPAIMIUT (Alaska, Sleetmute C-8) \nä pä´ myo͞ot\. From Yupik (Eskimo), meaning 'tree people', from *napa* 'tree' plus *-miut* 'people' (Orth 1967; Jacobson 1984).

NAPAKIAK (Alaska, Bethel C-8) \nə pak´ ē ak, nap´ ə kē yak\. From the Yupik (Eskimo) placename *naparyarraq,* containing *napa* 'tree' (Jacobson 1984).

NAPAKTUALUIT Mountain (Alaska, Chandler Lake A-3). The Iñupiaq (Eskimo) name was reported in 1956 (Orth 1967); cf. *napaaqtuq* 'tree' (MacLean 1980).

NAPANEE (Miss., Washington Co.) \nap´ ə nē\. Probably from a Choctaw (Muskogean) word meaning 'something to twist or braid', containing *ną-* 'something' and *panni* 'to braid' (Toomey 1917; P. Munro p.c.).

NAPANIK Creek (Alaska, Wainwright A-1). From Iñupiaq (Eskimo), the name of a local resident (Orth 1967).

NAPANOCH (N.Y., Ulster Co.) \nap´ ə nok\. Also written <Napanock>; probably from Munsee Delaware (Algonquian), perhaps meaning 'water-land' (Ruttenber 1906); cf. Munsee *mbuy* 'water', *áhkuy* 'land' (O'Meara 1996).

NAPAREAYAK Slough (Alaska, Hooper Bay C-3). The Yupik (Eskimo) name, reported in 1951, is said to mean 'little stakes' (Orth 1967).

NAPASKIAK (Alaska, Bethel C-8) \nə pas´ kē ak\. Yupik (Eskimo) *napaskiaq,* from *napa* 'tree' (Jacobson 1984).

NAPATOLIK Creek (Alaska, Selawik C-3). From Yupik (Eskimo), recorded in 1955 (Orth 1967); perhaps contains *napa* 'tree' (Jacobson 1984).

NAPAUTOKIK Creek (Alaska, Selawik D-3). The Yupik (Eskimo) name was obtained in 1955 (Orth 1967).

NAPAVINE (Wash., Lewis Co.) \nap´ ə vīn\. Said to mean 'little prairie'; perhaps a distortion of Upper Chehalis (Salishan) /náwaqʷəm/ 'big prairie' from which comes the name of the **Newaukum River,** on which **Napavine** is located (Hitchman 1985; D. Kinkade p.c.).

NAPAWALLA (Kans., Sumner Co.). From the name of a nineteenth-century Osage (Siouan) leader; the Native American term was /nǫ́hpe wáðe/ 'inspires fear' (R. Rankin p.c.). A variant is **Neptawah.**

NAPEAGUE (N.Y., Suffolk Co.) \nap´ əg\. Earlier written <Neapeague, Neppeage> (etc.); the SNEng. Algonquian placename may mean 'water land', containing <nepe> 'water' (Ruttenber 1906; Beauchamp 1907).

NAPEEQUA River (Wash., Chelan Co.) \nə pē´ kwə\. Perhaps a Moses/Columbian (Salishan) word meaning 'white water place', containing /na-/ 'place', /píq-/ 'white', and /-kʷ/ 'water' (Hitchman 1985; D. Kinkade p.c.).

NAPESTLE, Río de (Kans.). This Spanish name for the **Arkansas River** was formerly used in Colo. and Kans. (Rydjord 1968); a related name is **Nepesta** (Colo., Pueblo Co.). A possible origin is Comanche (Numic) /nɨpetsɨ/ 'wife' (J. McLaughlin p.c.).

NAPIAS Creek (Idaho, Lemhi Co.) \nap´ ē əs\. From Shoshoni (Numic) /nappias/ 'money', derived from Chinook Jargon, borrowed from French *la piastre,* referring to a unit of coinage (Crum and Dayley 1993). The placename also is found in Nev. (Eureka Co.).

NAPI Rock (Mont., Glacier Co.) \nä´ pē\. From Blackfoot (Algonquian) *náápi* 'old man', the creator/trickster figure of Native American myth (Holterman 1985, D. Franz p.c.).

NAPO Canyon (Idaho, Lemhi Co.) \nap´ ō\. Said to be named for an Indian resident, language not identified (Boone 1988).

NAPONEE (Neb., Franklin Co.) \nap´ ō nē, nap´ ə nē\. From the same source as **Nappanee** (Ind., Elkhart Co.); see below.

NAPOTOLI Creek (Alaska, Dillingham D-4). The Yupik (Eskimo) name was reported in 1930 (Orth 1967).

NAPOWAN, Lake (Wis., Waushara Co.). Probably from Ojibwa (Algonquian) <nibiwan> 'it is wet' (Vogel 1991); cf. *nibiiwan* 'be wet' (Nichols and Nyholm 1995).

NAPPANEE (Ind., Elkhart Co.) \nap ə nē\. Named for a town in Canada, also written <Napanee>, derived from a Missisauga (Algonquian) word for 'flour' (Baker 1995); cf. Ottawa *naapaane* 'flour' (Rhodes 1985). A related placename is **Naponee** (Neb., Franklin Co.); see above.

NARBONA Pass (N.Mex., San Juan Co.) \när bon´ ə\. Named for a Navajo (Athabaskan) leader. The pass was given this name, replacing earlier "Washington Pass," when it was realized in 1992 that the earlier name had commemorated not President George Washington but rather Colonel John Washington, whose soldiers scalped the Indian leader at this location in 1849; ironically, Narbona had been a proponent of peace (Julyan 1998). His personal name was derived from Spanish; his Navajo name was *hastiin naat'áanii,* lit. 'man chief' (Linford 2000). The Navajo name for the pass is *béésh łichíí'ii bigiizh* 'copper gap', containing *béésh łichíí'* 'copper' (*béésh* 'flint, metal' plus *łichíí'* 'it is red') and *bigiizh* 'its gap' (*bi-* 'its' plus *-giizh* 'cut, gap, pass') (Wilson 1995).

NARCOOSSEE (Fla., Osceola Co.). From Muskogee *nokose* /nokósi/ 'a bear' (Read 1934; Martin and Mauldin 2000).

NARIKSMIUT (Alaska, Nunivak Is. B-5). The Yupik (Eskimo) name was reported in 1949 (Orth 1967); the ending *-miut* means 'people'.

NARINGOLAPAK Slough (Alaska, Kwiguk C-5). The Yupik (Eskimo) name was recorded in 1951 (Orth 1967).

NARINO HONGUY Hill (Nev., Elko Co.) From Shoshoni (Numic) /nataannoo'aanko'ai/ 'saddlehorn', containing /nataanoo/ or /natɨnoo/ [narɨno:] 'saddle', /aan/ 'horn/, and /ko'ai/ 'peak, top' (J. McLaughlin p.c.).

NARKEETA (Miss., Kemper Co.) \när kē´ tə\. Perhaps from Choctaw (Muskogean) *naki itti* 'wood for arrows', from *naki* 'arrow' and *itti* 'wood' (Seale 1939; P. Munro p.c).

NAROKACHIK River (Alaska, Marshall A-8). The Yupik (Eskimo) name was reported in 1949 (Orth 1967).

NARRAGANSETT (R.I., Washington Co.) \nâr ə gan´ sit\. From SNEng. Algonquian <naiaganset> 'at or about a point of land', containing <nai-> 'a point or angle' (Huden 1962; W. Cowan p.c.).

NARRAGUAGUS (Maine, Hancock Co.) \nâr ə gwā´ gəs\. Previously written as <Arroguagus, Allaguagus>, perhaps containing Abenaki (Algonquian) <guagus> 'boggy place' (Eckstorm 1941:136). A possibly related placename is **Guagus Stream** (Maine, Hancock Co.).

NARRAGUINNEP Canyon (Colo., Dolores Co.) \nâr ə gwin´ əp\. The Ute (Numic) placename may reflect /naragwinap/ 'battleground' or /narɨgwinnap/ 'great power' (Bright 1993; J. McLaughlin p.c.).

NARRAMISSIC River (Maine, Hancock Co.) \nâr ə mis´ ik\. Probably from Abenaki (Algonquian), but the derivation is unclear (Rutherford 1970).

NARRASKATUCK Creek (N.Y., Nassau Co.) \nə ras´ kə tuk\. The SNEng. Algonquian name was earlier written <Warrasketuck>, apparently containing <wanashque> 'at the end of', <-tack> 'tidal stream' (Tooker 1911).

NARRATICON, Lake (N.J., Gloucester Co.). The name is probably from Delaware (Algonquian), but the derivation is not clear.

NARUNA (Va., Campbell Co.). Perhaps a CAC Algonquian name, but the derivation is unclear (Hagemann 1988).

NARVAK Lake (Alaska, Hughes D-6). From Iñupiaq (Eskimo) *narvaq* 'lake' (Orth 1967; MacLean 1980).

NARVAKRAK Lake (Alaska, Misheguk Mountain A-5). is said to mean 'great old lake' (Orth 1967).

NASAK, Mount (Alaska, Point Hope C-2). From Iñupiaq (Eskimo) *nasaq, nasraq* 'hood of a parka' (Orth 1967; Webster and Zibell 1970). Possibly related placenames include **Nasaurak Mountain** (Alaska, Chandler Lake B-3) and **Nasorak Creek** (Alaska, Point Hope C-2); see below.

NASAWAUPEE (WI, Door Co.) \naz ə wô´ pē\. A variant spelling of **Nasewaupee**; see below.

NASCHITTI (N.Mex., San Juan Co.) \näs´ chit ē\. Navajo (Athabaskan) *nahashch'idí* 'badger', lit. 'the one who digs or scratches around', from *nahashch'id* 'to dig around, scratch around' (Wilson 1995).

NASELLE (Wash., Pacific Co.) \nā sel´\. Earlier written <Nisal>, from the Lower Chinook placename \nísəl\. (Hitchman 1985; D. Kinkade p.c.).

NASEWAUPEE (Wis., Door Co.) \naz ə wô´ pē\. Also written as **Nasawaupee,** said to be named for a nineteenth-century Menominee leader (Vogel 1991).

NASHAMOIS Neck (Mass., Dukes Co.). The SNEng. Algonquian name apparently contains <nashue-> 'between' (Huden 1962; W. Cowan p.c.).

NASHAWANNUCK Pond (Mass., Bristol Co.) \nash ə wä´ nək\. The SNEng. Algonquian name contains <nashue-> 'between' and <-wonogq> 'hole' (W. Cowan p.c.).

NASHAWENA Island (Mass., Dukes Co.). The SNEng. Algonquian name apparently contains <nashue-> 'between' (W. Cowan p.c.).

NASHBITO (Ariz., Apache Co.) \nash´ bi tō, nash bē´ tō\. Navajo (Athabaskan) *na'shǫ́'ii bito'* 'lizard's spring', from *na'shǫ́'ii* 'lizard' (Wilson 1995).

NASHOBA (Okla., Pushmataha Co.) \nə shō´ bə\. From Choctaw (Muskogean) *nashobah* 'wolf' (Shirk 1974; P. Munro p.c.). A related placename is **Nashooba Bogue** (Ala., Green Co.) \nə sho͞o´ bə\, probably from Choctaw *nashobah book*, lit. 'wolf stream'.

NASHOBA Brook (Mass., Middlesex Co.). The SNEng. Algonquian name contains <nashue-> 'between' and <-pe> 'water' (Huden 1962; W. Cowan p.c.).

NASHOTAH (Wis., Waukesha Co.) \nə shō´ tä\. Probably from Ojibwa (Algonquian) *niiz-hoodenh* 'twin' (Vogel 1991; Nichols and Nyholm 1995). Related Wis. placenames are **Neshota** (Brown Co.), **Neshotah** (Manitowoc Co.), **Nijode Lakes** (Mich., Mecosta Co.), and **Shoto** (Wis., Manitowoc Co.).

NASHUA River (N.H., Hillsborough Co.; Mass., Middlesex Co.) \nash´ o͞o wə, nash´ wə\. The name was earlier written <Nashaway> and <Nashawake>; it is from SNEng. Algonquian <nashue-> 'between' (Huden 1962; W. Cowan p.c.) The placename also occurs as a transfer in Ill. (Ogle Co.), Iowa (Chickasaw Co.), and Mont. (Valley Co.).

NASHWAUK (Minn., Itasca Co.) \nash´ wäk\. Named after Nashwaak in New Brunswick, Canada; probably meaning 'land between', and related to **Nashua River** (Upham 2001).

NASJA Creek (Utah, San Juan Co.) \nas´ jä\. From Navajo (Athabaskan) *né'éshjaa'* 'owl' (Linford 2000).

NASKAK Camp (Alaska, St. Lawrence D-5). The Yupik (Eskimo) name was reported in 1932 (Orth 1967).

NASKEAG (Maine, Hancock Co.) \nas´ keg\. From Abenaki (Algonquian), meaning 'the end' (Eckstorm 1941); cf. *wanaskwa* 'the end of something' (Day 1994–95). The placename **Nasket** (Maine, Sagadahoc Co.) [nas´ kət] is also said to be from the Abenaki for 'at the end' (Huden 1962).

NASKETUCKET (Mass., Bristol Co.) \nas kə tuk´ ət\. The SNEng. Algonquian name means 'at the end of the tidal stream', from <(wa)nashque> 'at the end', <-tuck-> 'tidal stream', <-et> 'place' (Huden 1962; W. Cowan p.c.).

NASKONAT Peninsula (Alaska, Nunivak Is. D-1). The Yupik (Eskimo) name, obtained in 1951, is said to mean 'small hand' (Orth 1967).

NASOMA (Ore., Washington Co.) \nə sō´ mə\. The name is said to be from an unidentified Indian language of the area (McArthur 1992).

NASON Creek (Wash., Chelan Co.) \nā´ sən\. Named, with a change of spelling, after Charley Nasen, a Sahaptin Indian resident in the late nineteenth century (Hitchman 1985).

NASORAK Creek (Alaska, Point Hope A-2). The Iñupiaq (Eskimo) name is *nasauraq* 'little hood (for a parka)' (L. Kaplan p.c.). Possibly related Alaska placenames include **Nasaurak** (Chandler Lake B-3) and **Mount Nasak** (Point Hope C-2).

NASSAHEGAN (Conn., Hartford Co.). From a SNEng. Algonquian word meaning 'he has two houses', containing <neese> 'two' (Huden 1962; W. Cowan p.c.).

NASSAKEAG (N.Y., Suffolk Co.). Also written <Nesakak, Nasakake> etc., the name of a seventeenth century Indian leader and/or his place of residence (Tooker 1911).

NASSAWADOX (Va., Northampton Co.). Earlier written <Naswadux, Nasswatex>; the CAC Algonquian name may mean 'between the streams' (Kenny 1984). The name also occurs in Md. (Somerset Co.).

NASSAWANGO Creek (Md., Worcester Co.). The CAC Algonquian name may mean 'ground between the streams' (Kenny 1984).

NATAGA Creek (Alaska, Skagway C-3). The Tlingit name was recorded in 1883 (Orth 1967).

NATAHKI Lake (Mont., Glacier Co.) \nə tä´ kē\. Possibly from Blackfoot (Algonquian) *nataakii* 'fortunate woman', the name of the Piegan wife of the writer James Willard Schultz (Holterman 1985; D. Franz p.c.).

NATALBANY (La., Tangipahoa Par.) \nat ôl´ bə nē\. (A local pronunciation is \tô´ bə nē\.) Perhaps from Choctaw (Muskogean) *nita albani,* lit. 'bear-barbecued' (Read 1927; P. Munro p.c.).

NATANES Creek (Ariz., Graham Co.) \nə tan´ əs, nat ə nēz`\. Perhaps a Spanish plural from Western Apache (Athabaskan) *nadą́* 'corn' (Granger 1983; P. Greenfeld p.c.).

NATANNI NEZ School (N.Mex., San Juan Co.) \nə tä´ nē nez`\. Navajo (Athabaskan) *naat'áanii nééz* 'tall chief', from *naat'áanii* 'chief, leader' and *nééz* 'tall', referring to William T. Shelton, school superintendent at Shiprock (Wilson 1995).

NATAPOC Mountain (Wash., Chelan Co.) \nat´ ə pok\. Perhaps from Moses/Columbian (Salishan), said to be a name for **Nason Creek** (Hitchman 1985; D. Kinkade p.c.).

NATAROAROK Creek (Alaska, Flaxman Is. A-1). The Iñupiaq (Eskimo) name was reported in 1956 (Orth 1967).

NATAT Creek (Alaska, Nabesna C-6) \nä tat`\. From the Ahtna (Athabaskan) placename *nataeɬde* 'roasted salmon place' (J. Kari p.c.).

NATAZHAT, Mount (Alaska, McCarthy C-1) \nä tä zhät`\. The Upper Tanana (Athabaskan) name *naat'aayädi* refers to nearby Mt. Bona (J. Kari p.c.).

NATCHAUG River (Conn., Tolland Co.). From SNEng. Algonquian <nashauauke> 'land between (the rivers)', containing <nashau> 'between' and <-auke> 'land' (Trumbull 1881; W. Cowan p.c.).

NAT-CHE-LES Creek (Wash., Lewis Co.). From the Upper Chehalis (Salishan) placename /náč'alɬ/ (D. Kinkade p.c.).

NATCHES (Ariz., Graham Co.) \nach´ əz\. The name of a Chiricahua Apache (Athabaskan) leader (Granger 1983); also written as **Natchi Canyon** (Ariz., Coconino Co.). Not to be confused with **Nache,** from Northern Paiute (Nev., Pershing Co.); or with **Natchez**, a tribal name and placename from the southeastern United States.

NATCHEZ (Nev., Elko Co.) \nach´ əz\. From the same source as **Nache** (Nev., Pershing Co.), the name of a Northern Paiute (Numic) leader (Carlson 1974). The spelling is probably influenced by **Natchez**, a tribal name and placename from the southeastern United States. It is not to be confused with **Natches** (Ariz., Graham Co.) or **Natchi Canyon** (Ariz., Coconino Co.).

NATCHEZ \nach´ əz\. An Indian people who originally lived on the lower Mississippi River; sometimes pronounced \nä´ chē\. As a placename, the term occurs in Miss. (Adams Co.), La. (Natchitoches Par.), and Ala. (Monroe Co.). Not to be confused with **Natchez** in Nev. (Elko Co.), or with **Natches** in Ariz. (Graham Co.); see above.

NATCHI Canyon (Ariz., Coconino Co.). From the same source as **Natches** (Ariz., Graham Co.); see above.

NATCHITOCHES Parish (La.) \nak´ i tôsh, nak´ i tish\. Caddo /našit'usˀ/, the name of a tribal division, from /na-/ 'place' and /šit'usˀ/ 'pawpaw' (Read 1927; W. Chafe p.c.).

NATEEKIN River (Alaska, Unalaska C-2). The Aleut name was reported in 1826 as <Natyka> (Orth 1967).

NATHLIE Mountain (Alaska, Gulkana A-5) \nath´ lē\. Perhaps from the name of an Ahtna (Athabaskan) village *nataełde*; cf. **Natat** (J. Kari p.c.).

NATICK (Mass., Middlesex Co.) \nā´ tik\. The SNEng. Algonquian name may mean 'my home' (Huden 1962). The name also occurs in R.I. (Bristol Co.).

NATICOOK Brook (N.H., Hillsborough Co.) \nat´ i ko͝ok\. From Abenaki (Algonquian), meaning 'where the river flows downstream' (Huden 1962); cf. *naai(wi)-* 'downstream', *-tekw-* 'river', and *-k* 'place' (Day 1994–95).

NATINAKUNIT Pass (Alaska, Misheguk Mountain B-2). The Iñupiaq (Eskimo) name was reported in 1956 (Orth 1967).

NATIVE \nā´ tiv\. This term is widely used in referring to American Indians and is found in placenames throughout the United States: for example, in **Native Creek** (Mich., Ontonagon Co.).

NATMOTIRAK Creek (Alaska, Ambler River D-5). The Iñupiaq (Eskimo) name is *natmutigruaq*, said to mean 'old pack route' (Orth 1967; Burch 1998).

NATNOHOKA Creek (Alaska, Melozitna C-6). The Koyukon (Athabaskan) name was recorded in 1956 (Orth 1967).

NATOA Island (Alaska, Blying Sound C-7). The Yupik (Eskimo) word, reported in 1912, is said to mean 'summit' (Orth 1967).

NATOAS Peak (Mont., Glacier Co.) \nä tō´ əs\. Blackfoot (Algonquian) *naatówa's* 'sacred Indian-turnip', containing *ma's, a's* 'an edible root, *Psoralea esculenta,* locally called Indian turnip' (Holterman 1985; D. Franz p.c.).

NATOHONA Creek (Alaska, Tanacross A-6) \nä tə hō´ nə\. The Ahtna (Athabaskan) name does not have a clear derivation (J. Kari p.c.).

NATOMA (Calif., Sacramento Co.) \nə tō´ mə\. Nisenan (Southern Maidu) /notoma/ 'east place, upstream place', from /noto/ 'east, upstream' (Gudde 1998). The name was later the title of an opera by Victor Herbert. As a placename, it appears as a transfer in Kans. (Osborne Co.) In Alaska (Dixon Entrance D-2), **Natoma Bay** was named after a steamship called *Natoma*.

NATRAHAZUIVUN Lake (Alaska, Fort Yukon C-1). The Gwich'in (Athabaskan) name is *zhrąįį van* 'black-wolverine lake' (Caulfield et al. 1983).

NAT-SOO-PAH Warm Spring (Idaho, Twin Falls Co.) \nät so͞o´ pä\. Bannock (Numic) /nattsuappaa/ 'medicine springs', from /nattsua/ 'medicine' and /-paa/ 'water' (Boone 1988; J. McLaughlin p.c.).

NATVAKRAK Lakes (Alaska, Utukok River D-3). The Iñupiaq (Eskimo) name is *narvaksraq* 'something that will be a lake' (L. Kaplan p.c.). cf. *narvaq* 'lake' (MacLean 1980). A related name is **Natvakruak Creek** (Alaska, Chandler Lake C-4), said to be from *narvaġruaq* 'old lake' (Orth 1967). Other related names include **Neruokpuk Lakes** (Alaska, Mt. Michelson B-2).

NATVATCHIAK Hill (Alaska, Umiat A-4). The Iñupiaq (Eskimo) name *narvatchiaq* 'new lake' (L. Kaplan p.c.).

NATZUHINI Bay (Alaska, Craig B-3). The Indian name, probably Tlingit, *narvatchiaq* 'new lake' (L. Kaplan p.c.).

NAUBINWAY (Mich., Mackinac Co.) \nô´ bin wā\. Probably the name of an Ojibwa (Algonquian) leader of the early nineteenth century; his name is also written <Nabunway, Aubunway, Naw-aw-bun-way> (Vogel 1986).

NAUBUC (Conn., Hartford Co.). The SNEng. Algonquian name may contain <upauk> 'flooded' (Trumbull 1881, W. Cowan p.c.).

NAUCESTAARWIKCAK Point (Alaska, Cordova B-7). The name, perhaps from Yupik (Eskimo), was reported in BGN 1990 and said to mean 'garden point' (Orth 1967).

NAUFABA Creek (Ala., Lee Co.) \nô fä´ bə\. Perhaps from Hitchiti (Muskogean) /nof-a:pi/ 'beech tree', from /nofi/ 'beech' and /a:pi/ 'tree' (Read 1984; J. Martin p.c.).

NAUFUS Creek (Calif., Trinity Co.) \nā´ fəs\. From Wintu /norboos/ 'those living to the south', containing /nor/ 'south' and /boh-/ 'to live' (Gudde 1998).

NAUGATUCK (Conn., New Haven Co.) \nô´ gə tuk\. Earlier written as <Nawcatuck>; SNEng. Algonquian <neguttuck> 'one tree', from <negut-> 'one' and <-tugk> 'tree' (Hughes and Allen 1976, W. Cowan p.c.).

NAUGOLKA Point (Alaska, Kodiak D-4). The name, probably from Alutiiq (Eskimo), was published in 1943 (Orth 1967).

NAUKATI Bay (Alaska, Craig D-4). The Tlingit name was reported in 1904 as <Naukatee> (Orth 1967).

NAURAUSHAUN (N.Y., Rockland Co.). The name is probably from Munsee Delaware (Algonquian), with the earlier writings <Naurashank, Narrasunck> (Beauchamp 1907).

NAUSAUKET (R.I., Bristol Co.) \nô sô´ kət\. Also written as <Nausaucat>; perhaps SNEng. Algonquian for 'between outlets' (Huden 1962).

NAUSET Bay (Mass., Barnstable Co.) \nô´ sət\. Perhaps SNEng. Algonquian for 'place between' (Huden 1962).

NAVAHO \nä´ və hō, nav´ ə hō\. From the same origin as **Navajo**; occurring not only in the Southwest, but also in the placename **Navaho Lake** (Ore., Deschutes Co.).

NAVAJO \nä ´və hō, nav ´ə hō\. A people and language of the Athabaskan linguistic family, living in Ariz., N.Mex., and Utah. The English term is from Spanish *Navajó,* used in the seventeenth century for the area of northwestern N.Mex., and said to mean 'large planted fields' in an Indian language. The source is probably Tewa (Tanoan) /navahu:/, from /nava/ 'field' plus /hu:/ 'valley'. The spelling **Navajo,** instead of **Navaho,** was officially adopted by the Navajo Nation in 1969 (*HNAI* 10:496). As a placename, **Navajo** is the name of a county in Ariz. and a town in N.Mex. (Rio Arriba Co.); it occurs as a transfer name in Calif., San Luis Obispo Co.; Colo., Boulder Co.; Ill., Cook Co.; and Okla., Jackson Co.).

NAVASHAK Lake (Alaska, Howard Pass A-4). The Iñupiaq (Eskimo) name was reported in 1956, said to mean 'to call for' (Orth 1967).

NAVASOTA (Tex., Grimes Co.) \nav ə sō´ tə\. Said to be from an Indian word <Nabatoto> 'muddy waters', language not identified (Tarpley 1980).

NAVESINK (N.J., Monmouth Co.) \nā´ və singk\. From <newesink>, the name of a Munsee Delaware (Algonquian) band (*HNAI* 15:237). A related placename is **Neversink** (N.Y., Sullivan Co.; Pa., Berks Co.).

NAWADAHA Falls (Mich., Gogebic Co.). From the name of a story-teller who figures in

Longellow's *Hiawatha.* The word may be Ojibwa (Algonquian), but the derivation is not clear (Vogel 1986).

NAWAGO Creek (Wis., Ashland Co.). Perhaps from the same source as **Newaygo County** (Mich.); see below.

NAWAKWA Lake (Mich., Alger Co.). From Ojibwa (Algonquian) *naawaakwaa* 'in the middle of the woods' (Nichols and Nyholm 1995). The placename also occurs in Minn. (Lake Co.).

NAWTAWAKET Creek (Calif., Shasta Co.) \nô´ tə wä kət\. From Wintu /noti waqat/, lit. 'south creek', containing /nor/ 'south' and /waqat/ 'creek' (Gudde 1998).

NAWT VAYA (Ariz., Pima Co.) \nôt vä´ yə\. O'odham (Piman) *noḍ wahia* 'pampas-grass well', from *noḍ* 'pampas grass', *wahia* 'well' (J. Hill p.c.).

NAYANQUING Point (Mich., Bay Co.). Perhaps from Ojibwa (Algonquian), of unclear derivation (Vogel 1986).

NAYANTOVOY Creek (Nev., Elko Co.). Said to be Shoshoni (Numic) for 'standing Indian' (Carlson 1974); cf. /nɨmɨ/ 'person, Indian', /topo'i/ [tovo'i] 'they stand' (J. McLaughlin p.c.).

NAYA NUKI Peak (Mont., Gallatin Co.). Named by schoolchildren for a character in a book, described as a Shoshoni (Numic) Indian (BGN 8702, 8804:17).

NAYATT (R.I., Bristol Co.) \nā´ ət\. The SNEng. Algonquian name means 'corner place', from <nai> 'corner', <-att> 'place' (Huden 1962; W. Cowan p.c.).

NAY AUG (Pa., Lackawanna Co.). Probably from Delaware (Algonquian); said to be the name of Roaring Creek (Donehoo 1928).

NAYAUG (Conn., Hartford Co.) Formerly written <Nayage>; from SNEng. Algonquian <nayaug> 'corner' (Trumbull 1881; W. Cowan p.c.).

NAYLOX (Ore., Klamath Co.) \nā´loks\. From the Klamath placename /ni:ɬaqs/ 'sunrise', containing /ni:ɬɢ/ 'sun rises' (McArthur 1992; Barker 1963).

NAYORURUN River (Alaska, Goodnews Bay B-3). The Yupik (Eskimo) name was reported in 1965 (Orth 1967).

NAYUKA River (Alaska, Melozitna C-6) \nä yuk´ ə\. The Koyukon (Athabaskan) name was obtained in 1956 (Orth 1967).

NAZAN Bay (Alaska, Atka C-1). From the Aleut placename *ngazang,* perhaps from *na-, nga-* 'south' (Bergsland 1994).

NAZLINI (Ariz., Apache Co.) \näz lē´ nē\. From Navajo (Athabaskan) *názlíní* 'where the water makes a turn as it flows', containing *názlį́* 'to flow in a circle, to turn flowing' (Wilson 1995).

NAZURUK Channel (Alaska, Selawik C-5). The Iñupiaq (Eskimo) name is *nasruuraq* (Burch 1998).

NEACOLA River (Alaska, Tyonek A-8) \nē ə kō´ lə\. From Dena'ina (Athabaskan) *nikugh betnu* 'big-island river' (Kari and Fall 1987:44).

NEACOXIE Creek (Ore., Clatsop Co.) \nē ə kok´ sē\. From Clatsop (Chinookan) /niak'ák^{W}si/ 'where the little pines are' (D. Kinkade p.c.).

NEAH Bay (Wash., Clallam Co.) \nē´ ə\. From the Makah (Nootkan) placename /di:ya/ (W. Jacobsen p.c.) The alternation of *d* with *n* is characteristic of the region.

NEAHKAHNIE Creek (Ore., Tillamook Co.) \nē ə kä´ nē\. Supposedly the name of a deity in Tillamook (Salishan) or Lower Chinook (D. Kinkade p.c.). A related placename is **Nakarna Mountain** (Idaho, Benewah Co.).

NEAKOK Island (Alaska, Wainwright B-2) \nē´ ə kōk\. The Iñupiaq (Eskimo) name is *niaquq* 'head, skull' (Orth 1967; MacLean 1980). Probably related Alaska placenames are **Nakolik Mountain** (Baird Mountains D-4), **Naokok** (Point Lay B-2), **Niak Creek** (Point Hope D-2), and **Niakuk Islands** (Beechey Point B-3).

NEAWANNA Creek (Ore., Clatsop Co.). Said to be from an unidentified Indian language (McArthur 1992). A related placename is **Wahanna Lake** (Ore., Lane Co.).

NEBISH (Minn., Beltrami Co.) \nē´ bish\. From Ojibwa (Algonquian) *aniibiish, niibish* 'leaf, tea' (Rhodes 1985; Nichols and Nyholm 1995). The name also occurs in Wis. (Vilas Co.); cf. also **Neebish** below.

NEBRASKA \nə bras´ kə\. The name of the state represents the Omaha or Oto (Siouan) term for the Platte River; the Omaha form is /nį braska/, lit. 'water flat', while the Oto form is /nį bráθge/. The name of the Platte River is from French *rivière platte,* also meaning 'flat river'. There are also places called **Nebraska** in Iowa (Page Co.) and Ill. (Livingston Co.).

NECANICUM (Ore., Clatsop Co.) \nē kan´ i kəm\. From the Clatsop (Chinookan) village name /nikánikm/ (D. Kinkade p.c.).

NECEDAH (Wis., Juneau Co.) \nə sē´ dä\. Probably from Winnebago (Siouan) *niiziira* 'water-yellow', from *nį́į* 'water', *zíi* 'yellow', and *-ra* 'nominalizer'. The Native American name for the town of Necedah, however, is in fact *xeešúč* 'hill-red' (K. Miner p.c.).

NECHE (N.Dak., Pembina Co.) \nē´ chē\. Probably from Ojibwa (Algonquian) *niijii* 'my friend!', generally used between men (Wick 1988; Nichols and Nyholm 1995).

NECHELIK Channel (Alaska, Harrison Bay B-2). The Iñupiaq (Eskimo) name was reported in 1951 as meaning 'new deep channel' (Orth 1967).

NECKSHORTKA Lake (Alaska, Kenai D-2). Perhaps from Dena'ina (Athabaskan); the derivation is not clear (Orth 1967).

NECONISH, Lake (Wis., Shawano Co.) \nə kon´ ish\. From a Menominee (Algonquian) personal name, <neka-nes> 'little leader' (Vogel 1991).

NECONS River (Alaska, Lime Hills A-3) \nē´ konz\. Perhaps from Dena'ina (Athabaskan) (J. Kari p.c.).

NEDDICK, Cape (Maine, York Co.) \ned´ ik\. Perhaps from Micmac (Algonquian) *newte:jk* 'one, alone' (Eckstorm 1941:178–79; DeBlois 1996).

NEEBISH (Mich., Chippewa Co.) \nē´ bish\. Probably from Ojibwa (Algonquian) *aniibiish, niibish* 'leaf, tea' (Rhodes 1985; Nichols and Nyholm 1995). The name occurs elsewhere as **Nebish** (Wis., Vilas Co.; Minn., Beltrami Co.).

NEEGRONDA Reservoir (Colo., Kiowa Co.) \nē gron´ də\. Probably from Osage (Siouan) /nį kðąðe/, lit. 'water broad' (D. Rood p.c.).

NEENACH (Calif., Los Angeles Co.) \nē´ nəch\. Probably of Takic (Uto-Aztecan) origin, but the meaning is not known (Gudde 1998).

NEENAH (Wis., Winnebago Co.) \nē ´ nə\. From Winnebago (Siouan) *nįįną́* 'the water', from *nįį* 'water' (K. Miner p.c.). The name occurs, perhaps as a transfer, in several other states (e.g. Neb., Colfax Co.).

NEENOSHE Reservoir (Colo., Kiowa Co.) \nē nō´ shə\. Probably from Osage (Siouan) /nį ožo/, lit. 'water principal'; perhaps then from the same source as the town of **Neosho** in Mo. (D. Rood p.c.).

NEEPIKON Falls (Mich., Gogebic Co.). Perhaps from the same source as **Point Nipigon**; see below.

NEESEPONSETT Pond (Mass., Worcester Co.). Perhaps contains CNEng. Algonquian <neese-> 'two', <-s> 'small', <-et> 'place' (W. Cowan p.c.).

NEESKAH Reservoir (Colo., Kiowa Co.) \nē´ skə\. Probably from Osage (Siouan) /nį ska/, lit. 'water white' (D. Rood p.c.).

NEESOPAH Reservoir (Colo., Kiowa Co.) \nē sō´ pä\. Perhaps from Osage (Siouan) /nį shüpe/, lit. 'water entrails' (D. Rood p.c.).

NEGAUNEE (Mich., Marquette Co.) \nə gô´ nē\. The town was named by white inhabitants who wanted an Indian name referring to 'pioneers'; they chose Ojibwa (Algonquian) *niigaanii* 'to go ahead, to lead' (Vogel 1986; Nichols and Nyholm 1995).

NEGIT Island (Calif., Mono Co.) \neg´ it\. From Eastern Mono (Numic) /nɨkɨtta/ 'goose' (J. McLaughlin p.c.).

NEGOTSENA Creek (Alaska, Nulato D-4). The Koyukon (Athabaskan) name was reported in 1954 (Orth 1967).

NEGUKTHLIK River (Alaska, Hagemeister Is. D-1). The Yupik (Eskimo) was reported in the form <Ungulukthluk> in 1951 (Orth 1967).

NEHALEM (Ore., Tillamook Co.) \nē hā´ ləm\. From Tillamook (Salishan) or perhaps from Lower Chinook, /nəʔí:ləm/, the Nehalem people's name for themselves (D. Kinkade p.c.).

NEHANTIC State Forest (Conn., New London Co.). A written variant of **Niantic**; see below.

NEHAWKA (Neb., Cass Co.) \nē hôk´ ə\. Said to be an Indian name, but of unknown origin (Perkey 1995).

NEHENTA Bay (Alaska, Ketchikan A-6). Reported in 1922 as a Tlingit term meaning 'copper ore' (Orth 1967).

NEHUMKEAG (Maine, Kennebec Co.) \nə hum´ keg\. Perhaps from an Abenaki (Algonquian) name meaning 'eels run out' (Eckstorm 1941:143–44); cf. *nahômo* 'eel' (Day 1994–95).

NEKAKTE Creek (Alaska, Ambler River B-5). The Iñupiaq (Eskimo) name was reported in 1956 (Orth 1967).

NEKA River (Alaska, Juneau A-6). The name, perhaps Tlingit, was reported in 1951 (Orth 1967).

NEKEELIT Point (Alaska, St. Lawrence D-6). From St. Lawrence Is. Yupik (Eskimo) *elqiiq* 'visor' (Orth 1967; Jacobson 1987).

NEKETA Creek (Alaska, Chignik B-2). The name, perhaps Aleut, was reported in 1951 (Orth 1967).

NEKIMI (Wis., Winnebago Co.) \nə kē´ mē\. Perhaps from Menominee (Algonquian), but of unclear derivation (Vogel 1991).

NEKOMA (Ill., Henry Co.) \nə kō´ mə\. Perhaps from the same source as **Nokomis;** see below. The name **Nekoma** also occurs elsewhere (Kans., Rush Co.; N.Dak., Cavalier Co.; Ore., Lane Co.).

NEKOOSA (Wis., Wood Co.) \nə ko͞o´ sə\. From Winnebago (Siouan) *nį̨kúsa, nį̨kúse,* probably referring to some large stream; containing *nį̨* 'water' (Vogel 1991; K. Miner p.c.).

NEKUTAK Lake (Alaska, Kenai D-2). Perhaps a Dena'ina (Athabaskan) name, officially bestowed around 1963 (Orth 1967).

NELAGONEY (Okla., Osage Co.) \nē lag´ ə nē, nē lä´ gə nē\. A post office existed here from December 11, 1906, to February 28, 1959. The name is from Osage (Siouan) /ni ðákðį/, lit. 'water-good'; the modern form is /ni ðá:lį/ (R. Rankin p.c.).

NELCHINA (Alaska, Talkeetna Mountains A-1) \nel chē´ nə\. From Ahtna (Athabaskan) *neltsii na'* 'yellow stream' (Kari and Kari 1982:39).

NELSALUK (Alaska, Barter Is. A-5). The Iñupiaq (Eskimo) name is said to mean 'big Nelson's place' (Orth 1967).

NELTUSHKIN (Alaska, Sitka B-2). The Tlingit name was recorded in 1885 as <Neltuschkan> and later as <Naltuck-an> (Orth 1967).

NELUTAHALIK Creek (Alaska, St. Michael A-3). The Yupik (Eskimo) name was reported in 1899 as <Nehlutahalik> (Orth 1967).

NEMADJI River (Minn., Carlton Co.; Wis., Douglas Co.) \nə maj´ ē\. Said to be from an Ojibwa (Algonquian) word meaning 'left hand' (Upham 2001); cf. *namanjii* 'to be left-handed' (Nichols and Nyholm 1995).

NEMAHA County (Kans.) \nē´ mə hä\. Probably from Ioway-Otoe (Siouan) /nį maha/ 'muddy river', from /nį/ 'water, river' plus /maha/ 'dirt, mud' (Vogel 1983; R. Rankin p.c.). **Nemaha** is also the name of a county in Neb., and occurs elsewhere as well (Iowa, Sac Co.; Mo., Holt Co.).

NEMAHBIN Lakes (Wis., Waukesha Co.). Perhaps from the Potawatomi (Algonquian) for 'sucker', the fish (Vogel 1991); cf. Ojibwa *namebin* (Nichols and Nyholm 1995).

NEMASKET (Mass., Plymouth Co.) \nə mas´ kət\. The NEng. Algonquian name may mean 'at the fishing place' (Huden 1962).

NENA Creek (Ore., Wasco Co.) \nē´ nə\. From Sahaptin /niní, ni:ní/ 'quaking aspen' (McArthur 1992; D. Kinkade p.c.).

NENAMUSA (Ore., Tillamook Co.) \nē nə myo͞o´ sə\. The placename may be from an unidentified Indian language (McArthur 1992).

NENANA (Alaska, Fairbanks C-5) \nə nan´ ə\. From Lower Tanana (Athabaskan) *neenano'*, lit. 'stopping-while-migrating stream', containing *no'* 'stream' (Kari 1999:127).

NENEVOK Lake (Alaska, Goodnews Bay D-3). From Yupik (Eskimo) *nanvaq* 'lake' (Orth 1967; Jacobson 1984). Related Alaska placenames include **Nanvak Bay** (Hagemeister Is. C-6) and **Nanvaranak Slough** (Kwiguk C-4).

NEODESHA (Kans., Wilson Co.) \nē ō də shā´\. Perhaps from Osage (Siouan) /nį oðížąka/ 'fork in a stream', containing /nį/ 'water, river' (Rydjord 1968; R. Rankin p.c.).

NEOGA (Ill., Cumberland Co.) \nē ō´ gə\. Perhaps from a Seneca (Iroquoian) word for 'deer', though it is not clear how the word found its way to Ill.; cf. Seneca *(o)neokę'* 'deer' (Chafe 1967). The name **Neoga** occurs elsewhere in Fla. (Flagler Co) and Colo. (Hinsdale Co.).

NEOLA (Kans., Stafford Co.) \nē ō´ lə\. Perhaps from Osage (Siouan) /nįolą/ 'between the waters', from /nį/ 'water, river' plus /-olą/ 'inside, between' (R. Rankin p.c.). There is also a **Neola** in Utah (Duchesne Co.).

NEONGWAH (Mo., Camden Co.) \nē ong´ gwä\. Probably a Siouan name containing *ni-* 'water' (Ramsay 1952).

NEOPIT (Wisc., Menominee Co.) \nē ō´ pit\. From Menominee (Algonquian) /ni:wapet/, /nayi:wapet/ a nineteenth-century tribal leader (Vogel 1991; Bloomfield 1975:163).

NEOSHO County (Kans.) \nē ō´ shō\. From Siouan origin; cf. Osage /nį óžo/ 'principal river', from /nį/ 'water, river' plus /óžo/ 'principal' (Rydjord 1968; R. Rankin p.c.). The name also occurs elsewhere (e.g., Mo., Newton Co.; and Wis, Dodge Co.); see **Neenoshe Reservoir** (Colo., Kiowa Co.) above.

NEOTA, Mount (Colo., Larimer Co.) \nē ō´ tə\. An adaptation of Arapaho (Algonquian) *hóte'* 'bighorn sheep' (A. Cowell p.c.).

NEOTSU (Ore., Lincoln Co.) \nē ōt´ so͞o\. From the Tillamook (Salishan) placename [nəʔəhso, naʔahso] (D. Kinkade p.c.).

NEOUTAQUET River (Maine, York Co.). Said to be from an Abenaki (Algonquian) name meaning 'at the solitary river' (Huden 1962).

NEPAUG (Conn., Litchfield Co.). Perhaps a contraction of SNEng. Algonquian <nunnipaug> 'fresh pond' (Trumbull 1881).

NEPESSING Lake (Mich., Lapeer Co.) \nə pes´ ing\. Perhaps from an Ojibwa (Algonquian) name meaning 'little water place' (Vogel 1986); cf. *nibi* 'water' (Nichols and Nyholm 1995).

NEPESTA (Colo., Pueblo Co.) \nə pes´ tə\. From a Spanish name for the Arkansas River, *Río Nepesta* (Bright 1993); possibly from Comanche (Numic) /nɨpetsɨ/ 'wife' (J. McLaughlin p.c.). A related form is **Río de Napestle** (Kans.).

NEPEUSKUN (Wis., Winnebago Co.) \nə po͞os´ kən\. From Menominee (Algonquian) /nepiaskon/ 'cattail reed' (Vogel 1991; Bloomfield 1975).

NEPONSET (Mass., Suffolk Co.) \nə pon´ sət\. Perhaps from SNEng. Algonquian <nepun> 'summer', <-s> 'small', <-et> 'place' (Huden 1962). **Neponset** is also found as a transfer name (Ill., Bureau Co.; Calif., Monterey Co.).

NEPP Point (Maine, Washington Co.). Perhaps from Abenaki (Algonquian) *nebi* 'water' (Huden 1962; Day 1994–95).

NEPTAWAH (Kans., Sumner Co.). A variant of **Napawalla**; see above.

NEQUASSET (Maine, Sagadahoc Co.). Said to be related to Abenaki (Algonquian) <nequassebem> 'a pond' (Eckstorm 1941:138).

NERAGON Island (Alaska, Hooper Bay D-3). Perhaps from Yupik (Eskimo), reported in 1919 (Orth 1967).

NERELNA Creek (Alaska, Valdez B-1) \nə rel´ nə\. The Ahtna (Athabaskan) name is *nagael na'*, the name for the nearby Teday River (J. Kari p.c.).

NERUOKPUK Lakes (Alaska, Mt. Michelson B-2). The Iñupiaq (Eskimo) name means 'big lake'; cf. *narvaq* 'lake', *-(q)pak* 'big' (MacLean 1980). Other related names include **Natvakrak Lake** (Alaska, Utukok River D-3).

NESCATUNGA (Kans., Comanche Co.) \nē skə tung´ gə\. Perhaps from an Osage (Siouan) name meaning 'big white river', from /nį/ 'river', /ska/ 'white', and /htąka/ 'big'; or reduced from a term meaning 'big salty river', containing /nįsküye/ 'salt' (Rydjord 1968; R. Rankin p.c.).

NESCOPECK (Pa., Luzerne Co.) \nes´ kə pek\. Perhaps from Delaware (Algonquian) *niskëpèk* 'dirty water' (Kraft and Kraft 1985); cf. Unami Delaware /ní:ske/ 'it is dirty' (Blalock et al. 1994).

NESENKEAG Brook (N.H., Hillsborough Co.). Said to be from Abenaki (Algonquian), perhaps meaning 'they come two by two' (of eels; Huden 1962); cf. *nizi* 'two' (Day 1994–95). Possibly related names include **Nashotah** (Wis., Waukesha Co.), **Neshota** (Wis., Brown Co.), and **Nijode** (Mich., Mescosta Co.).

NESHAMMINY (Pa., Bucks Co.) \nə sham´ i nē\. Perhaps from Delaware (Algonquian), meaning 'two streams' (Donehoo 1928); cf. <nischa> 'two' (Brinton and Anthony 1888), Unami Delaware /ní:ša:/ 'two' (Blalock et al. 1994).

NESHANNOCK (Pa., Mercer Co.) \nə shan´ ək\. Perhaps from Delaware (Algonquian) <nishannok> 'two streams' (Donehoo 1928).

NESHKORO (Wis., Marquette Co.) \nesh kō´ rō\. From Winnebago (Siouan), meaning 'salt river' (Vogel 1991).

NESHOBA County (Miss.) \nə shō´ bə\. From the same source as **Nashoba** (Okla., Pushmataha Co.); see above.

NESHONOC (Wis., La Crosse Co.) \nə shon´ ək\. Perhaps a transfer from **Neshannock** (Pa., Mercer Co.); see above.

NESHOTA (Wisc., Brown Co.) \nə shō´ tä\. From Ojibwa (Algonquian) *niizhoodenh* 'twin' (Vogel 1991; Nichols and Nyholm 1995). Related placenames include **Neshotah** and **Neshoto** (Wis., Manitowoc Co.); possibly also related placenames are **Nashotah** (Wis., Waukesha Co.), **Nesenkeag Brook** (N.H., Hillsborough Co.), **Neshamminy** (Pa., Bucks Co.), **Nijode Lakes** (Mich., Mecosta Co.), and **Shoto** (Wis., Manitowoc Co.).

NESIKA Park (Ore., Coos Co.) \nes ē´ kə\. Chinook Jargon <ne-si´-ka> [nəsáikə] 'we, us, our, ours', perhaps from Lower Chinook [nčaika] 'we, exclusive' (D. Kinkade p.c.).

NESKOWIN (Ore., Tillamook Co.) \nes´ kō win\. Tillamook (Salishan), meaning 'plenty fish' (D. Kinkade p.c.).

NESOWADNEHUNK Falls (Maine, Piscataquis Co.). Perhaps from an Abenaki (Algonquian) name meaning 'swift stream between mountains' (Huden 1962); cf. *-aden-* 'mountain' (Day 1994–95).

NESPELEM (Wash., Okanogan Co.) \nes pē´ ləm\. Okanagan (Salishan) [nspíləm] 'flat country, level place, prairie', from /n-/ 'place', /s-/ 'nominalizer', /píl-/ 'flat', and /-m/ 'middle voice' (Hitchman 1985; D. Kinkade p.c.).

NESTOCTIN (Ore., Tillamook Co.) \nes tok´ tən\. A variant spelling of **Nestocton** (Ore., Tillamook Co.) \nes tok´ tən\. This is perhaps from a Tillamook (Salishan) placename [nəšdzáq'tən, nəšdzák'tən] (D. Kinkade p.c.).

NESTUCCA River (Ore., Tillamook Co.) \nes tuk´ ə\. From Tillamook (Salishan) [ksta?gʷə́hwəš] 'Nestucca (River) people' (D. Kinkade p.c.).

NESUFTANGA (Ariz., Navajo Co.). Hopi (Uto-Aztecan) *naqsöptanga* 'deafness medicine', from *naqsöp-, naqsövi* 'deaf', *-ta* 'causative', and *nga(-hu)* 'root, medicine' (K. Hill p.c.).

NESUNTABUNT Mountain (Maine, Piscataquis Co.). Said to be Abenaki (Algonquian) for 'three heads', referring to mountain peaks (Huden 1962); cf. *nas* 'three', *-mdeb-* 'head' (Day 1994–95).

NETARTS (Ore., Tillamook Co.) \nē´ tärts\. From the Tillamook (Salishan) village name /ni:ta:c/ (D. Kinkade p.c.).

NETAWAKA (Kans., Jackson Co.). The name is said to be Potawatomi (Algonquian), perhaps meaning 'fine view' (Rydjord 1968).

NETHKAHATI Creek (Alaska, Tanana D-6). The Koyukon (Athabaskan) name, recorded in 1956, is said to mean 'stream junction' (Orth 1967).

NETHOLZENDE Lake (Alaska, Kateel River C-1). The Koyukon (Athabaskan) name was reported in 1955 (Orth 1967).

NETLETNA River (Alaska, Ophir A-6) \net let´ nə\. Deg Hit'an (Athabaskan) *sigidaletno'* (J. Kari p.c.).

NETT Lake (Minn., Koochiching Co.). From an Ojibwa (Algonquian) placename <Asubikone>, said to mean 'taken in the net' (Upham 2001); cf. *asabikone* 'Nett Lake', *asab* 'net' (Nichols and Nyholm 1995).

NEUSE River (N.C., Pamlico Co.). Said to be named for an Indian group called <Neusiok>, not otherwise identified (Powell 1968). A related name is **Newasiac** (N.C., Craven Co.).

NEVA, Mount (Colo., Boulder Co.) \nē´ və\. Said to have been named for an Arapaho (Algonquian) leader (Bright 1993).

NEVAHBE Ridge (Calif., Mono Co.) \nə vä´ bē\. From Mono (Numic) /nɨpapi/ [nɨvávi] 'snow' (J. McLaughlin p.c.).

NEVERSINK (N.Y., Sullivan Co.) \nev´ ər singk\. A folk-etymology from <newesink>, the name of a Munsee Delaware (Algonquian) band (*HNAI* 15:237). The placename also occurs in Pa. (Berks Co.). A related name is **Navesink** (N.J., Monmouth Co.).

NEVER SUMMER Mountains (Colo., Jackson Co.) is a translation of Arapaho (Algonquian) *niicíibiicéí'* 'it is never summer' (A. Cowell p.c.).

NEWAGEN (Maine, Lincoln Co.). The name is shortened from **Cape Newagen,** earlier written <Capamanwagan, Capanawhagan, Capanewagen>, perhaps an Abenaki (Algonquian) name meaning 'interrupted route' (Eckstorm 1941: 123–24); cf. *gebem* 'it is closed', *gebinigen* 'it is shut; a dam' (Day 1994–95).

NEWALLA (Okla., Oklahoma Co.) \nə wô´ lə\. This represents the Osage (Siouan) name for the Canadian River, from /nį/ 'water, river' and /bðáða, bráða/ 'wide' (R. Rankin p.c.).

NEWASIAC (N.C., Craven Co.). The name is also written **Newasiwac;** it refers to an Indian group called <Neusiok>, not otherwise identified (Powell 1968). A related name is **Neuse River** (N.C., Pamlico Co.).

NEWAUKUM River (Wash., Lewis Co.) \nōō wô´ kəm\. Upper Chehalis (Salishan) /náwaqʷəm/ 'big prairie', with /náwa-/ 'big' and /-qʷ/ 'prairie' (D. Kinkade p.c.). A possibly related placename is **Napavine** in the same county; see above.

NEWAYGO County (Mich.) \nə wä´ gō\. Named for an Ottawa (Algonquian) leader of the early nineteenth century. The term has also been written as <Nuwagon, Neh-way-go, Ningwegon> (etc.) (Vogel 1986); cf. *n-ningwiihgan* 'my wing' (Rhodes 1985).

NEWDICK Point (Maine, Lincoln Co.) \nōō´ dick\. The name is said to represent a Malecite (Algonquian) word meaning 'alone' (Rutherford 1970).

NEWHALEN (Alaska, Iliamna C-6) \nōō hā´ lən, nōō´ hā lən\. Probably from Dena'ina

(Athabaskan) *nughilen* [nuɣilən] 'flows down' (Kari and Kari 1982:17). The Yupik (Eskimo) name is *nuurileng* [nu:ɣləŋ] (Jacobson 1984), probably a borrowing from Athabaskan.

NEW KNOCKHOCK (Alaska, Kwiguk D-6) \no͞o nok´ hok\. An Eskimo village, replacing an abandoned site now called simply "Knockhock" (Orth 1967). This is a folk-etymology from Yupik (Eskimo) *nunaqerraq,* from *nuna* 'land' (Jacobson 1984).

NEWTOK (Alaska, Baird Inlet D-8) \no͞o´ tok\. Yupik (Eskimo) *niugtaq,* from *niuk* 'rustling sound' (Jacobson 1984).

NEW YORKA (Ga., Heard Co.) \no͞o yôrk´ ə\. From Muskogee *nuyakv* /nuyá:ka/, this site of a former Indian village was perhaps named after a delegation of Muskogee leaders who visited New York to negotiate a treaty in 1790 (Goff 1975; Martin and Mauldin 2000). A variant writing is **New Yaucau.** Apparent transfers of the name are found in **Niuyaka** (Ala., Tallapoosa Co.) and **Nuyaka** (Okla., Okmulgee Co.).

NEZINSCOT River (Maine, Androscoggin Co.). Said to be Abenaki (Algonquian) for 'place of going downriver' (Huden 1962); cf. *naaijoan* [na:idzoan] 'it flows down' (Day 1994–95).

NEZ PERCE (Idaho) \nez pûrs´\. A people and language, belonging to the Sahaptian linguistic family. The term is derived from French *nez percé* 'pierced nose', referring to an early custom of piercing the nasal septum in order to wear shell ornaments (*HNAI* 12:437). The name of the people was given to **Nez Perce County** in Idaho.

NEZ Spring (Ariz., Coconino Co.) \nez\. From Navajo (Athabaskan) *-neez* 'long, tall' (Young and Morgan 1987), also used in English as a Navajo family name.

NIAGARA Falls (N.Y.) \nī ag´ rə\. The name is derived from an Iroquoian language, perhaps meaning 'a neck' (i.e., a channel connecting two lakes) (Beauchamp 1907). As a placename, it is found in **Niagara County** (N.Y.), and as a transfer in Iowa (Winneshiek Co.), Kans. (Piscataquis Co.), Ore. (Marion Co.), and Wis. (Marinette Co.). A related placename is **Niagra Reef** (Ohio, Ottawa Co.). Regarding the historical pronunciation of this name, see A. Read (2001:227–36).

NIAK Creek (Alaska, Point Hope D-2). Probably from Iñupiaq (Eskimo) *niaquq* 'head' (Orth 1967; MacLean 1980). Possibly related Alaska placenames are **Niakogon Buttes** (Umiat A-3) and **Niaktuvik River** (Ambler River A-5) (Orth 1967). Clearly related is **Niakuk Islands** (Beechey Point B-3) (Orth 1967).

NIANGUA (Mo., Webster Co.) \nī ang´ gwə\. The name, also recorded as <Neongwah, Niangura>, may be from Oto (Siouan) /ni ágwe/, lit. 'water to-bring'; cf. /agúre/ 'to bring' (R. Compton p.c.).

NIANTIC (Conn., New London Co.) \nī an´ tik\. The SNEng. Algonquian name may mean 'those who live at the point' (Trumbull 1881). A variant is **Nehantic.** The placename occurs as a transfer in Pa. (Montgomery Co.) and Ill. (Macon Co.).

NIAVI Wash (Nev., Nye Co.) \nī´ vē\. Probably from Shoshoni (Numic) /naipin/ [naivi] 'teenage girl' or /nai'pin/ [nai'vi] 'little girl' (J. McLaughlin p.c.).

NIAWIAKUM River (Wash., Pacific Co.). From the Lower Chehalis (Salishan) placename \náywəq^{w}əm\. 'Niawiakum River' (D. Kinkade p.c.).

NICABOYNE Lake (Wis., Burnett Co.) \nik´ ə boin\. The term is the surname of an Ojibwa (Algonquian) family; the further derivation is not clear (Vogel 1991).

NICATOU Island (Maine, Penobscot Co.) \nik´ ə tou\. From Abenaki (Algonquian), meaning 'fork of a river' (Huden 1962); cf. *nigidaw-* 'forked' (Day 1994–95). A related placename is **Nicatous Lake** (Maine, Hancock Co.) \nik ə tou´ is\, probably a diminutive.

NICHAWAK Mountain (Alaska, Bering Glacier A-8). The name, perhaps from Tlingit, was reported in 1903 (Orth 1967).

NICHENTHRAW Mountain (Alaska, Arctic B-3). The Gwich'in (Athabaskan) name is *nitsii ddhaa* 'big mountain' (Caulfield et al. 1980).

NICHEWAUG (Mass., Worcester Co.) \nich´ ə wôg\. The SNEng. Algonquian name contains <nashue-> 'between' and <-auke> 'land' (Huden 1962; W. Cowan p.c.).

NICHIN Cove (Alaska, Craig D-4). The name, perhaps from Tlingit, was reported in 1964 (Orth 1967).

NICHOMUS Run (N.J., Salem Co.). The name is probably from Delaware (Algonquian), but the derivation is not clear (Becker 1964).

NICKJACK (Ga., Cobb Co.) \nik´ ə jak\. Perhaps from a Cherokee (Iroquoian) word meaning 'old creek place' (Krakow 1975). The spelling **Nickajack** also occurs (Ga., Cobb Co.; Tenn., Marion Co.).

NICOLIN (Maine, Hancock Co.). Said to be an Indian word, language not identified, meaning 'wolves run in packs' (Huden 1962).

NIGAG Mountain (Alaska, Goodnews Bay C-4). The Yupik (Eskimo) name was reported in 1954 (Orth 1967).

NIGAKTOVIAKVIK Creek (Alaska, Killik River B-2). The Iñupiaq (Eskimo) name was reported in 1956 (Orth 1967).

NIGAKTUKVIK Creek (Alaska, Killik River A-2). The Iñupiaq (Eskimo) name is *nigaqtuġvik*, said to mean 'place where wild sheep are snared' (Orth 1967; Burch 1998); cf. *nigaq* 'a snare', *nigaqtuq* 'is snared' (Webster and Zibell 1970).

NIGATUK Creek (Alaska, Kateel River B-2). The Koyukon (Athabaskan) name was reported in 1955 (Orth 1967).

NIGERUK Creek (Alaska, Baird Mountains A-1). The Iñupiaq (Eskimo) name was reported in 1901 (Orth 1967).

NIGHTMUTE (Alaska, Baird Inlet B-8) \nīt´ myo͞ot\. From Yupik (Eskimo) *negtemiut,* perhaps containing *negte-* 'to press down on'; the suffix *-miut* means 'people' (Jacobson 1984).

NIGIKMIGOON River (Alaska, Candle A-3). The Iñupiaq (Eskimo) name was reprorted in 1949 (Orth 1967).

NIGIKTLIK Creek (Alaska, Point Hope D-1). The Iñupiaq (Eskimo) name was reported in 1956 (Orth 1967).

NIGISAKTUVIK River (Alaska, Meade River C-3). The Iñupiaq (Eskimo) name was reported as <Nigisakfogvik>, said to mean 'place where east wind blows', in 1923 (Orth 1967); cf. *nigiq, nigikpaq* 'northeasterly wind' (Webster and Zibell 1970).

NIGLAKTAK Lake (Alaska, Selawik C-2). The Iñupiaq (Eskimo) name is *niglaaqtuq,* apparently from *nigraq* 'tassel, fringe' (Burch 1998).

NIGTUN Lake (Alaska, Howard Pass A-2). From Iñupiaq (Eskimo) *niuqtuun* 'a drill, an oil rig' (Orth 1967, MacLean 1980).

NIGUANAK Ridge (Alaska, Demarcation Point D-4). The Iñupiaq (Eskimo) name, recorded in 1952, refers to an 'attempt to see animals' (Orth 1967).

NIGU Bluff (Alaska, Howard Pass B-1). From an Iñupiaq (Eskimo) word for 'rainbow' (Orth 1967); cf. *nigak* 'rainbow' (Webster and Zibell 1970).

NIGUEL Hill (Calif., Orange Co.) \ni gel´\. The place was earlier called *Nigüili* in Spanish and appears to be from Juaneño (Takic) /nawil/ 'young girl' (Gudde 1998). The city of **Laguna Niguel** is now located in the area.

NIITLTOKTALOGI Mountain (Alaska, Hughes B-2). The Koyukon (Athabaskan) name was published in 1956 (Orth 1967).

NIJODE Lakes (Mich., Mecosta Co.). From Ojibwa (Algonquian) *niizhoodenh* 'twin' (Vogel 1986; Nichols and Nyholm 1995). Related placenames are **Nashotah** (Wis., Waukesha Co.), **Neshota** (Wis., Brown Co.), **Neshotah** (Wis., Manitowoc Co.), and **Shoto** (Wis., Manitowoc Co.).

NIKABUNA Lake (Alaska, Lake Clark A-7) \nē kə bo͞o´ nə\. From Dena'ina (Athabaskan) *nikugh vena* 'big-island lake', with *vena* 'lake' (Kari and Kari 1982:22). Probably related is **Nikadavna Creek** (Alaska, Lake Clark B-7).

NIKISHKA (Alaska, Kenai C-4) \ni kis´ kə\. Probably from Dena'ina (Athabaskan); the name was reported in 1912. It is also written **Nikiski** (Orth 1967, BGN 8504).

NIKLAVIK Creek (Alaska, Point Lay D-2). The Iñupiaq (Eskimo) name was reported in 1923 (Orth 1967).

NIKOK River (Alaska, Baird Mountains B-2). The Iñupiaq (Eskimo) name may be from *niaquq* 'head' (L. Kaplan p.c.).

NIKONDA Creek (Alaska, Nabesna A-4) \nē kon´ də\. The Upper Tanana (Athabaskan) name is *nihxį̨ǫ nda* 'blue mud creek', the name for nearby Orange Hill Creek (J. Kari p.c.).

NILIKLUGUK (Alaska, Nunivak Is. C-1). The Yupik (Eskimo) name was reported in 1937 (Orth 1967).

NILIK River (Alaska, Point Hope C-1). From Iñupiaq (Eskimo) *niliq* 'fart' (Burch 1998; MacLean 1980).

NILILAK (Alaska, Kwiguk C-6). The Yupik (Eskimo) name was obtained in 1948 (Orth 1967).

NILLIK (Alaska, Selawik C-1). The Iñupiaq (Eskimo) name was reported in 1954 (Orth 1967).

NILUNORAT Hills (Alaska, Hughes D-5). The Koyukon (Athabaskan) name was reported in 1956 (Orth 1967).

NIMGUN Creek (Alaska, Goodnews Bay B-5). The Yupik (Eskimo) name is *nimrun* 'device for winding' (L. Kaplan p.c.).

NIMHAM, Mount (N.Y., Putnam Co.). Named for an Indian leader, language not identifed, who fought for the Americans in the Revolution (Beauchamp 1907).

NIMIKON Falls (Mich., Ontonagan Co.). Probably from the same source as **Namakan Lake** (Minn., St. Louis Co.); see **Namagosh Lake** above.

NIMIUK (Alaska, Survey Pass D-2). From Iñupiaq (Eskimo) *ninŋuq* 'cottonwood tree' (Burch 1998; Webster and Zibell 1970). Probably related is **Nimiuktuk River** (Alaska, Misheguk Mountain A-2). Also related is **Ningyoyak Creek** (Alaska, Ambler River D-1); see below.

NIMSHEW (Calif., Butte Co.) \nim´ sho͞o\. From Konkow (Northwestern Maidu) /nem sewi/ 'big stream', containing /sew/ 'creek, river' (Gudde 1998). A related placename is the nearby **Kimshew Creek.**

NINAGIAK Island (Alaska, Mt. Katmai B-1). The Yupik (Eskimo) name was published in 1852 (Orth 1967).

NINGEENAK Beach (Alaska, St. Lawrence D-6). The Yupik (Eskimo) name was reported in 1965 as meaning 'little camp' (Orth 1967).

NINGLICK River (Alaska, Nunivak Is. D-1). The Yupik (Eskimo) name was reported in 1949 as <Ningaluk> (Orth 1967).

NINGYOYAK Creek (Alaska, Ambler River D-1). The Iñupiaq (Eskimo) name was reported in 1956 as meaning 'little cottonwood' (Orth 1967); cf. *ninŋuq* 'cottonwood tree' (Webster and Zibell 1970). A related placename is **Nimiuk** (Alaska, Survey Pass D-2).

NINIGRET Pond (R.I., Washington Co.). From the name of a seventeenth-century SNEng. Algonquian leader (Huden 1962).

NINILCHIK (Alaska, Kenai A-5) \ni nil´ chik\. From Dena'ina (Athabaskan) *niqnalchint* 'a lodge is built' (Kari and Kari 1982:30).

NINNEKAH (Okla., Grady Co.) \nin´ ə kä\. Perhaps shortened from Chickasaw (Muskogean) *hashi' ninak ąa* 'the moon', lit. 'sun that goes around by night', from *hashi'* 'sun', *ninak* 'night', *ąa* 'go around' (P. Munro p.c.).

NINNESCAH River (Kans., Sumner Co.) \nin´ ə skə\. Perhaps from an Osage (Siouan) term meaning 'white spring', from /nį-hnį/ 'spring' and /ska/ 'white, clear'; or perhaps 'salty river', from /nį/ 'water, river' and /nįskü´e/ 'salt' (Rydyord 1968, R. Rankin p.c.).

NIN Ridge (Alaska, Talkeetna A-4) \nin\. From Dena'ina (Athabaskan) *nen* 'land' (Kari 1999:78).

NINULUK Creek (Alaska, Umiat A-5). The Iñupiaq (Eskimo) name was reported in 1901 (Orth 1967).

NIOBRARA River (Wyo., Neb., S.Dak.) \nī ō brâr´ ə\. Perhaps from Omaha (Siouan) /nį obrara/, lit. 'water spreading' (Urbanek 1974, J. Koontz p.c.). The river gives its name to **Niobrara County** in Wyo., and to a place in Neb. (Knox Co.).

NIOTA (Ill., Hancock Co.) \nī ō´ tə\. Perhaps from Ioway (Siouan), meaning 'water remaining', containing *nį* 'water, river' (Vogel 1963; R. Rankin p.c.). The name also occurs in Neb. (York Co.) and Tenn. (McMinn Co.). A related name is **Niotaze** (Kans., Chautauqua Co.) \nī ō tāz\, a name created by the postmaster, who added the meaningless *ze* to **Niota** (Rydjord 1968).

NIOTCHE Creek (Utah, Sevier Co.) \nē ō´ chē\. Perhaps from Ute (Numic) /nuutsi/ 'Ute, Indian, human being' (J. McLaughlin p.c.).

NIPIGON, Point (Mich., Cheboygan Co.) \nip´ i gon\. Probably from Ojibwa (Algonquian) *nibi* 'water', but of uncertain derivation (Vogel 1986; Nichols and Nyholm 1995). A possibly related placename is **Neepikon Falls** (Mich., Gogebic Co.).

NIPINNAWASEE (Calif., Madera Co.) \nip´ in ə wä´ sē\. The name is said to have been transferred from Mich., where it meant 'plenty of deer' in an Indian language (Gudde 1998); cf. Ojibwa (Algonquian) *niibowa* 'many' and *waawaashkeshi* 'deer' (Nichols and Nyholm 1995).

NIPMOOSE Brook (N.Y., Rensselaer Co.) \nip´ mōōs\. Probably from a Munsee Delaware (Algonquian) word <nip-mo-osh>, of unclear derivation (Beauchamp 1907).

NIPMUC Hill (R.I., Providence Co.) \nip´ muk\. From the same source as **Nipmuck Pond** (Mass., Worcester Co.); this is the name of a SNEng. Algonquian group, derived from <nip> 'water' (Trumbull 1881; W. Cowan p.c.). The placename **Nipmuck** is also found in Conn. (Tolland Co.).

NIPOMO (Calif., San Luis Obispo Co.) \ni pō´ mō\. Obispeño (Chumashan) /nipumu'/ 'house-place, village', from /(q)nipu/ 'house' (Gudde 1998).

NIPPENICKET Lake (Mass., Bristol Co.) \nip´ ə nik ət\. Earlier written <Nippaniquet>; from SNEng. Algonquian, containing<nip> 'water' and <-et> 'place' (Huden 1962; W. Cowan p.c.).

NIPPENOSE Mountain (Pa., Clinton Co.) \nip´ ə nōz\. Said to be named for a Delaware (Algonquian) Indian resident named <Nippenucy>, perhaps derived from <ni-pen> 'summer' (Donehoo 1928); cf. Unami Delaware /ní:pən/ (Blalock et al. 1994), Munsee *níipun* (O'Meara 1996).

NIPPERSINK Creek (Ill., McHenry Co.) \nip´ ər singk\. Perhaps from Potawatomi (Algonquian), meaning 'at the small lake' (Vogel 1963). The name also occurs in Wis. (Walworth Co.).

NIPPO Hill (N.H., Strafford Co.) \nip´ ō\. Probably from Abenaki (Algonquian) *nebioo* 'it is wet' (Day 1994–95).

NIPSACHUCK Hill (R.I., Providence Co.) \nip´ sə chuk\. From SNEng. Algonquian, containing <nippe> 'water', <-s-> 'little' (W. Cowan p.c.).

NIPSIC Bog (Conn., Hartford Co.) \nip´ sik\. Earlier written as <Nipsuck>, probably from SNEng. Algonquian <nippisauke> 'place by a small pool', containing <nip-> 'water', <-s-> 'small', <-auke> 'land' (Trumbull 1881; W. Cowan p.c.).

NISA, Mount (Colo., Grand Co.) \nē´ sə\. From Arapaho (Algonquian) /nîissóo/ 'twin', because of the double peak (Salzmann 1983).

NISHCOBA (Kans., Dickinson Co.) \nish kō´ bə\. From Kansa (Siouan) /nį/ 'water' and /škóbe/ 'deep' (Rydjord 1968; R. Rankin p.c.).

NISHISAKAWICK Creek (N.J., Hunterdon Co.). Perhaps from a Delaware (Algonquian) name meaning 'two outlets' (Becker 1964); cf. **Nishuane Park,** below.

NISHLIK Lake (Alaska, Taylor Mountains B-8) \nish´ lik\. The Yupik (Eskimo) name was reported in 1915 (Orth 1967).

NISHNA (Iowa, Audubon Co.) \nish´ nə\. An abbreviation of **Nishnabotna River** (Iowa, Fremont Co.) \nish nə bot´ nə\. This is perhaps from Osage (Siouan) /nį̨šni/ 'wellspring' plus /pošta/ 'spouting' (Vogel 1983; J. Koontz p.c.). The placename also occurs in Mo. (Atchison Co.) and Neb. (Otoe Co.). The related form **Nishnabotny** is found in Iowa (Crawford Co.).

NISHUANE Park (N.J., Essex Co.). Perhaps from Delaware (Algonquian), meaning 'two streams' (Becker 1964); cf. Unami Delaware /ni:ša:/ 'two' (Blalock et al. 1994), Munsee *níisha* (O'Meara 1996).

NISHU Bay (N.Dak., McLean Co.). Named for Floyd Bear, an Arikara (Caddoan) man; his Native American name was /niišu/ 'arrow' (Wick 1988; D. Parks p.c.).

NISKA Island (N.Y., Schenectady Co.) \nis´ kə\. Probably an abbreviation of **Niskayuna** (N.Y., Schenectady Co.) \nis kə yōō´ nə\. The name was formerly written <Conistigione, Nistigioone, Niskayune> (Beauchamp 1907); it is probably from Mohawk (Iroquoian) *ó:nvste* \ó:nę̨ste\. 'corn' (M. Mithun p.c.).

NISQUALLY (Wash., Thurston Co.) \ni skwä´ lē\. The name refers to a Southern Coast Salishan group, the Lushootseed name of which is /dx^{w}sq^{w}ə́liabš/ (*HNAI* 7:487). The meaning is 'people of /sq^{w}əlíʔ/ or Frank's Landing', from /q^{w}áliʔ-/ 'hay, grass' (D. Kinkade p.c.). The English form of the name shows the alternation of *d* and *n* that is characteristic in languages of the area. A related placename is **Squally** (Wash., Pierce Co.).

NISSEQUOGUE (N.Y., Suffolk Co.) \nis´ ə kwōg\. Earlier written as <Nesequake, Nessequack, Nissequage> (etc.); from SNEng. Algonquian, perhaps meaning 'clay country' (Tooker 1911).

NISSITISSIT Hills (Mass., Middlesex Co.) \nis i tis´ it\. The SNEng. Algonquian name may mean 'two brooks', with <nissi> 'two' (Huden 1962; W. Cowan p.c.). In N.H. (Hillsborough Co.), **Nissitissit River** is perhaps from Abenaki (Algonquian); cf. *nizi* 'two' (Day 1994–95).

NISSWA (Minn., Crow Wing Co.) \nis´ wə\. Perhaps from Ojibwa (Alonquian) *niswi* 'three' (J. Nichols. p.c.). A possibly related placename is **Niswi Lake** (Minn., St. Louis Co.).

NITACHUCKY (Miss., Itawamba Co.) \nit ə chuk´ i\. Probably from Choctaw (Muskogean) *nita-chuka,* lit. 'bear house' (Seale 1939).

NITAK (Alaska, Anchorage B-8). The Dena'ina (Athabaskan) name means 'among islands' (J. Kari p.c.).

NITA Lake (Miss., Itawamba Co.) \nē´ tə\. From Choctaw (Muskogean) *nita* 'a bear' (Toomey 1917; P. Munro p.c.).

NITSIN Canyon (Ariz., Coconino Co.). The Navajo (Athabaskan) name is said to refer to an 'antelope drive', but the derivation is unclear (Granger 1983; Linford 2000).

NITTANY (Pa., Centre Co.) \nit´ nē\. Probably of Delaware (Algonquian) origin, but the derivation is not clear (Donehoo 1928).

NITTA YUMA (Miss., Sharkey Co.) \nit ə yōō´ mə\. Probably from a Choctaw (Muskogean) personal name, *nita homma* 'red bear', from *nita* 'bear' and *homma* 'red' (Seale 1939; P. Munro p.c.).

NIUKLUK River (Alaska, Solomon D-3). The Iñupiaq (Eskimo) name is *niiqḷiq* 'northern one' (L. Kaplan p.c.).

NIUYAKA (Ala., Tallapoosa Co.) \nyōō yä´ kə\. Apparently from the same source as **New Yorka** (Ga., Heard Co.); see above.

NIVAT Point (Alaska, Wainwright B-4). The Iñupiaq (Eskimo) name was made official in BGN 7802.

NIWOT (Colo., Boulder Co.) \nī´ wot\. Named for an Arapaho (Algonquian) leader, whose name was said to mean 'left-handed'; cf. /nowóoθ/ 'left side', /noowôothinoo/ 'I am left-handed' (Salzmann 1983). But Lefthand Creek, in the same area, was named years earlier for a left-handed fur trader of European origin (Bright 1993).

NIXON Fork (Alaska, Medfra A-6) \nik´ sən\. An adaptation of an Upper Kuskokwim (Athabaskan) placename *nets'in* 'from upstream' (J. Kari p.c.).

NIYGHAPAK Point (Alaska, St. Lawrence B-0). The Yupik (Eskimo) name was reported in 1932 (Orth 1967).

NIYIKLIK Creek (Alaska, Point Hope A-2). The Iñupiaq (Eskimo) name was reported in 1962 (Orth 1967).

NIYKHAPAKHIT Lake (Alaska, St. Lawrence B-2). The Yupik (Eskimo) name was reported in 1949 (Orth 1967).

NIYRAKPAK Lagoon (Alaska, St. Lawrence C-5). The Yupik (Eskimo) name was reported as <naivakhpak> 'big lake' (Orth 1967); cf. St. Lawrence Yupik *naayvaq* 'lake', *-ghpak* [-ʀpak] 'big' (Jacobson 1987).

NIZHONI Point (Ariz., Apache Co.) \ni zhō´ nē\. From Navajo (Athabaskan) *nizhóní* 'it is beautiful' (A. Wilson p.c.). The placename also occurs in N.Mex. (Santa Fe Co.).

NIZINA River (Alaska, McCarthy B-6) \nē zē´ nə\. From Ahtna (Athabaskan) *nizii na'*, with *na'* 'stream' (Kari 1990).

NJOO Mountain (Alaska, Philip Smith Mtns. B-1). The Gwich'in (Athabaskan) name is *njoo ddhaa* 'black-duck (scoter) mountain' (J. Kari p.c.).

NOAK, Mount (Alaska, Noatak A-3). From Iñupiaq (Eskimo) *nuvuk* 'tip, point' (Orth 1967; MacLean 1980). Possibly related Alaska placenames include **Nuvagapa Point** (Demarcation Point D-3) and **Nuwuk** (Barrow B-4); see below.

NOANET Peak (Mass., Norfolk Co.). Perhaps from SNEng. Algonquian <noonuat> 'to suck' (W. Cowan p.c.).

NOANK (Conn., New London Co.). From SNEng. Algonquian, perhaps meaning 'it is a point' (Huden 1962).

NOATAK (Alaska, Noatak C-2) \nō´ ə tak\. From the Iñupiaq (Eskimo) placename *nuataaq* (Orth 1967; *HNAI* 5:318).

NOAUKTA Slough (Alaska, Tyonek A-5). From Dena'ina (Athabaskan) *nughi'ukda* 'extends down poorly' (Kari and Kari 1982:29).

NOBONNI DAHNA'A (N.Mex., Cibola Co.). The Zuni name may contain /noponni/ 'face' and /tahna/ 'to be sticking out' (Ferguson and Hart 1985; Newman 1958).

NOBSCOT (Mass., Middlesex Co.) \nob´ skət\. The SNEng. Algonquian name may mean 'at the rocky place' (Huden 1962).

NOBSCUSSET Point (Mass., Barnstable Co.). The SNEng. Algonquian name may mean 'at the place of small rocks' (Huden 1962).

NOBSKA Point (Mass., Plymouth Co.) \nob´ skə\. The SNEng. Algonquian name may mean 'rocks' (Huden 1962).

NOC, Bay de (Mich., Delta Co.) \bā də nok´\. Earlier written as <Noquet>, the term may be from Ojibwa (Algonquian) /nookkee/, a name for the Bear Clan (Vogel 1986; *HNAI* 15:770). Related placenames are **Lake Nocquebay** (Wis., Marinette Co.) and **Nokay Lake** (Minn., Crow Wing Co.).

NOCATEE (Fla., DeSoto Co.) \nok´ ə tē\. Perhaps from a Seminole (Muskogean) expression <nakiti> 'what is it?' (Read 1934).

NOCKAMIXON Township (Pa., Bucks Co.). A proposed derivation is from Delaware (Algonquian) <nochanichsink> 'where there are three houses' (Donehoo 1928); cf. Unami Delaware /na:xá:/ 'three' (Blalock et al. 1994), Munsee *nxáh* (O'Meara 1996).

NOCKUM Hill (R.I., Bristol Co.). Perhaps from a SNEng. Algonquian word meaning 'sandy' (Huden 1962).

NOCONA (Tex., Montague Co.) \nō kō´ nə\. Named for a Comanche (Numic) man, Pete

Nocona; his name was also written <Nookoni>. The term is from /noohkoni/, the name of a Comanche band, meaning 'wandering around', lit. 'moving camp around in circles', from /noo-/ 'to haul' plus /kooni/ 'to turn around' (J. McLaughlin p.c.). A related placename is **Nokoni Lake** (Colo., Grand Co.).

NOCQUEBAY, Lake (Wis., Marinette Co.) \nok ə bā\. From the same source as **Bay de Noc** (Mich., Delta Co.); also written **Noquebay.** Related placenames are **Nocquet** (Mich., Delta Co.) and **Nokay Lake** (Minn., Crow Wing Co.).

NODAWAY (Iowa, Adams Co.) \nod´ ə wā\. From an Algonquian term referring to neighboring Iroquoian and Siouan peoples, reconstructed as proto-Algonquian */na:towe:wa/ (*HNAI* 15:289); cf. Ojibwa /naadwe/ (Rhodes 1985). The placename also occurs in Mo. (Andrew Co.). Related placenames include **Nadawah** (Ala., Monroe Co.), **Nadoway Point** (Mich., Chippewa Co.), **Nottawa** (Mich., St. Joseph Co.), **Nottoway County** (N.C., Hertford Co.), and **Nottoway** (La., Iberville Par.).

NODODEHON Lake (Alaska, Melozitna D-6). The Koyukon (Athabaskan) name was reported in 1956 (Orth 1967).

NOGADANEODA Lake (Alaska, Kateel River B-3). The Koyukon (Athabaskan) name was recorded in 1955 (Orth 1967).

NOGAHABARA Sand Dunes (Alaska, Kateel River C-3) \nō gə hə bä´ rə\. The Koyukon (Athabaskan) name is *nokk'et hubaaghe* 'edge of mineral lick' (J. Kari p.c.).

NOGAK Creek (Alaska, Killik River C-4). From Iñupiaq (Eskimo) *nuġġaq* 'young caribou' (Orth 1967; Webster and Zibell 1970).

NOGAMUT (Alaska, Sleetmute A-5) \nō´ gə myo͞ot\. The Yupik (Eskimo) name is perhaps from *nuraq* 'young caribou' plus *-miut* 'people' (Jacobson 1984).

NOGGAI (Alaska, Nulato D-4). The Koyukon (Athabaskan) name is of unclear derivation (Orth 1967).

NOGOYALNA Slough (Alaska, Melozitna D-6). The Koyukon (Athabaskan) name was reported in 1955 (Orth 1967).

NOGRILENTEN Lake (Alaska, Hughes B-1). From Koyukon (Athabaskan) *nogheelenh denh* 'waterfall', containing *len* 'current flows' and *denh* 'place' (Jetté and Jones 2000).

NOHARTS Creek (Neb., Richardson Co.; Kans., Brown Co.) \nō´ härts\. Probably for a possessive, "No-Heart's Creek", said to refer to an Ioway (Siouan) leader (Perkey 1995).

NOHOKOMEEN Glacier (Wash., Whatcom Co.). Probably an Interior Salish placename, made official in BGN 7302.

NOHOOLCHINTNA (Alaska, Bettles C-4). The Koyukon (Athabaskan) name is of unclear derivation (Orth 1967).

NOIPA KAM (Ariz., Pima Co.). From the O'odham (Piman) placename *nowipakam* (J. Hill p.c.).

NOJOGUI Falls (Calif., Santa Barbara Co.) \nō´ hō wē\. The Purisimeño (Chumashan) placename was recorded by the Spanish as *Nojogüe, Nojoque* (etc.), perhaps from a Native American placename <Onohwi> (Gudde 1998).

NOK (Alaska, Nulato D-4). The Koyukon (Athabaskan) name is of unclear derivation.

NOKAI Canyon (Ariz., Navajo Co.) \nä kī´, nə kī´, nō´ kī\. From the same origin as **Naakai Canyon** (Utah, San Juan Co.), the Navajo (Athabaskan) word for 'Mexican' (Young and Morgan 1987). A related placename is **Nakai Peak** (Colo., Grand Co.); see above. **Nokaito Bench** (Ariz., Apache Co.; Utah, San Juan Co.) is from Navajo (Athabaskan) *naakai tó,* lit. 'Mexican water, Mexican spring', with *tó* 'water' (Linford 2000).

NOKASIPPI River (Minn., Crow Wing Co.) \nō kə sip´ ē\. The Ojibwa (Algonquian) name probably means 'Bear-Clan river', from *nooke* 'Bear Clan' and *ziibi* 'river' (Nichols and Nyholm 1995).

NOKAY Lake (Minn., Crow Wing Co.) \nō´ kā\. Refers to an Ojibwa leader of the late eighteenth century, sometimes called "Old Noka"; his name contains the same stem as in **Nokasippi River** above (Upham 2001). Related placenames are **Bay de Noc** (Mich., Delta Co.) and **Nocquebay Lake** (Wis., Marinette Co.).

NOKETCHEE Creek (Ga., Clarke Co.). This may be "a pseudo-Indian name suggesting poor fishing" (Krakow 1975).

NOKHU Crags (Colo., Jackson Co.) \nō´ ko͞o\. From Arapaho (Algonquian) *nohúúx* 'nest' (A. Cowell p.c.).

NOKOGAMIUT (Alaska, St. Michael A-6). The Yupik (Eskimo) name was reported in 1899 (Orth 1967). The suffix *-miut* means 'people'.

NOKOMIS \nō kō´ mis, nə kō´ mis\. This name, given to the hero's grandmother in Longfellow's *Hiawatha,* is from Ojibwa (Algonquian) *nookoomis* 'my grandmother' (Nichols and Nyholm 1995). The popularity of the poem led to its use as a placename in Iowa (Buena Vista Co.), Maine (Penobscot Co.), Fla. (Sarasota Co.), and elsewhere. Names probably from the same source include **No-Ko-Mos Lake** (Mich., Kent Co.), **Nekoma** (Ill., Henry Co.), and **Nakomis** (Ga., Crawford Co.).

NOKONI Lake (Colo., Grand Co.) \nō kō´ nē\. From /noohkoni/, the name of a Comanche (Numic) band, meaning 'wandering around', lit. 'moving camp around in circles', from /noo-/ 'to haul' plus /kooni/ 'to turn around' (Bright 1993; J. McLaughlin p.c.). A related placename is **Nocona** (Tex., Montague Co.).

NOKOTLEK River (Alaska, Wainwright B-4). The Iñupiaq (Eskimo) name was reported in 1923 (Orth 1967).

NOKROT (Alaska, St. Michael A-2) \nok´rot\. The Yupik (Eskimo) name was reported in 1898 (Orth 1967).

NOLAMATTINK (Pa., Northampton Co.). The Delaware (Algonquian) name has been said to mean 'where the silkworm spins' (Donehoo 1928).

NOLIC (Ariz., Pima Co.) \nō´ lik\. From O'odham (Piman) *nolik* 'the bend' (Granger 1983; J. Hill p.c.).

NOLICHUCKY River (Tenn., Unicoi Co.) \nō´ li chuk ē\. Perhaps from the name of a Cherokee (Iroquoian) town, <Na-na-tsu-gun>, meaning 'spruce tree place' (M. Toomey p.c.). The name occurs in abbreviated form as the **Little Chucky River** (N.C., Greene Co.).

NOLITNA Creek (Alaska, Bettles A-5) \nō lit´ nə\. An incorrect copying of *Notina,* recorded in 1958, reflecting Koyukon (Athabaskan) *notəyə no'* 'activity-place creek' (Kari 2000:195).

NOLLESEMIC Lake (Maine, Penobscot Co.). Said to be from Abnaki (Algonquian), meaning 'resting place at falls above the long stretch' (Huden 1962).

NOMAHEGAN Brook (N.J., Union Co.). Probably from Delaware (Algonquian), but the derivation is not clear (Becker 1964).

NOME (Alaska, Nome C-1). Perhaps from Iñupiaq (Eskimo) *nuum,* relative case of *nuuk,* an old village site, meaning 'point'; expressions relating a place to *nuuk* would use the form *nuum* plus a positional noun (L. Kaplan p.c.). A competing story is that it is an error for English *name,* written where a name was to be inserted on a map.

NOME-LACKEE (Calif., Tehama Co.) \nōm lä´ kē\. Also written <Nomlaki>, the name of a people also called the Central Wintun. The term is probably from /nom/ 'west' plus a form of the verb 'speak' (Gudde 1998).

NOMINI (Va., Westmoreland Co.). The name refers to a CAC Algonquian subgroup (Hagemann 1988).

NOMWAKET Creek (Calif., Shasta Co.) \nōm´ wä kət\. Wintu /nomwaqat/, lit. 'west creek', from /nom/ 'west' and /waqa̩t/ 'creek' (Gudde 1998).

NONACOICUS Brook (Mass., Middlesex Co.). The SNEng. Algonquian name may mean 'dry earth' (Huden 1962); cf. <nunoh> 'dry' (W. Cowan p.c.).

NONAMESSET Island (Mass., Dukes Co.) \non´ ə mes ət\. From SNEng. Algonquian, of unclear derivation (Huden 1962).

NONANTUM (Mass., Middlesex Co.) \nō nan´ tum\. Said to be from SNEng. Algonquian, meaning 'I rejoice' (Huden 1962). The same name is apparently reflected in the writing **Nonatum Mills** (Del., New Castle Co.).

NONDALTON (Alaska, Iliamna D-5) \non däl´ tən\. From Dena'ina (Athabaskan) *nuvendaltun, nuvendaltin, nundaltin* 'lake extends across' (Kari and Kari 1982:17).

NONEWAUG River (Conn., Litchfield Co.). Also written as <Nunnawauk, Nanawaug> (etc.); the SNEng. Algonquian name may be from <nunohohke> 'dry land', derived from <nunoh> 'dry' and <-ohke> 'land' (Trumbull 1881; W. Cowan p.c.).

NONOTUCK Park (Mass., Bristol Co.). Probably from SNEng. Algonquian <noe-> 'middle' (reduplicated) plus <-tuck> 'tidal stream' (Huden 1962; W. Cowan p.c.).

NONQUIT Pond (R.I., Newport Co.). Formerly written <Nonequit>; perhaps from SNEng. Algonquian *nannogkuit* 'southwest' (W. Cowan p.c.).

NONQUITT (Mass., Bristol Co.). Perhaps from SNEng. Algonquian, meaning 'dry place' (Huden 1962).

NONVIANUK Lake (Alaska, Mt. Katmai D-5). The Yupik (Eskimo) name was reported in 1951 (Orth 1967).

NOOKACHAMPS Creek (Wash., Skagit Co.). Lushootseed (Salishan) /dúq^{w}əčàbš/ 'people of the Nookachamps River', from /dúq^{w}ač/, the name of the river (D. Kinkade p.c.); the English name shows the alternation of *n* with *d* that is characteristic of languages in the area.

NOOKATI Creek (Alaska, Baird Mountains A-5). The Iñupiaq (Eskimo) name was reported in 1955 (Orth 1967).

NOOKSACK (Wash., Whatcom Co.) \nŏŏk´ sak\. From the Nooksack (Salishan) placename [nəx^{w}sə́ʔeq], [nəx^{w}sə́:q], [x^{w}sə́:q] 'place of bracken roots', containing /nəx^{w}-/ 'place' and /sə́ʔeq/ 'bracken roots' (Hitchman 1985; D. Kinkade p.c.).

NOONDAY, Chief (Mich., Barry Co.). This was the English name of an Ottawa (Algonquian) leader in the early nineteenth century. His Native American name was represented as <Nau-on-qual-que-zhick, Nau-qua-ga-sheek, Nawequa Geezhig> (etc.) (Vogel 1986); cf. Ottawa /naawkweg/ 'be noon' (Rhodes 1985).

NOONUKLOOK Mountain (Alaska, De Long Mountains D-4). Iñupiaq (Eskimo) *nunagluk* 'bad land', from *nuna* 'land' plus *-luk* 'bad' (Orth 1967; Webster and Zibell 1970).

NOORAVLOAKSMIUT Island (Alaska, Nunivak Is. A-2). The Yupik (Eskimo) name was obtained in 1949 (Orth 1967). The suffix *-miut* means 'people'.

NOORVIK (Alaska, Selawik D-5) \nŏŏr´ vik\. Iñupiaq (Eskimo) *nuurvik,* lit. 'moving place', from *nuut-* 'move to another dwelling' plus *-vik* 'place' (L. Kaplan p.c.).

NOOSENECK (R.I., Bristol Co.). The SNEng. Algonquian name may mean 'place of the beaver' (Huden 1962).

NOOTAS Hill (R.I., Newport Co.). Probably from SNEng. Algonquian <m'nootash> 'baskets' (Huden 1962, W. Cowan p.c.).

NOPAH Range (Calif., Inyo Co.) \nō´ pä\. Said to mean 'no water', a hybrid of English *no* and Southern Paiute (Numic) *paa-* 'water' (Gudde 1998). Similar names include **Weepah** and **Windypah** (both in Nev., Esmeralda Co.).

NOPAL (Tex., Presidio Co.) \nō´ pal\. The Mexican Spanish word refers to the prickly pear cactus, from Nahuatl (Aztecan) *nopalli* (Tarpley 1980). **Nopaleras Creek** (Tex., Jim Wells Co.) \nō pə lâr´ əs\. is Spanish for 'little patches of prickly pear cactus'.

NOQUEBAY Lake (Wisc., Marinette Co.). A variant of **Nocquebay** (Wis., Marinette Co.); cf. also **Noquet** below.

NOQUET \nok ā\. A French spelling for a division of the Ojibwa (Algonquian) people, probably from /nookkee/ 'Bear Clan' (Vogel 1986; *HNAI* 15:770). The term is no longer used as a placename, but see **Bay de Noc** (Mich., Delta Co.) and **Nocquebay Lake** (Wis., Marinette Co.) above.

NOQUOCHOKE Lake (Mass., Bristol Co.). Probably contains SNEng. Algonquian <nohk-> 'soft' and <-auke> 'land' (Huden 1962; W. Cowan p.c.).

NORAK (Alaska, Kenai D-2). Perhaps from Dena'ina (Athabaskan); the name became official in 1936 (Orth 1967).

NORKOK Butte (Wyo., Fremont Co.). Named for a Shoshoni (Numic) man called <Noikot> 'black hawk' (Urbanek 1974).

NORMANOCK (N.J., Sussex Co.). Perhaps from a Delaware (Algonquian) word meaning 'fishing place' (Becker 1964). Variant writings are **Namanock Island** and **Normanook.**

NORONEKE Lake (Conn., Fairfield Co.). Perhaps from Mahican (Algonquian), meaning 'dry land' (Huden 1962).

NOROTON (Conn., Fairfield Co.). The SNEng. Algonquian name has the related forms **Roawayton** or **Roatan**, of unclear derivation (Trumbull 1881).

NORRIDGEWOCK (Maine, Somerset Co.) \nôr´ ij wok\. Perhaps from Abenaki (Algonquian), 'where a swift river descends' (Huden 1962). The placename is also found in N.Y. (Herkimer Co.).

NORUMBEGA (Maine, Hancock Co.) \nôr əm bā´ gə\. The name was used by Europeans as early as 1550 to label a large area of New England; this resembles a Latinized form of the name *Norway* (Huden 1962). An even earlier recording of 1524, however, shows it as <Aranbega>, probably from Penobscot (Algonquian) /alɑ́məpek^{W}/ 'underneath a body of water', containing /-pek^{W}/ 'body of water' (Siebert 1943:504). The placename **Norumbega** also occurs in Mass. (Middlesex Co.).

NORUTAK, Lake (Alaska, Hughes D-3). The Iñupiaq (Eskimo) name is *nauyatuuq* 'gull lake' (Orth 1967; Burch 1998); cf. *nauyaq* 'gull' (MacLean 1980).

NORWALK (Conn., Fairfield Co.) \nôr´ wôk\. Perhaps from SNEng. Algonquian <naiaug> 'a point of land', containing <nai-> 'corner, angle', <auke> 'land' (W. Cowan p.c.); cf. Proto-Algonquian */ne:ya:-/ 'to be pointed' (I. Goddard p.c.). The name **Norwalk** has been transferred to several other states (e.g., Iowa, Warren Co.; Calif., Los Angeles Co.). Possibly related forms are **Noyack** (N.Y., Suffolk Co.) and **Nyack** (N.Y., Rockland Co.).

NORWOTTOCK, Mountain (Mass., Bristol Co.). Probably SNEng. Algonquian, meaning 'in the middle of the tidal river', from <nawa-> 'middle', <-tuk> 'tidal river' (W. Cowan p.c.).

NOSEUM (Wisc., Menominee Co.) \nō sē´ əm\. From the same source as **No-see-um**. The word is from American Indian Pidgin English, meaning 'you don't see them', referring to tiny, nearly invisible flying insects. The term has been applied in several spellings to placenames in several states: for example, **No-see-um** in Idaho (Idaho Co.) and Minn. (Lake Co.) and **Noseeum** or **Nosseum** or **Nosseeum** (Wis., Vilas Co.).

NOSONI Creek (Calif., Shasta Co.) \nə sō´ ne\. From Wintu /nosono/ 'south peak', containing /nor/ 'south' and /sono/ 'nose, peak' (Gudde 1998).

NOSSEEUM (Wisc., Vilas Co.) \nō sē ´ əm\. From the same source as **Noseum**; see above. Another variant spelling is **Nosseum**.

NOSSUK BAY (Alaska, Craig C-5). The name, probably Tlingit, was assigned in 1914 (Orth 1967).

NOTAKOK Mountain (Alaska, Nulato B-6). The Yupik (Eskimo) name was reported in 1939 (Orth 1967).

NOTASULGA (Ala., Macon Co.) \nō tə sul´ gə\. Possibly from Muskogee *nute-sulke* /notisólk-i/, lit. 'teeth-many', or from *notoss-vlke* /notoss-âlki/, lit. 'angelica-group', from *notossa* 'angelica' (Read 1984; Martin and Mauldin 2000).

NOTCH (Alaska, Nabesna A-3) \noch\. Perhaps an abbreviation from Upper Tanaina (Athabaskan) *nach'itąy niig,* lit. 'trail-across stream' (J. Kari p.c.).

NOTCHAWAY (Ga., Baker Co.) \noch´ ə wā\. Probably a shortening of **Ichawaynochaway** (Ga., Baker Co.), perhaps from Muskogee, meaning 'deer sleeping' (Martin and Mauldin 2000).

NOTONIONO Creek (Alaska, Hughes A-1). The Koyukon (Athabaskan) name is probably *notonee'o no'* 'water-extends-across stream' (J. Kari p.c.).

NOT TAK Tank (Ariz., Pima Co.). Probably from O'odham (Piman) *nod̦* 'prickly poppy' plus *tak* 'sitting' or *tatk* 'root' (J. Hill p.c.).

NOTTAWA (Mich., St. Joseph Co.) \not´ ə wā, not´ ə wä, not´ ə wə\. From an Algonquian term referring to neighboring Iroquoian and Siouan peoples, reconstructed as proto-Algonquian */na:towe:wa/ (*HNAI* 15:289); cf. Ojibwa /naadwe/ (Rhodes 1985). **Nottaway River** (N.C., Hertford Co.; Va., Southampton Co.) specifically reflects an Algonquian name for an Iroquoian group of N.C.; a variant spelling is **Nottoway.** Related placenames are **Nodaway** (Iowa, Adams Co.), **Nadawah** (Ala., Monroe Co.), and **Nadoway Point** (Mich., Chippewa Co.).

NOTTELY River (Ga., Union Co.; N.C., Cherokee Co.). From a Cherokee (Iroquoian) village name, <Naduhli> (Read 1949–50).

NOTTOWAY County (Va.) \not´ ə wā\. From the same source as **Nottawa** (Mich., St. Joseph Co.); see above. The name **Nottoway** also occurs in N.C. (Hertford Co.) and La. (Iberville Par.).

NOVAKAKET Island (Alaska, Ruby D-3) \nō´ vē kak ət\. The Koyukon (Athabaskan) placename, probably meaning 'mouth of the Nowitna River', was reported around 1952 (Orth 1967); cf. *nogheet no'* 'Nowitna River', lit. 'frog river', *-kaakk'et* 'mouth of stream' (Jetté and Jones 2000). Related placenames include **Nowi** and **Nowitna River** (Alaska, Ruby D-3); see below.

NOVATAK Glacier (Alaska, Yakutat B-2). The word was coined from Latin *nova* 'new' plus *nunatak* 'glacier island', borrowed into English from West Greenlandic Eskimo (Orth 1967; *RHD* 1987). A related placename is **Nunatak Cove** (Alaska, Mt. Fairweather D-1); see below.

NOWADAGA Creek (N.Y., Herkimer Co.) \nō´ wə dô gə\. Perhaps shortened from Iroquoian <Canowedage> 'village of mud turtles' (Beauchamp 1907); cf. Seneca *ka'no:wa'* 'turtle rattle' (Chafe 1967).

NOWATA County (Okla.) \nō´ wä tə, nō wä´ tə\. The name is said to be from a Unami Delaware (Algonquian) expression meaning 'welcome'; the Native American form may be /no:wi:t:i/ 'come here, little one' (I. Goddard p.c.).

NOWI (Alaska, Ruby D-3) \nō´ vē\. An abbreviation of **Novakaket Island**; see above.

NOWISKAY Cove (Alaska, Craig A-1). Said to be named in 1897 for an Indian, perhaps Tlingit, named <Nowisk-Kay> (Orth 1967).

NOWITNA River (Alaska, Ruby D-3) \nō wit´ nə\. Koyukon (Athabaskan) *nogheet no',* perhaps meaning 'frog river' (Jetté and Jones 2000). A related place name is **Novakaket Island** (Alaska, Ruby D-3); see above.

NOXAPAGA River (Alaska, Bendeleben B-5). The Iñupiaq (Eskimo) name is *naqsram paaga* 'mouth of the *naqsraq* river' (L. Kaplan p.c.).

NOXAPATER (Miss., Winston Co.) \nok sə pā´ tə\. Perhaps from Choctaw (Muskogean) *naki-chipi̱to* 'bullet', from *naki* 'lead, bullet' plus *chipi̱to* 'small', as contrasted with *naki-chitto* 'big bullet, i.e. cannonball' (Seale 1939; P. Munro p.c.).

NOXOBE (Ark., Columbia Co.). From the same source as **Noxubee County** (Miss.); see below.

NOXUBEE County (Miss.) \nok´ sə bē\. Perhaps shortened from Choctaw (Muskogean) *oka nakshobi* 'stinking water', from *oka* 'water' and *nakshobi* 'to stink' (Seale 1939; P. Munro p.c.). The placename also occurs in Ala. (Sumter Co.), where the pronunciation [nok´ shoo͞ob ē] is reported.

NOYACK (N.Y., Suffolk Co.) \noi´ ak\. Probably from SNEng. Algonquian <naiag> 'point, corner' (Tooker 1911); cf. Proto-Algonquian */ne:ya:-/ 'to be pointed' (I. Goddard p.c.). Perhaps related placenames are **Norwalk** (Conn., Fairfield Co.) and **Nyack** (N.Y., Rockland Co.).

NOYO (Calif., Mendocino Co.) \noi´ yō\. From a Northern Pomo village name, containing /nó/ 'dust, ashes' and /yow/ 'under, in' (Gudde 1998).

NUAKFUPPA Creek (Miss., Jasper Co.). Perhaps from Chickasaw (Muskogean) *nokfapa'* 'mudcat, a kind of fish' (P. Munro p.c.).

NUBANUSIT Brook (N.H., Hillsborough Co.) \noo͞ bə noo͞´ sit\. Perhaps from Abenaki (Algonquian), containing <niben-> 'summer' (Huden 1962; W. Cowan p.c.).

NUCEFAPPA (Miss., Jasper Co.). Possibly from Choctaw (Muskogean) *nossassapi* 'oak trees' (Seale 1939; P. Munro p.c.).

NUCHEK (Alaska, Cordova B-8) \noo͞´ chek\. From the Alutiiq (Eskimo) placename *nuuciq* (Kari 1983:2).

NUEKSHAT Island (Alaska, Harrison Bay B-1). The Iñupiaq (Eskimo) name is probably *nuiqsat* 'things that were speared' (L. Kaplan p.c.).

NUGNUGALUKTUK River (Alaska, Kotzebue A-5). The Iñupiaq (Eskimo) name is *liġliġnaqtuuġvik* (Burch 1998).

NUHINIK Creek (Alaska, Killik River A-2). The Iñupiaq (Eskimo) name was recorded in 1956 (Orth 1967).

NUIGALAK Lake (Alaska, Marshall C-8). The Yupik (Eskimo) name was reported in 1951 as <Nu-ig-ga-luk> (Orth 1967).

NUIQSUT (Alaska, Harrison Bay A-2). From the Iñupiaq (Eskimo) placename *nuiqsat*, probably with the original meaning of 'trident bird-spear' (L. Kaplan p.c.).

NUITA Lake (N.Dak., Dunn Co.). From Mandan (Siouan) /rų́'eta/ [nų́ʔeta], a subgroup that lived on the west bank of the Missouri in the early nineteenth century. In the late twentieth century the name was generalized to designate the entire Mandan people on the Fort Berthold Reservation (D. Parks p.c.).

NUKA Bay (Alaska, Seldovia B-2) \noo͞´ kə\. From Alutiiq (Eskimo), 'young caribou' (Orth 1967; Jacobson 1984).

NUKATPIAT Mountain (Alaska, Killik River A-5). The Iñupiaq (Eskimo) name is *nukatpiat* 'young men' (L. Kaplan p.c.).

NUKDIK Point (Alaska, Skagway A-2). The Tlingit name, published in 1923, is said to mean 'young grouse' (Orth 1967); cf. *núkt* 'male grouse' (Davis and Leer 1976).

NUKLAUKET Pass (Alaska, Tanana C-6). From Koyukon (Athabaskan) <Nyklukayet>. The modern form was reported in 1956 (Orth 1967); it is related to **Nuklukayet**, below.

NUKLUGALUK Creek (Alaska, Goodnews Bay C-6). The Yupik (Eskimo) name was published in 1951 (Orth 1967).

NUKLUKAYET (Alaska, Tanana A-5). The Koyukon (Athabaskan) name is *noo chugh loghoyet* 'end of the big island' (Jetté & Jones 2000).

NUKLUK Creek (Alaska, Goodnews Bay C-6). The Yupik (Eskimo) name was recorded in 1898 as <Nuchluk> (Orth 1967).

NUKLUNEK Mountain (Alaska, Goodnews Bay D-4). The Yupik (Eskimo) name was reported in 1898 (Orth 1967).

NUKOLOWAP Point (Wash., Jefferson Co.). From the Twana (Salishan) placename /dəx^{w}1əwáp/, lit. 'place of the inlet', containing /dəx^{w}-/ 'locative', /láw-/ 'enter', and /-ap/ 'end' (D. Kinkade p.c.). The English form shows the alternation of *n* and *d* that is characteristic of Indian languages in the region.

NUKSHAK Island (Alaska, Mt. Katmai B-1). The Yupik (Eskimo) name was published by Russians in 1847 as <Nukhshak> (Orth 1967).

NULARVIK River (Alaska, Mt. Michelson D-3). The Iñupiaq (Eskimo) name was reported in 1956 as meaning 'place where a tent stood' (Orth 1967); cf. *nullaq-* 'to set up camp for the night', *-vik* 'place' (MacLean 1980). Possibly related placenames iinclude **Nulavik** (Alaska, Barrow A-5); see below.

NULATO (Alaska, Nulato C-5) \noo lä´ tō, noo lat´ ō\. Koyukon (Athabaskan) *noolaaghe doh* 'preceding the dog-salmon' (i.e., a fish camp for dog-salmon), from *noolaaghe* 'dog-salmon' (Orth 1967; Jetté and Jones 2000).

NULAVIK (Alaska, Barrow A-5). The Iñupiaq (Eskimo) name was recorded around 1950 as meaning 'camping place' (Orth 1967); cf. *nullaq-* 'to set up camp' (MacLean 1980). A possibly related placename is **Nullaq Lake** (Alaska, Misheguk Mountain D-2). Other possibly related placenames include **Nularvik River** (Alaska, Mt. Michelson D-3).

NULEARGOWIK River (Alaska, Selawik C-2). The Iñupiaq (Eskimo) name is *nuliaġvik*, said to be the eleventh month of the Iñupiaq year, when deer cohabit (Orth 1967; Burch 1998).

NULHEDUS Mountain (Maine, Somerset Co.). The Abenaki (Algonquian) name is said to mean 'fall on each side' (Huden 1962).

NULHEGAN (Vt., Essex Co.). The Abenaki (Algonquian) name is said to mean 'my log-trap' or 'deadfall' (Huden 1962); cf. *gelahigan* 'deadfall trap' (Day 1994–95).

NULITNA River (Alaska, Kateel River D-2). The Koyukon (Athabaskan) name was obtained in 1955 (Orth 1967).

NULLAQ Lake (Alaska, Misheguk Mountain D-2). The Iñupiaq (Eskimo) name, made official in BGN 8402, is said to mean 'this is the place we stay or camp tonight'; cf. *nullaq-* 'to set up camp' (MacLean 1980). A possibly related placename is **Nulavik** (Alaska, Barrow A-5); see above.

NULUK River (Alaska, Teller D-4). The Iñupiaq (Eskimo) name was reported in 1901 as <Nooluk> (Orth 1967).

NULVORORОК Lake (Alaska, Selawik D-6). The Iñupiaq (Eskimo) name was reported in 1955 (Orth 1967).

NUMA Creek (Mont., Flathead Co.) \noo´ mə\. Perhaps from the surname of a Kutenai family, but ultimately from Kutenai <numa> 'thunder' (Holterman 1985).

NUMANA (Nev., Washoe Co.). From Northern Paiute (Numic), perhaps meaning 'the people's father', containing /nɨmɨ/ 'person, Indian' and /naa/ 'father' (Carlson 1974; J. McLaughlin p.c.).

NUMMY Island (N.J., Cape May Co.). Said to be named for a Delaware (Algonquian) leader; his name was also written <Na-mahomie> (Becker 1964).

NUNABIKLU Slough (Alaska, Kwiguk D-4). The Yupik (Eskimo) name was recorded in 1948 (Orth 1967).

NUNACHIK Pass (Alaska, Kwiguk D-4). The Yupik (Eskimo) name was reported in 1899 (Orth 1967).

NUNACHUAK (Alaska, Dillingham C-3) \noo nə choo´ äk\. The Yupik (Eskimo) name was reported in 1930 (Orth 1967).

NUNACHUK (Alaska, Baird Inlet D-2). The Yupik (Eskimo) name was reported in 1950 (Orth 1967).

NUNA Creek (Alaska, Ambler River B-5) \noo´ nə\. The Iñupiaq (Eskimo) name, reported in 1877, may be a shortening of a word beginning with *nuna* 'land, earth' (Orth 1967; MacLean 1980).

NUNAKA Valley (Alaska, Anchorage A-8) \noo nak´ ə\. The Dena'ina (Athabaskan) name is *nungge* 'upland area' (J. Kari p.c.).

NUNAKOGOK River (Alaska, St. Michael A-1). The Yupik (Eskimo) name was reported in 1952 (Orth 1967).

NUNAKTUK Island (Alaska, St. Michael A-6). The Yupik (Eskimo) name was reported in 1952 (Orth 1967).

NUNAMIUT (Alaska, Kodiak A-5). The Alutiiq (Eskimo) name consists of *nuna* 'land' plus *-miut* 'people' (Orth 1967; Leer 1978). A probably related placename is **Nunamuit Mountain** (Alaska, Chandler Lake A-4), for Iñupiaq (Eskimo) *nunamiut* 'land people', from *nuna* 'land' plus *-miut* 'people' (MacLean 1980).

NUNAPITCHUK (Alaska, Baird Inlet D-2) \no͞o nup´ i cho͞ok\. Yupik (Eskimo) *nunapicuaq,* lit. 'little tundra', from *nunapik* 'tundra' (Jacobson 1984).

NUNAPITSINCHAK (Alaska, Bethel D-7). Yupik (Eskimo) *nunapic'ngaq* 'little tundra', from *nunapik* 'tundra' (Jacobson 1984).

NUNATAK Cove (Alaska, Mt. Fairweather D-1). The word means 'glacier island', borrowed into English from West Greenlandic Eskimo *nunataq* (Orth 1967; *RHD* 1967). A related placename is **Novatak Glacier** (Alaska, Yakutat B-2).

NUNATHLOOGAGAMIUT (Alaska, Cape Mendenhall D-3). The Yupik (Eskimo) name was reported in 1942 (Orth 1967). The suffix *-miut* means 'people'. A related placename is the nearby **Nunathloogagamiutbingoi Dunes.**

NUNAVACHAK Lake (Alaska, Hagemeister Is. D-1). The Yupik (Eskimo) name, reported in 1948, means 'small lake' (Orth 1967); cf. *nanvaq* 'island' (Jacobson 1984).

NUNAVAKANUK Lake (Alaska, Kwiguk A-6). The Yupik (Eskimo) name was reported in 1948 (Orth 1967); perhaps a derivative of *nanvaq* 'island' (Jacobson 1984). An apparently related name, **NUNAVAKANUKAKSLAK Lake** (Alaska, Baird Inlet D-1) was reported in 1949 (Orth 1967).

NUNAVAK Bay (Alaska, Barrow B-4). The Iñupiak (Eskimo) word, reported in 1950, is said to mean 'big land' (Orth 1967), from *nuna* 'land' (Webster and Zibell 1970).

NUNAVAKPAK Lake (Alaska, Baird Inlet D-2). The Yupik (Eskimo) name was reported in 1949 (Orth 1967), probably derived from *nanvaq* 'island' (Jacobson 1984).

NUNAVIKSAK Creek (Alaska, Misheguk Mountain B-4). The Iñupiaq (Eskimo) name was reported in 1956 (Orth 1967).

NUNDA (N.Y., Livingston Co.) \nun´ dā\. Perhaps from Seneca (Iroquoian) <nun-da´-o> 'hilly' (Beauchamp 1907). The placename occurs as a transfer in Ill. (McHenry Co.), Mich. (Cheboygan Co.), and Minn. (Freeborn Co.).

NUNDEI Cave (Alaska, Craig D-4). The Tlingit name was published in 1964 (Orth 1967).

NUNGATAK River (Alaska, Marshall C-8). The Yupik (Eskimo) name was reported in 1949 (Orth 1967).

NUNGEE Brook (Mass., Bristol Co.). Probably from SNEng. Algonquian <nunnuke> 'he trembles' (Huden 1962; W. Cowan p.c.).

NUNICA (Mich., Ottawa Co.). The name has been said to come from Ojibwa (Algonquian) <menonica> 'clay for pottery', but the derivation has not been confirmed (Vogel 1986).

NUNIVACHAK Island (Alaska, Nunivak Is. D-1). The Yupik (Eskimo) name was recorded in 1951 (Orth 1967); it is probably derived from **Nunivak;** see below.

NUNIVAK (Alaska, Nunivak Is. A-4) \no͞o´ ni vak\. From the Yupik (Eskimo) placename *nunivaaq* (Jacobson 1984). **Nunivak Slough** (Alaska, Fairbanks C-5) is named for a boat called the *Nunivak,* named in turn after the island (Orth 1967).

NUNNA (Okla., McCurtain Co.) \nun´ ə\. From Choctaw (Muskogean) *nona* 'cooked' (Shirk 1974; P. Munro p.c.).

NUNNEPOG (Mass., Dukes Co.). Probably from SNEng. Algonquian <nanni-> 'fresh water' plus <-pog> 'pond' (Trumbull 1879; W. Cowan p.c.).

NUNSATUK River (Alaska, Iditarod B-1) \nun´ sə tuk\. From Deg Hit'an (Athabaskan) *nents'ididikno'* 'where we spend time' (Kari 1999:84).

NUNTRAGUT Slough (Alaska, Fort Yukon C-4). The Gwich'in (Athabaskan) name was reported in 1956 (Orth 1967).

NUNVOTCHUK Lake (Alaska, Russian Mission D-7). The Yupik (Eskimo) name was recorded in 1949 (Orth 1967).

NUOK Spit (Alaska, Hooper Bay B-3). The Yupik (Eskimo) name was reported in 1951 (Orth 1967).

NURIVA (W.Va., Wyoming Co.) \nōō rī´ və\. This is locally thought to be an Indian name, but the language of origin has not been identified (Kenny 1945).

NUSHAGAK River (Alaska, Dillingham A-7) \nōō´ shə gak\. The Yupik (Eskimo) name was recorded around 1809 (Orth 1967).

NUSHKA Lake (Minn., Cass Co.) \nŏŏsh´ kə\. The word occurs in Longfellow's *Hiawatha* and is said to be an Ojibwa (Algonquian) exclamation, meaning 'look!' (Upham 2001); cf. *nashke* 'look!' (Nichols and Nyholm 1995).

NUSHKOLIK Mountain (Alaska, Marshall C-8). The Yupik (Eskimo) name was reported in 1951 (Orth 1967).

NUSHRALUTAK Creek (Alaska, Ambler River D-1). The Iñupiaq (Eskimo) name is *naqsraġluqtuaq*, said to mean 'rough divide in the mountains' (Orth 1967; Burch 1998).

NUSKEALIK Lake (Alaska, Marshall B-7). The Yupik (Eskimo) name was reported in 1951 (Orth 1967).

NUTIRWIK Creek (Alaska, Chandalar D-6). Said to be the name of an Iñupiaq (Eskimo) man, known in English as Harry Snowden (Orth 1967).

NUTKWA Point (Alaska, Craig A-2). The Tlingit name was reported in 1897 (Orth 1967).

NUTMOYUK Creek (Alaska, Bendeleben B-1). The Iñupiaq (Eskimo) name was published in 1903 (Orth 1967).

NUTUVUKTI Lake (Alaska, Hughes D-4). The Koyukon (Athabaskan) name was published in 1900 as <Now-tow-vuk-toy>, and in 1887 as <Nor-to-rok-tee> or <Nor-tah-rok-tah> (Orth 1967).

NUTZOTIN (Alaska, Nabesna A-2) \nōō zō´ tin, noot´ sə tin\. From an Athabaskan ethnonym *nuuts'e hwt'een* 'people from upstream' (J. Kari p.c.).

NUVAGAPAK Point (Alaska, Demarcation Point D-3). The Iñupiaq (Eskimo) name, recorded in 1952, is said to mean 'big point' (Orth 1967); cf. **Nuwuk** below.

NUWUK (Alaska, Barrow B-4) \nōō´ wuk\. From Iñupiaq (Eskimo) *nuvuk* 'tip, point' (Orth 1967; MacLean 1980). Probably related placenames include **Noak** (Alaska, Noatak A-3).

NUYAKA (Okla., Okmulgee Co.) \nōō yä´ kə\. From Muskogee *nuyakv* /nuyá:ka/ (Martin and Mauldin 2000). The name represents a transfer of **New Yorka** (Ga., Heard Co.), the site of a Muskogee village, perhaps named after New York City. A related placename is **Niuyaka** (Ala., Tallapoosa Co.).

NUYAKUK River (Alaska, Dillingham D-4). The Yupik (Eskimo) name was reported in 1910 (Orth 1967).

NUZIAMUND Lake (Alaska, Tanacross A-4) \nōō zē ä´ mund\. From Upper Tanana (Athabaskan) *nuudh'ąą mënn'*, lit. 'timber-grove-is-there'. A related name is **Nuziamundcho Lake** (Alaska, Tanacross A-3), with added *choh* 'big' (J. Kari p.c.).

NYACK (N.Y., Rockland Co.) \nī´ ak\. Perhaps from Munsee Delaware (Algonquian), meaning 'a point, a corner' (Ruttenber 1906); cf. Proto-Algonquian */ne:ya:-/ 'to be pointed' (I. Goddard p.c.). The placename **Nyack** occurs as a transfer in several states (e.g., Kans., Crawford Co.; and Mont., Flathead Co.). Possibly related placenames are **Norwalk** (Conn., Fairfield Co.) and **Noyack** (N.Y., Suffolk Co.).

O

OACOMA (S.Dak., Lyman Co.) \ō ə kō´ mə\. From Lakhota (Siouan) *okó ogná* 'in between', lit. 'in the space' (Sneve 1973; B. Ingham p.c.).

OAHE (S.Dak., Hughes Co.) \ō wä´ hē\. From Dakota (Siouan) *oáhe, owáhe* 'foundation, something to stand on' (Sneve 1973; Riggs 1890).

OAHU Island (N.Y., Warren Co.) \ō ä´ hōō\. Probably named for the island in Hawai'i; the Hawai'ian name is *O'ahu* (Pukui et al. 1974). The placename also occurs in Mich. (Oakland Co.).

OAKACHICKAN (Miss., Yalobusha Co.). A variant of **Okachickima Creek** (see below) as well as of **Oka Achukma** (Okla., McCurtain Co.), both from Choctaw (Muskogean) for 'good water' (Seale 1939).

OAKACHOY Creek (Ala., Coosa Co.) \ō kə choi´\. Perhaps from the same source as **Oakchia** (Ala., Choctaw Co.); see **Oakchi Landing** below.

OAKAHALLA (Ala., Walker Co.). Perhaps from Choctaw (Muskogean) *oklah* 'people' (P. Munro p.c.).

OAKAHAY Creek (Miss., Covington Co.). A variant of **Oakohay Creek;** see below.

OAKCHICKAMAU (Miss., Yalobusha Co.) \ōk chik´ ə mô\. A variant of **Okachickima Creek;** see below.

OAKCHIHOOLA (Ala., Talladega Co.) \ōk chē hōō´ lə\. Perhaps from Muskogee *okcaye* /okčá:yi/, a tribal town (cf. **Oakchi Landing,** below), plus <yahola>, the 'black drink' (Read 1984; Martin and Mauldin 2000).

OAKCHI Landing (Ala., Marengo Co.). Perhaps from the same source as **Oakchia** (Ala., Choctaw Co.). This is probably from Muskogee *okcaye* /okčá:yi/, the name of a tribal town (Read 1984; Martin and Mauldin 2000). A possibly related placename is **Oakachoy Creek** (Ala., Coosa Co.).

OAKCHINAWA Creek (Ala., Talladega Co.). From Muskogee *okcvnwv* /okčánwa/ 'salt' (Martin and Mauldin 2000).

OAKCHOY (Ala., Coosa Co.). Perhaps from the same source as **Oakchia** (Ala., Choctaw Co.); see **Oakchi Landing** above.

OAKFUSKEE (Ala., Cleburne Co.) \ōk fus´ kē\. From Muskogee *akfvske* /akfáski/, the name of a tribal town, perhaps meaning 'a point of land between streams' (Read 1984; Martin and Mauldin 2000). The placename also occurs in Ga. (Pike Co.). A related form is **Okfuskee County** (Okla.). A related placename is **Oakfuskudshi** (Ala., Tallapoosa Co.), the Muskogee diminutive, with *oce* /očí/'little' (Martin and Mauldin 2000).

OAKLASAUSA (Ala., Tallapoosa Co.) \ōk lə sô´ sə\. Perhaps from the same source as **Oaktasasi;** see below.

OAKLIMETAL (Miss., Benton Co.). A variant of **Oaklimeter Creek** (Miss., Benton Co.). This is from Choctaw (Muskogean), meaning 'young people', from *oklah* 'people', *himmita* 'young' (Seale 1939; P. Munro p.c.).

OAKMULGEE (Ala., Perry Co.) \ōk mul´ gē\. Probably from Hitchiti (Muskogean) /oki/ 'water' plus /molki/ 'boiling, bubbling' (Read 1984; J. Martin p.c.). Related placenames are **Ocmulgee** (Ga., Pulaski Co.) and **Okmulgee County** (Okla.).

OAKOHAY Creek (Miss., Covington Co.) \ō´ kə hā\. From Choctaw (Muskogean), meaning 'water potato', perhaps referring to a wild edible root or tuber; from *oka* 'water' and *ahi* 'potato' (Seale 1939; P. Munro p.c.). Variant spellings include **Oakahay** and **Okahay.**

OAK Ridge (Ariz., Apache Co.). Corresponds to Navajo (Athabaskan) *tséch'il yílk'id,* lit. 'oak hill', from *tséch'il* 'oak' (*tsé* 'rock', *ch'il* 'plant') plus *yiílk'id* 'hill' (Wilson 1995).

OAKTARK, Bayou (Miss., Oktibbeha Co.). Perhaps from Choctaw (Muskogean) <hohtak> 'pond' (Seale 1939; Byington 1918).

OAKTASASI (Ala., Tallapoosa Co.) \ōk tə sä´ sē\. From Muskogee *oktahv-sasv* /okta:ha-sá:sa/ 'where there is some sand', from *oktahv* 'sand' (Read 1984; Martin and Mauldin 2000). A probably related placename is **Oaklasausa**. Also probably related is the nearby placename **Oaktazaza**.

OAKTOMIE (Miss., Covington Co.). Perhaps from Choctaw (Muskogean) *oktohbi* 'fog' (Cushman 1899, P. Munro p.c.).

OATKA (N.Y., Wyoming Co.) \ō at´ kə\. Said to be from Iroquoian, meaning 'the opening' (Beauchamp 1907).

OBADASH Lake (Wis., Iron Co.). Apparently abbreviated from Ojibwa (Algonquian) *oboodashkwaanishiinh* 'dragonfly' (Vogel 1991; Nichols and Nyholm 1995). A related placename is **Bobidosh Lake** (Wis., Vilas Co.).

OBION County (Tenn.) \ō´ bē on\. Named after the **Obion River,** said to be an Indian word meaning 'many forks', from an unidentified language (McClaren 1991:19).

OBI Point (Ariz., Coconino Co.) \ō´bē\. Southern Paiute (Numic) /opi/ [ovi] 'wood, trees' (J. McLaughlin p.c.).

OBLARON Creek (Alaska, Selawik C-3). The Iñupiaq (Eskimo) name was recorded in 1955 (Orth 1967).

OBWEBETUCK (Conn., Windham Co.). Earlier forms are <Ocquebituck, Auquebatuck, Owibetuck>, perhaps from a SNEng. Algonquian word meaning 'top of a tree' (Trumbull 1881).

OCALA (Fla., Marion Co.). Perhaps from a village name of the Timucua people (Read 1934). The name also occurs in Miss. (Tippah Co.). The possibly related name **Okalla Station** is found in Ind. (Putnam Co.).

OCAW (Tex., McLennan Co.) \ō kou`\. A backward spelling of **Waco,** from the name of a Caddoan group (Tarpley 1980).

OCCANUM (N.Y., Broome Co.) \ə kan´ əm\. Perhaps an Indian name, of unclear derivation (Beauchamp 1907).

OCCOHANNOCK Creek (Va., Accomack Co.). The placename is probably from the CAC Algonquian language, but its derivation is not clear (Hagemann 1988).

OCCOM Pond (N.H., Grafton Co.) \ok´ əm\. Probably from the same source as **Occum** (Conn., New London Co.); see below.

OCCONEECHEE Creek (N.C., Northampton Co.). The name of an Indian group; possibly from Tutelo (Siouan) <yuhkañ> 'man' (Powell 1968). The placename also occurs in Va. (Mecklenburg Co.).

OCCOOCH Pond (Mass., Dukes Co.). Perhaps from a SNEng. Algonquian word meaning 'small' (Huden 1962).

OCCOQUAN (Va., Prince William Co.). The name of a CAC Algonquian town, perhaps meaning 'at the end of the water' (Hagemann 1988).

OCCUM (Conn., New London Co.) \ok´ əm\. Named for Samson Occum (1723–92), a SNEng. Algonquian man who became a Christian preacher and worked for Indian education (Huden 1962). A related form is **Occom Pond** (N.H., Grafton Co.). The name may represent the traditional English surname *Ockham.*

OCELICHEE (Ala., Chambers Co.) \ō si lī´ chē\. An earlier writing is <O-so-li-gee>, perhaps from Muskogee *vsse* /ássi/ 'dried leaf, yaupon holly' and *licetv* /leycitá/ 'to set, to place' (Read 1984; Martin and Mauldin 2000).

OCEOLA Lake (N.Y., Westchester Co.) \ō sē ō´ lə\. From the same source as **Osceola,** the name of a famous Seminole (Muskogean) leader. The placename **Oceola** is also found in Ohio (Crawford Co.) and Ore. (Washington Co.).

OCHEDA Lake (Minn., Nobles Co.). From the same source as **Ocheyedan** (Iowa, Osceola Co.; Minn., Nobles Co.); see below. A variant is **Ocheeda.**

OCHEESEE (Fla., Calhoun Co.) \ō chē´ sē\. From Seminole (Muskogee) *ocēse* /očí:si/, the name of a village. In the related Hitchiti language, /oči:si/ means 'a Muskogee Indian' (Read 1934; J. Martin p.c.). A related name is **Ocheeseulga** (Fla., Calhoun Co.), perhaps meaning 'Ocheesee people'.

OCHELATA (Okla., Washington Co.) \ō shə lā´ tə\. Named for a nineteenth-century Cherokee (Iroquoian) leader; his English name was Charles Thompson (Shirk 1974).

OCHEYEDAN (Iowa, Osceola Co.) \ō chē´ dən\. From Dakota (Siouan) *očhéya* 'where they weep' (from *čhéya* 'to weep') plus *-dą* 'diminutive', referring to a place of mourning (Vogel 1983; J. Koontz p.c.). The placename also occurs in Minn. (Nobles Co.), sometimes written **Ocheda.** A related placename is **Okshida** (Minn., Murray Co.).

OCHILLEE (Ga., Chattahoochee Co.). Perhaps from Muskogee, meaning 'dead hickory', containing *ocē* /očí:/ 'hickory' and *elē* /ilí:/ 'dead' (Read 1949–50, Martin and Mauldin 2000); however, early records show the writings <Nochillee, Nochille> (etc.), of unclear derivation (Goff 1975). There is also an **Ochillee** in Ore. (Crook Co.).

OCHLAWILLA (Ga., Brooks Co.). Perhaps an invented term, combining Hitchiti (Muskogean) /okla/ 'people' with the *willa-* of **Willacoochee** (Ga., Atkinson Co.) (Goff 1975), from Muskogee /wi:łak-očí/ 'river-small' (Martin and Mauldin 2000); see also **Withlacoochee** (Ga., Lowndes Co.) below.

OCHLOCKNEE (Ga., Thomas Co.) \ok lok´ nē\. Hitchiti (Muskogean) /oki-lakni/ 'yellow/brown water', from /oki/ 'water' and /lakni/ 'yellow/brown' (Read 1949–50; J. Martin p.c.). The placename is also found in Fla. (Leon Co.).

OCHOCO Creek (Ore., Crook Co.) \ō´ chə kō\. Named for a Northern Paiute (Numic) leader of the nineteenth century; his name has also been written as <Ochiho> and <Hudziu> (T. Thornes p.c.).

OCHOPEE (Fla., Collier Co.) \ō chä´ pē\. From Muskogee /oča:pi/ 'field' (Read 1934; J. Martin p.c.).

OCHWALKEE (Ga., Wheeler Co.). A variant form of **Okeewalkee**; see below.

OCILLA (Ga., Irwin Co.) \ō sil´ ə\. The name of a Seminole (Muskogean) town (Goff 1975). A related placename is **Aucilla** (Ga., Thomas Co.).

OCKLAU Creek (Ga., Pulaski Co.). Perhaps shortened from Muskogee *aklowvhē* /aklowáhi:/ 'muddy' (Read 1949–50:131; Martin and Mauldin 2000). A probably related form is **Ocklawaha** (Fla., Marion Co.). From Muskogee *aklowvhē* /aklowáhi:/ 'muddy' or /aklowahí:/ 'mud' (Read 1934; Martin and Mauldin 2000).

OCKOOCANGANSET Hill (Mass., Middlesex Co.). The SNEng. Algonquian name may mean 'plowed fields place' (Huden 1962).

OCLA Draw (Wyo., Fremont Co.) \ōk´lə\. Perhaps an abbreviation of a transfer name from the southeastern United States; cf. Choctaw (Muskogean) *okla* 'water' (Urbanek 1974).

OCMULGEE (Ga., Pulaski Co.) \ōk mug´ ē, ōk mul´ gē\. Probably from Hitchiti (Muskogean) /oki/ 'water' plus /molki/ 'boiling, bubbling' (Read 1984; J. Martin p.c.). Related placenames are **Oakmulgee** (Ala., Perry Co.) and **Okmulgee County** (Okla.).

OCOBLA (Miss., Neshoba Co.). Perhaps from Choctaw (Muskogean) <akobvla> 'a bush called bird's-eye' (Seale 1939).

OCOEE River (Tenn., Polk Co.) \ō kō´ ē\. Said to be from a Cherokee (Iroqoian) placename <uwagahi> 'apricot-vine place' (Read 1934). The placename also occurs in Fla. (Orange Co.) and Ark. (Washington Co.). A related placename is **Okoee** (Okla., Craig Co.).

OCOLAKSUK Lake (Alaska, Russian Mission D-7). The Yupik (Eskimo) name was reported in 1949 (Orth 1967).

OCOME (Pa., Lycoming Co.). Perhaps from the same source as **Oconee County** (Ga.); see below.

OCONALUFTEE River (N.C., Swain Co.) \ə kon ə luf´ tē\. Said to be from the Cherokee (Iroquoian) village name <Egwanulti>, from *equoni* 'river' plus <nulati> 'near' (Powell 1968; Alexander 1971).

OCONEE County (Ga.) \ō kō´ nē\. Perhaps from a Muskogee placename written as <Oconi, Ekwoni> (etc.), said to mean 'place of springs' (Krakow 1975); cf. *uekiwv* /oykéywa/ 'a spring' (Martin and Mauldin 2000). Possibly of a separate origin is **Oconee County** in S.C.; this is said to be derived from a Cherokee (Iroquoian) village name <Ukwû´-ni> (Pearson 1978). These names seem to have been transferred to several other states (e.g., Ark., Randolph Co.; Ill., Shelby Co. \ō´ kə nē\; and Okla., Coal Co.). Possibly related placenames are **O-Co-Nee Lake** in N.Y. (Suffolk Co.), **Okome** in Pa. (Lycoming Co.), and **Okoni** in Ala. (Russell Co.).

OCONOMOWOC (Wis., Waukesha Co.) \ō kon´ ə mə wok\. Perhaps from Ojibwa (Algonquian) <okonimawag> 'beaver dam' (Vogel 1991).

OCONTO County (Wis.) \ō kon´ tō\. Menomini (Algonquian) /oka:ʔtow/ 'place of the pike (a fish)', from /oka:w/ 'pike' (Vogel 1991; Bloomfield 1975:172).

OCOTILLO (Calif., Imperial Co.) \ok ə til´ ō, ō kə tē´ yō\. Named for a desert shrub, Mexican Spanish *ocotillo* (Fouquieria splendens). The Spanish word is a diminutive of Mexican Spanish *ocote* 'pine tree', itself a borrowing from Nahuatl (Aztecan) *ocotl* (Gudde 1998).

OCOYA (Ill., Livingston Co.). From Miami/Illinois (Algonquian) /oohkoowia/ 'whippoorwill' (D. Costa p.c.).

OCQUEOC (Mich., Presque Isle Co.). Perhaps from an Ojibwa (Algonquian) placename <Wauk-Wa-Auk> or <We-Que-Og> (Vogel 1986); possibly related to *waaggid* 'to grow crooked' (Rhodes 1985).

OCQUIONIS Creek (N.Y., Otsego Co.) \ok wē on´ is\. Said to be from an Iroquoian language, meaning 'he is a bear' (Beauchamp 1907).

OCQUITTUNK, Lake (N.J., Sussex Co.). Perhaps from a Delaware (Algonquian) term meaning 'place of the wild pig' (Becker 1964).

OCTAHATCHEE (Fla., Hamilton Co.). Muskogee *oktah-hvcce* /okta:h-háčči/ 'sand creek', from *oktahv* /oktá:ha/ 'sand' plus *hvcce* /háčči/ 'stream' (Read 1934; Martin and Mauldin 2000). Related placenames are **Oktaha** (Okla., Muskogee Co.) and **Oktamulke** (Ala., Elmore Co.).

OCTORARO (Md., Cecil Co.; Pa., Chester Co.). Possibly from Tuscarora (Iroquoian) /yohtawakarera/ 'the sound of rushing water' (Kenny 1984).

ODAKOTA Mountain (S.Dak., Pennington Co.). Perhaps from Dakota (Siouan) *odákhota* 'friendship, peace treaty' (B. Ingham p.c.). Related placenames are **Dakota** and **Lakota.**

ODANAH (Wis., Ashland Co.) \ō dā´ nə\. From Ojibwa (Algonquian) *oodena* 'village, town' (Vogel 1991; Nichols and Nyholm 1995).

ODIAK Channel (Alaska, Cordova C-5). Probably from Yupik (Eskimo); reported in 1897 (Orth 1967).

ODODIKOSSI Lake (Minn., Cass Co.). Perhaps from the Ojibwa (Algonquian) for 'kidney'; cf. *indoodikosiw* 'my kidney' (Nichols and Nyholm 1995).

ODSHIAPOFA (Ala., Elmore Co.). Perhaps from Muskogee, meaning 'hickory grove', containing *ocē-vpe* /oči:apí/ 'hickory tree' (*ocē* /oči:/ 'hickory', *vpe* /apí/ 'tree') and *ofv* /ó:fa/ 'inside' (Toomey 1917; Martin and Mauldin 2000).

OFAHOMA (Miss., Leake Co.) \ō fə hō´ mə\. Said to be named for a Choctaw (Muskogean) man whose name was *ofi homma* 'red dog', from *ofi* 'dog' and *homma* 'red' (Seale 1939; P. Munro p.c.).

OGALLAH (Kans., Trego Co.) \ō gä´ lə\. Probably from the same source as **Oglala**

(S.Dak., Shannon Co.); see below. A related placename is **Ogallala** (Neb., Keith Co.) \ō gə lä´ lə\.

OGECHIE Lake (Minn., Mille Lacs Co.). Said to be named from the Ojibwa (Algonquian) word for an intestinal worm (Upham 2001).

OGEECHEE (Ga., Screven Co.) \ō gē´ chē\. Perhaps from Muskogee, meaning 'river of the Uchees', referring to a neighboring people called **Uchee, Euchee,** or **Yuchi** (Krakow 1975); cf. Muskogee *yocce* /yó:čči/ 'Yuchi' (Martin and Mauldin 2000). The name also occurs in Okla. (Ottawa Co.).

OGEMA (Minn., Becker Co.) \ō´ gə mä\. Said to be from Ojibwa (Algonquian) *ogimaa* 'a chief' (Upham 2001; Nichols and Nyholm 1995). The name also occurs in Wis. (Price Co.). Related placenames include **Ogima Lake** (Mich., Gogebic Co.) and **Ogimakwe Falls** (Mich., Gogebic Co.); the second may be from *ogimaa-kwe* 'chief-woman, chief's wife' (Vogel 1991). Also related to this last may be **Ogemaga** (Wis., Oneida Co.). Among other cognate placenames, **Ogemaw County** (Mich.) \ō´ gə mô\ is said to be an abbreviation of <Ogema-kegato>, the name of an Ojibwa (Algonquian) leader of the early nineteenth century, said to mean 'chief speaker'; cf. *giigido* 'to speak' (Vogel 1986; Nichols and Nyholm 1995). Another related name is **Okemah** (Okla., Okfuskee Co.).

OGISHKEMUNCIE Lake (Minn., Lake Co.). From Ojibwa (Algonquian) *ogiishkimanisii* 'kingfisher' (a bird) (Upham 2001; Nichols and Nyholm 1995).

OGLALA (S.Dak., Shannon Co.) \ō glä´ lə, ō gə lä´ lə\. A branch of the Teton Lakhota (Siouan) people, from *oglála* 'he scatters his own' (Sneve 1973; *HNAI* 13:756–57). The placename also occurs in Neb. (Sioux Co.). Related placenames are **Ogallah** (Kans., Trego Co.) and **Ogallala** (Neb., Keith Co.).

OGONTZ (Mich., Delta Co.) \ō´ gons\. Ojibwa (Algonquian) *ogaans* 'young pickerel', diminutive of *ogaa* 'pickerel, walleye' (Vogel 1986; Nichols and Nyholm 1995). As the name of a leader in the related Ottawa people during the early nineteenth century, the term seems to have been applied to a place in Ohio (Erie Co.) and transferred to other states (e.g., Maine, Somerset Co.; N.H., Grafton Co.; and Pa., Montgomery Co.).

OGUNQUIT (Maine, York Co.) \ō gung´ kwit\. From Abenaki (Algonquian) *ôgwaomkwid* 'sand lies drifted as dunes at river mouth' (Eckstorm 1941:176–77, Day 1994–95).

OHANAPECOSH (Wash., Lewis Co.) \ō han´ ə pi kosh\. From the Sahaptin placename /áw-xanapaykaš/ 'standing at the edge' (D. Kinkade p.c.).

OHATCHEE (Ala., Calhoun Co.) \ō hach´ ē\. Perhaps from Muskogee *ohhvcce* /oh-háčči/ 'upper stream' (Read 1984; Martin and Mauldin 2000).

OHIOPYLE (Pa., Fayette Co.) \ō hī´ ō pīl\. Earlier written <Ohiopehelle>; said to be from an Indian name, language not identified, meaning 'water whitened by froth' (Donehoo 1928).

OHIO River \ō hī´ ō\. From Seneca (Iroquoian) *ohi:yo'*, a proper name derived from *ohi:yo:h* 'good river'. The term is used by the Seneca not only for the **Ohio River** but also for the Allegheny or Allegany River, which they consider to be the headwaters of the Ohio (W. Chafe p.c.). The placename **Ohio,** apart from designating the state, is found in N.Y. (Herkimer Co.) and as a transfer in other areas (e.g., R.I., Bristol Co.; Vt., Windsor Co.; and Ill., Bureau Co.).

OHOOPEE (Ga., Toombs Co.) \ō hōō´ pē\. Perhaps named after a Muskogee leader, but the derivation is not clear (Goff 1975).

OHOP (Wash., Pierce Co.) \ō´ hop\. Said to be from an Indian language, not identified, meaning 'pleasant'. The nearby site **Ohop Bob** contains a Scottish term *bob* meaning 'hill' (Hitchman 1985).

OJAI (Calif., Ventura Co.) \ō´ hī\. From Ventureño (Chumashan) [a'hwai] 'moon' (Gudde 1998).

OJALA (Calif., Ventura Co.) \ō häl´ ə\. Probably from Ventureño (Chumashan), but the derivation has not been confirmed (Gudde 1998).

OJATA (N.Dak., Grand Forks Co.). From Dakota (Siouan) *ožáte* 'fork in a road or stream' (Wick 1988; B. Ingham p.c.).

OJIBWA \ō jib´ wā, ō jib´ wə\. The name of an Algonquian people and language, called /očipwe/ by themselves; the term may be connected with a root meaning 'puckered up', referring to the form of Ojibwa moccasins. Variants are **Ojibway** and **Ojibwe.** The related form **Chippewa** is preferred for groups in the United States and in southern Ontario, and **Ojibwa** (or Ojibway) for those elsewhere in Canada (*HNAI* 15:768). The **Ottawa** people and language are closely related. As a placename, the form **Ojibwa** is found in Wis. (Sawyer Co.); the form **Ojibway** occurs in Minn. (Lake Co.), Mo. (Wayne Co.), and Wash. (Pend Oreille Co.). A term used by the Ojibwas for themselves is *anishinaabe,* which has the more general meanings 'Indian, human being' (*HNAI* 15:768; Nichols and Nyholm 1995).

OJUS (Fla., Dade Co.). Perhaps from a Seminole (Muskogean) term meaning 'plentiful', but the derivation is not clear (Read 1934).

OKA ACHUKMA (Okla., McCurtain Co.). From the same source as **Okachickima Creek**; see below.

OKABENA (Minn., Jackson Co.). From the same source as **Okamanpeedan Lake** (Iowa, Emmet Co.; Minn., Martin Co.); see below.

OKACHICKIMA Creek (Miss., Yalobusha Co.) \ōk ə chik´ i mä\. From Choctaw (Muskogean) for 'good water', containing *oka* 'water', *achukma* 'good' (Seale 1939; P. Munro p.c.). Related forms are nearby **Oakachickan** and **Oakchickamau** as well as **Oka Achukma** (Okla., McCurtain Co.).

OKAHANIKAN Cave (Md., Dorchester Co.). Earlier writings are <Occahannock, Onkanikan, Hanikan>; perhaps from a CAC Algonquian name meaning 'winding river' (Kenny 1984).

OKAHATTA Creek (Miss., Newton Co.) \ō kə hat´ ə\. From Choctaw (Muskogean) *oka hata* 'white water', containing *oka* 'water' and *hata* 'white' (Seale 1939; P. Munro p.c.).

OKAHAY (Miss., Covington Co.). A variant of **Oakohay Creek**; see above.

OKAHOLA (Miss., Lamar Co.) \ō kə hō´ lə\. From Choctaw (Muskogean) *oka hollo* 'sacred water', containing *oka* 'water' and *hollo* 'sacred, taboo, beloved' (P. Munro p.c.). A related placename is **Oka Hullo** (Miss., Newton Co.).

OKAHUMPKA (Fla., Lake Co.) \ō kə hump´ kə\. Probably from Hitchiti (Muskogean) *okihampi,* lit. 'water-bad' (Read 1934; J. Martin p.c.).

OKAKAPASSA (Ala., Colbert Co.). From Choctaw (Muskogean) <oka-kuppissa> 'water-cold', from *oka* 'water' and *kapassa* 'cold' (Toomey 1917; P. Munro p.c.).

OKAK Bend (Alaska, Howard Pass A-5). From Iñupiaq (Eskimo) *uqaq* 'tongue' (Orth 1967; MacLean 1980). Related Alaska placenames are **Okalik Lake** (Teshekpuk D-1) and **Okok** (St. Lawrence B-5).

OKALEE Channel (Alaska, Cordova A-1). The name is from Eyak /'aax̲dalih/.

OKALIK Lake (Alaska, Teshekpuk D-1). From Iñupiaq (Eskimo), meaning 'having a tongue', reported in 1956 (Orth 1967); cf. *uqaq* 'tongue', *-lik* 'supplied with' (Webster and Zibell 1970). Related Alaska placenames include **Okak Bend** (Howard Pass A-5) and **Okok** (St. Lawrence B-5).

OKALLA Station (Ind., Putnam Co.). Perhaps from the same source as **Ocala** (Fla., Marion Co.); see above.

OKALOACOOCHEE Slough (Fla., Hendry Co.). Earlier writings are <Oc-hol-wa-coochee, Ok-hol-oa-coochee>; perhaps from Muskogee *akholwakuce* /ak-holwa:k-očí/ 'small bad water', from /ak-/ 'in water', /holwa:k-/ 'bad', and /-oči/ 'small' (Read 1934; J. Martin p.c.).

OKALOO (Fla., Okaloosa Co.) \ō´ kə lo͞o\. Probably an abbreviation of **Okaloosa County** (Fla.) \ō kə lo͞o´ sə\. This is from Choctaw (Muskogean) *oka losa,* lit. 'water-black' (Read 1934; P. Munro p.c.). The placename also occurs in La. (Ouachita Par.).

OKAMANPEEDAN Lake (Iowa, Emmet Co.; Minn., Martin Co.). From Dakota (Siouan) *hok'ámąpidą* 'little heron's nest', containing *hok'á* 'heron', *mą* 'to build a nest and hatch chicks' (Vogel 1983; Riggs 1890). A related placename is **Okabena** (Minn., Jackson Co.).

OKANOGAN County (Wash.) \ō kə nog´ ən\. From the Okanagan (Salishan) placename [ukʷnaqín] (D. Kinkade p.c.). The placename also occurs in Ore. (Baker Co.). In the adjacent area of Canada it is spelled **Okanagan**.

OKAPILCO Creek (Ga., Brooks Co.). Perhaps from Muskogee *tokperkv* /tokpíłka/ 'nighthawk' (Read 1949–50:131; Nichols and Nyholm 1995).

OKARCHE (Okla., Canadian Co.). Coined from elements of the words **Oklahoma, Arapaho,** and **Cheyenne,** all of Indian origin (Shirk 1974).

OKATEE River (S.C., Beaufort Co.) \ō´ kə tē\. Perhaps from an unidentified Indian language (Pickens 1961:7). A probably related placename is **Okatie** (S.C., Jasper Co.).

OKATIBBEE (Miss., Lauderdale Co.) \ō kə tib´ ē\. Probably from Choctaw (Muskogean) *oka aa-ittibi* 'fight at the water', from *oka* 'water', *aa-* 'place', *ittibi* 'to fight' (Toomey 1917; P. Munro p.c.).

OKATIE (S.C., Jasper Co.) \ō´ kə tē\. Probably from the same source as **Okatee** (S.C., Beaufort Co.); see above.

OKATOMA Creek (Miss., Covington Co.) \ō kə tō´ mə\. Perhaps from Choctaw (Muskogean) *oka aa-toomi* 'water where it shines', containing *oka* 'water', *aa-* 'place', *toomi* 'shine (of the sun)' (Toomey 1917; P. Munro p.c.).

OKATUPPA (Ala., Choctaw Co.) \ō kə tup´ ə\. Probably from Choctaw (Muskogean) *oktapa* 'dam' or *oka tapa* 'water dammed-up' (Read 1984; P. Munro p.c.).

OKAUCHEE (Wis., Waukesha Co.) \ō kô´ chē\. Perhaps from Ojibwa (Algonquian) <okitchi> 'the right side of something' (Vogel 1991); cf. *gichinik* 'right hand' (Nichols and Nyholm 1995).

OKAW Township (Ill., Shelby Co.) \ō´ kô\. Perhaps from French *aux Kas* [ō kä] 'to the Kaskakias', referring to a branch of the Miami/Illinois (Algonquian) people (Vogel 1963). Such abbreviations for the names of Indian groups were often used by early French explorers in the Midwest; cf. also **Kaskaskia.** But the French also used *aux Kas* to refer to the Kansa (Siouan) people, whence other occurrences of the placename **Okaw** (Mo., Kansas Co.; Kans., Harper Co.). A derived placename is **Okawville** (IL, Washington Co.) \ō´ kə vil\.

OKEAFENOKE Swamp (Fla., Baker Co.) \ō kē fə nō´ kē\. From the same source as **Okefenokee Swamp** (Ga., Charlton Co.); see below.

OKEANA (Ohio, Butler Co.). Said to be named for the daughter of Kiatte, an Indian leader (language not identified) of the early nineteenth century (Miller 1996).

OKEE (Wis., Columbia Co.) \ō kē\. Probably from an Algonquian word meaning 'land' (e.g., Ojibwa *aki*) (Nichols and Nyholm 1995).

OKEECHOBEE County (Fla.) \ō kē chō´ bē, ō kə chō´ bē\. Hitchiti (Muskogean) /oki-čo:bi/ 'big water', from /oki/ 'water' and /čo:bi/ 'big' (Read 1934; J. Martin p.c.).

OKEELALA Creek (Miss., Lee Co.) \ō kə lal´ ə\. Perhaps from Choctaw (Muskogean) *oka lawa* 'water-much' (Seale 1939; P. Munro p.c.). A possibly related placename is **Kolola Springs.**

OKEELANTA (Fla., Palm Beach Co.). Perhaps a blend of **Okeechobee** with *Atlantic* (Read 1934).

OKEENE (Okla., Blaine Co.) \ō kēn\. Coined from elements of the words **Oklahoma, Cherokee,** and **Cheyenne,** all of Indian origin (Shirk 1974).

OKEEWALKEE (Ga., Wheeler Co.) \ō kē wäl´ kē\. From Hitchiti (Muskogean), meaning 'dirty water', containing *oki* 'water' and <holwaki> 'dirty' (Read 1949–50). A variant is **Ochwalkee.**

OKEFENOKEE Swamp (Ga., Charlton Co.) \ō kē fə nō´ kē\. Perhaps from Hitchiti (Muskogean) /oki-fino:ki/ 'quivering water', containing /oki/ 'water' and /fino:ki/ 'quivering' (Goff 1975; J. Martin p.c.). The placename also occurs in Fla. (Taylor Co.). A related placename is **Okeafenoke Swamp** (Fla., Baker Co.).

OKEHOCKING Run (Pa., Chester Co.). The name of a Delaware (Algonquian) Indian village, of unclear derivation (Donehoo 1928).

OKEMAH (Okla., Okfuskee Co.) \ō kē´ mə\. From Ojibwa (Algonquian) *ogimaa* 'chief' (Nichols and Nyholm 1995). The placename also occurs in Ariz. (Maricopa Co.). Perhaps related placenames are **Okemo Mountain** (Vt., Windsore Co.) and **Okemos** (Mich., Ingham Co.) \ō´ kə məs\, the name of an Ojibwa (Algonquian) leader of the early nineteenth century, containing *-s* 'diminutive' (Vogel 1986). Other related names include **Ogema** (Minn., Becker Co.).

OKENOK Neck (N.Y., Suffolk Co.) \ō´ kē nōk\. Earlier written < Oquonock>, perhaps from SNEng. Algonquian, meaning 'burial place', or perhaps a borrowing from English *Oak Neck* (Tooker 1911). A variant is **Oquenok.**

OKEROKOVIK River (Alaska, Demarcation Point D-5). The Iñupiaq (Eskimo) name, reported in 1919, is said to mean 'place where there is a blubber cache' (Orth 1967); cf. *uqsruq* 'oil', *-vik* 'place' (MacLean 1980).

OKESA (Okla., Osage Co.) \ō kē´ sə\. From Osage (Siouan) /ohkísa/ 'half of something, halfway' (Shirk 1974; R. Rankin p.c.).

OKETO (Kans., Marshall Co.) \ō kē´ tō\. Said to be derived from the name of an Oto (Siouan) leader, recorded as <Ar-ke-kee-tah> 'stay by it' (Rydjord 1968). This may represent /akíkita/ 'looks after himself, sees to his own welfare' (R. Rankin p.c.).

OKFAUCHAVUK Slough (Alaska, Kwiguk C-4). The Yupik (Eskimo) name was reported in 1899 (Orth 1967).

OKFUSKEE County (Okla.) \ōk fus´ kē\. From the same source as **Oakfuskee** (Ala., Cleburne Co.); see above.

OKHAKONKONHEE (Fla., Polk Co.). Probably from Muskogee, containing the element /konkoh/, from /konh/ 'crooked' with reduplication (Read 1934; J. Martin p.c.).

OKI (Ga., Effingham Co.) \ō´ kē\. From Hitchiti (Muskogean) *oki* 'water' (Krakow 1975; J. Martin p.c.).

OKIKAK Mountain (Alaska, St. Lawrence B-2). The Yupik (Eskimo) name was reported in 1932 (Orth 1967).

OKIOTAK Peak (Alaska, Mt. Michelson B-2). From Iñupiaq *ukiuqtaq* 'gyrfalcon' (L. Kaplan p.c.).

OKISKO (N.C., Pasquotank Co.). Said to be named for a leader of the Yeopim group; the linguistic identification is unclear (Powell 1968).

OKLAHOMA \ōk lə hō´ mə\. The name of the state was coined by Allen Wright, a Choctaw scholar, and means 'red people', from Choctaw (Muskogean) *oklah* 'people' plus *homma* 'red' (P. Munro p.c.). The placename is found as a transfer in many states (e.g., Ill., St. Clair Co.; Mass., Dukes Co.; and Ore., Clatsop Co.).

OKMOK, Mount (Alaska, Umnak B-1). Aleut *unmagim anatuu* 'Okmok Caldera, lit. the stout one (roundish mountain) of Umnak', from *unmax, umnax* 'Umnak Island', perhaps from *una* 'out there on the sea' (Bergsland 1994).

OKMULGEE County (Okla.) \ōk mul´ gē\. Probably from Hitchiti (Muskogean) /oki/ 'water' plus /molki/ 'boiling, bubbling' (Read 1984; J. Martin p.c.). Related placenames are **Ocmulgee** (Ga., Pulaski Co.) and **Oakmulgee** (Ala., Perry Co.).

OKOBOJI (Iowa, Dickinson Co.) \ō kə bō´ jē, ō kə bō´ jə\. Perhaps from Dakota (Siouan), meaning ‘spreading to the south’, from *okax-bog-ya* (Vogel 1983; J. Koontz p.c.). A possibly related placename is **Okobojo** (S.Dak., Sully Co.).

OKOBOJO (S.Dak., Sully Co.). Probably from Dakota (Siouan) *okówožu* ‘to plant in spaces’ (Sneve 1973; A. Taylor p.c.).

OKOEE (Okla., Craig Co.) \ō kō´ ē\. From the same source as **Ocoee River** (Tenn., Polk Co.); see above.

OKOK (Alaska, St. Lawrence B-5) \ok´ ok\. From Yupik (Eskimo) *uqaq* ‘tongue’ (Orth 1967; Webster and Zibell 1970). Related Alaska placenames are **Okak Bend** (Howard Pass A-5) and **Okalik Lake** (Teshekpuk D-1).

OKOKLIK Lake (Alaska, Misheguk Mountain A-1). From Iñupiaq (Eskimo), reported in 1956, said to mean ‘it is warm’ (Orth 1967); see **Okotak Creek** (Alaska, Misheguk Mountain A-4) below.

OKOKMILAGA River (Alaska, Killik River D-1). The Iñupiaq (Eskimo) name was reported about 1946 (Orth 1967).

OKOLONA (Miss., Chickasaw Co.). Perhaps from Choctaw (Muskogean) *oklah-lokoli* ‘people gathered-together’ (Cushman 1899; P. Munro p.c.). The name also occurs in Ark. (Clark Co.), Ohio (Henry Co.), and Okla. (McCurtain Co.).

OKOME (Pa., Lycoming Co.). Perhaps a variation of **Oconee County** (Ga.); see above.

OKONAGUN Creek (Alaska, Killik River C-1). Reported around 1950 as <Okonagoon>, said to be from Iñupiaq (Eskimo) (Orth 1967); however, the similarity of **Okanogan County** (Wash.) is suspicious.

OKONI (Ala., Russell Co.). Perhaps from the same source as **Oconee County** (see above), transferred either from Ga. or S.C.

OKONOKA (Mich., Wayne Co.). Perhaps from the same source as **Okonoko** (W.Va., Hampshire Co.); see below.

OKONOKO (W.Va., Hampshire Co.). Perhaps an Indian name, but of unclear origin (Kenny 1945).

OKOTAK Creek (Alaska, Misheguk Mountain A-4). Said to be from Iñupiaq (Eskimo) *uquuttaq* ‘shelter from wind’ (L. Kaplan p.c.).

OKPIKRUAK River (Alaska, Killik River C-1). The Iñupiaq (Eskimo) name was reported in 1951 (Orth 1967); cf. *ukpik* ‘snowy owl’ (MacLean 1980). Possibly related is **Okpiksak River** (Alaska, Meade River C-2). Note the distinction between Iñupiaq *ukpik* ‘snowy owl’ and *uqpik* ‘willow’.

OKPIKSUGRUK Creek (Alaska, Noatak D-6). The Iñupiaq (Eskimo) name is said to be *uqpigruaq* ‘old willow’ (L. Kaplan p.c.). Probably related placenames are **Okpilak River** (Alaska, Flaxman Is. A-1), said to mean ‘no willows’, recorded in 1919 (Orth 1967); and **Okpirourak Creek** (Alaska, Demarcation Point C-5); see below.

OKPILATOK Bluff (Alaska, Point Hope D-2). The Iñupiaq (Eskimo) name was reported in 1950 as meaning ‘red appearing’ (Orth 1967).

OKPIROURAK Creek (Alaska, Demarcation Point C-5). The Iñupiaq (Eskimo) name, said to mean ‘a few willows’, was reported in 1919 (Orth 1967); cf. *uqpik* ‘willow’ (MacLean 1980). Probably related placenames include **Okpiksugruk Creek** (Alaska, Noatak D-6); see above.

OKRACOKE (N.C., Hyde Co.) \ok´ rə kōk\. Earlier written <Wococon, Woccock, Ocacock, Ocacock> (etc.); said to be from CAC Algonquian <waxkahikani, waxihikani> ‘fort, stockade’ (Powell 1968; Payne 1985).

OKROKNAKPAK Lakes (Alaska, Howard Pass D-2). The Iñupiaq (Eskimo) name is *ugrugnaqpak* ‘big shrew’ (L. Kaplan p.c.).

OKRURAT Creek (Alaska, Point Hope C-3). The Iñupiaq (Eskimo) name was reported in 1950 as <Oak-wroo-rut> ‘white rocks’ (Orth 1967).

OKSHIDA (Minn., Murray Co.). From the same source as **Ocheda Lake** (Minn., Nobles Co.) and **Ocheyedan** (Iowa, Osceola Co.).

OKSHOKWEWHIK Pass (Alaska, St. Michael A-4). The Yupik (Eskimo) name was reported in 1899 (Orth 1967).

OKSIK Creek (Alaska, Selawik D-4). The Iñupiaq (Eskimo) name was recorded in 1955 (Orth 1967).

OKSOTALIK Creek (Alaska, Taylor Mountains D-6). The Yupik (Eskimo) name was recorded in 1945 as meaning 'place of heads' (Orth 1967); cf. *uqsuq* 'head' (Jacobson 1984).

OKSRUKUYIK (Alaska, Philip Smith Mountains D-3). The Iñupiaq (Eskimo) name was reported in 1956 (Orth 1967).

OKSTUKUK Lake (Alaska, Dillingham C-7). The Yupik (Eskimo) name was reported as <Ok-so-kok> in 1910 (Orth 1967).

OKTAHA (Okla., Muskogee Co.) \ōk tä´ hä\. Abbreviated from the name of Oktaha-sars Harjo, a Muskogee leader of the nineteenth century; contains *oktahv* /oktá:ha/ 'sand' (Shirk 1974; Martin and Mauldin 2000). A related placename is **Octahatchee** (Fla., Hamilton Co.); see above.

OKTAMULKE (Ala., Elmore Co.) \ok tə mul´ kē\. Possibly from Muskogee *oktahv-morke* /okta:ha-mó:łki/ 'boiling sand' (Read 1984; Martin and Mauldin 2000).

OKTIBBEHA County (Miss.) \ok tib´ i hô\. Perhaps from Choctaw (Muskogean), meaning 'blocks of ice are in it', from *okti* 'snow, ice' and *abiha* 'be in, go in (pl. subj.)' (Seale 1939; P. Munro p.c.). A possibly related placename is **Tibbee** (Miss., Clay Co.).

OKTOC (Miss., Oktibbeha Co.). From Choctaw (Muskogean) *oktaak* 'prairie' (Toomey 1917; P. Munro p.c.).

OKUMIAK, Mount (Alaska, Russian Mission D-8). The Yupik (Eskimo) name was reported in 1916 (Orth 1967).

OKWEGA Pass (Alaska, St. Michael A-4). The Yupik (Eskimo) name was recorded in 1898 (Orth 1967).

OLALIE Lake (Ore., Jefferson Co.). From the same source as **Olalla** (Wash., Kitsap Co.) \ō lal´ ə, ō lä´ lə\. This represents Chinook Jargon <o´-lal-lie> [oláli, ólæli] 'salmon berries, berries in general, fruit', from Lower Chinook [ólili] 'salmon berries' (Hitchman 1985; D. Kinkade p.c.). The placename also occurs in Ore. (Douglas Co.) Related forms include **Olallie** (Ore., Linn Co.), **Olele Point** (Wash., Jefferson Co.), and **Ollala Canyon** (Ore., Lincoln Co.).

OLAMON (Maine, Penobscot Co.) \ō lem´ ən\. From Abenaki (Algonquian) *olaman* 'vermillion, red ochre' (Ekstorm 1941:41–42; Day 1994–95). Perhaps related is **Olentangy** (Ohio, Franklin Co.).

OLANCHA (Calif., Inyo Co.) \ō lan´ chə\. The term was applied in 1860 to a Panamint (Numic) village or band (Gudde 1998).

OLATHE (Kans., Johnson Co.) \ō lā´ thə\. Said to be Shawnee (Algonquian), meaning 'beautiful' (Rydjord 1968). The placename has also been transferred to Colo. (Montrose Co.).

OLDFIELD (Md., Frederick Co.). This term was used in frontier days to describe cleared land, once cultivated by Indians but then left fallow (Kenny 1984). The related form **Old Fields** occurs in W.Va. (Hardy Co.).

OLD LODGE Creek (S.Dak., Tripp Co.). So named when an abandoned tipi was found nearby or else named for a Lakhota (Siouan) man, Joe Old Lodge (Sneve 1973).

OLD MAN Mountain (Colo., Larimer Co.) is based on Arapaho (Algonquian) *hinén tahthi'ókut* 'old-man where he sits' (A. Cowell p.c.).

OLDTOWN (Md., Allegany Co.). The term was applied in frontier days to the abandoned site of an Indian village (Kenny 1984). The adaptation **Old Town** is found in Pa. (Cumberland Co.).

OLD WOMAN Creek (Alaska, Mt. McKinley D-5). A literal translation of Upper Koyukon (Athabaskan) *tsooch'aal no'* (J. Kari p.c.).

OLELE Point (Wash., Jefferson Co.). From the same source as **Olalla** (Wash., Kitsap Co.) and **Olallie** (Ore., Linn Co.); see **Olalie Lake** above.

OLEMA (Calif., Marin Co.) \ō lē´ mə\. The name of a Coast Miwok village, formerly written <Olemos, Olemus>; probably from /óle/ 'coyote' (Gudde 1998). The placename also occurs, perhaps as a transfer, in Wash. (Okanogan Co.).

OLENE (Ore., Klamath Co.) \ō lēn´\. From Klamath 'off the edge, off the side' (Barker 1963).

OLENTANGY (Ohio, Franklin Co.) \ō lən tan´ jē\. Perhaps from Delaware (Algonquian) <olam´-taámse> 'face-paint now and then', containing <olam´-> 'paint, (red) face paint' and <-taámse> 'now and then' (Mahr 1959:372). Perhaps related to the placename **Olamon** (Maine, Penobscot Co.).

OLEQUA (Wash., Cowlitz Co.) \ō´ lə kwä\. Probably from a Salishan word for 'snake'; cf. note Upper Chehalis /ʔúq'^{w}a/, Lower Chehalis /ʔúlq'/, Quinault /ʔúlq'aʔ/. The Chinook Jargon word for 'snake' is <oluk> [ólək], but this is probably a borrowing from Lower Chehalis rather than being the source of the English word (D. Kinkade p.c.).

OLEY (Pa., Berks Co.) \ō´ lē\. Perhaps from Delaware (Algonquian) <Olink, Wahlink, Woalac> 'a hole, a cove' (Donehoo 1928); cf. Munsee Delaware *waalakw* 'hole, pit' (O'Meara 1996).

OLIGAVIK Creek (Alaska, Point Hope C-1). The Iñupiaq (Eskimo) name was reported in 1955 to mean 'flood' (Orth 1967); cf. *uliqtuk* 'is flooded' (Webster and Zibell 1970). Perhaps related is **Olikatuk Channel** (Alaska, Selawik C-6).

OLIKTOK Point (Alaska, Beechey Point C-5). From Iñupiaq (Eskimo) *uulik-* 'to shiver, tremble' (Orth 1967; MacLean 1980).

OLJATO Wash (Ariz., Navajo Co.; Utah, San Juan Co.) \ōl jā´ tō\. Navajo (Athabaskan) *ooljéé'tó,* from *ooljéé'* 'moon' and *tó* 'water, spring' (Granger 1983; Wilson 1995). An alternative spelling is **Oljeto.**

OLLALA Canyon (Wash., Chelan Co.) \ō´ lä lə\. From the same source as **Olalla** (Wash., Kitsap Co.) and **Olallie** (Ore., Linn Co.); see **Olalie Lake** above. The placename also occurs in Ore. (Lincoln Co.).

OLLOKOT Campgound (Ore., Wallowa Co.). From Nez Perce /álok'at/ '(young) male mountain sheep' (Aoki 1994).

OLNGOOSEENUK Mountain (Alaska, St. Lawrence C-5) Said to be from Yupik (Eskimo) <otnosirnak>, containing <sirnak> 'walrus stomach' (Orth 1967); cf. St. Lawrence Island Yupik *siighnaq* [siiʀnaq] 'walrus stomach' (Jacobson 1987).

OLO (Ariz., Coconino Co.) \ō´ lō\. From Havasupai (Yuman) /olo/ 'horse', perhaps from Spanish *caballo* (Brian 1992).

OLOMPALI (Calif., Marin Co.) \ə lom´ pə lē, ō ləm pä´ lē\. From a Coast Miwok village called /óolum pálli/, apparently containing /ólom/ 'south' (Gudde 1998).

OLUMAGWILUTE River (Alaska, Goodnews Bay C-5). The Iñupiaq (Eskimo) name was recorded in 1898 (Orth 1967).

OLUSTEE (Fla., Baker Co.) \ō lus´ tē\. From Muskogee *ue-lvste* /oy-lásti/, lit. 'water-black' (Martin and Mauldin 2000). The name was transferred to Ala. (Pike Co.) and to Okla. (Jackson Co.). A possibly related placename is **Weolustee Creek** (Ala., Russell Co.).

OMAHA \ō´ mə hô, ō´ mə hä\. The name of a Siouan people and language; the Native American term is *umą́hą,* perhaps meaning 'upstream, against the flow' (*HNAI* 13:413). As a placename, the word is best known in Neb. (Douglas Co.); it also occurs, for example, in Iowa (Dickinson Co.) and Tex. (Morris Co.).

OMAK (Wash., Okanogan Co.) \ō´ mak\. From the Okanagan (Salishan) placename [umák] (D. Kinkade p.c.).

OMAKSTALIA Point (Alaska, Naknek C-3). The Yupik (Eskimo) name was reported in 1952 (Orth 1967).

OMALIK Creek (Alaska, Point Lay A-3). The Iñupiaq (Eskimo) name, reported in 1949, may be a family name (Orth 1967). A related placename is **Oumalik River** (Alaska, Teshekpuk B-4).

OMALURUK Creek (Alaska, Ambler River A-5). The Iñupiaq (Eskimo) name was reported in 1955 (Orth 1967).

OMEMEE (N.Dak., Bottineau Co.) \ō mē´ mē\. From Ojibwa (Algonquian) *omiimii* 'dove' (Wick 1988; Nichols and Nyholm 1995).

OMENA (Mich., Leelanau Co.) \ō mē´ nə\. Perhaps from Ojibwa (Algonquian) <ominan> 'he gives it to him' (Vogel 1986).

OMENOKU (Calif., Humboldt Co.) \om ə nō´ ko͞o\. From Yurok /o-menokw/ 'where it projects' (Gudde 1998).

OMIAKTALIK, Lake (Alaska, Teller A-1). The Iñupiaq (Eskimo) name was reported in 1908 (Orth 1967).

OMIKMAK Creek (Alaska, Wainwright C-2). The Iñupiaq (Eskimo) name is perhaps *umiŋmak* 'musk ox' (L. Kaplan p.c.).

OMIKMUKTUSUK River (Alaska, Utukok River D-2). The Iñupiaq (Eskimo) name was recorded in 1956 (Orth 1967).

OMILAK (Alaska, Bendeleben A-2) \o͞o´ mi lak\. The Iñupiaq (Eskimo) name was reported in 1881 (Orth 1967).

OMJUMI Mountain (Calif., Plumas Co.) \ōm jo͞o´ mē\. Contains Maidu /om/ 'rock' (Gudde 1998).

OMO Ranch (Calif., El Dorado Co.) \ō´ mō\. Perhaps an abbreviation of Northern Sierra Miwok /oomu' a' koča/ 'menstrual hut' (Gudde 1998).

OMOCHUMNES (Calif., Sacramento Co.). Probably a Spanish plural from Plains Miwok /omuučaïmni/ 'people of winter', containing /omuuča/ 'winter' (Gudde 1998).

OMOGAR Creek (Calif., Humboldt Co.) \om´ ə gär\. From the Yurok placename /omega'a/ (Gudde 1998).

OMPOMPANOOSUC River (Vt., Windsor Co.). Probably from Western Abenaki *bemômanosek* \bəmǫmanosək\. 'where there is frequent fishing'; cf. *ôma* 'he fishes' (Day 1994–95). A related form is **Pompanoosuc.**

OMUSEE Creek (Ala., Houston Co.) \ō mus´ ē\. Probably from the same source as the tribal name **Yamassee** (Fla., Jackson Co.), perhaps from Muskogee *yvmvsē* /yamási:/ 'tame, quiet' (Read 1984; Martin and Mauldin 2000). Another related form is **Yemassee** (S.C., Hampton Co.).

ONA (Ore., Lincoln Co.) \ō´ nə\. Chinook Jargon <o´-na> [óna, úna] 'clams', from Lower Chinook <e-ó-na> 'razor clam' (McArthur 1992; D. Kinkade p.c.).

ONAGA (Kans., Pottawatomie Co.) \ō nā´ gə\. Said to be from the name of a Potatwatomi (Algonquian) man, <Onago> (Rydjord 1968). A possibly related name is **Onarga** (Ill., Iroquois Co.).

ONAHU Creek (Colo., Grand Co.) \on´ ə ho͞o\. Said to be Arapaho for 'warms himself', referring to a horse that on cold evenings came up to the campfire to get warm (Bright 1993).

ONAKA (S.Dak., Faulk Co.) \ō nä´ kə\. From Dakota (Siouan) <oyanka> 'place' (Sneve 1973; Riggs 1890).

ONALASKA (Wis., Lacrosse Co.) \un ə las´ kə, on ə las´ kə\. The name is modified from <Oonalaska>, a former spelling of **Unalaska** (Alaska, Analaska C-2), shortened from Aleut *nawan-alaxsxa* 'the mainland along there' (Vogel 1991; Bergsland 1994). The placename **Onalaska** also occurs in Wash. (Lewis Co.), Ark. (Ouachita Co.), and Tex. (Polk Co.) A related placename is **Alaska.**

ONAMIA (Minn., Mille Lacs Co.). Perhaps from Ojibwa (Algonquian) <onamani> 'vermilion, red pigment' (Upham 2001).

ONANCOCK (Va., Accomack Co.). The name of a CAC Algonquian village, said to mean 'foggy place' (Hagemann 1988).

ONANDAGA (Pa., Luzerne Co.) \on ən dä´ gə, ō nən dä´ gə\. A term related to **Onondaga,** the name of an Iroquoian people; see below.

ONAPA (Okla., McIntosh Co.). From Muskogee *onvpv* /onápa/ 'above, upper' (Shirk 1974; Martin and Mauldin 2000).

ONAQUI (Utah, Tooele Co.) \ə nô´ kwə\. The Goshute (Numic) name is derived from <ona> 'salt' (Van Cott 1990); cf. Shoshoni /ona-pin/ 'salt' (Miller 1972).

ONARGA (Ill., Iroquois Co.) \ō när´ gə\. Perhaps from the same origin as **Onaga** (Kans., Pottawotomie Co.), said to be a Potawatomi (Algonquian) personal name (Vogel 1963).

ONAWA (Iowa, Monona Co.) \on´ ə wä\. From "Onaway" in Longfellow's *Hiawatha,* perhaps as the name of a mythical being (Vogel 1983). The placename **Onawa** also ocurs in Mich. (Presque Isle Co.) \on´ ə wä\, Maine (Piscataquis Co.); and Pa. (Monroe Co.). A related placename is **Onaway** (Wis., Waupaca Co.; and Idaho, Latah Co.).

ONCHIOTA (N.Y., Franklin Co.) \on chī ō´ tə\. Perhaps from Onondaga (Iroquoian) *o'h-nyooda'* 'rainbow' (Beauchamp 1907; H. Woodbury p.c.).

ONDAIG Island (Wis., Douglas Co.). From Ojibwa (Algonquian) *aandeg* 'a crow' (Vogel 1991; Nichols and Nyholm 1995).

ONDERIGUEGON (N.Y., Washington Co.). Probably Mohawk (Iroquoian) *ontarakwé:kon* 'blocked-up lake', containing /-ontar-/ 'lake', /-kwek-/ 'blocked up' (Lounsbury 1960:54; M. Mithun p.c.).

ONEATTA (Ore., Lincoln Co.) \ō nē et´ ə\. Said to be an Indian name, but no derivation is known (McArthur 1992).

ONECO (Conn., Windham Co.) \ō nē´ kō\. Named for a Mohegan (SNEng. Algonquian) leader of the late seventeenth century; his name is also written <Oweneco, Owaneco> (Huden 1962). The placename also occurs in Fla. (Manatee Co.). Possibly related placenames include **Onego** (W.Va., Pendleton Co.), **Oneka Lake** (Minn., Washington Co.), and **Owaneco** (Ill., Christian Co.).

ONEGA Lake (Mich., Schoolcraft Co.). Perhaps adapted from Cayuga (Iroquoian) <Oneaga>, referring to the Niagara River in N.Y. state (Vogel 1986).

ONEGO (W.Va., Pendleton Co.) \wun´ gō\. Perhaps from the same source as **Oneco** (Conn., Windham Co.) or perhaps from an Iroquoian source comparable to that of **Onega Lake** (Mich., Schoolcraft Co.) (Kenny 1945).

ONEIDA \ō nī´ də\. An Iroquoian people, originally of upper N.Y. state, who later moved in part to Wis. In the **Oneida** language, the people are called /onęyote'a:kâ:/ 'people of /onę:yóte'/ the standing stone'. The term contains /-nęy-/ 'stone' and /-ot-/ 'to stand' (*HNAI* 15:489, M. Mithun p.c.). As a placename, **Oneida** is not only a county in N.Y. but has been transferred to many other states (e.g., Ill., Knox Co.; Kans., Nemaha Co.; and Okla., Kingfisher Co.). In some areas it is pronounced \ō nē´ də\. A probably related placename is **Onida** (S.Dak., Sully Co.).

ONEKA Lake (Minn., Washington Co.). Perhaps from the same source as **Oneco** (Conn., Windham Co.); see above.

ONEKAMA (Mich., Manistee Co.) \ō nek´ ə mə\. Perhaps from Ojibwa (Algonquian) <onikama> 'an arm' (Vogel 1986); cf. *ninik* 'my arm' (Nichols and Nyholm 1995).

ONEONTA (N.Y., Otsego Co.) \on ē on´ tə\. From Onondaga (Iroquoian) /onęyǫ́:ta'/ 'protruding stone', containing /-nęy-/ 'stone' and /-ǫt-/ 'to protrude' (M. Mithun p.c.). The placename occurs as a transfer (e.g., Calif., Los Angeles Co.; Kans., Cloud Co.; and Wis., Marinette Co.).

ONGIVINUK Lake (Alaska, Goodnews Bay C-1). The Yupik (Eskimo) name was reported in 1898 (Orth 1967).

ONGOKE River (Alaska, Goodnews Bay A-1). The Yupik (Eskimo) name was reported around 1949 (Orth 1967).

ONGORAKVIK River (Alaska, Wainwright B-4). The Iñupiaq (Eskimo) name is *uŋuraġvik* 'place where animals are driven' (L. Kaplan p.c.).

ONGOVEYUK River (Alaska, St. Lawrence C-2). The Yupik (Eskimo) name was reported in 1949 (Orth 1967).

ONGUTVAK Mountain (Alaska, Taylor Mountains A-8). The Yupik (Eskimo) name was recorded in 1932 (Orth 1967).

ONIDA (S.Dak., Sully Co.) \ō nī´ də\. Probably from the same origin as **Oneida,** the name of an Iroquoian people in N.Y. state; see above.

ONKLAT Creek (Alaska, Yakutat C-5). From Eyak /'ą:tłahd/ 'head of river' (De Laguna 1972:79).

ONNUTESCHUIK Creek (Alaska, Teller B-6). The Iñupiaq (Eskimo) name was published in 1908 as <Onuntasekwik> (Orth 1967).

ONOLAVIK Lake (Alaska, Russian Mission D-7). The Yupik (Eskimo) name was reported in 1949 (Orth 1967).

ONONDAGA \on ən dä´ gə, ō nən dä´ gə\. The name of an Iroquoian people of northern N.Y. state, from /onõtá'ke/ 'place of the hill or mountain', containing /-nõt-/ 'hill, mountain' (*HNAI* 15:499; M. Mithun p.c.). As a placename, it refers to **Onondaga County** (N.Y.) and is found as a transfer name in Mich. (Ingham Co.). A related form is **Onandaga** (Pa., Luzerne Co.).

ONOTA (Mich., Alger Co.). Perhaps a misspelling of the title of H. R. Schoolcraft's book *Oneota, or the Red Race in America* (1845); in that work, the word is from the same source as **Oneida,** an Iroquoian people (Vogel 1986). Alternatively, Onota may be a transfer from **Onota Lake** (Mass., Berkshire Co.); this is perhaps from Mahican (Algonquian), meaning 'blue' or 'deep' (Huden 1962).

ONTARIO, Lake \on târ´ ē ō\. The name of the lake, lying between the United States and Canada, is from Mohawk (Iroquoian) /ǫtarí:io/ 'beautiful lake' or perhaps 'great lake', from /-ǫtar-/ 'lake, river' (Lounsbury 1960:51; M. Mithun p.c.). As a placename, the term applies not only to a province in Canada but to a county in N.Y. state and occurs as a transfer name throughout the United States (e.g., Calif., San Bernardino Co.; Ill., Knox Co.; and Kans., Nemaha Co.).

ONTELAUNEE (Pa., Berks Co.). The name is probably from Delaware (Algonquian) and is said to mean 'little daughter of a great mother', the mother being the Schuylkill River (Donehoo 1928).

ONTEORA Mountain (N.Y., Greene Co.) \on tē ôr´ ə\. Perhaps an adaptation by H. R. Schoolcraft from an Iroquoian name for the Catskills, said to mean 'very high mountain' (Beauchamp 1907).

ONTONAGAN River (Wis., Vilas Co.) \on tə nä´ gən\. Perhaps contains Ojibwa (Algonquian) *onaagan* 'bowl, dish' (Vogel 1986; Nichols and Nyholm 1995); or it may mean 'fishing place'. The placename also occurs in Mich. (Ontonagan Co.) and in the related form of **Oteneagen** (Minn., Itasca Co.).

ONTWA Township (Mich., Cass Co.). Probably after the fictional hero of a poem, *Ontwa, the Son of the Forest,* by Harry Whiting, published in 1823 (Vogel 1986).

OOCHEE Creek (Ga., Marion Co.) \o͞o´ chē\. Probably from the same source as **Euchee** or **Yuchi**, the name of a people once politically affiliated with the Muskogees in Ga., but speaking a distinct language. Related placenames are **Eucha** (Okla., Delaware Co.) and **Eucheee Valley** (Fla., Walton Co.).

OOLAGAH (Okla., Rogers Co.) A variant of **Oologah**; see below.

OOLAH Mountain (Alaska, Chandler Lake A-1) \o͞o´ lə\. From Iñupiaq (Eskimo) *ulu* 'woman's knife, a curved knife used for scraping hides' (Orth 1967; MacLean 1980).

OOLAHPUK Mountain (Alaska, St. Lawrence A-2). From St. Lawrence Island Yupik (Eskimo) *ulaaq* 'woman's knife, curved knife' plus *-ghpak* [-ʀpak] 'big' (Orth 1967, Jacobson 1987).

OOLAMNAGAVIK River (Alaska, Killik River D-2). The Iñupiaq (Eskimo) name was recorded about 1946 (Orth 1967).

OOLAMUSHAK Hill (Alaska, St. Lawrence A-2). The Yupik (Eskimo) name was reported in 1949 (Orth 1967).

OOLENOY River (S.C., Pickens Co.). Perhaps from Cherokee (Iroquoian), but the derivation is not clear (Pickens 1961–62:20).

OOLOGAH (Okla. Rogers Co.) \o͞o´ lə gä\. Said to have been named for Oologah or Dark Cloud, a Cherokee (Iroquoian) leader; cf. *ulogili* 'cloud' (Feeling 1975).

OOLTEWAH (Tenn., Hamilton Co.). Said to be from Cherokee (Iroquoian) <ultiwa'i> 'owl's nest' (M. Toomey p.c.).

OOMEYALUK Bay (Alaska, St. Lawrence B-3). The Yupik (Eskimo) name was reported in 1949 (Orth 1967).

OOMYOUSIK Point (Alaska, St. Lawrence C-2). The Yupik (Eskimo) name was reported in 1932 as <Oonyousik> (Orth 1967).

OONALASKA (Alaska). A variant writing of **Unalaska** (Alaska, Unalaska C-2), derived from Aleut. A related placename is **Onalaska** (Wash., Lewis Co.; Wis., Lacrosse Co.).

OONGALAMBINGOI Dunes (Alaska, Cape Mendenhall D-3). The Yupik (Eskimo) name was recorded in 1949 (Orth 1967).

OONGAYUK Hill (Alaska, St. Lawrence B-5). The Yupik (Eskimo) name was recorded in 1949 (Orth 1967).

OOSKAN (Ore., Lake Co.) \o͞o´ skən\. Chinook Jargon <oos´-kan> [úskən] 'cup, bowl', from Lower Chinook [-cgan] 'bucket, cup' (McArthur 1992; D. Kinkade p.c.).

OOSTANAULA (Ga., Gordon Co.) \o͞o stə nô´ lə\. The Cherokee (Iroquoian) name, which has also been written <Ústanali, Estanola> (etc.), may mean 'shoaly river' (Goff 1975). Related placenames are **Eastanola** (Ga., Stephens Co.) and **Ustanali** (Ga., Franklin Co.).

OOTHKALOOGA Creek (Ga., Gordon Co.). Perhaps from Cherokee (Iroquoian) <tsutygi-lagi> 'beaver' (Krakow 1975). Another form of the name is **Oothcaloga** (Ga., Calhoun Co.).

OOWAH, Lake (Utah, Grand Co.) \o͞o wä´\. Perhaps from Ute (Numic) /uu-pa/ [uu-va] 'arrow-water', with /uu-/ 'arrow'; or from Ute /oo-pa/ [oo-va] 'bone-water', with /oo-/ 'bone' (J. McLaughlin p.c.).

OOWALA (Okla., Rogers Co.) \o͞o wä´ lə\. Said to be the name of a Cherokee (Iroquoian) family, known in English as "Lipe" (Shirk 1974).

OOYNIK Point (Alaska, St. Lawrence D-6). The Yupik (Eskimo) name was reported in 1932 (Orth 1967).

OPAGYARAK River (Alaska, Hooper Bay A-2). The Yupik (Eskimo) name was recorded in 1951 (Orth 1967).

OPAH (Okla., Osage Co.) \ō´ pä\. From Choctaw (Muskogean) *opah* 'owl' (Shirk 1974; P. Munro p.c.).

OPAHWAH Butte (Calif., Modoc Co.) \ō pä´ wä\. Said to be an Indian name, in an unidentified language, of a mountain also called Rattlesnake Butte (Gudde 1998).

OPA-LOCKA (Fla., Dade Co.) \ō pə lok´ ə\. From Muskogee *opel-rakko* /opil-łákko/ 'big swamp', from *opelwv* /opílwa/ 'swamp' plus *-rakko* /-łakko/ 'big' (Read 1934; Martin and Mauldin 2000). Possibly related names are **Opelika** (Ala., Lee Co.) and **Opintlocco Creek** (Ala., Macon Co.).

OPATA (Calif., San Diego Co.) \ō´ pə tə\. From Spanish *Ópata,* the name of an Indian people, belonging to the Sonoran branch of the Uto-Aztecan language family and living in northwestern Mexico (Gudde 1998).

OPECHEE Point (Mich., Houghton Co.) \ō pē´ chē\. From Ojibwa (Algonquian) *opichi* 'robin', used in Longfellow's *Hiawatha* (Vogel

1986; Nichols and Nyholm 1995). The name occurs as a transfer in Maine (Hancock Co.), N.H. (Belknap Co.), and Mont. (Carter Co.).

OPEKISKA (W.Va., Monongalia Co.). Named for an Indian leader, perhaps from an Algonquian group, also known as **White Day** (Kenny 1945).

OPELIKA (Ala., Lee Co.) \ō pi lī´ kə\. Perhaps from the same source as **Opa-Locka** (Fla., Dade Co.); see above. The form **Opeleika** occurs in Ga. (Catoosa Co.).

OPELOUSAS (La., St. Landry Par.) \op ə lo͞o´ səs\. Perhaps from Choctaw (Muskogean) *apilosa* 'stalk-black' (Read 1927; P. Munro p.c.).

OPENAKA Lake (N.J., Morris Co.). Also written <Openaki>; probably from Delaware (Algonquian), but of unclear derivation (Becker 1964).

OPINTLOCCO Creek (Ala., Macon Co.). Perhaps from the same source as **Opa-Locka** (Fla., Dade Co.); see above.

OPOSSUM \ō pos´ əm\. The name of this marsupial animal is from CAC Algonquian <opassom>, equivalent to a proto-Algonquian term meaning 'white dog' (*RHD* 1987). As a placename, it occurs in many states (e.g., Ill., Shelby Co.; La., East Feliciana Par.; and Okla., Oklahoma Co.). The less formal equivalent **Possum** also occurs in many placenames.

OQUAGA Creek (N.Y., Broome Co.; Pa., Wayne Co.) \ō kwä´ gə\. Earlier forms are <Aughquagey, Onohaghquage, Ocquango> (etc.); the name is probably Iroquoian and has been said to mean both 'place of hulled-corn soup' (Beauchamp 1907) and 'place of wild grapes' (Donehoo 1928). A variant spelling is **Ouaquaga.** A possibly related placename is **Oquawka**; see below.

OQUAWKA (Ill., Henderson Co.) \ō kwô´ kə\. Perhaps named for a Sauk (Algonquian) leader, <Uc-quaw-ho-ko> or <O-quaw-ho-ko>, known in English as 'gray eyes' (Vogel 1963); or perhaps a transfer name from **Oquaga Creek** (N.Y., Broome Co.); Pa., Wayne Co.).

OQUENOC (N.Y., Suffolk Co.) \ō´ kē nōk\. A variant of **Okenock,** perhaps from SNEng. Algonquian (Tooker 1911).

OQUIRRH (Utah, Salt Lake Co.) \ō´ kər\. From Gosiute (Numic) /uukkatɨ/ [uukkaRɨ̥] 'wood sitting', containing /uu-/ 'wood' and /katɨ/ 'sit' (J. McLaughlin p.c.).

OQUOSSOC (Maine, Franklin Co.) \ō kwos´ ək\. From Abenaki (Algonquian), meaning place of the trout', from <oquassa> 'a type of trout' (Huden 1962).

ORAIBI (Ariz., Navajo Co.) \ō rī´ bē, ə rī´ bē\. Hopi (Uto-Aztecan) *orayvi* [ožáivi] from *oray,* the name of a rock at the site, plus *-vi* 'place' (*HNAI* 9:552, K. Hill p.c.).

ORANGE (N.J., Essex Co.). Perhaps from the name of a Delaware (Algonquian) leader or village or perhaps named after the Dutch prince William of Orange, who became King William III of England (Becker 1964).

ORANOAKEN Creek (N.J., Cumberland Co.) \ôr ə nō´ kən\. Perhaps from Delaware (Algonquian), but the derivation is not clear (Becker 1964). Also written as **Oranoken.**

OREGON \ôr´ ə gon, ôr´ ə gən, är´ ə gən\. The name is recorded from 1765 as referring to a large river of the West, probably the Columbia; early spellings were <Ouragon, Ourigan>. The term was later used for the northwestern region in general and finally for the present state. The origin of the word is obscure and controversial (McArthur 1992). One view is that it is from Cree (Algonquian) <orâgan> 'wooden bowl', a term brought west by French Canadian trappers (Vogel 1968). An alternative view is that it arose from a miswriting of the name of the <Ouisconsink> or **Wisconsin River;** the error resulted in <Ouaricon-sint>, which then lost its final syllable to become <Ouaricon> (Stewart 1967). More recently it has been established that the name is ultimately from Mohegan (Algonquian), meaning 'beautiful river', parallel to the Iroquoian name **Ohio** (I. Goddard p.c.).

OREIDA Spring (Ore., Malheur Co.) \ôr ī´ də\. A combination of elements from the state names **Oregon** and **Idaho,** both of probably Indian origin.

ORENAUG Hills (Conn., Litchfield Co.). Perhaps from a SNEng. Algonquian word meaning 'pleasant land', containing <-auke> 'land' (Huden 1962; W. Cowan p.c.).

ORESTIMBA Creek (Calif., Stanislaus Co.) \ôr əs tēm´ bə\. Probably from a Costanoan language, containing <ores> 'a bear' (Gudde 1998).

ORICK (Calif., Humboldt Co.) \ôr´ ik\. From the Yurok placename /oo'rekw/ (Gudde 1998).

ORISKA (N.Dak., Barnes Co.) \ō ris´ kə\. Perhaps named for the Indian heroine of a poem by Lydia H. Sigourney (1791–1865) (Wick 1988); she may have taken the name from <Orisca>, representing the placename **Oriskany** (N.Y., Oneida Co.).

ORISKANY (N.Y., Oneida Co.) \ō ris´ kə nē\. Earlier spellings are <Ochriskeny, Oriskeni, Orisca>; the term is from an Iroquoian word for 'nettle'; cf. Seneca <o-his´-heh>, Mohawk <ole-his´-ka> (Beauchamp 1907).

ORIZABA (Miss., Tippah Co.) \ôr i zä´ bə\. From the name of a mountain in the state of Veracruz, Mexico; from Nahuatl (Aztecan) *ahuilizapan,* perhaps containing *ahuilia* 'to irrigate' and *-pan* 'place' (Peñafiel 1897).

ORONIKOWAKTALIK Rock (Alaska, Nunivak Is. B-5). The Yupik (Eskimo) name was recorded in 1949 (Orth 1967).

ORONO (Maine, Penobscot Co.) \ôr´ ə nō\. For an Abenaki (Algonquian) leader, Joseph Orono, who died in 1801 (Eckstorm 1941). The name occurs as a transfer in Minn. (Hennepin Co.).

ORONOCO (Minn., Olmsted Co.) \ôr ə nō´ kō\. For the Orinoco river in Venezuela. Another spelling is found in **Oronoko Township** (Mich., Berrien Co.). The term may have become familiar through the name of the British play *Orinoko,* published in 1696; this was in turn based on the novel *Oroonoko,* published in 1688 (Vogel 1986).

ORONOQUE (Conn., Fairfield Co.) \ôr´ ə nōk\. The term is perhaps from SNEng. Algonquian <woronoke> 'turning place', containing <-auke> 'land, place' (Huden 1962; W. Cowan p.c.). There may be influence from the name of the Orinoco River in Venezuela, however. The placename **Oronoque** occurs as a transfer in Kans. (Norton Co.). Possibly related forms are **Woronock** (Conn., New Haven Co.) and **Woronoco** (Mass., Hampden Co.).

OROWOC Creek (N.Y., Suffolk Co.). Alternative writings are <O-ro-wuc, Orewake>; perhaps from SNEng. Algonquian for 'vacant land' (Beauchamp 1907).

ORSON Island (Maine, Penobscot Co.) \ôr´ sən\. Named for an eighteenth-century Abenaki (Algonquian) resident whose name was *azô* [azǫ], from French *Jean* [žã] (Eckstorm 1941; Day 1994–95).

ORUKTALIK Lagoon (Alaska, Barter Is. A-4). The Iñupiaq (Eskimo) name was reported in 1952 (Orth 1967).

OSAGE \ō sāj´, ō´ sāj\. A people and language belonging to the Dhegiha division of the Siouan language family, living in the lower Missouri River valley. The term is adapted, through French *osage* [ozáž] from the Native American term /wažáže/, which referred to clan groups in several Dhegiha tribes (*HNAI* 13:493; R. Rankin p.c.). As a placename, **Osage** occurs in several states (e.g., Ark., Carroll Co.; Kans., Osage Co.; and Okla., Osage Co.).

OSAGO Township (N.Dak., Nelson Co.). Perhaps from the same source as **Osage**; see above.

OSAHATCHEE Creek (Ga., Harris Co.) \ō sə hach´ ē\. A variant of **Ossahatchie**; see below.

OSAKIS (Minn., Douglas Co.). Probably from Ojibwa (Algonquian) /osa:ki:/, lit. 'person of the outlet', with a prefix /o-/ marking ethnic groups, a stem /sa:ki:/ 'mouth of a river', and either Ojibwa /-s/ 'diminutive' or French *-s* 'plural' (*HNAI* 16:654). The term may refer to the **Sac** or **Sauk** Indian people, who supposedly originated at the outlet of the **Saginaw River** (Mich.); or it may refer to Indians from some other 'outlet'. A related placename is **Ozaukee County** (Wis.).

OSANIPPA (Ala., Chambers Co.) \ō sə nip´ ə\. The Muskogee name may be from *asunwv* /a:sónwa/ 'moss' and *vpe* /apí/ 'tree' (Read 1984); or it may be from <asun-onvpv> /a:son-onápa/, lit. 'moss-upper' (Martin and Mauldin 2000).

OSAWATOMIE (Kans., Miami Co.) \ō sə wä´ tə mē\. Coined out of elements from the names of two Indian peoples, the **Osage** and the **Pottawatomi** (Rydjord 1968).

OSCALOOSA (Ky., Letcher Co.) \os kə lo͞o´ sə\. From the same source as **Oskaloosa,** see below.

OSCAR BOGUE (Miss., Newton Co.) \äs´ kə bōg\. From Choctaw (Muskogean) *oski* 'cane, reed' and *book* 'stream' (Seale 1939; P. Munro p.c.).

OSCAWANA (N.Y., Westchester Co.). Said to be named for a local Indian, presumably of the Munsee (Delaware) people, with earlier writings <Weskora, Weskheun, Weskomen>; the term may mean 'young' or 'green grass' (Ruttenber 1906; Beauchamp 1907).

OSCEOLA \os ē ō´ lə, ō sē ō´ lə\. The name is that of a Seminole (Muskogean) leader who led his people against U.S. forces during the Seminole War in Fla. in the early nineteenth century. The term is from Muskogee *vsse yvholv* /assi-yahó:la/, from /ássi/ 'leaves used for tea', especially leaves of the yaupon holly (used to prepare a beverage called the 'black drink') plus /yahó:la/ 'shouter', used in "war names" (Read 1934; Martin and Mauldin 2000). The bravery and military skill of **Osceola** made him a national hero, and places were named after him in many parts of the United States (e.g., Fla., Osceola Co.; Ill., Stark Co.; and Mass., Berkshire Co.). Related placenames include **Oceola Lake** (N.Y., Westchester Co.) and **Osseola** (Miss., Washington Co.).

OSCO (N.Y., Cayuga Co) \os´ kō\. Said to be from Onondaga (Iroquoian), meaning 'bridge' (Beauchamp 1907; Vogel 1963); cf. Seneca *waskóǫh* 'bridge' (Chafe 1967). Probably related placenames are **Owasco** and **Wasco** (N.Y., Cayuga Co.).

OSCODA (Mich., Iosco Co.) \os kō´ də\. Apparently a shortening of Ojibwa (Algonquian) *mashkode* 'prairie, meadow' (Vogel 1986; Nichols and Nyholm 1995). Related placenames are **Muscoda** (Wis., Grant Co.), **Muskoda** (Minn., Clay Co.); **Lake Muskoday** (Mich., Wayne Co.), **Mascouten Forest, Muscatine County,** and **Mascoutah.**

OSEETAH Lake (N.Y., Franklin Co.) \ə sē´ tə\. Perhaps from an Iroquoian word for 'willow' (Beauchamp 1907); cf. Seneca *oséhta'* 'willow' (Chafe 1967).

OSELIGEE Creek (Ala., Chambers Co.) \ō sə lē´ gē\. Earlier written as <Oselichee>; this may be from Muskogee *vsse-lecv* /assi-líča/, lit. 'leaves-under', from /ássi/ 'leaves used for tea' and /líča/ 'under' (Read 1984; Martin and Mauldin 2000).

OSEUMA (Okla., Ottawa Co.) \os ē o͞o´ mə\. Said to be from Cherokee (Iroquoian) <a'siyu ama> 'good water' (Shirk 1974).

OSHAWA (Minn., Nicollet Co.) \osh´ ə wä\. A transfer name from **Oshawa** in Canada (northwestern shore of Lake Ontario), said to mean 'ferry him over' (Upham 2001); cf. Ojibwa (Algonquian) *aazhawa'o* 'go across by boat' (Nichols and Nyholm 1995).

OSHETNA River (Alaska, Talkeetna Mountains C-1) \ō shet´ nə\. Dena'ina (Athabaskan) *q'usatnu* 'quiver stream', or perhaps 'cliff stream', with *-tnu* 'stream' (Kari and Fall 1987: 190).

OSHKOSH (Wis., Winnebago Co.) \osh´ kosh\. From Menominee (Algonquian) *oskas,* the name of a leader who lived from 1795 to 1850. His name may have meant 'claw' (Vogel 1991; Bloomfield 1975). The placename occurs as a transfer (e.g., Minn., Yellow Medicine Co.; Ore., Lane Co.; and La., Natchitoches Par.).

OSHOTO (Wyo., Crook Co.) \ə shō´ tō\. Said to be from an unidentified Indian language, meaning 'bad weather' (Urbanek 1974).

OSHTEMO (Mich., Kalamazoo Co.) \osh´ tə mô\. The name, supposedly meaning 'headwaters', may have been coined by H. R. Schoolcraft, combining elements of Ojibwa (Algonquian) <oshtigwânima> 'head' and <mokidjiwanibig> 'source, spring' (Vogel 1986); cf. *nishtigwaan* 'my head', *mookijiwanibiig* 'a spring' (Nichols and Nyholm 1995).

OSKALOOSA (Iowa, Mahaska Co.) \os kə lo͞o´ sə\. Supposedly named after a wife of **Osceola,** the Seminole leader (Vogel 1963); her name is perhaps from Choctaw (Muskogean) *oski* 'reed, cane' plus *losa* 'black' (P. Munro p.c.). The placename also occurs in Ill. (Clay Co.), Kans. (Jefferson Co.), and Mo. (Barton Co.). A related placename is **Oscaloosa** (Ky., Letcher Co.).

OSKAWALIK (Alaska, Sleetmute C-6) \os kə wä´ lik\. The Yupik (Eskimo) name, reported in 1898, is said to mean 'shoestring, thong' (Orth 1967).

OSOBAVI Peak (Ariz., Pima Co.). O'odham (Piman) *o:so waw* 'scythe bedrock', from *o:so* 'scythe' (borrowed from Spanish *hoz*) plus *waw* 'bedrock' (J. Hill p.c.).

OSOWAW Junction (Fla., Okeechobee Co.). A name taken from an 1896 Muskogee wordlist that erroneously gives <o-so-waw> 'bird', intending *osahwv* /osáhwa/ 'a crow' (Read 1934; Martin and Mauldin 2000).

OSOYOOS Lake (Wash., Okanogan Co.) \ō soi´ yo͞os\. From the Okanogan (Salishan) placename /suʔíw's/ (A. Mattina p.c.).

OSPOOK Creek (Alaska, Lake Clark A-3). The local name, perhaps from Dena'ina (Athabaskan), was reported in 1954 (Orth 1967).

OSSAGON Creek (Calif., Humboldt Co.) \os´ ə gən\. From the Yurok placename /osegen/ (Gudde 1998).

OSSAHATCHIE (Ga., Harris Co.) \os ə hach´ ē\. Muskogee /osa:-háčči/ 'pokeweed stream', from *osa* /osá:/ 'pokeweed' plus *hvcce* /háčči/ 'stream' (Read 1949–50; Martin and Mauldin 2000). Variants are **Osahatchie and Osahatchee.** Possibly related names include **Sawhatchee** and **Sowhatchee** (Ga., Early Co.).

OSSAWINAMAKEE Beach (Mich., Schoolcraft Co.). Perhaps named after a nineteenth-century Ojibwa (Algonquian) leader, <O-saw-waw-ne-me-ke>, possibly meaning 'yellow-painted land' (Vogel 1986); cf. *ozaawi-* 'yellow', *aki* 'land' (Nichols and Nyholm 1995). A related placename is **Ossawinnamakee** (Minn., Crow Wing Co.).

OSSEO (Mich., Hillsdale Co.) \os´ ē ō\. Named for a character in Longellow's *Hiawatha* (Vogel 1986), of unknown origin. The placename also occus in Minn. (Hennepin Co.) and Wis. (Trempealeau Co.).

OSSEOLA (Miss., Washington Co.) \os ē ō´ lə\. From the same source as **Osceola**; see above.

OSSINEKE (Mich., Alpena Co.). Ojibwa (Algonquian) *asiniika* 'there are many stones', from *asin* 'stone' (Vogel 1986; Nichols and Nyholm 1995). A related placename is **Assinika Creek** (Minn., Cook Co.).

OSSINING (N.Y., Westchester Co.) \os´ i ning\. Earlier written as <Ossinsing>, perhaps Munsee Delaware (Algonquian) for 'stone upon stone' (Beauchamp 1907); cf. Munsee *asún* 'stone' (O'Meara 1996). A related placename is nearby **Sing Sing Prison;** other possibly related names are **Assiniboine Creek** (Mont.), **Assonet** (Mass., Bristol Co.), **Assunpink Creek** (N.J., Mercer Co.), **Stoney Indians Lake** (Mont., Glacier Co.), and **Rocky Mountains.**

OSSIPEE (N.H., Carroll Co.) \os´ i pē\. Perhaps from Abenaki (Algonquian), containing *zibo* 'river' (Day 1994–95). The name occurs in other states (e.g., Maine, Oxford Co.; and N.C., Alamance Co.). **Ossippee Channel** in Alaska (Petersburg A-3) was named for a ship, which was in turn named for the New England location (Orth 1967).

OSVIAK (Alaska, Hagemeister Is. D-4) \os´ vē ak\. The Yupik (Eskimo) name was first recorded by Russian travelers as <Azvichvyak> and <Azi-avik> (Orth 1967).

OSWAYO (N.Y., Cattaraugus Co.; Pa., Potter Co.) \os wā´ yō\. Possibly from Seneca (Iroquoian) *o'só̜æyę'* "place of pines"; cf. *o'sóæ'* 'pine' (Donehoo 1928; W. Chafe p.c.).

OSWEGATCHIE (N.Y., St. Lawrence Co.) \os wē gä´ chē\. Perhaps from Ononadaga (Iroquoian) *oshwɛ'gaaji'* 'black lumber', containing *-shwɛ'gar-* 'lumber' and *-ji-* 'be black' (H. Woodbury p.c.). The placename also occurs in Conn. (New London Co.).

OSWEGO County (N.Y.) \os wē´ gō\. Possibly from Onondaga (Iroquoian) *deyoshweegɛ'* 'splitting waters' (H. Woodbury p.c.). The placename occurs as a transfer in Ill. (Kendall Co.), Kans. (Labette Co.), N.J. (Burlington Co.), and Ore. (Clackamas Co.). A possibly related name is **Swago Creek** (W.Va., Pocahontas Co.).

OSWICHEE (Ala., Russell Co.) \os wich´ ē\. From Muskogee *osuce* /o:sočí:/, the name of a tribal town (Read 1984; Martin and Mauldin 2000). The name also occurs in Ga. (Chattahoochee Co.).

OSYKA (Miss., Pike Co.). Perhaps from Choctaw (Muskogean) *ǫssi* 'eagle', but the derivation is not clear (Seale 1939; P. Munro p.c.).

OTAHKI Lake (Mo., Wayne Co.) \ō tä´ kē\. The name is associated with a legend about a Cherokee (Iroquoian) woman who is supposed to have died here on the "Trail of Tears" during the forced migration from Ga. to Okla. in the nineteenth century (D. Lance p.c.).

OTAPASSO Creek (Miss., Pike Co.). Perhaps from the Choctaw (Muskogean) for 'chinquapin bush', for *otapi* 'chestnut tree' plus *osi* 'little' (Seale 1939; P. Munro p.c.).

OTATSO Creek (Mont., Glacier Co.). Said to be from Blackfeet (Algonquian) *áótahsoowa,* lit. 'one who walks bending', a name given to President John F. Kennedy (Holterman 1985; D. Franz p.c.).

OTAY (Calif., San Diego Co.) \ō tī´, ō´ tī\. Perhaps from Diegueño (Yuman) *'etaay* 'big' (Gudde 1998).

OTEEN (N.C., Buncombe Co.). Said to be from an unidentified Indian language, meaning 'chief aim' (Powell 1968).

OTEGO (N.Y., Otsego Co.) \ō tē´ gō\. Probably related to Mohawk (Iroquoian) *yotékha* 'it is burning', from *-atek-* 'to be burning' (Beauchamp 1907; Michelson 1973). The name occurs as a transfer in Ill. (Fayette Co.), Kans. (Jewell Co.), and Okla. (Payne Co.).

OTEX (Okla., Texas Co.) \ō´teks\. The name was coined form elements of the placenames **Oklahoma** and **Texas**, both of Indian origin; it is adjacent to **Texhoma** (Shirk 1974).

OTIPALIN (Ala., Calhoun Co.). Muskogee <otē palen> /otí: pá:lin/, lit. 'ten islands', referring to a shoal in the Coosa River (J. Mauldin p.c.).

OTIPOBY Comanche Cemetery (Okla., Comanche Co.) \ō ti pō´ bē\. From Comanche (Numic) /otɨ-paapi/ [otɨpaaβi], lit. 'brown water' (J. McLaughlin p.c.).

OTIRGON Creek (Alaska, Killik River A-5). The Iñupiaq (Eskimo) name, published in 1954, is said to mean 'backward creek' (Orth 1967).

OTISCO (N.Y., Onondaga Co.) \ō tis´ kō\. Earlier written as <Otskah, Ostisco>, perhaps from an Iroquoian word meaning 'waters much dried away' (Beauchamp 1907). The placename is found as a transfer in Minn. (Waseca Co.), Mich. (Ionia Co.), Ind. (Clark Co.), and Ga. (Decatur Co.).

OTKURAK Creek (Alaska, Survey Pass C-5). From Iñupiaq (Eskimo) *utkusik* 'cooking pot' (Orth 1967; MacLean 1980).

OTO \ō´ tō\. The name of a people and language, in the Chiwere branch of the Siouan linguistic family. The term was earlier recorded as <Wah-toh-ta-na>, which may be from /watúhtaną/ 'to copulate', or this may be a folk-etymology within the original language (Vogel 1983; *HNAI* 13:460). As a placename, **Oto**

occurs in Iowa (Woodbury Co.); and in the spelling **Otoe** in Kans. (Russell Co.), Neb. (Otoe Co.), and Okla. (Noble Co.).

OTOKOMI (Mont., Glacier Co.). From Blackfoot (Algonquian) *otahko-omii*, lit. 'yellowfish', the name of a man also known as Charles Rose (Holterman 1985; D. Franz p.c.).

OTOMAKUST Flat (Nev., Elko Co.). Perhaps from Northern Paiute or Shoshoni (Numic), but the derivation is not clear (McLaughlin p.c.).

OTOUCALOFA (Miss., Lafayette Co.) \ō tuk´ ə lō fə\. Earlier written as <Otocluffa, Otoclaffah>; perhaps from Choctaw (Muskogean), meaning 'many prairies', from *oktaak* 'prairie' and *lawa* 'many' (Cushman 1899; P. Munro p.c.).

OTOWI (N.Mex., Santa Fe Co.) \ō tō´ wē, ō´ tə wē\. Said to be from Tewa (Tanoan), meaning 'gap where water sinks' (Julyan 1998).

OTSDAWA (N.Y., Otsego Co.) \ots´ dô wə\. Perhaps from an Iroquoian language, but of unclear derivation (Beauchamp 1907); cf. Ononadaga /osdɛhæ'/ (H. Woodbury p.c.).

OTSEGO County (N.Y.) \ot sē´ gō\. Perhaps from Onondaga (Iroquoian) /otji'go'/ 'misty place, clouds in water', containing /-atji'gr-/ 'cloud' (H. Woodbury p.c.). The placename occurs as a transfer in Mich. (Allegan Co.) and Minn. (Wright Co.). In Ohio (Muskingum Co.), the pronunciation \ot sā´ gō\ is reported.

OTSELIC (N.Y., Chenango Co.) \ot sē´ lik\. Probably from an Iroquoian language, but the derivation is not clear (Beauchamp 1907).

OTSIKITA Lake (Mich., Lapeer Co.). Perhaps from Wyandot (Iroquoian) <ochsheetau> 'foot' (Vogel 1986).

OTSQUAGO Creek (N.Y., Montgomery Co.) \ots kwä´ gō\. Perhaps from an Iroquoian language, meaning 'under a bridge' (Beauchamp 1907).

OTTARNIC Pond (N.H., Hillsborough Co.) \ə tär´ nik\. Perhaps from Abenaki (Algonquian) *odanak* 'at the village', from *odana* 'village' (Huden 1962; Day 1994–95).

OTTAWA \ot´ ə wə, ot´ ə wä\. The name of an Algonquian people, closely related to the **Ojibwa** people, living in Mich. and in the Canadian province of Ontario. Their Native American name is /ota:wa:/, sometimes said to be from <adawe> 'to trade' (Vogel 1986; *HNAI* 15:785); cf. *adaawe* 'to buy' (Nichols and Nyholm 1995). The spelling **Odawa** is preferred by Canadian Indians of the group. As a placename, **Ottawa** is not only the capital of Canada but also occurs in several parts of the United States (e.g., Ill., La Salle Co.; Kans., Franklin Co.; and Okla., Ottawa Co.). Probably related placenames include **Ottaway Hollow** (Mo., Dent Co.), **Tawas** (Ohio, Summit Co., Mich., Iosco Co.), **Tawatown** (Ohio, Allen Co.), and **Trade River** (Wis., Polk Co.).

OTTAWANAH (Nev., Elko Co.). Probably Shoshoni (Numic), meaning 'dust trap', from /ota-ppɨh/ 'dust' and /wana/ 'net, trap' (J. McLaughlin p.c.).

OTTAWAY Hollow (Mo., Dent Co.) \ot´ ə wā\. Perhaps from the same source as **Ottawa**; see above.

OTTER Creek (Alaska, Mt. McKinley Qu. D-2). Corresponds to Upper Koyukon (Athabaskan) *bezeye no'*, literally 'otter creek' (J. Kari p.c.). In Ind. (Ripley Co.) **Otter Creek** corresponds to Unami Delaware (Algonquian) /kwənúmuxkw/ 'otter' (McCafferty 2002).

OTTER TAIL County (Minn.). Corresponds to Ojibwa (Algonquian) *nigigwaanowe,* from *nigig, nigigw-* 'otter' plus *-aanow* 'tail' (J. Nichols p.c.) A related placename is **Ottertrack Lake** (Minn., Lake Co.), translating Ojibwa (Algonquian) <nigig-bimi-kawed sagaiigun> 'the lake where the otter made tracks', perhaps referring to places where otters slide over mud or snow into water (Upham 2001); cf. *nigig* 'otter', *bimikawe* 'go along leaving tracks', *zaaga'igan* 'lake' (J. Nichols p.c.).

OTTOKEE (Ohio, Fulton Co.) \ot´ ə kē\. Said to be the name of a Potawatomi (Algonquian) man (Miller 1996).

OTTUMWA (Iowa, Wapello Co.) \ə tum´ wə\. The name of a Meskwaki (Algonquian) village, earlier written <Ottumwah-noc, Ottumwano>. The derivation is not clear (Vogel 1983). The placename occurs as a transfer in Kans. (Coffey Co.).

OTUK Creek (Alaska, Killik River C-5). The Iñupiaq (Eskimo) name was reported around 1950 (Orth 1967).

OUABACHE State Park (Ind., Wells Co.). From the same source as **Wabash County.**

OUACHITA River (La., Union Par.; Ark., Dallas Co.) \wosh´ i tô\. The name is that of a Caddoan people (Read 1927); the term is more familiar as **Wichita** (Kans., Sedgwick Co.). The placename **Ouachita** also occurs in Ark. (Ouachita Co.) and Okla. (Le Flore Co.).

OUAQUAGA (N.Y., Broome Co.) \ō kwä´ gə\. A variant spelling of **Oquaga Creek,** perhaps Iroquoian (Beauchamp 1907).

OUCHKLUNE Range (Alaska, Goodnews Bay D-3). The Yupik (Eskimo) name was recorded in 1898 (Orth 1967).

OULEOUT Creek (N.Y., Delaware Co.) \ō´ lē o͞ot\. Perhaps from Munsee Delaware (Algonquian), meaning 'a continuing voice' (Beauchamp 1907).

OUMALIK River (Alaska, Teshekpuk B-4). The Iñupiaq (Eskimo) name is probably from the same source as **Omalik Creek** (Alaska, Point Lay A-3); see above.

OURAY County (Colo.) \o͞o rā´, yo͞o rā´\. Named for a Ute (Numic) leader of the nineteenth century, called /ɨti/ [ɨri] 'main pole of tipi'; the word for 'king', borrowed from Spanish *rey,* is pronounced the same (Bright 1993; J. McLaughlin p.c.). The placename also occurs in Utah (Uintah Co.).

OUTAGAMIE County (Wis.) \ou tə gam´ ē\. From Ojibwa (Algonquian) /otaka:mi:k/ 'people of the other shore', used to refer to the **Meskwaki** or **Fox** (Algonquian) people (*HNAI* 15:646); cf. *agaami-* 'across' (Nichols and Nyholm 1995).

OUTUCHIWENAT Mountain (Alaska, Goodnews Bay D-3). The Yupik (Eskimo) name was reported in 1898 (Orth 1967).

OUX-KANEE Overlook (Ore., Klamath Co.). Klamath /ʔewksikni:/ 'people of Klamath Marsh', from /ʔewksi/ 'Klamath Marsh' plus /kni:/ 'person or people from' (Barker 1963). **Ouxy** (Ore., Klamath Co.) \ouk´ sē\. is also from the name for Klamath Marsh (Barker 1963).

OVAPA (W.Va., Clay Co.). Composed of elements from the placenames **Ohio,** Virginia, and Pennsylvania (Kenny 1945).

OWACHOMO Bridge (Utah, San Juan Co.). This natural arch was given a name borrowed from the Hopi (Uto-Aztecan) language of Arizona: *owatsmo* 'rocky hill', from *owa* 'rock' and *tsomo* 'hill' (Van Cott 1990, K. Hill 1998).

OWALIT Mountain (Alaska, St. Lawrence C-6). The Yupik (Eskimo) name, reported in 1949, is said to mean 'the north one' (Orth 1967).

OWANECO (Ill., Chistian Co.) \ō wə nē´ kō\. Probably from the same origin as **Oneco** (Conn., Windham Co.); see above.

OWANKA (Minn., Murray Co.) \ə wäng´ kə\. From Dakota (Siouan) *ową́ka* 'a camping place' (Upham 2001; A. Taylor p.c.). The name also occurs in S.Dak. (Pennington Co.).

OWASA (Iowa, Hardin Co.) \ō wä´ sə\. Perhaps from the name *Owaissa,* used in Longfellow's *Hiawatha* to mean 'bluebird' (Vogel 1983); but the derivation of the word is not clear.

OWASCO (N.Y., Cayuga Co.) \ō wä´ skō\. Said to be from Onondaga (Iroquoian), meaning 'bridge' (Beauchamp 1907; Vogel 1963); cf. Seneca *waskǫ́ǫh* 'bridge' (Chafe 1967). The name **Owasco** occurs as a transfer in Ind. (Carroll Co.) and Mo. (Sullivan Co.). Probably related placenames are **Osco** and **Wasco** (N.Y., Cayuga Co.).

OWASIPPE Lake (Mich., Muskegon Co.) \ō wə sip´ ē\. From French <Ouabisipi>, probably from Ottawa (Algonquian) *waab-* 'white' and *ziibi* 'river' (Vogel 1986, Rhodes 1985). The spelling **Owasippi** also occurs.

OWASSA, Lake (N.J., Sussex Co.) \ō wä´ sə\. The name may be from Delaware (Algonquian), but the derivation is not clear (Becker 1964). This placename also occurs in Pa. (Tioga Co.).

OWASSO Lake (Minn., Ramsey Co.) \ō wä´ sō\. Perhaps from an Algonquian word for 'bear' (Upham 2001); cf. Abenaki *awasos* (Day 1994–95). A possibly related placename is **Wauseon** (Ohio, Fulton Co.). **Owasso** (Okla., Tulsa Co.) is perhaps from Osage (Siouan), meaning 'the end' (Shirk 1974).

OWATONNA (Minn., Steele Co.). From Dakota (Siouan) *owótąna* 'straight' (Upham 2001; Riggs 1890). The name also occurs in N.Y. (St. Lawrence Co.), and the alternative spelling **Owattonna** is found in S.Dak. (Potter Co.).

OWEEP Creek (Utah, Duchesne Co.) \ō´ wēp\. Perhaps from Ute (Numic) /uippi/ 'canyon' (J. McLaughlin p.c.).

OWEGO (N.Y., Tioga Co.) \ə wē´ gō\. Perhaps from an Iroquoian language, meaning 'where the valley widens' (Beauchamp 1907). The place name also occurs in Pa. (Pike Co.), and as a transfer in N.Dak. (Ransom Co.).

OWENYO (Calif., Inyo Co.) \ō´ wən yō\. Created out of a combination of elements from two placenames, Owens Lake and **Inyo** (Gudde 1998).

OWHI Creek (Wash., Okanogan Co.) \ou´ hī\. From Yakima (Sahaptian) [ʔáwx̣ay], the name of a nineteenth-century leader (D. Kinkade p.c.). A related placename is **Owyhigh Lakes** (Wash., Pierce Co.).

OWINZA (Idaho, Lincoln Co.) \ō win´ zə\. Perhaps from a Numic (Uto-Aztecan) language, said to mean 'to use as a bed'; but the derivation is not clear (Boone 1988).

O-WI-YU-KUTS Plateau (Colo., Moffat Co.) \ō wī´ yə kuts\. Named for a Ute (Numic) leader; his name may have been /uwáayɨkats/ 'he isn't arriving', from /uwa-/ 'to arrive' (Bright 1993; J. McLaughlin p.c.).

OWL Creek (S.Dak., Meade Co.). Corresponds to Dakota (Siouan), meaning 'owl feathers' (Sneve 1973); cf. *wíyaka* 'feather', *hįhą́* 'owl' (Riggs 1890).

OWOSSO (Mich., Shiawassee Co.) \ō wos´ ō\. Apparently named after <Wasso>, an Ojibwa (Algonquian) leader of the early nineteenth century, from *waasa* 'far' (Vogel 1986; Nichols and Nyholm 1995). A possibly related name is **Wausau** (Wis., Marathon Co.).

OWUNNEGUNSET Hill (Conn., New London Co.). Perhaps from a SNEng. Algonquian word meaning 'at the place of the portage' (Huden 1962).

OWYHEE County (Idaho) \ō wī´ hē, ə wī´ hē\. From Chinook Jargon [owáihi] 'Sandwich Islands, Hawai'i', borrowed either from English or from the Hawai'ian form *Hawai'i,* at a time in the early nineteenth century when a number of Hawai'ians had settled in the Pacific Northwest (D. Kinkade p.c.). The placename **Owyhee** also occurs in Ore. (Malheur Co.).

OWYHIGH Lakes (Wash., Pierce Co.). From Yakima (Sahaptian) [ʔáwx̣ay], the name of a nineteenth-century leader (D. Kinkade p.c.). A related placename is **Owhi Creek** (Wash., Okanogan Co.).

OXADAK Mountain (Alaska, Chandler Lake A-1). The Iñupiaq (Eskimo) name, reported in 1956, is said to be that of an elderly resident (Orth 1967).

OXOBOXO Creek (Conn., New London Co.) \ok sō bok´ sō\. Perhaps from SNEng. Algonquian, meaning 'a small pond' (Huden 1962).

OYACHEN Creek (Wash., Stevens Co.). Perhaps from Spokane (Salishan); the derivation is not clear (D. Kinkade p.c.).

OYAGARUK Creek (Alaska, Wainwright A-1). The Iñupiaq (Eskimo) name, recorded in 1956, is said to mean 'rocky' (Orth 1967); cf. *uyaġak* 'rock' (MacLean 1980). The same root may occur in **Oyagatut Creek** (Alaska, Meade River D-4).

OYAK Creek (Alaska, Goodnews Bay D-8). The Yupik (Eskimo) name was reported in 1898 (Orth 1967).

OYHUT (Wash., Grays Harbor Co.) \oi´ hut\. Chinook Jargon <o´ihat, way´-hut, wee-hut> [óyhət, óyhut] 'road, path, trail', from Lower Chinook <ó-e-hut> 'road, trail' (Hitchman 1985; D. Kinkade p.c.). A related placename is **Wayhut Lake** (Wash., Snohomish Co.).

OYUKAK Mountain (Alaska, Survey Pass C-6). The Iñupiaq (Eskimo) name is *auyuukkaaq,* said to refer to the glacier or snowcap on top of the mountain (Orth 1967; Burch 1998).

OZA Butte (Ariz., Coconino Co.) \ō´ zə\. From Southern Paiute (Numic) /ottsa/ 'water jar', a basket lined with gum to hold water (Granger 1983; J. McLaughlin p.c.).

OZARK Mountains (Mo., Ark., Okla.) \ō´ zärk\. From French *aux Arcs* \ō zärk´\, short for *aux Arcansas* 'to the Arkansas [Indians]' (i.e., to the **Quapaw** people, in the Dhegiha branch of the Siouan family); this group at one time occupied the Ark. area. *Arcansas* (a French plural) was in turn borrowed from Central Algonquian /akansa/ 'Quapaw', derived from Siouan /kką́:ze/, a term referring to the Dhegiha branch; this is the source of the name of the **Kansa** people and of the placename **Kansas** (Dickinson 1995). **Ozark** as a placename occurs in the name of the **Ozark Plateau** (Ark., Mo., Okla.), and by transfer in Kans. (Anderson Co.) and Mich. (Mackinac Co.).

OZA TANKA Lakebed (Minn., Faribault Co.) \ō zə täng´ kə\. The Dakota (Siouan) word apparently contains *thą́ka* 'big' (Upham 2001; Riggs 1890). The spelling **Ozahtanka** also occurs.

OZAUKEE County (Wis.) \ō zô´ kē\. Probably from Ojibwa (Algonquian) /osa:ki:/, lit. 'person of the outlet', with a prefix /o-/ marking ethnic groups plus /sa:ki:/ 'mouth of a river' (*HNAI* 15:654). The term may refer to the **Sac** or **Sauk** people, and to their supposed origin at the mouth of the **Saginaw River** (Mich.); or it may refer to Indians from some other 'outlet'. The placename was transferred to Kans. (Jefferson Co.) as **Ozawkie.** A related term is **Osakis** (Minn., Douglas Co.).

OZETTE (Wash., Clallam Co.) \ō zet´\. From the Makah (Nootkan) placename /ʔuse:ʔiɬ/, which refers literally to a woman's living separately from her husband (W. Jacobsen p.c.).

P

PA-AKO Ruins (N.Mex., Bernalillo Co.) \pə ä´ kō\. Perhaps from Tiwa (Tanoan), meaning 'root of the cottonwood' (Julyan 1998).

PACHALKA Spring (Calif., San Bernardino Co.) \pə chäl´ kə\. Named for a Southern Paiute (Numic) leader (Gudde 1998).

PACHAPPA (Calif., Riverside Co.) \pə chä´ pə, pə chap´ ə\. Perhaps a Gabrielino (Takic) placename (Gudde 1998).

PACHAUG (Conn., New London Co.). SNEng. Algonquian <pachauauke> 'turning place', from <pachau> 'it turns aside' plus <-auke> 'land, place' (Trumbull 1881; W. Cowan p.c.).

PACHET Brook (R.I., Newport Co.). Probably from SNEng. Algonquian <pache> 'up to, as far as' plus <-et> 'place' (Huden 1962; W. Cowan p.c.).

PACHITLA (Ga., Randolph Co.). From Muskogee, perhaps meaning 'pigeon town', from *pace* /pačí/ 'pigeon' plus *tvlwv* /tálwa/ 'town' (Read 1949–50:131, Martin and Mauldin 2000). A possibly related placename is **Pachuta** (Miss., Clarke Co.) \pə cho͞o´ tə\, from Choctaw (Muskogean), meaning 'a pigeon roosts there', from *pachi* 'pigeon', *aay-* 'place', and *atta* 'to live (sg.)' (Seale 1939; P. Munro p.c.).

PACKANACK (N.J., Passaic Co.). Probably from the same source as **Pequannock** (N.J., Morris Co.); see below.

PACKWAUKEE (Wis., Marquette Co.) \pak wô´ kē\. Perhaps from Ojibwa (Algonquian); cf. *bashkw-* 'base, bottom' (J. Nichols p.c.).

PACOIMA (Calif., Los Angeles Co.) \pə koi´ mə\. From Gabrielino (Takic), perhaps meaning 'running water' (Gudde 1998).

PACWAWONG Lake (Wis., Sawyer Co.). Perhaps from Ojibwa (Algonquian) *baagwaa* 'shallow' (Vogel 1991; Nichols and Nyholm 1995).

PADSHILAIKA Creek (Ga., Macon Co.). From Muskogee, said to mean 'pigeon roost'; cf. *pace* /pačí/ 'pigeon', *liketv* /leykitá/ 'to sit' (Krakow 1975; Martin and Mauldin 2000).

PADUCAH (Ky., McCracken Co.) \pə do͞o´ kə, pə dyo͞o´ kə\. Not named for a "Chief Paducah," as claimed by local folkore, but rather from French *Padouca,* a term referring to a number of peoples in the southern plains, first the Plains Apaches and later the Comanches (Dyson 1994). The name may come from a Siouan word referring in general to enemy groups (e.g., Quapaw /ppattookka/, Osage /ppátǫkka/, and Oto /phadų́kha/) (*HNAI* 13:903). As a placename, **Paducah** is found also in Tex. (Cottle Co.). Perhaps related names are **Patocca Lake** (Ark., Lincoln Co.) and **Patoka** (Ill., Marion Co.).

PAD WO'O Tank (Ariz., Pima Co.). O'odham (Piman) *paḍ wo'o* 'evil pond', from *paḍ* 'bad, evil' plus *wo'o* 'pond' (J. Hill p.c.).

PAFALLAYA (Ala., Greene Co.). Perhaps from Choctaw (Muskogean) <pvffvloha> 'a swelling, a bump' (Toomey 1917; Byington 1915).

PAGAHRIT, Lake (Utah, San Juan Co.) \pä´ gə rit\. Perhaps from Southern Paiute (Numic) /paa-kati-ti/ [páaɣaritɨ] 'water standing', containing /paa/ 'water', /kati/ 'stand', and /-ti/ 'participle' (Van Cott 1990; J. McLaughlin p.c.).

PAGILAK River (Alaska, Demarcation Point B-1). The Iñupiaq (Eskimo) name was reported in 1952 (Orth 1967).

PAGOSA Springs (Colo., Archuleta Co.) \pə gō´ sə\. Ute (Numic) /pagósa/ 'sulfur-spring water', from /pa-/ 'water' plus /kwasi/ 'to cook' (Bright 1993; J. McLaughlin p.c.).

PAGUEKWASH Point (Ariz., Mohave Co.). Southern Paiute (Numic) /pakɨu-kwasi/ 'fish-tail' (J. McLaughlin p.c.).

PAGUNA Arm (Alaska, Seldovia C-1). The Athabaskan name is perhaps from Dena'ina *begguna* 'his arm' (J. Kari p.c.).

PAHA (Wash., Adams Co.) \pä´ hä\. Perhaps from Northern Paiute (Numic), meaning 'big water' (Hitchman 1985).

PAHAPESTO Township (S.Dak., Tripp Co.). From Lakhota (Siouan) *pahá-phesto* 'hill-sharp' (A. Taylor p.c.).

PAHAQUARRY (N.J., Warren Co.). Probably from Delaware (Algonquian), but the derivation is not clear (Becker 1964).

PAHA SAPA Trail (S.Dak., Custer Co.). From Lakhota (Siouan) *pahá-sapa* 'Black Hills', lit. 'hill-black' (A. Taylor p.c.).

PAHASKA (Wyo., Park Co.) \pə has´ kə\. From Lakhota (Siouan) *pha-hą́ska* 'hair-long', a name applied to Buffalo Bill Cody (Urbanek 1974; J. Koontz p.c.); cf. *pháha* 'hair of the head', *hą́ska* 'long' (Buechel and Manhart 2002).

PAH Canyon (Nev., Nye Co.) \pä\. Probably from Shoshoni (Numic) /paa/ 'water' (J. McLaughlin p.c.).

PAHE (Okla., Osage Co.) \pä hē`\. Named for an Osage (Siouan) leader, called "Pretty Hair" in English (Shirk 1974); cf. /hpahü´/ 'hair' (R. Rankin p.c.).

PAHLONE Peak (Colo., Chaffee Co.) \pä lōn´, pä lō´ nē\. The name of a Ute (Numic) man, from *paarunu'ni* 'thinder while raining', containing *paa-* 'water' and *tunu'ni* 'thunder' (J. McLaughlin p.c.).

PAHOKEE (Fla., Palm Beach Co.) \pə hō´ kē\. From Hitchiti (Muskogean) /pahi-oki/, lit. 'grass-water', referring to the Everglades (Read 1934; J. Martin p.c.).

PAHRANAGAT Creek (Nev., Lincoln Co.) \pə ran´ ə gət\. From Southern Paiute (Numic) /patanikittsiŋwi/ [paráníɣittsiŋwɨ] 'people who stick their feet in water', containing /pa-/'water',

/ta-/ 'foot', and /nikki/ 'to stick in' (Carlson 1974; J. McLaughlin p.c.).

PAH River (Alaska, Shungnak D-1) \pä\. From Iñupiaq (Eskimo) *paa* 'stream mouth' (Orth 1967; MacLean 1980).

PAHROC Canyon (Nev., Lincoln Co.) \pä´ rok\. Southern Paiute (Numic) /pa-tukkwa/ [parukkwA] 'under the water', from /pa-/ 'water' and /-tukkwa/ 'under' (J. McLaughlin).

PAHRON (Alaska, Lookout Ridge C-3). The Iñupiaq (Eskimo) name was reported in 1949 (Orth 1967).

PAH-RUM Peak (Nev., Washoe Co.) \pä´ rum\. Perhaps from Shoshoni (Numic) /pa-tɨmpi/ 'water-rock' (Carlson 1974; J. McLaughlin p.c.). A related name is **Pahrump Valley** (Calif., Inyo Co.; Nev., Nye Co.) \pä´ rump\, from Southern Paiute (Numic) /pa-tɨmpi/ [parɨ́mpI] 'water-rock' (Gudde 1998).

PAHSIMEROI Mountains (Idaho,Custer Co.) \pə sim´ ə roi\. From Shoshoni (Numic), meaning 'one coming out of the water', from /paa-/ 'water', /sɨmmɨ/ 'one', and /to'i/ 'to emerge' (J. McLaughlin p.c.).

PAHSUPP Mountain (Nev., Pershing Co.) \pä´ səp\. Possibly from Northern Paiute (Numic) /pa'asuuppi'a/ 'higher', containing /pa'a-/ 'high' and /-suuppi'a/ 'more' (J. McLaughlin p.c.).

PAHUTE Lake (Nev., Nye Co.) \pī´ yōōt\. From the same source as **Paiute** or **Piute;** see below.

PAHVANT Butte (Utah, Millard Co.) \pə vänt´\. From Ute (Numic) /paa-pantɨ/ [páavantɨ] 'at the water' (BGN 8304), from /paa/ 'water' (J. McLaughlin p.c.). A variant spelling is **Pavant Butte.**

PAIA Island (Wash. , Cowlitz Co.) \pä´ yə\. Perhaps from Chinook Jargon <pi´-ah, pa´ya, paia, pire> [pə́ya, pə́yə] 'fire', borrowed from English *fire* (D. Kinkade p.c.). A possibly related placename is **Piah Creek** (Idaho, Latah Co.).

PAIAWISIT, Lake (Wis., Oconto Co.). Named for a Menominee (Algonquian) man, /payɛ:wehseh/, said to mean 'bird settling down' (Bloomfield 1975:205). A related placename is **Pywaosit Lake** (Wis., Menominee Co.).

PAICINES (Calif., San Benito Co.) \pī sē´ nəs\. Perhaps from Mutsun (Costanoan) /pay-sen/ 'to get pregnant' (Gudde 1998).

PAIMIUT (Alaska, Hooper Bay C-3) \pī´ myōōt\. Yupik (Eskimo) *paimiut* 'people of the mouth (of a river or tributary)', from *pai-* 'mouth, outlet' (Jacobson 1984). A related placename is **Bimiut.**

PAINGAKMEUT (Alaska, Baird Inlet D-1) \pān gak´ myōōt\. The Yupik (Eskimo) name was reported in 1950; it probably contains *-miut* 'people' (Orth 1967).

PAINOROUYUN Slough (Alaska, Hooper Bay B-3). The Yupik (Eskimo) name was reported in 1951 (Orth 1967).

PAINT Creek (Pa., Cambria Co.). Placenames with **Paint** are likely to refer to locations where Indians obtained pigments for decoration (especially vermillion) or used such pigments to make drawings on trees or rocks. In Pa., the name probably reflects Delaware (Algonquian) <olomoni siipunk>, lit. 'face-paint stream' (Mahr 1959:372–73), or a comparable form in Shawnee (Algonquian). Other placenames in this category occur in Mich. (Iron Co.), Wis. (Chippewa Co.), and Tex. (Concho Co.).

PAIOTA Falls (Mont., Glacier Co.) \pä yō´ tə\. From Blackfoot (Algonquian) *ipottaa, payóttaa* 'to fly; flyer' (Holterman 1985; D. Franz p.c.).

PAISEWA GOEI (Nev., Elko Co.). From Shoshoni (Numic), perhaps meaning 'louse summit', containing /posia/ 'louse' and /ko'i/ 'summit' (J. McLaughlin p.c.).

PAIUTE \pī´ yōōt\. The term is applied to a number of Numic (Uto-Aztecan) peoples living in the Great Basin. The Northern Paiutes, also called Paviotsos, live in northwestern Nev. and adjacent areas, and are closely related to the **Bannock** of Idaho. The Southern Paiute live in southern Nevada and Utah; they are closely related to the **Chemehuevis** of Calif. and to the

Utes of Utah and Colo. **Paiute** is not derived from **Ute** but was borrowed into English from Spanish *payuchis,* which in turn may be from Southern Paiute /paiyuutsiŋwɨ/ 'those who go and return', from /paiyu/ 'to go and return' (Bright 1993; J. McLaughlin p.c.). As a placename, **Paiute** occurs in several states (e.g., Colo., Boulder Co.; Nev., Washo Co.; and Ore., Lake Co.). Alternative spellings are **Pahute Lake** (Nev., Nye Co.) and **Piute** (Ariz., Navajo Co.).

PAIYUN Creek (Alaska, Goodnews Bay D-4). The Yupik (Eskimo) name was reported in 1951 (Orth 1967).

PAKACHOAG (Mass., Worcester Co.). The SNEng. Algonquian name may be from <pahke-> 'clear', <-achu-> 'hill', and <auke> 'land' (Huden 1962; W. Cowan p.c.).

PAKANASINK Creek (N.Y., Orange Co.) \pə kan´ ə singk\. Earlier written as <Pekadasank, Pakasank>; perhaps a Munsee Delaware (Algonquian) name (Beauchamp 1907).

PAKAN TALAHASSI (Ala., Chilton Co.) \pə kän´ tal ə has´ ē\. Perhaps from Muskogee *pvkanv* /paká:na/ 'may-apple, peach>, *tvlwv* /tálwa/ 'town', *vhassē* 'ancient, rancid' (Toomey 1917; Martin and Mauldin 2000).

PAKATAKAN Mountain (N.Y., Delaware Co.) \pə kat´ ə kən\. Earlier written as <Pa-ka-tagh-kan>; perhaps from Munsee Delaware (Algonquian) (Beauchamp 1907).

PAKIM Pond (N.J., Burlington Co.). Perhaps from Delaware (Algonquian) *pakim* 'cranberry' (Kraft and Kraft 1985); cf. Munsee Delaware *páakiim* (O'Meara 1996.) A possibly related placename is **Peckman River** (N.J., Passaic Co.).

PAKOMET Spring (Mass., Norfolk Co.). From SNEng. Algonquian, perhaps containing <pahke-> 'clear' (Huden 1962; W. Cowan p.c.).

PAKOON Springs (Ariz., Mohave Co.). From Southern Paiute (Numic), perhaps meaning 'bubbling water', containing /paa-/ 'water' (Granger 1983; J. McLaughlin p.c.).

PALA (Calif., San Diego Co.) \pä´ lə\. From Luiseño (Takic) *páala* 'water' (Gudde 1998).

PALANUSH Butte (Ore., Deschutes Co.) \pal´ ə nōōsh\. Klamath /palan ʔews/ 'dried up lake, dried up water', containing /pal-/ 'dry up' and /ʔews/ 'lake' (McArthur 1992; D. Kinkade p.c.).

PALATKA (Fla., Putnam Co.). Perhaps from Muskogee *perro-tiketv* /piɬɬo-teykitá/ 'ferry', containing *perro* /piɬɬo/ 'boat' and *tiketv* /tey-kitá/ 'to cross water' (Read 1934; Martin and Mauldin 2000). The placename also occurs in Ark. (Clay Co.), and the related term **Palatkee** is found in Ga. (Evans Co.).

PALATLAKAHA River (Fla., Lake Co.) \pə lat lə kä´ hä\. Perhaps from Muskogee /pil-ak-laká:hi/ 'spotted swamp', from *opelwv* /opílwa/ 'swamp', *ak-* /ak-/ 'in water', and *lvkahē* /laká:hi/ 'spotted' (J. Martin p.c.).

PALELA (Wash., Mason Co.). From Southern Lushootseed (Salishan) /plilaʔ/ 'bitter cherry', perhaps borrowed from /palilaʔ/ of the related Upper Chehalis language (BGN 8301; D. Kinkade p.c.).

PALICHUCOLA Bluff (S.C., Jasper Co.) \pal ə chōōk´ lə\. Also written <Pallachucola>; of unclear origin (Goff 1975:442).

PALIX River (Wash., Pacific Co.) \pä´ liks\. From Lower Chinook [ɬ'píləqs] (Hitchman 1985; D. Kinkade p.c.).

PALOUSE (Wash., Whitman Co.) \pə lōōs´\. From Sahaptin /palús/ 'what is standing up in the water', apparently referring to a large rock in the middle of the Snake River, near the mouth of the **Palouse River** (D. Kinkade p.c.). The placename also occurs in Idaho (Latah Co.) and Ore. (Coos Co.).

PALOWALLA (Calif., Riverside Co.) \pä´ lō wä lə\. Perhaps of Chemehuevi (Numic) origin (Gudde 1998).

PALUGVIK Creek (Alaska, Cordova B-6). The Yupik (Eskino) name was made official in BGN 7403.

PALUXY (Tex., Hood Co.) \pə luk´ sē\. Perhaps from the same source as **Biloxi,** a Siouan people of the lower Mississippi River.

PALWAUKEE (Ill., Cook Co.). Made up by combining elements from the names of **Milwaukee** Avenue and Palatine Road (Vogel 1963).

PAMAS Creek (Idaho, Benewah Co.). This is said to be named by the Forest Service from a Chinook Jargon word meaning 'gold' (Boone 1988), but apparently it is in fact from <pamas'> [pamás] 'cold', from Lower Chehalis (Salishan) /pamás/ 'cold' (D. Kinkade p.c.).

PAMEACHA Pond (Conn., Middlesex Co.). From SNEng. Algonquian, perhaps meaning 'crooked mountain' (Huden 1962).

PAMET River (Mass., Barnstable Co.) \pam´ ət\. From SNEng. Algonquian, perhaps meaning 'wading place' (Huden 1962).

PAMICHTUK Lake (Alaska, Wiseman D-5). The Iñupiaq (Eskimo) name, reported in 1932, is said to mean 'other' (Orth 1967).

PAMLICO County (N.C.) \pam´li kō\. Named for a local Indian group, probably speakers of a CAC Algonquian language (Powell 1968). Possible related forms are **Pamplico** (S.C., Florence Co.) and **Pimlico** (S.C., Berkeley Co.).

PAMOLA Peak (Maine, Piscataquis Co.) \pə mō´lə\. Perhaps from an Abenaki (Algonquian) name for the spirit of the mountain (Rutherford 1970).

PAMO Valley (Calif., San Diego Co.) \pä´ mō\. From the Diegueño (Yuman) placename *paamuu* (Gudde 1998).

PAMPA (Tex., Gray Co.) \pam´ pə\. From Quechua, spoken in the Andean region of South America, meaning 'a plain' (*RHD* 1987). The placename also occurs in Wash. (Whitman Co.).

PAMPLICO (S.C., Florence Co.) \pamp´ li kō\. Probably from the same source as **Pamlico County** (N.C.); see above.

PAMUNKEY (Va., New Kent Co.) \pə mung´ kē\. This term, apparently from the CAC Algonquian language, was applied by the British in the seventeenth century to a number of local groups (Hagemann 1988).

PANA (Ill., Christian Co.) \pā´ nə, pan´ ə\. Named for the <Pani> or **Pawnee** people, of the Caddoan language family (E. Callary p.c.).

PANACA (Nev., Lincoln Co.) \pə nak´ ə\. Earlier written <Panacker>; from Southern Paiute (Numic) /pannakkatɨ/ [pannákkarɨ] 'metal, iron, money' (Carlson 1974; J. McLaughlin p.c.).

PANAKANIC (Wash., Klickitat Co.). The Sahaptin name is of unknown derivation (D. Kinkade p.c.).

PANAMA \pan´ ə mô\. From the name of the Central American nation, said to be an Indian word meaning 'place of many fish'. As a placename, it is widespread in the United States, probably because of the interest aroused by the Panama Canal (e.g., Calif., Kern Co.; Fla., Bay Co.; and Iowa, Shelby Co.).

PANAMETA Point (Ariz., Coconino Co.). Said to be named for a Havasupai (Yuman) man; his name has been given as [apá nahamída] 'man feels glad' (Granger 1983).

PANAMINT Valley (Calif., Inyo Co.) \pan´ ə mint\. From /panɨmɨnt/, a name applied by the Southern Paiute (Numic) Indians of Nev. to the Kawaiisu Indians who lived in the valley (*HNAI* 11:282); the word may be for /pa-/ 'water' plus /nɨwɨntsi/ 'person' (P. Munro p.c.). **Panamint** is also used to refer to a Shoshoni (Numic) group of the same area; they are also called *Koso* (cf. **Coso** above) or Tümpisa.

PANASOFFKEE, Lake (Fla., Sumter Co.) \pan ə sof´ kē\. Muskogee for 'deep valley', from *pvne* /paní/ 'small valley' plus *sofke* /-sófki/ 'deep' (Read 1934; Martin and Mauldin 2000).

PANGNIK, Mount (Alaska, Mt. Michelson A-2). The Iñupiaq (Eskimo) name was made official by BGN 1992.

PANGUIPA Creek (Nev., Elko Co.). Shoshoni (Numic) for 'fish water', from /pankwi/ 'fish' and /paa/ 'water' (Carlson 1974; J. McLaughlin p.c.).

PANGUITCH (Utah, Garfield Co.) \pang´ gwich\. From Southern Paiute (Numic) /pakɨuci/ [paɣɨucI] 'fish person' (i.e., a member of the Panguitch Lake band), from /pakɨu/ 'fish' (Sapir 1930:638).

PANIKPIAK Creek (Alaska, Point Lay A-3). The Iñupiaq (Eskimo) name was that of a former resident of the area (Orth 1967).

PANNAWAY Manor (N.H., Rockingham Co.) \pan´ ə wā\. Perhaps from Abenaki (Algonquian), meaning 'where water spreads out' (Huden 1962).

PAN NEPODK (Ariz., Pima Co.). Perhaps O'odham (Piman) for 'shaped like a loaf of bread', from *pa:n* 'bread' (a borrowing from Spanish *pan*) plus *ñepodk* 'loaf-shaped' (J. Hill p.c.).

PANOCHE Creek (Calif., Fresno Co.) \pə nō´ chē, pə nōch´\. From Mexican Spanish *panoche, panocha* 'raw sugar', sometimes made from wild plant foods. The term may be from Nahuatl (Aztecan) (Gudde 1998).

PANOLA County (Miss.) \pan ō´ lə, pə nō´ lə\. From Choctaw (Muskogean) *ponǫla* or *ponoola* 'cotton' (Seale 1939; P. Munro p.c.). The placename is widespread in the southeastern United States (e.g., Ga., DeKalb Co.; La., East Carroll Par.; Okla., Latimer Co.) and as a transfer name elsewhere (e.g., Ill., Woodford Co.; and Mich., Iron Co.), because of a Civil War battle at Panola, Miss. Probably related placenames are **Penola** (Ala., Sumter Co.) and **Pinola** (Miss., Simpson Co.).

PANOWAT Spit (Alaska, Hooper Bay C-4). The Yupik (Eskimo) name, reported in 1951, is said to mean 'at the end of the hills' (Orth 1967).

PAN TAK (Ariz., Pima Co.). From O'odham (Piman) *ban dak,* lit. 'coyote sitting' (J. Hill p.c.).

PANTHER \pan´ thər\. This term has been used in some parts of the United States to refer to the large feline otherwise known as 'mountain lion', 'cougar', or 'puma'. The word is occasionally found in placenames (e.g., Iowa, Clayton Co.), where it may represent a translation of an Indian name.

PANTIGO (N.Y., Suffolk Co.). Also written <Pantego>; perhaps a SNEng. Algonquian placename (Tooker 1911).

PANUM Crater (Calif., Mono Co.) \pan´ əm\. Perhaps derived from a Numic (Uto-Aztecan) language (Gudde 1998).

PANWAUCKET Creek (Calif., Trinity Co.) \pan´ wô kət\. From Wintu /paani waqat/; /paan-/ is a tree similar to the yew, and /waqat/ is 'creek' (Gudde 1998).

PANYA Point (Ariz., Coconino Co.). From the surname of a Havasupai (Yuman) family (Granger 1983).

PAOHA Island (Calif., Mono Co.) \pä ō´ hə, pā ō´ hə\. From Eastern Mono (Numic) *pa-ohaa* 'water baby' (J. McLaughlin p.c.), referring to a dangerous supernatural creature supposed to live in bodies of water.

PAOLA (Kans., Miami Co.). From the same source as **Peoria**; see below.

PAPAGO \pä´ pə gō, pap´ ə gō\. The term refers to an Indian people and language of the Piman (Uto-Aztecan) linguistic family. The word is from local Spanish *Pápago,* from earlier *Pápabos* and still earlier *Papabi-Ootam*, from Native American *ba:bawĭ-'o"odham* 'people of the tepary beans' (a wild plant food of the Southwest), containing *ba:bawĭ* 'tepary beans' (sg. *ba:wĭ*) plus *'o"odham* 'people' (*HNAI* 10:134). A derivative placename is **Papagueria** (Ariz., Pima Co.) \pā pə gə rē´ ə\, from Spanish *Papaguería* 'place of the Papagos'. At present the people are officially called *Tohono 'O'odham,* lit. 'desert people'.

PAPAKATING (N.J., Sussex Co.) The Delaware (Algonquian) name is possibly from <papaches, papachk> 'woodpecker' plus <atin> 'hill' (Becker 1964).

PAPAKEECHIE Lake (Ind., Kosciusko Co.) \pä pə kē´ chē\. Named after a Miami/Illinois (Algonquian) leader of the early nineteenth century, called "Flat Belly" in English (McPherson 1993); the Native American name was /peepakicia/, also meaning 'bedbug' (M. McCafferty p.c.).

PAPALOTE Creek (Tex., Refugio Co.) \pä pə lō´ tē\. From Mexican Spanish *papalote* 'butterfly, kite, windmill' (Tarpley 1980), from Nahuatl (Aztecan) *papalotl* 'butterfly'. The placename also occurs in Ariz. (Pima Co.).

PAPAW Bayou (La., Morehouse Par.) \pô´ pô, pup´ ô\. From the same source as **Pawpaw,** a type of fruit; see below.

PAPIAK Point (Alaska, Naknek C-3). The Yupik (Eskimo) name was reported in 1952 (Orth 1967).

PAPIGAK Creek (Alaska, Meade River D-4). The Iñupiaq (Eskimo) name was reported in 1950 (Orth 1967).

PAPIOK, Mount (Alaska, Survey Pass C-4). From Iñupiaq (Eskimo) *papiġuq* 'tail of a fish' (Orth 1967; MacLean 1980).

PAPKA (Alaska, Baird Inlet A-2). The Yupik (Eskimo) name was recorded in 1898 (Orth 1967).

PAPOOSE \pap o͞os´, pə poos´\. This NEA Algonquian word for 'child' was recorded in 1643 as <papoòs> and has been widely used to mean 'Indian child' (*RHD* 1987); at present, however, like the word *squaw,* it is considered offensive. As a placename, it has been used throughout the United States (e.g., Conn., New London Co.; Iowa, Warren Co.; and Calif., Trinity Co.).

PAPSCANEE Island (N.Y., Rensselaer Co.) \pap´ skə nē\. The name may be from Mahican (Algonquian); earlier writings are <Papskanee, Poepskenekoes, Papakenea, Popsheny> (Beauchamp 1907).

PAQUANTUCK Brook (R.I., Providence Co.). The SNEng. Algonquian name seems to contain <pahke> 'clear' and <-tuk> 'stream' (Huden 1962; W. Cowan p.c.). A probably related name is **Paqua Pond** (Mass., Dukes Co.); see below.

PAQUA Pond (Mass., Dukes Co.) \pak´ wə\. From SNEng. Algonquian <pahke> 'clear' (Huden 1962; W. Cowan p.c.). The placename also occurs in Wash. (Pend Oreille Co.).

PAQUIAC (N.C., Dare Co.). This may be a CAC Algonquian word meaning 'it is shallow' (Powell 1968). A variant writing is **Paquiwock.**

PARAGONAH (Utah, Iron Co.) \pär ə go͞o´ nə\. From Southern Paiute (Numic) /patookwanna/ [paróoɣwanna] 'fighting water', with /pa-/ 'water' and /tookwa/ 'fight' (J. McLaughlin p.c.). A related placename is **Parowan** (Utah, Iron Co.).

PARAMUS (N.J., Bergen Co.). The Delaware (Algonquian) derivation is not clear (Becker 1964).

PARASHANT Canyon (Ariz., Mohave Co.) \pâr´ ə shant, pär ´ ə shant\. Probably from Southern Paiute (Numic) /pa-tasɨantɨ/ [paráŠɨantɨ], lit. 'water-dawn', containing /paa-/ 'water' and /tasɨa/ 'dawn' (J. McLaughlin p.c.). A variant writing is **Parashont.**

PARGON River (Alaska, Solomon D-3). The Iñupiaq (Eskimo) name was established in 1910 (Orth 1967).

PARIA River (Ariz., Coconino Co.; Utah, Kane Co.) \pə rē´ ə\. From Southern Paiute (Numic) /pa-tɨkia/ [parɨ́ɣia, parɨ́ia] 'elk' (Granger 1983; J. McLaughlin p.c.).

PARIKA Peak (Colo., Jackson Co.) \pə rē´ kə\. From Pawnee (Caddoan) /paariíku'/ 'horn', perhaps because of its shape (Bright 1993).

PARISSAWAMPITTS Canyon (Ariz., Coconino Co.). Southern Paiute (Numic) /patɨsɨŋwan-pittsi/ [parɨ́sɨŋwampittsI], lit. 'sand-gravel-little' (J. McLaughlin p.c.).

PARMACHENEE Lake (Maine, Oxford Co.). Said to be the name of the daughter of an Abenaki (Algonquian) leader, meaning 'across the usual path' (Huden 1962).

PARMICHO (Okla., Coal Co.). Choctaw (Muskogean) *palah mishsha* 'light in the distance', from *palah* 'light', *mishsha* 'far off' (Shirk 1974; P. Munro p.c.).

PAROWAN (Utah, Iron Co.) \pâr´ ə wän\. From the same source as **Paragonah** (Utah, Iron Co.); see above.

PARSIPPANY (N.J., Morris Co.). Earlier written <Parcipponong, Percypenny>; the Delaware (Algonquian) name is of unclear derivation (Becker 1964).

PARTRIDGE Creek (Ill., Woodford Co.). Named for a Potawatomi (Algonquian) leader, known in English as **Black Partridge** (Vogel 1963).

PARUNUWEAP Canyon (Utah, Washington Co.) \pə ro͞o´ nə wēp\. From Southern Paiute (Numic) /patunoippɨ/ [parúnoippɨ] 'whitewater canyon'; cf. /pa-/ 'water', /tusa/ 'white', and /noippɨ/ 'canyon containing water' (J. McLaughlin p.c.).

PASADENA (Calif., Los Angeles Co.) \pas ə dē´ nə\. One of the founders of the community wrote to a friend who was a missionary to the Ojibwa (Algonquian) Indians in Minn., and requested that he suggest an Indian name. The result was *basadinaa* 'valley' (Gudde 1998; Nichols and Nyholm 1995). The placename occurs as a transfer in Ohio (Montgomery Co.) and Tex. (Harris Co.).

PASAGSHAK Bay (Alaska, Kodiak B-2). The Alutiiq (Eskimo) name was published in 1943 (Orth 1967).

PASCACK Brook (N.J., Bergen Co.). Perhaps from Munsee Delaware (Algonquian) *pasíikaxkw* 'board, plank' (Becker 1964; O'Meara 1996). The name also occurs in N.Y. (Rockland Co.).

PASCAGOULA (Miss., Jackson Co.) \pas kə go͞o´ lə\. From the name of a group referred to in Choctaw (Muskogean) as *paska-oklah,* lit. 'bread people' (Seale 1939; P. Munro p.c.). The placename also occurs in La. (Caddo Par.).

PASCO (Wash., Franklin Co.) \pas´ kō\. Said to be named for the *Cerro de Pasco,* a mountain in Peru (Hitchman 1985); the name may then be of Quechua origin. Compare, however, the English surname *Pascoe.*

PASCOAG (R.I., Providence Co.). From SNEng. Algonquian, perhaps meaning 'the dividing place' (Huden 1962).

PASKAMANSET River (Mass., Bristol Co.) \pas kə man´ sət\. From SNEng. Algonquian, perhaps meaning 'at the fork in the path' (Huden 1962).

PASKENTA (Calif., Tehama Co.) \pas ken´ tə\. From Wintu /phas kenti/ 'under the cliff', containing /phas/ 'cliff', or from a similar form in the related Nomlaki (Central Wintun) language (Gudde 1998).

PASPAHEGH (Va., Charles City Co.). The name of a CAC Algonquian subgroup living near the Jamestown settlement (Hagemann 1988).

PASQUAHANZA Clreek (Md., Charles Co.). From CAC Algonquian, perhaps meaning 'forked stream' (Kenny 1984).

PASQUISET Brook (R.I., Washington Co.). Probably from SNEng. Algonquian <pissag> 'mud', <-s-> 'little', <-et> 'place' (Huden 1962; W. Cowan p.c.).

PASQUOTANK County (N.C.). Said to be from an Indian placename <pāsk-e'tan-ki> 'where the current divides'; the language is not identified (Powell 1968).

PASSACONAWAY (N.H., Carroll Co.) \pas ə kon´ ə wā\. Named for an Abenaki (Algonquian) leader. The name may represent <papisse-conwa> 'child-bear' (i.e., 'bear cub') (Julyan and Julyan 1993). The name also occurs in Maine (Somerset Co.).

PASSADUMKEAG (Maine, Penobscot Co.) \pas ə dum´ keg\. From Penobscot (Algonquian) /pasítɑmkik/ 'at the place beyond the gravel bar' (Eckstorm 1941:47–48, Siebert 1943:505).

PASSAGASSAWAKEAG River (Maine, Waldo Co.). Perhaps from Maleseet (Algonquian), said to mean 'place for spearing sturgeon by torchlight' (Huden 1962).

PASSAIC County (N.J.) \pə sā´ ik\. Perhaps from Munsee Delaware (Algonquian) *pahsaèk* 'valley' (Kraft and Kraft 1985); cf. <pachsegink> 'in the valley' (Brinton and Anthony 1888). A possibly related placename is **Passyunk** (Pa., Philadelphia Co.).

PASSAMAGAMET Falls (Maine, Piscataquis Co.). Perhaps from Abenaki (Algonquian), meaning 'place of many fish' (Huden 1962).

PASSAMAQUODDY (Maine, Washington Co.) \pas ə mə kwod´ ē\. The name of an Algonquian people; the Native American form is /pestəmohkatíyək/ (singular /pestə́mohkat/). The original meaning seems to have been 'those of the place of many pollock' (a type of fish); cf. Micmac (Algonquian) /pestəm/ 'pollock' (Rutherford 1970; HNAI 15:135).

PASSAQUA (Mass., Essex Co.) \pas´ ə kwä\. From SNEng. Algonquian; the derivation is unclear (Huden 1962).

PASSAYUNK (Pa., Philadelphia Co.) \pas´ ə yungk\. A variant spelling of **Passyunk**; see below.

PASSEONKQUIS Cove (R.I., Bristol Co.). The SNEng. Algonquian name probably contains <pissag> 'mud' (Huden 1962; W. Cowan p.c.).

PASSUMPSIC (Vt., Caledonia Co.). From Abenaki (Algonquian) *basômkasek* 'where there is puffy sand'; cf. *basômka* 'puffy sand', *basosa* 'it becomes puffy' (Huden 1962; Day 1994–95).

PASSYUNK (Pa., Philadelphia Co.) \pas´ ə yungk, pas´ yungk\. Perhaps from Unami Delaware (Algonquian) *pahsayung* 'in the valley' (Kraft and Kraft 1985); cf. <pachsegink> 'in the valley' (Brinton and Anthony 1888). A variant spelling is **Passayunk**; a possibly related placename is **Passaic County** (N.J.).

PASTOLIK (Alaska, St. Michael A-3) \pas tō´ lik\. Yupik (Eskimo) *pastuliarraq, pastuliq*, from *paste-* 'to become set in position' (Jacobson 1984).

PASUP Spring (Wyo., Fremont Co.). Shoshoni (Numic) /pasappɨ/ 'dried up', from /pasa/ 'dry' (J. McLaughlin p.c.).

PATAGUANSET Lake (Conn., New London Co.). From SNEng. Algonquian, perhaps meaning 'small round place' (Trumbull 1881). A variant is **Pattaquonsett.**

PATAGUMKIS (Maine, Penobscot Co.). A variant of **Pattagumkus**; see below.

PATAHA (Wash., Garfield Co.) \pə tä´ hə, pə tä´ hä\. From the Nez Perce (Sahaptian) placename /patáha/, possibly based on /pátan/ 'bush, brush' (Hitchman 1985; Aoki 1994). The placename also occurs in Ore. (Lane Co.), where it is said to be pronounced \pat´ ə hā\.

PATANGVOSTUYQA (Ariz., Navajo Co.). Hopi (Uto-Aztecan) *patangvostuyqa* 'pumpkin seed point', from *patang-, patnga* 'pumpkin, squash', *-vos-, poosi* 'seed', *tuyqa* 'point' (K. Hill p.c.).

PATAPSCO (Md., Carroll Co.) \pə tap´ skō\. From CAC Algonquian, perhaps meaning 'at the rocky point' (Kenny 1984).

PATASKALA (Ohio, Licking Co.) \pə tas´ kə lə\. Said to be the Delaware (Algonquian) name for the Licking River; the Native American form is <pət-as-əkuə-ələw> 'up to some point a swell of water always exists', from <pət> 'up to a point', <-as-> 'always', <-əkuə-> 'a swell of water', and <-ələw> 'it exists in motion' (Mahr 1959:366).

PATASSA, Bayou (La., Avoyelles Par.) \pä tä sä\. From Louisiana French *patassa* 'bream', a kind of fish; from Choctaw (Muskogean) *nani patassa*, lit. 'fish-flat' (Read 1927; P. Munro p.c.).

PATAULA (Ga., Clay Co.). Perhaps from Choctaw (Muskogean) <patvla> 'flat' (Goff 1975; Byington 1915).

PATAWA Creek (Ore., Umatilla Co.) \pat ə wä\. From the surname of a Umatilla (Sahaptian) Indian family (McArthur 1992).

PATCHOGUE River (Conn., Middlesex Co.). Probably from SNEng. Algonquian <pohshaog>

'place where two rivers divide'; cf. <pachau> 'it turns aside', <-auke> 'land, place' (Tooker 1911; W. Cowan p.c.). The placename is also found in N.Y. (Suffolk Co.).

PATCONG Creek (N.J., Atlantic Co.). The Delaware (Algonquian) name is of unclear derivation (Becker 1964).

PATIT (Wash., Columbia Co.). From Nez Perce (Sahaptian) /pé:tit/ 'branch, rind, bark' (Hitchman 1985; Aoki 1994).

PATO (Wash., Yakima Co.). From Sahaptin /pátu/ 'snow-capped peak', specifically Mt. Adams, lit. 'sitting there (sg. inanaimate)' (N. Rude p.c.).

PATOCCA Lake (Ark., Lincoln Co.). Probably from the same source as **Paducah** (Ky., McCracken Co.) or **Patoka** (Ill., Marion Co.).

PATOKA (Ill., Marion Co.) \pə tō´ kə\. Perhaps named for a Miami/Illinois (Algonquian) leader of the eighteenth century. The term may be from French *Padouca* (Vogel 1963), a Siouan word referring to Southern Plains peoples such as the Comanches and the Plains Apaches. The placename **Patoka** also occurs in Ind. (Gibson Co.). Probably related placenames are **Paducah** (Ky., McCracken Co.) and **Patocca Lake** (Ark., Lincoln Co.).

PATOWMACK Island (Va., Fairfax Co.) \pə tō´ mək\. From the same source as **Potomac River;** see below.

PATSALIGA Creek (Ala., Covington Co.) \pat sə lī´ gə\. From Muskogee *pvce-like* /paciléyki/, lit. 'pigeon-sitting', referring to the now extinct passenger pigeon (Read 1984; Martin and Mauldin 2000). A related form is **Patsiliga** (Ga., Taylor Co.).

PATTAGUMKUS (Maine, Penobscot Co.). Perhaps from Maliseet (Algonquian), meaning 'gravelly bend' (Eckstorm 1941); a variant spelling is **Patagumkis.**

PATTAQUATTIC Hill (Mass., Hampden Co.) \pat ə kwä´ tik\. From SNEng. Algonquian, perhaps containing <petukqui> 'round' (Huden 1962; W. Cowan p.c.).

PATTAQUONSETT (Conn., New London Co.). The SNEng. Algonquian name may mean 'small round place', with the written variant **Pataguanset Lake** (Trumbull 1881).

PATTERSQUASH Island (N.Y., Suffolk Co.) \pat´ ər skwäsh\. Earlier written as <Paterquos, Paterquas> (etc.); from SNEng. Algonquian, of unclear derivation (Tooker 1911).

PATTOWATOMIE Creek (Tex., Henderson Co.) \pä tə wä´ tə mē\. From the same source as **Potawatomi**; see below.

PATTYMOCUS (Calif., Tehama Co.) \pat´ ē mok əs\. Said to be a Wintu name referring to a tipped-over basket; apparently contains the element /muk-/ (Gudde 1998).

PATUISSET (Mass., Barnstable Co.). The SNEng. Algonquian name probably contains <pat-> 'falls', <-s> 'small', <-et> 'place' (Huden 1962; W. Cowan p.c.).

PATUXENT (Md., Charles Co.) \pə tuk´ sənt\. From CAC Algonquian, perhaps meaning 'at the falls' (Kenny 1984).

PAUBA (Calif., Riverside Co.) \pô´ bə\. Perhaps from a Luiseño (Takic) placename (Gudde 1998).

PAUCATUCK (Mass., Hampden Co.). Probably from SNE (Algonquian) <pahke-> 'clear' and <tuck> 'tidal stream' (W. Cowan p.c.).

PAUCAUNLA (Okla., Bryan Co.). Perhaps from Choctaw (Muskogean) *pakąli* 'to bloom, to flower' (Shirk 1974; P. Munro p.c.).

PAUCHAUG Brook (Mass., Franklin Co.) \pô´ chôg\. From SNEng. Algonquian, perhaps meaning 'at the turning place' (Huden 1962). The placename also occurs in N.H. (Cheshire Co.).

PAUGUS Bay (N.H., Belknap Co.) \pô´ gəs\. Probably SNEng. Algonquian for 'small pond', from <bagw-> 'pond', <-s> 'small' (Huden 1962; W. Cowan p.c.). A possibly related placenames is **Paugussett** (Conn., Fairfield Co.), perhaps SNEng. Algonquian for 'small pond place' (Huden 1962).

PAUGWAUNK (Conn., New London Co.). From SNEng. Algonquian, of unclear derivation (Trumbull 1881).

PAULALUK River (Alaska, Demarcation Point B-1). The Iñupiaq (Eskimo) name was reported in 1922 (Orth 1967).

PAULINA (Ore., Crook Co.) \pô lī´ nə\. Named for a leader of the Northern Paiute (Numic) people (McArthur 1992). Since there is no *l* sound in Northern Paiute, **Paulina** may be a modification of the related name **Paunina** (Ore., Klamath Co.).

PAUMANOK (N.Y., Suffolk Co.) \pä´ mə nōk\. The SNEng. Algonquian name, also written as <Paumanack> and <Pommanock>, is of unclear derivation (Tooker 1911).

PAUMA Valley (Calif., San Diego Co.) \pô´ mə\. Possibly Luiseño (Takic) *páa-may* 'little water', from *páa(-la)* 'water' (Gudde 1998).

PAUNAGAKTUK Bluff (Alaska, Umiat A-3). The Iñupiaq (Eskimo) name is *pauŋġaqtuuq* 'lots of blackberries' (Burch 1998); cf. *pauŋġaq* 'blackberry' (Webster and Zibell 1970).

PAUNINA (Ore., Klamath Co.) \pô nī´ nə\. Named for a leader of the Northern Paiute (Numic) people (McArthur 1992). Related names are **Paulina** (Ore., Crook Co.) and **Ponina Creek** (Ore., Klamath Co.).

PAUNSAUGUNT Plateau (Utah, Garfield Co.) \pôn´ sə gənt\. Southern Paiute (Numic) /pauntsikantɨ/ 'has beaver', from /pauntsi/ 'beaver' (J. McLaughlin p.c.).

PAUPACK (Pa., Pike Co.) \pô´ pak\. A shortened form of **Wallenpaupack Creek** (Pa., Pike Co.).

PAUPORES (Minn., St. Louis Co.) \pə pôrz´\. This is a possessive, "Paupore's," from <Paupore> or <Paupori>, the surname of an Ojibwa (Algonquian) family; perhaps from French (Upham 2001).

PAUTIPAUG Hill (Conn., New London Co.). From SNEng. Algonquian <pootupaug> 'a bay', containing <pootu> 'recessed area' and <-paug> 'pond' (W. Cowan p.c.).

PAUTO Lake (Wis., Vilas Co.) \pot´ ō\. Of unclear derivation; but possibly a transfer from **Pato** (Wash., Yakima Co.).

PAVANT Butte (Utah, Millard Co.). Probably from Ute (Numic) /paapantɨn/ [paavantƗ] 'being at the water', with /paa/ 'water' (J. McLaughlin p.c.). A variant spelling is **Pahvant Butte.**

PAVITS Spring (Nev., Nye Co.) \pä´ vits\. Shoshoni (Numic) /papittsi/ [pavíttsI] 'elder brother' (J. McLaughlin p.c.).

PAVO KUG Wash (Ariz., Pima Co.). Perhaps from O'odham (Piman) *waw ke:g,* lit. 'bedrock-standing' (J. Hill p.c.).

PAWCATUCK (Conn., New London Co.) \pô´ kə tuk\. From SNE <pauquatuck> 'clear river', containing <pahke-> 'clear' and <-tuck> 'tidal river' (Huden 1962; W. Cowan p.c.). The placename also occurs in R.I. (Washington Co.).

PAWHUSKA (Okla., Osage Co.) \pô hus´ kə, pə hus´ kə\. Named for an Osage (Siouan) leader of the early nineteenth century; the meaning of the term is 'white hair', from /hpahü´/ 'hair of the head' and /ska/ 'white' (Shirk 1974; R. Rankin p.c.) The term is also applied to a place in Kans. (Neosho Co.; cf. Rydjord 1968). A related placename is **Pahaska** (Wyo., Park Co.).

PAWNEE County (Kans.) \pô nē´, pô´ nē\. The name of an Indian people of the Caddoan family, once living in the central plains. They now live in Okla., and use the term /paári/ in their own language; both this and the English term apparently originate in neighboring Siouan languages (e.g., Omaha /ppáði̯/, Oto /pányi/) (*HNAI* 13:543). The placename occurs, for example, in Colo. (Weld Co.), Ga. (Grady Co.), and Ill. (Sangamon Co.).

PAWN Run (Md., Garrett Co.). Perhaps from the same source as **Pone Island** (Md., Dorchester Co.), from a CAC Algonquian word meaning 'corn cake' (Kenny 1984). A possibly related placename is **Half Pone Point** (Md., St. Mary's Co.).

PAWPAW \pô´ pô\. This name for a native bush and its fruit was borrowed from Spanish *papaya,* referring to a fruit of quite a different kind. The origin is probably a Caribbean language. As a placename, **Pawpaw** occurs in Kans. (Elk Co.) and Ohio (Fairfield Co.). In the spelling **Paw Paw,** it is more widespread (e.g., Ky., Pike Co.; Ill., Lee Co.; and Mich., Van Buren Co.). Possibly related placenames include **Papaw Bayou** (La., Morehouse Par.) and **Poppaw Creek** (N.C., Alamance Co.).

PAWTICFAW Creek (Miss., Kemper Co.) \pô tik´ fô\. Perhaps from Choctaw (Muskogan) *poa aa-tikafa* 'place where wild animals shed their hair', from *poa* 'wild animal', *aa-* 'place', *tikafa* 'to shed hair' (Seale 1939; P. Munro p.c.).

PAWTUCKAWAY Mountains (N.H., Rockingham Co.) \pô tuk´ ə wā, pə tuk´ ə wā\. Perhaps from SNEng. Algonquian <bôn-> 'tall', <-tegw-> 'in the river' (W. Cowan p.c.).

PAWTUCKET (Conn., Windham Co.) \pə tuk´ it\. Perhaps from SNEng. Algonquian <pawtuck> [pąwhtəkw-] 'waterfall' plus <-et> [-ət] 'at' (Trumbull 1881; I. Goddard p.c.). The placename also occurs in Mass. (Middlesex Co.) and R.I. (Providence Co.).

PAWTUXET (R.I., Bristol Co.) \pə tuk´ sit\. From SNEng. Algonquian, meaning 'at the small falls', from <pawtuck> 'waterfall', <-s> 'small', and <-et> 'at' (Huden 1962; W. Cowan p.c.).

PAW WAH Pond (Mass., Barnstable Co.). A variant writing of **Pow-wow**; see below.

PAXICO (Kans., Wabaunsee Co.) \pak´ si kō\. Said to have been named for a nineteenth-century Indian leader called <Pashqua>, perhaps of the Potawatomi (Algonquian) people (Rydjord 1968; R. Rankin p.c.).

PAXINOS (Pa., Northumberland Co.). Named for an eighteenth-century leader of the Shawnee (Algonquian); also written as **Paxinous** and **Paxinosa** (Donehoo 1928).

PAXTANG (Pa., Dauphin Co.) \pak´ stang\. Earlier written as <Peshtang, Paxton, Pechston> (etc.); the name is probably from Delaware (Algqonquian), but the derivation is not clear (Donehoo 1928).

PAYA Point (Ariz., Coconino Co.). The surname of a Havasupai (Yuman) family (Granger 1983).

PEAHALA Park (N.J., Ocean Co.). The Delaware (Algonquian) name is of unclear derivation (Becker 1964).

PEAPACK (N.J., Somerset Co.) \pē´ pak\. The Delaware (Algonquian) name is of unclear derivation (Becker 1964).

PEBOAMAUK Fall (N.H., Coös Co.). Perhaps Abenaki (Algonquian) for 'winter place' (Huden 1962); cf. *bebon* 'winter' (Day 1994–95).

PEBOAN Creek (Mich., Gogebic Co.). The word is used in Longellow's *Hiawatha* to mean 'winter'; cf. Ojibwa (Algonquian) *biboon* 'be winter' (Vogel 1986; Nichols and Nyholm 1995).

PECAN \pi kän´, pi kan´, pē´ kan\. The term refers to a kind of tree and its nuts, growing primarily in the southeastern United States. But the word entered English via French *pacane,* from a generic term for 'nut' that occurs in many Algonquian languages. It may have first entered French from Illinois/Miami <pacana, pacane> (Vogel 1963); cf. also Fox /paka:ni/ 'nut' (Goddard 1994), Ojibwa *bagaan* (Nichols and Nyholm 1995), and Abnaki *bagôn* [bagǫn] (Day 1994–95). As a placename, **Pecan** occurs in La. (Vermilion Par.), Ill. (Fayette Co.), and Iowa (Muscatine Co.). A possibly related placename is **Wawpecong** (IN, Miami Co.).

PECATONE Neck (Va., Westmoreland Co.). Named for a CAC Algonquian leader in the colonial period (Hagemann 1988).

PECATONICA River (Wis., Green Co.; Ill., Winnebago Co.) \pek ə ton´ i kə\. Perhaps inspired by Miami/Illinois (Algonquian) <pekitanoui>, said to mean 'muddy river' (I. Goddard p.c.).

PECAUSETT Pond (Conn., Middlesex Co.). From SNEng. Algonquian, perhaps meaning 'a small clearing' (Huden 1962).

PECHUCK Lookout (Ore., Clackamas Co.) \pə chuk′\. Chinook Jargon <pe-chugh> [pəčə́k] 'green', from Lower Chinook [pčix] 'green' (D. Kinkade p.c.).

PECKERWOOD Creek (Ala., Talladega Co.). The term is used in the South as a variant of *woodpecker*. The placename is probably a translation of *cvkvlv* /čakála/ 'red-headed woodpecker' (Martin and Mauldin 2000).

PECKMAN River (N.J., Passaic Co.). Perhaps from Delaware (Algonquian) <pakihm> 'cranberry' (Becker 1964); cf. Munsee Delaware *páakiim* (O'Meara 1996.) Possibly related placenames are **Pakim Pond** (N.J., Burlington Co.) and **Perkiomen** (Pa., Montgomery Co.).

PECONIC (N.Y., Suffolk Co.) \pē kon′ ik\. From SNEng. Algonquian, perhaps meaning 'a small plantation' (Tooker 1911).

PECONOM Creek (Calif., Lassen Co.) \pə kō′ nəm\. Named for a Maidu Indian woman, Roxie Peconom (1854–1962); the word is probably from Maidu /pekúnim/ 'mountain lion' (Gudde 1998).

PECOS River (N.Mex., Reeves Co.; Tex., Val Verde Co.) \pā′ kōs, pā′ kəs\. From Spanish *Pecos,* from Santo Domingo (Keresan) [p'æyok'ona], the name of **Pecos Pueblo** (N.Mex., Eddy Co.). This term is perhaps from the Jemez (Tanoan) name [p'akyula] (Harrington 1916:475; Julyan 1998). The name is also applied to **Pecos County** in Tex.

PECOUSIC Brook (Mass., Hampden Co.). From SNEng. Algonquian, perhaps meaning 'where the river widens' (Huden 1962).

PECUMSAUGAN Creek (Ill., La Salle Co.). Perhaps from Potawatomi (Algonquian) <pikúmisâgusin> 'hatchets' (Vogel 1963); or from Ojibwa (Algonquian) *apaakozigan* 'kinnikinnick, tobacco mixed with herbs' (Nichols and Nyholm 1995).

PECWAN (Calif., Humboldt Co.) \pek′ wän\. From the Yurok village name /pekwan/ (Gudde 1998).

PEDEE (Ore., Polk Co.) \ped′ ē\. From the same source as **Pee Dee River**; see below. There is also a **Pedee** in Okla. (Noble Co.).

PEE DEE River (N.C., Anson Co.; S.C., Marion Co.). From the name of a people, possibly from Catawban (Siouan) /bé'ire:/ 'they gather pot clay' (B. Rudes p.c.); also written **Peedee.** A related placename is **Pedee** (Ore., Polk Co.; Okla., Noble Co.).

PE ELL (Wash., Lewis Co.) \pē el′\. After Pierre Charles, a man of mixed French and Indian descent; the placename represents an Indian pronunciation of French *Pierre* (Hitchman 1985). Most of the Indian languages of the Northwest do not have an *r* sound and substitute *l*.

PEENPACK Trail (N.Y., Orange Co.). Perhaps of Delaware (Algonquian), of unclear derivation; or perhaps from Dutch (Ruttenber 1906).

PEGAN Hill (Mass., Worcester Co.). From SNEng. Algonquian, perhaps meaning 'bare' (Huden 1962).

PEGATI Lake (Alaska, Goodnews Bay D-3). The Yupik (Eskimo) name was reported in 1898 (Orth 1967).

PEGEELUK Creek (Alaska, Survey Pass C-3). The Iñupiaq (Eskimo) name is *pigiiḷyaq* 'something not good' (L. Kaplan p.c.).

PEIRO (Iowa, Woodbury Co.). From the same source as **Peoria;** see below.

PEJEPSCOT (Maine, Sagadahoc Co.). From Abenaki (Algonquian), said to mean 'long rocky rapids part' (Eckstorm 1941:150–52).

PEJUNKWA Ruin (N.Mex., Sandoval Co.). Jemez (Tanoan) /peejunkwa/ 'heart hill place', containing /peel/ 'heart, soul', /šuun/ 'hill', /-kwa/ 'place' (Y. Yumitani p.c.).

PEKTOTOLIK Slough (Alaska, Kwiguk B-5). The Yupik (Eskimo) name was recorded in 1899 (Orth 1967).

PELAHATCHIE (Miss., Rankin Co.) \pē lə hach′ ē\. From Choctaw (Muskogean), perhaps meaning 'hurricane creek', from *apihli* 'hurricane' and *hachcha* 'stream' (Seale 1939; P. Munro p.c.).

PELAZUK (Alaska, Teller C-6). Previously written <Palazruk>; from Iñupiaq (Eskimo), reported in 1907 (Orth 1967).

PELICAN Township (Minn., Crow Wing Co.). Corresponds to Ojibwa (Algonquian) *zhede-zaaga'igan,* lit. 'pelican-lake' (Upham 2001; Nichols and Nyholm 1995).

PELON Creek (Tex., Dimmit Co.) \pē lōn´\. Spanish *pelón* 'bald' may refer here to Indian groups that shaved their heads; however, the alternative form **Pilon** can also mean 'a loaf of sugar' or 'a gratuity' (Tarpley 1980).

PELTON Creek (Wash. Chelan Co.) \pel´ tən\. Chinook Jargon <pel´ ton, pehlten> [péltən] 'fool, foolish, crazy, insane', from an Anglo resident of Astoria around 1812 who was said to be deranged (Hitchman 1985; D. Kinkade p.c.). **Pelton** (Ore., Jefferson Co.) may be independently named for a family of that name (McArthur 1992).

PELUCIA Bayou (Miss., Leflore Co.) \pə lo͞o´ shə\. Probably from Choctaw (Muskogean), meaning 'flying squirrels are there', from *palih* 'flying squirrel' and *asha* '(pl.) to be there' (Seale 1939; P. Munro p.c.).

PELUK Creek (Alaska, Nome B-1). The Iñupiaq (Eskimo) name, also written as <Peeluk>, was reported in 1902 (Orth 1967).

PEMADUMCOOK Lake (Maine, Piscataquis Co.). Perhaps from Maliseet (Algonquian), meaning 'extended sandbar place' (Huden 1962).

PEMAQUID (Maine, Lincoln Co.) \pem´ ə kwid\. Perhaps from Micmac (Algonquian), meaning 'extended land' (Eckstorm 1941:102–3).

PEMBINA (N.Dak., Pembina Co.) \pem´ bi nə\. From Ojibwa (Algonquian) <anepeminan, nepin ninan> 'cranberry', lit. 'summer berry' (Wick 1988); cf. *aniibiiminagaawanzh* 'high-bush cranberry bush' (Nichols and Nyholm 1995). The placename also occurs in Minn. (Mahnomen Co.). Perhaps related is **Pembine** (Wis., Marinette Co.) \pem´ bīn\.

PEMEBONWON (Wisc., Marinette Co.) \pem ə bon´ won\. Probably from Ojibwa (Algonquian); perhaps related to **Pembina** or to **Pemene Falls** (Vogel 1991).

PEMENE Falls (Wis., Marinette Co.) \pem´ ə nē\. Perhaps from Ojibwa (Algonquian) <biminik> 'elbow' (Vogel 1991). The placename is also found in Mich. (Menominee Co.).

PEMETIC Mountain (Maine, Hancock Co.). Also written <Pem-etnic>; from Abenaki (Algonquian), perhaps meaning 'range of mountains' (Huden 1962); cf. *bemaden* 'mountain range' (Day 1994–95).

PEMIGEWASSET River (N.H., Belknap Co.) \pem i jə wä´ sət\. From Abenaki (Algonquian) *bemijijoasek* [bəmidzidzoasək] 'where side (entering) current is'; cf. *bemijin* 'an angle' (Day 1994–95). A probable variant is **Pemingewasset.**

PEMISCOT County (Mo.) \pem´ i skot, pem´ i skō\. Said to be named for a band of Abenaki (Algonquian) Indians who moved to Mo. in colonial times from their home on what was once called the Pemiscot River in Maine; the name is given as <penoonskeook> 'at the fall of the rocks' (Dickinson 1995:155). The placename also occurs in Ark. (Mississippi Co.).

PEMMAQUAN (Maine, Penobscot Co.). From Abenaki (Algonquian), meaning 'sloping ridge of maple trees' (Eckstorm 1941). Possibly related names are **Penman Rips** (Maine, Washington Co.) and **Pennamaquan Lake** (Maine, Washington Co.).

PEMMICAN \pem´ i kən\. The word refers to a food made by pounding meat together with dried berries, used on long journeys. It probably first entered English in Canada, from Cree (Algonquian) /pimihka:n/, derived from /pimihke:w/ 'he makes pemmican' (*RHD* 1987). As a placename, **Pemmican** occurs in Minn. (Cook Co.), Calif. (Fresno Co.), and Wash. (Snohomish Co.).

PENACOOK (Miss., Worcester Co.) \pen´ ə ko͝ok\. From the same source as **Pennacook** (N.H., Merrimack Co.); see below.

PENANTLY (Miss., Jasper Co.). Perhaps from Choctaw (Muskogean), meaning 'boat-standing place', from *piini* 'boat', *aay-* 'place', *talaya* '(sg.) to stand' (Seale 1939; P. Munro p.c.).

PENASA Lake (Mich., Osceola Co.). From Ojibwa (Algonquian), said to mean 'little partridge' (Vogel 1986); cf. *bine* 'partridge', *binesi* 'thunderbird' (Vogel 1986; Nichols and Nyholm 1995). Possibly related placenames are **Alpena County** (Mich.), **Bena** (Minn., Cass Co.), and **Bina** (N.C., Ashe Co.).

PENATAQUIT Creek (N.Y., Suffolk Co.) \pə nat´ ə kwit\. From SNEng. Algonquian, perhaps meaning 'crooked creek place'; cf. <penayi> 'crooked', <-tukq> 'tidal stream', <-ut> 'place' (Tooker 1911).

PENAWAWA (Wash., Whitman Co.). The name is probably Sahaptin, of unclear derivation (D. Kinkade p.c.).

PEND OREILLE River (Idaho, Bonner Co.; Wash., Pend Oreille Co.) \pän´ də rā, pän də rā`\. From the name of a Salishan Indian people. The English term is adapted from French *pend d'oreilles,* lit. 'hangs from the ears', referring to ear pendants (Hitchman 1985; *HNAI* 12:296). Related placenames are **Pondera County** (Mont.) and **Ponderay** (Idaho, Bonner Co.).

PENHOLOWAY Creek (Ga., Wayne Co.) \pen hol´ ə wā\. Perhaps from Muskogee *fenv* /finá/ 'foot log' (i.e., a log used as a footbridge) plus *hvlwe* /-hálwi/ 'high' (Read 1949–50:203; Martin and Mauldin 2000). A variant is **Phenholoway**; a related placename is **Fenholloway** (Fla., Taylor Co.).

PENIKESE Island (Mass., Dukes Co.). From SNEng. Algonquian, of unclear derivation (Huden 1962).

PENINGO Neck (N.Y., Westchester Co.). Previously also writen <Poningoe>; probably from Munsee Delaware, of unclear derivation (Beauchamp 1907).

PENISTAJA (N.Mex., Sandoval Co.) \pen i stä´ hä\. Perhaps a Spanish adaptation of Navajo (Athabaskan) *bíniishdáhí* 'where I sit leaning against it', containing *binii* 'against it' and *shdá* (*sédá*) 'I sit' (Wilson 1995, Linford 2000).

PENJAJAWOC Stream (Maine, Penobscot Co.). From Abenaki (Algonquian), perhaps meaning 'current falling down raggedly' (Huden 1962).

PENMAN Rips (Maine, Washington Co.) \pen´ mən\. Perhaps a variant writing of **Pennaman Brook, Pennamaquan Lake,** from Abenaki (Algonquian), meaning 'extensive area covered by maple trees' (Huden 1962).

PENNACOOK (N.H., Merrimack Co.) \pen´ ə ko͝ok\. From the Abenaki (Algonquian) village site at Concord, N.H.; the Native American term is *benôkoik* [bənɔ̨koik] 'among the falling-hill people', from *benegôkw, benôko* 'a hill or bank that moves down' (*HNAI* 15:159; Day 1994–95). A related placename is **Penacook** (Mass., Worcester Co.).

PENNAHATCHEE Creek (Ga., Dooly Co.) \pen ə hach´ ē\. From Muskogee, perhaps 'turkey creek', from *penwv* /pínwa/ 'turkey' plus *hvcce* /háčči/ 'stream' (Read 1949–50:131, Martin and Mauldin 2000).

PENNAMAN Brook (Maine, Washington Co.). Perhaps a variant of **Pennamaquan Lake** (Maine, Washington Co.). The name is from Abenaki (Algonquian), perhaps meaning 'extensive area covered by maple trees' (Huden 1962). Possibly related names are **Pemmaquan** (Maine, Penobscot Co.) and **Penman Rips** (Maine, Washington Co.).

PENNESSEEWASSEE Lake (Maine, Oxford Co.). Perhaps from SNEng. Algonquian; it has been translated 'a strange, shining-then-fading light' (Huden 1962).

PENNICHAW (Fla., Volusia Co.). Based on a word taken from a Muskogee wordlist, *penvca* /pinačá:/ 'turkey gobbler' (Martin and Mauldin 2000).

PENNICHUCK (N.H., Hillsborough Co.) \pen´ i chuk\. Probably from Abenaki (Algonquian) *benijoak* meaning 'a rapids, a falls' (Huden 1962; Day 1994–95).

PENNSAUKEN (N.J., Camden Co.). Earlier writings include <Pemsokin, Pimsaquim, Pemisawkin>; probably from Delaware (Algonquian), but of unclear derivation (Becker 1964).

PENNYMOTLEY Creek (Ala., Coosa Co.) \pen i mot´ lē\. Perhaps from Muskogee *penemarv* /pin-imá:ɬa/, possibly a man's "war name", from *penwv* /pínwa/ 'turkey' plus *emarv* /imá:ɬa/ 'a title', sometimes translated 'assistant chief' (Read 1984; Martin and Mauldin 2000).

PENNYPACK (Pa., Philadelphia Co.) \pen´ ē pak\. Early writings were <Pemecaeka, Pemapeck, Pemecacka> (etc.); from Delaware (Algonquian), perhaps meaning 'lake land' (Donehoo 1928).

PENNY POT (N.J., Atlantic Co.). Perhaps a folk-etymology from Delaware (Algonquian), but the derivation is not clear (Becker 1964).

PENOBSCOT (Maine, Hancock Co.) \pə nob´ skot\. Abenaki (Algonquian) *benapskak* 'at down-sloping rocks', from *benapskw* 'sloping rock' (Eckstorm 1941:1–2, Day 1994–95). The name occurs as a transfer in Pa. (Luzerne Co.).

PENOKEE (Kans., Graham Co.) \pə nō´ kē\. Perhaps from an unidentified Indian language; the placename was also formerly reported from Wis. (Rydjord 1968).

PENOLA (Ala., Sumter Co.) \pə nō´ lə\. From the same source as **Panola County** (Miss.); see above. There is also a **Penola** in Ore. (Grant Co.).

PENSACOLA (Fla., Escambia Co.) \pen sə kō´ lə\. The name of a Muskogean group, a Choctaw term meaning 'hair people', from *pąshi* 'hair of the head' plus *oklah* 'people' (Read 1934; P. Munro p.c.) The placename occurs as a transfer in N.C. (Yancey Co.) and Okla. (Mayes Co.).

PENSAUKEE (Wis., Oconto Co.) \pen sô´ kē\. Perhaps from Ojibwa (Algonquian) <pindsagi> 'inside the mouth of a river' (Vogel 1991).

PENTOGA (Mich., Iron Co.). Named for Pentoga Edwards, an Ojibwa (Algonquian) woman (Vogel 1986).

PENTUCKET Lake (Mass., Essex Co.) \pen tuk´ ət\. From SNEng. Algonquian, meaning 'crooked river place', from <penayi-> 'crooked', <-tuck-> 'tidal stream', <-et> 'place' (Huden 1962; W. Cowan p.c.).

PEOA (Utah, Summit Co.) \pē ō´ ə\. Perhaps derived from Ute (Numic) /piwati/ [piwárI] 'get married' (Van Cott 1990; J. McLaughlin p.c.).

PEOGA (Ind., Monroe Co.) \pē ō´ gə\. Perhaps from an Indian word for 'village', language not identified (Baker 1995).

PEORIA (Ill., Peoria Co.) \pē ôr´ ē ə\. The name of a subdivision of the Miami/Illinois (Algonquian) people, recorded in 1673 as <Peoualen> (*HNAI* 15:680); the Native American name is /peewaareewa, peewaalia/ (Costa 2000:48). The placename **Peoria** also occurs in other states (Iowa, Mahaska Co.; Okla., Ottawa Co.). Possibly also related are **Paola** (Kans., Miami Co.), **Peola Branch** (Mo., Reynolds Co.), and **Peiro** (Iowa, Woodbury Co.) (Scheetz 2000:56).

PEOSTA (Iowa, Dubuque Co.) \pē os´ tə\. Said to be the name of a Meskwaki (Algonquian) man who lived in the eighteenth century; but the derivation is not clear (Vogel 1983).

PEOTONE (Ill., Will Co.) \pē´ ə tōn\. Perhaps from Potawatomi (Algonquian) <petone> 'bring here'; cf. Ojibwa (Algonquian) *biidoon* 'bring' (Vogel 1963; Nichols and Nyholm 1995). The name also occurs in Kans. (Sedgwick Co.).

PEPACTON Reservoir (N.Y., Delaware Co.) \pə pak´ tən\. Also written <Pepachton>; perhaps from Munsee Delaware (Algonquian), but the derivation is not clear (Beauchamp 1907).

PEPCHILTK (Ariz., Pinal Co.). From O'odham (Pima) *pi:pcul* 'concave' (Granger 1983; J. Hill p.c.).

PEQUABUCK (Conn., Litchfield Co.). From SNEng. Algonquian <pehquapaug> 'clear pond', containing <pehke> 'clear' and <-paug> 'pond' (Huden 1962; W. Cowan p.c.).

PEQUAMING (Mich., Baraga Co.). Probably from Ojibwa (Algonquian), meaning 'shallow place' (Vogel 1986).

PEQUANNOCK (N.J., Morris Co.) Earlier written as <Pachquakonck, Paqunneck> (etc.);

perhaps Delaware (Algonquian) for 'cleared land' (Ruttenber 1906). A probable related placename is **Packanack** (N.J., Passaic Co.).

PEQUAWKET Pond (Maine, Oxford Co.) \pə kwä´ kət\. From Abenaki (Algonquian) /apíkʷahki/ 'land of hollows' (*HNAI* 15:146). The placename also occurs in N.H. (Carroll Co.). A variant is **Pigwacket.**

PEQUAYWAN Township (Minn., St. Louis Co.) \pə kwā´ ən\. An Ojibwa (Algonquian) name of unclear derivation (Upham 2001).

PEQUEA (Pa., Lancaster Co.). From Shawnee (Algonquian) /pekowe/, a tribal subdivision (*HNAI* 15:634; M. McCafferty p.c.). A related placename is **Pickaway County** (Ohio).

PEQUEST (N.J., Warren Co.). Probably from Delaware (Algonquian), but the derivation is not clear (Becker 1964).

PEQUID Brook (Mass., Norfolk Co.). From SNEng. Algonquian, perhaps meaning 'cleared land' (Huden 1962). A possibly related name is **Pequoig** (Mass., Worcester Co.).

PEQUOD (Conn., New London Co.) \pē´ kwod\. A variant of **Pequot,** from SNEng. Algonquian; see below.

PEQUOIG (Mass., Worcester Co.). From SNEng. Algonquian, perhaps meaning 'cleared land' (Huden 1962); a possibly related placename is **Pequid Brook** (Mass., Norfolk Co.).

PEQUONNOCK River (Conn., Fairfield Co.). From SNE Alonquian, perhaps meaning 'a small plantation' (Huden 1962).

PEQUOP (Nev., Elko Co.) \pē´ kwop\. Shoshoni (Numic) /pikkwappi/ 'something broken', from /pikkwa/ 'to break, to shatter' (J. McLaughlin p.c.).

PEQUOT (Conn., New London Co.) \pē´ kwot\. The name of a SNEng. Algonquian people, from <pequttoog> 'destroyers' (Trumbull 1881; W. Cowan p.c.). The name also occurs in Mass. (Hampden Co.), N.Y. (Westchester Co.), and Ill. (Grundy Co. The placename **Pequotsepos Brook** (Conn., New London Co.) means 'little river of the Pequot'.

PERCOSIN Creek (Ga., Dougherty Co.) \pə kō´ sin\. A variant writing of **Pocosin,** a CAC Algonquian word for 'swamp, marsh'; see below.

PERITSA Creek (Mont., Big Horn Co.). From an Indian word, language not identified, said to mean 'crow' or 'bird' (Cheney 1984).

PERKIOMEN (Pa., Montgomery Co.) \pər kē ō´ mən, pər kī´ ə mən\. Said to be from Delaware <pakihmomink> 'where there are cranberries' (Donehoo 1928); cf. Munsee Delaware *páakiim* 'cranberry' (O'Meara 1996). Possibly related placenames are **Pakim Pond** (N.J., Burlington Co.) and **Peckman River** (N.J., Passaic Co.).

PERMETER Creek (Ala., St. Clear Co.). Perhaps from Muskogee, meaning 'owl's wood'; cf. *opv* /opá/ 'owl' and *eto* /itó/ 'tree' (Read 1984; Martin and Mauldin 2000). A variant is **Permita.**

PEROTE Lake (Wis., Menominee Co.). Named for Sabatis Perrote, a Menominee (Algonquian) leader in the early twentieth century (Vogel 1991).

PERQUIMANS County (N.C.). Said to be named for an Indian group, perhaps of CAC Algonquian affiliation (Powell 1968).

PERSIMMON \pər sim´ ən\. The name of the fruit was first recorded from CAC Algonquian as <pessemmins> (etc.), containing proto-Algonquian */-min-/ 'fruit, berry' (*RHD* 1987). As a placename, the term occurs in Md. (St. Mary's Co.), S.C. (Saluda Co.), and Okla. (Woodward Co.).

PERU \pə rōō´, pē rōō´\. From Spanish *Perú,* the South American nation, said to be from Quechua <pelu> 'river' As a placename, the term occurs in many U.S. states (e.g., Ill., La Salle Co.; Mass., Berkshire Co.; and N.Y., Clinton Co.).

PESABIC Lake (Wis., Lincoln Co.). Probably from an unidentified Indian language (Vogel 1991). The spelling **Pesobic** and pronunciation \pə sō´ bik\. are also recorded.

PESHASTIN (Wash., Chelan Co.) \pə shas´ tən\. From Moses-Columbian (Salishan) /npspísaʔstn/ [npšpíšaʔštən], perhaps meaning 'flat rock' (D. Kinkade p.c.).

PESHAWBE (Mich., Leelanau Co.) \pə shō´ bē\. Named for an Ottawa (Algonquian) leader of the late nineteenth century; the name is also preserved in the form **Peshawbestown** or **Peshabestown** \pə shô´ bē toun\. (Vogel 1986), in which the *s* is not customarily pronounced.

PESHEKEE RIVER (Mich., Marquette Co.). Named for an Ojibwa (Algonquian) leader of the early nineteenth century, from *bizhiki* 'buffalo' (Vogel 1986; Nichols and Nyholm 1995).

PESHLAKAI Point (Ariz., Coconino Co.). Shortened from Navajo (Athabaskan) *beesh łikaiitsidí* 'silversmith', containing *beesh łikaii* 'silver' (*beesh* 'flint', *łikaii* 'white') (A. Wilson p.c.). The related placename **Peshlaki** (Ariz., Coconino Co.; Utah, Garfield Co.) reflects the Navajo word for 'silver' by itself.

PESHTIGO (Wis., Marinette Co.) \pesh´ ti gō\. Perhaps from Menominee (Algonquian) <pasatiko>, of unclear derivation (Vogel 1991).

PESKEOMSKUT Island (Mass., Franklin Co.). From SNEng. Algonquian, meaning 'split rock place', containing <pek(hommin-)> 'to split', <-ompsk> 'rock', <-ut> 'place' (Huden 1962; W. Cowan p.c.).

PESOTUM (Ill., Champaign Co.). Named for a Potawatomi (Algonquian) leader of the early nineteenth century; also written <Pee-so-sum> (Vogel 1963).

PESPATAUG (Conn., New London Co.). From SNEng. Algonquian, also written <Passpatanage> (Trumbull 1881).

PETALUMA (Calif., Sonoma Co.) \pet ə lo͞o´ mə\. From Coast Miwok /péta lúuma/ 'hillside ridge' (Gudde 1998). The placename occurs as a transfer in Fla. (Read 1934).

PETEETNEET Creek (Utah, Utah Co.) \pə tēt´ nēt\. The name of a nineteenth-century Numic (Uto-Aztecan) leader (Van Cott 1990).

PETER, Saint (Wash., Ferry Co.). This name of a creek is from the surname of an Indian family at the Colville Reservation (Hitchman 1985). A related placename is **Pe Ell** (Wash., Lewis Co.).

PETIT MANAN Point (Maine, Washington Co.) \pə tēt´ mə nan\. Meaning 'small island', from French *petit* 'small' and Abenaki (Algonquian) *menahan, menaan* 'island' (Day 1994–95). Possibly related placenames are **Manana Island** (Maine, Lincoln Co.), **Manhan River** (Mass., Bristol Co.), **Manhannock** (Conn., Hartford Co.), **Manhanock Pond** (Maine, Piscataquis Co.), and **Manhasset** (N.Y., Nassau Co.).

PETOBEGO Pond (Mich., Grand Traverse Co.). From Ojibwa <bitobig> 'pond, pool' (Vogel 1986).

PETOSKEY (Mich., Emmet Co.) \pə tos´ kē, pə tok´ ē\. Named for an Ottawa (Algonquian) resident of the nineteenth century; the name is also written <Petosegay> (Vogel 1986).

PETTAQUAMSCUTT River (R.I., Washington Co.). The SNEng. Algonquian name may mean 'round rock place' (Huden 1962).

PETTICOCOWAH (Miss., Grenada Co.) \put ə kə kō´ ə\. Choctaw (Muskogean), meaning 'broken sumac', from <bvti> 'a type of sumac' and <kakoa> 'broken' (Seale 1939; Byington 1915).

PEULIK, Mount (Alaska, Ugashik C-2). Perhaps Alutiiq (Eskimo) for 'smoking mountain' (Orth 1967).

PEWABECK Falls (Mich., Ontonagan Co.) \pə wä´ bik\. From Ojibwa (Algonquian) *biiwaabik* 'iron' (Vogel 1986; Nichols and Nyholm 1995). Related placenames include **Pewabic** (Mich., Houghton Co.) and **Bewabic Park** (Mich., Iron Co.).

PEWAMO (Mich., Ionia Co.) \pə wä´ mō\. Named for an Ojibwa (Algonquian) leader; the term is perhaps from <biwamo> 'the trail diverges' (Vogel 1986).

PEWAUKEE (Wis., Waukesha Co.) \pē wô´ kē\. Probably from an Algonquian language, of unclear derivation (Vogel 1991).

PEWAWAI (Wash., Garfield Co.). Said to be from Nez Perce (Sahaptian), meaning 'small creek' (BGN 7904).

PHALIA, Bogue (Miss., Washington Co.) \fə lī´ ə\. From Choctaw (Muskogean) *book* 'creek', *falaya* 'long' (Seale 1939; P. Munro p.c.).

PHENATCHIE Creek (Ala., Pickens Co.) \fē nach´ ē\. From Choctaw *fani* 'squirrel(s)' and *asha* 'are there' (Read 1984; P. Munro p.c.). The spellling **Fenache Creek** is used elsewhere (Ala., Sumter Co.). Related placenames are **Fannegusha Creek** (Miss., Holmes Co.) and **Funny Creek** (Miss., Pontotoc Co.).

PHENHOLOWAY (Ga., Wayne Co.) \fen hol´ ə wā\. A Muskogee word meaning 'high bridge', from *fenv* /finá/ 'foot-log, bridge', *hvlwe* /hálwi/ 'high' (Read 1934; Martin and Mauldin 2000). A variant is **Penholoway**; a related placename is **Fenholloway** (Fla., Taylor Co.).

PHILEMA (Ga., Lee Co.). Named for a leader of the Chehaw town of the Creek (Muskogean) Confederacy; his name was also written <Fullemy> (Krakow 1975). The name is said to be pronounced locally as [flim´ me] or [fil´ mē] (Goff 1975).

PIAH Creek (Idaho, Latah Co.) \pī´ yə\. Chinook Jargon <pi´-ah> [páia] 'fire, burned, cooked, ripe', from English *fire*; so named by the Forest Service because timber in the area had been burned off (Boone 1988, D. Kinkade p.c.). A probably related name is **Paia Island** (Wash., Cowlitz Co.).

PIA Mission (Wash., Ferry Co.). From Okanagan (Salishan) /pəʕa/ 'red-tailed hawk' (A. Mattina p.c.).

PIANKASHAWTOWN (Ill., Edwards Co.). The Piankashaws were an Algonquian group associated with the Miami/Illinois (*HNAI* 15:689). The name was /peeyaankihšiiwa, peeyankihšia/, probably meaning 'having torn or slit ears' (Costa 2000:49).

PIANKATANK (Va., Gloucester Co.). Probably from CAC Algonquian; of unclear derivation (Hagemann 1988).

PIANUM (Nev., White Pine Co.). Perhaps from Shoshoni (Numic) /paiyan/ 'bee' or /paihyɨn/ 'kangaroo rat' (J. McLaughlin p.c.).

PIA OIK (Ariz., Pima Co.) \pē ə oik\. From O'odham (Piman) *pi 'o'oik,* lit. 'not striped' (J. Hill p.c.).

PIAPI Canyon (Nev., Nye Co.). Perhaps from Shoshoni (Numic) /piappɨh/ 'big' (J. McLaughlin p.c.).

PIASA (Ill., Macoupin Co.) \pī´ sä\. From Miami/Illinois (Algonquian) /payiihsa/ 'legendary dwarf' (D. Costa p.c.).

PIASUK River (Alaska, Teshekpuk D-3). The Iñupiaq (Eskimo) name was reported in 1951 (Orth 1967).

PIATO VAYA (Ariz., Pima Co.). The O'odham (Piman) name contains *wahia* 'well' (J. Hill p.c.).

PICABO (Idaho, Blaine Co.) \pē´ kə bo͞o\. Perhaps a Numic (Uto-Aztecan) name, of unclear derivation (Boone 1988).

PICATINNY Lake (N.J., Morris Co.). From Delaware (Algonquian), perhaps from <peek, pic> 'still water' plus <atin> 'hill' (Becker 1964).

PICCOWAXEN Creek (Md., Charles Co.). The CAC Algonquian name has also been written <Pukewaxen, Pickyawaxent, Piciowaxon>, perhaps meaning 'broken shoe' (Kenny 1984).

PICEANCE Creek (Colo., Rio Blanco Co.) \pē´ ans\. Perhaps Shoshoni (Numic) /piasonittsi/ 'tall grass', with /pia-/ 'big' and /soni-/ 'grass' (J. McLaughlin p.c.); the discrepancy between the spelling and the pronunciation has not been explained (Bright 1993).

PICKAWAY County (Ohio) \pik´ ə wā\. From /pekowe/, a division of the Shawnee (Algonquian) people; earlier writings are <Peckawee, Pecowick> (etc.) (*HNAI* 15:634; M. McCafferty p.c.). The name **Pickaway** also occurs in W.Va. (Monroe Co.), and Ill. (Shelby Co.). Related placenames are **Pequea** (Pa., Lancaster Co.) and **Piqua** (Ohio, Miami Co.).

PICK-AW-ISH Campground (Calif., Siskiyou Co.) \pik ä´ wish\. From Karuk *pikyávish,* a term used to refer to the world renewal ceremony held every fall near this site. The term is not originally Karuk, but rather is a white simplification of *ithívthaaneen upikyávish* 'he will re-make the world', referring to the ceremonial actions of the Karuk priest (Gudde 1998).

PICKENS (Okla., McCurtain Co.). Named for Edmond Pickens, a prominent Chickasaw (Muskogean) (Shirk 1974).

PICKWACKET Pond (N.Y., Hamilton Co.) \pik wak´ ət\. Perhaps from the same source as **Pequawket Pond** (Maine, Oxford Co.); see above.

PICOLATA (Fla., St. Johns Co.) \pik ə lä´ tə\. A Spanish spelling for the name of an Indian settlement, perhaps Seminole (Muskogean); of unclear derivation (Read 1934).

PICURIS (N.Mex., Taos Co.) \pik yo͞o rēs´\. Spanish *Picurís,* perhaps from Keres <pee-koo-ree-a> 'those who paint', referring to the Tiwa (Tanoan) pueblo (Julyan 1998).

PIEGAN (Mont., Glacier Co.) \pā´ gan\, formerly pronounced \pē ä´ gan, pē ä´ gən\. The name of this Blackfoot (Algonquian) people is French *Piégane,* from Cree (Algonquian) /piye:kano-iyiniw/ 'Piegan people', from Blackfoot /pi:(ʔ)káni/, plural /pi:(ʔ)kániwa/, said to be from /apiikani/ 'people with scabby robes (from poorly processed hides)' (*HNAI* 13:627, D. Franz p.c.).

PIENELUK Island (Alaska, St. Michael A-4). The Yupik (Eskimo) name was reported in 1952 (Orth 1967).

PIESTEWA Peak (Ariz., Maricopa Co.) \pī ´ es tə wä\. Named in 2003 for Army PFC Lori Piestewa, the first female American Indian soldier to die in combat; she was killed during the Iraq invasion. Her Hopi (Uto-Aztecan) family name was shortened from *polìipayestiwa,* from *polìi-, povolhoya* 'butterfly' (E. Sekaquaptewa p.c.). This mountain was previously called **Squaw Peak;** American Indian groups had campaigned for a replacement of this term, which was found offensive by some (see **Squaw** below).

PIGEON River (Ind., Lagrange Co.). A translation of Potawatomi (Algonquian) /wabmimi/ 'white pigeon', for a Native American leader by that name (McCafferty 2002). Another **Pigeon River** (Minn., Cook Co.) corresponds to Ojibwa (Algonquian) *omiimii-ziibi,* lit. 'pigeon-river' (Upham 2001; Nichols and Nyholm 1995); a related placename is **Omemee** (N.Dak., Bottineau Co.).

PIGWACKET (Maine, Oxford Co.). A variant of **Pequawket Pond**; see above.

PIK Dunes (Alaska, Teshekpuk A-1). From Iñupiaq (Eskimo) <piq> 'dish, pot'; reported in 1956 (Orth 1967).

PIKMIKTALIK River (Alaska, St. Michael B-2). Yupik (Eskimo) *petmigtalek* 'place with many pit traps', from *petmik* 'pit trap' (Jacobson 1984).

PIKONIK Mound (Alaska, Harrison Bay B-1). Perhaps from Iñupiaq (Eskimo) <pingoqneg> 'high lookout place' (Orth 1967).

PIKROKA Creek (Alaska, Meade River B-2). The Iñupiaq (Eskimo) name was reported in 1956 (Orth 1967).

PIKSIKSAK Creek (Alaska, Meade River A-2). The Iñupiaq (Eskimo) name is probably *pisiksaġiaġvik* 'place to go shoot' (L. Kaplan p.c.).

PILCHUCK (Wash., Snohomish Co.) \pil´ chuk\. Chinook Jargon <pil chuck>, lit. 'red water', from <pil´-pil> [pílpɪl] 'blood, red', from Lower Chinook [tɬpɪl] 'red'; and <chuck> [čʌk] 'water, river', from Nootka /č'aʔak/ 'water, river' or Lower Chinook [-čúq^{W}] (Hitchman 1985; D. Kinkade p.c.). Related placenames are **Pilpil Butte** (Ore., Deschutes Co.) and **Skookum Chuck Creek** (Ore., Baker Co.).

PILDISH Spit (Wash., Jefferson Co.). Twana (Salishan) /sp'əlíč/ 'pond on dry land', containing /p'íl-/ 'pond' (D. Kinkade p.c.).

PILLAGER (Minn., Cass Co.). The English term, meaning 'person who pillages or robs', refers to an Ojibwa (Algonquian) band; cf. *makandwe* 'to pillage' (J. Nichols p.c.).

PILON Creek (Tex., Dimmit Co.) \pi lōn\. Perhaps from Spanish *pelón* 'bald', which may refer to Indian groups that shaved their heads (Tarpley 1980); but see the alternative form **Pelon Creek,** above.

PILPIL Butte (Ore., Deschutes Co.) \pil´ pil\. Chinook Jargon <pil´-pil> [pîlpɪl] 'blood, red', from Lower Chinook [tɬpɪl] 'red' (McArthur 1992; D. Kinkade p.c.). A related placename is **Pilchuck** (Wash., Snohomish Co.).

PIMA \pē´ mə\. The name refers to a Uto-Aztecan people of central Ariz.; **Piman** includes them along with the closely related **Papago** people as well as related groups in northwest Mexico. The Native American term is probably from *pi ma:c* '(I) don't know', mistaken by the Spanish for a tribal name; or from *pima* 'no', as used by southern Piman speakers in Mexico (*HNAI* 10:134, J. Hill p.c.). As a placename, the term is applied to **Pima County** (Ariz.). The related placename **Pimeria Alta** (Pima Co.) \pē mə rē´ ə äl´ tə, al´ tə\. is Spanish *Pimería Alta* 'upper Pima country', referring to territory occupied by Piman speakers in Ariz., as opposed to others in Mexico.

PIMLICO (S.C., Berkeley Co.) \pim´ li kō\. Perhaps from the same source as **Pamlico County** (N.C.) or **Pamplico** (S.C., Florence Co.); influenced by *Pimlico,* the name of a district in London, England.

PIMUSHE Lake (Minn., Beltrami Co.) \pi mo͞osh\. The Ojibwa (Algonquian) name is of unclear derivation (Upham 2001).

PINACATE (Calif., Riverside Co.) \pē nə kä´ tē, pin ə kä´ tē\. Mexican Spanish for a type of black beetle locally called 'stink bug', from Nahuatl (Aztecan) *pinacatl* (Gudde 1998). The term also occurs in Ariz. (Yuma Co.) A related placename is **Pinecate Peak** (Calif., San Benito Co.).

PINALENO Mountains (Ariz., Graham Co.) \pin ə lā´ nō\. From Spanish *pinaleño,* referring to an Apachean (Athabaskan) band; perhaps from Western Apache *bįįh* 'deer' (Granger 1983; Bray 1998). Alternatively, the term may be Spanish for 'belonging to the pine grove', from *pinal* 'pine grove' (*pino* 'pine') (Granger 1983).

PINCHONA (Ala., Baldwin Co.) \pin chō´ nə\. Perhaps from Muskogee, containing *penwv* /pínwa/ 'turkey' (Read 1984; Martin and Mauldin 2000). The possibly related name **Pinchoulee Creek** (Ala., Coosa Co.) reflects Muskogee *pen-vcule* /pin-ačól-i/ 'old turkey', with *vculē* /ačóli/ 'old' (Read 1984; Martin and Mauldin 2000).

PINCONNING (Mich., Bay Co.) \pin kon´ ing\. From Ojibwa (Algonquian), meaning 'place of the wild potato', referring to *opin,* originally an edible native root or tuber (Vogel 1986; Nichols and Nyholm 1995).

PINECATE Peak (Calif., San Benito Co.). From the same source as **Pinacate** (Calif., Riverside Co.); see above.

PINE Creek (Pa., Lycoming Co.). Corresponds to Delaware (Algonquian) <Cuwenhanne> (Donehoo 1928); cf. Unami Delaware /kú:we:/ (Blalock et al. 1994).

PINE Island (Minn., Goodhue Co.). A translation of Dakota (Siouan) *wazí-wita* (Upham 2001; Riggs 1890).

PINE Lake (Minn., Cook Co.). A translation of Ojibwa (Algonquian), from *zhingwaak* 'white pine' plus *zaaga'igan* 'lake' (Upham 2001; Nichols and Nyholm 1995).There is a similarly named **Pine Lake** in Wis. (St. Croix Co.). **Pine River** (Minn., Crow Wing Co.) corresponds to Ojibwa (Algonquian) *zhingwaako-ziibi* (Upham 2001; Nichols and Nyholm 1995).

PINE LOG Creek (Ga., Cherokee Co.). Corresponds to a Cherokee (Iroquoian) name meaning 'pine footlog', from *nohji* 'pine' and *asvhdlv'i* 'footlog, bridge' (Goff 1975; Feeling 1975).

PINE RIDGE (S.Dak., Shannon Co.). A translation of Lakhota (Siouan) *wazí-paha* 'pine hill' (Sneve 1973; A. Taylor p.c.).

PINGALUK (Alaska, Survey Pass B-2) \ping´ gə luk\. The Iñupiaq (Eskimo) name, reported in 1900, means 'bad hill'; cf. *pinguq* 'individual round hill', *-lluk* 'bad' (Orth 1967; Webster and Zibell 1970); see also **Pingo Lake,** below. Perhaps from the same root are the Alaska placenames **Pingaluligit Mountain** (Killik River C-2), **Pingaluruk Creek** (Noatak D-2), and **Pingasagruk** (Wainwright D-1) (Orth 1967).

PINGO Lake (Alaska, Baird Inlet D-7) \ping´ gō\. The term is used in Alaskan English to mean 'a mound formed by frost or freezing above the permafrost' (Orth 1967). It entered English from Iñupiaq (Eskimo) *pinguq* 'individual round hill' (*RHD* 1987; Webster and Zibell 1970); but cf. Yupik *penguq* 'hill' (Jacobson 1984). Other Alaska placenames also probably containing the Iñupiaq word are **Pingok Island** (Beechey Point C-5), **Pingokraluk Point** (Demarcation Point C-1) (Orth 1967), **Pingorarok Hill** (Wainwright B-3), **Pingu Bluff** (Point Hope B-3), **Pingucheak** (Point Hope B-3), **Pinguk River** (Teller D-5), and **Pungokosit Spit** (St. Lawrence C-5).

PINGOOTIKOOK Bay (Alaska, St. Lawrence A-2). The Yupik (Eskimo) name was reported in 1949 (Orth 1967); perhaps from *penguq* 'hill' (Jacobson 1987); cf. **Pingo Lake** above.

PINGORA Peak (Wyo., Fremont Co.) \ping gôr´ ə\. Perhaps from Shoshoni (Numic) /piaŋkuta/ 'mother's neck', from /pia/ 'mother' and /kuta/ 'neck' (J. McLaughlin p.c.).

PINGORAROK Hill (Alaska, Wainwright B-3). From Iñupiaq (Eskimo), reported in 1923, meaning 'many hills' (Orth 1967); cf. **Pingo Lake,** above. Alaska placenames from the same root are **Pingu Bluff** (Point Hope B-3); **Pingucheak** (Point Hope B-3), meaning 'little hill'; and **Pinguk River** (Teller D-5) (Orth 1967).

PINGURBEK Island (Alaska, Kuskokwim Bay D-6). The Yupik (Eskimo) name was reported in 1950 (Orth 1967); cf. **Pingo Lake,** above.

PIN HOOK Bridge (La., Lafayette Par.). Perhaps from Choctaw (Muskogean) *panashshok, pishannok* 'linden tree, basswood' (Read 1927; Byington 1915).

PINICON Ridge (Iowa, Linn Co.) \pin´ i kon\. Shortened from **Wapsipinicon River** (Iowa, Scott Co.), from Meskwaki (Algonquian) /wa:pesi:hpenihka:hi/ 'arrowhead', a plant with an edible root (Vogel 1983; I. Goddard p.c.).

PINK Creek (Ga., Heard Co.). From the same source as **Punk Creek** 'rotten wood, tinder' (Goff 1975); see below.

PINKIDULIA (Alaska, Iliamna A-4). The name, perhaps from Alutiiq (Eskimo), was reported in 1923 (Orth 1967).

PINNEBOG (Mich., Huron Co.). Perhaps from Ojibwa (Algonquian) <binebag> 'partridge leaf' (Vogel 1986).

PINNICKINNICK Mountain (W.Va., Harrison Co.). Perhaps from the same source as **Kinnickinnick** 'herbal mixture used for smoking' (Kenny 1945), from Delaware (Algonquian) (*RHD* 1987).

PINNYANAKTUK Creek (Alaska, Wiseman D-2). The Iñupiaq (Eskimo) name has been translated as 'absolute perfection of beauty' (Orth 1967).

PINOLA (Miss., Simpson Co.) \pə nō´ lə\. From the same source as **Panola County;** see above.

PINOLE (Calif., Contra Costa Co.) \pi nōl´\. Mexican Spanish 'ground and toasted grain', from Nahuatl (Aztecan) *pinolli* (Gudde 1998).

PINTHLOCCO (Ala., Coosa Co.) \pinth lok´ ō\. The Muskogee name may mean 'large turkey' (Toomey 1917); cf. *penwv* /pínwa/ 'turkey', *-rakko* /ɬákko/ 'large' (Martin and Mauldin 2000).

PINTLALA (Ala., Montgomery Co.) \pint lä´ lə\. Earlier written <Pa-thlau-la, Pilth-lau-le>; perhaps from Muskogee (Read 1984).

PINUSUK Island (Alaska, Stepovak Bay D-4). The name, perhaps Aleut, was reported in 1875 (Orth 1967).

PIOCHE Creek (Utah, Grand Co.). Perhaps from Numic (Uto-Aztecan) (Van Cott 1990).

PIPE Creek (Ind., Madison Co.). Named for "Captain Pipe," a Unami Delaware (Algonquian) leader in the late eighteenth century; his Native American name was /hupɔ́:kkan/ 'tobacco pipe' (McPherson 1993; Brinton and Anthony 1888). Cf. also **Hoboken**.

PIPESTONE County (Minn.). The name corresponds to Ojibwa (Algonquian) *opwaagan* 'tobacco pipe' (Upham 2001; Nichols and Nyholm 1995). The placename **Pipestone** also occurs in Mich. (Berrien Co.); **Pipestone Creek** is in Wis.

PIPSUK Point (Alaska, Barter Is. A-5). The Iñupiaq (Eskimo) name was reported in 1952 (Orth 1967).

PIPYAK (Ariz., Pima Co.). Perhaps from Papago (Piman), of unclear derivation (Granger 1983).

PIQUA (Ohio, Miami Co.) \pik´ wā, pik´ wə\. The name refers to a band of the Shawnee (Algonquian) people (*HNAI* 15:634); the Native American term is /pekowe/ (M. McCafferty p.c.). The name also occurs in other states (Ky., Robertson Co.; Kans., Woodson Co.). Related placenames are **Pequea** (Pa., Lancaster Co.) and **Pickaway County** (Ohio).

PIRU (Calif., Ventura Co.) \pi ro͞o´, pē´ ro͞o, pī ro͞o´\. From Tatavyam (Takic) [pi'idhu-ku], the name of a plant (Gudde 1998).

PISCASAW Creek (Wis., Walworth Co.; Ill., Boone Co.) \pis´ kə sô\. Perhaps from Potawatomi (Algonquian) <pesheka> 'buffalo' (Vogel 1991); cf. Ojibwa *bizhiki* (Nichols and Nyholm 1995).

PISCASSIC River (N.H., Rockingham Co.) \pi skas´ ik\. From Abenaki (Algonquian) *beska-* 'branch (of a river)' (Huden 1962; Day 1994–95). Probably containing the same root, with <-tekw> 'river', are **Piscataqua River** (Maine, Cumberland Co.; N.H., Rockingham Co.) \pi skat´ ə kwä\; **Piscataquis County** (Maine, Eckstorm 1941:255) \pi skat´ ə kwis\; and **Piscataquog Mountain** (N.H., Hillsborough Co.) \pi skat´ ə kwog\.

PISCATAWAY (N.J., Middlesex Co.) \pi skat´ ə wā\. Perhaps from Delaware (Algonquian), meaning 'branching of a stream' (Becker 1964); cf. **Piscassic River** (N.H., Rockingham Co.) and **Pikscataqua River** (Maine, Cumberland Co.) above. The name also occurs in Md. (Prince George's Co.) and Va. (Essex Co.).

PISCOE Creek (Wash., Yakima Co.) \pis´ kō\. From Sahaptin /písxu/ 'sage-brush, *Artemisia*' (D. Kinkade p.c.).

PISCOLA (Ga., Thomas Co.). Perhaps from Muskogee *pesē* /pisí:/ 'milk' and *kvlv* /kalá/ 'white oak' (Read 1949–50:131; Martin and Mauldin 2000).

PISECO (N.Y., Hamilton Co.) \pi sē´ kō\. The name of an Indian resident, derived from an Algonquian language; earlier written <Peezeko, Pezeeko> (Beauchamp 1907).

PISHAK Island (Alaska, Port Alexander D-5). Perhaps a Tlingit name, reported in 1919 (Orth 1967).

PISINIMO (Ariz., Pima Co.). O'odham (Piman) *pisinmo'o* 'bison head', from *pisin* 'bison, buffalo' plus *mo'o* 'head' (J. Hill p.c.).

PISMO Beach (Calif., San Luis Obispo Co.) \piz´ mō\. Obispeño (Chumashan) /pismu'/ 'tar, asphalt', lit. 'dark place, dark stuff', from /piso'/ 'to be black, dark' (Gudde 1998).

PISTAKEE (Ill., McHenry Co.) \pis tak´ ē\. Perhaps from Ojibwa (Algonquian) *bizhiki* 'buffalo' (Nichols and Nyholm 1995). The placename also occurs in Wis. (Kenosha Co.).

PISTAPAUG Mountain (Conn., Middlesex Co.). SNEng. Algonquian <pissagkipaug> 'muddy pond', from <pissagki> 'mud' and <-paug> 'pond' (Trumbull 1881; W. Cowan p.c.).

PISTUK Peak (Alaska, Goodnews Bay C-2). The Yupik (Eskimo) name was reported as <Piskut> in 1898, and as <Piskuk> in 1900 (Orth 1967).

PITA (N.Mex., Harding Co.) \pē´ tə\. The American Spanish word means both 'fiber, twine' and 'century plant', from which such fiber is extracted; it may be from a Latin American Indian language (Julyan 1998).

PITAHAYA Canyon (Ariz., Pima Co.) \pē tə hä´ yə\. The American Spanish word, referring to a type of cactus and its edible fruit, is from the Taino language of the Caribbean (*RHD* 1987).

PITAMAKAN Lake (Mont., Glacier Co.). Named for a Blackfoot (Algonquian) woman warrior called /píítaomahkaan/ 'eagle running', from /píítaa/ 'eagle' and /omahkaa-/ 'to move on foot' (Holterman 1985; D. Franz p.c.).

PITCHUK Lake (Alaska, Bettles D-4). The Native American name, probably from Iñupiaq (Eskimo), was reported in 1956 (Orth 1967).

PITHLACHASCOTEE River (Fla., Pasco Co.) Possibly from Muskogee *perro* /piłło/ 'canoe, boat' plus *cvskvtē* /časkati:/ 'chopped', referring to a place where canoes were made (Read 1934; Martin and Mauldin 2000).

PITHLACHOCCO (Fla., Alachua Co.). Muskogee *perro-cuko* /piłło-čóko/ 'ship', lit. 'boat-house' (Read 1934; Martin and Mauldin 2000).

PITKIK Creek (Alaska, Shungnak D-4). The Iñupiaq (Eskimo) name was reported in 1927 (Orth 1967).

PITMEGEA River (Alaska, De Long Mountains D-5). The Iñupiaq (Eskimo) name was reported in 1888 (Orth 1967).

PITOIKAM (Ariz., Pima Co.). From Papago (Piman), perhaps meaning 'sycamore place' (Granger 1983).

PITSUA Butte (Ore., Deschutes Co.) \pits´ wä\. Perhaps from a Klamath placename or from Northern Paiute <wapota pitsua> 'kangaroo rat' (McArthur 1992).

PITTALUKRUAK Lake (Alaska, Teshekpuk D-4). The Iñupiaq (Eskimo) name, said to mean 'old coming-through place', was reported in 1951 (Orth 1967).

PIUTE \pī´ yo͞ot\. A variant of **Paiute** (see above), a term applied to several Numic (Uto-Aztecan) peoples of the Great Basin. The word is not derived from the tribal name **Ute** but from local Spanish *payuchis,* probably borrowed from a Southern Paiute term. The spelling **Piute** is used for places in Ariz. (Navajo Co.), Calif. (Fresno Co. and elsewhere), Nev. (Lander Co.), Ore. (Lake Co.), and Utah (Piute Co.). Another related form is **Pahute Lake** (Nev., Nye Co.).

PIYUKENUK River (Alaska, Hooper Bay C-1). The Yupik (Eskimo) name was reported in 1951 (Orth 1967).

PLANTATION Lake (Wis., Iron Co.) **Plantation,** now used to refer to a type of large-scale agriculture, was also used earlier to refer to small plots where corn and other vegetables were grown by Indians of the eastern United States (Vogel 1991). A related usage is found in **Planting Ground Lake** (Wis., Oneida Co.).

PLAQUEMINE (La., Iberville Par.) \plak´ ə min, plak´ min, plak´ mən\. The term is La. French for 'persimmon', probably from Miami/Illinois (Algonquian) <piakimina> (Read 1927). Related La. placenames are **Plaquemines Parish** and **Bayou Plaquemine Brulé** (Acadia Par.) \bro͞o´ lē\, French for 'burnt persimmon (tree)'.

PLATTE River (Colo., Neb.) \plat\. The stream was named *Rivière Platte* 'flat river' by French explorers in 1739 because of its shallowness. This corresponds to its Omaha (Siouan) name /ne-braska/ 'water-flat', whence the word **Nebraska** (Bright 1993).

PLAUSAWA Hill (N.H., Merrimack Co.) \plôz´ ə wä\. Named for an eighteenth-century Abenaki

(Algonquian) warrior; probably contains *belaz* 'passenger pigeon' (Huden 1962; Day 1994–95).

PLEHNAM, Lake (Wash., Yakima Co.). Perhaps from a Sahaptin placename /ptɪxnam/ (D. Kinkade p.c.). A related placename is **Taneum Creek** (Wash., Kittitas Co.).

PLENTY COUPS Peak (Wyo., Park Co.) \plen´ tē ko͞o\. Named for a Crow (Siouan) leader. French *coup* 'a stroke, a blow' was borrowed into English to refer to the act of striking or killing an enemy among Plains Indians warriors (Whittlesey 1988). An alternative spelling is **Plentycoos.**

PLUM Creek (Pa., Armstrong Co.). Corresponds to Delaware (Algonquian) <sipuas-hanne> 'plum-stream' (Donehoo 1928); cf. Unami Delaware /sí:pu:wa:s/ (Blalock et al. 1994).

PLUSH (Ore., Lake Co.). Named after a Northern Paiute (Numic) resident, supposedly for his pronunciation of English *flush,* referring to a hand in poker (McArthur 1992).

POCA (W.Va., Putnam Co.) \pō´ kə\. An abbreviation of **Pocatalico** (W.Va., Kanawha Co.); see below.

POCAHANTAS (Conn., Fairfield Co.). A variant of **Pocahontas** \pō kə hon´ təs\. The daughter of the CAC Algonquian leader **Powhatan;** her Native American name has been given as <Pokachantesu> 'she is playful' (Vogel 1983). The placename **Pocahontas** is widespread (e.g., Va., Tazewell Co.; W.Va., Pocahontas Co.; and Ill., Bond Co.). Related forms include **Pocahuntas** (N.C., Swain Co.). Pocahontas was also called **Matoaca,** with a similar meaning, and that too appears as a placename (e.g., Va., Chesterfield Co.).

POCALLA Creek (S.C., Sumter Co.) \pō kal´ ə\. Perhaps an abbreviaton of **Pocataligo** (S.C., Jasper Co.).

POCANTICO River (N.Y., Westchester Co.) \pō kən tē´ kō\. Earlier written <Pocanteco, Puegkandico, Perghanduck, Pecantico> (etc.); perhaps from Munsee Delaware (Algonquian) <pohki-tuck-ut> 'clear-stream-place' (Ruttenber 1906; Beauchamp 1907).

POCASSE, Lake (S.Dak., Campbell Co.). Named for an Arikara (Caddoan) leader; his Native American name was /pákʌs/ 'straw, oats' (D. Parks p.c.).

POCASSET (Mass., Barnstable Co.) \pə kas´ ət\. SNEng. Algonquian, perhaps from <pokshau> 'it divides' plus <-et> 'place' (W. Cowan p.c.). The name also occurs in R.I. (Providence Co.), Maine (Kennebec Co.), and Okla. (Grady Co.). A variant is **Pucasset River**. Possibly related placenames are **Pochassic** (Mass., Hampden Co.) and **Pocksha Pond** (Mass., Plymouth Co.).

POCATALICO (W.Va., Kanawha Co.) \pō kə tal´ i kō\. Perhaps from an Algonquian language, said to mean 'plenty of fat doe' (Kenny 1945). A perhaps related placename is **Pocotalaco** (Fla., St. Johns Co.) It is not clear whether this term is related to **Pocotaligo** (S.C., Jasper Co.).

POCATALIGO (S.C., Jasper Co.). A variant of **Pocotaligo**; see below.

POCATAW (Fla., Orange Co.) \pō´ kə tô\. A word chosen from a Muskogee wordlist, based on *vpoktv* /(a)pó:kta/ 'twins' (Read 1934; Martin and Mauldin 2000).

POCATELLO (Idaho, Bannock Co.) \pō kə tel´ ō\. Said to be named for a Shoshoni (Numic) leader; perhaps /paakatɨtɨ/ 'sitting water', from /paa/ 'water' and /katɨ/ 'one sits' (J. McLaughlin p.c.). The placename occurs as a transfer in N.Y. (Orange Co.).

POCCOSIN Swamp (S.C., Dillon Co.) \pə kō´ sin\. From the same source as **Pocosin,** a generic term for 'swamp'; see below.

POCHASSIC (Mass., Hampden Co.). The SNEng. Algonquian name is perhaps from <pokshau> 'it divides' (W. Cowan p.c.). Possibly related placenames are **Pocasset** (Mass., Barnstable Co.) and **Pocksha Pond** (Mass., Plymouth Co.).

POCHET Island (Mass., Barnstable Co.). The SNEng. Algonquian name may mean 'narrow place' (Huden 1962).

POCHUCK Creek (N.Y., Orange Co.) \pō chuk\. Probably from Munsee Delaware (Algonquian), perhaps meaning 'a corner or recess' (Ruttenber 1906). The placename also occurs in N.J. (Sussex Co.). Possibly related names are **Lake Pochung** (N.J., Sussex Co.) and **Pojac Point** (R.I., Washington Co.).

POCKOY Island (S.C., Charleston Co.). Perhaps from an unidentified Indian language (Pickens 1963:40).

POCKSHA Pond (Mass., Plymouth Co.). Perhaps from SNEng. Algonquian <pokshau> 'it divides' (W. Cowan p.c.). Possibly related placenames are **Pocasset** (Mass., Barnstable Co.) and **Pochassic** (Mass., Hampden Co.).

POCKWOCKAMUS Falls (Maine, Piscataquis Co.). From Abenaki (Algonquian), perhaps meaning 'little muddy pond' (Huden 1962).

POCOCHICHEE Creek (Mont., Powder River Co.). The Indian name, of unclear origin, was earlier written <Pocochedie>; the present form was made official in BGN 7903.

POCOLA (Okla., Le Flore Co.) \pə kō´ lə\. From Choctaw (Muskogean) *pokkooli* 'ten' (Shirk 1974; P. Munro p.c.).

POCOMO (Mass., Nantucket Co.). Earlier written as <Pakummohquoh>, <Paquomoquat>, <Pocomock>, <Pohcomo> (Little 1984). Probably from SNEng. Algonquian, perhaps containing <pahke-> 'clear' (Huden 1962; W. Cowan p.c.). A possibly related placename is **Pocumtuck Mountain** (Mass., Franklin Co.).

POCOMOKE River (Del., Sussex Co.) \pō´ kə mōk\. From Delaware (Algonquian), perhaps meaning 'clam fishing place' (Heck et al. 1966). The placename also occurs in Md. (Worcester Co.), Va. (Accomack Co.), and N.C. (Franklin Co.).

POCOMOONSHINE Lake (Maine, Piscataquis Co.) \pō kə mo͞on´ shīn\. Probably from Abenaki (Algonquian), perhaps containing *bokwjanakw* 'stump' and *msôgama* 'big lake' (Eckstorm 1941:221; Day 1994–95). Variants are **Pokomoonshine, Poke-o-moonshine, Pokemoonshine.** A related placename is **Pokamoonshine Brook** (N.H., Strafford Co.); and the form **Poky Moonshine** is a transfer in Mo. (Franklin Co.).

POCONO (Pa., Carbon Co.) \pō´ kə nō\. Delaware (Algonquian), perhaps from <Pocohanne> 'stream between mountains' (Donehoo 1928). The placename also occurs in Conn. (Fairfield Co.) and Idaho (Shoshone Co.).

POCOPSON (Pa., Chester Co.) \pə kop´ sən\. Perhaps from Delaware (Algonquian), said to mean 'roaring creek' (Donehoo 1928).

POCOSIN \pə kō´ sin, pō´ kə sin\. This generic term is used in several southeastern states to mean 'swamp, marsh'; it may be from CAC Algonquian <pakwesan> 'swamp' (Kenny 1945). As a specific placename, it occurs in **Pocosin Creek** (Va., Greene Co.) and in similar names elsewhere (N.C., Jones Co.; Ga., Dooly Co.; La., Vernon Par.). Related forms include **Percosin Creek** (Ga., Doughterty Co.), **Poccosin Swamp** (S.C., Dillon Co.), and **Pocoson** (Fla., Dixie Co.).

POCOTALACO (Fla., St. Johns Co.) \pō kə tal´ ə kō\. Probably from the same source as **Pocatalico** (W.Va., Kanawha Co.) or **Pocotaligo** (S.C., Jasper Co.).

POCOTALIGO (S.C., Jasper Co.) \pōk ə tal´ i gō\. Perhaps a placename from the Yamassee variety of Muskogee. The placename also occurs in Ga. (Madison Co.); the variant spelling **Pocataligo** occurs in both S.C. and Ga. It is not clear whether this term is related to **Pocatalico** (W.Va., Kanawha Co.).

POCOTOPAUG Creek (Conn., Middlesex Co.). SNEng. Algonquian <pohqutaepaug> 'divided pond', from <pohqutae> 'divided' and <-paug> 'pond' (Trumbull 1881; W. Cowan p.c.).

POCQUAYAHWAN Lake (Wis., Douglas Co.). The Ojibwa (Algonquian) name may contain *baagwaa* 'be shallow' (Vogel 1991; Nichols and Nyholm 1995).

POCUMCUS Lake (Maine, Washington Co.). Perhaps from Micmac (Algonquian), meaning 'gravelly place' (Huden 1962).

POCUMTUCK Mountain (Mass., Franklin Co.). The SNEng. Algonquian name may contain <pahke-> 'clear' and <-tuck> 'tribal stream' (Huden 1962; W. Cowan p.c.). A possibly related placename is **Pocomo** (Mass., Nantucket Co.).

POCWOCK Stream (Maine, Aroostook Co.). Perhaps from Abenaki (Algonquian) *bôkwod* 'it is shallow' (Rutherford 1970; Day 1994–95).

PODICKERY Point (Md., Anne Arundel Co.). The name is probably from CAC Algonquian; cf. <pawcohiccora> 'hickory' (Kenny 1984). A possibly related placename is **Pohick** (Md., Talbot Co.).

PODUNK (Conn., New Haven Co.) \pō´ dungk, pō dungk´\. Probably from SNEng. Algonquian <pautaunke> 'a boggy place' (Huden 1962; A. Read 1980; Cutler 1996; W. Cowan p.c.). **Podunk** has come to be a metaphor for any remote, rustic locale. The placename appears in several other states (e.g., Mass., Worcester Co.; Mich., Barry Co.; and Utah, Kane Co.). Possibly related placenames include **Potunk** (N.Y., Suffolk Co.) and **Poudunk Swamp** (Ohio, Cuyahoga Co.).

POGA (Tenn., Carter Co.) \pō´ gə\. Perhaps an Indian name of unknown origin (Miller 2001).

POGIK Bay (Alaska, Harrison Bay D-5). The Iñupiaq (Eskimo) name, reported in 1950, is said to refer to 'the white belly fur of the caribou' (Orth 1967).

POGOLIMI (Calif., Sonoma Co.). Apparently a placename from an unidentified Indian language (Gudde 1998).

POGONIP (Nev., White Pine Co.) \pō´ gə nip\. From Shoshoni (Numic) /pakɨnappɨ/ [paɣɨ́nappɨ̥] 'fog' (Carlson 1974; J. McLaughlin p.c.). It has been assigned as a transfer name in **The Pogonip** (Calif., Santa Cruz Co.).

POGOPUK Creek (Alaska, Mt. Michelson B-5). The Iñupiaq (Eskimo) name was assigned in the 1950s (Orth 1967).

POGUE, The (Vt., Windsor Co.) \pōg\. The name of this lake may be from SNEng. Algonquian <pog, poag> 'pond' (Huden 1962).

POGY Brook (Maine, Piscataquis Co.). Perhaps from Abenaki (Algonquian), meaning 'pond' (Rutherford 1970).

POHATCONG Township (N.J., Warren Co.). Probably from Delaware (Algonquian), but of unclear derivation. There is also a **Pohatcong Lake** in another part of N.J. (Ocean Co.).

POHETA (Kans., Saline Co.). Possibly from Osage (Siouan), meaning 'at the fire', from /hpü´e/ 'fire' and /-hta/ 'place' (Rydjord 1968; R. Rankin p.c.).

POHICK (Md., Talbot Co.). The CAC Algonquian term may be related to <pawcohiccora> 'hickory' (Kenny 1984). The placename also occurs in Va. (Fairfax Co.) and W.Va. (Wood Co.). A possibly related name is **Podickery Point** (Md., Anne Arundel Co.).

POHOCCO Township (Neb., Saunders Co.) \pō hō´ kō\. Perhaps from Pawnee (Caddoan) <pahuk> 'headland, promontory' (Perkey 1995).

POHOPOCO Creek (Pa., Carbon Co.). Earlier writings are <Pocho, Pochto, Poopoko>; said to be from Delaware (Algonquian), perhaps meaning 'two mountains bearing down on each other' (Donehoo 1928).

POIA Lake (Mont., Glacier Co.). Named after a legendary Blackfoot (Algonquian) hero, called Scarface in English; the Native American term is /(oh)payoo/ 'lumpy scar tissue (n.)' (D. Franz p.c.).

POINTE AUX CHENES (Mich., Mackinac Co.). French *Pointe aux Chênes* 'oak point' corresponds to the Ojibwa (Algonquian) <nemitigomishking> (Vogel 1986); cf. Ojibwa *mitigomizh* 'oak' (Nichols and Nyholm 1995).

POISON IVY Canyon (AZ, Apache Co.). Corresponds to Navajo (Athabaskan) *ashíshjíízh sikaad nástł'ah* 'poison ivy sands spread out cove' (Linford 2000); cf. *íshíshjį́į́zh* 'poison ivy' (Young and Morgan 1987).

POJAC Point (R.I., Washington Co.). From SNEng. Algonquian <pachaak> 'corner' (W. Cowan p.c.). Perhaps related placenames are **Pochuck Creek** (N.Y., Orange Co.) and **Lake Pochung** (N.J., Sussex Co.).

POJOAQUE (N.Mex., Santa Fe Co.) \pō hwä´ kā\. Tewa (Tanoan) [p'osų̨ŋwæ̨ɣe] 'drink water place', from [p'o] 'water', [sų̨ŋwæ̨] 'to drink', [-ɣe] 'down at' (Harrington 1916:334; Julyan 1998).

POKAGON (Mich., Cass Co.) \pō´ kə gon, pō kä´ gən\. Named for a Ojibwa (Algonquian) leader of the eighteenth–nineteenth centuries. His Native American name was *bookoganaam* 'he breaks something in two by hitting' (McCafferty p.c.; Nichols and Nyholm 1995). The placename also occurs in Ill. (Steuben Co) as \pō kag´ ən\.

POKAMOONSHINE Brook (N.H., Strafford Co.) \pō kə mo͞on´ shīn\. From the same origin as **Pocomoonshine Lake** (Maine, Piscataquis Co.); see above. The placename also occurs in N.Y. (Essex Co.).

POKATA Creek (Md., Dorchester Co.). Probably from Delaware (Algonquian), perhaps containing <pok> 'open, clear> (Kenny 1984).

POKEBERRY Creek (Ind., Warrick Co.) The term refers to the *pokeweed,* a source of red dye; this word, like American English *puccoon,* may be from CAC Algonquian <poughkone> 'red dye' (*RHD* 1987). The placename also occurs in Mo. (Barry Co.) and N.C. (Chatham Co.). The term **Pokepatch** also occurs in placenames (Ohio, Gallia Co.; Tenn., Cumberland Co.). A possibly related placename is **Puckum Branch** (Md., Dorchester Co.).

POKEGAMA (Wis., Douglas Co.) \pō keg´ ə mə\. From Ojibwa (Algonquian) <bakegama> 'where a lake is divided in two branches by a projecting point' (Vogel 1991). The placename is also found in Minn. (Itasca Co.) and Ore. (Klamath Co.).

POKE-MOONSHINE (Maine, Piscataquis Co.). A variant of **Pocomoonshine**; see above. Another spelling is **Poke-o-moonshine.**

POKER JIM Lake (Ore., Lake Co.). Said to be named for an Indian resident (McArthur 1992).

POKETO Creek (Pa., Allegheny Co.). A variant of **Pucketa Creek;** see below.

POKEY Dam (Maine, Washington Co.). Perhaps from Abenaki (Algonquian) *bôkwad* 'it is shallow' (Huden 1962; Day 1994–95).

POKOK Lagoon (Alaska, Barter Is. A-3). The Iñupiaq (Eskimo) name was reported as <Pokang> in 1853 (Orth 1967).

POKOMOONSHINE (Maine, Piscataquis Co.). A variant of **Pocomoonshine Lake**; see above.

POKTOVIK Creek (Alaska, Misheguk Mountain A-4). The Iñupiaq (Eskimo) name was reported in 1956 (Orth 1967).

POKY MOONSHINE (Mo., Franklin Co.). Probably a transfer of **Pocomoonshine Lake** (Maine, Piscataquis Co.).

POKYWAKET Creek (Calif., Shasta Co.) \pō´ kē wak ət\. From Wintu /puki waqat/ 'unripe creek', containing /puk-/ 'unripe' and /waqat/ 'creek' (Gudde 1998).

POLACCA (Ariz., Navajo Co.) \pō lä´ kə, pō lak´ ə, pə lak´ ə\. Named for Tom Polacca, a member of the Hopi-Tewa (Tanoan) community.

POLALLIE Creek (Ore., Lane Co.) \pō´ lä lē\. Chinook Jargon <po´-lal-lie> [pólali] 'gunpowder, dust, sand', from French *poudre* 'powder' (McArthur 1992; D. Kinkade p.c.). The placename also occurs in Wash. (Kittitas Co.) A related name is **Pulali Point** (Wash., Jefferson Co.).

POLAWANA Island (S.C., Beaufort Co.). An earlier writing is <Palawana>. The term may be borrowed from a word for 'turkey', probably Algonquian in origin but borrowed into languages of the Southeast (Pickens 1961–62:21). Algonquian examples include Fox /pene:wa/ (Goddard 1994), Shawnee *peleewa* 'chicken' (Pearson 1995); Muskogean examples include Muskogee *penwv* /pínwa/ (Martin and Mauldin 2000).

POLE Creek (Wyo., Albany Co.). A translation of Shoshoni (Numic) /poton/ [porọ] 'tepee pole, staff, digging stick'. In spite of the accidental phonetic similarity, no borrowing is involved here; the Shoshoni word is a native Numic term (Urbanek 1974; J. McLaughlin p.c.).

POLLOCONA Creek (Miss., Lafayette Co.). Perhaps from Choctaw (Muskogean) *palih* 'flying squirrel' plus *okhina* 'creek' (Seale 1939; P. Munro p.c.). A variant is **Potlockney.**

POLPIS (Mass., Nantucket Co.) Earlier written <Poatpes>, <Podpis>. From SNEng. Algonquian (Little 1984).

POMERAUG (Conn., Litchfield Co.). Perhaps a variant of **Pomperaug River**; see below.

POMHAM Rocks (R.I., Providence Co.). Named for a SNEng. Algonquian leader of the seventeenth century; the name may mean 'he travels by sea' (Huden 1962).

POMME DE TERRE Township (Minn., Grant Co.) \pom´ də ter\. French *pomme de terre* 'potato', lit. 'apple of earth', is applied in North America to a variety of roots and tubers eaten by Indians. Like **Potato,** it appears in placenames as a translation of various Native American terms; in the present case, it corresponds to Dakota (Siouan) *típsi̧na* 'the Dakota turnip' (Upham 2001; Riggs 1890). The placename also occurs in Wis. (Buffalo Co.).

POMO (Calif., Mendocino Co.) \pō´ mō\. From Northern Pomo /phóomóo/ 'at red-earth hole', from /phóo/ 'red earth, magnesite'. As the name of a major language family of Indian peoples in north central Calif., **Pomo** has a different derivation, from Northern Pomo /phó'ma'/ 'inhabitant', from /phó/ 'to live, inhabit' (Gudde 1998).

POMONKEY (Md., Charles Co.). Earlier writings are <Pamaunke, Pamunkey>; the CAC Algonquian derivation is not clear (Kenny 1984).

POMPANOOSUC (Vt., Windsor Co.) \pom pə noo͞´ sək\. Probably from Western Abenaki (Algonquian) *bemômanosek* [bəmǫmanosək] 'where there is frequent fishing'; cf. *ôma* 'he fishes' (Day 1994–95). A related form is **Ompompanoosuc River.**

POMPERAUG River (Conn., Litchfield Co.). The SNEng. Algonquian name may mean 'place of offering' (Trumbull 1881).

POMPESTON Creek (N.J., Burlington Co.). Probably from Delaware (Algonquian), but the derivation is not clear (Becker 1964).

POMPTON (N.J., Passaic Co.). Perhaps from the same Delaware (Algonquian) source as **Pymatuning Creek** (Pa., Mercer Co.), referring to a sweathouse (Mahr 1959:373); see below.

PONAGANSET River (R.I., Providence Co.). The SNEng. Algonquian name may mean 'oyster processing-place' (Huden 1962).

PONCA \pong´ kə\. This name applies to a people and language in the Dhegiha group of the Siouan linguistic family; in historic times, they have lived in Neb. and in Okla. The name used by the people was /ppą́kka/ (R. Rankin p.c.). As a placename, the term is found in Ark. (Newton Co.), Neb. (Dixon Co.), Okla. (Kay Co.), and S.Dak. (Gregory Co.).

PONCHA Mountain (Colo., Chaffee Co.) \pon´ chə\. Perhaps from New Mexican Spanish *ponche* 'tobacco', possibly a derivative of Nahuatl (Aztecan) *poctli* 'smoke' (Bright 1999b, 1999c).

PONCHANTOULA Lake (N.J., Salem Co.) \pon chən too͞´ lə\. Perhaps a transfer from **Ponchatoula** (La., Tangipahoa Par.); see below.

PONCHATOULA (La., Tangipahoa Par.) \pon chə too͞ ´ lə\. Probably Choctaw (Muskogean), perhaps meaning 'falling hair', from *(i)pąshi* 'hair' plus *(it)tola* 'to fall' (Read 1927; P. Munro p.c.). A probably related name **Ponchitolawa Creek** (La., St. Tammany Par.) \pon chə tal´ ə wä\, also written <Ponchatalawa>, which is probably Choctaw, perhaps 'singing hair', from *(i)pąshi* 'hair' plus *taloowa* 'to sing' (Read 1927; P. Munro p.c.).

PONCHO Creek (Wis., Portage Co.) \pon´ chō\. The English term, referring to a type of sleeveless overgarment, was borrowed from Spanish, which borrowed it in turn from the Araucanian language of Peru and Bolivia (*RHD* 1987). The word is often confused by English speakers with Spanish *Pancho,* a nickname for *Francisco.*

PONCK HOCKIE (N.Y., Ulster Co.). Perhaps from Munsee Delaware (Algonquian), meaning 'dry land', from <ponkque> 'dry' and <hacky> 'land' (Beauchamp 1907); cf. Munsee *peengwi-* 'dried', *ahkuy* 'land' (O'Meara 1996). Alternatively, the term may be from Dutch *punthoekje* 'point-hook' (Ruttenber 1906).

PONDERA County (Mont.) \pän´ də rā, pän də rā´\. From the same source as **Pend Oreille River,** the name of a Salishan people, from French *pend d'oreilles,* lit. 'hangs from the ears', referring to ear pendants. A related form is **Ponderay** (Idaho, Bonner Co.).

PONE Island (Md., Dorchester Co.). The term, surviving in English *corn pone,* refers to a type of bread made by Indians from cornmeal, derived from CAC Algonquian <appoan> (Kenny 1984). Possibly related placenames are **Half Pone Point** (Md., St. Mary's Co.) and **Pawn Run** (Md., Garrett Co.).

PONEMAH (Ill., Warren Co.) \pō nē´ mə\. The term is used in Longfellow's *Hiawatha* to refer to the home of departed souls; it may be a spelling of Ojibwa (Algonquian) *paanimaa* 'later', wrongly taken as 'the hereafter' (I. Goddard p.c.). The placename also occurs in Mich. (Genesee Co.), Minn. (Beltrami Co.), and N.H. (Hillsborough Co.).

PONGLEVIK River (Alaska, Kwiguk B-6). The Yupik (Eskimo) name was reported in 1948 (Orth 1967).

PONINA Creek (Ore., Klamath Co.). A variant of **Paunina** or **Paulina,** the name of a Northern Paiute (Numic) leader in the nineteenth century; see above.

PONKA BOK Creek (Okla., McCurtain Co.) \pong´ kə bok\. Perhaps Choctaw (Muskogean) *pąkki book,* lit. 'grape creek' (P. Munro p.c.). A possibly related placename is **Ponkabia Creek** (Ala., Sumter Co.) \pong´ kə bī ə\; the Choctaw (Muskogean) name perhaps means 'grapes are in it', with *abiha* 'be inside' (Read 1984; P. Munro p.c.) Another possibly related placename is **Pontotoc**; see below.

PONKAPOAG (Mass., Norfolk Co.) \pong kə pō´ əg\. The SNEng. Algonquian name may be from <ponque-> 'fording place' and <-poag> 'pond' (W. Cowan p.c.).

PONLUKTULE Creek (Alaska, Unalakleet C-5). The Eskimo word, reported in 1952, is said to mean 'blackberry' (Orth 1967); cf. Iñupiaq *pauŋġak* 'blackberry' (Webster and Zibell 1970).

PONQUOGUE (N.Y., Suffolk Co.). The SNEng. Algonquian name perhaps means 'cleared land' (Tooker 1911).

PONSET (Conn., Middlesex Co.) \pon´ sət\. A shortening of **Cockaponset,** a SNEng. Algonquian name, perhaps meaning 'boundary-falls-place' (Trumbull 1881; Huden 1962).

PONTA Creek (Ala., Sumter Co.) \pon´ tə\. Perhaps from Choctaw (Muskogean) *pąti* 'cattail' (Read 1984; P. Munro p.c.). The placename also occurs in Miss. (Lauderdale Co.).

PONTAG Creek (Alaska, Medfra B-2) \pun´ tag\. From an Upper Kuskokwim (Athabaskan) name (J. Kari p.c.).

PONTATOC Canyon (Ariz., Pima Co.) \pon´ tə tok\. Probably a transfer from **Pontotoc County** (Miss.); see below.

PONTIAC \pon´ tē ak\. The name of an Ottawa (Algonquian) leader of the eighteenth century; the Native American form has been given as <bwandiag> (Vogel 1986). As a placename, the word is widespread (e.g., Mich., Oakland Co.; Ill., St. Clair Co.; Kans., Butler Co.; N.Y., Erie Co.; Ohio, Huron Co.; and R.I., Bristol Co.).

PONTOCOLA (Miss., Lee Co.). From Choctaw (Muskogean), meaning 'hanging grapes', from *pąkki* 'grape' and *takohli* '(pl.) to hang' (Toomey 1917; P. Munro p.c.). Possibly related placenames include **Ponka Bok Creek** and **Pontotoc County;** see above and below.

PONTOOK Reservoir (N.H., Coös Co.) \pon´ to͞ok\. Abenaki (Algonquian), abbreviated from <Pontoocook> 'falls-river-place', from *bôn-* 'a falls', *-tegw-* 'river', *-k* 'place' (Julyan and Julyan 1993; Day 1994–95).

PONTOOSUC (Conn., Hartford Co.). The SNEng. Algonquian name may mean 'falls on the brook' (Trumbull 1881). The name also occurs in Mass. (Berkshire Co.) and Ill. (Hancock Co.).

PONTOTOC County (Miss.) \pon´ tə tok\. Earlier written <Punkatuckahly>; probably from Choctaw (Muskogean), meaning 'hanging grape', from *pąkki* 'grape' and *takaali* '(sg.) to hang' (Seale 1939; P. Munro p.c.). The place-name also occurs in Okla. (Johnston Co.) and Tex. (Mason Co.). Possibly related forms include **Ponka Bok Creek** and **Pontocola**; see above.

PONUNTPA Springs (Wyo., Park Co.). Perhaps for Shoshoni (Numic) /puha-kantɨn-pa/ [puhağandɨmba] 'water having power', from /puha/ 'power', /kantɨn/ 'to have', and /paa/ 'water' (Whittlesey 1988; J. McLaughlin p.c.).

PONUS (Conn., Fairfield Co.) The name of SNEng. Algonquian leader in the seventeenth century (Huden 1962).

POONKINY Creek (Calif., Mendocino Co.) \po͞on´ kin ē\. From Yuki /p'unkini/ 'wormwood' (Gudde 1998).

POOSHEEPATAPA Creek (La., Washington Par.). A variant writing of **Pushepatapa Creek;** see below.

POOSPATUCK Creek (N.Y., Suffolk Co.) \po͞os´ pə tuk\. From SNEng. Algonquian, perhaps meaning 'where a creek flows out' (Tooker 1911).

POOTATUCK River (Conn., Fairfield Co.). From SNEng. Algonquian, perhaps meaning 'falls in river' (Huden 1962).

POOVOOKPUK Mountain (Alaska, St. Lawrence C-6). The Yupik (Eskimo) name is said to mean 'big Poovoot' (Orth 1967); cf. *-ghpuk* [-ʀpuk] 'big' (Jacobson 1987). The **Poovoot Range** was reported with this Yupik (Eskimo) name in 1949 (Orth 1967).

POPASQUASH Neck (R.I., Bristol Co.). Perhaps from SNEng. Algonquian, meaning 'partridges' (Huden 1962). **Popasquash Island** (Vt., Franklin Co.) is said to be from Abenaki (Algonquian) *wábeskwasék* 'where the bladder is', from *wabeskwá* 'bubble, bladder', *-sek* 'place' (Day 1981:156).

POPHANDUSING Brook (N.J., Warren Co.). Probably from Delaware (Algonquian), of unclear origin (Becker 1964).

POPHERS Creek (Tex., Angelina Co.) \pō´ fərz\. For an Indian resident named Popher, Native American group not identified (Tarpley 1980).

POPO AGIE River (Wyo., Fremont Co.) \pə pō´ zhə\. Said to be an Indian name referring to the disappearance and reemergence of the river; cf. Crow (Siouan) *a'asha* 'river' (R. Graczyk p.c.).

POPOCATEPETL, Mount (Ore., Lane Co.) \pō pō kat´ ə pet əl\. Named for a volcano in Mexico, Nahuatl (Aztecan) *popoca-tepetl* 'smoking mountain'; cf. *poc-tli* 'smoke', *tepetl* 'mountain' (McArthur 1992).

POPONOMING Lake (Pa., Monroe Co.). Perhaps from Delaware (Algonquian) <papennamink> 'where we were gazing' (Donehoo 1928).

POPPASGUASH Swamp (Mass., Bristol Co.). The SNEng. Algonquian name may mean 'partridges' (Huden 1962); also written **Poppasquash.**

POPPAW Creek (N.C., Alamance Co.) \pop´ ô\. Perhaps related to **Pawpaw,** a type of fruit; see above.

POPPONESSET Bay (Mass., Barnstable Co.) \pop ə nes´ ət\. The SNEng. Algonquian name may be from <popon-> 'winter' (W. Cowan p.c.).

POPSQUATCHET Hills (Mass., Nantucket Co.). The SNEng. Algonquian name may mean 'rocky hills' (Huden 1962).

POQUANTICUT Brook (Mass., Bristol Co.). The SNEng. Algonquian name may mean 'clear-stream-place' (Huden 1962).

POQUESSING Creek (Pa., Bucks Co.). Perhaps from Delaware (Algonquian) <poquesink> 'place of mice', from <ach-po-quees> 'mouse' (Donehoo 1928); cf. Unami Delaware /pu:kwetət/, Munsee Delaware *aapíikwus* (O'Meara 1996).

POQUETANUCK (Conn., New London Co.). From SNEng. Algonquian <puccatannock> 'plowed land' (Trumbull 1881; W. Cowan p.c.).

POQUIANT Brook (R.I., Washington Co.). From SNEng. Algonquian, perhaps meaning 'clear place' (Huden 1962).

POQUODENAW Hill (Minn., Aitkin Co.). From Ojibwa (Algonquian) <pikwadina> 'it is hilly' (Upham 2001). A probably related form is nearby **Quadna Mountain**.

POQUONOCK (Conn., Hartford Co.). From SNEng. Algonquian, perhaps meaning 'cleared land' (Huden 1962).

POQUOSON County (Va.) \pə kō´ sin\. Probably related to **Pocosin,** a generic term for 'marsh, swamp', of CAC Algonquian origin (Hagemann 1988). This form of the placename also occurs in N.C. (Camden Co.).

POQUOTT (N.Y., Suffolk Co.). Probably from SNEng. Algonquian, perhaps meaning 'clear land' (Tooker 1911).

POQUOY Brook (Mass., Bristol Co.). Probably from SNEng. Algonquian <pukquee> 'miry place' (W. Cowan p.c.).

PORCUPINE Creek (S.Dak., Shannon Co.). Corresponds to a Dakota (Siouan) placename referring to *phahį́* 'porcupine' (Sneve 1973; A. Taylor p.c.). **Porcupine Mountains** (Mich., Ontonagon Co.) corresponds to an Ojibwa (Algonquian) word <kagwadjiw>, perhaps meaning 'porcupine quills'; cf. *gaag* 'porcupine', *gaaway* 'quill' (Vogel 1986; Rhodes 1985).

PORGO Creek (Alaska, Baird Mountains D-5). The Iñupiaq (Eskimo) name was reported in 1955 (Orth 1967).

POROPOTANK River (Va., Gloucester Co.). From a CAC Algonquian placename reported in 1640 (Hagemann 1988).

PORTAGE \pôr´ tij, pôr tāj´\. This term for a place where canoes and baggage are carried across land, between two waterways, is French for 'carrying', from *porter* 'to carry'; this was an important feature of Native American transportation. As a placename, **Portage** occurs in several states; for example, in **Portage County** (Wis.), it may be a translation of Ojibwa (Algonquian) <onigam> (Vogel 1991). The placename **Portage Des Sioux** (Mo., St. Charles Co.) \por´ tij də sōō´\. means 'portage of the Sioux' (Ramsay 1952).

PORTE DES MORTS (Wis., Door Co.). Because of a legend about a flotilla of Indian canoes sunk at this point, the channel was called 'door of the dead' by the French. This term was adapted by Anglos as the name of **Door County** (Vogel 1991).

PORTOBAGO (Va., Caroline Co.). The term is from CAC Algonquian, of unclear derivation (Kenny 1984). Related placenames are **Potopaco** (Md., Charles Co.) and **Port Tobacco** (Md., Charles Co.; see **Tobacco**).

PORTOHONK Creek (N.C., Camden Co.). The name probably represents a placename in an unidentified Indian language (Powell 1968).

PORUM (Okla., Muskogee Co.). Named for J. Porum Davis, usually called Dave Porum, an Indian leader (group not identified) (Shirk 1974).

POSE'UINGE Archaeological Distrct (N.Mex., Rio Arriba Co.) Tewa (Tanoan) [p'osi'ǫŋwįkeyi] 'greenness pueblo-ruin', from [p'osi(wi'i)] 'greenness' and [ǫŋwįkeyi] 'pueblo ruin' ([ǫŋwį] 'pueblo', [keyi] 'old'; Harrington 1916:162, 165).

POSEY (Okla., Creek Co.) \pō´ zē\. Named for Alexander Posey, a nineteenth-century Muskogee poet and journalist; the surname may be from pose /pó:si/ 'cat' (from Eng. *pussy*) (Shirk 1974; Martin and Mauldin 2000).

POSEY Canyon (Utah, San Juan Co.) \pō´ zē\. Named for a Ute (Numic) leader of the early twentieth century (Van Cott 1990). A related placename is **Posy Lake** (Utah, Garfield Co.).

POSNEGANSET Pond (R.I., Bristol Co.). The SNEng. Algonquian name is of unclear derivation (Huden 1962).

POSOLMI (Calif., Santa Clara Co.) \pō sōl´ mē\. Perhaps from Mutsun (Costanoan) /pusluhmin/ 'person with a big belly' (Gudde 1998).

POSSUM \pos´ əm\. A shortening of **Opossum,** the name of a native marsupial mammal, from CAC Algonqian <opassom>, equivalent to a proto-Algonquian term meaning 'white dog' (*RHD* 1987). The placename occurs in several states: for example, in **Possum Creek** (Ill., Jersey Co.), **Possum Hollow** (Ohio, Scioto Co.), **Possum Tank** (Ariz., Coconino Co.), and the widespread **Possum Trot** (e.g., Ala., Calhoun Co.).

POSY Lake (Utah, Garfield Co.) \pō´ zē\. From the same source as **Posey Canyon,** the name of a Ute (Numic) leader; see above.

POTAGANNISSING Bay (Mich., Chippewa Co.). Said to be an Ojibwa (Algonquian) word meaning 'gaps' (Vogel 1986).

POTAKE Pond (N.J., Passaic Co.). From Delaware (Algonquian), but of unclear derivation (Becker 1964).

POTANAPA (NH, Hillsborough Co.). A variant writing of **Potanipo Pond**; see below.

POTANIPO Pond (N.H., Hillsborough Co.). From Abenaki (Old Algonquian), perhaps meaning 'cove in the pond' (Huden 1962). A variant is **Potanapa.**

POTAPO Creek (Okla., Atoka Co.) \pō tā´ pō, pō tap´ ō\. Perhaps from Choctaw (Muskogean) *pataapo* 'floor, bridge' (P. Munro p.c.).

POTATO \pə tā´ tō, pə tā´ tə\. This name for an edible tuber is borrowed from Spanish *batata* 'sweet potato', which was in turn borrowed from the Taino (Arawakan) language of the Caribbean (*RHD* 1987). In North America "Indian potato" or "wild potato" refers to several types of edible tubers or roots. In placenames, **Potato** typically has this reference; thus **Potato Creek** (Ind., St. Joseph Co.) corresponds to a reconstructed Miami/Illinois (Algonquian) /mihk-ohpina siipiiwi/, lit. 'red-potato creek', where 'red potato' is the wild sweet potato vine (McCafferty 2002). See also **Pomme de Terre Township** above.

POTAWATOMI \pot ə wä´ tə mē\. The name of an Algonquian people living around Lake Michigan, and during more recent times in Kans. and Okla.; their self-designation is /potewatmi/. There is a tradition that this means 'people of the place of the fire' (cf. Ojibwa *boodawe* 'makes a fire') (Nichols and Nyholm 1995), but this is likely to be a folk-etymology (*HNAI* 15:725). The placename **Potawatomi** is found in several states (e.g., Wis., Walworth Co.; Ill., Cook Co.; Ind., Cass Co.; Mich., Gogebic Co.; Okla., Comanche Co.). Alternative spellings are found in **Pottawatomie County** (Okla.), **Pottawattamie County** (Iowa), and **Pottawattomie Bayou** (Mich., Ottawa Co.).

POTAYWADJO Ridge (Maine, Piscataquis Co.). Perhaps a variant writing of **Potowadjo Hill** (Huden 1962); see below.

POTEM Creek (Calif., Shasta Co.) \pot´ əm\. Perhaps from Wintu /patem/ 'mountain lion' (Gudde 1998).

POTICAW Bayou (Miss., Jackson Co.). Perhaps from Choctaw (Muskogean), but of unclear derivation (BGN 8001).

POTIC Creek (N.Y., Greene Co.). Perhaps from Munsee Delaware (Algonquian) <petuhqui> 'it is round' (Beauchamp 1907); cf. Munsee *ptúkweew* 'to be round' (O'Meara 1996).

POTLATCH \pot´ lach\. The English term refers to a type of ceremony characteristic among the native peoples of the Northwest, in which gifts were exchanged. It is from Chinook Jargon <pot´-latch, paht-latsh> [pɔ́tlæč, pátlæc) 'give, gift', from Nootka /p'aƛp'a-/, reduplication of /p'a-/ 'make ceremonial gifts in potlatch', plus /-č/, a suffix marking iterative aspect (*RHD* 1987). As a placename, **Potlatch** occurs in Idaho (Latah Co.), Ore. (Gilliam Co.), and Wash. (Mason Co.).

POTLOCKNEY (Miss., Lafayette Co.). A variant of **Pollocona Creek;** see above.

POTOMAC River (W.Va., Md., Va., D.C.) \pə tō´ mak, pə tō´ mik\. From CAC Algonquian <Patowmeck>, the name of an Indian village in Va., perhaps meaning 'something brought' (Kenny 1984). As a transfer name, **Potomac** occurs in Ill. (Vermilion Co.),

POTONIEK Lake (Alaska, Selawik D-6). The Iñupiaq (Eskimo) name was reported in 1955 (Orth 1967).

POTOPACO (Md., Charles Co.). The name has the same origin as **Portobago** (Va., Caroline Co.); see above.

POTOSI \pō tō´ sē, pə tō´ sē\. From Spanish *Potosí,* originally the Aymara name for a famous silver mine in Bolivia, later transferred to San Luis Potosí in Mexico. The term came to be a metaphor for 'untold riches'. In the United States the placename occurs in several states (e.g., Colo., Ouray Co.; Kans., Linn Co.; and Wis., Grant Co.). In Idaho (Shoshone Co.) the pronunciation \pə tō´ zī\. is reported.

POTOWADJO Hill (Maine, Piscataquis Co.). The Abenaki (Algonquian) name may mean 'wind blows over the mountain' (Huden 1962). A variant is **Potaywadjo Ridge.**

POTOWOMUT (R.I., Bristol Co.). The SNEng. Algonquian name may mean 'low meadow land' (Huden 1962).

POTS SUM PA Spring (Utah, Beaver Co.). The name is from ą Numic (Uto-Aztecan) language (Van Cott 1990).

POTTAPAUG Hill (Mass., Worcester Co.). The SNEng. Algonquian name is from <pootuppog> 'a bay' (W. Cowan p.c.).

POTTAWATOMIE (Kans., Coffey Co.) \pot ə wä´ tə mē\. From the same source as **Potawatomi**; see above. The present spelling is also found elsewhere (e.g., Ill., Kane Co.; Okla., Pottawatomie Co.; and Tex., Henderson Co.). The spelling **Pottawattamie** occurs in Iowa (Pottawattamie Co.) and Ind. (La Porte Co.); and **Pottawattomie Bayou** is found in Mich. (Ottawa Co.).

POTTERCHITTO Creek (Miss., Newton Co.) \pot ə chit´ ə\. Perhaps from Choctaw (Muskogean) *book patha chito* 'big wide creek', containing *patha* 'wide' and *chito* 'big' (Seale 1939; P. Munro p.c.).

POTUCK Reservoir (N.Y., Greene Co.) \pō tuk\. Perhaps from Delaware (Algonquian) <petukqui> 'round' (Beauchamp 1907).

POTUNK (N.Y., Suffolk Co.). Perhaps from the same source as **Podunk** (Conn., New Haven Co.).

POTWISHA (Calif., Tulare Co.) \pot wish´ ə\. Named for a branch of the Monache (Numic) Indian people (Gudde 1998).

POUDUNK Swamp (Ohio, Cuyahoga Co.). Probably from the same source as **Podunk** (Conn., New Haven Co.).

POUGHKEEPSIE (N.Y., Dutchess Co.) \pō kip´ sē\. Early recordings of the name include <Apokeepsing, Pooghkeepesingh, Pokeapsinck> (etc.); perhaps from Munsee Delaware, meaning 'cattail water place', containing <uppuqui> 'cattail reeds' (Reynolds 1924).

POUGHQUAG (N.Y., Dutchess Co.) \pō´ kwāg\. Probably from Munsee Delaware (Algonquian), perhaps from <Apoquague> 'meadow of reeds or rushes', from <uppuqui> 'cattail reeds' (Ruttenber 1906).

POUPART Lake (Wis., Vilas Co.) \pōō´ pärt\. The surname of an Ojibwa (Algonquian) family; the name is of French origin (Vogel 1991).

POWAY (Calif., San Diego Co.) \pou´ wā, pou´ wī\. From Diegueño (Yuman); cf. *pawiiy* 'arrowhead' (Gudde 1998).

POWESHIEK County (Iowa) \pou´ ə shēk\. Named for a Meskwaki (Algonquian) leader; the Native American term is /pawišika/ '(bear that) shakes himself', a Bear Clan name (Vogel 1983; I. Goddard p.c.).

POWHATAN \pou´ ə tan, pou hat´ ən, pō hä´ tən\. The name of a CAC Algonquian village in Va., probably from <pawat-> 'falls' plus <-hanne> 'river' (Trumbull 1879; W. Cowan p.c.). The name was also applied to the leader of that village and of an associated confederacy of peoples; he was the father of **Pocahontas**. As a placename, **Powhatan** occurs, for example, in Va. (Powhatan Co.); W.Va. (McDowell Co.); and La. (Natchitoches Par.). A related form is **Powhattan** (Kans., Brown Co.) \pou hat´ ən\; this spelling also occurs in Ohio (Champaign Co.). Possibly related is **Purtan Bay** (Va., Gloucester Co.).

POWISSET (Mass., Norfolk Co.). A variant spelling for **Powissett Pond** (Mass., Norfolk Co.). The SNA Algonquian name may mean 'at the small, low field' (Huden 1962).

POWOOILIAK Camp (Alaska, St. Lawrence B-5). The Yupik (Eskimo) name was reported in 1849 as <Puguviliak> (Orth 1967).

POW WAH KEE Creek (Wash., Asotin Co.) \pou wä´ kē\. From Nez Perce /pawá:ki/, a personal name (N. Rude p.c.). Alternative forms are **Powahkee, Powaukie.**

POWWATKA (Ore., Wallowa Co.) \pou wat´ kə\. Said to be from an Indian placename <Paw-wa-ka> 'high, cleared ground', language not identified (McArthur 1992).

POW-WOW \pou´wou\. From SNEng. Algonquian <powwaw> 'Indian priest', from Proto-Algonquian **pawe:wa* 'he dreams; one who dreams'. The term was adopted in English to mean 'medicine man' and then came to be used in the sense 'council, conference' (*RHD* 1987). Spelled both **Powwow** and **Pow Wow,** it is widespread in placenames (e.g., Mass., Essex Co.; N.H., Rockhinghm Co.; Wis., Tremapealeau Co.; Wash., Stevens Co.).

POXABOGUE Pond (N.Y., Suffolk Co.). Also written **Poxabog**; from SNEng. Algonquian <Paugasa-baug> 'widening pond' (Tooker 1911).

POYGAN Lake (Wis., Winnebago Co.) \poi ´ gən\. Menominee (Algonquian) /pawa:hekan/ 'place for knocking down wild rice' (Afable & Beeler 1996:191).

POYSIPPI (Wis., Waushara Co.) \poi sip´ ē\ contains *ziibi* 'river' (Vogel 1991; Nichols and Nyholm 1995).

PRAIRIE DOG Creek (Kans., Phillips Co.). Corresponds to Pawnee (Caddoan) <uskuts> 'prairie dog' (Rydjord 1968).

PRAIRIE DU CHIEN (Wis., Crawford Co.) \prâr ē do͞o shēn\. The French name means 'prairie of the dog', perhaps derived from the personal name of a Meskwaki (Algonquian) Indian (Vogel 1991).

PRAIRIE DU SAC (Wis., Sauk Co.) \prâr ē do͞o sak\. The French name means 'prairie of the Sauk', referring to an Algonquian people (Vogel 1991); see **Sauk** below.

PRESCOTT (N.J., Hunterdon Co.). Probably an English adaptation of Delaware (Algonquian) <Piskot>, said to be the name of an Indian resident (Becker 1964).

PRESIDIO Bar (Calif., Siskiyou Co.) \prə sid´ ē ō\. The Spanish term *presidio* is used elsewhere in Calif. to designate a military headquarters; but in the present case it is an anglicization of *pasirú'uuvree,* a Karuk village site (Gudde 1998).

PRESUMPSCOT River (Maine, Cumberland Co.) \prə zump´ skot\. Earlier writings are <Pesumpsca, Presumskeag> (etc.), from Abenaki (Algonquian), perhaps meaning 'ledges in channel' (Eckstorm 1941).

PROMISE (S.Dak., Dewey Co.). The name refers to a Lakhota (Siouan) minister called *wahóyapi* 'promised' (Sneve 1973; A. Taylor p.c.).

PROPHETSTOWN (Ill., Whiteside Co.). Named for White Cloud (1794–1841), a religious leader of Sauk (Algonquian) and Winnebago (Siouan) descent; his Sauk name has been given as <Wabokischick>, lit. 'white cloud' (Vogel 1963).

PUALE Bay (Alaska, Karluk C-5). The name, perhaps Alutiiq (Eskimo), was recorded in 1836 (Orth 1967).

PUARAY (N.Mex., Sandoval Co.) \pōō´ ə rā\. The name of the ancient Tiwa (Tanoan) village is perhaps from a word meaning 'woman' (Harrington 1916; Julyan 1998).

PUBLITUK Creek (Alaska, Wiseman D-5). The Iñupiaq (Eskimo) word, recorded in 1930, is said to mean 'the hollow, drumlike sound one hears while walking on shell ice' (Orth 1967).

PUCASSET River (Mass., Barnstable Co.) \pə kas´ ət\. A variant of **Pocasset**; see above.

PUCHSHINNUBIE Creek (Miss., Carroll Co.) Probably of Choctaw (Muskogean) origin. A variant is **Puckshunnubbe**.

PUCHYAN River (Wis., Green Lake Co.). Perhaps from a Winnebago (Siouan) word meaning 'heron' (Vogel 1991).

PUCKAWAY Lake (Wis., Green Lake Co.) \puk´ ə wā\. From an Ojibwa (Algonquian) word, forms of which have been recorded as <apakwa> 'rush', <apakwei> 'mat, lodge mat' (Vogel 1991). Related forms in present-day Ojibwa are *apakwe* 'to put on a roof', *apakweshkway* 'cattail mat, cattail' (Nichols and Nyholm 1995). Related placenames are **Apukwa** and **Apeekwa Lake.**

PUCKETA Creek (Pa., Allegheny Co.). Perhaps from Delaware (Algonquian) <pock-a-tes> 'little creek' (Donehoo 1928). Another writing is **Poketo Creek.**

PUCKSHUNNUBBE Creek (Miss., Carroll Co.). A variant of **Puchshinnubie Creek.**

PUCKUM Branch (Md., Dorchester Co.). Perhaps from CAC Algonquian <poughkone> 'red dye' (Kenny 1984), from whence also comes English *puccoon* 'a plant used for red dye'; cf. Unami Delaware /pé:kɔ:n/ 'bloodroot' (*RHD* 1987). A possibly related placename is **Pokeberry Creek** (Ind., Warrick Co.).

PUEBLITO (N.Mex., Socorro Co.) \pweb lē´ tō\. Spanish for 'little pueblo, little village', referring to an extension of San Juan Pueblo, a Tewa (Tanoan) settlement (Julyan 1998).

PUEBLO \pweb´ lō\. The Spanish word for 'village, town' has come to be used to refer to the compact Indian settlements in Ariz. and N.Mex., and to the peoples that occupy them: the Hopi (Uto-Aztecan), Zuni, Keres, and Tanoan peoples; they are thus distinguished from more nomadic groups of the area such as the Navajos and Apaches. The placename **Pueblo Una Vida** (N.Mex., San Juan Co.) \pweb´ lō ōō´ nə vē´ də\, lit. 'one-life town', perhaps refers to a living tree stump growing in this archaeological site (Julyan 1998).

PUGUTAK Lake (Alaska, Point Lay C-1). Perhaps from Iñupiaq (Eskimo) *puggutaq* 'pot, pan, plate' (L. Kaplan p.c.). A perhaps related Alaska placename is **Pusaluk Lagoon** (Noatak D-7).

PUGWASH Pond (Maine, Piscataquis Co.) \pug´ wäsh\. Perhaps Abenaki (Algonquian) for 'pond at the end' (Rutherford 1970); cf. *pôbagw* 'pond' (Day 1994–95).

PUIVLIK Bluff (Alaska, Ikpikpuk River A-2). The Iñupiaq (Eskimo) name was reported in 1956 (Orth 1967).

PUKNIKRUK (Alaska, Wainwright B-2). The Iñupiaq (Eskimo) name was reported in 1955 (Orth 1967).

PUK PALIK Lake (Alaska, Marshall A-4). The Yupik (Eskimo) name was recorded in 1949 (Orth 1967).

PUKWANA Beach (Wis., Fond du Lac Co.). This is the form given in Longfellow's *Hiawatha* for Ojibwa (Algonquian) *bakwene* 'to be smoky' (Vogel 1991; Nichols and Nyholm 1995). The placename also occurs in S.Dak. (Brule Co.).

PULALI Point (Wash., Jefferson Co.). From the same source as **Polallie Creek** (Ore., Lane Co.), from Chinook Jargon, meaning 'powder, dust, sand', from French *poudre* (Hitchman 1985).

PUMA \po͞o´ mə, pyo͞o´ mə\. This term refers to the large native feline also called "mountain lion, cougar, panther"; it is borrowed, through Spanish, from the Quechua language of Peru (*RHD* 1987). As a placename, it occurs in Colo. (Park Co.) and Ore. (Lane Co.).

PUMAKNAK Pond (Alaska, Point Hope A-2). The Iñupiaq (Eskimo) name was reported in 1962 (Orth 1967).

PUMPKIN Creek (Kans., Montgomery Co.). Probably a loan translation from the Osage (Siouan) name <Watunk-a-kashink>, containing /watxą́/ 'pumpkin' (R. Rankin p.c.).

PUMPKIN HOOK (N.Y., Washington Co.). A folk etymology from an Abenaki (Algonquian) placename <pompanuck>, perhaps 'place for sports' (Beauchamp 1907); cf. *bapi* 'to play' (Day 1994–95).

PUMPKIN Ridge (Ore., Washington Co.). Probably a popular etymology from [pánaxtin] or [č^{h}apánaxtin], a Tualatin (Kalapuyan) village (H. Zenk p.c.).

PUNCHE Valley (Colo., Conejos Co.) \po͝on´ chē\. Perhaps a Spanish adaptation of a Ute (Numic) name (Bright 1993).

PUNELOK Bay (Alaska, St. Lawrence D-3). The Yupik (Eskimo) name was reported in 1949 (Orth 1967).

PUNGO (N.C., Beaufort Co.). A shortening of <Machapunga>, a town of North Carolina Algonquians.

PUNGO Creek (Idaho, Boise Co.). From Shoshoni (Numic) /punku/ [pungu] 'dog, pet animal, horse' (Boone 1988; J. McLaughlin p.c.).

PUNGOKEPUK Creek (Alaska, Goodnews Bay B-4). The Yupik (Eskimo) name was reported in 1949 as <Pangokeput> (Orth 1967).

PUNGOKOSIT Spit (Alaska, St. Lawrence C-5). The Yupik (Eskimo) name was recorded in 1965, said to mean 'always a mound' (Orth 1967); cf. *penguq* 'hill' (Jacobson 1987). Other possibly related Alaska placenames include **Pingaluk** (Survey Pass B-2) and **Pingo Lake** (Baird Inlet D-7).

PUNGOTEAGUE (Va., Accomack Co.). The CAC Algonquian placename may mean 'fine sand place' (Hagemann 1988).

PUNISHED WOMANS Lake (S.Dak., Codington Co.). A translation of Santee Dakota (Siouan) *wí-'iyópheya mde* 'woman-punished lake', referring to the legend of a young woman who was punished for rejecting the advances of a tribal leader (Sneve 1973; A. Taylor p.c.).

PUNK Creek (Ga., Heard Co.). Perhaps a translation of Muskogee *tokpafkv* /pokpá:fka/ 'punk, tinder' (Goff 1975; Martin and Mauldin 2000).

PUNOARAT Point (Alaska, Hooper Bay B-3). The Yupik (Eskimo) name was reported in 1951 (Orth 1967).

PUNUK Creek (Alaska, De Long Mountains D-4). The Iñupiaq (Eskimo) name is *pannaq* 'skinny person or animal' (L. Kaplan p.c.).

PUNUK Islands (Alaska, St. Lawrence A-0). The Yupik (Eskimo) name was reported in 1886 as <Poonook> (Orth 1967).

PUNXSUTAWNEY (Pa., Jefferson Co.) \pungk sə tô´ nē\. From Delaware (Algonquian) <punkəs-utènai> 'gnat town', from <punkəs> 'a stinging gnat' plus <-utènai> 'town' (Mahr 1959:369).

PUPIK Hills (Alaska, Howard Pass A-3). From Iñupiaq (Eskimo) *papik* 'bird tail' (Orth 1967; MacLean 1980).

PUPOSKY (Minn., Beltrami Co.) \pə pos´ kē\. The Ojibwa (Algonquian) name has been translated as both 'the end of the shaking lands' (i.e., the swamps) and 'mud lake' (Upham 2001).

PURTAN Bay (Va., Gloucester Co.). Perhaps from the same source as **Powhatan**; see above. A variant is **Purton.**

PUSALUK Lagoon (Alaska, Noatak D-7). The Iñupiaq (Eskimo) name, reported in 1950, is said to mean 'old bag' (Orth 1967); cf. *pu(g)uq* 'sack' (Fortescue et al. 1994), *-łuk* 'old and used' (Webster and Zibell 1970). A perhaps related placename is **Pugutak Lake** (Alaska, Point Lay C-1).

PUSHAWALLA Canyon (Calif., Riverside Co.) \po͝osh´ wä lə\. Perhaps of Indian origin, but its derivation is not clear (Gudde 1998).

PUSHEPATAPA Creek (La., Washington Par.) \po͝osh´ pə tap ə\. Perhaps from Choctaw (Muskogean) *poshi* 'powder' plus *pataapo* 'floor, bed', suggesting 'sandy bottom' (Read 1927; P. Munro p.c.). From the same source source is **Poosheepatapa Creek** (La., Washington Par.); see above.

PUSHMATAHA (Ala., Choctaw Co.) \po͝osh mə tô´ hô\. The name of a Choctaw (Muskogean) leader, perhaps from <vpushi> 'sprout, sapling' plus <imvlhtaha> 'prepared, stored', also a war title (Read 1984; Byington 1915). The placename also occurs in Miss. (Coahoma Co.) and Okla. (Pushmataha Co.).

PUSIGRAK Lagoon (Alaska, Point Hope A-1). The Iñupiaq (Eskimo) name was reported in 1960 as <Poohseegrux> (Orth 1967).

PUSKUS Creek (Miss., Lafayette Co.) \pus´ kəs\. From Choctaw (Muskogean) *poskos* 'baby' (Seale 1939; P. Munro p.c.). The placename occurs as **Pusscuss Creek** in Ala. (Choctaw Co.).

PUTAH Creek (Calif., Lake Co.) \po͞o´ tä\. From Lake Miwok /puṭa wuwwe/ 'grassy creek'; there is no connection with Spanish *puta* 'whore' (Gudde 1998).

PUTESOY Canyon (Ariz., Coconino Co.). From the surname of a Havasupai (Yuman) family (Brian 1992). The spelling **Puteosi** also occurs.

PUTGUT Plateau (Alaska, St. Lawrence C-5). The Yupik (Eskimo) name was reported in 1949 (Orth 1967).

PUTU Creek (Alaska, Marshall B-1). Perhaps from Yupik (Eskimo) *putu* 'to make a hole; a leather piece on a skin boot, with a hole for the bootlace' (Orth 1967; Jacobson 1984).

PUTUGOOK Creek (Alaska, Demarcation Point C-1). The Iñupiaq (Eskimo) name is *putuguq* 'big toe' (L. Kaplan p.c.).

PUTULIGAYUK River (Alaska, Beechey Point B-3). Named for an Iñupiaq (Eskimo) resident, and reported in 1949 (Orth 1967).

PUUTIK Mountain (Alaska, Misheguk Mountain A-4). The Iñupiaq (Eskimo) name was reported in 1956 (Orth 1967).

PUVAKRAT Mountain (Alaska, Howard Pass C-1). The Iñupiaq (Eskimo) name is probably *puvaksrat* 'things which could become lungs' (L. Kaplan p.c.).

PUXICO (Mo., Stoddard Co.) \puk´ si kō\. Said to be named for a Native American leader, language not identified (Ramsay 1952).

PUYALLUP (Wash., Pierce Co.) \pyo͞o al´ əp, pyo͞o ä´ ləp\. From Southern Coast Salishan; the Lushootseed name is /puy'áləp/, perhaps meaning 'crooked stream' (D. Kinkade p.c.).

PUYE (N.Mex., Rio Arriba Co.) \po͞o´ yā\. Tewa (Tanoan) [puye], perhaps from [pu] 'cottontail rabbit', [ye] 'to assemble' (Harrington 1916:236; Julyan 1998).

PUYUK Lake (Alaska, St. Michael C-1). From Yupik (Eskimo) *puyuq* 'smoke' (BGN 8002; Jacobson 1984).

PUYULIK Mountain (Alaska, Goodnews Bay A-7). The Yupik (Eskimo) name, said to mean 'always smoking', was reported in 1951 (Orth 1967).

PYMATUNING Creek (Ohio, Trumbull Co.; Pa., Mercer Co.) \pī´ mə to͞o ning\. Perhaps from Delaware (Algonquian) <piim-hattoonənk> 'it is put there for sweating oneself', referring to a sweathouse; it contains <piim-> 'going to sweat', <-háttoon-> 'it is put there', and <-ənk> 'place' (Mahr 1959:373). A possibly related name is **Pompton** (N.J., Passaic Co.).

PYMOSA Township (Iowa, Cass Co.) \pī mō´ sə\. From a Meskwaki (Algonquian) personal name, either male /pe:mose:ha/ 'walker' or female /pe:mosaha:ha/, perhaps 'one caused to walk' (Vogel 1983; I. Goddard p.c.).

PYOTE (Tex., Ward Co.) \pī´ ōt\. From Spanish *peyote* 'a type of hallucinatory cactus', from Nahuatl (Aztecan) *peyotl* (Tarpley 1980).

PYSHT (Wash., Clallam Co.) \pisht\. From Clallam (Salishan) /pə́šc't/, perhaps meaning 'against the wind or current' (D. Kinkade p.c.).

PYWAOSIT Lake (Wis., Menominee Co.). From the same source as **Lake Paiawisit** (Wis., Oconto Co.), the name of a Menominee (Algonquian) man (Vogel 1991).

PYWIACK Cascade (Calif., Mariposa Co.) \pī´ wē ak\. Southern Sierra Miwok /paywayak/, from /paywa/ 'chaparral' (Gudde 1998).

Q

QENGNASWIK Point (Alaska, Cordova B-7). The Alutiiq (Eskimo) name, meaning 'crowded point', was made official in BGN 1990.

QIKUTULIG Bay (Alaska, Seldovia A-4). The Alutiiq (Eskimo) name was made official in BGN 1990.

QUABOAG Pond (Mass., Worcester Co.) \kwā´ bôg\. The SNEng. Algonquian name is perhaps from <m'squ'boag> 'red pond', containing <(mis)qi-> 'red' plus <-paug> 'pond' (Huden 1962; W. Cowan p.c.).

QUACKCOHOWAON (Va., King William Co.). Probably from CAC Algonquian, of unclear derivation (Huden 1962).

QUACUMQUASIT Pond (Mass., Worcester Co.). Perhaps from the name of a SNEng. Algonquian leader (Huden 1962).

QUADDICK (Conn., Windham Co.). Probably a shortening of SNEng. Algonquian <Pattaquottuck>, perhaps meaning 'bend in river' (Trumbull 1881; Huden 1962).

QUADNA Mountain (Minn., Aitkin Co.) \kwäd´ nə\. From the same source as **Poquodenaw Hill**, Ojibwa (Algonquian) *bikwadinaa* 'it is hilly' (Upham 2001; Nichols and Nyholm 1995).

QUAHAUG Point (R.I., Washington Co.). From the same source as **Quahog Pond;** see below.

QUAHOG Pond (Mass., Barnstable Co.) \kwô´ hog, kwō´ hog, kō´ hog\. The term refers to a type of shellfish, sometimes called 'round clam', from Narragansett (SNEng. Algonquian) <poquaûhock> (*RHD* 1987). A related placename is **Quahaug Point** (R.I., Washington Co.).

QUAISE (Mass., Nantucket Co.) Earlier written <Masquetuck>, <Quaus>. From SNEng. Algonquain (Little 1984).

QUAKAKE (Pa., Schuylkill Co.) \kwā´ kāk\. Perhaps from Delaware (Algonquian) <Cuwenkeek> 'pine lands' (Donehoo 1928); cf. Unami Delaware /kú:we:/ 'pine' (Blalock et al. 1994). Possibly related placenames are **Queponco Station** (Md., Worcester Co.), **Quecreek** (Pa., Somerset Co.), and **Quemahoning** (Pa., Somerset Co.).

QUAKET Creek (R.I., Newport Co.). A shortening of <Nannequaket>, SNEng. Algonquian for 'narrow swampy place' (Huden 1962).

QUALACU (N.Mex., Socorro Co.) \kwä´ lə sōō\. From Spanish <Qualacú> or <Cuelaqu>, a Piro (Keresan) placename (Julyan 1998; *HNAI* 9:241); perhaps a miscopying of something like <Cualaçú> (i.e., *Cualazú*).

QUALLA (N.C., Jackson Co.) \kwä´ lə\. From Cherokee (Iroquoian) <kwalli> 'old woman' (Powell 1968); cf. *agayvli* 'old', *agayvligehi* 'old woman' (Feeling 1975).

QUAMBAUG (Conn., New London Co.). From SNEng. <qunnipaug> 'long pond', containing

<qunni> 'long' and <-paug> 'pond' (Huden 1962; W. Cowan p.c.). A related placename is **Quinebaug** (Conn., Windham Co.).

QUAMPHEGAN Brook (Maine, York Co.). From Abenaki (Algonquian), meaning 'dip net' (Huden 1962).

QUANADUCK Cove (Conn., New London Co.). The SNEng. Algonquian name means 'long tidal stream', from <qunni> 'long' and <-tuck> 'tidal stream' (Huden 1962; W. Cowan p.c.).

QUANAH (Tex., Hardeman Co.) \kwä´ nə\. Named for Quanah Parker, a Comanche (Numic) leader; his Native American name was /kwana/ 'a smell, an odor' (Tarpley 1980; J. McLaughlin p.c.) The name also occurs in Okla. (Comanche Co.).

QUANAI Canyon (Calif., San Diego Co.) \kwə nī´\. From Diegueño (Yuman) *kwa'naay* 'wire grass', a plant used in basket-making (Gudde 1998).

QUANDOCK Brook (Conn., Windham Co.). Probably a shortening of SNEng. Algonquian <Poquannatuck, Poquantuck>, perhaps meaning 'shallow stream' (Huden 1962). The placename **Quanduck** also occurs in R.I. (Providence Co.).

QUANICASSEE (Mich., Tuscola Co.). Possibly from the name of an Ottawa (Algonquian) man, <Aughquanahquosa> 'stump-tail bear' (Vogel 1986).

QUANKEY Creek (N.C., Halifax Co.). Tuscarora (Iroquoian) *kwęhtkye* 'red ochre place', from *kwęht* 'red ochre, vermillion' (B. Rudes p.c.).

QUANNAPOWITT Lake (Mass., Middlesex Co.). The SNEng. Algonquian name perhaps contains <qunni-> 'long', <-apow> 'he sits', and <-it> 'place' (W. Cowan p.c.).

QUANSET Pond (Mass., Barnstable Co.). Probably from the same source as **Quonset Point** (R.I., Washington Co.); see below.

QUANSOO (Mass,, Dukes Co.). Perhaps from SNEng. Algonquian <qunni-> 'long' plus <-sa(g)> 'outlet of a river' (Huden 1962; W. Cowan p.c.).

QUANTABACOOK Lake (Maine, Waldo Co.). From Abenaki (Algonquian), said to mean 'plenty of game animals' (Rutherford 1970).

QUANTICO (Va., Prince William Co.) \kwän´ ti kō\. From CAC Algonquian, perhaps meaning 'by the long stream' (Hagemann 1988). The placename also occurs in Md. (Wicomico Co.).

QUANTUCK Bay (N.Y., Suffolk Co.) \kwän´ tuk\. A shortening of <Quaquanantuck, Quaquantuck>, perhaps SNEng. Algonquian for 'long tidal stream'; cf. <qunni-> 'long', <-tuck> 'tidal stream' (Tooker 1911). Possibly related placenames are nearby **Quintuck Creek**, **Quioque**, and **Quogue.**

QUAPAW (Okla., Ottawa Co.) \kwô´ pô\. An Indian people of the Dhegiha group of the Siouan linguistic family, now living in Okla. The Native American name is /okáxpa/ 'downstream' (i.e., farther south in the Mississippi Valley than other Siouan groups). In an earlier period the Quapaws were called the **Arkansas** (*HNAI* 13:511). **Quapaw** occurs as a placename in several states (e.g., Ark., Lonoke Co.; La., Caddo Par.; and Tex., Harris Co.). A related placename is **Capaha Village** (Mo., New Madrid Co.).

QUARAI (N.Mex., Torrance Co.) \kwôr´ ī\. Said to be from Tiwa (Tanoan) <kuah-aye> 'bear place' (Julyan 1998).

QUARTERLIAH Creek (Miss., Jasper Co.) \kwâ tə lī´ ə\. Perhaps from Choctaw (Muskogean) *oka talaya* 'standing water', from *oka* 'water' and *talaya* '(sg.) to stand' (Seale 1939; P. Munro p.c.).

QUASHNET River (Mass., Barnstable Co.). From SNEng. Algonquian, 'at the wet place', containing <ogqushki-> 'it is wet', <-et >'place' (W. Cowan p.c.). A possibly related placename is **Acushnet** (Mass., Bristol Co.).

QUASSAIC Creek (N.Y., Orange Co.) \kwä sā´ ik\. Perhaps from Delaware (Algonquian), meaning 'stone-place' (Ruttenber 1906).

QUASSAPAUG, Lake (Conn., New Haven Co.). From SNEng. Algonquian, perhaps representing <k'chepaug> 'biggest pond', from <k'che> 'big' and <-paug> 'pond' (Trumbull 1881; W. Cowan p.c.).

QUATAL Canyon (Calif., Santa Barbara Co.) \kwə täl\. California Spanish *guatal* 'place where *guata* "juniper" grows', from Luiseño or Gabrielino (Takic) *wáa'at* (Gudde 1998).

QUATAMA (Ore., Washington Co.) \kwə tä´ mə\. The name of a band of Tututni (Athabaskan), from /gwada-meʔ/ 'in the valley of /gwada/' (D. Kinkade p.c.).

QUATEATA (Wash., Clallam Co.). From the Quileute (Chemakuan) placename /qʷá:tila/ (D. Kinkade p.c.).

QUATSAP Point (Wash., Jefferson Co.). Twana (Salishan) /kwacáp/, from /kʷac-/ 'between' and /-ap/ 'end' (D. Kinkade p.c.).

QUEBEC \kə bek´, kwə bek\. The Canadian placename, French *Québec,* is from Micmac (Algonquian) /kepe:k/ 'strait, narrows' (HNAI 17:191). As a U.S. placename, it occurs, for example, in N.Y. (St. Lawrence Co.), Va. (Smyth Co.), and La. (Madison Par.). The spelling **Quebeck** occurs in Tenn. (White Co.) (Miller 1972).

QUECREEK (Pa., Somerset Co.) \kyōō´ krēk\. Perhaps contains Delaware (Algonquian) /kú:we:/ 'pine tree' (Blalock et al. 1994). Possibly related names are **Quakake** (Pa., Schuylkill Co.), **Queponco Station** (Md., Worcester Co.), and **Quemahoning** (Pa., Somerset Co.).

QUEECHY (N.Y., Columbia Co.) \kwē´ chē\. Perhaps a shortening of <Quis-sich-kook>, possibly an Algonquian placename (Beauchamp 1907).

QUEETS (Wash., Jefferson Co.) \kwēts\. From Quinault (Salishan) \q'ʷícx̣ʷ\. 'dirt' (Hitchman 1985; D. Kinkade).

QUEKILOK Creek (Alaska, Unalakleet B-6). The Yupik (Eskimo) name was reported in 1952 (Orth 1967).

QUELITES (N.Mex., Valencia Co.) \kə lē´ tās\. Spanish *quelite* refers to a kind of edible leafy plant; the word is from Nahuatl (Aztecan) *quilitl* (Karttunen 1983).

QUEMAHONING Creek (Pa., Somerset Co.). From Delaware (Algonquian) <cuwei-mahoni> 'pine-tree salt-lick' (Donehoo 1928); cf. Unami Delaware /kú:we:/ 'pine tree' (Blalock et al. 1994). Possibly related placenames are **Quakake** (Pa., Schuylkill Co.), **Quecreek** (Pa., Somerset Co.), and **Queponco Station** (Md., Worcester Co.).

QUENEMO (Kans., Osage Co.) \kwin´ ə mō\. From a personal name used among the "Sac and Fox" (i.e., the Sauk and Meskwaki) (Algonquian) peoples (Rydjord 1968).

QUEONEMYSING (Pa., Delaware Co.). A former Unami Delaware (Algonquian) village site (Donehoo 1928).

QUEPONCO Station (Md., Worcester Co.). Earlier written <Capomco, Quapanquah, Quapomquah>; perhaps containing Delaware (Algonquian) /kú:we:/ 'pine tree' (Kenny 1984; Blalock et al. 1994). Possibly related placenames are **Quakake** (Pa., Schuylkill Co.), **Quecreek** (Pa., Somerset Co.), and **Quemahoning Creek** (Pa., Somerset Co.).

QUERECHO Plains (N.Mex., Lea Co.) \kə rā´ chō\. The Spanish name *Querecho* was given to nomadic peoples encountered in N.Mex.; it is probably from the Pecos equivalent of Jemez (Tanoan) /k'ʸǽlǽcoš/ 'Navajos, Apaches' (*HNAI* 10:387).

QUETZAL, Point (Ariz., Coconino Co.) \ket säl\. The name of a colorful bird found in Mexico and Central America; derived from Nahuatl (Aztec) *quetzaltototl* 'bird of beautiful plumage', from *quetzalli* 'beautiful plumage' plus *tototl* 'bird'.

QUIAMBOG Cove (Conn., New London Co.). SNEng. Algonquian <quomphauauke> 'place where nets are drawn', from <quomphau> 'he dips (water) up, he fishes with a drawnet' plus <-auke> 'land, place' (W. Cowan p.c.).

QUIBURI Mission (Ariz., Cochise Co.) \kē´ bə rē\. Earlier written as <Giburi, Guibore> (etc.); perhaps contains the world <ki> 'house' from Nevome (Piman), a language of northwest Mexico (Granger 1983).

QUICHAPA Creek (Utah, Iron Co.) \kwich´ ə pə\. From Southern Paiute (Numic) /kwitsappa/ 'excrement water', with /kwitsa-/ 'excrement' and /pa/ 'water' (J. McLaughlin p.c.). Probably related placenames are **Quitchampau Canyon** (Utah, Duchesne Co.), **Quitchupah Creek** (Utah, Emery Co.), and **Quichupah Creek** (Utah, Sevier Co.).

QUIDNESSETT (R.I., Washington Co.). Earlier written <Aquidnesit>; the SNEng. Algonquian name probably means 'at the small island', from <acquidne> 'island', <-s> 'small', and <-et> 'place' (Huden 1962; W. Cowan p.c.).

QUIDNET (Mass., Nantucket Co.). Probably from SNEng. Algonquian <aquidnet> 'island place', from <acquidne> 'island' and <-et> 'place' (Huden 1962; W. Cowan p.c.); cf. **Aquidneck**.

QUIGMY River (Alaska, Hagemeister Is. D-2). The Yupik (Eskimo) name was reported in 1948 as being from <kuikime> 'in the river' (Orth 1967); cf. *kuik* 'river', *-mi* 'place' (Jacobson 1984). Probably related Alaska placenames include **Kwichlowak Pass** (St. Michael A-4), **Kwigillingok** (Kuskokwim Bay D-4), **Kwiguk** (Kwiguk D-6), **Kwikpak** (St. Michael A-5), and **Quinhagak** (Goodnews Bay C-8).

QUIGUI (N.Mex., Sandoval Co.) \kē´ wē\. For a Spanish spelling *Quigüi,* from /dyîiwi/, the name for Santo Domingo pueblo in some Keresan dialects (other than that of Santo Domingo itself, in which the name is /dyîiwa/) (Julyan 1998; I. Davis p.c.). A probably related placename is **El Guique** (N.Mex., Rio Arriba Co.).

QUIHI (Tex., Medina Co.) \kwē´ hē\. Probably from the same source as **Keatchie** (La., De Soto Par.), referring to a group of the Caddoan language family.

QUIJOTOA (Ariz., Pima Co.) \kē hō tō´ ə, kē hi tō´ ə\. From O'odham (Piman) *giho do'ag,* lit. 'burden-basket mountain' (Granger 1983; J. Hill p.c.).

QUIKTALIK Creek (Alaska, Solomon C-1). Probably from Yupik (Eskimo) *kuigtalek,* from *kuik* 'river' (L. Kaplan p.c.).

QUILBY (Ala., Sumter Co.) \kwil´ bē\. Earlier written <Koilbah>; perhaps from Choctaw (Muskogean), meaning 'where the panther was killed', from <koi> 'panther' and <vlbi> 'killed' (Read 1984).

QUILCEDA Creek (Wash., Snohomish Co.) \kwil sē´ də\. From the Lushootseed (Salishan) placename /q^{W}əl'sídəʔ/ (D. Kinkade p.c.).

QUILCENE (Wash., Jefferson Co.) \kwil´ sēn\. From Twana (Salishan) /q^{W}əʔlsíd/, the name of a tribal group (Hitchman 1985; D. Kinkade p.c.). The name shows the alternation of *n* and *d* that is typical of Native American languages in the area.

QUILEUTE (Wash., Clallam Co.) \kwil´ ə yōōt\. The name of an Indian people and language, of the Chimakuan linguistic family; their Native American name is Quileute /k^{W}oʔlí:yot'/, perhaps derived from /k^{W}olí:/ 'wolves' (D. Kinkade p.c.). An alternative spelling is **Quillayute.**

QUILLISASCUT Creek (Wash., Stevens Co.). Okanagan (Salishan) /q'^{W}ləʔsásq't/, the name of a nineteenth-century Colville leader, lit. 'singed sky'; cf. /q'^{W}l-/ 'to roast', /-asq't/ 'sky, day' (A. Mattina p.c.).

QUILOMENE Creek (Wash., Kittitas Co.) \kwil´ ə mēn\. Moses-Columbian (Salishan) /(s)nq'^{W}əlq'^{W}əlmín/, lit. 'place of roasting spits', from /s-/ 'nominalizer', /na-/ 'locative, in, at', /q'^{W}əl-/ 'roast over a fire' (reduplicated), /-min/ 'instrument' (D. Kinkade p.c.).

QUINABY (Ore., Marion Co.) \kwin´ ə bē\. The name of an Indian once well known around Salem, from Santiam (Kalapuyan) [k^{wh}ínapi] (H. Zenk p.c.).

QUINADO Canyon (Calif., Monterey Co.) \kē nä´ dō\. Probably a Spanish adaptation from the name of an Indian village, Mutsun (Costanoan) /kináw/ (Gudde 1998).

QUINAPOXET (Mass., Worcester Co.). The SNEng. Algonquian name means 'little long pond place', from <qunni-> 'long', <-paug> 'pond', and <-s> 'small', and <-et> 'place' (Huden 1962; W. Cowan p.c.).

QUINAULT (Wash., Grays Harbor Co.) \kwi nôlt'\. The name of a Salishan language and people; the Native American term is [k^{W}ínayɬ] (Hitchman 1985; D. Kinkade p.c.).

QUINCOSIN Swamp (N.C., Johnston Co.). Probably from a CAC Algonquian placename; the name was made official in BGN 7503. See also **Quioccasin** (Va., Essex Co.) below.

QUINDARO (Kans., Wyandotte Co.). Named for a Wyandot (Iroquoian) woman; the name supposedly referred to a woman of the Turtle Clan (Rydjord 1968).

QUINDOCQUA (Md., Somerset Co.). Earlier writings are <Quindooque, Condocua, Quindoxua>; from CAC, of unclear derivation (Kenny 1984).

QUINEBAUG (Conn., Windham Co.) \kwin´ ə bôg\. From SNE <Qunnubbâgge, Quinibauge> (etc.), meaning 'long pond', from <qunni-> 'long' and <-paug> 'pond' (Trumbull 1881, W. Cowan p.c.). The name also occurs in Mass. (Worcester Co.). Possibly related placenames are **Quambaug** (Conn., New London Co.), **Quonnipaug Lake** (Conn., New Haven Co.), and **Quonopaug Brook** (R.I., Providence Co.).

QUINHAGAK (Alaska, Goodnews Bay C-8) \kwin´ hə gak, kwin´ ə häk\. The Yupik (Eskimo) name is *kuinerraq* 'new river', from *kuik* 'river' (Jacobson 1984). Probably related Alaska placenames include **Kwichlowak Pass** (St. Michael A-4), **Kwigillingok** (Kuskokwim Bay D-4), **Kwiguk** (Kwiguk D-6), **Kwikpak** (St. Michael A-5), and **Quigmy River** (Hagemeister Is. D-2).

QUININE Hill (S.C., Richland Co.) \kwī´ nīn, kwin´ īn\. The antimalarial drug, discovered in South America, takes its name, through Spanish *quina,* from Quechua *kina* 'bark' (*RHD* 1987).

QUINNATISSET Brook (Conn., Windham Co.). The SNEng. Algonquian name probably contains <qunni-> 'long' (Huden 1962; W. Cowan p.c.).

QUINNESEC (Mich., Dickinson Co.) \kin´ ə sek\. Perhaps from Ojibwa (Algonquian) <kiwanis> 'noise' and <aki> 'place' (Vogel 1986).

QUINNIPIAC (Conn., New Haven Co.) \kwi nip´ ē ak\. Earlier written <Quillipiac>, <Quiripeys>; from SNEng. Algonquian.

QUINSIGAMOND (Mass., Worcester Co.) \kwin sig´ ə mond\. Perhaps SNEng. Algonquian for 'pickerel fishing place'; cf. <-amaug> 'fishing place' (Trumbull 1879; W. Cowan p.c.).

QUIN SINS Ridge (Wash., Yakima Co.). Perhaps Sahaptin /k'^{W}ɨnčinš/, from /k'^{W}inč/ 'black-pine lichen' and /-inš/ 'having' (N. Rude p.c.).

QUINSNICKET Hill (R.I., Providence Co.). Perhaps SNEng. Algonquian for 'at my stone house' (Huden 1962).

QUINTUCK Creek (N.Y., Suffolk Co.) \kwin´ tuk\. Perhaps from the same source as nearby **Quantuck Bay;** see above.

QUIOCCASIN Creek (Va., Essex Co.). Probably from CAC Algonqian, of unclear derivation. A related placename is **Quioccosin** (N.C., Bertie Co.); see also **Quincosin Swamp** (N.C., Johnston Co.) above.

QUIOQUE (N.Y., Suffolk Co.). Perhaps from SNEng. Algonquian <Quaquanantuck, Quaquantuck>; see also **Quantuck Bay,** above.

QUIOTA Creek (Calif., Santa Barbara Co.) \kē ō´ tə\. Spanish *quiote,* a type of yucca, from Nahuatl (Aztecan) *quiotl* 'sprout' (Gudde 1998).

QUIRAUK Mountain (Md., Washington Co.). Earlier written as <Cwareuuoc, Quowaughkutt> (etc.); perhaps from CAC Algonquian <quiyough> 'gull' (Kenny 1984).

QUISSETT (Mass., Barnstable Co.) \kwis´ ət\. The SNEng. Algonquian name means 'small pine place', from <koowa-> 'pine tree', <-s> 'small', and <-et> 'place' (Huden 1962; W.

Cowan p.c.). A probably related placename is **Coös County** (N.H.).

QUITAQUE (Tex., Briscoe Co.) \kit´ ə kwē\. Perhaps from an obscure Indian source (Tarpley 1980); cf. Mexican Spanish *cuita* 'excrement', from Nahuatl (Aztecan) *cuitlatl* (Santamaría 1959).

QUITNESSET (Mass., Barnstable Co.). The SNEng. Algonquian name is of unclear derivation; it was made official in BGN 6704.

QUITO (Kans., Butler Co.) \kē´ tō\. Perhaps named for the capital city of Ecuador; the name is originally from Quechua. Another **Quito** is in N.Mex. (Taos Co.).

QUITOBAQUITO (Ariz., Pima Co.) \kē tō bə kē´ tō, kwē tō bä kwē´ tō\. A Spanish diminutive (with *-ito* 'little') from <Quitovac>, from O'odham (Piman) *gi'ito wa:k*, containing *wa:k* 'standing water' (Granger 1983; J. Hill p.c.).

QUITSNA (N.C., Bertie Co.) From Tuscarora (Iroquoian) *khwihsne'* 'I am strong' (Powell 1968; B. Rudes p.c.).

QUITTAPAHILLA Creek (Pa., Lebanon Co.). Said to be from Delaware (Algonquian) <cuwepehelle> 'pine spring' (Donehoo 1928); cf. Munsee Delaware /kú:we:/ 'pine' (Blalock et al. 1994).

QUIVIRA Lake (Kans., Johnson Co.) \kwi vēr´ ə\. This name was given to Wichita (Caddoan) settlements by the Spanish Coronado expedition in 1541, It is probably of Native American origin, but it is doubtful whether it is from the modern Wichita self-designation /kirikiʔi:s/ 'raccoon-eye(s)' (*HNAI* 13:566); see **Gran Quivira** (N.Mex., Torrance Co.) above.

QUODDY (Maine, Washington Co.) \kwod´ ē\. A shortening of Abenaki (Algonquian) **Passamaquoddy;** see above.

QUOGUE (N.Y., Suffolk Co.) \kwōg\. Perhaps a shortening of SNEng. Algonquian <Quaquanantuck> (Tooker 1911). A possibly related name is nearby **Quantuck Bay;** see above.

QUONNIPAUG Lake (Conn., New Haven Co.). Perhaps from the same source as SNEng. Algonquian **Quinebaug** 'long pond' (Conn., Windham Co.).

QUONOCHONTAUG (R.I., Washington Co.). Perhaps SNEng. Algonquian for 'the long, long pond' (Huden 1962).

QUONOPAUG Brook (R.I., Providence Co.). Perhaps from the same source as **Quinebaug** (Conn., Windham Co.).

QUONSET Point (R.I., Washington Co.) \kwon´ sət\. The SNEng. Algonquian name may mean 'small long place', from <qunni-> 'long', <-s> 'small', <-et> 'place' (Huden 1962; W. Cowan p.c.). It gave its name to the "Quonset hut," a type of prefabricated housing developed during World War II; and from that use the term was also applied to **Quonset Lake** (Alaska, Rat Is. A-3) (Orth 1967). A related placename is **Quanset Pond** (Mass., Barnstable Co.).

QUOSATANA Creek (Ore., Curry Co.) \kwō sāt´ nə\. From a Tututni (Athabaskan) placename, perhaps /gwəseʔdən/ 'camas place', from /gwəseʔ/ 'camas', or possibly from /gwəsaʔdən/ 'mussel place', from /gwəsaʔ/ 'mussel' (McArthur 1992; D. Kinkade p.c.).

QUOTONSET Beach (Conn., Middlesex Co.). From SNEng. Algonquian, perhaps meaning 'gravel-place' (Huden 1962).

R

RABBIT BRUSH (N.Mex., McKinley Co.). Perhaps corresponds to Navajo (Athabaskan) *k'iiɫ tsoii,* a plant called 'rabbit brush' in English; the Navajo term means 'alder that is yellow', from *k'ish, k'iish* 'alder' and *ɫtso* 'yellow' (A. Wilson p.c.).

RABBIT Creek (Alaska, Anchorage A-8). Probably a translation of Dena'ina (Athabaskan) *ggeh betnu* (Kari and Fall 1987:296). The name **Rabbit Lake** (Minn., Lake Co.) corresponds to Ojibwa (Algonquian) *waaboozo-waakaa'iganizaaga'igan,* lit. 'rabbit-house-lake' (J. Nichols p.c.).

RABBIT EAR Mountain (N.Mex., Union Co.). Said to have been the personal name of an Indian, of an unidentified ethnic group (Julyan 1998).

RACCOON \rak o͞on´, rə ko͞on\. The name of the animal is derived from CAC Algonquian <aroughcun> (*RHD* 1987). As a placename, it is widespread, e.g. in Va. (Sussex Co.), Md. (Dorchester Co.), Iowa (Polk Co.), Ill. (Clay Co.), and La. (Placquemines Par.). **Raccoon Creek** in Pa. (Beaver Co.), may be a translation of Delaware (Algonquian) <nachenum-hanne> (Donehoo 1928); cf. Unami Delaware /ná:hanam/ 'raccoon' (Blalock et al. 1994). In Ind. (Boone Co.) **Big Raccoon Creek** corresponds to Miami/Illinois (Algonquian) /eehsipana siipi-iwi/, lit. 'raccoon stream', named for an Indian leader called "Raccoon" (McCafferty 2002).

RACE TRACK (Wash., Skamania Co.). An area where Indians of the Yakima and Klickitat (Sahaptian) peoples once held horse races (Hitchman 1985).

RACINE County (Wis.) \rə sēn\. From the French word for 'root', referring to the Root River, and corresponding to Potawatomi (Algonquian) <che-pe-kat-aw sebe> 'root river' (Vogel 1991); cf. Ojibwa (Algonquian) *ojiibik* 'root', *ziibi* 'river' (Nichols and Nyholm 1995).

RAGGED Island (Maine, Cumberland Co.) \rag´ əd\. Earlier **Ragged Ass,** from Abenaki (Algonquian) <raggertask> 'island rocks' (Rutherford 1970).

RAHWAY (N.J., Union Co.) \rä ´ wā\. Earlier written <Rachaneak, Rahawack, Rawack> (etc.); probably from Delaware (Algonquian), but of unclear derivation (Becker 1964).

RAMAPO (N.Y., Rockland Co.) \ram´ ə pō\. Earlier writings are <Ramepogh, Ramopock> (etc.); the Munsee Delaware (Algonquian) name may mean 'slanting rock', with <-apughk> 'rock' (Ruttenber 1906). The placename also occurs in N.J. (Passaic Co.), N.Y. (Rockland Co.), and Ore. (Multnomah Co.).

RAMONA \rə mō´ nə\. This Spanish name for a woman, the feminine counterpart of *Ramón* 'Raymond', was given to the heroine of Helen Hunt Jackson's nineteenth-century romantic novel *Ramona*; she was modeled on Ramona Lubo, a member of the Cahuilla (Takic) people. **Ramona** became widely used as a placename (e.g., Calif., San Diego Co.; Kans., Marion Co.; Mich., Newaygo Co.; and Okla., Washington Co.).

RANCHEREE Canyon (Ore., Umatilla Co.). From the same source as **Rancheria Creek** (Ore., Jackson Co.) \ran chə rē´ ə\. From Spanish *ranchería,* referring to an Indian village (McArthur 1992). A related placename is **Rancherie Creek** (Ore., Josephine Co.) \ran chə rē´ ə\.

RANCOCAS (N.J., Burlington Co.). Perhaps the name of a Delaware (Algonquian) village (Becker 1964).

RANEGAS Plain (Ariz., Yuma Co.). From Hualapai (Yuman) <hanagas> 'good' (Granger 1983).

RAPIDAN River (Va., Culpeper Co.). Probably from the same source as **Rappahannock River** (Va., Lancaster Co.); see below. The name also occurs in Minn. (Blue Earth Co.) and Ore. (Marion Co.).

RAPID Creek (S.Dak., Pennington Co.). Probably a translation of Lakhota (Siouan) *mni-lúza wakpála* 'water-fast creek' (Sneve 1973; A. Taylor p.c.).

RAPPAHANNOCK River (Va., Lancaster Co.) \rap ə han´ ək\. From Delaware (Algonquian), perhaps meaning 'tidewater' (Hagemann 1988). Probably related names are **Rapidan** (Va., Culpeper Co.) and **Tappahannock** (Va., Essex Co.).

RARITAN (N.J., Somerset Co.) \râr´ i tan\. The name is from Delaware (Algonquian), of unclear derivation (Becker 1964; Grumet 1981). It also occurs in other states (e.g., N.Y, Richmond Co.; Ill., Anderson Co.; and N.Dak., Barnes Co.).

RAT. In historical documents, the word *rat* sometimes refers not to the domestic rat or the wood rat but to the **Muskrat;** see below. Thus

Rat Portage (Minn., Koochiching Co.), probably translates Ojibwa (Algonquian) *wazhashk* 'muskrat' (Upham 2001). **Rat Root Lake** (Minn., Koochiching Co.) similarly refers to an Ojibwa term for roots eaten by muskrats.

RATHLATULIK River (Alaska, Solomon D-3). The Iñupiaq (Eskimo) name was reported in 1908 as <Arathlatuluk> (Orth 1967).

RAT Island (Alaska, Rat Is. C-6). Pehaps a translation, through Russian *krysi,* of Aleut <ayugadak> 'rat' (Orth 1967).

RATTLESNAKE Butte (S.Dak., Ziebach Co.). A translation of Lakhota (Siouan) *pahá sįtéhla* 'hill [of the] rattlesnake' (Sneve 1973; A. Taylor p.c.).

RAWAH Peaks (Colo., Larimer Co.) \rä´ wä\. Perhaps from Ute (Numic) /urá'wa/ 'crest of a mountain ridge' (Bright 1993).

RAYADO (N.Mex., Colfax Co.) \rä yä´ dō\. The Spanish word means 'striped, streaked'; it may refer here to an Indian who wore painted lines on his face (Julyan 1998),

RECONOW Creek (Md., Wicomico Co.). From CAC Algonquian; the derivation is not clear (Kenny 1984).

RED BLANKET Creek (Ore., Jackson Co.). Perhaps named for a Klamath leader, called Red Blanket by whites, who died in 1848 (H. Zenk p.c.).

RED Butte (S.Dak., Harding Co.). Corresponds to Lakhota (Siouan) *pahá-šaša* 'red hill', from *pahá* 'hill' plus *šašá* 'red' (Sneve 1973; B. Ingham 2001). Similarly, **Red Canyon** (S.Dak., Custer Co.) is probably a translation of Lakhota (Siouan) <Imnizaisecašaša> (Sneve 1973); cf. Dakota *imníža* 'rock', *šašá* 'red' (Riggs 1890). **Red Lake** in Ariz. (Coconino Co.) is from Navajo (Athabaskan) *be'ek'id ha-lchíí',* lit. 'lake area-red' (Wilson 1995). **Red Mountain** in Idaho (Idaho Co.) corresponds to Nez Perce /mé·x̣sem ʔilp'ílp/ 'mountain red' (Aoki 1994). **Red River** in N.Mex. (Taos Co.) is a translation of the Taos (Tanoan) name for this stream (Julyan 1998).

RED CLOUD (S.Dak., Lyman Co.). Named for a Teton Lakhota (Siouan) leader of the nineteenth century; his Native American name was *mahpíya-lúta* 'red cloud, red sky' (Sneve 1973; A. Taylor p.c.). Another **Red Cloud,** in Wis. (La Crosse Co.), was named for Mitchell Red Cloud Jr., a Winnebago (Siouan) hero of the Korean War (Vogel 1991).

RED COAT Creek (S.Dak., Ziebach Co.). Corresponds to Lakhota (Siouan) *ógle-šašá* or *ógle-lúta,* both meaning 'coat-red' (Sneve 1973; A. Taylor p.c.).

RED EAGLE (Okla., Osage Co.). Named for Paul Red Eagle, an Osage (Siouan) leader (Shirk 1974).

RED IRON Lake (S.Dak., Marshall Co.). Named for a Santee Dakota (Siouan) leader of the nineteenth century; his Native American name was *máza-dúta,* lit. 'iron-red' (A. Taylor p.c.).

RED LAKE County (Minn.) Corresponds to Ojibwa (Algonquian) <misquagumiwi sagaiigun> 'red-water lake' (Upham 2001); cf. *misko-* 'red', *zaaga'igan* 'lake' (Nichols and Nyholm 1995).

REDMANS Tooth (Ore., Douglas Co.). The name given to this prominent rock likens it to the tooth of an Indian (McArthur 1992).

REDMOON (Okla., Roger Mills Co.). Named for a Cheyenne (Algonquian) leader, called Red Moon by whites; his Native American name was probably /ese'he ohma'aestse/, from /ese'he/ 'moon, sun' plus /ohma'aestse/ 'that which is red' (Shirk 1974; W. Leman p.c.).

RED ROCK (Iowa, Marion Co.). The portion of the Des Moines River now covered by the Red Rock Reservoir had the Meskwaki (Algonquian) name /e:hmeškosiči ši:kona/ 'where there is a red cliff' (I. Goddard p.c.).

RED SCAFFOLD (S.Dak., Ziebach Co.). Corresponding to Lakhota (Siouan) *čówahe-ša,* lit. 'scaffold-red', referring to a framework on which the bodies of the dead were placed

(Sneve 1973); cf. Dakota *čówahe* 'scaffold' (Riggs 1890).

RED SHIRT (S.Dak., Shannon Co.). Named for Frederick Red Shirt, a (Siouan) leader (Sneve 1973).

REDSTONE Creek (Pa., Fayette Co.). Probably a translation of Delaware (Algonquian) <machkachsen-hanne> (Donehoo 1928); cf. Unami Delaware /maxk-/ 'red', /a:hsə́n/ 'stone' (Blalock et al. 1994).

RED WING (Minn., Goodhue Co.). Named for a family of Dakota (Siouan) leaders; the Native American term is *ȟupáhu-ša* 'wing-red' (Upham 2001; Riggs 1890). The placename occurs elswhere, perhaps under the influence of a popular song about an Indian girl called 'pretty Redwing'; cf. **Redwing Creek** (Wis., Waukesha Co.).

REDWOOD River (Minn., Redwood Co.). A translation of Dakota (Siouan) *čą-šá yápi* perhaps referring to a tree that was painted red; cf. *čą* 'tree, wood', *ša* 'red', *yápi* 'they go' (Upham 2001; Riggs 1890). In Ind. (Warren Co.) **Redwood Creek** corresponds to Potawatomi (Algonquian) /mskwawak/ 'red tree' (i.e., red cedar) (McCafferty 2002).

REE Creek (S.Dak., Hand Co.) \rē\. From the same source as **Arikaree** (S.Dak., Campbell Co.) or **Arikara**, the name of a Caddoan people. The placename also occurs in N.Dak. (Ward Co.).

REELFOOT Creek (Tenn., Obion Co.). Said to be named for a legendary Chickasaw (Muskogean) leader who walked wth a reeling gait because of a clubfoot (McClaren 1991).

RENVILLE County (Minn.) \ren´ vil\. Named for Joseph Renville, a man of mixed French and Dakota (Siouan) ancestry, born around 1779 (Upham 2001).

REPAUPO (N.J., Gloucester Co.). Probably from Delaware (Algonquian), of unclear derivation (Becker 1964).

REPUBLIC County (Kans.) Named for the **Republican River** (Kans., Geary Co.); this in turn was named for a band of the Pawnee (Caddoan) people called <kitkahahki>, whom the French called *les Pahni républicaines* because they had declared a "republic" independent of other Pawnee groups (Rydjord 1968; *HNAI* 13:545).

REQUA (Calif., Del Norte Co.) \rek´wä\. From Yurok /rek'woy/ 'river mouth' (Gudde 1998). There may be some influence here from the Norwegian surname *Requa,* which has given its name to a place in Wis. (Jackson Co.).

RESERVATION Creek (Wash., Skagit Co.). So called because it is near the Swinomish (Salishan) Indian Reservation (Hitchman 1985).

RESOOTSKEH (N.C., Bertie Co.). A Tuscarora (Iroquoian) village site, also written <resootska>, said to mean 'to our grandfather' (Powell 1968).

REWASTICO (Md., Wicomico Co.). The CAC Algonquian name may mean 'weedy stream'; cf. Delaware (Algonquian) <liwasquall> 'weeds' (Kenny 1984); cf. Munsee Delaware *laawáskwe* 'in the middle of the high weeds' (O'Meara 1996).

RIB River (Wis., Marathon Co.). A translation of Ojibwa (Algonquian) <o-pik-wun-a se-be> (Vogel 1991); cf. *opikwan* 'back', *ziibi* 'river' (J. Nichols p.c.).

RICAHOKENE (N.C., Perquimans Co.). Perhaps from the same source as **Rickahake** (Va., Norfolk Co.); see below.

RICE Lake (Mich., Houghton Co.). The reference is to wild rice, called *manoomin* in Ojibwa (Algonquian), /mano:mɛh/ in Menominee; cf. **Menominee** above. The placename **Rice** also occurs in Wis. (Menominee Co.). Other related placenames include **Meno** (Ore., Hood River Co.) and **Menomin Lake** (Minn., Crow Wing Co.).

RICKAHAKE (Va., Norfolk Co.). Perhaps the name of an Iroquoian group (Hagemann 1988). Other possibly related names are **Ricahokene** (N.C., Perquimans Co.), **Rickahock** (Va., King and Queen Co.), **Ricohoc** (La., St. Mary Par.), **Righkahauk** (Va., New Kent Co.), and **Rockyhock** (N.C., Chowan Co.).

RICKAHOCK (Va., King and Queen Co.). Perhaps from the same origin as **Rickahake** (Va., Norfolk Co.); see above.

RICKREALL Creek (Ore., Polk Co.) \rik´ rē ôl, rik´ rē əl\. The origin of this name has been disputed, but it is unlikely to be from a local Indian language, since none of them contain the sound *r*. The name of the creek in the local Luckamiute (Kalapuyan) language is [čhínchel]. It is more likely that **Rickreall** reflects an earlier writing <La Creole>, from French *la créole* (fem.) or *le créole* (masc.) 'the native' (McArthur 1992; H. Zenk p.c.).

RICOHOC (La., St. Mary Par.) \rik´ ō hok, rik´ ə hok\. Perhaps a transfer of **Rickahake** (Va., Norfolk Co.) or **Rickahock** (Va., King and Queen Co.); see above. Another possibly related name is **Righkahauk** (Va., New Kent Co.).

RIPOGENUS Gorge (Maine, Piscataquis Co.) \rip ə jē´ nəs\. Perhaps from Abenaki (Algonquian), meaning 'small rocks, gravel' (Rutherford 1970).

RIPPOWAM River (N.Y., Westchester Co.). Probably from Munsee Delaware (Algonquian), of unclear derivation (Beauchamp 1907).

RISING FAWN (Ga., Dade Co.). Perhaps adapated from Cherokee (Iroquoian) <Kunnateetah, Kinnetehee, Agi-na-gi-li>, translated as 'young he-is-rising' (Goff 1975); cf. *awi-agina* 'fawn' (Alexander 1971), as well as *ahawi* 'deer', *agina* 'young animal' (Feeling 1975).

ROANOAKE (Ohio, Tuscarawas Co.). A name related to **Roanoke County** (Va.) \rō´ ə nōk\. This term reflects the name of Sir Walter Raleigh's "lost colony" in N.C., perhaps a CAC Algonquian placename, recorded in 1584. This may be the same as <rawranock> 'shells used for money' which, in the form **Roanoke,** also came to be used in this sense in English during colonial times (Kenny 1945). As a placename, **Roanoke** occurs in several states (e.g., N.Y., Genesee Co.; W.Va., Lewis Co.; and La., Jefferson Davis Par.). The pronunciation \rō´ nōk\. is reported from Tex. (Denton Co.) The related form **Roanoake** occurs in Neb. (Douglas Co.) and Ohio (Tuscarawas Co.).

ROATAN (Conn., Fairfield Co.) \rō´ ə tan\. From SNEng. Algonquian; it is perhaps an abbreviation of **Noroton** (see above), of unclear derivation. A variant writing is **Roawayton.** A perhaps related placename is **Rotan** (Tex., Fisher Co.).

ROBINSON Woods (Ill., Cook Co.). Named for Alexander Robinson, a resident of mixed Potawatomi (Algonquian) and European descent (Vogel 1963).

ROCKABEMA Lake (Maine, Aroostook Co.) \rok ə bē´ mə\. Perhaps Abenaki (Algonquian) for 'woodpecker' (Rutherford 1970).

ROCKAHOCK Bar (Va., New Kent Co.). Perhaps from the same source as **Rickahake** (Va., Norfolk Co.) or **Rickahock** (Va., King and Queen Co.). The variant **Ricohoc** also occurs in La. (St. Mary Par.).

ROCKAWAY Beach (N.Y., Queens Co.) \rok´ ə wā\. Probably from Munsee Delaware (Algonquian), meaning 'sand-place' (Tooker 1911, Grumet 1981); cf. Munsee *léekuw* 'sand' (O'Meara 1996). The placename **Rockaway** occurs in several other states (e.g., N.J., Morris Co.; and Wis., Winnebago Co.).

ROCK Creek (Ind., Carroll Co.). Corresponds to Miami/Illinois (Algonquian) /aašipehkwa/ 'rock face, cliff' (McCafferty 2002).

ROCK EXTENDING INTO WATER (Ariz., Apache Co.). Corresponds to Navajo (Athbaskan) *tsé táá'á* 'rock extending-into-water' (Linford 2000).

ROCK Point (Ariz., Apache Co.). Translation of Navajo (Athabaskan) *tsé łichii' deez'áhí* 'pointed or extended red rock', containing *tsé* 'rock', *łichii'* 'it is red', *deez'á* 'it is pointed, it extends' (Granger 1983; Wilson 1995).

ROCK River (Iowa, Sioux Co.). A translation of Dakota (Siouan) *íyą ȟeyáka,* from *íyą* 'rock' plus *ȟeyáka* 'river' (Vogel 1983; J. Koontz p.c.). In Ill. (Rock Co.), the **Rock River** is probably translated from Miami/Illinois (Algonquian)

/ahseni-šiipi/, lit. 'rock river' (McCafferty 2002). A related placename is **Sinnissippi River** (Ill., Winnebago Co.).

ROCK STRUCK BY LIGHTNING (AZ, Apache Co). Corresponds to Navajo (Athabaskan) *tsé bí'oosní'í* 'rock struck-by-lightning' (Linford 2000).

ROCK THAT PEOPLE TURNED INTO (Ariz., Apache Co.). The Navajo (Athabaskan) name, *tsé ná'áz'élí,* has been mistakenly translated as 'rock that they (people) turned into' but is actually 'rock that water flows around' (Linford 2000).

ROCK THEY RAN INTO (Ariz., Apache Co.). Corresponds to Navajo (Athabaskan) *tsé biih ńjíjahí* 'where people repeatedly run into the rock' (Linford 2000).

ROCKYHOCK (N.C., Chowan Co.). Perhaps the name of an Iroquoian group; see **Rickahake, Rickahock** and **Rockahock Bar** above.

ROCKY Mountains (Idaho, Mont., Wyo., Colo., N.Mex.). Named with a translation of French *Montagnes Rocheuses,* first applied to the Canadian Rockies. One theory is that French Canadians first applied the name not because the mountains were rocky but rather with reference to the "Rock" or Assiniboin (Siouan) people. These Indians were called /assiniipwaan/, lit. 'stone Sioux', by their Cree (Algonkian) neighbors (Stewart 1945:136; *HNAI* 13:590; cf. also Read 1969). Probably related placenames are **Assiniboine Creek** (Mont., Phillips Co.) and **Stoney Indian Lake** (Mont., Glacier Co.).

RODO River (Alaska, Nulato B-6) \rō´ dō\. The term represents a French missionary's spelling of Koyukon (Athabaskan) <khotol> (Orth 1967); cf. *hotol-no',* with *-no'* 'river' (Jetté and Jones 2000:251). The derived placename **Rodokakat** is from Koyukon *hudokkaakk'et* 'Rodo river-mouth' (J. Kari p.c.).

ROGEO Point (Vt., Chittenden Co.). Perhaps from Mohawk (Iroquoian) *rotsî:'yo* 'coward', the name of a mythic being (Lounsbury 1960:60ff.).

ROGUE River (Ore., Curry Co). A translation of French *Rivière aux Coquins* 'river of the rogues', because early French explorers found the local Indians to be "troublemakers" (McArthur 1992).

ROMAN NOSE (Okla., Blaine Co.). For Henry C. Roman Nose, a Cheyenne (Algonquian) leader (Shirk 1974); his Native American name was /vohko'xenehe/ or /voo'xenehe/, literally 'crooked-faced-one' (W. Leman p.c.).

RONCO Brook (Maine, Piscataquis Co.). Named for Ed Ronco, an Abenaki (Algonquian) guide (Rutherford 1925).

RONDOWA (Ore., Wallowa Co.) The name was coined by combining elements of the placenames *Grande Ronde* and **Wallowa County;** see below.

RONKONKOMA (N.Y., Suffolk Co.) \ron kong´ kə mə\. Earlier written <Raconkumake, Raconkamuck> (etc.); the SNEng. Algonquian name may mean 'boundary fishing-place' (Tooker 1911).

ROOTOK Island (Alaska, Unimak A-5) \ro͞o´ to͝ok\. Earlier recorded <Aektok, Ouektock> (Orth 1967); from Aleut *ayx̂alix* 'to travel' (Bergsland 1994).

ROOT River (Wis., Kenosha Co.). A translation of French *Rivière Racine,* corresponding to Potawatomi (Algonquian) <che-pe-kat-aw sebe> 'root river' (Vogel 1991); cf. Ojibwa *ojiibik* 'root', *ziibi* 'river' (Nichols and Nyholm 1995).

ROSEAU County (Minn.) \rō´ zō\. The French word for 'a reed, a rush' corresponds to Ojibwa (Algonquian) *anaakanashk* 'reed' (Nichols and Nyholm 1995).

ROSSAKATUM Branch (Del., Sussex Co.). Perhaps of Delaware (Algonquian) origin (Heck et al. 1966).

ROTAN (Tex., Fisher Co.) \rō tan`\. Perhaps a transfer of **Roatan** (Conn., Fairfield Co.); see above.

ROUGH Rock (Ariz., Apache Co.). A translation of Navajo (Athabaskan) *tséch'ízhí* 'rock that is rough', containing *tsé* 'rock' and *ch'ízh, ch'íízh* 'rough' (Granger 1983; Wilson 1995).

ROUND Lake (Alaska, Gulkana A-4). A translation of Ahtna (Athabaskan) *ben deldziidi,* lit. 'lake round' (J. Kari p.c.) Elsewhere, **Round Rock** (Ariz., Apache Co.) is perhaps an adaptation of Navajo (Athabaskan) *tsé nikáni* 'bowl-shaped rock', *tsé* 'rock' and *niką́* 'concave, bowl-shaped' (Wilson 1995). The placename **Round O** (S.C., Colleton Co.) is said to refer to a circle painted on the breast of an Indian who was met here (Pickens 1961–62:21).

RUM River (Minn., Mille Lacs Co.). This is apparently a jocular adaptation of the name *Spirit Lake,* a translation of Dakota (Siouan) <mde wakan>, lit. 'lake-sacred' (Upham 2001); cf. Dakota *mde* 'lake', *wakhą́* 'sacred, holy' (Riggs 1890; Ingham 2001). Related placenames are the nearby **Spirit Lake** and **Wahkon.**

RUMSON (N.J., Monmouth Co.). Earlier writen <Navaarumsun, Narumson> (etc.); the Delaware (Algonquian) derivation is unclear (Becker 1964).

RUSH Lake (Wis., Winnebago Co.). Corresponds to Menominee (Algonquian) /nepiaskon/ 'reeds, bulrushes' (Vogel 1991, Bloomfield 1975). **Rush River** (Minn., Sibley Co.) is a translation of Dakota (Siouan) <wayecha oju> 'river of reeds or rushes' (Upham 2001); cf. *wąyéča* 'reeds' (Riggs 1890). **Rushseba Township** (Minn., Chisago Co.) \rush sē´ bə\ is a combination of English *rush* 'a water plant' with Ojibwa (Algonquian) *ziibi* 'river' (Upham 2001; Nichols and Nyholm 1995).

RUSSIAVILLE (Ind., Howard Co.) \roo͞´ shə vil\. A folk-etymology from the surname of Jean Baptiste Richardville (1761–1841), a resident of mixed Miami/Illinois (Algonquian) and French ancestry (McPherson 1993).

S

SAA BETOH (Ariz., Navajo Co.) \sā´ bi tō\. From Navajo (Athabaskan), perhaps representing *tsah bito'* 'water of the needle', from *tsah* 'awl, needle' (Young and Morgan 1987).

SABA CHIBO (Miss., Neshoba Co.) \sab ə chib´ ə\. Perhaps from Choctaw (Muskogean) *osaapa chito* 'big cornfield', from *osaapa* 'field, cornfield' and *chito* 'big' (Seale 1939, P. Munro p.c.). A related placename is **Sapa** (Miss., Webster Co.).

SABAO Mountain (Maine, Hancock Co.) \sab´ ē ō\. Said to be from Maliseet (Algonquian), meaning 'passage' or 'almost through' (Eckstorm 1941:222–23).

SABATTIS (N.Y., Hamilton Co.) \sə bat´ is\. Named for an Indian man, tribal affiliation unknown; the term represents an Indian pronunciation of French *Jean Baptiste* '[Saint] John the Baptist' (Beauchamp 1907). A related name is **Sabattus** (Maine, Androscoggin Co.), which also occurs in N.H. (Merrimack Co).

SABINO (Maine, Sagadahoc Co.). Named for an Abenaki (Algonquian) leader (Huden 1962).

SABLE Creek (Mich., Alger Co.) \sā´ bəl\. An adaptation of French *grand sable* 'great sand-dune', corresponding to Ojibwa (Algonquian) <nagawadjing> 'at the sand mountain (Vogel 1986); cf. *negaw* 'sand' (Rhodes 1985).

SABOUGLA (Miss., Calhoun Co.). Probably from Choctaw (Muskogean) *shobolli, shobohli* 'smoke' (Read 1984; P. Munro). A variant is **Sobola.** The placename is perhaps related to **Sepulga** (Ala., Conecuh Co.) and/or **Sawokla** (Okla., Muskogee Co.); see below.

SAC \sak\. The term refers to a Central Algonquian people of the Midwest; from the French abbreviation *Saki,* probably from Ojibwa (Algonquian) /osa:ki:/ 'person of the outlet', with /o-/ marking ethnic groups (Vogel 1983; *HNAI* 15:654). The 'outlet' referred to is probably that of the **Saginaw River** in Wisconsin (see **Saginaw County** below). The Sauk's name for themselves is /asa:ki:waki/ (*HNAI* 15:648), with /a-/ marking ethnic groups. As a placename, **Sac** occurs in Iowa (Sac Co.), Mich. (Delta Co.), and Kans. (Anderson Co.). The **Sac** people have long been associated, linguistically and culturally, with the **Fox** group, and the phrase **Sac and Fox** is applied to placenames in Iowa (Tama Co.) and Okla. (Lincoln Co.). An alternative writing is **Sauk**; see below. Probably related placenames include **Osakis** (Minn., Douglas Co.) and **Ozaukee County** (Wis.).

SACAGAWEA \sak ə gə wē´ ə\. This is one form of the name of the Shoshoni (Numic) woman, also known as **Sacajawea** (see below), who accompanied the Lewis and Clark Expedition; it has also been written as <Sakakawea> and <Tsakakawea>. She had been a captive among the Hidatsas (a Siouan people), and her Hidatsa name was *tsaka'aka wi'a,* lit. 'bird woman' (Hartley 2002). Her Shoshoni name, rendered as **Sacajawea** and translated 'boat-launcher', may have been a folk-etymological transformation of the Hidatsa term (Shaul 1972). As a placename, **Sacagawea** also occurs in Wyo. (Fremont Co.) and Mont. (Petroleum Co.). The related placename **Sakakawea** is found in S.Dak. (Corson Co.).

SACAHUISTE Draw (N.Mex., Eddy Co.) \sā kə wē´ stā\. The Mexican Spanish name, also written *zacahuiste* and *zacahuistle,* refers to the nolina, a type of yucca; it is from Nahuatl (Aztecan) *zacahuitztli,* lit. 'grass-thorn', from *zacatl* 'grass', *huitztli* 'thorn' (Santamaría 1959). Related placenames are **Zacahuistle Pasture** (Tex., Brooks Co.) and **Zacaweista River** (Tex., Wilbarger Co.).

SACAJAWEA \sä kə jə wē´ ə, sak ə jə wē´ ə\. This is one form of the name of the Shoshoni (Numic) woman, also known as **Sacagawea** (see above), who accompanied the Lewis and Clark Expedition. She had been a captive among the Hidatsas (a Siouan group); the form **Sacajawea,** said to be Shoshoni for 'boat launcher', may represent a folk-etymological transformation of a Hidatsa original (Shaul 1972); cf. Shoshoni /saikki/ 'boat' (Miller 1972). The placename **Sacajawea** occurs in Idaho (Custer Co.), Mont. (Cascade Co.), Ore. (Wallowa Co.), Wash. (Cowlitz Co.), and S.Dak. (Corson Co.).

SACANDAGA River (N.Y., Saratoga Co.) \sak ən dôg´ ə\. Perhaps an Iroquoian name, of unclear derivation (Beauchamp 1907). The placename also occurs in Ore. (Lane Co.).

SACATE (Calif., Santa Barbara Co.) \sä kä´ tā\. The Mexican Spanish word, usually spelled *zacate,* means 'grass, hay'; it is from Nahuatl (Aztecan) *zacatl* (Gudde 1998).The placename also occurs in N.Mex. (Socorro Co.) Related placenames are **Sacaton Flat** (Calif., Riverside Co.), **Zacata Creek** (Tex., Webb Co.), and **Arroyo Zacatoso** (Tex., Zapata Co.).

SACATON Flat (Calif., Riverside Co.) \sä kə tōn´\. The Mexican Spanish word, usually spelled *zacatón,* refers to a type of fodder grass, lit. 'big grass', from *zacate* 'grass, hay', derived from Nahuatl (Aztecan) *zacatl* 'grass' (Gudde 1998). The placename also occurs in N.Mex. (Grant Co.). A related placename is **Sacate** (Calif., Santa Barbara Co.).

SACATOSA Mesa (N.Mex., San Miguel Co.) \sä kə tō´ zə\. The Mexican Spanish word, usually spelled *zacatosa,* means 'full of grass', from *zacate* 'grass, hay', derived from Nahuatl (Aztecan) *zacatl* 'grass'. A related placename is **Arroyo Zacatoso** (Tex., Zapata Co.).

SACCARAPPA Falls (Maine, Cumberland Co.). Probably from Abenaki (Algonquian), of unclear derivation (Eckstorm 1941:162–63).

SACHEEN Lake (Wash., Pend Oreille Co.) \sash´ ēn\. From Spokane (Salishan) /soʔc'im/, /coʔc'im/ 'to trap' (D. Kinkade p.c.).

SACHEM \sāch´ əm\. This word, referring to an Indian leader, is borrowed from SNEng. Algonquian <sâchim> 'chief'. **Sagamore** is distantly related, through Proto-Algonquian */sa:kima:wa/ (*RHD* 1987) As a placename, **Sachem** occurs in N.H. (Grafton Co.), N.Y. (Suffolk Co.), and Wash. (Skagit Co.).

SACO (Maine, York Co.) \sä´ kō, sô´ kō\. Probably from Eastern Abenaki (Algonquian) [sákohki] 'land where the river comes out', with an element [-ohki] meaning 'land' (I. Goddard p.c.) The placename also occurs in N.H. (Coös

Co.) and Mont. (Phillips Co.). Probably related placenames include **Saugus** (Maine, Essex Co.).

SADATANAK Island (Alaska, Atka C-2). Aleut *sadatanax̂* 'outside island', from *sada-* 'outside', *tanax̂* 'island' (Bergsland 1994).

SADAWGA Lake (Vt., Windham Co.). Perhaps from Mohawk (Iroquoian), of unclear derivation (Huden 1962).

SADLEROCHIT River (Alaska, Flaxman Is. A-1). The Iñupiaq (Eskimo) name was reported in 1855 as <Shud-ta-ro-shik> 'area outside the mountains' (Orth 1967).

SAGADAHOC County (Maine) \sag ə də hok´\. Perhaps a shortening of Abenaki (Algonquian) *zawakwtegw* 'river that throws out wood', from *zawaka* 'to throw out', *-tegw* 'river' (Day 1994–95). Possibly related placenames include **Saugus** (Mass., Essex Co.).

SAGAIGAN Creek (Mich., Gogebic Co.). From Ojibwa (Algonquian) *zaaga'igan* 'lake' (Vogel 1986; Nichols and Nyholm 1995), perhaps derived from <sâgi> 'mouth of a river' (Baraga 1880); a perhaps related name is **Saganing** (Mich., Arenac Co.).

SAGAK, Cape (Alaska, Samalga Is. D-4). Reported in 1836; from Aleut *sagax̂* 'sleep' (Orth 1967, Bergsland 1994).

SAGAMORE \sag´ ə môr\. A term designating an Indian leader, perhaps from Abenaki (Algonquian) *zôgemô* [sǫgəmǫ] 'chief' (Day 1994–95); it is distantly related to the word **Sachem**, through Proto-Algonquian */sa:kima:wa/ (*RHD* 1987). As a placename, **Sagamore** is widespread (e.g., Maine, Cumberland Co.; N.Y., Hamilton Co.; and Ga., Hall Co.).

SAGANAGA Lake (Minn., Cook Co.) \sag´ ə nə gä, sag ə nä´ gə\. Perhaps from Ojibwa (Algonquian) *zagaanaga* 'there are small passages between islands' (Upham 2001; J. Nichols p.c.).

SAGANASHKEE Slough (Ill., Cook Co.). From Potawatomi (Algonquian) <Ausagaunaskee>, perhaps meaning 'tall grass valley' (Vogel 1963).

SAGANING (Mich., Arenac Co.). Perhaps from Ojibwa (Algonquian) <sâgi> 'mouth of a river', <sâging> 'at the mouth' (Baraga 1880), *zaagiing* 'at the inlet' (or outlet?) (Vogel 1986; Nichols and Nyholm 1995). Probably related placenames include **Saginaw County** (Mich.).

SAGAPONACK (N.Y., Suffolk Co.) \sä gə pə näk´, sə gap´ ə nak\. From a SNEng. Algonquian word referring to a type of edible root or tuber (Tooker 1911). An abbreviated form of the name is found in **Sag Harbor.**

SAGAVANIRKTOK River (Alaska, Beechey Point B-2) \sag ə və nûrk´ tuk\. Iñupiaq (Eskimo) *saġvaġniqtuuq* 'strong current', from *saġvaq-* 'to flow (L. Kaplan p.c.).

SAGCHUDAK Island (Alaska, Atka C-2). The Aleut name was published in 1852 (Orth 1967).

SAGE Creek (S.Dak., Fall River Co.). A translation of Lakhota (Siouan) *makhá čheyaka* 'lance-leafed sage' (Sneve 1973; Ingham 2001).

SAGEEYAH (Okla., Rogers Co.) \sə gē´ yə\. Named for a Cherokee (Iroquoian) resident, Sageeyah Saunders; the given name is a Cherokee rendering of the Biblical name *Zaccheus* (Shirk 1974).

SAGHALIE Creek (Wash., Jefferson Co.) \sə hä´ lē\. Chinook Jargon <sagh-a-lie, sahhali> [səháli, sáhali] 'up, above, high, top, heaven, sky', from Lower Chinook [kw-šáxale] 'above' (D. Kinkade p.c.). A related placename is **Sahale Falls** (Ore., Hood River Co.); see below.

SAG Harbor (N.Y., Suffolk Co.) \sag\. An abbreviation of **Sagaponack** (see below), from SNEng. Algonquian, referring to a kind of edible root or tuber (Tooker 1911). There is a **Sag Pond** in Maine (Aroostook Co.).

SAGIGIK Island (Alaska, Seguam C-4). From Aleut *saĝuugax̂* 'rookery, bird colony' (Bergsland 1994).

SAGINAW County (Mich.) \sag´ i nô\. From Ojibwa (Algonquian) /sa:ki:na:ŋ/ 'in the **Sauk** country', referring to /osa:ki:/ 'Sauk, people of the outlet' (of the **Saginaw River**) (I. Goddard p.c.). The placename **Saginaw** has been transferred to several states (e.g., Minn., St. Louis Co.; N.J., Sussex Co.; and Alaska, Port Alexander D-1). Probably related placenames include **Osakis** (Minn., Douglas Co.) and **Ozaukee County** (Wis.).

SAGTIKOS (N.Y., Suffolk Co.). Earlier written <Saghtekoos, Sagtakos>; perhaps originally a possessive, <Saghtekoo's>, from a SNEng. Algonquian personal name (Ruttenber 1906; Tooker 1911).

SAGUACHE County (Colo., Saguache Co.) \sə wăch\. From Ute (Numic) *sagwách,* referring to the color range that includes both green and blue (Bright 1993). An alternative spelling is used in the name of the **Sawatch Range.**

SAGUARO National Park (Ariz., Pima Co.) \sə wä´ rō\. From the Mexican Spanish name for a type of cactus, perhaps from the Yaqui (Sonoran) language of northwestern Mexico; the modern Yaqui form is *sauwo* (Molina et al. 1999). A related form is **Sahuaro Tank** (Ariz., Yavapai Co.).

SAGWON (Alaska, Sagavanirktok B-3). Probably an abbreviation of **Sagavanirktok River;** see above (L. Kaplan p.c.).

SAHALE Falls (Ore., Hood River Co.) \sə hä´ lē\. Chinook Jargon <sagh-a-lie, sahhali> [səháli, sáhali] 'up, above, high, top, heaven, sky', from Lower Chinook [kw-šáxale] 'above' (McArthur 1992; D. Kinkade p.c.). The placename also occurs in Wash. (Chelan Co.). A related placename is **Saghalie Creek** (Wash., Jefferson Co.); see above. **Sahalee Tyee** (Wash., Skamania Co.) has the Chinook Jargon name for 'the Lord above', from <sahalee> 'above, sky' plus <tyee> 'chief' (Hitchman 1985); cf. **Sahale Tyee** (Wash., Chelan Co.). Another related form is **Sahalie Falls** (Ore., Linn Co.).

SAHAPTIN \sə hap´ tin\. This term is applied to a group of linguistically related peoples living in eastern Wash. and Ore., including the **Yakima** and **Umatilla** divisions. Along with Nez Perce, the Sahaptin language belongs to the **Sahaptian** family. The origin of the word **Sahaptin** is in Interior Salishan words referring to the Nez Perce, such as Columbian /sḥáptnəx^{w}/ (*HNAI* 12:58). A placename deriving from this is **Shahapta** (Ore., Multnomah Co.).

SAH-DA-PED-THL (Wash., Clallam Co.). This group of rocks appears to have a Makah (Nootkan) name (Hitchman 1985).

SAHUARITA (Ariz., Pima Co.) \sä wä rē´ tə, sä wə rē´ tə\. Originally Spanish *sahuarito* or *saguarito* 'little saguaro', from **Saguaro** (see **Saguaro National Park** above) or **Sahuaro,** a type of cactus. A related placename is **Sahuaro Tank** (Ariz., Yavapai Co.).

SAINT. For placenames beginning with **Saint** (e.g., **St. Tammany Parish**, La.), look under the name of the saint (in this case **Tammany**).

SAITCHUCK, The (Alaska, Dixon Entrance D-1). The name of this bay seems to be a typographic error for **Saltchuck** (Alaska, Craig C-2), Chinook Jargon for 'salt water' (Orth 1967).

SAJAKA, Cape (Alaska, Gareloi Is. C-1). From the Aleut placename *sa(m)yaaĝa*, perhaps 'front point' (Bergsland 1994).

SAKAKAWEA, Lake (N.Dak., McLean Co.) \sə kā kə wē´ ə\. From the same source as **Sacagawea** or **Sacajawea,** the name of the Shoshoni (Numic) woman who accompanied the Lewis and Clark expedition. The name also occurs in S.Dak. (Corson Co.).

SAKETON (N.Mex., San Juan Co.) \sak ə tōn\. Represents Mexican Spanish *zacatón* 'a type of grass' (Julyan 1998), from *zacate* 'grass, hay', from Nahuatl (Aztecan) *zacatl* 'grass'. Related placenames are **Sacate** (Calif., Santa Barbara Co.) and **Sacaton Flat** (Calif., Riverside Co.).

SAKLOLIK Mountain (Alaska, Point Hope A-1). The Iñupiaq (Eskimo) name was reported in 1960 (Orth 1967).

SAKONNET (R.I., Newport Co.). From SNEng. Algonquian; cf. <sauki> 'outlet' (Huden 1962; W. Cowan p.c.). Possibly related placenames include **Saugatuck** (Conn., Fairfield Co.) and **Saugus** (Mass., Essex Co.).

SAKONOWYAK River (Alaska, Beechey Point B-4). The Iñupiaq (Eskimo) name is said to mean 'twisting waters' (Orth 1967); cf. *saqu-* 'to turn, change direction' (MacLean 1980). Perhaps from the same root is **Sakoonang Channel** (Alaska, Harrison Bay B-2), translated 'big curves' (Orth 1967).

SAKPIK Mountain (Alaska, Point Hope B-1). From Iñupiaq (Eskimo) *saqpik* 'whale's tail' (L. Kaplan p.c.).

SAKRORAK Mountain (Alaska, Noatak D-7). The Iñupiaq (Eskimo) name was recorded in 1950 as meaning 'stretched out' (Orth 1967).

SAKSAIA Glacier (Alaska, Skagway B-4). The name, perhaps from Tlingit, was reported in 1883 (Orth 1967).

SAKTUINA Point (Alaska, Harrison Bay C-4). The Iñupiaq (Eskimo) name, reported in 1854, is said to mean 'waiting place' (Orth 1967).

SAKVELAK Creek (Alaska, Point Hope C-1). The Iñupiaq (Eskimo) name is *saġvaiḷaq* 'no current' (L. Kaplan p.c.).

SAK'YAYA YALANNE (N.Mex., McKinley Co.). The Zuni name contains /yala-nne/ 'mountains' (Ferguson and Hart 1985; Newman 1958).

SALACOA (Ga., Cherokee Co.). Said to be from Cherokee (Iroquoian) < sălikwəyĭ> 'bear grass, silk grass' (Goff 1975).

SALAHKAI (Ariz., Apache Co.). Navajo (Athabaskan) *tséligai* 'white rock(s)', from *tsé* 'rock' and *ɬigai* 'it is white' (Wilson 1995).

SA'LAKO (Ariz., Navajo Co.). This stone pillar was named for the Hopi (Uto-Aztecan) kachina *Sa'lako,* borrowed from the Zuni *Sha'lako* (K. Hill p.c.). A related placename is **Shalako Ski Trail** (N.Mex., Taos Co.).

SALAL Creek (Ore., Lane Co.) \sə lal´\. The name of a berry and the bush on which it grows, Chinook Jargon <sal-lal´> [səlǽl] from Lower Chinook *sálal* (McArthur 1992; *RHD* 1987). The placename **Salal** also occurs in Calif. (Siskiyou Co.) and Wash. (Lewis Co.). A related form is **Sallal Prairie** (Wash., King Co.).

SALAMONIA (Ind., Blackford Co.) \sal ə mō´ nē, sal ə mōn´ yə\. Said to represent Miami/Illinois (Algonquian) /oonsaalamooni/ 'the bloodroot plant', lit. 'yellow vermilion', from /oonsaa- 'yellow' plus /alamooni/ 'paint, vermilion' (Vogel 1986; M. McCafferty p.c.); cf. Ojibwa (Algonquian) *ozaawi-* 'yellow, brown' (Nichols and Nyholm 1995) and <onaman, osânaman> 'vermillion, yellow clay' (Baraga 1880). Probably related names include **Salamonie River** (Ind., Blackford Co.) and **Saunemin** (Ill., Livingston Co.).

SALCHA River (Alaska, Big Delta B-6) \säl´ chə\. Reported in 1898 as <Salchaket> (Orth 1967); from Middle Tanana (Athabaskan) *saal cheeget*, with *cheeget* 'river mouth' (J. Kari p.c.). **Salchaket Slough** (Alaska, Fairbanks C-3) \säl´ chak it\. has the same origin.

SALGHAT Beach (Alaska, St. Lawrence B-1). The Yupik (Eskimo) name was reported in 1949 (Orth 1967).

SALIGVIK Creek (Alaska, Point Hope B-1). The Iñupiaq (Eskimo) name is *salikvik* 'place to travel quickly' (L. Kaplan p.c.).

SALINA (Ariz., Apache Co.) \sə lē´ nə\. From Spanish *salina* 'salt spring, salt flat', a folk-etymology from Navajo (Athabaskan) *tsélání* 'many rocks', from *tsé* 'rock' plus *ɬání* 'many' (Wilson 1995). Elsewhere the placename **Salina** is simply from Spanish (e.g., Kans. and Utah) and is often pronounced \sə lī´ nə\; but in Calif., **Salinas** is always \sə lē´ nəs\.

SALISH \sā´ lish\. The self-designation of the Flathead (Salishan) people of Mont.; the Native American term is [sǽliš], containing [-iš] 'people' (D. Kinkade p.c.). The English derivative **Salishan** \sā´ lish ən\. has been formed to refer to the language family to which Flathead belongs and also occurs as a placename (Ore., Lincoln Co.; Wash., Pierce Co.), usually pronounced \sal´ i shan\. A related placename is **Selish** (Mont., Flathead Co.).

SALITPA (Ala., Clarke Co.) \sə lit´ pə\. From the same source as **Satilpa Creek** (Read 1984); see below.

SALKEHATCHIE (S.C., Colleton Co.). Probably from Muskogee, containing *hvcce* /háčči/ 'river' (Pearson 1978; Martin and Mauldin 2000).

SALKUM (Wash., Lewis Co.) \sal´ kəm, sôl´ kəm\. From the Sahaptin placename /sálkum/ (Hitchman 1985; Kinkade p.c.).

SALLAL Prairie (Wash., King Co.) \sə lal´\. From the same source as **Salal Creek**; see above.

SALMONBERRY Lake (Alaska, McGrath D-4). Corresponds to Upper Kuskokwim (Athabaskan) *nikotl' mina'*, with *mina'* 'lake' (J. Kari p.c.).

SALMON LA SAC (Wash., Kittitas Co.) \sam ən lə sak´\. The name is intended to mean 'salmon bag', referring to a woven container for holding salmon. It consists of English *salmon* plus Chinook Jargon <le-sack, le-sak´> [lisák] 'bag, sack', from French *le sac* 'the sack' (Hitchman 1985; D. Kinkade p.c.).

SALOFKA (Fla., Osceola Co.) \sə lof´ kə\. The placename was taken from a published Muskogee vocabulary; it represents *eslafkv* /islá:fka/ 'knife' (Read 1934; Martin and Mauldin 2000).

SALT Creek (Ala., Talladega Co.). Probably corresponds to Muskogee *okcvnwv* /okčánwa/ 'salt' (Read 1984, Martin and Mauldin 2000). Elsewhere (Ind., Brown Co.), **Salt Creek** corresponds to reconstructed Shawnee (Algonquian) */nepipemii-θiipi/, lit. 'salt stream' (McCafferty 2002). **Salt** in many other U.S. placenames is similarly likely to be a translation of a Native American prototype. **Salt Chuck** (Alaska, Craig C-2) \sôlt´ chuk\ is Chinook Jargon for 'salt water', combining English *salt* with Jargon <chuck> /čʌk/ 'water' (Orth 1967); a related placename is **The Saitchuck** (Alaska, Dixon Entrance D-1). **Salt Lick** (Pa., Fayette Co.) refers to a natural saline spring, frequented by deer and cattle, and may be a translation of Delaware (Algonquian) <sikheunk> 'at the salt spring' (Brinton and Anthony 1888); cf. Unami Delaware /sí:khay/ 'salt' (Blalock et al. 1994). **Salt Trail Canyon** (AZ, Coconino Co.) corresponds to Navajo (Athabaskan) *áshįįh nabitiin* 'salt trail' (Linford 2000), containing *ashiih* 'salt' and *bitiin* 'trail' (Young and Morgan 1987).

SALTESE (Wash., Spokane Co.) \səl tēs´\. From Coeur d'Alene (Salishan) /sl'tís/, the name of a man known in English as Andrew Seltice (Hitchman 1985; D. Kinkade p.c.). The placename **Saltese** is also found in Mont. (Mineral Co.). The name also occurs as **Saltice.**

SALUDA County (S.C.) \sə lo͞o´ də\. Said to be the name of an Indian band, perhaps belonging to the Shawnee (Algonquian) people (Pearson 1978). It may come from an Indian word <salutah>, meaning 'corn river' (Powell 1968); cf. Cherokee (Iroquoian) *selu* 'corn' (Feeling 1975). The placename also occurs in N.C. (Polk Co.) and Va. (Middlesex Co.) and as a transfer name in Ill. (Knox Co.) and Ind. (Jefferson Co.).

SALUNGA (Pa., Lancaster Co.) \sə lung´ gə\. Abbreviated from an earlier <Chiquesalunga>, from Delaware (Algonquian) <chickiswalungo> 'place of the crawfish' (Donehoo 1928). A related placename is **Chickies** (Pa., Lancaster Co.).

SAMAGATUMA Valley (Calif., San Diego Co.) \sä mə gə to͞o´ mə\. The Diegueño (Yuman) village name was given in 1845 as <Jamatayune>, perhaps from 'water place spread-in-the-sun' (Gudde 1998).

SAMAK (Utah, Summit Co.). A backward spelling of the nearby placenames **Kamas,** from the same source as **Camas**, referring to an edible root (Van Cott 1990), see above.

SAMALGA Island (Alaska, Samalga Is. D-4). From the Aleut placename *samalĝa* (Orth 1967; Bergsland 1994).

SAMALOGH Ridge (Alaska, Pribilof Is. A-3). From Aleut *saamlax̂* 'egg', named in 1903 (Orth 1967; Bergsland 1994).

SAMBO Gulch (Calif., Siskiyou Co.) \sam´ bō\. Named for a Shasta Indian family that settled here in 1870 (BGN 8101). A member of the family, Sargent Sambo, was one of the last surviving speakers of the Shasta language in the mid 1900s.

SAM Creek (Ore., Lincoln Co.). Named for an Indian leader, called in English "Chief Sam," of the Rogue River peoples (McArthur 1992).

SAMISH (Wash., Skagit Co.) \sam´ ish\. The name of a Central Coast Salishan people and language of the Puget Sound area; the Native American form is /sʔéməš/, from /s-/ 'nominalizer', /ʔé/ 'be there', and /-məš/ 'people' (*HNAI* 7:455, D. Kinkade p.c.).

SAMIS River (Wash., Jefferson Co.). Said to be from <Samms-mish>, a division of the Quinault (Salishan) people (Hitchman 1985). A variant is **Sams River.**

SAMMAMISH (Wash., King Co.) \sə mam´ ish\. From the name of a Southern Coast Salish subgroup, Lushootseed /sc'ababš/, with the alternation of *m* and *b* that is characteristic of languages in the Puget Sound area (*HNAI* 7:487).

SAMOSET Lake (Mass., Worcester Co.) \sam´ ə set\. Named for the SNEng. Algonquian leader who greeted the Pilgrims in 1620 (Huden 1962). The placename **Samoset** has also been transferred to Fla. (Manatee Co) and Wis. (Bayfield Co.).

SAMP (W.Va., Webster Co.) \samp\. The word refers to a kind of porridge made of coarsely ground corn; it is from SNEng. Algonquian <nasàump> 'cornmeal mush' (*RHD* 1987). The placename **Samp Mortar Reservoir** occurs in Conn. (Fairfield Co.).

SAMPALA Lake (Fla., Madison Co.) \sam pä´ lə\. Possibly from Muskogee *svmpv* /sámpa/ 'basket' (Read 1934; Martin and Mauldin 2000).

SAMPAWAMS Neck (N.Y., Suffolk Co.). Probably from SNEng. Algonquian, of unclear derivation (Tooker 1911).

SAMS River (Wash., Jefferson Co.). A variant of **Samis River**; see above.

SAMS Valley (Ore., Jackson Co.). Named in the nineteenth century for an Indian leader from the Rogue River area, known as "Chief Sam" (McArthur 1992).

SANAGUICH River (Alaska, Shishmaref A-2). The Iñupiaq (Eskimo) name was reported in 1901 (Orth 1967).

SANAK (Alaska, False Pass B-3) \sə nak´\. From the Aleut placename *sanaĝax, sanax̂ax* (Bergsland 1994).

SANATAG Creek (Okla., Cotton Co.). Perhaps from an unidentified Indian language (BGN 8801).

SAND PILLOW (Wis., Jackson Co.) A translation of a Winnebago (Siouan) name, referring to people who were said to be "so poor that they use sand for pillows" (Vogel 1991).

SANDUSKY (Ohio, Erie Co.) \san´ dus kē, san dus´ kē, sən dus´ kē\. Earlier written <Sandouske>; perhaps from Wyandot (Iroquoian) /sa'ndesti/ 'water' (Mahr 1957:153). The placename occurs as a transfer in other states (e.g., Iowa, Lee Co.; Ill., Alexander Co.; and Mich., Sanilac Co.).

SANEL Mountain (Calif., Mendocino Co.) \sə nel´\. From the name of a Central Pomo village; the Native American form is /šane-l/ 'at the ceremonial house', from /šane/ 'ceremonial house' (Gudde 1998).

SANENEHECK Rock (Ariz., Navajo Co.). Navajo (Athabaskan) *tsé ani'įįhí* 'thief rock' (Linford 2000), containing *tsé* 'rock' and *ani'įįhí* 'thief' (Young and Morgan 1987).

SANGAINA Creek (Alaska, McCarthy B-8) \san gī´ nə\. Ahtna (Athabaskan) *saen k'ena'* 'summer creek', containing *saen* 'summer' and *-na'* 'stream' (Kari 1990).

SANGAMON County (Ill.) \sang´ gə mon, sang´ gə mən\. The name was written by a French explorer in 1721 as <Saguimont>; it may be related to Ojibwa (Algonquian) *zaagiing* 'at the inlet' (Vogel 1963; Nichols and Nyholm 1995).

SANHICKAN Creek (N.J., Mercer Co.). Perhaps from Delaware (Algonquian) *sànghikàn* 'fire-drill', i.e. implement for making fire (Kraft and Kraft 1985); cf. <sankhikan> 'gun lock' (Brinton and Anthony 1888).

SANIGARUAK Island (Alaska, Barrow A-2). The Iñupiaq (Eskimo) name is *saniŋaruaq* 'placed crosswise' (L. Kaplan p.c.).

SANILAC County (Mich.) \san´ i lak\. Named for a literary figure, supposed to be a Wyandot (Iroquoian) leader, in the poem *Sannilac* by Henry Whiting, published in 1831 (Vogel 1986).

SANISH (N.Dak., Mountrail Co.) \san´ ish\. From the Arikara (Caddoan) self-designation *sáhniš* 'person, human being, Arikara' (Wick 1988; D. Parks p.c.).

SANKANAC (Pa., Chester Co.). Said to be from Delaware (Algonquian) <sankhanne> 'flint stream' (Donehoo 1928).

SANKATY Head (Mass., Nantucket Co.). Earlier written <Sanckatanck>, <Sankata> (Little 1984). From SNEng. Algonquian, perhaps containing <sonqui-> 'it is cold' (Huden 1962; W. Cowan p.c.).

SANKIN Island (Alaska, False Pass D-4). The Aleut name was given as <Sankik> in 1847 (Orth 1967).

SANONA Creek (Alaska, Talkeetna Mountains C-1) \sə nō´ nə\. Ahtena (Athabaskan) *snuu na'*, from *snuu* 'brush area along river bottom' plus *na'* 'stream' (Kari 1990).

SANOOSE Creek (Miss., Kemper Co.). Perhaps from Choctaw (Muskogean) *issi aanosi* 'where deer sleep', containing *issi* 'deer', *aa-* 'place', and *nosi* 'to sleep' (Seale 1939, P. Munro p.c.). A related name is **Sanusi Creek** (Ala., Sumter Co.).

SANOSTEE (N.Mex., San Juan Co.) \sə nos´ tē\. Navajo (Athabaskan) *tsé ałnáozt'i'í* 'where rocks overlap or are layered', containing *tsé* 'rock(s)' and *ałnáozt'i'* 'they overlap' (Wilson 1995). The placename also occurs in Ariz. (Apache Co.) \san´ əs tē\.

SANPETE County (Utah) \san pēt´\. From Ute (Numic) /saimpitsi/ 'people of the tules', containing /saimpivɨ/ 'tule, bulrush' (J. McLaughlin p.c.) A related form is found in the name **San Pitch Creek** \san pich´\. in the same area.

SANPOIL River (Wash., Ferry Co.) \san pō el´\. From Okanagan (Salishan) [snpʕ^{w}ílx] 'gray as far as one can see' (Hitchman 1985; D. Kinkade p.c.). The term seems to have been folk-etymologized in the direction of French *sans poil* 'without fur'.

SANSARC (S.Dak., Stanley Co.). French *sans arc* 'without a bow', a translation of Lakhota (Siouan) *itázibčho,* the name of a Teton clan; cf. *itázipa* 'a bow', *-čho* 'without' (Sneve 1973; Ingham 2001).

SANSAVILLA Bluff (Ga., Wayne Co.). From the name of an Indian town, language not identified; early Spanish records show apparently folk-etymologized forms such as <Santa Savilla> (Goff 1975; Krakow 1975).

SANTABARB Creek (La., Sabine Par.) \san´ tə bärb\. Choctaw (Muskogean) for 'snake creek', from *sįti* 'snake' and *book* 'creek' (Seale 1939; P. Munro p.c.). Probably related forms are **Santa Bogue** (Ala., Washington Co.) and **Senter Bogue Creek** (Miss., Wayne Co.).

SANTA BOGUE (Ala., Washington Co.) \san´ tə bōg\. Choctaw (Muskogean) for 'snake creek', from *sįti* 'snake' and *book* 'creek' (Seale 1939; P. Munro p.c.). Probably related forms are **Senter Bogue Creek** (Miss., Wayne Co.), **Santabarb Creek** (La., Sabine Par.), and **Sintabogue** (Ala., Washington Co.).

SANTAN (Ariz., Pinal Co.) \san tan´, san´tan\. An O'odham (Piman) adaptation of Spanish *Santa Ana* 'St. Anne' (Granger 1983; J. Hill p.c.).

SANTANTA Peak (Colo., Grand Co.) Named for a nineteenth-century Kiowa leader better known as **Satanta;** see below.

SANTAPOGUE Neck (N.Y., Suffolk Co.) \san´ tə pōg\. The SNEng. Algonquian name may mean 'cool water' (Tooker 1911).

SANTAQUIN (Utah, Utah Co.) \san´ tə kwin\. Said to have been named for a Southern Paiute (Numic) Indian leader (Van Cott 1990).

SANTEE \san tē´\. The term designates the eastern division of the Dakotan (Siouan) people, living mainly in Minn., and in N.Dak. and S.Dak. east of the Missouri River. The early French spelling <Izatys> represents the term *isą́'athi* or *isą́yathi,* apparently from *isą́* 'knife' and *athí* 'to make camp (at a place)' (*HNAI* 13:751–52). As a placename, **Santee** occurs in Neb. (Knox Co.) and as a transfer name elsewhere (e.g., Ind., Decatur Co.).

SANTEE River (S.C., Orangeburg Co.) \san´ tē\. Probably from Catawban (Siouan) /są́ta:/ 'swift, of a current' (B. Rudes p.c.). A possible transfer occurs in Miss. (Jefferson Davis Co.).

SANTEETLAH (N.C., Graham Co.). Perhaps from Cherokee (Iroqoian), but of unclear derivation (Powell 1968).

SANTIAM Lake (Ore., Linn Co.) \san tē am´, san´ tē am\. Named for the Santiam (Kalapuyan) people, from the name [santyám] (McArthur 1992; H. Zenk p.c.). A variant is **Santyam,** in the same area. The placename **Santiam** occurs as a transfer in Idaho (Idaho Co.).

SANTUIT (Mass., Barnstable Co.). From SNEng. Algonquian, perhaps meaning 'cool water place' (Huden 1962).

SANUSI Creek (Ala., Sumter Co.) \san (h)o͞o´ chē\. Perhaps from Choctaw (Muskogean) *issi aanosi* 'deer sleep there', from *issi* 'deer', *aa-* 'there', *nosi* 'to sleep'; also written **Sanhoochee** (Read 1984). A related name is **Sanoose Creek** (Miss., Kemper Co.).

SAN XAVIER DEL BAC, Mission (Ariz., Pima Co.) \san hə vēr´ del bak´, san hə vēr´ del bäk´\. Spanish *San Xavier* (modern *Javier*) *del Bac,* after St. Francis Xavier, with reference to O'odham (Piman) *wa:k* 'standing water' (J. Hill p.c.).

SANYA (Alaska, Prince Rupert D-3). From the name of the Tlingit village [sa:n'ya: q^{W}á:n], containing [q^{W}á:n] 'village' (*HNAI* 7:227).

SAOOK Bay (Alaska, Sitka B-4). The Tlingit name was reported in 1895 as <sa-uk> (Orth 1967).

SAPA (Miss., Webster Co.) \sä´ pə\. From Choctaw (Muskogean) *osaapa* 'field, cornfield' (Seale 1939; P. Munro p.c.). A related placename is **Saba Chibo** (Miss., Neshoba Co.).

SAPANA VAYA (Ariz., Pima Co.). Perhaps from O'odham (Piman) *ṣapan wahia* 'soap well'; cf. modern *ṣawon* 'soap', *wahia* 'well' (J. Hill p.c.). Both forms of the word for 'soap' are from Spanish *jabón.*

SAPAWE (N.Mex., Rio Arriba Co.). This archaeological site is named for a Pueblo village, perhaps of the Tewa (Tanoan) language family (*HNAI* 9:250).

SAPELLO (N.Mex., San Miguel Co.) \sä´ pē yō\. Perhaps from earlier <Shapellote, Chaptellote>; cf. <Chapalote>, the name of an early French-Kiowa resident of Taos (Julyan 1998).

SAPELO Island (Ga., McIntosh Co.) \sap´ ə lō\. From Spanish *Zapala,* perhaps derived from an Indian word (Krakow 1975). There is a place called *Zapala* in Argentina, where it may also be from a local Indian language.

SAPINERO (Colo., Gunnison Co.) \sap i nâr´ ō\. Named for a Ute (Numic) leader; the name is apparently Spanish, perhaps from *sabino* 'juniper' (Bright 1993).

SAPOKESICK Lake (Wis., Menominee Co.). Perhaps from Menominee (Algonquian), but of unclear derivation (Vogel 1991).

SAPOLIL (Wash., Walla Walla Co.) \sap´ ə lil\. Chinook Jargon <sap-a-lil, shappleel> [sápolil] 'wheat, flour, bread', perhaps from Chinookan /a-sáblal/ 'bread'.

SAPONAC (Maine, Penobscot Co.) \sə pon´ ək\. Earlier written <Chibanook>, probably from Abenaki (Algonquian), said to mean 'big opening' (Eckstorm 1941).

SAPONY Creek (N.C., Nash Co.). Named for an Siouan group, also written as **Saponi,** which merged with the Cayuga (Iroquoian) in 1753 (Powell 1968; *HNAI* 15:501). A related form is **Sappony Creek** (Va., Chesterfield Co.).

SAPOWET Creek (R.I., Newport Co.). From SNEng. Algonquian, probably representing <seipu> 'river' and <-et> 'place' (Huden 1962; W. Cowan p.c.).

SAPPA Creek (Kans., Decatur Co.) \sap´ ə\. Probably from Lakhota (Siouan) *sápa* 'black' (Rydjord 1968; Ingham 2001).

SAPPONY Creek (Va., Chesterfield Co.) \sap ō nī´\. Named for an Siouan group, also written as **Saponi,** which merged with the Cayuga (Iroquoian) in 1753 (Hagemann 1988; *HNAI* 15:501). A related form is **Sapony Creek** (N.C., Nash Co.).

SAPULPA (Okla., Creek Co.) \sə pul´ pə\. Named for a nineteenth-century Muskogee leader <Sus-pul-ber> or for his family (Shirk 1974); perhaps from *isvpvlpakē* /(i)s-apalpakí:/ 'wrapped with' (J. Martin p.c.).

SAPUMIK Ridge (Alaska, Point Hope D-1). The Iñupiaq (Eskimo) name was reported in 1966 (Orth 1967).

SAPUN Creek (Alaska, Baird Mountains D-3). The Inupiaq (Eskimo) word is *sapun* 'fish weir' (L. Kaplan p.c.).

SAQUATUCKET Harbor (Mass., Barnstable Co.). From SNEng. Algonquian, perhaps containing <sagket-> 'it pours out', <-tuck-> 'tidal stream', and <-et> 'place' (Huden 1962; W. Cowan p.c.).

SAQUISH Neck (Mass., Plymouth Co.). From SNEng. Algonquian, perhaps representing <sickis> 'clam' (Huden 1962; W. Cowan p.c.).

SARANAC (N.Y., Clinton Co.) \sâr´ ə nak\. Abenaki (Algonquian) *zalônaktegw* 'sumac-cone river', containing *zalôn* 'sumac cone' and *-tegw-* 'river' (Day 1994–95). The name occurs as a transfer in other states (e.g., Alaska, Sumdum A-4; Ga., Clay Co.; and Mich., Ionia Co.).

SARASOTA County (Fla.) \sâr ə sō´ tə\. A Spanish spelling of an Indian placename, language not identified (Stewart 1970).

SARASSA (Ark., Lincoln Co.). Probably from <Sarasin>, a Quapaw (Siouan) leader; this in turn may be from the French surname *Sarasin* or *Sarrazin* (Dickinson 1995),.

SARATOGA County (N.Y.) \sâr ə tō´ gə\. The name was earlier written as <Saraghtoge, Saraghtogo> (etc.); it is apparently from an Iroquoian language but is of unclear derivation. The term occurs as a transfer name in many states (e.g., Calif., Santa Clara Co.; Iowa, Howard Co.; and Wis., Wood Co.).

SARCEE Mountain (Mont., Glacier Co.) \sär´ sē\. The name of an Athabaskan people living in Alberta, Canada; also spelled **Sarsi.** The term is possibly derived from *sa:hsí:wa*, the name applied by the Blackfoot (Algonquian) to the Sarcee people (Holterman 1985; *HNAI* 13:636).

SARCOXIE Township (Kans., Jefferson Co.) \sär kok´ sē\. Named for a Delaware (Algonquian) leader; his name has also been written as <Sah-coc-sa> (Rydjord 1968). The name also occurs in Mo. (Jasper Co.).

SARHEEN Cove (Alaska, Petersburg A-4). The Tlingit name, reported in 1902, probably contains *héen* \hi:n\. 'river' (Orth 1967; Davis and Leer 1976:5).

SARKAR Creek (Alaska, Craig D-4). The Tlingit name was reported in 1897 (Orth 1967).

SARSAPKIN Creek (Wash., Okanogan Co.). Probably from the Okanagan (Salishan) placename \səsáʕpqən\. (D. Kinkade p.c.).

SARVORUM Mountain (Calif., Humboldt Co.) \sär vôr´ əm\. Karuk *sahvúrum,* apparently containing *sah-* 'downhill' and *vur-* 'to flow' (Gudde 1998).

SASABE (Ariz., Pima Co.) \sä´ sə bē, sas´ ə bē\. From O'odham (Piman) *ṣaṣawk* 'echo' (Granger 1983; Saxton et al. 1983).

SASACAT Creek (Wis., Langlade Co.). Perhaps from Ojibwa (Algonquian) <sasaga> 'it is full of brushwood' (Baraga 1880; Vogel 1991).

SASAKWA (Okla., Seminole Co.) \sə sä´ kwə\. From Muskogee *sasakwv* /sâ:sákwa/ 'goose' (Shirk 1974; Martin and Mauldin 2000).

SASANOA River (Maine, Lincoln Co.). Named for <Sasanou> or <Sasano>, an Abenaki (Algonquian) leader in the seventeenth century (Huden 1962).

SASCO Brook (Conn., Fairfield Co.). The SNEng. Algonquian name may be from <wososki> 'marshland, mud' (Trumbull 1881; W. Cowan p.c.). A related name is **Sasqua Hill** (Conn., Fairfield Co.).

SASE NASKET (Ariz., Coconino Co.). Said to be from Navajo (Athabaskan), but of unclear derivation (Brian 1992).

SASETANHA Mesa (Ariz., Apache Co.). Also written <Sastanha>; perhaps from Navajo (Athabaskan), but the derivation is not clear (Linford 2000).

SASHABAW Creek (Mich., Oakland Co.) \sash´ i bô\. Probably named for an Ojibwa (Algonquian) leader, <Sassaba>, of the early nineteenth century (Vogel 1986).

SASKA Peak (Wash., Chelan Co.). Shortened from **Silicosaska Park** (see below), from Moses-Columbian (Salishan) /c'ə́lxʷuʔsásq't/, the name of a leader of the Entiat people in the nineteenth century; meaning 'standing in the middle of the sky', from /c'líx/ 'stand', /-aw's/ 'middle', and /-asq't/ 'sky, day' (D. Kinkade p.c.).

SASMIK, Cape (Alaska, Adak B-6). From the Aleut placename *sasmiix* (Orth 1967; Bergsland 1994).

SASQUA Hill (Conn., Fairfield Co.). A related name is nearby **Sasco Brook**; see above.

SASQUATCH Steps (Wash., Skamania Co.) \sas´ kwäch\. The name refers to a giant being from Northwestern Indian legend, also called "bigfoot" (BGN 8401). The term is from Halkomelem (Salishan) [sǽsq'əc] (D. Kinkade p.c.).

SASSAQUIN Pond (Mass., Bristol Co.). From SNEng. Algonquian, perhaps reflecting <sassagus> 'it is slow' (Huden 1962; W. Cowan p.c.).

SATAILAK Creek (Alaska, Killik River A-2). The Iñupiaq (Eskimo) name was reported in 1956 (Orth 1967).

SATANK (Colo., Garfield Co.) \sə tangk\. Named for a nineteenth-century Kiowa leader, also known as <Setangya>, said to mean 'bear-sitting' (Rydjord 1968; Bright 1993); cf. [seit] 'bear', [ʔæ̨:'gyæ] 'to sit' (Harrington 1916). The name has sometimes been confused with that of **Satanta**, another Kiowa leader.

SATANTA (Kans., Haskell Co.) \sə tan´ tə\. Named for a nineteenth-century Kiowa leader; the name has been given as <set-tainte> 'bear-white' (Rydjord 1968); cf. [seit] 'bear', [t'ę̨ę] 'white' (Harrington 1916). The placename **Satanta** also occurs in Colo. (Grand Co.). The name has sometimes been confused with that of **Satank,** another Kiowa leader.

SATARTIA (Miss., Yazoo Co.\. \sä tä´ shə\. Choctaw (Muskogean) *issito asha* 'pumpkins are there', from *issito* 'pumpkin', *asha* 'they are there' (Seale 1939; P. Munro p.c.).

SATICOY (Calif., Ventura Co.) \sat´ i koi\. The name of a Ventureño (Chumashan) village (Gudde 1998).

SATILLA (Ga., Jeff Davis Co.) \sə til´ ə\. Earlier written as <St. Illa>, sometimes said to be a Spanish surname, but perhaps a borrowing from an unidentified Indian language (Krakow 1975).

SATILPA Creek (Ala., Clarke Co.) \sə til´ pə\. Perhaps from Choctaw (Muskogean) *isito* 'pumpkin' plus *ilhpa* 'provisions' (Read 1984; Byington 1915). A related form is **Salitpa**, in the same area.

SATOLAH (Ga., Rabun Co.). From Cherokee (Iroquoian) *sudali* 'six' (Krakow 1975; Feeling 1975).

SATSOP (Wash., Grays Harbor Co.) \sat´ səp\. From Upper Chehalis (Salishan) /sə́capš/, lit. 'made stream', from /sə́ʔa-/ 'make, do', plus /cápš/ 'stream' (D. Kinkade p.c.).

SATUCKET (Mass., Barnstable Co.). From SNEng. Algonquian, probably containing <-tuck-> 'tidal stream', and <-et> 'place' (Huden 1962; W. Cowan p.c.).

SATUIT Brook (Mass., Plymouth Co.). The SNEng. Algonquian name may mean 'cold brook' (Huden 1962).

SATULICK Mountain (Wash., Pierce Co.). Named for a local Indian, also known as <Sotolick>, language not identified (Hitchman 1985).

SATUS (Wash., Yakima Co.) \sā´ təs\. From Yakima (Sahaptian) /sátas/, /šátas̓/, /šátaaš/ 'gathering place' (D. Kinkade p.c.).

SAUBEE Lake (Mich., Eaton Co.). Probably named for <Sawba>, an Ottawa (Algonquian) leader in the early nineteenth century (Vogel 1986).

SAUCON (Pa., Northampton Co.) \sô´ kən\. Earlier written <Sakunk>, perhaps Delaware (Algonquian) for 'outlet'; cf. Unami Delaware <sakuwit> 'mouth of a stream' (Donehoo 1928; Brinton and Anthony 1888), Munsee Delaware *saak-* 'out' (O'Meara 1996). The name **Saucon** also occurs in Wash. (Pend Oreille Co.). A variant writing is nearby **Saucona**; a related placename is **Saucony** (Pa., Berks Co.). Other probably related names include **Saugus** (Mass., Essex Co.) and **Sawkunk** (Pa., Washington Co.).

SAUGAGE Lake (Mich., Kent Co.). Perhaps from Ojibwa (Algonquian) <sâgaki> 'it comes out of the ground' (Baraga 1880; Vogel 1986); cf. *zaag-* 'out' (Nichols and Nyholm 1995). Probably related placenames include **Saginaw County** (Mich.).

SAUGANASH (Ill., Cook Co.). Named for a Potawatomi (Algonquian) leader known in English as Billy Caldwell. He was of mixed English and Indian descent, and the Native American form of his name meant 'Englishman' (Vogel 1963); cf. Ojibwa (Algonquian) *zhaaganaash* 'Englishman' (Nichols and Nyholm 1995). A related placename is **Sogonosh Valley** (Mich., Emmet Co.).

SAUGA Point (R.I., Washington Co.). SNEng. Algonquian; cf. <sauki> 'outlet' (Huden 1962; W. Cowan p.c.). Probably related names include **Saugus** (Mass., Essex Co.).

SAUGATUCK (Conn., Fairfield Co.) \sô´ gə tuk\. From SNEng. Algonquian <saukituck>, probably containing <sauki> 'outlet' and <-tuck> 'tidal stream' (Huden 1962; W. Cowan p.c.). The name **Saugatuck** occurs as a transfer in Mich. (Allegan Co.). **Saugatucket Pond** (R.I., Washington Co.) contains the same elements, plus <-et> 'place'. Probably related placenames include **Sagadahoc County** (Maine) and **Saugus** (Mass., Essex Co.).

SAUGEP Creek (Calif., Del Norte Co.) \sô´ gep\. Perhaps from Yurok /segep/ 'coyote' (Gudde 1998).

SAUGUS (Mass., Essex Co.) \sô´ gəs\. From SNEng. Algonquian; cf. <sauki> 'outlet' and <-s> 'diminutive' (Huden 1962; W. Cowan p.c.). The placename occurs as a transfer in Calif. (Los Angeles Co.). Probably related placenames include **Saco** (Maine, York Co.).

SAUK \sôk\. An alternative writing of **Sac** (see above), a Central Algonquian group. As a placename, Sauk occurs in Ill. (Cook Co.), Mich. (Branch Co.), Minn. (Benton Co.), and Wis. (Sauk Co.). Probably related placenames include **Osakis** (Minn., Douglas Co.) and **Ozaukee County** (Wis.).

SAUK (Wash., Skagit Co.) \sôk´\. From the name of a Southern Coast Salishan subgroup, locally called the Sauk people; the Lushootseed name is /sáʔk^{w}bìk^{w}/ (Hitchman 1985; *HNAI* 7:487); probably folk-etymologized in English pronunciation to resemble the name of the Algonquian people called the **Sac** or **Sauk,** native to the midwestern United States.

SAUNEMIN (Ill., Livingston Co.). Said to be named after a Kickapoo (Algonquian) leader whose name was <osanamon> 'yellow ochre, vermillion' (Vogel 1963; McPherson 1993); cf. Ojibwa (Algonquian) *ozaawi-* 'yellow, brown' (Nichols and Nyholm 1995) and <onaman, osânaman> 'vermillion, yellow clay' (Baraga 1880). A probably related placename is **Salamonia** (Ind., Blackford Co.).

SAUQUOIT (N.Y., Oneida Co.) \sə kwoit´\. The name was earlier written <Sadachqueda, Sadaquoit> (etc.); it is probably from an Iroquoian language, but the derivation is not clear (Beauchamp 1907). A related placename is **Sequoit Creek** (Ill., Lake Co.).

SAURA (N.C., Rockingham Co.). From Catawba (Siouan) *saaraa'* 'peninsula, point of land', the name of one of the two Catawban groups that came together to form the modern Catawba Nation (B. Rudes p.c.).

SAUTA (Ala., Jackson Co.) \sô´ tə\. Said to be from a Cherokee (Iroquoian) placename <itsati> (Read 1984). **Sautee** (Ga., White Co.) is related to the same word (Krakow 1975).

SAVANNA (Ill., Carroll Co.) \sə van´ ə\. From the same source as **Savannah River** (see below), from Spanish *sabana* 'a type of grassland' (Vogel 1963). The spelling **Savanna** also occurs in Md. (Dorchester Co.).

SAVANNAH River (Ga., S.C.) \sə van´ ə\. The placename is derived from <Savana>, a name applied to Indians in the area; and some writers have held that the term is derived from /šaawanwa/, the self-designation of the **Shawnee** (Algonquian) Indians. Pearson (1974–76), however, has argued that the tribal designation is in fact derived from the English topographic term *savannah* 'a type of tropical grassland', which was borrowed by English from Spanish *sabana* in the 1500s and has been used in the southeastern United States since that time. The Spanish term was in turn borrowed in the West Indies from Taino (Arawakan) *zabana* (*RHD* 1987). The placename **Savannah** also occurs in other states (e.g., Iowa, Davis Co.).

SAVAYEIT Lake (Alaska, Beaver B-5) \sä´ və yēt\. Koyukon (Athabaskan) *ts'ebaa yeet mene'* 'spruce-in lake' (Kari 2000); contains *ts'ebaa* 'spruce tree' and *ben, men* 'lake' (Jetté and Jones 2000).

SAVIOYOK Creek (Alaska, Wiseman D-4). The Iñupiaq (Eskimo) name was obtained in 1956 (Orth 1967).

SAVIUKVIAYAK River (Alaska, Sagavanirktok A-2). The Iñupiaq (Eskimo) name was reported in 1956 (Orth 1967).

SAVONOSKI (Alaska, Naknek C-3) \sav ə nos´ kē\. The Yupik (Eskimo) name was reported in 1919 (Orth 1967).

SAVOONGA (Alaska, St. Lawrence D-3) \sə vōōng´ gə\. From the St. Lawrence Is. Yupik (Eskimo) placename *sivungaq* (Jacobson 1987).

SAVUKAHUK Point (Alaska, St. Lawrence C-6). Said to be Yupik (Eskimo), meaning 'material for a harpoon head' (Orth 1967); cf. St. Lawrence Is. Yupik (Eskimo) *savek* 'harpoon' (Jacobson 1987).

SAWACKLAHATCHEE Creek (Ala., Lee Co.) \sə wäk lə hach´ ē\. Muskogee *svwoklehacce* /sawakli-háčči/ 'Sawakli stream', referring to *svwokle,* a tribal town, and *hacce* 'stream' (Read 1984; Martin and Mauldin 2000). Related placenames are **Sawokla** (Okla., Muskogee Co.) and **Sawokli** (Ala., Russell Co.).

SAWAMISH County (Wash.). This county in western Wash. was formed in 1854, but its name was changed to Mason County in 1964 (Reese 1996). The name is from Lushootseed (Salishan) /səhíʔwəbš/, the name of a band also known as <Sahewamish> (D. Kinkade p.c.). The term shows the alternation of *m* and *b* that is characteristic of Indian languages in the Puget Sound area.

SAWATCH Range (Colo., Saguache Co.) \sə wäch´\. From the same source as **Saguache County** (Bright 1993); see above.

SAWHATCHEE (Ga., Early Co.) \sē hach´ ē\. Perhaps from Muskogee *osa-hacce* /osa:-háčči/, lit. 'pokeweed stream' (Martin and Mauldin 2000). Possibly related placenames include **Sowhatchee** (Ga., Early Co.) and **Ossahatchie** (Ga., Harris Co.).

SAWIK Mountain (Ariz., Maricopa Co.). From O'odham (Piman) *ṣawikuḍ* 'rattle' (J. Hill p.c.).

SAWKUNK (Pa., Washington Co.). Probably from Delaware (Algonquian), meaning 'stream mouth'; cf. Unami Delaware (Algonquian) <sakuwit> 'mouth of a stream' (Donehoo 1928:203; Brinton and Anthony 1888), Munsee Delaware *saak-* 'out' (O'Meara 1996). A likely related placename is **Saucon** (Pa., Northhampton Co.).

SAWOKLA (Okla., Muskogee Co.) \sə wōk′ lə\. From Muskogee *svwokle* /sawókli/, the name of a tribal town (Martin and Mauldin 2000). Related placenames include **Sawokli** (Ala., Russell Co.), as well as **Sawacklahatchee Creek** (Ala., Lee Co.).

SAXAPAHAW (N.C., Alamance Co.). Catawban (Siouan) /sak 'yápha:/ 'piedmont, foothill', from /sak/ 'hill' plus /'yápha:/ 'step' (B. Rudes p.c.).

SAYALIK Creek (Alaska, Goodnews Bay C-8). The Yupik (Eskimo) name was published in 1951 (Orth 1967).

SAYDATOH (N.Mex., Sandoval Co.) \sā′ də tō\. Perhaps from Navajo (Athabaskan), containing *tó* 'water, spring' or *tooh* 'body of water' (Young and Morgan 1987).

SCABBY Creek (S.Dak., Todd Co.). Corresponds to Lakhota (Siouan) *hąyuȟpu* 'scabby', referring to a herd of horses with scabby skins (Sneve 1973; Buechel and Manhart 2002).

SCAJAQUADA Creek (N.Y., Erie Co.) \skaj′ ə kwä də\. Probably from an Iroquoian language but of unclear derivation.

SCAMMON Pond (Maine, Hancock Co.). Perhaps from Abenaki (Algonquian) *skamon* 'maize, corn' (Huden 1962; Day 1994).

SCANAWAH Island (S.C., Charleston Co.). Perhaps from an unidentified Indian language (Pickens 1963:38).

SCANEWA, Lake (Wash., Lewis Co.). Named for Chief Scanewa Wahawah, a leader of the Cowlitz (Sahaptian) people (BGN 1995).

SCANTIC (Mass., Hartford Co.) \skan′ tik\. Reduced from SNEng. Algonquian <peskatuk> (Trumbull 1881). A related placename may be **Scitico** (Conn., Hartford Co.).

SCAPPOOSE (Ore., Columbia Co.) \skap o͞os′, skə po͞os\. Said to mean 'gravelly plain' in an unidentified Indian language (McArthur 1992).

SCARGO Hill (Mass., Barnstable Co.) \skär′ gō\. Perhaps from SNEng. Algonquian, meaning 'it flows out' (Huden 1962).

SCATCHET Head (Wash., Island Co.) \skach′ it\. From the name of the **Skagit** (Salishan) Indian people (Phillips 1971); see **Skagit County** below.

SCHAGHTICOKE (Conn., Litchfield Co.) \skat′ ē ko͞ok, shat′ ē ko͞ok\. Perhaps from Mahican (Algonquian), meaning 'where the river branches', from earlier <Pishgachtigok, Pachgatgoch> (Trumbull 1881; Ruttenber 1906). The placename also occurs in N.Y. (Rensselaer Co.). Possibly related names are **Piscataqua River** (N.H., Rockingham Co.) and **Piscataway** (N.J., Middlesex Co.).

SCHATULGA (Ga., Muscogee Co.). Perhaps from Muskogee *sakco* /sákčo/ 'crawdad' plus *vlkē* /álki:/ 'only, nothing but' (Martin and Mauldin 2000).

SCHENECTADY (N.Y., Schenectady Co.) \skə nek′ tə dē\. From Mohawk (Iroquoian) *skahnéhtati* 'on the other side of the pines', containing *-hneht-* 'pine tree'. This was originally the Mohawk name for Albany and is still so used by Mohawks in Canada (M. Mithun p.c.).

SCHENEVUS (N.Y., Otsego Co.) \skə nē′ vəs\. Probably from an Iroquoian language, of unclear derivation (Beauchamp 1907).

SCHENOB Brook (Conn., Litchfield Co.). An alternative writing is <Kisnop>; the name may be from Mahican (Algonquian) <k'chenups> 'greatest pond' (Trumbull 1881).

SCHODACK (N.Y., Rensselaer Co.) \skō′ dak, skō′ dək\. Perhaps from Mahican (Algonquian), meaning 'fire-location' (Ruttenber 1906).

SCHOHARIE County (N.Y.) \skə hâr′ ē\. Probably from a Iroquoian language, meaning 'floodwood, driftwood' (Ruttenber 1906; Beauchamp 1907). The placename **Schoharie** occurs as a transfer in Kans. (Ness Co.). The alternative spelling **Schoharrie** is found in Ill. (Williamson Co.).

SCHONCHIN Butte (Calif., Siskiyou Co.) \skon´shin\. Named for a nineteenth-century leader of the Modoc people (Gudde 1998).

SCHONOWE (N.Y., Schenectady Co.). Probably from an Iroquoian language, said to mean 'great flat' (Beauchamp 1907).

SCHONTHDA Hill (Alaska, Nabesna D-2). The Upper Tanana (Athabaskan) name was reported in 1955 (Orth 1967).

SCHOODAC Brook (N.H., Merrimack Co.) \sko͞o´ dak\. Probably from the same origin as **Schoodic;** see below.

SCHOODIC (Maine, Hancock Co.) \sko͞o´ dik\. Probably from Abenaki (Algonquian) *skotam* 'speckled trout' (Huden 1962; Day 1994–95).

SCHROON Lake (N.Y., Essex Co.) \skro͞on\. From Mohawk (Iroquoian) *skanyatarowá:nę* 'longest lake', noun form *kanyá:tare'* 'lake', from *-nyatar-* 'lake' (Beauchamp 1907; Lounsbury 1960:51).

SCHUCHK (Ariz., Pima Co.). O'odham (Piman) *scuck* 'black ones' (i.e., 'black hills'), from *s-* 'adjective', *cu-* 'reduplication', and *cuk* 'black' (Granger 1983; J. Hill p.c.).

SCHUCHULI (Ariz., Pima Co.). O'odham (Piman) *s-cuculig* 'many chickens', from *cucul* 'chicken' (J. Hill p.c.).

SCHUK COWLIK (Ariz., Pima Co.). O'odham (Piman) *scuk kawlik* 'black hill', from *s-cuk* 'black' and *kawlik* 'hill' (J. Hill p.c.).

SCHUNNEMUNK Mountain (N.Y., Orange Co.) \sho͞o´ mungk\. Earlier written <Skoonemoghky, Choonnenoghky, Sononaky> (etc.); the name may be Munsee Delaware but is of unclear derivation (Ruttenber 1906).

SCHUNYAK (Ariz., Pima Co.). Said to be from O'odham (Piman), meaning 'much corn' (Granger 1983), but of unclear derivation.

SCIOTA (Ill., McDonogh Co.) \sī ō´ tə\. A transfer name and alternative form of **Scioto** (Ohio, Delaware Co.); see below. The placename **Sciota** also occurs in Mich. (Shiawassee Co.), Minn. (Dakota Co.), and Pa. (Monroe Co.).

SCIOTO (Ohio, Delaware Co.) \sī ō´ tō\. Said to be from Wyandot (Iroquoian) <och-skəonto> 'a deer' (Mahr 1957:140); cf. Mohawk *oskęnǫ́:tǫ'* 'deer' (Michelson 1973). As a transfer name, **Scioto** occurs in Ill. (Stephenson Co.). The related form **Sciota** occurs in other states; see above. Possibly related placenames also include **Sconondoa** (N.Y., Oneida Co.) and **Scononton** (N.Y., Clinton Co.).

SCITICO (Conn., Hartford Co.). Perhaps reduced from SNEng. Algonquian <peskatuk> 'river branch' plus <ohke> 'land' (Trumbull 1881). A related placename may be **Scantic** (Mass., Hartford Co.).

SCITTERYGUSSET Creek (Maine, Cumberland Co.) \skit´ ə rē gus ət\. Perhaps from <Squidrayset>, the name of an Abenaki (Algonquian) leader (Huden 1962).

SCITUATE (Mass., Plymouth Co.) \sit´ yo͞o ət\. From SNEng. <(ku)ssitchuwa(n)' 'it flows swiftly', plus <-at> 'place' (W. Cowan p.c.). The placename **Scituate** also occurs in Maine (York Co.) and R.I. (Providence Co.).

SCOBEY (Miss., Yalobusha Co.) \skō´ bē\. Perhaps from Choctaw (Muskogean) *oskoba* 'small cane', containing *oski* 'cane, reed' and *holba* 'like' (Seale 1939, Byington 1915). A possibly related placename is **Scooba** (Miss., Kemper Co.).

SCONONDOA (N.Y., Oneida Co.) \skon ən dō´ ə\. Perhaps from the same source as **Cape Scononton** (N.Y., Clinton Co.) \skə non´ tən\. From an Iroquoian word for 'deer', probably Mohawk *oskęnǫ́:tǫ'* (Lounsbury 1960:64). Possibly related placenames include **Sciota** (Ill., McDonogh Co.), **Scioto** (Ohio, Delaware Co.), and **Shenandoah** (N.Y., Dutchess Co.).

SCONTICUT Neck (Mass., Bristol Co.) \skon´ ti kət\. From SNEng. Algonquian, perhaps containing <squan(tam)-> 'door', <-tuck-> 'tidal stream', and <-ut> 'place' (Huden 1962; W. Cowan p.c.).

SCOOBA (Miss., Kemper Co.) \skōō´ bə\. Perhaps from Choctaw *oskoba* 'small cane, reed', containing *oski* 'reed' plus *holba* 'similar' (Seale 1939; Byington 1915). A possibly related placename is **Scobey** (Miss., Yalobusha Co.).

SCOOTANAY (Wash., Franklin Co.) \skōō´ tə nā\. A variant of **Scooteney Reservoir**; see below. Another variant spelling is **Scootenay.**

SCOOTENEY Reservoir (Wash., Franklin Co.) \skōō´ tə nā\. Named for an Indian subgroup of the area, not further identified. Variant spellings are **Skootenay** and **Scootanay.** A related placename is **Scootney** (Wash., Adams Co.).

SCOWHEGAN (Maine, Sagadahoc Co.). Earlier written as <Erascohegan, Rasthegan, Reskeghan>; perhaps from Abenaki (Algonquian), meaning 'place to watch for fish' (Eckstorm 1941:126–27); cf. *skawôda* 'to watch out for something' (Day 1994–95).

SCRAPER (Okla., Cherokee Co.) \skrā´ pər\. Named for Capt. Archibald Scraper, a Union officer of Indian ancestry during the Civil War (Shirk 1974).

SCUMA Creek (Ala., Sumter Co.) \skōō´ mə\. Possibly from Choctaw (Muskogean) *iskona* 'guts' (P. Munro p.c.).

SCUPPERNONG (N.C., Washington Co.) \skup´ ər nong\. The name was written in the eighteenth century as <Cascoponung, Cuscopang>, from an unidentified Indian source; the placename is also applied to a type of grape. There is a transfer name, **Scuppernong River,** in Wis. (Jefferson Co.).

SCUSSET Beach (Mass., Barnstable Co.) \skus´ ət\. From a SNEng. Algonquian word, perhaps meaing 'at the wading place' (Huden 1962).

SEABECK (Wash., Kitsap Co.) \sē´ bek\. Twana (Salishan) /ɬqábaqʷ/, from /ɬ-/ 'far', /qab/ 'smooth, calm', and /-aqʷ/ 'water' (Hitchman 1985; D. Kinkade p.c.).

SEAHPO Peak (Wash., Whatcom Co.) \sē ä´ pō\. Chinook Jargon <se-áh-po, se-áh-pult> [siápo, siyapó, sɪyápuɬ] 'cap', from French *chapeau* 'hat' (D. Kinkade p.c.).

SEAKOOVOOK Bay (Alaska, St. Lawrence B-3). The Yupik (Eskimo) name was reported in 1949 (Orth 1967).

SEAMA (N.Mex., Cibola Co.) \sā ä´ mə\. From Laguna (Keresan) /ts'íyâama/ 'doorway, passageway' or by extension 'mountain gap' (Julyan 1998; I. Davis p.c.).

SEAPUIT River (Mass., Barnstable Co.). From SNEng. Algonquian, perhaps meaning 'in the current' (Huden 1962).

SEATAC (Wash., King Co.) \sē´ tak\. Composed from elements of **Seattle** and **Tacoma,** both names of Native American origin (Reese 1996).

SEATCO (Wash., Thurston Co.). From Upper Chehalis (Salishan) /c'iátkʷ/, the name of a legendary creature with supernatural powers, sometimes referred to as a 'giant', 'devil', 'stick Indian', or 'Sasquatch' (Hitchman 1985; D. Kinkade p.c.).

SEATTLE (Wash., King Co.) \sē at´ əl\. From Lushootseed (Salishan) /siʔáɬ /, the personal name of an Indian leader referred to in English as Noah Sealth or "Chief Seattle" (Hitchman 1985; D. Kinkade p.c.). The placename **Seattle** also occurs in Alaska (Hagemeister Is. D-6).

SEATUCK Creek (N.Y., Suffolk Co.) \sā´ tuk\. From SNEng. Algonquian, perhaps containing <-tuck> 'tidal stream' (Tooker 1911; W. Cowan p.c.).

SEAWARRIOR Creek (Ala., Choctaw Co.). A folk-etymology; said to be from Choctaw *isawaya* 'crouching deer' (Read 1984); cf. *isi* 'deer' (Byington 1915).

SEBA DALKAI (Ariz., Navajo Co.) \sā bə däl´ kī\. Navajo (Athabaskan) *séí bídaagai* 'sand piled against the ridge' (Linford 2000); cf. *séí* 'sand' (Young and Morgan 1987).

SEBAGO Lake (Maine, Cumberland Co.) \si bā´ gō\. From earlier <Mesibegat>, Abenaki

(Algonquian) for ‘big lake’ (Eckstorm 1941: 161–62); cf. *masabagw* ‘big lake or bay’ (Day 1994–95). The name **Sebago** also occurs in N.Y. (Rockland Co.).

SEBASCO (Maine, Sagadahoc Co.) \sə bas´ kō\. Perhaps a shortening of **Sebascodegan**; see below.

SEBASCODEGAN (Maine, Cumberland Co.). Earlier written <Sebascoe Diggine, Sebascoa Diggin>; perhaps from Passamaquoddy (Algonquian), meaning ‘almost-through passage’ (Eckstorm 1941:154–56).

SEBASTICOOK (Maine, Penobscot Co.) \sə bas´ ti ko͝ok\. Also written as <Sebestegook, Sebestocook> (etc.); from Abenaki (Algonquian), perhaps meaning ‘almost-through river’ (Eckstorm 1941:11–12). Cf. *sibategw* ‘river channel, trickling river’, locative *sibategok* (Day 1994–95:322).

SEBEC (Maine, Piscataquis Co.). From Abenaki (Algonquian), perhaps meaning ‘much water’ (Huden 1962); cf. *msebaga* ‘it is big water’ (Day 1994–95:439).

SEBEKA (Minn., Wadena Co.) \sə bē´ kə\. Ojibwa (Algonquian) *ziibiikaa* ‘there are (many) rivers’, from *ziibi* ‘river’ (Upham 2001; J. Nichols p.c.).

SEBEWAING (Mich., Huron Co.) \sē´ bə wing\. From Ojibwa (Algonquian), meaning ‘where the river is’ (Vogel 1986) from *ziibi* ‘river’ (Nichols and Nyholm 1995).

SEBEWA Township (Mich., Ionia Co.) \sē´ bə wä\. Perhaps from Ojibwa (Algonquian) *ziibiwan* ‘rivers’, from *ziibi* ‘river’ (Vogel 1986; Nichols and Nyholm 1995).

SEBOEIS (Maine, Penobscot Co.). From Abenaki (Algonquian), perhaps meaning ‘small lake’ (Huden 1962).

SEBONAC Creek (N.Y., Suffolk Co.) Earlier written <Seabamuck>; from SNEng. Algonquian, perhaps meaning ‘river fishing-place’ (Tooker 1911).

SEBOOMOOK (Maine, Somerset Co.) \si bo͞o´ mo͝ok\. From Abenaki (Algonquian), perhaps meaning ‘at the large stream’ (Huden 1962).

SEBOYETA (N.Mex., Cibola Co.) \seb ō yet´ ə\. From Spanish *cebolleta* ‘wild onion’, a diminutive of *cebolla* ‘onion’. The name corresponds to Navajo (Athabaskan) *tł’ohchin* ‘onion’, from *tł’oh* ‘grass’ (Wilson 1995); cf. *halchin* ‘to have an odor’ (Young and Morgan 1987). The spelling **Cebolleta** is also used.

SECANE (Pa., Delaware Co.) \sē´ kān\. Named for a seventeenth-century Delaware (Algonquian) leader (Donehoo 1928).

SECATOGUE (N.Y., Suffolk Co.). Earlier written <Secoutagh, Secontok, Sequatogue> (etc.); from SNEng. Algonquian, perhaps meaning ‘dark land’ (Tooker 1911).

SECAUCUS (N.J., Hudson Co.) \sə kô´ kəs\. Earlier <Siskakes>; from Delaware, perhaps meaning ‘salt-sedge marsh’ (Becker 1964).

SECESAKUT Hill (R.I., Providence Co.). From SNEng. Algonquian, perhaps containing <seckesu> ‘black, dark’ (Huden 1962; W. Cowan p.c.).

SECONA (S.C., Pickens Co.) \sə kō´ nə\. Said to be be from Cherokee (Iroquoian), meaning ‘blue, green’ (Pickens 1961–62:22); cf. *sagonige* ‘blue’ (Alexander 1971).

SECONSETT Island (Mass., Barnstable Co.) \sə kon´ sət\. From SNEng. Algonquian, perhaps containing <sequan-> ‘springtime’ (W. Cowan p.c.). A possibly related placename is **Segwun** (Mich., Kent Co.).

SECOTAN (N.C., Beaufort Co.). From a CAC Algonquian placename, perhaps meaning ‘town at the bend of a river’ (Powell 1968). The term occurs as a transfer in Fla. (Taylor Co.).

SEDANKA Island (Alaska, Unalaska C-1). From Aleut *sidaanax̂* ‘graphite’ (Bergsland 1994).

SEDAYE Mountains (Nev., Nye Co.). Perhaps an adaptation of **Desatoya Peak** (Nev., Lander Co.), representing Shoshoni (Numic) /tɨasɨ-toya/

'frozen mountain', from /tɨasɨ/ 'to be frozen', /toya(pi)/ 'mountain' (J. McLaughlin p.c.).

SEDGEUNKEDUNK Stream (Maine, Penobscot Co.). Also written <Sedunkehunk>; from Abenaki (Algonquian), perhaps meaning 'rapids at mouth' (Huden 1962).

SEEDSHADEE Park (Wyo., Sweetwater Co.). From the same source as **Seedskedee**; see below; the form with *sh* originated as an error.

SEEDSKEDEE (Wyo., Lincoln Co.) \sēd´ skə dē\. Said to be an Indian name, language not known, meaning 'sage hen river', referring to the Green River (Urbanek 1974).

SEEKONK (Mass., Bristol Co.) \sē´ kongk\. Perhaps from SNEng. Algonquian <seqwonk> 'skunk' (Trumbull 1879; W. Cowan p.c.). The name **Seekonk** also occurs in R.I. (Providence Co.).

SEEKSEEQUA Creek (Ore., Jefferson Co.) \sēk sē´ kwə\. Probably from Sahaptin /si:k^{w}sí:k^{w}/ 'horsetail fern' (D. Kinkade p.c.).

SEELOCU (N.Mex., Socorro Co.). The name of a Piro (Tanoan) pueblo, abandoned during the period of Spanish rule (Julyan 1998).

SEEMALIK Butte (Alaska, Nunivak Is. A-6). The Yupik (Eskimo) name was reported in 1949 (Orth 1967).

SEEPANPAK Lagoon (Alaska, St. Lawrence B-1). The Yupik (Eskimo) name was recorded in 1932 (Orth 1967).

SEEVOOKHAN Mountain (Alaska, St. Lawrence B-0). The Yupik (Eskimo) name was reported in 1949 (Orth 1967). Perhaps related is **Seevoonah Mountain** (St. Lawrence A-2).

SEEVOO Point (Alaska, St. Lawrence B-0). The Yupik (Eskimo) name is *sivu* 'front' (L. Kaplan p.c.).

SEGEKE Butte (Ariz., Navajo Co.). Said to be Navajo (Athabaskan) for 'square rock' (Granger 1983); containing *tsé* 'rock' (Young and Morgan 1987).

SEGETOA Spring (Ariz., Apache Co.). From the same source as **Tsegito Spring,** from Navajo (Athabaskan) *tsiyi' tóhí* 'spring in the forest', containing *tsiyi'* 'forest' (Linford 2000; Young and Morgan 1987).

SEGIHATSOSI Canyon (Ariz., Navajo Co.) \seg ē hə tso´ sē\. Navajo (Athabaskan) *tséyi' hats'ózí* 'canyon that is narrow', containing *tséyí'* 'canyon', *ha-* 'area', *ts'óz* 'narrow' (Wilson 1995). An alternative spelling is **Tseye Ha Tsosi.**

SEGI Mesas (Ariz., Navajo Co.) \seg´ ē\. Navajo (Athabaskan) *tséyí'* 'canyon', lit. 'inside the rocks', from *tsé* 'rock' and *yi'* 'inside' (Wilson 1995). The placename is also written **Tsegi Canyon.**

SEGO Springs (Colo., Conejos Co.) \sē´ gō, sā´ gō\. Probably from Northern Ute (Numic) /siku'a/ [siɣú'a] 'sego lily, mariposa lily', a flower with an edible bulb (Bright 1993; J. McLaughlin p.c.). The placename **Sego** also occurs in Utah (Grand Co.) and as a transfer in Kans. (Reno Co.), Ohio (Perry Co.), and S.Dak. (Yankton Co.).

SEGREGANSET (Mass., Bristol Co.). From SNEng. Algonquian, perhaps meaning 'place of hard rocks' (Huden 1962).

SEGUAM (Alaska, Seguam D-2) \sē´ gwəm\. Aleut *saĝuugamax,* from *saĝuugax̂* 'rookery, bird colony' (Bergsland 1994).

SEGUIN Island (Maine, Sagadahoc Co.). Earlier written as <Sutquin, Satquin> (etc.); perhaps from Abenaki (Algonquian) <sigan> 'hump' (Eckstorm 1941).

SEGULA Island (Alaska, Rat Is. D-6). Earlier written <Chugul> (Orth 1967); represents Aleut *chiĝulax̂* 'chasing (in a skin boat)'; cf. *chiĝulix* 'to chase (a sea lion) in a skin boat' (Bergsland 1994).

SEGWUN (Mich., Kent Co.) \sē´ gwən\. The name is used in Longfellow's *Hiawatha* to mean 'springtime'; cf. Ojibwa (Algonquian) *ziigwan* 'be spring' (Vogel 1986; Nichols and Nyholm

1995). A possibly related name is **Seconsett Island** (Mass., Barnstable Co.).

SEHILI (Ariz., Apache Co.). A variant of the Navajo (Athabaskan) name otherwise written as **Tsaile;** see below.

SEHOME Hill (Wash., Whatcom Co.) \sē´ hōm\. From Lummi (Salishan) [sixʷóm], a man's name (Hitchman 1985; D. Kinkade p.c.).

SEIAD (Calif., Siskiyou Co.) \sī´ ad\. Earlier written <Sciad>; perhaps from a village name of the Shasta people (Gudde 1998).

SEI DEELZHA (Ariz., Apache Co.) \sā dāl´ zhä\. Navajo (Athabaskan) *séí deelzha* 'jagged sand dune' (Linford 2000); cf. *séí* 'sand', *deelzhah* 'undulating line' (Young and Morgan 1987). Related placenames are **Sei Be Toh Well** (Ariz., Coconino Co.) \sā´ bi tō\, from Navajo *séí bii' tó* 'spring in the sand', with *bii'* 'in it', and *tó* 'water'; and **Sei Haasgaii Wash** (Ariz., Coconino Co.) \sā häs´ gī\. , from Navajo *séí haasgai* 'sand slopes upward white', containing *haasgai* 'it slopes upward white', from *lgai* 'to be white' (Young and Morgan 1987).

SEKINAK Lagoon (Alaska, St. Lawrence A-2). The Yupik (Eskimo) name was reported in 1949 (Orth 1967).

SEKIU (Wash., Clallam Co.) \sē´ kyōō\. From a Makah (Nootkan) placename [sí:kiyu:ʔ] (W. Jacobsen p.c.). Also written as **Sekui.**

SELAH (Wash., Yakima Co.) \sē´ lə\. From Sahaptin [síla] 'still water, smooth water' (Hitchman 1985; D. Kinkade p.c.). The choice of the name and spelling may have been influenced by use as a liturgical term in the Psalms. In Ariz. (Apache Co.), **Selah Springs** is said to be named for a Navajo (Athabaskan) man called *síílah* (Jett 2001:99).

SELATNA River (Alaska, McGrath C-6) \sə lat´ nə\. From Deg Hit'an (Athabaskan) *tsalatno'* 'killing-beaver creek' (Kari 1999:85).

SELAWIK (Alaska, Selawik C-3) \sel´ ə wik\. Represents the Iñupiaq (Eskimo) placename *siilivik,* apparently derived from *siilik* 'northern pike, shee-fish' (*HNAI* 15:319, Webster and Zibell 1970:iv).

SELIN Creek (Alaska, Point Hope D-2). The Iñupiaq (Eskimo) name, said to mean 'canyon', was reported in 1950 (Orth 1967).

SELISH (Mont., Flathead Co.) \sā´ lish\. From the same source as **Salish** (see above), the name of the Flathead (Salishan) Indian people.

SELTICE (Wash., Whitman Co.) \səl tēs`\. From Coeur d'Alene (Salishan) /sl'tís/, the name of a man known in English as Andrew Seltice (Hitchman 1985; D. Kinkade p.c.). The name also occurs as **Saltese** (Wash., Spokane Co.).

SEMIAHMOO (Wash., Whatcom Co.) \sem ē am´ ōō\. From a Lummi (Salishan) placename [səmyámə] (Hitchman 1985; D. Kinkade p.c.).

SEMICHI Islands (Alaska, Attu B-1). From the Aleut placename *samiyan*; cf. also **Shemya** (Bergsland 1994); or perhaps from Russian *semik* 'feast on the 7th Thursday after Easter' (Orth 1967).

SEMINO Creek (Wyo., Converse Co.) \sem´ i nō\. Perhaps from the same source as the **Seminoe Mountains** (Wyo., Carbon Co.). Named for Basil Cimineau Lajeunesse, a French trapper who had combined the name of his Indian wife, *Cimineau*, with his own surname (Urbanek 1974). The term may be derived from **Shamineau**, an Ojibwa (Algonquian) personal name which occurs as a placename in Minn. (Morrison Co.).

SEMINOLE \sem´ i nōl\. The term refers to Indians of the Muskogean language family, originally living in southern Ala. and Ga., who moved to Fla. during the eighteenth and nineteenth centuries to escape European domination. The word is derived from Muskogee *semvnole* /simanó:li/, from *semvlone* /simaló:ni/ 'untamed', from Spanish *cimarrón* 'untamed'. Subsequently a portion of the Fla. Seminoles moved to Okla. At present some of the Fla. Seminoles use the Hitchiti (or Mikasuki) language; others use a variety of Muskogee (or Creek). The Okla.

Seminoles use their own variety of Muskogee (Read 1934; Martin and Mauldin 2000). As a placename, **Seminole** occurs in Fla. (Seminole Co.), Ga. (Seminole Co.), Ala. (Baldwin Co.), and Okla. (Seminole Co.) and as a transfer name in several other states (e.g., Iowa, Linn Co.; Tex., Gaines Co.).

SEMIUTAK Bend (Alaska, Ikpikpuk River D-3). Said to be from Iñupiaq (Eskimo) *simiataq-* 'to plug' (L. Kaplan p.c.).

SENACHWINE Creek (Ill., Peoria Co.). Named for a Potawatomi (Algonquian) leader of the early nineteenth century, also written <Ce-na-ge-wine, Che-nau-che-wine> (etc.) (Vogel 1963).

SENATI (Alaska, Tanana B-3) \sen´ ə tē\. The name was that of *shahnyaati'*, a Gwich'in (Athabaskan) leader (Orth 1967). A related name is nearby **Senatis Mountain** \sen´ ə tis\, containing the possessive "Senati's."

SENATOBIA (Miss., Tate Co.) \sen ə tō´ bē ə\. Choctaw (Muskogean) *sinih tohbi* 'white sycamore', from *sinih* 'sycamore' and *tohbi* 'white' (Seale 1939; P. Munro p.c.).

SENEACQUOTEEN (Idaho, Bonner Co.) \sin ē ak´ ə tēn\. Pend d'Oreille (Salishan) /s-n-yeʔk'ʷ-tín/ 'place to cross a river or ford a stream', from the root /yék'ʷ-/ 'to cross' (Boone 1988; D. Kinkade p.c.). The spelling **Seneaquoteen** also occurs.

SENECA \sen´ ə kə\. An Indian people of the Iroquoian family, living in upper N.Y. state. The term was earlier written as <Sinnekens, Senakees> (etc.) and was also applied to the Oneidas (another Iroquoian group). It has been proposed that **Seneca** is from a Mahican (Algonquian) word meaning 'people of the place of the stone', but this has not been confirmed (*HNAI* 15:515). As a placename, **Seneca** occurs not only in N.Y. (Seneca Co.) but also as a transfer name in many states (e.g., Fla., Lake Co.; Iowa, Kossuth Co.; and S.C., Oconee Co.)—probably with influence from the name of the ancient Roman philosopher and dramatist. In N.Mex. (Union Co.), however, the placename **Seneca** is said to be a distortion of Spanish *ciénega* 'marsh, meadow' (Julyan 1998).

SENECU (N.Mex., Socorro Co.). The site of a Piro (Tanoan) pueblo, destroyed in the colonial period; the placename was also written as <Tze-no-que> and <She-an-ghua> (Julyan 1998).

SENGEKONTACKET Pond (Mass., Dukes Co.). From SNEng. Algonquian, perhaps meaning 'at the cold, long creek' (Huden 1962).

SENIX Creek (N.Y., Suffolk Co.). From SNEng. Algonquian, perhaps named after an Indian man called Sinnekes (Tooker 1911).

SENNEBEC Pond (Maine, Knox Co.) \sen´ ə bek\. Perhaps from Abenaki (Algonquian), meaning 'rocks in the pond' (Huden 1962); cf. *sen* 'a stone' (Day 1994–95).

SENOIA (Ga., Coweta Co.) \sə noi´ ə\. Perhaps from <Shenoywa>, a possible Indian title of the nineteenth-century Muskogee leader William McIntosh (Krakow 1975).

SENTER BOGUE Creek (Miss., Wayne Co.) \sin tə bōg´\. Choctaw (Muskogean) for 'snake creek', from *sįti* 'snake' and *book* 'creek' (Seale 1939; P. Munro p.c.).

SEPASCO Lake (N.Y., Dutchess Co.). Earlier written <Sepeskenot>, perhaps a Mahican (Algonquian) placename (Beauchamp 1907).

SEPO (Ill., Fulton Co.) \sē´ pō\. Probably from Meskwaki (Algonquian) /si:po:wi/ 'river' (Vogel 1963; Goddard 1994). A possibly related name is **Sippo** (Ohio, Stark Co.).

SEPULGA (Ala., Conecuh Co.) \sə pul´ gə\. Perhaps from Muskogee *svwokle* /sawókli/, the name of a tribal town (Read 1984; Martin and Mauldin 2000).

SEQUALITCHEW Creek (Wash., Pierce Co.) \sə kwäl´ i cho͞o\. From the Lushootseed (Salishan) placename [sigʷáličču] (Hitchman 1985; D. Kinkade p.c.).

SEQUATCHIE County (Tenn.) \sə kwä´ chē\. Perhaps the name of a Cherokee (Iroquoian) leader, of unclear derivation (Miller 2001:186).

SEQUIM (Wash., Clallam Co.) \skwim\. From the Clallam (Salishan) placename variously recorded as /sčq^{w}éʔyəŋ/, /sx^{w}čk^{w}iə́ŋ/, /sx^{w}čk^{w}íyəŋ/ (D. Kinkade p.c.).

SEQUO (Okla., Sequoyah Co.). An abbreviation of **Sequoyah County** (Shirk 1974); see below.

SEQUOIA \sə kwoi´ yə\. From the same source as **Sequoyah,** the inventor of the Cherokee (Iroquoian) alphabet (see **Sequoyah County** below), was adopted in 1847 as the genus name for the two species of redwood trees native to California—the 'coast redwood', *Sequoia sempervirens,* and the 'big tree' of the Sierras, *Sequoia giganteum.* As a placename, the term is applied to **Sequoia National Park** (Calif., Tulare Co.) and to other places in the state. The placename also occurs in Tenn. (Bradley Co.).

SEQUOIT Creek (Ill., Lake Co.). An adaptation of **Sauquoit** (N.Y., Oneida Co.) (Vogel 1963); see above.

SEQUOYAH County (Okla.) \sē kwoi´ yə\. Named for the Cherokee (Iroquoian) man, known in English as George Guess or George Gist, who in the early nineteenth century invented a syllabic writing system for his language; his Native American name has been given as <Sikwayi>, with no known etymology. The placename also occurs in several other states (e.g., Ala., Etowah Co.; Kans., Johnson Co.; and N.C., Swain Co.). A related placename is **Sequoia**; see above.

SERPENT Lake (Minn., Crow Wing Co.). Corresponds to Ojibwa (Algonquian) *newe zaaga'igan,* lit. 'blowsnake lake' (Upham 2001; Nichols and Nyholm 1995).

SESACHACHA (Mass., Nantucket Co.) \sə kach´ ə\. Earlier written <Sisackochat>, <Sasagacha>, <Sasacha> (Little 1984). The SNEng. Algonquian name has been translated 'boulder hill here' (Huden 1962).

SESPE (Calif., Ventura Co.) \ses´ pē\. From the Ventureño (Chumashan) village name <sek-pe>, probably meaning 'knee pan' (Gudde 1998).

SETAUKET (N.Y., Suffolk Co.) \sə tô´ kət\. Earlier written <Siketeuhacky, Seatauke, Setokett> (etc.), from SNEng. Algonquian; cf. <sauki> 'outlet', <-tuck> 'tidal stream', <-haki> 'land', <-t> 'place' (Beauchamp 1907a; Tooker 1911). A perhaps related name is **Seatuck Creek** (N.Y., Suffolk Co.); see above.

SETHKOKNA River (Alaska, Kantishna River B-6) \seth kok´ nə, seth kōt´ nə\. Koyukon (Athabaskan) *seł kaakk no', seł kuh no',* lit. 'ridge-surface stream' (Kari 1999:105), containing *-yeł, seł* 'ridge', *kkaa* 'surface', and *no'* 'stream' (Jetté and Jones 2000).

SETSILTSO Springs (Ariz., Apache Co.) \set silt´ sō\. Navajo (Athabaskan) for 'big oak', from *tséch'il, chéch'il* 'oak' (*tsé, ché* 'rock' plus *ch'il* 'plant') and *-tsoh* 'big' (Young and Morgan 1987).

SETTICO (Tenn., Monroe Co.) \set´ i kō\. A variant of **Citico**; see above.

SEUL CHOIX Point (Mich., Schoolcraft Co.). French for 'only choice', perhaps folk-etymologized from Ojibwa (Algonquian) <shashoweg> 'straight line' (Vogel 1986); cf. *zhyaaw* 'straight' (Rhodes 1985).

SEVAK Camp (Alaska, St. Lawrence B-1). The Yupik (Eskimo) name was reported in 1932 (Orth 1967).

SEVEN LAKES (N.Mex., McKinley Co.). Corresponds to Navajo *tsosts'id be'ek'id* 'seven lakes', from *tsosts'id* 'seven' and *be'ek'id* 'lake' (Julyan 1998; Wilson 1995).

SEVEN UTES Mountain (Colo., Jackson Co.). From Arapaho (Algonquian) *nı́ísootoxúthi' wo'téeneihíthi'* 'seven Utes' (A. Cowell p.c.).

SEVISOK Slough (Alaska, Noatak B-2). The Iñupiaq (Eskimo) name is *siviisuuq,* said to mean 'long way to go by' (Burch 1998; Orth 1967).

SEVUOKUK Mountain (Alaska, St. Lawrence D-6). From St. Lawrence Yupik (Eskimo) *sivuqaq,* the name for the village of Gambell (Orth 1967; Jacobson 1987).

SEWAMMOCK Neck (Mass., Bristol Co.). From SNEng. Algonquian, perhaps from <seah-ham-> 'he scatters' (W. Cowan p.c.).

SEWANHAKA (N.Y., Nassau Co.). Earlier written <Sewanhackey, Sewanhacky>; said to be a SNEng. Algonquian name for Long Island, perhaps meaning 'land of scattered shell beads' (Beauchamp 1907).

SEWEE Bay (S.C., Charleston Co.). Earlier written <Suye>, <Xoye>, <Sowee> (Waddell 1980). From the Catawban (Siouan) for 'island'; cf. modern Catawba /sá:wę̨/ (Pickens 1961–62:22; B. Rudes p.c.).

SEWICKLEY (Pa., Allegheny Co.) \zwik´ lē\. Said to be from <Asswekales> or <Hatha-wekela>, a subgroup of the Shawnee (Algonquian) people (Donehoo 1928), also referred to as <Qawakila> (*HNAI* 15:634).

SEYOUYAH Creek (Ala., Choctaw Co.) \sə yo͞o´ yə\. Perhaps a garbled version of **Sequoyah;** see above. Or perhaps from Choctaw (Muskogean) *issi yaaya* 'crying deer', from *issi* 'deer', *yaaya* 'to cry, weep' (Read 1984; Munro p.c.).

SHABAKUNK Creek (N.J., Mercer Co.). From Delaware (Algonquian), of unclear derivation (Becker 1964).

SHABBONA Creek (Ill., Fulton Co.) \shab´ nə\. Named for a Potawatomi (Algonquian) leader of the early nineteenth century; the name was also written as <Chamblee, Shaubenee> (etc.) (Vogel 1963). The placename also occurs in Iowa (Mills Co.) and Mich. (Sanilac Co.).

SHABIKESHCHEE (N.Mex., San Juan Co.) \shə bik´ ə shē\. Navajo (Athabaskan) *shá bik'e'eshchį́* 'the sun is written or carved upon it', containing *shá* 'sun' and *bik'e'eschchį́* 'it is carved on it' (*bi-* 'its', *k'e, k'i* 'upon', *eshchį́* 'it is written or carved') (A. Wilson p.c.).

SHABODOCK Creek (Wis., Forest Co.) \shab´ ə duk\. Named for John Shabbodock, a Potawatomi (Algonquian) resident (Vogel 1991). The placename is also written **Shabbodock.**

SHACKALOA Creek (Miss., Amite Co.) \shak´ ə lō\. From Choctaw *shąkolo* 'cypress tree' (Seale 1939; P. Munro p.c.). Related placenames include **Shockaloo Creek** (Miss., Scott Co.) and **Shongaloo** (La., Webster Par.).

SHACKAMAXON Lake (N.J., Union Co.) \shak´ ə mak sən\. From Delaware (Algonquian) <schachamek> 'eel' (Brinton and Anthony 1888; Becker 1964); cf. Unami Delaware /sɔ́:x:ame:kw/ 'eel', lit. 'slippery fish' (M. McCafferty p.c.). Perhaps related placenames are **Lake Shakamak** (Ind., Sullivan Co.) and **Shamokin** (Pa., Northumberland Co.).

SHADAGEE Brook (Maine, Franklin Co.). Perhaps from the same source as **Chateaugay** (N.Y., Franklin Co.). Other possibly related placenames are **Shadigee** (N.Y., Orleans Co.) and **Shadogee** (N.H., Carroll Co.).

SHAGAK Bay (Alaska, Adak C-3). From Aleut *chaxchix̂,* referring to the narrow entrance; cf. *chaxsix* 'to split, crack' (Bergsland 1994).

SHAGELUK (Alaska, Holy Cross C-2) \shag´ ə lo͞ok, shag´ ə luk\. Perhaps borrowed, via Yupik (Eskimo), from Deg Hit'an *łeggi jit',* lit. 'rotten fish' (J. Kari p.c.), with influence of Yupik pronunciation.

SHAGWONG Point (N.Y., Suffolk Co.) \shag´ wong\. From SNEng. Algonquian, perhaps meaning 'on a hillside' (Tooker 1911).

SHAHAPTA (Ore., Multnomah Co.) \shə hap´ tə\. The term is related to **Sahaptin** (see above), a people and language of eastern Wash. and Ore., derived from an Interior Salishan term for the Nez Perce (*HNAI* 12:58).

SHAH-BUSH-KUNG Point (Minn., Mille Lacs Co.) \shə bosh´ kung\. Probably named for an Ojibwa (Algonquian) leader whose name has been translated 'who passes under' (Upham 2001); cf. *zhaabose* 'to pass through' (Nichols and Nyholm 1995).

SHAHEEN Creek (Alaska, Craig C-4) \shə hēn\. The Tlingit name was recorded in 1949 (Orth 1967); cf. *héen* [hí́in] 'river' (Davis and Leer 1976:5).

SHAHEEYA (Mont., Glacier Co.) \shə hē´ yə\. This is a term applied to Plains Cree (Algonquian) of Canada by the Siouan groups to the south of them, such as the Assiniboines /šahíya/ (Holterman 1985; *HNAI* 13:650).

SHAIAK Island (Alaska, Hagemeister Is. C-5). The Yupik (Eskimo) name was reported in 1826 (Orth 1967).

SHAKAMAK, Lake (Ind., Sullivan Co.) \shak´ ə mak\. From Unami Delaware (Algonquian) /sɔ́:x:ame:kw/ 'eel', lit. 'slippery fish' (McCafferty 2002). Perhaps related placenames are **Shackamaxon Lake** (N.J., Union Co.) and **Shamokin** (Pa., Northumberland Co.).

SHAKAN (Alaska, Petersburg A-5) \shak´ ən\. The Tlingit name may be derived from <Shakes>, the name of a local leader, plus *aan* 'town' (Orth 1967; Davis and Leer 1976).

SHAKOPEE (Minn., Scott Co.) \shä´ kə pē\. Named for a Dakota (Siouan) leader; the Native American term is *šákpe* 'six' (Upham 2001; Riggs 1890).

SHAKTOOLIK (Alaska, Norton Bay B-5) \shak to͞o´ lik\. From the Yupik (Eskimo) placename *cagtulek* (Jacobson 1984); cf. *cagte-* 'be spread out' (L. Kaplan p.c.).

SHAKUN Rock (Alaska, Afognak C-6). The Alutiiq (Eskimo) name was recorded by Russians in 1852 as <Shakhun> (Orth 1967).

SHAKUSEYI Creek (Alaska, Skagway B-2). The Tlingit name, published in 1923, is said to mean 'mountain-foot' (Orth 1967); cf. *shaa* 'mountain' (Davis and Leer 1976).

SHA'LAK'ONA:WA (N.Mex., Cibola Co.). The name of a Zuni sacred spring, probably from *Sha'lako,* the name of a kachina (Ferguson and Hart 1985).

SHALAKO Ski Trail (N.Mex., Taos Co.) \shal´ ə kō\. From Zuni *Sha'lako,* the name of a kachina. A related placename is **Sa'lako** (Ariz., Navajo Co.).

SHALERUCHIK Mountain (Alaska, Shungnak D-4). The Iñupiaq (Eskimo) name is *saliagutiik* (Burch 1998).

SHAMAN Island (Alaska, Juneau B-3) \shä´ mən, shā´ mən\. The English word refers to a traditional Native American healer; it is not an American Indian term but is borrowed through German and Russian, in the use of anthropologists, from a language of Siberia (*RHD* 1987).

SHAMBIP County (Utah) \sham´ bip\. This political unit was formed in 1856 and absorbed into Tooele County in 1862. The name is said to be from Goshute (Numic), meaning 'rushes, reeds' (Van Cott 1990); cf. Shoshoni /saippɨh/ 'tule, bulrush' (Miller 1972).

SHAMINEAU Lake (Minn., Morrison Co.) \sham´ i nō\. A French spelling of an Ojibwa (Algonquian) personal name (Upham 2001). A possibly related placename is **Seminoe Mountains** (Wyo., Carbon Co.).

SHAM-NA-PUM (Wash., Benton Co.). From Sahaptin /pšwánwapam/, a term referring to the Kittitas band, derived from /pšwá-/ 'rock' (D. Kinkade p.c.).

SHAMOKIN (Pa., Northumberland Co.) \shə mō´ kin\. The Unami Delaware (Algonquian) name has been given as <Schahamokink> 'place of eels' (Donehoo 1928); cf. Unami /sɔ́:x:ame:kw/ 'eel', lit. 'slippery fish' (M. McCafferty p.c.). The placename **Shamokin** also occurs in S.C. (Kershaw Co.). Perhaps related placenames are **Shackamaxon Lake** (N.J., Union Co.) and **Lake Shakamak** (Ind., Sullivan Co.).

SHAMONG Township (N.J., Burlington Co.). From Delaware, perhaps meaning 'horn-place', from <wschummo> 'horn' (Brinton and Anthony 1888; Becker 1964).

SHANDAKEN (N.Y., Ulster Co.) \shan dā´ kən\. Perhaps from Mahican (Algonquian), perhaps meaning 'hemlock place' (Ruttenber 1906).

SHANIKO (Ore., Wasco Co.) \shan´ i kō\. The name is said to represent an Indian pronunciation of the name of pioneer settler August Scherneckau (McArthur 1992).

SHANINGAROK Creek (Alaska, Lookout Ridge C-3). The Iñupiaq (Eskimo) placename was reported in 1956 (Orth 1967).

SHANKATANK Creek (Ind., Rush Co.) \shang´ kə tangk\. Possibly from reconstructed Munsee Delaware (Algonquian) /šaaxkihtank/ 'it flows straight' (McCafferty 2002). An alternative form is **Shankitunk** \shang´ ki tungk\

SHANNOCK (R.I., Washington Co.) \shan´ ək\. From SNEng. Algonquian, perhaps 'place between (streams)' (Trumbull 1881; Huden 1962). There is also a **Shannock** in Pa. (Armstrong Co.). A possibly related placename is **Shunock River** (Conn., New London Co.).

SHANNOPIN (Pa., Beaver Co.) \shan´ ə pin\. Named for a Delaware (Algonquian) leader (Doneho 1928).

SHANTAPEDA Lake (N.Dak., Morton Co.) Lakhota (Siouan) *čhąté pheta* 'heart-fire', from *čhąté* 'heart' plus *phéta* 'fire' (Wick 1988; Ingham 2001). Cf. also **Chanta Peta**.

SHANTATALIK Creek (Alaska, Kenai B-3) \shan tə tä´ lik\. Dena'ina (Athabaskan) *shanteh k'eleht* 'where fish spawn in summer' (Kari and Kari 1982:30).

SHANTOK Brook (Conn., New London Co.) \shan´ tək\. Abbreviated from SNEng. Algonquian <Mashantackack, Mashantucket>, perhaps meaning 'big wood place', containing <missi> 'big', <-htugk> 'tree, wood', and <-et> 'place' (Trumbull 1881; W. Cowan p.c.). An alternative spelling is **Shantuck.**

SHANUB Point (Ariz., Mohave Co.) \shə nub´\. From a Southern Paiute (Numic) family name, derived from /sɨnna'api/ [šɨnná'avI] 'dog, wolf' (J. McLaughlin p.c.).

SHAOKATAN (Minn., Lincoln Co.) \shok´ ə tan\. From Dakota (Siouan), of unclear derivation (Upham 2001).

SHAOTKAM (Ariz., Pima Co.). From O'odham (Piman) *ṣa:ḍkam* 'wild sweet-potato' (J. Hill p.c.).

SHAPLISH Canyon (Ore., Umatilla Co.) \shap´ lish\. Named for a Sahaptin shaman called *šápliš,* called "Doctor Whirlwind" in English (D. Kinkade p.c.).

SHAPNACK Island (Pa., Pike Co.). Perhaps from Delaware (Algonquian), of unclear derivation (Becker 1964).

SHASHAMUND Lake (Alaska, Tanacross A-2) \shə shä´ mund\. From Upper Tanana (Athabaskan) *shahsąąy männ',* lit. 'widgeon lake' (J. Kari p.c.).

SHASKET Creek (Wash., Ferry Co.). Perhaps from Okanagan (Salishan) (D. Kinkade p.c.).

SHASTA, Mount (Calif., Siskiyou Co.) \shas´ tə\. Named for the Shasta Indian tribe of the region; early recordings of the term include <Sastise, Saste, Shaste> (Gudde 1998). The placename also occurs in Alaska (Valdez A-7), Fla. (Levy Co.), Ill. (Alexander Co.), and Ore. (Malheur Co.). **Shasta Bally Mountain** (Calif., Shasta Co.) combines **Shasta** with Wintu *boli* 'mountain' (Gudde 1998). **Shasta Costa Bar** (Ore.) has nothing to do with **Mount Shasta;** the name refers to a band of the Tututni (Athabaskan) group, also called **Chasta Costa** (McArthur 1992); the Native American name is /šista q'wə́sta/ (D. Kinkade p.c.).

SHASTINA (Calif., Siskiyou Co.) \shas tē´ nə\. This playful diminutive form of **Shasta** has been applied to the west peak of **Mount Shasta** (Gudde 1998).

SHATTERACK Mountain (Mass., Hampden Co.). Perhaps from Abenaki (Algonquian); the name may mean 'where two streams meet' (Huden 1962). The placename **Shatterack** also occurs in Vt. (Windham Co.).

SHAUNTIE (Utah, Beaver Co.) \shôn´ tē\. From Southern Paiute (Numic), perhaps meaning 'much' (Van Cott 1990); cf. Shoshoni /soontɨ/ 'many' (J. McLaughlin p.c.).

SHAUPANEAK Mountain (N.Y., Ulster Co.). Perhaps from Munsee Delaware (Algonquian), but the derivation is unclear (Beauchamp 1907).

SHAVANO, Mount (Colo., Chaffee Co.) \shav´ ə nō\. Named for a Ute (Numic) leader; his name, however, seems to be related to **Shawano** (see below), an Algonquian term meaning 'southerner' (Bright 1993). The placename **Shavano** also occurs in Tex. (Bexar Co.).

SHAVEHEAD Lake (Mich., Cass Co.). Named for a Potawatomi (Algonquian) leader (Vogel 1986).

SHAVIOVIK River (Alaska, Beechey Point A-1). The Iñupiaq (Eskimo) name was reported in 1901, said to mean 'where there is iron' (Orth 1967); cf. *saviksraq* 'iron' (Webster and Zibell 1970).

SHAWAN (Md., Baltimore Co.) \shə wän´\. Probably a reference to the **Shawnee** (Algonquian) people; see below.

SHAWANEE (Tenn., Clairborne Co.) \shə wä´ nē\. Perhaps a variant of **Shawnee**; see below.

SHAWANGUNK (N.Y., Ulster Co.) \shong´ əm\. Also written <Skonemoghky, Schunemunk> (etc.); perhaps from Munsee Delaware (Algonquian), but of unclear derivation (Ruttenber 1906; Beauchamp 1907). A possibly related placename is **Shongum** (N.J., Morris Co.).

SHAWANNI, Lake (N.J., Sussex Co.). Perhaps from the Delaware (Algonquian) word for 'south' (Becker 1964); cf. Unami Delaware /ša:o:né:yu:nk/ 'south' (Blalock et al. 1994). Possibly related names include **Shawano County** and **Shawnee**; see below.

SHAWANO County (Wis.) \shä´ wə nō\. Named for a leader of the Menominee (Algonquian) people in the eighteenth century; he was called *Chawanon* by the French (Vogel 1991). Compare Menominee /sa:wanoh/ 'in the south', /sa:wanow/ 'southerner'; also /osa:wanow, osa:wanoh/ as a personal name (Bloomfield 1975). The placename **Shawano** also occurs in Fla. (Palm Beach Co.) and **Shawano** (N.C., Swain Co.) Probably related names are **Mount Shavano** (Colo., Chaffee Co.) and **Shawnee** (see below).

SHAWKEMO (Mass., Nantucket Co.). From SNEng. Algonquian, perhaps meaning 'place of springs' (Huden 1962).

SHAWME Lake (Mass., Barnstable Co.). From SNEng. Algonquian, perhaps meaning 'the neck' (Huden 1962). A perhaps related placename is **Shawmut.**

SHAWMUT (Mass., Suffolk Co.) \shô´ mət\. From SNEng. Algonquian <Mushauwomuk>, referring to the estuary of the Charles River (I. Goddard p.c.). As the name of a street and a bank in Boston, it was transferred to several other states (e.g., Ark., Pike Co.; Ill., Cook Co.; and Mich., Kent Co.). Possibly related placenames are **Shawme** (Mass., Barnstable Co.) and **Shawomet** (R.I., Bristol Co.).

SHAWNEE \shô´ nē, shô nē´\. The name of an Algonquian people; they were probably once concentrated in southern Ohio but later moved to such areas as Pa., Ky., Ala., Kans., and Okla. They were referred to by the French in 1648 as *Ouchaouanag,* corresponding to their self-designation /ša:wanwa/, lit. 'person of the south' (*HNAI* 15:622, 634). As a placename, **Shawnee** occurs in many states (e.g., Ark., Mississippi Co.; Ill., Gallatin Co.; and Okla., Pottawatomie Co.). Probably related placenames are **Mount Shavano** (Colo., Chaffee Co.), **Shawano County** (Wis.), and **Shawnette** (Tenn., Wayne Co.).

SHAWOMET (R.I., Bristol Co.). Probably from SNEng. Algonquian, meaning 'a neck of land' (Huden 1962). Related placenames are **Shawme** (Mass., Barnstable Co.) and **Shawmut** (Mass., Suffolk Co.).

SHAWONDASSE (Iowa, Dubuque Co.). An adaptation of *Shawondasee,* the name of the South Wind in Longfellow's *Hiawatha* (Vogel 1983). The poet may have taken the name from Ojibwa (Algonquian), but it is no longer attested in that language; cf. Meskwaki (Algonquian) /ša:watesiwa/ 'snow fog' (I. Goddard p.c.).

SHAWSHEEN River (Mass., Essex Co.) \shô´ shēn\. Named after a SNEng. Algonquian man, also known as Shoshanim or Sagamore Sam (Huden 1962).

SHEBEON Creek (Mich., Huron Co.). Ojibwa (Algonquian) *ziibiwan* 'rivers', from *ziibi* 'river, stream' (Vogel 1986; Nichols and Nyholm 1995).

SHEBOYGAN County (Wis.) \shə boi´ gən\. Menominee (Algonquian) /sa:pi:we:hekaneh/ 'at calling distance' (Afable & Beeler 1996: 192). The same form appears in Mich. as **Cheboygan County.**

SHEENJEK River (Alaska, Fort Yukon C-2) \shēn´ jik\. The Gwich'in (Athabaskan) name is *khiinjik* 'dog-salmon river' (J. Kari p.c.).

SHEEP. The domestic sheep was introduced to North America from Europe; however, the word *sheep* sometimes occurs in placenames with reference to the native 'bighorn' or 'mountain sheep'. **Sheepeater Canyon** (Wyo., Park Co.) corresponds to Shoshoni (Numic) /tukkutɨkka/ [tukkurɨkkA] 'sheepeater', the name of a tribal division, from /tukku/ 'mountain sheep' and /tɨkka/ 'eat' (J. McLaughlin p.c.).

SHEEPSCOT (Maine, Lincoln Co.) \shēp´ skot\. Perhaps an abbreviation of an Abenaki (Algonquian) placename; it may have meant 'many rocky channels' (Eckstorm 1941:113–16).

SHEHAWKEN (Pa., Wayne Co.) \shə hä´ kən\. Also written <Chechocton, Shehocking> (etc.); probably from Delaware (Algonquian), but of unclear derivation (Donehoo 1928).

SHEKLUKSHUK Range (Alaska, Shungnak C-3). The Iñupiaq (Eskimo) name was reported in 1901 (Orth 1967).

SHEKOMEKO (N.Y., Dutchess Co.) \shi kom´ i kō\. The Mahican (Algonquian) name, also written <Chicomico>, is of unclear derivation (Ruttenber 1906). The name also occurs in Conn. (Litchfield Co.).

SHELOCTA (Pa., Indiana Co.) \shə lok´ tə\. Perhaps from Delaware (Algonquian), but of unclear derivation (Donehoo 1928).

SHELOKUM, Lake (Alaska, Ketchikan D-5). Perhaps from a Chinook Jargon word for 'mirror' (Orth 1967). The placename also occurs in Wash. (Okanogan Co.).

SHEMYA (Alaska, Attu B-0) \shēm´ yə\. From the Aleut placename *samiyax̂*; cf. **Semichi Islands** (Bergsland 1994).

SHENANDOAH (N.Y., Dutchess Co.) \shen ən dō´ ə\. From the Oneida (Iroquoian) family name <Skenondoah> or <Skenandore>, that is, *skę̄nǫtǫ́ha'*, shortened from *oskę̄nǫtǫ́ha'*, derived from *oskę̄nǫ́:tǫ'* 'deer' (Lounsbury 1960:66). The name was apparently transferred to the **Shenandoah River** and **Valley** in Va. and from there to other states (e.g., Iowa, Page Co.; and Ohio, Richland Co.). Possibly related placenames are **Scononton** (N.Y., Clinton Co.) and **Sherando** (Va., Augusta Co.).

SHENANGO (Pa., Mercer Co.) \shə nang´ gō, shə näng´ gō\. Said to be from Onondaga (Iroquoian) <otseningo>, from <o-che-nang> 'bull thistles' (Beauchamp 1907; Donehoo 1928). The term occurs as a transfer name in Minn. (St. Louis Co.), Ohio (Ashtabula Co.), and W.Va. (Wetzel Co.). A related placename is **Chenango County** (N.Y.).

SHENECOSSET (Conn., New London Co.). A variant spelling of **Shennecossett Beach;** see below.

SHENIPSIT Lake (Conn., Tolland Co.) \shə nip´ sət\. Probably an abbreviation of Mohegan (SNEng. Algonquian) <meshenipset> 'big-water-place', from <missi> 'big', <nip> 'water', <-s> 'small', and <-et> 'place' (Huden 1962; W. Cowan p.c.).

SHENNECOSSETT Beach (Conn., New London Co.). From SNEng. Algonquian, perhaps meaning 'level land' (Huden 1962); a variant spelling is **Shenecosset.**

SHEOSH Creek (Wis., Douglas Co.) \shē´ osh\. Perhaps from an unidentified Indian language (Vogel 1991).

SHEPAUG River (Conn., Litchfield Co.) \shə pôg´\. From SNEng. Algonquian, probably corresponding to <missipaug> 'big pond', containing <missi-> 'big' and <-paug> 'pond' (Trumbull 1881; W. Cowan p.c.).

SHEQUAGA Falls (N.Y., Schuyler Co.) \shə kwô´ gə\. Perhaps from an Iroquoian placename (Beauchamp 1907).

SHERANDO (Va., Augusta Co.). Perhaps from the same origin as **Shenandoah** (Hagemann 1988); see above.

SHESHALIK (Alaska, Kotzebue D-2) \shi shä´ lik\. From Iñupiaq (Eskimo) *sisualik* 'one that has beluga whales', from *sisuaq* 'beluga' and *-lik* 'one that has' (L. Kaplan p.c.).

SHESHEEB, Lake (Mich., Keweenaw Co.) \shə sheb´\. From Ojibwa *zhiishiib* 'a duck' (Vogel 1986; Nichols and Nyholm 1995).

SHESHEQUIN (Pa., Bradford Co.) \shə shē´ kwin\. Perhaps from Delaware <tschech-schequqannink> 'gourd-rattle place' (Donehoo 1928); cf. Unami Delaware /xkaná:khakw/ 'gourd' (Blaylock 1994).

SHESHOK Creek (Alaska, Shungnak D-3). The Iñupiaq (Eskimo) name was reported in 1954 (Orth 1967).

SHETEK Township (Minn., Murray Co.) \shə tek´\. Probably from Ojibwa (Algonquian) *zhede* 'pelican', plural *zhedeg* (Nichols and Nyholm 1995).

SHETIPO Creek (Wash., Chelan Co.). Probably a misspelling of Chinook Jargon [she´-lĭ-po] 'ice, frozen' (D. Kinkade p.c.); see **Shillapoo Lake** (Wash., Clark Co.) below.

SHETUCKET River (Conn., New London Co.). From Mohegan (SNEng. Algonquian), perhaps from <nashauetuckit> 'land between rivers', containing <nashue> 'between', <-tuck> 'tidal stream', and <-et> 'place' (Trumbull 1881; W. Cowan p.c.).

SHEYENNE River (N.Dak., Eddy Co.; Minn., Clay Co.) \shī an´\. Named for the **Cheyenne** (Algonquian) people (Upham 2001; Wick 1988). The term is from Dakota (Siouan) *šahíyena*, a diminutive of *šahíya*, referring to the Cree (Algonquian) people (*HNAI* 13:880).

SHIAWASSEE County (Mich.) \shī ə wä´ sē\. Perhaps named for a nineteenth-century Ottawa (Algonquian) leader (Vogel 1986).

SHICK SHACK Hill (Ill., Cass Co.) \shik´ shak\. Perhaps named for a nineteenth-century Potawatomi (Algonquian) leader (Vogel 1963).

SHICKSHINNY (Pa., Luzerne Co.) \shik shin´ ē\. Perhaps from Delaware (Algonquian), recorded in 1848 (Donehoo 1928).

SHIEKUK Creek (Alaska, St. Lawrence D-4). The Yupik (Eskimo) name was reported in 1949 (Orth 1967).

SHIKAT Point (Alaska, Craig D-4). The Tlingit name was published in 1964 (Orth 1967).

SHIKELLAMY (Pa., Dauphin Co.) \shi kel´ ə mē\. Said to be named for an eighteenth-century Oneida (Iroquoian) leader (Donehoo 1928). A variant writing is **Shikellimy**.

SHIKOSI Island (Alaska, Skagway A-1). The Tlingit name was published in 1923 (Orth 1967).

SHILIAK Creek (Alaska, Noatak A-1). From Iñupiaq (Eskimo) *siġḷuaq* 'storage space' (Orth 1967; MacLean 1980).

SHILLAPOO Lake (Wash., Clark Co.) \shil´ ə pōō\. Chinook Jargon <she´-lĭ-po> [šɛ́ləpo] 'ice, frozen', perhaps from Kathlamet Chinook [ičélpo-ix̣] 'it was cold' (Reese 1996; D. Kinkade p.c.). A probably related name is **Shetipo Creek** (Wash., Chelan Co.).

SHILSHOLE Bay (Wash., King Co.) \shil shōl´, shil´ shōl\. From the Lushootseed (Salishan) placename \šəlšúl\, lit. 'pass beneath, put beneath' (Hitchman 1985; D. Kinkade p.c.).

SHIMHI (Utah, Iron Co.). From Numic (Uto-Aztecan), of unclear derivation (Van Cott 1990).

SHIMMO (Mass., Nantucket Co.). Earlier written <Shuakimmo>, <Shouahkemmuck>, <Showakemmo>. Probably from SNEng. Algonquian, perhaps meaning 'a spring' (Huden 1962); but cf. <showaucamor> 'the middle field of land' (Little 1984). The spelling **Shimmoah** also occurs.

SHINAKU Creek (Alaska, Craig C-4). The Tlingit name was reported in 1961 (Orth 1967).

SHINANGUAG Lake (Mich., Genesee Co.). Probably of Indian origin, but of unclear derivation (Vogel 1986).

SHINARUMP Cliffs (Ariz., Coconino Co.) \shin´ ə rump\. Probably from Southern Paiute (Numic) /sɨnna'a-rɨmpi/ [šɨnná'arɨmpI] 'dog rock', from /sɨnna'a-/ 'wolf, dog, coyote' plus /tɨmpi/ 'rock' (J. McLaughlin p.c.).

SHINDATA Creek (Alaska, Tanacross A-6) \shin dä´ tə\. Perhaps an Ahtna (Athabaskan) name, reported in 1936 (Orth 1967).

SHINGASS (Pa., Washington Co.). Named for <Shingas>, an eighteenth-century Indian leader; cf. Delaware (Algonquian) <schingaskunk> 'bog meadow' (Brinton and Anthony 1888; Donehoo 1928). Variant spellings include **Shingiss.**

SHINGOB Lake (Minn., Hubbard Co.). From Ojibwa (Algonquian) *zhingob* 'balsam fir' (Upham 2001; Nichols and Nyholm 1995). A related placename is that of the **Shingobee River** (Minn., Cass Co.) \shin´ gō bē\.

SHINILIKROK Creek (Alaska, Shungnak B-3). The Iñupiaq (Eskimo) name was reported in 1927 (Orth 1967).

SHINNECOCK (N.Y., Suffolk Co.) \shin´ ə kok\. Earlier written <Shinacau, Shinacaugh>; from SNEng. Algonquian, but of unclear derivation (Ruttenber 1906; Tooker 1911).

SHINOB-KIAB (Utah, Washington Co.). A variant of **Shinob Kibe** \shi nob´ kīb\. This represents Southern Paiute (Numic) /sɨnna'a-kaipa/ [šɨnná'a-kaivA] 'dog mountain', from /sɨnna'a-/ 'wolf, dog, coyote' and /kaipa/ [kaivA] 'mountain' (Van Cott 1990; J. McLaughlin p.c.).

SHINUMO Creek (Ariz., Coconino Co.). Said to be from a Southern Paiute (Numic) term referring to 'ancient people, cliff dwellers' (Granger 1983).

SHIOC (Wis., Outagamie Co.) \shī´ ok\. Perhaps an abbreviation of the Menominee (Algonquian) placename /mɛ:nomehsa:yak/, cf. /mano:mɛh/ 'wild rice' (Vogel 1991; Bloomfield 1975). A derived placename is nearby **Shiocton** \shī ok´ tən\.

SHIPETAUKIN Creek (N.J., Mercer Co.). Probably from Delaware (Algonquian), of unclear derivation (Becker 1964).

SHIPOLOVI (Ariz., Navajo Co.) A variant of **Shipaulovi** (Ariz., Navajo Co.) \shi pou´ lə vē, shi pol´ ə vē\. This is from the Hopi (Uto-Aztecan) placename *supawlavi*, containing *-vi* 'place'; the translation 'mosquito-place', which has often been given, cannot be confirmed (*HNAI* 9:552; K. Hill p.c.) A variant is **Sipaulovi.**

SHIPPAN Point (Conn., Fairfield Co.). Perhaps from SNEng. Algonquian, possibly meaning 'shore' (Huden 1962; W. Cowan p.c.).

SHIPSHEWANA (Ind., Lagrange Co.) \ship shē wä´ nə\. From Potawatomi (Algonquian) /mšə-bži-wanə-k/, lit. 'great-cat-den-place' (McCafferty 2002).

SHIRTEE Creek (Ala., Talladega Co.) \shûr´ tē\. Perhaps from Muskogee *catē* /čá:ti:/ 'red' (Read 1984; Martin and Mauldin 2000).

SHIRUKAK Lake (Alaska, Umiat C-2). Perhaps from Iñupiaq (Eskimo) <sirukak> 'ice house' (Orth 1967).

SHISHAKSHINOVIK Pass (Alaska, Ambler River B-1). The Iñupiaq (Eskimo) name may be from *sisuuk* 'snowslide' (L. Kaplan p.c.).

SHISHALDIN Volcano (Alaska, False Pass D-6) \shi shäl´ din\. A Russianized version of the Aleut placename *sisagux̂*, perhaps from *sisa-* 'to get lost' (Bergsland 1994); see **Sisaguk** below.

SHISHEBOGAMA Lake (Wis., Vilas Co.) \shish ə bog´ ə mə\. From Ojibwa (Algonquian), said to mean 'lake with arms running in all directions' (Vogel 1991).

SHI-SHI Beach (Wash., Clallam Co.) \shī´ shī\. From the Makah (Nootkan) placename /ša:ša:yi:s/, /šayšayi:s/ (W. Jacobsen p.c.).

SHISLOISO Hills (Alaska, Mt. McKinley D-5) \shish loi´ sə\. From Koyukon (Athabaskan) *ses loy yese'*, lit. 'ridge-end ridge' (Kari 1999: 103).

SHISNONA River (Alaska, Medfra B-1) \shish nō´ nə\. From Upper Kuskokwim (Athabaskan) *shisr nu no'*, lit. 'bear island stream' (Kari 1999:101).

SHITAMARING Creek (Utah, Garfield Co.) \shit´ ə mə ring\. Perhaps from Numic (Uto-Aztecan), but the derivation is not clear (Van Cott 1990).

SHITIKE Creek (Ore., Jefferson Co.) \shi tīk´\. From the Klamath placename /sidayksdi/ (Barker 1963).

SHIVUGAK Bluff (Alaska, Umiat B-3). Said to be from Iñupiaq (Eskimo) <sivugak> 'first' (Orth 1967); cf. *sivulliq* 'first one' (MacLean 1980).

SHIVWITS Plateau (Ariz., Mohave Co.) \shiv´wits\. The name of a Southern Paiute (Numic) band, /sipici-mɨ/ [šivítsɨwɬ], perhaps originally meaning 'easterners' (Sapir 1930:656; *HNAI* 11:396).

SHLOKOVIK Point (Alaska, St. Lawrence C-6). The Yupik (Eskimo) name, reported in 1932, is said to mean 'place where sling is used for getting birds' (Orth 1967).

SHOBAN Lake (Idaho, Lemhi Co.). Named for the **Shoban** team of Indian firefighters, coined from the names of two Numic (Uto-Aztecan) peoples, the **Shoshonis** and the **Bannocks** (Boone 1988).

SHOBONIER (Ill., Fayette Co.). Named for a Potawatomi (Algonquian) leader of the early nineteenth century; the word is derived from the French surname *Chevalier,* lit. 'horseman' (Vogel 1963).

SHOCCO Mountain (Ala., Talladega Co.) \shok´ ō\. Probably a shortening of **Choccolocco** (Ala., Calhoun Co.), from Muskogee *cahkē-rakko* /čahki:-ɬákko/, lit. 'shoal-big' (Read 1984; Martin and Mauldin 2000). It is also possible, however, that there is influence from the name of **Shocco Creek** in N.C. (Franklin Co.), which may reflect Catawba (Siouan) *suk'aa* 'our house', from *suk* 'house' (B. Rudes p.c.). A similar name is **Shoccoe** (Miss., Madison Co.), perhaps from Muskogee *cuko* /čokó:/ 'house' (Toomey 1917; Martin and Mauldin 2000).

SHOCKALOO Creek (Miss., Scott Co.) \shok´ ə lōō\. From Choctaw *shąkolo* 'cypress tree' (Seale 1939; P. Munro p.c.). A variant form is **Shongaloo,** and a related placename is **Shackaloa Creek** (Miss., Amite Co.).

SHOCKUM Mountains (Alaska, Cordova B-1). Named after a Dena'ina (Athabaskan) resident, as reported in 1905 (Orth 1967).

SHOGVIK Lake (Alaska, Selawik C-3). The Iñupiaq (Eskimo) name is *suaġvik* 'scolding place' (Burch 1998); cf. *suak-* 'to scold' (MacLean 1980).

SHOHOLA (Pa., Pike Co.) \shō hō´ lə\. Perhaps from Delaware (Algonquian) <schauwihilleu> 'it is weak' (Brinton and Anthony 1888; Donehoo 1928); cf. Unami Delaware /ša:w-/ 'weak' (Blalock et al. 1994).

SHOKOKON (Ill., Anderson Co.). Perhaps from Meskwaki (Algonquian) <Shock-o-con> 'flint' (Vogel 1963); cf. /ša:kohka:ni/ 'piece of flint' (Goddard 1994).

SHOKUM Creek (Alaska, Bering Glacier A-3). The Tlingit name was reported in 1904 (Orth 1967).

SHOMO Creek (Ala., Monroe Co.) \shō´ mō\. Named for Dr. Joseph Shomo, of Muskogee descent; the name, however, may be from Choctaw *shumo* (Read 1984; Byington 1915).

SHONGALO (Miss., Carroll Co.). From the same source as **Shongaloo** (La., Webster Par.) \shäng´ gə lōō\. This represents Choctaw *shąkolo* 'cypress tree' (Seale 1939; P. Munro p.c.). It also occurs as a variant of **Shockaloo Creek** (Miss., Scott Co.), and related placenames include **Shackaloa Creek** (Miss., Amite Co.), **Shangalo** (Miss., Caroll Co.), and **Shongelo** (Miss., Smith Co.).

SHONGUM (N.J., Morris Co.). Probably from the same source as **Shawangunk** (N.Y., Ulster Co.), which is also pronounced \shong´ gəm\.

Perhaps from Delaware (Algonquian), but of unclear derivation (Becker 1964).

SHONIKTOK Point (Alaska, Selawik C-3). The Iñupiaq (Eskimo) name is *sauniqtuuq* (Burch 1998).

SHONIP Creek (Idaho, Boise Co.). Named by the Forest Service, from Shoshoni (Numic) /sonippɨh/ 'grass' (Boone 1988; J. McLaughlin p.c.).

SHONTO (Ariz., Navajo Co.) \shon´ tō, shōn´ tō\. Navajo (Athabaskan) *sh*ą́ą́*'tóhí* 'where the spring is in the sunshine', containing *sh*ą́ą́*'* 'in the sunshine' and *tó* 'water' (Granger 1983; Wilson 1995).

SHOOTING ARROWS IN THE ROCK (Ariz., Apache Co.). A translation of Navajo (Athabaskan) *tsé né'eltoho* 'shooting arrows into the rock', referring to archery competitions; cf. *tsé* 'rock' (Linford 2000).

SHO-PAI Marina (Nev., Elko Co.) \shō´ pī\. Probably a blend of elements from the names of two Numic (Uto-Aztecan) peoples, **Shoshonis** and **Paiutes** (J. McLaughlin p.c.).

SHOPISHK (Ariz., Pinal Co.). Perhaps from O'odham (Piman) *ṣowick* 'narrow passage' (Granger 1983; J. Hill p.c.).

SHOSHONE \shō shōn´, shō shō´ nē\. The name of a people and language of the Great Basin, of the Numic (Uto-Aztecan) linguistic family; the spelling **Shoshoni** \shō shō´ nē\ is also used, and is preferred in this book. The term was first applied in the nineteenth century to the Eastern Shoshonis of Wyoming; its origin is not known (*HNAI* 11:334). The placename **Shoshone** occurs in several states (e.g., Idaho, Shoshone Co.; Nev., White Pine Co.; and Wyo., Big Horn Co.); the spelling **Shoshoni** also occurs in Wyo. (Fremont Co.) and Colo. (Grand Co.).

SHOTO (Wis., Manitowoc Co.) \shō´ tō\. An abbreviation of **Neshotah** or **Neshoto** (also in Manitowoc Co.), from Ojibwa (Algonquian) *niizhoodenh* 'twin' (Vogel 1991; Nichols and Nyholm 1995).

SHOTUIH Hill (Alaska, Fort Yukon D-3). The Gwich'in (Athabaskan) name is *shoh t*ą̨*i* 'black-bear hill' (Caulfield et al. 1980).

SHOVUN Lake (Alaska, Fort Yukon D-3) \shō´ vən\. The Gwich'in (Athabaskan) name is *shoh van* 'black-bear lake' (Caulfield et al. 1980).

SHOYA K'OSKWI'A (N.Mex., Cibola Co.). The Zuni name may contain /k'oskwi/ 'to stick out' (Ferguson and Hart 1985; Newman 1958).

SHUBLIK Island (Alaska, Mt. Michelson B-4). The Iñupiaq (Eskimo) name, reported in 1819, means 'a spring' (Orth 1967).

SHUBUTA (Miss., Clarke Co.) \shōō bōō´ tə\. From Choctaw (Muskogean) *shobota* 'smoke' (Seale 1939; P. Munro p.c.).

SHUKOK Creek (Alaska, Wiseman C-6). The name, of unclear origin, was reported in 1932 as meaning 'a kind of black rock' (Orth 1967). A perhaps related name is **Shukokluk** (Alaska, Wiseman C-5), made official in BGN 8802.

SHUKSAN (Wash., Whatcom Co.)) \shuk´ sən, shuk´ san\. From Lummi (Salishan) [šə́qsən], said to mean 'high peak' (D. Kinkade p.c.).

SHUKTUSA Creek (Alaska, Petersburg C-1). The Tlingit name was recorded in 1953 (Orth 1967).

SHULAKPACHAK Peak (Alaska, Survey Pass B-6). The Iñupiaq (Eskimo) name is said to mean 'like a big feather' (Orth 1967); cf. Siglit Inuvialiut dialect *suluk* 'feather' (Lowe 1984a).

SHULIN Lake (Alaska, Talkeetna A-2) \shōō´ lin\. Dena'ina (Athabaskan) *chulyin bena,* lit. 'raven lake' (Kari and Fall 1987:146).

SHULUNARURAK Creek (Alaska, Misheguk Mountain D-5). The Iñupiaq (Eskimo) name was reported in 1956 (Orth 1967).

SHUMATUSCACANT River (Mass., Plymouth Co.). From SNEng. Algonquian, of unclear derivation (Huden 1962).

SHUMULLA Creek (Ala., Sumter Co.) \shōō mul´ ə\. From Choctaw (Muskogean) *ashǫbala* 'cottonwood tree' (Read 1984; P. Munro p.c.).

SHUMUNKANUC Hill (R.I., Washington Co.). From SNEng. Algonquian, perhaps meaning 'high enclosed place' (Huden 1962).

SHUNGANUNGA Creek (Kans., Shawnee Co.) \shung gə nung´ gə\. From Kansa (Siouan) /šǫ́ge nǫ́ge/, lit. 'horse running' (Rydjord 1968; R. Rankin p.c.).

SHUNGNAK (Alaska, Shungnak D-3) \shung´ nak\. From Iñupiaq (Eskimo) *isingnaq* 'jade' (Webster and Zibell 1970).

SHUNGOPAVI (Ariz., Navajo Co.) \shung gop´ ə vē, shəng gō´ pə vē, shi mō´ pə vē\. Hopi (Uto-Aztecan) *songòopavi* 'sand-grass spring', from *songòo-, songowu* 'sand grass, a type of reed', *-pa-, paa-hu* 'water, spring', and *-vi* 'place' (*HNAI* 9:552; K. Hill p.c.).

SHUNKAWAKAN (N.C., Polk Co.). Apparently adapted from Dakota (Siouan) *šų́ka-waką* 'horse', from *šų́ka* 'dog' plus *wak ą́* 'sacred' (Riggs 1890).

SHUNOCK River (Conn., New London Co.). From SNEng. Algonquian, perhaps meaning 'where streams join' (Huden 1962). A possibly related placename is **Shannock** (R.I., Washington Co.).

SHUNTAVI Butte (Utah, Washington Co.). Probably from Southern Paiute (Numic), but the derivation is unclear.

SHUQUALAK (Miss., Noxubee Co.) \shoo͝g´ ə läk\. Perhaps from Choctaw (Muskogean) *shikalla* 'bead, necklace' (Seale 1939; P. Munro p.c.).

SHUSHALLUK Creek (Alaska, Wiseman D-2). The Iñupiaq (Eskimo) term is said to be a personal name (Orth 1967).

SHUSH BE TOU (Ariz., Apache Co.) \shush´ bi tō, shoo͞sh bi too͞\. Navajo (Athabaskan) *shash bito'* 'bear's spring', from *shash* 'a bear' and *bito'* 'its water' (*bi-* 'its', *to'* 'water, spring') (Young and Morgan 1987).

SHUSHUSKIN (Wash., Kittitas Co.). From the Sahaptin placename [šúšusqən], perhaps a personal name (Hitchman 1985; D. Kinkade p.c.).

SHUTISPEAR Creek (Miss., Calhoun Co.) \shoo͞´ ti spēr\. Probably a folk-etymology from Choctaw (Muskogean) *shoti ishpiha* 'pot ladle', from *shoti* 'pot' and *ishpiha* 'ladle' (from *piha* 'be scooped') (Seale 1939; P. Munro p.c.).

SHUWAH (Wash., Clallam Co.). From the Quileute (Chimakuan) village name /šó:waq^{W}/ (D. Kinkade p.c.).

SHUYAK Island (Alaska, Afognak C-2). The Alutiiq (Eskimo) name was reported in 1785 (Orth 1967).

SIA (N.Mex., Sandoval Co.) \sē´ ə\. A variant writing of **Zia,** the name of a Keresan pueblo in the Rio Grande Valley.

SIAH Butte (Ore., Deschutes Co.) \sī´ ə\. Named by the U.S. Forest Service, from Chinook Jargon <si-ah'> [sayá] 'distant', from Nootka /sayaa/ 'distant' (D. Kinkade p.c.). The placename **Siah** also occurs in Idaho (Valley Co.).

SIAKTAK Hills (Alaska, Noatak D-6). Iñupiaq (Eskimo), meaning 'extending in a straight line' (orth 1967).

SIASCONSET (Mass., Nantucket Co.) \skon´ sət\. From SNE Algonquian, perhaps meaning 'at the place of many bones', from <(mis)si-> 'many', <-skon> 'bone', <-s> 'small', and <-et> 'place' (Huden 1962; W. Cowan p.c.).

SIAVLAT Mountain (Alaska, Killik River A-5). The Iñupiaq (Eskimo) name was reported in 1956 (Orth 1967).

SIBONEY (Okla., Tillman Co.). Named after a town in Cuba, captured by U.S. forces in 1898 (Shirk 1974); the term is derived from the Taino (Arawakan) language.

SICHOMOVI (Ariz., Navajo Co.) \si chom´ ə vē\. Hopi (Uto-Aztecan) *sitsom'ovi* 'flower-hill high-place', from *si-, sihu* 'flower', *-tsom-, tsomo* 'hill', *-'o-* 'high', and *-vi* 'place' (K. Hill p.c.).

SICOMAC (N.J., Bergen Co.). Probably from Delaware (Algonquian), perhaps from <Shickamack> 'cemetery' (Becker 1964).

SIDIK Lake (Alaska, Howard Pass A-5). The Iñupiaq (Eskimo) name was obtained in 1956 (Orth 1967).

SIDWALTER Buttes (Ore., Wasco Co.) \sid´ wäl tər\. From the surname of a Wasco (Chinookan) family (also written <Sidwallo> etc.) (McArthur 1992; D. Kinkade p.c.).

SIF VAYA (Ariz., Pinal Co.). O'odham (Piman) *siw wahia* 'bitter well', from *siw* 'bitter' and *wahia* 'well' (J. Hill p.c.).

SIGEAKRUK Point (Alaska, Wainwright C-2). The Iñupiaq (Eskimo) name was reported in 1955 (Orth 1967).

SIGINAKA Islands (Alaska, Sitka A-5). The Tlingit name was reported in 1848 (Orth 1967).

SIGNAL Hill (Ill., St. Clair Co.). Supposedly so named because the hill was used by the Potawatomi (Algonquian) people as a signal station (Vogel 1963). Similarly, **Signal Peak** (Wash., Yakima Co.) is supposed to have used in this way by local Indians.

SIGRIKPAK Ridge (Alaska, Point Hope A-1). From Iñupiaq (Eskimo) *siksrikpak* 'marmot' (Orth 1967; MacLean 1980). Related placenames include **Siksikpak Ridge** (Alaska, Ikpikpuk River A-1).

SIKANASANKIAN (Alaska, Juneau A-1). The Tlingit name supposedly means 'small-black-bear town' (Orth 1967); cf. *s'eek* [s'i:k] 'black bear', *aan* 'town' (Davis and Leer 1976).

SIKETI Point (Alaska, Craig B-5). The Tlingit name, reported in 1923, is said to mean 'sea otter' (Orth 1967).

SIKIK Lake (Alaska, Howard Pass A-4). The Iñupiaq (Eskimo) name, reported in 1956, is said to mean 'deep water' (Orth 1967).

SIKNIK Cape (Alaska, St. Lawrence B-3). The Yupik (Eskimo) name was reported in 1932 (Orth 1967).

SIKOKINI Springs (Mont., Flathead Co.). From Blackfoot (Algonquian) *síikokiini(s)* 'birch tree' (Holterman 1985; D. Franz p.c.).

SIKOLIK Lake (Alaska, Wainwright A-5). The Iñupiaq (Eskimo) name is *sikulik* 'has ice' (L. Kaplan p.c.). Possibly related Alaska names are **Sikrelurak River** (Demarcation Point D-3) and **Siku Point** (Demarcation Point D-2).

SIKONSINA Pass (Alaska, Tanacross A-6). From Ahtna (Athabaskan), etymology unknown.

SIKORT CHUAPO (Ariz., Pima Co.). From O'odham (Piman) *sikol ce:po,* lit. 'round bedrock-mortar' (Granger 1983; J. Hill p.c.).

SIKRELURAK River (Alaska, Demarcation Point D-3). The Iñupiaq (Eskimo) name was reported in 1952; it may contain *siku* 'ice' (MacLean 1980). A possibly related name is **Sikolik Lake** (Alaska, Wainwright A-5).

SIKSIKA Falls (Mont., Glacier Co.) \sik si kä´\. Blackfoot (Algonquian) *siks-iká,* the name of the people, lit. 'black-foot' (*HNAI* 13:623; D. Franz p.c.). The placename **Siksikaikwan Glacier** (Mont., Glacier Co.) reflects the personal name *siksikáíkoan,* lit. 'Blackfoot man', a famous Indian scout who was called William Jackson in English (Holterman 1985; D. Franz p.c.).

SIKSIKPAK Ridge (Alaska, Ikpikpuk River A-1). From Iñupiaq (Eskimo) *siksrikpak* 'marmot' (Orth 1967, MacLean 1980). A related Alaska placename is **Sigrikpak Ridge** (Point Hope A-1). Other related Alaska names are **Siksikpalak River** (Alaska, Demarcation Point C-2), **Siksikpuk** (Chandler Lake D-4), and **Siksrikpak** (Point Lay C-2).

SIKSIK River (Alaska, Demarcation Point D-3) \sik´ sik\. From Iñupiaq (Eskimo) *siksrik* 'ground squirrel' (Orth 1967; MacLean 1980). Note, however, that **Siksik Lake** (Alaska, Healy B-2) is from Ahtna (Athabaskan).

SIKUL HIMATK (Ariz., Pima Co.). O'odham (Piman) *sikol himadek* 'whirling' (of water), from *sikol* 'round' and *himadk* 'going' (Granger 1983; J. Hill p.c.).

SIKULIK Lake (Alaska, Barrow A-4). The Iñupiaq (Eskimo) name was recorded in 1956 as meaning 'having ice' (Orth 1967); cf. *siku* 'ice'

(MacLean 1980). Related Alaska names include **Siku Point** (Demarcation Point D-2), **Sikolik Lake** (Wainwright A-5), and **Siku Point** (Demarcation Point D-2).

SIKU Point (Alaska, Demarcation Point D-2). From Iñupiaq (Eskimo) *siku* 'ice' (MacLean 1980). Possibly related Alaska placenames include **Sikolik Lake** (Wainwright A-5), **Sikulik Lake** (Barrow A-4), and **Sikrelurak River** (Demarcation Point D-3).

SIKYATKI Ruins (Ariz., Navajo Co.) \sik yät´ kē\. From Hopi (Uto-Aztecan) *sikyatki,* with *sikya* 'ravine' and *-tki, tuki* 'cut' (K. Hill p.c.).

SI Lake (Ore., Marion Co.) \sē\. Chinook Jargon <tsee> [tsi] 'sweet', perhaps from Lower Chinook [(í-)ts'emən] 'sweetness' (H. Zenk p.c.).

SILAK Island (Alaska, Adak C-1). From the Aleut placename *silax̂,* perhaps meaning 'approach' (Bergsland 1994).

SILALINIGUN Creek (Alaska, Killik River B-2). The Iñupiaq (Eskimo) name is *siḷalliñġun* 'exposed slope' (L. Kaplan p.c.).

SILCO (Ga., Camden Co.). Perhaps from Muskogee <silkosi> 'narrows, narrow place' (Goff 1975); cf. *selke* 'sliced', *selkuse* 'something small that is sliced' (J. Martin p.c.).

SILESIA Creek (Wash., Whatcom Co.) \sə lē´ zhə\. A folk-etymology from Chilliwack (Upriver) Halkomelem (Salishan) [səlísi], meaning either 'fang' or 'leaning mountain', the latter from /ləlís-/ 'to lean' (D. Kinkade p.c.); the form has been changed to resemble **Silesia,** a region of central Europe, now part of Poland.

SILETZ (Ore., Lincoln Co.) \si lets´, sī lets`\. The name of the site of a reservation where Indians from all over central and southern Ore. were settled may be from a Tillamook (Salishan) placename [nš(ə)lǽč'] (McArthur 1992; D. Kinkade p.c.).

SILICOSASKA Park (Wash., Chelan Co.) \sil i kə sas´ kə\. From Moses-Columbian (Salishan) /c'ə́lx^{w}uʔsásq't/, the name of a leader of the Entiat people in the nineteenth century; meaning 'standing in the middle of the sky', from /c'líx/ 'stand', /-aw's/ 'middle', and /-asq't/ 'sky, day' (D. Kinkade p.c.). A related placename is **Saska Peak** (Wash., Chelan Co.).

SILLYASHEEN Mountain (Alaska, Wiseman D-6). The Iñupiaq (Eskimo) name was reported in 1932 (Orth 1967).

SILLYCOOK Mountain (Ga., Habersham Co.). Said to be from Cherokee (Iroquoian) <saligugi> 'turtle' (Goff 1975).

SIL MURK (Ariz., Maricopa Co.). O'odham (Piman) *si:l mek* 'burnt saddle', from *siil* (from Spanish *silla*) 'saddle' plus *mek* [mɨk] 'burnt' (Granger 1983; J. Hill p.c.).

SIL NAKYA (Ariz., Pima Co.). O'odham (Piman) *si:l naggia* 'hanging saddle', from *si:l* (from Spanish *silla*) 'saddle' plus *naggia* 'hanging' (Granger 1983; J. Hill p.c.).

SILTCOOS (Ore., Lane Co.) \silt´ ko͞os\. From the Lower Umpqua (Siuslaw) placename [tš^{h}ïltɬk^{h}us] (D. Kinkade p.c.). A variant is used for the nearby **Camp Tsiltcoos.**

SIMAX Bay (Ore., Klamath Co.) \sī´ maks\. Perhaps an Indian term for 'landing place', language unknown (McArthur 1992).

SIMCOE Creek (Wash., Yakima Co.) \sim´ kō\. Perhaps from Sahaptin /sɨmk'wí:/ 'saddle' (speaking of a mountain) (Hitchman 1985; D. Kinkade p.c.).

SIMI (Calif., Ventura Co.) \si mē´, sē´mē\. From the Ventureño (Chumashan) village name <simiyi>, of no known etymology (Gudde 1998).

SIMIK Mountain (Alaska, Noatak A-3). The Iñupiaq (Eskimo) name is *simik* 'stopper, plug' (Burch 1998).

SIMILKAMEEN (Wash., Okanogan Co.) \si mil´ kə mēn\. Said to be named for an Indian group called <Similkameigh>, translated as 'treacherous waters' (Hitchman 1985).

SIMILK Bay (Wash., Skagit Co.) \sī´ milk\. Perhaps an Indian word for 'salmon', language not identified (Phillips 1971).

SIMNASHO (Ore., Wasco Co.) \sim nash´ ō, sim näsh´ ō\. Earlier <Sinemasho>, from Sahaptin [išnɨma:šu] 'black hawthorn bush', from [išnɨ́m] 'black hawthorn' and [-á:šu] 'tree, bush' (McArthur 1992; D. Kinkade p.c.).

SIMSQUISH Brook (Maine, Washington Co.) \sim´ skwish\. Perhaps from Abenaki (Algonquian), meaning 'dip up a drink' (Huden 1962).

SIMTUSTUS (Ore., Jefferson Co.) \sim tus´tus, sim tus´ təs\. Named for Kyuslute Simtustus, a Sahaptin leader (McArthur 1992; D. Kinkade p.c.).

SINAMOX (Ore., Wasco Co.) \sin´ ə moks\. The railway station was given the Chinook Jargon name <sin´-a-mokst, sin´-a-moxt> [sínəmaks, sínamɔkst] 'seven', because it the seventh station on the line; perhaps from Lower Chinook [sínamɔkšt] 'seven' (McArthur 1992; D. Kinkade p.c.).

SINARURUK River (Alaska, Wainwright C-2). The Iñupiaq (Eskimo) name is *siŋiaġrum kuugauraŋa* (Burch 1998).

SIN-AV-TO-WEAP (Utah, Garfield Co.). From Southern Paiute (Numic), perhaps meaning 'wolf canyon', from /sɨna'api/ [šiná'avI] 'wolf, dog' plus /uippi/ 'canyon' (Sapir 1930). See also **Temple of Sinawava**, below.

SINAWAVA, Temple of (Utah, Washington Co.). Perhaps from Southern Paiute (Numic) /sɨna'api/ [šiná'avI] 'coyote' (Sapir 1930). The stem is related to that meaning 'wolf' in **Sin-av-to-weap**; see above.

SINEAK River (Alaska, Norton Bay B-5). The Eskimo name was reported about 1954 (Orth 1967).

SINEPUXENT (Md., Worcester Co.). Earlier written <Cinnepuxon, Senepuchen> (etc.); perhaps from Delaware (Algonquian), but the derivation is unclear (Kenny 1984).

SINGAC (N.J., Passaic Co.). The term is probably from Delaware (Algonquian), but the derivation is unclear (Becker 1964).

SINGA Island (Alaska, Craig D-5). Perhaps from Haida <shing-ia> 'night' (Orth 1967).

SINGARUAK Creek (Alaska, Barrow A-5). The Iñupiaq (Eskimo) name, reported as <Sinrarua> in 1853, is said to refer to the estuary-like mouth of the stream (Orth 1967).

SINGAUK Entrance (Alaska, Noatak C-5). The Iñupiaq (Eskimo) name, recorded in 1950, is said to mean 'separating entrance' (Orth 1967).

SINGAURUK Point (Alaska, Selawik C-4). The Iñupiaq (Eskimo) name was reported in 1955 (Orth 1967).

SINGAYOAK Creek (Alaska, Misheguk Mountain D-1). The Iñupiaq (Eskimo) name, said to mean 'loaded', was reported in 1953 (Orth 1967).

SINGEAK (Alaska, Kotzebue C-6). The Iñupiaq (Eskimo) name was reported in 1940 (Orth 1967). Probably related is **Singeakpuk River** (Alaska, Kotzebue B-6); cf. *-qpak* 'big'.

SINGIGRAK Spit (Alaska, Noatak C-5). The Iñupiaq (Eskimo) name is probably *siŋiksraq* 'material for bootlace' (L. Kaplan p.c.). A perhaps related name is **Sinigrok Point** (Alaska, Point Hope B-3).

SINGIGYAK (Alaska, Nome D-3). The Iñupiaq (Eskimo) name was reported around 1940 (Orth 1967).

SINGIKPO Cape (Alaska, St. Lawrence C-3). Perhaps from Yupik (Eskimo) *cingig-* 'sharp' (Orth 1967; Jacobson 1984); cf. **Singik,** above.

SINGIK Point (Alaska, St. Lawrence D-6). From St. Lawrence Island Yupik (Eskimo) *singik* 'point' (Orth 1967; Jacobson 1987). The related name **Singikpak** (Alaska, St. Lawrence B-5) means 'big point' (Orth 1967); cf. *-ghpak* [-ʀpak] 'big' (Jacobson 1987).

SING SING Prison (N.Y., Westchester Co.) \sing´ sing\. Probably related to the name of nearby **Ossining,** perhaps from Munsee Delaware (Algonquian) <assin> 'stone' (Ruttenber 1906);

cf. Munsee *asún* 'stone' (O'Meara 1996). There is also a **Sing Sing Pond** in Maine (Piscataquis Co.). Possibly related names include **Assiniboine Creek** (Mont., **Assonet** (Mass., Bristol Co.), **Assunpink Creek** (N.J., Mercer Co.), **Stoney Indians Lake** (Mont., Glacier Co.), and **Rocky Mountains.**

SINIGROK Point (Alaska, Point Hope B-3). The Iñupiaq (Eskimo) name, reported in 1956, is said to mean 'shoe-lace, thong' (Orth 1967); cf. *siŋiq* 'bootlace' (MacLean 1980). A perhaps related Alaska placename is **Singigrak Spit** (Noatak C-5).

SINIKTANEYAK Creek (Alaska, Point Hope C-3). The Iñupiaq (Eskimo) name is *siñiktaġnaiḷaq*, which may mean 'some way or reason for not sleeping' (Burch 1998; Orth 1967); cf. *siñik-* 'to sleep' (MacLean 1980). The apparently related **Siniktanneyak** (Alaska, Howard Pass B-5) is translated 'place where cannot sleep' (Orth 1967).

SINIOGAMUTE (Alaska, Teller B-4). The Iñupiaq (Eskimo) name was reported in 1880 (Orth 1967); cf. *-miut* 'people'.

SIN-I-ROCK (Alaska, Teller D-6). The Iñupiaq (Eskimo) name is probably *sinġaq* 'channel' (L. Kaplan p.c.).

SINKYONE (Calif., Humboldt Co.) \sing´ ki yōn\. The name of an Athabaskan people of Calif.; derived from the name applied to them by the related Kato Indians: /sin-kiyahan/ 'coast tribe' (Gudde 1998).

SINLAHEKIN Creek (Wash., Okanogan Co.) \sin lə hik´ ən\. Perhaps from an Okanagan (Salishan) placename (Hitchman 1985; D. Kinkade p.c.).

SINNEMAHONING (Pa., Cameron Co.) \sin ə mə hō´ ning\. Probably from Delaware (Algonquian) <achsinni-mahoni> 'stony salt-lick', from <achsin> 'stone' and <mahoning> 'salt-lick' (Donehoo 1928); cf. Unami Delaware /a:hsə́n/ 'stone' (Blalock et al. 1994). A related placename is **Mahoning** (Pa., Fayette Co.).

SINNISSIPPI River (Wis., Rock Co.; Ill., Winnebago Co.) \sin ə sip´ ē\. From an Algonquian language, meaning 'rock river' (Vogel 1963; 1991); the specific source may be Miami/Illinois /(a)hseni-siipi/ 'rock river' (M. McCafferty p.c.). The translation **Rock River** also occurs as a placename in the area.

SINNONDOWAENE (N.Y., Livingston Co.). Said to represent earlier <Sonnontouan> 'great hill' (Beauchamp 1907).

SINONA Creek (Alaska, Gulkana C-2). Ahtna (Athabaskan) *snuu na'* 'brushy creek', from *snuu* 'brushy area along river bottom' and *na'* 'stream' (Kari 1990).

SINOPAH Mountain (Mont., Glacier Co.). From Blackfoot (Algonquian) *sinopáá* 'a type of fox' (Holterman 1985; D. Franz p.c.).

SINRAZAT (Alaska, Shishmaref A-4). The Iñupiaq (Eskimo) name is probably from *sinġaq* 'channel' (L. Kaplan p.c.).

SINSINAWA River (Ill., Jo Daviess Co.) \sin si nä´ wä\. From Ojibwa (Algonquian), perhaps meaning 'rocky in the middle' (Vogel 1963). The placename **Sinsinawa** in Wis. (Grant Co.) is said to be pronounced \sin sin´ ə wä\.

SINTABOGUE (Ala., Washington Co.) \sin´ tə bōg\. Choctaw (Muskogean) for 'snake creek', from *sịti* 'snake' and *book* 'creek' (Seale 1939; P. Munro p.c.). Probably related forms are **Senter Bogue Creek** (Miss., Wayne Co.), **Santabarb Creek** (La., Sabine Co.), and **Santa Bogue** (Ala., Washington Co.).

SINTE GALESKA College (S.Dak., Todd Co.). Named for a nineteenth-century leader of the Lakhota (Siouan) people. The Native American name consists of *sịté* 'tail' plus *gleškā́* 'spotted' (Ingham 2001).

SINUK Creek (Alaska, Killik River A-3) \sē´ nuk\. From Iñupiaq (Eskimo) *sinġaq* 'inlet; lagoon on the coast' (L. Kaplan p.c.).

SINYALAK Creek (Alaska, Hughes C-1). The Iñupiaq (Eskimo) name, recrded in 1956, is said to mean 'all split up' (Orth 1967).

SINYALA Tank (Ariz., Coconino Co.). A variant of **Sinyella Canyon**; see below.

SINYELLA Canyon (Ariz., Coconino Co.). Named for a Havasupai (Yuman) leader of the nineteenth century; cf. **Sinyala Tank** (Granger 1983).

SIOTUKUYUK Bluff (Alaska, Umiat C-2). The Iñupiaq (Eskimo) name was reported in 1956 (Orth 1967).

SIOUAN \so͞o´ ən\. The name of a language family that includes the **Dakotan** dialects; see **Sioux** below.

SIOUX \so͞o\. An abbreviation of French <Nadouessioux>, from early Ottawa (Algonquian) singular /na:towe:ssi/, plural /na:towe:ssiwak/ 'Sioux'. The term is apparently related to words in other Algonquian languages that mean 'Northern Iroquoian', derived from a verb meaning 'to speak a foreign language' (*HNAI* 13:749). It is commonly applied to a group of related peoples, mostly located in the upper Midwest, who are also called **Dakotan**; this includes dialect groups called **Dakota** (mostly east of the Missouri River), **Lakhota** (mostly west of the Missouri River), and **Nakota** (mostly in Canada). The Dakotan languages—along with other languages such as **Crow, Hidatsa, Mandan, Omaha, Osage, Kansa, Ioway-Oto, Winnebago,** and **Quapaw**—form the **Siouan** linguistic family (*HNAI* 13:94). As a placename, **Sioux** is widespread in Dakotan territory (e.g., Iowa, Sioux Co.; Minn., Itasca Co.; and Neb., Sioux Co.). It also occurs as a transfer name in other states (e.g., Ohio, Pike Co.).

SIOVI SHUATAK (Ariz., Pima Co.). O'odham (Piman) *si'i'owĭ su:dagĭ,* lit. 'sweet water' (Granger 1983; J. Hill p.c.).

SIPAPU \sē pä po͞o´\. The English term refers to an opening in the kiva or ceremonial chamber of the Pueblo peoples, which is believed to connect with the supernatural world. It may be derived from Keresan /šíp'áap'I/, but related words occur in other Pueblo languages (I. Davis p.c.). As a placename, **Sipapu** is found in Ariz. (Coconino Co.), N.Mex. (Taos Co.), and Utah (San Juan Co.).

SIPAULOVI (Ariz., Navajo Co.) \si pol´ ə vē\. A variant of **Shipolovi**; see above.

SIPPEWISSET (Mass., Barnstable Co.) From SNEng. Algonquian, perhaps 'little river place', containing <sepu> 'river', <-s> 'small', and <-et> 'place' (Huden 1962, W. Cowan p.c.).

SIPPICAN River (Mass., Plymouth Co.). From SNEng. Algonquian, perhaps 'long stream', containing <sepu> 'river' (Huden 1962; W. Cowan p.c.).

SIPPO (Ohio, Stark Co.) \sē´ pō\. Probably from Delaware (Algonquian) <sipo> 'river' (Brinton and Anthony 1888); cf. Unami Delaware /sí:pu:/ (Blalock et al. 1994).

SIP Pond (N.H., Cheshire Co.). Perhaps from SNEng. Algonquian; cf. <sib(es)> 'bird' (Huden 1962; W. Cowan p.c.).

SIPSEY (Ala., Walker Co.) \sip´ sē\. Perhaps from Choctaw (Muskogean) *sipsi* 'poplar tree' (Read 1984; P. Munro p.c.). The name **Sipsey** also occurs in Miss. (Scott Co.).

SIRUK Creek (Alaska, Hughes C-1). The Iñupiaq (Eskimo) name was reported in 1901 (Orth 1967).

SISAGUK (Alaska, False Pass C-4). From the Aleut placename *sisagux̂,* perhaps from *sisa-* 'to get lost' (Bergsland 1994). A related Alaska placename is **Shishaldin Volcano** (False Pass D-6).

SISAR Creek (Calif., Ventura Co.). \si sär´\. From Ventureño (Chumashan) *Sisá,* a village name (Gudde 1998).

SISCHU Mountain (Alaska, Kantishna River A-6). Upper Kuskokwim (Athabaskan) *sis chwh* [səs čʊh], lit. 'ridge big' (Kari 1999:103).

SISCOWIT Reservoir (Conn., Fairfield Co.) \sis´ kə wit\. Perhaps a transfer of **Siskiwit River**, also spelled **Siskowit** (Mich., Keweenaw Co.); see below.

SISEK Cove (Alaska, Unalaska C-1). From the Aleut placename *sisan,* perhaps meaning 'losing one's way'; cf. *sisa-lix* 'to lose one's way, to get lost' (Bergsland 1994).

SISGRAVIK Lake (Alaska, Meade River D-1). The Iñupiaq (Eskimo) name was recorded in 1956 (Orth 1967).

SISIAK Creek (Alaska, Misheguk Mountain A-5). The Iñupiaq (Eskimo) name is *sisigaq* 'fox den' (Burch 1998); cf. *sisi* 'burrow, den' (MacLean 1980).

SISI Creek (Ore., Clackamas Co.) \sē´ sē, sī´ sī\. Perhaps from Chinook Jargon <pasisi> [pasísi] 'blanket, cloth' (McArthur 1992; D. Kinkade p.c.).

SISKIWIT River (Mich., Keweenaw Co.) \sis´ ki wit\. Named for a fish otherwise known in English as *siscowet, cisco,* or 'lake trout'; from Ojibwa (Algonquian) /pe:mite:wiskowe:t/ 'that which has oily flesh', from /pe:mite:w-/ 'oil' (Vogel 1986; *RHD* 1987). A variant form is the nearby **Siskowit**. The name **Siskiwit** also occurs in Wis. (Bayfield Co.). Possibly related placenames include **Cisco** (Mich., Gogebic Co.) and **Siscowit Reservoir** (Conn., Fairfield Co.).

SISKIYOU County (Calif.) \sis´ ki yo͞o\. From a Chinook Jargon word meaning 'a bobtailed horse', from Cree (Algonquian) *kîskâyowêw* 'bobtailed', containing *kîsk-* 'cleanly cut off' and *-âyow-* 'tail' (Gudde 1998). The name **Siskiyou** also occurs in Ore. (Jackson Co.).

SISNATHYEL Mesa (N.Mex., Sandoval Co.). Navajo (Athabaskan) *sis naateel* 'wide belt', containing *sis* 'belt', *naa-* 'across', and *-teel* 'wide' (Wilson 1995).

SISQUOC River (Calif., Santa Barbara Co.) \sis kwok´\. From Barbareño (Chumashan), perhaps meaning 'quail' (Gudde 1998).

SISSABAGAMA Creek (Wis., Sawyer Co.) \sis ə bag´ ə mə\. From Ojibwa (Algonquian), said to mean 'lake with arms running in all directions' (Vogel 1991). A related name is **Shishebogama Lake** (Wis., Sawyer Co.).

SISSETON Lake (Minn., Martin Co.) \sis´ ə tən\. From Dakota (Siouan) *sisíthųwą,* the name of a tribal division, containing *thųwą́* 'village' (Upham 2001; *HNAI* 13:753). The name **Sisseton** also occurs in S.Dak. (Roberts Co.).

SITAKADAY Narrows (Alaska, Mt. Fairweather C-1). From Tlingit, said to mean 'icy bay', referring to Glacier Bay (Orth 1967). A probably related Alaska name is **Sitth-gha-ee** (Skagway A-3).

SITCHIAK Lake (Alaska, Chandler Lake D-2). The Iñupiaq (Eskimo) name, recorded in 1956, may mean 'new ice' (Orth 1967); cf. *siku* 'ice' (MacLean 1980).

SITEELUK Bay (Alaska, St. Lawrence B-6). The Yupik (Eskimo) name was reported in 1949 (Orth 1967).

SITHDONDIT Creek (Alaska, Tanana D-6). The Koyukon (Athabaskan) name was obtained in 1956 (Orth 1967).

SITHYLEMENKAT Lake (Alaska, Bettles A-3). The Koyukon (Athabaskan) name was reported in 1956 (Orth 1967).

SITKA (Alaska, Sitka A-4) \sit´ kə\. From the Tlingit placename /ši:t'ká/ (Orth 1967; *HNAI* 7:227). The name **Sitka** has been transferred to several states (e.g., Ark., Sharp Co.; Kans., Clark Co.; and Ohio, Washington Co.).

SITKAGI Bluff (Alaska, Yakutat C-8). From Tlingit [sɪt' x'ayi] 'glacier point' (De Laguna 1972:97).

SITKALIDAK Island (Alaska, Kodiak A-4) \sit´ kə lē dak\. The Alutiiq (Eskimo) name was first recorded in 1794 as <Salthidack>, and in 1805 as <Syakhlidok> (Orth 1967).

SITKALIDA Lagoon (Alaska, Kodiak A-4). A variant writing of **Sitkalidak Island**; see below.

SITKINAK (Alaska, Trinity Islands C-1) \sit´ ki nak\. The Alutiiq (Eskimo) name was published in 1826 as <Sitkhunak> (Orth 1967).

SITKLAN Island (Alaska, Prince Rupert C-3). The Tlingit name was reported in 1869 (Orth 1967).

SITKOH Creek (Alaska, Sitka C-3). The Tlingit name was reported in 1883 (Orth 1967).

SITKOK Point (Alaska, Point Lay C-2). From Iñupiaq (Eskimo) *sitquq* 'knee' (Orth 1967; MacLean 1980).

SITKUM (Ore., Coos Co.) \sit´ kəm\. Chinook Jargon <sit´-kum> [sítkəm] 'half, part, middle', perhaps from Lower Chinook [čítkum, šítkum] 'half' (D. Kinkade p.c.). The name **Sitkum** also occurs in Alaska (Wiseman A-1) and Wash. (Clallam Co.).

SITNAZUAK (Alaska, Nome C-2). The Iñupiaq (Eskimo) name is *sitnazuaq*, from *sinġaq* 'channel' (L. Kaplan p.c.).

SITTA (Alaska, St. Lawrence C-5). The Yupik (Eskimo) name was recorded in 1932 (Orth 1967).

SITTAKANAY River (Alaska, Taku River C-6). The Tlingit name was published in 1895 (Orth 1967).

SITTH-GHA-EE Peak (Alaska, Skagway A-3). The Tlingit name, recorded in 1879, is said to mean 'great cold lake', referring to Glacier Bay (Orth 1967). A probably related Alaska name is **Sitakaday Narrows** (Mt. Fairweather C-1).

SITTING BULL. This was the English name of the Lakhota (Siouan) chief <Tatanka Yotanka>, lit. 'buffalo-bull sitting' (Sneve 1973), containing *thathą́ka* 'buffalo bull' and *íyotaka* 'to sit down' (Ingham 2001). As a placename, **Sitting Bull** is found in S.Dak. (Corson Co.), and as a transfer name in other states (e.g., N.Mex., Eddy Co.; and Wash., Snohomish Co.).

SITTING GOD (Ariz., Apache Co.). Navajo (Athabaskan) *yé'ii dah sidáí* 'the god sits at an elevation', containing *yé'ii* 'divine being' (Linford 2000).

SITTING ROCK (Ariz., Canyon de Chelly, Apache Co.). A translation of Navajo (Athabaskan) *tsé sí'ání* 'rock sits', containing *tsé* 'rock' (Linford 2000).

SITUK (Alaska, Yakutat B-5). From Tlingit [sɪtʌk], said to have been pronounced earlier as [ts'ʌtʌġ]; no etymology is known (De Laguna 1972:78).

SITUKUYOK River (Alaska, Noatak A-3). The Iñupiaq (Eskimo) name is *siutuquuyuk* 'spiral seashell' (L. Kaplan p.c.).

SIUSLAW River (Ore., Lane Co.) \sī yo͞o´ slô\. The term also refers to an Indian group; the name is from Siuslaw [šáʔyú:štl'a:], the name of the region (D. Kinkade p.c.).

SIVILI CHUCHG (Ariz., Pima Co.). O'odham (Piman) *siwol cu:ck* 'onions standing', with *siwol* 'onion' from Sp. *cebolla* (J. Hill p.c.).

SIVNEGHAK Lagoon (Alaska, St. Lawrence B-0). The Yupik (Eskimo) name was reported in 1949 (Orth 1967).

SIVOGAKRUAK Bluff (Alaska, Killik River C-1). The Iñupiaq (Eskimo) name is *sivuġaġruaq* 'big front tooth or leg' (L. Kaplan p.c.).

SIVUGAK Hill (Alaska, Noatak D-4). The Iñupiaq (Eskimo) name is *sivuġaq* 'space in front, bow of a boat' (Burch 1998; MacLean 1980); cf. *sivu* 'front part, bow'.

SIVUKAT Mountain (Alaska, Noatak D-2). The Iñupiaq (Eskimo) name is *sivuqqat* 'front teeth or legs' (L. Kaplan p.c.).

SIWANOY (N.Y., Westchester Co.). The term refers to an Indian group, perhaps speakers of Munsee Delaware (Algonquian), who once lived on the north shore of Long Island Sound. The name may be from a SNE Algonquian term meaning 'southerners' (Grumet 1981). Possibly related names are **Shawano County** and **Shawnee.**

SIWASH \sī´ wäsh\. This term represents a word for 'Indian' once commonly used in the English of the Pacific Northwest but now considered offensive. It represents Chinook Jargon <si´wash> [sáiwaš], from French *sauvage* 'wild' (D. Kinkade p.c.). As a placename, it occurs in Alaska (Talkeetna C-3), Idaho (Clearwater Co.), Ore. (Douglas Co.), and Wash. (Lewis Co.).

SIWUKVA (Ariz., Navajo Co.). Represents the Hopi placename *siwukva,* perhaps from *siwuk-* 'solids fall out' plus *-va, paa-hu* 'water, spring' (K. Hill p.c.).

SIXES (Ga., Cherokee Co.) \sik´ səz\. A translation of Cherokee (Iroquoian) *sudali* 'six' (Goff 1975; Feeling 1975).

SIXES (Ore., Curry Co.) \sik´ səz\. Tututni Athabaskan /səgweče?/ 'wide-open river mouth', from /səgwe/ 'wide open' and /-če-?/ 'its tail' (i.e., 'its [a river's] mouth'); possibly reinforced by Chinook Jargon <sikhs, six> [sɪks, šɪks] 'friend', perhaps from Lower Chinook [-šikš] 'friend' (McArthur 1992; D. Kinkade p.c.).

SIX NATIONS Hill (N.Y., Schuyler Co.). The term refers to the confederacy formed by Iroquoian peoples in upper N.Y. state (Beauchamp 1907).

SIYEH Creek (Mont., Glacier Co.). Perhaps a shortening of Blackfoot (Algonquian) /saayiiwa/ 'is rabid; one who is rabid', from /saayii/ 'be rabid' (Holterman 1985; D. Franz p.c.).

SKADULGWAS Peak (Wash., Skagit Co.). Probably from an unidentified Salishan language (BGN 8804).

SKAGIT County (Wash.) \skaj´ it\. The Lushootseed (Salishan) name is /sqádžət/, referring to a Southern Coast Salishan subgroup (Hitchman 1985; *HNAI* 7:487). The name also occurs in Ore. (Douglas Co.).

SKAGUL Island (Alaska, Gareloi Island B-2). From the Aleut placename *sxaĝulax̂* (Bergsland 1994).

SKAGWAY (Alaska, Skagway B-1) \skag´ wā\. The Tlingit name was first recorded in 1883 as <Schkague> (Orth 1967). The name is also found in Ore. (Grant Co.) and Wash. (Whatcom Co.).

SKAKET Beach (Mass., Barnstable Co.). From SNEng. Algonquian, perhaps meaning 'at the fishing place' (Huden 1962).

SKALABATS Creek (Wash., Snohomish Co.). Perhaps from a Lushootseed (Salishan) placename (D. Kinkade p.c.).

SKAMANIA County (Wash.) \skə mā´ nē ə\. From Cascades Chinook /sk'mániak/ 'obstructed' (D. Kinkade p.c.).

SKAMOKAWA (Wash., Wahkiakum Co.) \skə mok´ ə wā, skə mok´ ə wä\. From the Kathlamet (Chinookan) placename [sqəmáq^{w}əyə], sometimes said to mean 'smoke on the water' (Hitchman 1985; D. Kinkade p.c.). The name also occurs in Ore. (Clatsop Co.).

SKANAWAN Creek (Wis., Lincoln Co.) \skā´ nə wän\. Perhaps from Ojibwa (Algonquian) *oshkinawe* 'young man' (Vogel 1991; Nichols and Nyholm 1995). A related placename is **Skinaway Lake** (Wis., Barron Co.).

SKAN Bay (Alaska, Unalaska B-4). From the Aleut placename *sxaanan* (Bergsland 1994).

SKANEATELES (N.Y., Onondaga Co.) \sken ē at´ ə lēz, sken ē at´ ləs\. This is 'long lake', in Oneida (Iroquoian) *skanyátales* 'long lake', conaining *-nyatal-* 'lake' (Beauchamp 1990; M. Mithun p.c.).

SKANNATATI, Lake (N.Y., Orange Co.). Said to be a Mohawk (Iroquoian) term for the Hudson River, also written <Skanetade> (Grumet 1981).

SKANNAYUTENATE (N.Y., Seneca Co.). From an Iroquoian language, said to mean 'on the other side of the lake' (Beauchamp 1907); cf. Mohawk *kanyá:tareh* 'lake', *skanyá:tara'* 'one lake' (Kanatawakhon-Maracle 2001).

SKANODARIO (N.Y., Niagara Co.). Said to be from Mohawk (Iroquoian), meaning 'beautiful lake' (Beauchamp 1907); cf. *yóhskats* 'beautiful', *kanyá:təreh* 'lake' (Kanatawakhon-Maracle 2001).

SKANONDAGA Heights (N.Y., Onondaga Co.). Probably from an unidentified Iroquoian language (Beauchamp 1907).

SKATE Creek (Wash., Lewis Co.) \skāt\. From the Sahaptin placename [č'qé:t, čqé:t], of unknown etymology (D. Kinkade p.c.).

SKATUTAKEE (N.H., Cheshire Co.) \skə to͞o´ tə kē\. From Abenaki (Algonquian), perhaps referring to fire (Huden 1962); cf. *skweda* 'fire', *-aki* 'land' (Day 1994–95).

SKEDEE (Okla., Pawnee Co.) \skid´ ē, ski dē´, skē´ dē\. Named for the <Skidi> band of the Pawnee (Caddoan) people (Shirk 1974). The related placename **Skeedee** occurs in Neb. (Nance Co.).

SKEENAH Creek (N.C., Macon Co.) \skē´ nə\. From Cherokee (Iroquoian) *asgina* 'demon, devil' (Powell 1968; Feeling 1975). The name also occurs in Ga. (Fannin Co.).

SKEGEMOG Lake (Mich., Kalkaska Co.). Perhaps from an Algonquian source, but the language has not been identified (Vogel 1986).

SKELL Head (Ore., Klamath Co.) \skel\. From Klamath /sqel/ 'Old Marten', a mythic character (McArthur 1992; Barker 1963).

SKIATOOK (Okla., Osage Co.) \skī´ ə to͞ok\. Named for <Skiatooka>, an Osage (Siouan) leader (Shirk 1974).

SKIDAWAY Island (Ga., Chatham Co.) skid´ ə wā\. The placename, apparently a folk-etymology, is said to be from Yamacraw, a little-known Indian language (Krakow 1975).

SKIHI Creek (Alaska, Talkeetna D-1). Perhaps an Ahtna (Athabaskan) name, published in 1940 (Orth 1967).

SKILAK Lake (Alaska, Kenai B-1). From Dena'ina (Athabaskan) *sqilant* 'ridge place' (*HNAI* 6:639).

SKILLIKALIA Bayou (Miss., Warren Co.) \skil´ ə kal ē\. From Choctaw (Muskogean), perhaps representing *shilaklak aay-aala* 'geese get here', or *shikalilli* 'small white beads', or *shikkiliklik, sikkiliklik* 'sparrow-hawk' (Seale 1939; P. Munro p.c.).

SKIMO Creek (Alaska, Chandler Lake B-4). A shortening of the word **Eskimo** (Orth 1967).

SKINAWAY Lake (Wis., Barron Co.) \skin´ ə wā\. Probably from Ojibwa (Algonquian) *oshkinawe* 'young man' (Vogel 1991; Nichols and Nyholm 1995). A related placename is **Skanawan Creek** (Wis., Lincoln Co.).

SKINEQUIT Pond (Mass., Barnstable Co.). From SNEng. Algonquian, perhaps meaning 'at the salmon fishing place' (Huden 1962).

SKIOU Point (Wash., Snohomish Co.). Said to be from an Indian word meaning 'dead body', language not identified (Hitchman 1985). Probably related is **Skiyou Island** (Wash., Skagit Co.).

SKIPANON River (Ore., Clatsop Co.) \skip´ ə nun, skip´ ə non\. From the Clatsop (Chinookan) village name /sqipanáwunx/ (D. Kinkade p.c.). A variant is **Skipannon.**

SKIPPACK (Pa., Montgomery Co.) \skip´ ek\. Perhaps from Delaware (Algonquian), of unclear derivation (Donehoo 1928).

SKITACOOK Lake (Maine, Aroostook Co.) \skit´ ə ko͞ok\. From Abenaki (Algonquian), perhaps meaning 'dead water' (Huden 1962).

SKITCHEWAUG (Vt., Windsor Co.). Probably from Abenaki (Algonquian), perhaps meaning 'big mountain' (Huden 1962).

SKITTOK (Alaska, Kenai C-4). From Dena'ina (Athabaskan) *shk'ituk't* 'where we slide down' (Kari and Kari 1982:31).

SKITWISH Creek (Idaho, Kootenai Co.) \skit´ wish\. From a name applied to the Coeur d'Alene Indians (Salishan) by other Salishan peoples, perhaps meaning 'the discovered people'; cf. Moses-Columbian /skícəʔəx^{W}/ (*HNAI* 12:325; D. Kinkade p.c.).

SKIUMAH Creek (Mont., Flathead Co.). Said to be from Kutenai /sq'umu/ 'service-berry' (Holterman 1985).

SKIYOU Island (Wash., Skagit Co.). Probably related to **Skiou Point** (Wash., Snohomish Co.); see above.

SKOI-YASE (N.Y., Seneca Co.). Earlier written <Schoyerre, Scawyace, Shaiyus>, from an Iroquoian language, perhaps meaning 'long falls' (Beauchamp 1907).

SKOKIE (Ill., Cook Co.) \skō´ kē\. Perhaps a shortening of Potawatomi (Algonquian) <Kitchi-wâp´chkôkú> 'great marsh' (Vogel 1963); cf. Ojibwa *miishkooki* 'marsh' (Rhodes 1985). A possibly related term is **Muskeg.**

SKOKOMISH River (Wash., Mason Co.) \skō kō´ mish\. From the name of a Southern Coast Salishan subgroup, Twana /sqʷuqʷóʔbəš/ 'river people', containing /qʷúʔ/ 'water' (*HNAI* 7:488; D. Kinkade p.c.).

SKOKSONAK (Ariz., Pima Co.). O'odham (Piman) *skoksonag* 'full of woodrats', containing *ksona* 'woodrat' (J. Hill p.c.).

SKOLAI Pass (Alaska, McCarthy C-3). The name is said to represent an Upper Tanana (Athabaskan) version of the Russian personal name *Nikolai* (Orth 1967).

SKOOKOLEEL (Mont., Flathead Co.). Perhaps from a Flathead (Salishan) placename, but the derivation is not clear (Cheney 1984).

SKOOKUM Creek (Ore., Clatsop Co.) \skōō´ kəm\. Chinook Jargon <skookum, skoo´-koom> [skúkəm] 'strong, powerful; supernaturally dangerous', from Lower Chehalis (Salishan) /skʷəkʷúm/ 'devil, anything evil' (McArthur 1992; D. Kinkade p.c.). The placename **Skookum** also occurs in Alaska (Nabesna A-2), Wash. (Pierce Co.) and Idaho (Kootenai Co.), and as a transfer name in Mich. (Lake Co.). A related placename is **Skukum** (Alaska, Eagle A-1). The derived placename **Skookum Chuck Creek** (Ore., Baker Co.) \skōō´ kəm chuk\ is from Chinook Jargon, meaning 'powerful water', from **Chuck** (D. Kinkade p.c.); the name also occurs in Alaska (Craig D-4), Idaho (Idaho Co.), Wash. (Thurston Co.), and as a transfer name in far-away N.H. (Grafton Co.). The placename **Skookum Puss Mountain** (Wash., Chelan Co.) reflects a Chinook Jargon word for 'cougar', lit. 'strong cat', from Eng. *puss* (D. Kinkade p.c.). The placename **Skookumhouse Butte** (Ore., Curry Co.) represents a Chinook Jargon word for 'fort, jail' (McArthur 1992; D. Kinkade p.c.).

SKOOKWAMS Creek (N.Y., Suffolk Co.). Earlier written <Skook-quams, Schook-waumes>; from SNEng. Algonquian, perhaps meaning 'snake neck' (Tooker 1911).

SKOOTENAY (Wash., Franklin Co.). A variant of **Scooteney Reservoir**; see above.

SKOOTS Creek (Utah, Iron Co.) \skōōts\. From Southern Paiute (Numic) /sikkutsi/ 'squirrel' (J. McLaughlin).

SKOWHEGAN (Maine, Somerset Co.). From Abenaki (Algonquian), perhaps meaning 'a fish-spearing place' (Huden 1962).

SKOWL Arm (Alaska, Craig B-2). From Tlingit <sqaoal>, the name of a local leader (Orth 1967).

SKUG River (Mass., Essex Co.). Probably from SNEng. Algonquian <askook> 'snake' (Huden 1962; Trumbull 1903).

SKUKUM (Alaska, Eagle A-1). From Chinook Jargon <skookum> 'powerful'; see **Skookum Creek**, above.

SKULL Cliff (Alaska, Meade River D-3). Said to be a translation of an Iñupiaq (Eskimo) placename (Orth 1967). Elsewhere, **Skull Creek** (Alaska, McCarthy B-8) corresponds to Ahtna (Athabaskan) *netsits'ene' na',* lit. 'our-skull creek' (J. Kari p.c.). Again, **Skull Butte** (S.Dak., Corson Co.) corresponds to Lakhota (Siouan) <paha pahupi> 'hill of the skull' (Sneve 1973); cf. *pahá^* 'hill', *phahú* 'skull' (Ingham 2001).

SKULLYVILLE (Okla., Le Flore Co.) \skul´ ē vil\. From Choctaw (Muskogean), said to mean 'money town' (Shirk 1974); cf. *iskali, skali* 'a bit (12½ cents), a dime; money', perhaps from French *escalin* 'shilling' (P. Munro p.c.).

SKUMPAH Creek (Utah, Sevier Co.) \skōōm´ pä\. From Southern Paiute (Numic) /sikkumpɨ/ 'rabbitbrush' (J. McLaughlin p.c.). A related placename is **Skutumpah Creek**; see below.

SKUNGAMAUG River (Conn., Tolland Co.). Also written <Skunkamug>; from SNE Algonquian, said to mean 'eel fishing here' (Trumbull 1881; Huden 1962).

SKUNK. The name of this native American mammal is from Massachusett (SNEng. Algonquian), derived from Proto-Algonquian */šeka:kwa/, from */šek-/ 'to urinate' plus */-a:kw/ 'fox' (*RHD* 1987). As a placename, the term is widespread in the United States (e.g., Mass., Hampden Co.; Iowa, Monona Co.; and Mich., Rusk Co.).

SKUTHAZIS (Maine, Penobscot Co.). Also written <Escutossis, Skutahzis> (etc.); probably contains Eastern Abenaki (Algonquian) <skoo´tam> 'trout' (Eckstorm 1941); cf. Western Abenaki *skotam* 'trout' (Day 1994–95).

SKUTUMPAH Creek (Utah, Sevier Co.) \skōō´ təm pä\. From Southern Paiute (Numic) /sikku-tɨmpaya/ 'rabbitbrush canyon-mouth', containing /sikkumpɨ/ 'rabbitbrush' and /tɨmpaya/ 'canyon mouth' (J. McLaughlin p.c.). A related placename is **Skumpah Creek**; see above.

SKWA-KWE-I (Wash., Jefferson Co.). From the Clallam (Salishan) placename /sq'ʷaq'ʷéʔyəɬ, sq'ʷaq'ʷíʔiɬ/ (D. Kinkade p.c.).

SKWENTNA (Alaska, Tyonek D-4) \skwent´ nə\. Dena'ina (Athabaksan) *shqitnu,* possibly 'sloping-ridge stream', containing *-tnu* 'stream' (Kari and Fall 1987:119).

SKYCO (N.C., Dare Co.). Said to be named for a member of the Choanoke (CAC Algonquian) people (Payne 1985).

SKYKOMISH (Wash., King Co.). From Northern Lushootseed (Salishan) /sq'íxʷəbš/ 'upriver people', from /q'íxʷ/ 'upstream', the name of a Southern Coast Salishan group (D. Kinkade p.c.). The name shows the alternation of *m* with *b* that is characteristic in the Puget Sound area.

SKYMO Creek (Wash., Whatcom Co.). Perhaps a Lushootseed (Southern Coast Salishan) placename (D. Kinkade p.c.).

SKYO Mountain (Wash., Lewis Co.). Sahaptin /tiskáya/ 'Skunk (in myths)', from /tiskáy/ 'skunk' and /-ya/ 'honorific' (Hitchman 1985; D. Kinkade p.c.).

SKYUKA Creek (N.C., Polk Co.). Said to be named for the son of a Cherokee (Iroquoian) leader (Powell 1968). The name also occurs in Ga. (Dade Co.).

SLANA (Alaska, Nabesna C-6) \slan´ ə\. Ahtna (Athabaskan) *stl'aa na'* 'rear river'; cf. *tl'aa* 'rear, bottom, headwaters', *na'* 'stream' (Kari 1990).

SLATHTOUKA Creek (Alaska, Hughes A-1). The Koyukon (Athabaskan) name, recorded in 1956, is said to mean 'trapping' (Orth 1967).

SLATKA Creek (Alaska, McCarthy C-8). The Ahtna (Athabaskan) name was reported in 1900 (Orth 1967).

SLEEPING BEAR Dunes (Mich., Leelanau Co.). Corresponds to an earlier French name, *l'ours qui dort* 'the bear that sleeps' and supposedly to an Indian name, perhaps in the Ojibwa (Algonquian) language (Vogel 1986).

SLEEPING DUCK Rock (Ariz., Apache Co.). A translation of Navajo *tsé naal'eełí sitíní* 'lying-down duck rock', containing *tsé* 'rock' and *naal'eełí* 'duck, goose' (Linford 2000; Young and Morgan 1987).

SLEEPY EYE (Minn., Brown Co.). Named for a Dakota (Siouan) leader, <Ish-tak-ha-ba>; cf. *ištá* 'eye', *ȟba* 'sleepy' (Sneve 1973; Riggs 1890).

SLEETMUTE (Alaska, Sleetmute C-4) \slēt´ myōōt\. Represents the Yupik (Eskimo) placename *cellitemiut,* perhaps meaning 'whetstone people', containing *celli-* 'to whet, to sharpen' and *-miut* 'people' (Orth 1967; Jacobson 1984).

SLEITAT Mountain (Alaska, Taylor Mountains A-3). The Yupik (Eskimo) name is said to mean 'whetstone' (Orth 1967); cf. *cellin* 'whetstone' (Jacobson 1984).

SLICKPOO (Idaho, Lewis Co.) \slik´ pōō\. This was named for Josué Slickpoo, a Nez Perce (Sahaptian) leader; his Native American name has been written as <Zimcklixpusse> (Boone 1988).

SLIDING OFF Rock (Ariz., Apache Co.). Corresponds to Navajo (Athabaskan) *tsé naashzhoojí* 'sliding-off rock', containing *tsé* 'rock' (Linford 2000).

SLIDING ROCK Ruins (Ariz., Apache Co.). A translation of Navajo (Athabaskan) *kin náázhoozhí* 'the house that slid down', containing *kin* 'house, building' and *náázhoozh* 'it slid down' (Wilson 1995).

SLIKOK Creek (Alaska, Kenai B-3). Dena'ina (Athabaskan) *shla kaq* 'little mouth' (Kari and Kari 1982:31).

SLIM Buttes (S.Dak., Harding Co.). Corresponds to Lakhota (Siouan) <cistalahanska> 'slim, thin' in a vertical sense (Sneve 1973); cf. *cístila* 'small', *hą́ska* 'be long' (Ingham 2001).

SLIPPERY ROCK (Pa., Lawrence Co.). Said to be from Delaware (Algonquian) <Weschachachapochka> 'slippery rock', containing <w'schacheu> 'slippery' (Donehoo 1928); cf. Munsee Delaware *wsháaxsuw* 'slippery' (O'Meara 1996).

SLO DUC (Alaska, Petersburg D-6). Perhaps a transfer and misspelling of the placename **Sol Duc River** (Wash., Clallam Co.).

SLOKHENJIKH Creek (Alaska, Tanana D-6). The Koyukon (Athabaskan) name was recorded in 1956 (Orth 1967).

SLUISKIN Falls (Wash., Pierce Co.). Named for an Indian guide, language not identified (Hitchman 1985).

SLUP-PUKS (Wash., Snohomish Co.). From the Lushootseed (Salishan) placename /sɬə́p'qs/, containing /-ɬə́p'-/ 'hang over (as clothes thrown over a line)' and /-qs/ 'nose, point' (D. Kinkade p.c.).

SNAHAPISH River (Wash., Jefferson Co.). Said to have been named for a subgroup of the Quinault (Salishan) Indians (Hitchman 1985).

SNAKE Butte (S.Dak., Hughes Co.). A translation of the Dakota (Siouan) name, from *pahá* 'hill, butte' and *zuzéča* 'snake' (Sneve 1973; Riggs 1890). Elsewhere, the placename **Snake Creek** (S.Dak., Ziebach Co.) corresponds to Lakhota (Siouan) *sįtéȟla* 'rattlesnake' (Sneve 1973; Ingham 2001). The well-known **Snake River** (Wyo., Idaho, Ore., Wash.) is named after the Indians called the **Snakes,** corresponding to French *Les Serpents*; the term was applied by whites to various groups of the Shoshoni (Numic) people. A number of Plains peoples referred to the Shoshonis by terms meaning 'snake people', such as Lakhota (Siouan) *zuzéča wičháša* (*HNAI* 11:334). Another **Snake River** (Minn., Marshall Co.) represents a translation from Ojibwa (Algonquian) <ginebigo zibi>; cf. *ginebig* 'snake', *ziibi* 'snake' (Nichols and Nyholm 1995).

SNASS Creek (Wash., Skamania Co.). From Chinook Jargon <snass, snas> [snæs, snas] 'rain', of unknown origin (D. Kinkade p.c.).

SNATELUM Point (Wash., Island Co.). Named for /sníƛ'əm/, a Lushootseed (Salishan) man also called Long Charlie (Hitchman 1985; D. Kinkade).

SNEE-OOSH Point (Wash., Skagit Co.) \snē´ ōsh\. The name of a Swinomish (Salishan) village (Hitchman 1985).

SNIPATUIT Brook (Mass., Plymouth Co.). From SNE, said to mean 'log palisade' (Huden 1962).

SNOHOMISH County (Wash., Snohomish Co.) \snō hō´ mish\. From Lushootseed (Salishan) /sduhúbš/, the name of a Southern Coast Salish subgroup (Hitchman 1985; *HNAI* 7:487). The alternation of *m* and *b* is characteristic of Native American languages in the Puget Sound area. The name **Snohomish** also occurs in Alaska (Mt. McKinley D-6).

SNOQUALMIE (Wash., King Co.) \snō kwäl´ mē\. From Lushootseed (Salishan) /sduk^{w}álbix^{w}/, the name of a Southern Coast Salish subgroup, perhaps from /duk^{w}(u)-/ 'to change, transform' (Hitchman 1985; D. Kinkade p.c.). Note that *n* and *d* interchange in the Puget Sound languages.

SNOQUERA (Wash., Pierce Co.) Perhaps an artificial name based on **Snoqualmie;** see above.

SNOWSHOE Lake (Wis., Polk Co.). The snowshoe was an invention of Indians who inhabited northern regions; some placenames that include the word may have been translations of Native American terms such as Ojibwa (Algonquian) *aagim* (Vogel 1991; Nichols and Nyholm 1995). The placename **Snowshoe** also occurs in other states (e.g., Mich., Keweenaw Co.; Colo., Gunnison Co.; and Alaska, Nome C-2).

SNOWSNAKE Mountain (Mich., Clare Co.). The term refers to a game played by American Indians, in which players propel a long straight stick over snow or ice, to see whose stick will go the farthest (Vogel 1986).

SOAKPAK Mountain (Alaska, Chandler Lake A-4). Named for an Iñupiaq (Eskimo) man (Orth 1967).

SO-BAHLI-ALHI Glacier (Wash., Snohomish Co.). Probably from an unidentified Salishan language (Hitchman 1985).

SOBOBA (Calif., Riverside Co.) \sə bō´ bə\. From a Gabrielino (Takic) placename *shovóvanga,* perhaps related to Luiseño /ṣuvó-ya/ 'be cold', /ṣuvóo-wut/ 'winter' (Gudde 1998).

SOBOLA (Miss., Calhoun Co.). A variant of **Sabougla**; see above.

SOCAPATOY (Ala., Coosa Co.) \sok ə pə toi´\. From Muskogee <Sakapatayi>, a village name (Read 1984).

SOCASTEE (S.C., Horry Co.) \sok´ əs tē\. Perhaps from an unidentified Indian language, meaning 'house' (Pickens 1961–62:22); a possibly related name is **Soccee Swamp** (S.C., Florence Co.).

SOCATEAN Bay (Maine, Piscataquis Co.). From Abenaki (Algonquian), perhaps meaning 'divided into two parts' (Huden 1962).

SOCCEE Swamp (S.C., Florence Co.). Perhaps from an unidentified Indian language, meaning 'house' (Pickens 1961–62:22); a possibly related name is **Socastee** (S.C., Horry Co.).

SOCKANOSSET (R.I., Providence Co.). Named for a Narraganssett (SNE Algonquian) leader (Huden 1962).

SOCKEYE Creek (Alaska, Ketchikan A-3) \sok´ ī\. Named for a type of salmon; the term is from /sθə́qə'y/ in the Halkomelem (Salishan) language of Wash. (*RHD* 1987). The placename also occurs in Idaho (Custer Co.) and Minn. (Becker Co.).

SOCKOROCKETS Ditch (Del., Sussex Co.). Probably named for a Delaware (Algonquian) leader of the seventeenth century (Heck et al. 1966).

SOCKS Island (Maine, Penobscot Co.) \soks\. This represents the possessive, "Sock's Island." The term is from Abenaki (Algonquian), named for an eighteenth-century Indian resident and is a modification of French *Jacques* (Eckstorm 1941:39).

SOCO Falls (N.C., Jackson Co.). Perhaps from Cherokee (Iroquoian) *sagwu* 'one' (Powell 1968; Feeling 1975).

SOCOHACHEE Creek (Ga., Randolph Co.) \sō kə hach´ ē\. Perhaps from Muskogee, meaning 'hog stream', from *sukhv* /sókha/ 'hog' plus *hvcce* /háčči/ 'stream' (Read 1949–50; Martin and Mauldin 2000).

SOCTAHOMA Creek (Miss., Chickasaw Co.) \sok tə hō´ mə\. Choctaw (Muskogean), meaning 'red bluff', from *saktih* 'bank of a stream, bluff' and *homma* 'red' (Seale 1939; P. Munro p.c.). A related name is **Soctum Creek** (Ala., Sumter Co.).

SOCTISH Creek (Calif., Humboldt Co.) \sok´ tish\. Named for a Hupa (Athabaskan) family; said to be from *sawhjich* 'I put (seeds, granular substance) into my mouth' (Gudde 1998).

SOCTUM Creek (Ala., Sumter Co.) \sok´ təm\. Shortened from Choctaw (Muskogean) *saktih* 'bank of a stream, bluff' plus *homma* 'red' (Read 1984; P. Munro p.c.); a related placename is **Soctahoma Creek** (Miss., Chickasaw Co.).

SODA Lake (La., Caddo Par.) \sō´ də\. Earlier written <Sheodo, Sodo>; from the Caddo language (Read 1927). As a placename in the western states, **Soda** is more likely to refer to bubbling springs or to alkaline lakebeds.

SODUS (N.Y., Wayne Co.) \sō´ dəs\. Earlier written <Aserotus>; perhaps from an Iroquoian language, but the derivation is not clear. **Sodus** also occurs as a transfer in Mich. (Berrien Co.) and Minn. (Lyon Co.).

SOFKA (Okla., Creek Co.) \sof´ kə\. Perhaps shortened from *hvcce-sofke,* a tribal town; this apparently consists of *hvcce* /háčči/ 'river' plus *osafke, safke* /sá:fki/ 'sofkee, sofkey, a type of corn gruel' (Shirk 1974; Martin and Mauldin 2000). The related name **Sofkahatchee** (Ala., Elmore Co.) is apparently an inversion of the elements in the Muskogee name (Read 1984). The placename **Sofkee** (Ga., Bibb Co.) was probably shortened from some such compound of the Muskogee word for corn gruel (Goff 1975; Martin and Mauldin 2000). A related placename is **Tobesofkee** (Ga., Bibb Co.).

SOFTUK Bar (Alaska, Cordova A-2). The Alutiiq (Eskimo) name was reported in 1903 (Orth 1967).

SOGONOSH Valley (Mich., Emmet Co.) \sog´ ə nosh\. From Ojibwa (Algonquian) *zhaaganaash* 'Englishman' (Vogel 1986; Nichols and Nyholm 1995). A related placename is **Sauganash** (Ill., Cook Co.).

SOHU Park (Ariz., Maricopa Co.). From Hopi (Uto-Aztecan) *soohu* 'star' (K. Hill p.c.).

SOKKWI'A (N.Mex., Cibola Co.). This is the name of a Zuni campsite (Ferguson and Hart 1985).

SOKOKIS Brook (N.H., Coös Co.). From the plural or possessive of **Sokoki,** a Western Abenaki (Algonquian) group, from their own name *ozokwaki,* plural *ozokwakiak* 'the ones who broke up, broke away' (*HNAI* 15:159). A perhaps related placename is **Lake Sokokis** (Maine, York Co.).

SOLDIER Creek (Ill., Iroquois Co.). Named for a nineteenth-century Potawatomi (Algonquian) leader; his Native American name was /šəmakənəš/ 'soldier' (Vogel 1963). In areas occupied by Siouan peoples, the English word *soldier* often refers to the Native American "hunt police" or members of a military society; this often turns up both in personal names and in placenames; an example is **Soldier Creek** in S.Dak. (Buffalo Co.), reflecting Lakhota (Siouan) *akíčhita* 'soldier' (Sneve 1973; J. Koontz p.c.).

SOLDOTNA (Alaska, Kenai B-3) \sōl dot´ nə\. From Dena'ina (Athabaskan) *ts'eldatnu* 'trickles-down creek' (Orth 1967; Kari and Kari 1982).

SOL DUC River (Wash., Clallam Co.) \sōl´ duk\. From Quileute /só:liłt'aq^{W}/, the name of the **Sol Duc River** (D. Kinkade p.c.). An alternative spelling is **Soleduck.** A possibly related name is **Slo Duc** (Alaska, Petersburg D-6).

SOLGOHACHIA (Ark., Conway Co.). Probably named for **Sougahatchee Creek** (Ala., Tallapoosa Co.), a Muskogee village; from *svokv* /sáwka/ 'a rattle' plus *hvcce* /háčči/ 'stream' (Dickinson 1995; Martin and Mauldin 2000).

SOLIVIK Island (Alaska, Wainwright A-6). The Iñupiaq (Eskimo) name is probably *sulivik* 'sewing place' (L. Kaplan p.c.).

SOLLEKS Creek (Wash., Chelan Co.) \sol´ əks\. Chinook Jargon <saleks, sul-luks, salux, sa´lix> [sáləks, sóləks, sə́ləks] 'fight, anger, hate'; origin unknown (Hitchman 1985; D. Kinkade p.c.).

SOLOLA Valley (N.C., Swain Co.) \sə lō´ lə\. From Cherokee (Iroquoian) *saloli* 'squirrel' (Feeling 1975).

SOLOMAN Butte (Ore., Klamath Co.). Named for Sam Soloman Lalakes, a Klamath Indian (McArthur 1992).

SOLSMUNKET Lake (Alaska, Shungnak A-10). The Koyukon (Athabaskan) name was reported in 1952 (Orth 1967).

SOLUKA Creek (Alaska, Mt. Katmai A-3). The Alutiiq (Eskimo) name was reported in 1898 (Orth 1967).

SOMIS (Calif., Ventura Co.) \sō´ mis\. The name of a Ventureño (Chumashan) village (Gudde 1998).

SOMONAUK (Ill., Fulton Co.) \som´ ə näk, sam´ ə näk\. Probably from <As-sim-in-eh-kon>, a Potawatomi (Algonquian) village, lit. 'paw-paw grove', referring to a native fruit tree (Vogel 1963); cf. Ojibwa (Algonquian) <as-seme-nun> 'paw-paw'.

SONGO Lock (Maine, Cumberland Co.). Perhaps from Abenaki (Algonquian), meaning 'the outlet' (Rutherford 1970).

SONIELEM (Mont., Lake Co.). Also written <Sinyalemin>; from Flathead (Salishan) (D. Kinkade p.c.).

SONOITA (Ariz., Santa Cruz Co.) \sō noi´ tə, sə noi´ tə\. O'odham (Piman) *ṣon 'oidag* 'spring field', from *ṣon* 'a spring' plus *'oidag* 'field' (J. Hill p.c.). The related form **Sonoyta Mountains** also occurs (Ariz., Pima Co.).

SONOMA County (Calif.) \sə nō´ mə\. Apparently from the name of an Indian group called <sonomas> or <sonomi>, of unclear origin (Gudde 1998). The placename **Sonoma** also occurs in Mich. (Calhoun Co.).

SONORA (Calif., Tuolumne Co.) \sə nôr´ ə\. Named for the state in northwestern Mexico, which in turn perhaps got its name from an Ópata (Sonoran) word. The placename **Sonora** also occurs in Alaska (Nome C-2), Ariz. (Pinal Co.), Calif. (Tuolumne Co.), and elsewhere.

SONOYTA Mountains (Ariz., Pima Co.) \sə noi´ tə\. Probably from the same source as **Sonoita** (Ariz., Santa Cruz Co.); see above.

SONSELA Buttes (Ariz., Apache Co.) \sun sel´ ə\. Navajo (Athabaskan) *sǫ' silá* 'a pair of sitting stars', from *sǫ'* 'star' and *silá* 'they two sit' (Granger 1983; Wilson 1995). A variant is **Sunsela Saddle.**

SONYAKAY Ridge (Alaska, Sitka D-3). The Tlingit name was reported in 1951 (Orth 1967).

SONYEA (N.Y., Livingston Co.) \son´yā, sōn´ yā\. Perhaps from an Iroquoian language, but the derivation is not clear (Beauchamp 1907).

SOOES (Wash., Clallam Co.). From the Makah (Nootkan) placename /c'u:yas/ 'hole dug in the ground' (W. Jacobsen).

SOOGHMEGHAT (Alaska, St. Lawrence B-1). The Yupik (Eskimo) name was published in 1948 (Orth 1967).

SOOKATONCHIE (Miss., Clay Co.) \so͞o kə tôn´ chē\. Choctaw (Muskogean) *shukha-tąchi,* lit. 'hog corn' (i.e., beech mast prized as food for hogs), from *shukha* 'pig' and *tąchi* 'corn' (Seale 1939; P. Munro p.c.). A related placename is **Chuquatonchee Creek** (Miss., Chickasaw Co.).

SOOMAGHAT Mountain (Alaska, St. Lawrence B-1). The Yupik (Eskimo) name was reported in 1949 (Orth 1967).

SOONAKAKAT River (Alaska, Nulato C-5). The Koyukon (Athabaskan) name was published in 1898 as <Junekaket> (Orth 1967); cf. *-kaakk'et* 'mouth of stream' (Jetté and Jones 2000). A variant is **Soonkakat River.**

SOONGLAGHAK Creek (Alaska, St. Lawrence B-0). The Yupik (Eskimo) name was reported in 1932 (Orth 1967).

SOONKAKAT River (Alaska, Nulato C-5). A variant of **Soonakakat River**; see above.

SOOSAP Peak (Ore., Clackamas Co.) \so͞o´ sap\. Named for a local Indian whose English name was Joe Suisap, perhaps from an Indian pronunciation of *Joseph* (McArthur 1992; D. Kinkade p.c.).

SOOS Creek (Wash., Lewis Co.). Probably from a Salishan language.

SOPCHOPPY (Fla., Wakulla Co.). From Muskogee *lakcvpe* /lakčapí/ 'oak tree', from *lakcv* /lákča/ 'acorn' and *vpe* /apí/ 'tree' (Read 1934; Martin and Mauldin 2000).

SOPORI Wash (Ariz., Santa Cruz Co.). Perhaps from <Sobaipuri>, the name of an O'odham (Piman) subgroup (Granger 1983; *HNAI* 10:319).

SOQUEE River (Ga., Habersham Co.). From Cherokee (Iroquoian) <Sakwiyi>, a village name (Krakow 1975).

SOQUEL (Calif., Santa Cruz Co.) \sō kel´\. From a Costanoan language, perhaps meaning 'willow' or 'laurel' (Gudde 1998).

SOTOYOME (Calif., Sonoma Co.). Perhaps a Lake Miwok village name, containing <soto>, the name of an Indian leader, and /yomi/ 'village' (Gudde 1998).

SOUADABSCOOK Stream (Maine, Penobscot Co.). Probably from Abenaki (Algonquian), but the derivation is not clear.

SOUBUNGE Mountain (Maine, Piscataquis Co.). Also written <Sowbungy>; probably from Abenaki (Algonquian), but of unclear derivation (BGN 6902).

SOUCOOK River (N.H., Merrimack Co.) \sōō´ kŏŏk, sou´ kŏŏk\. Perhaps from Abenaki (Algonquian), meaning 'rocky place' (Huden 1962).

SOUENLOVIE Creek (Miss., Clarke Co.) \sōō in luv´ ē\. Perhaps from Choctaw (Muskogean) *halǫlabi* 'bullfrog' 'bullfrog' (Seale 1939; P. Munro p.c.).

SOUGAHATCHEE Creek (Ala., Tallapoosa Co.) \sô gə hach´ ē\. From Muskogee *svokv* /sáwka/ 'a rattle' plus *hvcce* /háčči/ 'stream' (Dickinson 1995; Martin and Mauldin 2000). A related placename is **Solgohachia** (Ark., Conway Co.).

SOUHEGAN River (N.H., Hillsboro Co.) \sōō hē´ gən, sou hē´ gən\. Also written <Souheganock>; perhaps Abenaki (Algonquian) for 'watching place; still-water fishing' (Huden 1962).

SOULAJULLE (Calif., Marin Co.) \sōō lə hōō´ lē\. Probably from Coast Miwok /sówlas/ 'laurel' and /húyye/ 'promontory' (Gudde 1998). The spelling **Soulajoule** also occurs.

SOUWILPA (Ala., Choctaw Co.) \sōō wil´ pə\. Perhaps from Choctaw, meaning 'where raccoons are killed', containing *shawi* 'raccoon' and *albi* 'to be killed' (Read 1984; P. Munro p.c.).

SOVWALK Creek (Alaska, St. Lawrence D-3). The Yupik (Eskimo) name was reported in 1949 (Orth 1967).

SOWATS Canyon (Ariz., Coconino Co.). Said to be from Southern Paiute (Numic) <showap> 'tobacco' (Granger 1983), but this has not been confirmed.

SOWHATCHEE (Ga., Early Co.) \sou hach´ ē\. Perhaps from Hitchiti (Muskogean) /sawi/ 'raccoon' and /hahči/ 'creek' (Read 1949–50); or from Muskogee *osa-hacce* /osa:-háčči/, lit. 'pokeweed stream' (Martin and Mauldin 2000). Possibly related placenames include **Sawhatchee** (Ga., Early Co.), **Souwilpa** (Ala., Choctaw Co.), and **Ossahatchie** (Ga., Harris Co.).

SOWISH Lake (Maine, Aroostook Co.). Probably from Abenaki (Algonquian), perhaps meaning 'sluggish' (Rutherford 1970).

SOZAVARIKA Island (Alaska, False Pass D-2). The Aleut name was assigned in 1916 (Orth 1967).

SPAK Point (Wash., Clallam Co.). Probably from Chinook Jargon <spāk, spo´oh, spo´eh, spock> [spuk, spak] 'blue, gray, pale', probably from Lower Chinook [špeq] 'gray' (Hitchman 1985; D. Kinkade p.c.).

SPANAWAY (Wash., Pierce Co.). Perhaps from an Indian placename <Spannuch> 'on the shore of the lake', language not identified (Hitchman 1985).

SPANISH Trail (Ariz., Apache Co.). Navajo (Athabaskan) *naakaii adáánání ha'atiin* 'where Spaniards descended trail-up-out', containing *naakai* 'Spaniard, Mexican' (Linford 2000).

SPEARFISH (S.Dak., Lawrence Co.). A translation of Lakhota (Siouan) <ho-wohukeza>, literally 'fish-spear' (Sneve 1973); cf. *ho(ǧą́)* 'fish' and *wahúkheza* 'spear', (Sneve 1973; Ingham 2001).

SPEDIS (Wash., Klickitat Co.). Named for Bill Spedis, a Wishram (Chinookan) resident (Hitchman 1985).

SPEDNIC Falls (Maine, Washington Co.) \sped´ nik\. From Abenaki (Algonquian), perhaps meaning 'visible, but shut in by mountains' (Huden 1962).

SPEE-BI-DAH (Wash., Snohomish Co.). The Lushootseed (Salishan) placename is from /sbíbədaʔ/ 'small child', containing /bədáʔ/ 'child, offspring' (Reese 1996; D. Kinkade p.c.).

SPEELYAI Creek (Ore., Clatsop Co.) \spē´ lē ī\. Although the place is not in Sahaptin territory, the name represents Sahaptin /spilyáy/ 'coyote' (myth character), from /spilyá/ 'coyote' (animal). The written variant **Speelyais** \spē´ lē īs\. also occurs, perhaps originally a possessive. The placename **Speelyai** also is found in Wash. (Cowlitz Co.).

SPEONK (N.Y., Suffolk Co.) \spē´ ongk\. From SNE Algonquian, of unclear derivation (Tooker 1911).

SPIDER Rock (Ariz., Apache Co.). Corresponds to Navajo (Athabaskan) *tsé na'ashjé'ii* 'spider rock' (Linford 2000), containing *tsé* 'rock' and *na'ashjé'ii* 'spider' (Young and Morgan 1987).

SPINO Spring (Ore., Umatilla Co.). Named with the surname of an Indian family, affiliation not known (McArthur 1992).

SPIRIT. The term is widely used in English as an equivalent of Indian words translatable as 'god, divine spirit, sacred', such as Ojibwa (Algonquian) *manidoo*—often also adapted to English as **Manitou** in placenames—and Dakota (Siouan) *wakhą́,* often adapted as **Wakan.** Examples of the latter are **Spirit Lake** (Iowa, Dickinson Co.), from Dakota *mniwákhą,* lit. 'lake-sacred' (Vogel 1983; J. Koontz p.c.); and **Spirit Mound,** from *wakhą́-šiča,* lit. 'spirit-bad' (SD, Clay Co.) In Idaho **Spirit Lake** (Kootenai Co.) translates the Indian name <Tesemini>, language not identified (Boone 1988). Cf. also **Rum River** and **Wahkon**, both in Minn. (Mille Lacs Co.).

SPOKANE County (Wash.) \spō kan´\. From the Spokane dialect of Interior Salishan; the Native American name is [spoqín] (Hitchman 1985; D. Kinkade p.c.). The placename also occurs, for example, in Alaska (Juneau C-6), Ore. (Curry Co.), and S.Dak. (Custer Co.).

SPOON River (Ill., Champaign Co.). Probably translated from a Miami/Illinois (Algonquian) word meaning 'spoon' (Vogel 1963); cf. Ojibwa (Algonquian) *emikwaan* 'ladle' (Nichols and Nyholm 1995). A related placename is **Maquon** (Ill., Knox Co.).

SPRUCEFISH Lake (Alaska, Mt. McKinley C-6). Corresponds to Upper Kuskokwim (Athabaskan) *ts'ima łuk'a mina',* lit. 'spruce salmon lake' (J. Kari p.c.).

SPUNK Creek (Minn., Stearns Co.). The term is equivalent here to 'tinder, punk' and translates Ojibwa (Algonquian) *zagataagan* 'tinder' (Upham 2001; Nichols and Nyholm 1995).

SPUNKWUSH (Wash., Pierce Co.). From Klikitat (Sahaptian), said to mean 'a large number of small streams' (Hitchman 1985).

SQUACONNING Creek (Mich., Bay Co.). Perhaps from an American Indian language, which has not been identified (Vogel 1986).

SQUAG City (N.H., Sullivan Co.) \skwäg\. An abbreviation of of the SNEng. Algonquian placename **Piscataquog Mountain** (N.H., Hillsborough Co.), perhaps meaning 'at the river branch' (Huden 1962).

SQUAK Mountain (Wash., King Co.). From the Southern Lushootseed (Salishan) placename /sq^{w}ásx^{w}/ (D. Kinkade p.c.). A related placename is **Issaquah Creek** (Wash., King Co.).

SQUALICUM (Wash., Whatcom Co.). The Lummi (Salishan) placename [x^{w}k'^{w}ál'əx^{w}əm] means 'dog-salmon place', containing /k'^{w}ál'əx^{w}/ 'dog salmon' (Hitchman 1985; D. Kinkade p.c.).

SQUALLY (Wash., Pierce Co.) \skwä´ lē\. Named for Charley Squally, a member of a Southern Coast Salishan subgroup. The Native American name is /sq^{w}əlíʔ/, a place called "Frank's Landing" in English, from /q^{w}áliʔ-/ 'hay, grass' (D. Kinkade p.c.). The placename **Squally** also occurs in Ore. (Wasco Co.). A related placename is **Nisqually** (Wash., Thurston Co.).

SQUAMISH Harbor (Wash., Jefferson Co.) \skwä´ mish\. From the same source as **Suquamish** (see below).

SQUAM River (Mass., Essex Co.) \skwäm\. From SNEng. Algonquian, perhaps meaning 'at the summit' (Huden 1962). In Maine (Lincoln Co.) **Squam Creek** is perhaps from Abenaki (Algonquian) *mskwamagw* 'salmon'; this name also occurs in N.H. (Belknap Co.). The possibly also related name **Squamanagonic** (N.H., Strafford Co.) \skwä mə nə gon´ ik\. is from Abenaki, said to mean 'salmon spearing place' (Huden 1962); it is abbreviated in the nearby placename **Gonic.**

SQUAMSCOT Bog (N.H., Hillsborough Co.) \skwäm´ skot, skwäm´ skət\. Perhaps from Abenaki (Algonquian) *skwamiskw* 'female beaver' (Day 1994–95). The spelling **Squamscott** occurs in Rockingham Co., N.Y.

SQUANKIN Pond (Maine, Piscataquis Co.). Perhaps from Abenaki (Algonquian), of unknown derivation (Rutherford 1970).

SQUANKUM (N.J., Monmouth Co.). Probably from Delaware (Algonquian), but the derivation is not clear (Becker 1964).

SQUANNACOOK River (Mass., Middlesex Co.). From SNEng. Algonquian, perhaps meaning 'green place' (Huden 1962). The spelling **Squannakonk** occurs in Bristol Co.

SQUANTUM (Mass., Norfolk Co.) \skwän´ təm\. Perhaps from a seventeenth-century SNEng. Algonquian man, also called <Squanto>; or directly from Natick (SNEng. Algonquian) *squóntam* 'door' (Huden 1962; Trumbull 1903). The name also occurs in R.I. (Providence Co.), N.H. (Cheshire Co.), and Maine (Hancock Co.).

SQUA PAN (Maine, Aroostook Co.) \skwä´ pan\. Perhaps from Abenaki (Algonquian), said to mean 'bear's den' (Huden 1962).

SQUARE Butte (Ariz., Coconino Co.). Corresponds to Navajo (Athabaskan) *tsé dik'ání* 'square rock', with *tsé* 'rock' (Linford 2000).

SQUASH \skwôsh\. The name of this native vegetable is shortened from Narragansett (SNEng. Algonquian) <askútasquash> 'squashes' (*RHD* 1987). As a placename, the word is widespread (e.g., Mass., Dukes Co.; N.Y, Herkimer Co.; and Wis., Oneida Co.).

SQUASSUX Landing (N.Y., Suffolk Co.) \skwä´ səks\. Probably a possessive from the name of a SNEng. Algonquian resident named <Wesquassuck>, perhaps meaning 'pot-maker' (Tooker 1911).

SQUAW \skwô\. This word, referring to an Indian woman, was borrowed from SNEng. Algonquian <squa> 'woman' (*RHD* 1987). Over the years it has come to have a derogatory sense and is now considered offensive by many Native Americans (Bright 2000c). It is widespread in placenames, including **Squaw Island** (Mass., Barnstable Co.), **Squaw Creek** (Iowa, Franklin Co.), and **Squaw Valley** (Calif., Placer Co.). **Squawbetty Hill** (Mass., Bristol Co.) was named after a seventeenth-century SNEng. Algonquian woman; her Native American name was <Sausaman>. **Squaw Teat Butte** is in S.Dak. (Ziebach Co.), and the name also occurs in Mont. (Meagher Co.) and Wyo. (Sublette Co.). The spelling **Squaw Tit** occurs in Ariz. (Maricopa Co.) and four other states. **Squaw-Humper Creek** (S.Dak., Shannon Co.) translates Lakhota Siouan <wašičuwikiyuha>, said to refer to a white man who cohabited with Indian women (Sneve 1973). The term seems actually to contain the noun *wašíču* 'white person', however, with the prefix *wi-* 'woman', and the verb *khiyúha* 'to copulate with' (B. Ingham p.c.); so perhaps it means 'a white person copulates with women'.

SQUAXIN Island (Wash., Mason Co.) \skwôk´ sin\. From the Lushootseed (Salishan) placename /sq^{w}áx̣səd/ (D. Kinkade p.c.).

SQUETEAGUE Harbor (Mass., Barnstable Co.) From SNEng. Algonquian, perhaps meaning 'weakfish' (Huden 1962).

SQUIBNOCKET (Mass., Dukes Co.). From SNEng. Algonquian, perhaps meaning 'place of red rocks' (Huden 1962).

SQUILCHUCK Creek (Wash., Chelan Co.) From Moses-Columbian (Salishan) /sk^{w}əltak^{w}-

cín/, lit. 'warm shore', containing /k^{W}əl-/ 'warm', /-atk^{W}/ 'water', and /-cin/ 'mouth, edge, shore'; the *-chuck* in English is probably from the Chinook Jargon word for 'water' (Hitchman 1985; D. Kinkade p.c.).

SQUIRREL River (Alaska, Selawik D-3). Corresponds to Iñupiaq (Eskimo) *sikskrik* 'ground squirrel' or *siksrikpak* 'marmot' (Orth 1967; MacLean 1980). In Ariz. (Apache Co.), **Squirrel Rock** corresponds to Navajo (Athabaskan) *hazéí łání* 'many squirrels' (Linford 2000), with *hazéí* 'squirrel' (Young and Morgan 1987).

SQUITCH Lake (Wash., Kitsap Co.). From Chinook Jargon <skwich, skutch> [skwəč] 'vagina' (D. Kinkade p.c.).

STAHAHE Brook (N.Y., Orange Co.). From Onondaga (Iroquoian), perhaps /osdɛhee'/ 'rocks or ledge in water', or perhaps /osdɛhæhæ'/ 'rocks on top', both with /-sdɛhr-/ 'rock' (Beauchamp 1907; H. Woodbury p.c.).

STANDING BEAR LAKE (Neb., Douglas Co.). Named for a Ponca (Siouan) leader (BGN 7904).

STANDING COW Ruin (Ariz., Apache Co.). A translation of Navajo (Athabaskan) *béegashii siziní kits'iil* 'standing cow ruin' (Linford 2000), containing *béegashii* 'cow' (from Spanish *vacas* 'cows').

STANDING INDIAN (N.C., Macon Co.). Corresponds to an Indian term <yunwitsulenunyi> 'where the man stood', perhaps from Cherokee (Iroquoian) (Powell 1968).

STANDING RED ROCKS (Ariz., Apache Co.). A translation of Navajo *tsé łichii 'íí'áhí* '(two) standing red rocks' (Linford 2000), with *tsé* 'rock'. **Standing Rock** (Ariz., Apache Co) is a translation of Navajo *tsé 'íí'áhí* 'standing rocks' (Linford 2000); the name also occurs in N.Mex. (McKinley Co.). The name **Standing Rock Tribe Dam** (S.Dak., Corson Co.) was given by the government in 1873.

STAND WATIE, Mount (N.C., Swain Co.). Named for General Stand Watie (1806–1871), a Cherokee (Iroquoian) man who was the only Indian general in the Confederate Army (BGN 7402).

STANISLAUS County (Calif., Stanislaus Co.) \stan´ is lô, stan´ is lôs\. The name is the English equivalent of Spanish *Estanislao,* the baptismal name of a Costanoan Indian who ran away from San José Mission in 1828 and organized a resistance movement against the Spanish (Gudde 1998).

STAN SHUATUK (Ariz., Pima Co.). O'odham (Piman) *ston ṣu:dagĭ,* lit.'hot water' (Granger 1983; J. Hill p.c.).

STAPALOOP Creek (Wash., Okanogan Co.). Perhaps from an Okanagan (Salishan) placename (Hitchman 1985).

STARRUCCA (Pa., Wayne Co.). Probably an Indian name, from an unidentified language (Donehoo 1928).

STARVED ROCK (Ill., La Salle Co.). Supposedly named because a band of Miami/Illinois (Algonquian) Indians suffered hunger when besieged here by other tribes in 1769 (Vogel 1963).

STARWEIN Flat (Calif., Humboldt Co.) \stär´ win, stär´ wīn\. From the Yurok village name /stowen/ (Gudde 1998).

STECOAH (N.C., Graham Co.) \stə kō´ ə\. Perhaps from a Cherokee (Iroquoian) placename <stika'yi> (Powell 1968). A related name is **Stekoa Creek** (Ga., Rabun Co.).

STEDATNA Creek (Alaska, Tyonek A-5). Dena'ina (Athabaskan) *sdidahtnu,* containing *-tnu* 'stream' (Kari and Fall 1987:44).

STEESTACHEE Bald (N.C., Haywood Co.). Said to be from Cherokee (Iroquoian) *tsisdetsi* 'rat' (Powell 1968).

STEHEKIN (Wash., Chelan Co.). From Moses-Columbian (Salishan) /stx^{W}íkn'/ [stx^{W}íkən'] (Hitchman 1985; D. Kinkade p.c.).

STEILACOOM (Wash., Pierce Co.). From Lushootseed (Salishan) /č'tílq^{W}əbš/, referring to a Southern Coast Salishan subgroup (Hitchman 1985; *HNAI* 7:487).

STEINHATCHEE (Fla., Taylor Co.). Perhaps from Muskogee *este enhvcce* /ísti in-háčči/ 'person's stream', from *isti* 'human being' and *hacce* 'stream' (Read 1934; Martin and Mauldin 2000).

STEKOA Creek (Ga., Rabun Co.). Perhaps from a Cherokee (Iroquoian) placename <stika'yi/; see the related name **Stecoah** (N.C., Graham Co.).

STELIKO (Wash., Chelan Co.). Moses-Columbian (Salishan) /cílk^{W}u/, a man's name (D. Kinkade p.c.).

STEMILT (Wash., Chelan Co.). Moses-Columbian (Salishan) /stmílx^{W}/ [stəmílx^{W}], a man's name (Reese 1996; D. Kinkade p.c.).

STEQUALEHO Creek (Wash., Jefferson Co.). From a Quinault (Salishan) placename (D. Kinkade p.c.).

STETATTLE Creek (Wash., Whatcom Co.). From a Salishan placename, not further identifiable (Hitchman 1985).

STIKINE (Alaska, Petersburg B-2) \sti kēnˈ\. From Tlingit \štax'hín\. (Orth 1967; *HNAI* 7:227).

STILLAGUAMISH River (Wash., Snohomish Co.). From Northern Lushootseed (Salishan) /stuləg^{W}ábš/, lit. 'river people' (containing /túlək^{W}-/ 'river'), referring to a Southern Coast Salishan subgroup (Hitchman 1985; D. Kinkade p.c.).

STILLIPICA (Fla., Madison Co.). Muskogee *estelepikv* /(i)stilipéyka/ 'shoe', from *estele* /istilí/ 'a foot' (Read 1934; Martin and Mauldin 2000).

STINKING Lake (N.Mex., Rio Arriba Co.). Probably a translation of the Tewa (Tanoan) name, meaning 'smelly lake' (Julyan 1998).

STISSING (N.Y., Dutchess Co.). Earlier written <Teesink, Tishasinks>; perhaps from Mahican (Algonquian), of unclear derivation (Beauchamp 1907).

STITCHIHATCHIE Creek (Ga., Laurens Co.). Perhaps from Muskogee *vtēkē* /ati:kí:/ 'edge' plus *hvcce* /háčči/ 'stream' (Read 1949–50; Martin and Mauldin 2000).

STOA PITK (Ariz., Pima Co.). O'odham (Piman) *stoha bidk* 'white mud', from *s-toha* 'white' and *bidk* 'mud' (Granger 1983; J. Hill p.c.). **Stoa Tontk Well** (Pima Co.) is O'odham *stoha ta:nk* 'white bank' (J. Hill p.c.). **Stoa Vaya** (Pima Co.) is O'odham *stoha wahia* 'white well' (J. Hill p.c.).

STOCKBRIDGE (Mass., Berkshire Co.). A mission community of Mahican (Algonquian) Indians, as well as people from SNEng. Algonquian tribes, existed here in the eighteenth century; and they became known as the "Stockbridge Indians." In 1746 they moved to Bethlehem, Pa., where they merged with Munsee Delaware (Algonquian) Christians, and in 1786 to New Stockbridge, N.Y. (*HNAI* 15:207–9). In 1822–33 the group was transported to Wis., where their descendants live at what is called the **Stockbridge Indian Reservation** (Shawano Co.) (Vogel 1991).

STOCKING Branch (Ga., Burke Co.). Names used earlier are **Stalking Creek, Stocking Creek,** and **Stockinghead Creek.** Apparently the original reference is to a "stalking head": a decoy deer head worn by Indian hunters (Goff 1975). Related placenames occur elsewhere in Ga. (Candler Co, Jasper Co.).

STOGGNANG Creek (Alaska, Goodnews Bay D-8). The Yupik (Eskimo) name was published in 1951 (Orth 1967).

STONEY INDIAN Lake (Mont., Glacier Co.). The term **Stoney** is applied to a branch of the **Assiniboine** (Siouan) people. It corresponds to Ojibwa (Algonquian) *assini:pwa:n* 'stone Sioux' (Holterman 1985; *HNAI* 13:602). A possibly related term is **Rocky Mountains.**

STONO (S.C., Charleston Co.). Reported in 1609 as Ostano; perhaps a subgroup of the Cusabo tribe (Pickens 1961–62:22; B. Rudes p.c.).

STONY CREEK (Pa., Somerset Co.). Corresponds to Delaware (Algonquian) <achsinnehanne> 'stony stream' (Donehoo 1928); cf. <achsin> 'stone' (Brinton and Anthony 1888), modern Unami Delaware /a:hsə́n/ 'stone' (Blalock et al. 1994).

STOTONIC (Ariz., Pinal Co.). O'odham (Piman) *s-totoñigk* 'many ants' (J. Hill p.c.), from *totoñ* 'ant' (Saxton et al. 1983). **Stotonyak** (Ariz., Pima Co.) is from the same source.

STOVE (S.Dak., Dewey Co.). A translation from Lakhota (Siouan) *mazóčheti* 'cookstove', from *máza* 'iron, metal' and *očhéti* 'stove, hearth' (Sneve 1973; Ingham 2001).

STRAIGHT River (Minn., Rice Co.). A translation of Dakota (Siouan) *owótąna* 'straight' (Upham 2001; Riggs 1890).

STRANGER Creek (Kans., Leavenworth Co.). A translation from Kansa (Siouan) /okkü´čče, okkíčče/ 'enemy, stranger' (Rydjord 1968; R. Rankin p.c.). In Wash. (Stevens Co.) **Stranger Creek** is an adaptation of **Strensgar Creek,** named for John Strensgar, an Indian of the Colville Reservation (D. Kinkade p.c.).

STREAKED Rock (Ariz., Apache Co.). From Navajo (Athabaskqan) *tséndíłkéłí* 'streaked rock', with *tsé* 'rock' (Linford 2000).

STRELNA Creek (Alaska, Valdez C-1) \strel´ nə\. From Ahtna (Athabaskan) *staghael na'*, with *na'* 'stream' (Kari 1983:7).

STRELSHLA Mountain (Alaska, Anchorage D-3). From the Ahtna (Athabaskan) placename *hwdghelsle* (Kari 1983:40).

ST. TAMMANY Parish (La.) \tam´ ə nē\. An adaptation of **Tamanend,** the name of a Delaware (Algonquian) leader of the seventeenth century (Read 1927).

STUCK River (Wash., Howell 1948). From Lushootseed (Salishan) /stə́q/ 'log jam' or /stə́x̣/ 'gouged through' (Hitchman 1985; D. Kinkade p.c.).

STURGEON Bay (Wis., Door Co.). Corresponds to Menominee (Algonquian) /namɛ:w-wi:hkit/, from /namɛ:w/ 'sturgeon' plus /wi:hkit/ 'bay' (Vogel 1991; Bloomfield 1975).

STUYAHOK (Alaska, Dillingham D-2) \sto͞o´ yə hok\. From the Yupik (Eskimo) placename *cetuyaraq,* containing *cetu-* 'to go with the river current' (Jacobson 1984). The spelling **Stuyarok** also occurs.

SUAGEE (Okla., Delaware Co.). Named for Wilson Suagee, a Cherokee (Iroquoian) leader (Shirk 1974).

SUCARNOOCHEE River (Ala., Sumter Co.) \so͝ok ər noch´ ē\. Probably from Choctaw (Muskogean), meaning 'hog's stream', from *shokha* 'hog' and *hachcha* 'stream' (Read 1984; P. Munro p.c.). The name also occurs in Miss. (Kemper Co.).

SUCATOLBA Creek (Miss., Lauderdale Co.). From Choctaw (Muskogean), 'where possums are killed', with *shokhata* 'possum' and *alba* 'be killed' (Seale 1939; P. Munro p.c.).

SUCCASUNNA (N.J., Morris Co.). Probably from Delaware (Algonquian), perhaps containing <sukeu> 'black' (Brinton and Anthony 1888; Becker 1964); cf. Unami Delaware /sə́ke:/ 'it is black' (Blalock et al. 1994).

SUCCONNESSET Point (Mass., Barnstable Co.). From SNEng. Algonquian, perhaps meaning 'black shell place' (Huden 1962).

SUCCOTASH Point (R.I., Washington Co.) \suk´ ə tash\. From a SNEng. Algonquian term meaning 'boiled whole kernels of corn'; cf. Narragansett <msíckquatash> (*RHD* 1987). The name also occurs in Wash. (Pierce Co.), where it may be a folk-etymology based on a local Indian word <so-ho-tash> 'place of the wild strawberry' (Reese 1996).

SUCKATUNKANUC Hill (R.I., Providence Co.). From Narragansett (SNEng. Algonquian), perhaps meaning 'dark-colored earth' (Huden 1962).

SUCKER Creek (Minn., St. Louis Co.). A translation of Ojibwa (Algonquian) *namebin ziibi,* from *namebin* 'sucker (fish)' (Upham 2001; Nichols and Nyholm 1995). Elsewhere, **Sucker Lake** (Alaska, Gulkana A-5) corresponds to Ahtna (Athabaskan) *dahwts'adyeh bene',* with *bene'* 'lake' (J. Kari p.c.).

SUDAK, Cape (Alaska, Adak C-5). From the Aleut placename *sudux̂*, perhaps meaning 'easy taking' (Bergsland 1994).

SUEY Creek (Calif., Santa Barbara Co.) \sōō ā\. From Ventureño (Chumashan), perhaps meaning 'tarweed' (Gudde 1998).

SUGAKUIK Creek (Alaska, Killik River A-2). The Iñupiaq (Eskimo) name, reported in 1956, is said to mean 'resting place' (Orth 1967).

SUGAR Creek (Ind., Clinton Co.). In a number of areas, placenames containing English *sugar* refer to sugar maple groves maintained by Indians, and the English placenames may be translations of those used by Indians; the Miami/Illinois (Algonquian) name for this creek was /(ah)senaamiši siipiiwi/ 'maple-sugar-tree river' (M. McCafferty p.c.). Other states in which similar names occur include Iowa (Cedar Co.), Ill. (Franklin Co.), and Mich. (Wayne Co.). In N.C. (Mecklenburg Co.), however, **Sugar Creek** is probably a folk-etymology from **Sugaw Creek**; see below. In Miss. (Scott Co.) **Sugar Bogue** is a folk-etymology from Choctaw (Muskogean) *shokha book,* lit. 'hog creek' (Seale 1939; P. Munro p.c.).

SUGARITE (N.Mex., Colfax Co.) \shōōg´ ə rēt\. The name has nothing to do with *sugar* but is a folk-etymology from **Chicorica Creek,** from Spanish *Chicorico,* perhaps a folk-etymology ('small-rich') from an Apachean (Athabaskan) word for 'turkey' (Bright & de Reuse 2002).

SUGAW Creek (S.C., York Co.) \shōō´ gə\. Probably from Catawban (Siouan) /suk'aa/ 'our house' (B. Rudes p.c.).

SUGTUTLIG Mountain (Alaska, Goodnews Bay B-7). The Yupik (Eskimo) name was recorded in 1951 as meaning 'old high mountain' (Orth 1967). Probably related is **Sugtutlik Peak** (Alaska, Goodnews Bay A-1).

SUHTI Island (Alaska, Craig D-4). The Tlingit name was published in 1964 (Orth 1967).

SUIATTLE River (Wash., Skagit Co.). From the name of a Southern Coast Salishan subgroup; the Lushootseed term is /suyátł'/ (Hitchman 1985; D. Kinkade p.c.).

SUISE Creek (Wash., King Co.). From the Lushootseed (Salishan) placename [sús] (Hitchman 1985; D. Kinkade p.c.).

SUISUN (Calif., Contra Costa/Solano Cos.) \sə sōōn\. Named for a Patwin (Wintuan) subgroup or village (Gudde 1998).

SUKAKPAK Mountain (Alaska, Chandalar C-6). The Iñupiaq (Eskimo) word is *sukaqpak*, of uncertain origin (L. Kaplan p.c.).

SUKKWAN (Alaska, Craig A-3) \sə kwän\. From Tlingit /suq^{W}kaʔa:n/ 'town on the fine underwater grass', containing /ʔa:n/ 'town' (Orth 1967; *HNAI* 7:258).

SUKOK Lake (Alaska, Barrow A-4). Perhaps a mistranscription of Iñupiaq (Eskimo) <Sikolik>, recorded in 1950 as meaning 'having ice' (Orth 1967); cf. *siku* 'ice' (MacLean 1980).

SULAKPOATOKVIK Creek (Alaska, Hughes D-5). The Iñupiaq (Eskimo) name, reported in 1956, is said to mean 'place where grayling (fish sp.) are caught' (Orth 1967); cf. *sulukpaugaq* 'grayling' (MacLean 1980). A related Alaska placename is **Sulupoagaktak Channel** (Point Hope B-3).

SULATNA River (Alaska, Ruby C-3). The Koyukon (Athabaskan) name was reported in 1908 (Orth 1967).

SULTAN (Wash., Snohomish Co.). A folk-etymology based on <Tseul-tud>, the name of a Snohomish (Salishan) leader (Hitchman 1985).

SULUA Bay (Alaska, Kaguyak D-6). Reported in 1934 as being from an Alutiiq (Eskimo) word meaning 'cabin' (Orth 1967).

SULUAK Creek (Alaska, Killik River A-2). The Iñupiaq (Eskimo) word is *suluk* 'wing feather' (L. Kaplan p.c.).

SULUGIAK Creek (Alaska, Killik River A-1). The Iñupiaq (Eskimo) name was reported in 1956 (Orth 1967).

SULUKNA River (Alaska, Ruby A-3). From Koyukon (Athabaskan) *soolaah no'*, with *no'* 'river'; perhaps reduced from an expression meaning 'martens are caught' (Kari 1999:105).

SULUKPUK Creek (Alaska, Iliamna A-4). The Alutiiq (Eskimo) name was published in 1926 (Orth 1967).

SULUNGATAK Ridge (Alaska, Misheguk Mountain C-5). The Iñupiaq (Eskimo) name was published in 1962 (Orth 1967).

SULUPOAGAKTAK Channel (Alaska, Point Hope B-3). The Iñupiaq (Eskimo) name, reported in 1950, is said to mean 'it abounds with grayling (fish sp.)' (Orth 1967); cf. *suluk-paugaq* 'grayling' (MacLean 1980). A related Alaska placename is **Sulakpoatokvik Creek** (Hughes D-5).

SULUTAK Creek (Alaska, Goodnews Bay A-5). From Yupik (Eskimo) *suulutaaq* 'gold' (Orth 1967; Jacobson 1984).

SUMAS (Wash., Whatcom Co.). From Chilliwack Halkomelem (Salishan) [səméθ], perhaps containing /méθ/ 'flat, level' (Hitchman 1985; D. Kinkade p.c.).

SUMAVA (Ind., Newton Co.) \sə mä´ və\. Supposedly from a Native American word meaning 'progress, success', but the language has not been identified (Baker 1995).

SUMDUM (Alaska, Sumdum C-5) \sum´ dum\. From the Tlingit placename \s'awdá:n\. (Orth 1967; *HNAI* 7:227).

SUNAPEE (N.H., Sullivan Co.) \sun´ ə pē\. Perhaps from Western Abenaki (Algonquian) *seninebi* [səninəbi] 'rock water'; cf. *sen* 'rock', *nebi* 'water' (Day 1994–95).

SUNCOOK (N.H., Merrimack Co.) \sun´ ko͞ok\. Perhaps from Abenaki (Algonquian), meaning 'rocky place'; cf. *sen* 'rock' (Huden 1962; Day 1994–95).

SUNDANCE (Wyo., Crook Co.). The term refers to an annual ceremony held by a number of Plains tribes. The name also occurs as a transfer in Mich. (Gogebic Co.).

SUNEVA Lake (Alaska, Kenai D-4). The name may be from Dena'ina (Athabaskan); its derivation is unclear (Orth 1967).

SUNE Well (Ariz., Yuma Co.) \sho͞o´ nē\. Named for Chico Sune, a leader of the Sand Papago (O'odham, Piman); perhaps from *ṣon* 'spring' (J. Hill p.c.).

SUNGIC Point (N.Y., Suffolk Co.). From SNEng. Algonquian, perhaps meaning 'stony' (Tooker 1911).

SUNKHAZE Stream (Maine, Penobscot Co.) \sungk´ hāz\. Early written <Saquaische>; from Abenaki (Algonquian), of unclear derivation (Eckstorm 1941).

SUN Lake (Alaska, Tanacross A-4). Corresponds to Upper Tanana (Athabaskan) *saa nah männ'*, lit. 'sun sign lake' (J. Kari p.c.).

SUNQUAM (N.Y., Suffolk Co.). From SNEng. Algonquian, perhaps meaning 'cool place' (Beauchamp 1907).

SUNRISE River (Minn., Chisago Co.). Corresponds to Ojibwa (Algonquian) <memokage zibi>, lit. 'keep-sunrising river' (Upham 2001).

SUNSELA Saddle (Ariz., Apache Co.). A variant of **Sonsela Buttes**; see above.

SUNSHINE Spring (Ariz., Apache Co.). A translation of Navajo (Athabaskan) *shą́ą́'tóhí* 'sunshine water' (Linford 2000); cf. *shą́ą́'* 'sunshine' (Young and Morgan 1987).

SUNTAHEEN Creek (Alaska, Juneau A-4). The Tlingit name, reported in 1959, perhaps means 'middle creek' (Orth 1967); cf. *héen* [hí:n] 'creek' (Davis and Leer 1976).

SUNTAUG Lake (Mass., Essex Co.). From SNEng. Algonquian, perhaps meaning 'stony ground' (Huden 1962).

SUNTRANA (Alaska, Healy D-4) \sun tran´ ə\. From Lower Tanana (Athabaskan) *sen' trona* 'coal', lit. 'star excrement' (Kari 1999:129).

SUPAI (Ariz., Coconino Co.) \so͞o´ pī\. A shortening of the name of **Havasupai** (Yuman) Indians;

the longer term means 'blue-water people' (*HNAI* 10:23).

SUPI OIDAK (Ariz., Pima Co.). O'odham (Piman) *s-he:pi oidag* 'cold field', from *s-he:pi* 'cold' plus *oidag* 'field' (J. Hill p.c.).

SUQUALENA (Miss., Lauderdale Co.) \so͝ok ə lē´ nə\. Perhaps from Choctaw *saktih-abina* 'a camp on the bluffs', from *saktih* 'a bank, a bluff' plus *abina* 'a camp' (Seale 1939; P. Munro p.c.).

SUQUAMISH (Wash., Kitsap Co.) \so͞o kwä´ mish\. The name of a Southern Coast Salishan subgroup, from Lushootseed /xʷsə́q'ʷəb/ (Hitchman 1985; *HNAI* 7:487). The alternation of *m* and *b* is characteristic of Native American languages in the Puget Sound area. A related placename is **Squamish Harbor** (Wash., Jefferson Co.).

SURGONE (Calif., Humboldt Co.) \sûr´ gôn\. From the Yurok village name /sregon/ (Gudde 1998).

SURKU Cove (Alaska, Craig D-4). The Tlingit name was published in 1964 (Orth 1967).

SURPUR Creek (Calif., Humboldt Co.) \sûr´ pûr\. From the Yurok village name /srpr/ (Gudde 1998).

SURRY County (N.C.). Probably from Catawban (Siouan) /saaraa'/ 'peninsula, point of land', the name of one of the two groups that form the modern Catawba Nation; influenced by the English placename *Surrey* (Powell 1968; B. Rudes p.c.).

SUSCOL Creek (Calif., Napa Co.) \sus´ kəl\. The name of a Patwin (Wintuan) Indian village (Gudde 1998).

SUSHANA River (Alaska, Fairbanks A-6) \sho͞o shä´ nə\. The name may be from Lower Tanana (Athabaskan); it was reported in 1910 (Orth 1967).

SUSHGITIT Hills (Alaska, Hughes A-1). The Koyukon (Athabaskan) name is said to mean 'cache hill' (Orth 1967).

SUSITNA (Alaska, Tyonek C-2) \so͞o sit´ nə\. From Dena'ina (Athabaskan) *susitnu* 'sand river', containing *-tnu* 'river' (Kari and Fall 1987:69; Kari 1990).

SUSKARALOGH Point (Alaska, Pribilof Islands A-3). From the Aleut placename *sasxaĝilux̂*, perhaps from *sasxa-lix* 'to be in good condition' (Bergsland 1994).

SUSLOSITNA Creek (Alaska, Nabesna D-6). Perhaps from Ahtna (Athabaskan) *tsek'ohwtsedl na'*, with *na'* 'creek' (Kari 1983:91).

SUSLOTA (Alaska, Nabesna C-6). From Ahtna (Athabaskan) *sas luugge* [lu:ɢe] 'small sockeye salmon' (Kari 1990).

SUSQUEHANNA County (Pa.) \sus kwə han´ ə\. An Algonquian name for an Iroquoian people; it has been translated as 'people at the falls' or 'roily water people' (*HNAI* 15:362–63). The placename **Susquehanna** occurs in other states (e.g., Md., Cecil Co.; and N.Y., Broome Co.). A related placename is **Susquehannock State Forest** (Pa., Potter Co.).

SUSQUETONSCUT Brook (Conn., New London Co.). From Mohegan (SNEng. Algonquian), of unclear derivation (Trumbull 1881).

SUSSAYMIN Lakes (Alaska, Beaver A-6). From Koyukon (Athabaskan) *səsiy bənə'* 'widgeon lake' (Kari 2000).

SUSULATNA River (Alaska, Medfra D-4). The Koyukon (Athabaskan) name was reported in 1915 (Orth 1967).

SUTAMACHUTE Hill (R.I., Providence Co.). From Narragansett (SNEng. Algonquian), perhaps meaning 'at the great stony hill' (Huden 1962).

SUTWIK Island (Alaska, Sutwik Island C-4). The Alutiiq (Eskimo) name was published in 1827 (Orth 1967).

SUVALOYUK Creek (Alaska, Misheguk Mountain C-1). The Iñupiaq (Eskimo) is said to mean 'waster of food' (Orth 1967).

SUWANEE (Ga., Gwinnett Co.) \swä´ nē\. A onetime Cherokee (Iroquoian) village, <Sawani>

(A. Read 2001). This site seems to have given its name to the **Suwannee River** (Ga., Fla.), also written **Swanee.** The name has been transferred to other states, probably because of the popularity of Stephen C. Foster's song, "Old Folks at Home" ("Way down upon the Swannee River"). The form **Suwanee** is used for placenames in Calif. (Tulare Co.), Ky. (Lyon Co.), and N.Mex. (Valencia Co.).

SUWUK TONTK (Ariz., Pima Co.) \sə wuk tontk\. O'odham (Piman) *swegĭ ta:nk* 'red bank', from *s-wegĭ* 'red' and *ta:nk* 'bank'. A related name is **Suwuki Chuapo** (Ariz., Maricopa Co.), representing O'odham (Piman) *swegĭ ce:po* 'red bedrock-mortar', with *ce:po* 'bedrock mortar' (Granger 1983; J. Hill p.c.).

SWADHUMS Creek (Wash., Pierce Co.). Probably from Lushootseed (Salishan) */s-wada-bš/, referring to the **Wanapum**, a Sahaptian subgroup. The term consists of Lushootseed /š-/ 'nominalizer', Sahaptin /wána-/ 'water' (with a common Lushootseed sound change of *n* to *d*), and Lushootseed /-abš/ 'people'. It is thus an adaptation of the native Sahaptian name /wána-pam/ 'water-people' (Hitchman 1985; D. Kinkade p.c.).

SWAGO Creek (W.Va., Pocahontas Co.) \swā´ gō\. Perhaps derived from the name of **Oswego County** (N.Y.), of Iroquoian origin (Kenny 1945).

SWAKANE Creek (Wash., Chelan Co.). Moses-Columbian (Salishan) /sx^{W}ər'qín/ "holes in heads; saddle or gap on a ridge', from /s-/ 'nominalizer', /x^{W}ər'-/ 'hole, gap', and /-qin/ 'head' (D. Kinkade p.c.).

SWAMPSCOTT (Mass., Essex Co.) \swämp´ skot\. From SNEng. Algonquian, probably containing <-mpsk-> 'rock' (Huden 1962; W. Cowan p.c.).

SWANEE River (Ga., Fla.) \swä´ nē\. A variant of **Suwanee** or **Suwannee**; see above. The name **Swanee** is given to places in Colo. (Mesa Co.) and Wash. (Adams Co.).

SWAN Lake (Iowa, Carroll Co.). Perhaps a translation of Meskwaki (Algonquian) /e:he:wa/ 'swan' (Vogel 1983; I. Goddard p.c.). In Alaska one of several places called **Swan Lake** (Tanacross A-3) corresponds to Upper Tanana (Athabaskan) *taagoh männ'*, lit. 'swan lake' (J. Kari p.c.). In Minn. (Itasca Co.) the **Swan River** corresponds to Ojibwa (Algonquian) *waabizii* 'swan' (Upham 2001; Nichols and Nyholm 1995). Elsewhere in Minn. (Nicollet Co.) another **Swan River** corresponds to Dakota (Siouan) *maǧá-tąka* 'swan', lit. 'goose-big', from *maǧá* 'goose' and *tą́ka* 'big' (Upham 2001; Riggs 1890).

SWANNANOA (N.C., Buncombe Co.) \swä nə nō´ ə\. From Cherokee (Iroquoian) <suwali-nunna> 'trail of the Suwali people'; cf. *nvnohi* 'road' (Feeling 1975). The term refers to a Catawban (Siouan) subgroup who called themselves /yį saaraa'/ 'peninsula people' (B. Rudes p.c.). The placename **Swannanoa** also occurs in Va. (Augusta Co.) and N.J. (Morris Co.).

SWATARA (Pa., Dauphin Co.) \swə tä´ rə\. Earlier written <Sawhatara, Swehatara> (etc.); probably of Indian origin, but the language is not identified (Donehoo 1928).

SWAUK Creek (Wash., Kittitas Co.). Probably of Sahaptian or Salishan origin, but the language has not been identified (Hitchman 1985).

SWEATHOUSE Canyon (Ore., Jackson Co.). The term is commonly used to refer to a structure built by Indians for the purpose of taking sweatbaths. As a placename, it occurs in several states (e.g., Ariz., Navajo Co.; Calif., Humboldt Co.; and Va., Amelia Co.).

SWEETWATER Creek (Idaho, Nez Perce Co.). Probably a translation from Nez Perce (Sahaptian); cf. /cicyúkis/ 'sweet' and /kú:s/ 'water' (Aoki 1994). In Tenn. (Monroe Co.) the placename **Sweetwater** is said to correspond to Cherokee (Iroquoian) <culla saga> (McClaren 1991); but this has not been confirmed.

SWIFT BIRD Creek (S.Dak., Dewey Co.). Named for a Lakhota (Siouan) chief who was called "Swift Bird" in English (Sneve 1973).

SWIKSHAK (Alaska, Afognak C-6). The Alutiiq (Eskimo) placename was published in 1952 (Orth 1967).

SWIMPTKIN Creek (Wash., Okanogan Co.). Perhaps from an Okanagan (Salishan) placename \swə́mptqən\. (D. Kinkade p.c.).

SWINOMISH (Wash., Skagit Co.) \swin´ ə mish\. The name of a Southern Coast Salishan subgroup, from Lushootseed /swə́dəbš/ (Hitchman 1985; *HNAI* 7:487). The alternation of *n* with *d,* and of *m* with *b,* is characteristic of Lushootseed.

SYCAMORE (Ill., DeKalb Co.). Perhaps a translation of a Meskwaki (Algonquian) term that also yields the placename **Kishwaukee** (Ill., Winnebago Co.); cf. /ki:šowa:hkowiwa/ 'he is a sycamore' (Goddard 1994).

SYCAN Marsh (Ore., Klamath Co.). From Klamath /sa:yk'a(n)/ 'plain, clearing' (McArthur 1992; Barker 1963).

SYCUAN Creek (Calif., San Diego Co.) \sə kwän\. From Diegueño (Yuman) <sekwan>, a kind of bush (Gudde 1998).

SYLACAUGA (Ala., Talladega Co.) \sil ə kô´ gə\. Muskogee *sule-kake* /soli-ká:k-i/ 'sitting buzzards', from *sule* /solí/ 'buzzard' plus *kake* /ká:ki/ 'sitting (of two)' (Read 1984; Martin and Mauldin 2000).

SYLOPASH Point (Wash., Jefferson Co.). From a Twana (Salishan) placename /duswáylupš/ (Reese 1996; D. Kinkade p.c.). A related placename is **Dosewallips River** (Wash., Jefferson Co.).

SYMPAUG Brook (Conn., Fairfield Co.). From SNEng. Algonquian <sumhupaog> 'beavers' (Huden 1962; W. Cowan p.c.).

SYOSSET (N.Y., Nassau Co.) \sī os´ ət\. Earlier written <Siocits>; perhaps from a Munsee Delaware (Algonquian) pronunciation of Dutch *schout* 'bailiff, sheriff' (Beauchamp 1907).

SYPAH Gulch (Idaho, Latah Co.). Chinook Jargon <si´-pah> [sâipa] 'straight'; cf. Wasco (Chinookan) /sáiba/ 'straight' (Boone 1988).

SYSLADOBSIS Lake (Maine, Washington Co.) \sis´ ə lə dob sis\. Also written <Sycledobscus, Sekledobscus, Sikladapskesk> (etc.); from Malecite (Algonquian), perhaps meaning 'shark-shaped rock' (Eckstorm 1941:234). It is familiarly called \dob´ sē\ by locals.

T

TAAIN Creek (Alaska, Petersburg C-3). Named in 1933 for a Tlingit resident (Orth 1967).

TAAWAKI (Ariz., Navajo Co.) \tä´ wä kē\. Hopi (Uto-Aztecan) *taawaki* 'house of the sun', from *taawa* 'sun' plus *-ki, kii-hu* 'house' (K. Hill p.c.).

TABASCO Creek (Alaska, Russian Mission A-2) \tə bas´ kō\. Named after Tabasco sauce, a spicy condiment (Orth 1967), which was named in turn for the state of *Tabasco* in Mexico. The term is derived from an unidentified Mexican Indian language. There is also a **Tabasco** in N.Y. (Ulster Co.). A related placename is **Tobasco** (Ohio, Clermont Co.).

TABASECA Tank (Calif., Riverside Co.) \tä bə sā´ kə\. From Cahuilla (Takic) *távish héki'* 'home of the flicker', containing *távish* 'flicker (bird)', *he-* 'its', and *-ki, kish* 'house, home' (Gudde 1998).

TABBY Creek (Utah, Duchesne Co.) \tab´ ē\. Said to be named for <Tava>, a Ute (Numic) leader (Van Cott 1990). Perhaps related is **Tabbyune Creek** (Utah, Utah Co.) \tab´ ē yo͞on\, from a Numic language (Van Cott 1990). A related placename is **Tabiona**; see below.

TABEASCOT Lake (Alaska, Bettles C-6). The Koyukon (Athabaskan) language was recorded in 1956 (Orth 1967).

TABEGUACHE Peak (Colo., Chaffee Co.) \tab´ ə wäch, tab´ wäch\. Shortened from Southern Ute (Numic) /mogwátavi'waachi/, a name for the Northern Utes. The term means 'walking /mogwáchi/', referring to a Ute subgroup; cf. /taví'way/ 'to step toward' (Givón 1979; *HNAI* 11:366).

TABERNASH (Colo., Grand Co.) \tab´ ər nash\. Named for a Ute (Numic) Indian killed here by a white man; the Native American name was perhaps /tapö´n'aci/ 'having a cramp' (Bright 1993).

TABIONA (Utah, Duchesne Co.) \tab ē ō´ nə\. A combination of the names of two Ute (Numic) leaders, Tabby or <Tava> and <Tayneena> (Van Cott 1990); see **Tabby Creek,** above.

TABIRA Ruin (N.Mex., Torrance Co.) \tə bē´ rə\. From Spanish *Tabirá,* the site of a Tompiro pueblo, destroyed in Spanish colonial times (Julyan 1998). The Tompiro language is now unknown.

TABOOK Point (Wash., Jefferson Co.). From the Twana (Salishan) placename /tá?bəx^{w}/ (D. Kinkade p.c.) A probably related name is **Dabob** (Wash., Jefferson Co.).

TABOOSE Creek (Calif., Inyo Co.) \tə bo͞os´\. From Mono or Northern Paiute (Numic) /tɨpattsi/, diminutive of /tɨpa/ 'pine nut' (J. McLaughlin p.c.).

TABYAGO Canyon (Utah, Uintah Co.). Probably from a Numic (Uto-Aztecan) language (Van Cott 1990).

TACALEECHE (Miss., Benton Co.) \tak ə lē ´ chē\. From Choctaw (Muskogean) *takaalichi* 'to hang' (P. Munro p.c.). A variant writing is nearby **Tacalichi.**

TACCOA River (Ga., Fannin Co.). A variant spelling of **Toccoa River**; see below.

TACHANLOWA Lake (Alaska, Kateel River B-3). The Koyukon (Athabaskan) name was reported in 1955 (Orth 1967).

TACHEVAH Canyon (Calif., Riverside Co.) \tä chē´ vä\. Said to mean 'a plain view' in the Cahuilla (Takic) language (Gudde 1998).

TACHINISOK Inlet (Alaska, Meade River D-4). The Iñupiaq (Eskimo) name was reported in 1850 (Orth 1967).

TACKOBE Mountain (Idaho, Elmore Co.) \tak´ ə bē\. From Shoshoni (Numic) *takkapi* [takkavi] 'snow' (J. McLaughlin p.c.).

TACLODAHTEN Lake (Alaska, Bettles B-4). The Koyukon name was obtained in 1956 (Orth 1967).

TACOA (Ala., Shelby Co.). From the same source as **Toccoa River** (Ga., Fannin Co.); see below.

TACOMA (Wash., Pierce Co.) \tə kō´ mə\. From Lushootseed (Salishan) /təq^{w}úbə?, təqúbəd/ 'snow-covered mountain', or specifically Mt. Rainier (Howell 1948; D. Kinkade p.c.). The name has been adopted as a transfer in other states (e.g., N.Y., Delaware Co.; Ohio, Belmont Co.; and Ore., Curry Co.); see also **Takoma Park** (Md., Montgomery Co.). Elsewhere in Wash. **Tacoma Creek** (Pend Oreille Co.) probably takes its name from the Kalispel placename [ckúmən] (D. Kinkade p.c.). A related placename is **Tahoma Creek** (Wash., Pierce Co.); see below.

TACONIC Range (Mass., Berkshire Co.) \tə kon´ ik\. Perhaps from Mahican (Algonquian) */ta:hkənək/ 'in the woods'; cf. Unami Delaware (Algonquian) /tékən/ 'woods', /tekə́nink/ 'in the woods' (Blalock et al. 1994), /té:kəne/ 'in the woods' (I. Goddard p.c.). Other possibly related names include **Taghkanic** (N.Y., Columbia Co.), **Ticonic** (Iowa, Monona Co.), and **Tokeneke** (Conn., Fairfield Co.).

TACONY (Pa., Philadelphia Co.). Perhaps from Delaware (Algonquian) *tèkhane* 'cold river' (Kraft and Kraft 1985); cf. Unami Delaware *theew* 'cold' (O'Meara 1996).

TACOOSH River (Mich., Delta Co.) \tə ko͞osh´\. Perhaps from Ojibwa (Algonquian) *dakoozi* 'be short' (Vogel 1986; Nichols and Nyholm 1995).

TADLUK, Cape (Alaska, Atka C-3). The Aleut name was published in 1852 (Orth 1967).

TADMUCK Brook (Mass., Middlesex Co.) \tad´ muk\. From SNEng. Algonquian, perhaps meaning 'wading place' (Huden 1962).

TAGAGAWIK River (Alaska, Selawik B-1). The Iñupiaq (Eskimo) name is *taġraġviim kuuŋa* (Burch 1998).

TAGAKVIK Lake (Alaska, Noatak D-1). The Iñupiaq (Eskimo) name, obtained in 1956, is said to mean 'shadowy place' (Orth 1967); cf. *taġġaq* 'shadow', *-vik* 'place' (MacLean 1980).

TAGALAK (Alaska, Atka B-6). Aleut *tagalax̂*, perhaps meaning 'alighting in several places', referring to waterfowl, from *tagalix* 'to alight, to land' (Bergsland 1994); see **Tagadak Islands** above.

TAGAYARAK River (Alaska, Baird Inlet A-2). The Yupik (Eskimo) name was reported in 1949 (Orth 1967).

TAGHKANIC (N.Y., Columbia Co.) \tə kon′ ik\. Probably from the same origin as **Taconic Range** (Ruttenber 1906); see above.

TAGHUM Butte (Ore., Deschutes Co.) \tä′ gəm\. Named by the U.S. Forest Service, from Chinook Jargon <tagh′-um, to′-hum> [táhəm] 'six', perhaps from Lower Chinook \tə́xəm\. 'six' (McArthur 1992; D. Kinkade p.c.).

TAG Islands (Alaska, Gareloi Island B-2). Aleut *tagachaluĝis* 'alighting places', from *tagalix* 'to alight, to land', referring to waterfowl (Bergsland 1994). A related name is **Tagadak Islands** (Alaska, Adak C-1), from Aleut *tanadax*, perhaps replacing *tagadax* 'continuous alighting', referring to waterfowl, from *tagalix* 'to alight, to land' (Bergsland 1994). Cf. also **Tagalak** below.

TAGIUNITUK (Alaska, Noatak D-6). The Iñupiaq (Eskimo) name is perhaps *taġiuniktuaq* 'has gotten salty' (L. Kaplan p.c.). A possibly related Alaska name is **Tahinichok Mountains** (Noatak C-4).

TAGOOMENIK River (Alaska, Norton Bay B-5). From Iñupiaq (Eskimo) <Tagumanik>, reported in 1867 (Orth 1967).

TAHAMUND Lake (Alaska, Nabesna D-2) \tä hä′ mund\. From Upper Tanana (Athabaskan) *t'üüh männ'* 'cottonwood lake' (J. Kari p.c.).

TAHANTO Point (Mass., Worcester Co.) \tə hän′ tō\. From SNEng. Algonquian, named for George Tahanto, a leader of the Nashaway subgroup in 1700 (Huden 1962).

TAHAWUS (N.Y., Essex Co.) \tə hô′ wəs, tə hôz′\. Perhaps from an Iroquoian language, referring to the concept 'to pierce' (Beauchamp 1907); cf. Mohawk /-ahwe'eh-/ 'to pierce', /tekahwe'éhstha/ 'I pierce' (Michelson 1973).

TAH Bay (Alaska, Dixon Entrance D-1) \tä\. The Tlingit placename was published in 1943 (Orth 1967). A perhaps related name is **Tahini River** (Skagway C-3).

TAH CHEE (Ariz., Apache Co.) \tä′ chē, tä shā′\. From Navajo (Athabaskan) *táchii'* 'red streak running into water' (Linford 2000).

TAH HA BAH Well (N.Mex., McKinley Co.) \tä′ hä bä\. Perhaps Navajo (Athabaskan) *táhabąąh* 'spacious shore, edge', from *tá-* 'water', *ha-* 'space, area', and *bąąh* 'shore' (A. Wilson p.c.).

TAHINICHOK Mountains (Alaska, Noatak C-4) The Iñupiaq (Eskimo) name is probably *taġiunitchuaq* 'tastes salty' (L. Kaplan p.c.). A possibly related name is **Tagiunituk** (Noatak D-6).

TAHINI River (Alaska, Skagway C-3). The Tlingit name was reported in 1883 (Orth 1967); cf. *heen* /hiin/ 'river' (Davis and Leer 1976). A perhaps related name is **Tah Bay** (Alaska, Dixon Entrance D-1).

TAHKA Point (Alaska, Craig D-4). The Tlingit name was published in 1964 (Orth 1967).

TAHKENITCH Creek (Ore., Douglas Co.) \tak′ ə nich\. From Lower Umpqua (Siuslawan) [tsá:xínɪtš] 'having arms running out like a crab, tributaries' (McArthur 1992; D. Kinkade p.c.).

TAHKODAH, Lake (Wis., Bayfield Co.) \tə kō′ dä\. Perhaps related to Dakota (Siouan) *thakhódaku* 'his friend' (Riggs 1890; Ingham 2001). Possibly related placenames include **Dakota** and **Lakhota.**

TAH KUM WAH Creek (Ind., Huntington Co.) \tä kum′ wä\. Named for a Miami/Illinois (Algonquian) woman (BGN 7001). The writing **Tah Kun Wah** also occurs.

TAHLEQUAH (Okla., Cherokee Co.) \tal´ ə kwä\. From <Talikwa, Tellico>, a Cherokee (Iroquoian) town (Shirk 1974); a related name is **Tellico River** (N.C., Tenn.). In Wash. (King Co.) **Tahlequah** may be an Indian name, recorded in 1841, language not identified (Reese 1996; D. Kinkade p.c); a possibly related name is **Point Dalco** (Wash., King Co.).

TAHNETA Pass (Alaska, Anchorage D-1) \tä nē´ tə\. The Dena'ina (Athabaskan) name was reported in 1900 (Orth 1967).

TAHO (Ore., Coos Co.) \tä´ hō\. Perhaps from Chinook Jargon <tah-oo> 'away, far' (D. Kinkade p.c.). In Mich. (Clare Co.), **Lake Taho** is probably a transfer name from **Lake Tahoe** (Calif., Nev.).

TAHOE, Lake (Calif., Nev.) \tä´ hō\. From Washo /dá'aw/ 'lake' (Gudde 1998). The term occurs as a transfer name in Idaho (Idaho Co.) and Wis. (Iron Co.).

TAHOKA (Tex., Lynn Co.) \tə hō´ kə\. Said to be from an unidentified Indian language, translated 'clear water' or 'deep water' (Tarpley 1980).

TAHOLAH (Wash., Grays Harbor Co.) \tə hō´ lə\. Named for a Quinault (Salishan) leader called [t'x^{W}úlə] or [tax̹^{W}úləʔ] (Hitchman 1985; D. Kinkade p.c.).

TAHOMA Creek (Wash., Pierce Co.) \tə hō´ mə\. From Lushootseed (Salishan) /təq^{W}úbəʔ, təqúbəd/ 'snow-covered mountain', or specifically Mt. Rainier (Hitchman 1985; D. Kinkade p.c.). **Tahoma** was formerly well known as a name for Mt. Rainier, and as such it seems to have spread as a transfer to other states (e.g., Calif., Placer Co.; Ga., Richmond Co.; and N.C., McDowell Co.). In the Aleutian Islands (Alaska), **Tahoma Reef** was named for a U.S. Coast Guard ship lost here in 1914 (Orth 1967). A related placename is **Tacoma** (Wash., Pierce Co.); see above.

TAHOSA Valley (Colo., Larimer Co.) \tə hō´ sə\. Perhaps the name of a nineteenth-century Kiowa leader (Bright 1993).

TAHQUAMENON Falls (Mich., Chippewa Co.) \tə kwä´ mə non, tə kwä´ mə nən\. The name appears in Longfellow's *Hiawatha* as "Taquamenaw." It may be from Ojibwa (Algonquian), but the derivation is not clear (Vogel 1986).

TAHQUITZ Peak (Calif., Riverside Co.) \tä´ kwits, tä´ kēts\. From the name of a supernatural being said to manifest itself as a fireball in the mountains. The name is similar in two Takic languages, Luiseño *táakwish* and Cahuilla *tákush* (Gudde 1998).

TAHUACHAL, Banco (Tex., Cameron Co.) \tä wä chäl\. The name of this levee is probably a Mexican Spanish word meaning 'possum-place', from *tahuache, tacuache, tlacuache* 'possum', from Nahuatl (Aztecan) *tlacuatzin* 'little possum', from *tlacuatl* 'possum' (Santamaría 1959). The nearby **Banco Tahuachalito** \tä wä chä lē´ tō\. is the diminutive, meaning 'little possum-place'.

TAHUTA Point (Ariz., Coconino Co.) \tə hōō´ tə\. Named for Eunice Tahota Jones, a Havasupai (Yuman) basketmaker; her Native American name was [tahóta], perhaps meaning 'something concealed' (L. Hinton p.c.).

TAHUYA (Wash., Mason Co.) \tə hōō´ yə\. From the name of a Southern Coast Salish subgroup, Twana /taxúya/ (Hitchman 1985; *HNAI* 7:488).

TAIBAN (N.Mex., DeBaca Co.) \tī´ ban\. Said to be a loanword from an unidentified Indian language (Julyan 1998).

TAIGUD Islands (Alaska, Port Alexander D-5). The Tlingit name was published in 1826 (Orth 1967).

TAIHOLMAN Lake (Alaska, Bettles A-4). The Koyukon (Athabaskan) name was obtained in 1956 (Orth 1967).

TAIXTSALDA Hill (Alaska, Nabesna D-3) From Upper Tanana (Athabaskan) *shah tsäl* 'little house' (J. Kari p.c.).

TAIYA Inlet (Alaska, Skagway B-1) \tä´ yə\. The Tlingit name was published in 1870 (Orth

1967). Perhaps related is **Taiyasanka Harbor** (Alaska, Skagway B-2).

TAJANTA (Calif., Los Angeles Co.) \tä hän´ tä\. Perhaps from Gabrielino (Takic), of unknown derivation (Gudde 1998).

TAJIGUAS Creek (Calif., Santa Barbara Co.) \tə hig´ wəs, tə hē´ wəs\. A Spanish spelling for the name of a Barbareño (Chumashan) village. Perhaps from <tayiyas>, referring to a native plant called, in California Spanish, *islay* 'holly-leafed cherry' (Gudde 1998).

TAJIQUE (N.Mex., Torrance Co.) \tä hē´ kā, tə hē´ kē\. A Spanish spelling, also written <Taxique>, for a Tiwa (Tanoan) village; the Native American name was <Tüsh-yit-yay> (Harrington 1916:533).

TAJITTRO Creek (Alaska, Fort Yukon B-5). The Gwich'in (Athabaskan) name was reported in 1956 (Orth 1967).

TAKAHULA River (Alaska, Survey Pass B-2). The Iñupiaq (Eskimo) name was recorded in 1886 (Orth 1967).

TAKAIAK (Alaska, Nulato B-3). From Koyukon (Athabaskan); the derivation is not clear (Orth 1967).

TAKANASSEE, Lake (N.J., Monmouth Co.) \tak ə nas´ ē\. Perhaps from Delaware (Algonquian), but of unclear derivation (Becker 1964).

TAKANIS Bay (Alaska, Sitka D-8). The Tlingit name was published in 1852 (Orth 1967).

TAKATZ Bay (Alaska, Sitka A-3). The Tlingit name was reported in 1895 (Orth 1967).

TAKAYOFO Creek (Alaska, Naknek A-1). From Yupik (Eskimo) *taryaqvak* 'king salmon' (Orth 1967; Jacobson 1984).

TAKEENA Pensinsula (Alaska, Sitka C-7). Named for Jacob Takeena, a Tlingit man (Orth 1967).

TAKELMA Gorge (Ore., Jackson Co.) \tə kel´ mə\. The name of an Indian people of southwestern Ore., reflecting their self-designation /ta:kelmàʔn/ 'person from Rogue River', from /ta:kelám/ 'Rogue River' (D. Kinkade p.c.). A related placename is **Takilma** (Ore., Josephine Co.).

TAKEMMY (Mass., Dukes Co.) \tə kem´ ē\. From SNEng. Algonquian; cf. <togguhhum> 'he grinds corn' (Huden 1962; W. Cowan p.c.).

TAKENA Park (Ore., Linn Co.) \tə kē´ nə\. From Central Kalapuyan [čhanthíkini], a village name; cf. Tualatin (Kalapuyan) [tíkana] 'hummingbird' (H. Zenk p.c.).

TAKHAKHDONA Hills (Alaska, Melozitna C-4). The Koyukon (Athabaskan) name was obtained in 1956 (Orth 1967).

TAKHIN River (Alaska, Skagway B-2). The Tlingit name was reported in 1880 (Orth 1967). Perhaps related is the name of the **Takhinsha Mountains** (Alaska, Skagway A-3).

TAKHLAKH (Wash., Skamania Co.). The name probably originated as a misprint for **Takh Takh Meadow** (Hitchman 1985; D. Kinkade p.c.).

TAKH TAKH Meadow (Wash., Skamania Co.). Sahaptin /ta:ktá:k/ 'meadows', reduplication of /tá:k/ 'meadow' (D. Kinkade p.c.).

TAKILMA (Ore., Josephine Co.) \tə kil´ mə\. From the same source as **Takelma Gorge** (Ore., Jackson Co.); see above.

TAKLI Islands (Alaska, Mt. Katmai A-2). The Alutiiq name was published in 1847 (Orth 1967).

TAKOKA Creek (Alaska, Lake Clark A-4). The Dena'ina (Athabaskan) name was reported in 1954 (Orth 1967).

TAKOMAHTO Lake (Alaska, Nabesna C-2) \tä kə mä´ tō\. The Upper Tanana (Athabaskan) name is *taagoh naat'oh männ* 'swan nest lake' (J. Kari p.c.).

TAKOMA Park (Md., Montgomery Co.) \tə kō´ mə\. Named for **Mt. Tacoma**, an earlier name of Mt. Rainier (Wash., Pierce Co.); see **Tacoma** above.The placename **Takoma** also occurs in Alaska (Charley River B-6). Another related placename is **Tahoma Creek** (Wash., Pierce Co.).

TAKONAK Creek (Alaska, Marshall D-4). The Yupik (Eskimo) name was reported in 1951 (Orth 1967).

TAKOTNA (Alaska, Iditarod D-1) \tä kōt´ nə\. From Athabaskan, perhaps Upper Kuskokwim *tochotno'* or Deg Hit'an *tokotno'*, lit. 'open-water stream' (J. Kari p.c.).

TAKRAK Lake (Alaska, Wainwright A-1). From Iñupiaq (Eskimo) *taki-* 'to be long' (Orth 1967; MacLean 1980).

TAKSAKWIVIK Slough (Alaska, Kwiguk D-5). The Yupik (Eskimo) name was obtained in 1948 (Orth 1967).

TAKSHAK (Alaska, Marshall D-1) \tak´ shak\. The Yupik (Eskimo) name is *taksruk* 'long narrow lake' (L. Kaplan p.c.).

TAKSHANUK Mountains (Alaska, Skagway B-3). The Tlingit name was reported in 1952 as meaning 'water falls' (Orth 1967).

TAKSHILIK Creek (Alaska, Goodnews Bay C-6). The Yupik (Eskimo) name was reported in 1898 (Orth 1967).

TAKSLESLUK Lake (Alaska, Marshall A-3). Also called Long Lake. The Yupik (Eskimo) name was obtained in 1948 (Orth 1967); cf. Yupik *take-* 'be long' (Jacobson 1984).

TAKTALURAK Rocks (Alaska, Noatak D-6). The Iñupiaq (Eskimo) name is *taaqtaaluuraq* 'little black rock' (L. Kaplan p.c.).

TAKTELAK Creek (Alaska, Point Hope B-2). The Iñupiaq (Eskimo) name was recorded in 1960 as <Daktaeluk> (Orth 1967).

TAKTUSAK Hill (Alaska, Marshall C-5). The Yupik (Eskimo) name, obtained in 1965, is said to mean 'kidney-like' (Orth 1967); cf. *tartuq* 'kidney' (Jacobson 1984).

TAKUAK Creek (Alaska, Killik River B-1). The Iñupiaq (Eskimo) name is probably *taquaq* 'trail provisions' (L. Kaplan p.c.).

TAKUKAK Lake (Alaska, Kenai D-2) \tä ko͞o´ käk\. Perhaps from Dena'ina (Athabaskan); assigned about 1963 (Orth 1967).

TAKUP Point (Wash., Clallam Co.). Chinook Jargon <tŭkōpe, t'kópe, tekope> etc. [t^{h}kop] 'white', perhaps from Lower Chinook [tk'op] 'white' (Hitchman 1985; D. Kinkade p.c.).

TAKU River (Alaska, Juneau A-1) \tak o͞o´\. From a Tlingit placename [t'a:qú] (Orth 1967; *HNAI* 6:479).

TAKWAKLANUK Slough (Alaska, Kwiguk C-5). The Yupik (Eskimo) name was obtained in 1899 (Orth 1967).

TALA APOPKA (Fla., Orange Co.) \tä´ lə ə pop´ kə\. Perhaps from the same source as **Lake Tsala Apopka** (Fla., Citrus Co.); see below.

TALACHE (Idaho, Bonner Co.) \tə lä´ chē\. From Mexican Spanish *talache* or *talacha*, meaning 'pick-ax', perhaps from Nahuatl (Aztecan) *tlalli* 'earth' plus Spanish *hacha* 'ax' (Boone 1988; Santamaría 1959).

TALACHULITNA River (Alaska, Tyonek D-4) \tal ə cho͞o lit´ nə\. Dena'ina (Athabaskan) *tununiłch'ulyutnu* 'people-killed-each-other-in-water river', with *-tnu* 'river' (Kari and Fall 1987:120).

TALADEGA (Miss., Noxubee Co.) \tal ə dē´ gə\. From the same source as **Talladega County** (Ala.); see below.

TALAHOGAN Canyon (Ariz., Navajo Co.) \tal ə hō´ gən\. From Navajo (Athabaskan) *táala hooghan* 'flat-topped hogan (native house)' (Linford 2000).

TALALA (Okla., Rogers Co.) \tə lä´ lə\. Named for a Cherokee (Iroquoian) officer in the Civil War, known in English as Captain Talala (Shirk 1974); or perhaps from Unami Delaware (Algonquian) *talalakw* 'white cedar tree' (J. Rementer p.c.). Possibly related forms include **Talle** (Ala., Montgomery Co.).

TALAMANTES Creek (Colo., Moffat Co.) \tal ə man´ tēz\. Said to be the name of an

Indian leader but originally a Spanish family name (Bright 1993).

TALA Point (Wash., Jefferson Co.) \tä´ lə\. From a placename of an unidentified language; perhaps from Chinook Jargon <tala, dol-la> [tála] 'money', from English *dollar* (Kinkade p.c.).

TALAPUS Butte (Ore., Deschutes Co.) \tal´ ə pəs\. Chinook Jargon <t´al-a-pus> [tə́ləpəs, tálapəs], perhaps from Lower Chinook [i-t'a:lapas] 'coyote' (McArthur 1992; D. Kinkade p.c.). The name **Talapus** also occurs in Idaho (Latah Co.) and Wash. (King Co.).

TALARHUN River (Alaska, Baird Inlet C-7). The Yupik (Eskimo) name was reported in 1949 as meaning 'rot' or 'die' (Orth 1967).

TALAWA Lake (Calif., Del Norte Co.) \tä´ lə wə\. From the name of the **Tolowa** (Athabaskan) Indians of the area (Gudde 1998).

TALBIKSOK River (Alaska, Russian Mission C-6). The Yupik (Eskimo) name was reported in 1844, in Russian, as <Talgaksyuak> (Orth 1967).

TALIAH, Bayou (Miss., Attala Co.) \tə lī´ ə\. From Choctaw (Muskogean) <talaia> 'stagnant' (Seale 1939; Byington 1915).

TALIHINA (Okla., Le Flore Co.) \tal ə hē´ nə\. Choctaw (Muskogean) *tali-hina* 'railroad', from *tali* 'rock, metal' and *hina* 'road' (Shirk 1974; P. Munro p.c.).

TALIKOOT (Alaska, Noatak A-4) \tä lē´ ko͞ot\. The Iñupiaq (Eskimo) name, reported in 1925, is said to mean 'seal's forepaws' (Orth 1967).

TALIK Ridge (Alaska, Candle B-3). The Iñupiaq (Eskimo) name was reported in 1949 (Orth 1967).

TALISHEEK (La., St. Tammany Par.) \tal´ i shēk\. Probably from Choctaw *talǫshik* 'pebbles, gravel' (Read 1927; P. Munro p.c.).

TALISI (Ala., Lowndes Co.) \tal´ i sē\. Perhaps from the same origin as **Tallahassee,** from Muskogee *etvlwv* /(i)tálwa/ 'tribal town' and *vhassē* /ahá:ssi/ 'old, rancid' (Toomey 1917; Martin and Mauldin 2000). Other related placenames are **Tullahassee** (Okla., Wagoner Co.) and **Tulsa County** (Okla.).

TALKEETNA (Alaska, Talkeetna B-1) \täl kēt´ nə, tal kēt´ nə\. Dena'ina (Athabaskan) *k'dalkitnu* 'food-is-stored river', with *-tnu* 'river' (Orth 1967; Kari and Fall 1987:199).

TALLA Bayou (Miss., Jackson Co.) \tä´ lə\. From Choctaw (Muskogean) *talah* 'palmetto' or *tali* 'rock' (Toomey 1917; P. Munro p.c.).

TALLA BENA (La., Madison Par.) \tal ə bē´ nə\. From Choctaw (Muskogean) *talah* 'palmetto' or *tali* 'rock' plus *albina, abina* 'a camp', *abina* 'to camp' (Read 1927; P. Munro p.c.).

TALLABINNELA Creek (Miss., Monroe Co.) \tal ə bi nē´ lə\. From Choctaw (Muskogean), probably meaning 'where there is a rock', from *tali* 'rock', *aa-* 'place', and *binili, binniili* '(singular) to sit' (Seale 1939; P. Munro p.c.).

TALLABOGUE (Miss., Scott Co.) \tal ə bōg´\. From Choctaw *talah-book,* lit. 'palmetto creek' (Seale 1939; P. Munro p.c.).

TALLAC, Mount (Calif., El Dorado Co.) \tə lak´\. From Washo /dalá'ak/ 'mountain' (Gudde 1998).

TALLADEGA County (Ala.) \tal ə dē´ gə, tal ə dig´ ə\. Muskogee *tvlvtēke* /talatí:ki/, a tribal town, from *etvlwv* /(i)tálwa/ 'tribal town' plus *vtēke* /-atí:ki/ 'at the edge, border' (Read 1984; Martin and Mauldin 2000). The name **Talladega** also occurs in Ark. (Jefferson Co.).

TALLAHA, Lake (Miss., Tallahatchie Co.). Probably an abbreviation of **Tallahatchie County**; see below.

TALLAHAGA Creek (Miss., Winston Co.) \tal ə hā´ gə\. Perhaps from Choctaw (Muskogean), meaning 'a rock stands', from *tali* 'rock' and *hikiya* '(singular) to stand' (Seale 1939; P. Munro p.c.).

TALLAHALA (Miss., Perry Co.) \tal ə hal´ ə\. Perhaps from Choctaw (Muskogean), meaning 'rocks stand', from *tali* 'rock' and *hiili* '(plural) to stand' (Seale 1939; P. Munro. p.c.). A probably related name is **Tallahaly** (Ala., Sumter Co.; Read 1984).

TALLAHASSEE (Ga., Jeff Davis Co.) \tal ə has´ ē\. Muskogee *tvlvhasse* /talahá:ssi/, the name of a tribal town, perhaps from *etvlwv* /(i)tálwa/ 'tribal town' and *vhassē* /ahá:ssi/ 'old, rancid' (Goff 1975; Martin and Mauldin 2000). The name also occurs in Fla. (Leon Co.) and was first reported there in 1799, in the form "Sim-e-no-le-tallau-has-see," meaning 'Seminole Tallahassee' (Read 1934). The placename **Tallahassee** also occurs in Fla. (Leon Co.) and Mich. (Branch Co.). Possibly related placenames are **Talisi** (Ala., Lowndes Co.), **Tullahassee** (Okla., Wagoner Co.) and **Tulsa County** (Okla.).

TALLAHATCHIE County (Miss.) \tal ə hach´ ē\. Perhaps from Choctaw *tali* 'rock' plus *hachcha* 'river' (Seale 1939; P. Munro p.c.). A related placename is **Lake Tallaha** (Miss., Tallahatchie Co.).

TALLAHATTA Creek (Ala., Clarke Co.) \tal ə hat´ ə\. Probably from Choctaw (Muskogean) *tali-hata* 'silver', lit. 'rock-white' (Read 1984; P. Munro p.c.). The placename **Tallahatta** also occurs in Miss. (Lauderdale Co.). A related form is **Tallahattah Creek** (Miss., Jasper Co.).

TALLAHOMA (Miss., Jasper Co.) \tal ə hō´ mə\. Perhaps from Choctaw (Muskogean) *tali-homma* 'copper', lit. 'rock-red' (Seale 1939; P. Munro p.c.). A related placename is **Tallahomo** (Miss., Jones Co.).

TALLALOOSA (Miss., Marshall Co.) \tal ə lo͞o´ sə\. From Choctaw (Muskogean) *tali-losa,* lit. 'rock-black' (Seale 1939; P. Munro p.c.).

TALLAPOOSA County (Ala.) \tal ə po͞o´ sə\. Perhaps from Choctaw *tali* 'rock' plus *poshi* 'pulverized material' (Read 1984; P. Munro p.c.). The name also occurs in Ga. (Haralson Co.) and Alaska (Kodiak A-5).

TALLASEEHATCHEE (Ala., Talladega Co.) \tal ə sē hach´ ē\. From Muskogee *tvlvhasse* /talahá:ssi/, a tribal town, plus *hvcce* /hačči/ 'stream' (Martin and Mauldin 2000). The name of the tribal town is also the source of the modern placenames **Tallahassee** (Fla., Leon Co.), **Tullahassee** (Okla., Wagoner Co.), and **Tallassee** (Ala., Elmore Co.); see also **Tallasseehatchee** (Ala., Calhoun Co.).

TALLASHUA Creek (Miss., Newton Co.). Probably from Choctaw (Muskogean), meaning 'palmettos are there', from *talah* 'palmetto' and *asha* '(pl.) to be there' (Seale 1939; P. Munro p.c.).

TALLASSEE (Ala., Elmore Co.) \tal´ ə sē\. From Muskogee *tvlvhasse* /talahá:ssi/, a tribal town (Read 1984; Martin and Mauldin 2000). The placename also occurs in Tenn. (Blount Co.), where it is pronounced \tə las´ ē\, and in Ga. (Dougherty Co.). Probably related placenames include **Tallahassee** (Fla., Leon Co.), **Talsse** (Ala., Macon Co.), and **Tullahassee** (Okla., Wagoner Co.).

TALLATCHEE Creek (Ala., Monroe Co.) \tə lach´ ē\. Perhaps from Choctaw (Muskogean) *tali* 'rock' and *hachcha* 'stream' (Read 1984; P. Munro p.c.).

TALLATIKPI (Ala., Clarke Co.) \tal ə tik´ pē\. Perhaps from Choctaw (Muskogean) *tali* 'rock' and *tikpi* 'knob' (Read 1984).

TALLAWAMPA Creek (Ala., Choctaw Co.) \tal ə wäm´ pə\. From Choctaw (Muskogean), perhaps meaning 'to sing and eat (something)', from *taloowa* 'to sing' and *apa, ąpa* 'to eat' (Read 1984; P. Munro p.c.).

TALLAWASSEE Creek (Ala., Lowndes Co.) \tal ə wä´ sē\. Possibly derived from Muskogee *tvlvhasse* /talahá:sse/, a tribal town (Read 1984; Martin and Mauldin 2000); this also yields the placenames **Tallahassee** (Fla., Leon Co.), **Tullahassee** (Okla., Wagoner Co.), and others.

TALLAWYAH Creek (Ala., Sumter Co.). Perhaps from Choctaw (Muskogean) *tala* 'rock' and *waiya* 'leaning' (Read 1984).

TALLE (Ala., Montgomery Co.) \tal´ ē\. Probably from the same source as **Talala** (Okla., Rogers Co.); see above.

TALLEQUAH Landing (Miss., Holmes Co.) \tal´ ə kwä\. From the same origin as **Tahlequah** (Okla., Cherokee Co.); see above.

TALL Mountain (Ariz., Navajo Co.). Corresponds to Navajo (Athabaskan) *dził* 'mountain' plus *-neez* 'long, tall' (Granger 1983; Young and Morgan 1987).

TALLOKAS (Ga., Brooks Co.) Possibly from Muskogee *tvlako* /talá:ko/ 'bean' (Goff 1975; Martin and Mauldin 2000).

TALL PRAIRIE CHICKEN Creek (S.Dak., Dewey Co.). Named for a Lakhota (Siouan) resident who was called "Tall Prairie Chicken" in English (Sneve 1973).

TALLULA (Miss., Issaquena Co.) \tə lo͞o´ lə\. Choctaw (Muskogean) *talola* 'a bell', from *tali* 'rock, metal' plus *ola* 'to make a noise' (Read 1984; P. Munro p.c.). The placename **Tallula** also occurs in Ill. (Menard Co.).

TALLULAH Falls (Ga., Habersham Co.) \tə lo͞o´ lə\. The term is said to have a different origin from **Tallula** in Miss.; the Ga. name may refer to a Cherokee (Iroquoian) village, <talulu> or <taruri>. The actress Tallulah Bankhead was named after these falls (Goff 1975). The name **Tallulah** occurs in other states as a transfer (e.g., Calif., Tuolumne Co.; La., Madison Co.; and Mont., Lincoln Co.).

TALOFA (Fla., Putnam Co.) \tə lō´ fə\. From Muskogee *(e)tvlofv* /(i)taló:fa/ 'town' (Read 1934; Martin and Mauldin 2000).

TALOGA (Okla., Dewey Co.) \tə lō´ gə\. Perhaps from Choctaw (Muskogean), of unclear derivation; cf. *tali* 'rock'. The name **Taloga** also occurs in Kans. (Morton Co.).

TALOWAH (Miss., Lamar Co). From Choctaw (Muskogean), perhaps meaning 'many rocks', from *tali* 'rock' and *lawa* 'many' (Seale 1939); or perhaps a personal name, *taloowa* 'singer' (P. Munro p.c.).

TALPA (N.Mex., Taos Co.) \täl´ pə, tal´ pə\. From Mexican Spanish *Talpa,* a placename in Jalisco, Mexico (Julyan 1998); this is a dialect variant of Nahuatl (Aztecan) *tlalpan* 'on the earth, on the shore', from *tlalli* 'earth'. The name **Talpa** also occurs in Tex. (Coleman Co.).

TALPACATE Creek (Tex., Bee Co.) \tal´ pə kat\. Perhaps from Karankawa, meaning 'tadpole' (Tarpley 1980).

TALSSE (Ala., Macon Co.) \tal´ sē\. Probably from the same origin as **Tallassee** (Ala., Elmore Co.); see above.

TALTHEADAMUND Lake (Alaska, Tanacross A-4). From Upper Tanana (Athabaskan) *talttheedn männ'*, perhaps 'water-level-drops lake' (J. Kari p.c.).

TALTLINKHO Creek (Alaska, Hughes B-4). The Koyukon (Athabaskan) name, recorded in 1956, is said to mean 'always flowing' (Orth 1967).

TALUCAH (Ala., Morgan Co.) \tə lo͞o´ kə\. Perhaps from Toluca, a city in Mexico (Read 1984); see **Toluca Lake** below.

TALUGA (Fla., Liberty Co.) \tə lo͞o´ gə\. Perhaps from Muskogee *tvlako* /talá:ko/ 'pea' (Read 1934; Martin and Mauldin 2000).

TALUM Glaciers (Wash., Whatcom Co.). The personal name of an Indian guide, language not identified (BGN 7301).

TALURAREVUK Point (Alaska, Nunivak Island C-1). The Yupik (Eskimo) name, obtained in 1951, is said to mean 'where nets are placed' (Orth 1967).

TALUYETLEK Creek (Alaska, Goodnews Bay C-8). The Yupik (Eskimo) name was published in 1951 (Orth 1967).

TAMA County (Iowa) \tä´ mə\. Named for a Meskwaki (Algonquian) leader of the early nineteenth century; from Meskwaki /te:wame:ha/, a man's name of the Thunder Clan (Vogel 1983; I. Goddard p.c.). The placename **Tama** also occurs in Fla. (Liberty Co.), and S.Dak. (Meade Co.). In Idaho (Clearwater Co.) **Tama Creek** may be a shortening of the name of nearby **Tamarack Creek.**

TAMAHA (Okla., Haskell Co.) \tä mä´ hä, tä´ mə hä\. Perhaps from Choctaw (Muskogean) *tamaha* 'town' (Shirk 1974; P. Munro p.c.). Possibly related is **Tamahaw Peak** (Okla., Haskell Co.).

TAMALPAIS, Mount (Calif., Marin Co.) \tam əl pī´ əs\. From Coast Miwok /tamal páyis/, lit. 'coast mountain'; *tamal* means 'west, west coast' (Gudde 1998).

TAMANAWAS Falls (Ore., Hood River Co.) \tə man´ ə wäs\. Chinook Jargon <ta-mah-no-us> \tamánoəs\. 'guardian spirit, magic, luck, supernatural power'; probably from Sahaptin, containing /tama-/ supernatural power' (McArthur 1992; D. Kinkade p.c.).

TAMANEND (Pa., Schuylkill Co.) \tam´ ə nend\. Named for a Delaware leader of the seventeenth century, also called **Tammany;** see below.

TAMANOS Mountain (Wash., Pierce Co.). Probably from the same origin as **Tamanawas Falls** (Hitchman 1985); see above.

TAMANTALOI Hill (Alaska, Nulato B-6). The Koyukon (Athabaskan) name was reported in 1954 (Orth 1967).

TAMAQUA (Pa., Schuylkill Co.) \tə mak´ wə\. Perhaps from Delaware (Algonquian) *tëmakwe* 'beaver' (Kraft and Kraft 1985); cf. Unami Delaware /təmá:kwe:/ 'beaver' (Blalock et al. 1994). A probably related name is **Tamaques** (N.J., Union Co.).

TAMARAC River (Minn., Marshall Co.). A translation of Ojibwa (Algonquian) *mashkiigwaatig* 'tamarack tree' (Upham 2001; Nichols and Nyholm 1995). **Tamarac** is an alternative spelling of **Tamarack** \tam´ ə rak\. The name of this native coniferous tree is perhaps from Algonquian, but the derivation is not clear; cf. Canadian French *tamarac* (*RHD* 1987). As a placename, the term **Tamarack** occurs in many states (e.g., Conn., New Haven Co.; Ill., Will Co.; and Mont., Lincoln Co.).

TAMARAWA Ridge (Ill., Monroe Co.). Perhaps from the same source as **Tamaroa** (Ill., Perry Co.); see below.

TAMAROA (Ill., Perry Co.) \tam ə rō´ ə\. The term refers to a Miami-Illinois (Algonquian) subgroup (*HNAI* 15:680). Possibly related placenames are **Tamarawa Ridge** (Ill., Monroe Co.) and **Maroa** (Ill., Macon Co.).

TAMASSEE (S.C., Oconee Co.) \tə mas´ ē, tə mä´ sē\. Perhaps the name of a Cherokee (Iroquoian) town (Pearson 1978).

TAMAYARIAK River (Alaska, Flaxman Island A-3). The Iñupiaq (Eskimo) name, reported in 1912, is said to mean 'route where some people were lost' (Orth 1967); cf. *tammaq-* 'to get lost' (MacLean 1980). A probably related name is **Tamayayak Channel** (Alaska, Harrison Bay B-2), said to mean 'it is lost' (Orth 1967).

TAMBO (Calif., Yuba Co.). This Spanish-American word for 'hotel, inn' (borrowed from Quechua) was applied to the railroad station here (Gudde 1998).

TAMETT Brook (Mass., Plymouth Co.). From SNEng. Algonquian, perhaps meaning 'flooded place' (Huden 1962).

TAMGAS Harbor (Alaska, Ketchikan A-5). Perhaps an alternative form of **Tongass** (Alaska, Prince Rupert D-3).

TAMINAH, Lake (Wyo., Teton Co.) \tam´ i nä\. From Shoshoni (Numic) /tahmani/ 'springtime' (Urbanek 1974; J. McLaughlin p.c.).

TAMMANY \tam´ ə nē\. See **St. Tammany.** The name **Tammany,** without **Saint,** occurs, for example, in Idaho, Shoshone Co.; and N.J., Warren Co.). A related name is **Tamanend**; see above.

TAMOLA (Miss., Kemper Co.) \tə mō´ lə\. Perhaps from Choctaw (Muskogean); cf. *tamoli* 'to scatter', *tamowa* '(pl.) to get lost' (Seale 1939; P. Munro p.c.).

TAMOLITCH Falls (Ore., Linn Co.) \tam´ ō lich\. Chinook Jargon <ta-mo´-litsh, ta-mow´-litsh> [tamólɪc] 'tub, barrel, bucket', said to come from Sahaptin (McArthur 1992; D. Kinkade p.c.).

TAMPA (Fla., Hillsborough Co.) \tam´ pə\. Probably the name of a Calusa village, of unclear derivation (Read 1934). The placename also occurs in Kans. (Marion Co.).

TAMPICO (Ill., Whiteside Co.) \tam pē´ kō\. Named for a city in Tamaulipas state, western Mexico. The origin of the name is Huastec (Mayan) /tampik'o'/ 'place of dogs', from /pik'o'/ 'dog' (Vogel 1963; Larsen 1955). The placename also occurs in other states (e.g., Mont., Valley Co.; N.Mex., McKinley Co.; and Ohio, Darke Co.).

TANAAK, Cape (Alaska, Afognak B-4). From Aleut *tanax̂* 'land' (Bergsland 1994).

TANACROSS (Alaska, Tanacross B-5) \tan´ ə kros\. The name originated from "Tanana crossing", the place where telegraph lines crossed the **Tanana River** (Orth 1967). The name has also been applied to an Athabaskan people and language of the area.

TANADA Creek (Alaska, Nabesna C-6) \tə nä´ də\. From Ahtna (Athabaskan) *tanaadi menn'* 'moving-water lake', with *menn'* 'lake' (Kari 1990).

TANADAK Islands (Alaska, Gareloi Island A-4) \tan´ ə dak\. From the Aleut placename *tanaadax̂*, perhaps 'the island opposite' (Bergsland 1994).

TANAGA Islands (Alaska, Adak C-6). From the Aleut placename *tanax̂ax, tanagax̂*, with *tanax̂* 'land' (Bergsland 1994).

TANAINA Peak (Alaska, Anchorage A-7) \tə nī´ nə\. Named for the local Athabaskan Indian group also called Dena'ina; the Native American name is /dənaʔina/ 'the people' (*HNAI* 6:638). The term should not be confused with the tribal name and placename **Tanana River**; see below.

TANAK, Cape (Alaska, Unalaska B-6). Aleut *tanax̂siqax̂* 'made into land', from *tanax̂* (Bergsland 1994). A related name is **Tanaklak Islands** (Alaska, Adak C-1), from Aleut *tanaqlax̂*.

TANAKOT (Alaska, Unalakleet D-1). The Koyukon (Athabaskan) name was reported in 1880 as <Tanakhotkhaik> (Orth 1967).

TANALIAN River (Alaska, Lake Clark A-4) \tä nä´ lē ən\. From Dena'ina (Athabaskan) *tanilen vetnu* 'flows-into-water river', with *vetnu* 'river' (Kari and Kari 1982:20).

TANANA River (Alaska, Tanana A-5) \tan´ ə nä\. From Koyukon (Athabaskan) *tene no', tenene,* lit. 'trail river' (Kari 1999:104); the term is also applied to an Athabaskan Indian group (*HNAI* 6:575). It should not be confused with **Tanaina** or Dena'ina, which also refers both to a place and to an Athabaskan group.

TANANI (Alaska, Skagway B-2). The Tlingit name was reported in 1883 as meaning 'leaping place' (Orth 1967).

TANA Point (Alaska, Adak C-1) \tan´ə\. An abbreviation of **Tanaga Islands**; see below.

TANA River (Alaska, McCarthy A-5). From Ahtna (Athabaskan) *łtaan na'*, lit. 'bagged-object-is-in-position river', with *na'* 'stream' (Kari 1983:10).

TANASBOURNE (Ore., Washington Co.) \tan´ əs bôrn\. A compound of Chinook Jargon <ten´-as, tan´as> 'small, few, child' (see **Tenas Lakes,** below) with dialectal English *burn, bourne* 'brook' (McArthur 1992; D. Kinkade p.c.).

TANASEE Creek (N.C., Jackson Co.). Perhaps from an unidentified Indian language (Powell 1968).

TANASKAN Bay (Alaska, Unalaska B-2). From Aleut *tanasxa* 'field, camping area' (Orth 1967; Bergsland 1994).

TANAWASHER Spring (Ore., Wasco Co.) \tan´ ə wä shə\. Probably from <tăniwášĕ>, the name of a Wishram (Chinooan) man (D. Kinkade p.c.).

TANDY (Okla., Hughes Co.) \tan´ dē\. Said to be named for Tandy Walker, a Cherokee (Iroquoian) leader (Shirk 1974).

TANEUM Creek (Wash., Kittitas Co.) \tan´ əm\. From the Sahaptin placename /ptɨxnam/ (D. Kinkade p.c.).

TANGASCOOTACK Creek (Pa., Clinton Co.). Earlier recorded as <Tingascoutack, Tingascon-

tack> (etc.); perhaps from Delaware (Algonquian), but of unclear derivation (Donehoo 1928).

TANGIK (Alaska, Unimak A-5). From the Aleut placename *tan'gax̂* (Bergsland 1994).

TANGINAK Islands (Alaska, Unimak A-4). Derived from Aleut *tanĝix* 'island' (Bergsland 1994).

TANGIPAHOA Parish (La.) \tan ji pä hō´, tan ji pə hō´ (ə)\. Earlier written <Tandgepao, Tangipaos> (etc.). Perhaps contains Choctaw (Muskogean) *tąchapi* 'corncob' (from *tąchi* 'corn') and *ayowa* 'gather' (Read 1927; P. Munro p.c.). The placename also occurs in Miss. (Amite Co.).

TANIGNAK Lake (Alaska, Kodiak D-2). The Alutiiq (Eskimo) name was published in 1943 (Orth 1967).

TANIMA Peak (Colo., Boulder Co.) \tə nī´ mə\. Named for a Comanche (Numic) subgroup called /tanɨmɨtɨhka/ 'liver-eaters' (Bright 1993); cf. /nɨɨmɨ/ 'liver' (Robinson and Armagost 1990).

TANIS River (Alaska, Yakutat A-2). From Tlingit [tanís], of unknown etymology (De Laguna 1972:83).

TANJOGA Lake (Alaska, Beaver B-4). Koyukon (Athabaskan) *tonjəgə mənə'*, borrowed form Gwich'in (Athabaskan), meaning 'slough lake' (Kari 2000); cf. Gwich'in *van* 'lake' (Peter 1979).

TANKUSIM Hill (Calif., Plumas Co.) \täng kə sim`\. Probably from Maidu /t'am-k'ɨsím/, lit. 'butterfly ridge' (W. Shipley p.c.). The name was made official by the BGN in 1999.

TANNAMUS, Lake (Wash., Lewis Co.). An alternative form of **Tamanawas Falls**; see above.

TANNAWASHA Pasture (Wash., Yakima Co.). Perhaps an alternative form of **Tanawasher** (Ore., Wasco Co.).

TANOGTUKAN Lake (Alaska, Pribilof Islands A-2). The Aleut name was recorded in 1897 (Orth 1967).

TANO Point (N.Mex., Santa Fe Co.) \tä´ nō\. The Spanish form was applied in colonial times to the Tewa Indians of the Rio Grande Valley, from a probable Native American form [tʰáno, tʰá:nu] This is the origin of the name **Tanoan** \tə nō´ ən\, applied by anthropologists to the language family in which Tewa is included (*HNAI* 9:234–35, 601). Another related placename is **Hano** (Ariz., Navajo Co.).

TANOS, Los (N.Mex., Guadalupe Co.) \lōs tä´ nōs\. The Spanish name may be a plural of **Tano**; see **Tano Point** above.

TANTABOGUE Creek (Tex., Trinity Co.). Perhaps from Choctaw (Muskogean), but of unclear derivation.

TANTASQUA (Mass., Worcester Co.) \tän tä´ skwə\. From SNEng. Algonquian, but the derivation is not clear (Huden 1962).

TANUNAK (Alaska, Nunivak Island C-1) \tə nōō´ nak\. Probably from the same source as **Tununak**; see below.

TANWAX (Wash., Pierce Co.) \tan´waks\. The placename, said to mean 'neck of land', is in Lushootseed (Salishan) territory, but the term does not appear to be either from Salishan or from Chinook Jargon. A possible source is Sahaptin <tanwet> 'neck' (Reese 1996; D. Kinkade p.c.).

TAOPI (Minn., Mower Co.) \tā ō´ pē\. Named for a nineteenth-century Dakota (Siouan) leader; his Native American name was *thaópi* 'wounded' (Upham 2001; Riggs 1890). The placename also occurs in S.Dak. (Minnehaha Co.).

TAOS County (N.Mex.) \tä´ ōs\. The name of the pueblo and of the Tanoan Indian community is from /tə̂otho/ 'in the village' (*HNAI* 9:267). The local placename **Cerro de los Taoses** means 'hill of the Taos Indians'.

TAPAGHTALGHEE Bay (Alaska, St. Lawrence A-1). The Yupik (Eskimo) name was reported in 1949 (Orth 1967).

TAPEATS Creek (Ariz., Coconino Co.) \tap´ əts\. Said to be the name of a Southern Paiute (Numic) resident (Granger 1983).

TAPHOOK Point (Alaska, St. Lawrence C-5). From Yupik Eskimo, reported in 1932, perhaps from <taphak> 'barrier bar' (Orth 1967).

TAPIOCA Creek (Alaska, Teller C-5) \tap ē ō´ kə\. The place was named for the familiar dessert, made from the cassava root; the word is from *tipioca* 'juice squeezed out' in the Tupí language of Brazil (*RHD* 1987).

TAPISAGHAK River (Alaska, St. Lawrence B-0). The Yupik (Eskimo) name was reported in 1949 (Orth 1967).

TAPKALUK Islands (Alaska, Barrow B-3). The Iñupiaq (Eskimo) name was recorded in 1914 (Orth 1967).

TAPKAURAK Spit (Alaska, Barter Island A-4). The Eskimo name is *tapqauraq* 'little spit' (L. Kaplan p.c.).

TAPO Canyon (Calif., Ventura Co.) \tap´ ō\. From a Ventureño (Chumashan) name, perhaps referring to a sulphur deposit (Gudde 1998).

TAPPAHANNA Ditch (Del., Kent Co.) \tap ə han´ ə\. From Delaware (Algonquian), perhaps meaning 'stream that ebbs and flows' (Heck et al. 1966). Probably related placenames are **Tappahannock** (Va., Essex Co.), said to be a CAC Algonquian word meaning 'rise and fall of water'; and **Rappahannock** (Va., Lancaster Co.).

TAPPAN, Lake (N.J., Bergen Co.). Said to be an abbreviation of a Delaware (Algonquian) name such as <Thuphanne, Tuppeekhanne>; of unclear derivation (Becker 1964). The placename also occurs in **Tappan Zee** (N.Y., Rockland Co.), with Dutch *zee* 'lake'.

TAPPGHAPPAGHAK (Alaska, St. Lawrence D-3). The Yupik (Eskimo) name was reported in 1932 (Orth 1967).

TAQUACHE Creek (Tex., Zapata Co.) \tə kwä´ chē\. Mexican Spanish *tlacuache* 'possum', from Nahuatl (Aztecan) *tlacuatzin* (Santamaría 1959; Karttunen 1983).

TARAL (Alaska, Valdez B-2) \tə ral´\. From Ahtna (Athabaskan) *taghael* 'weir in water' (J. Kari p.c.).

TARANCAHUAS Creek (Tex., Duval Co.) \tə räng´ kə wäs\. Perhaps a Spanish plural, reflecting an alternative form of Karankawa, the name of an Indian group that once lived in Tex.

TARANOVOKCHOVIK Pass (Alaska, Kwiguk C-6). This watercourse has a Yupik (Eskimo) name, recorded in 1899 (Orth 1967).

TARBOO Creek (Wash., Jefferson Co.) \tär´ bo͞o\. Perhaps from the Twana (Salishan) placename /táʔbəx^{W}/ (D. Kinkade p.c.). Possibly related placenames are nearby **Dabob** and **Tabook Point** (Wash., Jefferson Co.).

TARGHEE (Idaho, Fremont Co.) \tär´ gē\. Named for a nineteenth-century Bannock (Numic) leader (Boone 1988). The placename **Targhee** also occurs in Wyo. (Lincoln Co.).

TARITSI Gulch (Calif., Siskiyou Co.) \tä rit´ sē\. Formerly called Squaw Gulch; renamed by BGN 1997 with Shasta /taríc'i'/ 'woman'.

TARKIO (Mo., Atchison Co.) \tär´ kē ō\. Perhaps from an unidentified Indian language (Ramsay 1952).

TARLECHIA Creek (Miss., Prentiss Co.) \tä lē´ chē\. Probably from Choctaw (Muskogean) *talah aa-chiiya* 'where two palmettos sit', containing *talah* 'palmetto'', *aa-* 'place', and *chiiya* 'two sit' (Seale 1939; P. Munro p.c.).

TARLOW Creek (Miss., Newton Co.) \tä´ lō\. Earlier written as <Tala>; probably from Choctaw (Muskogean) *tala* 'palmetto' (Seale 1939; P. Munro p.c.).

TAROKA Arm (Alaska, Seldovia C-1). Probably from Alutiiq (Eskimo) *takuka'aq* 'brown bear' (Orth 1967; Leer 1978).

TAROLKES (Calif., Trinity Co.) \tə rōl´ kəs\. From Wintu /toror kelas/, lit. 'long ridge' (Gudde 1998).

TARPISCAN Creek (Wash., Kittitas Co.) \tär pis´ kən\. From the Moses-Columbian (Salishan) placename /tạpíṣqn/ [tạpíṣqən] (D. Kinkade p.c.).

TARRATINE (Maine, Somerset Co.) \târ´ ə tēn\. Said to be the name of a Micmac (Algonquian) subgroup (Huden 1962).

TASAYCHEK Lagoon (Alaska, Noatak B-4). The Iñupiaq (Eskimo) is perhaps *tasitchiaq* 'new lagoon' (L. Kaplan p.c.). A related Alaska placename is **Tasikpak Lagoon** (Noatak D-7); see below.

TASCALA Canyon (Ariz., Santa Cruz Co.) \tä skä´ lə\. Perhaps an alternative form of Mexican Spanish *Tlaxcala,* the name of a city and state in central Mexico; from Nahuatl (Aztecan) *tlaxcallan* 'place for making tortillas', from *tlaxcalli* 'tortilla' (Granger 1983).

TASCO (Kans., Sheridan Co.) \tä´ skō\. An alternative spelling of Taxco, a town in Mexico, from Nahuatl (Aztecan) *tlachco* 'ball-court place', from *tlachtli* 'ball court' (Rydjord 1968).

TASHALICH River (Alaska, Bering Glacier A-8). The Tlingit name was reported in 1904 (Orth 1967).

TASHMOO Lake (Mass., Dukes Co.). From SNEng. Algonquian, perhaps meaning 'big spring' (Huden 1962).

TASHOSHGON (Alaska, Nulato D-3). The Koyukon (Athabaskan) is of unclear derivation (Orth 1967).

TASHUA Hill (Conn., Fairfield Co.). A shortening of <Tamtashua>, from SNEng. Algonquian, perhaps meaning 'summit of the mountain' (Huden 1962).

TASIGHOOVIK Bay (Alaska, St. Lawrence A-2). The Yupik (Eskimo) name was reported in 1949 (Orth 1967).

TASIKPAK Lagoon (Alaska, Noatak D-7). The Iñupiaq (Eskimo) name, said to mean 'big lagoon', was reported in 1950 (Orth 1967); cf. *tasiq* 'lagoon', *-(q)pak* 'big' (Webster and Zibell 1970). A related Alaska placename is **Tasaychek Lagoon** (Noatak B-4); see above.

TASISWANE Lake (Alaska, Bettles C-6). The Koyukon (Athabaskan) name was reported in 1956 (Orth 1967).

TASKA (Miss., Marshall Co.) \tas´ kə\. Perhaps from Choctaw (Muskogean) *tashka* 'warrior' (Seale 1939; P. Munro p.c.). A possible alternative form is **Taskee** (Mo., Wayne Co.) \tas´ kē\.

TASKIGI (Ala., Elmore Co.). Probably an alternative form of **Tuskeegee**; see below.

TASNUNA Glacier (Alaska, Cordova D-5) \taz nōō´ nə\. From Ahtna (Athabaskan) *t'aghes nuu na'*; cf. *nuu* 'river island', *na'* 'stream' (Kari 1990).

TATAHATSO Wash (Ariz., Coconino Co.). Perhaps from Navajo (Athabaskan) *bidáá hatsoh* 'big rim', with the English influenced by the nearby placename **Tatahoysa Wash** (Linford 2000).

TATAHOYSA Wash (Ariz., Coconino Co.). Perhaps from Navajo (Athabaskan), but the derivation is unclear (Linford 2000).

TATAI TOAK (Ariz., Pima Co.). From O'odham (Piman) *taḍai do'ag,* lit. 'roadrunner mountain' (J. Hill p.c.).

TATALINA River (Alaska, McGrath D-6) \tat ə lē´ nə\. From Upper Kuskokwim (Athabaskan). Another **Tatalina River** (Livengood A-5) is from Lower Tanana *tat'ali no'* 'middle Washington Creek', with *no'* 'stream' (J. Kari p.c.).

TATAMY (Pa., Northampton Co.) \tat´ ə mē\. Named for a seventeenth-century Delaware (Algonquian) leader, known to white settlers as Moses Fonda Tatemy—also Titamy, Totami, and Tundy (Donehoo 1928).

TATANKA Lake (S.Dak., Corson Co.). From Lakhota (Siouan) *thathą́ka* 'buffalo bull', with *thą́ka* 'big' (Ingham 2001).

TATASCO (Alaska, Dixon Entrance C-3). Perhaps a Tlingit name, reported in 1795 (Orth 1967).

TATEGNAK Point (Alaska, St. Lawrence D-6). From St. Lawrence Island Yupik (Eskimo) *tatek* 'bridge of the nose' (Orth 1967; Jacobson 1987). A probably related form is **Tatik Point** (Alaska, St. Lawrence C-6).

TATER (Idaho, Lemhi Co.) \tā´ tər\. Colloquial English for *potato,* from Spanish *batata* 'sweet potato', from the Taino (Arawakan) language of the West Indies. The placename **Tater** is also found in N.C. (Macon Co.).

TATETUCK (Conn., Fairfield Co.). From SNEng. Algonquian, perhaps meaning 'principal stream' (Huden 1962).

TATIGIROK Creek (Alaska, Noatak D-6). The Iñupiaq (Eskimo) name is *tatikkiraq* 'little thing to brush against' (Burch 1998); cf. *tatigaa* 'touches it' (Webster and Zibell 1970).

TATIK Point (Alaska, St. Lawrence C-6). Probably from the same origin as **Tategnak Point**; see above.

TATINA River (Alaska, Talkeetna B-6) \tä tē´ nə\. From Upper Kuskokwim (Athabaskan) *tatinu,* containing *-nu* 'river' (Kari and Fall 1987: 130).

TATITLEK (Alaska, Cordova D-8) \tə tit´ lek\. Perhaps an Ahtna (Athabaskan) name, of unclear derivation (Orth 1967).

TATK KAM VO (Ariz., Pima Co.). O'odham (Piman) *ta:tad wo'o* 'pond of the feet', from *ta:tad* 'feet' (*tad* 'foot') plus *wo'o* 'pond' (J. Hill p.c.). An alternative form of the placename is **Tatkum Vo.**

TATLALINGUK Pass (Alaska, St. Michael A-3). The Yupik (Eskimo) name was obtained in 1899 (Orth 1967).

TATLANIKA Creek (Alaska, Fairbanks C-4) \tat əl nē´ kə\. Lower Tanana (Athabaskan) *tl'aɬ nik'a,* lit. 'fire-drill stream', with *nik'a* 'secondary stream' (Kari 1999:135).

TATLAWIKSUK River (Alaska, Sleetmute D-1). Perhaps from Athabaskan; cf. Upper Kuskokwim *tolghwtno', tilghutno'* or Deg Hit'an *tilighutno',* containing *no'* 'stream' (J. Kari p.c.).

TATLIGNAGPEKE Mountains (Alaska, Goodnews Bay B-7). The Yupik (Eskimo) name was reported in 1954 (Orth 1967).

TAT MOMOLI (Ariz., Pinal Co.). O'odham (Piman) *taḍ memelĭ* 'footrace', from *taḍ* 'foot' plus *memelĭ* 'running' (J. Hill p.c.). A related placename in the same area is **Tat Momolikot Dam,** with *memelĭkuḍ* 'place of the footrace'.

TATNIC Brook (Conn., Windham Co.) \tat´ nik\. Perhaps a shortening of a SNEng. Algonquian name meaning 'big hill place' (Trumbull 1881). The name **Tatnic** also occurs in Maine (York Co.). A possibly related placename is **Tatnuck** (Mass., Worcester Co.) \tat´ nək\.

TATOMUCK Brook (Conn., Fairfield Co.). From SNEng. Algonquian, perhaps meaning 'trembling meadow' (Huden 1962).

TATONDAN Lake (Alaska, Anchorage D-3) \tə ton´ dən\. Perhaps from Ahtna (Athabaskan) *taɬtaan bene'* 'water-extends lake', with *bene'* 'lake' (Kari and Fall 1987:266).

TATONDUK River (Alaska, Eagle D-1) \tə ton´ duk\. Probably from Han (Athabaskan) *tthee t'aw ndëk* (J. Kari p.c.).

TATONKA (Kans., Ellsworth Co.). Perhaps from a Kansa (Siouan) word meaning 'big deer', from /ttá/ 'deer' plus /ttǫ́ga/ 'big' (Rydjord 1968; R. Rankin p.c.).

TATOOSH Creek (Wash., Lewis Co.) \ta to͞osh´\. Chinook Jargon <ta-toosh´, to-toosh´> [tætúš] 'nipple, breast, milk', probably from Ojibwa (Algonquian) *doodoosh* 'nipple, breast' (D. Kinkade p.c.; Rhodes 1985). The placename also occurs in Alaska (Ketchikan C-6). A related name is **Tatouche Peak** (Ore., Jackson Co.). Distinct from the above is **Tatoosh Island** (Wash., Clallam Co.), from Makah (Nootkan) /tutu:tš/ 'thunderbird'. This is probably a borrowing from the related Nootka language of British Columbia (W. Jacobsen).

TATOW Knob (Utah, Millard Co.) \tə tou´\. From Ute (Numic), said to mean 'big toe' (Van Cott 1990).

TATSIMISA (Alaska, Noatak D-6). The Iñupiaq (Eskimo) name was reported in 1966 (Orth 1967).

TATSOLO Point (Wash., Pierce Co.). Perhaps from an unidentified Indian language (Hitchman 1985).

TATTILABA (Ala., Clarke Co.) \tat ə lā´ bə\. Perhaps from Choctaw (Muskogean) *itti hata* 'whitewood tree', *illi* 'dead', and *aba* 'above' (P. Munro p.c.).

TATTITGAK Bluff (Alaska, Umiat B-4). From Iñupiaq (Eskimo) *tatirgaq* 'crane' (bird) (Orth 1967; Webster and Zibell 1970).

TATUGH (Wash., Kitsap Co.). From Lushootseed (Salishan) [tátču], the name for Blake Island; this is the diminutive of [táču'], the name of Vashon Island (D. Kinkade p.c.).

TAUGHANNOCK Creek (N.Y., Tompkins Co.) \tə gan´ ək\. Perhaps a transferred alternative form of **Taconic Range**; see above.

TAUKOMAS (N.Y., Suffolk Co.). From SNEng. Algonquian, of unclear derivation (Tooker 1911).

TAULAGEE (Ga., Sumter Co.). Perhaps from Muskogee *tvlako* /talá:ko/ 'bean' (Goff 1975; Martin and Mauldin 2000).

TAUM SAUK Mountain (MO, Iron Co.) \tam´ sôk, tôm´ sôk, täm´ suk\. Perhaps from an unidentified Indian language (Ramsay 1952).

TAUPA (Okla., Comanche Co.). Said to be a Comanche (Numic) personal name (Shirk 1974).

TAUPAWSHAS Swamp (Mass., Nantucket Co.) For the possessive <Towpusher's>, referring to a Wampanoag (SNEng. Algonquian) man living in 1723 (F. Karttunen p.c.).

TAUROMA (Kans., Pottawatomie Co.). Named for a Wyandot (Iroquoian) leader in the nineteenth century (Rydjord 1968); also written **Tauromee.**

TAVAPUTS Plateau (Utah, Carbon Co.). Ute (Numic) /tapappɨttsi/ [tavάppɨttsI], diminutive of /tapappɨ/ 'shield' (J. McLaughlin p.c.).

TAVEELUK Point (Alaska, St. Lawrence B-6). The Yupik (Eskimo) name was reported in 1949 (Orth 1967).

TAWAH Creek (Alaska, Yakutat B-5). From Tlingit [t'áwàł], of unknown etymology (De Laguna 1972:74).

TAWAKONI Causeway (Tex., Hunt Co.). Said to be the name of a Caddoan subgroup, related to the Wacos and the Wichitas (Wright 1951). The placename **Tawakoni** also occurs in Kans. (Butler Co.).

TAWAK Passage (Alaska, Sitka C-7). From Tlingit *t'aawáq* 'Canada goose' (Orth 1967; Davis and Leer 1976).

TAWAPA Spring (Ariz., Navajo Co.) \tə wä´ pə\. Hopi *taawapa* 'sun spring', from *taawa* 'sun' plus *-pa, paa-hu* 'water, spring' (K. Hill p.c.). There is also a **Tawapa** in N.Mex. (Sandoval Co.).

TAWA Point (Ariz., Apache Co.) \tä´ wə\. From Hopi (Uto-Aztecan) *taawa* 'sun' (K. Hill p.c.). There is also a **Tawa** in N.Mex. (Rio Arriba Co.).

TAWAS (Ohio, Summit Co.) \tä´ wäs, tä´ wəs\. Probably from Miami-Illinois /ta:wa:wa/ 'person of the Ottawa (Algonquian) people' (M. McCafferty p.c.); the placename also occurs in Mich. (Iosco Co.). See also **Ottawa** above. Related placenames are **Tawatown** (Ohio, Allen Co.) and **Tawawa** (Ohio, Shelby Co.).

TAWASA (Ala., Montgomery Co.). Also written <Tawasha> and <Toucha>, the name of an Indian group of uncertain identification (Read 1984:70).

TAWASENTHA Hill (Mass., Barnstable Co.). Formerly the name of a place in Albany Co., N.Y.; perhaps of Algonquian origin, but of unclear derivation (Beauchamp 1907).

TAWATOWN (Ohio, Allen Co.). From the same source as **Tawas**; see above. Probably of the same origin is **TAWAWA** (Ohio, Shelby Co.).

TAWAWAG (Conn., New London Co.). From SNEng. Algonquian, perhaps meaning 'abandoned land' (Tooker 1911).

TAWAWE Lake (Alaska, Gulkana A-6) \tə wä´ wā\. From Ahtna (Athabaskan) *taghaaghi bene'* 'next-to-the-water lake' (Kari 1983:37); cf. *ben, -bene'* 'lake' (Kari 1999:34).

TAWCAW Creek (S.C., Clarendon Co.). Perhaps from an unidentified Indian language (Pickens 1963:38).

TAXAHAW (S.C., Lancaster Co.). Perhaps from Catawba (Siouan), meaning 'wild dog, wolf' (Pickens 1961–62:22).

TAYCHEEDAH (Wis., Fond du Lac Co.) \tā chē´ də\. From Winnebago (Siouan) *teechíra* 'lake camp', containing *tée* 'lake', *chíi* 'dwell', and *-ra* 'nominalizer' (Vogel 1991; K. Miner p.c.).

TAYWA Creek (N.C., Swain Co.). Said to have been named for a Cherokee (Iroquoian) leader (Powell 1968).

TAZCOL Peak (Alaska, Valdez B-7). A name composed from parts of **Tazlina** (see below) and *Columbia,* the names of two glaciers (Orth 1967).

TAZIMINA (Alaska, Iliamna D-5) \taz i mē´ nə, tə zim´ nə\. From Dena'ina (Athabaskan) *taz'in vena* 'fish-trap lake' (Kari and Kari 1982:17); cf. *ven, -vena* 'lake' (Kari 1999:34).

TAZLINA (Alaska, Gulkana A-3) \taz lē´ nə\. From Ahtna (Athabaskan) *tezdlen na'* 'swift-current river', from *tezdlen* 'it is flowing swiftly' and *na'* 'stream' (J. Kari p.c.).

TCHEFUNCTA (La., St. Tammany Par.) \chə fungk´ tə\. From Choctaw (Muskogean) <hachofakti> 'chinquapin nut' (Byington 1915; Read 1927). The spelling **Tchefuncte** is also used.

TCHOUPITOULAS (La., Jefferson Par.) \chop i to͞o´ ləs\. Perhaps the name of a Choctaw (Muskogean) subgroup, meaning 'those who live by the stream', from *haccha* 'stream', *pit-* 'there', and *tǫla* 'to lie' (Read 1927; P. Munro p.c.).

TCHOUTACABOUFFA River (Miss., Harrison Co.). From Choctaw (Muskogean), possibly meaning 'where pottery is broken', from *shoti* 'earthen pot', *aa-* 'place', and *kobafa* 'broken' (Seale 1939; P. Munro p.c.).

TCHULA (Miss., Holmes Co.) \cho͞o´ lə\. Probably from Choctaw (Muskogean) *cholah* 'fox' (Seale 1939; P. Munro p.c.).

TCHULKADE Lake (Alaska, Black River B-5). The Gwich'in (Athabaskan) name is *chuu k'aadlaii* 'water is there' (J. Kari p.c.).

TEA Bar (Calif., Siskiyou Co.) \tē\. From Karuk *tíih,* the name of a village, of no known etymology (Gudde 1998).

TEAHWHIT Head (Wash., Jefferson Co.). Chinook Jargon <te-áh-wit, tee-owitt, te-yah´-wit> [tiáwɪt] 'foot, leg', perhaps from Kathlamet (Chinookan) [tiáqo-it] 'his feet, his legs'. This placename is not derived, as has sometimes been said, from Quileute (Salishan) /cix̣á:taloq^{W}/ 'at the waterfall place' (Hitchman 1985; D. Kinkade p.c.).

TEAKEAN (Idaho, Clearwater Co.). From Nez Perce (Sahaptian) /té:kin/ 'meadow, swamp' (Aoki 1994).

TEANAWAY (Wash., Kittitas Co.) \tē an´ ə wā\. From Sahaptin, possibly representing /tyawnawí-ins/ 'drying place' (Hitchman 1985; D. Kinkade p.c.).

TEATICKET (Mass., Barnstable Co.) \tē´ tik ət\. From SNEng. Algonquian, perhaps meaning 'great tidal-stream place', from <k'te-, te-> 'great', <-tuck> 'tidal stream', and <-et> 'place' (Huden 1962; W. Cowan p.c.). A related placename is **Titicut** (Mass., Plymouth Co.).

TEBAY River (Alaska, McCarthy B-8) \tē´ bā\. From Ahtna (Athabaskan) *debae* 'Dall sheep' (J. Kari p.c.).

TECATE (Calif., San Diego Co.) \ti kä´ tē\. From Spanish *Tecate*; the name is better known as applying to a city just across the Mexican border in Baja Calif. It is probably Diegueño (Yuman), perhaps derived from *tuukatt* 'to cut with an ax' (Gudde 1998).

TECHEVA Creek (Miss., Yazoo Co.) \tə chē´ və\. Perhaps abbreviated from Choctaw *isht-achifa* 'what one washes with' (with *achifa* 'to wash') or *isht-ahchifa* 'soap', lit. 'what something is washed with' (P. Munro p.c.). An alternative spelling is **Tesheva Creek.**

TECHUMTAS Island (Ore., Umatilla Co.) \tē kum´ təs\. Perhaps a name given by the Cayuse (Sahaptian) Indians to J. B. Switzler, the owner of the island (McArthur 1992).

TECOLOTE \tek ə lō´ tē\. This Mexican Spanish word for 'owl' is from Nahuatl (Aztecan) *tecolotl.* It is widely used as a placename (e.g., Calif., Santa Barbara Co.; and N.Mex., Lincoln Co.). The related name **Tecoloteños** (N.Mex., San Miguel Co.) \tek ə lō tā´ nyōs\. means 'owl-people'. Another related placename, **Tecolotito** \tek ə lō tē´ tō\, could be the Spanish diminutive, meaning 'little owl', but it is more likely to mean 'the small place founded as an offshoot of the place called **Tecolote**' (Julyan 1998); the name is found in Calif. (Santa Barbara Co.) and N.Mex. (San Miguel Co.).

TECOMA (Nev., Elko Co.) \tə kō´ mə\. Named in 1869 for the **Tecoma Mines** in the region (Carlson 1974). The origin of the name is unclear, but it may be derived from **Tacoma,** the term formerly applied to Mt. Rainier (Wash., Pierce Co.) There is also a **Tecoma** in Utah (Box Elder Co.).

TECOPA (Calif., Inyo Co.) \tə kō´ pə\. Said to have been named for a Southern Paiute (Numic) elder, /tuku-pɨda/ 'wildcat-arm' (Gudde 1998).

TECTAH Creek (Calif., Humboldt Co.) \tek´ tä\. From the Yurok village name /tektoh/ 'log' (Gudde 1998).

TECUMSEH \tə kum´ sē, tə kum´ sə\. Named for a Shawnee (Algonquian) leader who tried to unite Indian peoples in the early nineteenth century. His Native American name may have been /tkamʔθe/ 'flies across' (I. Goddard p.c.); cf. the Menominee (Algonquian) equivalent /tahkamehsɛ:w/ 'flies straight across' (Bloomfield 1975). As a placename, **Tecumseh** has been adopted in many states (e.g., Ind., Vigo Co.; Kans., Shawnee Co.; and Mo., Ozark Co.). A related form is found in **Tecumsey Lake** (Ohio, Perry Co.).

TECUYA (Calif., Kern Co.) \tə ko͞o´ yə\. Perhaps for <Tokya>, a term applied by the Yokuts Indians to the Chumashan Indians; possibly from Yokuts <tʰoxil> 'west' (Gudde 1998).

TEDOC (Calif., Tehama Co.). A variant spelling of **Tidoc Mountain**; see below.

TEEC-NI-DI-TSO Wash (N.Mex., San Juan Co.) \tēk ni dit´ sō\. Navajo (Athabaskan) *t'iis niditso* 'cottonwood trees beginning to descend yellow', containing *t'iis* 'cottonwood', *ni-* 'earth', *di-* 'beginning', and *-tso* 'yellow, light green' (A. Wilson p.c.).

TEEC NOS POS (Ariz., Apache Co.) \tēk nōs pos´, tēs nōs pos ˋ\. Navajo (Athabaskan) *t'iis názbąs* 'cottonwoods in a circle', from *t'iis* 'cottonwood trees' plus *názbąs* 'circle, circular' (Granger 1983; Wilson 1995). A related place name is **Tees Toh** (Ariz., Navajo Co.).

TEEKALET (Wash., Kitsap Co.). This represents the Lushootseed (Salishan) placename /ti q'íɬt'/, referring to Port Gamble, from /ti/ 'the' and /q'íɬt'/ 'skunk cabbage' (D. Kinkade p.c.).

TEEPEE \tē´ pē\. An alternative spelling of **Tepee;** see below. The spelling **Teepee** occurs as a placename in several states (e.g., N.Dak., McKenzie Co.; S.Dak., Harding Co.; and Ore., Wallowa Co.). **Tepee Flats** is in Idaho (Idaho Co.). The spelling **Tee Pee** also occurs (e.g., Ga., Oconee Co.; Tex., Motley Co.; and Alaska, Nome C-1). The name **Teepeeota Point** (Minn., Wabasha Co.), also written **Tepeeota,** means 'many houses'; cf. *óta* 'many'.

TEES TOH (Ariz., Navajo Co.) \tēs tō ˋ\. From Navajo (Athabaskan) *t'iis tó,* lit. 'cottonwood water' (Linford 2000). Related placenames include **Teec Nos Pos** (Ariz., Apache Co.); see above.

TEETHCANOE Lake (Alaska, Kateel River B-2). Apparently a folk-etymology, probably from Koyukon (Athabaskan), obtained in 1955 (Orth 1967).

TEE WEES Butte (Ore., Jefferson Co.) \tē´ wēz\. Perhaps from an unidentified Indian language (D. Kinkade p.c.).

TE'EWI (N.Mex., Rio Arriba Co.). Also written **Teewi**; an abandoned pueblo once occupied by speakers of the Tewa (Tanoan) language (*HNAI* 9:250).

TEEWINOT Mountain (Wyo., Teton Co.) \tē´ wi not\. Shoshoni (Numic) /tɨwɨnɨtɨ/ 'Teton Range', lit. 'standing rock', containing /tɨm-/ 'rock' and /wɨnɨ/ 'stand' (J. McLaughlin p.c.).

TEGUA (Ariz., Navajo Co.) \tā´ gwə, tā´ wə\. From Spanish *Tegua,* referring to the **Tewa** (Tanoan) Indians who live on the Hopi First Mesa. An alternative spelling is **Tequa.**

TEHACHAPI (Calif., Kern Co.) \tə hach´ ə pē\. Kawaiisu (Numic) /tɨhačɨpía/, perhaps meaning 'hard climbing'; cf. /tɨhaa/ 'difficult' plus /čipii-/ 'to climb' (Gudde 1998).

TEHAMA County (Calif.) \tə hā´ mə\. The name of a Wintun village, of unclear derivation (Gudde 1998). The name **Tehama** also occurs in Kans. (Cherokee Co.).

TEHIPITE Dome (Calif., Fresno Co.) \tə hip´i tē\. Perhaps from Monachi (Numic), of unclear derivation (Gudde 1998).

TEHUACANA (Tex., Limestone Co.) \ti wô´ kə nə\. A Spanish spelling for the name of a Wichita (Caddoan) subgroup; also written <Tawakoni, Tewockony> (Tarpley 1980).

TEHUA Hills (Ariz., Navajo Co.) \tā´ wə\. The Spanish spelling comes from the same origin as **Tewa** and **Tegua.**

TEKAKWITHA \tek ə kwith´ ə\. A seventeenth-century Iroquoian woman, Kateri Tekakwitha, was converted to Catholicism and is venerated by many Catholics. Her surname has been given to places in S.Dak. (Roberts Co.) and Wis. (Langlade Co.).

TEKAMAH (Neb., Burt Co.) \tə kā´ mə\. Perhaps from Omaha (Siouan) <te-ka-mah> 'cottonwood tree' (Perkey 1995).

TEKAPO (N.Mex., McKinley Co.). Perhaps from Zuni /tek'appowa/ 'hill' (Ferguson and Hart 1985; Newman 1958).

TEKEAKSAKRAK Lake (Alaska, Shungnak D-3). The Iñupiaq (Eskimo) lake was reported in 1954 (Orth 1967).

TEKEGAKROK Point (Alaska, Barrow B-4). The Iñupiaq (Eskimo) is probably *tikiġaġruaq* 'big point' (L. Kaplan p.c.). cf. *tikiq* 'index finger' (Fortescue et al. 1994).

TEKENI Lake (N.Y., Herkimer Co.) \ti kē´ nē\. Probably from Delaware <tekene> 'forest' (Brinton and Anthony 1888).

TEKIU Point (Wash., Kitsap Co.). From Twana or Lushootseed (both Salishan) /stiqíw/ 'horse' or perhaps from Lushootseed /stiqáyuʔ/ 'wolf' (D. Kinkade p.c.).

TEKLANIKA River (Alaska, Fairbanks B-5) \tek lə nē´ kə\. From Lower Tanana (Athabaskan) *toch'edha* 'water-amulet' plus *nik'a* [ni:k'a] 'river' (Kari 1999:125).

TEKOA (Wash., Whitman Co.) \tē´ kō\. From the biblical placename *Tekoah*; the Coeur d'Alene (Salishan) name for the place is /t'ík'ʷut/ 'elder tree', probably folk-etymologized on the basis of the English term (D. Kinkade p.c.).

TEKONSHA (Mich., Calhoun Co.) \tə kon´ shə\. Named for a Potawatomi (Algonquian) leader, <Tekonquasha> (Vogel 1986).

TELAQUANA River (Alaska, Lime Hills A-4) \tə lak´ wə nə\. From Dena'ina (Athabaskan) *dilah vena* 'fish-swim-in lake' (Kari and Kari 1982:35); cf. *ven, -vena* 'lake' (Kari 1999:34).

TELAVIRAK Hills (Alaska, Point Hope A-2). The Iñupiaq (Eskimo) name was reported in 1962 (Orth 1967).

TELEMITZ Islands (Alaska, False Pass B-2). Perhaps from Aleut, reported in 1901 (Orth 1967).

TELIAMINA Lake (Alaska, Medfra C-1) \tə lī´ mi nə\. Cf. Upper Kuskokwim (Athabaskan) *tilaydi mina',* lit. 'broad whitefish lake', with *mina'* 'lake' (Kari 1999:100).

TELICO Township (Ark., St. Francis Co.) \tel´ i kō\. Probably from the same origin as **Tellico**

River; see below. The name **Telico** also occurs in Tex. (Ellis Co.).

TELIDA (Alaska, Medfra B-1) \tə lī´ də\. From Upper Kuskokwim (Athabaskan) *tilaydi* 'broad whitefish place'. A related name is **Telidaside Creek** (Alaska, Medfra B-1), abbreviated from *tilaydits'i noghwdl no'* 'to-broad-whitefish-place crooked creek' (J. Kari p.c.).

TELLICO River (N.C., Tenn.) \tel´ i kō\. From the name of a Cherokee (Iroquoian) village, also written <Talikwa, Telliquo> (Powell 1968; Booker et al. 1992:444, fn. 35). A related placename is **Tahlequah** (Okla., Cherokee Co.); see above.

TELOCASET (Ore., Union Co.) \tel´ ō kas ət\. Said to be from a Nez Perce (Sahaptian) word meaning 'a thing at the top' (McArthur 1992).

TELOGA (Ga., Chattooga Co.) \tē lī´ gə\. From Muskogee *tvlako* /tala:ko/ 'bean' (Goff 1975; Martin and Mauldin 2000). A related placename is **Telogia** (Fla., Liberty Co.; Read 1934).

TELSITNA River (Alaska, Ruby B-1) \tel sit´ nə\. The Koyukon (Athabaskan) name was reported in 1915 (Orth 1967); cf. /-no:'/ 'river' (Kari 1999).

TELUKHTI Creek (Alaska, Melozitna C-5). The Koyukon (Athabaskan) name was obtained in 1956 (Orth 1967).

TELULAH Park (Wis., Outagamie Co.) \tə lo͞o´ lə\. Probably a transfer from **Tallula** (Miss., Issaquena Co.) or **Tallulah Falls** (Ga., Habersham Co.).

TEMECULA (Calif., Riverside Co.) \tə mek´ yo͞o lə, tem ə kyo͞o´ lə\. From <Temeku>, the name of a Luiseño (Takic) village (Gudde 1998).

TEMESCAL, Lake (Calif., Alameda Co.) \tem ə skal´, tem´ ə skal\. From Mexican Spanish *temescal* 'sweathouse, a structure used by Native Americans for sweat-baths', from Nahuatl (Aztecan) *temaxcalli* 'sweathouse', containing *tema* 'to bathe' and *calli* 'house'. The placename is used widely in California (Gudde 1998).

TEMETATE Creek (Calif., San Luis Obispo Co.) \tem ə tä´ tē\. The name apparently reflects Mexican Spanish *temetate* 'stone slab used for grinding corn' or its Nahuatl (Aztecan) prototype *temetlatl,* from *tetl* 'stone' and *metlatl* 'grinding slab'. This is probably a folk-etymology, however, distorting the original Obispeño (Chumashan) placename /stemeqtatimi/ (Gudde 1998).

TEMNAC Bay (Alaska, Attu C-3). Named for an Aleut resident in the eighteenth century (Orth 1967).

TE-MOAK Well (Nev., Elko Co.). From Western Shoshoni (Numic) /tɨmukkun/ 'rope' (J. McLaughlin p.c.).

TEMPA Mine (Nev., Lincoln Co.) \tem´ pə\. From Southern Paiute (Numic) /tɨm-paa/, lit. 'rock water', from /tɨm(pi)/ 'rock' and /paa/ 'water' (J. McLaughlin p.c.). The apparently related name **Tempiute** (Nev., Lincoln Co.) \tem pī yo͞ot´\ contains /tɨm-/ 'rock' plus the name of the **Piute** or **Paiute** Indians; see above; a variant spelling is **Timpahute Range.**

TENABO (N.Mex., Torrance Co.) \ten´ ə bō\. From Spanish *Tenabó,* from the name of an abandoned Tompiro (Tanoan) pueblo (Julyan 1998; *HNAI* 9:351). In Nev. (Lander Co.) **Tenabo** may be a transfer name from N.Mex.; or it may be from Southern Paiute (Numic) /tɨnna-pa/ [tɨnna-va] 'stump water', containing /tɨnna/ 'stump, base' (J. McLaughlin p.c.).

TENAHA (Tex., Shelby Co.) \ten´ ə hô\. Said to be from from an unidentified Indian language, meaning 'muddy water' (Tarpley 1980); however, another possible source is Spanish *tinaja* 'large jar; rock waterhole' (Cobos 1983).

TENAKEE (Alaska, Sitka D-4) \ten´ ə kē\. Probably a Tlingit placename, of unclear derivation (Orth 1967).

TENALQUOT Prairie (Wash., Thurston Co.). From an unidefntified Indian language, said to mean 'the best yet' (Hitchman 1985).

TENASKET Mountain (Wash., Ferry Co.) \tə nas´ kət\. A variant writing of **Tonasket**; see below.

TENAS Lakes (Ore., Lane Co.) \tə nas\. The name means 'small lakes', from Chinook Jargon <ten´-as, tan´as> [ténəs, tənǽs] 'baby, child, small, few', from Nootka /t'an'eʔis, t'an'aʔis/ 'young child' (McArthur 1992; D. Kinkade p.c.). The placename **Tenas** also occurs in Wash. (Chelan Co.) and Alaska (Valdez B-2). The name of **Tenas George Canyon** (Wash., Chelan Co.) refers to an Indian resident, 'little George' (Hitchman 1985). The placename **Tenas Illahe** (Ore., Clatsop Co.) \ten äs´ il´ ə hē\ means 'little land' (McArthur 1992). Another related name is **Tenass Islands** (Alaska, Craig D-4); see below.

TENASS Islands (Alaska, Craig D-4). From the same source as **Tenas Lakes** (Ore., Lane Co.); see above.

TENAYA Lake (Calif., Mariposa Co.) \tə nī´ yə\. Southern Sierra Miwok /ṭïyenna/ 'sleeping place', from /ṭïye-/ 'to sleep' (Gudde 1998).

TENHASSEN Township (Minn., Martin Co.) \ten has´ ən\. Earlier written <Chanhassen>, from Dakota (Siouan), meaning 'sugar maple tree' (Upham 2001); cf. *čhąhá* 'tree bark', *są* 'whitish' (Riggs 1890, Ingham 2001). Related placenames in Minn. are **Hassan Township** (Hennepin Co.) and **Chanhassen** (Carver Co.).

TENINO Creek (Ore., Jefferson Co.) \tē nī´ nō, tə nī´ nō\. From the Sahaptin placename /tináynu/; cf. Chinook Jargon <ta-ni´-no> [tənáino] 'canyon, crevasse, vulva' (McArthur 1992; D. Kinkade p.c.). The name **Tenino** also occurs in Wash. (Thurston Co.), where it is probably derived from Chinook Jargon, not from Sahaptin.

TENISLANDS (Ala., Calhoun Co.) For *Ten Islands*, a translation of Muskogee *otē palen* /otí: pá:lin/; cf. *otē* 'ten' and *palen* 'island' (Read 1984; Martin and Mauldin 2000).

TENKILLER Ferry (Okla., Sequoyah Co.). Named for a Cherokee (Iroquoian) man who lived nearby (Shirk 1974).

TENNELINA (N.C., Madison Co.). The name is made up from parts of the placenames **Tennessee** and Carolina (Powell 1968).

TENNEMO (Tenn., Dwyer Co.). Probvably a combination of **Tennessee** and **Mo** (for **Missouri**); both parts are Native American names.

TENNESSEE \ten ə sē\. The name of the state and of the river is derived from the Cherokee (Iroquoian) village name <tă´năsī´, tănsī´>, of no known etymology (Vogel 1963). This placename has been transferred to other states (e.g., Ark., Drew Co.; and Ill., McDonough Co.).

TENNGA (Ga., Murray Co.). A combination of the first syllable of **Tennessee** with Ga., the abbreviation for *Georgia* (Goff 1975).

TENSAS Parish (La.) \ten´ sô\. Also written <Taensa>; from the name of a small Indian group, associated with the Natchez (Read 1927). The name **Tensas** also occurs in Alaska (Chicot Co.). A related placename is **Tensaw** (Ala., Baldwin Co.).

TENSAWATTEE (Ga., Dawson Co.). The name of a Cherokee (Iroquoian) village, perhaps related to the name of **Tennessee** (Goff 1975).

TENSLEEP Creek (Wyo., Washakie Co.). From an Indian village that was said to be "ten sleeps" (i.e., ten days' travel) from Fort Laramie (Urbanek 1974); the Cheyenne (Algonquian) name was /mahtohtohee'ese/, lit. 'ten days' (W. Leman p.c.).

TEOC (Ala., Sumter Co.). From Choctaw (Muskogean) *tiyak* 'pine tree' (Read 1984; P. Munro p.c.). The name **Teoc** also occurs in Miss. (Carroll Co.). Related placenames include **Teock** (Miss., Smith Co.) and **Tiak Lake** (Miss., Perry Co.).

TEOCALLI MOUNTAIN (Colo., Gunnison Co.) \tē ō kä´ lē\. Nahuatl (Aztecan) *teocalli* 'temple', lit. 'god-house', from *teo(-tl)* 'god' plus *calli* 'house' (Bright 1993). The placename **Teocalli** also occurs in Alaska (McGrath A-1).

TEOCK (Miss., Smith Co.) \tē´ ok\. Probably from Choctaw (Muskogean) *tiyak* 'pine tree'; see **Teoc**, above. The placename **Teoctalia** (Miss., Carroll Co.) \tē ok tə lī´ ə\ is Choctaw (Muskogean) for 'pine grove'; cf. *tiyak* 'pine tree', *talaya* 'to stand' (Seale 1939; P. Munro p.c.).

TEPEE \tē´ pē\. The term is used for a type of house, made of poles and animal hides, characteristic of Plains Indian culture; the origin is Dakota (Siouan) *thípi* 'house' (A. Taylor p.c.); the related Lakhota has the same word. As a placename, **Tepee** occurs in many states (e.g., Colo., Grand Co.; Mont., Flathead Co.; and N.Dak., Heltinger Co.). An alternative spelling is **Teepee**; see above. The placename **Tepeeota** (Minn., Wabasha Co.) is a variant of **Teepeeota Point.** The name **Tepeetonka** (S.Dak., Roberts Co.) is from Dakota *thípi thą́ka* 'big house' (A. Taylor p.c.).

TEPEH (Wash., Skagit Co.). Chinook Jargon <te-péh> [tipíʔ] 'feather, wing', from Lower Chinook [təpé] (?) (D. Kinkade p.c.).

TEPEHEMUS Brook (N.J., Monmouth Co.). Probably from Delaware (Algonquian), of unclear derivation (Becker 1964).

TEPETATE (La., Acadia Par.) \tep ə tä´ tē\. Mexican Spanish, referring to a type of rock, derived from Nahuatl (Aztecan) *te-petlatl,* containing *te(-tl)* 'rock' and *petatl* 'mat' (Santamaría 1959).

TEPONA Point (Calif., Humboldt Co.) \ti pō´ nə\. A Yurok placename /tepoona/, from /tepoo/ 'tree' (Gudde 1998).

TEPO Ridge (Calif., Del Norte Co.) \ti pō´\. From Yurok /tepon-/ 'to stand, be vertical' (Gudde 1998).

TEPUSQUET Creek (Calif., Santa Barbara Co.) \tep´ əs kē\. From Mexican Spanish *tepuzque* 'a small copper coin', from Nahuatl (Aztecan) *tepuztli* 'copper' (Gudde 1998).

TEQUA (Ariz., Navajo Co.). Probably a mistranscription of Spanish *Tegua* or *Tehua,* referring to the **Tewa** (Tanoan) Indians; see below. There is also a **Tequa** in Kans. (Osage Co.).

TEQUEPIS Canyon (Calif., Santa Barbara Co.) \tek´ ə pis\. Probably from a Barbareño (Chumashan) placename (Gudde 1998).

TEQUESQUITE Slough (Calif., San Benito Co.) \tek əs kē´ tē\. Spanish for 'alkali, saltpeter', from Nahuatl (Aztecan) *tequixquitl,* containing *te(-tl)* 'rock' and *quixquitl* 'efflorescent' (Gudde 1998). The name **Tequesquite** also occurs in N.Mex. (Harding Co.) and Tex. (Maverick Co.).

TERBILON Islands (Alaska, Port Alexander D-5). The Tlingit name was recorded in 1809 (Orth 1967).

TERLINGUA (Tex., Brewster Co.) \tər ling´ gwə, tər ling´ gə\. Of obscure origin, but perhaps from Spanish *tres lenguas,* referring to the Spanish, English, and Indian languages (Tarpley 1980).

TERRAMUGGUS, Lake (Conn., Hartford Co.). Named after a SNEng. Algonquian leader (Huden 1962).

TERRAPIN \ter´ ə pin\. This word for a type of turtle was borrowed from CAC Algonquian; cf. Munsee (Delaware) /tó:lpe:w/ (*RHD* 1987). As a placename, **Terrapin** occurs in several states (e.g., Md., Howard Co.; and Ill., Jo Daviess Co.).

TERRA TOMAH Mountain (Colo., Larimer Co.) \târ´ ə tō´ mə\. Named by a mountaineer, using words supposedly taken from a song of the Cahuilla (Takic) Indians in California (Bright 1993).

TERWAH Creek (Calif., Del Norte Co.) \tûr´ wä\. From the Yurok village name /trwr:/ (Gudde 1998).

TESBITO (Ariz., Navajo Co.) \tēs´ bi tō, tes bē´ tō\. Navajo (Athabaskan) *t'iis bitó* 'cottonwood spring', containing *t'iis* 'cottonwood tree', *bi-* 'its', and *tó* 'water, spring' (Linford 2000). Related placenames include **Teec Nos Pos** and **Tes Nez Iah**; see below.

TESHEKPAK Lake (Alaska, Point Hope B-3). From Iñupiaq (Eskimo) *tasiqpak* 'big lagoon', from *tasiq* 'lagoon' plus *-(q)pak* 'big' (L. Kaplan p.c.). A related placename is **Teshekpuk** (Alaska, Teshekpuk C-1) (Orth 1967).

TESHEVA Creek (Miss., Yazoo Co.) \tə shē´ və\. A variant spelling of **Techeva Creek**; see above.

TESHIM Butte (Ariz., Navajo Co.). From Navajo (Athabaskan), of unclear derivation (Linford 2000).

TESNATEE (Ga., White Co.). Perhaps from Cherokee (Iroquoian), of unclear derivation (BGN 7804); a probably related name is **Tessentee Creek** (N.C., Macon Co.).

TES NEZ IAH (Ariz., Apache Co.) \tēs nez ē´ yə\. From Navajo (Athabaskan) *t'iis nééz íí'á* 'tall cottonwood stands', containing *t'iis* 'cottonwood tree' (Linford 2000). Related placenames include **Tesbito**; see above.

TESSENTEE Creek (N.C., Macon Co.). Perhaps from Cherokee (Iroquoian), of unclear derivation (Powell 1968); a probably related name is **Tesnatee** (Ga., White Co.).

TESUQUE (N.Mex., Santa Fe Co.) \ti sōō´ kē\. From Tewa (Tanoan) /t'athų̨ŋɣe/, perhaps 'down at the dry spotted place', from /t'a/ 'dry', /thų̨/ 'spotted', and /-ɣe/ 'down at' (Julyan 1998; Harrington 1916:387).

TES YAHZ LANI (Ariz., Coconino Co.) \tēs yäz lä´ nē\. From Navajo *t'iis yáázh łání* 'many little cottonwoods', containing *t'iis* 'cottonwood tree' (Linford 2000). Related placenames include **Tesbito** aand **Tes Nez Iah**; see above.

TETAGOUCHE (Minn., Lake Co.) \tet´ ə gōōch\. Perhaps from Ojibwa (Algonquian), of unclear derivation (Upham 2001). Also written as **Tettegouche Lake.**

TETESEAU Lake (Mo., Saline Co.) \tē´ tə sô\. From French *petit Osage* 'little Osage', referring to a Siouan Indian group (D. Lance p.c.).

TETILESOOK Creek (Alaska, Baird Mountains A-2). The Iñupiaq (Eskimo) name was obtained in 1955 (Orth 1967).

TETLIN (Alaska, Tanacross A-4) \tet´lin\. From the Upper Tanana (Athabaskan) placename /te:łą̨y/ 'current flows' (J. Kari p.c.), or from Ahtna (Athabaskan) *tezdlende* 'swift current place' (Kari 1983:104).

TETON County (Mont.) \tē´ ton\. The term refers collectively to western subgroups of the Dakotan (Siouan) peoples, who use the Lakhota language. The native word is *thíthų̨wą̨*, perhaps from *thį̨ta* 'plains' (*HNAI* 13:755); there is no connection with the placename *Grand Teton*, which is French for 'big breast'. The placename **Teton** also occurs in S.Dak. (Stanley Co.).

TETONKA Township (S.Dak., Spink Co.) \tē tong´ kə\. Dakota (Siouan) *thí-thąka* 'house-big'; cf. *thípi* 'house' (A. Taylor p.c.) The name **Tetonka** is also found in Minn. (Le Sueur Co.). A related name is **Tetonkaha Lake** (S.Dak., Brookings Co.), from Dakota (Siouan) *thí-thąka hą́* 'house-big stand' (Sneve 1973; B. Ingham p.c.).

TETRAVUN Lakes (Alaska, Christian A-5). The Gwich'in (Athabaskan) name is *teetree van* (J. Kari p.c.).

TETSYEH Lake (Alaska, Arctic B-2). The Gwich'in (Athabaskan) name was reported in 1956 (Orth 1967).

TETTEGOUCHE Lake (Minn., Lake Co.). A spelling variant of **Tetagouche**; see above.

TETTHAJIK Creek (Alaska, Black River C-2). The Gwich'in (Athabaskan) name was recorded in 1956 (Orth 1967).

TEVYARAQ Lake (Alaska, Sleetmute B-6). Yupik (Eskimo) *tevyaraq* 'portage', from *teve-* 'to go over or through a portage' (Schorr 1974; Jacobson 1984).

TEWA \tā´ wə\. The name refers to speakers of a Tanoan language, originally living in several pueblos in the Rio Grande Valley of N.Mex., such as Santa Clara and San Juan. After the Pueblo Rebellion in 1680, some Tewas fled westward and settled among the Hopis in Ariz.; this group is now called "Hopi-Tewa" (Granger 1983; *HNAI* 9:601). As a placename, **Tewa** refers to the settlement in Ariz. (Navajo Co.); other spellings, based on Spanish, are **Tehua** and **Tegua.**

TEWAUKON Township (N.Dak., Sargent Co.). Perhaps Dakota (Siouan) *thíwakhą* 'church', from *thí(pi)* 'house' and *wakhą́* 'holy' (D. Parks p.c.).

TEXANA (Tex., Jackson Co.) \tek san´ ə\. Originally named Santa Anna, for Antonio López de Santa Anna, a nineteenth-century Mexican leader; later changed to **Texana** in honor of the independence of **Texas;** see below. A related placename is **Texanna** (Okla., McIntosh Co.).

TEXARKANA (Tex., Bowie Co.) \tek sär kan´ ə\. The name was created by combining elements from the placenames **Texas, Arkansas,** and *Louisiana* (Tarpley 1980).

TEXAS \tek´ səs\. From Caddo /táyšaʔ/ 'friend, ally', written by the Spanish as plural *Texas, Tejas* (W. Chafe p.c.). As a placename, **Texas** has been transferred to many other states (e.g., Mich., Ontanagan Co.; Pa., Lycoming Co.; and Wis., Marathon Co.).

TEXHOMA (Okla., Texas Co.; Tex., Sherman Co.) \teks hō´ mə\. Coined from the placenames **Texas** and **Oklahoma** (Shirk 1974).

TEXICO (Ill., Jefferson Co.) \tek´ si kō\. Coined from the placenames **Texas** and **Mexico** (Vogel 1963). In N.Mex. (Curry Co.) the name **Texico** refers to **Texas** and **New Mexico** (Julyan 1998).

TEXLA (Tex., Orange Co.) \teks´ lə\. A blend of elements from the placenames **Texas** and Louisiana (Tarpley 1980).

TEXMO (Okla., Roger Mills Co.) \teks´ mō\. Coined from elements of **Texas** and **Missouri** (Shirk 1974).

TEXOKLA (Okla., Beckham Co.) \tek sō´ klə\. Coined from elements of **Texas** and **Oklahoma** (Shirk 1974). Similar nearby names are **Texola** \tek sō´ lə\. and **Lake Texoma** \tek sō´ mə\.

TEXOWA (Okla., Tillman Co.). Coined from the placename **Texas** and the name of the **Kiowa** (Kiotanoan) Indian people (Shirk 1974).

TEYPAMA (N.Mex., Socorro Co.) \ti pä´ mə\. An archaeological site once occupied by the Piro (Tanoan) Indians; also written as <Teypana> (Julyan 1998; *HNAI* 9:241).

TEZAH Mountain (N.Mex., McKinley Co.) \tez´ ä\. Probably from Navajo (Athabaskan) *deez'á* 'it extends a ridge, bluff, point' (A. Wilson p.c.).

THADLTHAMUND Lake (Alaska, Nabesna D-3). The Upper Tanana (Athabaskan) name, obtained in 1962, is said to mean 'lily pads on lake' (Orth 1967).

THAZZIK Mountains (Alaska, Chandalar B-1). The Gwich'in (Athabaskan) name was reported in 1956 (Orth 1967).

THIEF River (Minn., Madison Co.). Corresponds to Ojibwa (Algonquian) <kimodakiwi zibi> 'stealing-earth river' (Upham 2001); cf. *gimoodi* 'to steal' (Nichols and Nyholm 1995).

THINGS FLOW AROUND THE STONE (Ariz., Apache Co.). From Navajo (Apache) *tsé biná'áz'éí* 'rock around which floating took place' (Linford 2000).

THIRTYTWO KAZYGA Slough (Alaska, Russian Mission C-7). So called because a village of thirty-two *kayzgas* (Native American buildings) is supposed to have been located here once (Orth 1967). The term *kazyga* is a Russian adaptation of Yupik (Eskimo) *qasgiq* 'men's community house, steambath house' (Jacobson 1984).

THLUICHOHNJIK Creek (Alaska, Christian B-1). The Gwich'in (Athabaskan) name is of unclear derivation (Orth 1967).

THOHEDLIH (N.Mex., San Juan Co.). Navajo (Athabaskan) *tó aheedlį́* 'waters converge, flow together', from *tó* 'water', *ahee (ahi)* 'convergent', and *(d)lį́* 'flow' (Wilson 1995).

THONOTOSASSA (Fla., Hillsborough Co.). The Muskogee name means 'some flint', from *ronoto* /ɬonóto/ 'flint' and *sasv* /sá:sa/ 'some' (Read 1934; Martin and Mauldin 2000).

THORKONA (Alaska, Mt. Hayes B-3) \thôr kō´ nə\. A blend of elements from a place called "The Thorn" plus the name of **Mt. Gakona** (BGN 1999).

THORNTOWN (Ind., Boone Co.). Corresponds to Miami/Illinois (Algonquian) /kaawinšaahkionki/ 'in the thorn land' (McCafferty 2002).

THROAT River (Alaska, Selawik C-2). A translation of Iñupiaq (Eskimo) *iggiaq* 'throat' (Orth 1967, MacLean 1980).

THUNDERBIRD. Among many Northern American peoples, thunder was said to be caused by this legendary bird; the English word corresponds to Native American terms such as Ojibwa (Algonquian) *animikii* (Nichols and Nyholm 1995), Lakhota (Siouan) *wakį́yą* (Ingham 2001), and Klamath /lmelmnis/ (Barker 1963).

THUNDER Butte (S.Dak., Ziebach Co.). Probably from Lakhota (Siouan) *wakį́yą hothų́*, lit. 'the thunderbirds call', the usual expression for thunder (Sneve 1973; B. Ingham p.c.). In Idaho (Nez Perce Co.) **Thunder Hill** is named for a Nez Perce (Sahaptian) leader, Big Thunder; his Native American name has been reconstructed as /hinmetu:tqekeʔéykt/ 'thunder rushing over', containing /hinmétu/ 'thunder', /teqe/ 'suddenly', and /keʔéy/ 'to move' (D. Kinkade p.c.).

THUNDER HAWK (S.Dak., Corson Co.). Named for a Lakhota (Siouan) leader who once lived here (Sneve 1973).

THUNDER Pass (Colo., Jackson Co.). A translation of Arapaho (Algonquian) *bonoh'óoníthesóó'* 'thunder pass' (A. Cowell p.c.).

THUNDER WOMAN County Park (Iowa, Black Hawk Co.). Named for a Winnebago (Siouan) woman who lived in the area (Vogel 1983).

TIADAGHTON (Pa., Tioga Co.) \tī ə däk´ tən\. Earlier written <Tyadaghton>; probably of Iroquoian origin, but the derivation is not clear (Donehoo 1928).

TIAK Lake (Miss., Perry Co.). From Choctaw (Muskogean) *tiyak* 'pine tree' (Read 1984; P. Munro p.c.). Related placenames include **Teoc** (Ala., Sumter Co.) and **Teock** (Miss., Smith Co.).

TIANA (N.Y., Suffolk Co.) \tē ä´ nə\. Perhaps from SNEng. Algonquian, but the derivation is not clear (Tooker 1911).

TIASQUAM River (Mass., Dukes Co.). Named for a SNEng. Algonquian man, also known as <Tiashq> or <Tuspaquin> (Huden 1962).

TIAWAH (Okla., Rogers Co.) \tī´ ə wä, tī´ wä\. Said to be named for an Indian mound in Ga.; the language of origin is not known (Shirk 1974).

TIBBEE (Miss., Clay Co.) \tib´ ē\. Perhaps an abbreviation for **Oktibbeha County** (Miss.). Related names are **Tibbie** (Ala., Washington Co.) and **Tibby** (Miss., Noxubee Co.).

TICABOO (Utah, Garfield Co.) \tik´ ə boo\. Probably from Southern Paiute (Numic) /tɨkkap-pɨh/ 'food', from /tɨkka/ 'eat' (J. McLaughlin p.c.) A related placename is **Ticapoo Spring** (Nev., Lincoln Co.), with the variant form **Tikaboo**.

TICETONYK Mountain (N.Y., Ulster Co.) \tī sə ton´ ik\. Perhaps from an Iroquoian word referring to a steep ascent (Beauchamp 1907).

TICHIGAN (Mich., Racine Co.) Perhaps shortened from Ojibwa (Algonquian) <tchigi-kitchi-gama> 'along the great lake' (Vogel 1991); cf. *jiigew* 'along the shore', *gichi-* 'big', *-gami* 'lake' (Nichols and Nyholm 1995). Probably related names include **Lake Gitchegumee** (Mich., Wexford Co.) and **Michigan.**

TICKANETLEY (Ga., Gilmer Co.). From the name of a Cherokee (Iroquoian) village (BGN 7803).

TICKFAW River (Miss., La.) Perhaps from Choctaw (Muskogean) *tiyak* 'pine' and *foha* 'a rest' (Read 1927; P. Munro p.c.). There is also a **Tickfaw** in Ala. (Russell Co.).

TICONDEROGA (N.Y., Essex Co.) \tī kon də rō´ gə\. From Mohawk (Iroquoian) *tekǫtaró:kę* 'branching or confluence of waters', containing the root *-ǫtar-* 'large river, lake' (Lounsbury 1960:46; M. Mithun p.c.).

TICONIC (Iowa, Monona Co.) \tə kon´ ik\. Probably from the same source as **Taconic Range** (Mass., Berkshire Co.), from an Algonquian element meaning 'forest' (Vogel 1983).

TIDGITUK Islands (Alaska, Gareloi Island B-1). From the Aleut placename *tidĝitux̂* (Bergsland 1994).

TIDIOUTE (Pa., Warren Co.) \tid´ ē ōōt, tid ē ōōt\. Probably from Delaware (Algonquian), but the derivation is not clear (Donehoo 1928).

TIDOC Mountain (Calif., Tehama Co.) \tē´ dok\. From Wintu *t'idooq* 'red ant' (Gudde 1998); also written **Tedoc.**

TIECHOVUN Lake (Alaska, Black River B-6). The Gwich'in (Athabaskan) name was reported in 1956 (Orth 1967); cf. *van* 'lake' (Peter 1979).

TIEKEL (Alaska, Valdez B-4) \tē´ kəl\. Perhaps from Ahtena (Athabaskan) (Orth 1967).

TIENASHEAVUN Slough (Alaska, Black River C-4). The Gwich'in (Athabaskan) name was reported in 1956 (Orth 1967); cf. *van* 'lake' (Peter 1979).

TIERRA AMARILLA (N.Mex., Rio Arriba Co.) \tyâr´ ə ä mə rē´ ə\. The Spanish name, meaning 'yellow earth', corresponds to Navajo *łitsooí* 'yellow place' (Linford 2000). The Tewa name for the place has the same meaning.

TIETON River (Wash., Yakima Co.) \tī´ ə tən\. From the Sahaptin placename /táytɨn, tá:ytɨn/ (Hitchman 1985; D. Kinkade p.c.).

TIFALLILI Creek (Ala., Sumter Co.; Miss. Kemper Co.). From Choctaw (Muskogean), perhaps meaning 'tall dead tree', from *itti* 'tree', *falaya* 'tall', and *illi* 'die' (Read 1984; P. Munro p.c.). A possibly related placename is **Tillatoba** (Miss., Yalobusha Co.).

TIFLIGHAK Bay (Alaska, St. Lawrence D-6). The Yupik (Eskimo) name was reported in 1955, perhaps from <tivlarak> 'portage' (Orth 1967). A spelling variant is **Dovelawik Bay.**

TIGALDA Bay (Alaska, Unimak A-3) \ti gäl´ də\. From the Aleut placename *qigalĝan* (Bergsland 1994).

TIGARA (Alaska, Point Hope B-3) \tē gä´ rə\. From Iñupiaq (Eskimo) *tikiġaq* 'point of land' (L. Kaplan p.c.). A related placename is **Tigaraha Mountains** (Alaska, Nome D-1; Orth 1967). Another related name is **Tikigaruk Point** (Alaska, Barrow B-4).

TIGEE Lake (Wyo., Fremont Co.) \tī´ gē\. Perhaps Shoshoni (Numic) /taitsi/ [taiči] 'brother-in-law' (J. McLaughlin p.c.).

TIGER (Okla., Creek Co.). Named for Billy Tiger, a prominent Muskogee (G. Shirk p.c.). The English word *tiger* is used locally to mean 'cougar, mountain lion', corresponding to Muskogee *kaccv* /ká:čča/ (Martin and Mauldin 2000).

TIGIWON (Colo., Eagle Co.) \tig´ i won\. From Ute (Numic) /tɨgɨ́vɨn/ 'friend' (Bright 1993).

TIGLUKPUK Creek (Alaska, Chandler Lake C-4). The Iñupiaq (Eskimo) name, reported in 1950, is said to mean 'moose' (Orth 1967).

TIGNAGVIK Point (Alaska, Iliamna B-2). The Alutiiq (Eskimo) name was published in 1915 (Orth 1967).

TIGUA Pueblo (Tex., El Paso Co.) \tē´ wə\. An alternative name of **Ysleta (del Sur),** a settlement of **Tiwa** (Tanoan) Indians who originally lived in **Isleta** (N.Mex., Bernalillo Co.). A related but distinct Indian group are the **Tewa** people; see above.

TIGVARIAK Islands (Alaska, Beechey Point A-1). From Iñupiaq (Eskimo), said to mean 'portage' (Orth 1967); cf. *itivyaaq* 'portage' (Fortescue et al. 1994:119).

TIHONET (Mass., Plymouth Co.). The SNEng. Algonquian placename has been said to mean 'at the abode of crane or bittern' (Huden 1962).

TIINKDHUL Lake (Alaska, Black River C-5). The Gwich'in (Athabaskan) name was obtained in 1956 (Orth 1967).

TIIS NDIITSOOI Wash (Ariz., Apache Co.). From Navajo (Athabaskan), with *t'iis* 'cottonwood' (Young & Morgan 1987).

TIJUANA River (Calif., San Diego Co.) \tē wä´ nə\. From the name of a Diegueño (Yuman) village, written as <Tiajuan> in 1829. The name of the city on the Mexican side of the border has often been folk-etymologized as *Tía Juana* 'Aunt Jane' (Gudde 1998).

TIKABOO Range (Nev., Lincoln Co.). A written variant of **Ticaboo**; see above.

TIKAGHAPUK Point (Alaska, St. Lawrence C-6). The Yupik (Eskimo) name, reported in 1949, is said to mean 'big point of land' (Orth 1967); cf. St. Lawrence Island Yupik *tekeghaq* 'point of land', *-ghpak* [-ʀpak] 'big' (Jacobson 1987).

TIKAN Creek (Alaska, Black River A-1). The Gwich'in (Athabaskan) name was reported in 1908 (Orth 1967).

TIKCHIK Lake (Alaska, Dillingham D-7). The Yupik (Eskimo) name was reported in 1880 (Orth 1967).

TIK Hill (Alaska, Marshall B-5). From Yupik (Eskimo) *teq* 'anus' (Orth 1967; Jacobson 1984).

TIKIGARUK Point (Alaska, Barrow B-4). From Iñupiaq (Eskimo) *tiqiq* 'index finger' (Orth 1967; Fortescue et al. 1994:338). A related placename is **Tigara** (Alaska, Point Hope B-3). A possibly related placename is **Tikikluk** (Alaska, Meade River B-3) \ti kik´ luk\, perhaps meaning 'big finger'; cf. *-aluk* 'big' (Webster and Zibell 1970).

TIKISHLA (Alaska, Anchorage A-8). From Dena'ina (Athabaskan) *ghedishla* 'black bear' (Kari and Fall 1987:296).

TIKIZAT (Alaska, Noatak A-4) \tik´ ē zat\. The Iñupiaq (Eskimo) name is said to mean 'other sides of the bend' (Orth 1967).

TIKMIAKPALIK (Alaska, Killik River B-1). The Iñupiaq (Eskimo) name is said to mean 'golden eagle's nest' (Orth 1967); cf. *tiŋmiaqpak* 'eagle' (MacLean 1980). A related Alaska placename is **Tingmerkpuk River** (De Long Mountains D-10); see below.

TIKUGHA Point (Alaska, St. Lawrence C-4). The Yupik (Eskimo) name, reported in 1949, is said to mean 'pointer' (Orth 1967); cf. St. Lawrence Island Yupik *tekeq* 'index finger' (Jacobson 1987).

TILIKUM Lake (Ore., Yamhill Co.) \til´ i kəm\. From the same origin as **Tillicum Creek**; see below.

TILLAMOOK County (Ore., Tillamook Co.) \til´ ə mŏŏk\. The name refers to a Salishan people living in the area; early spellings include <Callemex> and <Killamook> (McArthur 1992). The origin is Lower Chinook /tʔilimuks/ 'those of /niʔilim/'; the Chinook placename also has the variants /-ʔilim/ and /-qilim/ (D. Kinkade p.c.).

TILLANGORA Creek (Ore., Clatsop Co.) \til´ əng gôr ə\. Probably a combination of **Tillamook** plus *Angora*, a breed of goat that may have been raised here (D. Kinkade p.c.).

TILLATOBA (Miss., Yalobusha Co.) \til ə tō´ bə\. Perhaps from Choctaw (Muskogean), meaning 'white dead tree', containing *itti* 'tree', *illi* 'die', and *tohbi* 'white' (Seale 1939; P. Munro p.c.). A possibly related placename is **Tifallili Creek** (Ala., Sumter Co.).

TILLICUM Creek (Ore., Lane Co.) \til´ i kəm\. Chinook Jargon <til´-i-kum, tilakum> [tíləkəm] 'people, person, relative(s), family, friend(s)', probably used here in the meaning 'friend'; from Lower Chinook [télxəm] 'people' (McArthur 1992; D. Kinkade p.c.). The name **Tillicum** is also used in Wash. (Pierce Co.) A related form is **Tilikum Lake** (Ore., Yamhill Co.).

TILTILL (Calif., Tuolumne Co.). From Southern Sierra Miwok /tiltilna/ 'tarweed' (Gudde 1998).

TIMALULA Falls (Calif., Mariposa Co.) \ti mä´ lōō lə\. Probably from Southern Sierra Miwok /temaalɨ-la/ 'trading place', from /temaalɨ/ 'to trade' (Gudde 1998).

TIMBER Lake (S.Dak., Dewey Co.). Corresponds to Santee Dakota (Siouan) *mdé-čhą* 'lake [of] wood'; cf. *mde* 'lake', *čhą* 'lake' (Sneve 1973; A. Taylor p.c.).

TIMENTWA Flat (Wash., Okanogan Co.) \tī´ mən twä\. From Moses-Columbian (Salishan) [čməntwáxʷ], the surname of a Native American family (Reese 1996; D. Kinkade p.c.

TIMICO Lake (Wyo., Sublette Co.) \tim´i kō\. Probably from the same source as **Timmoco Creek**; see below.

TIMMILICHEES Ford (Ala., Sumter Co.). Named for Timmillichee, a Choctaw (Muskogean) leader; his Native American name was <tammalichi> 'he who strikes once with the heel of the hand' (Read 1984).

TIMMOCO Creek (Wyo., Fremont Co.) \tim´ ə kō\. Said to be Shoshoni (Numic), meaning 'windy, blustery' (Urbanek 1974).

TIMOTHY, Chief (Wash., Asotin Co.). The state park was named for a Nez Perce (Sahaptian) leader (D. Kinkade p.c.).

TIMPANOGAS Lake (Ore., Douglas Co.) \tim pə nō´ gəs\. A transfer name derived from **Timpanogos** (Utah, Utah Co.), once used to refer to Great Salt Lake (McArthur 1992). The earlier form of the name occurs as **Mount Timpanogos** (Utah, Utah Co.) \tim pə nō´ gəs\, from Ute (Numic), perhaps meaning 'rock river'; the term was once applied to Great Salt Lake, and before that to what is now called Provo Creek (Van Cott 1990).

TIMPAS (Colo., Otero Co.) \tim´ pəs\. Perhaps a Spanish plural from a Ute (Numic) form cognate with Southern Paiute /tɨmpi/ [tɨmpI] 'stone'; or from Spanish *timpa,* English *tymp* 'bar of stone or iron in a blast furnace' (Bright 1993). Possibly related placenames are **Timp Canyon**, **Timpanogas Lake**, and **Timpi Canyon.**

TIMP Canyon (Ariz., Coconino Co.) \timp\. From Southern Paiute (Numic) /tɨmpi/ [tɨ́mpI] 'rock'. Related placenames include **Timpa** (Idaho, Elmore Co.) \tim´ pə\, from Shoshoni (Numic) /tɨmpi/ [tɨ́mpI] 'rock' (J. McLaughlin p.c.), and **Timpahute Range** (Nev., Lincoln Co.) \tem pī yo͞ot´\, a variant writing of **Tempiute**; see **Tempa Mine** above.

TIMPI Canyon (Nev., Nye Co.). From Southern Paiute or Shoshoni (both Numic) /tɨmpi/ 'rock' (J. McLaughlin p.c.). A related form is **Timpie** (Utah, Tooele Co.), probably from the Goshute dialect of Shoshoni (Van Cott 1990).

TIMPOONEKE Campground (Utah, Utah Co.). From the same origin as **Mount Timpanogos** (Utah, Utah Co.); see **Timpanogas Lake** above.

TIMUCUAN School (Fla., Duval Co.). The name is based on Spanish *Timuqua,* the name of an Indian people living in Fla. during colonial times. A related name is that of nearby **Timuquana Park**. Another related name is **Tomoka River** (Fla., Volusia Co.).

TINAQUAIC (Calif., Santa Barbara Co.). From the name of a Barbareño (Chumashan) village (Gudde 1998).

TINAYGUK River (Alaska, Wiseman C-3). From Iñupiaq (Eskimo) *tinniikaq* 'moose' (Orth 1967; Webster and Zibell 1970).

TINDIR Creek (Alaska, Charley River B-1). Perhaps a Han (Athabaskan) word for 'moose' (Orth 1967); cf. Gwich'in (Athabaskan) *dinjik* 'moose', *ch'izhir* 'bull moose' (Peter 1979). Possibly related is **Tinjik Lake** (Alaska, Arctic B-3); see below.

TINEMAHA, Mount (Calif., Inyo Co.) \tin´ ə mə hä\. Named after a Paiute (Numic) leader, also known as <Tinemakar> (Gudde 1998).

TINGMEACHSIOVIK River (Alaska, Harrison Bay B-3). The Iñupiaq (Eskimo) name is probably *tiŋmiaqsiuġvik* 'place to hunt ducks or geese' (L. Kaplan p.c.).

TINGMERKPUK River (Alaska, De Long Mountains D-10). From Iñupiaq (Eskimo) *tiŋmiaqpak* 'golden eagle' (Orth 1967; MacLean 1980). A related Alaska placename is **Tikmiakpalik** (Killik River B-1); see above.

TINGUK Ridge (Alaska, Point Hope A-1). From Iñupiaq (Eskimo) *tiŋuq* 'liver' (Orth 1967; MacLean 1980).

TINICUM (Pa., Bucks Co.) \tin´ i kəm\. From Delaware (Algonquian), but the derivation is unclear (Donehoo 1928). The name **Tinicum** also occurs in N.J. (Hunterdon Co.).

TINJIK Lake (Alaska, Arctic B-3) \tin´ jik\. The Gwich'in (Athabaskan) name is *dinjik van* 'moose lake' (J. Kari p.c.). Probably related is the name of **Tinjikvun Lake** (Alaska, Christian A-6); cf. *van* 'lake' (Peter 1979). Possibly also related is **Tindir Creek** (Alaska, Charley River B-1); see above

TINTAH (Minn., Traverse Co.) \tin´ tä\. From Dakota (Siouan) *thį́ta* 'prairie' (Upham 2001; Riggs 1890).

TINTIC Mountain (Utah, Juab Co.) \tin´ tik\. Named for a Goshute Shoshoni (Numic) leader (Van Cott 1990).

TIOGA (N.Y., Tioga Co.) \tī ō´ gə\. From Mohawk (Iroquoian) *teyó:kę* 'junction or fork' or from *teyaó:kę* 'having a junction or fork', from the root *-okę-* 'to be Y-shaped' (Lounsbury 1960:53). The name **Tioga** has been transferred to other states (e.g., Calif., Mono Co.; Kans., Neosho Co.; and La., Rapides Par.).

TIOGUE Lake (R.I., Bristol Co.). Perhaps from Massachusett (SNEng. Algonquian) *tiohquonkque* 'it is low' (Huden 1962; W. Cowan p.c.).

TIONA (Pa., Warren Co.) \tī on´ ə\. An abbreviation of **Tionesta**; see below.

TIONESTA (Pa., Forest Co.) \tī ə nes´tə\. Perhaps from Seneca (Iroquoian) *dyone:sdœ'* 'where there is a board' (W. Chafe p.c.); cf. *gané:sdœ'* 'board' (Chafe 1967). A variant spelling is **Tyonesta.**

TIORATI, Lake (N.Y., Orange Co.). Perhaps from older Onondaga (Iroquoian) *dyorade'* 'where it is windy', corresponding to modern Onondaga *dyowœœde'* (H. Woodbury p.c.).

TIOSA (Ind., Fulton Co.) \tī ō´ sə\. Said to be from the name of a Potawatomi (Algonquian) leader in the early nineteenth century (McPherson 1993); the derivation is not clear.

TIOUGHNIOGA River (N.Y., Broome Co.) \tī ō nē ō´ gə, tī ō nō´ gə\. The Iroquoian name, earlier written <Te-ah-hah-hogue> or <Te-yogh-a-go-ga>, may refer to the forks of rivers (Beauchamp 1907); cf. **Tioga** above.

TIPOOKTULEARUK River (Alaska, Norton Bay D-4). The Iñupiaq (Eskimo) name is probably *tipuktuliaġruk*, from *tipuk* 'whitefish' (L. Kaplan p.c.).

TIPPAH County (Miss.) \tip´ ə\. Perhaps named for a Choctaw or Chickasaw (Muskogean) woman; her Native American name may have been Choctaw *tapa* 'separated' (Seale 1939; Munro and Willmond 1994). A probably related name is **Tippo** (Miss., Tallahatchie Co.).

TIPPECANOE County (Ind.) \tip ē kə noo͞´\. From a Miami/Illinois (Algonquian) word for 'buffalo fish', reconstructed as */kiteepihkwana/ (McCafferty 2002). The placename **Tippecanoe** has been transferred to other states (e.g., Ohio, Harrison Co.; Pa., Fayette Co.; and Wis., Vilas Co.).

TIPPECANSETT Pond (R.I., Washington Co.) \tip ə kan´ sət\. From SNEng. Algonquian, perhaps meaning 'at the great clearing' (Huden 1962).

TIPPIPAH Point (Nev., Nye Co.) \tip´ i pä\. From Northern Paiute (Numic), meaning 'rock water' or 'rock springs', consisting of /tippi/ 'rock' plus /paa/ 'water' (Carlson 1974; McLaughlin p.c.).

TIPPITY WICHITY Island (Md., St. Mary's Co.) \tip´ i tē wich´ i tē\. From a word <tĭtĭpĭwĭtshik> 'Venus fly-trap, a carnivorous plant', used in regional English, and derived from CAC Algonquian (Kenny 1984).

TIPPO (Miss., Tallahatchie Co.). Probably from Choctaw (Muskogean) *tapa* 'separated' (Seale 1939; P. Munro p.c.). A probably related placename is **Tippah County.**

TIPSOO Creek (Ore., Lane Co.) \tip´ soo͞\. Chinook Jargon <tup-so, tip´-so> [tə́pso] 'leaf, grass, feathers, fur, hair', perhaps from Lower Chinook [tə́pšo] 'grass' (McArthur 1992; D. Kinkade p.c.). The name **Tipsoo** also occurs in Wash. (Pierce Co.) A related placename is **Tupso Creek** (Wash., Snohomish Co.).

TISHABEE (Ala., Greene Co.) \tish´ bē\. From a Choctaw (Muskogean) war name, meaning 'killer of an assistant chief', containing *tishu* 'assistant chief' and *abi* 'killer' (Read 1984).

TISHDOGATUMINA Lake (Alaska, Beaver B-5). From Koyukon (Athabaskan) *təsh t'oghə mənə'* 'beneath-hill lake' (Kari 2000).

TISHIMNA Lake (Alaska, Sleetmute B-1). From Athabaskan, meaning 'lowland lake'; cf. Deg Hit'an *htset vina,* Dena'ina *htsit vena* (J. Kari p.c.).

TISHLARA Creek (Ala., Choctaw Co.). Perhaps an Indian name; otherwise not identified (Read 1984).

TISHOMINGO County (Miss.) \tish ə ming´ gō\. Named for a Chickasaw (Muskogean) leader; his Native American name was *tishoh' minko,* containing *tisho'* 'assistant to an Indian doctor' and *minko* 'chief' (Seale 1939; P. Munro p.c.). The name also occurs in Okla. (Johnston Co.).

TISH-TANG-A-TANG Creek (Calif., Humboldt Co.) \tish täng´ ä tin\. From the Hoopa (Athabaskan) village name *diysh-taang'aading,* probably meaning 'grouse-promontory' (Gudde 1998). The nearby placename **Tish-Tang Point** has the same origin.

TISKEET Lake (Alaska, Kateel River B-3). The Koyukon (Athabaskan) name was reported in 1955 (Orth 1967).

TISKILWA (Ill., Bureau Co.) \tis´ kil wä\. Perhaps from Ojibwa (Algonquian) <tchitchwishkiwê> 'plover' (Vogel 1963; Baraga 1880); or from Cherokee (Iroquoian) *tsisqua* 'bird', *tsigilili* 'chickadee' (Alexander 1971).

TISPAQUIN Pond (Mass., Plymouth Co.). Named after a SNEng. Algonquian leader of the seventeenth century, also called <Watuspaquin>, perhaps meaning 'black plume' (Huden 1962).

TISUK River (Alaska, Nome D-3). The Iñupiaq (Eskimo) name was reported in 1900 (Orth 1967).

TITACOCLOS Falls (Wash., Clallam Co.). From Makah (Nootkan) /tit'aq'atu:s/ 'water falling down onto the beach' (W. Jacobsen p.c.).

TITALUK River (Alaska, Ikpikpuk River D-3). The Iñupiaq (Eskimo) name is *tittaaliq* 'ling cod' (L. Kaplan p.c.).

TIT Butte (S.Dak., Ziebach Co.). Probably corresponds to Lakhota (Siouan) *pahá makhú thawíču,* lit. 'his wife's breast hill' (A. Taylor); cf. *pahá* 'hill', *makhú* 'breast, chest', *thawíču* 'his wife' (Ingrham 2001).

TITHUMIJI (Ariz., Coconino Co.). The term is the surname of a local Havasupai (Yuman) family (Granger 1983).

TITI Branch (Ala., Washington Co.) \tī´ tī\. Perhaps a placename from the now extinct Timucua language (Read 1984).

TITICACA Creek (Wash., King Co.) \tit ē kä´ kä\. Named for the large lake between Peru and Bolivia; the term is from a South American Indian language (Hitchman 1985).

TITICUS River (Conn., Fairfield Co.; N.Y., Westchester Co.) \tit´ i kəs\. Perhaps from Mahican (Algonquian), meaning 'place without trees' (Ruttenber 1906; Huden 1962).

TITICUT (Mass., Plymouth Co.) \tit´ i kət\. From SNEng. Algonquian, perhaps meaning 'great tidal-stream place', from <k'te-, te-> 'great', <-tuck-> 'tidal stream', and <-et> 'place' (Huden 1962; W. Cowan p.c.).

TITNA River (Alaska, Ruby B-2) \tit´ nə, tēt´ nə\. From Koyukon (Athabaskan) *teet no'* [ti:t no:'], with *no'* 'river' (Kari 1999:105).

TITNUK Creek (Alaska, Sleetmute B-3) \tēt´ no͝ok\. From Deg Hit'an (Athabaskan) *tetno'* 'pike creek' (J. Kari p.c.).

TITONKA (Iowa, Kossuth Co.) \tī tong´ kə\. This has the same origin as **Tetonka Township** (Minn., Le Sueur Co.), from Dakota (Siouan), meaning 'big house' (Vogel 1983).

TITTABAWASSEE River (Mich., Saginaw Co.) \tit ə bə wä´ sē\. Said to be from Ojibwa (Algonquian) <ta-tu-ba-war-say> 'the river running parallel with the shore' (Vogel 1986); cf. *ditibise* 'to roll, go around' (Nichols and Nyholm 1995).

TITUNA Spit (Ore., Curry Co.). Perhaps from the same origin as **Tututni,** the name of an Athabaskan group (D. Kinkade); see below.

TIURPA Islands (Alaska, Port Alexander D-5). The Tlingit name was reported in 1809 (Orth 1967).

TIVA Canyon (Nev., Nye Co.) \tē´ və\. From Southern Paiute or Shoshoni (both Numic) /tɨpa/ [tɨ́va] 'pinyon pine' (Carlson 1974; J. McLaughlin p.c.).

TIVEHVUN Lake (Alaska, Fort Yukon D-3). The Gwich'in (Athabaskan) name was reported in 1956 (Orth 1967); cf. *van* 'lake' (Peter 1979).

TIVYAGAK Creek (Alaska, Goodnews Bay A-7). The Yupik (Eskimo) name was reported in 1954 (Orth 1967).

TIWA \tē´ wə\. A linguistic grouping within the Tanoan family; it includes the people of **Taos, Picuris,** Sandia, and **Isleta** pueblos in New Mexico (*HNAI* 9:171). See also **Tigua Pueblo** (Tex., El Paso Co.).

TIYAKTALIK Mountains (Alaska, Noatak A-3). The Iñupiaq (Eskimo) name is probably *tiġiaqtalik*, from *tiġiaq* 'weasel' (L. Kaplan p.c.).

TIYE Point (Wash., Pierce Co.) \tī´ yē\. Perhaps from the same origin as **Tyee** (Ore., Douglas Co.), from the Chinook Jargon word for 'chief'.

TIYO Point (Ariz., Coconino Co.) \tē´ yō\. From Hopi (Uto-Aztecan) *tiyo* 'young man' (K. Hill p.c.).

TIZ NA TZIN Trading Post (N.Mex., San Juan Co.) \tiz nä´ tsin\. Perhaps from Navajo (Athabaskan) *t'iis náshjin* 'black cottonwood circle' (Linford 2000).

TLATL Hills (Alaska, Ophir D-4). The Koyukon (Athabaskan) name was reported in 1954 (Orth 1967).

TLA-XAGH Island (Alaska, Yakutat C-5). The Tlingit name was reported in 1928 (Orth 1967).

TLECHEGN Lake (Alaska, Tanacross A-3). From Upper Tanana (Athabaskan) *łeecheegn männ'*, lit. 'joined-confluences lake' (J. Kari p.c.).

TLEGON (Alaska, Ophir A-6) \tlā´ gōn\. The Deg Hit'an (Athabaskan) name is *łeghunh*, perhaps 'by the ice' (J. Kari p.c.).

TLEVAK Narrows (Alaska, Craig B-4). The Tlingit name was reported in 1952 (Orth 1967).

TLIALIL (Alaska, Nulato C-5). The Koyukon (Athabaskan) name is of unclear derivation (Orth 1967).

TLIKAKILA River (Alaska, Lime Hills A-2) \tlē kə kē´ lə\. The Dena'ina (Athabaskan) name was reported in 1902 (Orth 1967); the Native American term is *łiq'a qilanhtnu* 'salmon-are-there river'.

TLINGIT \tliŋ´ git, tliŋ´ kit; kliŋ´ git, kliŋ´ kit\. The name of an Indian group living in southwestern Alaska and adjacent Canada. The term is from Tlingit /łi:ngít/ 'human being(s)' (*HNAI* 6:479).

TLOCOGN Lake (Alaska, Tanacross A-3). The Tanacross (Athabaskan) name was published in 1964 (Orth 1967).

TLOZHAVUN Lake (Alaska, Fort Yukon B-4). The Gwich'in (Athabaskan) name is *tloojaa van* (Caulfield et al. 1980); cf. *van* 'lake' (Peter 1979).

TLUNA Icefall (Alaska, Mt. McKinley A-3) \tlo͞o´ nə\. From Koyukon (Athabaskan) *łoo no'*, lit. 'glacier stream' (Kari 1999:118).

TOADLENA (N.Mex., San Juan Co.) \tō ad lē´ nə, tōd lē´ nə\. Navajo (Athabaskan) *tó háálį* 'it flows up and out', from *tó* 'water, spring', *há(á-)* 'up and out', and *lį́'* 'it flows' (A. Wilson p.c.).

TOANDOS Peninsula (Wash., Jefferson Co) \tō än´ dōs\. From the same source as **Twana,** the name of a Southern Coast Salishan language, and **Twanoh State Park** (Wash., Mason Co.); see below.

TOANO (Nev., Elko Co.) \tō ä´ nō\. From Shoshoni (Numic) /toi/ 'pipe' and /no/ 'camp' (Carlson 1974, McLaughlin p.c.).

TOANO (Va., James City Co.). Supposedly named for an Indian resident, language not identified (Hagemann 1988).

TOATS COULEE Creek (Wash., Okanogan Co.). A folk-etymologized form of Okanagan (Salish) \tuc'kʷúl'axʷ, tuʔckʷúlaʔxʷ\, containing /-ulaʔxʷ/ 'earth, ground' (Hitchman 1985; D. Kinkade p.c.).

TOAWLEVIC Point (Alaska, Kotzebue A-2). The Iñupiaq (Eskimo) name is *tauġaaluuvik* (Burch 1998).

TOBACCO \tə bak´ ō\. The name of the herb widely used for smoking is from Spanish *tabaco,* perhaps from an Arawakan language of the Caribbean area (*RHD* 1987). In placenames it is widespread (e.g., S.Dak., Gregory Co.; and Va., Brunswick Co.). In Md. (Charles Co.) **Port Tobacco** is a folk-etymological version of a name earlier written as <Portobacke>; the term is from CAC Algonquian, of unclear derivation. Related placenames are **Portobago** (Va., Caroline Co.) and **Potopaco** (Md., Charles Co.).

TOBANNEE Creek (Ga., Quitman Co.). Also written <Tobenanee>; perhaps from Muskogee, meaning 'tree with a crooked trunk', containing *eto* 'tree, *vpe* 'trunk, stalk', and *yvnahi* 'crooked' (Read 1949–50).

TOBASCO (Ohio, Clermont Co.) \tə bas´ kō\. Named for the state of Tabasco on the Caribbean coast of Mexico, derived from an Indian language of that area; or else named for the spicy sauce of the same name. The placename also occurs in Wash. (Pend Oreille Co.). A related placename is **Tabasco Creek** (Alaska, Russian Mission A-2).

TOBATOKH Creek (Alaska, Tanana D-6). The Koyukon (Athabaskan) name was obtained in 1956 (Orth 1967).

TOBESOFKEE (Ga., Bibb Co.). Perhaps from Muskogee, meaning 'sofkee stirrer', from *vtapv* /atá:pa/ 'wooden stirring ladle' plus *osafke* /(o)sá:fke/ 'sofkee, corn gruel' (Read 1949–50; Martin and Mauldin 2000). Related placenames are **Sofka** (Okla., Creek Co.) and **Sofkee** (Ga., Bibb Co.).

TO BILA'I (N.Mex., San Juan Co.). Navajo (Athabaskan) *tó bíla'í'* water fingers' (Linford 2000).

TO-BIL-HASK-IDI Wash (N.Mex., San Juan Co.). Navajo (Athabaskan) *tó bił hask'idí* 'water with a hill', containing *tó* 'water', *bił* 'with it', and *hask'id* 'it mounds, makes a hill' (A. Wilson p.c.).

TOBOGGAN \tə bog´ ən\. This word for a type of sled was borrowed from Maleseet (Algonquian) /tʰapákən/ (*RHD* 1987). As a placename, it occurs in several states (e.g., Idaho, Clearwater Co.; N.Mex., Otero Co.; and Wyo., Sublette Co.).

TOBONA (Alaska, Tyonek A-4) \tə bō´ nə\. From Dena'ina (Athabaskan) *tubughnenq'* 'beach land'; cf. *tuvugh* 'beach', *nen* 'land' (Kari and Fall 1987:45; Kari and Kari 1982:30). A related placename is **Tyonek** (Alaska, Tyonek A-4).

TOBOXKY (Okla., Pittsburg Co.) \tə boks´ kē\. From Choctaw (Muskogean) *tobaksi* 'coal' (Shirk 1974; P. Munro p.c.).

TOBUK Creek (Alaska, Survey Pass A-1). Named in 1931 for an Iñupiaq (Eskimo) resident called *tuvaaq* (L. Kaplan p.c.).

TOBY Creek (Alaska, McCarthy B-4). Perhaps from a Tanana (Athabaskan) word, meaning 'a variety of sheep' (Orth 1967).

TOBY Creek (Pa., Clarion Co.). Perhaps from Delaware (Algonquian) <topi-hanna> 'alder stream'; cf. <topi> 'alder tree' (Brinton and Anthony 1888; Donehoo 1928).

TOBYHANNA (Pa., Monroe Co.) \tō bē han´ ə\. Perhaps from Delaware *tëpihane* 'cold water creek' (Kraft and Kraft 1985); or perhaps related to **Toby Creek;** see above.

TOBY TUBBY Creek (Miss., Lafayette Co.). From a Choctaw (Muskogean) personal name, probably a "war name" of the form *atobbitabi* 'he pays and kills', containing *atobbi* 'to pay' and *abi* 'to kill' (Seale 1939; P. Munro p.c.).

TOCALOMA (Calif., Marin Co.) \tō kə lō´ mə\. From Coast Miwok, perhaps containing /lúme/ 'willow' (Gudde 1998).

TOCCOA River (Ga., Fannin Co.). From Cherokee (Iroquoian), meaning 'Catawba place', referring to the Catawba (Siouan) Indians; cf. <atagwa, tagwa> 'Catawba Indian' (Read 1984). A variant spelling is **Taccoa River.** A related placename is **Tacoa** (Ala., Shelby Co.); see above.

TOCCOPOLA (Miss., Pontotoc Co.) \tok ə pō´ lə\. Perhaps from Choctaw (Muskogean) *itti aay-okpolo* 'where trees are destroyed', from *itti* 'tree', *aay-* 'place', and *okpolo* 'to be destroyed' (Seale 1939; P. Munro p.c.).

TOCITO (N.Mex., San Juan Co.) \tō sē´ tō\. A Spanish-appearing spelling for Navajo (Athabaskan) *tó sido* 'hot spring, hot water', from *tó* 'water' and *sido* 'it is hot' (Julyan 1998; A. Wilson p.c.).

TOCKSHISH (Miss., Pontotoc Co.). From Choctaw (Muskogean), meaning 'tree roots', containing *itti* 'tree' and *hakshish* 'root' (Seale 1939; P. Munro p.c.).

TOCKWOTTON Park (R.I., Providence Co.). From Narragansett (SNEng. Algonquian), perhaps meaning 'frozen'; cf. <seip taquattin> 'the river is frozen' (W. Cowan p.c.).

TOCOI (Fla., St. Johns Co.). Probably a village name in Timucua, a language now extinct (Read 1934).

TOCOWA (Miss., Panola Co.). Perhaps from Choctaw (Muskogean) *ittaakowa* 'where trees are broken', from *itti* 'tree', *aa-* 'place', and *kowa* 'broken'; or from *ittakowa* 'firewood', from *itti* 'tree', *aa-* 'from', and *kowa* 'broken' (Seale 1939; P. Munro p.c.).

TOCWOGH (Md., Queen Anne's Co.). The name of a CAC Algonquian subgroup and/or their village (Kenny 1984).

TODACHEENE Lake (N.Mex., San Juan Co.). Navajo (Athabaskan) *tó dích'íi'nii* 'bitter water, alkaline water', with *tó* 'water' and *dích'íí'* 'it is bitter, sour' (A. Wilson p.c.).

TODASTONI Spring (Ariz., Apache Co.). A variant spelling of **Toh Dahstini Spring**; see below.

TODATONTEN, Lake (Alaska, Bettles A-6). The Koyukon (Athabaskan) name is *todaatl-tonhdenh* 'enclosed lake place' (J. Kari p.c.).

TO-DIL-HIL Wash (N.Mex., San Juan Co.). Navajo (Athabaskan) *tódiłhił* 'dark water, whiskey', from *tó* 'water' and *diłhił* 'it is dark'; also called "Whiskey Creek" in English (Young and Morgan 1987:706; Wilson 1995). A possibly related name is **Tol Dohn Spring** (N.Mex., McKinley Co.).

TODILTO Park (N.Mex., McKinley Co.) \tō dēl´ tō\. Navajo (Athabaskan) *tó dildǫ'* 'water that pops, sounding water', from *tó* 'water, spring' and *dildǫ'* 'it pops, explodes' (Wilson 1995). Possibly related placenames **Tohdildonih Wash** and **Tol Dohn Spring** (both in N.Mex., McKinley Co.); see below.

TODOKOZH (Ariz., Navajo Co.). A variant spelling of **Toh De Coz**; see below.

TOE Rock (N.Mex., Sandoval Co.). Said to be a translation of a Tiwa (Tanoan) placename (Julyan 1998).

TOGIAK (Alaska, Goodnews Bay A-4) \tō´ gē ak\. From the Yupik (Eskimo) placename *tuyuryaq* (Orth 1967; Jacobson 1984).

TOGOYE Lake (N.Mex., McKinley Co.). Probably from Navajo (Athabaskan) *tóyéé'* 'scarce water', from *tó* 'water' and *yéé'* 'scarce' (Linford 2000). A related placename is **Tuye Spring** (Ariz., Apache Co.).

TOGOYUK Creek (Alaska, Killik River A-2). The Iñupiaq (Eskimo) name was reported in 1956 (Orth 1967).

TOGUE Pond (Maine, Aroostook Co.) \tōg\. The word *togue* is used in local English for the 'lake trout' (Huden 1962); it may be a shortening of Micmac (Algonquian) /atoɣwa:su/ 'trout' (*RHD* 1987).

TOGUS (Maine, Kennebec Co.) \tō´ gəs\. From Abenaki (Algonquian), perhaps meaning 'brook (entering cove)' (Huden 1962).

TOGWOTEE Pass (Wyo., Teton Co.) \tō´ gə tē\. Named for a Shoshoni (Numic) leader, /tɨkwɨtti/ [tɨɣwɨtl] 'thrower' (i.e., 'spear-thrower') (Urbanek 1974; J. McLaughlin p.c.).

TOHACHE Wash (N.Mex., San Juan Co.) \tō hach´ ē\. From Navajo (Athabaskan) *tóhaach'i'*; a related name is **Tohatchi,** see below. The name **Tohache** also occurs in Ariz. (Apache Co.) \tō hä´ chē\. The spelling **Toh Ah Chi** also occurs in Ariz. (Navajo Co.).

TOHAKUM Peak (Nev., Washoe Co.) \tō hä´ kəm\. Northern Paiute (Numic) /toha-kkammɨ/ 'winter phase of jackrabbit', from /toha/ 'white' plus /kammɨ/ 'jackrabbit' (Carlson 1974; J. McLaughlin p.c.).

TOHASGED Spring (N.Mex., McKinley Co.). Navajo (Athabaskan) *tó haasgeed* 'water is dug out', from *tó* 'water' and *haasgeed* 'is dug out' (A. Wilson p.c.).

TOHATCHI (N.Mex., McKinley Co.) \tō´ hach ē\. Navajo (Athabaskan) *tóhaach'i'* 'water is scratched out', from *tó* 'water' and *haach'i'* 'it is scratched out' (Julyan 1998; Wilson 1965). A related placename is **Tohache Wash** (N.Mex., San Juan Co.); see above.

TOH ATIN Mesa (Ariz., Apache Co.). Shortened from Navajo (Athabaskan) *tó ádin dah azką́* 'no-water mesa' (Linford 2000); cf. *tó* 'water', *ádin* 'non-existent', *dah* 'above', *asgą'* 'something dried up' (Young and Morgan 1987).

TOH CHIN LINI Canyon (Ariz., Apache Co.). Navajo (Athabaskan) *tó ch'ínlíní* 'water flowing out' (Linford 2000).

TOH DAHSTINI Spring (Colo., Montezuma Co.; Utah, San Juan Co.; Ariz., Apache Co.). Navajo (Athabaskan) *tó dah da'aztání* 'fingers of water here and there above' (Granger 1983; Linford 2000). Alternative spellings are **Todastoni Spring** and **Tohdenstani.**

TOH DE COZ (Ariz., Navajo Co.) \tō´ di kōz\. From Navajo (Athabaskan) *tó dík'ǫ́ǫ́zhí* 'bitter water', with *tó* 'water' and *dík'ǫ́ǫ́zh* 'salty, sour, bitter' (Granger 1983; Wilson 1995). Variants are **Todokozh** and **Tudecoz Spring.**

TOHDENSTANI Spring (Ariz., Apache Co.). A variant writing of **Toh Dahstini Spring**; see above.

TOHDILDONIH Wash (N.Mex., McKinley Co.). From the same origin as **Todilto Park**; see above.

TOHEE Township (Okla., Lincoln Co.) \tō´ hē\. Named for an Iowa (Siouan) leader (Shirk 1974). It is not clear whether this name has anything to do with *towhee,* the name of a bird.

TOHICKON (Pa., Bucks Co.). Said to be from Delaware <tohick-hanne> 'driftwood stream' (Donehoo 1928).

TOHITKAH Mountains (Alaska, Skagway C-3). The Tlingit name was published in 1952 (Orth 1967).

TOHLAKAI (N.Mex., McKinley Co.). Navajo (Athabaskan) *tó łigaaí* 'white water', from *tó* 'water, spring' plus *łigaaí* 'it is white' (Julyan 1998; A. Wilson p.c.).

TOHNALI Mesa (Ariz., Coconino Co.). Navajo (Athabaskan) *tó náálíní* 'water flowing downward' (Linford 2000).

TOH-NI-TSA Lookout (N.Mex., San Juan Co.). Navajo (Athabaskan) *tónitsaa* 'big water', from *tó* 'water' plus *nitsaa* 'big' (Wilson 1995).

TOHNOKALONG (Alaska, Ruby B-3). The Koyukon (Athabaskan) language is of unclear derivation (Orth 1967).

TOH-NOZ-BOSA Well (N.Mex., McKinley Co.). Navajo (Athabaskan) *tó názbąsí* 'round water, circular water', with *tó* 'water' and *názbąs* 'round, circular' (A. Wilson p.c.).

TOHOPEKA (Ala., Tallapoosa Co.) \tō hə pē´ kə\. From Muskogee *tohopke* /tohó:pki/ 'fence, fort' (Read 1984; Martin and Mauldin 2000). A related placename is **Lake Tohopekaliga** (Fla., Osceola Co.), from Muskogee *tohopke* /tohó:pki/ 'fence, fort' plus *likv* /léyk-a/ 'site' (Read 1934; Martin and Mauldin 2000); a variant spelling is **Tohopikaliga.**

TOHOPKEE (Fla., Osceola Co.). From Muskogee *tohopke* /tohó:pki/ 'fence, fort' (Read 1934; Martin and Mauldin 2000). A related placename is **Tohopeka** (Ala., Tallapoosa Co.).

TOIK Hill (Alaska, Unalakleet B-5). The Yupik (Eskimo) name was reported in 1898 (Orth 1967).

TOIKIMING (Mass., Dukes Co.). From SNEng. Algonquian, perhaps meaning 'at the gushing spring' (Huden 1962).

TOISNOT Swamp (N.C., Wilson Co.). From Tuscarora (Iroquoian) *teyuynuukt* 'next to two rivers' (B. Rudes p.c.).

TOIYABE Peak (Nev., Lander Co.) \toi yä´ bē\. From Shoshoni (Numic) /toyapi/ [toyavi] 'mountain' (Carlson 1974; J. McLaughlin p.c.). The name **Toiyabe** also occurs in Calif. (Mono Co.).

TOKAINA Creek (Alaska, Valdez D-7) \tō kī´ nə\. From Ahtna (Athabaskan) *tahwghi'aayi na',* lit. 'one-that-stands-in-the-water creek' (Kari 1983:35).

TOKATEE Lakes (Ore., Lane Co.) \tō´ kə tē\. Chinook Jargon <t'oke-tie> [tókti] 'good, nice, pretty, handsome', perhaps from Lower Chinook [tgt'ókti] 'good' (D. Kinkade p.c.).

TOKATJIKH Creek (Alaska, Melozitna C-1). The Koyukon (Athabaskan) name was obtained in 1956 (Orth 1967).

TOKAWANA Peak (Utah, Summit Co.) \tō kə wä´ nə\. Perhaps from Ute (Numic), said to mean 'peace' (Van Cott 1990). A variant spelling is **Tokewanna Peak.**

TOKEBA Bayou (Miss., Yazoo Co.). Perhaps from Choctaw (Muskogean), meaning 'tree frog', from *itti* 'tree' and *kiba* 'frog' (Seale 1939; P. Munro p.c.).

TOKEEN (Alaska, Craig D-5) \tō kēn´\. The Tlingit name was recorded in 1901 (Orth 1967).

TOKEENA Point (S.C., Oconee Co.). Perhaps from a Cherokee (Iroquoian) word meaning 'giant fish' (Pickens 1961–62:22).

TOKENEKE (Conn., Fairfield Co.). Perhaps named for a Mahican (Algonquian) leader; cf. also <touuhkomuk(w-)> 'wilderness', from /taw-/ 'open' and /-ahkaməkw/ 'land' (Huden 1962; I. Goddard p.c.).

TOKE Point (Wash., Pacific Co.) \tōk\. Named for a Lower Chinook man called [túq] (Hitchman 1985; D. Kinkade p.c.). A placename derived from this is nearby **Tokeland**.

TOKETA Creek (Ore., Lincoln Co.). From the same origin as **Tokatee Lakes**; see above. Related placenames include **Toketee Falls** (Ore., Douglas Co.) \tō´ ki tē\, **Lake Toke Tie** (WA, Skamania Co.), and **Toketie Creek** (Wash., Chelan Co.).

TOKEWANNA Peak (Utah, Summit Co.). Perhaps from Ute (Numic), meaning 'peace' (Van Cott 1990). A variant spelling is **Tokawana Peak.**

TOKHAKLANTEN Lake (Alaska, Hughes A-4). The Koyukon (Athabaskan) name was recorded in 1956 (Orth 1967).

TOKHINI Creek (Alaska, Petersburg A-4). The Tlingit name was reported in 1897 (Orth 1967).

TOKIO (Okla., Kiowa Co.). Supposedly from Kiowa (Kiotanoan) <towkyowy> 'long building' (Shirk 1974). The placename also exists in Ark. (Hempstead Co.), Miss. (Wayne Co.), N.Dak. (Benson Co.), Tex. (Terry Co.), and Wash. (Adams Co.); some of these may be from an alternative spelling of *Tokyo* in Japan.

TOKLAT (Alaska, Kantishna River B-1) \tōk´ lat\. From Lower Tanana (Athabaskan) *tutl'ot* 'headwaters' (Kari 1999:123).

TOKLIK (Alaska, Russian Mission C-8). The Yupik (Eskimo) village was reported in 1943 as <Tochtlik> (Orth 1967).

TOKOMARIK Mountains (Alaska, Hagemeister Island C-6). The Yupik (Eskimo) name was published in 1948 (Orth 1967).

TOKOP (Nev., Esmeralda Co.) \tok´ əp, tō´ kop\. From Shoshoni (Numic) /takkappi/ 'snow' (Carlson 1974; J. McLaughlin p.c.).

TOKOPAH Falls (Calif., Tulare Co.) \tō´ kə pä\. Perhaps from Yokuts, meaning 'high mountain valley' (Gudde 1998).

TOKOSHA Mountains (Alaska, Talkeetna C-2) \tə kosh´ ə\. The Dena'ina (Athabaskan) name is *tuqashi* 'things fall in water' (J. Kari p.c.).

TOKOSITNA River (Alaska, Talkeetna D-2) \tō kə sit´ nə\. Dena'ina (Athabaskan) *tuqashitnu* 'stream of things that fall into water', with *-tnu* 'stream' (Kari and Fall 1987:176).

TOK River (Alaska, Tanacross B-4) \tōk\. Probably from Athabaskan, reported as <Tokai> in 1887 (Orth 1967).

TOKSOOK (Alaska, Baird Inlet C-8) \tuk´ sōōk\. The Yupik (Eskimo) name was reported in 1949 (Orth 1967).

TOKUL (Wash., King Co.) From an Indian word <tu-kwa-l>, language not identified, said to mean 'very dark water' (Hitchman 1985).

TOKUN Lake (Alaska, Cordova B-1). The Eyak name is */tugun/*.

TOKUSATATQUATEN Lake (Alaska, Bettles A-3). The Koyukon (Athabaskan) name was obtained in 1956 (Orth 1967).

TO-KWAK-SOSE (Wash., Clallam Co.). From Makah (Nootkan) /t'ukaqsuwis/, meaning 'small mouth' or 'narrow channel', with the root /t'uk-/ 'small' (W. Jacobsen p.c.).

TOLAGEAK (Alaska, Wainwright A-6). The Iñupiaq (Eskimo) name is from *tulak-* 'to land a boat' (L. Kaplan p.c.). Probably related is **Tolaktovut Point** (Alaska, Harrison Bay B-2), said to mean 'where boats are landed' (Orth 1967).

TOLANI Lake (Ariz., Coconino Co.). Navajo (Athabaskan) *tółání* 'much water, many bodies of water', from *tó* 'water" plus *łání* 'many, much' (Granger 1983; Wilson 1995).

TOLAY Creek (Calif., Sonoma Co.) \tō´ lā\. Said to be the name of an Indian leader, language not identified (Gudde 1998).

TOLCHACO Gap (Ariz., Coconino Co.). Probably a variant writing of **Tolchico**; see below.

TOLCHICO (Ariz., Coconino Co.). Navajo (Athabaskan) *tółchí'íkooh* 'red-water wash', from *tó* 'water', *-łchí'í, łichíí'* 'red', and *kooh* 'a wash, an arroyo' (Wilson 1995).

TOL DOHN Spring (N.Mex., McKinley Co.). Perhaps from the same origin as **Todilto Park** (N.Mex., McKinley Co.); see above.

TOLEAK Point (Wash., Jefferson Co.) \tō´ lē ak\. Quileute (Chemakuan) /łoloq'^{W}ayá:x̣iq^{W}/ 'hole-in-the-rock place', from /łiló:q'^{W}a/ 'tunnel, cave, hole', /-yax̣i/ 'rock', and /-q^{W}/ 'place' (Parratt 1984; D. Kinkade p.c.).

TOLENAS Creek (Calif., Solano Co.) \tə lē´ nəs\. Said to be the name of a Patwin (Wintuan) village (Gudde 1998).

TOLICHA (Nev., Nye Co.) \tō lē´ chə\. Perhaps an Indian name, but from an unidentified language (Carlson 1974).

TOLISHDEN Slough (Alaska, Harrison Bay B-2). The Koyukon (Athabaskan) name was reported in 1955 (Orth 1967).

TOLLER BOGUE (Ala., Washington Co.) \tol ə bōg\. From Choctaw (Muskogean) *taala-book* 'palmetto stream', with *taala* 'palmetto' and *book* 'stream' (Read 1984; P. Munro p.c.).

TOLMAN, Mount (Wash., Ferry Co.). From Okanagan (Salishan) [kłtúl'mən] 'piece of red ochre paint' (D. Kinkade p.c.).

TOLOKA (Okla., Haskell Co.) \tə lō´ kə\. Perhaps from Choctaw (Muskogean), but the derivation is not clear (Shirk 1974; P. Munro p.c.).

TOLO Lake (Idaho, Idaho Co.) \tō´ lō\. Named for a Nez Perce (Sahaptian) woman in the late nineteenth century; she was also called <Alablernot> or <Too-lah> (Boone 1988). The name may have the same Chinook Jargon origin as **Tolo** in Wash. (Kitsap Co.); cf. Jargon <to´-lo> 'to earn, to gain', perhaps from Kalapuyan [tú:lu:ʔ] 'to win' (Reese 1996; D. Kinkade p.c.). There is also a **Tolo Creek** in Ore. (Douglas Co.), which is said to represent a deliberate change and transfer of the placename **Yolo County** (Calif.) (McArthur 1992).

TOLONO (Ill., Champaign Co.) \tə lō´ nō\. Perhaps from <Tolony>, a seventeenth-century SNEng. Algonquian man (Vogel 1963).

TOLOVANA (Alaska, Fairbanks D-6) \tō lə van´ ə\. From Lower Tanana (Athabaskan) *tolba no'*, lit. 'pale-water stream' (J. Kari p.c.). The name **Tolovana** also occurs as a transfer in Ore. (Clatsop Co.).

TOLSONA (Alaska, Gulkana A-4) \tol sō´ nə\. From Ahtena (Athabaskan) *taltsogh na'*, lit. 'yellow-water stream' (Kari 1983:34).

TOLSTOI Creek (Alaska, Ophir B-3). Possibly from Deg Hit'an (Athabaskan) *toltsiyhno'*, containing *no'* 'stream' (J. Kari p.c.).

TOLTEC (Colo., Huerfano Co.) \tol´ tek\. From Nahuatl (Aztecan) *tolteca*, designating an ancient people of Mexico. The literal meaning is 'people of the tules or cat-tail reeds' (Bright 1993). The placename **Toltec** also occurs in N.Mex. (Cibola Co.).

TOLT River (Wash., King Co.) \tōlt\. From the Lushootseed (Salishan) village name /túlq/ (Hitchman 1985; D. Kinkade p.c.).

TOLU (Ky., Crittenden Co.) \to͞o´ lo͞o\. From a whiskey-based tonic made with tolu resin, named after the town of *Tolú* in Columbia; that placename is derived for a South American Indian language (Rennick 1984; *RHD* 1987). The name **Tolu** also occurs in Ark. (Washington Co.).

TOLUCA Lake (Calif., Los Angeles Co.) \tō lo͞o´ kə, tə lo͞o´ kə\. A transfer from the name of a city in Mexico, orginally *Tolocan* in Nahuatl (Aztecan) (Gudde 1998). The name **Toluca** also occurs in Ill. (Marshall Co.) and Kans. (Haskell Co.).

TOMAH (Maine, Washington Co.) \tō´ mə\. Said to be named for an Abenaki (Algonquian) leader, perhaps from the French given name *Thomas* \tō mä`\. (Eckstorm 1941). In Wis. (Monroe Co.), **Tomah** \tō´ mä\. was named for Thomas Carron, an eighteenth-century Menominee leader of French ancestry (Vogel 1991).

TOMAHA Point (S.Dak., Pennington Co.) Also written <Tomahaw>; named for Tamaha, a Santee Dakota (Siouan) leader in the early nineteenth century (Sneve 1973).

TOMAHAWK \tom´ ə hôk\. A type of hatchet used in warfare; from Va. Algonquian <tamahaac> 'hatchet' (*RHD* 1987). As a placename, it occurs in many states (e.g., Kans., Johnson Co.; Mich., Presque Isle Co.; and N.J., Sussex Co.).

TOMAKOKIN Creek (Md., St. Mary's Co.). From CAC Algonquian, of unclear derivation (Kenny 1984).

TOMALES Bay (Calif., Marin Co.) \tə mä´ ləs\. From the Spanish plural *Tamales*, having nothing to do with the popular Mexican food, but designating a Miwokan subgroup; derived from Coast Miwok /támal/ 'west, west coast' (Gudde 1998).

TOMAQUAG Brook (R.I., Washington Co.). From SNEng. Algonquian, probably meaning 'beavers'; cf. Narragansett <tummock> 'beaver' (Huden 1962; W. Cowan p.c.).

TOMAR (Wash., Benton Co.). Named for a leader of the Walla Walla (Sahaptian) Indians (Hitchman 1985).

TOMASAKI, Mount (Utah, Grand Co.) \tom ə sä´ kē, tō mə sä´ kē\. Named for an Indian guide in an 1875 survey; the term is probably from a Numic language (Van Cott 1990).

TOMATO Creek (Alaska, Eagle A-3). Named for the vegetable; from Spanish *tomate*, from Nahuatl (Aztecan) *tomatl*. The placename **Tomato** also occurs in Ark. (Mississippi Co.) and Idaho (Idaho Co.). In S.Dak. (Butte Co.) we also find the **Tomato Can Buttes.**

TOMBIGBEE (Ala., Marengo Co.) \tom big´ bē\. Choctaw (Muskogean) *itumbi ikbi* 'box maker, coffin maker', from *itumbi* 'box, coffin' and *ikbi* 'maker' (Read 1984; P. Munro p.c.). The name **Tombigbee** also is found in Miss. (Lowndes Co.).

TOMB OF THE WEAVER (Ariz., Apache Co.). Navajo (Athabaskan) *hastiin tł'ó bitséyaa* 'mister weaver's cave' (Linford 2000).

TOMHANNOCK (N.Y., Rensselaer Co.) \tom han´ ək\. Perhaps from Mahican (Algonquian), of unclear derivation (Beauchamp 1907).

TOMHEGAN Cove (Maine, Piscataquis Co.) \tom hē´ gən\. From Abenaki (Algonquian) *demahigan* 'axe, hatchet' (Huden 1962; Day 1994–95).

TOMICHI Dome (Colo., Gunnison Co.) \tō mē´ chē\. Probably from Ute (Numic) *tumúchich* 'dome-shaped rock' (Bright 1993).

TOMKA Valley (Calif., San Diego Co.) \tom´ kə\. Probably from Luiseño (Takic), but of unclear derivation (Gudde 1998).

TOMKI Creek (Calif., Mendocino Co.) \tôm´ kī\. From Northern Pomo /mitʰhóm kʰáy/, lit. 'splash valley' (Gudde 1998).

TOMLIKE Mountain (Ore., Hood River Co.) \tom´ līk\. Named after a Chinookan leader, <Tomlike> (etymology unknown), known in English as "Indian George" (McArthur 1992).

TOMNAME Point (Alaska, St. Lawrence B-1). The Yupik (Eskimo) name was reported in 1932 (Orth 1967).

TOMOKA River (Fla., Volusia Co.). An alternative form of **Timucua**, an Indian group that once inhabited much of Fla. (Read 1934).

TOMYHOI Creek (Wash., Whatcom Co.). From Halkomelem (Salishan) /t'emiyə-há:y/, lit. 'hermaphrodite's end', from /t'émiye/ 'wren, hermaphrodite' (D. Kinkade p.c.).

TONACANA Creek (Miss., Newton Co.) \tō´ ni kan i\. Perhaps from Choctaw (Muskogean), meaning 'posts standing' (Seale 1939); cf. *tonnik* 'post', *hiili* 'stand' (P. Munro p.c.).

TONAHUTU Creek (Colo., Grand Co.) \ton ə hōō´ tōō\. From Arapaho (Algonquian) *toonóó xuuté'* 'meadow' (A. Cowell p.c.).

TONALEA (Ariz., Coconino Co.) \tō nə lē´ ə\. Navajo (Athabaskan) *tó nehelį́į́h* 'water flows to a point', from *tó* 'water', *nehe, nihi* 'to a point', and *lį́į́h, lį́* 'flow' (Wilson 1995).

TONASKET (Wash., Okanogan Co.) \tə nas´ kət\. Named for an Okanagon (Salishan) leader called [tunásq't] 'short day', with /twn-/ 'short' and /-asq't/ 'sky, day' (Hitchman 1985; D. Kinkade p.c.). Related placenames are **Tomasket** and **Tenasket Mountain** (Wash., Ferry Co.).

TONAWANDA (N.Y., Erie Co.) \tun ə wän´ də\. Probably from an Iroquoian source, but of unclear derivation (Beauchamp 1907). The name **Tonawanda** is found in several states (e.g., Alaska, Tanana A-2; Mich., Grand Traverse Co.; and Ga., Jones Co.).

TONCLANUKNA Creek (Alaska, Medfra B-2). Perhaps from Upper Kuskokwim (Athabaskan) *toneł'ono,* lit. 'where-water-extends creek', with *no'* 'stream' (Kari 1999:99).

TONGANOXIE (Kans., Leavenworth Co.) \tong gə nok´ sē\. Named for a Delaware (Algonquian) leader of the nineteenth century (Rydjord 1968).

TONGASS (Alaska, Prince Rupert D-3) \tong´ gas, tong´ gəs\. The Tlingit name /t'anga:s/ was adopted in 1868 (Orth 1967; *HNAI* 7:227).

TONGUE River (Wyo., Sheridan Co.). Corresponds to Cheyenne (Algonquian) /vetanoveo'he/, where /vetanove/ is 'tongue' and /o'he'e/ is 'river' (Urbanek 1974; W. Leman p.c.).

TONICA (Ill., La Salle Co.) \ton´ i kə\. Of unclear derivation (Vogel 1963); perhaps from the same origin as **Tunica** (La., West Feliciana Par.).

TONIGUT Spring (Utah, Duchesne Co.). Probably from a Numic (Uto-Aztecan) language; the derivation is not clear (Van Cott 1990).

TO-NIL-CHONI Wash (N.Mex., San Juan Co.). Navajo (Athabaskan) *tónììłchxoní* 'stinking water', with *tó* 'water' and *niłchxon* 'it stinks' (A. Wilson p.c.).

TONIQUINT (Utah, Washington Co.) \tō´ nə kwint\. Named for a Southern Paiute (Numic) subgroup (Van Cott 1990).

TONITLEAGMUND Lake (Alaska, Tanacross A-4). From Upper Tanana (Athabaskan) *too-niitleeg männ'*, perhaps meaning 'mushy lake' (J. Kari p.c.).

TONKA (Nev., Elko Co.) \tong´ kə\. Named for the tropical tonka bean, used to flavor snuff (Carlson 1974); the original form in Tupí, a language of Brazil, is /tǫka/. The placename **Tonka** also occurs in Alaska (Alaska, Petersburg C-3). In Minn. (Hennepin Co.) **Tonka Bay** is said to be abbreviated from **Minnetonka,** in the same area (Upham 2001).

TONKAWA (Okla., Kay Co.) \tong´ kə wə, tong´ kə wä, earlier tong´ kə wā\. The name of a Texas Indian tribe. Doubtfully derivable from Waco (Caddoan) <tonkawéya> 'they all stay together' (*HNAI* 13:962). The name also occurs in Tex. (Cooke Co.). Related placenames are **Tonkaway Lake** (Tex., Brazos Co.) and **Tonkowa Lake** (Mich., Marquette Co.) (Vogel 1986). Another related name is **Tonk Creek** (Tex., Throckmorton Co.).

TONK Creek (Tex., Throckmorton Co.). An abbreviation of **Tonkawa,** a Texas Indian people (Tarpley 1980); see above.

TONOKA Valley (Ariz., Pima Co.). From O'odham (Piman) *to:nk* 'dike, hill' (Granger 1983; J. Hill p.c.).

TONOLOWAY Creek (Pa., Fulton Co.; Md., Washington Co.). Earlier written <Canallowais, Conolloway> (etc.); perhaps from Shawnee (Algonquian), but of unclear derivation (Donehoo 1928; Kenny 1984). The name **Tonoloway** also occurs in W.Va. (Morgan Co.). A probably related placename is **Conoloway** (Ky., Grayson Co.).

TONOPAH (Nev., Nye Co.) \tō´ nə pä\. Shoshoni (Numic) /tonoppaa/ 'greasewood spring', from /tonoppi/ 'greasewood' and /paa/ 'water, spring' (Carlson 1974; J. McLaughlin p.c.). The name **Tonopah** also occurs in Ariz. (Maricopa Co.) (Granger 1983) \tō nə pä´\; it is perhaps to be derived independently from Southern Paiute /tonnoppaa/ 'greasewood spring', from /tonno/ 'greasewood' and /paa/ 'water' (J. McLaughlin p.c.).

TONOWEK Bay (Alaska, Craig C-5). The Tlingit name was reported in 1853 (Orth 1967).

TONQUA Creek (Tex., DeWitt Co.). Perhaps from the **Tonkawa** Indian people; see above.

TONQUE, Arroyo (N.Mex., Sandoval Co.) \tong´ kā\. Probably from Spanish *Tunque,* a precolonial pueblo; perhaps from Tewa (Tanoan) [t'ųɣe] 'down at the basket', from [t'ųŋy] 'basket', [-ɣe] 'down at' (Julyan 1998; Harrington 1916). The spelling variant **Tunque Pueblo** also occurs.

TONQUISH Creek (Mich., Wayne Co.) \tong´ kwish\. Also written <Tonguish>; perhaps the name of a Potawatomi (Algonquian) leader in the early nineteenth century (Vogel 1986).

TONSET (Mass., Barnstable Co.). From SNEng. Algonquian, perhaps meaning 'hill place' (Huden 1962).

TONSINA (Alaska, Valdez C-4) \ton sē´ nə\. Ahtna (Athabaskan) *kentsii na',* said to be derived from *kentsaadi* 'spruce-bark boat' and *na'* 'stream' (Kari 1990).

TONSOL Lake (Alaska, Tanacross A-4). From Upper Tanana (Athabaskan) *taaniitsoh männ',* lit. 'yellow-water lake' (J. Kari p.c.).

TONTETHAIMUND Lake (Alaska, Nabesna D-2). From Upper Tanana (Athabaskan) *tǫht'ayh männ',* lit. 'pulling-in-the-water lake' (J. Kari p.c.).

TONTO (Ariz., Gila Co.) \ton´ tō\. The Spanish word means 'foolish', but reference here is probably to the **Tonto Apaches,** a term formerly used to refer to the Western Apaches (Athabaskan). This probably represents a Spanish translation of Chiricahua Apache /bini:'édiné/ or Mescalero Apache /bini:'édinendé/ 'people without minds', terms that they used to designate the Western Apaches (*HNAI* 10:488).

TONTOGANY (Ohio, Wood Co.) \ton tō gā´ nē\. Said to be named for an Indian leader, language not identified (Miller 1996).

TONUCO (N.Mex., Doña Ana Co.) \tə nōō´ kō\. Perhaps an Indian placename, language not identified (Julyan 1998).

TONUK VO (Ariz., Pima Co.). O'odham (Piman) *to:nk wo'o,* lit. 'dike pond' (Granger 1983; J. Hill p.c.).

TONYTANK (Md., Wicomico Co.). Earlier written <Tundotenake, Tundotanck> (etc.); probably from CAC Algonquian, but the derivation in unclear (Kenny 1984).

TONZONA River (Alaska, Medfra A-2) \ton zō´ nə\. Upper Kuskokwim (Athabaskan) *tonilt-s'uno', tondzuno',* with *-no'* 'river' (Kari 1999: 96).

TOOELE County (Utah) \tə wil´ ə\. From Shoshoni (Numic) /tuuwɨɨta/ [tuuwɨɨra] 'black bear', containing /tuu-/ 'black' and /wɨɨta/ 'bear' (J. McLaughlin p.c.).

TOOGOODOO Creek (S.C., Charleston Co.) \to͞o´ gə do͞o\. Earlier written <Tobedo>, Tubedoo>, <Tukatu> (Waddell 1980); perhaps from an unidentified Indian language (Pickens 1963:38).

TOOIE Creek (Alaska, Iliamna D-1). The local name, perhaps from Dena'ina (Athabaskan), was reported in 1951 (Orth 1967).

TOOK TAY Hill (S.Dak., Charles Mix Co.). From Dakota (Siouan) *tukté* 'where' (D. Parks p.c.).

TOO KUSH Creek (Idaho, Idaho Co.). Possibly from Nez Perce (Sahaptian) /tú·k'es/ 'digging stick, cane' (Aoki 1994).

TOOLIK River (Alaska, Sagavanirktok D-5) \to͞o´ lik\. From Iñupiaq (Eskimo) *tuutlik* 'loon (bird)' (Orth 1967; Webster and Zibell 1970).

TOOMSET Lake (Utah, Summit Co.). Perhaps from from an unidentified Numic (Uto-Aztecan) language (Van Cott 1990).

TOOMSUBA (Miss., Lauderdale Co.) \to͞om´ so͝ob ə\. From Choctaw (Muskogean) *tǫsubi* 'fish-hawk' (Seale 1939; P. Munro p.c.).

TOO MUCH BEAR Lake (Ore., Lane Co.). Supposedly an American Indian Pidgin English phrase, warning of bears in the locality (McArthur 1992).

TOONIGH (Ga., Cherokee Co.). Perhaps from the same origin as **Toonowee Mountain** (Ga., Fannin Co.); see below.

TOONOWEE Mountain (Ga., Fannin Co.). May be from Cherokee (Iroquoian) <too-ni>, probably a personal name or title (Goff 1975).

TOOTOOSAHATCHEE Creek (Fla., Orange Co.). Perhaps from Muskogee *tottolose* /tot-tolô:si/ 'chicken' plus *hvcce* /háčči/ 'stream' (Read 1934; Martin and Mauldin 2000).

TOOWA Range (Calif., Tulare Co.) \to͞o´ wä\. Perhaps of Numic (Uto-Aztecan) origin, but the derivation is not clear (Gudde 1998).

TOPACHE Peak (Utah, Beaver Co.) \tə pä´ chē\. Perhaps from Numic (Uto-Aztecan), but of unclear derivation (Van Cott 1990).

TOPACOBA Hilltop (Ariz., Coconino Co.). A spelling variant of **Topocoba Hilltop**; see below.

TOPAGORUK River (Alaska, Teshekpuk D-5). The Iñupiaq (Eskimo) name, reported in 1965, is said to mean 'place for tent' (Orth 1967); cf. *tupiq* 'tent' (MacLean 1980).

TOPANEMUS, Lake (N.J., Monmouth Co.). Probably from Delaware (Algonquian), but of unclear derivation (Becker 1964).

TOPANGA Canyon (Calif., Los Angeles Co.) \tō pang´ gə, tə pang´ gə\. From the Gabrielino (Takic) placename *topa'nga,* with the locative ending *-nga* (Gudde 1998; McLendon & Johnson 1999).

TOPASHAW Creek (Miss., Chickasaw Co.) \top´ ə shô\. Perhaps from Choctaw (Muskogean) *otapi* 'chestnut tree' plus *-osi* 'little' (Seale 1939; P. Munro p.c.); or perhaps from the same origin as **Topisaw;** see below.

TOPATOPA Mountains (Calif., Ventura Co.) \tō pə tō´ pə\. Possibly from Barbareño (Chumashan) /tɨptɨp/ 'brushy place', reduplication of /tɨp/ 'brush, wild vegetation' (Gudde 1998).

TOPAWA (Ariz., Pima Co.) \tō pä´ wə, tə pä´ wə\. Perhaps from O'odham (Piman) *oḍ bawe* 'it is a tepary bean' (Granger 1983; J. Hill p.c.).

TOPEKA (Kans., Shawnee Co.) \tō pē´ kə, tə pē´ kə\. From a Kansa (Siouan) name meaning 'a good place to dig potatoes', referring to the 'Indian potato', the root or tuber of an edible native plant (Rydjord 1968). The Native American term consists of /dó/ 'wild potato', /ppi/ 'good', and /kʔe/ 'to dig' (R. Rankin p.c.). The name occurs in other states (e.g., Alaska, Mt. Fairweather D-4; Ill., Mason Co.; and Ind., Langrange Co.).

TOPINABEE (Mich., Cheboygan Co.) \top´ i nə bē\. Named for a Potawatomi (Algonquian) leader of the early nineteenth century; his name was also written <Topenebee, Thupenebu> (etc.) (Vogel 1986).

TOPISAW (Miss., Pike Co.). Perhaps from Choctaw (Muskogean) *ittaapisa* 'where (they) saw each other', containing *itti-* 'each other', *aa-* 'place', and *pisa* 'to see' (Toomey 1917; P. Munro p.c.); or perhaps from the same origin as **Topashaw Creek;** see above.

TOPKOK (Alaska, Solomon C-4). The Iñupiaq (Eskimo) name is *tapqaaq* (L. Kaplan p.c.).

TOPOCK (Calif., San Bernardino Co.) \tō´ pok\. From Mojave (Yuman) *tuupák,* derived from the verb *tapák-* 'to drive piles' (Gudde 1998). The name also occurs in Ariz. (Mohave Co.).

TOPOCOBA Hilltop (Ariz., Coconino Co.). From the Havasupai (Yuman) placename <Tovokyóva> (Granger 1983; L. Hinton p.c.).

TOPONAS (Colo., Routt Co.) \tə pō´ nəs\. From a Ute (Numic) word, of uncertain derivation (Bright 1993).

TOPONIS (Idaho, Gooding Co.) \tə pon´ is\. From a Shoshoni (Numic) word of unclear derivation (Boone 1988).

TOPOPAH Spring (Nev., Nye Co.) \tō´ pə pä\. Probably a variant of **Tupapa Seep**; see below.

TOPPENISH (Wash., Yakima Co.) \top´ ə nish\. Sahaptin /txápniš/, referring to a landslide, from /txá-/ 'accidentally', /-pni-/ 'to launch, to take forth and out', and /-ša/ 'continuative present tense' (D. Kinkade p.c.).

TOPSY (Ore., Klamath Co.). Said to be named for a Shasta man, otherwise called <Thipsi>, a word of no known etymology (McArthur 1992).

TOQUAMSKE (Conn., Middlesex Co.). From SNEng. Algonquian, perhaps an abbreviation of a word meaning 'round rock' (Tooker 1911).

TOQUA Township (Minn., Big Stone Co.) \tō´ kwə\. Earlier written <Taqua, Ta Kara>; said to be from Dakota (Siouan) *ta* 'moose' plus <Kahra>, a Dakota band (Upham 2001).

TOQUERVILLE (Utah, Washington Co.) \tō´ kər vil\. From Southern Paiute (Numic) /tookkatɨ/ [tóokkarɨ̥] 'black sitting (place)', referring to the lava flows; the form contains /too-/ 'black' and /katɨ/ 'sit' (J. McLaughlin p.c.).

TOQUIMA Range (Nev., Nye Co.) \tō kē´ mə\. The name refers to a Monache (Numic) subgroup; the name is said to mean 'black backs' (Carlson 1974).

TORCH River (Mich., Kalkaska Co.). The name refers to the use of torches by Indians for fishing at night (Vogel 1986); some places named with this term may be translations of Indian words such as Ojibwa (Algonquian) *waaswaagan* (Nichols and Nyholm 1995). The placename **Torch Lake** also occurs in Wis. (Vilas Co.). A related name is **Flambeau River** (Wis., Iron Co.).

TORDRILLO Mountains (Alaska, Tyonek B-7). The word appears Spanish but cannot be identified in a Spanish dictionary. It may be an adaptation of a Dena'ina (Athabaskan) placename including the word *dghelay* 'mountain' (Kari and Fall 1987:123).

TOREVA (Ariz., Navajo Co.) \tō rē´ və, tə rē´ və\. Hopi (Uto-Aztecan) *toriva* 'twisted spring', from *tori* 'twist' and *-va, paa-hu* 'water, spring' (K. Hill p.c.).

TORODA (Wash., Ferry Co.). This may represent an Indian placename <To-ro-tee>, language not identified (Hitchman 1985).

TORONTO \tə ron´ tō\. The name of the Canadian city is from an Iroquoian language, but the derivation is unclear. As a placename in the United States it occurs in many states (e.g., Fla., Orange Co.; Iowa, Clinton Co.; and Ill., Sangamon Co.).

TOROWEAP Valley (Ariz., Mohave Co.) \tō rə wēp\. Probably from Southern Paiute (Numic) /tutu-uippi/ [turú-uippI] 'whirling canyon', from /tutu/ 'to whirl' plus /uippi/ 'canyon' (J. McLaughlin p.c.).

TORSAR Islands (Alaska, Port Alexander D-5). The Tlingit name was reported in 1809 (Orth 1967).

TOSI Creek (Wyo., Sublette Co.) \tō´ zē\. Named for a Shoshoni (Numic) man (Urbanek 1974).

TOTACON (Ariz., Apache Co.) From Navajo (Athabaskan), meaning 'sweet water' (Granger 1983); cf. *tó* 'water', *łikan* 'be sweet' (Young and Morgan 1987).

TOTAGATIC Lake (Wis., Bayfield Co.) \tō täg´ ə tik\. Probably from Ojibwa (Algonquian), but the derivation is not clear (BGN 7204).

TOTARO (Va., Brunswick Co.). From a CAC Algonquian placename; the derivation is not clear (Hagemann 1988).

TOTASKWINU Ruin (N.Mex., Sandoval Co.). From a Jemez (Tanoan) placename /tootakwinun/, perhaps containing /-kwi/ 'to be standing' and /-nun/ 'place' (Y. Yumitani p.c.).

TOTATLANIKA River (Alaska, Fairbanks C-4) \tō tat əl nē´ kə\. From Lower Tanana (Athabaskan) *tutadlnik'a*; cf. *nik'a* 'secondary stream' (Kari 1999:134).

TOTAVI (N.Mex., Santa Fe Co.). Perhaps from a Tewa (Tanoan) word meaning 'quail' (Julyan 1998).

TOTCHAKET Slough (Alaska, Fairbanks D-5) \tō chak´ ət\. From Lower Tanana (Athabaskan) *tochaget,* lit. 'water mouth' (Kari 1999:132).

TOTEK Hills (Alaska, Fairbanks B-6). From a Lower Tanana (Athabaskan) placename (Orth 1967).

TOTEM (Alaska, Petersburg B-5) \tō´ təm\. The name refers to the totem poles constructed by Indians of the Northwest Pacific coast to display symbols of families and clans. The word *totem* is from Ojibwa (Algonquian) *-doodem* 'totem' (*in-doodem* 'my totem or clan') (Nichols and Nyholm 1995).

TOTI Islands (Alaska, Craig B-4). The Tlingit name, applied in 1779, is said to mean 'robber' (Orth 1967).

TOT Mountain (Ore., Deschutes Co.) \tot\. From Chinook Jargon <tot>, probably [tat, tɔt] 'uncle', probably based on Lower Chehalis (Salishan) /táʔt'/ 'uncle' (McArthur 1992; D. Kinkade p.c.).

TOTO (Ind., Starke Co.) \tō´ tō\. Perhaps from an Algonquian word for 'bullfrog' (Baker 1995); cf. Meskwaki /to:to:wa/ 'bullfrog' (Goddard 1994).

TOTOILON Mountains (Alaska, Lime Hills D-1). The Dena'ina (Athabaskan) name is of unclear derivation (Orth 1967).

TOTOKET (Conn., New Haven Co.). From SNEng. Algonquian <k'tetuckete> 'on the great tidal stream', from <k'te> 'great', <-tuck-> 'tidal stream', and <-et> 'place' (Huden 1962).

TOTONTEAC Mountain (Ariz., Maricopa Co.) \tō ton´ tē äk\. A name assigned by Spanish explorers to the area of Ariz. (Granger 1983); perhaps from Nahuatl (Aztecan) *totonqui* 'hot'.

TOTOPITK (Ariz., Maricopa Co.). Perhaps from O'odham (Piman) <top't> 'crooked, lopsided' (Granger 1983).

TOTOPOTOMOI Creek (Va., Hanover Co.). Named for a seventeenth-century CAC Algonquian leader (Hagemann 1988). Also written **Totopotomoy.**

TOTOWA (N.J., Passaic Co.). Also written <Totohaw, Totoa>; perhaps from Delaware (Algonquian) <tetauwi> 'it is between' (Becker 1964).

TOTSCHUNDA Creek (Alaska, Nabesna B-4) \tə cho͞on´ də\. Perhaps from an Upper Tanana (Athabaskan) name meaning 'red stone' (Orth 1967).

TOTSON Mountains (Alaska, Nulato B-3). The Koyukon (Athabaskan) name was reported in 1927 (Orth 1967).

TOTUCK Lake (Alaska, Anchorage C-7). Perhaps from Koyukon (Athabaskan), made official in BGN 8002.

TOUCHET (Wash., Walla Walla Co.) \to͞o´ shē\. From the Sahaptin placename /tú:šа, táwaša/, perhaps meaning 'broiling' (Phillips 1971; D. Kinkade p.c.).

TOUGALOO (Miss., Hinds Co.) \tug´ ə lo͞o\. Probably shortened from Choctaw (Muskogean) *book-atokla* 'second stream', containing *book* 'stream' and *atokla* 'second' (Seale 1939; P. Munro p.c.).

TOUGHKENAMON (Pa., Chester Co.) \tuf ken´ ə mən\. Probably from Delaware (Algonquian), but of unclear derivation (Donehoo 1928).

TOUGLAALEK Bay (Alaska, Seldovia A-4). The Alutiiq (Eskimo) name was made official in BGN 1990.

TOUISSET Highlands (Mass., Bristol Co.). Perhaps from SNEng. Algonquian <touishin> 'it is deserted land' (W. Cowan p.c.). The name also occurs in R.I. (Bristol Co.). A probably related placename is **Toweset Point** (R.I., Bristol Co.).

TOULOU Creek (Wash., Stevens Co.). This is the surname of a local Salishan Indian family (Hitchman 1985).

TOUTLE (Wash., Cowlitz Co.) \to͞o´ təl\. Said to be from the name of an Indian subgroup, language not identified, who were called <Hullooetell> by Lewis and Clark (Phillips 1971). Although **Toutle** is in Cowlitz (Salishan) territory, the name is not from the Cowlitz language.

TOVAKWA Ruin (N.Mex., Sandoval Co.). From the Jemez (Tanoan) placename *túuva-kwa* (Y. Yumitani p.c.).

TOWACO (N.J., Morris Co.). Perhaps from Delaware (Algonquian) <towako>, referring to a legendary figure called 'Father Snake' (Becker 1964).

TOWAGO Point (Ariz., Coconino Co.). This is the surname of a Havasupai (Yuman) family, perhaps from <tahwága> 'to have two wives' (Granger 1983; L. Hinton p.c.).

TOWAHMINA Lake (Alaska, Medfra B-2). Perhaps from Upper Kuskokwim (Athabaskan) *tomo mina'*, lit. 'swan lake' (Kari 1999:99).

TOWAK Creek (Alaska, Hooper Bay D-3). The Yupik (Eskimo) name was reported in 1952 (Orth 1967).

TOWALAGA (Ga., Spalding Co.). From the same source as **Towaliga River**; see below.

TOWALIGA River (Ga., Monroe Co.) \tī wi lag´ ē, tī wi lī´ gē\. Perhaps Muskogee, meaning 'sumac place', from *tvwv* /tawá/ 'sumac' and *like* /leyki/ 'place' (Read 1949–50; Martin and Mauldin 2000).

TOWAMENCIN Township (Pa., Montgomery Co.). From the same source as **Towamensing Township**; see below.

TOWAMENSING Township (Pa., Carbon Co.). Perhaps from Delaware (Algonquian) <Towsissinck> 'at the ford' (Donehoo 1928); cf. <towin> 'to wade, to ford' (Brinton and Anthony 1888).

TOWANDA (Pa., Bradford Co.) \tə wän´ də\. Perhaps from Delaware (Algonquian) <tawunde-unk> 'where we bury the dead' (Donehoo 1928), cf. <tauwunnasin> 'to be buried' (Brinton and Anthony 1888). The name has been transferred to several other states (e.g., Ill., McLean Co.; N.Mex., Union Co.; and Wis., Vilas Co.).

TOWANTA Flat (Utah, Duchesne Co.). Perhaps an adaptation of **Towanda**; see above.

TOWANTIC Brook (Conn., New Haven Co.). From SNEng. Algonquian, perhaps meaning 'wading place, ford' (Huden 1962). A possibly related name is **Towamensing Township**; see above.

TOWAOC (Colo., Montezuma Co.) \tō´ wä ok, toi´ ok\. From Southern Ute (Numic) /tɨwáyak/ 'all right', also used to mean 'thank you'; cf. /tɨ̈ɨ́'ay/ 'it's good' (Bright 1993).

TOWD Point (N.Y., Suffolk Co.). Perhaps from SNEng. Algonquian, but the derivation is not clear (Tooker 1911).

TOWESET Point (R.I., Bristol Co.). Perhaps from SNEng. Algonquian <touishin> 'it is deserted land' (W. Cowan p.c.). A probably related placename is **Touisset Highlands** (Mass., Bristol Co.).

TOWESIC, TOWESICK, or **TOWESSEK Neck** (Maine, Sagadahoc Co.). Probably from Abenaki (Algonquian), perhaps meaning 'broken passage' (Huden 1962).

TOWN Creek (Md., Allegany Co.). Abbreviated from **Oldtown Creek,** referring to a former Indian settlement (Kenny 1984).

TOXAWAY River (N.C., Transylvania Co.). Perhaps from Cherokee (Iroquoian) *daksi* 'terrapin' plus English *way* (Feeling 1975; B. Rudes p.c.). The placename also occurs in S.C. (Anderson Co.).

TOYATTE Glacier (Alaska, Mt. Fairweather D-4). Said to be named after a leader of the Stickeen division of the Tlingit Indians (Orth 1967).

TOYEI (Ariz., Apache Co.) \toi ā´\. An alternative form of **Tuye Spring,** from Navajo (Athabaskan) *tó-yéé,* lit. 'water-scarce' (Linford 2000).

TOYON (Calif., Calaveras Co.) \toi´ on\. The word refers to the California holly bush, from Costanoan [totčon] (Gudde 1998).

TOYONAK (Alaska, Kenai D-5). The Dena'ina (Athabaskan) name is a variant of **Tyonek** (see below).

TOZI, Mount (Alaska, Tanana C-2) \tō´ zē\. Perhaps an abbreviation of **Tozitna River** (Tanana A-5), from the Koyukon (Athabaskan) *tozeetno'* 'current-near-bark stream' (Jetté & Jones 2000). A related name is **Tozikakat** (Alaska, Tanana A-5) \tō zē kak´ ət\, from <tozi> plus *cha:get* 'stream mouth' (Kari 1999:34). Also related is **Tozimoran** (Alaska, Tanana B-5), an English combination of *Tozi* plus the placename *Moran Dome*. All these are linked to **Tozitna River** (Alaska, Tanana A-5) \tō zit´ nə\, from <tozi> plus Tanana (Athabaskan) *-no:'* 'river'.

TRADE River (Wis., Polk Co.). Corresponds to Ojibwa (Algonquian) <Attanwa Sibi> (Vogel 1991); cf. *adeaawe* 'to buy' (Nichols and Nyholm 1995). Related placenames include **Ottawa** (Kans., Franklin Co.).

TRAIL Creek (Ind., La Porte Co.). A translation of Potawatomi (Algonquian) /myewes zibiwe/ 'trail creek' (McCafferty 2002).

TRAIL THE MEXICANS CAME DOWN Canyon (Ariz., Apache Co.). From Navajo (Athabaskan) *naakaii adáánání* 'trail the Mexicans came down', containing *naakaii* 'Spaniard, Mexican' (Linford 2000).

TRAIL WHERE THE ENEMY WALKED UP SINGING (Ariz., Apache Co.). Navajo *anaa' sin yił haayáhí* 'where the enemy [a Hopi woman] walked up singing', containing *anaa'* 'enemy' (Granger 1983; Linford 2000).

TRALEIKA Glacier (Alaska, Mt. McKinley A-2) \trə lā´ kə\. Said to be from a Dena'ina (Athabaskan) name for Mt. McKinley, meaning 'the high one' (Orth 1967).

TRANQUILLON Mountain (Calif., Santa Barbara Co.) \trang kwil´ yən\. Perhaps from Barbareño (Chumashan), but the derivation is not clear (Gudde 1998).

TRANSQUAKING River (Md., Dorchester Co.). Earlier written <Tramasquecook, Tresquaquin> (etc.); a folk-etymology from CAC Algonquian, of unclear derivation (Kenny 1984).

TRAVERSE City (Mich., Grand Traverse Co.). From French *travers* 'a crossing, a shortcut'; in some placenames, the word may be a translation of Ojibwa (Algonquian) *niminâgan* (Baraga 1880). In Minn., **Traverse Co.** corresponds to

Dakota (Siouan) Santee *mde-hdákiya*, lit. 'lake-crosswise' (A. Taylor p.c.).

TRELIPE Township (Minn., Cass Co.) \trel´ i pē\. The name is an adaptation of English *tullibee,* earlier *tellibee,* from French *toulibi* 'a type of whitefish', from early Ojibwa (Algonquian) */oto:lipi:/ (*RHD* 1987); cf. present-day Ojibwa *odoonibii* (Nichols and Nyholm 1995).

TREMPEALEAU County (Wis.) From French *montagne qui trempe à l'eau* 'mountain that soaks in the water', said to be a translation of an Ojibwa (Algonquian) name (Vogel 1991).

TRIMOKISH Hills (Alaska, McGrath A-3). From Upper Kuskokwim (Athabaskan) *tr'emo k'esh, ts'emo kesh* 'grieving birch' (Kari 1999:92).

TROGSHAK (Alaska, Kwiguk C-5). The Yupik (Eskimo) name was reported in 1899 (Orth 1967).

TROUT Lake (Minn., Itasca Co.). A translation of Ojibwa (Algonquian) <namêgoss> (Baraga 1880; Upham 2001); cf. *namegos* 'lake trout' (J. Nichols p.c.).

TRUCKEE River (Calif., Nevada Co.; Nev., Washoe Co.) \truk´ ē\. Named for a Northern Paiute (Numic) leader; the term supposedly means 'all right' (Gudde 1998).

TRUULI Peak (Alaska, Seldovia D-2) \tro͞o´ lē\. From Dena'ina (Athabaskan) *dghili,* not a placename but simply the word for 'mountain' (Kari and Kari 1982).

TSADAKA Canyon (Alaska, Anchorage C-6) \tsə dak´ ə\. Dena'ina (Athabaskan) *tsideq'atnu* 'grandmother's-place stream' (J. Kari p.c.).

TSAH TAH Trading Post (N.Mex., San Juan Co.). Navajo (Athabaskan) *ts'ahtah* 'among the sagebrush', from *ts'ah* 'sagebrush, Artemesia' plus *-tah* 'among' (A. Wilson p.c.).

TSAILE (Ariz., Apache Co.) \sā lē´\. Navajo *tsééhílį́* 'it flows into a canyon', from *tsééh* 'into rock, into a canyon' plus *(y)ílį́* 'it flows' (Granger 1983; Wilson 1995). Related terms include **Tsai Skizzi Rock** (Ariz., Coconino Co.); see below.

TSAI SKIZZI Rock (Ariz., Coconino Co.) \sā skē´ zē\. Navajo (Athabaskan) *tsé k'izí* 'rock cleft', containing *tsé* 'rock' (Linford 2000). Related terms include **Tsaile** (Ariz., Apache Co.), **Tsaya** (N.Mex., San Juan Co.), and **Tseanazti** (N.Mex., San Juan Co.).

TSALA APOPKA Lake (Fla., Citrus Co.). Muskogee *calo apapkv* 'where trout are eaten', from *calo* /čá:lo/ 'trout', *apapkv* /a:pá:pka/ 'eating there'; cf. *pvpeta* /papitá/ 'to eat (something)' (Read 1934; Martin and Mauldin 2000). A related form is **Charley Apopka Creek** (Fla., Hardee Co.).

TSA LA GI Indian Village (Okla., Cherokee Co.). From Cherokee (Iroquoian) *jalagi* 'Cherokee' (Feeling 1975). For related placenames, see **Cherokee** above.

TSAMA Archaeological District (N.Mex., Rio Arriba Co.). A variant of **Chama** from Tewa (Tanoan) *tsąmą* 'to wrestle' (Harrington 1916).

TSANKAWI Ruins (N.Mex., Santa Fe Co.) \tsäng´ kə wē\. Tewa (Tanoan) [sæ̨k'wewi] 'gap of the sharp round-cactus', from [sæ̨] 'round cactus', [k'e] 'sharp', and [wi'i] 'gap' (Julyan 1998; Harrington 1916).

TSAYA (N.Mex., San Juan Co.). Navajo (Athabaskan) *tséyaa* 'beneath the rock', from *tsé* 'rock' plus *yaa* 'beneath' (Julyan 1998; Wilson 1995). Related placenames include **Tsayatoh** (N.Mex., McKinley Co.), **Tseanazti Creek** (N.Mex., San Juan Co.), and names listed below beginning with **Tse.**

TSAYAGTULEK Creek (Alaska, Goodnews Bay D-4). The Yupik (Eskimo) name was reported in 1954 (Orth 1967).

TSAYATOH (N.Mex., McKinley Co.). From Navajo (Athabaskan) *tséyaa tó* 'rock-beneath spring' (Julyan 1998; Linford 2000). Related placenames include **Tsaya** (N.Mex., San Juan Co.) and **Tseyah** (Ariz., Apache Co.) Another related name is **Tsay-Yah-Kin** (Ariz., Navajo Co.) \tsā´ yä kin\, from *tséyaa kin* 'house under the rock', with *kin* 'house, building' (Granger 1983; Linford 2000).

TSBANTOTLODEN Lake (Alaska, Kateel River A-1). The Koyukon (Athabaskan) name is of unclear derivation (Orth 1967).

TSEANAZTI Creek (N.Mex., San Juan Co.). A variant of **Sanostee,** Navajo (Athabaskan) *tsé ałnáozt'i'í* 'where rocks overlap', containing *tsé* 'rock' and *ałnáozt'i'* 'they overlap' (Wilson 1995). Many Navajo placenames, as listed below, begin with the same element *tsé* 'rock'.

TSE BINAAYOLI (N.Mex., McKinley Co.). From Navajo (Athabaskan) *tsé binááyołí* 'rock [that] wind blows around' (Linford 2000).

TSE BITA'I (N.Mex., San Juan Co.). From Navajo (Athabaskan) *tsé bit'a'í* 'winged rock' (Linford 2000); cf. *bit'a'* 'its wings' (Young and Morgan 1987:729).

TSE BIYI (Ariz., Navajo Co.) \sā bi yä \. From Navajo (Athabaskan) *tsé biyi* 'rock canyon' (Linford 2000). A nearby placename is **Tse Biyi Yazzi**, from *tsé biyi yázhí* 'little rock-canyon' (Linford 2000).

TSE BONITA Wash (Ariz., Apache Co.; N.Mex., McKinley Co.). A variant writing of **Tse Bonito Wash;** see below.

TSE BONITO Wash (Ariz., Apache Co.; N.Mex., McKinley Co.) \sā bə nē´ tə\. Navajo (Athabaskan) *tsé binii' tó* 'rock-face water, water on the face of the rock', containing *tsé* 'rock', *binii'* 'its face' (*bi-* 'its', *-nii'* 'face'), and *tó* 'water'. The placename has been folk-etymologized to suggest Spanish *bonito* 'pretty' (Wilson 1995). A written variant is **Tse Bonita Wash.**

TSE CHIZZI Wash (Ariz., Navajo Co.) \sā chē´ zē\. From Navajo (Athabaskan) *tsé ch'ízhí* 'rough rock' (Linford 2000).

TSE-CLANI-TO Wash (N.Mex., San Juan Co.). From Navajo (Athabaskan) *tsé łání* 'much water' plus *tó* 'water' (Young and Morgan 1987).

TSEDAATAH Canyon (N.Mex., Apache Co.). Navajo (Athabaskan) *tsédáá'tah* 'among the rock edges', with *dáá'* 'rim, edge' and *tah* 'among' (Wilson 1995). A related name is **Tseda Hwidezohi Peak** (Ariz., Apache Co.) from Navajo (Athabaskan) *tsédáá' hwiidzohí* 'the place where marks or lines are carved into the edge of the rock', containing *dáá'* 'edge, rim', *hwii, ho* 'space, area', and *dzoh* 'draw a line or mark' (Wilson 1995).

TSEDOLALINDIN Lake (Alaska, Kateel River C-2). The Koyukon (Athabaskan) name was reported in 1955 (Orth 1967).

TSEGAHODZANI Canyon (Ariz., Apache Co.). Navajo (Athabaskan) *tséghá hoodzání* 'rock with a hole in it', containing *tsé* 'rock', *ghá* 'through', and *hoodzą́* 'be a perforated area or space' (Wilson 1995).

TSEGI Canyon (Ariz., Navajo Co.) \tə sā´ gē\. Navajo (Athabaskan) *tséyi'* 'canyon', lit. 'inside the rocks', with *-yi'* 'inside' (Granger 1983; Young and Morgan 1987:259). The related name **Tsegihatsoso** (Ariz., Apache Co.) means 'tight canyon'; cf. *hatsoh* 'be tight' (Granger 1983; Young and Morgan 1987:422).

TSEGITO Spring (Ariz., Apache Co.). Navajo (Athabaskan) *tsiyi' tóhí* 'spring in the forest' (Granger 1983; Linford 2000); cf. *tsiyi'* 'forest' (Young and Morgan 1987). A variant is **Segetoa Spring.**

TSEHSO (N.Mex., San Juan Co.). Navajo (Athabaskan) *tsétsoh* 'big rock', from *tsé* 'rock' plus *tsoh* 'big' (Wilson 1995).

TSEH-YA-KIN Canyon (Ariz., Apache Co.). From Navajo (Athabaskan) *tséyaa kin* 'house under the rock' (Linford 2000).

TSE'II'AHI (N.Mex., McKinley Co.). Navajo (Athabaskan) *tsé íi'áhí* 'rock spire', containing *tsé* 'rock' and *íí'á* 'it stands up, sticks up' (Wilson 1995).

TSE LIGAI (Ariz., Apache Co.). Navajo (Athabaskan) *tsé łigai* 'white rock' (BGN 8302; Young and Morgan 1987). A related name is **Tseligaideeza Canyon** (Ariz., Apache Co.), meaning 'white rock extends'; cf. *tsé* 'rock', *łigai* 'white', *deez'á* 'it extends' (Young and Morgan 1987).

TSE-NAS-CHII Wash (N.Mex., San Juan Co.). Navajo (Athabaskan) *tsé náshchii'*, with *náshchii'* 'red in a circle, red ring' (Young and Morgan 1987:731).

TSE-NI-CHA Pillar (N.Mex., San Juan Co.). Navajo (Athabaskan) *tsé nitsaa* 'big rock' (Young and Morgan 1987).

TSE TAA Ruins (Ariz., Apache Co.). Navajo (Athabaskan) *tsé táá'á* 'rock extending into water' (Linford 2000).

TSE-YAA-TOHI Wash (N.Mex., San Juan Co.). Navajo (Athabaskan) *tséyaatóhí* 'where there is water beneath the rocks', containing *yaa* 'beneath' and *tó* 'water' (A. Wilson p.c.).

TSEYAH (Ariz., Apache Co.). Probably from Navajo (Athabaskan) *tséyaa* 'beneath the rocks' (Young and Morgan 1987). A related name is **Tsay-Yah-Kin** (Ariz., Navajo Co.); see **Tsayatoh** above.

TSE YA TOE Spring (Ariz., Navajo Co.). Probably Navajo (Athabaskan) *tséyaa tó* 'water under rock', with *yaa* 'under' and *tó* 'water' (Young and Morgan 1987).

TSHACHALING-ATACHTOLI Lake (Alaska, Goodnews Bay D-3). The Yupik (Eskimo) name was reported in 1898 (Orth 1967).

TSILCHIN Lake (Alaska, Tanacross A-3) \tsil chin\. From Upper Tanana (Athabaskan) *tsiił chinn' männ'*, lit. 'bridge meadow lake' (J. Kari p.c.).

TSILTCOOS, Camp (Ore., Lane Co.) \chilt´ ko͞os\. From the Lower Umpqua (Siuslaw) place-name [tš^hîltłk^hus], of no known etymology (D. Kinkade p.c.). A variant is the nearby **Siltcoos.**

TSIMPSHIAN Point (Alaska, Icy Bay D-2). A variant spelling of **Tsimshian,** an Indian group of British Columbia. The term is derived from /c'msyan/, lit. 'inside the Skeena River', the designation the Coast Tsimshian and Southern Tsimshian people use for themselves (BGN 8001; *HNAI* 7:282).

TSINA River (Alaska, Valdez B-4) \tsē´ nə\. From Ahtna (Athabaskan) *łts'aay na'*; cf. *na'* 'stream' (Kari 1990).

TSINAT Mesa (NM, Santa Fe Co.). Probably from Keresan /tsínãuta/, a form of the verb meaning 'to finish, to come to the end', applied to a mounain summit or the edge of a cliff (I. Davis p.c.).

TSINGIGKALIK Lake (Alaska, Goodnews Bay C-8). The Yupik (Eskimo) name was published in 1951 (Orth 1967).

TSIN KLETZIN (N.Mex., San Juan Co.) \tsin klet´sin\. Navajo (Athabaskan) *tsinłizhin* 'charcoal', from *tsin* 'wood, tree' plus *łizhin* 'black' (A. Wilson p.c.).

TSIN LANI Creek (Ariz., Apache Co.). From Navajo (Athabaskan) *tsin łání* 'many trees' (Linford 2000).

TSIN-NAS-KID Summit (N.Mex., San Juan Co.). Navajo (Athabaskan) *tsin násk'id* 'trees ringed about with hills', from *tsin* 'tree(s)', *ná(s)* 'encircling, around', and *-k'id* 'hill, hump, mound' (A. Wilson p.c.).

TSIN SIKAAD (Ariz., Apache Co.). From Navajo (Athabaskan) *tsin sikaad* 'clumps of trees', from *tsin* 'wood, tree' plus *sikaad* 'they sit in clumps' (Granger 1983; Wilson 1995).

TSIPING (N.Mex., Rio Arriba Co.). Tewa (Tanoan) [tsip'i̜ŋy] 'Pedernal Mountain', from [tsi'i] 'flaking stone, obsidian' and [p'i̜ŋy] 'mountain' (Julyan 1998; Harringon 1916).

TSIRKU River (Alaska, Skagway B-3) \sûr´ ko͞o\. The Tlingit name was reported in 1883 (Orth 1967).

TSISI Creek (Alaska, Talkeetna Mtns. C-2) \tsē´ sē\. The Ahtna (Athabaskan) name is of unclear derivation (Orth 1967).

TSISNAATEEL (N.Mex., San Juan Co.). Navajo (Athabaskan) *tsis naateel* 'wide hill extending downward', from *sis, tsis* 'hill, mountain' plus *naateel* 'it is wide downward' (Linford 2000; Young and Morgan 1987:688, 738).

TSITAH Wash (Ariz., Apache Co.). Navajo (Athabaskan) *tsiitah* 'among the hair', from *tsii'* 'hair' and *tah* 'among' (Linford 2000; Young and Morgan 1987).

TSIU River (Alaska, Bering Glacier A-6). The Eyak name is *ts'iyuh*.

TSIVAT River (Alaska, Bering Glacier A-6). The Tlingit name was reported in 1852 (Orth 1967).

TS'IYA'A:WA (N.Mex., Sandoval Co.). Perhaps contains Zuni /ts'iya/ 'to cut, to tear' (Ferguson and Hart 1985; Newman 1958).

TSIYEEHVUN Lake (Alaska, Fort Yukon C-1). The Gwich'in (Athabaskan) name was obtained in 1956 (Orth 1967); cf. *van* 'lake' (Peter 1979).

TSKAWAHYAH Island (Wash., Clallam Co.). From the Makah (Nootkan) placename /čaka:wakt/ (W. Jacobsen p.c.).

TSO-DZIL Ranch (N.Mex., McKinley Co.) \tso͞o´ tsil\. Navajo (Athabaskan) *tsoodził* 'tongue mountain', from *(a)tsoo'* 'tongue' plus *dził* 'mountain' (Wilson 1995).

TSOKTUI Hill (Alaska, Black River C-6). The Gwich'in (Athabaskan) name is *tsuk-tą̨ih* 'marten hill' (J. Kari p.c.).

TSOLMUND Lake (Alaska, Nabesna D-2). The Upper Tanana (Athabaskan) name is *tsa'ol männ* 'beaver dam lake' (J. Kari p.c.).

TSOSIE Well (Ariz., Navajo Co.) \sō´ sē\. From Navajo (Athabaskan) *ts'ozí* 'long-haired' (Young and Morgan 1987); frequently used as a family name.

TSUKON (Alaska, Fort Yukon D-4). The Gwich'in (Athabaskan) name is *tsuk kon* (J. Kari p.c.).

TSUN-JE-ZHIN (N.Mex., San Juan Co.). Navajo (Athabaskan) *tsin ch'ézhin* 'trees extending out black', from *tsin* 'tree', *ch'é-, ch'í-* 'extending out horizontally', and *(łi-)zhin* 'black' (A. Wilson p.c.).

TSUROTLUMA Slough (Alaska, Nulato B-5). The Koyukon (Athabaskan) name was reported in 1935 (Orth 1967).

TSUSENA Creek (Alaska, Talkeetna Mtns. D-4) \tso͞o sā´ nə\. Ahtna (Athabaskan) *nts'ezi na'*, with *na'* 'creek' (Kari and Fall 1987:189).

TSYOOKTUIHVUN Lake (Alaska, Christian B-5). The Gwich'in (Athabaskan) name was obtained in 1956 (Orth 1967); cf. *van* 'lake' (Peter 1979).

TUALATIN (Ore., Washington Co.) \to͞o ä´ lə tin, twä´ lə tən\. From the name of a Northern Kalapuyan subgroup, called [at^hfálat'i], of no known etymology (H. Zenk p.c.). From the same origin is the name of **Tuality Plains** (Ore., Washington Co.).

TUAPAKTUSHAK Creek (Alaska, Meade River D-3). The Iñupiaq (Eskimo) name was reported in 1950 (Orth 1967).

TUBAC (Ariz., Santa Cruz Co.) \to͞o bak´, to͞o´ bäk\. A Spanish spelling corresponding to O'odham (Piman) *cewagĭ* [čɨwakI] 'cloud' (J. Hill p.c.). The name was recorded as <Tubac> in the eighteenth century; subsequently, O'odham [t] was replaced by [č] before high vowels; cf. **Tucson** below.

TUBA City (Ariz., Coconino Co.) \to͞o´ bə\. From Hopi *tuuvi*, the nickname of Qötswayma, the founder of Tuba City. It is possibly a shortened form of an alternative personal name, *tuuvi'yma* 'go to throw out', containing *tuuv-, tuuva* 'throw' (K. Hill p.c.).

TUBBALUBBA Creek (Miss., Monroe Co.) \tub ə lub´ ē\. Also written <Tubbalubby>; from Choctaw (Muskogean) *tobi aa-lobbi* 'where beans are rooted up', from *tobi* 'beans', *aa-* 'where', and *lobbi* 'root up' (Seale 1939; P. Munro p.c.).

TUBBY Creek (Miss., Benton Co.). Probably a shortened form for a Choctaw (Muskogean) "war name" ending in *abi* 'to kill' (P. Munro p.c.); see **Moshulitubbees Prairie** (Miss., Noxubee Co.) above.

TUBUNGALUK Creek (Alaska, Bethel D-7). The Yupik (Eskimo) name was reported in 1951 (Orth 1967).

TUBUTULIK River (Alaska, Norton Bay C-6). The Iñupiaq (Eskimo) name was reported in 1844 (Orth 1967).

TUCALOTA Creek (Calif., Riverside Co.) \too̅ kə lō´ tə\. Perhaps from Mexican Spanish *tecolote* 'buzzard', reflecting Nahuatl (Aztecan) *tecolotl* (Gudde 1998).

TUCANNON (Wash., Columbia Co.) \too̅ kan´ ən\. Nez Perce (Sahaptian) /tuké:nen/ (placename) 'digging'; cf. /tukumné:/ 'to go dig camas', an edible root or bulb (Hitchman 1985; Aoki 1994).

TUCHO (Calif., Monterey Co.). Perhaps from the Rumsen (Costanoan) name of a certain plant; but the derivation is not clear (Gudde 1998).

TUCK, Mount (Maine, Waldo Co.). Perhaps from Abenaki (Algonquian), meaning 'a tree' (Huden 1962).

TUCKABATCHEE Church (Okla., Hughes Co.). Perhaps from **Tuckabatchie**; see below.

TUCKABATCHIE (Ala., Elmore Co.). A Muskogee tribal town, *tokepahce* [tokipáhči] (Martin and Mauldin 2000).

TUCKABUM Creek (Miss., Lauderdale Co.). Probably from Choctaw (Muskogean), perhaps containing *tikbi* 'river bend' (Seale 1939; P. Munro p.c.).

TUCKAHOE \tuk´ ə hō\. An edible root native to the eastern United States; from CAC Algonquian <tockwhogh, tockawhouge, taccaho> (*RHD* 1987). As a placename, the term occurs in several states (e.g., Md., Talbot Co.; N.J., Cape May Co.; and N.Y., Suffolk Co.).

TUCKALUGE Creek (Ga., Rabun Co.). Probably an Indian name, but the language has not been determined (BGN 7804).

TUCKANUCK Ledge (Maine, Knox Co.). From SNEng. Algonquian; the term has been translated 'a round loaf of bread' (Rutherford 1970). A possibly related placename is **Tuckernuck Island** (Mass., Nantucket Co.).

TUCKAPAHWOX Point (Wash., Mason Co.). Perhaps from the Skwaksnamish variety of Salishan, representing <tcpa'wax> 'a crane' (the bird) (BGN 8301).

TUCKASEEGEE (Ga., Towns Co.) \tuk ə sē´ gē\. Perhaps from Cherokee (Iroquoian) *daksi* 'terrapin' (Feeling 1975). Probably from the same origin is **Tuckasegee** (N.C., Jackson Co.).

TUCKASEE KING Landing (Ga., Effingham Co.) \tuk´ sē king\. From an unidentified Indian language (BGN 7801).

TUCKERNUCK Island (Mass., Nantucket Co.) \tuk´ ər nuk\. Earlier written <Petockenock>, <Tuckanuck>, <Tuckanuckett> (Little 1984). From SNEng. Algonquian, perhaps meaning 'a round loaf of bread' (Huden 1962). A possibly related placename is **Tuckanuck Ledge** (Maine, Knox Co.).

TUCKI Mountain (Calif., Inyo Co.) \tuk´ ī, tuk´ ē\. Perhaps from Shoshoni (Numic) /tukku/ 'mountain sheep' (J. McLaughlin p.c.).

TUCKSEL Point (Wash., Mason Co.). Said to be from the Skwaksnamish variety of Salishan, meaning 'rocks arranged like a man lying on his stomach' (BGN 8301).

TUCKTA Trail (Ore., Lane Co.). The surname of an Indian family at Warm Springs Reservation, perhaps from Chinook /-t'úkti/ 'good' (H. Zenk p.c.); see **Tokatee Lakes** (Ore., Lane Co.) above.

TUCQUALA Lake (Wash., Kitsap Co.). Probably from Sahaptin /tkála/ 'trout' (D. Kinkade p.c.).

TUCQUAN Creek (Pa., Lancaster Co.). Probably from Delaware (Algonquian), perhaps meaning 'a winding stream' (Donehoo 1928).

TUCSON (Ariz., Pima Co.) \too̅´ son\. Spanish *Tucsón* \too̅k sōn´, too̅ sōn´\, formerly also written *Chuk Son,* from O'odham (Piman) *cukṣon* 'black base' (Granger 1983, J. Hill p.c.), containing *cuk* 'black' and *ṣon* 'base'. The alternation between *t* and *ch* represents a change within O'odham since the eighteenth century (Bright

2000b); cf. **Tubac** above. There is also a **Tucson Mountain** in N.Mex. (Lincoln Co.).

TUCUMCARI (N.Mex., Quay Co.) \tōō´ kəm kâr ē\. Probably from Comanche (Numic) /tɨkamɨkarɨ/ 'to lie in wait for someone or something to approach' (Julyan 1998; Robinson & Armagost 1990).

TUCUPIT Point (Utah, Washington Co.). Probably from Southern Paiute (Numic) (Van Cott 1990).

TUDECOZ Spring (Ariz., Apache Co.). Probably from the same origin as **Toh De Coz** (Ariz., Navajo Co.); see above. Other probably related placenames include **Todokozh.**

TUEEULALA Falls (Calif., Tuolumne Co.) \tōō ē lä´ lə\. Perhaps from Sierra Miwok /tɨ"elela'/ 'shallow place' (Gudde 1998).

TUFTI Creek (Ore., Lane Co.) \tuf´ tē\. Said to be named for Charlie Tufti, a Molala man at the Warm Springs Reservation (McArthur 1992; H. Zenk p.c.).

TUGAK Peak (Alaska, Mt. Michelson B-1). From Iñupiaq (Eskimo) *tuugaaq* 'walrus tusk' (Orth 1967, MacLean 1980). Elsewhere in Alaska (Noatak D-6) **Tugak Lagoon** may be from Yupik (Eskimo) *tugkar* 'walrus ivory' (Orth 1967; Jacobson 1984).

TUGALOO River (S.C., Anderson Co.; Ga., Habersham Co.) \tōōg´ ə lōō, tug´ ə lōō\. Probably from Choctaw (Muskogean) *toklo* 'two' (Neuffer and Neuffer 1983; P. Munro p.c.) or Chickasaw *toklo* 'two' (Munro and Willmond 1994). A related placename is **Tuklo Creek** (Okla., Bryan Co.).

TUGAMAK Range (Alaska, Unimak D-2). From the Aleut placename *tugamax̂* (Bergsland 1994).

TUGIDAK (Alaska, Trinity Islands C-2) \tōō´ gi dak\. The Alutiiq (Eskimo) placename was reported in 1906 (Orth 1967).

TUG Mountain (Maine, Washington Co.) \tug\. Perhaps from an Abnaki (Algonquian) word for 'tree' (Huden 1962).

TUJUNGA (Calif., Los Angeles Co.) \tə hung´ gə\. Probably from the name of a Gabrielino (Takic) village (Gudde 1998).

TUKALLAH Lake (Alaska, Tyonek A-3). From Dena'ina (Athabaskan) *tuk'eleh bena* 'spawning lake' (Kari and Fall 1987:53).

TUKGAHGO Mountains (Alaska, Skagway B-2). The Tlingit name was published in 1952 (Orth 1967).

TUKINGAROK Creek (Alaska, Point Hope B-1). The Iñupiaq (Eskimo) name was reported in 1960 as <Tukingnuwa> (Orth 1967).

TUKLO Creek (Okla., Bryan Co.) \tōō´ klō\. From Choctaw (Muskogean) *toklo* 'two' (Shirk 1974; P. Munro p.c.). A related name is **Tugaloo River** (S.C.).

TUKLOMARAK Lake (Alaska, Selawik B-3). The Iñupiaq (Eskimo) name is *tuqłumaaġruk* (Burch 1998).

TUKLUNG (Alaska, Nushagak Bay D-4). The Yupik (Eskimo) name was reported in 1952 (Orth 1967).

TUKMAKNA Creek (Alaska, Anchorage D-3). The Ahtna (Athabaskan) name was reported in 1932 (Orth 1967).

TUKPAHLEARIK Creek (Alaska, Baird Mountains B-4). The Iñupiaq (Eskimo) name was obtained in 1955 (Orth 1967).

TUKROK River (Alaska, Noatak A-3). The Iñupiaq (Eskimo) name is *tuqsruk* 'narrow entrance' (L. Kaplan p.c.).

TUKSUK Channel (Alaska, Teller A-3). The Iñupiaq (Eskimo) name is *tuqsruk* 'narrow entrance' (L. Kaplan p.c.).

TUKTU Bluff (Alaska, Chandler Lake C-4). The Iñupiaq (Eskimo) name was reported in 1944 (Orth 1967).

TUKUHNIKIVATZ, Mount (Utah, San Juan Co.) \tōō kə nik´ ə väts\. From Southern Paiute (Numic), said to mean 'where the sun sets last' (Orth 1967).

TUKUKAPAK (Alaska, Kwiguk C-5). The Yupik (Eskimo) name was obtained in 1899 (Orth 1967).

TUKUTO Creek (Alaska, Howard Pass C-1). The Iñupiaq (Eskimo) name, reported in 1925, may be related to *taktuk* 'fog' or to *taqtu* 'kidney' (Orth 1967; MacLean 1980).

TUKWILA (Wash., King Co.) \tuk wil´ ə\. Chinook Jargon <tuk´-wil-la> [tʌkwílə] 'nut, hazelnut', from Kathlamet Chinook [tə́qula] 'nuts' (D. Kinkade p.c.).

TUL, Laguna del (N.Mex., Guadalupe Co.). The Spanish name means 'lake of the tule, the cat-tail reed', from Spanish *tul, tule* 'cat-tail reed', from Nahuatl (Aztecan) *tollin* (Santamaría 1959).

TULA (Miss., Lafayette Co.) \tyōō´ lə\. Perhaps from Muskogee *tola* /tó:la/ 'red bay tree' (Seale 1939; Martin and Mauldin 2000); or perhaps from Spanish *Tula,* the name of a city in central Mexico, representing Nahuatl (Aztecan) *tollan* 'place of the tules', from *tolli* 'tule, cat-tail reed'.

TULAGEAK Point (Alaska, Barrow A-3). The Iñupiaq (Eskimo) name was reported in 1951 as <Tulakgeak> 'landing place' (Orth 1967).

TULAINYO Lake (Calif., Tulare Co.) \tōō lə in´ yō\. The name was coined because the lake almost touches the boundary of **Tulare County** and **Inyo County** (Gudde 1998).

TULALIP (Wash., Snohomish Co.) \tə lā´ lip\. Northern Lushootseed (Salishan) /dx^{w}lílap/ 'distant bottom', referring to the head of **Tulalip Bay,** from /dx^{w}-/ 'place', /líl-/ 'far, distant', and /-ap/ 'bottom, base' (Hitchman 1985; D. Kinkade p.c.).

TULAPAI Creek (Ariz., Gila Co.) \tōō lə pī´\. Said to refer, in a unidentified Indian language, to a kind of 'beer' made from agave cactus (Granger 1983).

TULAR, El (Tex., Cameron Co.) \tōō lär´\. Mexican Spanish for 'a patch of tules or cat-tail reeds', from *tule* 'cat-tail reed, tule' (see **Tule** below). A probably related name is **Tolar** (N.Mex., Roosevelt Co.) **Tularcitos Creek** (Calif., Monterey Co.) represents a diminutive plural form, meaning 'little patches of tules' (Gudde 1998). **Tulare County** (Calif.) \tōō lâr´ ē\ is an English name formed by deleting the final *-s* 'plural' of Spanish *tulares* 'patches of cat-tail reeds' (Gudde 1998); the placename also occurs in S.Dak. (Spink Co.) and Wash. (Snohomish Co.). **Tularosa** (N.Mex., Otero Co.) \tōō lə rō´ sə\. is the feminine form of a Spanish adjective meaning 'reedy, having many patches of tules or cat-tail reeds' (Julyan 1998). The feminine form of the adjective may come from a phrase like *tierra tularosa* 'reedy land'. A name derived from **Tularosa** is nearby **Alamorosa**; see above.

TULE (Calif., Tulare Co.) \tōō´ lē\. From Mexican Spanish *tule* 'cat-tail reed', from Nahuatl (Aztecan) *tolli* (Gudde 1998). The phrase "in the tules" has come to mean 'in a remote rural area'. As a placename, **Tule** occurs in many western states (e.g., Calif., Mono Co.; N.Mex., Eddy Co.; and Tex., Briscoe Co.). Related placenames include **El Tular** (Tex., Cameron Co.) and **Tulare County** (Calif.); see above. Another probably related name is **Tulia** (Tex., Swisher Co.) (Tarpley 1980).

TULEBAGH Lake (Alaska, Beaver B-4) \tōō´ lē bä\. Koyukon (Athabaskan) *təli bəghə',* borrowed from Gwich'in (Athabaskan); the derivation is not clear (Kari 2000).

TULIA (Tex., Swisher Co.) \tōōl´ yə\. An adaptation of **Tule** (Tarpley 1980); see above.

TULIK Volcano (Alaska, Umnak B-1). Perhaps from Yupik (Eskimo) *tuullek* 'loon' (Orth 1967; Jacobson 1984).

TULILIK Lake (Alaska, Killik River A-2). From Iñupiaq (Eskimo) *tuullilik* 'has loons', from *tuullik* 'loon' (L. Kaplan p.c.).

TULIMANIK Islands (Alaska, Barrow A-1). The Iñupiaq (Eskimo) name was recorded in 1854 as <toolemina> 'whale rib' (Orth 1967); cf. *tulimaaq* 'rib' (MacLean 1980).

TULIUMNIT Point (Alaska, Chignik A-1). The Alutiiq (Eskimo) name was reported in 1847 (Orth 1967).

TULLAHASSEE (Okla., Wagoner Co.) \tul ə has´ ē\. From Muskogee *tvlvhasse* /talahá:ssi/, name of a tribal town; perhaps containing *etvlwv* /(i)tálwa/ 'tribal town' and *vhassē* /ahá:ssi:/ 'rancid, stale, old' (Shirk 1974; Martin and Mauldin 2000). A related placename is **Tallahassee** (Fla., Leon Co.).

TULLAHOMA (Miss., Jones Co.) \tul ə hō´ mə\. Earlier <Tul-i-hum–ma>; from Choctaw *tali-homma,* lit. 'rock-red' (Toomey 1917; P. Munro p.c.). The name also exists in Tenn. (Coffee Co.).

TULOSA (N.Mex., San Miguel Co.). The Spanish adjective means 'reedy, full of tules or cat-tail reeds'; it is derived from *tule* 'cat-tail reed', from Nahuatl (Aztecan) *tolli* (Julyan 1998). The feminine form may mean that the name was abbreviated from a phrase like *tierra tulosa* 'reedy land'. A possible related form is **Tuloso** (NM, San Miguel Co.), apparently the masculine form of the adjective. Possibly related placenames include **Laguna del Tul** (N.Mex., Guadalupe Co.), **Tula** (Miss., Lafayette Co.), **El Tular** (Tex., Cameron Co.), and **Tule** (Calif., Tulare Co.); see above.

TULOT (AR, Poinsett Co.) \to͞o´ lət\. Said to have been the name of an Indian man, tribe not identified (Deane 1986).

TULPEHOCKEN Creek (N.J., Burlington Co.). From Delaware (Algonquian) <tuulpe-wi-hákki-ənk> 'land abounding in turtles', from <tuulpe-> 'turtle', <-wi-> 'connective', <-hakki-> 'land', and /əŋk/ 'place' (Mahr 1959:370). The name **Tulpehocken** also occurs in Pa. (Berks Co.).

TULSA County (Okla.) \tul´ sə, tul´ sē\. From the same source as **Tulse** (Ala., Shelby Co.), a former Muskogee village in Ala. (Shirk 1974; Martin and Mauldin 2000); see below.

TULSE (Ala., Shelby Co.) \tul´ sē\. Also written <Tulsey>; perhaps a shortening of Muskogee *lucv-pokv tulse* /loča-po:ka-tálsi/, the name of a tribal town. This itself may mean 'turtles-sitting old-town', from *lucv-pokv* /loca-pó:ka/ 'turtles sitting' plus *tvlvhassē* /talahá:ssi/ 'old town' (Read 1984; Martin and Mauldin 2000). Booker et al. (1992:431) note that the etymology is unclear. Possibly related names are **Tallahassee** (Fla., Leon Co.), **Tullahassee** (Okla., Wagner Co.), and **Tulsa County** (Okla.).

TULSONA Creek (Alaska, Gulkana B-3) \tul sō´ nə\. From Ahtna (Athabaskan) *taltsogh na'* 'yellow-water creek'; cf. *tsogh* 'yellow-brown', *na'* 'stream' (Kari 1990).

TULUCAY Creek (Calif., Napa Co.) \to͝ol´ ə kā\. Probably from Patwin (Wintuan) [tu'luka] 'red' (Gudde 1998).

TULUGA River (Alaska, Umiat B-2). From Iñupiaq (Eskimo) *tulugaq* 'raven' (Orth 1967; MacLean 1980). Probably related Alaska placenames include **Tulukak Creek** (Noatak D-5) and **Tuluvak Bluffs** (Umiat A-3). Another related placename is **Tulugak**, which occurs in several areas of Alaska (e.g., Baird Mountains D-6) (Orth 1967).

TULUKAK Creek (Alaska, Noatak D-5). From Iñupiaq (Eskimo) *tulugaq* 'raven' (Orth 1967; MacLean 1980). Probably related Alaska placenames include **Tuluga River** (Umiat B-2) and **Tuluvak Bluffs** (Umiat A-3).

TULUK Creek (Alaska, Sagavanirktok C-4). The Iñupiaq (Eskimo) name was made official in BGN 7903.

TULUKSAK (Alaska, Russian Mission A-6) \to͞o lo͝ok´ sak\. From the Yupik (Eskimo) placename *tuulkessaaq,* not necessarily related to *tulukaruq* 'raven' (Jacobson 1984).

TULULA (N.C., Graham Co.). Said to be from Cherokee (Iroquoian) <talulu> 'the cry of the frog' (Powell 1968). See also **Tallulah Falls** (Ga., Habersham Co.).

TULUVAK Bluffs (Alaska, Umiat A-3). Probably from Iñupiaq (Eskimo) *tulugaq* 'raven' (Orth 1967, MacLean 1980). Probably related

Alaska placenames include **Tuluga River** (Umiat B-2) and **Tulukak Creek** (Noatak D-5).

TUMACACORI (Ariz., Santa Cruz Co.) \too mə kak´ ə rē, too mə kä´ kə rē\. Perhaps from O'odham (Piman) *cemagĭ gakolig* 'caliche bending' (Granger 1983), where *caliche* refers to 'alkali'; *cemagĭ* 'caliche' is not current, but cf. *gakodk* 'to be bent' (Saxton et al. 1983). Or perhaps from *cem ko'okolig* 'place of little chili', with *cem* 'insufficient' and *ko'okol* 'chili' (O. Zepeda p.c.).

TUMALO (Ore., Deschutes Co.) \tum´ ə lō\. Perhaps from Klamath /dmolo/ 'wild plum' (McArthur 1992; Barker 1963).

TUMALT Creek (Ore., Multnomah Co.) \too´ môlt\. Named for an Indian man, of unknown affiliation, killed by U.S. troops in 1856 (McArthur 1992).

TUMALUM (Ore., Umatilla Co.). Perhaps from Sahaptin /tamalám/ 'rocks (in the water)' (D. Kinkade p.c.). The name also occurs in Wash. (Garfield Co.) (McArthur 1992).

TUMAMOC Hill (Ariz., Pima Co.) \too mə mok`\. O'odham (Piman) *cemamagĭ* 'horned lizard' (Granger 1983; J. Hill p.c.).

TUMBALOO Creek (Miss., Rankin Co.). From Choctaw (Muskogean) *hatǫbalaha* 'beech tree' (Seale 1939; P. Munro p.c.).

TUMIA (Ore., Umatilla Co.) \too´ mē ə\. Named for <Toom-hi-ya>, an Indian woman, language not identified (McArthur 1992).

TUMI Creek (Alaska, Point Hope A-2). From Iñupiaq (Eskimo) *tumi* 'track, footprint', reported in 1962 (Orth 1967; MacLean 1980). A probably related name is **Tumit Creek** (Alaska, Misheguk Mountain A-2).

TUMIT Creek (Alaska, Misheguk Mountain A-2). From Iñupiaq (Eskimo) *tumi* 'track' (Orth 1967; MacLean 1980). A probably related name is **Tumi Creek** (Alaska, Point Hope A-2).

TUMKEEHATCHEE Creek (Ala., Elmore Co.) \tum kē hach´ ē\. A shortening of Muskogee *ue-tumhkv-hvcce* /oy-tomhka-háčči/ 'sounding-water stream', from *ue* 'water', *tomhka* 'sounding', and *hacce* 'stream' (Read 1984; Martin and Mauldin 2000).

TUM Lake (Ore., Deschutes Co.) \tum\. Chinook Jargon <tum> [tʌm] 'noise, thump', probably from Lower Chinookan [təmm, tumm] 'noise' (H. Zenk p.c.). Possibly related placenames include **Tumtum River** (Ore., Lincoln Co.) and **Tumwata Creek** (Wash., Jefferson Co.).

TUMTUM River (Ore., Lincoln Co.) \tum´tum\. From Chinook Jargon <tum´-tum> [tʌ́mtʌm] 'noise, thump, heart, mind, memory etc.', reduplicated from Lower Chinook [təmm, tumm] 'noise, thump' (McArthur 1992; D. Kinkade p.c.). The placename also occurs in Wash. (Stevens Co.) and Alaska (Unalaska A-5). Probably related placenames include **Tum Lake** (Ore., Deschutes Co.) and **Tumwata Creek;** see above and below.

TUMWATA Creek (Wash., Jefferson Co.) \tum wä´ tə\. Chinook Jargon <tum-wa´-ta> [təmwɔ́tə, təmwátə] 'waterfall, cascade', from Chinook Jargon <tum> [tʌm] 'thump, noise' and English *water* (D. Kinkade p.c.). The name also occurs in Wash. (Jefferson Co.) (Parratt 1984). The related name **Tumwater** \tum´ wä tər\. is found in Ore. (Wasco Co.) and Wash. (Thurston Co.) (Hitchman 1985). Another related name is **Tum Lake** (Ore., Deschutes Co.).

TUNA (Pa., McKean Co.) A shortening of <Tuneungwant>, perhaps from Iroquoian, said to mean 'an eddy, not strong' (Donehoo 1928). Related names include **Tunungwant Creek** (N.Y., Cattaraugus Co.).

TUNA Canyon (Calif., Los Angeles Co.) \too´ nə\. From Mexican Spanish *tuna* 'fruit of the prickly pear cactus', orginally from the Taino (Arawakan) language of the West Indies (Gudde 1998). A related name is **Arroyo Las Tunas**; see below.

TUNALIK River (Alaska, Wainwright A-5). The Iñupiaq (Eskimo) word is *tunulliq* 'back-most one' (L. Kaplan p.c.).

TUNALKTEN Lake (Alaska, Hughes A-3). The Koyukon (Athabaskan) name is said to mean 'hot spring' (Orth 1967).

TUNAS, Arroyo Las (N.Mex., Rio Arriba Co.). The Spanish name means 'creek [of] the prickly-pears'; see **Tuna** above.

TUNAWEE Canyon (Calif., Inyo Co.) \tun´ ə wē\. From Panamint (Numic) /tɨnapi/ [tɨnávI] 'mountain mahogany' (J. McLaughlin p.c.).

TUNE Creek (Calif., Shasta Co.) \to͞o´ nē, tō´ nə\. From Wintu /tune/ 'forward, front' (Gudde 1998).

TUNGAICH Point (Alaska, Point Lay D-2). The Iñupiaq (Eskimo) name is from *tuunġaich* 'shaman's helping spirits; devils' (L. Kaplan p.c.). A probably related name is **Tungak Creek** (Alaska, Point Lay D-2) (Orth 1967). Another **Tungak Creek** (Alaska, Kuskokwim Bay D-1) is from Yupik, rather than Iñupiaq, but also means 'shaman's familiar spirit; devil' (Orth 1967; Jacobson 1984). The related term **Tungaluk Slough** (Alaska, Hooper Bay B-1) is perhaps from Yupik *tuunralek* 'one who has a familiar spirit, i.e., a shaman' (Orth 1967; Jacobson 1984).

TUNGA Inlet (Alaska, Craig D-4). From Haida <tanga> 'sea, salt', recorded in 1932 (Orth 1967).

TUNGNAK Hill (Alaska, Point Hope C-1). The Iñupiaq (Eskimo) name, reported in 1956, is said to mean 'resembles back fat, as on a caribou' (Orth 1967).

TUNGPUK River (Alaska, Hooper Bay D-1). The Yupik (Eskimo) name was reported in 1949 (Orth 1967).

TUNGULARA Mountains (Alaska, Trinity Islands D-1). The Alutiiq (Eskimo) name was reported in 1934 (Orth 1967).

TUNIAK, Cape (Alaska, Kodiak C-1). Said to be related to **Chiniak Bay,** an Alutiiq (Eskimo) name (Orth 1967). The related Yupik name **Tuniakpuk** (Alaska, Goodnews Bay B-4) was reported in 1880 as meaning 'big *tuniak*' (Orth 1967); the meaning is otherwise unknown.

TUNICA County (Miss.) \tyo͞o´ ni kə, to͞o´ ni kə\. The name of an Indian people; the Native American term is /tónika/ 'the people', from /ta-/ 'the', /ʔóni/ 'people', and /-ka/ 'noun suffix' (Seale 1939; Haas 1953). The placename also occurs in La. (West Feliciana Par.).

TUNICHA Mountains (Ariz., Apache Co.; N.Mex., San Juan Co.). A variant spelling of **Tunitcha Mountains**; see below.

TUNILKHANTEN Lake (Alaska, Hughes A-4). The Koyukon (Athabaskan) name, recorded in 1956, is said to mean 'clear-water lake' (Orth 1967).

TUNIPUS Pond (R.I., Newport Co.). SNEng. Algonquian, perhaps from <toonupas> 'turtle' (Huden 1962; W. Cowan p.c.).

TUNITCHA Mountains (Ariz., Apache Co.; N.Mex., San Juan Co.) \to͞o ni chä´\. Navajo (Athabaskan) *tón(i)tsaa'* 'big water', from *tó* 'water' and *n(i)tsaa* 'big' (Granger 1983; Wilson 1995). Also written **Tunicha Mountains.**

TUNKALESHNA Creek (Alaska, Lime Hills A-4). The Dena'ina (Athabaskan) name is *duuk'elushtnu* 'he-carries-thing-in stream' (J. Kari p.c.).

TUNKHANNOCK (Pa., Wyoming Co.) \tungk han´ ək\. Perhaps from Delaware (Algonquian) *tànkhanèk* 'small stream' (Kraft and Kraft 1985).

TUNK Lake (Maine, Hancock Co.) \tungk\. Abenaki (Algonquian), perhaps abbreviated from <k't-hunk> 'large swift stream' (Huden 1962). The name also occurs in Wash. (Okanogan Co.).

TUNNABORA Peak (Calif., Inyo Co.) \to͞o nə bôr´ ə\. The name is probably from Panamint (Numic) /tuu/ 'black' plus /napatɨn/ 'canyon' (J. McLaughlin p.c.).

TUNQUE Pueblo (N.Mex., Sandoval Co.). A variant of **Arroyo Tonque**; see above.

TUNRAVIK Creek (Alaska, Dillingham B-4). The Yupik (Eskimo) name was obtained in 1930 (Orth 1967).

TUNTSA Creek (Ariz., Apache Co.). A variant of **Tunitcha Mountains**; see above. The name **Tuntsa** also occurs in N.Mex. (San Juan Co.).

TUNTUNGUAK Mountains (Alaska, Goodnews Bay C-5). The Yupik (Eskimo) name was reported in 1951 as meaning 'deer-like' (Orth 1967).

TUNTUTULIAK (Alaska, Baird Inlet B-2) \to͞on tə to͞o´ lē ak\. From Yupik (Eskimo) *tuntutuliaq* 'many caribou' (reindeer), from *tuntu* 'caribou' (Jacobson 1984).

TUNUGARAT Hill (Alaska, Howard Pass D-3). The Iñupiaq (Eskimo) name, reported in 1956, is said to mean 'to turn aside, to turn away' (Orth 1967).

TUNUIGAK Slough (Alaska, Kwiguk C-6). The Yupik (Eskimo) name is in the Yukon-Kuskokwim Delta (Orth 1967).

TUNUING River (Alaska, Nushagak Bay D-4). The Yupik (Eskimo) name was reported in 1952 (Orth 1967).

TUNUKUCHIAK Creek (Alaska, Ambler River D-1). The Iñupiaq (Eskimo) name, reported in 1956, is said to mean 'to go or sneak behind' (Orth 1967); cf. *tunu* 'back part' (MacLean 1980). A possibly related name is **Tunusiktok Lake** (Alaska, Point Lay C-1). Another probably related name is **Tunulik River** (Alaska, Goodnews Bay A-7), from Yupik (Eskimo), said to mean 'one that has the back' (Orth 1967); cf. *tunu-* 'area in back of' (Jacobson 1984).

TUNUNAK (Alaska, Nunivak Island C-1) \tə no͞o´ nak\. The Yupik (Eskimo) name was reported as <Tununuk> in 1878, said to mean 'behind one's back' (Orth 1967); cf. the village name *tununeq,* from *tunu-* 'behind' (Jacobson 1984). A probably related placename is **Tanunak**; see above.

TUNUNGWANT Creek (N.Y., Cattaraugus Co.) \tə nung´ wənt\. Earlier written <Tu-ne-un´-gwan, Tu-ne-ga´-want> (etc.); perhaps from Iroquoian, translated as 'an eddy not strong' (Beauchamp 1907). The name also occurs in Pa. (McKean Co.), along with the shortened variant **Tuna.**

TUNUROKPAK Channel (Alaska, Kwiguk B-4). The Yupik (Eskimo) name, obtained in 1899, has been translated 'big slough' (Orth 1967); cf. *tunuirun* 'slough' (Jacobson 1984).

TUNUSIKTOK Lake (Alaska, Point Lay C-1). The Iñupiaq (Eskimo) name, obtained in 1956, may mean 'it lies behind' (Orth 1967); cf. *tunu* 'back part' (MacLean 1980). A possibly related name is **Tunukuchiak Creek** (Alaska, Ambler River D-1).

TUNUTUK Creek (Alaska, Ambler River A-5). The Iñupiaq (Eskimo) name was obtained in 1902 (Orth 1967).

TUOLUMNE County (Calif.) \to͞o ol´ ə mē\. Probably from Central Sierra Miwok /ṭaawa-lɨmni/ 'squirrel place', contining /ṭaawalɨ/ 'squirrel' (Gudde 1998).

TUPAPA Seep (Nev., Nye Co.). Southern Paiute (Numic) /tuppappaa/ 'emerging water', from /tuppa/ 'emerge' and /paa/ 'water' (J. McLaughlin p.c.). A probable variant form is **Topopah Spring.**

TUPELO \to͞o´ pə lō\. The term refers to a tree called the *tupelo gum tree,* perhaps from Muskogee *eto* /itó/ 'tree' plus *opelwv* /opílwa/ 'swamp' (*RHD* 1987; Martin and Mauldin 2000). As a placename, it occurs in several southeastern states (e.g., Ala., Jackson Co.; Miss., Lee Co.; and Okla., Coal Co.).

TUPICHALIK Creek (Alaska, Howard Pass B-5). The Iñupiaq (Eskimo) name is *tupiqchialik* 'new tent place' (Burch 1998); cf. *tupiq* 'tent' (MacLean 1980). Related Alaska names include **Tupik Creek** (Misheguk Mountain C-4) and **Tupikchak Creek** (De Long Mountains D-2), meaning 'new tent' (Orth 1967).

TUPKAK Bar (Alaska, Wainwright C-2). The Iñupiaq (Eskimo) name <tapqaq> 'sand spit' was published in 1955 (Orth 1967).

TUPSHIN Peak (Wash., Chelan Co.). Chinook Jargon <tup´-shin, tip´-sin, tŭp-shin> [tʌpšɪn] 'needle; to patch'; cf. Lower Chehalis (Salishan) /t'ə́lpšn/ 'she patched it' (D. Kinkade p.c.).

TUPSO Creek (Wash., Snohomish Co.). From Chinook Jargon <tupso> 'grass'; the same origin as **Tipsoo Creek;** see above.

TUPUKNUK Slough (Alaska, Bethel C-8). The Iñupiaq (Eskimo) name was reported in 1951 (Orth 1967).

TURKEY. The name of this native American fowl occurs in U.S. placenames, often of translating Indian names for the places concerned. In Ala. (Choctaw Co.) **Turkey Creek** corresponds to Choctaw (Muskogean) *fakit chipǫta* 'little turkey' (Read 1984; P. Munro p.c.); see **Fakit Chipunta** (Ala., Clarke Co.). In Iowa (Clayton Co.) **Turkey River** corresponds to Meskwaki (Algonquian) /pe:ne:hka:hi/, lit. 'abounding in turkeys', with /pene:wa/ (Vogel 1983, I. Goddard p.c.). In Kans. (Labette Co.) **Turkey Creek** translates the Osage (Siouan) word, consisting of /süˊhka/ 'chicken' plus /htǫ́ka/ 'big' (Rydjord 1968; R. Rankin p.c.). In S.Dak. (Yankton Co.) **Turkey Creek** corresponds to Dakota (Siouan) *zičá-thąka* 'turkey', lit. 'partridge-big', from *zíča* 'partridge' and *thą́ka* (Riggs 1890; A. Taylor p.c.).

TURNIPTOWN Mountain (Ga., Gilmer Co.). From Cherokee (Iroquoian) <ulunyi> 'tuber place', referring to an edible native root or tuber (BGN 7803).

TURPENTINOM Creek (Calif., Shasta Co.) \tûr pən tĭˊnəm\. A folk-etymological transformation of Wintu /čur-pantinom/; cf. /čur-/ 'spawn', /pan-/ 'top', and /nom/ 'west' (Gudde 1998).

TURTLE. The term is often used in placenames to translate Indian words referring to the turtle. Thus **Turtle Lake** (Minn., Cass Co.) translates Ojibwa (Algonquian) *mikinaako-zaaga'igan* 'snapping-turtle lake' (Upham 2001; Nichols and Nyholm 1995). In Pa. (Allegheny Co.) **Turtle Creek** corresponds to Delaware (Algonquian) <tulpewi-sipu> 'turtle-stream' (Donehoo 1928). In Ind. (Sullivan Co.) **Turtle Creek** was named for a Miami/Illinois (Algonquian) leader called /mihšihkina/ 'painted terrapin' (McCafferty 2002). In S.Dak. (Ziebach Co.) **Turtle Butte** translates Lakhota (Siouan) *khéya pahá* (A. Taylor p.c.).

TURUP Creek (Calif., Del Norte Co.) \to͞oˊ rəp\. For the Yurok village /turip/ (Gudde 1998).

TUSAS (N.Mex., Rio Arriba Co.) \to͞oˊ səs\. Mexican Spanish *tuzas* 'wood-rats, prairie dogs', from singular *tuza,* corresponding to Nahuatl (Aztecan) *tuzan* 'wood-rat' (Cobos 1983). There is also a placename **Las Tusas** (San Miguel Co.), meaning 'the prairie dogs' (Julyan 1998).

TUSAYAN (Ariz., Coconino Co.) \to͞oˊ sä yän, to͞o sä yänˊ, tusˊ ə yan\. From Spanish *Tusayán,* used by the early explorers to designate the area of the Hopi (Uto-Aztecan) pueblos (*HNAI* 9:551).

TUSCAHOMA (Miss., Grenada Co.) \tus kə hōˊ mə\. From Choctaw (Muskogean) *tvshka-homma,* lit. 'warrior-red' (Seale 1939; P. Munro p.c.). The placename also occurs in Ala. (Choctaw Co.) Perhaps related placenames include **Tuskahoma** (Okla., Pushmataha Co.), **Tuscaloosa County** (Ala.), and others listed below.

TUSCALOOSA County (Ala.) \tus kə lo͞oˊ sə\. This was originally the Choctaw (Muskogean) name for the river that is now called the **Blackwarrior River.** The term **Tuscaloosa** was first recorded by Spanish explorers as *Tascaluza* (Booker et al. 1992:435); it is from *tashka-losa,* lit. 'warrior-black' (Read 1984; P. Munro p.c.). Possibly related placenames include **Tuscahoma** (Miss., Grenada Co.) and others listed below.

TUSCARAWAS (Ohio, Tuscarawas Co.) \tusk ə rôrˊ əs\. Perhaps from the same source as **Tuscarora**; see below. Note that the name of the Ohio county is apparently formed from a plural, **Tuscarawas.**

TUSCARORA \tus kə rôrˊ ə\. The name of an Iroquoian Indian group who once lived in N.C. During the colonial period, they migrated north to join the Iroquoians in N.Y. state. The term entered English from Catawban (Siouan) /taskarúde:/, lit. 'dry salt eater', a folk-etymology containing /tas/ 'salt', /karu/ 'dry', and /-de:/ 'devour'; based on the Tuscarora (Iroquoian) self-designation /skarù:rę?/ 'hemp-gatherer' (B. Rudes p.c.). As a placename, **Tuscarora** occurs in several states (e.g., N.C., Craven Co.; N.Y., Livingston Co.; and Mich., Cheboygan Co.).

TUSCATUCKET Brook (R.I., Bristol Co.). From SNEng. Algonquian, perhaps containing <tiusk> 'bridge', <-tuk> 'tidal stream', and <-et> 'place' (Huden 1962; W. Cowan p.c.).

TUSCAWILLA Lake (Fla., Alachua Co.) \tus kə wil´ ə\. Probably from Choctaw (Muskogean) *tashka-hullo,* lit. 'sacred warrior', from *tashka* 'warrior' plus *hollo* 'sacred, taboo, beloved' (Read 1934; P. Munro p.c.). Perhaps related placenames include **Tuscahoma** (Miss., Grenada Co.) and others listed above.

TUSCOBIA (Wis., Barron Co.) \tus kō´ bē ə\. Perhaps a name coined by whites, combining elements from various Indian placenames; cf. **Tuscola** (Miss., Leake Co.) and **Tuscumbia** (Ala., Colbert Co.), both containing Choctaw (Muskogean) *tashka* 'warrior' (Vogel 1991). Another probable coined name is **Tuscohatchie Lake** (Wash., King Co.); cf. Choctaw *tashka* 'warrior' and *hachcha* 'stream' (P. Munro p.c.). Related names include **Tuscahoma** (Miss., Grenada Co.) and others listed above.

TUSCOLA (Miss., Leake Co.\. \tus kō´ lə\. Probably an abbreviation of **Tuscolameta**; the name **Tuscola** also occurs in Ill. (Douglas Co.), Mich. (Tuscola Co.), and Tex. (Taylor Co.). The name of **Tuscolameta Creek** (Miss., Leake Co.) \tus kə lə mē´ tə\. is probably from Choctaw (Muskoean) *tashka-himmita,* lit. 'warrior-young' (Seale 1939; P. Munro p.c.).

TUSCUMBIA (Ala., Colbert Co.) \tus kum´ bē ə\, commemorating an Indian leader who is variously identified as being Cherokee (Iroquoian) or Chickasaw (Muskogean); however, his name appears to be Choctaw (Muskogean), meaning 'warrior-killer', containing *tashka* 'warrior' and *abi, ąbi* 'kill' (Read 1984; P. Munro p.c.). The placename **Tuscumbia** also occurs in Miss. (Alcorn Co.) and Tenn. (McNairy Co.). Other related placenames include **Tuscahoma** (Miss., Grenada Co.) and others listed above.

TUSERO Windmill (N.Mex., San Miguel Co.). Mexican Spanish *tucero* 'prairie-dog colony' (Cobos 1983) cf. **Tusas** above.

TUSHAR Mountains (Utah, Piute Co.) \tush´ ər\. From Ute (Numic) /tosatɨ/ [tosáRɨ] 'white thing', containing /tosa/ 'white' (J. McLaughlin p.c.).

TUSHKA (Okla., Atoka Co.) \tush ´ kə\. From Choctaw (Muskogean) *tashka* 'warrior' (Shirk 1974; P. Munro p.c.).

TUSHTENA Pass (Alaska, Tanacross B-6). The Tanacross (Athabaskan) name was reported in 1936 (Orth 1967).

TUSIK, Cape (Alaska, Adak B-4). The Aleut name was published in 1852 (Orth 1967).

TUSIKPAK, Cape (Alaska, Point Hope B-2). From Iñupiaq (Eskimo) *tasiqpak* 'big lagoon' (L. Kaplan p.c.). A related term is **Tusikvoak Lake** (Alaska, Barrow A-3), meaning 'old lagoon' (Orth 1967).

TUSKAHOMA (Okla., Pushmataha Co.) \tus kə hō´ mə\. From Choctaw (Muskogean) *tashka-homma,* lit. 'warrior-red' (Shirk 1974; P. Munro p.c.). A variant spelling is **Tushkahomma.** Related placenames include **Tuscahoma** (Miss., Grenada Co.) and others listed above.

TUSKAN (Ore., Wasco Co.) \tus´ kən\. From an Indian placename <Tush-kan-ee>, language not identified (McArthur 1992).

TUSKEEGEE (N.C., Graham Co.). Probably from the same origin as **Tuskegee** (Ala., Macon Co.); see below.

TUSKEEGO (Iowa, Decatur`Co.). Probably a transfer and adapted spelling of **Tuskegee** (Ala.,Macon Co.); see below.

TUSKEGEE (Ala., Macon Co.) \tus kē´ gē\. The name of a Muskogee tribal town, *taskēke* /ta:skí:ki/ (Read 1984; Martin and Mauldin

2000). According to Booker et al. (1992:429–30), the town was in the chiefdom of Coosa, a part of the Creek Confederacy; its name was first recorded by Spanish explorers as *Tasquiqui,* from dialectal Koasati (Muskogean) /taskiki/ 'warriors'. The placename **Tuskegee** also occurs in Okla. (Creek Co.). Related placenames include **Tuscaloosa County** (Ala.); see above.

TUSQUITEE (N.C., Clay Co.). Said to be from Cherokee (Iroquoian) <tusquitta> 'rafters' (Powell 1968).

TUSSAHAW Creek (Ga., Butts Co.). Said to be from a Muskogee word indicating 'ability to inflect pain or to sting' (Goff 1975).

TUSTUMENA Glacier (Alaska, Seldovia D-1) \to͞o stə men´ ə\. From Dena'ina (Athabaskan) *dusdubena* 'peninsula lake', with *-bena* 'lake' (Kari and Kari 1982:28).

TUTAGO (Alaska, Unalakleet B-1). The Koyukon (Athabaskan) name is of unclear derivation (Orth 1967).

TUTAK Creek (Alaska, Noatak D-4). From Iñupiaq (Eskimo) *tuutaq* 'labret, lip ornament' (Orth 1967; Webster and Zibell 1970).

TUTAKOKE River (Alaska, Hooper Bay B-2). The Yupik (Eskimo) name was reported in 1951 (Orth 1967).

TUTALOSI (Ala., Russell Co.). Perhaps from Muskogee *tottolose* /tottolô:si/ 'chicken' (Read 1984; Martin and Mauldin 2000). The name also occurs in Ga. (Lee Co.).

TUTELO (N.Y., Chemung Co.) \to͞o´ tə lō\. Named for a Siouan people of Va. and N.C. who migrated to N.Y. state during colonial times (Beauchamp 1907). An alternative form of the name is found in **Tutelow Creek** (Pa., Bradford Co.).

TUTKA Bay (Alaska, Seldovia B-4). From Dena'ina (Athabaskan) *tut' ka'a,* lit. 'big enclosed water' (Kari and Kari 1982:30).

TUTKAIMUND Lake (Alaska, Tanacross A-3). From Upper Tanana (Athabaskan) *tutk'ąąy männ',* lit. 'scaup lake' (J. Kari p.c.).

TUTLUT (Alaska, Fairbanks C-6). The Koyukon (Athabaskan) name is of unclear derivation (Orth 1967).

TUTNA Lake (Alaska, Lake Clark B-7) \do͞ot´ nə\. Dena'ina (Athabaskan) *dutna vena* 'Yupik (Eskimo) lake' (J. Kari p.c.).

TUTOLIVIK (Alaska, Wainwright C-2). The Iñupiaq (Eskimo) name was reported in 1955 (Orth 1967).

TUTUILLA Creek (Ore., Umatilla Co.) \tō tō il´ ə\. Perhaps from a Umatilla (Sahaptin) placename, derived from <tutuilla> 'thorn bush' (McArthur 1992).

TUTUSIROK Lake (Alaska, Misheguk Mountain A-2). The Iñupiaq (Eskimo) name is *tut-tusiruaq* 'he meets a caribou'. A probably related name is **Tututalak Mountains** (Alaska, Baird Mountains D-5), said to mean 'caught a caribou' (Orth 1967).

TUTUTNI Pass (Ore., Klamath Co.) \to͞o to͞ot´ nē\. This is the self-designation of an Athabaskan subgroup, /dotodəni/, from /doto/, a village name, and /dəni/ 'people' (D. Kinkade p.c.).

TUVAK Lake (Alaska, Meade River C-5). The Iñupiaq (Eskimo) name is *tuvaq* 'shorefast ice' (L. Kaplan p.c.).

TUWA Canyon (Utah, San Juan Co.). From Southern Paiute (Numic) but of unclear derivation (Van Cott 1990).

TUWEEP (Ariz., Mohave Co.) \to͞o´ wēp\. A variant of **Toroweap Valley**; see above.

TUXACHANIE Creek (Miss., Harrison Co.) \tuk sə chā´ ni\. Choctaw (Muskogean) *taksho aa-chiiya* 'boiler fragments are sitting there', referring to fragments of the pots in which corn is boiled; from *taksho* 'boiler pot', *aa-* 'place', *chiiya* 'two objects sit' (Seale 1939; P. Munro p.c.).

TUXEDNI Bay (Alaska, Kenai A-8) \to͞ok sed´ nē\. From Dena'ina (Athabaskan) *tuk'ezitnu* 'fish-stranded-in-tide river' (Kari and Kari 1982:17).

TUXEDO (N.Y., Orange Co.) \tuk sē´ dō\. Probably from Munsee Delaware (Algonquian), perhaps from <p'tuck-sepo> 'crooked river' (Ruttenber 1906). The status of the town as a resort gave rise to the use of the term *tuxedo* for a man's formal jacket. The placename **Tuxedo** also occurs in other states (e.g., Ala., Jefferson Co.; Md., Prince George's Co.; and Mo., St. Louis Co.). In Tex. (Jones Co.) it is said to be pronounced \tuk´ si dō\.

TUXEKAN (Alaska, Craig D-4) \tuk sē´ kan\. From the name of a Tlingit village (Orth 1967).

TUYE Spring (Ariz., Apache Co.). From the same origin as **Toyei**; see above.

TUZIGOOT National Monument (Ariz., Yavapai Co.) \to͞o zi go͞ot´, to͞o´ zi go͞ot\. Said to be Western Apache (Athabaskan) for 'crooked water' (Granger 1983); cf. /tó/ 'water' and /-god/ 'something bent, a knee' (P. Greenfeld p.c.).

TVATIVAK Bay (Alaska, Nushagak Bay D-5). The Yupik (Eskimo) name was reported in 1952 (Orth 1967).

TWALITY (Ore., Wash.) \twä´ li tē\. This was the historical name of an administrative district in the Oregon Territory; it once included much of western Wash. and Ore. The term has the same origin as **Tualatin** (Ore., Washington Co.); see above.

TWANA \twä´ nə\. The term applies to a division of the Coast Salishan people, living in the Puget Sound area. The Native American term is /tuwáduq/ 'people from down below', containing /tu-/ 'from', /wə́d/ 'down, below', and /-q/ 'voice, language' (D. Kinkade p.c.). A placename derived from this is **Twanoh State Park** (Wash., Mason Co.).

TWIGHTWEE (Ohio, Hamilton Co.). From Unami Delaware (Algonquian) /tuwéhtuwe/, applied to the Miami/Illinois (Algonquian) Indians; it is said to be derived from the cry of the crane (*HNAI* 15:688; M. McCafferty p.c.).

TWIN Rivers (Wis., Manitowoc Co.). The names of the East Twin River and the West Twin River may correspond to Ojibwa (Algonquian) *niizhoodenh* 'twin' (Vogel 1991; Nichols and Nyholm 1995). A related term is **Two Rivers** (Wis., Manitowoc Co.).

TWISP (Wash., Okanogan Co.) \twisp\. From the Okanagan (Salishan) placename [tx^{w}ə́c'p] (Hitchman 1985; D. Kinkade p.c.).

TWO HEARTED River (Mich., Luce Co.). Perhaps a translation of Ojibwa (Algonquian) *niizhoodenh-ziibi,* lit. 'twin river', containing *niizh* 'two', *-de'-* 'heart', and *ziibi* 'river' (Vogel 1986; Nichols and Nyholm 1995).

TWO LICK (Pa., Indiana Co.). Said to be a translation from an unidentified Algonquian language, in which <nischa-honi> 'two licks' refers to salt-licks or saline springs (Donehoo 1928).

TWO RIVERS (Minn., Kittson Co.). Said to correspond to Ojibwa (Algonquian) <ganijoshino zibi>, lit. 'the river that lies two together as in a bed' (Upham 2001). In Wis. (Manitowoc Co.) the town of **Two Rivers** is named for the East Twin River and the West Twin River, from Ojibwa (Algonquian) *niizhooshin* 'to lie as two'; cf. *niizhi-* 'two', *-shin* 'to lie' (J. Nichols p.c.).

TYBO (Nev., Nye Co.) \tī´ bō\. From Shoshoni (Numic) /taipo/ 'white man' (Carlson 1974; J. McLaughlin p.c.).

TYEE (Ore., Douglas Co.) \tī´ ē\. Chinook Jargon <ty´-ee> [táyi] 'chief, boss', from Nootka /taayii/ 'older brother, senior' (McArthur 1992; D. Kinkade p.c.). The placename **Tyee** also occurs in Alaska (Bradfield Canal A-5), Idaho (Boise Co.), and Wash. (Chelan Co.).

TYENDE Creek (Ariz., Apache Co.). From Navajo (Athabaskan) *téé'ndééh* '(animals) fall into the water' (Wilson 1995). A related placename is **Kayenta** (Ariz., Navajo Co.).

TYEWHOPPETY (Ky., Todd Co.) \tī hwop´ ə tē\. Perhaps from a Shawnee (Algonquian) word meaning 'place of no return' (Rennick 1984). Possibly related names are **Tywappity** (Mo., Mississippi Co.) and **Zewapeta** (Mo., Scott Co.).

TYGEE Creek (Idaho, Caribou Co.) \tī´ jē\. Said to be named for a Bannock (Numic) leader whose name was also written <Tyhee, Terghee>

(Boone 1988; Urbanek 1974). The probably related placename **Tygee** in Wyo. (Lincoln Co.) is reported as being pronounced \tī´ gē\. Other probably related placenames are **Targhee** (Idaho, Fremont Co.) and **Tyhee** (Idaho, Bannock Co.).

TYGH Valley (Ore., Wasco Co.) \tī\. From the Sahaptin placename /táyx̣/ (McArthur 1992; D. Kinkade p.c.).

TYHEE (Idaho, Bannock Co.) \tī´ hē\. Named for a Bannock (Numic) leader; the term is said to mean 'swift' (Boone 1988). Probably related placenames are **Targhee** (Idaho, Fremont Co.) and **Tygee Creek** (Idaho, Caribou Co.).

TYMOCHTEE (Ohio, Wyandot Co.) \tī mok´ tē\. Said to be Wyandot (Iroquoian) for 'the stream around the plains' (Miller 1996).

TYNBITO Spring (N.Mex., McKinley Co.). From Navajo (Athabaskan), perhaps from *tin bito'* 'the spring of ice', from *tin* 'ice', *bi-* 'its', and *to'* 'water, spring' (A. Wilson p.c.).

TYONEK (Alaska, Tyonek A-4) \tī ō´ nik\. From Dena'ina (Athabaskan) *tubughnenq'* 'beach land', containing *nen* 'land' (Kari and Fall 1987:45).

TYONE River (Alaska, Talkeetna Mountains C-1). The name was reported in 1906; it is said to be an "Alaska jargon word for 'chief'" (Orth 1967); cf. Chinook Jargon **Tyee** 'chief'.

TYONESTA (Pa., Forest Co.). A variant of **Tionesta**; see above.

TYUONYI (N.Mex., Sandoval Co.) \chō´ nyē\. From the Cochiti (Keresan) placename [tyo'onye], not necessary related to [tyú'uni] 'pottery' (Harrington 1916; I. Davis p.c.).

TYWAPPITY Township (Mo., Mississippi Co.) \tī wä´ pi tē, tə wä´ pi tē\. Perhaps from Shawnee (Algonquian), meaning 'place of no return' (Ramsay 1952; Rennick 1984). Possibly related placenames are **Tyewhoppety** (Ky., Todd Co.) and **Zewapeta** (Mo., Scott Co.).

TZABACO (Calif., Sonoma Co.). The name of the Spanish land grant probably referred to a Coast Miwok subgroup, perhaps meaning 'sweat people' (Gudde 1998).

TZUSE Shoal (Alaska, Yakutat C-5). The Tlingit name was published in 1959 (Orth 1967).

U

UALIK Lake (Alaska, Goodnews Bay A-2) \yōō´ ə lik\. The Yupik (Eskimo) name was recorded in 1898 as <Oaleek> (Orth 1967).

UBEHEBE Peak (Calif., Inyo Co.) \yōō bē hē´ bē\. Perhaps from Owens Valley Paiute (Numic) /hibi-bici/ 'woman's breasts' (Gudde 1998).

UBLUTUOCH River (Alaska, Harrison Bay B-3). The Iñupiaq (Eskimo) name, reported in 1951, is said to mean 'fat fish' (Orth 1967).

UCETA Yard (Fla., Hillsborough Co.). This represents the name of a sixteenth-century Timucua leader, also written *Ocita, Ecita* (Read 1934).

UCHEE Creek (Ga., Columbia Co.) \ōō´ chē, yōō´ chē\. This represents the name of a tribe also known as **Yuchi,** politically associated with the Muskogee people but speaking a separate language (Goff 1975); they originally lived in Ga., but their descendants are now in Okla. The Muskogee form of the name is *yocce* /yó:čči/ (Martin and Mauldin 2000). Related placenames are **Eucha** (Okla., Delaware Co.) and **Euchee Valley** (Fla., Walton Co.).

UCHUGRAK Hills (Alaska, Misheguk Mtn. A-5). The Iñupiaq (Eskimo) term, reported in 1956, is said to mean 'old vulva' (Orth 1967); cf. *utchuk* 'vulva' (Webster and Zibell 1970).

UCOLO (Utah, San Juan Co.). Coined by combining elements from the names **Utah** and Colorado (Van Cott 1990).

UDAGAK Strait (Alaska, Unalaska B-1). From Aleut *udagax* 'going out in the open sea' (Bergsland 1994).

UDAK, Cape (Alaska, Samalga Island D-3). From Aleut *udax* 'two bays', referring to Traders

Cove; this is the dual form of *udax̂* 'bay'. The Aleut name for the cape is *sax̂ax* 'big scarp', from *sax̂* 'scarp, steep promontory' (Bergsland 1994). A related name is **Udamak Cove** (Alaska, Unalaska B-3), Aleut *udamax* 'large bay', from *udax̂* 'bay' (Bergsland 1994). Another probably related name is **Udamat Bay** (Alaska, Unalaska C-1), reported in 1888 (Orth 1967).

UDRIVIK, Lake (Alaska, Killik River C-2). The Iñupiaq (Eskimo) name was reported in 1956 (Orth 1967).

UEBRA (Mont., Garfield Co.). Said to be a garbling and shortening of **Nebraska** (Cheney 1984); see above.

U-FISH Creek (Calif., Siskiyou Co.) \yo͞o´ fish\. Karuk *yufísh-thuuf* 'salt creek', from *yúfish* 'salt' plus *thúuf* 'creek' (Gudde 1998).

UGADAGA Bay (Alaska, Unalaska C-2). From the Aleut placename *uugadaga* (Bergsland 1994).

UGAIUSHAK Island (Alaska, Sutwik Island D-3). From Alutiiq (Eskimo), published in 1827 (Orth 1967).

UGAK Bay (Alaska, Kodiak B-3). From Aleut *qugax̂* 'shaman's assistant spirit' (Orth 1967; Bergsland 1994).

UGAKLIK River (Alaska, Bethel A-8). The Yupik (Eskimo) name was reported in 1951 (Orth 1967).

UGALAK Creek (Alaska, Point Hope A-2). The Iñupiaq (Eskimo) name was reported in 1962 as <Ooghaluk> (Orth 1967).

UGAMAK Island (Alaska, Unimak A-3) From the Aleut placename *ugangax̂* (Bergsland 1994).

UGANIK (Alaska, Kodiak D-5) \yo͞o´ gə nik\. The Alutiiq (Eskimo) name was reported in 1805 as <Oohanick> (Orth 1967).

UGASHIK (Alaska, Ugashik C-5) \yo͞o gash´ ik\. The Yupik (Eskimo) name was reported in 1828 as <Ougatchik> (Orth 1967).

UGCHIRNAK, Mount (Alaska, Nunivak Island C-1). The Yupik (Eskimo) name, obtained is 1951, is said to mean 'it goes on top' (Orth 1967).

UGIDAK Island (Alaska, Gareloi Island B-2). The Aleut placename is said to refer to 'steep cliffs' (Bergsland 1994).

UGNURAVIK River (Alaska, Beechey Point B-5). The Iñupiaq (Eskimo) name is *uŋuraġvik* 'place where animals are driven' (L. Kaplan p.c.).

UGRURAK Bluff (Alaska, Noatak B-4). The Iñupiaq (Eskimo) name is *uġruuraq* 'little piece of blubber' (L. Kaplan p.c.).

UHANA'A (N.Mex., Cibola Co.). The Zuni name of a sacred spring (Ferguson and Hart 1985).

UHS KUG (Ariz., Pima Co.). From O'odham (Piman) *u:s ke:k*, lit. 'stick standing' (J. Hill p.c.).

UINKARET Mountains (Ariz., Mohave Co.). From Southern Paiute (Numic) /yɨpinkatɨtɨ/ [yɨvínkarɨRƗ] 'Mt. Trumbull', lit. 'pine peak' (*HNAI* 11:396); cf. /yɨpim-pɨ/ [yɨvímpƗ] 'pine tree', /katɨtɨ/ [qarɨ́RƗ] 'peak', from /katɨ-/ 'to sit' (Sapir 1930).

UINTA Range (Utah, Colo.) \yo͞o in´ tə\. From Northern Ute (Numic) /yɨvintɨ/ [yɨvíntƗ] 'pine canyon-mouth' (Bright 1993). The spelling **Uintah** also occurs.

UIVAKSAK Creek (Alaska, Howard Pass B-5). The Iñupiaq (Eskimo) name is *uivaqsaat* 'follow the bend' (Burch 1998); cf. *uivaqsaaq-* 'to round a point of land, when traveling by boat' (MacLean 1980).

UKAK (Alaska, Baird Inlet C-8). The Yupik (Eskimo) name was reported in 1878 as <Ookagamiut>, with the ending *-miut* 'people' (Orth 1967). Perhaps related is the name of the **Ukak River** (Alaska, Mt. Katmai C-5), reported in 1917, probably from Alutiiq (Eskimo) (Orth 1967).

UKALIKCHIK (Alaska, Hooper Bay B-1). The Yupik (Eskimo) name was reported in 1951 (Orth 1967).

UKAWUTNI Creek (Alaska, Ruby D-4). The Koyukon (Athabaskan) name was reported in 1869 (Orth 1967).

UKFIGAG Creek (Alaska, Goodnews Bay A-7). The Yupik (Eskimo) name, said to mean 'little trees', was reported around 1951 (Orth 1967); cf. *uqvik* 'tree, willow' (Jacobson 1984).

UKIAH (Calif., Mendocino Co.) \yo͞o kī´ ə\. Earlier written <Yokaya>, from Central Pomo /yó-qhaaya/, lit. 'south valley' (Gudde 1998).

UKINREK Crater (Alaska, Ugashik D-2). The Yupik (Eskimo) name is said to mean 'two holes' (Orth 1967); cf. *ukinek* 'hole' (Jacobson 1984).

UKINYAK Creek (Alaska, Point Hope C-2). The Iñupiaq (Eskimo) name, recorded in 1956, is said to mean 'cut', because "the stream cuts into the mountains" (Orth 1967).

UKIVOK (Alaska, Nome D-7) \yo͞o kē´ vok, o͞o´ kē vuk\. The Iñupiaq (Eskimo) name was reported in 1880 as <Ookivok> (Orth 1967).

UKNAVIK (Alaska, Russian Mission B-5). The Yupik (Eskimo) name was recorded in 1893 as <Ougavik> (Orth 1967).

UKONOM Creek (Calif., Siskiyou Co.) \yo͞o´ kə nom\. From the Karuk village *yuhnaam,* which may be from *yu-* 'downriver' plus *naam* 'a flat' (Gudde 1998).

UKPIKSUK (Alaska, Noatak D-6). Probably Iñupiaq (Eskimo) *uqpiksuuq* 'lots of willows,' from *uqpik* 'willow' (L. Kaplan p.c.).

UKSHIVIK (Alaska, Kodiak A-5). The Alutiiq (Eskimo) name, recorded in 1849, may mean 'winter village' (Orth 1967); cf. *uksuq* 'winter' (Leer 1978).

ULAH (Ill., Henry Co.) \yo͞o´ lə\. Probably named for the heroine of a pseudo-Indian legend, invented by whites (Vogel 1963).

ULAKAIA Hill (Alaska, Pribilof Islands A-2). From Aleut *ulax̂* 'house' plus *qayax̂* 'high' (Orth 1967; Bergsland 1994).

ULAK Island (Alaska, Atka C-6) \o͞o´ lək\. From the Aleut placename *uulax* (Bergsland 1994). Of separate origin, on the Gareloi Island A-3 quadrangle, is **Ulak Island** \yo͞o´ lək\, from Aleut *yuulax̂,* perhaps meaning 'creased, wrinkled'; cf. *yun* 'pleats, creases' (Bergsland 1994).

ULAKTA Head (Alaska, Unalaska C-2). The Aleut name, reported in 1869, is said to be an accidental mistranscription of <Udakta> 'Dutch Harbor' (Orth 1967).

ULANEAK Creek (Alaska, Ambler River B-2). The Iñupiaq (Eskimo) name is said to mean 'wrong route' or 'blind pass' (Orth 1967).

ULATIS Creek (Calif., Solano Co.) \yo͞o lat´ is\. A shortening of <Ululatos>, a term applied by the Spanish to a Patwin (Wintuan) subgroup (Gudde 1998).

ULCOHATCHEE Creek (Ga., Crawford Co.). From Muskogee *orko-hvcce* 'pawpaw stream', from *orko* /óɬko/ 'pawpaw' plus *hvcce* /háčči/ 'stream' (Read 1949–50; Martin and Mauldin 2000).

ULIAGA Pass (Alaska, Umnak A-6). From the Aleut placename *ulaĝa,* cf. *hulax̂, ulax̂* 'bearberry' (Bergsland 1994).

ULISTAC (Calif., Santa Clara Co.) \o͞o li stäk\. The name of the Mexican land grant dated 1845 is from an Ohlone (Costanoan) placename, perhap from <uli, uri> 'head, hair' plus <-tak> 'place' (Gudde 1998).

ULOKAK (Alaska, Sleetmute C-7). Probably from Yupik (Eskimo) *uluarkaq* 'material for an *ulu,* a woman's semicircular knife' (*HNAI* 6:600). A related name is that of **Ulokat Hills** (Marshall D-8), reported in 1899 (Orth 1967). Other related Alaska names include **Uluksrak Bluff** (Umiat C-3) and **Uluruk Point** (Nunivak Island C-1).

ULPINOS (Calif., Solano Co.) \o͞ol pē´ nōs\. The Spanish plural form, also written <Julpones>, refers to a Patwin (Wintuan) subgroup (Gudde 1998).

ULUKLUK Creek (Alaska, Candle D-3). The Iñupiaq (Eskimo) name was reported in 1949 (Orth 1967).

ULUKSIAN Creek (Alaska, Baird Mountains D-3). The Iñupiaq (Eskimo) name is *uliksaun* 'hammerstone' (Burch 1998).

ULUKSRAK Bluff (Alaska, Umiat C-3). The Iñupiaq (Eskimo) name is *uluksraq* 'material for an *ulu*, a woman's semicircular knife' (Orth 1967; MacLean 1980). Probably related Alaska placenames include **Ulokak** (Sleetmute C-7) and **Uluruk Point** (Nunivak Island-C-1).

ULURUK Point (Alaska, Nunivak Island C-1). The Yupik (Eskimo) name probably means 'old *ulu*', a woman's semicircular knife (Orth 1967). Related Alaska placenames include **Ulokak** (Sleetmute C-7) and **Uluksrak Bluff** (Umiat C-3).

UMAGATSIAK Hill (Alaska, Noatak C-4). The Iñupiaq (Eskimo) name is *uummagatchiaq,* perhaps meaning 'new heart' (Burch 1998; Orth 1967); cf. *uumman* 'heart' (MacLean 1980). A probably related name is **Umarachek Peak** (Alaska, Noatak D-6).

UMAGVIRAK (Alaska, Noatak C-5). The Iñupiaq (Eskimo) name was recorded in 1966 (Orth 1967).

UMAK Island (Alaska, Adak C-1). From Aleut *uhmax̂, luhmax̂* 'flank' (Bergsland 1994).

UMANANGULA Bluffs (Alaska, Pribilof Islands A-2). The Aleut name, reported in 1903, is said to mean 'cannot be seen' (Orth 1967).

UMAPINE (Ore., Umatilla Co.) \yo͞o´ mə pīn\. Named for a Cayuse (Sahaptian) leader; but the term itself is from Nez Perce (Sahaptian) /hiyúumepeyme/ 'grizzly-bear toes', containing /hiyúum/ 'grizzly bear' and /héepeyme/ 'toes' (Aoki 1994; D. Kinkade p.c.).

UMARACHEK Peak (Alaska, Noatak D-6). The Iñupiaq (Eskimo) name may be a variant of **Umagatsiak**, above.

UMATILLA County (Ore.) \yo͞o mə til´ ə\. From Sahaptin /ímatilam/ 'lots of rocks, rocky bottom', the name of a village (McArthur 1992; D. Kinkade p.c.). The placename **Umatilla** also occurs in Idaho (Idaho Co.) and Wash. (Benton Co.) and as a transfer name in Fla. (Lake Co.).

UMBAGOG Lake (Maine, Oxford Co.; N.H., Coös Co.) \o͞om bā´ gog, um bā´ gog, um´ bə gog\. Western Abenaki (Algonquian) *wôbagok* [wą̄bagok] 'at the clear lake'; cf. *wôba* 'it is white water', *wôbi* 'white' (Day 1994–95).

UMGA Island (Alaska, False Pass D-3). The Aleut name was reported in 1847 (Orth 1967).

UMIAK Bend (Alaska, Noatak D-5) \o͞o´ mē ak\. From Iñupiak (Eskimo) *umiaq* 'skin boat, women's boat' (*RHD* 1987). A related name is **Umiat** (Alaska, Umiat B-4) \o͞o´ mē at\ 'skin boats', the plural of *umiaq* (Orth 1967). Also related is **Ungyat Point** (Alaska, St. Lawrence C-6), from the Yupik (Eskimo) for 'boats' (Orth 1967).

UMKUMIUT (Alaska, Nunivak Island B-1) \o͞om´ kə myo͞ot\. The Yupik (Eskimo) name was reported in 1950 (Orth 1967).

UMLA Island (Alaska, False Pass B-2). The Aleut name was reported in 1901 (Orth 1967).

UMNAK Island (Alaska, Umnak A-2) \yo͞om´ nak, o͞om´ nak\. From the Aleut placename *umnax, unmax,* perhaps from *un-* 'out there on the sea' (Bergsland 1994).

UMPACHENE River (Mass., Berkshire Co.). Named after a Mahican (Algonquian) leader and translated as 'conqueror' (Huden 1962).

UMPCOOS Ridge (Ore., Coos Co.) \ump´ ko͞os\. Apparently coined from elements in the names **Umpqua River** (Ore., Douglas Co.) and **Coos County** (Ore.) (D. Kinkade p.c.).

UMPQUA River (Ore., Douglas Co.) \ump´ kwô\. From Tututni (Athabaskan) /ąkwa/ 'the Upper Umpqua River' (McArthur 1992; D. Kinkade p.c.).

UMPTANUM (Wash., Kittitas Co.) \ump tā´ nəm\. From Sahaptin, probably /ɨmtanam/, possibly 'taste' or 'mouth full', based on /ɨm/ 'mouth' (Hitchman 1985; D. Kinkade p.c.). A variant is **Umtanum.**

UMTUCH, Chief (Wash., Clark Co.). Named for a Sahaptin leader (D. Kinkade p.c.). A related form is **Lake Umtux** (Wash., Skamania Co.).

UMUNHUM, Mount (Calif., Santa Clara Co.) \yo͞o´ mə num\. Perhaps from a Costanoan word for 'hummingbird' (Gudde 1998).

UNADILLA (N.Y., Otsego Co.) \yo͞o nə dil´ ə, un´ ə dil ə\. Said to be Oneida (Iroquoian), meaning 'place of meeting' (Beauchamp 1907). The name also occurs as a transfer in Ga. (Dooly Co.) and Mich. (Livingston Co.).

UNAKA (N.C., Cherokee Co.) \yo͞o nā´ kə\. From Cherokee (Iroquoian) /uuneega/ 'white' (Powell 1968; B. Rudes p.c.). The placename also occurs in Tenn., in **Unicoi County**; see below.

UNAKSERAK River (Alaska, Survey Pass C-3). The Iñupiaq (Eskimo) name is probably *unaq-siuraq* 'little piece of wood' (L. Kaplan p.c.).

UNAKWIK Inlet (Alaska, Anchorage A-2). The Alutiiq (Eskimo) name was recorded in 1898 (Orth 1967).

UNALAKLEET (Alaska, Unalakleet D-4) \yo͞o´ nə lə klēt\. This settlement is on the boundary between the two major Eskimo languages, Yupik and Iñupiaq, so its name has two forms: Yupik *ungalaqliit,* from *ungalaq* 'south', so called from an Inupiaq viewpoint because it is their southernmost village (Jacobson 1984); and Iñupiaq *uŋallaqłiit,* from *uŋalak, uŋallaq* 'southwesterly wind' (Webster and Zibell 1970).

UNALASKA (Alaska, Unalaska C-2) \un ə las´ kə\. A shortening of Aleut *nawan-alaxsxa* 'the mainland along there', referring to **Unalaska Island;** cf. *nawa* 'along there', *alaxsxa* 'mainland' (Bergsland 1994). The latter element, referring to the Alaskan Peninsula, also gives its name to the state of **Alaska.** Another related placename is **Onalaska** (Wis., Lacrosse Co.).

UNALGA Island (Alaska, Unalaska C-1). Aleut *unalĝa* 'the seaward one', from *una* 'out there on the sea' (Bergsland 1994). Another island (Alaska, Gareloi Island B-4) has the same name.

UNALUK River (Alaska, Hagemeister Island D-5). The Yupik (Eskimo) name was reported in 1938 (Orth 1967).

UNAMI Creek (Pa., Montgomery Co.) \o͞o nä´ mē\. The term refers to a division of the Delaware (Algonquian) people. It comes from Munsee Delaware /wə̆ná:mi:w/ or from Unalachtigo Delaware /wəna:mi:w/, and means 'person from downriver' (*HNAI* 15:236–37). The placename **Unami** also occurs in N.J. (Union Co.).

UNANA, Mount (Alaska, Yakutat D-4). The Tlingit name was reported in 1892 (Orth 1967).

UNANGASHAK River (Alaska, Chignik C-4). The Yupik (Eskimo) name was reported in 1880 as <Oonongashik> (Orth 1967).

UNATLOTLY Creek (Alaska, Bettles C-6). The Koyukon (Athabaskan) name is of unclear derivation (Orth 1967).

UNA VIDA, Pueblo (N.Mex., San Juan Co.). This ancient Indian village is called in Spanish 'one life', perhaps referring to a living tree stump growing in the archaeological site (Julyan 1998).

UNAVIKSHAK Island (Alaska, Sutwik Island B-6). The Alutiiq (Eskimo) name was published in 1847 as <Unavikhshak> (Orth 1967).

UNAWATTI Creek (Ga., Franklin Co.) \yo͞o nə wä tē\. The name is said to be Cherokee (Iroquoian) <unawatti> 'a flat creek' (i.e., a shallow stream); or perhaps from an earlier English <Yonawattee>, reflecting Cherokee <yonawattee> 'old bear', from *yona* 'bear' plus *uweti* 'old' (Goff 1975; Feeling 1975).

UNAWEEP Canyon (Colo., Mesa Co.) \yo͞o´ nə wēp\. From Ute (Numic) *kuná-wiiyapi* 'fire canyon', because of the red color (Bright 1993).

UNCANOONUC Mountains (N.H., Hillsborough Co.) \un kə no͞o´ nək\. From Abenaki (Algonquian), perhaps meaning 'a breast' (Huden 1962); cf. *nonoz* 'nipple' (Day 1994–95).

UNCAS \ung´ kəs\. The name of a seventeenth-century Mohegan (SNEng. Algonquian) leader, derived from <wonkus> 'fox' (Huden 1962; *HNAI* 15:90); the name was made well known through James Fenimore Cooper's novel *The Last of the Mohicans*. As a placename, **Uncas** occurs in many states (e.g., Conn., New London Co.; Mass., Norfolk Co.; and N.Y., Warren Co.).

UNCATENA Island (Mass., Dukes Co.). From SNEng. Algonquian, perhaps meaning 'like a hill' (Huden 1962).

UNCHACHOGUE Creek (N.Y., Suffolk Co.) \ung´ kə chog\. The SNEng. Algonquian name was earlier written <Uncachaug, Unquachage>, of unclear derivation (Beauchamp 1907).

UNCHUKA (Okla., Coal Co.) \un cho͞o´ kə\. From Choctaw (Muskogean) *ą-chokka* 'my house' (Shirk 1974; P. Munro p.c.).

UNCOA (Conn., Fairfield Co.). From SNEng. Algonquian, perhaps meaning 'beyond' (Trumbull 1881; Huden 1962).

UNCOMPAHGRE River (Colo., Delta Co.) \un kəm pä´ grē\. Spanish records of 1776 show this as *Ancapagari,* translated 'red lake'. A present-day Southern Ute (Numic) pronunciation is /aká-paagarɨr/, containing /aká(-gar)/ 'red' and /páagarɨr/ 'lake' (Bright 1993). The name **Uncompahgre** occurs as a transfer in Alaska (Charley River A-4).

UNEVA Peak (Colo., Summit Co.) \yo͞o nē´ və\. Perhaps from Ute (Numic) *yunáv* 'mountainous country' (Bright 1993).

UNGA (Alaska, Port Moller A-2) \ung´ gə\. A shortening of Aleut *uĝnaasaqax̂* 'warmed, sheltered'; cf. *uĝnat-, uĝnasix* 'to warm oneself', *ħuĝnaa, uĝnaa* 'lee side' (Bergsland 1994).

UNGALAK, Mount (Alaska, Russian Mission C-7). The Yupik (Eskimo) name was reported in 1948 (Orth 1967).

UNGALIK River (Alaska, Norton Bay C-4) \ung gä´ lik\. The name ws reported in 1844 as <Ounag-touli> (Orth 1967).

UNGALIKTHLUK (Alaska, Hagemeister Island D-1). The Yupik (Eskimo) name was reported in 1948 (Orth 1967).

UNGINA WONGO (Nev., Elko Co.). The Shoshoni (Numic) name apparently contains /wonko-pin/ 'pine tree' (J. McLaughlin p.c.).

UNGLUAYAGAT, Mount (Alaska, Goodnews Bay B-5). The Yupik (Eskimo) name, obtained in 1951, is said to mean 'little nest' (Orth 1967); cf. *unglu* 'nest' (Jacobson 1984).

UNGULUNGWAK Hill (Alaska, Kwiguk B-5). The Yupik (Eskimo) name was obtained in 1899 (Orth 1967).

UNGYAT Point (Alaska, St. Lawrence C-6). The St. Lawrence Island Yupik (Eskimo) name is *angyat* 'boats'. A probably related name is **Umiat** (Alaska, Umiat B-4), from the corresponding Iñupiaq form meaning 'boats'.

UNICOI County (Tenn.) \yo͞o´ ni koi\. From Cherokee (Iroquoian) *unega* 'white' (Krakow 1975; Feeling 1975). The placename Unicoi also occurs in Ga. (White Co.). A related name is **Unaka** (N.C., Cherokee Co.).

UNIKTALI Bay (Alaska, Unalaska C-2). From the Aleut placename *ungixtála* (Bergsland 1994).

UNIMAK Bight (Alaska, Unimak C-1) \yo͞o´ ni mak\. From the Aleut placename *unimax* (Bergsland 1994).

UNKAR Creek (Ariz., Coconino Co.) \un´ kär\. Perhaps from Southern Paiute (Numic), meaning 'red creek' (Granger 1983); cf. /anka-/ 'red' (Sapir 1930).

UNKETY Brook (Mass., Middlesex Co.) \ung´ kə tē\. From SNEng. Algonquian, perhaps meaning 'boundary' (Huden 1962).

UNKPAPA Peak (S.Dak., Custer Co.) \o͝ongk´ pä pə\. From /hų̃kpapha/, a subgroup of the Teton or Lakhota (Siouan) Indians (Sneve 1973). A more familiar form of the name is **Hunkpapa Peak** (S.Dak., Custer Co.).

UNMANOKUK Creek (Alaska, Selawik D-3). The Iñupiaq (Eskimo) name was obtained in 1955 (Orth 1967).

UNQUA Point (N.Y., Nassau Co.) \ung´ kwə\. Earlier written <Onqua, Unkway> (etc.); perhaps from Munsee Delaware (Algonquian), meaning 'beyond' (Beauchamp 1907).

UNQUITY Brook (Mass., Norfolk Co.). From SNEng. Algonquian, perhaps meaning 'boundary' (Huden 1962).

UNQUOMONK Brook (Mass., Bristol Co.). From SNEng. Algonquian, perhaps meaning 'at the end place' (Huden 1962).

UNROOJITHOK Lake (Alaska, Nunivak Island A-6). The Yupik (Eskimo) name, reported in 1949, is said to mean 'stomach' (Orth 1967).

UNSHAGI Ruin (N.Mex., Sandoval Co.). Jemez (Tanoan) /unšaagi/ 'place surrounded by cedar trees', with /un/ 'cedar', /šaa/ 'to surround', and /-gi / 'place' (Y. Yumitani p.c.).

UNUK River (Alaska, Bradfield Canal A-4). The Tlingit name was recorded in 1906 as <Junuk> (Orth 1967).

UPAPAK Point (Alaska, St. Lawrence D-6). From Yupik (Eskimo) <apapak> 'potlatch' (Orth 1967).

UPATOI (Ga., Muscogee Co.) \yōō´ pə toi\. Earlier written <au-put-taue, apatoi> (etc.), translated 'a covering' (Goff 1975); cf. Muskogee *vpvtake* /apatá:ki/ 'up against a hill', *vpvtvtakēn* /apatatáki:n/ 'up against each other' (Martin and Mauldin 2000). A possibly related placename is **Cohobadiah Creek** (Ala., Randolph Co.) from *kohv-apvtake* /koha-apatá:ki/ 'cane up against a hill' (Martin and Mauldin 2000).

UPKUAROK Creek (Alaska, Teller D-4). The Iñupiaq (Eskimo) name was published in 1956 (Orth 1967).

UPNUK Lake (Alaska, Teller D-4) The Yupik (Eskimo) name was reported in 1915 (Orth 1967).

UPPER KUSKOKWIM \kus´ kō kwim\. The term is now often used to refer to the Athabaskan people and language of the upper Kuskokwim River drainage, in western Alaska, otherwise known as **Kolchan.** See also **Kuskokwim River.**

UQUALLA Point (Ariz., Coconino Co.) \ōō´ kwä lə, uk´ wä lə\. The surname of a Havasupai (Yuman) family that lives in the area (Granger 1983; L. Hinton p.c.).

URADO (Utah, San Juan Co.). The name was coined from elements of **Utah** and *Colorado* (Van Cott 1990).

URAHAW Swamp (N.C., Northampton Co.). Probably an Indian name, but the source language has not been identified (Powell 1968).

URANATINA River (Alaska, Valdez B-2). From Ahta (Athabaskan) *ighenetina'* 'bend creek', with *-na'* 'stream' (Kari 1983:4).

URUMANGNAK River (Alaska, Baird Inlet C-7). The Yupik (Eskimo) name, reported in 1949, is said to mean 'very warm' (Orth 1967); cf. *maqaq* 'warmth', *matneq* 'warmth' (Jacobson 1984).

USAL (Calif., Mendocino Co.) \yōō´ sôl\. From Northern Pomo /yoosal/, perhaps containing /yoo/ 'south' (Gudde 1998).

USHAGAT Island (Alaska, Afognak D-1). The name is perhaps from Aleut, published in 1852 (Orth 1967).

USHK Point (Alaska, Sitka C-5). The Tlingit name was recorded in 1895 (Orth 1967).

USKI (Alaska, Kodiak D-2). Perhaps from Aleut *usxix̂* 'willow bush' (Orth 1967; Bergsland 1994), although the local population speaks the Alutiiq (Eskimo) language.

USQUEPAUG (R.I., Washington Co.). SNEng. Algonquian, perhaps meaning 'at the end of the pond' (Huden 1962).

USTANALI (Ga., Franklin Co.). The Cherokee (Iroquoian) name, which as also been written <Ustanali, Estanola> (etc.), may mean 'shoaly river' (Goff 1975). Related placenames are **Eastanola** (Ga., Stephens Co.) and **Oostanaula** (Ga., Gordon Co.).

USTAY River (Alaska, Yakutat A-3). The Tlingit name was reported in 1901 (Orth 1967).

USUKTUK River (Alaska, Meade River C-3). Derived from Iñupiaq (Eskimo) <esuktu> 'penis', reported in 1885 (Orth 1967); cf. *usuk* 'penis' (Webster and Zibell 1970).

UTAH \yo͞o´ tô\. From Spanish *yuta,* applied to the Ute (Numic) people; this was perhaps a borrowing from Western Apache (Athabaskan) *yúdah* 'high' (i.e., 'in the mountains') (*HNAI* 11:364; Bray 1998). As a placename, **Utah** occurs in Alaska (Eagle C-2), Idaho (Idaho Co.), and Ill. (Warren Co.). A related name is **Utahn** (Utah, Duchesne Co.) \yo͞o´ tän\, an English derivative from **Utah,** designating a person from the state (Van Cott 1990). Related terms include **Ute** (see below), **Utida** (Utah, Cache Co.), and **Uvada** (Utah, Iron Co.).

UTAKAHT Slough (Alaska, Kwiguk C-5). The Yupik (Eskimo) name was obtained in 1899 (Orth 1967).

UTALUG, Cape (Alaska, Atka C-1). Aleut *utalux̂,* from *ut-* 'to go down to the beach' (Bergsland 1994).

UTE \yo͞ot\. The name of Numic (Uto-Aztecan) people, living in Colo. and Utah; they are now often distinguished as the Northern Utes, in northern Utah, and the Southern Utes, in southern Colo. The term is from Spanish *yuta,* perhaps a borrowing from Western Apache *yúdah* 'high' (i.e., 'in the mountains') (*HNAI* 11:364; Bray 1998). As a placename, **Ute** occurs in Colo. (Montrose Co.), N.Mex. (Mora Co.), and Utah (Daggett Co.) and as a transfer in others states (e.g., Iowa, Monon Co.; and Kans., Sheridan Co.). Related terms include **Utah** (see above), **Utida** (Utah, Cache Co.), and **Uvada** (Utah, Iron Co.).

UTEVAK (Ariz., Pima Co.). From O'odham (Piman) *uḍuwhag* 'cat-tail reed' (Saxton et al. 1983:135; J. Hill p.c.).

UTIDA (Utah, Cache Co.). A coinage made by combining parts of the placenames **Utah** and **Idaho**.

UTKUSIKRAK Hill (Alaska, Noatak D-7). The Iñupiaq (Eskimo) name is *utkusigraq* 'place where there is pottery clay' (Burch 1998); cf. *utkusik* 'cooking pot' (MacLean 1980).

UTOWANA Lake (N.Y., Hamilton Co.) \yo͞o tō wä´ nə\. Perhaps from Onondaga (Iroquoian) /odo'dowaanɛ/ 'big wave', containing /-owanɛ-/ 'be large' (Beauchamp 1907; H. Woodbury p.c.).

UTOY Creek (Ga., Fulton Co.). Named for an Indian subgroup whose language has not been identified; the term has been translated as 'final people' (Krakow 1975).

UTSALADY (Wash., Snohomish Co.) \ut sə lad´ ē\. From the Lushootseed (Salishan) placename /ʔəcəládiʔ/, which is not analyzable (Hitchman 1985; D. Kinkade p.c.).

UTSAYANTHA Lake (N.Y., Schoharie Co.) \o͝ot si yan´ thə\. Also written <Ote-se-ont-e-o>, said to be from an Iroquoian language, meaning 'beautiful spring' (Beauchamp 1907).

UTUKAKARVIK (Alaska, Marshall D-8). The Yupik (Eskimo) name, reported in 1948, is said to mean 'where slate for making *ulus* is found', referring to the women's semicircular knives (Orth 1967).

UTUKOK (Alaska, Wainwright A-6) \o͞o to͞o´ kok\. From Iñupiaq (Eskimo) *utuqqaq* 'old thing' (Orth 1967; L. Kaplan p.c.).

UVADA (Utah, Iron Co.). A coinage using elements from the placenames **Utah** and *Nevada* (Van Cott 1990).

UVGOON Creek (Alaska, Noatak C-1). The Iñupiaq (Eskimo) name may be from *avgun* 'boundary' (L. Kaplan p.c.). A related placename is **Avgun River** (Alaska, Noatak D-1).

UWHARRIE (N.C., Montgomery Co.). From Catawban (Siouan) /wą̂ri:/ 'lance, spear' (Powell 1968; B. Rudes p.c.).

UWIK Slough (Alaska, St. Michael A-5). The Yupik (Eskimo) name was reported in 1899 as <Oowik> (Orth 1967).

UYAK (Alaska, Kodiak C-6) \o͞o´ yak\. The Alutiiq (Eskimo) name was reported in 1884 as <Ooiak> (Orth 1967).

UYAK Island (Alaska, Atka C-1). From the Aleut placename *uuyax* (Bergsland 1994).

UYAKTUROK Creek (Alaska, Point Hope C-1). The Iñupiaq (Eskimo) name was recorded in 1960 (Orth 1967).

UYARAKSIVIK Hill (Alaska, Noatak D-5). The Iñupiaq (Eskimo) name, reported in 1966, is said to mean 'where things are buried under stones' (Orth 1967); cf. *uyaġak* 'stone' (MacLean 1980).

UYON Lakes (Alaska, Baird Mountains D-3). The Iñupiaq (Eskimo) name was obtained in 1955 (Orth 1967).

V

VACAHANYANDE Mountain (Alaska, Black River C-4). The Gwich'in (Athabaskan) name was obtained in 1956 (Orth 1967).

VAKEEKALIK Creek (Alaska, Nunivak Island B-3). The Yupik (Eskimo) name was reported in 1937 (Orth 1967).

VANTICLESE Creek (Alaska, Christian D-1). The Gwich'in (Athabaskan) name is of unclear derivation (Orth 1967).

VEAHNA Creek (Alaska, Sleetmute C-7). Cf. Deg Hit'an (Athabaskan) *viyan* 'no' (J. Kari p.c.).

VEDAUWOO Glen (Wyo., Albany Co.) \vē´ də vo͞o\. From Arapaho (Algonquian) *bí:to'ówu'* 'earth' (Urbanek 1974; Salzmann 1983).

VENANGO County (Pa.) \və nang´ gō\. Probably from Delaware (Algonquian), perhaps reflecting <onenge, winingus> 'mink' (Donehoo 1928). A variant is **Wenango,** in the same county.

VENETIE (Alaska, Christian A-5) \vē´ nə tī, ven´ ə tī\. The Gwich'in (Athabaskan) placename is *vįįhtąįį* 'trail comes from hills' (Caulfield et al. 1980).

VERMILION or **VERMILLION.** The name refers to a type of reddish earth, used as pigment, and often equated with red ochre; it was widely used by Native Americans to decorate their faces and bodies. In many placenames, it corresponds to Indian words such as Ojibwa (Algonquian) <onaman> (Baraga 1880) and Dakota (Siouan) *įyą́-šaša* 'stone-red', from *į́yą* 'stone' and *šašá* 'red' (Riggs 1890). The English spelling **Vermilion** is used for a county in Ill. as well as for a place in Mich. (Chippewa Co.). The spelling **Vermillion** is used for places in Minn. (Dakota Co.), S.Dak. (Clay Co.), and Wis. (Barron Co.). In Ind. **Vermillion County** corresponds to reconstructed Potawatomi (Algonquian) */osaanaman/ 'bloodroot', a plant also used for a reddish pigment (McCafferty 2002).

VERSIPPI (N.Dak., Stark Co.). A blend of French *vert* 'green' and Ojibwa (Algonquian) *ziibi* 'river' (Wick 1988).

VETENJERLO Lakes (Alaska, Fort Yukon D-4). The Gwich'in (Athabaskan) name is of unclear derivation (Orth 1967).

VETTATRIN Lake (Alaska, Arctic B-2). The Gwich'in (Athabaskan) name was obtained in 1956 (Orth 1967).

VETTEKWI Lake (Alaska, Arctic A-3). The Gwich'in (Athabaskan) name was recorded in 1956 (Orth 1967).

VICKS Peak (N.Mex., Socorro Co.) \viks\. Named for the Apache leader **Victorio**; see **Victorio Mountains** below.

VICTOR (S.Dak., Roberts Co.). Named for Victor Renville, a man of mixed Sisseton Dakota (Siouan) and French ancestry who lived in the late nineteenth century (Sneve 1973).

VICTORIO Mountains (N.Mex., Luna Co.) \vik tôr´ ē ō\. The Spanish name of a Mimbreño Apache (Athabaskan) leader (Julyan 1998). It is said that he was known in Apache as *bidóóya*; the relation between the Spanish and the Apache forms is not clear (W. de Reuse p.c.). In Tex. (Culberson Co.), **Victorio Peak** is also named for the Apache warrior (BGN 7504).

VIENNA (Md., Dorchester Co.) \vī an´ ə, vē an´ ə\. Probably a popular etymology based on the initial syllables of <Unnacocassinon> or

<Vnnacocassinon>, a CAC Algonquian leader who lived in the seventeenth century (Kenny 1984).

VIEUX DESERT, Lac (Mich., Gogebic Co.; Wis., Vilas Co.). The French name, meaning 'lake [of the] old deserted-place', corresponds to Ojibwa <Ketekitiganing> 'old field place', because Indians once planted crops here (Vogel 1991); cf. *gete-* 'old', *gitigaan* 'field' (Nichols and Nyholm 1995).

VILLISCA (Iowa, Montgomery Co.). Also written <Villiska>, earlier <Valiska>; probably from Meskwaki (Algonquian) /wa:waneška:ha, wa:neška:/ 'rascal, naughty one, evil one', with *n* for earlier *l* (Vogel 1983; I. Goddard p.c.).

VINASALE (Alaska, McGrath C-6) \vē´ nə sāl, vē nə sal´ ē\. From the Deg Hit'an (Athabaskan) placename *venisale, minisale* (Kari 1999:85).

VIROQUA (Wis., Vernon Co.) \vī rō´ kwə\. Probably named for the heroine of a novel, *Viroqua; or, The Flower of the Ottawas,* published in 1848 (Vogel 1991).

VORZUI Mountain (Alaska, Arctic A-2). The Gwich'in (Athabaskan) name was obtained in 1956 (Orth 1967).

VUKPALIK Creek (Alaska, Taylor Mountains A-4). The Yupik (Eskimo) name was reported in 1931 (Orth 1967).

VUNDIK Lake (Alaska, Coleen B-6). The Gwich'in (Athabaskan) name is *vandik* 'edge of lake' (Caulfield et al. 1980). A possibly related placename is **Vunikth Lakes** (Alaska, Fort Yukon D-5). Other possibly related Alaska names include **Vunittsieh Lakes** (Chandalar C-1); **Vunlui Lake** (Fort Yukon D-6); **Vunvekottlui Lake** (Black River A-2); and **Vunzik Lake** (Fort Yukon D-6). Also perhaps related is **Venetie**; see above.

W

WAACKAACK Creek (N.J., Monmouth Co.) \wā´ kāk\. Probably from Delaware (Algonquian), but of unclear derivation (Becker 1964). A variant spelling is **Waycake Creek.**

WAADAH Island (Wash., Clallam Co.) \wə had´ ə, wä yad´ ə\. From the Makah (Nootkan) placename /waʔadʔa/, perhaps meaning 'echo island' (W. Jacobsen p.c.). Variant spellings are **Waada** and **Waaddah.**

WAATCH (Wash., Clallam Co.) \wä´ yach\. From the Makah (Nootkan) village name /waʔač'/, said to mean 'bundling up cedar to make a torch' (W. Jacobsen p.c.).

WABAKWA Ruin (N.Mex., Sandoval Co.). From the Jemez (Tanoan) placename *waabakwa,* with *-kwa* 'place' (Y. Yumitani p.c.).

WABAN (Mass., Middlesex Co.) \wô´ ban\. Name of a Massachusett (SNEng. Algonguian) leader and early convert; probably reflecting <waban> 'wind' (Huden 1962; W. Cowan p.c.). The name **Lake Waban** occurs in Ore. (Klamath Co.).

WABANA Lake (Minn., Itasca Co.) \wä ban´ ə\. Perhaps from Ojibwa (Algonquian) *waaban* 'be dawn', *waabanong* 'in/to the east' (Upham 2001; Nichols and Nyholm 1995); or from <wâbanow> 'be a sorcerer' (Baraga 1880). A variant is **Wabano.** Probably related placenames include **Wabeno Creek** (Wis., Forest Co.), **Wauban Beach** (Mich., Cheboygan Co.), **Waubun** (Minn., Mahnomen Co.), and **Waupun** (Wis., Fond du Lac Co.).

WABANG Lake (Minn., St. Louis Co.). Perhaps from the Ojibwa (Algonquian) for 'dawn, east'; see **Wabana Lake,** above. A variant is **Wabun.**

WABANICA Creek (Minn., Lake of the Woods Co.). Perhaps from Ojibwa (Algonquian) *waaban* 'east'; or perhaps from *wabaanagaa* 'island at the narrows', from *wab-* 'narrows, channel' (J. Nichols p.c.).

WABANINGO (Mich., Muskegon Co.). Named for a late-nineteenth-century Ottawa (Algonquian) leader, from <wabananang> 'morning star' (Vogel 1986); cf. Ojibwa *waaban* 'be dawn' (Nichols and Nyholm 1995).

WABANO (Minn., Itasca Co.). A spelling variant of **Wabana Lake**; see above.

WABASCAN Creek (Mich., Kalamazoo Co.). Perhaps from Potawatomi (Algonquian) *wapshkyak* 'white' (Vogel 1986; Kansas 1997). An alternative form is **Wabascon.**

WABASHA County (Minn.) \wä´ bə shô\. Supposedly named for a Dakota (Siouan) chief, *wápahaša* or *wápaša,* lit. 'red cap', from *wapáha* 'cap, hat' plus *ša* 'red' (Upham 2001; Riggs 1890).

WABASH County (Ind.) \wô´ bash\. From French *Ouabache*; named for the **Wabash River,** from Miami/Illinois (Algonquian) /waapaahšiiki/ 'it shines white', referring to the limestone bed of the stream's middle course (McCafferty 2000). The placename **Wabash** also occurs in **Wabash County** (Ill.) and in several other states (e.g., Mass., Worcester Co.; Mich., Luce Co.; and Wash., King Co.).

WABASIS Creek (Mich., Montcalm Co.). Said to be named for a Potawatomi (Algonquian) leader, meaning 'little swan' (Vogel 1986); cf. Ojibwa (Algonquian) *waabizii* 'swan', *-s* 'diminutive' (Nichols and Nyholm 1995).

WABASSO Lake (Wis., Vilas Co.) \wä bas´ ō\. The term is used to mean 'rabbit' in Longfellow's *Hiawatha*; cf. Ojibwa (Algonquian) *waabooz* 'rabbit' (Nichols and Nyholm 1995). The name also occurs in Fla. (Indian River Co.) and Minn. (Redwood Co.). Perhaps related are **Waboo Creek** (Wis., Ashland Co.) and **Waboose Lake** (Minn., Hubbard Co.).

WABASSUS Lake (Maine, Washington Co.). Perhaps from Maliseet (Algonquian), meaning 'shining' (Huden 1962).

WABAUNSEE County (Kans.) \wä bun´ sē\. Named for a Potawatomi (Algonquian) leader, said to mean 'dawn of day' (Rydjord 1968); cf. Ojibwa (Algonquian) *waaban* 'be dawn' (Nichols and Nyholm 1995). Possibly related placenames are **Wapaunsie** (Calif., Plumas Co.), **Waubansee** (Ill., Kane Co.), **Waubonsie** (Iowa, Fremont Co.), and **Wauponsee** (Ill., Grundy Co.).

WABBASEKA (Ark., Jefferson Co.). Perhaps from Quapaw (Siouan), but of unclear derivation (Dickinson 1995); cf. /pazikka/ 'to whittle, sharpen to a point' (R. Rankin p.c.).

WABEDO (Minn., Cass Co.) \wä´ bə dō\. Said to be from Ojibwa (Algonquian) <wabudo> 'a type of mushroom', translated literally as 'white gore' (Upham 2001); cf. *waabishki* 'white' (and *waaban* 'be dawn') plus *wado* 'blood clot' (Nichols and Nyholm 1995).

WABEEK Lake (Mich., Oakland Co.) \wô bēk\. Perhaps from an Ojibwa (Algonquian) word meaning 'rock', popularized as <wawbeek> in Longfellow's *Hiawatha* (Vogel 1986); cf. *âjibik* 'rock' (Baraga 1880). Possibly related forms include **Wabek** (N.Dak., Mountrail Co.), **Waubeek** (Wis., Pepin Co.), and **Wawbeek** (N.Y., Franklin Co.).

WABEE Lake (Ind., Kosciusko Co.) \wô´ bē\. Probably an abbreviation from the name of a Miami/Illinois (Algonquian) leader, also written <Wah-we-as-see> and translated 'round one; full moon' (McPherson 1993); the Native American name was /waawiyasita/ 'the one who is round' (M. McCafferty p.c.).

WABEGON Lake (Minn., Cass Co.) \wä´ bə gon\. Perhaps from Ojibwa (Algonquian) *waabigan* 'clay'; the place is also known as "Mud Lake" (Upham 2001:785; Nichols and Nyholm 1995). Not related to Garrison Keillor's "Lake Wobegon." A related placename is **Wahbegon Lake** (Minn., Becker Co.).

WABEK (N.Dak., Mountrail Co.) \wä´ bek\. Perhaps from the same origin as **Wabeek Lake**; see above.

WABENO Creek (Mich., Gogebic Co.) \wä bē´ nō\. Perhaps from the Ojibwa (Algonquian) word for 'sorcerer' (Vogel 1986). The placename also occurs in Wis. (Forest Co.) Possibly related names are **Wabena Creek** (Calif., Placer Co.) and **Witch Lake** (Mich., Marquette Co.).

WABIGON Lake (Wis., Bayfield Co.) \wä´ bə gon\. Perhaps from the same origin as **Wabegon** (Minn., Cass Co.). Probably related is **Wabikon Lake** (Wis., Forest Co.) \wa´ bi kon\.

WABOO Creek (Wis., Ashland Co.) \wä´ bo͞o\. Perhaps from Ojibwa (Algonquian) *waabooz* 'snowshoe hare, rabbit' (Vogel 1991; Nichols and Nyholm 1995). Perhaps related are **Waboose Lake** (Minn., Hubbard Co.) \wä´ bo͞os\ and **Wabosons Lake** (Minn., Lake Co.) \wä´ bə sənz\; cf. the Ojibwa diminutive *waaboozoons* (Upham 2001:785; J. Nichols p.c.). Also possibly related is **Wabasso Lake** (Wis., Vilas Co.).

WABUN (Minn., St. Louis Co.). A variant of **Wabang Lake**; see above.

WABUSKA (Nev., Lyon Co.) \wə bus´ kə\. Perhaps from an unidentified Indian language (Carlson 1974).

WACAHOOTA, Fort (Fla., Alachua Co.) \wä kə ho͞o´ tə\. From Muskogee *wakv-hute* /wa:ka-hóti/ 'cow-barn', containing *wakv* /wá:ka/ 'cow' (from Spanish *vaca*) and *(e)hute* /(i)hóti/ 'home of an animal' (Read 1934; Martin and Mauldin 2000). A variant is **Wacahotta.** Related placenames are **Wacca Station** and **Waccasassa** (both in Fla., Levy Co.).

WACCABUC (N.Y., Westchester Co.). Also written <Waccaback>; perhaps from Munsee Delaware (Algonquian), of unclear derivation (Beauchamp 1907).

WACCAMAW (N.C., Brunswick Co.). Probably refers to a Catawban (Siouan) subgroup; the term may have been /wahką́ ma:/, lit. 'sacred place' (Powell 1968; B. Rudes p.c.). The name also occurs in S.C. (Georgetown Co.).

WACCASASSA River (Fla., Levy Co.) \wä kə sä´ sə\. From Muskogee, meaning 'some cows', containing *wakv* /wá:ka/ 'cow' (from Spanish *vaca*) plus *sasv* /sá:sa/ 'some' (Read 1934; Martin and Mauldin 2000). A variant spelling is **Wakasassa.** Related placenames are **Fort Wacahoota** (Fla., Alachua Co.) and **Wacca Station** (Fla., Levy Co.).

WACCA Station (Fla., Levy Co.) \wä´ kə\. Abbreviated from **Waccasassa River;** see below.

WACHAPREAGUE (Va., Accomack Co.). From a CAC Algonquian village name (Hagemann 1988).

WACHIPAUKA Pond (N.H., Grafton Co.). Probably from Abenaki (Algonquian), meaning 'mountain pond' (Huden 1962), containing *wajo-* 'mountain' and *-bagw* 'pond' (Day 1994–95).

WACHOCASTINOOK Creek (Conn., Litchfield Co.). From SNEng. Algonquian, perhaps containing <wadchu> 'mountain' (Huden 1962; W. Cowan p.c.).

WACHUSETT (Mass., Worcester Co.) \wä cho͞o´ sət\. SNEng. Algonquian, perhaps meaning 'small mountain place', from <wadchu> 'mountain', <-s> 'small', and <-et> 'place' (Huden 1962; W. Cowan p.c.). In Alaska (Mt. Fairweather D-1) **Wachusett Inlet** is named for the U.S.S. *Wachusett,* which explored the area in 1881.

WACISSA (Fla., Jefferson Co.) \wä sis´ ə\. Perhaps a Timucua placename, of unclear derivation (Read 1934).

WACO (Tex., McLennan Co.) \wā´ kō\. From Wichita (Caddoan) /wi:ko/, referring to a tribal subgroup. The term was earlier written <Wico> by Anglo-Americans and <Hueco> by the Spanish (*HNAI* 13:565). The name also occurs in several other states (e.g., Kans., Sedgewick Co.; Ky., Madison Co.; and Okla., Grady Co.). Possibly related placenames include **Hico** (Tex., Hamilton Co.) and **Wego-Waco** (Kans., Sedgwick Co.).

WACONDA (Minn., St. Louis Co.) \wä kon´ də, wə kon´ də\. Dakota (Siouan) *wakhą́da* 'to worship' (Upham 2001), from *wakhą́* 'sacred, spirit' (Riggs 1890). The placename **Waconda** occurs in several states (e.g., Kans., Mitchell Co.; Neb., Cass Co.; and Ore., Marion Co.). Related names include **Wahkon** (Minn., Mille Lacs Co.), **Wakonda** (S.Dak., Clay Co.), and **Waukon** (Minn., Norman Co.).

WACONIA (Iowa, Linn Co.). Perhaps from Dakota (Siouan) *wakhóniya* 'fountain, spring' (Vogel 1983; J. Koontz p.c.). The name also occurs in Minn. (Carver Co.).

WACOOCHEE Creek (Ala., Lee Co.) \wə ko͞o´ chē\. Probably from Muskogee *wakuce*

/wa:koči/ 'calf', containing *wakv* /wá:ka/ 'cow' (from Spanish *vaca*) plus *-uce* /-oči/ 'little' (Read 1984; Martin and Mauldin 2000).

WACOTA (Wash., Franklin Co.). Perhaps a transfer from **Wacouta** (Minn., Goodhue Co.); see below.

WACOUSTA Township (Iowa, Humboldt Co.). Named for a fictional character in a novel called *Wacousta; or, The Prophecy,* published in 1832. In the story, Wacousta is a white "renegade" who becomes an advisor to Pontiac, the famous Ottawa (Algonquian) leader (Vogel 1983). The name **Wacousta** also occurs in Mich. (Clinton Co.), Wis. (Fond du Lac Co.), and W.Va. (Hampshire Co.). A related placename is **Wahcousta** (Wis., Fond du Lac Co.).

WACOUTA (Minn., Goodhue Co.). From Dakota (Siouan) *wakhúte* 'shooter, he who shoots' (Upham 2001; Ingham 2001). A probably related placename is **Wahcoutah Island** (Wis., Pepin Co.).

WADBOO (S.C., Berkeley Co.) \wäd´ bo͞o\. Earlier written <Watbu>, <Watbooe> (Waddell 1980). Perhaps from Catawba (Siouan) /widebuuye/ 'deer' (Pickens 1961–62:24; B. Rudes p.c.). A variant is **Wedboo Creek.**

WADE (Okla., Bryan Co.). Named for Alfred Wade, a prominent Choctaw (Muskogean) man (Shirk 1974).

WADENA County (Minn.) \wä dē´ nə, wə dē´ nə\. Said to have been named for an Ojibwa (Algonquian) leader in the early nineteenth century (Upham 2001). This may be a shortened form of a name ending in *-adinaa* 'hill' (I. Goddard p.c.). The placename also occurs in Ind. (Benton Co.) and Iowa (Fayette Co.). A related placename is **Pasadena** (Calif., Los Angeles Co.).

WADING River (N.Y., Suffolk Co.). Said to correspond to a SNEng. Algonquian placename referring to 'wading', because Indians waded there to collect shellfish (Ruttenber 1906).

WADMALAW Island (S.C., Charleston Co.). Earlier written <Wadmelaugh>, <Wadmilaw> (Waddell 1980). Perhaps from an unidentified Indian language (Pickens 1963:39).

WAHA (Idaho, Nez Perce Co.) \wā´ hô\. Said to be an Indian word, from an unidentified language (Boone 1988).

WAHABONCEY Lake (Iowa, Fremont Co.). From the same origin as **Waubonsie** (Iowa, Fremont Co.); see **Waubonsee Creek** below.

WAHACHEE (Ga., Dade Co.). A spelling variant of **Wauhatchie Branch**; see below.

WAHAGHBONSY (Iowa, Mills Co.). From the same origin as **Waubonsie** (Iowa, Fremont Co.); see **Waubonsee Creek** below.

WAHAK HOTRONTK (Ariz., Pima Co.). O'odham (Piman) *wo:g huḍuñĭk* 'a dip in the road', from *wo:g* 'road' plus *huḍuñĭk* 'a dip' (Granger 1983; J. Hill p.c.).

WAHALAK (Ala., Kemper Co.) \wô´ hä läk, wô´ hə läk\. Earlier written <Wahloh>; perhaps from Choctaw (Muskogean) <wahhaloha> 'to branch out' (Read 1984; Byington 1915). The name also occurs in Mich. (Kemper Co.).

WAHANNA Lake (Ore., Lane Co.) \wä´ nə\. A shortening for the name of **Neawanna Creek** (Ore., Clatsop Co.); see above (McArthur 1992).

WAHATCHIE (Ga., Dade Co.). A spelling variant of **Wauhatchie Branch**; see below.

WAHATIS Peak (Wash., Grant Co.). From Sahaptin /wá:taš/ 'place for seeking spirit power' (Hitchman 1985; D. Kinkade p.c.).

WAHATOYA Creek (Colo., Huerfano Co.) \wä hä toi´ yə\. An alternative form of **Guajatoyah Creek** from Comanche (Numic), meaning 'two mountains' (J. McLaughlin p.c.).

WAHBAY Township (S.Dak., Day Co.) \wô bā`\. A spelling variant of **Waubay**; see below.

WAHBEGON Lake (Minn., Becker Co.) \wä´ bə gon\. Probably from the same origin as **Wabegon Lake** (Minn., Cass Co.); see above. Not related to Garrison Keillor's "Lake Wobegon." The placename **Wahbegon** also occurs in Wis. (Douglas Co.).

WAHB Springs (Wyo., Park Co.). Named for a fictional animal, the protagonist of Ernest Thompson Seton's book *Biography of a Grizzly* (1900). According to Seton, the name is Shoshoni (Numic) for 'white bear' (Urbanek 1974), but it has not been possible to confirm this.

WAHCHEECHEE Mountain (Mont., Glacier Co.). Perhaps a misspelling of Cree (Algonquian) <ochichak> 'sandhill crane' (Holterman 1985); cf. Ojibwa *ajijaak* 'sandhill crane' (Nichols and Nyholm 1995).

WAHCLELLA (Ore., Multnomah Co.) \wä klel´ ə\. From Kiksht (Chinookan) /wałála/ 'small lake (place)', with /wa-/ 'feminine singular' and /-łála/ 'lake' (McArthur 1992; D. Kinkade p.c.). The name also occurs in Wash. (Skamania Co.).

WAHCONAH Falls (Mass., Berkshire Co.) \wə kō´ nə\. Perhaps from Mahican (Algonquian), of unclear derivation (Huden 1962).

WAHCOUTAH Island (Wis., Pepin Co.) \wä kō´ tə\. Probably from the same origin as **Wacouta** (Minn., Goodhue Co.).

WAHGUYHE Peak (Nev., Nye Co.) \wä´ gī\. The Panamint (Numic) name for the Grapevine Mountains was /waakko'i/, from /waa-/ 'pinyon tree' and /-ko'i/ 'summit' (Carlson 1974; J. McLaughlin p.c.).

WAH GWIN GWINN (Ore., Hood River Co.) \wä gwin´gwin\. Said to mean 'tumbling waters' in an unidentified Indian language (McArthur 1992). An alternative spelling is **Wahgwingwin Falls.**

WAHKEENA Creek (Ore., Multnomah Co.) \wä kē´ nə\. Said to be from Yakima (Sahaptian), meaning 'most beautiful' (McArthur 1992). The placename also is found in Ohio (Fairfield Co.).

WAHKIACUS (Wash., Klickitat Co.) \wä kī´ ə kəs\. Said to be from the name of a Klickitat (Sahaptian) leader of the late nineteenth century or from the surname used by his descendants (Reese 1996); perhaps from the Sahaptin village name /wakáykas/ (D. Kinkade p.c.).

WAHKIAKUM County (Wash.) \wə kī´ ə kəm\. From Cathlamet (Chinookan) /wáqayqam/; cf. /qáiqamix/ 'region downriver' (D. Kinkade p.c.).

WAHKON (Minn., Mille Lacs Co.) \wä´ kon\. From Dakota (Siouan) *wakhą́* 'sacred, spiritual' (Upham 2001; Riggs 1890). A related placename is nearby **Rum River;** see above. Other related names include **Waconda** (Minn., St. Louis Co.), **Wakonda** (S.Dak., Clay Co.), and **Waukon** (Minn., Norman Co.).

WAHKONSA (Iowa, Webster Co.). Named for a Dakota (Siouan) warrior; the Native American term may have been *wakǫ́ze* 'influence; spirit helper' (Vogel 1983; Riggs 1890).

WAHKPA CHUG'N (Mont., Hill Co.). The name refers to an old "buffalo jump," where buffalo were killed by driving them over a bluff. The name contains Lakhota (Siouan) *wakpá* 'stream, river' and English *chugging,* referring to the sound of the buffalo falling (Cheney 1984; Ingham 2001). Related placenames include **Chug Spring** (Wyo., Sweetwater Co.).

WAHLUKE (Wash., Benton Co.) \wä lo͞ok´\. From the Sahaptin placename /walú:k/, possibly meaning 'watering hole', from /wána-/ 'water, to flow' (Hitchman 1985; D. Kinkade p.c.).

WAHMONIE (Nev., Nye Co.) \wä mō´ nē\. From Panamint (Numic) /oammoni/ 'money', consisting of /oa-/ 'yellow' plus English *money* (J. McLaughlin p.c.).

WAHNENA Township (Minn., Cass Co.) \wä nē´ nə\. Said to have been named for an Ojibwa (Algonquian) leader of the late nineteenth century (Upham 2001).

WAHNESHIN Lake (Minn., Cass Co.) \wä´ nə shin, wä nē´ shin\. Formerly called Lost Lake; from Ojibwa (Algonquian) *wanishin* 'be lost' (Upham 2001; Nichols and Nyholm 1995).

WAHNOOWISHA River (Wash., Kittitas Co.). From the Sahaptin placename /wanawíš/, perhaps containing /wána-/ 'water; to flow' (D. Kinkade p.c.).

WAHOO (Ga., Lumpkin Co.) \wä´ hōō\. The name refers to various native trees, such as the winged elm (*RHD* 1987). It is from Muskogee *vhahwv* /ahá:hwa/ 'walnut' (Martin & Mauldin 2000). There is also a Wahoo in Fla. (Sumter Co.).

WAHOO (Neb., Saunders Co.) \wä hōō\. The term refers to a bush also called *Euonymus* or 'burning bush'; from Dakota (Siouan) *wąhu*, equivalent to *wą-* 'arrow' plus *-hu* 'wood' (*RHD* 1987). The placename also occurs in Mich. (Monroe Co.), Mont. (Flathead Co.), and Ohio (Madison Co.).

WAHPETON (Iowa, Dickinson Co.) \wä´ pə tən\. The name refers to a subgroup of the Dakota (Siouan) people; the Native American form is *wahpé-thųwą*, lit. 'leaf-village' (Vogel 1983; *HNAI* 13:753). The placename also occurs in N.Dak. (Richland Co.). A related name is **Waupeton** (Iowa, Dubuque Co.).

WAHPOO Creek (Alaska, Russian Mission D-8) \wä´ pōō\. A "prospectors' name," perhaps from Koyukon (Athabaskan), reported in 1916 (Orth 1967).

WAHSATCH (Utah, Summit Co.) \wä´ sach\. An alternative form of **Wasatch**; see below.

WAHSEEJA Lake (Mont., Glacier Co.) \wä sē´ jə\. Said to be from Assiniboine (Siouan) <washeeju> 'white person' (Holterman 1985); cf. Lakhota (Siouan) *wašíču* 'white person' (Ingham 2001).

WAHTOKE (Calif., Fresno Co.) \wä´ tōk\. Perhaps from Yokuts [watak] 'pine nut' (Gudde 1998).

WAHTUM Lake (Ore., Hood River Co.) \wä´ təm\. Probably from Sahaptin /watám/ 'lake' (McArthur 1992; D. Kinkade p.c.). The name also occurs in Wash. (Yakima Co.).

WAH WAH Mountains (Utah, Beaver Co.) \wä´ wä\. Said to be from a Numic (Uto-Aztecan) language, meaning 'good clear water' (Van Cott 1990).

WAHWEAP (Ariz., Coconino Co.) \wä´ wēp\. Perhaps from Southern Paiute (Numic) /wa'a-uippi/ 'cedar canyon', from /wa'a-/ 'cedar, pinyon pine' plus /uippi/ 'canyon' (Granger 1983; J. McLaughlin p.c.). The name **Wahweap** in Utah (Kane Co.), however, may be from Ute (Numic) /oa-uippɨ/, lit. 'salt canyon' (J. McLaughlin p.c.).

WAIILATPO or **WAIILATPU** (Wash., Walla Walla Co.) \wä lät´ pōō\. Nez Perce /weyí:letpu:/ 'Cayuse people', from /weyí:let-/ 'Cayuse' and /-pu:/ 'people' (Hitchman 1985; Aoki 1994)' The term for 'Cayuse' is apparently from /weyíletn/ 'wave, undulate', as of rye grass waving in the wind (D. Kinkade p.c.).

WAIKIKI Springs (Wash., Spokane Co.) \wī kē kē\. Named for Waikiki Beach in Hawai'i, from Hawai'ian *waikīkī* 'shooting water, spouting water', containing *wai* 'fresh water' and *kīkī*, reduplication of *kī* 'to shoot, to squirt' (Pukui et al. 1974).

WAINSCOTT (N.Y., Suffolk Co.) \wānz´ kot\. Perhaps from SNEng. Algonquian, in a folk-etymology based on English *wainscot* 'wood paneling'; but the origin is unclear (Beauhamp 1907).

WAISKA River (Mich., Chippewa Co.) \wī´ skə\. Named for an Ojibwa (Algonquian) leader whose name was also written as <Waiskee, Wayishkey, Waishkee>, translated 'first' (Vogel 1986); cf. Ojibwa *wayeshkad* 'at first' (Vogel 1986; Nichols and Nyholm 1995).

WAITISAW (Calif., Shasta Co.) \wē´ ti sô\. From Wintu /wayti sawal/, perhaps meaning 'north pond', containing /way/ 'north' and /saaw-/ 'pond' (Gudde 1998).

WAKA (Tex., Ochiltree Co.) \wä´ kə\. Said to be shortened from <Wawaka>, meaning 'wet or swampy ground' in an unidentified Indian language (Tarpley 1980).

WAKANDA Park (Wis., Dunn Co.) \wə kän´ də\. From the same origin as **Waconda**: Dakota (Siouan) *wakǫ́da* 'to worship' (Vogel 1991); see above.

WAKARUSA (Ind., Elkhart Co.) \wä kə roo͞´ sə\. Probably from Shawnee (Algonquian), but of unclear derivation. The name also occurs as a transfer in Kans. (Shawnee Co.).

WAKASASSA (Fla., Levy Co.) \wä kə sä´ sə\. A variant spelling of **Wacasassa River**; see above.

WAKATOMIKA (Ohio, Coshocton Co.) \wā´ kə tō mē´ kə, wā´ kə tom´i kə\. Probably from an unidentified Indian language.

WAKE Butte (Ore., Deschutes Co.) \wāk\. Named by the U.S. Forest Service, from Chinook Jargon wake [wek] 'no, not, none'; cf. Nootka /wik/ 'not, nothing' (McArthur 1992; D. Kinkade p.c.). Related names are **Wakepish Creek** (Wash., Skamania Co.) and **Waketickeh Creek** (Wash., Mason Co.).

WAKEMUP (Minn., St. Louis Co.) \wä´ kə mup\. The folk-etymologized name of an Ojibwa (Algonquian) leader, also written <Way-ko-mah-wub> (Upham 2001).

WAKENDA (Mo., Carroll Co.) \wô´ kən dô, wä´ kin dä, wä ken´ də\. From the same origin as **Waconda**: Dakota (Siouan) *wakhą́da* 'to worship' (Picinich 1951); see above.

WAKEPISH Creek (Wash., Skamania Co.) \wāk´ pish\. A combination of Chinook Jargon elements, intended to mean 'no fish', from **Wake** 'no, not' (see **Wake Butte** above) and <pish> [pɪš] 'fish' (D. Kinkade p.c.).

WAKESHMA Township (Mich., Kalamazoo Co.) \wä kesh´ mə\. Perhaps an adaptation of Ojibwa (Algonquian) <wâkeshka> 'it is shining', or a corresponding form in Potawatomi (Baraga 1880; Vogel 1986).

WAKETICKEH Creek (Wash., Mason Co.) \wāk tik´ ē\. A combination of Chinook Jargon elements, intended to mean something like 'we don't like it', from **Wake** 'no, not' (see **Wake Butte** above) and <tickey, tu-kégh, ti-k´-eh> [tikέɣ], later [tíki] 'want, wish, like, love', perhaps from Lower Chinook [tq'éx] 'to like' (Hitchman 1985; D. Kinkade p.c.).

WAKITA (Okla., Grant Co.) \wä kē´ tə\. Said to be Cherokee (Iroquoian), meaning 'water collected in a depression, such as a buffalo wallow' (Shirk 1974).

WAKLAROK (Alaska, Black C-1). The Yupik (Eskimo) name was obtained in 1899 (Orth 1967).

WAKOFUDSKY Creek (Ga., Clay Co.) \wä kə fud´ skē\. Perhaps referring to a type of heron, from Muskogee *wvko* /wáko/ 'heron' plus *fvskē* /fáski/ 'sharp-pointed' (Read 1950–50; Martin and Mauldin 2000). A variant spelling is **Waukeefriskee Creek.**

WAKONDA (S.Dak., Clay Co.) \wə kon´ də\. From the same origin as **Waconda;** see above. The placename **Wakonda** also occurs as a transfer in Ore. (Lincoln Co.). Related placenames include **Wahkon** (Minn., Mille Lacs Co.).

WAKOPA Creek (N.Dak., Rolette Co.). Perhaps from Dakota (Siouan) *wakpá* 'creek' (D. Parks p.c.).

WAKPALA (S.Dak., Corson Co.) \wäk pä´ lə\. Probably from Lakhota (Siouan) *wakpála* 'creek' (Sneve 1973; Ingham 2001).

WAKPAMANI (S.Dak., Shannon Co.). Probably from Lakhota (Siouan) *wékpamni* 'to distribute', *owákpamni* 'Indian agency', composed of *wa-* 'things' and *kpamní* 'to distribute' (D. Parks p.c.; Ingham 2001).

WAKULLA (N.C., Robeson Co.). Perhaps from Tuscarora (Iroquoian) /aweekarih/ 'boiling liquid', because of the springs in the area (Powell 1968; B. Rudes p.c.).

WAKULLA County (Fla.) \wä kul´ ə\. Perhaps from Muskogee *wahkolv* /wahkó:la/ 'whippoorwill' (Read 1934; Martin and Mauldin 2000).

WALAKPA Bay (Alaska, Barrow A-5) \wä läk´ pə\. The Iñupiaq (Eskimo) name has been translated as 'big village' (Orth 1967); cf. *-qpak* 'big' (MacLean 1980).

WALAPAI (Ariz., Mohave Co.) \wä´ lə pī\. From the same origin as **Hualapai,** a Yuman people (Granger 1983).

WALESKA (Ga., Cherokee Co.) \wä les´ kə\. Said to be named after <Warluskee> or <Walaska>, a Cherokee (Iroquoian) personal name (Goff 1975). *Waleska* is also a woman's name in English, however, perhaps derived from Slavic.

WALHONDING (Ohio, Coshocton Co.) \wôl hon´ ding\. Perhaps from Delaware <woaləanti-nk/ 'ravine' (Mahr 1957).

WALIK Creek (Alaska, Meade River D-5). The Iñupiaq (Eskimo) name was reported in 1950 (Orth 1967).

WALKER'S Station (Okla., Le Flore Co.). Said to be named for Tandy Walker, a Choctaw (Muskogean) leader (Shirk 1974). The name may be derived from *waaka* 'cow', reflecting Spanish *vaca* (P. Munro p.c.). But *Walker* is also a common Creek surname, again perhaps from *wakv* /wá:ka/ 'cow' (Martin and Mauldin 2000).

WALLACUT River (Wash., Pacific Co.) \wä´ lə kut\. From the Lower Chinook placename /wálxat/ (Hitchman 1985; Kinkade p.c.).

WALLAGRASS (Maine, Aroostook Co.) \wä´ lə gras\. Perhaps from Abenaki (Algonquian), of unclear derivation (Rutherford 1970).

WALLAHATCHEE Creek (Ala., Elmore Co.) \wä lə hach´ ē\. Possibly from Muskogee *rewahle* /ɬiwáhli/, a tribal town, plus *hvcce* /háčči/ 'stream' (Read 1984; Martin and Mauldin 2000).

WALLALUTE Falls (Ore., Hood River Co.) \wäl´ ə lo͞ot\. Said to be from Wasco (Chinookan), meaning 'strong water' (McArthur 1992).

WALLAMANUMPS Falls (Mass., Hampden Co.). From SNEng. Algonquian, perhaps meaning 'red cliffs' (Huden 1962).

WALLAMATOGUS Mountain (Maine, Hancock Co.). Perhaps from Abenaki (Algonquian), meaning 'coves in a little river' (Huden 1962).

WALLAMETTE (Ore., Clackamas Co.) \wä´ lə met\. From the same origin as **Willamette**; see below.

WALLA Valley (Ariz., Coconino Co.) \wä´ lə\. From Hopi (Uto-Aztecan) *waala* 'gap' (Granger 1983; K. Hill p.c.).

WALLA WALLA (Wash., Walla Walla Co.) \wä lə wä´ lə, wä´ lə wä lə\. From Sahaptin /walawála/ 'little rivers or streams', diminutive of /wána/ 'river' (Hitchman 1985; D. Kinkade p.c.). The placename **Walla Walla** occurs in several other states (e.g., Alaska, Solomon C-1; Ill., Cumberland Co.; and Wis., Waupaca Co.).

WALLENPAUPACK Creek (Pa., Pike Co.). Perhaps from Delaware (Algonquian) <walinkpa-peek> 'a deep spring' (Donehoo 1928).

WALLOOMSAC (N.Y., Rensselaer Co.) \wä lo͞om´ sak\. Earlier written <Wallumschack>; perhaps from Mahican (Algonquian), of unclear derivation (Ruttenber 1906). The name also occurs in Vt. (Bennington Co.).

WALLOOSKEE River (Ore., Clatsop Co.) \wä lo͞os´ kē\. Said to be the name of a Chinookan subgroup (McArthur 1992).

WALLOWA County (Ore.) \wä lou´ ə\. From Nez Perce (Sahaptian) /wal'áwa/ 'Wallowa River' (McArthur 1992; Aoki 1994).

WALLPACK (N.J., Sussex Co.). Probably from Delaware (Algonquian), of unclear derivation (Becker 1964). The name also occurs in Pa. (Monroe Co.).

WALLULA (Wash., Walla Walla Co.) \wä lo͞o´ lə, wə lo͞o´ lə\. From the Northeastern Sahaptin placename /walúula/, equivalent to /walawála/ 'lots of little streams or rivers', from /wána/ 'river' (Hitchman 1985; D. Kinkade p.c.). The placename **Wallula** also occurs in Kans. (Wyandotte Co.) and Ore. (Umatilla Co.). A related placename is **Walla Walla.**

WALLUM Lake (Mass., Worcester Co.; R.I., Providence Co.) \wô´ ləm\. Earlier written <Allum>; perhaps from SNEng. Algonquian *allum* 'dog' (Huden 1962; W. Cowan p.c.). The placename **Wallum** also occurs in Mont. (Golden Valley Co.).

WALLUPA Creek (Ore., Wallowa Co.) \wä lo͞o´ pə\. Perhaps a word meaning 'wildcat' in an unidentified Indian language (McArthur 1992).

WALPI (Ariz., Navajo Co.) \wäl´ pē\. From Hopi (Uto-Aztecan) *wàlpi* 'place of the gap', containing *waala* 'gap' (*HNAI* 9:551; K. Hill p.c.).

WALUGA Park (Ore., Clackamas Co.) \wä lo͞o´ gə\. Clackmas (Chinookan) *waluga* 'swan', from *wa-* 'feminine' plus *-luga* 'swan' (McArthur 1992; D. Kinkade p.c.).

WALUPT Creek (Wash., Lewis Co.). From the Sahaptin placename /wálupt, wálpt/ (Hitchman 1985; D. Kinkade p.c.).

WAMBA (S.C., Chesterfield Co.) \wäm´ bə\. Said to be from Cherokee <wambee> 'ground tuber, wild turnip' (Pickens 1961–62:23). An apparently related placename is **Wambaw Creek** (S.C., Charleston Co.).

WAMDUSKA Township (N.Dak., Nelson Co.). Probably from Dakota (Siouan) *wamdúška* 'snakes' (Wick 1988; Riggs 1890).

WAMEGO (Kans., Pottawatomie Co.) \wä mē´ gō\. Perhaps from the surname of a Potawatomi (Algonquian) family, written <Wam-me-go> (Rydjord 1968).

WAMELO Rock (Calif., Madera Co.) \wä´ mə lō\. Said to be called <Wamello> in an unidentified Indian language (Gudde 1998).

WAMESIT (Mass., Middlesex Co.). From SNEng. Algonquian, perhaps meaning 'there is room for all'. A variant form is **Wamoset.**

WAMPANOAG Lake (Mass., Worcester Co.) \wäm pə nō´ əg\. The name of a SNEng. Algonquian subgroup, perhaps meaning 'easterner' (Huden 1962; *HNAI* 15:175). The placename also occurs in R.I. (Providence Co.).

WAMPATUCK Hill (Mass., Norfolk Co.) \wôm´ pə tuk\. From SNEng. Algonquian, perhaps meaning 'white river', from <wompum> 'white' and <-tuck> 'tidal stream' (Huden 1962; W. Cowan p.c.).

WAMPECACK Creek (N.Y., Rensselaer Co.) \wäm´ pi kak\. Perhaps from Mahican (Algonquian), meaning 'place of chestnuts' (Beauchamp 1907).

WAMPEE (S.C., Horry Co.). Perhaps from an unidentified Indian language, meaning 'pickerel weed' (Pickens 1964:33). The name Wampee also occurs in Fla. (Baker Co.).

WAMPEE Pond (Conn., Litchfield Co.) \wäm´ pē\. Perhaps from SNEng. Algonquian <wompi> 'bright, white' (Huden 1962; W. Cowan p.c.).

WAMPENUM Brook (Mass., Berkshire Co.). From SNEng. Algonquian, perhaps containing <wompum> 'white' (Huden 1962; W. Cowan p.c.).

WAMPHASSUC Point (Conn., New London Co.). Earlier written <Wamphasset, Wampashuck> (etc.), perhaps from SNEng. Algonquian <wompaskit> 'marsh' (Huden 1962; Trumbull 1881).

WAMPUM Rock (Mass., Norfolk Co.) \wäm´ pəm\. The word refers to strings of seashells used as money; it is short for SNEng. Algonquian <wampumpeag>, equivalent to a combination meaning 'white string' (Huden 1962; *RHD* 1987). The name also occurs in Ill. (Cook Co.) and Pa. (Lawrence Co.).

WAMPUS River (N.Y., Westchester Co.) \wäm´ pəs\. Perhaps from Delaware (Algonquian) <woapink> 'possum' (Brinton and Anthony 1888; Beauchamp 1907); cf. Unami Delaware /ópi:nkw/ (Blalock et al. 1994). The placename **Wampus** also occurs in Minn. (Lake Co.).

WAMSUTTA (Mass., Bristol Co.) \wäm sut´ ə\. The name of a SNEng. Algonquian leader who died in 1662 (Huden 1962). The placename also occurs in N.H. (Coös Co.). A probably related form is **Wamsutter** (Wyo., Sweetwater Co.) \wäm´ sut ər\.

WAMUL Tank (Ariz., Pima Co.) \wa´ məl\. From O'odham (Piman) *wamel* [wámɨl] 'swamp' (J. Hill p.c.).

WANACUT Creek (Wash., Okanogan Co.) \wä´ nə kət\. Named for George Wanacut, an Okanogan (Salishan) Indian (BGN 7901). A variant spelling is **Wannacut Creek.**

WANADOGA Creek (Mich., Calhoun Co.). Perhaps an adaptation of **Onondaga** (see above), an Iroquoian people of N.Y. state (Vogel 1986).

WANAGAN Creek (Mich., Gogebic Co.) \wä´ nə gən\. The term is used by lumberjacks to mean what is locally called a trap, that is, 'a supply chest, a temporary shelter, a commissary or food wagon'; from Ojibwa (Algonquian) *waanikaan* 'an excavated hole', from *waanike* 'to dig a hole' (*RHD* 1987; Nichols and Nyholm 1995). Related placenames include **Wannagan Creek** (N.Dak., Billings Co.), **Wannigan Rapids** (Wis., Sawyer Co.), and **Wanoka Lake** (Wis., Bayfield Co.).

WANAKAH (N.Y., Erie Co.) \wə nä´ kə\. Perhaps from Iroquoian, but of unclear derivation (Beauchamp 1907).

WANAKENA (N.Y., St. Lawrence Co.) \wä nə kē´ nə\. Perhaps from Abenaki (Algonquian), meaning 'good or pleasant place' (Beauchamp 1907).

WANAKSINK Lake (N.Y., Sullivan Co.). Perhaps from Munsee Delaware (Algonquian) <winak> 'sassafras' derivation (Ruttenber 1906). Possibly related names are **Wanaque** (N.J., Passaic Co.) and **Wanaksink** (N.Y., Rockland Co.).

WANAMASSA (N.J., Monmouth Co.). Perhaps named for a Delaware (Algonquian) leader called <Wanamasoa> (Becker 1964).

WANAMIE (Pa., Luzerne Co.) \wä´ nə mē\. A variant of **Unami,** a division of the Delaware (Algonquian) Indians (Donehoo 1928). It comes from Munsee Delaware /wə̆ná:mi:w/ or from Unalachtigo Delaware /wəna:mi:w/ and means 'person from downriver' (*HNAI* 15:236–37).

WANAMINGO (Minn., Goodhue Co.) \wä nə ming´ gō\. Perhaps named for the Indian heroine of a popular novel (Upham 2001).

WANANGO (Pa., Venango Co.). A variant of **Venango**; see **Venango County** above.

WANANISH (N.C., Columbus Co.). Also written <Ouaniche>; said to be a word for 'landlocked salmon' in an unidentified Indian language (Powell 1968).

WANAPUM Lake (Wash., Kittitas Co.) \wä´ nə pəm\. From Sahaptin [wánapam] 'river people', containing [wána] 'river' and [-pam] 'people' (Hitchman 1985; D. Kinkade p.c.).

WANAQUE (N.J., Passaic Co.). Perhaps from Delaware (Algonquian) <winak> 'sassafras' (Brinton and Anthony 1888; Becker 1964). Possibly related names are **Wanoksink Lake** (N.Y., Rockland Co.) and **Wanaksink Lake** (N.Y., Sullivan Co.).

WANATA State Park (Iowa, Clay Co.) \wə nä´ tə\. Named for a Dakota (Siouan) leader, probably from *wa-nátą* 'he attacks' (Vogel 1983; J. Koontz p.c.). The name is written **Wanatah** in Ind. (La Porte Co.) and Neb. (Dawes Co.). A related name is **Waneta** (S.Dak., Potter Co.).

WANBLEE (S.Dak., Jackson Co.). From Lakhota (Siouan) *wąblí* 'eagle' (Sneve 1973; Ingham 2001).

WANCHESE (N.C., Dare Co.). Named for a CAC Algonquian man who was taken to England in 1584 (Payne 1985).

WANDAWEGA, Lake (Wis., Walworth Co.) \wän də wē´ gə\. Perhaps related to Winnebago (Siouan) <wah-wen-da> 'she-bear' (Vogel 1991).

WANDO (S.C., Berkeley Co.). Perhaps from Catawba (Siouan) /widebuuye/ 'deer' (Pickens 1961–62:23; B. Rudes p.c.). Cf. **Awendaw, Wadboo.**

WANESKA Park (N.Dak., Stutsman Co.). From Ojibwa (Algonquian) <wanashkobia> 'there is a reservoir or basin of water' (Baraga 1880; Wick 1988). A possibly related term is **Wannaska** (Minn., Roseau Co.).

WANETA (Iowa, Davis Co.). Supposedly the name of an Indian woman (Vogel 1983). The name may be a respelling of the Spanish *Juanita,* familiar from a popular song of the nineteenth century (Bright 1993). Related placenames include **Waunita** (Colo., Gunnison Co.) and **Wauneta** (Kans., Chautauqua Co.).

WANGAN (Maine, Piscataquis Co.). Perhaps from Abenaki (Algonquian), translated as 'the bend' (Huden 1962).

WANGO (Md., Wicomico Co.). Probably a shortening of **Nassawango Creek,** a CAC Algonquian placename (Kenny 1984).

WANGO (N.Y., Chautauqua Co.) \wang´ gō\. A shortening of **Conewango,** perhaps an Iroquoian name, of unclear derivation (Beauchamp 1907).

WANGUMBAUG Lake (Conn., Tolland Co.). Also written <Wongumbaug>; said to be from SNEng. Algonquian, meaning 'crooked pond' (Trumbull 1881).

WANGUM Lake (Conn., Litchfield Co.). Also written <Wongum>; perhaps from SNEng. Algonquian <wangunk> 'a bend' (Trumbull 1881; W. Cowan p.c.). The name also occurs in Pa. (Wayne Co.).

WANGUNK Meadows (Conn., Middlesex Co.). Also <Wongunk>; from SNEng. Algonquian <wangunk> 'a bend' (Huden 1962).

WANIHIGAN Lake (Minn., Cook Co.). Perhaps from the same origin as **Wanagan Creek** (Mich., Gogebic Co.); see above.

WANKINCO River (Mass., Plymouth Co.). From SNEng. Algonquian, perhaps meaning 'bent stream' (Huden 1962).

WANMAYEE Creek (Alaska, St. Lawrence B-6). The Yupik (Eskimo) name was reported in 1949 (Orth 1967).

WANNACOMET (Mass., Nantucket Co.). Earlier written <Wannaconset> (Little 1984). From SNEng. Algonquian, perhaps meaning 'at the beautiful field' (Huden 1962).

WANNACUT Creek (Wash., Okanogan Co.) \wä´ nə kət\. A variant spelling of **Wanacut Creek**; see above.

WANNAGAN Creek (N.Dak., Billings Co.). Probably from the same origin as **Wanagan Creek** (Mich., Gogebic Co.); see above.

WANNASKA (Minn., Roseau Co.). Perhaps from the same origin as **Waneska Park** (N.Dak., Stutsman Co.); see above.

WANNEE (Fla., Gilchrist Co.) \wä´ nē\. A shortening of **Suwannee** (Read 1934); see **Suwanee** above.

WANNIGAN Rapids (Wis., Sawyer Co.) \wä´ nə gən\. The term is used by lumberjacks to mean what is locally called a trap, that is, 'a supply chest, a temporary shelter, a commissary or food wagon'; see **Wanagan Creek** (Mich., Gogebic Co.) above.

WANNUCHECOMECUT Brook (R.I., Washington Co.). From SNEng. Algonquian, perhaps meaning 'enclosed camping place' (Huden 1962).

WANNUPPEE Islands (Conn., Litchfield Co.). Perhaps from Mahican (Algonquian) <wunnenip> 'good water'; cf. <wunne> 'good', <nip> 'water' (Huden 1962, W. Cown p.c.).

WANOGA Butte (Ore., Deschutes Co.) \wə nō´ gə\. Klamath /wnaga/ 'son', objective form of /wnak/ (McArthur 1992; Barker 1963:452).

WANOKA Lake (Wis., Bayfield Co.). Perhaps from Ojibwa (Algonquian) *waanikaan* 'an excavated hole', from *waanike* 'to dig a hole' (Vogel 1991; Nichols and Nyholm 1995). The name **Wanoka** also occurs in Pa. (Wayne Co.). Possibly related terms are **Wanagan Creek** (Mich., Gogebic Co.) and **Wannigan Rapids** (Wis., Sawyer Co.).

WANOKSINK Lake (N.Y., Rockland Co.). Perhaps from Delaware (Algonquian) <winak> 'sassafras' (Brinton and Anthony 1888; Beauchamp 1907). Possibly related names are **Wanaque** (N.J., Passaic Co.) and **Wanaksink Lake** (N.Y., Sullivan Co.).

WANSHIP (Utah, Summit Co.) \wän´ ship\. Named for a Shoshoni (Numic) leader; his name was said to mean 'good man' (Van Cott 1990).

WANSKUCK (R.I., Providence Co.). From SNEng. Algonquian, perhaps meaning 'at the end-place' (Huden 1962).

WANTAGH (N.Y., Nassau Co.) \wän´ tô\. Perhaps from the same source as **Wyandanch**; see below.

WANTASTIQUET (N.H., Cheshire Co.) \wän tas´ ti kət\. From Abenaki (Algonquian), perhaps meaning 'lost river place', with *wantas* 'lost', *-tegw-* 'river', and *-et* 'place' (Huden 1962; W. Cowan p.c.). The name also occus in Vt. (Windsor Co.).

WANUNGATUCK Brook (Conn., Windham Co.). From SNEng. Algonquian, perhaps meaning 'winding river place' (Trumbull 1881; Huden 1962).

WA-PAI-SHONE (Nev., Carson City Co.) \wä pī shōn\. The name combines elements from the **Washoe, Paiute,** and **Shoshoni** tribal names (Carlson 1974).

WAPAKONETA (Ohio, Auglaize Co.) \wô pə kə net´ ə\. From the name of a Shawnee (Algonquian) leader and/or settlement (Miller 1996). The name is sometimes abbreviated locally to \wô´ päk\.

WAPALANNE, Lake (N.J., Sussex Co.). Probably from Delaware (Algonquian), but of unclear derivation (Becker 1964).

WAPAMA Falls (Calif., Tuolumne Co.) \wə pä´ mə\. Perhaps from a Sierra Miwok form such as /wepaama/, from /weepa/ 'uphill' (Gudde 1998).

WAPANACKI Lake (Vt., Lamoille Co.). Perhaps from Abenaki (Algonquian) *wôbanaki* 'dawnland, the east' (Huden 1962; Day 1994–95). A possibly related term is **Wapanocca Bayou** (Ark., Crittenden Co.). Perhaps a Central Algonquian word referring to Indians from the east coast, lit. 'easterners' (Dickinson 1995); cf. Ojibwa <wâban> 'east' (Baraga 1880). A perhaps related placename is **Wapanucka** (Okla., Johnston Co.) \wä pə no͞ok´ ə\. Both these seem to be related to the tribal name **Abenaki.**

WAPATA (Ore., Yamhill Co.) \wä´ pə tə\. A variant form of **Wapato** \wä´ pə tō\. From Chinook Jargon <wap´-pa-too, wap´-a-to> [wápato] 'arrowroot', an edible plant also locally called 'wild potato', first recorded in 1795. The derivation appears to be from Upper Chinook [wa-] 'prefix forming nouns' plus [-pato], borrowed from Kalapuyan [-pdóʔ] 'wild potato' (Berman 1990:54). The placename **Wapato** also occurs in Wash. (Yakima Co.). Related forms include **Wapito Point** (Idaho, Clearwater Co.) and **Wapatoo** (Ore., Washington Co.). Outside the Pacific Northwest, there are **Wapato Lakes** in Wis. (Oconto Co.) and **Wapato Creek** in Mich. (Gogebic Co.), also said to refer to an edible root. It has been speculated that this is an Algonquian word that was carried to the Pacific coast by Lewis and Clark in 1805 (Vogel 1986); but this has not been substantiated. A possibly relevant form is Menominee (Algonquian) /wa:patow/ 'mushroom' (Vogel 1991; Bloomfield 1975).

WAPAUNSIE (Calif., Plumas Co.) \wə pôn´ sē\. Probably a transfer from the name of a Potawatomi (Algonquian) leader in the Midwest; cf. **Wabaunsee County** (Kans.), as well as **Waubansee** (Ill., Kane Co.), **Waubonsie** (Iowa, Fremont Co.), and **Wauponsee** (Ill., Grundy Co.).

WAPELLA (Ill., De Witt Co.) \wä pel´ ə\. Named for a Meskwaki (Algonquian) leader of the early nineteenth century (Vogel 1963); his Native American name was perhaps /wa:pino:ha/, a type of small bird, with a historical replacement of *n* by *l* (I. Goddard p.c.). The placename **Wapello** occurs in Iowa (Louisa Co.). **Wapello** \wä pel´ ō\ is found in Idaho (Bingham Co.). A possibly related name is **Wappapello** (Mo., Wayne Co.).

WAPI (Idaho, Blaine Co.) \wä´ pī\. Said to be an Algonquian word, language and meaning not identified (Boone 1988).

WAPINITIA (Ore., Wasco Co.) \wä pi nish´ ə\. Earlier written <Wapinita>; perhaps a Sahaptin placename (McArthur 1992).

WAPITI \wä ´ pi tē\. This term, equivalent to 'elk', is from Shawnee (Algonquian) /wa:piti/

'white rump' (*RHD* 1987). The word occurs as a placename in several states (e.g., Colo., Gunnison Co.; Mont., Gallatin Co.; and Ore., Lane Co.); in Idaho (Idaho Co.) the pronunciation \wə pē´ tī\ is reported.

WAPITO Point (Idaho, Clearwater Co.) \wə pē´ tō\. From the same origin as **Wapato**, a Chinook Jargon word for 'wild potato'; see **Wapata** above.

WAPOGASSET Lake (Wis., Polk Co.) \wä pō gas´ ət\. From Ojibwa (Algonquian) <wapagessi> 'a type of large fish' (Baraga 1880; Vogel 1991).

WAPOOSE (Wis., Forest Co.) \wä po͞os´\. From an Algonquian word for 'rabbit'; cf. Menomini /wa:pos/ 'jackrabbit; a man's name' (Bloomfield 1975) and Ojibwa *waabooz* 'rabbit' (Vogel 1991; Nichols and Nyholm 1995). Perhaps related placenames include **Waboo Creek** (Wis., Ashland Co.) and **Wabasso Lake** (Wis., Vilas Co.).

WAPOWETY Cleaver (Wash., Pierce Co.). Named for an Indian guide, of unknown affiliation, who accompanied mountaineers in 1857 (Hitchman 1985).

WAPPAPELLO (Mo., Wayne Co.). Perhaps an alternative of **Wapello** (Ramsay 1952); see **Wapella** above.

WAPPAQUASSET Pond (Conn., Windham Co.).From SNEng. Algonquian, perhaps meaning 'at the place of cattails' (Huden 1962).

WAPPASENING Creek (N.Y., Tioga Co.; Pa., Bradford Co.). Perhaps from Delaware (Algonquian) <wapachsinnink> 'place of white stones', containing <woap-ach-sin> 'white stone; silver' (Donehoo 1928).

WAPPETOW (S.C., Charleston Co.). Perhaps from Catawba (Siouan) <wapito> 'sky' (Pickens 1961–62:23).

WAPPING (Conn., Hartford Co.) \wä´ ping\. From SNEng. Algonquian, perhaps referring to 'east' or 'dawn' (Huden 1962). The name also occurs in Mass. (Franklin Co.).

WAPPINGER (N.Y., Dutchess Co.) \wä´ pin jər\. Earlier written as <Wappinck, Wappings> (etc.); from Munsee Delaware (Algonquian) /wá:pi:nkw/ 'possum'. The name has nothing to do with the meaning 'east' (Grumet 1981; *HNAI* 15:238).

WAPPOCOMO (W.Va., Hampshire Co.). From a placename in an unidentified Algonquian language (Kenny 1945).

WAPPOO Creek (S.C., Charleston Co.) \wä´ po͞o\. Perhaps a word for 'water' in an unidentified Indian language (Neuffer and Neuffer 1983).

WAPPOOLAH (S.C., Berkeley Co.). An earlier writing is <Wapaoolah>; perhaps from an unidentified Indian language (Pickens 1961–62:23).

WAPPOQUIA Brook (Conn., Windham Co.). Earlier <Wappoquian's, Webaquian>, named for a SNEng. Algonquian Indian (Huden 1962; Trumbull 1881).

WAPREMANDER Creek (Md., Dorchester Co.). Earlier written <Wappermando, Whapplemander> (etc.); perhaps from a CAC Algonquian placename, of unclear derivation.

WAPSACONHAGAN (Maine, Washington Co.). Earlier written <Wapskenigan>; from Abenaki (Algonquian), perhaps meaning 'white-rock portage' (Eckstorm 1941:232–32); cf. Abenaki *wôbi* 'white', *-apskw* 'rock', and *onigan* 'a carry, a portage' (Day 1994–95).

WAPSHILLA Creek (Idaho, Nez Perce Co.) \wäp shil´ ə\. Said to be the surname of a Nez Perce (Sahaptian) family (Boone 1888).

WAPSIE (Iowa, Bremer Co.) An abbreviation for **Wapsipinicon River** (Vogel 1983); see below.

WAPSINONOC Creek (Iowa, Muscatine Co.). Perhaps from Meskwaki (Algonquian), meaning 'white men' (i.e., 'men who are white', not 'Europeans') (Vogel 1983); cf. /wa:pi-, wa:peški-/ 'white', /wa:pino:ha/ 'white person; a species of bird' (Goddard 1994).

WAPSIPINICON River (Minn., Mower Co.; Iowa, Scott Co.). Meskwaki (Algonquian) /wa:pesi:hpenihka:hi/ 'abounding in arrowhead plants'; cf. /wa:pesi:hpeny-e:ki/ 'arrowhead plants (pl.)' from /wa:pesiw-/ 'waterfowl', /-ihpeny/ 'tuber' and /-ihka:h/ 'abound with' (Vogel 1983; I. Goddard p.c.). A related placename is **Wapsie** (Iowa, Bremer Co.); see above.

WAPTI Creek (Md., Cecil Co.). Perhaps an alternative form of **Wapiti** 'elk'; see above.

WAPTUS River (Wash., Kittitas Co.). From Sahaptin /wáptas/ 'feather' (D. Kinkade p.c.).

WAPUNBEM Hill (Calif., Plumas Co.) \wä pun´ bem\. From Mountain Maidu /wapɨ́nbe/ 'little hopper-basket', from /wapɨ́n/ 'hopper basket' plus /-be/ 'diminutive' (BGN 1999; W. Shipley p.c.).

WAPWALLOPEN (Pa., Luzerne Co.) \wäp wä´ lə pən, wä´ pə lō pən\. Earlier written <Opolopona, Wambhallobank> (etc.); said to be from Delaware (Algonquian) <woap-hallack-pink> 'white hemp place', containing <woapeu> 'white' and <hallachpis> 'wild hemp' (Brinton and Anthony 1888; Donehoo 1928); cf. Munsee Delaware *wáapeew* 'be white' and *áhlap, ahlapiis* 'wild hemp' (O'Meara 1996).

WAQUOIT Bay (Mass., Barnstable Co.). From SNEng. Algonquian, perhaps meaning 'at the end' (Huden 1962).

WARACKAMAC Lake (N.Y., Dutchess Co.). Earlier written <Waraukameck, Warachkameek> (etc.); perhaps Munsee Delaware, of unclear derivation (Ruttenber 1906; Beauchamp 1907).

WARAMAUG, Lake (Conn., Litchfield Co.). Earlier written <Warramock>; perhaps from Mahican (Algonquian), meaning 'good fishing-place' (Huden 1962).

WARBA (Minn., Itasca Co.) \wôr´ bə\. Perhaps from Ojibwa (Algonquian) *wayiiba* 'soon' (Upham 2001; Nichols and Nyholm 1995).

WARBONNET Lake (Wyo., Sublette Co.). The term refers to the long feathered headdresses worn by Plains warriors (Urbanek 1974).

WAR EAGLE Park (Iowa, Woodbury Co.). Named for a Dakota (Siouan) leader of the early nineteenth century; this may have corresponded to *wąmdí-thąka,* lit. 'war-eagle big', from *wąmdí* 'war-eagle' (a Native American category of eagles) plus *tháka* 'large' (Vogel 1983; J. Koontz p.c.). In W.Va. (Mingo Co.) the town of **War Eagle** is said to have been named for the War Eagle Coal Company.

WARINANCO Park (N.J., Union Co.). Said to be named for a Delaware (Algonquian) leader (Becker 1974).

WARM CHUCK Inlet (Alaska, Craig C-5). A combination intended to mean 'warm water', from English *warm* and Chinook Jargon <chuck> [čʌk] 'water' (Orth 1967). Similar formations are **Salt Chuck** (Alaska, Craig C-2), **Whitechuck River** (Wash., Snohomish Co.), and **Winchuck** (Ore., Curry Co.).

WAR-RAS-KOY-ACK (Va., Isle of Wight Co.). Earlier written <Warescoyak> (etc.); the name of a CAC Algonquian village or subgroup (Hagemann 1988).

WARRIOR (Ala., Blount Co.). **Warrior,** referring to a Native American fighting man, is popular as a placename all over the United States, including Md. (Allegany Co.), Mont. (Flathead Co.), and Minn. (Roseau Co.).

WASAI, Baie de (Mich., Chippewa Co.). French, meaning 'bay of Wasai'; from Ojibwa (Algonquian) <awâssi>, perhaps from *awanzisii* 'bullhead' (J. Nichols p.c.).

WASATCH Mountains (Utah, Wasatch Co.) \wä´ sach\. Named for a Shoshoni (Numic) leader; the Native American term is /wasattsi/ 'blue heron' (J. McLaughlin p.c.). The placename also occurs in Colo. (San Miguel Co.), Idaho (Caribou Co.), and Wyo. (Uinta Co.).

WASCO (N.Y., Cayuga Co.) \wä´ skō\. Perhaps from an Iroquoian language, meaning 'bridge'; cf. Seneca *waskǫ́ǫh* 'bridge' (Chafe 1967). The placename **Wasco** occurs as a transfer in Ill. (Kane Co.). Probably related placenames are **Osco** and **Owasco** (N.Y., Cayuga Co.).

WASCO County (Ore.) \wä´ skō\. The name refers to a Chinookan subgroup and is derived from /wašq'ú/ 'small dipper', used as the name of a village (McArthur 1992; D. Kinkade p.c.). In Calif. (Kern Co.), **Wasco** occurs as a transfer name (Gudde 1998). Another name in Ore. (Wasco Co.), **Wascopam** \wä´ skō päm\, is a Sahaptin adaptation meaning 'Wasco people', with the suffix /-pam/ 'people' (D. Kinkade p.c.).

WASECA County (Minn.) \wä sē´ kə\. An adaptation of Dakota (Siouan) *wašéča* 'rich' (Riggs 1890; Upham 2001), with Riggs's Dakota orthography <waśeca> interpreted in terms of English pronunciation.

WASECK (Calif., Humboldt Co.) \wä´ sek\. From the Yurok village name /wahsek/ (Gudde 1998).

WASEKA Acres (Pa., Cumberland Co.). Perhaps an adaptation of **Watseka** (Ill., Iroquois Co.).

WASEPI (Mich., St. Joseph Co.) \wä sip´ ē\. A shortening of <Nottawassepee>, said to Potawatomi (Algonquian) for 'enemy river' (Vogel 1986); cf. the related Ojibwa (Algonquian) *naadwe* 'enemy', *ziibi* 'river'(Rhodes 1985).

WASEPKA Ranch (N.Dak., Golden Valley Co.). Perhaps from Lakhota (Siouan) *wasé-k'a* 'red-earth diggings', a word for a location where Indians dug for red paint (D. Parks p.c.); cf. *wasé* 'red earth, vermilion' (Ingham 2001).

WASHAKIE County (Wyo.) \wäsh´ ə kē\. Named for a nineteenth-century Shoshoni (Numic) leader; his Native American name was /wɨsayuki/ 'to rattle' (J. McLaughlin p.c.). The placename also occurs in Utah (Box Elder Co.).

WASHAPIE Mountains (Calif., Tulare Co.) \wä´ shə pī\. Named for a nearby Indian village, perhaps Yokuts-speaking (Gudde 1998).

WASHAQUA Hill (Mass., Dukes Co.). From SNEng. Algonquian, perhaps meaning 'at the end' (Huden 1962).

WASHAW Creek (S.C., Berkeley Co.). Said to be from Chickasaw (Muskogean), meaning 'hunting place' (Pickens 1961–62:23).

WASHIKI (Nev., Pershing Co.). The name is related to **Washakie County** (Wyo.); see above.

WASHINEE Lakes (Conn., Litchfield Co.). Perhaps from SNEng. Algonquian, of unclear derivation (Huden 1962; Trumbull 1881). A variant form is **Washining.**

WASHITA County (Okla.) \wäsh´ ə tä\. An alternative form of **Ouachita** (Shirk 1974). The name **Washita** also occurs in Ark. (Montgomery Co.).

WASKISH (Minn., Beltrami Co.) \wäsh´ kish\. From Ojibwa (Algonquian) *waawaashkeshi* 'deer' (Upham 2001; Nichols and Nyholm 1995). A variant is **Waskish**.

WASHLEY Creek (La., Tangipahoa Par.). Perhaps from Choctaw *wosholli* 'to ferment, to form a froth' (Read 1927; P. Munro p.c.). A possibly related placename is **Wauchula** (Fla., Hardee Co.); see below.

WASHOE County (Nev.) \wä´ sho͞o, wä´ shō\. From the name of the **Washo** Indian people; the Native American name is /wáašiw/ (W. Jacobsen p.c.). The placename also occurs in Calif. (Sonoma Co.) and Idaho (Payette Co.).

WASHOUGAL (Wash., Clark Co.) \wô´ sho͞o gəl\. From the Cascades Chinook placename /wašúxwal/ or /wašúxal/ (Hitchman 1985; D. Kinkade p.c.).

WASHTA (Iowa, Cherokee Co.) \wäsh´ tə\. From Dakota (Siouan) *wašté* 'good, pretty' (Vogel 1983; Riggs 1890). In Minn. (Lake Co.), **Washte** is from the same origin.

WASHTENAW County (Mich.) \wäsh´ tə nö\. Said to be from Ojibwa (Algonquian) <washtenong>, a name for the Grand River, perhaps from <wuste-nong> 'further district' (Vogel 1986); cf. *waasa* 'far' (Nichols and Nyholm 1995). The name is also preserved in the county as **Washtenong Park.**

WASHTUCNA (Wash., Adams Co.) \wäsh tuk´ nə\. Perhaps from Sahaptin /waštukna/, the name of a Palouse leader (Hitchman 1985; D. Kinkade p.c.).

WASHUNGA (Okla., Kay Co.) \wä sho͝ong´ gə\. Named for a Kansa (Siouan) leader; his Native American name was /wašų́ge/ (R. Rankin p.c.).

WASILLA (Alaska, Anchorage C-7) \wä sil´ ə\. From Russian *Vasilij,* the name of a Dena'ina (Athabaskan) leader (Orth 1967). The Russian name corresponds to English *Basil.*

WASIOJA (Minn., Dodge Co.) \wä sē ō´ jə\. Said to be from Dakota (Siouan) <wazi oju> 'pine-clad' (Upham 2001); cf. *wazí* 'pine', *óžu* 'to be full' (Riggs 1890). The name **Wasioja** \wä sē ō´ ə\ occurs as a transfer in Calif. (Santa Barbara Co.).

WASIOTO (Ky., Bell Co.) \wä sē ō´ tə\. Said to be from Cherokee (Iroquoian) <Ouasioto> 'mountain pass' (Rennick 1984).

WASKANARESKA Bay (Alaska, Afognak A-3). The Alutiiq (Eskimo) name was reported in 1952 (Orth 1967).

WASKISH (Minn., Beltrami Co.). A variant of **Washkish**; see above.

WASOLA (Mo., Ozark Co.) \was ō´ lə, wə sō´ lə\. Perhaps from an unidentified Indian language (Ramsay 1952).

WASQUE Point (Mass., Dukes Co.). Perhaps from SNEng. Algonquian <waskeke> 'whale-bone' (Huden 1962; W. Cowan p.c.).

WASSAIC (N.Y., Dutchess Co.). Perhaps from Mahican (Algonquian), but of unclear derivation (Ruttenber 1906; Beauchamp 1907). **Wassaic** occurs as a transfer name in N.Dak. (Mountrail Co.).

WASSAMASSAW (S.C., Berkeley Co.). Earlier written <Wassum Saw>, <Wausumsaw> (Waddell 1980). Perhaps from Catawba (Siouan), meaning 'cane-ground river' (Pickens 1961–62: 23).

WASSATAQUOIK Lake (Maine, Piscataquis Co.). From Abenaki (Algonquian), perhaps meaning 'clear shining lake' (Huden 1962); cf. **Wass Point** above.

WASSAW Creek (Ga., Chatham Co.). Perhaps from Muskogee *wēso* /wí:so/ 'sassafras' (Krakow 1975; Martin and Mauldin 2000).

WASSOOKEAG, Lake (Maine, Penobscot Co.). From Abenaki (Algonquian), perhaps meaning 'shining fishing-place' (Huden 1962).

WASS Point (Maine, Washington Co.). Perhaps from Abenaki (Algonquian) <wassa-> 'clear, bright' (Huden 1962; Day 1994–95). A possbily related name is **Wassataquoik Lake**, below.

WASSUC (Conn., Hartford Co.). A shortening of <Assawassuck>; perhaps from SNEng. Algonquian <nashaue-suck> 'between-brook' (Trumbull 1881). In Nev. (Mineral Range) **Wassuk** may be an adaptation of the same name.

WASSUMA Creek (Calif., Madera Co.) \wä so͞o´ mə\. The name of a Southern Sierra Miwok village, perhaps from *wassa* 'pine' or *wasayya-* 'mush-stirrer; coarse acorn flour' (Gudde 1998).

WASTA (S.Dak., Pennington Co.) \wäs´ tə\. From Lakhota (Siouan) *wašté* 'be good' (Sneve 1973; Ingham 2001). A related placename is **Washta** (Iowa, Cherokee Co.).

WASTINA (Ore., Lake Co.) \wä stē´ nə\. Said to be from an unidentified Indian language, meaning 'beautiful valley' (McArthur 1992). Perhaps a coinage from Sioux *wašté* 'good'; see **Wasta** above.

WATAB (Minn., Benton Co.) \wä´ tab\. From Ojibwa (Algonquian) <watab> 'roots used as threads for sewing canoes' (Baraga 1880; Upham 2001). A related placename is **Watap Lake** (Minn., Cook Co.).

WATABA Lake (Conn., Fairfield Co.). Perhaps from Mahican (Algonquian) <wottapp> 'root' (Huden 1962; W. Cowan p.c.).

WATAGA (Ill., Knox Co.) \wə tä´ gə\. Perhaps from the same source as **Watauga** (S.Dak., Corson Co.): from Lakhota (Siouan) *watháǧe* 'foam, froth' (Ingham 2001); or perhaps from the **Watauga River** in N.C. and Tenn. (Vogel 1963); see below. The placename **Wataga** also occurs in Mo. (Mercer Co.) and Mont. (Stillwater Co.).

WATAHOMIGIE Point (Ariz., Coconino Co.) \wä tə hō´ mi jē\. From the surname of a Havasupai (Yuman) family (Granger 1983). The Native American name is [watahómija], perhaps meaning 'stripped house'; cf. [wa] 'house', [tahómiga] 'to strip off' (L. Hinton p.c.).

WATANA Creek (Alaska, Talkeetna Mountains D-3) \wə tä´ nə\. Perhaps from Ahtna (Athabaskan) *debae-tse' na'*, lit. 'sheep-head creek' (Kari 1983).

WATANGA Mountain (Colo., Grand Co.) \wə täng´ gə\. Named for an Arapaho (Algonquian) leader; his Native American name is said to have been *wó'teen-koo'óh* 'black coyote' (A. Cowell p.c.). A related placename is **Watonga** (Okla., Blaine Co.).

WATAP Lake (Minn., Cook Co.). From the same origin as **Watab** (Minn., Benton Co.); see above.

WATAQUADOCK Hill (Mass., Worcester Co.). Perhaps from SNEng. Algonquian <wudtuckqu> 'piece of wood' (Huden 1962; W. Cowan p.c.).

WATASA Lake (Wis., Shawano Co.). From the name of a nineteenth-century Menominee (Algonquian) leader, also written <Way-taw-say> (etc.) (Vogel 1991). A related placename is **Watosah Lake** (Wis., Menominee Co.).

WATASSA Lake (Mich., Mason Co.). Perhaps shortened from Ojibwa (Algonquian) *waawaatesi* 'firefly' (Vogel 1986; Nichols and Nyholm 1995). Possibly related names are **Wauwatosa** (Wis., Milwaukee Co.) and **Wawatosa Island** (Minn., Hennepin Co.).

WATATIC Lake (Mass., Worcester Co.). From SNEng. Algonquian, perhaps meaning 'mountain stream' (Huden 1962).

WATAUGA River (Tenn., Johnson Co.; N.C., Watauga Co.) \wə tô´ gə\. Earlier written <Watagi, Watogo> (etc.); said to be the name of a Cherokee village, recorded in 1771. The placename appears in many states (e.g., Ky., Clinton Co.; N.Y., Delaware Co.; and Tex., Tarrant Co.). In S.Dak. (Corson Co.) the name **Watauga** may have a separate origin, from Lakhota (Siouan) *wathá̃ǧe* 'foam'; see **Wataga** above. Another probable transfer of **Watauga** is **Lake Watawga** (Pa., Wayne Co.).

WATCHAUG Brook (Conn., Tolland Co.). From SNEng. Algonquian, perhaps meaning 'hill country'; cf. <wadchu> 'hill', <-auke> 'land' (Trumbull 1881; W. Cowan p.c.). This placename also occurs in Mass. (Hampden Co.) and R.I. (Washington Co.). A possibly related name is **Watchogue Creek** (N.Y., Suffolk Co.).

WATCHEMOKET Cove (R.I., Providence Co.). Also written <Watchamoquot>; from SNEng. Algonquian, perhaps containing <wadchu> 'hill' (Huden 1962; W. Cowan p.c.).

WATCH Hill (R.I., Washington Co.). Perhaps from Narragansett (SNEng. Algonquian) <wadchu> 'hill' (W. Cowan p.c.). In Mass. (Dukes Co.), **Watcha Pond** may be from the same source.

WATCHIC Pond (Maine, Cumberland Co.). Perhaps from Abenaki (Algonquian), meaning 'at the mountain' (Huden 1962); cf. *wajo* 'mountain, hill' (Day 1994–95).

WATCHOGUE Creek (N.Y., Suffolk Co.) \wä´ chog\. Perhaps from SNEng. Algonquian, of unclear derivation (Tooker 1911); cf. **Watchaug Brook** above.

WATCHUNG (N.J., Somerset Co.). Perhaps from Delaware (Algonquian) *ohchung* 'hilly place' (Kraft and Kraft 1985); cf. <wachtschu> 'hill, mountain' (Brinton and Anthony 1888).

WATEREE (S.C., Richland Co.). From Catawban (Siouan) /wá:tiri:/ 'rapids' (Pearson 1978; B. Rudes p.c.).

WATERNOMEE, Mount (N.H., Grafton Co.) \wä tər nō´ mē\. Perhaps named for an Abenaki (Algonquian) leader killed in 1712 (Julyan and Julyan 1993).

WATHA Gulch (Colo., Larimer Co.) Perhaps from Arapaho *wóoxe* 'knife' (Bright 1993).

WATHENA (Kans., Doniphan Co.) \wô thē´ nə\. Said to be named for a nineteenth-century Potawatomi (Algonquian) leader; the name has also been written as <Wa-se-na, Wathene> (etc.) (Rydjord 1968).

WATNONG Mountain (N.J., Morris Co.). Probably from Delaware (Algonquian), but of unclear derivation (Becker 1964).

WATOGA (W.Va., Pocahontas Co.). Probably from the same origin as **Watauga River** (Tenn., Johnson Co.); see above.

WATONGA (Okla., Blaine Co.) \wä tong´ gə\. From the same origin as **Watanga Mountain** (Colo., Grand Co.); see above.

WATONWAN County (Minn.) \wä´ tən wən\. Said to be from Dakota (Siouan) <watanwan> 'fish bait' (Upham 2001); cf. *wat ą* 'bait' (Riggs 1890).

WATOPA Township (Minn., Wabasha Co.) \wä tō´ pə\. From Dakota (Siouan) *watópha* 'to paddle a canoe' (Upham 2001; Riggs 1890).

WATOSAH Lake (Wis., Menominee Co.) \wä tō´ sə\. From the same origin as **Watasa Lake** (Wis., Shawsano Co.); see above.

WATOVA (Okla., Nowata Co.) \wä tō´ və\. Named for an Osage (Siouan) leader; the term is said to mean 'spider' (Shirk 1974); but it is doubtful if this is an Osage name (R. Rankin p.c.).

WATSECO (Ore., Tillamook Co.). Perhaps a transfer of **Watseka** (Ill., Iroquois Co.) \wät sē´ kə\. This is said to have been named for a Potawatomi (Algonquian) woman of the early nineteenth century, whose name was also written <Watch-e-kee> (Vogel 1963). The name also occurs in Ala. (Blount Co.) and Mont. (Rochester Co.

WATSESSING Park (N.J., Essex Co.). Probably from Delaware (Algonquian), of unclear derivation (Becker 1964).

WATTAMUSE Creek (Alaska, Goodnews Bay B-6). Perhaps a folk-etymologized version of <Wahmus>, also <Watermouse>, recorded in 1919. The term may be from *Bartimeus,* the baptismal name of a Yupik (Eskimo) resident (Orth 1967).

WATTENSAW (Ark., Lonoke Co.). From earlier <Ouatensaw>; perhaps from the Quapaw (Siouan) language (Dickinson 1995).

WATULA Creek (Ala., Lee Co.) \wə to͞o´ lə\. Perhaps shortened from Muskogee *wvtolv-hake* /watola-há:ki/ 'sandhill crane', lit. 'whooping crane'; cf. *wvtolv* /watóla/ 'crane (bird)', *haketv* /ha:kitá/ 'to make a melodious animal noise' (Read 1984; Martin and Mauldin 2000).

WATUPPA Pond (Mass., Bristol Co.). From SNEng. Algonquian <wottapp> 'root' (Huden 1962; W. Cowan p.c.).

WAUBAN Beach (Mich., Cheboygan Co.). Probably from Ojibwa (Algonquian) *waaban* 'be dawn' (Nichols and Nyholm 1995); see **Wabana Lake** (Minn., Itasca Co.) above. There is also a **Wauban Pond** in Mass. (Franklin Co.).

WAUBAY (S.Dak., Day Co.) \wô bā\. Perhaps from Dakota (Siouan) *hoȟpí, wahóȟpi* 'bird's nest' (Sneve 1973; Riggs 1890). A spelling variant is **Wahbay Township.**

WAUBEEK (Wis., Pepin Co.) \wô bēk\. Probably adapted from <wawbeek>, a supposed Ojibwa (Algonquian) word for 'rock'; see **Wabek** above.

WAUBEEKA Lake (Conn., Fairfield Co.). Earlier written <Waubcoka>; perhaps from Mahican (Algonquian), meaning 'a crossing place' (Huden 1962).

WAUBEE Lake (Wis., Oconto Co.) \wô bē\. Perhaps shortened from an Ojibwa (Algonquian) word beginning with *waabi-* 'white' (Vogel 1991; Nichols and Nyholm 1995). Probably related placenames include the nearby **Waupee Creek** (Oconto Co.).

WAUBEESEE Lake (Wis., Racine Co.). Perhaps from the same origin as **Waubesa** (Wis., Dane Co.); see below.

WAUBEKA (Wis., Ozaukee Co.) \wô´ bē kə\. Said to be named for a nineteenth-century Potawatomi (Algonquian) leader (Vogel 1991).

WAUBESA, Lake (Wis., Dane Co.). Perhaps from Ojibwa (Algonquian) *waabizii* 'swan' (Vogel 1991; Nichols and Nyholm 1995). A related form is **Waubeesee** (Wis., Racine Co.).

WAUBONSEE Creek (Ill., Kane Co.) \wə bon´ zē\. From the same origin as **Wabaunsee County** (Kans.); see above. Another related placename is **Waubonsie** (Iowa, Fremont Co.); this name also occurs in Ill. (Kendall Co.).

WAUBUN (Minn., Mahnomen Co.). Probably from Ojibwa (Algonquian) *waaban* 'be dawn', the same origin as **Wabana Lake** (Minn., Itasca Co.).

WAUCAPENA (Neb., Cedar Co.). Perhaps named for a Potawatomi (Algonquian) leader (Perkey 1995).

WAUCEDAH (Mich., Dickinson Co.). Perhaps a transfer from a former Wis. placename of Siouan origin, referring to pine trees (Vogel 1986); cf. Dakota *wazí* 'pine', *wazí-ta* 'toward the pines, north', or Winnebago *waazí* 'pine' plus *-ra* 'nominalizer' (K. Miner p.c.). Probably related placenames include **Wayzata** (Minn., Hennepin Co.) and **Wazeda Lake** (Wis., Monroe Co.). **Wauzeka** (Wis., Crawford Co.) may be named after a person called 'Pine', from Winnebago *waazí* 'pine' plus *-ga* 'personal ending' (K. Miner p.c.); a possible variant is **Lake Wazeecha** (Wis., Wood Co.).

WAUCHEESI (Tenn., Monroe Co.) \wô ches´ ē\. Perhaps from an unidentified Indian language (Siler 1985).

WAUCHULA (Fla., Hardee Co.) \wä cho͞o´ lə\. Perhaps from Choctaw (Muskogean) *wosholli* 'to ferment, to form froth' (Read 1934; P. Munro p.c.). A possibly related placename is **Washley Creek** (La., Tangipahoa Par.).

WAUCOBA Canyon (Calif., Inyo Co.) \wə kō´ bə\. From Owens Valley Paiute /wokóbɨ/ or Northern Paiute (both Numic) /wogópi/ 'bull pine' (Gudde 1998).

WAUCOMA (Iowa, Fayette Co.) \wô kō´ mə\. Probably from the name of a nineteenth-century Meskwaki (Algonquian) leader; the Native American term may have been */wa:hkami:ha/, referring to 'clear water', from /wa:hkam-/ 'clean, clear' (Vogel 1983; I. Goddard p.c.). The placename also occurs in Ore. (Hood River Co.), but there it may be from Wishram (Chinookan) /wa-/ 'feminine gender' plus /-ikúma/ 'cottonwood tree' (D. Kinkade p.c.).

WAUCONDA (Ill., Lake Co.) \wô kon´ də, wə kon´ də\. From Dakota (Siouan) *wakhą́da* 'to worship' (Riggs 1890; Ingham 2001). The placename **Wauconda** is also found in Wash. (Okanogan Co.). This is from the same source as **Waconda, Wakanda Park, Wakonda** (etc.); see above.

WAUCOUSTA (Wis., Fond du Lac Co.) \wä ko͞os´ tə\. From the same origin as **Wacousta Township** (Iowa, Humboldt Co.); see above.

WAUGOSHANCE Point (Mich., Emmet Co.) \wä´ gə shäns\. Probably from an Ottawa (Algonquian) diminutive of 'fox' (Vogel 1986); cf. Ojibwa (Algonquian) *waagoshens* 'little fox', from *waagosh* 'fox' (Nichols and Nyholm 1995). Possibly related placenames include **Wayka Creek** (Wis., Menominee Co.).

WAUHATCHIE Branch (Ga., Dade Co.) \wô hach´ ē\. Perhaps from a Cherokee (Iroquoian) form which has been translated as 'terrible wolf' (Goff 1975; Krakow 1975); cf. Cherokee *wahya* 'wolf' (Feeling 1975). Variants are **Wahachee, Wahatchie.** The placename **Wauhatchie** also occurs in Tenn. (Hamilton Co.).

WAUHAUKAUPAUKEN Falls (Wash., Pierce Co.). The name, said to mean 'spouting water', is from an unidentified Indian language (Hitchman 1985).

WAUHILLAU (Okla., Adair Co.). Said to be from Cherokee (Iroquoian) <awa'hili> 'eagle' (Shirk 1974).

WAUKAU (Wis., Winnebago Co.) \wô´ kô\. From the surname of a Menominee (Algonquian) family (Vogel 1991); probably from Menominee /wa:kow/ 'fox' (Bloomfield 1975). Possibly related placenames include **Waugoshance Point** (MI, Emmet Co.) and **Wayka Creek** (Wis., Menominee Co.).

WAUKAZOO (Mich., Ottawa Co.). Probably named for an Ottawa (Algonquian) leader of the early nineteenth century. His name was also written <Wah-ka-zee, Wa-ke-zoo>, perhaps related to the village name <War-gun-uk-ke-zee>, in French *L'Arbre Croché,* in English 'crooked tree' (Vogel 1986); cf. Ottawa *waagzid* 'be crooked' (Rhodes 1985) as well as Ojibwa <wâgâkosi mitig> 'the tree is crooked' (Baraga 1880), *waaga* 'be bent' (Nichols and Nyholm 1995).

WAUKEAG (Maine, Hancock Co.). A shortening of <Adowaukeag>, perhaps from Abenaki (Algonquian) <adowaket> 'glacial ridge', locally called a 'horseback' (Eckstorm 1941:210–11).

WAUKECHON (Wis., Shawano Co.) \wô´ kə shon\. Named for a Menominee (Algonquian) leader (Vogel 1991). The Native American name is perhaps /wa:keca:na:pɛ:w/, lit. 'crooked beak man'; cf. /wa:kekew/ 'it is crooked' (Bloomfield 1975).

WAUKEE (Iowa, Dallas Co.) \wô´ kē\. A shortening of **Milwaukee County;** see above.

WAUKEEFRISKEE Creek (Ga., Clay Co.) A variant spelling of **Wakofudsky**; see above.

WAUKEENA Lake (N.H., Merrimack Co.) \wä kē´ nə\. Perhaps from Abenaki (Algonquian), of unclear derivation (Huden 1962). In Fla. (Jefferson Co.) **Waukeenah** is a possible transfer of **Waukeena.**

WAUKEGAN (Ill., Lake Co.) \wô kē´ gən\. Perhaps from Potawatomi (Algonquian) <wakāígín> 'fort'; cf. Ojibwa <wâkaigan> 'fort' (Baraga 1880; Vogel 1963).

WAUKELL Creek (Calif., Del Norte Co.) \wô kel`\. From the Yurok village name /wo'ke'l/ (Gudde 1998).

WAUKENABO (Minn., Aitkin Co.) Said to be from Ojibwa (Algonquian) <wakonabo> 'broth of moss growing on rocks or trees' (Upham 2001); cf. <wâkon> 'moss of cedar and some other trees', <-âbo> 'liquid, soup' (Baraga 1880).

WAUKESHA County (Wis.) \wô´ kə shä\. Probably from Ojibwa (Algonquian) *waagosh* 'fox' (Nichols and Nyholm 1995). The placename also occurs in Wash. (Lincoln Co.) \wô kē´ shə\ and in Pa. (Clearfield Co.).

WAUKOMIS (Okla., Garfield Co.) \wô kō´ mis\. Perhaps from an unidentified Indian language. The name also occurs in Miss. (Alcorn Co.) (Shirk 1974).

WAUKON (Iowa, Allamakee Co.) \wô kon`\. Probably named for a Winnebago (Siouan) leader, shortened from <Wau-kon-haw-kaw> 'snakeskin' (Vogel 1983). The Native American form is probably /wakahága/, from /waką́/ 'snake', /háa/ 'skin', and /-ga/ 'personal name ending' (K. Miner p.c.).

WAUKON (Minn., Norman Co.) \wô´ kon\. Probably from Dakota (Siouan) *wakhą́* 'a spirit, something sacred' (Upham 2001; Riggs 1890). The placename also occurs in Wash. (Lincoln Co.). Related placenames include **Wahkon** (Minn., Mille Lacs Co.), **Waconda** (Minn., St. Louis Co.), and **Wakonda** (S.Dak., Clay Co.).

WAUKSHA, Bayou (La., St. Landry Par.) \wôk´ shə\. The term refers to an Muskogean subgroup, called *wakse* /wáksi/ in Muskogee; the source may be Catawban (Siouan) /wátsa:'/ 'crest of hair' (B. Rudes p.c.). A variant is **Waxia.** Possibly related placenames are **Waxhaw** (N.C., Union Co.) and **Waxahatchee** (Ala., Shelby Co.).

WAUMANDEE (Wis., Buffalo Co.) \wô´ mən dē\. Probably an abbreviation of the name of a Dakota (Siouan) leader, <wa-man-de-tun-ka>; he was known in English as "Black Dog," but the Native American name means 'big eagle', from *wąmdí* 'a type of eagle' and *thą́ka* 'big' (Vogel 1991; Riggs 1890).

WAUMBEK, Mount (N.H., Coös Co.) \wôm´ bek, wäm´ bek\. Probably related to Abenaki (Algonquian) *wôbigen* [wǫbigən] 'white' (Julyan and Julyan 1993; W. Cowan p.c.).

WAU-ME-GAH Lake (Mich., Oakland Co.). Perhaps an Ojibwa (Algonquian) name, but of unclear derivation (Vogel 1986).

WAUNA (Ore., Clatsop Co.) \wô´ nə\. Perhaps from Sahaptin /wána/ 'river' (McArthur 1992; D. Kinkade p.c.). The placename also occurs in Wash. (Pierce Co.).

WAUNAKEE (Wis., Dane Co.) \wô´ nə kē\. Supposedly from Ojibwa (Algonquian) *wânaki* 'to live in peace' (Baraga 1880; Vogel 1991).

WAUNEKA Point (Ore., Multnomah Co.) \wô nē´ kə\. Said to be a placename in an unidentified Indian language (McArthur 1992).

WAUNETA (Kans., Chautauqua Co.) \wô nē´ tə\. Probably from the same source as **Waunita** (Colo., Gunnison Co.), supposedly the name of an Indian woman. The name may be a respelling of the Spanish *Juanita,* familiar from a popular song of the nineteenth century (Bright 1993). Related placenames include **Juanita** and **Waneta** etc.

WAUNONA Park (Wis., Dane Co.). Perhaps an alternative form of **Winona County;** see below.

WAUPACA County (Wis.) \wô pak´ ə\. Said to be named for a Potawatomi (Algonquian) man who lived in the early nineteenth century; the derivation of the name is not clear (Vogel 1991). In Ill. (Grundy Co.) the name of **Waupecan Creek** has similarly obscure Potawatomi associations (Vogel 1963).

WAUPAN Valley (Neb., Cherry Co.) \wô´ pan, wô´ pən\. Perhaps from the same source as **Waubun** (Mich., Mahnomen Co.; see above) or **Waupun** (Wis., Fond du Lac Co.).

WAUPEE Creek (Wis., Oconto Co.) \wô´ pē\. Perhaps an abbreviation of a Potawatomi (Algonquian) personal name beginning in <wabi-> 'white' (Vogel 1991). A probably related placename, also in Oconto Co., is **Waubee Lake**; see above.

WAUPETON (Iowa, Dubuque Co.) \wä´ pə tən\. From Dakota (Siouan) *wahpé-thų̧wą̧* 'leaf-people', the name of a tribal subgroup (Vogel 1983; HNAI 13:753). A related placename is **Wahpeton** (Iowa, Dickinson Co.).

WAUPONSEE (Ill., Grundy Co.). An alternative form of **Wabaunsee County** (Kans.); see above.

WAUPUN (Wis., Fond du Lac Co.) \wô pun´\. An alternative form of **Wauban Beach** (Mich., Cheboygan Co.) or **Waubun** (Minn., Mahnomen Co.); see above.

WAUREGAN (Conn., Windham Co.). From SNEng. Algonquian, perhaps meaning 'a good thing' (Trumbull 1881).

WAURIKA (Okla., Jefferson Co.) \wô rē´ kə\. Perhaps from Comanche (Numic) /wo'arɨhka/, the name of a tribal band; the term is literally 'worm eaters', from /wo'a/ 'worm' (J. McLaughlin p.c.).

WAUSA (Neb., Knox Co.) \wô´ sô, wô´ sə\. Perhaps an alternative form of **Wausau** (Wis., Marathon Co.) \wô´ sô\. This is from Ojibwa (Algonquian) *waasa* 'far, distant' (Vogel 1991; Nichols and Nyholm 1995). The placename also is found in Fla. (Washington Co.). A probably related name is **Wausaukee** (Wis., Marinette Co.) \wô sô´ kē\, said to mean 'far-away land' (Vogel 1991); cf. Ojibwa *aki* 'land' (Nichols and Nyholm 1995).

WAUSEON (Ohio, Fulton Co.) \wô´ sē on\. Said to be the name of a Potawatomi (Algonquian) leader in the early nineteenth century (Miller 1996); perhaps derived from a word for 'bear'. The placename also occurs in Fla. (Orange Co.). A possibly related placename is **Owosso Lake** (Minn., Ramsey Co.).

WAUSHACUM Pond (Mass., Worcester Co.). From SNEng. Algonquian, perhaps reflecting <wechekum> 'seacoast' (W. Cowan p.c.). A probably related name is **Waushakum Pond** (Mass., Middlesex Co.).

WAUSHARA County (Wis.) \wô shâr´ ə\. An abbreviation of Winnebago (Siouan) <Waushay-ray-kay-ga> (Vogel 1991), that is, /wašerekéga/ 'The Fox', from *wašereké* 'fox' (K. Miner p.c.). The placename also occurs in Kans. (Lyon Co.).

WAUTAUGA (Wash., Kitsap Co.). Perhaps an adaptation of **Watauga River** (Tenn., Johnson Co.); see above.

WAUTOMA (Wis., Waushara Co.) \wô tō´ mə\. Perhaps a coinage based on the placename **Waushara County,** from Winnebago (Siouan), plus a Menominee (Algonquian) personal name *Tomow,* originally /toma:wɛ:hsaw/ (Vogel 1991; Bloomfield 1975).

WAUTUBBEE (Miss., Clarke Co.). Probably named for a Choctaw (Muskogean) man, a "war name" meaning 'one who hunts and kills', from *owatta* 'to hunt', plus connective *-t-*, plus *abi* 'to kill' (Seale 1939; P. Munro p.c.).

WAUWATOSA (Wis., Milwaukee Co.) \wô wə tō´ sə\. Probably from Ojibwa (Algonquian) *waawaatesi* 'firefly' (Vogel 1991; Nichols and Nyholm 1995). Possibly related names are **Watassa Lake** (Mich., Mason Co.) and **Wawatosa Island** (Minn., Hennepin Co.).

WAUWINET (Mass., Nantucket Co.). From SNEng. Algonquian, perhaps containing <wauwau-> 'testify' (Huden 1962; W. Cowan p.c.).

WAUXAMAKA Creek (Ala., Macon Co.) \wôk sə mā´ kə\. Perhaps named for a Muskogee man called <woksi miko> (Read 1984); cf. *wakse* /wáksi/, a clan name, and *mēkko* /mí:kko/ 'chief' (Martin and Mauldin 2000). A possibly related placename is **Waxahatchee** (Ala.).

WAUZEKA (Wis., Crawford Co.) \wô zē´ kə\. Apparently from Winnebago (Siouan) *waaziga*; cf. *waazí* 'pine' (K. Miner p.c.). Possibly related placenames include **Waucedah** (Mich., Dickinson Co.), **Wayzata** (Minn., Hennepin Co.), **Wazeda Lake** (Wis., Monroe Co.), and **Lake Wazeecha** (Wis., Wood Co.).

WAWA Creek (Ore., Clatsop Co.) \wô´ wô\. Chinook Jargon <wawa, wau-wau> [wáwa, wɒ́wɒ] 'talk, speak, call, ask; speech, sermon, language', perhaps referring here to the sound of the creek, from Nootka /wawaa/ 'to say'; cf. also Kathlamet (Chinookan) [wáwa] 'talk, say' (McArthur 1992; D. Kinkade p.c.). The placename **Wawa Point** also occurs in Wash. (Jefferson Co.).

WAWAKA (Ind., Noble Co.) \wə wä´ kə\. The name is said to mean 'big heron' in an unidentified Indian language (Baker 1995).

WAWA Lake (Minn., Cass Co.). Earlier called "Goose Lake"; popularized by Longfellow, from Ojibwa (Algonquian) *we'we* 'snow goose' (I. Goddard p.c.). The term has been transferred to Pa. (Delaware Co.), where it is familiar as the name of a grocery chain.

WAWARSING (N.Y., Ulster Co.) \wə wôr´ sing\. Earlier written <Wawasink>; perhaps from Munsee Delaware (Algonquian), of unclear derivation (Beauchamp 1907).

WAWASEE (Ind., Kosciusko Co.) \wä´ wä sē\. Named for a Miami/Illinois (Algonquian) leader, <Wah-we-as-see>, translated 'full moon' or 'round one', from /waawiyasita/ 'he is round' (McCafferty 2002).

WAWASET (Pa., Chester Co.) \wə wä´ sət\. Perhaps from a Delaware (Algonquian) placename (Donehoo 1928). The name also occurs in Del. (New Castle Co.).

WAWATAM Township (Mich., Emmet Co.) \wä´ wə täm\. Named after an Ojibwa (Algonquian) man who lived in in the eighteenth century, also written <Wow-yat-ton> 'whirling eddy' (Vogel 1986); cf. <wanâtan> 'there is a whirlpool' (Baraga 1880).

WAWATOSA Island (Minn., Hennepin Co.) \wä wə tō´ sə\. Probably from the same source as **Wauwatosa** (Wis., Milwaukee Co.) A possibly related placename is **Watassa** (Mich., Mason Co.).

WAWAWAI Bay (Wash., Whitman Co.) \wə wä´ wē, wə wä´ ē, wə wī´\. From the Nez Perce (Sahaptian) placename /wawá:wi:/ (Aoki 1994).

WAWAYANDA (N.Y., Orange Co.) \wā wə yän´ də\. Perhaps a Munsee Delaware placename, of unclear derivation (Ruttenber 1906). The name also occurs in N.J. (Sussex Co.).

WAWBEEK (N.Y., Franklin Co.) \wô´ bēk\. An alternative form of an Ojibwa (Algonquian) word for 'rock'; see **Wabeek Lake** (Mich., Oakland Co.). The placename **Wawbeek** also occurs in N.H. (Carroll Co.).

WAWECUS Hill (Conn., New London Co.). From SNEng. Algonquian, the name of a Mohegan man who lived around 1600 (Huden 1962).

WAWELA Park (Mass., Worcester Co.). Perhaps from Abenaki (Algonquian), meaning 'white ducks' (Huden 1962).

WAWENOCK (Maine, Lincoln Co.). From Penobscot (Algonquian) /wɑ̃winak/, evidently meaning 'round or oval island' (*HNAI* 15:146).

WAWINA (Minn., Itasca Co.) \wä wē´ nə\. A railroad name, perhaps <wâwina> 'to name often, mention frequently', probably taken from Baraga's Ojibwa (Algonquian) dictionary (Baraga 1880; Upham 2001).

WAWONA (Calif., Mariposa Co.) \wä wō´ nə\. From Southern Sierra Miwok /wohwohna/ 'sequoia, redwood tree' (Gudde 1998).

WAWPECONG (Ind., Miami Co.) \wä´ pə kong\. Said to be from Miami/Illinois (Algonquian) <wa-pi-pa-ka-na> 'shell-bark hickories' (Baker 1995); cf. Ojibwa (Algonquian) *bagaan* 'nut' (Nichols and Nyholm 1995), Meskwaki (Algonquian) /paka:ni/ 'hickory nut' (Goddard 1994). Cf. **Pecan**.

WAXAHACHIE (Tex., Ellis Co.) \wäk sə hach´ ē\. Perhaps a transfer of **Waxahatchee** (Ala., Shelby Co.); see below. Or perhaps from something close to the Wichita (Caddoan) /waksʔashe:cʔa/ 'fat monster', containing /waks/ 'a mythical monster' and /he:c/ 'fat' (Bright 1999a; D. Rood p.c.).

WAXAHATCHEE (Ala., Shelby Co.) \waks ə hach´ ē\. Perhaps from Muskogee *wakse* /wáksi/, a clan name, plus *hvcce* /háčči/ 'stream' (Read 1984; Martin and Mauldin 2000). Possibly related placenames are **Waxhaw** (N.C., Union Co.) and **Bayou Wauksha** (La., St. Landry Par.).

WAXHAW (N.C., Union Co.). Perhaps from Catawban (Siouan) /wátsa:'/ 'crest of hair' (Powell 1968; B. Rudes p.c.). The placename also occurs in S.C. (Lancaster Co.) and Miss. (Bolivar Co.). Possibly related names are **Bayou Wauksha** (La., St. Landry Par.) and **Waxahatchee** (Ala., Shelby Co.).

WAXIA (La., St. Landry Par.). An alternate form of **Bayou Wauksha**; see above.

WAYAH Bald (N.C., Macon Co.). Perhaps from Cherokee (Iroquoian) *wahya* 'wolf' (Powell 1968; Feeling 1975).

WAYANITOKE (R.I., Washington Co.). From SNEng. Algonquian, perhaps meaning 'twisting current' (Huden 1962).

WAYCAKE Creek (N.J., Monmouth Co.) \wā´ kāk\. Probably from Delaware (Algonquian), but of unclear derivation (Becker 1964). A variant spelling is **Waackaack Creek.**

WAYEHUTTA Creek (N.C., Jackson Co.). Perhaps from a placename of an unidentified Indian language (Powell 1968).

WAYHUT Lake (Wash., Snohomish Co.) \wä´ hut\. Chinook Jargon <o´ihat, way´-hut, wee-hut> [óyhət, óyhʊt] 'road, path, trail', from Lower Chinook <ó-e-hut> 'road, trail' (Hitchman 1985; D. Kinkade p.c.). A related placename is **Oyhut** (Wash., Grays Harbor Co.).

WAYKA Creek (Wis., Menominee Co.) \wā´ kə\. A Menominee (Algonquian) personal name, from /wa:koh/ 'fox' (Vogel 1991; Bloomfield 1975). Possibly related placenames include **Waugoshance Point** (Mich., Emmet Co.) and **Waukau** (Wis., Winnebago Co.).

WAY LUWA (Wash., Asotin Co.). From the Nez Perce placename /wel'íwe/, related to /wal'áwa/ 'Wallowa River' (Aoki 1994; D. Kinkade p.c.).

WAYNOKA (Okla., Woods Co.) \wā nō´ kə, wə nō´ kə\. Said to be from Cheyenne (Algonquian) /tseve'eeno'e/ 'that which tastes sweet', containing /vé(k)e-/ 'sweet' and /-éno'e/ 'taste' (Shirk 1974; W. Leman p.c.). There is also a **Lake Waynoka** in Ohio (Brown Co.).

WAYZATA (Minn., Hennepin Co.) \wī zet´ ə\. Probably from Dakota (Siouan) *wazíyata* 'north', lit. 'at the pines', from *wazí* 'pine' (Riggs 1890; Upham 2001). A possibly related form is **Wazeda Lake** (Wis., Monroe Co.), which probably contains Winnebago (Siouan) *waazí* 'pine' (K. Miner p.c.). Perhaps from the same Siouan stem are **Wayzetta** (N.Dak.,

Mountrail Co.), **Waucedah** (Mich., Dickinson Co.), **Lake Wazeecha** (Wis., Wood Co.), and **Wazeka** (Wis., Jackson Co.).

WAZEECHA, Lake (Wis., Wood Co.) \wä zē´ chə\. Probably from Dakota (Siouan) *wazíčhą* 'pine tree', from *wazí* 'pine' plus *čhą* 'tree' (Vogel 1991; Williamson 1902). Probably containing the same stem is **Wazeka** (Wis., Jackson Co.) \wä zē´ kə\. Other related placenames include **Waucedah** (Mich., Dickinson Co.) and **Wayzata** (Minn., Hennepin Co.).

WEA Creek (Ind., Tippecanoe Co.) \wē´ ə\. The name of a Miami/Illinois (Algonquian) subgroup; an abbreviation of a term first noted in 1673 as <Ouaouiatanoukak>, perhaps meaning 'bend of stream' (McPherson 1993; *HNAI* 15:689). The placename **Wea** also occurs in Kans. (Miami Co.).

WEALAKA (Okla., Tulsa Co.). From Muskogee *ue-vlvkv* /oy-ʔalá:ka/, lit. 'water-rising' (Shirk 1974; Martin and Mauldin 2000). A possibly related placename is **Welaka** (Fla., Putnam Co.); see below.

WEANTINOCK (Conn., Fairfield Co.). From SNEng. Algonquian, of unclear derivation (Trumbull 1881).

WEASAW Creek (Ind., Miami Co.) \wē´ sô\. Named for a Miami/Illinois (Algonquian) leader; the term <wi-saw, we-saw> (etc.) may represent <wīnsi> 'gall, bile' (J. Nichols p.c.). A related name is **Weesaw Township** (Mich., Berrien Co.).

WEATOGUE (Conn., Litchfield Co.). From SNEng. Algonquian, of unclear origin (Trumbull 1881). A related placename is **Wetaug** (Ill., Pulaski Co.).

WEBATUCK (Conn., Litchfield Co.; N.Y., Dutchess Co.) \wē´bə tuk, web´ə tuk\. Perhaps from Mahican (Algonquian) <weepwoiutohke> 'place of the narrow pass', consisting of <weepwoiut> 'passage' plus <-ohke> 'land, place' (Trumbull 1881; W. Cowan p.c.).

WEBHANNET River (Maine, York Co.). From Abenaki (Algonquian), perhaps meaning 'clear stream' (Huden 1962).

WEBINGUAW Lake (Mich., Newaygo Co.). Perhaps from an unidentified Indian language (Vogel 1986).

WECHARTY (Okla., Hughes Co.) \wə chär´ tē\. Said to be named after a blacksmith shop, reflecting Muskogee *wecattetv* /wiča:ttitá/ 'to make sparks' (Shirk 1974; Martin and Mauldin 2000).

WECHES (Tex., Houston Co.) \wē´ chiz\. An adaptation of earlier **Neches**, of unknown origin.

WECOMA Beach (Ore., Lincoln Co.) \wə kō´ mə\. Chinook Jargon <wecoma, we-co´-ma>, probably [wikómə] 'sea', from Lower Chinook [wékua] 'ocean' (McArthur 1992; D. Kinkade p.c.).

WECOTA (S.Dak., Faulk Co.) \wə kō´ tə\. From Dakota (Siouan) *wičhóta* 'many persons, a crowd' (Sneve 1973; Riggs 1890). The town was probably named by whites who interpreted Dakota <wicota> in terms of English spelling.

WEDBOO Creek (S.C., Berkeley Co.). A variant of **Wadboo**; see above.

WEDOWEE (Ala., Randolph Co.) \wi dou´ ē\. Said to be named after an Indian man called <Wahdowwee>, perhaps from Muskogee, meaning 'water sumac'; cf. *uewv, ue-* /óywa, wi-/ 'water' plus *tvwv* /tawá/ 'sumac' (Read 1984; Martin and Mauldin 2000).

WEEHAWKEN (N.J., Hudson Co.) \wē´ hô kən\. From Delaware (Algonquian), of unclear derivation (Becker 1964).

WEEKAPAUG (R.I., Washington Co.). From SNEng. Algonquian, perhaps meaning 'at the end of the water'; cf. <wehque> 'ending at', <-paug> 'water' (Huden 1962; W. Cowan p.c.).

WEEKEEPEEMEE (Conn., Litchfield Co.). Said to be named for a Mahican (Algonquian) man whose name was also written <Wecuppemee, Wickapema> (etc.); perhaps from <wikopi> 'inner bark of the basswood tree' (Huden 1962; W. Cowan p.c.). A possibly related placename is **Wiccopee** (N.Y., Dutchess Co.).

WEEKI WACHEE (Fla., Hernando Co.). From Muskogee, meaning 'a small spring'; cf. *uekiwv* /oykéywa/ 'a spring', abbreviated to /wi:-/, plus *-uce* /-oči/ 'small' (Read 1934; Martin and Mauldin 2000).

WEEPAH (Nev., Esmeralda Co.) \wē´ pä\. From Shoshoni (Numic), meaning 'knife springs', containing /wihi/ 'knife' and /-paa/ 'water, springs' (Carlson 1974, J. McLaughlin p.c.). A related placename is **Wepah Creek** (Idaho, Latah Co.).

WEEPECKET Island (Mass., Dukes Co.). From SNEng. Algonquian, perhaps meaning 'osprey' (Huden 1962).

WEEQUAHIC Park (N.J., Essex Co.). From Delaware (Algonquian), perhaps meaning 'at the end or boundary' (Becker 1964); cf. <wiquajungo> 'at the end' (Brinton and Anthony 1888), Munsee Delaware *wíhkweew* 'to come to an end' (O'Meara 1996).

WEEQUAKUT (Mass., Barnstable Co.). From SNEng. Algonquian, perhaps meaning 'at the end' (Huden 1962).

WEESATCHE (Tex., Goliad Co.) \wē´ sach\. From Mexican Spanish *huisache* 'acacia', from Nahuatl (Aztecan) *huixachin* (Tarpley 1980; Santamaría 1959).

WEESAW Township (Mich., Berrien Co.) \wē´ sô\. Probably from the same source as **Weasaw Creek** (Ind., Miami Co.); see above.

WEESET (Mass., Barnstable Co.). From SNEng. Algonquian, perhaps meaning 'slippery place' (Huden 1962).

WEETAMOO Cliff (Mass., Essex Co.) \wē´ tə mo͞o\. Said to be named for a SNEng. Algonquian female chief, perhaps derived from <wetu-> 'house' (Huden 1962; W. Cowan p.c.). A related placename is **Mt. Weetamoo** (N.H., Grafton Co.), but in this case the term was adapted from John Greenleaf Whittier's poem "The Bridal of Penacook," in which he borrowed the name to refer to his Abenaki (Algonquian) heroine (Julyan and Julyan 1993).

WEGATCHIE (N.Y., St. Lawrence Co.) \wi gach´ ē\. An abbreviation of **Oswegatchie**; see above.

WEGEE Creek (Ohio, Belmont Co.). Supposedly from a word meaning 'winding, crooked' in an unidentified Indian language (Miller 1996); cf. Delaware (Algonquian) <waktscheu> 'crooked', Unami Delaware /wókče/ 'it has a crooked shape' (Blalock et al. 1994).

WEGO-WACO (Kans., Sedgwick Co.). Supposedly derived from an advertising sign that said "To Waco We Go," referring to **Waco** (Tex., McLennan Co.) (Rydjord 1968).

WEGWAAS Lake (Mich., Chippewa Co.). From Ojibwa (Algonquian) *wiigwaas* 'birch bark' (Vogel 1986; Nichols and Nyholm 1995). A related placename is **Wegwos** (Minn., Cass Co.). Another related name is **Wequos** (Mich., Otsego Co.).

WEHADKEE Creek (Ala., Randolph Co.; Ga., Troup Co.) \wi had´ kē\. From Muskogee *uehvtke* /wi:-hátki/, lit. 'water-white' (Read 1984; Martin and Mauldin 2000).

WEHAMBA Creek (Fla., Hillsborough Co.) \wē häm´ bə\. Perhaps from Hitchiti (Muskogean), meaning 'bad water'; cf. <hampi> 'bad' (Read 1934).

WEIMAR (Calif., Placer Co.) \wē´ mär\. Said to have been named for "old Weimah," a leader of an unidentified Indian group. The placename is spelled, though not pronounced, like the German city of *Weimar* (Gudde 1998).

WEIPPE (Idaho, Clearwater Co.) \wē´ īp\. From the Nez Perce placename /oyáyp/ (Aoki 1994).

WEITCHPEC (Calif., Humboldt Co.) \wich´ pek\. From Yurok /wecpek, wecpus/ 'confluence' (Gudde 1998).

WEKIVA (Fla., Lake Co.) \wə kī´ və\. From Muskogee *uekiwv* /oykéywa/ 'a spring' (Read 1934; Martin and Mauldin 2000). The placename also occurs in Okla. (Tulsa Co.). An alternate form is **Wekiwa.**

WELAGAMIKA (Pa., Northampton Co.). From Delaware (Algonquian), perhaps meaning 'best earth', containing <welhick> 'best' and <haki> 'earth' (Brinton and Anthony 1888, Donehoo 1928); cf. Munsee Delaware *wŭlút* 'good', *áhkuy* 'earth' (O'Meara 1996).

WELAKA (Fla., Putnam Co.). Perhaps from Muskogee *ue-vlakv* /oy-ʔalá:ka/ 'water-rising', or from *ue-rakko* /oy-ɬákko/ 'river' (Read 1934; Martin and Mauldin 2000). In the first case, a related placename is **Wealaka** (Okla., Tulsa Co.).

WELAUNEE Creek (Fla., Jefferson Co.) \wə lô´ nē\. Muskogee *ue-lane* /wi:-lá:ni/ 'yellow water', containing /lá:ni/ 'green, brown, yellow' (Read 1984; Martin and Mauldin 2000). An alternative form is **Welawnee.**

WELEETKA (Okla., Okfuskee Co.) \wə lēt´ kə\. From Muskogee *ueletkv* /wi:-lí:tka/, lit. 'water running' (Shirk 1974; Martin and Mauldin 2000).

WELLPINIT (Wash., Stevens Co.) \wel´ pin it\. Perhaps from Nez Perce (Sahaptian), containing /wé:l(e)-/ 'flowing' and /pn'it/ 'pouring out' (Aoki 1994; D. Kinkade p.c.).

WELLS County (Ind.). Named for William Wells, who was born of European ancestry in 1770, was adopted by Miami/Illinois (Algonquian) Indians at age eleven, and became a leader of that people. His Indian name was <Apekonit>, perhaps meaning 'wild carrot' (McPherson 1993).

WELONA (Ala., Coosa Co.) \wi lō´ nə\. Perhaps from the same Muskogee sources as **Welaunee Creek** (Fla., Jefferson Co.; see above). Or perhaps from Muskogee *welanv* /wilá:na/, the name of a plant (Read 1984; Martin and Mauldin 2000).

WEMINUCHE Creek (Colo., Hinsdale Co.) \wem i nōō´ chē\. Previously written <Weeminuche> (etc.); the term refers to a Ute (Numic) subgroup (*HNAI* 11:366). Utes nowadays use the pronunciation *wimɨnuchi* (Bright 1993), but the term may reflect older */wii-nɨŋwɨntsi/ 'canyon people', containing /wii-/ 'canyon' and /nɨŋwɨ(n)/ 'people' (J. McLaughlin p.c.).

WEMROCK Brook (N.J., Monmouth Co.). Perhaps from Delaware (Algonquian), of unclear derivation (Becker 1964).

WENAHA (Wash., Columbia Co.) \wə nä´ hä\. Perhaps from a Cayuse placename /winάha/ (D. Kinkade p.c.). The placename **Wenaha** \wen´ ə hä\ also occurs in Ore. (Wallowa Co.). The name **Wenaka** (also in Wallowa Co.) is said to have been the result of a miswriting.

WENANGO \wə nang´ gō\. A variant of **Venango** (see above), probably from Delaware (Algonquian), perhaps reflecting <onenge, winingus> 'mink' (Donehoo 1928).

WENAS (Wash., Yakima Co.) \wē´ nas\. From a Sahaptin placename /winás, winá:s/ (Hitchman 1985; D. Kinkade p.c.).

WENATCHEE (Wash., Chelan Co.) \wə nach´ ē\. From Sahaptin [wi:náča], said to mean 'river issuing from a canyon' (Hitchman 1985; D. Kinkade p.c.). A possibly related placename is **Menatchee Creek** (Wash., Asotin Co.).

WENAUMET Station (Mass., Barnstable Co.). From SNEng. Algonquian, of unclear derivation (Huden 1962).

WENONA (Ill., Marshall Co.) \wə nō´ nə\. From the same origin as **Winona County**; see below. A related placename is **Wenonah** (Ill., Montgomery Co.); the term also occurs in N.J. (Gloucester Co.) and W.Va. (Mercer Co.).

WEOGUFKA (Ala., Coosa Co.) \wē ō guf´ kə, wē ə guf´ kə\. Muskogee *ue-okofke* /wi:ʔokófki/, lit. 'water-muddy', a tribal town; also used to refer to the Mississippi River (Read 1984; Martin and Mauldin 2000). A related placename is **Weogufkee Church** in Okla. (McIntosh Co.).

WEOHYAKAPKA, Lake (Fla., Polk Co.). Muskogee *ue-ohyvkvpkv* /wi:-ʔoh-yakápka/ 'walking on the water', containing *uewv* /óywa/ 'water', *oh-* 'on', and *yvkvpkv* /yakapka/ 'walking' (Read 1934; Martin and Mauldin 2000).

WEOKA (Ala., Elmore Co.) \wē ō´ kə\. From Muskogee *ue-wohkv* /wi:wóhka/, the name of a tribal town, perhaps meaning 'barking water' or 'roaring water' (Read 1984; Martin and Mauldin 2000). A related placename is **Wewoka** (Ala., Talladega Co.).

WEOLUSTEE Creek (Ala., Russell Co.) \wē ə lus´ tē\. From Muskogee *ue-lvste* /oy-lásti/, lit. 'water-black' (Martin and Mauldin 2000); see **Olustee** (Fla., Baker Co.) above.

WEOTT (Calif., Humboldt Co.) \wē´ ot\. From the same origin as *Wiyot,* a local group of Indians (Gudde 1998).

WEPAH Creek (Idaho, Latah Co.). From the same source as **Weepah** (Nev., Esmeralda Co.); see above.

WEPAWAUG River (Conn., New Haven Co.). From SNEng. Algonquian; cf. <weepwoiauk> 'the passage, the crossing place' (Trumbull 1881; W. Cowan p.c.).

WEPO Village (Ariz., Navajo Co.) \wē´ pō, wā´ pō\. From Hopi (Uto-Aztecan) *wipho* 'cattail' (K. Hill p.c.).

WEQUAPAUG Brook (Conn., New London Co.). From SNEng. Algonquian, perhaps meaning 'at the end of the pond' (Trumbull 1881).

WEQUAPAUSET, Lake (Conn., New Haven Co.). From SNEng. Algonquian, perhaps meaning 'at the end of the small pond' (Trumbull 1881; W. Cowan p.c.).

WEQUAQUET Lake (Mass., Barnstable Co.). From SNEng. Algonquian, perhaps meaning 'shining place' (Huden 1962).

WEQUATUCKET River (Conn., New London Co.). From SNEng. Algonquian, perhaps meaning 'head of a tidal stream' (Trumbull 1881). A variant writing is **Wequetequock.**

WEQUETONSING (Mich., Emmet Co.) \wē kwə ton´ sing\. Said to be from Ojibwa (Algonquian) <wikwedonsing> 'at the little bay' (Vogel 1986); cf. <wikwed> 'bay', <wikwedong> 'in a bay' (Baraga 1880).

WEQUOBSQUE Cliffs (Mass., Dukes Co.). From SNEng. Algonquian, said to mean 'at the end of the rocks' (Huden 1962).

WEQUOS, Lake (Mich., Otsego Co.). From the same origin as **Wegwaas Lake** (Mich., Chippewa Co.); see above.

WERACOBA (Ga., Muscogee Co.). Perhaps from Muskogee, meaning 'big water' (Krakow 1975); cf. *uē-* /wi:-/ 'water', *-rakko* /ɬákko/ 'big' (Martin and Mauldin 2000). An alternative form is **Werocoda.**

WEROWACOMOCO (Va., Gloucester Co.). Said to be a CAC Algonquian village, meaning 'where the *werowances* live'; the term refers to war chiefs (Hagemann 1988).

WESCOGAME Point (Ariz., Coconino Co.). From the name of a Havasupai (Yuman) family (McNamee 1997).

WESCUTOGO Hill (Maine, Cumberland Co.). Perhaps from Abenaki (Algonquian), meaning 'at the mouth of the river' (Huden 1962). An alternative form is **Wesgustogo.**

WESHRINARIN Creek (Alaska, Charley River B-3). The Gwich'in (Athabaskan) name was recorded in 1898 (Orth 1967).

WESICKAMAN Creek (N.J., Burlington Co.). From Delaware (Algonquian), of unclear derivation (Becker 1964).

WESKEAG River (Maine, Knox Co.). A shortening of <Wessaweskeag>, perhaps meaning 'tidal stream at the peninsula' (Eckstorm 1941).

WESOBULGA Creek (Ala., Randolph Co.) Perhaps from Muskogee *wēs-vp-vlke* /wi:s-ap-âlki/ 'sassafras tree grove', containing *wēso* /wí:so/ 'sassafras', *vpe* /apí/ 'stem, tree', and *-vlke* /-âlki/ 'group' (Read 1984; Martin and Mauldin 2000).

WESO Creek (Wis., Oconto Co.). Perhaps from Menominee (Algonquian) /wa:sew/ 'large catfish, bullhead' (Vogel 1991; Bloomfield 1975).

WESQUAGE Pond (R.I., Washington Co.). From SNEng. Algonquian, perhaps meaning 'end place' (Huden 1962).

WESSAGUSSET Beach (Mass., Norfolk Co.) \wes ə gus´ ət\. From SNEng. Algonquian, perhaps meaning 'at the small saltwater cove' (Huden 1962).

WESSERUNSETT (Maine, Somerset Co.) \wes run´ sət\. Probably from Abenaki (Algonquian), perhaps meaning 'bitter water place' (Huden 1962).

WESTCONNAUG (R.I., Providence Co.). From SNEng. Algonquian, perhaps meaning 'where walnut trees grow on the hill' (Huden 1962).

WESTECUNK Creek (N.J., Ocean Co.). From Delaware (Algonquian), of unclear derivation (Becker 1964).

WESTOE (S.C., Dorchester Co.). Probably from Catawban (Siouan) /wéstuk/ 'shield' (B. Rudes p.c.).

WETA (S.Dak., Jackson Co.). From Lakhota (Siouan) *wíta* 'island' (Sneve 1973; Ingham 2001).

WETAPPO (Fla., Gulf Co.). Muskogee *ue-tapho* /wi:-tá:pho/ 'wide water', from /wi:-/ 'water' and *-tapho* /-tá:pho/ 'wide' (Read 1934; Martin and Mauldin 2000).

WETAUG (Ill., Pulaski Co.) \wē´ tog\. The name is re-spelled and transferred from **Weatogue** (Conn., Litchfield Co.) (Vogel 1963).

WETAUWANCHU Mountain (Conn., Litchfield Co.). From SNEng. Algonquian, of unclear derivation (Trumbull 1881).

WETHOCOUCHY (Fla., Wakulla Co.). From the same origin as **Withlacoochee River** (Fla., Citrus Co.); see above.

WETIPQUIN (Md., Wicomico Co.). Earlier recorded as <Tipquin, Wellipqueen, Wilipquin> (etc.); from CAC Algonquian, of unclear derivation (Kenny 1984).

WETONKA (S.Dak., McPherson Co.) \wə tông´ kə\. From Dakota (Siouan) *wi-thąka,* lit. 'sun-big' (Sneve 1973; Ingham 2001).

WETUMKA (Okla., Hughes Co.) \wē tum´ kə\. From the same source as **Wetumpka** (Ala., Elmore Co.) \wē tump´ kə\. The name is from Muskogee *wetumhkv* /wi:tómhka/, perhaps meaning 'tumbling water'; cf. *ue-* /wi:-/ 'water' (Read 1984; Martin and Mauldin 2000). The placename **Wetumpka** also occurs in Fla. (Gadsden Co.) and N.J. (Somerset Co.).

WEVOK (Alaska, Point Hope D-2). The Iñupiaq (Eskimo) name is *uivvaq* 'go around a point of land' (L. Kaplan p.c.).

WEWAHITCHKA (Fla., Gulf Co.) \wē wə hich´ kə\. Muskogee /oywa-híčka/ 'place where water is obtained or seen', from *uewv* /óywa/ 'water' and *heckv* /híč-ka/ 'seeing, obtaining' (Read 1934; Martin and Mauldin 2000).

WEWAHOTEE (Fla., Orange Co.) \wē wə hō´ tē\. A word chosen from a Muskogee wordlist, to designate a railroad stop; it is intended to mean 'water tank'. The term represents *uewv-hute* /oywa-hóti/ 'water container' (Read 1934; Martin and Mauldin 2000).

WEWEANTIC River (Mass., Plymouth Co.). From SNEng. Algonquian, perhaps meaning, 'cooked stream' (Huden 1962).

WEWEEDER Ponds (Mass., Nantucket Co.). Also written <Weweda>. From SNEng. Algonquian <wewedor> 'a pair of horns' (Little 1984).

WEWELA (S.Dak., Tripp Co.) \wē wē´ lə\. Lakhota (Siouan) *wiwíla* 'a spring', from *wiwi-* 'a spring' plus *-la* 'diminutive' (Sneve 1973; D. Parks p.c.).

WEWOKA (Ala., Talladega Co.). An alternative form of **Weoka** (Ala., Elmore Co.); see above. The placename **Wewoka** also occurs in Kans. (Rydjord 1968) and Okla. (Seminole Co.).

WEYAHOK River (Alaska, Survey Pass D-5). This was the Iñupiaq (Eskimo) name for the nineteenth-century artist and editor Howard Rock (BGN 7801).

WEYANOKE (Va., Charles City Co.) \wī´ ə nōk\. The name refers to a CAC Algonquian subgroup, also written <Weanoc, Wyanoke>

(etc.), perhaps from a word for 'sassafras' (Hagemann 1988); cf. Delaware <winak> 'sassafras' (Brinton and Anthony 1888). The placename is found in La. (West Feliciana Par.) and W.Va. (Mercer Co.).

WEYAUWEGA (Wis., Waupaca Co.) \wī ō wē´ gə\. Supposedly from a Menominee (Algonquian) personal name <Wey-au-wa-ya>, but perhaps actually a mistranscription of /we:yawakɛh/ 'old woman' (Vogel 1991; Bloomfield 1975).

WHAKATNA Creek (Alaska, Nulato D-2). The Koyukon (Athabaskan) name was recorded in 1905 (Orth 1967).

WHAT CHEER (Iowa, Keokuk Co.). This old English greeting was adopted by SNEng. Algonquian Indians from the Puritans and spread through Indian languages as far as the Cree (Algonquian) of Canada (Vogel 1983).

WHATCOM County (Wash.) \hwät´ kəm\. From the Lummi (Salish) placename [x̣^{w}átq^{w}əm], perhaps meaning 'noisy' with reference to a waterfall (Hitchman 1985; D. Kinkade p.c.).

WHEELING (W.Va., Logan Co.) \hwē´ ling\. Said to be from Delaware (Algonquian), meaning 'head-place', perhaps referring to a decapitation (Kenny 1945); cf. <wil> 'head' (Brinton and Anthony 1888), Unami Delaware /wil/ (Blalock et al. 1994). The placename **Wheeling** has been transferred to several other states (e.g., Ill., Cook Co.; Okla., Comanche Co.; and Pa., Washington Co.).

WHEETIP Creek (Idaho, Lemhi Co.). From Shoshoni (Numic) /kwitappɨh/ 'shit' (Boone 1988; J. McLaughlin p.c.).

WHERE THE YEI WENT UP (Ariz., Apache Co.). A translation of Navajo (Athabaskan) *yee'ii hadeeyáhí* 'where the yei went up and out'; the word *yei* refers to supernatural beings (Linford 2000).

WHETSTONE (Minn., Lac Qui Parle Co.). Perhaps a translation of Dakota (Siouan) *izúza* 'whetstone, grindstone' (Upham 2001; Riggs 1890).

WHIPPANY (N.J., Morris Co.). Also written as <Whipponong, Wipany> (etc.); probably from Delaware (Algonquian), but of unclear derivation (Becker 1964).

WHIRLWIND Cave (Ariz., Apache Co.). Corresponds to Navajo (Athabaskan) *tséyaa hahwiiyoolí* 'where the wind eddies under rock' (Linford 2000).

WHISKEAG Creek (Maine, Sagadahoc Co.). From Abenaki (Algonquian), perhaps referring to a tidal stream that runs nearly dry at low tide (Eckstorm 1941:134).

WHISKEY Bay (La., St. Martin Par.). The term did not originally contain the English word *bay* but was written <Oscabe, Oskibe, Oskibehat>, from Choctaw (Muskogean) *oski abiha* 'they are in the canes', containing *oski* 'cane' and *abiha* 'to be in, to go in' (Read 1927; P. Munro p.c.). A related placename in La. (Vernon Par.) is **Whiskey Chitto** \hwis kē chit´ ə\, from Choctaw *oski* 'cane' plus *chito* 'big' (Read 1927; P. Munro p.c.). Also related in La. (Perry Co.) is **Whiskey Creek,** probably shortened from a Choctaw placename beginning with *oski* 'reed'.

WHISKEY Creek (Ariz., Apache Co.). Corresponds to Navajo (Athabaskan) *tó diłhił bikooh,* from *tó diłhił* 'whiskey' plus *bi-kooh* 'its creek'. But *tó diłhił* probably meant 'dark water' originally; *diłhił* means both 'causes dizziness' and 'is dark-colored' (Granger 1983; Young and Morgan 1987). A related placename is **To-dil-hil Wash** (N.Mex., San Juan Co.).

WHISKINBOO Creek (S.C., Berkeley Co.). Perhaps from an unidentified Indian language (Pickens 1961–62:24).

WHITEAGLE (Okla., Kay Co.). A variant of **White Eagle**; see below.

WHITE BEAD (Okla., Garvin Co.). Named for a Caddo leader known as Chief White Bead (Shirk 1974).

WHITE BEAR (Minn., Pope Co.). Named for an Ojibwa (Algonquian) leader; his Indian name was given *waabi-makwa,* lit. 'white-bear' (Upham 2001; Nichols and Nyholm 1995). By contrast, **White Bear Township** (Minn., Ramsey Co.) corresponds to Dakota (Siouan) *mathó-mde,* lit. 'bear lake' (Upham 2001; Riggs 1890).

WHITE BIRD Creek (Idaho, Idaho Co.). Named for a Nez Perce (Sahaptian) leader; his Native American name was /piyó:piyo x̣ayx̣áyx̣/ 'bird-species white', where /piyó:piyo/ is a species of large white bird, while /x̣ayx̣áyx̣/ means 'white' (Aoki 1994).

WHITE BREAST Creek (Iowa, Marion Co.). Named for a Meskwaki (Algonquian) man called /wa:peškihka:hke:ha/, lit. 'white-breasted [eagle]' (Vogel 1983; I. Goddard p.c.).

WHITECHUCK River (Wash., Snohomish Co.) \hwīt´ chuk\. A combination of English *white* and Chinook Jargon <chuck> /čʌk/ 'water' (Hitchman 1985; D. Kinkade p.c.). For related placenames, see such names as **Skookum Chuck Creek** (Ore., Baker Co.), **Salt Chuck** (Alaska, Craig C-2), and **Warmchuck Inlet** (Alaska, Craig C-5).

WHITE CHURCH (Kans., Wyandotte Co.). Named for a Methodist church, built in 1832, which served the Delaware (Algonquian) community (Rydjord 1968).

WHITE CLAY Creek (S.Dak., Shannon Co.). Corresponds to Lakhota (Siouan) *makhá̆ği-ska,* lit. 'clay-white' (Sneve 1973; Ingham 2001). By contrast, **White Clay Wash** (Ariz., Apache Co.) is from Navajo (Athabaskan) *dleesh łigai,* lit. 'clay-white' (Linford 2000).

WHITE CLOUD (Iowa, Mills Co.). Named for an Iowa (Siouan) leader also known by his Native American name **Mahaska;** see **Mahaska County.** The placename **White Cloud** also occurs in Kans. (Doniphan Co.).

WHITEDAY Creek (W.Va., Marion Co.). Named for an Indian leader, perhaps from an Algonquian group, also known as **Opekiska** (W.Va., Monongalia Co.) (Kenny 1945).

WHITE DEER (Pa., Union Co.). Said to be a translation of Delaware (Algonquian) <woap'-tuchanne> 'white deer stream', containing <woap> 'white', <achtu> 'deer', and <hanne> 'stream' (Brinton and Anthony 1888; Donehoo 1928); cf. Unami Delaware /op-, o:p-/ 'white', /a:htú:/ 'deer' (Blalock et al. 1994).

WHITE EAGLE (Okla., Kay Co.). Named for a Ponca (Siouan) leader (Shirk 1974).

WHITE EARTH (Minn., Becker Co.). Said to be a translation of Ojibwa (Algonquian) <gawababigunikag> 'place of white clay' (Upham 2001); cf. *gaa-waabaabiganikaag* 'White Earth Reservation', *waabaabigan* 'white clay' (Nichols and Nyholm 1995).

WHITE EYE Branch (Ind., Scott Co.). Named for an eighteenth-century Indian leader, perhaps of the Delaware (Algonquian) people (McPherson 1993).

WHITE Lake (S.Dak., Bennett Co.). Corresponds to Lakhota (Siouan) *mní-ska,* lit. 'water-white' (Sneve 1973). **White Mesa** in Ariz. (Coconino Co.) is from Navajo (Athabaskan) *łigaii dah azkání* 'white mesa' (Linford 2000). In Ind. (Randolph Co.) **White River** is probably a translation of Miami/Illinois (Algonquian) /waapikamiki/ 'it is white water', referring to what is now called the West Fork of the **White River;** this contains /waap-/ 'white' and /-(i)kami/ 'water' (McCafferty 2002).

WHITE LICK Creek (Ind., Hendricks Co.). Corresponds to Miami/Illinois (Algonquian) /waapahkiwi/ 'it is a white field', referring to the salt lick rather than the stream (M. McCafferty p.c.).

WHITE OAK Point (Minn., Itasca Co.). Said to correspond to Ojibwa (Algonquian) <nemijimijikan> (Upham 2001); cf. <mishimij> 'white oak' (Baraga 1880), *miizmizh* (Rhodes 1985).

WHITE PIGEON (Mich., St. Joseph Co.). Named for a Potawatomi (Algonquian) prophet of the early nineteenth century. His Native American name is given as <Wapmeme> (Vogel 1986); cf. Ojibwa (Algonquian) *omiimiii* 'pigeon' (Nichols and Nyholm 1995). The placename **White Pigeon** also occurs in Ill. (Whiteside Co.).

WHITE SWAN (Wash., Yakima Co.). Named for a Sahaptin leader, translating his Native American name /qúyx wawqilúk/; whites called him Joe Stwire (Hitchman 1985; D. Kinkade p.c.).

WHITEWATER (Wis., Walworth Co.). Probably a translation from Menominee (Algonquian) /wa:peskiw/ 'it is white' plus /nepe:w/ 'water' (Vogel 1991; Bloomfield 1975). Elsewhere **Whitewater River** (Ind., Wayne Co.) may correspond to Miami/Illinois (Algonquian) */waapi-nepi/ 'white water' (McCafferty 2002). By contrast, **WHITEWATER River** (Minn., Winona Co.) may be a translation of Dakota (Siouan) *mní-ska,* lit. 'water-white' (Upham 2001). A related placename is **Minneiska** (Minn., Winona Co.).

WHONTLEYA (Alaska, Nulato D-3). The Koyukon (Athabaskan) name was reported in 1952 (Orth 1967).

WIANNO (Mass., Barnstable Co.). From the name of a SNEng. Algonquian leader; his name is also written <Iyannough> (Huden 1962).

WICCACON River (N.C., Hertford Co.). The name appears earlier as <Weecaunse> and <Veecaune>; it may be a placename from an unidentified Indian language (Powell 1968).

WICCOPEE (N.Y., Dutchess Co.) \wik´ ə pē\. Perhaps from Mahican (Algonquian) <wikopi> 'basswood or linden tree' (Ruttenber 1906). Possibly related placenames are **Weekeepeemee** (Conn., Litchfield Co.) and **Wickopee Hill** (Vt., Windham Co.).

WICHITA (Kans., Sedgwick Co.) \wich´ i tô\. A people and language of the Caddoan linguistic family, living in the southern Plains. **Wichita,** earlier written <Ouachita, Ousita> (etc.), was originally the name of a single village group but came to be applied to a group of related peoples, including the **Waco** and the **Kichai.** In the twentieth century the **Wichita** people came to call themselves /kirikirʔi:s/ 'raccoon-eye(s)', which was also originally the name of a single band (Rydjord 1968; *HNAI* 13:564). The placename **Wichita** also occurs in Okla. (Comanche Co.) and Ore. (Clackamas Co.). The related name **Ouachita** is found in La. (Union Par.), Ark. (Dallas and Ouachita Cos.), and Okla. (Le Flore Co.).

WICKAHONEY (Idaho, Owyhee Co.) \wik ə hō´ nē\. Possibly Shoshoni (Numic) /wɨkka'aa'nii/ 'chopping beavers' or 'beaver-chopped', from /wɨkka'a/ 'cut, chop' plus /a'nii/ 'beaver' (J. McLaughlin p.c.).

WICKAPOGUE Pond (N.Y., Suffolk Co.) \wik´ ə pog\. From SNEng. Algonquian, perhaps meaning 'end of the pond' (Tooker 1911).

WICKATUNK (N.J., Monmouth Co.). Perhaps from Delaware (Algonquian) *wikwètung* 'the finishing place' (Kraft and Kraft 1985).

WICKECHEOKE Creek (N.J., Hunterdon Co.). From Delaware (Algonquian), of unclear derivation (Becker 1964).

WICKIUP \wik´ ē up\. The term refers to an Indian dwelling house, especially of the hut-like type made of brushwood, covered with bark or mats; the word is from Meskwaki (Algonquian) /wi:kikya:pi/ 'house', distantly related to **Wigwam** (*RHD* 1987). It is found as a placename in several states, including Calif. (Shasta Co.), Idaho (Owhyhee Co.), and Ore. (Grant Co.). Possibly related placenames are **Wickup Hill** (Iowa, Linn Co.) and **Wikieup Spring.**

WICKOPEE Hill (Vt., Windham Co.). Perhaps from Abenaki (Algonquian) *wigebi* 'the inner bark of trees, from which cord is made' (Huden 1962; Day 1994–95). Possibly related names are **Wiccopee** (N.Y., Dutchess Co.), **Wico** (Mich., Gogebic Co.), and **Weekeepeemee** (Conn., Litchfield Co.).

WICKUP Hill (Iowa, Linn Co.). Perhaps from the same origin as **Wickiup**; see above.

WICKWAS Lake (N.H., Belknap Co.) \wik´wäs\. Perhaps from SNEng. Algonquian <wequash> 'swan' (Trumbull 1903; Huden 1962).

WICO (Mich., Gogebic Co.). Perhaps from Ojibwa (Algonquian) *wiigob* 'inner bark of basswood tree' (Vogel 1986). Probably related placenames include **Wickopee Hill** (Vt., Windham Co.); see above.

WICOMICO (Md., Charles Co.) \wī kom´ i kō, wī kō´ mi kō\. From CAC Algonquian, of unclear derivation (Kenny 1984). The name occurs also in Va. (Gloucester Co.). A possibly related placename is **Yeocomico River** (Va., Northumberland Co.).

WICONISCO (Pa., Dauphin Co.) \wik ə nis´ kō\. From Delaware (Algonquian), perhaps meaning 'muddy house' (Donehoo 1928).

WICOPEE (Ore., Lane Co.) \wik´ ə pē\. Probably transferred from **Wiccopee** (N.Y., Dutchess Co.), where the name refers to the 'basswood or linden tree' (McArthur 1992). Other related placenames include **Wico** (Mich., Gogebic Co.) and **Wickopee Hill** (Vt., Windham Co.).

WICOPESSET Island (N.Y., Suffolk Co.). From SNEng. Algonquian, perhaps meaning 'little thing at the end' (Ruttenber 1906; Tooker 1911).

WIDE RUINS (Ariz., Apache Co.). Corresponds to Navajo (Athabaskan) *kinteel* 'wide house' (Linford 2000), from *kin* 'house' and *-teel* 'wide' (Young and Morgan 1987). A related name is **Kin Teel** (N.Mex., McKinley Co.).

WIGWAM \wig´ wäm\. The term refers to an Indian dwelling house, particularly the type formed of poles overlaid with bark, mats, or skins; derived from Eastern Abenaki (Algonquian) /wìkəwɑm/ 'house', related also to **Wickiup** (*RHD* 1987). As a placename, **Wigwam** occurs in a number of states (e.g., N.Y., Allegany Co.; Conn., Middlesex Co.; and Ill., McDonough Co.).

WIJIJI (N.Mex., San Juan Co.) \wi jē´ jē\. From Navajo (Athabaskan) *diwózhiishzhiin* 'black greasewood', containing *diwózhii* 'greasewood' and *-(sh)zhiin* 'black' (Julyan 1998; Wilson 1995).

WIKIEUP Spring (Utah, Sevier Co.). An alternative form of **Wickiup**; see above.

WIKK'YAL'A (N.Mex., Cibola Co.). A Zuni site for ceremonial offerings (Ferguson and Hart 1985).

WILATSU'U:KW AN K'YAN'A (N.Mex., Cibola Co.). Contains Zuni /wilats'u:kwe/ 'Apache' (Ferguson and Hart 1985; Newman 1958).

WILDCAT Creek (Ind., Tippecanoe Co.). Corresponds to Miami/Illinois (Algonquian) /pinšiwa amootayi/ 'the bobcat's stomach, the bobcat's pouch' (McCafferty 2002). By contrast, **Wildcat Trading Post** (N.Mex., McKinley Co.) corresponds to Navajo (Athabaskan) *náshdóí ba'áan* 'wildcat's cave', from *náshdóí* 'wildcat' plus *ba'áán* 'its cave' (*ba-, bi-* 'its', *a'áan* 'cave') (Wilson 1995).

WILD CHERRY Canyon (Ariz., Apache Co.). Corresponds to Navajo (Athabaskan) *didzé sikaad* 'chokecherry (bush) sits', containing *didzé* 'chokecherry' (Young and Morgan 1987).

WILD RICE River (Minn., Norman Co.). Named for Ojibwa (Algonquian) *manoomin* 'wild rice' (Upham 2001; Nichols and Nyholm 1995). A related placename is **Menominee County** (Wis.).

WILLACOOCHEE (Ga., Atkinson Co.) \wil ə ko͞o´ chē\. An alternative form of **Withlacoochee River** (Fla., Citrus Co.); see below (Martin and Mauldin 2000). The name **Willacoochee** also occurs in Fla. (Gadsden Co.).

WILLAHA (Ariz., Coconino Co.) \wi lä´ hä\. Said to be Havasupai (Yuman) for 'watering place' (Granger 1983).

WILLAME Creek (Wash., Lewis Co.). From the same origin as **Willamette** (Ore., Clackamas Co.); see below.

WILLAMETTE (Ore., Clackamas Co.) \wi lam´ ət\. From the Clackamas (Chinookan) village name /wálamt/ (McArthur 1992; D. Kinkade p.c.). By contrast, **Willamette Slough** (Wash., Lewis Co.) is from the Upper Chehalis (Salishan) placename /wlámt/ [wəlámt] (D. Kinkade p.c.).

WILLAPA (Wash., Pacific Co.) \wil´ ə pə\. From the Kwalhioqua (Athabaskan) placename /wəlá:pəx̣yú/ (Hitchman 1985; D. Kinkade p.c.). A placename derived from Willapa is **Willapacific** (also in Pacific Co.).

WILLIMANSETT (Mass., Hampden Co.) \wil i man´ sət\. From SNEng. Algonquian, perhaps meaning 'red earth place' (Huden 1962). A variant is **Willmansett.**

WILLIMANTIC (Conn., Windham Co.) \wil i man´ tik\. From SNEng. Algonquian, perhaps meaning 'good cedar swamp' (Trumbull 1881). The placename also occurs in Maine (Piscataquis Co.).

WILLIWAKAS Creek (Wash., Lewis Co.). From Sahaptin [wilawáikaš] 'jump-across place' (Hitchman 1985; D. Kinkade p.c.).

WILLIWAW Point (Alaska, Unalaska A-4) \wil´ ə wô\. The term is used in Alaska to refer to violent gusts of wind; no etymology is known, though an Aleut origin is possible (Orth 1967).

WILLMANSETT (Mass., Hampden Co.). A variant of **Willimansett**; see above.

WILLOCHOCHEE Creek (Fla., Gadsden Co.) \wil ə ko͞o´ chē\. From Muskogee, literally meaning 'big small-river' (Read 1934:41; Martin and Mauldin 2000); see **Withlacoochee River** below.

WILLOWEMOC (N.Y., Sullivan Co.) \wil ō wē´ mək\. Also written <Williwemack>; perhaps from Munsee Delaware, of unclear derivation (Beauchamp 1907).

WILLOW Lake (S.Dak., Clark Co.). Corresponds to Dakota (Siouan) <mdewahopopa> (Sneve 1973); cf. *mde* 'lake', *waȟphópa* 'large species of willow' (Riggs 1890).

WILMETTE (Ill., Cook Co.) \wil met´\. Named for Archange Ouilmette, a Potawatomi (Algonquian) woman married to a French trader around 1800 (Vogel 1963).

WIMANBOWA YALANNE (N.Mex., Cibola Co.). The Zuni name contains /yala-nne/ 'mountains' (Ferguson and Hart 1985; Newman 1958).

WIMICO, Lake (Fla., Gulf Co.) \wi mē´ kō\. From Muskogee *uewv, we-* /óywa, wi:-/ 'water' plus *mēkko* /mí:kko/ 'chief' (Read 1934; Martin and Mauldin 2000).

WINAMAC (Ind., Pulaski Co.) \win´ ə mak\. Named for a Potawatomi (Algonquian) leader of the early nineteenth century. His name is said to mean 'catfish'; cf. Ojibwa (Algonquian) *men-meg* 'catfish' (McPherson 1993; Rhodes 1985). Related placenames include **Winameg** (Ohio, Fulton Co.) \win´ ə meg\ and **Winnemac** (Ill., Cook Co.).

WINBEAM Mountain (N.J., Passaic Co.) \win´ bēm\. Perhaps from Delaware (Algonquian), but of unclear derivation (Becker 1969).

WINCHECK Pond (R.I., Newport Co.) \win´ chek\. From SNEng. Algonquian, perhaps meaning 'at the pleasant place' (Huden 1962).

WINCHUCK River (Ore., Curry Co.) \win´ chuk\. Perhaps a name coined from Chinook Jargon <win> 'wind' (from English) plus Chinook Jargon <chuck> [čʌk] 'water' (McArthur 1992; D. Kinkade p.c.). Possibly related terms include **Warm Chuck Inlet** (Alaska, Craig C-5).

WINDAGA, Lake (Mich., Isabella Co.) \win´ də gə\. An alternative form of **Windigo**; see below.

WIND Cave (S.Dak., Custer Co.). Corresponds to Lakhota (Siouan) *thaté-wakq̨,* lit. 'sacred wind', from *thaté* 'wind' and *wakhą́* 'be sacred' (Sneve 1973; Ingham 2001).

WINDIGO (Mich., Keweenaw Co.) \win´ di gō\. From Ojibwa (Algonquian) *wiindigoo* 'winter cannibal monster' (Vogel 1986; Nichols and Nyholm 1995). The placename also occurs in Minn. (Beltrami Co.), Ore. (Douglas Co.), and Wis. (Sawyer Co.).

WINDOW ROCK (Ariz., Apache Co.). Corresponds to Navajo (Athabaskan) *tségh́áhoodzání* 'rock with a hole through it', containing *tsé* 'rock', *ghá* 'through', and *hoodzą́* 'perforated area or space' (Granger 1983; Wilson 1995:69).

WINDSWEPT TERRACE (Ariz., Navajo Co.). Corresponds to Hopi *huk'ovi* 'high windy place', from *huk-* 'wind', *-'o-* 'high', and *-vi* 'place' (Granger 1983; K. Hill p.c.).

WINDY Canyon (N.Mex., McKinley Co.). Navajo *tsé bii'naayolí* 'wind blowing around in the rocks', containing *tsé* 'rock', *bii'* 'in it/them', and *naayolí* 'wind blowing around' (Wilson 1995). The same Navajo name probably underlies the placename **Windy Rock** (Ariz., Apache Co.).

WINDYPAH (Nev., Esmeralda Co.) \win´ dē pä\. A combination of English *windy* plus Shoshoni (Numic) /-paa/ 'water' (Carlson 1974; J. McLaughlin p.c.). Related names include **Weepah** (Nev., Esmeralda Co.) and **Nopah Range** (Calif., Inyo Co.).

WINEMA (Ore., Klamath Co.) \wī nē´ mə\. Named for a Modoc woman who played an important role in the Modoc War of the late nineteenth century (McArthur 1992). In Calif. (Ventura Co.) this name, spelled **Wynema,** was formerly sometimes confused with the name **Hueneme.**

WINETKA Point (Mich., Benzie Co.) \wi net´ kə\. From the same source as **Winnetka** (Ill., Cook Co.); see below.

WINGINA (Va., Nelson Co.). Said to be named for a CAC Algonquian leader who lived in N.C. during the sixteenth century (Hagemann 1988).

WINGOHOCKING Creek (Pa., Philadelphia Co.) \wing´ gō hok ing\. Perhaps represents Delaware (Algonquian) <Wingehacking> 'sweet earth place', containing <wingan> 'sweet' and <haki> 'earth' (Brinton and Anthony 1888; Donehoo 1928).

WINGRA, Lake (Wis., Dane Co.) \wing´ grə\. Winnebago (Siouan) *wįįğrá* 'the duck', from *wį́įx* 'duck' (Vogel 1991; K. Miner p.c.).

WINGVA (Ariz., Navajo Co.). Earlier <Wein-Bahi>; perhaps from Hopi (Uto-Aztecan) (K. Hill p.c.).

WINIMUSSET Brook (Mass., Worcester Co.) \win i mus´ ət\. From SNEng. Algonquian, perhaps containing <wenomen-> 'grape' (W. Cowan p.c.).

WININO (Ore., Lane Co.) \wi nē´ nō\. Perhaps from an unidentified Indian language (McArthur 1992).

WINKUMPAUGH Brook (Maine, Hancock Co.) \wing´ kəm pô\. Perhaps from Abenaki (Algonquian), meaning 'good enclosed pond' (Huden 1962).

WINNABOW (N.C., Brunswick Co.) \win´ ə bō\. Perhaps from an unidentified Indian language (Powell 1968).

WINNAPAUG (R.I., Washington Co.) \win´ ə pôg\. Probably from SNEng. Algonquian <winne> 'good' plus <-paug> 'water' (Huden 1962; W. Cowan p.c.).

WINNEBAGO \win ə bā´ gō\. The name of a Siouan people, based in Wis.; a portion of the group now also lives in Neb. The term is derived from an Algonquian form, perhaps Potawatomi /winpyeko/ 'person of dirty water', referring to the fact that the lower Fox River was clogged every summer with dead fish. The Winnebagos' own name for themselves is /ho:čą́gra/, sometimes anglicized as *Ho-chunk,* with /ho/ meaning either 'fish' or 'voice', and /čąk/ meaning 'big' (*HNAI* 15:706). As a placename, **Winnebago** occurs in several states (e.g., Iowa, Winnebago Co.; Neb., Thurston Co.; and Wis., Winnebago Co.). Related placenames are **Winnibigoshish Reservoir** (Minn., Cass Co.), **Winnipeg** (Minn., Calhoun Co.), and *Winnipegosis* in Canada.

WINNEBOUJOU (Wis., Douglas Co.) \win ə bo͞o´ zho͞o\. The name of the legendary culture hero among several Algonquian groups of the Great Lakes region; cf. Ojibwa *wenabozho* or *nenabozho,* often anglicized as "Manabush, Manabozho, Nanabush" (etc.) (Vogel 1991; Nichols and Nyholm 1995).

WINNECOMAC (N.Y., Suffolk Co.) \win ə kō´ mak\. From SNEng. Algonquian, perhaps meaning 'good field' (Tooker 1911). A related form is **Commack** (N.Y., Suffolk Co.).

WINNECONNA (Ill., Cook Co.) \win ə kon´ ə\. From the same origin as **Winneconne** (Wis.,

Winnebago Co.) \win´ ə kon ē\. This is Menominee (Algonquian) /we:nekaneh/, from /we:nekan/ 'skull' (Vogel 1991; Bloomfield 1962:129).

WINNECOOK (Maine, Waldo Co.) \win´ ə ko͞ok\. Probably from Abenaki (Algonquian), perhaps meaning 'at the portage' (Huden 1962). The placename also occurs in Mont. (Wheatland Co.).

WINNECUNNET (Mass., Bristol Co.) \win ə kun´ ət\. The SNEng. Algonquian name is of unclear derivation (Huden 1962).

WINNEDUMAH (Calif., Inyo Co.) \win ə do͞o´ mə\. Named for a Paiute (Numic) medicine man; his name may contain Owens Valley Paiute /wɨnɨ/ 'to stand' or /wɨnɨdɨ/ 'tree' (Gudde 1998).

WINNEGANCE (Maine, Sagadahoc Co.) \win´ ə gans\. Perhaps Abenaki (Algonquian) for 'little portage' (Eckstorm 1941:136); cf. *onigan* 'portage' (Day 1994–95).

WINNEKEAG Lake (Mass., Worcester Co.) \win´ ə kēg\. From SNEng. Algonquian, of unclear derivation (Huden 1962).

WINNEMAC (Ill., Cook Co.) \win´ ə mak\. Named for a Potawatomi (Algonquian) leader of the early nineteenth century. The name is said to mean 'catfish' (Vogel 1963); cf. Ojibwa *menmeg* 'catfish' (Rhodes 1985). The name also occurs in Ohio (Marion Co.). A related placename is **Winamac** (Ind., Pulaski Co.).

WINNEMUC Hill (Nev., Clark Co.) \win´ ə muk\. Nevada old-timers used to speak of the *winnemucs* 'chills and fever' (Carlson 1974). This may be derived from **Winnemucca** (Nev., Humboldt Co.) \win ə muk´ ə\, the name of a Paiute (Numic) leader in the nineteenth century. His name may be related to /moko/ 'shoe' (Gudde 1998). The placename **Winnemucca** also occurs in Calif. (Alpine Co.), Idaho (Custer Co.), and Ore. (Harney Co.).

WINNEPESAUG Lake (Mich., Newaygo Co.) \win´ ə pə sôg\. Perhaps a shortening of **Winnepesaukee River** (N.H., Merrimack Co.); see below.

WINNEPESAUKA, Lake (Ga., Catoosa Co.) \win ə pə sô´ kē\. Also written **Winnespesaukau** (Krakow 1975). Perhaps a writing variant of **Winnepesaukee**; see below.

WINNEPESAUKEE River (N.H., Merrimack Co.) \win ə pə sô´ kē\. The name has been written over 100 different ways in English. It is possibly from Western Abenaki (Algonquian) *wiwninebesaki* 'land around-lakes'; cf. *wiwni* 'all around', *nebes* 'lake', *ki* 'land'; or possibly from *wiwnibizaga* 'brushy around', cf. *neskibizaga* 'thicket' (Huden 1962; Day 1994–95). A related form is **Winnipesaukee** (N.H., Carroll Co.).

WINNEPOCKET Lake (N.H., Merrimack Co.) \win i pok´ ət\. Perhaps from Abenaki (Algonquian), meaning 'at the portage by the pond' (Huden 1962); cf. *onigan* 'portage', *-bagw-* 'pond', *-et* 'place' (Day 1994–95).

WINNESHEIK (Kans., McPherson Co.) \win´ ə shēk\. An alternative form of **Winneshiek** (Iowa, Winneshiek Co.); see below.

WINNESHIEK County (Iowa) \win´ ə shēk\. Named for a Winnebago (Siouan) leader; however, the derivation of the name is unclear (Vogel 1983). The placename also occurs in Ill. (Stephenson Co.) and Minn. (Wright Co.),

WINNETKA (Ill., Cook Co.) \wi net´ kə\. The name is apparently an artificial coinage from elements in various Algonquian languages, including SNEng. Algonquian <winne> 'beautiful' (Vogel 1963). The placename also occurs in Calif. (Los Angeles Co.) and Minn. (Hennepin Co.).

WINNETOON (Neb., Knox Co.) \win´ ə to͞on\. Supposedly named after a site in Wis. (Dane Co.), now perhaps disappeared; it is from an unidentified Indian language (Perkey 1995).

WINNETUXET River (Mass., Plymouth Co.) \win ə tuk´ sət\. From SNEng. Algonquian, perhaps meaning 'at the good tidal-stream', containing <winne> 'good' and <-tuck-> 'tidal stream' (Huden 1962; W. Cowan p.c.).

WINNEWANA Lake (Mich., Washtenaw Co.) \win ə wä´ nə\. Perhaps an adaptation of <min-

newawa>, a word used in Longfellow's *Hiawatha* for 'a pleasant sound, as of wind in the trees' (Vogel 1986).

WINNEWISSA Falls (Minn., Pipestone Co.) \win ə wis´ ə\. Perhaps from Dakota (Siouan) *wínawizi* 'to be jealous, envious' (Riggs 1890; Upham 2001).

WINNIBIGOSHISH Reservoir (Minn., Cass Co.) \win i bi gosh´ ish\. Probably from Ojibwa (Algonquian), perhaps meaning 'miserable dirty water', containing <winipeg> 'dirty water', <-osh> 'miserable', and <-ish> 'diminutive' (Upham 2001); cf. *winad* 'it is dirty' (Baraga 1880). Probably related names include **Winnebago** (see above) and **Winnipeg Lake** (Minn., Calhoun Co.).

WINNIBULLI (Calif., Shasta Co.) \win´ē bo͞ol ē\. From Wintu *wenem buli,* lit. 'middle mountain' (Gudde 1998).

WINNICUT River (N.H., Rockingham Co.) \win´ i kut\. Perhaps Eastern Abenaki (Algonquian), 'at the portage' (Huden 1962); cf. Western Abenaki *onigan* 'portage' (Day 1994–95).

WINNIPAUK (Conn., Fairfield Co.) \win´ i pôk\. Probably from SNEng. Algonquian <winnipaug> 'fine pond', containing <winne> 'fine' and <-paug> 'pond' (Trumbull 1881; W. Cowan p.c.).

WINNIPEG Lake (Mich., Calhoun Co.) \win´i peg\. Probably from Ojibwa (Algonquian) <winipeg> 'dirty water' (Vogel 1986); cf. *winad* 'it is dirty' (Baraga 1880). The name **Winnipeg** also occurs in Minn. (Clay Co.), Mont. (Madison Co.), and Manitoba, Canada. Related names are **Winnebago** (see above) and **Winnibigoshish Reservoir** (Minn., Cass Co.).

WINNIPESAUKEE (N.H., Carroll Co.) \win ə pə sô´ kē\. From the same source as **Winnepesaukee River** (N.H., Merrimack Co.); see above.

WINNISQUAM (N.H., Belknap Co.) \win´ i skwäm\. Perhaps from Eastern Abenaki (Algonquian), referring to 'salmon fishing' (Huden 1962); cf. Western Abenaki *mskwamagw* 'salmon' (Day 1994–95).

WINNOCKS Neck (Maine, Cumberland Co.) \win´ əks\. Perhaps from Abenaki (Algonquian), meaning 'good place' (Huden 1962); cf. *wali* 'good' (Day 1994–95).

WINOLA, Lake (Pa., Wyoming Co.) \wī nō´ lə\. Said to mean 'water lily', the name of an "Indian princess" (O'Hara 2000); or perhaps a coinage based on **Wyoming** (Pa.). A possibly related placename is **Wynola** (Calif., San Diego Co.).

WINONA County (Minn.) \wi nō´ nə\. Perhaps named for a particular Dakota (Siouan) woman, but in any case derived from Dakota *winóna* 'first-born child, if a daughter' (Upham 2001; Riggs 1890). It was the name of Hiawatha's mother in Longellow's poem and became immensely popular in the nineteenth century both as a woman's given name and as a placename; it is found, for example, in Mont. (Flathead Co.), N.H. (Belknap Co.), and Ore. (Polk Co.). Sometimes (e.g., Wis., Pierce Co.), it is pronounced \wī nō´ nə\. Variant spellings are found in **Wenona** (Ill., Marshall Co.), **Wenonah** (Ill., Montgomery Co.), and **Wynonah** (Okla., Osage Co.).

WINOOSKI (Vt., Chittenden Co.) \wi no͞o´ skē\. Abenaki (Algonquian) *winoski* 'onion land', from *winós* 'onion', *ki* 'land' (Day 1981: 162).

WINOPEE Lake (Ore., Deschutes Co.) \win´ ō pē\. Chinook Jargon <win´-a-pie> [wínəpi] 'by-and-bye, presently; wait', from Nootka /wiinapi/ 'stopping, remaining' (McArthur 1992; D. Kinkade p.c.).

WINTECHOG Hill (Conn., New London Co.) \win´ tə chog\. Perhaps adapted from SNEng. Algonquian <Minnechog>, meaning 'berry place' (Huden 1962).

WINTU \win´ to͞o\. The term refers to a people and language of the northern Sacramento Valley in Calif., of the Wintuan linguistic family. The name represents Wintu /winthuun/ 'Indian', from /win-/ ‘person’ (Gudde 1998). The related form **Wintun** \win´ to͞on\ is also sometimes used, both for the Wintu people and for the Wintuan family to which they belong; it also occurs as a placename in **Wintun Butte** (Calif., Siskiyou Co.) (Gudde 1998).

WINTUCKET Cove (Mass., Dukes Co.) \win tuk´ ət\. From SNEng. Algonquian, perhaps meaning ‘good tidal-stream place’, from <winne> ‘good’, <-tuck> ‘tidal stream’, and <-et> ‘place’ (Huden 1962).

WINYAH Bay (S.C., Georgetown Co.) \win´ yä\. Probably from Catawban (Siouan) /wį́ya:/ ‘dye, paint’ (Pearson 1978; B. Rudes p.c.). The placename occurs as a transfer in Fla. (Orange Co.), Mass. (Dukes Co.), and Mich. (Alpena Co.).

WIONA Cliffs (Md., Anne Arundel Co.) \wī ō´ nə\. An adaptation of **Winona County**; see above. The placename **Wiona** also occurs in Ark. (Poinsett Co.) and Pa. (Northampton Co.).

WIONKHIEGE Hill (R.I., Providence Co.). Earlier written <Wayunkeag, Wayunkeke>; from SNEng. Algonquian, perhaps referring to ‘bending’ (Huden 1962); cf. <woonki, wâuki> ‘it bends’ (Trumbull 1903).

WIOTA (Iowa, Cass Co.) \wī ō´ tə\. Probably Dakota (Siouan) *wióta* ‘many moons, many months’, from *wi* ‘sun, moon, month’ plus *óta* ‘much, many’ (Vogel 1983; Riggs 1890). The placename also occurs in Mont. (Valley Co.). In Wis. (Lafayette Co.), the town of **Wiota** was named in the 1830s, perhaps an artificial coinage of literary origin (Vogel 1991).

WISACKY (S.C., Lee Co.) \wi sak´ ē\. Earlier written <Wisacke>; perhaps derived from Catawba (Siouan) *wasa* ‘cane’ (Pickens 1961–62:24; 1963:40).

WISCASSET (Maine, Lincoln Co.) \wis kas´ ət\. From Abenaki (SNEng. Algonquian), perhaps meaning ‘the outlet’ (Eckstorm 1941:118–20). The name also occurs in N.C. (Stanly Co.).

WISCONSIN \wi skon´sin\. The name was first applied to the **Wisconsin River,** earlier written as <Mescousing, Mishkonsing, Ouisconsing, Wishkonsing> (etc.). The Ojibwa (Algonquian) names <Wishkons> ‘Wisconsin’, <Wishkonsing> ‘in Wisconsin’, and <Wishkonsi-sibi> ‘Wisconsin River’ (Baraga 1880) are of unknown etymology. The placename **Wisconsin** also occurs in Minn. (Jackson Co.).

WISCOTTA (Iowa, Dallas Co.) \wis kot´ ə\. Probably from Dakota (Siouan) *wič-óta* ‘many raccoons’, from *wičá* ‘raccoon’ and *óta* ‘much, many’ (Vogel 1983; J. Koontz p.c.).

WISCOY (N.Y., Allegany Co.) \wis´ koi\. Earlier written <Owaiska>, said to mean ‘under the banks’, perhaps from an Iroquoian language (Beauchamp 1907). The placename has been transferred to Minn. (Winona Co.).

WISHKAH (Wash., Grays Harbor Co.) \wish´ kä\. Lower Chehalis (Salishan) [x^{W}ə́šqal’], lit. ‘stinking water’, from /x^{W}ə́š-/ ‘stink’ and /qál’/ ‘water’ (Hitchman 1985; D. Kinkade p.c.).

WISHRAM (Wash., Klickitat Co.) \wish´ rəm\. From Sahaptin /wíšxam/, a name applied to an Upper Chinookan village, called [nixlúidix] in Chinookan (Hitchman 1985; D. Kinkade p.c.).

WISSAHICKEN Brook (N.J., Passaic Co.) \wis ə hik´ ən\. From the same source as **Wissahickon**; see below.

WISSAHICKON (Pa., Philadelphia Co.) \wis ə hik´ ən\. Earlier called <Wiessahitkonk>; cf. Delaware (Algonquian) <wisamek> ‘catfish’ (Brinton and Anthony 1888; Donehoo 1928).

WISSINOMING (Pa., Philadelphia Co.) \wis i nō´ ming\. From Delaware (Algonquian), of unclear derivation (Donehoo 1928).

WISSOTA, Lake (Wis., Chippewa Co.) \wi sō´ tə\. Coined from parts of the Native American placenames **Wisconsin** and **Minnesota** (Vogel 1991).

WITA Lake (Minn., Blue Earth Co.) \wit´ ə\. From Dakota (Siouan) *wíta* ‘island’ (Upham 2001; Riggs 1890).

WITCH Lake (Mich., Marquette Co.). This may correspond to an Indian term for ‘sorcerer’, as in **Wabeno Creek** (Mich., Gogebic Co.).

WITCH WATER POCKET (Ariz., Mohave Co.). Perhaps a translation of Southern Paiute (Numic) <innupin picabu> (Granger 1983); cf. /ɨnɨppi-/ 'evil spirit, "devil," ghost' (Sapir 1930).

WITHLA (Fla., Polk Co.) \with´ lə\. An abbreviation of **Withlacoochee River**; see below.

WITHLACOOCHEE River (Ga., Lowndes Co.; Fla., Citrus Co.) \with lə ko͞o´ chē\. Muskogee *ue-rakkuce* /wi:łakk-očí/ 'small river', from *uerakko* /oy-łákko/ 'river' plus *-uce* /-oči/ 'small'. The word *uerakko* 'river' is itself from *uewv, ue-* /wi:-/ 'water' plus *rakko* /-łakko/ 'big'; thus **Withlacoochee** is literally 'little big-water' (Read 1934:41; Martin and Mauldin 2000). Related placenames include **Willacoochee** (Ga., Atkinson Co.; Fla., Gadsden Co.), **Wethocouchy** (Fla., Wakulla Co.), and **Withla** (Fla., Polk Co.).

WITOKA (Minn., Winona Co.) \wi tō´ kə\. From Dakota (Siouan) *withóka* 'female captive' (Upham 2001; Ingham 2001).

WIT-SO-NAH-PAH, Lake (Calif., Mono Co.) \wit sō nä´ pə\. Probably from a Numic (Uto-Aztecan) language, ending in /paa/ 'water' (Gudde 1998).

WITTAWAKET (Calif., Shasta Co.) \wī´ ti wä kət\. From Wintu /witee waqat/ 'turn creek', containing /wit-/ 'to turn' and /waqat/ 'creek' (Gudde 1998).

WIWONA Reservoir (Ore., Jackson Co.) \wə wō´ nə\. Probably an alternative of **Wawona**; see above.

WOAHINK (Ore., Lane Co.) \hō´ hingk\. Perhaps from Siuslaw [wa:xʸɪni:k] (D. Kinkade p.c.).

WOBIC (Mich., Marquette Co.) \wob´ ik\. An alternative form of **Waubeek**; see above.

WOCUS (Ore., Klamath Co.) \wō´ kəs\. From Klamath /wokas/ 'pond-lily seeds', used for food (McArthur 1992; Barker 1963).

WODO, Mount (Ariz., Coconino Co.) \wō´ dō\. This is the surname of a Havasupai (Yuman) family (Granger 1983; L. Hinton p.c.).

WOLF Creek (Ind., Marshall Co.). Corresponds to Potawatomi (Algonquian) /mkədemʔwe ziibi/ 'black wolf creek', named for the leader /mkədemʔwe/ 'Black Wolf' (McCafferty 2002). By contrast, **Wolf Creek** (Pa., Butler Co.) is perhaps a translation of Delaware (Algonquian) <Tummeink> 'wolf place', from <timmeu> 'wolf' (Brinton and Anthony 1888; Donehoo 1928); cf. Unami Delaware /tə́me/ 'wolf' (Blalock et al. 1994). Again, **Wolf Creek** (S.Dak., Shannon Co.) corresponds to Lakhota (Siouan) *šųgmánitu thą́ka* 'wolf', lit. 'big coyote', from *šųg-mánitu* 'coyote' plus *thą́ka* 'big'. The word for 'coyote' itself contains *šųka* 'dog'; cf. also *maníl* 'into the wilderness' (Sneve 1973; Ingham 2001). In Alaska (Tanacross B-5) **Wolf Lake** is a literal translation of Tanacross (Athabaskan) *s̲hos menn'* (J. Kari p.c.).

WOLF Point (Ill., Cook Co.). Perhaps named after a Potawatomi (Algonquian) Indian resident in the early nineteenth century, called <Moaway> 'wolf' (Vogel 1963); cf. Potawatomi <mwi> 'wolf' (Kansas 1997).

WOLF River (Wis., Eau Claire Co.). Perhaps a translation of Menominee (Algonquian) /mahwɛɛw/ 'wolf river' (Vogel 1991; Bloomfield 1975).

WOLLOCHET (Wash., Pierce Co.) \wō´ lō chet, wə loch´ ət\. The name, from an unidentified language, is said to mean 'squirting clams' (Hitchman 1985).

WOLOMOLOPOAG Pond (Mass., Norfolk Co.). Perhaps from Abenaki (Algonquian), meaning 'red paint pond' (Huden 1962); cf. *olaman* 'red ochre' (Day 1994–95).

WOMAN Lake (Minn., Cass Co.). Said to have been so named because women were once killed at this site when the Ojibwas were attacked by the Sioux (Upham 2001).

WONALANCET (N.H., Carroll Co.) \wun ə lan´ sət, won ə lan´ sət\. Named for an Abenaki (Algonquian) leader of the seventeenth century; the derivation of the word is not clear (Huden 1962).

WONEWOC (Wis., Juneau Co.) \won´ ə wok\. Perhaps from Ojibwa (Algonquian) <wo-no-waug> '(wolves) howl'; cf. <wonawin> 'howling' (Baraga 1880; Vogel 1991).

WONGA DOUYA (Nev., Elko Co.). From Shoshoni (Numic) /wonko-tɨhɨya/, lit. 'pine deer' (J. McLaughlin p.c.).

WONOGA Peak (Calif., Inyo Co.) \wō nō´ gə\. Perhaps contains Mono (Numic) /wono/ 'burden basket' (J. McLaughlin p.c.).

WONONPAKOOK Lake (Conn., Litchfield Co.). Perhaps from Mahican (Algonquian), meaning 'land at the bend of the pond' (Huden 1962).

WONONSKOPOMUC Lake (Conn., Litchfield Co.). Perhaps from Mahican (Algonquian), meaning 'rocks at the bend in the lake' (Huden 1962).

WONSITS Valley (Utah, Uintah Co.) \won´ sits\. From Ute (Numic) /wantsi-tsi/ 'antelope place' (J. McLaughlin p.c.) The name also occurs in Ariz. (Mohave Co.), where it is probably from the related Southern Paiute language.

WOODCHUCK. This native mammal is also called the *groundhog*; the term is borrowed, with folk-etymology, from a SNEng. Algonquian term (for example, Narragansett <ockqutchaun>). As a placename, **Woodchuck** occurs in many states (e.g., Alaska, Nome C-1; Calif., Fresno Co.; and Mich., Monroe Co.).

WOODENHAWK Pines (Md., Caroline Co.) \wo͞od´ ən hôk\. An alternative form of **Wootenaux Creek** (Md., Talbot Co.); see below.

WOOD Springs (Ariz., Apache Co.). Corresponds to Navajo (Athabaskan) *tsiyi' tóhi* 'where there is a spring in the woods', containing *tsi, tsin* 'wood(s)', *yi'* 'inside', and *tó* 'water, spring' (Wilson 1995).

WOONASQUATUCKET River (R.I., Providence Co.). From SNEng. Algonquian, perhaps meaning 'at the head of the tidal river' (Huden 1962).

WOONSOCKET (R.I., Providence Co.) \wo͞on´ sok ət\. From SNEng. Algonquian, perhaps meaning 'ravine, place of steep descent' (Huden 1962; W. Cowan p.c.). The placename also occurs in S.Dak. (Sanborn Co.).

WOOTENAUX Creek (Md., Talbot Co.) \wo͞od´ ən hôk\. Perhaps from a CAC Algonquian personal name or placename (Kenny 1984); see **Woodenhawk Pines**, above.

WOPOWOG (Conn., Middlesex Co.). Earlier written <Wepowage, Weepowaug>; from SNEng. Algonquian <weepwoiauk> 'a crossing-place, passageway' (Trumbull 1881; W. Cowan p.c.).

WOPSONONOCK (Pa., Blair Co.). Perhaps formed by combining elements from various Algonquian languages; the derivation is not clear (Donehoo 1928).

WORONOCK (CT, New Haven Co.) \wôr´ ə nok\. Perhaps an alternative form of **Woronoco** (Mass., Hampden Co.) \wôr ə nō´ kō\. This is possibly from SNEng. Algonquian, meaning 'winding about' (Huden 1962). The placename also occurs in N.Y. (Jefferson Co.). A possibly related form is **Oronoke** (Conn., New Haven Co.).

WORTHLA Creek (Calif., Del Norte Co.) \wûrth´ lə\. From the Yurok village name /wɹɬɹi/ (Gudde 1998).

WOUNDED KNEE (S.Dak., Shannon Co.) A translation of Lakhota (Siouan) *čhąkpé-opi,* from *čhąkpé* 'knee' and *ópi* 'wounded' (Sneve 1973; B. Ingham 2001).

WOVOKA Wash (Nev., Mineral Co.) \wō vō´ kə\. Named for a nineteenth-century Paiute (Numic) man who was the prophet of the Ghost Dance Religion (BGN 7504).

WOW, Mount (Wash., Pierce Co.) \wou\. From a word meaning 'mountain sheep' in an unidentified Indian language (Hitchman 1985).

WUH, Mount (Colo., Larimer Co.) \wo͞o\. From Arapaho (Algonquian) /wox/ 'bear' (Salzmann 1983).

WUKOKI Ruin (Ariz., Coconino Co.) \wo͞o kō´ kē, wə kō´ kē\. The name is apparently composed of Hopi (Uto-Aztecan) elements, supposedly meaning 'big house'; cf. *wuko-* 'big', *-ki, kii-hu* 'house' (K. Hill p.c.).

WUKOPAKABI (Ariz., Apache Co.) \wə kō´ pə kä bē\. Hopi (Uto-Aztecan) *wukovaqavi* 'big reed place', from *wuko-* 'big' plus *-vaqa-, paaqa* 'reed' and *-vi* 'place' (Granger 1983; K. Hill p.c.).

WUKSI Butte (Ore., Deschutes Co.) \wuk´ sē\. Perhaps from Molala [wakšúi] 'basket made of a single piece of bark' (H. Zenk p.c.).

WUKUKLOOK Creek (Alaska, Sitka D-3). Perhaps from Tlingit <wa-kak-luk> 'cliff' (Orth 1967).

WULIK River (Alaska, Noatak C-5). The Iñupiaq (Eskimo) name is *ualliik kuuŋak* (Burch 1998).

WUPATKI National Monument (Ariz., Coconino Co.) \wo͞o pät´ kē, wə pät´ kē\. Hopi *wupatki* 'long cut', containing *wupa-* 'long' and *-tki, tuki* 'to get cut', referring to a wash (K. Hill p.c.).

WUTCHUMNA Hill (Calif., Tulare Co.) \wə chum´ nə\. The name of a Yokuts subgroup, also written <Wukchumne, Wikchamni> (Gudde 1998).

WYACONDA River (Mo., Lewis Co.) \wô´ kən dô\. Probably an alternative form of **Wakanda Park** (see above), from Dakota (Siouan) *wakhą́da* 'sacred power'. The name of the town of **Wyaconda,** as opposed to the river, is pronounced \wī ə kon´ də\ (Don Lance, p.c.). In Iowa (Davis Co.) the placename **Wyacondah** has the same origin.

WYALOOSING Creek (Ind., Jennings Co.) \wī ə lo͞o´ sing\. From the same origin as **Wyalusing** (Pa., Bradford Co.) \wī ə lo͞o´ sing\. This is said to be from Munsee Delaware (Algonquian) <M'chwihillusink> 'old-man place' (Donehoo 1928); cf. <mihillusis> 'old man' (Brinton and Anthony 1888), *mihlóosus* (O'Meara 1996). The placename **Wyalusing** also occurs in Wis. (Grant Co.).

WYANDANCH (N.Y., Suffolk Co.) \wī´ ən danch, wīn´ danch\. Also written <Wyandance>; the name of a SNEng. Algonquian leader of the seventeenth century (Tooker 1911).

WYANDOCK Lake (Wis., Vilas Co.) \wīn´ dok\. Probably an adaptation of **Wyandot County**; see below.

WYANDOT County (Ohio) \wī ən dot´, wī´ ən dot, wīn´ dot\. The name of an Iroquoian people and language, closely associated with the Hurons; their self-designation was *wę́dat,* perhaps a shortening of a longer form corresponding to Mohawk (Iroquoian) *skawę́:nat* 'one language' or *tsha'tekawę́nat* 'the same language' (*HNAI* 15:405). Alternatively, the name may be related to Huron [wendat] 'forest' and/or [yandata] 'village' (B. Rudes p.c.). The placename **Wyandot** also occurs in Ind. (Tippecanoe Co.) and Calif. (Butte Co.). A related spelling is **Wyandotte** (Kans., Wyandotte Co.); this form also occurs in other states (e.g., Ind., Crawford Co.; and La., St. Mary Par.). A possibly related placename is **Yondota** (Ohio, Lucas Co.).

WYANET (Ill., Bureau Co.) \wī ə net´\. The name allegedly means 'beautiful' in Potawatomi (Algonquian); cf. *wèonuk* 'beauty' (Kansas 1997). A probable transfer name is **Wyanett** (Minn., Isanti Co.).

WYASSUP Lake (Conn., New London Co.). Earlier <Ahyosupsuck, Wyassupsuck>; from SNEng. Algonquian, perhaps containing <ashap> 'plant fiber for making nets' (Trumbull 1881; W. Cowan p.c.).

WYBEN (Mass., Hampden Co.) \wī´ bən\. From SNEng. Algonquian, perhaps meaning 'white stuff' (Huden 1962).

WYCO (W.Va., Wyoming Co.) \wī´ kō\. Said to be a combination of elements from the name **Wyoming** and the word *county* (Kenny 1945).

WY'EAST (Ore., Hood River Co.) \wī ēst´\. Said to be a "legendary" name for Mt. Hood, from an unidentified Indian language (McArthur 1992).

WYESOCKING Bay (N.C., Hyde Co.). A variant of **Wysocking Bay**; see below.

WYNEMA \wī nē´ mə\. A now obsolete variant of both **Hueneme** (Calif., Ventura Co.) and **Winema** (Ore., Klamath Co.); see above.

WYNOLA (Calif., San Diego Co.) \wī nō´ lə\. Perhaps from the same source as **Lake Winola** (Pa., Wyoming Co.); see above.

WYNONA (Okla., Osage Co.) \wī nō´ nə\. Probably adapted from **Winona** (Shirk 1974); see above. The name of **Lake WYNONAH** (Pa., Schuylkill Co.) may have a similar origin.

WYNOOCHEE River (Wash., Grays Harbor Co.) \wī no͞o´ chē\. From the Lower Chehalis placename [x^{W}ənúƚč] (Hitchman 1985; D. Kinkade p.c.).

WYNOOSKA Lake (Pa., Pike Co.) \wī no͞o´ skə\. Perhaps from Delaware (Algonquian), but the derivation is not clear (Donehoo 1928).

WYNOPITS Mountain (Utah, Washington Co.) \wə nop´ its\. Said to be Southern Paiute (Numic) name for a supernatural being (Van Cott 1990).

WYOCOLO (Wyo., Albany Co.) \wī ə kō´ lō\. Created by combining elements of **Wyoming** and *Colorado*. Similarly, **Lake Wyodaho** (Wyo., Teton Co.) combines elements of **Wyoming** and **Idaho** (Bright 1993; Urbanek 1974).

WYOLA (Pa., Delaware Co.) \wī ō´ lə\. Perhaps from Delaware (Algonquian), but the derivation is not clear (Donehoo 1928).

WYOMA (Mass., Essex Co.) \wī ō´ mə\. From SNEng. Algonquian, but the derivation is not clear (Huden 1962). The name also occurs in W.Va. (Mason Co.).

WYOMANOCK (N.Y., Rensselaer Co.) \wī ō man´ ək\. Perhaps from Mahican (Algonquian), but the derivation is not clear.

WYOMING (Pa., Luzerne Co.) \wī ō´ ming\. From Munsee Delaware (Algonquian) <chwewamink>, probably /xwé:wamənk/ 'at the big river flat', from /xw-/ 'big', /-e:wam-/ 'river flat', and /-ənk/ 'place' (Donehoo 1928; I. Goddard p.c.). The placename was made popular by an 1809 poem "Gertrude of Wyoming," commemorating a conflict between Indians and whites at the Indian site; during the nineteenth century, the name was assigned not only to the state but also to many other locations (e.g., Kans., Marshall Co.; Ohio, Hamilton Co.; and Wis., Iowa Co.).

WYOMISSING (Pa., Berks Co.) \wī ə mis´ ing\. Perhaps from Delaware (Algonquian), of unclear derivation (Donehoo 1928).

WYSOCKING Bay (N.C., Hyde Co.) \wī sok´ ing\. Earlier written as <Yesocking>; perhaps from a CAC Algonquian language (Powell 1968). A spelling variant is **Wyesocking Bay.**

WYSOX (Pa., Bradford Co.) \wī´ soks\. From earlier <Wysaukin> (etc.); of Delaware (Algonquian) origin, but the derivation is not clear (Donehoo 1928). The placename also occurs in Ill. (Carroll Co.).

WYTOPITLOCK (Maine, Aroostook Co.) \wit ə pit´ lok\. From Abenaki (Algonquian), perhaps meaning 'alder place'; cf. *odopi* 'alder tree' (Day 1994–95).

WYUTA (Utah, Rich Co.) \wī o͞o´ tə\. A combination of elements from **Wyoming** and **Utah.**

Y

YAAK (Mont., Lincoln Co.) The name is said to mean 'arrow' in an unidentified Indian language (Cheney 1984).

YACHATS (Ore., Lincoln Co.) \yä´ häts\. From the Alsea placename [yáx̣ayk^{y}] (McArthur p.c.; D. Kinkade p.c.).

YACHERK (Alaska, Goodnews Bay A-1). The Yupik (Eskimo) name was recorded in 1898 (Orth 1967).

YACKO Creek (Alaska, Talkeetna Mountains B-1). The Ahtna (Athabaskan) name was reported in 1915 (Orth 1967).

YACOLT (Wash., Clark Co.) \yä´ kôlt\. From an unidentified Indian language, perhaps meaning 'haunted place' (Hitchman 1985).

YADKIN (N.C., Rowan Co.). Earlier written <Atkin, Reatkin> (etc.); perhaps a placename from an unidentified Indian language (Powell 1968).

YAGANUDA Cove (Alaska, Pribilof Islands A-3). From Aleut *hyaagax̂, yaagax̂* 'wood, drift-wood' plus *udax̂* 'bay' (Bergsland 1994).

YAGHMELNGAK Mountain (Alaska, Lawrence C-5). The Yupik (Eskimo) name was reported in 1949 as meaning 'the lowest one' (Orth 1967).

YAHANY Inlet (S.C., Georgetown Co.) A variant of **Yauhannah**; see below.

YAHARA (Wis., Rock Co.) \yə hâr´ ə, yə hä´ rə\. Perhaps from Winnebago (Siouan), but the derivation is unclear (Vogel 1911).

YAHI Indian Camp (Calif., Tehama Co.) \yä´ hē\. For the local Yahi Indians, a subgroup of the Yana (Gudde 1998); see also **Ishi Caves.** The placename also occurs in Nev. (Pershing Co.).

YAHKU Cove (Alaska, Craig D-4). The Tlingit name was published in 1964 (Orth 1967).

YAHOLA (Okla., Muskogee Co.) \yə hō´ lə\. Supposedly named for a Muskogee Indian named Yahola Harjo (Shirk 1974). This may be an alternative form of **Yahoola Creek** (Ga., Lumpkin Co.), which has been said to be from a Cherokee (Iroquoian) personal name, perhaps based on <yahula> 'doodle bug' (Krakow 1975).

YAH-TA-HEY (N.Mex., McKinley Co.) \yä´ tə hā\. From the Navajo (Athabaskan) greeting *yá'át'ééh,* lit. 'it is good' (Julyan 1998; Wilson 1995).

YAHTSE River (Alaska, Icy Bay D-2). From Tlingit [yas'é] 'swampy ground' (De Laguna 1972:95).

YAINAX Butte (Ore., Klamath Co.) \yä´ naks\. Klamath /y'ayn'aks/ 'mountain place', from /y'ay'na/ 'mountain' (McArthur 1992; Barker 1963).

YAJOME (Calif., Napa Co.) \yä hō´ mā\. The name of an 1841 Mexican land grant, from an unidentified Indian language (Gudde 1998).

YAKAK Peninsula (Alaska, Adak B-3) Aleut *yax̂ax* 'great cape', from *yax̂* 'cape, point of land' (Bergsland 1994).

YAKALA Creek (Idaho, Latah Co.). Probably Chinook Jargon <yak´-a-la> [yákala] 'eagle', perhaps from Nisqually (Salishan) /yə́x^{W}la/ 'bald eagle' (D. Kinkade p.c.).

YAKATAGA (Alaska, Bering Glacier A-3) \yak´ ə tag ə\. From Tlingit [yak^{W} deyi] 'canoe road' (De Laguna 1972:100).

YAKIMA (Wash., Yakima Co.) \yak´ i mä\. Perhaps from Sahaptin /íyakima/ 'pregnant women' (Hitchman 1985; D. Kinkade p.c.).

YAKI Point (Ariz., Coconino Co.) \yä´ ke, yak´ ē\. Named for the Yaqui (Uto-Aztecan) Indians of Sonora, Mexico; many now live in Ariz. The term is from the self-designation /hiaki/ (*HNAI* 10:262). A related placename is **Yaqui Camp** (Calif., Calaveras Co.).

YAKINIKAK Creek (Mont., Flathead Co.). Perhaps from the Flathead (Salishan) language (BGN 6904).

YAKSO Falls (Ore., Douglas Co.) \yak´ sō\. Chinook Jargon <yak´-so> [yákso] 'hair of the head', perhaps from Lower Chinook [yákso] 'hair' (McArthur 1992; D. Kinkade p.c.).

YAKSON Canyon (Wash., Chelan Co.) \yak´ sən\. From Moses-Columbian (Salishan) /yáqsm/ [yáqsəm], a man's name (D. Kinkade p.c.).

YAKUTANIA Point (Alaska, Skagway B-1). The Tlingit name, published in 1923, is said to mean 'canoe-landing' (Orth 1967).

YAKUTAT (Alaska, Yakutat C-5) \yak´ o͞o tat\. From Tlingit [yak^{W}dat], of unclear etymology (De Laguna 1972:58).

YALAHA (Fla., Lake Co.). From Muskogee *yvlahv* /yalá:ha/ 'orange', from Spanish *naranja* (Read 1934; Martin and Mauldin 2000).

YALA ŁANA (N.Mex., Cibola Co.). The Zuni placename contains /yala-/ 'mountain' (Ferguson and Hart 1985; Newman 1958).

YALIK Bay (Alaska, Seldovia B-2). The Alutiiq (Eskimo) name was reported in 1880 (Orth 1967).

YALOBUSHA County (Miss.) From Choctaw (Muskogean) *yalooboshi* 'little tadpole', containing *yalooba* 'tadpole' and *-ushi* 'diminutive' (P. Munro p.c.).

YAMACRAW Bluff (Ga., Chatham Co.) \yam´ ə krô\. Named for an Indian group associated with the Muskogee (Krakow 1975); the term may be from Catawban (Siouan) /yį mikra:/ 'great people' (B. Rudes p.c.). The placename also occurs in Ky. (McCreary Co.), Miss. (Pearl River Co.), and N.C. (Pender Co.). A related name is **Yamacrow Creek** (Miss., Wilkinson Co.).

YAMACUTAH, Lake (Ga., Jackson Co.). Said to be the name of a Cherokee (Iroquoian) village, derived from the word 'to tumble' (Krakow 1975).

YAMASSEE (Fla., Jackson Co.) \yə mä´ sē\. The name of an Indian group, perhaps from Muskogee *yvmvsē* /yamási:/ 'tame, quiet' (Read 1984; Martin and Mauldin 2000); or perhaps from Catawban (Siouan) /yį musí:/, lit. 'people-ancient' (B. Rudes p.c.). Possibly related placenames are **Yemassee** (S.C., Hampton Co.) and **Omusee Creek** (Ala., Houston Co.).

YAMHILL County (Ore.) \yam´ hil\. From Kalapuyan [ayámhil], the name of a tribal subgroup (D. Kinkade p.c.).

YAMPA (Colo., Routt Co.) \yam´pə\. The term refers to a variety of roots or tubers used as food by the Numic (Uto-Aztecan) peoples; the Ute term is /yampa/ or /nanta/; the Shoshoni is /yampa/. In local English, the plant is called <yampa, yamp, yant, nant> (Bright 1993; J. McLaughlin p.c.) The placename also occurs in Utah (Uintah Co.) and Wyo. (Lincoln Co.). A related placename is **Yomba Indian Reservation** (Nev., Nye Co.).

YAMPAI (Ariz., Yavapai Co.) \yäm´ pī, yäm´ pē\. The name was earlier recorded both as **Yampa** and **Yampai** (Granger 1983). Thus the word may be related to **Yampa** (see above); or to **Yavapai County,** from the name of a Yuman people (see below).

YAMPO (Ore., Yamhill Co.). The name was coined by combining elements from **Yamhill County** and *Polk County* (McArthur 1992).

YAMSAY Mountain (Ore., Klamath Co.) \yam´ zē\. Klamath /y'amsii/ 'north wind place', from /yaama/ 'blows from the north' (Barker 1963). A variant spelling is **Yamsi.**

YANA Point (Nev., Pershing Co.) \yä´ nə\. Named for a group of Indian peoples who once lived in the Sacramento Valley of Calif. (BGN 7201).

YANKEE. This term for an Anglo-American, especially one from New England, is perhaps from Algonquian <yengees>, adapted from the word *English.* There may be influence from Cherokee (Iroquoian) <eankke> 'slave, coward, prisoner' (Masthay 2002), however; cf. modern Cherokee *ayvgi* [ayʌ̨gi] 'captive' (Alexander 1971). A derivation from a Dutch nickname *Jan Kees* 'John Cheese' is also possible (*RHD* 1987); for discussion of the alternative hypotheses, see A. Read (2001:75–86) and Masthay (2002). **Yankee** occurs in many U.S. placenames, such as **Yankeetown** (Fla., Levy Co.); as a personal nickname, it appears as **Yank** in placenames like **Yank's Canyon** (Ariz., Santa Cruz Co.).

YANKTONAI Creek (N.Dak., McLean Co.). The name of a Dakota (Siouan) subgroup, from *ihą́kthųwąna* 'little village on the end'; this is the same as **Yankton,** but with *-na* 'diminutive' added (Sneve 1973; *HNAI* 13:753).

YANKTON County (S.Dak.) \yängk´ tən\. The name of a Dakota (Siouan) subgroup, from *ihą́kthųwą* 'village on the end', from *ihą́ke* 'on the end' plus *thųwą́* 'village' (Sneve 1973; *HNAI* 13:754). The term also occurs as a placename in Neb. (Pierce Co.). In Ore. (Columbia Co.) the placename **Yankton** is said to be a contraction of *Yankeetown.*

YANTACAW Park (N.J., Essex Co.). Earlier written <Younticaw>; probably from Delaware (Algonquian), but of unclear derivation (Becker 1964).

YANT Flat (Utah, Washington Co.). An alternative form of **Yampa**; see above.

YANTLEY (Ala., Choctaw Co.) \yant´lē\. Perhaps from Choctaw <Bouk-Oké-Yannalé>

'creek of running water'; cf. *book* 'creek', *oka* 'water', *yanalli* 'to run' (Read 1984; P. Munro p.c.).

YANUSH (Okla., Latimer Co.) \yä´ nəsh\. From Choctaw (Mukskogean) *yanash* 'buffalo' (Shirk 1974; P. Munro p.c.).

YAPAHANK Creek (N.Y., Suffolk Co.). A variant of **Yaphank**; see below.

YAPASHI (N.Mex., Sandoval Co.) \yə pä´ shē\. A shortening of Cochiti (Keresan) [yapašenye] 'sacred enclosure' (Julyan 1998; Harrington 1916).

YAPHANK (N.Y., Suffolk Co.) \yap´ hangk\. Earlier written <Yamphank>; from SNEng. Algonquian, of unclear derivation (Tooker 1911). A variant is **Yapahank Creek.**

YAPOAH Lake (Ore., Deschutes Co.) \yä pō´ ə\. Possibly related to Tualatin (Kalapuyan) [ampúi'wa] 'island, small prairie in the woods' (McArthur 1992; H. Zenk p.c.).

YAPONCHA (Ariz., Coconino Co.). From Hopi (Uto-Aztecan) *yaapontsa,* the name of a supernatural being associated with windstorms (Granger 1983; K. Hill p.c.).

YAQUI Camp (Calif., Calaveras Co.) \yä´ kē\. Named for the Yaqui (Uto-Aztecan) Indians of Sonora, Mexico; many now live in Ariz. The term is from the self-designation /hiaki/ (*HNAI* 10:262). A related placename is **Yaqui Crater** (Ariz., Coconino Co.).

YAQUINA (Ore., Lincoln Co.) \yə kē´ nə, yə kwin´ ə, yak in´ ə\. From the Alsea placename /yaqúuna, yuqúuna/ (McArthur 1992; D. Kinkade p.c.).

YARMONY (Colo., Eagle Co.) \yär´ mə nē\. Named for a Ute (Numic) leader called *yáamani* 'quiet man' (Bright 1993).

YARNABY (Okla., Bryan Co.) \yä´ nə bē\. Perhaps from the "war name" of a Choctaw (Muskogean) man, meaning 'to go and kill', containing *iya* 'to go' and *abi* 'to kill' (Shirk 1974; P. Munro p.c.).

YASHAU Creek (Okla., McCurtain Co.) \yä´ shou\. Perhaps from Choctaw (Muskogean) *iyaasha* 'large kettle used for cooking hominy with pork' (P. Munro p.c.).

YATAMA Creek (Wash., Yakima Co.). Perhaps from Sahaptin /latáma, lantá:ma/ 'underground oven' (D. Kinkade p.c.).

YATUK Creek (Alaska, Craig D-4). The Tlingit name was recorded in 1949 (Orth 1967).

YAUHANNAH (S.C., Georgetown Co.). Perhaps from Catawban (Siouan) /yą́hare:/ 'it is a path', from /yą/ 'path' (Pickens 1961–62:24; B. Rudes p.c.).

YAUPON Beach (N.C., Brunswick Co.) \yô´ pon\. The English word *yaupon* refers to a plant, sometimes called *yaupon holly,* from Catawba (Siouan) /'yą́pą'/ (*RHD* 1987; B. Rudes p.c.). The placename also occurs in S.C. (Horry Co.). A related form is **Yupon** (Ala., Baldwin Co.).

YAVA (Ariz., Yavapai Co.) \yav´ ə, yä´ və\. Said to be an abbreviation of **Yavapai County** (Granger 1983); see below.

YAVAPAI County (Ariz.) \yä və pī´, yav´ ə pī\. The term refers to a Yuman people; this word is the plural of /yavpé/, the name for a member of the largest tribal subgroup (*HNAI* 10:52).

YAWBUCS Brook (Conn., New London Co.). From SNEng. Algonquian, pehaps meaning 'on one side of a small pond' (Trumbull 1881).

YAWGOO Pond (R.I., Washington Co.). From SNEng. Algonquian, of unclear derivation (Huden 1962).

YAWGUNSK (R.I., Washington Co.). From SNEng. Algonquian, perhaps meaning 'as far as that rock' (Huden 1962).

YA WHEE Plateau (Ore., Klamath Co.) \yä´ wē\. Klamath /yeewa/ 'blows from the southeast' (McArthur 1992; Barker 1963).

YAZZI Well (N.Mex., San Juan Co.) \yä´ zē, yaz ´ ē\. From Navajo Athabaskan) *yázhí* 'small (person)'. This is a very common Navajo surname, usually spelled in English as **Yazzie.** The placename **Yazzi** also occurs in Ariz. (Apache Co.). An adaptation of the same word is **Yazzie Mesa** (Ariz., Apache Co.).

YCATAPOM Peak (Calif., Shasta Co.) \wī kä´ tə pōm, wī kat´ ə pōm\. From Wintu /wayk'odipom/ 'north step place', containing /way/ 'north', /k'od-/ 'to step', and /-pom/ 'place' (Gudde 1998).

YCOTTI Creek (Calif., Shasta Co.) \wī kot´ ē\. Perhaps an abbreviation of **Ycatapom Peak**; see above.

YDALPOM (Calif., Shasta Co.) \wī dal´ pom\. From Wintu /waydalpom/ 'place to the north', from /way/ 'north', /-dal/ 'direction', and /-pom/ 'place' (Gudde 1998).

YEEHAW (Fla., Indian River Co.). From Muskogee *yvhv* /yahá/ 'wolf' (Read 1934; Martin and Mauldin 2000).

YEEK-SHA Mountain (Alaska, Sumdum C-6). The Tlingit name was reported in 1951 (Orth 1967).

YEI BICHEI (Ariz., Navajo Co.). From Navajo *ye'ii bicheii* 'grandfather of the ye'ii', referring to a type of supernatural beings (Granger 1983; Linford 2000).

YELDAGALGA Creek (Alaska, Skagway A-1). The Tlingit name was published in 1923 (Orth 1967).

YELKIS Creek (Ore., Clackamas Co.). Named for [yélqas], a nineteenth-century Molala leader (D. Kinkade p.c.).

YELLEPIT (Wash., Benton Co.)) \yel´ ə pit\. Named for a Walla Walla (Sahaptan) leader of the early nineteenth century; the term is said to mean 'trading partner' (Hitchman 1985; D. Kinkade p.c.).

YELLOWHAWK Creek (Wash., Walla Walla Co.). Corresponds to the name of a nineteenth-century Sahaptin leader, recorded as <Peo-Peo-Mox-Mox> (Hitchman 1985).

YELLOWHEAD Township (Ill., Kankakee Co.). Named for a Potawatomi (Algonquian) leader of the early nineteenth century; his Native American name may have been <Ozanatap> (Vogel 1963). Cf. <wizawa> 'yellow', <dup> 'head' (Kansas 1997).

YELLOW JACKET Canyon (Ariz., Coconino Co.) A translation of Navajo (Athabaskan) *tsís'nááłtsooí* 'yellowjacket, a kind of hornet', from *tsís'na* 'bee, wasp' and *-łtso-* 'yellow' (Granger 1983, Young and Morgan 1987).

YELLOW Lake (Wis., Burnett Co.). A translation of Ojibwa (Algonquian) *ozaawaagami* (Vogel 1991; Nichols and Nyholm 1995). Similarly, **Yellow River** (Ind., Starke Co.) corresponds to Potawatomi (Algonquian) /wezawgəmək/ 'at the yellow water' (McCafferty 2002).

YELLOW LEAF Creek (Ala., Chilton Co.). Corresponds to Muskogee *vsse-lanvpe* /assi-la:n-apí/, the name of a tribal town, literally 'leaf-yellow-tree' (Read 1984; Martin and Mauldin 2000).

YELLOW MEDICINE County (Minn.). A translation of Dakota (Siouan) *phežúta-zi*, containing *phežúta* 'medicine' and *zi* 'yellow', referring to a type of medicinal plant (Upham 2001; Riggs 1890).

YELLOW THUNDER Park (Wis., Sauk Co.). Named for a Winnebago (Siouan) leader of the early nineteenth century, whose Native American name has been written <Wau-kaun-zee-kaw> (Vogel 1991); a modern transcription is *wakąǰázigá*, from *wakąǰá* 'thunder,' *zíi* 'yellow or orange,' and *-ga* 'personal name ending' (K. Miner p.c.).

YELM (Wash., Thurston Co.) \yelm\. Said to be from a Salishan word <chelm> 'heat waves from the sun' (Hitchman 1985).

YELNU Islets (Alaska, Prince Rupert D-1). The Tlingit name was recorded in 1936 (Orth 1967).

YEMASSEE (S.C., Hampton Co.). An alternative form of **Yamassee** (Pearson 1978); see above.

YENITUK Creek (Alaska, Wiseman D-5). The Iñupiaq (Eskimo) name was reported about 1930 (Orth 1967).

YENLO Creek (Alaska, Talkeetna A-2) \yen´ lō\. From Dena'ina (Athabaskan) *yentl'u*, referring to the upper Yentna River area (Kari and Fall 1987:139).

YENSUS Lake (Alaska, Tyonek C-2) \yen´ səs\. Dena'ina *yen ses bena* 'backbone ridge lake' (J. Kari p.c.).

YENTNA (Alaska, Tyonek C-2) \yent´ nə\. From Dena'ina (Athabaskan) *yentnu*, perhaps 'backbone river' or 'straight river', containing *-tnu* 'river' (Kari and Fall 1987:107).

YEOCOMICO River (Va., Northumberland Co.). From CAC Algonquian, of unclear derivation (Hagemann 1988).

YEOMALT (Wash., Kitsap Co.). From a word <Yem-o-alt> in an unidentified Indian language, perhaps referring to storytelling (Hitchman 1985).

YEOMET Creek (Calif., Amador Co.) \yō´ mət\. Probably an Indian village name, from an unidentified language (Gudde 1998).

YEOPIM (N.C., Chowan Co.). The name of a CAC Algonquian subgroup (Powell 1968).

YES Bay (Alaska, Ketchikan D-6). From Tlingit *yées'* [yíis'] 'large mussel on stormy coast, used for scraping' (Orth 1967; Davis and Leer 1976:35).

YETNA River (Alaska, Ophir A-5) \yet´ nə\. From Deg Hit'an (Athabaskan) *yeq'itno'*, containing *no'* 'stream' (J. Kari p.c.). But the similarly named **Yetna Creek** (Alaska, Valdez D-4) is perhaps from Ahtna *tatsen na'*, lit. 'smelly-water creek' (Kari 1983:31).

YISTLETAW (Alaska, Nulato D-3). The Koyukon (Athabaskan) name was reported in 1952 (Orth 1967).

YNVEEGHIK River (Alaska, Lawrence C-4). From Yupik (Eskimo) <Ingresik> 'rising slope' (Orth 1967).

YOCANA (Ark., Polk Co.) \yok´ ə nə\. From Choctaw (Muskogean) *yaakni* 'land'. There is a **Yocana Lake** in Miss. (Pontotoc Co.). Related forms are **Yocona** (Miss., Lafayette Co.) and **Yocony** (Miss., Itawamba Co.). Perhaps from the same stem is **Yocanoocana** (Miss., Leake Co.); a variant is **Yockanookany**.

YOCKWAH Creek (Idaho, Valley Co.) Chinook Jargon <yuk´-wa, yah´-kwa> [yák^{w}a] 'here, this side', from Lower Chinook [yákwa] 'here' (D. Kinkade p.c.).

YOCONA (Miss., Lafayette Co.) \yok´ ə nə\. From the same source as **Yocana** (Ark., Polk Co.); see above. Another probably related form is **Yocony** (Miss., Itawamba Co.).

YOGO Creek (Utah, Sevier Co.) \yō´ gō\. Probably from Ute (Numic) /yoko/ [yóɣo] 'to copulate' (J. McLaughlin p.c.).

YOHOLA, Lake (Ga., Early Co.) \yə hō´ lə\. An alternative form of **Yahola**; see above.

YOKAKEK (Alaska, Nulato C-1). The Koyukon (Athabaskan) name is of unclear derivation (Orth 1967).

YOKNEDA Lake (Alaska, Gulkana B-2). The Ahtna (Athabaskan) name was reported in 1949 (Orth 1967).

YOKOHL Creek (Calif., Tulare Co.) \yō´kôl\. The name of a Yokuts subgroup (Gudde 1998).

YOKONTOH Slough (Alaska, Unalakleet B-1). The Koyukon (Athabaskan) name was reported in 1935 (Orth 1967).

YOKUM (Mass., Berkshire Co.) \yō´ kəm\. Said to be named for an eighteenth-century Mahican (Algonquian) leader (Huden 1962). The term is also written as **Yokun.**

YOLLA BOLLY Mountains (Calif., Trinity Co.) \yō´ lə bō lē, yō´ lə bō lə\. Represents Wintu /yoola buli/, lit. 'snow mountain' (Gudde 1998).

YOLO County (Calif., Yolo Co.) \yō´ lō\. Earlier recorded as <Yoloy, Yodoi, Ioleo, Dioleo> (etc.); from Patwin (Wintuan), perhaps meaning 'place abounding in cattails' (Gudde 1998). The placename also occurs in Wis. (Clark Co.).

YOMBA Indian Reservaton (Nev., Nye Co.) \yom´ bə\. From Shoshoni (Numic) /yampa/ 'wild carrot' (J. McLaughlin p.c.); see **Yampa** above.

YONAGUSKA, Mount (N.C., Haywood Co.). Named for a Cherokee (Iroquoian) leader of the nineteenth century (Powell 1968).

YONAH Mountain (Ga., White Co.) From Cherokee *yona* 'a bear' (Krakow 1975; Feeling 1975).

YONCALLA (Ore., Douglas Co.) \yon kä´ lə\. From Kalapuyan [yánkalat], the name of a tribal subgroup, perhaps contaiing [yank-] 'high' (H. Zenk p.c.).

YONCOPIN Lake (Ark., Independence Co.). Perhaps from Choctaw (Muskogean). Probably related names are **Yonkapin Lake** (Miss., Tallahatchie Co.) and **Yonkipin Lake** (Okla., Rogers Co.).

YONDOTA (Ohio, Lucas Co. \yon dot´ ə\. Probably from Huron/Wyandot (Iroquoian) [yandata] (B. Rudes p.c.). A possibly related name is **Wyandot County.**

YON DOT Mountains (Ariz., Coconino Co.). From Navajo (Athabaskan) *yaa ndee'nil* 'series of hills going down' (Linford 2000).

YONNA (Ore., Klamath Co.) \yon´ ə\. Perhaps from Klamath /yana:/ 'below' (Barker 1963; McArthur 1992).

YONTOCKETT (Calif., Del Norte Co.) \yon´ tok ət\. From the Tolowa (Athabaskan) village /yan'-dagəd/, lit. 'southward uphill' (Gudde 1998).

YOSEMITE Valley (Calif., Mariposa Co.) \yō sem´ i tē\. From Southern Sierra Miwok /yohhe'meti, yoṣṣe'meti/ 'they are killers', derived from /yoohu-/ 'to kill', evidently a name given to the Indians of the valley by those outside it (Gudde 1998). The placename also occurs in Ky. (Casey Co.), pronounced \yō´ sə mīt\. and in Utah (Salt Lake Co.).

YOUBA (Ohio, Athens Co.) \yo͞o´ bə\. Perhaps a transfer from **Yuba County** in Calif.; see below.

YOUGHAPOTIT Rocks (Alaska, Lawrence A-2). The Yupik (Eskimo) name, reported in 1949, has also been written <Ukhapatit> (Orth 1967).

YOUGHIOGHENY River (Md., Garrett Co.; Pa., Allegheny Co.) \yok ə hā´ nē, yok´ ə gā nē\. It is said that the name was applied first to the **Pamunkey River** in Va. In Md. and Pa. it was earlier written as <Ohio gani, Yoxhio geni> (etc.), perhaps meaning 'four rivers', referring to the main stream and three branches; cf. CAC Algonquian <yeough> 'four' (Kenny 1984). The name also occurs in W.Va. (Preston Co.).

YOUTLKUT Butte (Ore., Lake Co.) \you´ təl kət\. Chinook Jargon <youtl´-kut, yult-cut, yūlkat> [yútlkət] 'long, length'; cf. Kathlamet (Chinookan) [éyaƛqt] 'long' (D. Kinkade p.c.).

YOVIMPA Point (Utah, Kane Co.) \yō vim´ pə\. From Southern Paiute (Numic) /yɨpimpɨ/ [yɨvímpɨ̥] 'long-leafed pine' (Van Cott 1990; J. McLaughlin p.c.).

YREKA (Calif., Siskiyou Co.) \wī rē´ kə\. From Shasta /wáik'a/, the name for the nearby **Mt. Shasta** (Gudde 1998). The placename **Yreka** also occurs in Ore. (Wallowa Co.).

YSLETA (Tex., El Paso Co.) \is let´ ə\. This is a spelling variant of Spanish **Isleta** 'little island', as applied to a Tiwa (Tanoan) pueblo in N.Mex. (Bernalillo Co.); some Indians from this pueblo moved to the El Paso area. The Tex. site is also called **Ysleta del Sur** and **Tigua Pueblo** (*HNAI* 9:336).

YSLETAÑO Canyon (N.Mex., Otero Co.). The Spanish word means 'belonging to Ysleta', referring to **Isleta Pueblo** (N.Mex., Bernalillo Co.).

YUBA County (Calif.) \yo͞o´ bə\. From the name of a Maidu village, written as <Yubu, Yupu, Jubu>; cf. Nisenan (Maiduan) /yubuy/ 'shade, shadow' (Gudde 1998). The name **Yuba** also occurs in Mich. (Grand Traverse Co.), Okla. (Bryan Co.), and Wis. (Richland Co.).

YUCAIPA (Calif., San Bernardino Co.) \yo͞o kī´ pə\. Supposedly derived from a Serrano (Takic) word meaning ‘wet or marshy land’ (Gudde 1998).

YUCATAN (Minn., Houston Co.) \yo͞o´ kə tan\. From Spanish *Yucatán,* a peninsula in southeastern Mexico. The name may be from Yucatec (Mayan), but the derivation is not clear. The placename **Yucatan** also occurs in La. (Tensas Par.).

YUCCA \yuk´ ə\. A plant of the agave family, especially common in the southwestern states. The term is from Spanish *yuca*—which, however, referred originally to manioc, a very different plant. The Spanish term may come from a Cariban language of the West Indies (*RHD* 1987). As a placename, **Yucca** occurs in Calif. (San Bernardino Co.), Colo. (Montezuma Co.), and N.Dak. (Hettinger Co.).

YUCHI \yo͞o´ chē\. This represents the name of a people politically associated with the Muskogees but speaking a separate language (Goff 1975); they originally lived in Ga., but their descendants are now in Okla. The Muskogee form of the name is *yocce* /yó:čči/ (Martin and Mauldin 2000). As a placename, **Yuchi** occurs in Ala. (Russell Co.). Related placenames are **Eucha** (Okla., Delaware Co.), **Euchee Valley** (Fla., Walton Co.), and **Uchee Creek** (Ga., Columbia Co.).

YUFALI (Ala., Houston Co.) \yo͞o fä´ lē\. An alternative form of **Eufaula**; see **Eufala** above. Another related form is **Yufaula** (Ala., Talladega Co.).

YUGNAT Rocks (Alaska, Mt. Katmai B-1). Perhaps from Dena’ina (Athabaskan), reported in 1831 (Orth 1967).

YUGOK Lake (Alaska, Kenai D-2). The name is probably from Dena’ina (Athabaskan), of unclear derivation (Orth 1967).

YUHA Desert (Calif., Imperial Co.) \yo͞o´ hä\. Perhaps from an unidentified Indian language (Gudde 1998).

YUHWAMAI (Calif., San Diego Co.) \yo͞o wä´ mī\. Probably from Luiseño (Takic) /yuxwáamay/ ‘little mud’, from /yuxwáala/ ‘mud’ (Gudde 1998).

YUKANILUK Creek (Alaska, Russian Mission A-5). The Yupik (Eskimo) name was reported in 1948 (Orth 1967).

YUKI Cemetery (Calif., Mendocino Co.) \yo͞o´ kē\. From the name of the Yuki people, native to the area. A similar placename is the **Yuki River** in Alaska (Nulato C-1); it is probably from the Koyukon (Athabaskan) language (Orth 1967).

YUKLA, Mount (Alaska, Anchorage A-6) \yuk´ lə\. From Dena’ina (Athabaskan) nuk’elehitnu ‘fish run again river’ (J. Kari p.c.).

YUKMI Creek (S.Dak., Mellette Co.). From Dakota (Siouan) *yukmí* ‘to clear off (e.g., a field)’ (D. Parks p.c.).

YUKON River (Canada, Alaska) \yo͞o´ kon\. From Athabaskan, perhaps Koyukon *yookkene* or Lower Tanana *yookuna* (Orth 1967; Kari 1999:104, 123). As a placename, **Yukon** also occurs in Okla. (Canadian Co.), Ore. (Josephine Co.), and Wis. (Oneida Co.).

YUKUK Bay (Alaska, Afognak A-3). From Aleut *uxchux* ‘tufted puffin’ (Bergsland 1994).

YULUPA (Calif., Sonoma Co.) \yo͞o lo͞o´ pə\. Also written <Ulupa, Julupa>, a placename from an unidentified Indian language (Gudde 1998).

YUMA County (Ariz.) \yo͞o´ mə\. From the name of an Indian people of the Yuman language family. The term is probably from O’odham (Piman) *yu’mĭ,* the name that the Piman peoples applied to the Yuma people (*HNAI* 9:97). In recent years, the Yumas have restored their traditional self-designation *Quechan* or *Kwtsaan* \kwə chän\. As a placename, **Yuma** also occurs in other states (e.g., Calif., Imperial Co.; Colo., Yuma Co.; and Kans., Cloud Co.).

YUMTHESKA Mesa (Ariz., Coconino Co.). This is the surname of a Havasupai (Yuman) family (Granger 1983; L. Hinton p.c.).

YUNASKA Island (Alaska, Amukta C-3) \yo͞o nas´ kə\. From the Aleut placename *yunax̂sxa* (Bergsland 1994).

YUNOSI Point (Ariz., Coconino Co.). The surname of a Havasupai (Yuman) family (L. Hinton p.c.).

YUONGLIK River (Alaska, Solomon C-3). Also written <Youunglik>; the Iñupiaq (Eskimo) name was reported in 1909 (Orth 1967).

YUPON (La., West Baton Rouge Par.) \yōō´ pon\. An alternative form of **Yaupon Beach** (N.C., Brunswick Co.); see above. The name also occurs in Ala. (Baldwin Co.) and Tex. (Colorado Co.).

YUTAN (Neb., Saunders Co.) \yōō´ tan\. Named for an Oto (Siouan) leader; related forms are **Iatan** (Mo., Platte Co.) and **Iatt** (La., Grant Parish).

YUTOKH Hill (Alaska, Mt. McKinley D-5) \yōō´ tok\. From Koyukon (Athabaskan) *yo t'uh,* lit. 'sky nest' (Kari 1999:122).

Z

ZACA (Calif., Santa Barbara Co.) \zak´ ə\. Perhaps from Barbareño (Chumashan), said to mean 'quiet place' (Gudde 1998).

ZACAHUISTLE Pasture (Tex., Brooks Co.) \sä kä wēst´ lā\. Mexican Spanish, referring to a native plant; from Nahuatl (Aztecan) *zacahuitztli,* containing *zaca(tl)* 'grass' and *huitztli* 'thorn' (Santamaría 1959). A further adaptation is **Zacaweista Ranch**; see below.

ZACATA Creek (Tex., Webb Co.). An adaptation of **Zacate** \zə kä´ tē\, from Mexican Spanish *zacate* 'grass, hay, fodder', pronounced approximately \sä kä´ tā\; from Nahuatl (Aztecan) *zacatl* 'grass'. This term as such is not currently used as a placename, but it occurs in the nonstandard spelling **Sacate** (Calif., Santa Barbara Co.) and in many combinations such as **Sacaton** (Calif., Riverside Co.), **Zacates** (N.Mex., Bernalillo Co.), and **Arroyo Zacatoso** (Tex., Zapata Co.).

ZACATES (N.Mex., Bernalillo Co.). The plural of Mexican Spanish *zacate* 'grass'; see **Zacata Creek** above.

ZACATON (Calif., Riverside Co.). From Mexican Spanish *zacatón* 'big grass'; see **Zacata Creek** above. The term is also written **Sacaton.**

ZACATOSO, Arroyo (Tex., Zapata Co.). Spanish for 'grassy creek', from Mexican Spanish *zacate* 'grass, hay'; see **Zacata Creek** above.

ZACAWEISTA Ranch (Tex., Wilbarger Co.) \zak´ ə wis tə\. Derived from **Zacahuistle Pasture** (Tex., Brooks Co.); see above.

ZACKUSE Creek (Wash., King Co.). Named for James Zackuse, a nineteenth-century Snoqualmie (Salishan) resident (BGN 1994).

ZAYANTE Creek (Calif., Santa Cruz Co.) \zä yan´ tē\. Probably from Rumsen (Costanoan) /sayyan-ta/ 'at the heel' (Gudde 1998).

ZEKIAH Swamp (Md., Charles Co.) \zə kī´ ə\. Earlier written <Zachkia, Saccaia>; perhaps from CAC Algonquian (Kenny 1984).

ZELATCHED Point (Wash., Jefferson Co.). Perhaps from a Twana (Salishan) placename (Hitchman 1985; D. Kinkade p.c.).

ZEWAPETA (Mo., Scott Co.) \zə wä´ pə tə\. Perhaps an alternative form of **Tyewhoppety** (Ky., Todd Co.) and **Tywappity Township** (Mo., Mississippi Co.), said to be from Shawnee (Algonquian).

ZIA Pueblo (N.Mex., Sandoval Co.) \zē´ ə\. From Keresan *ts'îiya,* the Native American name (Julyan 1998; I. Davis 1998).

ZILBETOD Peak (Ariz., Apache Co.) \zil bā tōd´\. From Navajo (Athabaskan) *dził béét'óód* 'bald mountain' or *dził bét'ood* 'balding mountain', with *dził* 'mountain' (Granger 1983; Linford 2000). Several of the following names also contain *dził* 'mountain'.

ZILDITLOI Mountain (N.Mex., McKinley Co.) \zil´ di tloi\. Navajo (Athabaskan) *dził ditłoii* 'fuzzy mountain', with *ditł'o* 'it is fuzzy' (Julyan 1998; Wilson 1995).

ZILLESA Mesa (Ariz., Navajo Co.). From Navajo (Athabaskan) *dził deez'á* 'where the mountain range begins' (Linford 2000); cf. *deez'á* 'it extends' (Young and Morgan 1987).

ZILNEZ Mesa (Ariz., Navajo Co.) \zil nez´\. From Navajo (Athabaskan) *dziɫ ninééz* 'long mountain' (Linford 2000).

ZILTAHJINI Peak (Ariz., Navajo Co.). From Navajo (Athabaskan), meaning 'standing cranes' (Granger 1983); cf. *déétɫ* 'a crane (bird)' (Young and Morgan 1987).

ZILWAUKEE (Mich., Saginaw Co.) \zil wô´ kē\. An invented name modeled on **Milwaukee County** (Vogel 1986); see above.

ZITZIANA River (Alaska, Kantishna River D-2) \zit sē an´ ə\. Koyukon (Athabaskan) *ch'edzaaye' no'*, lit. 'heart river', with *no'* 'river' (Kari 1999:111).

ZOGLIAKHTEN (Alaska, Kateel River B-4). The Koyukon (Athabaskan) name is of unclear derivation. Perhaps related is the nearby **Zonagoliakten**, also unanalyzable.

ZUMA Creek (Ill., Rock Island Co.). Perhaps shortened from the name of the Aztec ruler **Montezuma** (Vogel 1963), as if it were "Monte Zuma," meaning 'Mt. Zuma'. There is also a **Zuma Beach** in Calif. (Los Angeles Co.).

ZUNI Pueblo (N.Mex., McKinley Co.) \zo͞o´ nē\. The name refers to the Indian people and language that are native to the pueblo; from Spanish *Zuñi*, from a Keresan name like Acoma /sî:ni/ [sî:ñi] 'Zuni Pueblo' (Julyan 1998; *HNAI* 9:479–80). The placename also occurs in Ariz. (Navajo Co.).

ZUZAX (N.Mex., Bernalillo Co.) \zo͞o´ zaks\. An name invented by a curio shop owner, intended to attract attention, but attributed by him to the "Zuzax Indians" (Julyan 1998).

References

Afable, Patricia O., and Madison S. Beeler. 1996. Place-names. In Goddard 1996:17–42.

Akrigg, G. P. V., and H. B. Akrigg. 1986. *British Columbia placenames.* Victoria: Sono Nis Press.

Alexander, J. T. 1971. *A dictionary of the Cherokee Indian language.* [Sperry, Okla.: The author.]

Aoki, Haruo. 1994. *Nez Perce dictionary.* University of California Publications in Linguistics, 122. Berkeley: University of California Press.

Aschbacher, Frances M. (ed.) 1978. *Pronouncing directory of cities, towns and counties in Texas.* [San Antonio:] The editor.

Ashley, Leonard R. N. 1996. Amerindian toponyms in the United States. In *Namenforschung: Ein internationales Handbuch zur Onomastik,* ed. Ernst Eichler et al., 2:1403–8. Berlin: de Gruyter.

Aubin, George F. 1975. *A Proto-Algonquian dictionary.* National Museum of Man, Mercury Series, Canadian Ethnology Service, Paper No. 29. Ottawa: National Museums of Canada.

Baker, Ronald L. 1995. *From Needmore to Prosperity: Hoosier place names in folk history.* Bloomington: Indiana University Press.

Baker, Ronald L., and Marvin Carmony. 1975. *Indiana place names.* Bloomington, Indiana University Press.

Baraga, Frederic. 1880. *A dictionary of the Otchipwe language.* 2 vols. Montreal: Beauchemin & Valois. [Reprinted as *A dictionary of the Ojibwe language.* St. Paul: Minnesota Historical Society, 1992.]

Barker, M. A. R. 1963. *Klamath dictionary.* University of California Publications in Linguistics, 31. Berkeley: University of California Press.

Barnes, Arthur M. 1959. *Pronunciation guide to names of places and state officeholders in Iowa.* 2nd ed. Iowa City: State University of lowa.

Barnes, William Croft. 1960. *Arizona place names.* Revised and enlarged by Byrd H. Granger. Tucson: University of Arizona Press.

Beauchamp, J. Larry. 1900. *A guide to the pronunciation of Indiana cities and towns.* [Lafayette, Ind.:] Purdue University.

Beauchamp, William M. 1907. *Aboriginal place names of New York.* New York State Museum, Bulletin 108. Albany: New York State Education Dept. Reprinted, Detroit, Grand River Books, 1971; Detroit: Gale, 1972; Temecula, Calif.: Reprint Services, 1993.

Becker, Donald William. 1964. *Indian place-names in New Jersey.* Cedar Grove, N.J.: Phillips-Campbell.

Bergsland, Knut. 1994. *Aleut dictionary / Unangam tunudgusii: An unabridged lexicon of the Aleutian, Pribilof, and Commander Islands Aleut language.* Fairbanks: Alaska Native Language Center, University of Alaska.

Berman, Howard. 1990. Kalapuya historical phonology. *International Journal of American Linguistics* 56:27–59.

Blalock, Lucy, Bruce Pearson, and James Rementer. 1994. *The Delaware language.* Bartlesville, Okla.: Delaware Tribe of Indians.

Bloomfield, Leonard. 1962. *The Menominee language.* New Haven: Yale University Press.

———. 1975. *Menominee lexicon.* Ed. Charles F. Hockett. Publications in Anthropology and History, 3. Milwaukee: Milwaukee Public Museum.

Booker, Karen M., Charles M. Hudson, and Robert L. Rankin. 1992. Place name identification and multilingualism in the sixteenth-century Southeast. *Ethnohistory* 19:399–451.

Boone, Lalia Phipps. 1988. *Idaho place names: A geographical dictionary.* Moscow: University of Idaho Press.

Bradfield, Bill. (ed.). N.d. *Texas towns from A to Z: Pronunciation guide.* Dallas: Three Forks Press.

Bray, Dorothy. (ed.). 1998. *Western Apache-English dictionary: A community-generated bilingual dictionary.* Tempe: Bilingual Press.

Brian, Nancy. 1992. *River to rim: A guide to place names along the Colorado River in Grand Canyon from Lake Powell to Lake Mead.* Flagstaff: Earthquest.

Bright, William. 1993. *Colorado place names.* Boulder, Colo.: Johnson. (Revised edition, 2004).

———. 1999a. From Poncha to Waxahatchie. *Society for the Study of the Indigenous Languages of the Americas, Newsletter* 18(3):9.

———. 1999b. The placename department [Mazama, Oregon]. *Society for the Study of the Indigenous Languages of the Americas, Newsletter* 17(4):7.

———. 1999c. The placename department: Is Idaho really in Colorado? *Society for the Study of the Indigenous Languages of the Americas, Newsletter* 18(1):8

———. 1999d. Two Numic (?) placenames. *Society for the Study of the Indigenous Languages of the Americas, Newsletter* 18(2):10.

———. 2000a. Hispanisms in southwest Indian languages. *Romance Philology* 53:259–88.

———. 2000b. The placename department: Tucson, Arizona, etc. *Society for the Study of the Indigenous Languages of the Americas, Newsletter* 19(2):9–10.

———. 2000c. The sociolinguistics of the "s-word": *Squaw* in American placenames. *Names* 48:207–16.

———. 2001a. The placename department: Must every name have an etymology? *Society for the Study of the Indigenous Languages of the Americas, Newsletter* 19(4):110–11.

———. 2001b. The placename department: Sacs, Sauks, and other ways out. *Society for the Study of the Indigenous Languages of the Americas, Newsletter* 20(3):9–10.

———. 2002. The NAPUS (Native American placenames of the United States) Project: Principles and problems. In *Making dictionaries: Preserving indigenous languages of the Americas,* ed. by William Frawley et al., 322–35. Berkeley: University of California Press.

Bright, William, and Willem de Reuse. 2002. The placename department: Chicorica, NM—'Little cup', 'spotted bird', 'rich child'? *Society for the Study of the Indigenous Languages of the Americas, Newsletter* 20:11–12.

Bright, William, and John McLaughlin. 2000. Inyo redux. Names 48:147–50.

Brinton, Daniel G., and Albert Seqaqkind Anthony. 1888. *A Lenâpé-English dictionary.* Philadelphia: Historical Society of Pennsylvania. Reprinted, New York: AMS Press, 1979.

Brokenshire, Doug. 1993. *Washington State place names: From Alki to Yelm.* Caldwell, Idaho: Caxton Printers.

Brown, Donald E., and Frank E. Schooley. 1957. *Pronunciation guide for Illinois place names.* Urbana: College of Journalism and Communications, University of Illinois.

Bue, Olaf J. 1959. *A guide to pronunciation of place names in Montana.* Missoula: School of Journalism, Montana State University.

Buechel, Eugene, and Paul Manhart. 1983. *Lakota dictionary: Lakota-English, English-Lakota.* New comprehensive edition. Lincoln: University of Nebraska Press.

Burch, Ernest S., Jr. 1998. *The Iñupiaq Eskimo nations of northwest Alaska.* Fairbanks: University of Alaska Press.

Byington, Cyrus. 1915. *A dictionary of the Choctaw language.* Washington, D.C.: Government Printing Office.

Callary, Edward. (ed.). 1985. *Festschrift in honor of Virgil J. Vogel.* Papers of the North Central Names Institute, 5. DeKalb: Illinois Name Society, 1985.

———. 2000 (ed.) *Place names in the midwestern United States.* Lewiston, N.Y.: Mellen.

Campbell, Lyle. 1997. *American Indian languages: The historical linguistics of Native America.* Oxford: University Press.

Canonge, Elliott. 1958. *Comanche texts.* Norman, Okla.: Summer Institute of Linguistics.

Carlson, Helen S. 1974. *Nevada place names; a geographical dictionary.* Reno: University of Nevada Press. Reprinted, Ann Arbor, Mich.: Books on Demand, 1985.

Cassidy, Frederic G. 1948. Koshkonong: A misunderstood place name. *Wisconsin Magazine of History* 31:429–40.

———. 1991. Miscousing, Wisconsin. *Names* 39:191–98.

Caulfield, Richard A., Walter J. Peter, and Clarence Alexander (eds.). 1983. *Gwich'in Athabaskan place names of the Upper Yukon-Porcupine region, Alaska.* Fairbanks: Alaska Dept. of Fish and Game.

Chafe, Wallace L. 1967. *Seneca morphology and dictionary.* Smithsonian Contributions to Anthropology, 4. Washington, DC: Smithsonian Press.

Chamberlain, Alexander F. 1902. Geographic terms of Kootenay origin. *American Anthropologist* n.s. 4:348–50.

Cheney, Roberta Carkeek. 1984. *Names on the face of Montana: The story of Montana's places.* Revised ed. Missoula: Mountain Press.

Christensen, Arved, et al. 1953. *A pronunciation guide to Nebraska place names.* University of Nebraska Publication No. 183. Lincoln: Dept. of Speech, University of Nebraska.

Cobos, Rubén. 1983. *A dictionary of New Mexico and southern Colorado Spanish.* Santa Fe: Museum of New Mexico Press.

Coggins, Allen, et al. 1999. *Place names of the Smokies.* Gatlinburg, Tenn.: Great Smoky Museum Natural History Association.

Colorado. 1976. *Elementary bilingual dictionary: English-Lakhóta, Lakhóta-English.* Boulder: Dept. of Linguistics, University of Colorado.

Costa, David. 2000. Miami-Illinois tribe names. In *Papers of the Thirty-first Algonquian Conference,* ed. by John D. Nichols, 30–53. Winnipeg: University of Manitoba.

Couro, Ted, and Christina Hutcheson. 1973. *Dictionary of Mesa Grande Diegueño.* Banning, Calif.: Malki Museum Press.

Cowan, William. 1987. Ojibwa vocabulary in Longfellow's *Hiawatha.* In *Papers of the Eighteenth Algonquian Conference,* 59–67. Ottawa: Carleton University.

Cresswell, Thomas J. 2000. The great vowel shift in *Chicago.* In Callary 2000:109–20.

Crum, Beverly, and John Dayley. 1993. *Western Shoshoni grammar.* Boise, Idaho: Boise State University.

Cushman, H. B. 1899. *History of the Choctaw, Chickasaw and Natchez Indians.* Greenville, Tex.: Headlight. Revised ed., ed. by Angie Debo: New York: Russell and Russell, 1972; reprinted, Norman: University of Oklahoma Press, 1999.

Cutler, Charles L. 1994. *O brave new words! Native American loanwords in current English.* Norman: University of Oklahoma Press.

———. 1996. Obscurely famous [concerning Podunk]. MS.

Davis, Henry, and Jeff Leer. 1976. *English–Tlingit dictionary: Nouns*. Sitka, Alaska: Sheldon Jackson College. Revised ed. of Constance Naish and Gillian Story, *The English–Tlingit noun dictionary*. College, Alaska: Summer Institute of Linguistics, 1996.

Day, Gordon M. 1961. The name Contoocook. *International Journal of American Linguistics* 27:168–71. Reprinted in Day 1998:61–64.

———. 1968. Iroquois: An etymology. *Ethnohistory* 15:389-402. Reprinted in Day 1998:109–15.

———. 1972. The name *Algonquin. International Journal of American Linguistics* 38:226–28. Reprinted in Day 1998:123–26.

———. 1981. Abenaki place-names in the Champlain valley. *International Journal of American Linguistics* 47:143–71. Reprinted in Day 1998:229–62.

———. 1994–95. Western Abenaki dictionary. Vol. 1, *Abenaki–English.* Vol. 2, *English–Abenaki.* Canadian Ethnology Service, papers 128–29. Ottawa: Canadian Museum of Civilization.

———. 1998. *In search of New England's native past: Selected essays.* Ed. by Michael K. Foster and William Cowan. Amherst: University of Massachusetts Press.

Dayley, Jon P. 1989. *Tümpisa (Panamint) Shoshone dictionary.* University of California Publications in Linguistics, 116. Berkeley: University of California.

Deane, Ernie. 1986. *Arkansas place names.* Branson, Mo.: Ozarks Mountaineer.

DeBlois, Albert D. 1996. *Micmac dictionary*. Canadian Ethnology Service, Paper 131. Ottawa: Canadian Museum of Civilization.

DeCamp, L. Sprague. 1944. Pronunciation of upstate New York place-names. *American Speech* 19:250–65.

De Laguna, Frederica. 1972. *Under Mount Saint Elias*. Smithsonian Contributions to Anthropology, 7:1. Washington, D.C.: Government Printing Office.

Dickinson, Samuel D. 1995. Indian signs on the land. *Cultural encounters in the early South: Indians and Europeans in Arkansas,* ed. by Jeannie Whayne, 142–57. Fayetteville: University of Arkansas Press.

Donehoo, George Patterson. 1928. *A history of the Indian villages and place names in Pennsylvania, with numerous historical notes and references.* Harrisburg, Pa.: Telegraph. Reprinted: Baltimore, Gateway, 1977.

Dorais, Louis-Jacques. 1990. *1000 Inuit words.* Inuit Studies, Occasional Papers, 3. Québec: Groupe d'Études Inuit et Circumpolaires, Université Laval.

Douglass, William A. 1979. On the naming of Arizona. *Names* 27:217–34.

Duncan, Tom, et al. 1975. *Alaska place names pronunciation guide.* Elmer E. Rasmuson Library, Occasional Papers, 4. [Fairbanks:] University of Alaska.

Dunlap, Arthur Ray. 1967. Two Delaware Valley Indian place names. *Names* 15:197–202

Dunlap, Arthur Ray, and Clinton Alfred Weslager. 1950. *Indian place names in Delaware.* Wilmington: Archaeological Society of Delaware.

Dunn, Jacob Piatt. 1908. *True Indian stories, with glossary of Indiana Indian names.* Indianapolis: Sentinel.

———. 1909. Glossary of Indian names and supposed Indian names in Indiana. In his *Indiana and Indianans,* 86–97 Chicago: American Historical Society.

Dyson, John P. 1994. The naming of Paducah. *Register of the Kentucky Historical Society* 92:149–74.

Eckstorm, Fannie Hardy. 1941. Indian place-names of the Penobscot Valley and the Maine coast. University of Maine Studies, 2nd series, no. 55; Maine Bulletin, 44:4. Orono, Maine: University Press

Ehrensperger, Edward C. (ed.). 1941. *South Dakota place names.* Compiled by workers of the Writers' Program of the Work Projects Administration in the State of South Dakota. Vermillion: University of South Dakota. Reprinted as Sneve 1973.

Engel, Harold A. 1969. *Wisconsin place names: A pronouncing gazetteer.* 3rd ed. Madison: University Extension, University of Wisconsin. 1st ed., 1938; 2nd ed., 1948.

Feeling, Durbin. 1975. *Cherokee–English dictionary.* Tahlequah: Cherokee Nation of Oklahoma.

Ferguson, T. J., and E. Richard Hart. 1985. *A Zuni atlas.* Norman: University of Oklahoma Press.

Fitzpatrick, Lilian Linder. 1960. *Nebraska place names.* 2nd ed. Including selections from *The origin of the place-names of Nebraska* by J. T. Link. Lincoln: University of Nebraska Press.

Fleisher, Mark S. 1979. A note on Schuhmacher's inference of wahú' in Colville Salish. *International Journal of American Linguistics* 45:279–80. [Response to Schuhmacher 1977; see also Hockett 1984.]

Flowers, Paul. 1960. Place names in Tennessee. *West Tennessee Historical Society Papers* 14: 113–23.

Fortescue, Michael, Steven Jacobson, and Lawrence Kaplan. 1994. *Comparative Eskimo dictionary, with Aleut cognates.* Fairbanks: Alaska Native Language Center, University of Alaska.

Foscue, Virginia. 1989. *Placenames in Alabama.* Tuscaloosa: University of Alabama Press.

Frantz, Donald G., and Norma Jean Russell. 1995. *Blackfoot dictionary of stems, roots, and affixes.* 2nd ed. Toronto: University of Toronto Press.

Froke, Marlowe D., and Warren G. Bodow. 1962. *Pronunciation guide to place names in Pennsylvania.* [Harrisburg:] Pennsylvania Association of Broadcasters.

Fullerton, Ralph O. 1974. *Place names of Tennessee.* Division of Geology, Bulletin No. 73. Nashville: Dept. of Conservation.

Geoghegan, Richard H. 1994. *The Aleut language.* Washington, D.C.: Dept. of the Interior.

Givón, Talmy. 1979. *Ute dictionary.* Ignacio, Colo.: Ute Press.

Goddard, Ives. 1977. Review of Trumbull 1974. *International Journal of American Linguistics* 43:157–59.

———. 1994. *Leonard Bloomfield's Fox lexicon.* Algonquian and Iroquoian Linguistics, Memoir 12. Winnipeg: [University of Manitoba.]

———. (ed.). 1996. *Handbook of North American Indians,* vol. 17: *Languages.* Washington, D.C.: Smithsonian Press.

Goff, John Hedges. 1975. *Placenames of Georgia.* Athens: University of Georgia Press.

Gómez de Silva, Guido. 1988. *Breve diccionario etimológico de la lengua española.* Mexico City: Fondo de Cultura Económica.

Gould, Charles Newton. 1933. *Oklahoma place names.* Norman: University of Oklahoma Press.

Granger, Byrd Howell. 1983. *Arizona's names: X marks the place.* Tucson: Falconer. Revised ed. of Barnes 1960.

Grumet, Robert Steven. 1981. *Native American place names in New York City.* New York: Museum of the City of New York.

Gudde, Erwin G. 1998. *California place names: The origin and etymology of current geographical names.* 4th ed. Revised and enlarged by William Bright. Berkeley: University of California Press.

Gudgel-Holmes, Dianne. (ed.). 1991. *Native place names of the Kantishna drainage, Alaska.* Anchorage: National Park Service, U.S. Dept. of the Interior.

A guide to pronunciation of place names in West Virginia. 1972. [Morgantown:] School of Journalism, West Virginia University.

Haas, Mary R. 1953. *Tunica dictionary.* Publications in Linguistics, 6:2. Berkeley: University of California.

Hagemann, James A. 1988. *The heritage of Virginia: The story of place names in the Old Dominion*. 2nd ed. West Chester, Pa.: Whitford Press.

Handbook of North American Indians. Ed. by William C. Sturtevant. Washington, D.C.: Smithsonian Institution, 1971–. [Eventually 20 volumes.]

Harder, Kelsie B. 1976. *Illustrated dictionary of placenames: US and Canada*. New York: Van Nostrand & Reinhold.

———. 1985. Names of major peaks in the Adirondacks. *Geolinguistic perspectives: Proceedings of the international conference celebrating the twentieth anniversary of the American Society of Geolinguistics 1985,* ed. by Jesse Levitt et al., 139–46. Lanham, Md.: University Presses of America.

Harrington, John Peabody. 1916. The ethnogeography of the Tewa Indians. In *Bureau of American Ethnology, Annual report,* vol. 29 [1907–8], 29–636. Washington, D.C.: Government Printing Office.

Hartley, Alan H. 2001. Camas. *Society for the Study of the Indigenous Languages of the Americas Newsletter* 20 (3): 10–11.

———. 2002. Sacagawea. *Society for the Study of the Indigenous Languages of the Americas Newsletter* 20 (4): 12–13.

Hartsook, Richard M. 1976. *A pronunciation guide to Alabama place names.* [Tuscaloosa:] School of Communication, University of Alabama.

Heck, L. W., et al. 1966. *Delaware place names*. US Geological Survey, Bulletin No. 1245. Washington, D.C.: Government Printing Office.

Heller, Murray. 1989. *Call me Adirondack: Names and their stories*. Saranac Lake, N.Y.: Chauncy.

Hickerson, R. B. 1979. *Texas pronunciation guide for unusual names.* College Station: Texas A&M University, Texas Agricultural Extension Service.

Hinton, Leanne, et al. 1984. *A dictionary of the Havasupai language*. Supai, Ariz.: Havasupai Tribe.

Hitchman, Robert. 1949. Onalaska, Washington. *Western Folklore* 8:368–69.

———. 1985. *Place names of Washington state*. Tacoma: Washington State Historical Society.

Hockett, Charles F. 1984. The word Hawaii. *International Journal of American Linguistics* 50:349–50. [Comment on Schuhmacher 1977 and Fleisher 1979.]

Holland, C. Joe. 1950. *A pronunciation guide to Oklahoma place names*. [Norman:] School of Journalism, University of Oklahoma, 1950.

Holterman, Jack. 1985. *Place names of Glacier/Waterton National Parks*. [West Glacier, Mont.]: Glacier Natural History Association.

Howell, Philip Hugh. 1948. *Dictionary of Indian geographic names: The origin and meaning of Indian names.* [Seattle:] The American Indian Historical Society.

Huden, John Charles. 1962. *Indian place names of New England.* New York, Museum of the American Indian, Heye Foundation.

Hughes, Arthur H., and Morse S. Allen. 1976. *Connecticut place names*. [Hartford:] Connecticut Historical Society.

Hunn, Eugene. 1990. *Nch'i-wana, "the big river": Mid-Columbia Indians and their land*. Seattle: University of Washington Press.

Ingham, Bruce. 2001. *English-Lakhota dictionary*. Richmond, Surrey, U.K.: Curzon.

Jacobson, Steven A. 1984. *Yup'ik Eskimo dictionary*. Fairbanks: Alaska Native Language Center, University of Alaska.

———. 1987. *A dictionary of the St. Lawrence Island / Siberian Yupik Eskimo language*. 2nd ed. Fairbanks: Alaska Native Language Center, University of Alaska.

Janssen, Quinith, and William Fernbach. 1984. *West Virginia place names: Origins and history*. Shepherdstown, W.Va.: J and F Enterprises.

Jett, Stephen C. 2001. *Navajo placenames and trails of the Canyon de Chelly system, Arizona.* New York: Peter Lang.

Jetté, Jules, and Eliza Jones. 2000. *Koyukon Athabaskan dictionary.* Fairbanks: Alaska Native Language Center, University of Alaska.

Julyan, Robert. 1998. *The place names of New Mexico.* 2nd ed. Albuquerque: University of New Mexico Press.

Julyan, Robert, and Mary Julyan. 1993. *Place names of the White Mountains.* 2nd ed. Hanover, N.H.: University Press of New England.

Kanatawakhon-Maracle, David. 2001. *A Mohawk thematic dictionary.* London, Ont., Canada: Kanyen'keha Books, University of Western Ontario.

Kansas. 1955. *A pronunciation guide to Kansas place names.* [Lawrence:] William Allen White School of Journalism and Public Information, University of Kansas.

———. Potawatomi dictionary. http://www.ukans.edu/~kansite/pbp/books/dicto/d_title.html.

Kari, James M. 1983 (ed.) *Ahtna place names lists.* [Fairbanks:] Alaska Native Language Center, University of Alaska.

———. 1990. *Ahtna Athabaskan dictionary.* Fairbanks: Alaska Native Language Center, University of Alaska.

———. 1999. *Draft final report: Native place names mapping in Denali National Park and Preserve.* N.p.: National Park Service.

———. 2000. Contributions of the United States Geological Survey to the documentation of Alaska native names, 1950–75. *Names* 48:193–98.

———. 1986. The Tenada–Denali–Mount McKinley controversy. *Names* 34:241–43.

Kari, James M., and James A. Fall. 1987. *Shem Pete's Alaska: The territory of the Upper Cook Inlet Dena'ina.* Fairbanks: Alaska Native Language Center, University of Alaska. Revised ed., 2002.

Kari, James M., and Priscilla Russell Kari. 1982. *Tanaina country = Dena'ina eɫaina.* Fairbanks: Alaska Native Language Center, University of Alaska.

Karttunen, Frances. 1983. *An analytical dictionary of Nahuatl.* Austin: University of Texas Press.

Kenny, Hamill. 1945. *West Virginia place names, their origin and meaning including the nomenclature of the streams and mountains.* Piedmont, W.Va.: Place Name Press.

———. 1950–51. The origin and meaning of the Indian place-names of Maryland. 2 vols. Thesis, University of Maryland, College Park.

———. 1961. *The origin and meaning of the Indian place names of Maryland.* Baltimore: Waverly Press.

———. 1967. Adena [ədínə]. *Names* 15:240.

———. 1984. *The placenames of Maryland: Their origin and meaning.* Baltimore: Museum and Library of Maryland History, Maryland Historical Society.

Kraft, Herbert C., and John Kraft. 1985. *The Indians of Lenapehoking.* South Orange, N.J.: Seton Hall University Museum. [Glossary on 44; Lenape placenames on 45.]

Krakow, Kenneth K. 1975. *Georgia place-names.* Macon, Ga.: Winship.

Kuethe, J. Louis. 1937. Pocosin. *Modern Language Notes* 52:210–11.

Lance, Donald M. 1999. The origin and meaning of *Missouri. Names* 47:109-18.

Larsen, Ramón. 1955. *Vocabulario huasteco del Estado de San Luis Potosí.* Mexico City: Instituto Lingüístico de Verano.

Lawrence, Erma. 1977. *Haida dictionary.* Fairbanks: Alaska Native Language Center, University of Alaska.

Leer, Jeff. 1978. *A conversational dictionary of Kodiak Alutiiq.* Fairbanks: Alaska Native Language Center, University of Alaska.

Leland, J. A. C. 1953. Indian names in Missouri. *Names* 1:266–73

Lenmark, Barbara. 1953. *A pronunciation guide to Minnesota place names.* [Minneapolis:] School of Journalism, University of Minnesota.

Linford, Laurance D. 2000. *Navajo places: History, legend, landscape.* Salt Lake City: University of Utah Press.

Little, Elizabeth A. 1984. Indian place names on Nantucket Island. *Papers of the Fifteenth Algonquian Conference*, ed. by William Cowan, 345–62. Ottawa: Carleton University.

Losk, Walter S. (ed.). 1951. *Pronunciation guide to North Dakota place names.* Grand Forks: Dept. of Journalism, University of North Dakota.

Lounsbury, Floyd G. 1960. Iroquois place-names in the Champlain Valley. In *Interstate Commission on the Lake Champlain Basin, Report,* 21–66. Albany: New York State Legislative Document, 1960, no. 9. Reprinted, Albany: University of the State of New York, State Education Dept., [1972?].

Lowe, Ronald. 1984a. *Basic Siglit Inuvialuit Eskimo dictionary.* Inuvik, NWT, Canada: Committee for Original Peoples Entitlement.

———. 1984b. Basic Uummarmiut Eskimo dictionary. Inuvik, NWT, Canada: Committee for Original Peoples Entitlement.

MacLean, Edna Ahgeak. 1980. *Iñupiallu tanŋiłłu uaqaluŋisa iłaŋich: Abridged Iñupiaq and English dictionary.* Fairbanks: Alaska Native Language Center, University of Alaska.

Mahr, August C. 1953. How to locate Indian places on modern maps. *Ohio Journal of Science* 53:129–37.

———. 1957. Indian river and place names in Ohio. *Ohio Historical Quarterly* 66:137–58.

———. 1959. Practical reasons for Algonkian Indian stream and place names. *Ohio Journal of Science* 59:365–74.

———. 1960. Shawnee names and migrations in Kentucky and West Virginia. *Ohio Journal of Science* 60:155–64.

Manguel, Alberto, and Gianni Guadalupi. 1987. *The dictionary of imaginary places.* 2nd ed. Orlando, Fla.: Harcourt Brace Jovanovich.

Martijn, Charles A. 1991. Gepèg (Québec): Un toponyme d'origine micmaque. *Recherches Amérindiennes au Québec* 21(3):51-64.

Martin, Jack B., & Mauldin, Margaret McKane. 2000. *A dictionary of Creek/Muskogee, with notes on the Florida and Oklahoma Seminole dialects of Creek.* Lincoln: University of Nebraska Press, 2000.

Masthay, Carl. 1987. New England Indian place names. In *Rooted like the ash trees: New England Indians and the land,* ed. by Richard G. Carlson, 13–17. Eagle Wing Press, 6:5. Naugatuck, Conn.: American Indians for Development.

———. 1991. *Schmick's Mahican dictionary.* American Philosophical Society, Memoirs, 197. Philadelphia: American Philosophical Society.

———. 2002. Yankee: A name with a problematic origin. *Society for the Study of the Indigenous Languages of the Americas, Newsletter,* 21(3):7–8.

Matthew, Margaret, et al. 1999. *Stevens Village land use plan, ethnogeography of ancestral lands, and integrated resource management plan.* Stevens Village, Alaska: Stevens Village Council.

McArthur, Lewis A. 1992. *Oregon geographic names.* 6th ed. Rev. and enlarged by Lewis L. McArthur. Portland: Oregon Historical Society Press. [7th ed., 2003.]

McCafferty, Michael. 2000. Wabash, its meaning and history. In *Papers of the Thirty-first Algonquian Conference,* ed. by John D. Nichols, 1–5. Winnipeg: University of Manitoba.

———. 2002. American Indian place-names in Indiana. MS.

———. 2003. On the birthday and etymology of the placename Missouri. *Names* 51:31–45.

McClaren, Adrian W. 1991. *What's in a name? Tennessee towns.* N.p.: Tennessee Council of Teachers of English.

McLendon, Sally, and John R. Johnson. 1999. Cultural affiliation and linear descent of Chumash peoples in the Channel Islands and the Santa Monica Mountains. 2 vols. Santa Barbara, Calif.: Santa Barbara Museum of Natural History.

McMullen, E. Wallace. (ed.). 1993. *Names new and old: Papers of the Names Institute (Fairleigh Dickinson University).* Lanham, Md.: University Press of America.

McNamee, Gregory. 1997. *Grand Canyon place names.* Seattle: The Mountaineers.

McPherson, Alan. 1993. *Indian names in Indiana.* N.p.: Blasted Works.

Michelson, Gunther. 1973. *A thousand words of Mohawk.* Ethnology Division, Papers, 5. Ottawa: National Museum of Man.

Miller, Larry L. 1996. *Ohio place names.* Bloomington: Indiana University Press.

———. 2001. *Tennessee place names.* Bloomington: Indiana University Press.

Miller, Wick R. 1972. *Newe natekwinappeh: Shoshoni stories and dictionary.* University of Utah anthropological papers, 94. Salt Lake City: University of Utah.

Mithun, Marianne. 1999. *The languages of Native North America.* Cambridge: Cambridge University Press.

Molina, Felipe S., et al. 1999. *Yoeme-English, English-Yoeme standard dictionary: A language of the Yaqui tribe in the American Southwest and northern Mexico.* New York: Hippocrene.

Monaghan, Robert R. 1961. *Pronunciation guide to Oregon place names.* Eugene: Oregon Association of Broadcasters.

Morrison, Alvin H. 1983. *The name "Canadaway."* Canadaway Creek Anthropology Project, Reports, 3. Fredonia: Dept. of Sociology & Anthropology, State University of New York.

Mott Wedel, Mildred. 1978. A synonymy of names for the Ioway Indians. *Journal of the Iowa Archeological Society* 25:49–77.

Munro, Pamela, and Catherine Willmond. 1994. *Chickasaw: An analytical dictionary.* Norman: University of Oklahoma Press.

Neuffer, Claude Henry, and Irene Neuffer. 1983. *Correct mispronunciations of some South Carolina names.* [Columbia:] University of South Carolina Press.

Newman, Stanley S. 1958. *Zuni dictionary.* Indiana University Research Center in Anthropology, Folklore, and Linguistics, Publications, 6; International Journal of American Linguistics, 24:1, part II. Bloomington: Indiana University.

Nichols, John D., and Earl Nyholm. 1995. *A concise dictionary of Minnesota Ojibwe.* Minneapolis: University of Minnesota Press.

O'Hara, Mike. 2000. Name origins of northeast PA towns. www/lastsite.com/towns.html.

O'Meara, John. 1996. *Delaware-English, English-Delaware dictionary.* Toronto: University of Toronto Press.

Orth, Donald J. 1967. *Dictionary of Alaska place names.* Geological Survey, Professional Papers, 567. Washington, D.C.: Government Printing Office.

———. 1990. *Potomac and Blue Ridge toponymic tour.* Reston, Va.: U.S. Board on Geographic Names.

Parratt, Smitty. 1984. *Gods and goblins: A field guide to place names of Olympic National Park.* Port Angeles, Wash.: C P Publications.

Payne, Roger L. 1985. *Place names of the Outer Banks.* Washington, N.C.: Thomas A. Williams.

Pearce, Thomas M. 1965. *Mexico place names: A geographical dictionary.* Albuquerque: University of New Mexico Press.

Pearson, Bruce L. 1974–76. Savannah and Shawnee: Same or different? *Names in South Carolina* 21:19–22, 23:20–22.

———. 1978. On the Indian place-names of South Carolina. *Names* 26:58–67.

———. 1995. *Shawnee language dictionary.* Shawnee, Okla.: Absentee Shawnee Tribe of Oklahoma.

Peñafiel, Antonio. 1897. *Nomenclatura geográfica de México: Etimologías de los nombres de lugar correspondientes a los principales idiomas que se hablan en la República.* Mexico City: Secretaría de Fomento.

Perkey, Elton. 1995. *Perkey's Nebraska place names.* 2nd ed. N.p.: J. & L. Lee.

Peter, Katherine. 1979. *Dinjii zhuh ginjik nagwan tr'iłtsąįį [Gwich'in junior dictionary].* Anchorage: University of Alaska.

Peters, Bernard C. 1996. *Lake Superior place names.* Marquette: Northern Michigan University Press.

Phillips, James Wendell. 1971. *Washington state place names.* 2nd ed. Seattle: University of Washington Press.

———. 1973. *Alaska-Yukon place names.* Seattle: University of Washington Press.

Picinich, Donald George. 1951. *A pronunciation guide to Missouri place names.* Revised by Robert Lee Ramsay. University of Missouri Bulletin, 52:3, Journalism. Columbia: University of Missouri.

Pickens, A. L. 1961–62. Indian place-names in South Carolina. *Names in South Carolina* 10(8):2–7, 10(9):20–24.

———. 1963. Indian place-names in South Carolina (largely from Muskhogean area). *Names in South Carolina* 10:35–40.

———. 1964. Aboriginal miscellany in placenames. *Names in South Carolina* 11:33.

Powell, Margaret, and Stephen D. Powell. 1990. Bibliography of placename literature, United States and Canada, 1980–1988. *Names* 28:49–141.

Powell, William S. 1968. *The North Carolina gazetteer.* Chapel Hill: University of North Carolina Press.

Press, Margaret L. 1979. *Chemehuevi: A grammar and lexicon.* University of California publications in linguistics, 92. Berkeley: University of California Press.

Prince, John Dyneley. 1900. Some forgotten Indian place names in the Adirondacks. *Journal of American Folklore* 13:123–28. Reprinted in his *Fragments from Babel,* 165–71. New York: Columbia University Press, 1939.

Pukui, Mary Kawena, Samuel Elbert, and Esther Mookini. 1974. *Place names of Hawaii.* Honolulu: University Press.

Ramos, Mary G. (ed.). 2001. *Texas almanac, 2000–2001.* Dallas: Dallas Morning News. ["Texas pronunciation guide," 623–28.]

Ramsay, Robert Lee. 1952. *Our storehouse of Missouri place names.* University of Missouri Bulletin, vol. 53, no. 34, Arts and science, no. 7; Missouri Handbook no. 2. Columbia: University of Missouri.

Randall, Richard R. 1993. Political changes and new names. In McMullen 1993:5–14. [Discussion of Chargoggagoggmanchauggagoggchaubunagungamaug, 12–13.]

Random House dictionary of the English language. Ed. by Stuart Berg Flexner. 2nd ed. New York: Random House. [American Indian etymologies by Ives Goddard.]

Ransom, J. Ellis. 1940. Derivation of the word *Alaska. American Anthropologist* 42:550–51.

Rayburn, Alan. 1997. *Dictionary of Canadian place names.* Toronto: Oxford University Press.

Read, Allen Walker. 1969. The rivalry of names for the Rocky Mountains of North America. In International Congress of Onomastic Sciences (Vienna), *Proceedings,* 10, 207–22. Vienna: Wiener Medizinische Akademie. [Also in McMullen 1993:47–60.]

———. 1980. An updating of research on the name *Podunk.* In *Names Northeast: Amerindian names,* ed. by Murray Heller, 86–99. Northeast Regional Names Institute, Publication no. 2. Saranac Lake, N.Y.: North Country Community College Press.

———. 1981. The pronunciation of the name *Illinois.* In *The dangerous, secret name of God; Fartley's Compressed Gas Company; the Barf'n'choke; and other matters onomastic,* ed. by

Laurence E. Seits, 38–51. Papers of the North Central Names Institute, 2. Sugar Grove, Ill.: Waubonsee Community College. [Reprinted in Callary 2000:81–96.]

———. 2001. *America—naming the country and its people*. Lewiston, N.Y.: Mellen.

Read, William Alexander. 1927. Louisiana place-names of Indian origin. University Bulletin, n.s., vol. 19. Baton Rouge: Louisiana State University. [A list of addenda and corrigenda was published in *Louisiana Historical Quarterly* 11 (1928):445–62.

———. 1934. *Florida place-names of Indian origin and Seminole personal names*. Baton Rouge: Louisiana State University Press.

———. 1938. Ten Alabama place names. *American Speech* 13:79–80.

———. 1940. Caxambas, a Florida geographic name. *Language* 16:210–13.

———. 1949–50. Indian stream-names in Georgia. *International Journal of American Linguistics* 15:128–32, 16:203–7.

———. 1984. *Indian place-names in Alabama*. 2nd ed., revised by James M. Macmillan. Tuscaloosa: University of Alabama Press, 1984. [First published, Baton Rouge: Louisiana State University Press, 1937.]

Reese, Gary Fuller. 1996. Washington place names. Tacoma Public Library. http://www.tpl.lib.wa.us/nwr.wanames.htm.

Rennick, Robert M. 1984. *Kentucky place names*. Lexington: University Press of Kentucky.

Reynolds, Helen Wilkinson. 1924. *Poughkeepsie: The origin and meaning of the word*. Poughkeepsie, N.Y.: Dutchess County Historical Society.

Rhodes, Richard A. 1985. *Eastern Ojibwa-Chippewa-Ottawa dictionary*. Trends in linguistics: Documentation, 3. The Hague: Mouton.

Richthofen, Erich von. 1975. Oregon: A still controversial toponym (Spanish, French, or American Indian?). In *Philologica Romanica*, ed. by Manfred Bambeck and Hans Helmut Christmann, 323–26. München: Fink.

Riggs, Stephen R. 1890. *A Dakota–English dictionary*. Washington, D.C.: Government Printing Office. Reprinted, St. Paul: Minnesota Historical Society, 1984.

Robinson, Lila W., and James Armagost. 1990. *Comanche dictionary and grammar*. Dallas: Summer Institute of Linguistics.

Room, Adrian. 1997. *Placenames of the world: Origins and meanings*. Jefferson, N.C.: McFarland.

Rudes, Blair A. 1998. Etymology of Tuscarora. *Maine History* 37(3):94–97.

Rundell, Hugh A. 1964. *Washington names: A pronunciation guide of Washington state place names*. 3d ed. Pullman: Radio Station KWSC and the Extension Service, Institute of Agricultural Sciences, Washington State University.

Rutherford, Phillip Roland. 1970. *The dictionary of Maine placenames*. Freeport, Maine: Bond Wheelwright.

Ruttenber, Edward Manning. 1906. *Indian geographical names in the Valley of Hudson's River, the Valley of the Mohawk, and on the Delaware: Their location and the probable meaning of some of them*. [Albany?:] New York State Historical Association.

Ryan, William J. 1975. *Pronunciation guide for the state of Idaho*. [Pocatello?:] Journalism Dept., Idaho State University Press.

Rydjord, John. 1968. *Indian place-names: Their origin, evolution, and meanings, collected in Kansas from the Siouan, Algonquian, Shoshonean, Caddoan, Iroquoian, and other tongues*. Norman: University of Oklahoma Press.

Salzmann, Zdenek. 1983. *Dictionary of contemporary Arapaho usage*. Wind River Reservation, Wyo.: Arapaho Language and Culture.

Santamaría, Francisco J. 1959. *Diccionario de mejicanismos*. Mexico City: Porrúa.

Sapir, Edward. 1930. *Southern Paiute dictionary*. American Academy of Arts and Sciences, Proceedings, 65:3. Boston: American Academy of Arts and Sciences. Reprinted in *Collected works of Edward Sapir,* 10: *Southern Paiute and Ute linguistics and ethnography,* ed. by William Bright. Berlin: Mouton de Gruyter, 1992.

Saxton, Dean, Lucille Saxton, and Susie Enos. 1983. *Dictionary: Papago/Pima-English, O'othham-Mil-gahn; English-Papago/Pima, Mil-gahn-O'othham.* Tucson: University of Arizona Press.

Scheetz, George H. 2000. Peoria. In Callary 2000:43-70.

Schooley, Frank E., & Brown, Donald E. 1948. *Pronunciation guide for Illinois towns and cities.* Urbana: School of Journalism, University of Illinois.

Schorr, Alan Edward. 1974. *Alaska place names.* Elmer E. Rasmuson Library, Occasional Papers, 2. Fairbanks: University of Alaska.

———. 1986. *Alaska place names.* 3rd ed. Juneau, Alaska: Denali Press. 4th ed., 1991.

Schuhmacher, W. W. 1977. Colville name for Hawaii. *International Journal of American Linguistics* 43:65–66. [See also Fleisher 1979, Hockett 1984.]

———. 1979. Honolulu, Alaska. *International Journal of American Linguistics* 43:27–78. [Also re Owyhee; see also White 1980.]

Seale, Lea L. 1939. Indian place names in Mississippi. Doctoral diss., Louisiana State University.

Sealock, Richard Burl, Margaret M. Sealock, and Margaret S. Powell. 1982. *Bibliography of place-name literature: United States and Canada.* 3rd ed. Chicago: American Library Association.

Shaul, David L. 1972. The meaning of the name Sacajawea. *Annals of Wyoming* 44:237–40.

Shipley, William F. 1963. *Maidu texts and dictionary.* University of California Publications in Lingustics, 33. Berkeley: University of California Press.

Shirk, George H. 1974. *Oklahoma place names.* 2d ed. Norman: University of Oklahoma Press.

Siebert, Frank T., Jr. 1943. Review of Eckstorm 1941. *New England Quarterly* 16:503–7.

Siler, Tom. 1985. *Tennessee towns: From Adams to Yorkville.* Knoxville: East Tennessee Historical Society.

Silver, Shirley, and Wick Miller. 1997. *American Indian languages: Cultural and social contexts.* Tucson: University of Arizona Press.

Smith, Grant. 1996. Amerindian place names: A typology based on meaning and form. *Onomastica Canadiana* 78:53–64.

Sneve, Virginia Driving Hawk. (ed.). 1973. *South Dakota geographic names.* Sioux Falls, S.Dak.: Brevet Press. Reprint ed. of Ehrensperger 1941.

South Dakota. 1963. *What's that name?: A pronunciation guide to South Dakota names.* Brookings: Dept. of Printing and Journalism, South Dakota State College of Agriculture and Mechanic Arts.

Stennett, William. 1908. *A history of the origin of the place names connected with the Chicago & North Western and Chicago, St. Paul, Minneapolis & Omaha Railways.* 2d ed. Chicago: n.p.

Stewart, George R. 1945. *Names on the land.* New York: Random House.

———. 1967. Ouaricon revisited. *Names* 15:166–68. [Response by Vogel 1968.]

———. 1970. *American place-names.* New York: Oxford University Press.

Stokes, George M. 1977. *A guide to the pronunciation of Texas towns.* Waco, Tex.: Stokes.

Story, Gillian L., and Constance M. Naish. 1973. *Tlingit verb dictionary.* College: Alaska Native Language Center, University of Alaska.

Swenson, John F. 1991. Chicagoua/Chicago: The origin, meaning, and etymology of a place name. *Illinois Historical Journal* 84:233–48.

Sylestine, Cora, et al. 1993. *Dictionary of the Alabama language.* Austin: University of Texas Press.

Tarpley, Fred. 1980. *1001 Texas place names.* Austin: University of Texas Press.

Teeter, Karl V. 1958. Notes on Humboldt County, California, place names of Indian origin. *Names* 6:55–56.

Thomas, Edward H. 1935. *Chinook: A history and dictionary of the Northwest Coast trade jargon.* Portland, Ore.: Metropolitan Press.

Thornton, Thomas F. 1995. Place and being among the Tlingit. Diss., University of Washington dissertation, Seattle.

Tooker, William Wallace. 1911. *The Indian place-names on Long Island and islands adjacent, with their probable significations.* New York: Putnam. Reprinted, Port Washington, N.Y.: Friedman, 1962.

Toomey, Noxon. 1917. *Proper names from the Muskhogean languages.* Hervas Laboratories of American Linguistics, Bulletin 3. St. Louis: Hervas Laboratories of American Linguistics.

Trager, George L. 1960. The name of Taos, New Mexico. *Anthropological Linguistics* 2(3):5–6.

Trumbull, James Hammond. 1879. *The composition of Indian geographical names, illustrated from the Algonkin languges.* Hartford, Conn.: Case, Lockwood & Brainard.

———. 1881. *Indian names of places etc., in and on the borders of Connecticut, with interpretations of some of them.* Hartford: Case, Lockwood & Brainard Co. Reprinted, Hamden, Conn.: Archon, 1974.

———. 1903. *Natick dictionary.* Bureau of American Ethnology Bulletin 25. Washington, D.C.: Government Printing Office.

Tynan, Trudy. 2000. Chargoggagoggmachauggagoggchaubunagungamaugg: A mouthful of a name, this Massachusetts lake has inspired poems, songs and tall tales. Associated Press, June.

Upham, Warren. 2001. *Minnesota geographic names: Their origin and historic significance.* 3rd ed. St. Paul: Minnesota Historical Society.

Urbanek, Mae Bobb. 1974. *Wyoming place names.* 3d ed. Boulder, Colo.: Johnson. Reprint, Missoula, Mont.: Mountain Press, 1988.

U.S. Board on Geographic Names. Decision lists. Washington, D.C.: Dept. of the Interior.

U.S. Geological Survey. 2002. Geographical Names Information System (GNIS). Reston, Va.: Board on Geographic Names, U.S. Geological Survey, Dept. of the Interior. Available on the Internet at http://geonames.usgs.gov/pls/gnis.

Van Cott, John W. 1990. *Utah place names: A comprehensive guide to the origins of geographic names.* Salt Lake City: University of Utah Press.

Vogel, Virgil J. 1960. The origin and meaning of "Missouri." *Missouri Historical Society, Bulletin* 16:213–22.

———. 1963. *Indian place names in Illinois.* Springfield: Illinois State Historical Library.

———. 1968. Oregon: A rejoinder. *Names* 16:136–40. Response to Stewart 1967.

———. 1980. Names that come in pairs. In *Papers of the North Central Names Institute, 1980,* ed. Laurence E. Seits 9–21. Sugar Grove, Ill.: Waubonsee Community College.

———. 1982a. Nishna and Botna: Fractionated names on the American map. In *Places, pets, and charactonyms,* ed. by Laurence E. Seits and Jean Divine, 19–29. Papers of the North Central Names Institute, 3. Sugar Grove, Ill.: Waubonsee Community College.

———. 1982b. Their name is on your waters: A narrative of Native American place names in the United States and Canada. Manuscript in the Newberry Library, Chicago.

———. 1983. *Iowa place names of Indian origin.* Iowa City: University of Iowa Press.

———. 1986. *Indian names in Michigan.* Ann Arbor: University of Michigan Press.

———. 1991. *Indian names on Wisconsin's map.* Madison: University of Wisconsin Press.

Waddell, Gene. 1980. *Indians of the South Carolina lowcountry, 1562–1751.* Columbia, S.C.: Southern Studies Program, University of South Carolina.

Waite, David L. 1973. *Broadcasters' pronunciation guide for geographical locations of the state of Mississippi.* Hattiesburg: Dept. of Communication, University of Southern Mississippi.

Wassillie, Albert. 1979. *Dena'ina Athabaskan junior dictionary.* Ed. by James Kari. Anchorage, Alaska: National Bilingual Materials Development Center.

Waterman, T. T. 1920. *Yurok geography*. University of California Publications in American Archaeology and Ethnology, 16, no. 5. Reprinted, Trinidad, Calif.: Trinidad Museum Society, 1993.

Webber, Bert. 1995. *Oregon's names, how to say them and where are they located?: An illustrated pronunciation guide*. Medford, Ore.: Webb.

Webster, Donald H., and Wilfried Zibell. 1970. *Iñupiat Eskimo dictionary*. Fairbanks, Alaska: Summer Institute of Linguistics.

West Virginia. 1995. *A guide to pronunciation of place names in West Virginia*. 5th ed. [Morgantown:] Office of Publications, West Virginia University.

Whaley, Storm. 1950. *They call it: Guide to the pronunciation of Arkansas place names*. N.p: Associated Press.

White, R. G. 1980. Owyhee recooked. *International Journal of American Linguistics* 46:318–19. [Response to Schuhmacher 1979.]

Whittlesey, Lee H. 1988. *Yellowstone place names*. Helena: Montana Historical Society Press.

Wick, Douglas A. 1988. *North Dakota place names*. Bismarck, N.Dak.: Hedemarken. Reprinted, Fargo, N.Dak.: Prairie House, 1989.

Williams, Mary Ann Barnes. 1973. *Origins of North Dakota place names*. [Washburn, N.Dak.:] McLean County Historical Society.

Williamson, John P. 1902. *An English–Dakota dictionary*. New York: American Tract Society. Reprinted, St. Paul: Minnesota Historical Society, 1984.

Wilson, Alan. 1995. *Navajo placenames: An observer's guide*. With audio cassette. Guilford, Conn.: Audio-Forum, 1995.

Wolfart, H. C., and Freda Ahenakew. 1998. *The student's dictionary of Literary Plains Cree*. Algonquian and Iroquoian Linguistics, Memoir 15. Winnipeg: University of Manitoba.

Wright, Muriel H. 1951. *A guide to the Indian tribes of Oklahoma*. Norman: University of Oklahoma Press.

Young, Robert W., & Morgan, William. 1987. *The Navajo language: A grammar and colloquial dictionary*. 2nd ed. Albuquerque: University of New Mexico Press.

Zawadzki, Paul A. 1982. *Pronunciation guide to place names in Pennsylvania*. 2nd ed. N.p.: Pennsylvania Association of Broadcasters.

Zygmond, Maurice L., Curtis G. Booth, and Pamela Munro. 1991. *Kawaiisu: A grammar and dictionary with texts*. University of California publications in linguistics, 119. Berkeley: University of California Press.